LAND LAW IN IRELAND

Second Edition

UNITED KINGDOM
Sweet & Maxwell
London

AUSTRALIA
LBC Information Services
Sydney

CANADA and the USA
Carswell
Toronto

NEW ZEALAND
Brooker's
Auckland

SINGAPORE and MALAYSIA
Thomson Information (S.E. Asia)
Singapore

Land Law in Ireland

Second Edition

Andrew Lyall
PhD (Lond) LLD (Lond)
of Gray's Inn, Barrister
Senior Lecturer, Faculty of Law, University College Dublin

Dublin
Roundhall Sweet & Maxwell
2000

Published in 2000 by
Round Hall Ltd
43 Fitwilliam Place
Dublin 2, Ireland.

Typeset by
Red Dot, Dublin

Printed by
MPG Books, Cornwall

ISBN 1-85800-186-2 pbk
ISBN 1-85800-199-4 hbk

A catalogue record for this book
is available from the British Library.

For David and Tom

FOREWORD

It is both a source of pleasure and an honour to have been asked to contribute a foreword to this remarkable work. A source of pleasure, because the law of real property, which constitutes an important part of the book, has always fascinated me. Even as a student it interested me, though students for the most part tend to shy away from it, and it increased its hold over me thanks to my having taught the real property course in UCD in the 1960s. It has, accordingly, given me enormous pleasure to be plunged once again into this area of law.

I feel also it is a considerable honour to be associated, even to this very minor extent, with a work which is so comprehensive and of such a high academic standard. In addition to covering the subject which one would normally expect to find in a textbook on land law, such as all aspects of the law of real property, registration of title, landlord and tenant etc., Dr Lyall has also chapters on planning law, housing law and the law relating to family property. In the latter chapter Dr Lyall analyses with admirable clarity the recent case law on the circumstances in which a wife may acquire a beneficial interest in the family home, the legal title to which is vested in the husband solely, and considers how the position has been affected by the powers given to the courts by the Judicial Separation and Family Law Reform Act, 1989 to make property orders when a judicial separation order has been made.

Practitioners and students should find the book invaluable, and the writing is so clear that even persons with no knowledge of the law may profit from it. I have always divided textbooks into two simple categories - those I can understand and those I cannot. I unhesitatingly put this work into the category of those I can understand.

Dr Lyall reserves some of the best wine to the end. In Appendix A, under the title "The Purchaser's Equity", he discusses in great detail the decision of the Supreme Court in *Tempany v. Hynes* [1976] IR 101, and makes a very strong case for its being reviewed by a full court (it is a majority decision of a court of three). If this should ever come about, the argument he advances will be of great assistance both to the counsel in the case and to the members of the Court (hopefully still including myself) who will have to decide it.

I have enjoyed very much reading Dr Lyall's book and it only remains for me to congratulate him on his achievement and to express my wish that his book will have the success it deserves.

John Blayney
Supreme Court
Dublin
October 1994

PREFACE TO THE FIRST EDITION

The object of this book, as the title suggests, is to explain land law in Ireland. The book is mainly concerned with land law in what is still referred to as the twenty-six counties or what may be described, with some possible constitutional impropriety, as the Republic of Ireland.[1] Since some reference is made throughout the book to the law in Northern Ireland, one must avoid the possibility of inaccuracy and so I have generally used "Ireland" to refer to both parts of Ireland, and "the Republic" to refer to "the twenty-six counties."

Land law is generally regarded by students as a difficult subject and is not a popular one for that reason. This is no doubt due to the complexity of the rules in some areas but also because of their seeming remoteness from actual practical problems. This apparent remoteness is, I believe, in part attributable to a phenomenon known as "reification" which presents property as a thing with inherent attributes, rather than as social relationship whose content is determined by judges with their own attitudes and values. It has become fashionable, particularly in England, to attempt to overcome the problems of exposition by treating the subject as if it started afresh from the 1925 reform legislation enacted in England. In Ireland there is no such clear divide between the "modern " law and the "old" law and so such an approach would not be as easy to achieve, even if it were desirable. However, such an approach tends to impoverish a subject which ought properly to be treated historically if its richness is to be brought out. Land law provides an opportunity to study law an evolving social context. In many of the rules one can detect a change in interpretation over time and one which can be related to changes in social conditions or in moral values. An important part of understanding the law as it is applied today is understanding how it is different from the past. The underlying attitude in this book can, in that sense, be described as post-modern.

Some areas of land law are of less practical importance now than in the past and this must affect the way the subject is taught. Future interests and the rule against perpetuities were at one time regarded as the heart of land law. They are certainly one of the most complex areas of law in any subject. Today they can probably be regarded as a specialist interest, although solicitors still need to know enough about them to recognise problems involving future interests. However, the task of a textbook writer is not the same as a teacher, and this book contains a thorough coverage of future interests for those who wish to

1 Under the Constitution of 1937 Article 4 the name of the State is "Ireland." The Republic of Ireland Act, 1948 s 2 declares that the "description of the State shall be the Republic of Ireland." However, it is arguable that this is inconsistent with Article 4, despite the attempt to distinguish between the "name" of the State and its "description". The drafters of the Act might have avoided this possible objection by spelling "Republic" with a small "r".

pursue the subject. Problems on perpetuities still arise, as in the case of the transfer of ownership of the common areas in blocks of flats, options in leases to purchase the freehold and shared ownership leases. Indeed, the whole of the law on future interests ought to be reformed, if only for the sake of students who may still have to grapple with its complexities. The need for reform is evident, and long overdue, in other areas as well, such as legal tenancies in common, and the Statute of Uses, 1634, which is still with us after more than three centuries.

A preface also provides an opportunity to an author to mention problems encountered in research. The Interpretation Act, 1937 makes it clear that where a statute repeals the whole or part of a previous statute, the repeal does not have the effect of reviving the earlier law which applied before the affected statute. Although the statute goes on to deal with some specific situations, there is no explicit provision as to the effect of repealing a statute which itself amends, rather than repeals, sections of an earlier statute. For example, the Housing Act, 1966 was extensively amended by the Housing Act, 1970. The Housing Act, 1970 was itself repealed by the Housing (Miscellaneous Provisions) Act, 1992. One assumes that the amendments to the 1966 continue in force, although the sections which enacted them are no longer themselves in force, and this is the implication of the general rule, but a specific rule on the point would be useful. Furthermore, in terms of legislative style, it would be preferable to leave the amending sections in place until a statute codifying the law in the area can be enacted. Another problem of legislative style is posed by the Housing (Private Rented Dwellings) Act, 1982. The statute repeals earlier rent restriction legislation, but reference still has to be made to the repealed sections in order to determine whether a "dwelling" comes within the 1982 Act. It should not be necessary to refer to repealed sections to establish the current law.

Anyone who writes on Irish land law must acknowledge a debt to John Wylie, whose book *Irish Land Law* first appeared in 1975. It is to be hoped that the subject will benefit from having more than one view on this area of law. The scope of the present work is somewhat different from Wylie's book. As to Northern Ireland, while the present book notes points of difference between the law in this jurisdiction and both Northern Ireland and England and Wales, it does not attempt a full statement of the law in Northern Ireland. On the other hand, it does cover the important area of family or domestic property law which is also a matter of current debate in this jurisdiction. I have also included chapters on planning and housing law, the latter being a somewhat neglected subject up to this point.

The law is that in force at 31st December 1993. One or two developments between then and the date of this preface are worth mentioning. The National Monuments (Amendment) Bill, 1993 has now been enacted as the National Monuments (Amendment) Act, 1994. Barr J in the High Court has delivered a landmark judgment in *Re the Sailing Vessels "La Lavia", "Juliana" and "Santa Maria de la Vision"*, unreported, July 26th, 1994 in which the judge holds that ancient wrecks belong in the realm of archaeological law rather than within commercial maritime law. Although a full consideration of the case would fall outside the scope of the present text, it deserves such consideration elsewhere.

I should like to thank Kenneth Casey and Tom Cooney for reading parts of the draft and for their comments, John O'Dowd, for many comments and suggestions made in the course of writing the book and my friend Victor Akonta for his encouragement over a long period. I should also like to thank Dr Christopher Sherrin for permission to quote from his PhD thesis, Kenneth Nicholls for references on Irish legal history, Dr Nicholas Williams for references to Irish linguistic materials and Alexei Sayle for permission to use his definition of a mortgage. Kenneth Detheridge kindly allowed me to use his set of the English Reports from time to time. Finally, I should like to thank Mr Justice Blayney for his kind remarks in his Foreword to the book.

Andrew Lyall
Cabinteely
4th October 1994.

PREFACE TO THE SECOND EDITION

In the six years that have passed since the first edition of this work there has been a steady accretion, in the metaphorical sense, of case and statute law. One has to note, so far as the Republic is concerned, that it has not been as radical as that in Northern Ireland, where the form of legislation though orders in council has not faced the same constraints as to parliamentary time as is the case in the Republic. New sections have been added to increase the coverage of Northern Ireland and to take account of the Property (Northern Ireland) Order 1997 and other orders such as the Children (Northern Ireland) Order 1995 and the Succession (Northern Ireland) Order 1996.

Nevertheless, the years since the last edition have seen much legislation which affect land law in the Republic, including the Family Law Act, 1995, the Domestic Violence Act, 1996 and the advent of divorce in the form of the Family Law (Divorce) Act, 1996. The important and long neglected area of cultural property law has seen the passing of the Heritage Act, 1995, the National Cultural Institutions Act, 1997, and the Architectural Heritage (National Inventory) and Historic Monuments (Miscellaneous Provisions) Act, 1999. The problems of the long-suffering travelling community have also been addressed by the Housing (Traveller Accommodation) Act, 1998. The habit of passing legislation which is to be brought into force by ministerial order increases problems of the legal researcher, particularly where different parts of an Act are brought into force at different times, the latter statute being a case in point. It also raises the awkward jurisprudential status of legislation that is an Act, not a Bill, since has been enacted, but is not in force until the orders are made.

A great improvement has nevertheless been made in solving the problems of the legal researcher by the issue by the Attorney General of all legislation and subsidiary legislation in the form of CD ROM. One also welcomes the proposal to incorporate amending legislation into an officially updated version, hopefully available on the Internet.

Some 250 case references have been added to the text, some older authorities and many new decisions. Areas such as landlord and tenant, registration, mortgages, easements and succession continue to generate case law. Proprietary estoppel now seems firmly established in the Republic by the decisions in *Smyth v. Halpin* [1997] I.L.R.M. 38 and *McCarron v. McCarron*, unreported, Supreme Court, 13 February 1997. Some new sections have been added, such as that on future easements. In Chapter 26 contracts, proprietary estoppel, the rule in *Strong v. Bird* and donatio mortis causa have been grouped together to form a new major subdivision of succession which has been called "informal or non-testamentary succession", as distinct from testamentary and intestate succession. Some pruning has been necessary to make room for the new material, since the book is already bulky enough. The former Appendix A, which was a reprint of an article I wrote on the purchaser's equity, has had to go, and the old Appendix B on future interests in Ireland before 1877 will not be missed by many.

The law is that force at the end of December 1999 as far as materials allow, although one or two changes since the end of 1999 have been incorporated, namely the Housing (Registration of Rented Houses) (Amendment) Regulations, 2000 (SI 12 of 2000) and the Housing (Traveller Accommodation) Act, (Commencement) Order, 2000 (SI 37 of 2000), which brings the last part of that Act into force. It has not been possible to wait for the Planning Bill, 1999 to complete its legislative stages, but proposals in the Bill as initiated have been included in Chapter 27 on planning law and Chapter 28 on housing law.

Many colleagues have contributed useful comments which have been taken into account in the preparation of the present edition. I should like to thank in particular John O'Dowd, Oonagh Breen and Kevin Costello of the Faculty of Law and those members of the legal profession who have written to me, sometimes to point out what I choose to regard as a few inevitable errors. It would be hypocritical to pretend that gratitude was the first feeling I experienced at such moments, but at least we are still on speaking terms. I am also grateful to the staff of the Library of University College Dublin, particularly Tony Eklof and Norma Jessop.

Andrew Lyall
Cabinteely
18 June 2000.

TABLE OF CONTENTS

CHAPTER 8

CHAPTER 9

CHAPTER 10

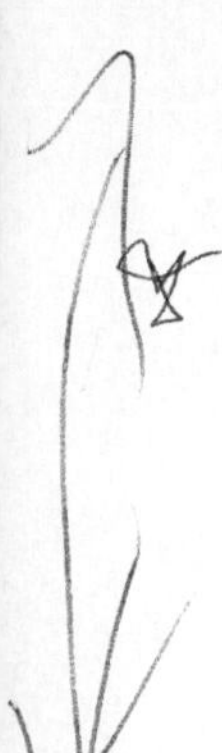

CHAPTER 11

CHAPTER 12

CHAPTER 13

CHAPTER 14

CHAPTER 15

CHAPTER 16

CHAPTER 17

CHAPTER 18

CHAPTER 19

CHAPTER 20

CHAPTER 21

CHAPTER 22

CHAPTER 24

CHAPTER 25

CHAPTER 26

CHAPTER 27

CHAPTER 28

TABLE OF STATUTES

STATUTES OF THE PARLIAMENT OF IRELAND (PRE-UNION)

[Note: Short titles are those given by the Short Titles Act, 1962, or, failing that, as where a statute was repealed before 1962, the short title is that conventionally employed in the past. Failing that, the regnal year citation is used, preceded by a description of the content of the statute. See also the Statute Law Revision (Pre-Union Irish Statutes) Act, 1962.]

STATUTES OF THE PARLIAMENTS OF ENGLAND & GREAT BRITAIN (PRE-UNION)

STATUTES OF THE PARLIAMENT OF THE UNITED KINGDOM OF GREAT BRITAIN & IRELAND (DURING THE UNION)

STATUTES OF THE OIREACHTAS OF SAORSTÁT ÉIREANN (IRISH FREE STATE) & THE OIREACHTAS (POST-1922 ACTS)

NORTHERN IRELAND LEGISLATION

[Note: The list includes statutes of the Parliament of Northern Ireland and Orders in Council made under the UK Northern Ireland (Temporary Provisions) Act, 1972, numbered as Statutory Instruments, which have effect as statutes of the Parliament of Northern Ireland. Northern Ireland subsidiary legislation made under Orders in Council, known as Statutory Rules, are included in the Table of Subsidiary Legislation]

STATUTES OF THE PARLIAMENT OF THE UNITED KINGDOM OF GREAT BRITAIN AND NORTHERN IRELAND (POST 1922 STATUTES)

LEGISLATION OF THE EUROPEAN UNION

OTHER LEGISLATION

GERMANY

NEW SOUTH WALES

SOUTH AUSTRALIA

SWITZERLAND

TABLE OF ARTICLES OF THE CONSTITUTION

ARTICLES OF THE CONSTITUTION OF 1922 (SAORSTÁT ÉIREANN: IRISH FREE STATE)

ARTICLES OF THE CONSTITUTION OF 1937

ALPHABETICAL LIST OF STATUTES

Note: Where the regnal year citation is not enclosed in brackets, there is no official short title of the statute. Where necessary, statutes are identified by the parliament which passed them, *e.g.* "Ir" (Pre-Union Irish parliament), "GB" (Pre-Union British parliament), "UK" (Post-1922 British parliament).

Accumulations Act, 1800 (39 & 40 Geo III c 98, GB)
Accumulations Act, 1892 (55 & 56 Vict c 58)
Acquisition of Land (Assessment of Compensation) Act, 1919 (9 & 10 Geo V c 57)
Act of Union (39 & 40 Geo III c 67)
Administration of Estates Act, 1833 (3 & 4 Wm IV c 104)
Administration of Estates Act, 1869 (32 & 33 Vict c 46) (Hinde Palmer's Act)
Administration of Estates Act, 1959 (No. 8)
Administration of Estates Act, 1955, NI
Administration of Estates Act, 1925, UK
Administration of Justice Act, 1707 (6 Anne c 10, Ir)
Administration of Justice Act, 1970, UK
Administration of Justice Act, 1973, UK
Administration of Justice Act, 1977, UK
Administration of Justice Act, 1982, UK
Adoption Act, 1952 (No. 25)
Age of Majority Act, 1985 (No. 2)
Aids, 1350, 25 Edw III st 5 c 11
Aids for Knighthood, Statute of Westminster I, 1275, c 36
Air Navigation and Transport Act, 1936 (No. 40)
Air Navigation and Transport Act, 1988 (No. 15)
Ancient Monuments Protection Act, 1882 (45 & 46 Vict c 73)
Appeal of Murder, 1819, 59 Geo III c 46
Appellate Jurisdiction Act, 1876 (39 & 40 Vict c 59)
Architectural Heritage (National Inventory) and Historic Monuments (Miscellaneous Provisions) Act, 1999 (No. 19)
Assignment of Leases, Ireland, 1832, 2 & 3 Wm IV c 17
Bill of Rights, 1689 (1 Wm & Mar sess 2 c 2, GB)
Building Control Act, 1990 (No. 3)
Building Societies, 1836, 6 & 7 Wm IV c 32
Building Societies (Amendment) Act, 1986 (No. 36)
Building Societies Act, 1874 (37 & 38 Vict c 42)
Building Societies Act, 1989 (No. 17)
Building Societies Act, 1967, NI
Casual Trading Act, 1980 (No. 43)
Cestui que Vie Act, 1665 (19 Chas II c 6, GB)
Cestui que Vie Act, 1707 (6 Anne c 72, GB)
Chancery (Ireland) Act, 1867 (30 & 31 Vict c 44)

Chancery Amendment Act, 1858 (21 & 22 Vict c 27)
Charities Act, 1960 (No. 17)
Chief Rents Redemption (Ireland) Act, 1864 (27 & 28 Vict c 38)
Church Temporalities Act, 1833 (3 & 4 Wm IV c 37)
City and County Management (Amendment) Act, 1955 (No. 12)
Civil Bill Courts, Ireland, 1851, 14 & 15 Vict c 57
Civil Evidence Act, 1968, UK
Common Law Procedure Act, 1852 (15 & 16 Vict c 76)
Common Law Procedure Amendment Act, Ireland, 1853 (16 & 17 Vict c 113)
Common Law Procedure Amendment Act, Ireland, 1870 (33 & 34 Vict c 109)
Companies (Amendment) Act, 1982 (No. 10)
Companies (Amendment) Act, 1983 (No. 13)
Companies Act, 1963 (No. 33)
Competition Act, 1991 (No. 24)
Competition (Amendment) Act, 1996 (No. 19)
Congested Districts Board (Ireland) Act, 1899 (62 & 63 Vict c 18)
Consumer Credit Act, 1974, UK
Consumer Credit Act, 1995 (No. 24)
Continental Shelf Act, 1968 (No. 14)
Contingent Remainders Act, 1877 (40 & 41 Vict c 33)
Conveyance by Release Act, 1841 (4 & 5 Vict c 21)
Conveyancing (Strata Titles) Act, 1961, Aus, NSW
Conveyancing Act, 1881 (44 & 45 Vict c 41)
Conveyancing Act, 1882 (45 & 46 Vict c 39)
Conveyancing Act, 1892 (55 & 56 Vict c 13)
Conveyancing Act, 1911 (1 & 2 Geo V c 37)
Conveyancing Act, 1919, Aus, NSW
Copyhold Act, 1841 (4 & 5 Vict c 35)
Copyhold Act, 1894 (57 & 58 Vict c 46)
Corruption of Blood Act, 1814 (54 Geo III c 145)
Council Directive 85/337/EEC OJ No L175/40, 5th July 1985, EU
Court of Probate Act (Ireland), 1859 (22 & 23 Vict c 31)
Courts Act, 1971 (No. 36)
Courts of Justice Act, 1924 (No. 10)
Courts of Justice Act, 1936 (No. 48)
Criminal Justice Act, 1953, NI
Criminal Law Act, 1997 (No. 14)
Criminal Law (Suicide) Act, 1993 (No. 11)
Criminal Procedure Act, 1951, NI
De Donis Conditionalibus, 1285, Statute of Westminster II, 1285 c 1
Deasy's Act, 1860, see Landlord and Tenant Law (Amendment) Act, 1860
Debt for Rent Service, 1710, 9 Anne c 8, Ir
Declaratory Act, 1719, 6 Geo I c 5, GB
Derelict Sites Act, 1990 (No. 14)
Distress for Rent Act, 1712 (11 Anne c 2, Ir)
Distress for Rent Act, 1741 (15 Geo II c 8, Ir)
Distress for Rent Act, 1751 (25 Geo II c 13, Ir)

Domestic Violence Act, 1996 (No. 1)
Domicile and Recognition of Foreign Divorces Act, 1986 (No. 24)
Dower Act, 1833 (3 & 4 Wm IV c 105)
Ejectment, 1731, 5 Geo II c 4, Ir
European Communities Act, 1972 (No. 27)
Evicted Tenants Act, 1907 (7 Edw VII c 56)
Exchequer Equitable Jurisdiction (Ireland) Act, 1850 (13 & 14 Vict c 51)
Executors Act, 1830 (11 Geo IV & 1 Wm IV c 40)
Factories Act, 1955 (No. 10)
Family Home (Protection of Spouses and Children) Act, 1981 (No. 21)
Family Home Protection Act, 1976 (No. 27)
Family Law (Divorce) Act, 1996 (No. 33)
Family Law (Maintenance of Spouses and Children) Act, 1976 (No. 11)
Family Law Act, 1981 (No. 22)
Family Law Act, 1995 (No. 26)
Fee Farm Rents (Ireland) Act, 1851 (14 & 15 Vict c 20)
Finance Act, 1894 (57 & 58 Vict c 30)
Finance Act, 1972 (No. 19)
Finance Act, 1994 (No. 13)
Fines and Recoveries (Ireland) Act, 1834 (3 & 4 Wm IV c 92)
Fisheries (Amendment) Act, 1997 (No. 23)
Fisheries (Consolidation) Act, 1959 (No. 14)
Fisheries and Foreshore (Amendment) Act, 1998 (No. 54)
Foreshore (Amendment) Act, 1992 (No. 17)
Foreshore Act, 1933 (No. 12)
Forestry Act, 1946 (No. 13)
Forfeiture Act, 1870 (33 & 34 Vict c 23)
Forfeiture Act, 1982 (UK)
Government of Ireland Act, 1920 (10 & 11 Geo V c 67)
Grantees of Reversions Act, 1540 (32 Hen VIII c 34) (Eng)
Grantees of Reversions Act, 1634 (10 Chas I sess 2 c 4) (Ir)
Ground Game Act, 1880 (43 & 44 Vict c 47)
Guardianship of Infants Act, 1964 (No. 7)
Heritage Act 1995 (No. 4)
Hinde Palmer's Act, see Administration of Estates Act, 1869
Housing (Gaeltacht) Act, 1929 (No. 41)
Housing (Gaeltacht) Act, 1934 (No. 29)
Housing (Ireland) Act, 1919 (9 & 10 Geo V c 45)
Housing (Miscellaneous Provisions) Act, 1979 (No. 27)
Housing (Miscellaneous Provisions) Act, 1992 (No. 18)
Housing (Miscellaneous Provisions) Act, 1997 (No. 21)
Housing (Private Rented Dwellings) Act, 1982 (No. 6)
Housing (Private Rented Dwellings) (Amendment) Act, 1983 (No. 22)
Housing Act, 1966 (No. 21)
Housing Act, 1969 (No. 16)
Housing Act, 1970 (No. 18)
Housing Act, 1984 (No. 1)
Housing Act, 1988 (No. 28)
Housing Finance Agency Act, 1981 (No. 37)
Illusory Appointments Act, 1830 (11 Geo IV & 1 Wm IV c 46)

Improvement of Land Act, 1864 (27 & 28 Vict c 114)
Incumbered Estates Act, 1848 (11 & 12 Vict c 48)
Incumbered Estates Act, 1849 (12 & 13 Vict c 77)
Inheritance Act, 1833 (3 & 4 Wm IV c 106)
Interest on Money, 1703, 2 Anne c 16, Ir
Interest on Money, 1721, 8 Geo I c 13, Ir
Interest on Money, 1731, 5 Geo II c 7, Ir
Intestates' Estates Act, 1890 (53 & 54 Vict c 29)
Intestates' Estates Act, 1954 (No. 12)
Intestates Estates Act, 1884 (47 & 48 Vict c 71)
Irish Appeals, 1783, 23 Geo III c 28, GB
Irish Church Act, 1869 (32 & 33 Vict c 42)
Irish Church Act (1869) Amendment Act, 1872 (35 & 36 Vict c 90)
Irish Church Act Amendment Act, 1881 (44 & 45 Vict c 71)
Irish Land Act, 1903 (3 Edw VII c 37)
Irish Land Act, 1907 (7 Edw VII c 38)
Irish Land Act, 1909 (9 Edw VII c 42)
Irish Land Commission (Dissolution) Act, 1992 (No. 25)
Judgment Mortgage (Ireland) Act, 1850 (13 & 14 Vict c 29)
Judgment Mortgage (Ireland) Act, 1858 (21 & 22 Vict c 105)
Judgments (Enforcement) Act, 1969, NI
Judgments (Ireland) Act, 1844 (7 & 8 Vict c 90)
Judgments (Ireland) Act, 1849 (12 & 13 Vict c 95)
Judicial Separation and Family Law Reform Act, 1989 (No. 6)
Labourers' Act, 1936 (No. 24)
Land Act, 1923 (No. 42)
Land Act, 1931 (No. 11)
Land Act, 1939 (No. 26)
Land Act, 1946 (No. 12)
Land Act, 1953 (No. 18)
Land Act, 1965 (No. 2)
Land Act, 1984 (No. 24)
Land Improvement Act, 1735 (9 Geo II c 7, Ir)
Land Law (Ireland) Act, 1881 (44 & 45 Vict c 49)
Land Law (Ireland) Act, 1896 (59 & 60 Vict c 47)
Land Registration Act, 1970, NI
Land Registration Act, 1925, UK
Land Registry Act, 1862 (25 & 26 Vict c 53)
Land Transfer (Ireland) Act, 1848 (11 & 12 Vict c 120)
Land Transfer Act, 1875 (38 & 39 Vict c 87)
Land Transfer Act, 1897 (60 & 61 Vict c 65)
Landed Estates Court, 1858, 21 & 22 Vict c 72
Landed Property (Ireland) Improvement Act, 1860 (23 & 24 Vict c 153)
Landed Property Improvement (Ireland) Act, 1847 (10 & 11 Vict c 32)
Landlord and Tenant (Amendment) Act, 1971 (No. 30)
Landlord and Tenant (Amendment) Act, 1980 (No. 10)
Landlord and Tenant (Amendment) Act, 1984 (No. 4)
Landlord and Tenant (Amendment) Act, 1989 (No. 2)

Landlord and Tenant (Amendment) Act, 1994 (No. 20)
Landlord and Tenant (Ground Rents) (No. 2) Act, 1978 (No. 16)
Landlord and Tenant (Ground Rents) Act, 1967 (No. 3)
Landlord and Tenant (Ground Rents) Act, 1978 (No. 7)
Landlord and Tenant (Ground Rents) (Amendment) Act, 1983 (No. 20)
Landlord and Tenant (Ground Rents) (Amendment) Act, 1987 (No. 12)
Landlord and Tenant (Ireland) Act, 1826 (7 Geo IV c 29)
Landlord and Tenant (Ireland) Act, 1870 (33 & 34 Vict c 46)
Landlord and Tenant (Reversionary Leases) Act, 1958 (No. 2)
Landlord and Tenant Act, 1851 (14 & 15 Vict c 25)
Landlord and Tenant Act, 1931 (No. 55)
Landlord and Tenant Law (Amendment) Act, 1860 (23 & 24 Vict c 154)
Law of Distress Amendment Act, 1908 (8 Edw VII c 53)
Law of Property (Amendment) Act, 1859 (22 & 23 Vict c 35)
Law of Property (Amendment) Act, 1860 (23 & 24 Vict c 38)
Law of Property (Miscellaneous Provisions) Act, 1989, UK
Law of Property Act, 1922, UK
Law of Property Act, 1925, UK
Leases Act, 1634 (10 Chas I sess 3 c 6, Ir)
Leases Act, 1849 (12 & 13 Vict c 26)
Leases Act, 1850 (13 & 14 Vict c 17)
Legal Practitioners (Ireland) Act, 1876 (39 & 40 Vict c 44)
Life Estates Act, 1695 (7 Wm III c 8, Ir)
Life Peerages Act, 1958, UK
Limitation Act, 1939, UK
Limitations, 1623, 21 Jas I c 16, GB
Local Government (Ireland) Act, 1898 (61 & 62 Vict c 37)
Local Government (No. 2) Act, 1960 (No. 40)
Local Government (Planning and Development) Act, 1963 (No. 28)
Local Government (Planning and Development) Act, 1976 (No. 20)
Local Government (Planning and Development) Act, 1982 (No. 21)
Local Government (Planning and Development) Act, 1983 (No. 28)
Local Government (Planning and Development) Act, 1990 (No. 11)
Local Government (Planning and Development) Act, 1992 (No. 14)
Local Government (Planning and Development) Act, 1993 (No. 12)
Local Government (Planning and Development), Act, 1999 (No. 17)
Local Government (Roads and Motorways) Act, 1974 (No. 6)
Local Government (Sanitary Services) Act, 1964 (No. 29)
Local Government Act, 1946 (No. 24)
Local Government Act, 1991 (No. 11)
Local Government Financial Provisions Act, 1978 (No. 35)
Local Registration of Title (Ireland) Act, 1891 (54 & 55 Vict c 66)
Locke King Acts, see Real Estate Charges Acts, 1854, 1867, 1877
Lord Cairns' Act: Chancery Amendment Act, 1858 (21 & 22 Vict c 27)
Lord Cranworth's Act, 1860 (23 & 24 Vict c 145)
Magna Carta, 1215 (16 John)
Magna Carta, 1225 (9 Hen III c 18)

Magna Carta Hiberniae (18 John c 39)
Manor Courts Abolition (Ireland) Act, 1859 (22 Vict c 14)
Manorial Courts, 1785, 25 Geo III c 44, Ir
Manorial Courts, 1787, 27 Geo III c 22, Ir
Manorial Courts, 1795, 36 Geo III c 25, Ir
Manorial Courts, 1804, 44 Geo III c 90
Married Women's Property Act, 1882 (45 & 46 Vict c 75)
Married Women's Status Act, 1957 (No. 5)
Master of the Rolls (Ireland) Act, 1801 (41 Geo III c 25)
Matrimonial Causes and Marriage Law (Ireland) Amendment Act, 1870 (33 & 34 Vict c 110)
Merchant Shipping (Salvage and Wreck) Act, 1993 (No.34)
Minerals Development Act, 1940 (No. 31)
Minerals Development Act, 1979 (No. 12)
Mining Leases Act, 1723 (10 Geo I c 5, Ir)
Moneylenders Act, 1900 (63 & 64 Vict c 51)
Moneylenders Act, 1933 (No. 36)
Mortmain (Repeal of Enactments) Act, 1954 (No. 32)
Mortmain (Repeals) Act, 1960, NI
National Cultural Institutions Act, 1997 (No. 11)
National Monuments (Amendment) Act, 1954 (No. 37)
National Monuments (Amendment) Act, 1987 (No. 17)
National Monuments Act, 1930 (No. 2)
Notices to Quit (Ireland) Act, 1876 (39 & 40 Vict c 63)
Office Premises Act, 1958 (No. 3)
Ormonde, Duke of, 8 & 9 Wm III c 5, 1697 (Eng) (private).
Partition, 1540, 32 Hen VIII c 32 (Eng)
Partition, 1542, 33 Hen VIII c 10 (Ir) Partition Act, 1868 (31 & 32 Vict c 40)
Partition Act, 1876 (39 & 40 Vict c 17)
Pawnbrokers Act, 1964 (No. 31)
Perpetuities Act, 1966, NI
Perpetuities and Accumulations Act, 1964, UK
Petroleum & Other Minerals Development Act, 1960 (No. 7)
Popery, 1703, 2 Anne c 6, Ir
Powers of Appointment Act, 1874 (37 & 38 Vict c 37)
Poyning's Act, 1495 (10 Hen VII c 22, Ir)
Prescription (Ireland) Act, 1858 (21 & 22 Vict c 42)
Prescription Act, 1832 (2 & 3 Wm IV c 71)
Probates and Letters of Administration Act (Ireland), 1857 (20 & 21 Vict c 79)
Prohibition of Forcible Entry and Occupation Act, 1971 (No. 25)
Public Health (Ireland) Act, 1878 (41 & 42 Vict c 52)
Quia Emptores, 1290, Statute of Westminster III, 1290 cc 1, 2
Real Actions, Statute of Gloucester, 1278 c 7
Real Estate Charges Act, 1854 (Locke King's Act) (17 & 18 Vict c 113)

Real Estate Charges Act, 1867 (Locke King Act) (30 & 31 Vict c 69)
Real Estate Charges Act, 1877 (Locke King Act) (40 & 41 Vict c 34)
Real Property Act, 1845 (8 & 9 Vict c 109)
Real Property Act, 1858, Aus, S Aus
Real Property Limitation Act, 1833 (3 & 4 Wm IV c 27)
Real Property Limitation Act, 1874 (37 & 38 Vict c 57)
Record of Title (Ireland) Act, 1865 (27 & 28 Vict c 88)
Redemption of Rent (Ireland) Act, 1891 (54 & 55 Vict c 57)
Registration of Deeds (Amendment) Act, 1967, NI
Registration of Deeds Act, 1707 (6 Anne c 2, Ir)
Registration of Deeds Act, 1709 (8 Anne c 10, Ir)
Registration of Deeds Act, 1721 (8 Geo I c 15, Ir)
Registration of Deeds Act, 1785 (25 Geo III c 47, Ir)
Registration of Deeds Act, 1970, NI
Registration of Title Act, 1942 (No. 26)
Registration of Title Act, 1964 (No. 16)
Registry of Deeds (Amendment) (Ireland) Act, 1822 (3 Geo IV c 116),
Registry of Deeds (Amendment) (Ireland) Act, 1832 (2 & 3 Wm IV c 87)
Renewable Leasehold Conversion (Ireland) Act, 1868 (31 & 32 Vict c 62)
Renewable Leasehold Conversion Act, 1849 (12 & 13 Vict c 105)
Rent Restrictions (Amendment) Act, 1967 (No. 10)
Rent Restrictions (Temporary Provisions) Act, 1981 (No. 26)
Rent Restrictions Act, 1946 (No. 4)
Rent Restrictions Act, 1960 (No. 42)
Repeal of Criminal Statutes, 1828, 9 Geo IV c 53
Repealing Act, 1782, 22 Geo III c 53, GB
Riot Act, 1787 (27 Geo III, c 15, Ir)
Roads Act, 1993 (No. 14)
Safety in Industry Act, 1980 (No. 9)
Satisfied Terms Act, 1845 (8 & 9 Vict c 112)
Settled Estates Act, 1856 (19 & 20 Vict c 120)
Settled Estates Act, 1876 (39 & 40 Vict c 30)
Settled Estates Act, 1877 (40 & 41 Vict c 18)
Settled Land Act, 1882 (45 & 46 Vict c 38)
Settled Land Act, 1884 (47 & 48 Vict c 18)
Settled Land Act, 1890 (53 & 54 Vict c 69)
Settled Land Act, 1925, UK
Settlement of Ireland Act, 1634 (10 Chas I c 3, Ir)
Settlement of Ireland Acts, 1634 (10 Chas I sess 3 cc 2, 3, Ir)
Settlement of Ireland Act, 1639 (15 Chas I sess 2 c 6, Ir)
Settlement of Ireland Act, 1665 (17 & 18 Chas II c 2, Ir)
Settlement of Ireland Act, 1695 (7 Wm III c 3, Ir)
Short Titles Act, 1962 (No. 5)
Shrubs and Trees, 1791 (31 Geo III c 40, Ir)
State Authorities (Development and Management) Act, 1993 (No. 1)
State Property Act, 1954 (No. 25)

Turf Development Act, 1946 (No. 10)
Usury Act, 1634 (10 Chas I sess 2 c 22, Ir)
Usury Laws Repeal Act, 1854 (17 & 18 Vict c 90)
Vendor and Purchaser Act, 1874 (37 & 38 Vict c 78)
Wills (Soldiers and Sailors) Act, 1918 (7 & 8 Geo V c 58)
Wills Act, 1837 (7 Wm IV & 1 Vict c 26)
Wills Act Amendment Act, 1852 (15 & 16 Vict c 24)

TABLE OF CASES

Stewart's Estate, Re (1893) 31 LR Ir 405. . . . 128, 129n., 130n., 498, 498n., 783n.

Stileman v Ashdown (1737) 2 Atk 477, 26 ER 688 . . . . 434n.

Stilwell v Blackman [1968] Ch 508 . . . . 700n.

Stoneham, Re [1919] 1 Ch 149. . . . . 994n.

Strangways, Re (1885) 34 Ch D 423 . . . . 390n.

Strathblaine Estates Ltd, Re [1948] Ch 228 . . . . 85n.

Stratheden and Campbell, Re Lord [1894] 3 Ch 265. 318

Street v Mountford [1985] 1 AC 809, [1985] 2 All ER 289, [1985] 2 WLR 877, 50 P & CR 258, 274 EG 821, [1985] 1 EGLR 128, [1985] Conv 328, [1986] Conv 39 . . . . 565, 575, 576

Strong, Re [1940] IR 382 . . . . 846n.

Strong v Bird (1874) LR 18 Eq 315. 988

Stroud's Case (1572) 3 Dyer 313a, 73 ER 709. 48n.

Stuart v Babington (1891) 27 LR Ir 551 . . . . 376n.

Stuart v Easton (1898) 170 US 383, 42 L Ed 1078, 18 S Ct 650 . . 82n., 87n.

Studdart v Von Steiglitz (1889) 23 LR Ir 564 . . . . 228n.

Sturge v Hackett [1962] 3 All ER 166 . . . . 38n.

Sturgeon v Wingfield (1846) 15 M & W 224, 15 LJ Ex 212, 153 ER 831 . . . . 593n

Sturolson & Co v Weniz (1984) 272 EG 326 . . . . 576n

Sugden v Lord St Leonards (1879) 1 PD 154 . . . . 930, 930n., 931, 931n.

Supatone (Eire) Ltd, Re [1973] ILTR 105. . . . . 265n

Sutton's Hospital, Case of (1612) 10 Co Rep 1a, 23a, 77 ER 937, 960. 109n

Sutton v Temple (1843) 12 M & W 52, 152 ER 1108. 613

Swanton v Gould (1860) 9 Ir CLR 234 . . . . 731n.

Sweeney v Denis (1883) 17 ILTR 76 589

Sweeney v Duggan [1997] 2 ILRM 211, Supreme Court 720

Sweeney v Powerscourt Shopping Centre, unreported, High Court, Carroll J, 6 June 1984 . . . . 633n

Sweet v Anderson (1772) 2 Bro PC 256, 430, 1 ER 927, 2 Eq Cas Abr 211, 477, 22 ER 180, 405. . . . . 255, 258, 330n.

Sweetman v Sweetman (1868) IR 2 Eq 141 . . . . 956n

Swift v Kelly (1889) 24 LR Ir 107, QB, 478. . . . . 218n., 759n.

Swiney, Re (1858) 6 Ir Ch R 455 . . . . 935n.

ABBREVIATIONS

Abr Cas	See Cr & Dix Ab Ca.
Al & N	Alcock & Napier's Reports, Irish King's Bench, Exchequer Chamber, 1831–33.
Alc & Nap	See Al & N.
All ER	All England Reports, 1936–(current).
All ER Reprint	All England Reports Reprint, 1558–1935.
Arm M & O	Armstrong Macartney & Ogle, Irish *Nisi Prius*, 1840–42.
B & B	Ball & Beatty's Reports, Irish Chancery, 1802–9.
Ba & B	See B & B
Ball & B	See B & B.
Bat	Batty's Reports, Irish King's Bench, 1825–26.
Beatty	Beatty's Reports, Irish Chancery, 1814–30.
Bl D & Osb	Blackham, Dundas & Osborne, Irish *Nisi Prius*, 1846–48.
CA	Court of Appeal.
Cal St Pap Ir	Calendar of State Papers of Ireland, London: HMSO. Various dates.
Camb L J	Cambridge Law Journal.
Co Litt	Coke on Littleton.
Colum L Rev	Columbia Law Review.
Cr & Dix	Crawford & Dix Circuit Reports, 1839–46
Cr & Dix Ab Ca	Crawford & Dix Abridged Notes of Cases, Law & Equity, 1837–38.
Davies	Davies Reports, Irish King's Bench, 1604–1612.

Drew	Drewry's Vice Chancellors' Reports, 1852–59.
Dru & Wal	Drury & Walsh's Reports, Irish Chancery during the time of Lord Chancellor Plunket, 1837–41.
Dru & War	Drury & Warren's Reports, Irish Chancery during the time of Lord Chancellor Sugden, 1841–43.
Dru t Nap	Drury *tempore* Napier: Drury's Reports at the time of Lord Napier, Irish Chancery, 1858–59.
Dru t P	Drury *tempore* Plunket: See Dru & Wal.
Dru t Sug	Drury *tempore* Sugden: Drury's Reports, Irish Chancery during the time of Lord Chancellor Sugden, 1843–44.
DULJ	Dublin University Law Journal (Trinity College Dublin).
EIAR	Environmental Impact Assessment Regulations.
EIS	Environmental impact statement.
Eng Hist Rev	English Historical Review.
F & S	Fox & Smith's Reports, Irish King's Bench, 1822–24.
FL	FirstLaw number (unreported judgments)(followed by number).
Fl & K	Flanagan & Kelly's Reports, Irish Rolls Court, 1840–42.
Frewen	Frewen's Reports, Court of Criminal Appeal, Ireland, 1924–89.
Glas	Glascock's Reports, 1831–32.
H & B	See Hud & Br.
H & J	Hayes & Jones' Reports, Irish Exchequer, 1832–34.
Harv LR	Harvard Law Review.
Hayes	Hayes' Reports, Irish Exchequer, 1830–32.
HEL	Holdsworth's *History of English Law*.
HL	House of Lords.

HLC	Clark's House of Lords Cases, 1847–66.
Hud & Br	Hudson & Brooke's Reports, Irish King's Bench, 1827–31.
ILRM	Irish Law Reports Monthly, 1980–(current).
ILTSJ	Irish Law Times and Solicitor's Journal.
IR	Irish Reports, 1894–(current)
IR [vol] CL	Irish Reports, Common Law Series, 1866–78.
IR [vol] Eq	Irish Reports, Equity Series, 1866–77.
Ir Ch R	Irish Chancery Reports, 1850–66.
Ir Cir Rep	Cases on the Six Circuits (Irish Circuit Reports), 1841.
Ir CLR	Irish Common Law Reports, 1849–66.
Ir Eq R	Irish Equity Reports, 1838–51.
Ir Jur (os)	Irish Jurist (old series), 1849–66.
Ir Jur Rep	Irish Jurist Reports, 1935–current.
Ir LR	Irish [Common] Law Reports, 1838–50.
Ir WLR	Irish Weekly Law Reports, 1895–1902.
J & B	Jebb & Bourke's Reports, Queen's Bench, 1841–2.
J & S	Jebb & Symes's Reports, Queen's Bench, 1838-41.
Jebb & B	See J & B.
Jebb & S	See J & S.
Jo	Jones's Reports, Irish Exchequer, 1834–38.
Jo & Ca	Jones & Carey's Reports, Irish Exchequer, 1838–39.
Jo & La T	Jones & La Touche's Reports, Irish Chancery, 1846–49.
L & T	Longfield & Townsend's Reports, Irish Exchequer, 1841–42.

Law Rec (ns) Irish Law Recorder, new series, 1833–38.

Law Rec (os) Irish Law Recorder, old series, 1827–31.

Ll & G t P Lloyd & Goold *tempore* Plunket: Lloyd & Goold's Irish Chancery Reports at the time of Lord Chancellor Plunket, 1834–39.

Ll & G t Sug Lloyd & Goold *tempore* Sugden: Lloyd & Goold's Irish Chancery Reports at the time of Lord Chancellor Sugden, 1835.

Longf & T See L & T

LQR Law Quarterly Review.

LR Ir Law Reports of Ireland, 1878–93.

Lyne Lyne's Leases for Lives, appendix, 1716–1837.

MacCarthy MacCarthy's Land Purchase Cases.

MacDevitt MacDevitt's Irish Land Cases , 1882–84.

Mich L Rev Michigan Law Review.

Minn L Rev Minnesota Law Review.

MLR Modern Law Review.

Moll Molloy's Reports, 1827–31, Irish Chancery.

NI Northern Ireland.

NIJB Northern Ireland Judicial Bulletin.

RI Republic of Ireland.

Ridg L & S Ridgway, Lapp and Schoales, Irish King's Bench, 1793–95.

Ridg P C Ridgway's Parliamentary Cases, Irish House of Lords, 1784–96.

Rowe Rowe's Interesting Cases (English & Irish), King's Bench, 1798–1823.

Sausse & Sc Sausse & Scully' Reports, Irish Chancery, 1837–40.

Sch & Lef Schoales & Lefroy's Reports, Irish Chancery, 1802–6.

Shepp Touch Sheppard's Touch-stone of Common Assurances, 6th edition, London: 1791.

SLRA Statute Law Revision Act.

Sm & Bat Smith & Batty's Reports, Irish King's Bench, 1830.

U Pa L Rev University of Pennsylvania Law Review.

Ver & Scr Vernon and Scriven's Reports, Irish King's Bench, 1786–88.

Wyl Cas Wylie *Cases*: J C W Wylie *A Casebook on Irish Land Law* Abingdon: Professional Books, 1984.

GLOSSARY

Note: Many phrases in land law are from Law French, the language of the courts until the seventeenth century. Law French, being medieval French with added legal vocabulary, did not use accents, but accents and modernised spellings have crept into some phrases. See J H Baker *A Manual of Law French* 2nd edition. 1990.

agistment a licence to use land for pastoral purposes.

alienate dispose of or create an interest in land by sale, lease, mortgage, etc.

base fee the estate which is produced when a fee tail is barred only as to the issue in tail but not as to the remainders or reversions due to take effect after the end of the entail. An estate which, like the fee simple, is alienable and will pass on intestacy to the intestate successors of the holder for the time being, but which will last only so long as the original entail would have lasted, *i.e.* until the issue in tail of the original donee in tail die out.

bona vacantia (Latin: "vacant goods"). Goods without an owner. At common law *bona vacantia* belonged by prerogative to the Crown. A similar right is assumed to vest such property in the State in the Republic.

cestui que use (Law French: the person who uses. Originally "cestuy") the person who is to have the use under a feoffment. The equivalent in the law of uses of a beneficiary under a trust.

cestui que vie (Law French: the person who lives) the person whose life is the measure of the duration of an estate *pur autre vie*.

common law remainder rules rules at common law applicable to freehold estates and controlling the types of remainders which can be created. They are mainly concerned to enforce the feudal policy that a lord should always be able to identify the tenant of the land. See "remainder."

conacre the right created by contract, and peculiar to Irish law, to till land owned by and in the possession of another, together with the right of access to the land. The owner has the right to retain the crop until payment by the conacre holder.

concurrent lease a lease granted to take effect at the same time as an existing lease and which has the effect of replacing the landlord/grantor with the grantee of the concurrent lease who therefore becomes the new landlord of the existing tenant. It has the same meaning as "lease of the reversion" and should not be confused with "reversionary lease", *q.v.*

cy-pres (Law French: "near to it"). The doctrine which allows a court to redraft a limitation which is void. Its main effect is in the law of charities, but it has a limited application in the Old Rule against perpetuities. It has not been applied in Ireland in the Modern Rule against perpetuities, although some States in the United States have done so.

disentailing assurance the conveyance still required in Ireland to turn a fee tail into a fee simple estate. If done successfully it bars the right of the issue in tail and any person entitled in remainder or reversion to inherit the estate and thus renders the land freely alienable. The deed is made under the Fines & Recoveries (Ireland) Act, 1834.

escheat right of a feudal lord to retake land when freehold tenure came to an end.

estoppel a doctrine, originally of the law of evidence, by which, on proof of certain facts, a party is debarred from pleading some further fact. Proprietary estoppel gives rise to property rights, for example, where A has led B to believe that A will confer a property interest on B and B has acted in reliance on the assurance in such a way that B will suffer a detriment if A is not compelled to make good the assurance. On proof of this, A is estopped from denying that B has the interest, and may be compelled to transfer the interest to B.

estate 1. interest in land considered from the point of view of its duration. Freehold estates are of uncertain duration measured by human lives. Leasehold estates are of certain duration, or consist of a succession of certain periods, such as a tenancy from week to week. 2. The property of a deceased person. 3. An area of land, as in "country estate" or "housing estate."

estate of inheritance a fee simple or fee tail estate.

executory interest future interest arising under the Statute of Uses and which is thereby exempt from the common law remainder rules.

fee farm grant, estate in fee farm a fee simple held subject to a rent. There are three kind kinds of such interests in Ireland: 1. Those which create freehold tenure between the grantor and successors in title and the grantee and successors in title (*i.e.* grants *non obstante Quia Emptores*, 1290), 2. Those which create leasehold tenure, and 3. Those which create no tenure at all, the rent being in the form of a separate rentcharge.

fee simple the largest of the freehold estates in land. On intestacy a fee simple devolves upon the intestate successor(s) (in the past, upon the "heirs") of the deceased holder, who may be descendants (children, grandchildren), ascendants (parents, etc), or collaterals (cousins) depending upon the situation at the death of the holder. The holder may, however, freely alienate the estate during his/her life or by will. Thus the intestate successors do not have a right to inherit (except that now the Succession Act, 1965, gives certain rights to spouses and children where a testator dies possessed of a fee simple or other property and the will cannot override them).

fee tail, or estate tail, or entail An estate which will pass to the descendants of the original donee. Descent is traced from the original donee in tail, who may not be the current holder of the estate. The donee may not alienate the estate during his/her life or by will. But fees tail may be "barred," *i.e.* turned into a fee simple, in most cases. In Ireland this cannot be done by will, but only by an *inter vivos* disentailing assurance (*qv*) under the Fines & Recoveries (Ireland) Act, 1834.

fine 1. a lump sum of money legally payable. 2. a collusive action used before the Fines & Recoveries (Ireland) Act, 1834 partially to bar an entail, resulting in a base fee. See "recovery."

foreclosure procedure whereby the equity of redemption of a mortgage is declared to be at an end, resulting in the mortgagee becoming entitled to the estate in the land free of the mortgage. It is never granted in Ireland .

gale, gale day the day on which a periodic payment of rent is due. The expression is peculiar to Irish law. A 'hanging gale' denotes payment in arrear. It became notorious in Ireland as a means by which landlord would hold the threat of eviction constantly over tenant farmers.

hereditament property passing to the heir-at-law at common law. Property held for an estate of inheritance.

inter vivos between living persons. Used to describe a disposition of property other than by will.

interesse termini (Latin: an "interest in the term"). At common law a leasehold estate did not vest in the tenant until he or she actually entered the land. Until then the tenant had a mere *interesse termini.* The doctrine may have been abolished by Deasy's Act, 1860.

issue in tail the descendants of the original donee of a fee tail, *i.e.* the persons who are entitled to inherit the fee tail.

laches (Law French: "delay". Pronounced "laychiz"). The equitable doctrine that "delay defeats equity" so that the court will not grant a remedy if the claimant has delayed for too long.

lease for lives an estate *pur autre vie* in which the measuring lives are plural and the holder pays a rent to the owner of the reversion in fee simple. Such leases in Ireland often had a covenant for perpetual renewal of the lives and for the payment of a fine by the tenant for lives on renewal. The Irish courts developed an equity to renew the lives even after the contractual date for doing so had passed. "Lease" is a misnomer as the estate is not leasehold, nor, on the better view, is the tenure. "Lease" is used because it had come to be associated with the holding of land at a rent and leases for lives were often held at a rent, *i.e.* they were commercial, not family, interests.

lease of the reversion See concurrent lease.

legal executory interest a new class of future interests made possible by the Statute of Uses, 1634 and which do not have to comply with the common law remainder rules.

limitation 1. words in a deed conferring interests in land. 2. the period within which an action must be brought in court.

nuncupative oral, of wills.

overreach the process by which certain interests affecting the title to land are converted, on sale of the land, into interests in the purchase money.

particular estate an estate less than a fee simple and which precedes a remainder. The phrase was originally used in connection with the common law remainder rules (*q.v.*) which required a remainder to follow immediately upon the end of the particular estate, *i.e.* normally the preceding life estate. It is now sometimes used to mean any estate less than a fee simple.

per stirpes (Latin: "by the stirrups"). It refers to a method of distribution of property where persons entitled die leaving issue entitled to divide their parent's share among them, rather than being entitled to share equally with all others entitled. Thus if A, B and C are entitled to property, but B dies leaving P, Q and R and C dies leaving issue X and Y, then distribution is *per stirpes* if P, Q and R divide B's share between them and X and Y divide C's share, rather than P, Q, R, X and Y all taking equal shares. The phrase comes from the shape which is made by a diagram of the relationship of X and Y to C. Contrast *per capita.*

per capita (Latin: "by the heads"). It refers to the method of dividing property equally among a group of people who are treated as a distinct class. Contrast *per stirpes.*

pernor of the profits (pernor is from French *prendre,* to take) old-fashioned phrase for the person taking the profits of land, used to refer to the person entitled to the profit of a rentcharge. See "terre tenant".

profit à prendre (modernised Law French: "a liberty to take [something]." Originally "profit apprendre") The right to enter someone's land and take from it something capable of ownership, such turf, fish from a river, or sand.

pur autre vie (modernised Law French: "for another life." Originally, and more correctly, "pur *auter* vie"). A freehold estate in which the land is held for the life of someone other than the holder of the estate, *e.g.* "to A for the life of B."

que estate (Law French "whose [or which] estate" pronounced "kway"). The estate for the benefit of which an easement is acquired by prescription, *i.e.* the dominant tenement. Easements, since they are property rights and not personal rights, must exist against a servient tenement for the benefit of a dominant tenement. A debased phrase derived from Law French – the prescriber acquires the easement for the benefit of the estate "que il ad" (*i.e.* "which he has").

recovery a collusive action used before the Fines & Recoveries (Ireland) Act, 1834 to bar an entail.

remainder an estate granted to begin after the first estate conferred by the same grant has come to an end.

rent seck (Law French: "dry" rent). A rent paid where there is no remedy of distress and therefore, originally, no tenure between the parties.

rent service Originally, the rent payable on freehold land to the feudal lord as the service of the tenure. By analogy it has been applied to the rent paid by a leasehold tenant to a landlord, and in this sense means a rent paid where the parties are in the relationship of landlord and tenant.

rentcharge an annual payment charged on land. It is a separate property interest and not part of any tenurial relationship between the holder of the land and the holder of the rentcharge.

reversion what is left of a fee simple after a lesser estate, such as a life estate, has been created out of it. It also refers to the rights of a freeholder after a lease has been created out of the freehold, or the right of a leaseholder after a sub-lease has been created out of the head lease. It therefore refers to the right to resume possession after a lesser estate has terminated, and also the rights which the holder of the greater estate enjoys in the meantime, *e.g.* rent.

reversionary lease a lease granted to take effect at the end of the present lease.

reversioner in fee person entitled to the freehold reversion.

seignory the interest of a feudal lord in land which is held in freehold tenure in fee simple from him. It included both the services and the incidents of tenure, especially the right of escheat (*q.v.*) *i.e.* the right to recover possession if the fee simple came to an end by the tenant dying without heirs or being convicted of felony.

tenure 1. a continuing relationship between the grantor of an interest in land and his or her successors and the grantee and his or her successors which involves mutual obligations, such as to pay rent or to repair, etc. Tenure in this sense is either freehold, which is now rarer, or leasehold. 2. In a looser sense, the conditions under or terms on which land is held, including national laws affecting land ownership.

terre tenant	(Law French "land" tenant). The freehold tenant in possession. The person liable to pay a rentcharge.
ventre sa mere, en	(Law French: "in his/her mother's womb"). Used of a child which is in the womb, but unborn.

CHAPTER 1
INTRODUCTION

"Whilst there is much appeal in the philosophy – From each according to his ability, to each according to his need", (Karl Marx – Criticism of the Gotha Programme) it is not an aid to statutory construction."

– McCarthy J in *Quirke v. Folio Homes Ltd* [1988] ILRM 496.

A. Land Law and Real Property

This is a book about land law. "Land" includes buildings and other things attached to land. Partly for that reason, this area of law is also known as the law of "real property", although the term is less common now than in the past. "Real" is from the Latin *res* meaning "thing". Real property, or as it is still called today, "realty", included freehold interests and leasehold interests in land while all other property, comprising moveables, was "personal property" or "personalty". In the past there were some important differences between real and personal property. Until the 19th century there were different writs which began actions in court. Real property descended to the heir-at-law of a deceased person on intestacy whereas personal property passed to the next-of-kin. Today, under the Succession Act, 1965 there is no such distinction and all property on intestacy passes to the intestate successors under Part VI of the 1965 Act.

According to the common law system, the subject of ownership is not land directly but estates and interests in land. One of the achievements of the common law system of land ownership is precisely this interposition of the doctrine of estates and interests between the owner and the physical object of ownership. It has given greater flexibility than systems based on the notion of a single "owner" with all other rights taking effect as rights less than ownership. At the same time, and this is a point which will be noted from time to time in the course of the book, there is a tendency to think of the estates and interests as if they were things and as having inherent qualities of their own.

Personal property is also sometimes called chattels, a word which has the same origin as the word "cattle." This is no accident, for cattle were the most important kind of personal property in the Middle Ages. Leasehold property developed at a later stage, in the Tudor period, and it came to be classified as chattels real, as opposed to personal property which is not land, and which, by contrast, is called pure personalty. A special action known as ejectment was introduced to allow a tenant who had been ousted to recover the leasehold. In the case of pure personalty it used to be the case that only its market value and not the property itself could be recovered, but this rule has been abolished and so there is less reason today to distinguish pure personalty from other kinds of property. Furthermore, the purely procedural distinctions between the different types of property are no longer significant.

B. Reification: From Explanation to Exposition

People, including judges, often speak as if property was a thing, or the attribute of a thing. We say "my book". The book has the quality of being mine, just as it has a certain colour or size. We might also say "my lease", or "X owned a lease of the house". In this case the lease appears to be a thing in itself, whereas a closer examination reveals that it is in reality a number of rights, duties or powers which a lessee has in relation to a landlord, and vice versa, and which may also affect third parties. Newspapers often have "Property supplements" which list houses as the "properties" for sale. Yet what we really mean is that X has certain rights in relation to that land. What is in reality a legal relationship is represented as if it were a thing, a distinct entity separate from X or the people in relation to whom X has these rights and powers. Property relations are represented as things and are thought of as if they were indeed things.

This tendency to reify interests, to represent them or think of them as things, is something to be resisted. Property law is not the study of things but of relationships: relationships of power between individuals in society. Property rights, whether in terms of private property or communal property, are essentially political in a broad sense. They represent a particular distribution of power over land. They therefore require to be justified on the basis of some wider political and moral theories. That is not to say that an examination of political theory is within the scope of this book, but those who study property law must be able to see through the illusion of reifying vocabulary so that they can be aware of the issues of justice and theories of distribution that lie beyond. It is then for the reader to decide whether the decisions of the judges in the case law is persuasive or is morally defensible or accords with the reader's own view of justice.

There is, it has to be admitted, a certain amount of explanation in this book which concentrates on the logical implications of rules and it is unavoidable if the rules themselves are to be understood. The book nevertheless aims to move from explanation to exposition, from explaining the rules in a technical sense to an exposition of the real issues that lie beneath them.

The tendency to reify interests in land also makes property law more difficult and less interesting for students to learn because it induces them to believe that they are trying to grasp by some intuitive process the inherent qualities of property concepts and that how well they deal with property problems is determined by how well they have grasped these essential qualities. In fact these "qualities" are no more than choices made by judges or legislators about how rights and duties should be distributed and choices necessarily involve social values. It disguises as facts what are in reality normative statements about how society ought to be organised. By disguising these choices reification has another effect. It serves to inculcate the political or moral values on which these choices are based in the student when he or she may not be fully aware that this is being done. It disarms a critical approach to the rules.

Many of these issues are in the realm of political theory and a full discussion of them lies outside the scope of this book. What this book does aim to do, however, is to indicate that such issues are immanent in property rules and principles, to show that issues of justice and social policy lie buried in rules that apparently have little or no relation to them. To expose the reified concepts in real property is to expose the real social issues that lie beneath them. This act of exposure naturally and properly leads to a discussion of issues of justice, to a critique of the way in which rights in property are distributed and therefore whether the law needs to be changed.

C. The Social Concept of Property and the Legal Concept

One of the contradictions in property concepts in Ireland is between, on the one hand, the concept of property as understood by most people in society – what we may call the "social concept of property" – and, on the other hand, the strictly legal concept of property as embodied in the rules of law applicable to land, buildings, etc. – what we may call the "legal concept of property."

The social concept of property is not something which came into being all at once. It is a product of the historical experience of Irish people. That historical experience is now just beyond living memory although it is a period which is painful to contemplate. It was nevertheless so powerful that the experience, and the reaction to it, has shaped the ideas which people have today about their homes or their farms. That experience was, until the end of the 19th century, the experience of insecure titles, of agricultural tenants who were mere "tenants at will" and of landlords who cared little about their tenants except for the rent they paid. It was an experience of lack of incentives to improve land and of no reward for doing so.

The reaction against this was naturally enough a demand for security of tenure, for substantial rights of ownership instead of the instability of tenancy at will. The reforms at the end of the 19th century, beginning effectively with Gladstone's Act, 1881[1], aimed to meet these demands by giving security of

1 Land Law (Ireland) Act, 1881.

tenure to tenants, and providing the alternative of voluntary sale of the freehold to the tenant with State aid. It also established the Irish Land Commission[2] to carry out the process. The popular concept of outright, or absolute, ownership of land as a desirable aim became a realistic one and took another major step forward after 1922 with the enactment of the Land Act, 1923 which vested compulsory powers of acquisition in the Land Commission.

This attitude, long felt in relation to agricultural land, has in recent years been transferred to the increasingly urban environment of property-owning today. This is reflected in the high percentage of home-ownership in Ireland. Many people wish to own their own home and are prepared to accept a considerable reduction in their disposable income in order to pay for it. Owning one's own home usually carries with it an expectation that one will acquire something in the nature of an absolute right, or at least a right free of other private interests. The legal position, however, does not necessarily accord with the aspiring home owner's expectations. Ground rents were unpopular for this reason. People moving from the rented sector to home ownership did not expect to continue paying rent, however small. Many people would also be surprised to learn that, while they are buying their house with a mortgage, the freehold interest is vested in the mortgagee until the end of the repayment period and that in the meantime they have only an equity of redemption. This divergence of the social concept of property from the prevailing legal concept may be a source of legal reform.

D. Private Property and Communal Property

When we talk of the legal concept of property it must be borne in mind that the actual rules in the statutes concerning property and the rules as contained in judgments delivered by the judges speak only occasionally in abstract terms like "common property" or "private property." More usually they use the technical language of property developed by lawyers over a long period of time. There is also a distinction between private property on the one hand and common or communal property on the other. Both of these concepts exist as social concepts and as legal concepts.

Everyone in our society is familiar with the notion of private property. But there are also forms of common or communal property. In one sense this is easy to grasp. Parks, botanical gardens etc. may be thought of as communal property and in some respects they are. But communal property also exists in another sense: in a way which only shows itself as a limitation on private property. One example is the powers of planning authorities. Another is the protection the law gives through various means to cultural property: archaeological artefacts and sites which people justifiably regard as in some sense theirs, but

2 See Chapter 15.

theirs not in the sense that they can take them home and use or study them exclusively: that would be private property. They regard it as theirs rather in the sense that they have some sort of right to see them displayed in a place to which the public has access, such as a museum, and to study them either personally, or through the work of scholars, and this also means that scholars must have access to them. They must be protected from destruction. These ideas can only be explained if we are treating them as having actual legal force, as a type of property qualifying or modifying the right of private property owners.

E. Basic Concepts in the Common Law System of Land Law

"It is one of the maxims of the civil law that definitions are hazardous."

– Dr Samuel Johnson, *Rambler* No. 125 p.1.

1. Ownership and Possession

The notion that there is only one true owner of land so that other persons necessarily have rights less than full ownership is absent from the common law system of land law.[3] One does not, in the common law system, own land, rather one may own various types of estates and other interests in law, and more than one such interests can exist in the same piece of land at the same time. This is probably the main advantage of the common law system. Interposing the concept of the estate between the legal subject and the land itself gives greater flexibility than a single-owner system.

The common law developed in a feudal system of land tenure. Under that system land was held in a series of hierarchical relations between lords and tenants. Everyone held land of someone else in return for services. When land changed hands it normally did so on the death of the tenant or of the lord and their interest passed to their relatives. Land tenure was therefore clearly seen for what it was, a relation between individuals, or, often, between families, consisting of mutual obligations and rights. It was difficult to think of property as a thing separate from these mutual obligations and so a concept of absolute ownership was largely absent.

As the market economy developed within feudal society the nature of land ownership changed. Land, which had previously passed from generation to generation on death or marriage now came more often to be sold. Land became progressively freed from the rights of the feudal superior and from the obligations of tenure. Over a long period of time the law of property became more adapted to market relations and the courts played their part in the change, alter-

3 In the past it may have been true to say that the Crown in England or Ireland owned land in the royal demesne. This topic is pursued in Chapter 3 Tenure.

ing or reinterpreting old rules. Thus, while the system of property law superficially remained the same, its substance changed to express and give effect to the new economic relations. It became easier to think and talk as if property were a thing, an attribute attaching itself to successive owners through market transactions. The vendor lost all contact with the land sold and the purchaser acquired rights in relation to the public at large rather than in relation to the feudal lord. With the decline of tenure the concept of estate became reified so that it became easier to think of a fee simple as a thing which one owns.

This mystification of property law also explains why land law is often not a popular subject with students. It is not popular because it is taught in a reified form. It all seems to be metaphysics with little or no relation to real life or to actual relations between people, detached from social life and from history. The solution is often seen as making land law more relevant to the modern world and in so doing ignoring or glossing over the historical aspects. Yet the result of ignoring the historical explanations if often to increase the sense of detachment. We therefore feel that the historical explanations have to be made and they have to be deciphered, that is to say, they have to be de-mystified, de-reified so that they can be seen in their true light as the solutions to the practical social problems even if they are the practical problems of past ages. The system of land law we have today would never have been produced by rational planning. It was produced by historical evolution and can only be understood by understanding its history.

"Substantive law", said Maine, is "secreted in the interstices of procedure".[4] Nowhere is this more true than in the concepts of possession and title at common law. Yet a study of this topic of procedures underlines many of the points we have just made. The actions in the courts were actual disputes between people to which the courts had to find solutions and the practical considerations of what effect a decision would have, of who would be bound by it, came first, and the abstract concepts of ownership came second and were framed by the practicalities.

2. Actions to Recover Land

The common law originally made a fundamental distinction in its remedies. If one sued to recover moveable objects then even if one succeeded the defendant was left with a choice: he or she could return the object or its equivalent in money. The law regarded money as the equivalent of the thing. It took no regard of sentimental value. It was economic value which it took to be real.

4 Sir Henry Maine, *Early Law and Custom* p.389: "So great is the ascendancy of the Law of Actions in the infancy of Courts of Justice, that substantive law has at first the look of being gradually secreted in the interstices of procedure." See also Maitland, *Forms of Action* p.1.

In this sense the common law from the earliest time regarded things a commodities. It regarded things as things-in-exchange, as the subject of exchange transactions of an economic nature. If you obtain the value of the thing, you could go out and buy an identical one. The liability was satisfied. This was the position in what were known as the personal actions, *i.e.* types of proceedings to recover personal property.

On the other hand when it came to land the common law recognised that land was different in that every plot of land occupies a unique space. It also varies in fertility, which was probably of more interest to the early common lawyers living as they did in an agricultural society. They therefore developed a distinct set of actions in which one sued to recover land, or rather interests in land, in which the right to possess the land could be recovered – the land itself in reified language. These were the real actions, so-called because they resulted in the return of the *res*, the thing.

a) The Real Actions

(1) Writ of Right

The first and most ancient of the real actions was the Writ of Right. It became increasingly encrusted with procedural complications over the centuries, which increased its cost and although this made it more attractive to lawyers, it made it less so for litigants. It also had some archaic indeed primitive features. Originally it had to be brought in the court of the lord of the tenure, not the King's court. The defendant could enter *essoins* or excuses for not appearing and these could be used to frustrate the *demandant*, as the plaintiff in a real action was known. Most serious of all, the defendant in the action could offer trial by battle as a means of resolving the dispute, a primitive rule which was not finally abolished until 1819.[5] In the reign of Henry II a more rational alternative to trial by battle was introduced. This was the grand assize in which the case was tried by twelve knights of the shire and was the origin of the jury.

The writ of right did have one characteristic that is still relevant to the question of possession and title. Although the demandant was allowed to delve back into the history of the title to prove his or her claim, the result of the action only bound the parties to it. This is fundamental, because when the procedure becomes abstracted into a concept it can be seen that title to land is relative. A decision in a dispute between A and B, to the effect that A has title and B does not, is only binding between A and B. It does not prejudice C who may at a

5 By 59 Geo III c.46 s.2. The statute was passed in response to *Ashford v. Thornton* (1818) 1 B & Ald 423, 106 ER 149. One Abraham Thornton claimed the right to trial by battle in an appeal of felony. Lord Ellenborough reluctantly held that the right still existed. The last case in which trial by battle was offered to settle a land dispute (writ of right) was *Claxton v. Lilbourn* (1638) Cro Car 522, 79 ER 1052. See Simpson, *History of Land Law* p.27.

later time be able to prove he or she has a title superior to that of A. In other words a decision between A and B in favour of A is only a decision that, as between A and B, A has a better title. It does not decide that A is the owner of the land in an absolute sense. In order to avoid the complications of the writ of right new forms of *possessory assizes* (or actions) were introduced in the reign of Henry II in the last quarter of the 12th century. The earliest of these was called *novel disseisin*. As the name suggests, it was based upon an allegation that the demandant had recently been dispossessed of his or her land. All the demandant had to do was to allege a possession prior to that of the tenant[6] and an act of dispossession, or *disseisin*, on the part of the tenant. It made no difference that the tenant was the true owner and had resorted to self-help to recover the land. Self-help was to be discouraged. It can be seen that the action had a public law function as well as a private law one in that it preserved the peace. This is also seen in the rule that the possessory assizes had to be brought in the royal courts.

(2) Novel Disseisin

Novel disseisin lay where the plaintiff personally had been disseised.[7] The plaintiff was essentially asserting that he or she had a *better right to possession* than the present tenant. The general replacement of the writ of right by novel disseisin as a means of vindicating rights to land therefore had as a consequence the establishment of the notion that right, or title, to land was not some absolute concept detached from factual possession, but consisted simply of a better right to possession.

(3) Mort d'Ancestor

Other possessory assizes were developed to protect possession in other situations and these also had effects upon the concept of title. *Mort d'ancestor* could be brought where the plaintiff had never possessed the land personally, but alleged that an ancestor had died and had been dispossessed by the defendant, the plaintiff claiming that they were rightfully entitled to possession having become entitled by inheritance to the title of their ancestor.[8] Thus, mort d'ancestor is the starting point of the notion that a title, as a right to possession, can be completely detached from any factual possession on the part of the claimant. In novel disseisin, the plaintiff was claiming that he or she ought to be put back into possession because they had in fact possessed the land before the defendant. In mort d'ancestor the plaintiff was claiming that he or she

6 The defendant was know as the tenant, since he or she was the person in possession.

7 The assize was provided for in Ireland in 1310 by 3 Edw II c.5 (Ir): "... that there shall be certain justices assigned to take the assizes of *mortdauncestor*, and of *novel disseisin*, in all the counties of Ireland...". For mention of the writ in Ireland, see *Calendar of State Papers, Ireland 1171–1251* No. 2379.

8 See footnote 7; *Calendar of State Papers, Ireland 1171–1251* p.344 No. 2314.

ought to be put into possession because they ought to have been in possession before the defendant. Possession as a fact and possession as title became truly distinct for the first time.

b) Seisin

The real actions were essentially actions to recover seisin. Seisin was the feudal concept of the right to possession. Only freeholders had seisin, even if the land was factually in the possession of an unfree tenant, such as a villein, or a tenant holding by an unfree tenure.[9] It followed that only freeholders could bring the real actions.[10] Those other than freeholders, who probably constituted the bulk of the population, were left to the lord's court. Since their claim might well be against the lord, this system effectively denied them access to an impartial tribunal. As we have seen, freeholders suffered from the same disability in actions over land before the assize of novel disseisin put them in the King's courts. Secondly, and this is of fundamental importance in the substantive law, the actions were tests of competing claims to seisin, and so only decided who, as between the parties to the dispute, had a better title. Seisin still remains part of the law in theory but to say today that someone is seised of land means little more than saying that no other person is in adverse possession.

c) Ejectment and Freeholders

The inconvenience of the real actions led freeholders to find ways in which they might avail of the more informal procedure by which to settle the claim of title. At first it seems that freeholders would actually grant leases in order to make use of the new procedure, but the court soon allowed an action by a fictitious leaseholder against a fictitious defendant. The creation of this fictitious action has been attributed to Chief Justice Rolle at the time of the Commonwealth.[11] The fiction was that the freehold plaintiff had granted a lease to one John Doe, the feigned lessee, who had then been evicted by Richard Roe, the casual ejector. In Ireland this character usually went under the alias of John Thrustout.

---

9 See below Chapter 3 Tenure.

10 See *Tamworth BC v. Fazeley T C* (1978) 77 LGR 238, Ch D; *Re Sirett (deceased)* [1968] 3 All ER 186, [1969] 1 WLR 60, 207 EG 527 Ch D.

11 Holdsworth 7 HEL 10; De Moleyns 8th ed. 432.

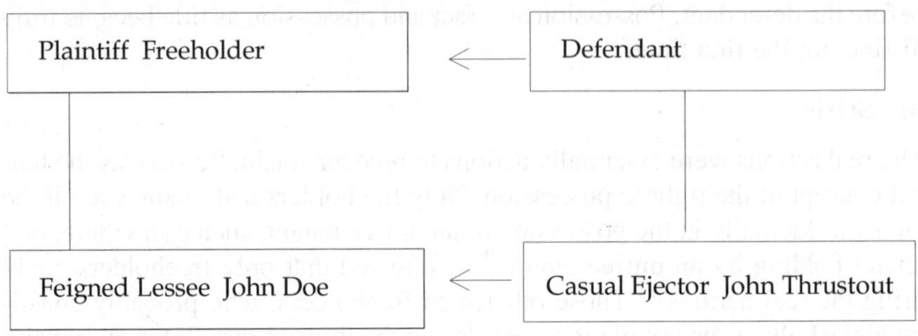

The plaintiff's solicitor began the action by sending a declaration in ejectment to the defendant's solicitor purporting to be an action by Doe against Thrustout alleging that Thrustout had ejected him from the land. To this declaration was attached a letter, purporting to be from Thrustout, to the defendant, advising him that he should defend the action in Thrustout's place, otherwise both Thrustout and he would be thrust out.[12] The freehold plaintiff was then permitted to defend the action in place of Thrustout but only if he admitted the lease, the entry of Doe and the ouster by Thrustout. The only issue at the trial was therefore whether Doe had a good title to the land and that resolved itself into whether the plaintiff, Doe's supposed landlord, had a better title than the defendant. The title of the action would be in the form *Doe* [fictitious lessee] on the demise of *A* [the true plaintiff] *v. B* [the true defendant], suing in place of Thrustout, the fictitious ejector. This was abbreviated to *Doe d A v. B*. But different styles existed. In Ireland it was common to refer to the plaintiff simply as the Lessee of A and the defendant as the Casual Ejector. It seems that in Ireland the fictitious action could be defended by a wider class of claimants than in England *i.e.* by anyone who had a legal or equitable estate, including an equity of redemption, in the land claimed,[13] probably for the reason that they could grant a lease. One of the drawbacks of the action was that it was not available to holders of a freehold interest, such as annuitants, who had less than an estate in the land.[14] The fictitious action was abolished from Trinity Term 1850 by two statutes.[15] The first Act provided that all personal actions should begin by a single writ of summons in the forms set out in the schedule. The writ

12 Forms of the documents are printed in Bl Com iii, appendix No. II.

13 *Boardman v. Greer* (1824) F & S (Ir) 55, notes; *Doe d Greene v. Casual Ejector* (1824) F & S (Ir) 56, notes.

14 *Lessee of Balfour v. Casual Ejector* (1786) Ver & Scr 98.

15 13 & 14 Vict. c.18 s.1 and 13 & 14 Vict. c.19 s.1. These statutes, dealing with procedure in the superior common law courts in Ireland, were never given official short titles. Furlong (1869) Vol. 2 p.956.

in the case of ejectment was simply to state "trespass and ejectment for non-payment of rent" or "on title" as the case might be. This reform on the face of it only affected the process by which personal actions should be started and the parties to them.

d) Abolition of the Forms of Action

(1) Real Actions

The real actions, with the exception of the writ of dower and related writs, were abolished in Ireland by the Real Property Limitation Act, 1833, section 36, which also abolished the mixed actions. The Act applied to Ireland except in relation to advowsons.[16] The writ of dower and related writs were abolished by the Common Law Procedure Amendment Act (Ireland), 1870.[17]

(2) Personal Actions

The next major step was that the personal actions themselves were abolished by the Common Law Procedure Amendment Act (Ireland), 1853. Section 5 abolished the old actions, while section 6 provided that there should be two forms of personal action in future, a general form and the action of ejectment.[18] The Act provided for the actions to be begun and tried in the manner set out in the Act.[19] Thus there remains in theory two separate forms of personal action in Ireland, but they are practically indistinguishable. One consequence of the reforms is that from 1853 onwards a plaintiff has not had to allege any fiction or engage in technical pleadings. All he or she has to do is to show a cause of action good in substance,[20] and it does not seem that the courts would strike down pleadings because they failed to state which of the two personal actions was being brought.[21] Although the old forms have been abolished, the substantive law has not fundamentally been affected, so that ejectment on title, or an action to establish title to land as it might now be called, still depends on trespass

16 *ibid.* s.44. For comments on the writ of assize see *Corporation of Dublin v. Herbert* (1863) 12 Ir CLR 502 at 512. At common law there was no action for debt to recover rent of land granted in freehold. A freehold rent service had to be recovered by the writ of assize or another real action. This made the recovery of rents difficult in the case of leases for lives which were popular – at any rate with landlords – in Ireland. The remedy was provided by 9 Anne c.8 (Ir), in England 8 Anne c.19. Thereafter the action of debt lay in such a case.

17 *Nolan v. Morgan* (1869) IR 4 CL 603; *Cranston v. Scott* (1869) IR 4 CL 481.

18 In England the Common Law Procedure Act, 1852 abolished the forms of action and replaced them by a single form of civil action. The 1852 Act did not apply to Ireland: s.236.

19 Section 6.

20 *Leslie v. Johnstone* (1861) 10 Ir CLR 83; *Gason v. Ryan* 7 Ir Jur 272.

21 *ibid.*

and prior possession. Prior possession is itself enough to sustain an action against a wrongful dispossessor.

> "In ejectment against a person who has entered forcibly without any title, evidence of possession is sufficient to entitle [the] Plaintiff to recover; and the plaintiff does not have to lose his right to recover possession by setting up a title which he fails to establish in proof."[22]

Prior possession is good against all who cannot show a better title.[23] Relativity of title still prevails in the action to recover land.

3. The Theory of Estates

Broadly speaking, tenure concerns the terms and conditions under which someone holds land; the doctrine of estates concerns the length or duration of the interest which a person has in land.

In the chapter on tenure we examine one kind of tenure: freehold tenure. The incidents and services of freehold tenure have declined to such an extent that it can hardly be detected at all. In most common law jurisdictions it has ceased to have significant practical effects. Much more common today is leasehold tenure or, which is perhaps a more accurate expression for the same thing, the modern relationship of landlord and tenant. Leasehold tenure or, which is the same thing, the relationship of landlord and tenant, may exist where there is a lease, *i.e.* a written document, but it may also exist where there is merely an oral agreement and then it usual to speak of a tenancy. Most books on the subject maintain the convention of using the expression "lord and tenant" to refer to freehold tenure and "landlord and tenant" or "the modern relationship of landlord and tenant" to refer to leasehold tenure.

Since estates concern the duration of an interest, the different estates can be ranked according to how long they are likely to last. The largest estate known to the common law, because it is the one which can last the longest time, is the *fee simple*. If A has a fee simple then when A dies (without making a will) it will pass to her intestate successors, *i.e.* the people designated by the Succession Act, 1965 to take the property on that event. Before the Succession Act,

---

22 *Davison v. Gent* (1857) 1 H & N 744, 156 ER 1400, per Bramwell B. Cited by Whiteside CJ in *Nagle v. Shea* (1875) IR 9 CL 389, Exch Ch affirming CP on the point on the will. Forcibly should be taken to mean without consent. There is no authority in the cases for a distinction between forcible entry and non-forcible but non-consensual entry. *Doe d Harding v. Cooke* (1831) 5 Moo & Pay 181, 131 ER 134; *Doe d Pitcher v. Anderson* (1816) 1 Stark 262, 171 ER 467. The majority judgment in the CP in *Nagle v. Shea* (1874) IR 8 CL 224, Monohan CJ dissenting, is at variance with authority. The majority held that the plaintiff could not bring ejectment because title was shown to be in a third party, thus allowing a *jus tertii* to succeed.

23 *Doe d Hughes v. Dyeball* (1829) Moo & Mal 346, 173 ER 1184; *Catteris v. Cowper* (1812) 4 Taun 547, 128 ER 444; *Roe d Haldane v. Harvey* (1769) 4 Burr 2484, 98 ER 302; *Doe d Johnson v. Baytup* (1835) 3 Ad & E 188, 11 ER 384.

1965 there were rules of the common law which designated the person or persons to take real property on intestacy known as the heir or heirs general. Personalty was inherited by the next-of-kin who might be a different person. The old rules also preferred males to females, so that if A has a son and two daughters, the son alone inherited the real property. Today, the rules as to intestate successors do not discriminate on grounds of sex and all children take equally. But to continue: when the intestate successor of A dies the fee simple will pass to that persons intestate successor, and so on, so long as the person holding the fee simple for the time being does not leave it by will or sell it. On the other hand A may leave her estate by will to X, in which case when X dies it will pass to X's intestate successors and so on. A may also alienate her estate, *i.e.* sell it, create leases out of it, etc. She may also create out of it either of the other two estates, the fee tail and the life estate. She may also create more than one these estates, or a combination of them, out of the fee simple. Such successions of estates, or settlements, are considered below.

The fee tail (from Law French *taillé* or cut down) is a lesser estate than the fee simple in a number of respects. First of all, if T is granted a fee tail it will pass on his death only to his children or, if they have died, to their children, *i.e.* to descendants only. These were known to the common law as heirs of the body and the old rules have been retained for the fee tail. A fee tail does not pass cousins or aunts or other collateral relatives. Thus a fee tail is a lesser estate because fees tail are, in general, of lesser duration than fees simple. Of course, a fee tail over plot A will not necessarily, as matters turn out, end before a fee simple over plot B, but it is, from the beginning, less likely to last as long. The fee tail estate is now rare. Its purpose was to facilitate landowning families keep land within their family over generations and played a central part in family settlements. For that reason so long as the fee tail remains unchanged it is inalienable. If T has a fee tail he may not sell it, nor can he dispose of it by will. As we shall see, methods were adopted by which a fee tail could be changed into a fee simple, *i.e.* barred, and so enable the holder of the land to alienate it again.

Even lower in the scale of estates is the life estate. Normally this exists, for example, when A holds for her own life. A modified form of life estate exists when A hold for the life of some other person, such as B. The law regards this as a lesser form of life estate known as an estate *pur autre vie*. In such a case B has no interest in the land. It is just that B's life is used as a measure of the duration of the estate. B is known as the *cestui que vie* (Law French for "the one who lives").

In addition to freehold estates, there are leasehold estates, but these are really only of two kinds: a definite period of time of any length in weeks, months or years, and periodic tenancies which are successive definite periods, such as a tenancy from week to week or from year to year, which will end when one party gives notice to the other. Lawyers often say that the difference between leasehold and freehold estates is that leasehold estates are for definite periods of time while freehold estates are for indefinite periods, *i.e.* human lives. But this neat distinction is not really true of periodic tenancies. Definitions are hazardous.

In most common law jurisdictions a freehold estate implies freehold tenure. Equally, in most common law jurisdictions a leasehold estate implies leasehold tenure, or a landlord and tenant relationship. The problem in Ireland is that it is possible to have hybrid interests in which a person has a freehold estate but leasehold tenure exists, an example being a leasehold fee farm grant in which the tenant has the fee simple estate but must still pay a rent to a person who in theory is a landlord. As we shall see, the relationship is in fact modified in such cases so that the landlord may not have all the remedies of an ordinary landlord, but the existence of such hybrid interests makes it difficult to define clearly the distinction between freehold and leasehold. This becomes easier, however, if one considers separately the estate and the tenure, and maintains the distinction in considering the various types of interests. One further cause of confusion is that one cannot even maintain strictly the notion that estate only concerns the duration of the interest while tenure concerns the quality of the interest, the terms and conditions under which it is held. For example, we shall see that a characteristic of the fee simple is that it is freely alienable and judges have stuck down conditions which attempt to restrict alienability of a fee simple, on the ground that this is repugnant to the estate. Yet alienability, *i.e.* the right to convey or dispose of property, is obviously something which affects the quality of ownership rights. Restrictions on alienability are more freely imposed by a landlord in a lease, since a landlord has a continuing and usually substantial interest in the land. The conflict between what is regarded as the quality of an estate and the nature of the tenure is again seen in Ireland in leasehold fee farm grants, and this controversy is dealt with in the section on fee farm grants.

One basic principle of estates is that there is always a fee simple in relation to any land. One minor possible exception is land held directly by the State in the Republic, and certainly land held by the Crown in Northern Ireland, but this point is pursued in the chapter on tenure. If, therefore, someone creates a fee tail, or a life estate, it is because they had a fee simple out of which the fee tail or life estate was created. This being so, since a life estate is a lesser estate than a fee simple, there remains a part of the fee simple vested in the grantor of the lesser estate. This is known as a *reversion*.[24] A reversion is a single interest in land, viewed in its reified form, but depending on the context the word may be used to refer to different aspects of such an interest. Thus it – the reified form – is in fact a number of different rights vested in the grantor. Thus even in its reified form it may be useful to represent it as having two different parts:

24 Co Litt 22b.

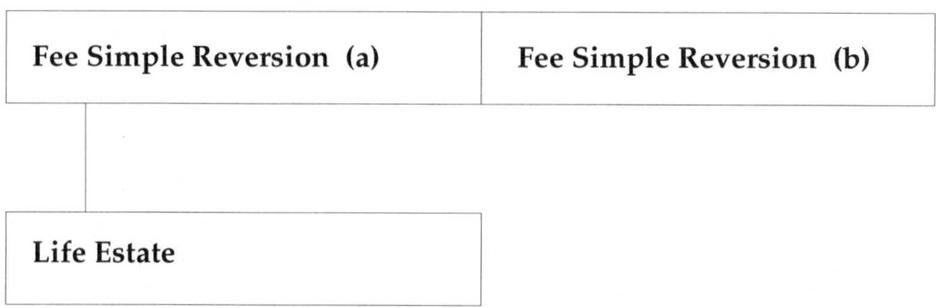

Reversion is sometimes used in sense (a) to mean the rights which the grantor has while the grantee (of the life estate in this example) is entitled to possession. This is seen as including the right to sell the reversion, to grant interests out of the reversion to take effect in possession after the life estate ends, and so on. In this sense, however, reversion is really the same thing as tenure. The grantor could, for example, reserve a rent on the grant of the life estate.[25] The rights to receive this rent is really a service of tenure. The right to sell the reversion in the sense of selling the right to possess the land at a future time is part of the reversion in the correct sense (b) and is the right to alienate a future interest.

Reversion in the sense of (b) would include the right to possession of the land when the life estate comes to an end. This is the accurate sense of reversion which does not confuse it with tenure. The land reverts to the grantor after the end of the life estate.

Again, the theory of estates is that a grantor can grant away any number of estates less than a fee simple and there still remains a part of the fee simple left over. So the grantor may grant a life estate followed by a fee tail, or a series of such estates to different people and, so long as the grantor does not end the series by a grant of the fee simple, the grantor retains a fee simple reversion:

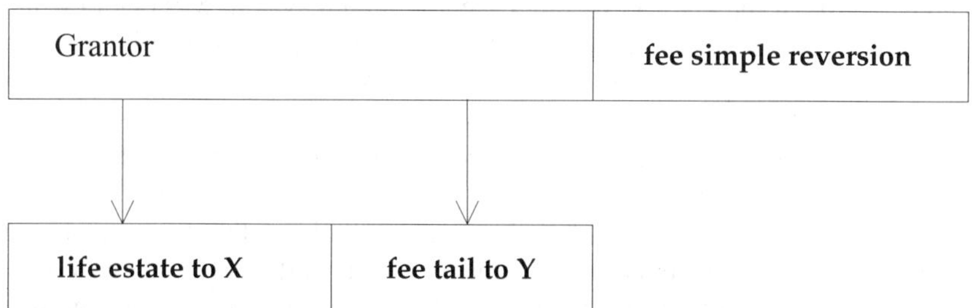

25 This would involve creating a layer of freehold tenure, one of the surviving examples of such tenure after the Statute *Quia Emptores*, 1290: see below Chapter 3 Tenure.

In this example there is a life estate to take effect at once, known as an estate in possession, or in old books, the *particular estate*, and a fee tail to take effect in future after the estate in possession, known as a *remainder*.[26] The word remainder is used in a technical sense: it is not necessarily all that remains of the fee simple. One can have more than one remainder, and a remainder or remainders followed by the reversion, as in this example. In fact the holder of a fee simple can grant any number of lesser estates, either retaining the fee simple reversion or ending with the grant of the fee simple in remainder. In this example, when X dies, the land goes to Y and his or her descendants. When they die out, the land goes to the grantor, or, since he or she will probably be dead, to the grantor's intestate successors, since the grantor's interest is a fee simple. In this example there is both a fee tail in remainder and a fee simple reversion.

The grantor may also grant away the fee simple in the same grant that creates the life estate and fee tail. If she does, then she has parted with all her estate. There will then be a remainder in fee simple to take effect after the prior estate has come to an end:

Grantor →	life estate to X	fee tail to Y	fee simple to Z

It follows from this that if there is a fee simple remainder there can be no reversion. There can be no reversion after a fee simple.[27]

4. Relativity of Title and Adverse Possession

We have already seen that the notion of a single owner is absent from the common law system of land law. The historical reasons for this may be found in the feudal origins of the law. As we shall see, the feudal system was one in which hierarchical social relations coincided with economic relationships to land. The legal expression of these relationships was found in the doctrine of tenure and estates. Although the feudal relations have gone, the basic concepts of land law are still marked by these basic concepts. The substance has changed, but many of the forms remain intact.

The common law system of land law is also relative rather than absolute in another sense and that concerns the concept of title. Title is the proof of one's right to a particular piece of land. If ownership was an absolute concept, then there would only be one title, the true title to the land. Legal disputes over title would simply be contests as to who could prove they had the true title. But the

26 Co Litt 49a.

27 Either before or after *Quia Emptores*, 1290: see Chapter 3 Tenure.

common law is not like this. It knows only relative titles to land.[28] If A sues B, claiming that B is occupying land that belongs to him, all that A has to prove is that he has a better title to the land than B. He does not have to show that he has the best or only title to it. Equally, B cannot resist A's claim merely by showing that C has the "true title." B cannot, in general, plead *jus tertii*, the right of a third party. The second point is that at common law titles are based ultimately upon the proof of prior possession. This has been consistently asserted by judges in Ireland:

> "The possession of land carries with it in general, by our law. . . in the absence of a better title elsewhere, the right to possess it also. . . the legal possession rests on a real *de facto* possession constituted by the occupier's general power and intent to exclude unauthorised interference."[29]

> "Possession, prima facie, is a title good against everyone who cannot prove a better title. . ." [30]

Suppose O occupies a piece of land. He is dispossessed by D. This can happen in a number of ways. Perhaps O has gone abroad and D is a squatter. Or a fence has been erected in the wrong place and D is occupying part of O's land. O can bring an action to claim back his land. To succeed all he has to prove is that he possessed the land before D and that D ousted him from possession.[31] But the law does not allow him to delay indefinitely. Under the Statute of Limitations, 1957 he has 12 years from the dispossession to claim his land back.[32] After that, his title to the land is extinguished.[33]

a) Before the Limitation Period Has Expired

We have seen that O can succeed in an action against D. But before that happens, what sort of right does D have in the land? None as against *O*. But as against Z, who comes along later and dispossesses D? The answer is that D can

---

28 *Perry v. Clissold* [1907] AC 73, 79; *Ocean Estates v. Pinder* [1969] 2 AC 19, [1969] 2 WLR 1359 (Privy Council). Kent McNeil, "Possession and Title to Land in English Law", Chapter 2, *Common Law Aboriginal Title* (Oxford: Clarendon, 1989).

29 Finlay CJ in *Webb v. Ireland* [1988] IR 353, [1988] ILRM 565, Henchy and Griffin JJ concurring. Citing *South Staffordshire Water Co v. Sharman* [1896] 2 QB 44, Lord Russell CJ in turn citing Pollock and Wright, *Possession in the Common Law.*

30 Palles CB in *Kennan v. Murphy* (1880) 8 LR Ir 285 at 293.

31 *Hamilton v. Marquess of Donegall* (1795) 3 Ridg PC 291, 323, Ir HL (possession alone allows a person to bring an action on the case); *Hume v. Tennyson* [1987] NI 139, [1987] 2 NIJB 12.

32 Statute of Limitations, 1957 s.13(2)(a).

33 *ibid.* s.24.

successfully bring trespass against Z,[34] because D has the better title. In an action based on trespass D only has to prove prior possession.[35]

The same is true of incorporeal hereditaments, such as a right of way: mere possession is enough to found an action against someone interfering with their exercise.[36] In an action of ejectment on title the defendant in possession can merely allege his possession and put the plaintiff to proof that he has a better right.[37] Possession is title as against someone with a lesser title.[38] D has an interest in land which he can dispose of,[39] either by will, or convey by deed if he can find someone willing to buy it or which will pass on D's intestacy to his intestate successors. If D conveys his possessory interest to Z, or if he leaves it to Z by will, or Z inherits it from D, or D abandons his rights in favour of Z, Z can add the period of D's possession to his own to make up 12 years' adverse possession, and bar O's title.[40] At common law D has a fee simple estate relative to everyone except O or anyone with an even better title than O.[41] To carry this further, we can also say that anyone who claims from O has a better title than anyone who claims through D, so long as the limitation period has not barred their title.[42] Furthermore, it also follows that D, or someone claiming through D, cannot defend an action by O, or anyone claiming through O, by pleading that a third party, X, has a better title than O. They cannot plead the *jus tertii*.[43]

---

34 *Matson v. Cook* (1838) 4 Bing NC 392.

35 *Hamilton v. Marquess of Donegal* (1795) 3 Ridg PC 291 at 323, Ir HL. *Williams v. Williams* (1861) 10 Ir CLR appx xxxvi, per Lefroy CJ (actual possession or the legal right to possession).

36 *Pullan v. Roughfort Bleaching & Dyeing Co Ltd* (1888) 21 LR Ir 73, V-C.

37 Palles CB in *Kennan v. Murphy* (1880) 8 LR Ir 285 at 293-4. The Common Law Procedure Amendment Act, Ireland, 1853 specifically preserved this defence by s.198, and sch B, form 16. See also Judicature Act, 1877 Order XVIII rule 8.

38 *Catteris v. Cowper* (1812) 4 Taun 547, 128 ER 444.

39 *Irish Land Commission v. Davies* (1891) 27 LR Ir 334, at 346 per Monroe J citing *Asher v. Whitlock* (1865) LR 1 QB 1.

40 *Clarke v. Clarke* (1868) IR 2 CL 395. *Mount Carmel Investments Ltd v. Peter Thurlow Ltd* [1988] 3 All ER 129, [1988] 3 WLR 1078, 57 P & CR 396, CA (Eng).

41 *Asher v. Whitlock* (1865) LR 1 QB 1; *Allen v. Roughly* (1955) 94 CLR 98 [1956] 29 ALJ 603; see Australian Digest and note of the case in [1956] CLJ 177 by H. Wade. Holdsworth, *History of English Law* Vol. VII, 1925 pp.62–69 maintained that judges in the nineteenth century had begun to allow the plea of *jus terii*, but this was largely refuted by Hargreaves, "Terminology and Title in Ejectment" (1940) LQR 376. And see Holdsworth's reply in (1940) 56 LQR 479.

42 This is the position at common law. But even before the limitation period has expired equitable principles, such as proprietary estoppel, may prevent O or a person claiming through O, from recovering possession. See *McMahon v. Kerry County Council* [1981] ILRM 419, below Proprietary Estoppel in Chapter 18.

43 *Rhatigan v. Gill*, unreported, High Court, O'Sullivan J, 16 February 1999, citing Salmond and Heuston on Tort 21st ed. p.47:

"The mere *de facto* and wrongful possession of land is a valid title of right against all

It is irrelevant as between O and D or persons claiming through them. Two cases illustrate these points.

In *Asher v. Whitlock*[44] L was dispossessed by H. H died and left his interest in the land by his will to his widow for life, or until she remarried. If she did so, the land was to go to his daughter. The widow remarried. After her death her husband remained in possession of the land. The heir of H's daughter brought an action against the husband to recover the land. The action was successful. The heir had succeeded to the daughter's title and it was a better title than that of the husband. L was not a party to the proceedings and it was not proved that his title had been barred by the Statute of Limitations, 1957. The issue was not relevant:

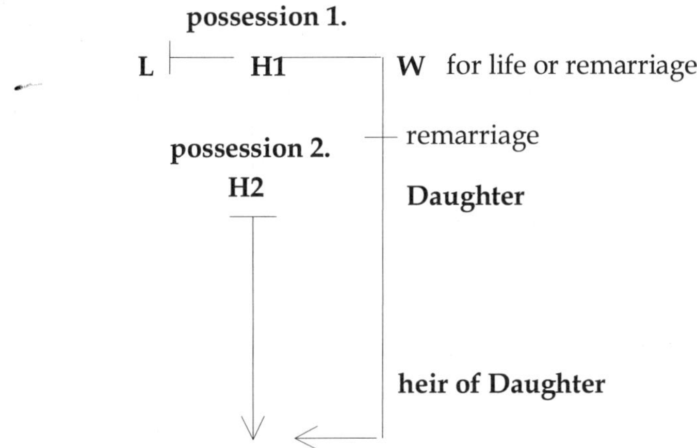

In *Lysaght v. Royse*[45] a lease for 500 years was granted in 1703. From 1725 to 1840 the representatives of the lessee dealt with it as if it were a fee simple. There then arose a dispute between two parties both of whom claimed to be entitled under a deed of 1770. It was held that as between those parties there was a presumption that a release of the freehold reversion had been executed. Such a presumption would not however, affect a person claiming to be entitled to the reversion on the lease. The case illustrates the relativity point well: even

persons who cannot show a better title in themselves, and is therefore sufficient to support an action of trespass against such persons. Just as a legal title to land without the possession of it is insufficient for this purpose, so conversely the possession of it without legal title is enough. In other words, no Defendant in an action of trespass can plead the *jus tertii* the right of possession outstanding in some third person – as against the fact of possession in the Plaintiff. It is otherwise, of course. if the Defendant is himself the lawful owner or has done the act complained of by the authority precedent or subsequent, of him who is thus rightfully entitled."

44 (1865) LR 1 QB 1.

45 (1862) 12 Ir Ch R 444.

though there was evidence that the title was not freehold, the court ignored it insofar as it was dealing with parties claiming from the same deed which purported to be conveying the fee simple. The court was concerned with the relative rights of the parties before the court, not absolute rights.

One of the reasons why the law of real property is still affected by this notion of possession and relative rights to possession is that it developed in feudal society. Feudal land law was obsessed with the idea of possession, or seisin to use the technical expression. Why was that so? Here again, the answer is not to be found by looking at the law itself but at the kind of society that produced the law. Feudal society was an agricultural society. And it was also a class society with a ruling class of nobles – feudal lords whose income came directly to them in the form of agricultural products – in grain and meat and the products of crafts such as cloth and domestic utensils. This income did not come to them through the economic mechanism of the market but directly as the tribute provided by the serfs or lesser lords as a condition of holding their land. A lord only had an income if he physically controlled an area of land cultivated by serfs and was able, through his agents, to enforce his right to tribute. He would actually live on part of it himself. Possession was therefore an important legal concept in such a society. It should be noticed that although more than one person can have a fee simple in the same land, relatively speaking, only one person could have seisin.[46]

b) After the Limitation Period Has Run

If the 12 year period has expired does it mean that there is no longer any such thing as relative titles, and that D's title is now absolute? The answer, perhaps surprisingly, is no. There is still such a thing as relativity of title even after the 12 years have elapsed. If a person dispossesses someone who only has a lease, then when the 12 years are up they have extinguished the title of the dispossessed lessee, but not of the landlord. The law has been unwilling to accept that a squatter on leasehold property could deprive the landlord of his title. Time does not begin to run against the landlord until his reversion has fallen in as property lawyers say, *i.e.* until the end of the lease, when the landlord will again be entitled to possession himself.[47] If we take this a bit further it means that V, the person who has inherited D's title, and who appears to all intents and purposes to have a fee simple, and who is trying to sell the land to P, may derive title from someone 120 years ago, D, who had dispossessed a tenant, T. Let us say that that lease was for a term of 150 years. T's title was barred after 12 years from the time D dispossessed T, but the title of the landlord, L, is not

46 See later for definition of seisin. Megarry & Wade (4th ed.) p.48–49.

47 *Perry v. Woodfarm Homes Ltd* [1975] IR 104 at 117 (ousted lessee cannot surrender the lease to the lessor and give immediate right to possession to lessor, because ousted lessee's title to lease barred after 12 years: Per Walsh J at 119, Griffin J at 130, Henchy J dissenting at 124).

barred. Thirty years from now the lease will come to an end and the reversion will fall in. There is someone, X, who is entitled to L's reversion, under a series of wills or conveyances or intestacies etc. X will acquire at that point a new right to possession which has not been barred and will not become barred for another 12 years from that point. Until it is barred, X has a better title than V or P. In relation to any title, therefore, it may be that the title of the current holder of the land is derived from a long lease the reversion on which has not yet fallen in and we have no means of knowing how long it will be before it does fall into possession, giving the holder of it the right to sue for possession, and a better right than current holder.

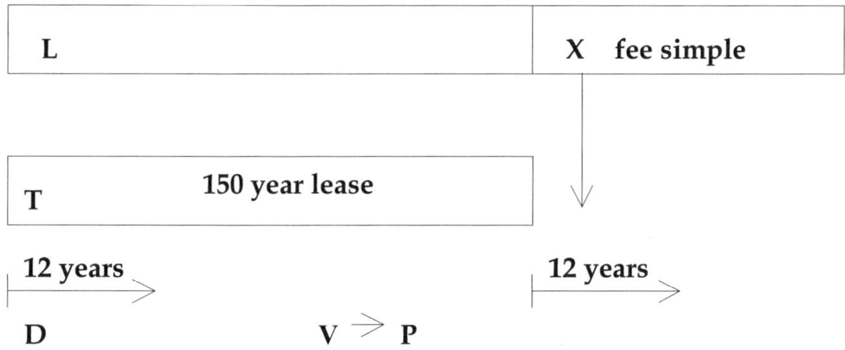

No one today who is selling land will investigate the title back 140 years. In unregistered conveyancing the investigation is to a good root of title[48] at least 40 years before, unless there is agreement to the contrary,[49] and it is usual for a purchaser to agree to go back only 20 years to a good root of title.[50] So it can be seen that this uncertainty as to title exists as to all titles.[51]

48 A good root of title is a document which conveys the whole legal and equitable estate which the vendor contracts to sell, such as a conveyance on sale, or a mortgage by conveyance of the fee simple. See Wylie *Conveyancing* para. 13.56.

49 Vendor and Purchaser Act, 1874 s.1, see Wylie *Conveyancing* para. 13.54–13.55. The period at common law was 60 years.

50 Wylie, *Conveyancing* para. 13.54. For leasehold the practice is to examine the original lease and then an assignment at least 15 years old.

51 The general position has been improved in some respects. The example of a reversion on a long lease appears to be the remaining instance of such a general defect, but there were others in the past which have been abolished. A reversion or remainder on a base fee is extinguished by the person entitled under the base fee remaining in possession for 12 years: Real Property Limitation Act, 1874 s.6, now s.19 of the Statute of Limitations, 1957; *Re Domvile* [1952] IR 37 (section does not apply if person in possession under the base fee is also the person who would have been entitled under the settlement).

There is one partial exception to this, namely land sold under the Land Purchase legislation in Ireland,[52] and one possible exception, namely registered land.[53]

52 Land Law (Ireland) Act, 1896 s.31(1) provides that where any land was sold under the Land Purchase Acts and an advance under the Acts was made for the purpose of the sale "or where a lessor or grantor has signified his consent to the redemption of a rent under the Redemption of Rent (Ireland) Act, 1891", the sale of the land or the redemption "shall be made discharged from all superior interests" as defined by the section. The land was to vest in the purchaser in fee simple, and the superior interests became a lien on the purchase money of the land, *i.e.* they were overreached. Section 31(8) defines superior interest as including any reversion "if such land is held under a lease for lives or years renewable forever, or for a term of years of which not less than 60 are unexpired at the date of the sale, and notwithstanding that such reversion or estate may be vested in [the Crown]". Where the term had less than 60 years unexpired it would, depending on when the land was sold, probably have fallen in by now. Thus, the defect in title described in the text above would have been cleared off such fees simple at the time of sale. This would not in itself prevent such defects arising in future if long leases were again granted over such land.

53 See Chapter 24 Registered Land: Absolute Title. In the past the Crown in Ireland owned land in the royal demesne as an absolute interest. Theoretically the State in the Republic may have succeeded to such land, if any existed in 1937. See Chapter 3 Tenure.

CHAPTER 2

OWNERSHIP ABOVE AND BELOW THE SURFACE

A. General Principles

It is sometimes said that the general principle is that the freehold owner owns all that is above the surface to an unlimited extent and owns all below the surface to the centre of the earth: *cujus est solum, ejus est usque ad coelum et usque ad inferos*. This, as we shall see, is not, however, accurate as far as airspace above the surface is concerned and has many qualifications as to the earth below the surface.

B. Things Found Below the Surface

In the English case of *Elwes v. Brigg*[1] land had been leased to a gas company. They were excavating on the land in order to erect a gasholder. While doing so they discovered a prehistoric boat six feet below the surface. It was held to be the property of the lessor although the lessor was ignorant of the existence of the boat at the time the lease was granted.[2] This case is one of a number of authorities in favour of the view that things found under the surface of land belong to the owner of the freehold, in the absence of the original owner, even if the owner of the freehold is not aware that they are there. This latter point was

1 (1886) 33 Ch D 562.

2 See also *Waverley Borough Council v. Fletcher* [1996] QB 334, [1995] All ER 756.

doubted in *Webb v. Ireland and Attorney General*[3] and may not represent the law in the Republic.

There are many qualifications on the principle that the freeholder has a superior title to things below the surface. Some of these, such as minerals and treasure trove, are dealt with below.

C. Things Found Above the Surface

When things are found above the surface of the land it is less likely that the owner of the land will be able to show both possession and an intention to possess such as to give him or her a better title than the finder of the objects.

In the famous case of *Armory v. Delamirie*[4] in 1722, a boy chimney sweep found a jewel in a chimney. He took it to a jeweller and offered it for sale. The jeweller took the jewel and then refused to pay for it. The boy, through an adult friend, sued the jeweller. The jeweller pleaded in the action that he was not under an obligation to return it because some third party evidently was the true owner and not the boy. In other words, the jeweller pleaded *jus tertii*. The court

---

3 [1988] IR 353, [1988] ILRM 565. In *Webb v. Ireland and Attorney General* [1988] IR 353, at 372, [1988] ILRM 565, Supreme Court Walsh J doubted whether the owner of land who was not aware of the existence of objects found under the land and buried for safekeeping, could claim the objects as against the original owner who placed them there:

> "In my opinion it would be a great injustice if the true owner of the chattels, having intentionally placed them in a particular place for safe keeping and then cannot recall where he placed them, or where he did not have an opportunity to come back to recover them, should be deemed to have lost his title in favour of the owner of the lands in which he placed them. Strictly speaking nothing can be said to be lost in the literal sense if it continues to exist even though its owner may be unknown or because it has been unknowingly misplaced. Notwithstanding the number and the weight of the authorities cited it is my opinion that the owner of the land upon which mislaid or unremembered chattels are intentionally placed for safe keeping, whether in or under the surface, cannot claim to be the owner of the chattels simply by reason of his being the owner of the land. To so hold would be to fail to vindicate the rights of property of the true owners of the chattels so placed and would permit the type of injustice which Article 40.3 of the Constitution is designed to prevent. The owner of such land is to be deemed to be in bare possession of the chattels even if he does not know of their existence on his lands. He can assert a good claim to possession, as distinct from ownership, against any claimant whether it be trespasser, or otherwise, whose claim is based on simply unearthing and removing the chattels in question."

However, it is doubtful if he authorities go that far: *Elwes v. Brigg* did not involve a claim by the original owner. Also, the judge does not seem to appreciate that in the common law a better right to possession is ownership as against those with a lesser right. It is doubtful if the owner of land would have a better right to possession as against an original owner of the articles who had not abandoned ownership.

4 (1722) 93 ER 664, [1558–1774] All ER Reprint 12; *Quinn v. Coleman* (1898) 33 ILTR 79.

held that he could not do so. As between the jeweller and the boy, the boy had the better title.

In *Hanna v. Peel*[5] the defendant was the owner of a house which he had never occupied. The house was requisitioned during the war to billet soldiers. The plaintiff, a soldier, found a brooch in a crevice on top of a window frame. The true owner was not known. There was no evidence that the owner of the house knew it was there. The police handed it over to the owner of the house. The plaintiff claimed that he was entitled to it. The English court held that the soldier was entitled to it as against everyone except the true owner. The court distinguished *Elwes v. Brigg* on the ground, apparently, that as to things above the surface of the land the title of an owner depends on the concept of possession which applies in relation to personal property. The owner only has a superior title to a finder if he has the requisite intention to possess the item. Such an intention could be of a general kind, as where there was evidence that he had intended to exercise control over everything on the land. They found that there was no such evidence here as the owner had never occupied the land.[6]

In *Parker v. British Airways*[7] Mr Parker found a gold bracelet lying on the floor in the international lounge, Terminal 1, Heathrow Airport in London. He handed it to a British Airways official with his name and address, saying that if it was not claimed by the true owner they should return it to him. The owner never came forward. British Airways sold the bracelet and kept the £800 they obtained for it. Mr Parker sued them for the money. The English Court of Appeal held that he was entitled to the money. Donaldson MR held, following *Hanna*, that a finder of an article who is lawfully on land and who finds an article on the land which is not attached to it or buried under it and who takes it into care and control has a title to it good against all except the true owner. It also held that where property is found in a building the owner of the building only has a superior right to the finder if the owner of the building has manifest an intention, before the finding, to exercise control over the building and arti-

---

5 [1945] KB 509

6 See also In *Re Cohen* [1953] Ch. 88 money was found hidden in a house after the owners had died. In an action brought by the executors of the surviving wife, the court held that in the absence of evidence as to who it belonged they had to fall back on the principle that the owner owns chattels found on land. The executors did not, of course, claim it as finders.

In *Grigsby v. Melville* [1973] 3 All ER 455 the English Court of Appeal held that in the absence of anything to the contrary a conveyance of land included not only the whole surface but the whole substratum. A basement to which there was no access from within the building was held included.

In *Mustafa v. Baptists Union Corporation Ltd* (1983) 266 EG 812 a similar situation arose in the case of a room above the surface but which was inaccessible from within the building. It was held that a person reading the particulars of sale would not have concluded that the room was excluded.

7 [1982] 1 All ER 834.

cles found in it. Where the thing is found under the surface then in order to obtain possession of it the finder would have to dig it up and in doing so would either be a trespasser, in which case the owner of the land would have a better title, or would do so under a licence from the owner, in which case whether the finder had a better title would depend on the terms of the licence.

D. Airspace

The supposed general principle is even less true of the airspace above the surface of land.

In *Bernstein v. Skyviews Ltd*[8] the defendants flew over the plaintiff's land to take an aerial photograph of his country house. They then offered it for sale to the plaintiff. He sued them for trespass.[9] Counsel for the defendants pointed out in the course of argument that the plaintiff, Lord Bernstein, had been the head of Granada Television at the time when a series of programmes had been made in which a helicopter flew from Land's End to John O'Groats and had shown aerial views of the land it passed over. The owners of the land over the route had not been asked for permission to fly over their land. This argument did not technically constitute a defence to the action, but it was persuasive in the sense that it bore on the reasonableness of the plaintiff's position. The English High court noted that the Latin maxim had been coined by Accursius of Bologna in the 13th century but could find no case in which it had been applied to uphold an indefinite right to the air space above land. They cited Lord Ellenborough *obiter* in *Pickering v. Rudd*[10] to the effect that it would not be a trespass to pass over someone's land in a balloon, nor to fire a bullet across it, unless the bullet fell on the ground. It would be absurd if it were a trespass every time a satellite passed over someone's land. They held that an owner's right extended to such a height as was necessary for the ordinary use and enjoyment of the land and the structures on it. Above that height the owner had no more right than anyone else.

The Supreme Court of the United States came to a similar conclusion in *US v. Causby*.[11] They held that:

1. The doctrine of the common law that ownership of land extends to the periphery of the universe has no place in the modern world.
2. The landowner owns at least as much of the space above the ground as he can occupy or use, even if he does not occupy it in the physical sense, by buildings.

---

8 (1977) 3 WLR 136.

9 He also sued in the alternative for breach of a right to privacy.

10 (1815) 4 Camp 219, 1 Stark 56, 171 ER 70, NP.

11 (1945) 328 US 256; 90 L ed. 1206.

In the Republic the Air Navigation and Transport Act, 1936 section 55[12] provides that no action shall lie for trespass or nuisance by reason only of the flight of aircraft over any property at a height above the ground which is reasonable in regard to wind, weather and all the circumstances.[13]

In *Bernstein* the court said that a person could not be held liable in tort if they were at a reasonable height and complying with air safety regulations, but flying below a reasonable level could give rise to an action in trespass and repeated flying causing noise is a nuisance.[14]

Loss or damage caused by anything falling from an aircraft is a trespass. In *Kelsen v. Imperial Tobacco Co Ltd*[15] a sign was erected which projected out over an adjoining shop leased to the plaintiff. It was held not to constitute a nuisance since damage has to be proved in that tort, but it was a trespass which is actionable without proof of special damage. Where the trespass is purely technical, however, courts today may postpone an injunction.[16]

E. Archaeological Objects

1. The Pre-1994 Law: Treasure Trove

Treasure trove was in origin a royal prerogative and was the right on the part of the Crown to the ownership of objects made substantially of gold or silver[17] which had been buried with the intention of recovering them[18] and which had no known owner.[19] The claim of the Crown, now of the State, yields to the claim of a person who can show they are the original owner of the objects or hold by a title derived from the original owner.[20] At common law there had to be an inquest by a coroner to establish the title to the treasure. It was also an of-

12 Air Navigation and Transport Act, 1988 s.47 (as amended).

13 There was no claim for nuisance in Bernstein because it could not be maintained that a single flight fell within that tort.

14 See *Roedean School Ltd v. Cornwall Aviation Co Ltd* (1926) The Times, London, 3 July 1926.

15 [1957] 2 All ER 334.

16 See *Woolerton & Wilson v. Costain Ltd* [1970] 1 WLR 411. But see also *Anchor Brewhouse Developments Ltd v. Berkeley House (Docklands Developments) Ltd* (1987) 38 Build LR 82, Ch D.

17 *Attorney General of Lancaster v. Overton Farms* (1982) 1 All ER 524. The case is discussed below.

18 *Attorney General v. Trustees of the British Museum* (1903) Ch D 598. The case is discussed below.

19 On the English doctrine see Emden, "The Law of Treasure Trove, Past and Present" (1926) CLXVII LQR at 368–381; Palmer, "Treasure Trove and the Protection of Antiquities" 44 MLR at 178–187.

20 *Webb v. Ireland* [1988] IR 353 at 390 per Walsh J.

fence on the part of the finder to conceal treasure trove.[21] It had also become the practice to give a reward to the finder, but it was *ex gratia* and was not the subject of a right.

a) Gold or Silver

The early commentator on English law, Bracton[22] only mentioned the title of the finder and did not confine the doctrine to objects made of gold or silver, although he did confine it to metal objects:

> "... treasure, that is, silver or gold or metal of some other kind... Treasure is any ancient store of money or other metal which has been forgotten so that it no longer has an owner; thus it belongs to the finder since it belongs to no one else."[23]

By the time of Sir Edward Coke, Chief Justice of the King's Bench until 1616, the royal prerogative had been established and the doctrine had also been confined to gold and silver:

> "Treasure Trove is when any gold or silver, in coin, plate, or bullyon hath been of ancient time hidden, wheresoever it be found, whereof no person can prove any property, it doth belong to the king, or to some lord or other by the king's grant, or prescription."[24]

Thus, by the time the doctrine had become part of a royal prerogative it had also become confined to gold and silver. The reason for the latter restriction was that the Crown regarded treasure trove as a useful source of metal for the Mint. Coins at that time were of gold or silver. This indicates that the origin of the doctrine had nothing to do with preserving objects of archaeological interest: on the contrary, it resulted in their destruction.

In *Attorney General of Lancaster v. Overton Farms*[25] the English Court of Appeal reaffirmed that the English doctrine was confined to objects of gold and silver. The case concerned a hoard of Roman coins in which silver had been mixed with base metal. This had been done due to inflation in Roman times. The silver content of the coins ranged from 0 per cent to 18 per cent. Most had between 1 per cent and 2 per cent silver. The English Court of Appeal reaffirmed that the prerogative extends only to gold and silver objects. Lord Denning MR held that the silver content must be 50 per cent or more before the

---

21 *R v. O'Toole* (1867) 11 Cox CC 75. The case concerned coins of the reigns of Elizabeth I, Charles I and the Commonwealth found at Booterstown, near Dublin. The judge directed the jury that if the accused did not know the coins were silver he should be acquitted. See also "Treasure Trove" (1894) ILTSJ 127, 10 March 1894.

22 Henry de Bracton, living in the period 1250–68. His book is entitled *De Legibus et Consuetudinibus Angliae*. See *Attorney General of Lancaster v. Overton Farms* (1982) 1 All ER 524, per Lord Denning MR at 526g.

23 Op cit vol. 2 p.338.

24 3 Co Inst 132.

25 [1982] 1 All ER 524.

objects qualify as treasure trove.[26] Dunn LJ concurred generally with Denning and, while declining to lay down a specific figure, held that the coins must contain a "substantial proportion" of silver or gold.[27] Oliver LJ concurred without expressing a definite view on the proportion. The *ratio decidendi* must therefore be, as the headnote in the All England Reports correctly states, that there must be a substantial proportion of silver or gold.

Why did the judges in modern times continue to restrict the doctrine to objects of gold and silver? Once it was accepted that the objects were handed over by the Crown in England to the British Museum and in Ireland to the Royal Irish Academy, it was clear that the basis of the doctrine had effectively been changed by social practice. The judges could have recognised this fact and reformulated the doctrine as they had done with many other doctrines of the law. It was surely open to them to say that the doctrine in its origin was confined to valuable objects – to treasure – and that value, or treasure, should now be understood in terms of archaeological or historical value. One reason why this change was not made, apart from failure of imagination, may have been that the doctrine of treasure trove itself constitutes a derogation from the rights of private ownership – generally the landowner. It expresses, in its new form, a notion of social or national property. In the 19th century the judges tended to adapt the law rather to the needs of private property. It may be that, while recognising as they had to do the existence of the doctrine, they resisted efforts to enlarge or extend it in any way. Efforts to increase the protection afforded to cultural property in the present century have encountered opposition from a similar quarter.

b) Intention to Recover

The common law right also applies only to objects buried with thought of recovery. If the ownership of the objects has been abandoned, then the landowner has a title probably superior to the finder.

It follows from the above that grave goods are not treasure trove even if they are gold or silver. An instance of this is provided by the Sutton Hoo treasure in England, which consisted of gold and silver Saxon objects found in a burial ship.[28] The finds, valued at several million pounds, were donated by the landowner, Mrs Pretty, to the British Museum and it was the largest single donation in its history.

A person who finds objects buried beneath land which does not belong to the finder is either a trespasser, in which case they could have no title as against the landowner, or they dug for them under a licence from the landowner, in

26 *ibid.* at p.530e.

27 *ibid.* at p.531g–h.

28 Charles Green, *Sutton Hoo: The Excavation of a Royal Ship-Burial* (London: Merlin Press, 1963).

which case whether the finder is entitled to anything they find will depend on the express or implied agreement with the landowner.

The leading case on the question of burial with intention of recovery is *Attorney General v. Trustees of the British Museum*[29] which concerned the Broighter Hoard. The hoard consists of a collection of objects including a gold model boat and a gold torque. The objects were turned up by a farmer when ploughing his field near Lough Foyle in Northern Ireland. The objects found their way by some questionable means[30] into the hands of an antiquary who sold them to the British Museum. The Royal Irish Academy, to whom the prerogative of treasure trove had been transferred or granted before 1922, claimed the hoard as treasure trove.

It was argued on behalf of the British Museum that the objects had been placed at the edge of an ancient lake which in the past had extended to the area where they were found, and that they were a votive offering to the Irish god of the sea and (evidently) of lakes, Manana Mac Lir. Thus, if this were so, they were not treasure trove since there had been no intention of recovery. A great deal of archaeological evidence was adduced[31] to prove the existence of an ancient beach at the site. However, it did not convince the judge. He also seems to have been impressed by the fact that all the objects were found together in the same place, whereas if they had been placed at the edge of a lake it would be more likely that the action of the water would have dispersed them.

The judge also held that once it was proved that the objects had been found buried and were of gold or silver there was a presumption that they were treasure trove and it was for those who denied this to prove from the circumstances of their burial that they were not. The British Museum had not rebutted the presumption.

c) Webb *v.* Ireland

(1) The High Court Decision

The whole issue of the application of the doctrine of treasure trove in the Republic was taken up in *Webb v. Ireland and Attorney General*[32] which concerned the Derrynaflan chalice and the other objects found with it, including a paten and a strainer, all of remarkable workmanship and beauty. The objects

---

29 [1903] Ch D 598.

30 See Praeger, *The Way That I Went: an Irishman in Ireland* (Dublin, 1969) pp. 63–7. Praeger relates that the ploughman sold them to his employer "for a few pounds" who in turn disposed of them to a Mr Robert Day of Cork, a collector of antiquities for a great deal more and Mr Day sold them to the British Museum for £600. The author also gives some account of the trial. Sir Edward (later Lord) Carson, as Solicitor-General, appeared for the Crown.

31 See (1904) XXV Sec C *Proceedings of the Royal Irish Academy* Nos. 5, 6 p.144 *et seq.*

32 [1988] IR 353, [1988] ILRM 565.

were found by Mr Webb and his son (the finders). They had approached the owners of the land and asked if they could visit the ruined Derrynaflan church. The owners gave them permission to do so. A preservation order under the National Monuments Acts had been made in relation to the land in 1935. The finders had not been given permission to dig on site by the owners and indeed no such permission would have been valid in view of the preservation order and also since digging for archaeological objects is made a criminal offence under the National Monuments Acts.[33] Despite this the finders proceeded to use on the site a metal detector which they had in their possession. The metal detector gave a positive signal near a depression in the ground close to the church. The finders proceeded to dig into the depression with implements which they had carried with them for just such a purpose. They uncovered a bowl and beneath the bowl what turned out to be the chalice and the other objects. Without informing the authorities immediately and without any proper scientific method being employed, they proceeded roughly to remove the objects. In doing so they irreparably damaged the paten. They then took the objects to their home, evidently with the intention of informing the authorities of the find. The finders subsequently took the objects to the National Museum. They were told they would be honourably treated. This representation was apparently made to the father but intended to be communicated to the son also.[34] The National Museum took the view that the objects were treasure trove, under the law as it was then understood, and that they therefore belonged to the State. The Chief Solicitor offered the finders £10,000 on behalf of the State. They thought it was not enough. The State, evidently in order to secure their position since the law was in some doubt, then offered to purchase whatever title the landowners might have in the objects. The landowners conveyed their interest to the Minister for Education in return for £25,000 each. The finders later sued for return of the objects, claiming that the State were mere bailees and that they, the finders, as bailors, were entitled to their return. The State argued first, that the landowners had a better title to the objects than the finders and that the State had acquired this better title by purchase. This argument, as the attentive reader will no doubt perceive, is open the objection that it is a plea of *jus tertii*. In the case of bailment there are exceptional cases where a plea of *jus tertii* may succeed and one issue in the case was whether the State's plea could be supported as an exception to the general rule. The State further argued that it had its own superior title by virtue of the doctrine of treasure trove.

In the High Court Blayney J held that the State were bailees and could not resist the claim of the bailors on the basis of a better title acquired after the bailment was entered into. The judge held that this fell outside of existing exceptions to the prohibition of pleas of *jus tertii*.

33 National Monuments Act, 1930 s.14.

34 See McMahon and Binchy, *Torts* p.156.

The judge further held that the doctrine of treasure trove, being a royal prerogative, had not survived the 1937 Constitution.

(2) The Supreme Court Decision

The Supreme Court did not uphold it. The court held that a doctrine of treasure trove, with the same limits as the common law doctrine, applied in the Republic, based not upon the survival of a prerogative power, but as part of the sovereign rights of the people established by the 1937 Constitution. The court also held that the doctrine included a power to provide a reward for the finder of the object. This did not of itself confer a right on the finder, but the court further held that the State, in the circumstances of the case, by assuring the finders that they would be treated honourably, had created a legitimate expectation which caused the assurance to become binding. The court held that any reward should be based not upon the market price of the objects, but for the finding. They were awarded £25,000 each.

Finlay CJ defined the Constitutional principle in the following terms:

> "It would, I think, now be universally accepted, certainly by the People of Ireland, and by the people of most modern States, that one of the most important national assets belonging to the people is their heritage and knowledge of its true origins and the buildings and objects which constitute keys to their ancient history."[35]

Finlay CJ went on to formulate the specific doctrine derived from, or based upon, the constitutional principle in the following terms:

> "If this be so, then it would appear to me to follow that a necessary ingredient of sovereignty in a modern State and certainly in this State, having regard to the terms of the Constitution, with an emphasis on its historical origins and a constant concern for the common good is and should be an *ownership by the State of objects which constitute antiquities of importance which are discovered and which have no known owner*."[emphasis supplied][36]

The judge went on to emphasise, perhaps surprisingly, that, notwithstanding that the specific doctrine was based upon the constitutional principle, it nevertheless extended only so far as the common law doctrine had done in 1922:

> ". . . *the much more limited right* of the prerogative of treasure trove known to the common law should be upheld not as a right derived from the Crown but rather as an inherent attribute of the sovereignty of the State which was recognised and declared by Article 11 of the 1922 Constitution. . . I would conclude that there does exist in the State a right or prerogative of treasure trove, *the characteristics of which are the characteristics of the prerogative of treasure trove at common law* which I have already outlined in this judgment *as they stood in 1922.*"[emphasis supplied][37]

35 [1988] IR 353 at 383.

36 *ibid.*.

37 *ibid.* and see also 385.

It was therefore clear beyond doubt that the State ownership in the Republic was still limited to items of gold and silver buried with thought or intention of recovery, and that grave goods, for example, were still outside the doctrine. Finaly CJ nevertheless indicated that it was open to the legislature to expand the doctrine to the extent defined by the constitutional principle and this has now been done.[38]

(a) "National" Heritage or Importance

One aspect of the judgment that attracted criticism was the introduction of a test of nationality into a doctrine from which it was previously absent. Kelly[39] argued that "national" can too readily be given a narrow or even bigoted meaning. Referring to the removal of statues of William III and George II and to the crowns from Kingsbridge, Professor Kelly continues:

> "This bridge, erected to commemorate the visit of George IV in 1821, recalled, like all the other monuments I mentioned, a national history which, if I could, I would turn back and reshape in a sense happier for the ancient Irish race, dispossessed in the 16th and 17th centuries of land, power, influence and self-respect; but I cannot do it, and it certainly cannot be done by such mean and spiteful acts of rage against inanimate objects. These objects, of course, did not belong to the category of things which *Webb* was about; but the sort of mentality which could violently or officially exclude objects of similar provenance from our national heritage is still with us, and I would be apprehensive, therefore, about anchoring in our constitutional law a concept so readily abused by the official or the unofficial bigot."[40]

One can also question whether it was wise to make the assumption that culture is national in character. Ancient Celtic cultures were not confined to Ireland; they stretched across Europe to the Mediterranean. People at that time may have had a concept of themselves as belonging to local groups but there is no reason to suppose that they identified themselves as Irish or French in the sense used today. The concept of the national state is modern. Moreover, evidence of many cultures exists in Ireland from the Stone and Bronze Ages onwards, including the pre-Celtic people of Newgrange and also Roman and Viking settlements. Would a piece of Roman silver, if it were to be found in Ireland, be excluded from treasure trove on the ground that it was not part of Irish culture? Furthermore, archaeologists, whose opinions and practice in this area should be taken seriously in framing the law, recognise that ancient artefacts produced in country A, but transported in ancient times to what is now country B to the site where they have been found, belong to country B and not to the country of their origin.

On the other hand, it is arguable that the concept may in future have at least one positive effect. One problem with the *Webb* case is that the limitations of

38 *ibid.* at pp. 386.

39 Kelly, "Hidden Treasure and the Constitution "(1988) 10 DULJ 5.

40 *ibid.* at p.18.

the common law doctrine were impossible to reconcile with the constitutional principle which the court in the *Webb* case held to be its new basis. Whether or not an object is of national importance in terms of its relation to Irish history clearly does not depend on its being made of gold or silver or whether it is contained in a grave or buried for later recovery.

(b) "Legitimate Expectation"

The doctrine of legitimate expectation expounded in the Webb case is so wide that it will no doubt be relied upon in future in a growing number of contexts. Indeed, unless limited in some way, it would replace the doctrine of proprietary estoppel, or promissory estoppel, with a doctrine of almost infinite extent.

A troubling aspect of the judgments is that there is no mention of a requirement, similar to that in proprietary estoppel, of detrimental reliance. It might be argued that the finders did rely upon the assurance by leaving the objects in the possession of the National Museum. However, it is difficult to see how this could be a detriment because the assurance appears to have been given after the objects were given into the care of the Museum. Furthermore, it is difficult to argue that the act of reliance was the leaving of the Museum by the finders without the objects. It was not known at that time whether they had a right to possess them or not. Nor is it true to say that the expectation had been created by a pattern of previous behaviour. It is true that it had been the practice in the past, especially under the doctrine of treasure trove at common law, to reward finders of such objects. Indeed it may well have been the intention of the finders when they set off that night to hand in anything valuable to the authorities and to claim a reward. The court held, however, that the expectation was created by the express assurance given to the finders and the judgments do not rest on the ground of past practice.[41] Indeed the court held that the common law practice of rewarding the finder was a matter of grace and did not give rise to a legal right in the absence of an assurance.

d) Detection Devices

The bill which became the National Monuments (Amendment) Act, 1987 was in its legislative stages when *Webb* was decided and was amended to include what is now section 2 of the Act. This makes it an offence to be in possession of a detection device at the site of a monument or within an archaeological area or to use it elsewhere for the purpose of searching for archaeological objects without a licence from the Minister.

41 See *Re "La Lavia"* [1996] ILRM 194, Supreme Court (O'Flahery J, Hamilton CJ, Egan and Blayney JJ concurring), High Court, unreported, Barr J, 26 July 1994. The Supreme Court rejected the argument, left undecided by W*ebb*, that a right to reward had arisen by legitimate expectation based upon the past practice of the State alone, as distinct from a promise or assurance given. Reward is now governed by s.10 of the National Monuments (Amendment) Act 1994; see below.

2. The National Monuments (Amendment) Act, 1994

(a) *Introduction*

The Supreme Court in *Webb* indicated that the specific doctrine of treasure trove applicable in this jurisdiction could be enlarged by the legislature to fill out the boundaries of the constitutional principle laid down in that case, and indeed invited the legislature to do so. The legislature could remove the limits of gold and silver, burial with intent to recover, etc. The doctrine could be expanded to include all "objects which constitute antiquities of importance which are discovered and which have no known owner" in the judge's phrase. This change was implemented by the National Monuments (Amendment) Act, 1994.[42]

(b) *Archaeological Objects*

Section 2 of the 1994 Act implements the suggestion in the *Webb* case by the following provision:

> 2.– (1) Without prejudice to any other rights howsoever arising in relation to any archaeological object[43] found before the coming into operation of this section, there shall stand vested in the State the ownership of any archaeological object found in the State after the coming into operation of this section where such object has no known owner at the time when it was found.
>
> (2) In this section "owner" means the person for the time being having such estate or interest in the archaeological object as entitles him to the actual possession thereof.

Sub-section 2 of the 1994 Act seems designed to exclude the finder from the term owner. Section 3 provides that the Director of the National Museum may waive the rights of the State. Section 5 creates offences of failing to report the possession of archaeological objects and failing to give information about them. It also establishes a record of monuments and places where there are believed to be monuments.

---

42 The Act came into force on 6 July 1994. In 1988 Professor Kelly, who was also a TD, asked the Taoiseach if there were plans to introduce legislation to amend the law and to regulate any reward to finders (Dáil Debates 377 cols 1–2, 3–5, 27 January 1988). The Taoiseach, Mr Haughey, stated that his department and that of the National Museum, the Office of Public Works and the Attorney General's Office were drawing up "the heads of the legislation" needed to deal with the matter (Dáil Debates 377 col 2, 27 January 1988). It was another five years before legislation was introduced.

43 Archaeological object is defined for the purpose of the the Act (by s.2 of the National Monuments (Amendment) Act, 1987 as amended by s.14 of the 1994 Act) as:

> any chattel whether in a manufactured or partly manufactured or an unmanufactured state which by reason of the archaeological interest attached thereto or of its association with any Irish historical event or person has a value substantially greater than its intrinsic (including artistic) value, and the said expression includes ancient human, animal or plant remains.

(c) Reward

Section 10 of the 1994 Act now provides that the State may pay a reward to the person who finds an archaeological object,[44] the owner of the land and the occupier of the land on or under which the object was found, where the object is retained by the State. In assessing the amount of the award the Director of the National Museum shall take into account any or all of the following criteria: the intrinsic value of the object, its general historical and archaeological importance, the circumstances of the finding and the amount of rewards paid by the State in the case of comparable archaeological objects.

F. Historic and National Monuments

The National Monuments Acts[45] give varying forms of protection to historic[46] and national[47] monuments,[48] including restrictions on altering them or damaging them. National monuments may be compulsorily acquired,[49] but historic monuments and national monuments which have not been so acquired are protected although the fee simple or other interest in the land on or in which they are located remains vested in a private owner.

One way of viewing such provisions is to see them as qualifications or reductions of private property rights which otherwise rightfully belong to the owners of the land and which therefore require compensation for their loss. Another view is that the protection of historic and national monuments is a more general form property, of a national, communal and cultural character and the detailed provisions of the law in this sphere serves to reconcile the two forms of property. On this basis, there is no reduction from an assumed prior and all-pervasive private property right and therefore no necessary right to compensation.

The Supreme Court in *O'Callaghan v. The Commissioners of Public Works*[50] seems to have adopted the latter view. In that case the plaintiff in 1977 bought land at Loughshinny on the coast of County Dublin which included a

44 See footnote 43.

45 National Monuments Act, 1930 as amended by the National Monuments (Amendment) Act, 1954 and the National Monuments (Amendment) Act, 1987.

46 Section 2 of the 1987 Act.

47 Section 2 of the 1930 Act. The definition includes every monument in Saorstát Éireann to which the Ancient Monuments Protection Act, 1882, applied immediately before the passing of the 1930 Act. Newgrange, Knowth and Dowth are scheduled in the 1882 Act together with several other sites in Ireland.

48 Monument is defined by the 1930 Act s.2 as amended (in fact replaced) by s.11 of the 1987 Act.

49 Section 11 of 1930 Act, as amended by s.6 of 1987 Act.

50 [1985] ILRM 364, Supreme Court.

38½-acre site occupied by a prehistoric promontory fort. In 1970 the latter had been listed for preservation under section 8 of the National Monuments (Amendment) Act, 1954, a section which also prohibited the owner from interfering with the site without giving prior notice to the Commissioners of Public Works. Soon after acquiring the land the plaintiff, who knew through his predecessor in title that the land contained an ancient monument, employed contractors to plough part of the area occupied by the fort. He failed to notify the Commissioners of his intention to undertake this work, and could not at the relevant time be found by the Commissioners and warned to desist. Accordingly the Commissioners, the defendants in the action, made a preservation order under section 8 of the National Monuments Act, 1930, as amended by section 3 of the 1954 Act, the effect of which was to apply to the site the extensive prohibitions listed in section 14 of the 1930 Act. In subsequent correspondence the defendants declined an application from the plaintiff to revoke the preservation order. The plaintiff sought a declaration from the High Court that the defendants, by failing to consult him prior to the making of the preservation order, had acted *ultra vires*; and that section 8 of the 1930 Act, which includes no provision for the payment of compensation to owners of land containing national monuments, was an unjust attack on the property rights of citizens within the meaning of Article 40.3.2 o of the Constitution. In the High Court 1982 McWilliam J refused to grant the declarations sought.

The Supreme Court held in two judgments, the first a judgment of the Court (delivered by O'Higgins CJ and pronounced in accordance with its practice when adjudicating on constitutional matters) that the impugned legislation was valid, and the second a unanimous decision that there had been no breach of natural justice. On the constitutional issue the court held that the property rights guaranteed by the Constitution are subject to regulation with reference to the common good, which plainly requires that national monument be preserved, and to social justice, which may or may not according to circumstances require the payment of compensation, citing *Dreher v. Irish Land Commission.*[51] They further held that section 8 of the National Monuments Act 1930, delimits not the right of private ownership but the user to which land, in the interests of the common good, may be put; and the preservation of national monuments should be regarded as the common duty of all citizens.

There is no doubt that on the facts of the case the property owner had no just claim to compensation since he clearly knew of the existence of the fort before he bought the land. It could, however, be otherwise. A monument might be discovered on land after an owner had acquired it and had paid a price based on the full use of the land. The case is less satisfactory in resolving such a problem. It may be regarded as unfair that in such a situation some citizens are called upon to bear the full loss. One method of dealing with it is to spread the

51 [1984] ILRM 94.

cost by a system of compensation. A free market-oriented solution, on the other hand, is to take into account that the risk of a monument being found on land is one which potentially affects all land and is a risk which prospective buyers could presumably insure against.

G. Horizontal Layers

Freehold land can be held in separate horizontal layers, each one being a separate fee simple estate.[52] These are known to lawyers as "flying freeholds". An obvious case where one might expect to find such freeholds in practice would be flats.[53]

There are, however, legal problems about subdividing a building in separate horizontal fees simple. Let us suppose that D, a developer, builds a block of flats on his land. He sells the ground floor flat to A in fee simple and the first floor flat to B in a separate horizontal fee simple. What B owns is a layer of air-space corresponding to the dimensions of his flat, but this in itself does not give him the right to support for the physical structure unless it is expressly granted to him and binding on A and, if it is to be of any value, binding on A's successors at law. There is a common law right of support, but this only gives a right to support for land in its natural state[54] and not to buildings and so this is

52 *Iredale v. Loudon* (1908) 40 SCR 313. I sold his interest in land with buildings to a co-owner and continued to occupy one room on the second floor. It was connected to the street by a landing staircase and a street door the key to which I had. At first he paid rent, but later stopped and he continued in occupation without paying rent. He claimed he had acquired title under Statute of Limitations. Held: he had acquired title. Duff J: "It is, I think, too late to dispute the proposition that an upper room not resting directly upon the soil but supported entirely by the surrounding parts of a building might at common law be the subject of a feoffment and livery as a corporeal hereditament, that is to say, as land.". *Doe d Freeland v. Burt* (1787) 1 Term 701: demise of premises and yard does not pass cellar under the yard in occupation of B, a tenant. Ashhurst J: "We know that in London different persons have several freeholds over the same spot: different parts of the house are let out to different people. That is the case in the Inns of Court.". *Prima facie* the cellar passes, but rebuttable and rebutted here; *Evans and Fitch's Case* (1597) Cro Car 340, 79 ER 1009.

53 See *Metropolitan Properties Ltd v. O'Brien* [1995] 2 ILRM 383 in which this passage was quoted in the Supreme Court by O'Flaherty J. George and George, *The Sale of Flats* (4th ed. 1978). Bodkin, "Rights of Support for Buildings & Flats" (1962) 26 Conv 210; Leyser "Ownership of Flats: Comparative Study" (1958) 7 ICLQ 31; Tolson "Land Without Earth: Freehold Flats in English Law" (1950) 14 Conv NS 350; Scamell, "Legal Aspects of Flat Schemes" (1961) 14 CLP 161; *Sturge v. Hackett* [1962] 3 All ER 166; *Gatehouse v. Vise* [1957] 2 All ER 183; *Penn v. Gatenex* [1958] 1 All ER 712; *Re Wonderland Cleethorpes* [1963] 2 All ER 775, HL; *Reilly v. Booth* (1890) 44 Ch D 12; *Harris v. Ryding* (1839) 5 M & W 60, 151 ER 29; *Yorkshire Insurance v. Clayton* (1881) 8 QBD 421; Watts 1927–28 1 Aust LJ.

54 *State (McGuiness) v. Maguire* [1967] IR 348; *Latimer v. Official Co-operative Society* (1885) 16 LR Ir 305. See Chapter 22 Incorporeal Hereditaments.

of no use to B. There is therefore no automatic right to support of B's flat. But surely B can bargain for such rights? B can indeed ensure that the conveyance from the developer grants him a legal easement of support binding on A and A's successors in title, but such an easement is ineffective without positive covenants of repair requiring A and A's successors positively – by expending money – to maintain support for the flat above. But the problem is that the law has developed the position that while the benefit of positive covenants runs at law,[55] so that B and his successors can enforce the covenants against A, the burden of positive covenants does not run at law or in equity,[56] so that B and his successors cannot enforce them against the successors of A. The law did not take this position deliberately to frustrate people in the position of B: it did so in the general context of defining land ownership and for the general policy reason that private owners should not be able to impose burdensome obligations on ownership. It did this in order that land – or rather fee simple estates in land – should not be rendered so unattractive as a commodity that land subject to such burdens would become unsaleable. Of course in the specific context of flying freeholds it appears absurd that a freehold flat can exist without an obligation on those beneath to support it, but one should remember that it is absurd from a social point of view. The absurdity is a product of a system of law based upon laissez-faire capitalism, on the restricted vision of leaving it to individuals to strike their own bargains and without concern for the general social effects this produced.

In Ireland these problems of horizontal titles have sometimes been avoided by the developer granting not fee simple estates but long leases and retaining a fee simple reversion. Covenants are then created between the developer and the various leaseholders of flats. This solves a technical problem but creates another: it conflicts with the popular concept of property. Most people who decide to buy flat are not satisfied with a mere lease even if it is for 999 years.

A more satisfactory solution is to be found in Australia. The New South Wales Strata Titles Act, 1973[57] creates a special regime in the case of flats and other similar situations. The area over which the special regime operates is registered as the strata plan. Each flat constitutes a three-dimensional lot and each lot bears a part of the burden of the cost of maintenance of the common areas in proportion to its volume. The lot owners for the time constitute a body corporate which owns the common property, defined as any part of the strata plan not comprised in any lot. The body corporate levies charges on the individual

55 *Shayler v. Woolf* [1946] Ch. 320, Eng CA; see Chapter 21 Covenants Between Freeholders.

56 *Haywood v. Brunswick Permanent Building Society* (1881) 8 QBD 403; see Chapter 21 Covenants Between Freeholders.

57 The Act replaced the earlier Conveyancing (Strata Titles) Act, 1961. See Simpson, *Land Law and Registration* paras. 14.5, 22.2.VA.

lot owners and pays these into an administration fund which is used to maintain and repair the common areas.

H. Foreshore

The foreshore is land between the high and low water marks and so intermittently covered by the tide. Under Article 10 of the Constitution and the Foreshore Act, 1933,[58] ownership of the foreshore is vested in the State. The State may grant licences to individuals to use the foreshore.[59] It may also may serve on any person a notice prohibiting the removal of beach material.[60]

Seaweed between the high and low water mark drifting and ungathered is not the property of the owner of the foreshore and is not the subject of larceny.[61] This rule probably gives effect to the common practice in certain parts of Ireland of gathering carrageen, a particular kind of seaweed,[62] also common on British coasts, from which is produced a jelly used in cooking and for medicinal purposes. It seems that the seaweed must be drifting in the sea and that the right is part of a more general public right to fish and gather other things from the sea.[63] The rule implies that at the time the seaweed is gathered the part of the foreshore concerned is covered by the sea. To enter dry foreshore and gather seaweed may be a trespass.

The right to all minerals under the foreshore is vested in the State.[64]

58 See also the Foreshore (Amendment) Act, 1992.

59 Foreshore Act, 1933 s.3; Fisheries (Consoldiation) Act, 1959 s.15; *Madden v. Minister for the Marine* [1993] ILRM 436, [1997] 1 ILRM 136 (Minister must act in accordance with constitutional justice). Applicant to furnish environmental impact statement and with notice: s.19 Foreshore Act, 1933; and s.19A of the Foreshore Act (inserted by Part III of the European Communities (Environmental Impact Assessment) Regulations, 1989); *Cobh Fishermen's Association Limited v. Minister for the Marine and Natural Resources,* unreported, High Court, O'Sullivan J, 29 August 1997; Fisheries (Amendment) Act, 1997; Fisheries and Foreshore (Amendment) Act, 1998 (aquaculture licences).

60 Foreshore Act, 1933 s.7 as amended by the Foreshore (Amendment) Act, 1992 s.4.

61 *The Queen v. Clinton* (1869) IR 4 CL 6, CCCR. But see *Brew v. Haren* (1878) IR 11 CL 198 affirming (1875) IR 9 CL 29 bound by *Clinton* but holds that a person taking it away liable in tort. This seems doubtful.

62 The species *chrondus crispus*. The Irish name comes from Carragheen in Waterford.

63 *Brew v. Haren* (1877) IR 11 CL 198 at 201–2 per Lawson J. Wylie, *Irish Land Law* para. 6.116.

64 Foreshore Act, 1933 s.2(1) as amended by the Minerals Develpment Act, 1940 s.55(d). See also the Foreshore (Amendment) Act, 1992.

An owners of land through which water flows is known as a riparian owner. Where an owner of land owns one bank of a river the owner's riparian rights are presumed to extend to the centre of the river.[65] A riparian owner has no absolute right to the water flowing in a defined channel,[66] but has rights of user set out below. There is no common law right to water percolating through the ground and not in a defined channel[67] and there is no right in A to prevent an adjoining owner, B, drawing off percolating water in a such a way as to reduce that available for A.[68]

1. Fishing

A riparian owner has the right to fish in the water, subject to private fishing rights which may exist as profits *a prendre* or in conjunction with ownership of the river bed.[69] The public has no right to fish except in tidal waters.[70]

2. Flow

The riparian owner may sue if the stream or river is diverted or dammed up[71] but at common law does not have an unrestricted right to draw off water.[72] A riparian owner has a right to the flow of water through the land unaltered in quality and quantity subject to the rights of user of riparian owners upstream and is bound by a corresponding obligation to riparian owners downstream. Obstruction of the flow of water is actionable per se by a riparian owner.[73] The rights of user are as follows:[74]

a) Ordinary Use

The riparian owner has the right to use water necessary for ordinary purposes connected with the riparian tenement, even though this exhausts the stream. Ordinary purposes include watering cattle, or domestic water supply. This may possibly have been extended in manufacturing areas to include manufacturing uses. This extension was to the benefit of manufacturers but at the cost of a greater adverse impact on the environment.

---

65 *Tennent v. Clancy* [1987] IR 15.

66 *Thompson v. Horner* [1927] NI 191.

67 *Black v. Ballymena Township Commissioners* (1886) 17 LR Ir 459.

68 *Chasemore v. Richards* (1859) 7 HLC 349, 11 ER 140.

69 *Gannon v. Walsh*, unreported, High Court, Keane J, 20 June 1996.

70 See Chapter 22.

71 *Massereene v. Murphy* [1931] NI 192.

72 *McCartney v. Londonderry & Lough Swilly Railway Co* [1904] AC 503. For an extensive discussion of common law riparian rights see Howarth, *Watercourses* Ch. 3.

73 *Palmer v. Persse* (1877) IR 11 Eq 616.

74 *ibid.*

The limitation here is that the use must be connected with the tenement and not to the advantage of other land nearby. In *McCartney v. Londonderry & Lough Swilly Railway Co*[75] a railway company wanted to extract water to be stored in tanks beside the line from which locomotives could refill their boilers. It was held that this was an illegal use to the extent that the water would be used to fill tanks not on the riparian tenement itself.

b) Extraordinary Use

The riparian owner has the right to use water necessary for extraordinary purposes connected with the riparian tenement provided the use is reasonable and the water is restored substantially undiminished in quality and quantity. Extraordinary purposes include irrigation and, in all areas, manufacturing purposes. Use in excess of the above limits can only be authorised by statute or acquired as easements.[76]

J. Accretion

Where a river adds soil to an adjoining bank the additions of soil belong to the owner of the bank provided the process is imperceptible in its progress, *i.e.* as it occurs.[77] The doctrine derives from the Roman law doctrine of *alluvion*.[78] If A owns land beside a river and B owns land on the other side and a sudden torrent rips off a part of A's land and deposits it on the opposite bank adjoining on B's land, the doctrine probably does not apply and A can follow the soil across the river.[79] So in the words of Callis:

> "The case was, that a river of water did run between two lordships. . . and the river, by little and little, did gather upon the soil of the other land, but so slowly, that if one had fixed his eye a whole day thereon together, it could not be perceived. By this petty and imperceptible increase the increasement was not to the owner of the river; but if the river, by a sudden and unusual flood, had gained hastily a great parcel of the other lord's ground, he should not thereby have lost the same. . ."[80]

75 [1904] AC 503.

76 *Pullan v. Roughfort Bleaching and Dyeing Co Ltd* (1888) 21 LR Ir 73; *Hanna v. Pollock* [1900] 2 IR 664; Wylie, *Cases* p.329.

77 Sir Matthew Hale, *De Jure Maris*; Callis, *On Sewers* p.51; *Gifford v. Yarborough (Lord)* (1824) 2 B & C 91, 107 ER 688 sub nom *Rex v. Yarborough (Lord)*, affirmed HL (1828) 5 Bing 163, 130 ER 1023 at 1024; *Attorney General v. McCarthy* [1911] 2 IR 260; *Southern Centre of Theosophy Inc v. South Australia* [1982] 1 All ER 283, PC; 1982 2 WLR 544. Lyall, "The Case of the Moveable Land" [1968] 1 EALR 95–100.

78 Inst 2.1.20–24, via Bracton and Hale. See footnote 77.

79 Inst 2.1.21. Callis, *On Sewers* p.51, quoted by Blackstone, 2 Bl Com 262.

80 Callis, *On Sewers* p.51, quoted by Blackstone, 2 Bl Com 262.

An increase is imperceptible as it occurs will become perceptible after a lapse of time, but this does not prevent the application of the doctrine, as Abbot CJ pointed out in *Gifford v. Yarborough*:[81]

> An accretion extremely minute, so minute as to be imperceptible even by known antecedent marks or limits at the end of four or five years, may become, by gradual increase, perceptible by such marks or limits at the end of a century, or even after 40 or 50 years. . . And considering the word "imperceptible" in this issue, we think it must be understood as expressive only of the manner of the accretion as the words undoubtedly are, and as meaning imperceptible in progress, not imperceptible after a long lapse of time.

This is also clearly the meaning of the Roman doctrine:

> Alluvion means latent increment, because what is added by alluvion is added so slowly that you cannot tell how much is added at any moment of time.[82]

Doubt was cast on this position in the 19th century by *Attorney General v. Chambers*[83] and *Hindson v. Ashby*[84] in which the idea gained ground that if land were laid out with precise boundary marks, the doctrine would not apply. This fallacy is based upon a misunderstanding of the Roman doctrine of *ager limitatus*. Maitland explains the doctrine and exposes the fallacy:

> "Even if Azo knew much about the meaning of this highly technical term, we may doubt whether Bracton understood it. The *agri limitati* were, we are told, land laid out by the *agrimensores* when captured territory was assigned or a new colony was founded. Their boundaries were fixed by rigid lines, and were not to be altered by alluvion. . . It is improbable, however, that he could have found in England any foundation of fact for the distinction between *agri limitati* and other lands."[85]

---

81 (1824) 2 B & C 91, 107 ER 688 *sub nom Rex v. Yarborough (Lord)*, affirmed HL (1828) 5 Bing 163, 130 ER 1023 at 1024.

82 Inst 2.1.20.

83 (1859) 4 De G & J 55, 45 ER 22 at 28 per Lord Chelmsford LC. Frederic Augustus Thesiger, later Lord Chelmsford, was born in 1794 in the West Indies at St Vincent, and was the son of the owner of a slave plantation. He entered the navy but in 1812 his father's planation was destroyed by a volcanic eruption. As a result of this decline in the family fortunes he resolved to become a barrister and was called to the bar of Gray's Inn in 1813. He became Attorney General in 1845 and Lord Chancellor in 1858. His chancellorship may be seen as one of the more unfortunate results of the explosion. His son and heir continued the family tradition by being in command of the British forces in 1879 at Ishandlwana when they were defeated by the Zulus.

84 [1896] 2 Ch. 1 at 13, per Lindley LJ.

85 Maitland, *Selden Society* Vol. 8 (1894) "Bracton and Azo" p.iii. And see Dig 41.1.16, 43.12.1.6. Such land formed by alluvion to *agri limitati* belonged to the first occupant.

K. Minerals

Before 1922 minerals became vested in the State primarily through the operation of the Land Purchase Acts.[86] When the Irish Land Commission acquired the fee simple from a landowner it then vested it in the tenant but reserved minerals to the State.[87] Article 11 of the Constitution of 1922 provided that:

> "... all the lands and waters, mines and minerals, within the territory of Saorstát Éireann hitherto vested in the State, or any department thereof, or held for the public use or benefit, and also the natural resources of the same territory (including the air and all forms of potential energy), and also all royalties and franchises. . . shall, from and after the date of coming into operation of this Constitution, belong to Saorstát Éireann, subject to any trusts, grants leases or concessions then existing in respect thereof, or any valid private interest therein. . ."

Article 43 of the present Constitution vests in the State mines and minerals vested in the State in 1922.[88]

The Minerals Development Act, 1979 vests in the Minister the exclusive right to work minerals.[89] This is apparently intended to be so even where minerals are privately owned, although the statute is open to Constitutional challenge on that ground. The right to explore and exploit minerals beneath the territorial seas of the State is vested in the Minister.[90] All rights to petroleum in the State and in designated areas of the continental shelf vest in the Minister.[91] All mines of gold and silver vest in the State[92] although this too is open to Constitutional challenge.

The extent of State ownership of minerals in unknown, but it is estimated that approximately 60 per cent to 65 per cent of potential mineral resources are state-owned.[93]

---

86 Especially the Irish Land Act, 1903; the Irish Land Act, 1907; the Irish Land Act, 1909; the Land Act, 1923 and the Minerals Development Act, 1940. See also *Webb v. Ireland* [1988] ILRM 565, [1988] IR 353. Donellan, *Energy Law* p.36.

87 Land Act, 1903 s.13(3) as amended by the Land Act, 1923 s.45(5). See Irish Land Commission (Dissolution) Act, 1992 s.4 (not yet in force); Minerals Development Act, 1999 s.2 (minerals vested in Land Commission vested in State).

88 Constitution of 1937, Art. 10; Minerals Development Act, 1940.

89 Section 12. The section is subject to s.14 which creates an exception where some other person was lawfully operating a mine before 15 December 1978.

90 Constitution, Art. 2.

91 Minerals Development Act, 1960 s.5(1); Continental Shelf Act, 1968 s.2(1) .

92 Minerals Development Act, 1940 s.5(e).

93 Donellan, *Energy Law* p.36 n.32.

CHAPTER 3

TENURE

"Well, this distinguished jurist has written to me asking whether an estate with remainders to the first and fourth sons in tail can be alienated without reversionary codicils terminating pro tanto all seignory advowsons in gross. . . Alas, the answer must be no. Any estate held as between coparceners without inseisinment of freebench copyholds must stand in feoffment pending escheat of all incorporeal rent-charge bars, subinfeudations in frankalmoin aperte, mesne rights, copycharges presented à prendre, or devises held by charterbrokers possessio fratris, pur autre vie, or even quousque. . . The under-copyholder has the advowson absolutely, with uncommuted scutage and burgage rights where the estate subsists in petty serjaunty. . . There, possibly, I might crave permission to leave the matter."

– Flann O'Brien, "The Plain People of Ireland", *The Best of Myles*

A. Introduction

In the common law the concept of estate defines the duration of a person's interest in land, while tenure (from Latin *tenere,* to hold) defines the terms upon which land is held. The system of land law in Ireland today is based upon the system of land tenure introduced into Ireland by the Anglo-Normans in the 12th century. It has been transformed by historical change to a system appropriate to a capitalist economy. To understand the modern law it is therefore necessary to appreciate the nature of this underlying change. To do that, it is necessary to have some appreciation of the feudal economy and how it differed from a capitalist one.

The system which was the economic basis of feudal land law was introduced in England with the Norman conquest in 1066 and, with some modifications, in Ireland with the establishment and spread of Anglo-Norman rule, a process of conquest which was initiated in Ireland about a hundred years later by Henry II in 1171–1172. The process of conquest was far more protracted in Ireland than in England and was not completed until the 17th century. This imposition took the form of Anglo-Norman lords being granted land already held by the indigenous population, and the superimposition of a ruling class on top of existing communities. By the 17th century a second form of the imposition of land law and of conquest was under way and had begun in the previous century. This was plantation, a word which in Irish history imports not so much the planting of land with crops, but the planting of land with people. It entailed the replacement of the indigenous population of cultivators with English and Scottish peasant farmers. We shall describe the characteristics of the initial form first and later deal with the second type.

B. The Manor

The manor was the basic unit of the Anglo-Norman economic system. Typically it would comprise the lord's fortified stockade or castle surrounded by the lord's own fields, or demesne which in turn would be surrounded by three great unenclosed fields. The serfs, or villeins, produced their own means of subsistence on these fields. Thus, they were unlike modern wage workers who work in return for wages with which they purchase items of subsistence through the mechanism of the market.

The technology of the time did not permit putting fields under permanent cultivation. Crop rotation was practised on two of the three fields while the third lay fallow. In the next year of cultivation the fallow field would be brought under cultivation again and one of the other two would lie fallow. On the fields that were cultivated in one year the villeins cultivated strips which they distributed among themselves, often by means of field juries chosen from among themselves. Each villein would have several strips in different parts of the cultivated fields so that fertile and infertile land was to some extent equitably distributed. The system of crop rotation meant that each villein only had temporary rights over the strips and these rights which would be lost when the field was left fallow.

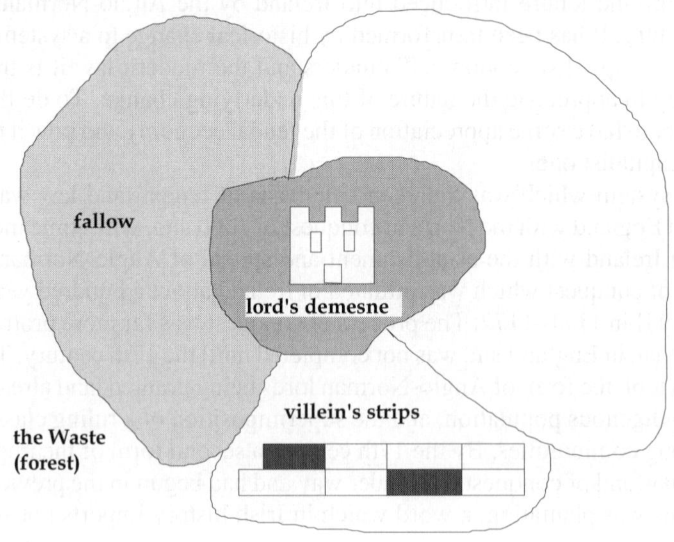

During the early period of feudalism villeins were personally unfree and could not leave the manor to move to another one. In addition to producing their own food on the strips of the three-field system, the villeins produced food for the lord and his household by working a number of days each year on the demesne. In Ireland unfree tenants were called betaghs[1] from the Irish word *biatach* meaning food-provider or food-rent provider.[2]

The working year was thus divided into distinct periods of subsistence production and periods in which the villeins produced a surplus product which was appropriated by the lord. Within the manor in addition to the villeins there were free tenants of the lord holding their land in one of the free tenures. Tenants who were personally free could hold land in villeinage tenure, but villeins could not hold in free tenure.

The villeins might exchange surplus products produced on their own strips in a local market, but the economic mechanism of the market did not distribute their labour-time or the product of the demesne. It was law, not economics, which distributed these, through the mechanism of the custom of the manor and the degree of respect which the lord paid to it. Custom determined the ratio of days in the year spent by the villein on working the demesne in relation to the days spent on working his strips. This absence of the market from the process of production itself meant that the land was cultivated to produce things which were valued for their useful qualities rather than their ability to be turned into cash profit. Land produced use-values rather than exchange-values. This affected in turn the legal concepts of feudal society, as we shall see.

C. The Hierarchy of Tenure

The manor stood at the base of the economic and social system. At its apex was the King. The King granted land containing manors to his immediate subordinates, the barons, to hold in tenure as tenants in chief. He would also retain some manors which he would hold directly and these would include the King's own demesne. Tenants in chief would in turn make grants of manors to their followers, retaining some manors for themselves. Their followers would do likewise. The common law therefore saw title to land as deriving typically from grant rather than from first occupation.[3]

It followed that feudal lords who were not tenants in chief were tenants of some other lord higher up the system. These intermediate holders of land were

---

1 Otway-Ruthven, *Medieval Ireland* p.110–11.

2 Probably from *bíathad,* food-rent, also used to mean the food provided by a *briugu* (hospitaller). See D.A. Binchy, *Críth Gablach Mediaeval and Modern Irish Series* (SO Dublin, 1941) p.76.

3 J.E. Hogg, "The Effect of Tenure on Real Property Law" 98 LQR 178.

called mesne[4] lords. The entire system was a pyramid with the King at the top and layers of tenure below him with the manor and its free and unfree tenants at the bottom. It was a maxim that there was no land which was *allodial*, *i.e.* without a lord. There was, however, some land that was not held in tenure, namely, land that the king held directly. Land held directly by the King was held in what we may call absolute ownership.[5] Neither the doctrine of estates nor the doctrine of tenure[6] applied to it. An example was royal demesne, the demesne in royal manors. These were manors of which the King was the lord of the manor. This is the only example of the concept of absolute ownership in medieval land law. This form of ownership survives in the United Kingdom. All other land was held in some kind of tenure with its mutual rights and obligations between lord and tenant.

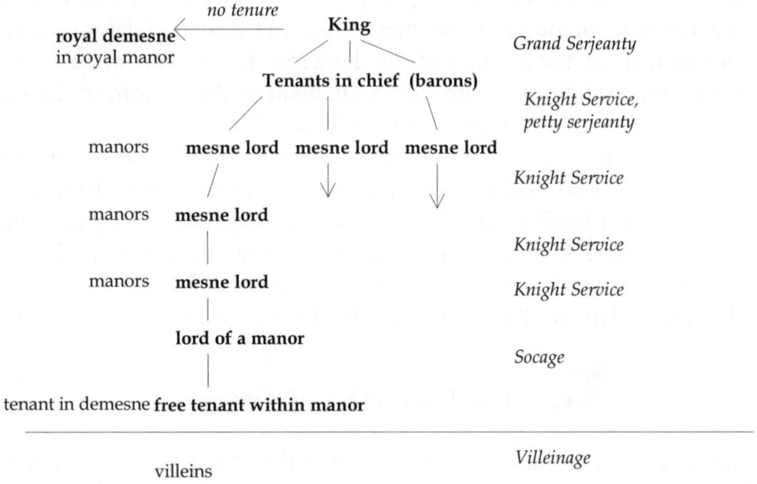

The concept of tenure was important in one other respect. It performed an ideological function. It brought some concept of unity to a society sharply and brutally divided by status and wealth. The tenants holding in free and unfree agricultural tenures actually provided the food and other necessities of life for the lords who provided none of these for themselves, but since the lords were

4 Pronounced main or mean, the latter probably being preferable since it indicates the connection with mean meaning intermediate.

5 Sir Edward Coke said: "All lands owned by subjects in England are holden of some lord, the King's lands are not holden of any superior, but he is lord paramount." Cited in J.E. Hogg "The Effect of Tenure on Real Property Law" (1909) 98 LQR 178 at p.182. As Hogg points out, this not quite the same as saying, as Blackstone did, that the King owned land allodially. Kent McNeil, "The Crown's Title to Lands in England" Chapter 3, *Common Law Aboriginal Title* (Oxford: Clarendon, 1989).

6 *Stroud's Case* (1572) 3 Dyer 313a, 73 ER 709; *Case of Tenures*, p.195: "So that it is clear, that only lands in the King's possession are free from tenure;..."

also under obligations under their tenure to provide valuable services to their superior lords, it appeared that everyone shared a common experience of being under obligations to those higher up the system in return for their land, and this obscured the reality that the wealth of society was produced only by those at the bottom of the tenurial system.

The tenurial system had implications for the concept of property in feudal society. It is sometimes said, inaccurately, that all land belonged to the King. This could only be said accurately of the royal demesne. Conversely there was no concept of absolute ownership of land except, again, in relation to the King's demesne. The concept was rather that land was held of someone else. The King's legal position as lord in relation to his immediate tenants did not differ from other lords in relation to their tenants except for a few special privileges. The main difference, which was political and economic rather than legal, was that the King was the only lord in the system who was not also a tenant of someone else.

D. Summary of Tenures

Tenures were classified according to their legal characteristics. These classifications changed over time, but it is as well to set out a simple classification before describing each of them in detail.

1. Free Tenures:
   - a) Military Tenures or Tenures in Chivalry
     - i) Knight Service
     - ii) Grand Serjeanty
   - b) Tenures in Socage
     - i) Common Socage
     - ii) Petty Serjeanty
     - iii) Burgage
   - c) Spiritual Tenures
     - i) Frankalmoin
     - ii) Divine Service
2. Unfree Tenures
   - a) Villeinage
   - b) Copyhold
3. Irish Laws Assimilated to Tenure
   - a) Irish Gavelkind
   - b) Rundale
   - c) Commonage

E. Free Tenures

Tenures had two main aspects: services and incidents. Services were the obligations which the tenant was to perform, the amount of which was the subject of agreement between the original parties to the charter creating the tenure. In the case of knight service, for example, the services involved military duties. In the case of socage the services were agricultural labour or the supply of agricultural products. Incidents were obligations attached to the tenure by the general law and whose nature depended on the type of tenure. Having chosen a particular tenure, the parties were powerless to alter the incidents. The existence of these obligations meant that voluntary agreement or contract was not the dominant legal idea in the feudal period.

1. Knight Service

Originally the service of this tenure was military.[7] The King made grants to tenants in chief and they in turn made grants in knight service. The tenant had to go himself and bring so many other knights with him. If the tenant held the land for the service of going himself and to take five knights with him, then he was said to hold the land for six knight's fees.[8] A knight's fee was not really a measure of land since services were a matter for agreement when the tenure was created and so could vary depending on the bargain struck.[9] Raising an army in this way had disadvantages as well as advantages for the King. Ambitious lords, particularly tenants in chief, might be tempted to turn their own knights into a private army and use it against the King. The feudal state based on military tenure was an inherently unstable political form. It became the practice therefore to commute the service to money and the King used the money to hire mercenaries, an early example of wage labour in feudal society. The commuted payments were called *scutage*, or in Ireland, royal service.[10] Otway-Ruthven gives an example of scutage in Rathfarnham near Dublin.[11] Since the payments were fixed, inflation reduced them over time to insignificant amounts. This was one of the factors in the decline of tenure itself.

---

7 Simpson, *Land Law* pp. 7–9; Baker (1st ed.) pp.123-4; (2nd ed.) pp.196–198; Pollock and Maitland, *History* 1: 252-282; Plucknett, *History* pp. 531–3; Wylie, *Irish Land Law* pp.16–17.

8 E. St. J. Brooks, *Knight's Fees in Counties Wexford, Carlow and Kilkenny* (1950); J Otway-Ruthven, "Knight's Fees in Kildare, Leix and Offaly" 91 JRSAI pp. 163–81. S Harvey, "The Knight and the Knight's Fee in England". 49 Past and Present 3.

9 Otway-Ruthven, *Medieval Ireland* pp. 104, 107–8.

10 Cosgrove ed, *New History of Ireland* II *Medieval Ireland* p.442.

11 Otway-Ruthven, *Medieval Ireland* p.103. In 1332 Geoffrey le Bret, tenant of Rathfarnham, was exempted from scutage as to part of the service. The arms of le Bret, or de la Brette, are also remarkable, being *gules plain, i.e.* a plain red shield: *Dictionary of British Arms*: H 58.

a) Tenant's Obligations to the Lord

The incidents of tenure varied according to the type of tenure. Those described below refer to knight service, but some were found in other tenures, as we shall see.

(1) Primogeniture

A characteristic shared by knight service, socage and serjeanties, and a peculiarity of Norman rule both in Ireland and England, was that if the tenant died the land passed to the eldest son by primogeniture. In knight service and socage if there was no son but there were daughters, all the daughters inherited in a form of co-ownership called coparcenary.[12]

(2) Fealty

This was the personal oath to perform the services of the tenure and applied even to unfree tenure.[13]

(3) Homage

Homage applied only to military tenures and was the oath of loyalty or allegiance to the lord to follow him in time of war.[14]

(4) Suit of court

This was the obligation to attend the lord's court and take part in its proceedings.[15]

(5) Wardship of the Tenement

A peculiar incident of knight service, and in Ireland also of socage, was wardship.[16] If a tenant died and the heir was under age, which was twenty-one for males and fourteen for females, the tenure was suspended and the feudal lord "dropped down" into the position of the former tenant until the heir came of age:

---

12 Co-parcenary was restated for Ireland in 1236: Otway-Ruthven, *Medieval Ireland* p.6, and see Chapter 16 Co-ownership.

13 Co Litt 67b.

14 Co Litt 64b, 65a.

15 Maitland, "Introduction to Selden Society" (1888) Vol. 1, *Select Pleas From Manorial Courts*; Pollock and Maitland, *History* 1:558 *et seq*; Williams, *Real Property* p.49. See footnote 101.

16 Pollock & Maitland, *History* 1: 318-329; Simpson, *Land Law* pp.16–19; Plucknett, *History* pp.534–5.

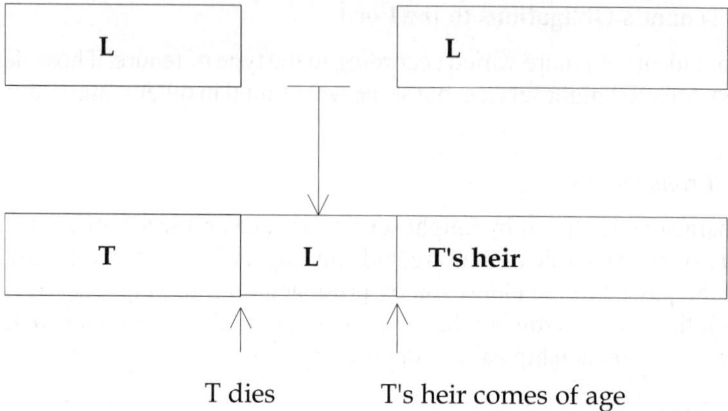

If T had subinfeudated to a subtenant, L became entitled to whatever services had been reserved on the sub-tenure. When the tenant attained majority he or she had a legal action to recover the land from the lord known as *ousterlemain* (*i.e.* "to oust the hand" of the lord).

(6) Wardship of the body

This was the lord's right to custody of the body of the person of the heir who was under age. With it went the profitable right of marriage *i.e.* the right to arrange the marriage of the minor tenant and receive payment from the other partner or their family.

(7) Aid

At first this was a form of private taxation levied by lords when they had particular need for cash, but tenants secured a limitation on the occasions which justified aids. Magna Carta of 1215 limited them to raising a ransom if the lord were captured in war or for the expenses incurred when the lord's son became a knight or his daughter married.

(8) Relief

If the heir was of full age when the former tenant died there was no wardship. Instead the heir had to pay a relief[17] before taking over the tenement. This shows that at first the heir of the deceased tenant was not entitled to the land purely by inheritance. Reliefs were often equal to one year's value of the land.[18]

17 Pollock & Maitland, *History* 1: 307–318; Simpson, *Land Law* pp. 16–17; Plucknett, *History* pp. 536.

18 Holdsworth, *HEL* 3: 60.

(9) Primer Seisin

If the land was held of the King the heir was not entitled to seisin by paying a relief. An inquest had to be held to determine who was the heir. In the meantime, which could be some time, the King had the right to the land, a right known as primer seisin.[19] It reflected the fact that, in the medieval period, a tenant in chief held a political position of great importance. For this reason it seems that, whether the practice had legal force or not, the King exercised a discretion in deciding whom to recognise as heir.

(10) Escheat

Escheat put an end to the tenure between the tenant and the tenant's immediate lord.

Escheat[20] caused the tenure to come to an end. The effect was to terminate both the layer of tenure and the fee simple estate for which it was held. The lord would then become entitled to the seisin of the land, or, if the former tenant was lord of a tenure below, the lord would drop into the position of the deceased tenant. There were several forms of escheat of which the more important were:

(a) Propter defectum sanguinis

This was escheat "due to a defect in the blood". This form of escheat occurred when a tenant died without heirs. In such a case the fee simple estate came to an end. It also meant that the layer of tenure came to an end.

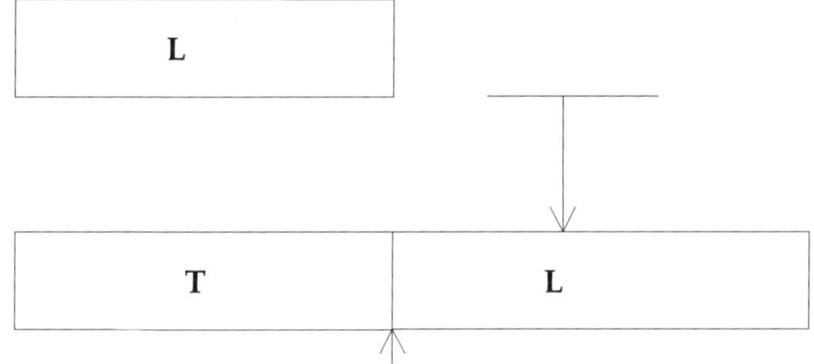

T dies without heirs

One should note that there was no reversion on a fee simple: there was an escheat. L would drop down into the position of T permanently and if T had subinfeudated L would become entitled to whatever services had been reserved

19 Pollock & Maitland, *History* 1: 307-318; Simpson, *Land Law* pp.16–17.

20 Simpson, *Land Law* pp.19–20; Pollock & Maitland, *History* 1: 351–356; Plucknett, *History* p.536.

on the sub-tenure. As we shall see later, this was to be a significant factor in the decline of tenure.

(b) Propter delictum tenentis

This was escheat "due to the tenant's wrong." If the tenant committed a felony and had either been convicted and executed for it, or had fled and been outlawed, the tenant's real property escheated.[21]

A felony was an offence against the King as representing public order and this was recognised in the King's entitlement to year, day and waste, *i.e.* the right to seisin and the right to commit waste[22] for a year and a day before the tenure escheated to the lord.[23]

This type of escheat is to be distinguished from forfeiture, mentioned in the next section.

(11) Forfeiture

Forfeiture occurred if the tenant committed treason. In this case the King was entitled to the land forever. It destroyed all tenures between the tenant and the King. The King could therefore make a new grant of the land.

b) Lord's Obligations to the Tenant

(1) Warranty

If someone brought an action against the tenant claiming a better title to the land, the tenant could vouch his lord to warranty and the lord would have to take over the defence.[24] If the claimant succeeded, *i.e.* he established a better title to the land than the lord, the tenant would also lose his right to the land. In such a case the tenant could enforce the warranty and his remedy was to claim land of equal value from the lord. This was the lord's duty of exchange.

(2) Lord could not Deny Tenure

The lord could not claim the land from the tenant himself, *i.e.* could not deny the tenure.

(3) Acquittance

The lord had to guarantee peaceful possession of the land by the tenant. A dis-

---

21 There is one example of escheat for felony in the Irish reports: *Anonymous* (1842) 4 Ir Eq R 701. The convict was transported for felony and the land vested in the Crown.

22 See Chapter 9 Life Estates.

23 Personal property could not be held in tenure and so escheated to the Crown permanently: *McDowell v. Bergen* (1861) 12 Ir CLR 391.

24 Williams, *Real Property* p.39, 647n.

turbance to possession was most likely to occur, as we shall see,[25] if the lord himself had failed to perform the services or incidents of his tenure to his own lord.

2. Grand and Petty Serjeanty

The main characteristic of these tenures was that the land was held for some personal service to be performed by the grantee for the lord.[26] At first there was no distinction between grand and petty serjeanty. The King commonly granted land to tenants in chief for some honorary service as a reward or political bribe. The service might be to present him with a lance or a sword once a year, or to lead his army into war, which could be a dubious honour, or to act as constable of one of his castles.[27] Land was also granted to those of lower status in return for more lowly services, such as to be the King's butler or cook.[28] In Ireland Richard le Latimer held land in County Dublin in 1207 for the service of acting as an interpreter.[29] In 1252 land was held of the Priory of Louth for the service of acting as its steward,[30] and there is mention in 1538 of land held for the service of acting as standard-bearer to the Lords of Trim.[31]

Tenants in chief and mesne lords also granted land in serjeanty, examples of service being to act as bodyguard, or to preside over the manorial court. In fact, serjeanty tenure was a method of providing services which came to provided under capitalism by wage labour or salaried employment. This kind became known as petty serjeanty. With the development of this economic form, the petty form of serjeanty tenure tended to decline. The fact that grand serjeanty was an honorary form of tenure and that petty serjeanty tended to be replaced by wage labour meant that neither form was likely to develop into the

---

25 See below, Subinfeudation.

26 Simpson, *Land Law* pp. 9–10, 13–14; Pollock & Maitland, *History* 1: 282–290.

27 *Duke of Buckingham's Case* (1569) Dy 285b, 72 ER 346, 73 ER 640 (Constable of England).

28 Blount's *Ancient Tenures* contains some amusing examples from the time of King John. One man held land for the service of holding the King's head on the ship from France while he was being sick. Another had to provide straw for the royal privy, while one Rolland had to entertain the King on Christmas Day by executing a "whistle, leap and fart."

29 *Calendar of State Papers, Ireland 1171–1251* No. 342, Charter 9 John m 5. The land was that of Tircahin and Killinglas and it was to be held of the King "*per servitium latimeriae faciendae*." The name Latimer means interpreter, "latimer" being a corruption of "latiner".

30 I have not found the source of this information at the present time. In 1333 Nicholas Taafe was granted a rentcharge of 100 shillings and two suits of clothes by the prior for acting as seneschal to the Priory of Louth: Archdall, *Monasticon Hibernicum* p.482.

31 I have not found the source of this information at the present time.

main form of tenure in the future. In the 13th century serjeanty came to be confined to tenants in chief in which case it was always grand serjeanty.

The legal characteristics of the tenure came to reflect this. These characteristics were as follows:

a) Primer Seisin

Since grand serjeanty was a tenure in chief the incident of primer seisin necessarily applied to it.

b) No Relief

Relief did not apply to grand serjeanty. After the King's primer seisin the heir entered without payment as a privilege of the tenure.

c) Inalienable

Serjeanties involved a personal relationship and, in the case of grand serjeanty, a political one also. For this reason they were held to be inalienable.

d) Impartible

Probably for the same reason they were also held to be impartible *i.e.* they could not be held in co-ownership. If the tenant died leaving no sons but a number of daughters, there was no coparcenary. The eldest daughter inherited alone.

e) No Wardship

Petty serjeanty became increasingly assimilated to socage, except that one privilege of the tenure was that there was no incident of wardship of the tenement.[32] In petty serjeanty the lord was only the personal guardian of an under age heir.

The absence of wardship of the tenement in petty serjeanty meant that the tenure would decline in the long term. By the Tudor period financiers invested speculatively in land, or rather, in seignories. They bought lordships, not for the services they would be entitled to from the freehold tenants, since those services might have declined to money payments of little value, but in anticipation of a wardship occurring which entitle them to the services of the sub-tenure which they hoped, or calculated, would be of greater value. Obviously, since petty serjeanty did not offer this possibility, it was less desirable to the Tudor speculator.

32 See below page 57.

3. Socage

After the Norman invasion of England the Normans recognised some Anglo-Saxon peasantry as free men, as they had been before the conquest, and recognised therefore a free form of agricultural tenure.[33] This tenure was called socage which according to Bracton comes from the Norman French *soc* meaning plough.[34]

One characteristic which was supposed to indicate the free nature of the tenure was that the services consisted of a definite amount of agricultural labour. At first socage was free tenure within a manor, but in the course of time the tendency was for the service to be commuted to money payment and as this happened the tendency also was for the tenure to spread up the feudal ladder. It was to become the residual tenure of real property law.

a) Relief

Reliefs were payable in socage, but they may not have been legally enforceable.

b) Fee Farm

Where the rent was substantial, *i.e.* enough provide an income for the lord, it was known as fee farm. Originally fee farm may have been a distinct form of tenure, but it had become assimilated to socage during the reign of Edward I. In Ireland the term is still used to denote a fee simple estate held at a rent, a form which still survives in this jurisdiction.

c) Wardship of the Tenement

In England wardship in socage did not go to the lord, but to the nearest relative of the heir as guardian. He could not keep the profits.[35] In Ireland socage was militarised and lords in Ireland insisted on wardship even in socage tenure. In *Comyn's Case*,[36] which was before the courts from 1277 to 1294 and again in 1331, the Irish practice was upheld.

4. Frankalmoin

Frankalmoin, meaning free alms, was the tenure by which religious bodies held land[37]. Again, it was an extension of the concept of tenure to a situation which had little in common with the military and agricultural relationships on

---

33 Simpson, *History of the Land Law* pp.11–14; Plucknett, *History* p.537.

34 OED socage. It may also refer to the duty to attend the lord's court.

35 At least after the Statute of Marlbridge [Marlborough], 1267 which gave an action for account when the heir became 14.

36 Hand, *English Law In Ireland* pp.178–185.

37 Simpson, *Land Law* p.10.

which the feudal system had been established. Nevertheless, the medieval church was a powerful economic institution quite apart from any spiritual attributes it may have possessed, and frankalmoin tenure gave it something approaching absolute ownership in the land it held. Only ecclesiastic bodies could hold land in frankalmoin: monasteries, priories, convents, and individual clerics in right of their office: bishops, abbots, and parish priests. The motive for making a grant in frankalmoin was charitable or religious and often the grant was made nominally to God or a saint, the idea being that the religious body merely held it on behalf of the spiritual donee. The economic purpose was to provide an income to support the poor, or the religious body itself. The service of the tenure was an obligation to pray for the soul of the grantor, but it was indefinite and not legally enforceable. If the grantor's lord did not confirm the grant the lord retained the right to levy distress[38] on the land if the grantor failed to render his own service.

If the land was wrongfully occupied by some person, religious bodies enjoyed the privilege of a remedy in the King's court, similar to the writ of right, to recover land held in frankalmoin, called the assize of utrum.

In a variant of frankalmoin, known as divine service, the service was fixed, as a certain number of masses a week or a year and the obligation was enforceable in both the King's courts and the ecclesiastical courts. The existence of this variant may suggest that there was some abuse of the moral trust imposed by frankalmoin and that sometimes the services of that tenure were forgotten or neglected.

Because the service was nominal, frankalmoin tenure became a way by which religious institutions came to undermine the feudal system. What in form was a donation for charitable purposes sometimes became, in substance, a purchase of land by the religious body, the monastery or abbey, paying the donee a lump sum and so acquiring a virtually absolute right to the land. Frankalmoin was also free of some of the incidents of tenure which attached to other tenures:

a) No Wardship

There was no wardship in frankalmoin, since there was no heir to inherit.

b) No Escheat

There was no escheat for lack of heirs for the same reason.

If land was held by a corporation sole, such as the abbot of a monastery or the priest of a particular parish, and the individual cleric committed a felony, the land passed to his successor in office.

38 See page 72.

c) No Relief

Relief was not payable, again, because the religious body never died.

5. Burgage

This was the tenure by which free persons in towns or boroughs held their land.[39] As with socage, tenants held for the service of a money rent. Social relationships in the towns and cities in the Middle Ages differed considerably from that in the countryside. Work was governed less by the seasons or by the need for organised periodic activities, such as at harvest or during the division of strips in the common fields. Petty commodity production in the form of craft industry developed. Craftsmen, owning their own means of production, *i.e.* the tools of their trade, and often employing wage labourers, called journeymen, produced commodities for sale. The craftsmen did not provided their own subsistence as villeins did, directly in articles of consumption, but indirectly by selling the commodities they produced and then spending the money on the purchase of food. Although this was quite an un-feudal situation, the medieval lawyers was applied to it the dominant feudal legal concept, tenure, by analogy. They still thought of this new economic relation in terms of the old legal concepts. Nevertheless, the concept had to be adapted to fit the greater freedom of people in the towns. Burgage tenants, for example, had a freedom not achieved by tenants in socage or knight service until the 16th century, the freedom to leave their tenement by will.

F. Unfree Tenures

1. Villeinage

Villeinage was not only a tenure by which land was held, but also a status.[40] Villeins were bondsmen, bound to the manor in which they lived. Villeins necessarily held by unfree tenure, but freemen could hold land by villeinage tenure. Villeins did not have seisin of the land. The main service was labour in the direct form: the villein had to work two or three days a week on the lord's demesne and at times of the year such as at harvest when the needs of agriculture required a lot of work to be done, often by larger work teams, four or even six days in the week. In the time that was left he had to produce his own subsistence on the strips on the open fields. Villeins sometimes also had to pay rent in kind to the lord as well. The essential point is that the services were uncertain. The only restriction on the lord's power to set the number of days to be worked on his demesne was the custom of the manor. If any dispute arose it could only

39 Simpson, *Land Law* pp.14–15, 21.

40 Simpson, *Land Law* pp.145–150; Pollock and Maitland, *History* 1: 356. 383

be litigated in the lord's court. Villeins had no right to bring an action in the King's courts. The villein's unfree status meant that he had no rights against the lord: the relationship was one of power, the power of the lord over the tenant, rather than a relationship of law in which the parties had rights and duties in relation to each other.

Villein tenure changed in the course of time and so did villeinage status. The change was accelerated in England by the epidemic of bubonic plague known as the Black Death of 1349. It has been estimated that the epidemic killed about one third of the population but one consequence was that it strengthened the bargaining position of those who survived. The development of wage labour in new forms of employment also played a part. By the mid 15th century the services of villeinage had been commuted to money rent and villeins had become personally free.[41]

In England there was another form of unfree tenure known as ancient demesne.[42] This occurred in manors held by the Crown before the Norman Conquest of England by the Anglo-Saxons kings. The Normans recognised that tenants within these manors enjoyed certain privileges under the previous Anglo-Saxon law.[43]

No similar tenure, relating to land held from one of the Kings of the four Irish traditional kingdoms, was recognised in Ireland. For one thing, large parts of the country remained unconquered until the 17th century within those areas the indigenous law in Ireland remained untouched. The military suppression of the those remaining areas in the 17th century was accompanied by an ideology which was extremely hostile to indigenous Irish culture and had as its object the extirpation of the elements of it which remained.

2. Copyhold

Villeinage became known as copyhold, indicating that the tenant held by copy of the manorial roll. A copyhold tenant could not sell the land directly, but instead conveyed it by surrender and admittance. This involved surrendering the tenure to the lord who then admitted the person nominated by the former tenant as the new tenant of the land. Once the transformation from villeinage to copy-

41 Megarry & Wade, *Real Property* p.26. The last case in England concerning villein status was *Pigg v. Caley* (1618) Noy 27, 74 ER 997; Holdsworth, *HEL* 3:508; Hargrave, *Jurisconsult Excercitations* London: 1811–13 vol. 1, p.25.

42 A surviving example was to be found in *Merttens v. Hill* [1901] 1 Ch. 842 (Manor of Rothley, Leicestershire); *Stafford's Case* (1554) 2 Dyer 111b, 73 ER 245 (Bromsgrove, Worcestershire). Ancient demesne may have survived the 1922–25 legislation in England: see Megarry, *Manual* (3rd ed.) p.27.

43 One of these was access to the royal courts. While the manor was held by the King, this was logical, since the royal court was also the court of the lord of the manor, but the privilege was that access to royal courts still applied even if the King granted the manor to another lord.

hold had taken place, the lord no longer had any power to refuse such a transfer. Nevertheless, since the transfer was recorded in the court roll, the incidents of the tenure were often preserved. One of these was heriot, the right of the lord to take the tenant's best beast at his death.[44] A few examples of copyhold occurred in Ireland at the time of the Tudor settlements[45] but the tenure has long since become obsolete.[46]

G. Irish Laws Assimilated to Tenure

1. Irish Gavelkind

Under the Brehon laws which survived in Ireland until the 17th century there was no relationship which corresponded precisely to the Anglo-Norman concept of tenure. There were relationships involving the loan or grant of cattle which created patron/client relationships which had many similarities with tenure and similar[47] relationships in relation to land, but, since in the Gaelic communities the patrons and the clients, or lord and vassals, generally belonged to the same kinship group and claimed descent from a common ancestor, the purely economic relationship involving the land or cattle was mitigated and permeated by kinship ties.

The indigenous Irish laws of succession varied in a number of respects from that of the Anglo-Normans. The Anglo-Normans followed the practice of primogeniture, the land passing to the eldest son. The Irish divided land among all the sons equally. Originally the division was probably made by the father before his death. An interesting variant occurred, which ensured an equal division. The youngest son divided the land into equal parts. Then the eldest chose a piece for himself, then the second son, and so on until the youngest son took the last piece. It was thus in the youngest son's own interest to divide the land equally, for he would be left with the last piece. The ingenuity lies in the fact that equality does not depend upon altruism: equality is achieved if everyone

44 *Inchquin v. Burnell* (1795) 3 Ridg PC 425, Ir HL.

45 R. Dunlop, "The Plantation of Munster 1584-1589" (1888) 3 Eng Hist Rev 250–269 p.255; R. Dunlop, "The Plantation of Leix and Offaly"(1891) 6 Eng Hist Rev 61–96.

46 R. Dunlop, "The Plantation of Munster 1584–1589" (1888) 3 Eng Hist Rev 250–269 pp. 255–6. Manorial courts did exist, although they may have dated only from the pseudo-feudal tenures of the plantation period. See *Boyd v. Magee* (1849) 13 Ir LR 435 (appointment of coroner and seneschals); *Costelloe v. Hooks* (1848) 11 Ir CLR 294 (manor of Newry); but see *Herbert v. Maclean* (1862) 12 Ir Ch R 84 (covenant to attend manorial court in Merrion Square, Dublin); and see footnote 101.

47 *Case of Gavelkind* (1605) Dav 49, 80 ER 535; Hans Pawlisch, "The Cases of Gavelkind and Tanistry: Legal Imperialism in Ireland, 1603–1610" in *Sir John Davies and the Conquest of Ireland* (Cambridge: Cambridge UP); *Fauconberg (Earl) v. Kingsland (Viscount)* (1790) 2 Ridg PC 147.

acts in their own best interest. The rule was a product of legal skill of the highest order as well as a wordly-wise view of human nature.

The relationship of the variant rule to the rule of division by the father is not clear. The variant form may have been a local variation, or it may have taken place if the father died without being able to make a division. It may also have tended to replace the division by the father and become the general rule since it ensured greater equity among the sons: a father might show favouritism. At any rate, it is mentioned in surviving Chancery pleadings from Westmeath-Offaly in the 1590s.[48]

Gavelkind was the name given by the Anglo-Normans to this Irish inheritance law, which, since the Normans thought in terms of tenures, they saw as a separate tenure. Sometimes it is more correctly referred to as a custom in the nature of gavelkind. It reminded them of English gavelkind, a form of land holding found in Kent and which they had recognised. The English form, like the Irish form, was probably not really a tenure in the Norman sense, but a local Anglo-Saxon form of inheritance.[49]

The Irish law differed in two other respects from the Anglo-Norman law of succession: the Irish did not permit females to inherit in the absence of males[50] and did not exclude the sons resulting from informal sexual relationships: in fact the Gaelic Irish did not have a concept of illegitimacy as the Normans did. While the Gaelic system still survived, the Irish Chancery recognised gavelkind but by the 1590s had refused in a number of cases to recognise the exclusion of females from inheritance.[51] With the end of the Gaelic order at the end of the 16th century the process of physical colonisation was accompanied, as it invariably was, by attacks on the culture of the indigenous population. In the *Case of Gavelkind*[52] both the exclusion of females[53] and the inclusion of children considered illegitimate under the imposed law were used to denounce the Irish custom as barbaric and it was declared illegal.[54]

48 Nicholls, *Gaelic Ireland* p.61. See also Nicholls, "Some Documents on Irish Law and Custom in the Sixteenth Century" (1970) 26 Analecta Hibernica 105 p.106.

49 Pollock & Maitland, *History* vol. 2 p.269; Bl Com vol. 2.

50 Husbands could, however, give land acquired by them during their lifetime to their wives, and women also received land in pledge for their dowries: Nicholls, *Gaelic Ireland* p.60.

51 Nicholls, *Gaelic Ireland* p.60.

52 (1605) Dav 49, 80 ER 535; Hans Pawlisch, "The Cases of Gavelkind and Tanistry: Legal Imperialism in Ireland, 1603-1610" in *Sir John Davies and the Conquest of Ireland* (Cambridge: Cambridge UP). See footnote 54.

53 Nicholls "Some Documents on Irish Law and Custom in the Sixteenth Century" (1970) 26 Analecta Hibernica 105 p.107; Nicholls, "Irishwomen and Property in the Sixteenth Century" in MacCurtain and O'Dowd (1991).

54 As Pawlisch (footnote 52) points out, the case report is a fake and was invented for propaganda purposes. The land had already been recovered by an order in equity.

In one of those paradoxes which readily occurs when law is used as an oppressive instrument, the concept of an Irish form of gavelkind was actually revived during the period of the Penal Laws. The Gavelkind Act, in fact a section of a statute of Queen Anne,[55] was used to force Catholic Irish landowners to divide their land among their sons on their death. The evident purpose of this was to weaken the Catholic landowning class by reducing the size of holdings over a period.

2. Rundale

Again, this is not a tenure in the Anglo-Norman sense, but probably the survival of native Irish, *i.e.* Brehon law. Within the areas where rundale survives, which are the Western counties of Ireland, rights of pasture are held in common by local landowners, while arable plots are held individually but periodically redistributed among them.[56]

3. Commonage

These are common rights to pasture only vested in local landowners. There are no arable plots associated with the tenure and this distinguishes it from rundale. Rights of commonage exist on hill or mountain pasture.[57] These commonage rights are also, somewhat confusingly, referred to as rundale. Commonage survives today in parts of Ireland. There is provision for compulsory partition under section 24 of the Land Act, 1939.[58]

H. Introduction of Tenure into Ireland

1. The Establishment of Anglo-Norman Rule

The system of tenure was introduced into Ireland in the wake of the advent of Anglo-Norman rule in Ireland in the 12th century and the expansion of Anglo-Norman control in the 13th century. The process was slower than in England, due to the continued resistance of the indigenous Irish people. Some of the grants made were over territory that had not in fact been conquered and such grants were in substance a licence to subdue the land granted. Grants were in knight service except where churches or monasteries had held in the land before the conquest, in which case they were recognised as holding in frankalmoin.

55 Section 10 of 2 Anne c.6 (Ir).

56 Wylie, *Irish Land Law* para. 1.14.

57 *Re Commonage at Glennamaddoo* [1992] 1 IR 297; Wylie, *Irish Land Law* para. 1.14.

58 *ibid.*, and see Chapter 16 Co-Ownership.

The first grant was the entire Irish kingdom of Leinster by Henry II in 1171–72 to Richard de Clare, known as Strongbow, who had led the army which conquered it. The grant was for a service of a 100 knight's fees.

The next large grant was of the kingdom of Meath in 1172 by Henry II to Hugh de Lacy for 50 knight's fees. In 1177 King John made grants of the kingdoms of Cork to Robert fitz Stephen, and Limerick to Philip de Braose. In the 1190s the whole of Connaught was granted William de Burgo although it had not been conquered at the time. In 1185 King John made smaller grants of land to tenants in chief in knight service in County Clare, Offaly, Tipperary, Limerick, Louth, Armagh, Monaghan and also the Irish kingdom of Uriel. In 1205 Hugh de Lacy was granted the entire kingdom of Ulster, which had been partly conquered and ruled as an independent lordship by John de Courcy.

A special feature of the early grants in Ireland was that they were not, as had been the case in England, grants of territory which had already been conquered, but rather were authorisations to conquer and feudalise the areas concerned. Military service was nevertheless commuted to scutage at an earlier date than that in England.

2. The Tudor and Stuart Period

The expansion of feudal tenure during this period can be attributed to a distinct historical cause: the development of capitalism in England. Money, made in commerce or money rent itself, came to be invested in agricultural production and at the same time landlords, whose income was formed from rent rather than capital, sought capitalist farmers as tenants. The picture is further complicated by the fact that the income of the lords appears not to have come so frequently from the services of tenure as from the incidents. By the Tudor period in England the services of tenure had declined in importance while the incidents of tenure, especially wardship in knight service, remained of value. Indeed, it was often the case that lordships were now bought more for the incidents that went with them than for the services. It was probably the case that those who had made money in commerce or finance were buying lordships as a form of speculation in the hope or expectation that a wardship[59] would occur and thus the lordship would come to have a substantial value.[60] We shall now consider the different methods by which tenure came to be introduced in this period.

59 For wardship, see below.

60 Suppose L was the lord of T1. L had inherited the lordship which had been created generations ago. The services were now worth much less than in the past. More recently, T1 had subinfeudated to T2 for services that were worth much more than those he owed to L. If T1 died leaving an under-age heir, L would reap a profit until the heir came of age. L's seignory could be sold as a speculative investment.

a) Surrender and Regrant

In the 1540s officials of Henry VIII negotiated with previously independent lords, of both Irish and Anglo-Norman descent, to surrender their lands in return for regrants in knight service at a rent. This was part of a process which led to the decline of the Gaelic order of society and the replacement of Brehon law with Anglo-Norman law.

b) Plantations

The plantation process began in the reign of Mary I in the 1550s and continued until the reign of William III. It differed from the other methods in that the primary producers on the land were replaced with immigrants. In legal terms it involved a two-stage process. First, the previous lords or occupants of the land lost their rights by forfeiture for what the English Crown and the courts considered to be treason in resisting English rule. This act of forfeiture left the title in the Crown. A royal title might also be established by escheat or through special statutes providing that landowners who were absent from Ireland for a period forfeited their rights. In the latter case this meant that those who were ineffectual in conquering an area could be replaced by those who would be more effective. Secondly, new grants were made to settlers as quasi-feudal tenants of the Crown.

The first plantation took place in Leix and Offaly. In 1557 the Irish parliament was induced to declare lands including Leix and Offaly as belonging to Philip and Mary through forfeiture for treason.[61] Grants were made in knight service at a money rent. The tenants were of Irish as well as English descent who had participated in the conquest of the area.

The second area was Munster. The pretext was the rebellion of the Earl of Desmond, the lands being those of the Earl and his followers. Grants were made in socage (or fee farm) at a money rent. Each tenant was to retain some land himself as demesne and grant the rest out in freehold socage, or in leasehold tenure or on copyhold. In fact more land was leased than was granted out in other types of tenure, showing the growing importance of leasehold as expressing the increasingly commercial nature of landholding.

The largest area of plantation was, of course, Ulster. The area was forfeited and regranted after the Flight of the Earls in 1607. Most of the land in Armagh, Cavan, Donegal, Fermanagh, Tyrone and in Coleraine was held to have been forfeited to the Crown. Most of the land was granted to English and Scottish settlers in socage at a money rent, with further sub-grants by these tenants.

c) Composition

This was the method used in Connaught. A commission, established in 1585, inquired into the ownership of land in the area. The commission entered into

61 Hence they were named King's County and Queen's County.

agreements with persons successfully claiming land whereby they could have their titles confirmed and the Crown relinquished its right to cess, a type of tax used to pay for the military government of the area. Landowners usually agreed to hold their land in knight service from the Crown. Lesser landowners were acknowledged as holding in the same tenure from higher lords.

By 1640 most land in Ireland was subject to one kind of tenure or another. The few gaps that remained were filled during the Commonwealth and in the reign of William III, through confiscations and regrants. The Williamite regrants were in socage at a money or quit rent.

I. The Creation of a Layer of Tenure

A new tenure would come into existence when a landholder granted land to another person who would thereby become a tenant and the grantor would become a lord in relation to the new tenure. This process of creating a new layer of tenure was known as subinfeudation. In the 11th and 12th centuries most people including feudal lords were illiterate. An agreement creating tenure was not drawn up in the form of a document but took the form of a ceremony before witnesses. This was the *feoffment* (pronounced "feffment") and it consisted of a ceremony whereby the grantor of the land presented the grantee with a clod of earth or turf cut from the plot as a symbolic gesture. It was symbolic of the transfer of seisin. Seisin was the legal concept incorporating the notion of possession, but misrepresenting it at the same time. Since land produced use values for its lord, physical possession of the land in some sense was a necessary part of owning property in land. To be sure of receiving tribute payments the lord, through subordinates, would have to have means of enforcement at hand. The tenants themselves would have possession in an even more real sense in that they cultivated the soil. At this point, however, the law misrepresented reality because the King's courts did not recognise the possession of cultivators, *i.e.* the villeins, as seisin. Only freeholders had seisin and access to the King's courts. This was ensured by the system of forms of action.

In order to succeed in court a claimant had to prove that the facts of his case came within one of the recognised forms, and these generally specified that the claimant should be a freeholder. By the 13th century the feoffment was reduced to writing in a charter of feoffment. This would contain a statement of the services of the tenure which were, in amount, a matter for agreement between the grantor and the grantee. The incidents of tenure on the other hand were rights and duties which applied automatically and which depended on what type of tenure was created. The ceremony of feoffment was still performed and comprised three acts: an act of homage, in the case of military tenures, by which the grantee swore allegiance to the lord, to be loyal in time of war, an act of fealty, which was a personal oath to perform the services and applied even in unfree tenures, and an act of seisin where by it was transferred. The ceremony, and later its evidence in the form of the deed, was collectively called feoffment with livery of seisin[62] and was the oldest conveyance known to the common law.

J. Forms of Alienation and their Effects

1. Subinfeudation

The usual method of alienating, *i.e.* transferring an interest in land, until about 1200 was by subinfeudation. Suppose L, who held land in fee simple, granted land to T1 by knight service for an estate in fee simple. L constituted himself a lord and T1 as his freehold tenant. It can be said that while T1 held the land in fee simple, L held a *seignory*[63] or lordship in fee simple:

L - fee simple **(seignory)**
freehold tenure in knight service
T1 - fee simple

L had created a new layer of freehold tenure. L's seignory, his rights as lord of the tenure, entitled him to the services and the incidents of the tenure.

T1 in turn may have wished to grant land out to tenants in order to obtain services from them himself. Suppose T1 granted, *i.e.* subinfeudated, to T2 in knight service, for an estate in fee simple. A new layer of tenure was created. T1 made himself into a lord. He had created a seignory or lordship in himself. There were now three people to consider. L was still T1's lord, and he was the lord paramount of T2. T2 was T1's tenant, and in relation to L was a tenant paravail. T1 was a tenant in relation to L, but a lord in relation to T2:

62 Livery meaning delivery.

63 *Delacherois v. Delacherois* (1859) 8 Ir CLR 1, Exch Ch. per Pigot B: "On the other hand, a right remained in the lord (after a grant made) called a seignory consisting of services to be performed by the tenant and a right to have the land returned on the expiration of the grant... a right afterwards called an escheat." *Burgess v. Wheate* (1757–9) 1 Eden 128, 176, 28 ER 652; 3 Cruise Dig 491; Note in 5 M & R 157.

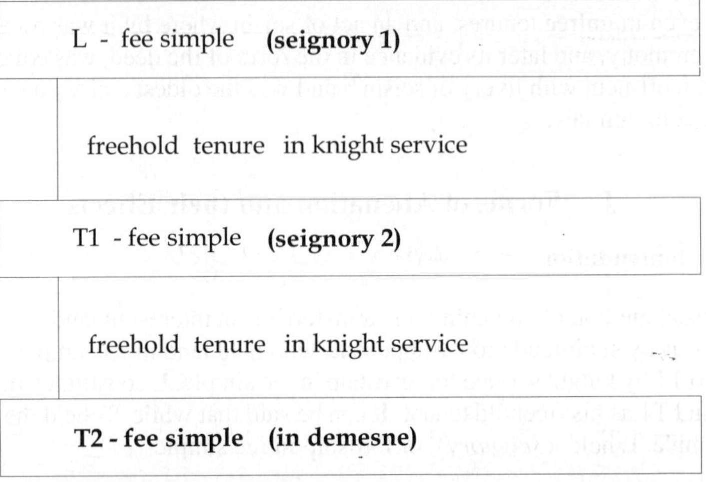

We have seen that the common law recognised title as relative rights to possession. Layers of tenure gave rise to relativity of rights in another aspect: the relativity of tenure. The new layer of tenure had no effect legally on the tenure between L and T1. T1 still owed the same services to L as before. He could not force L to accept some of the services direct from T2. Moreover, L still had his right of distress against the whole tenement which he granted to T1. L's right of distress entitled him to go onto the land and seize chattels on the land and hold them until T1 performed his service. L was entitled to seize chattels, even if the chattels in fact belong to T2. T2 could not legally resist the lord paramount[64]. But he did have a remedy against his own lord who had failed in his obligation of acquittance owed to his tenant through the tenure between them. T2 could bring a writ of mesne against T1, the mesne, or intermediate, lord.

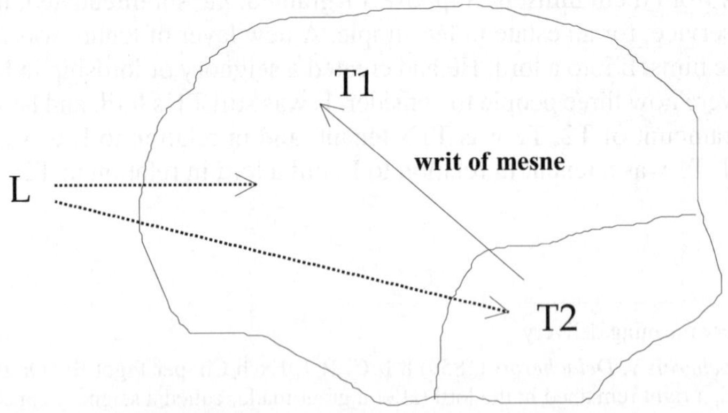

64 The same rule was applied to leasehold tenure by analogy: *Heawood v. Bone* (1884) 13 QBD 179, until reformed by the Law of Distress Amendment Act, 1908.

Thus, the obligations of the superior tenure were not merely personal rights as between the parties to the tenure, they were burdens on the land.[65] The two private individuals, as we would think of them, T1 and T2, had made an agreement between themselves, but could not do so without involving legal relations with L who was not a party to the agreement. The relationship was quite different, therefore, to a modern contract. T2 could not enter into an agreement with T1 without being subjected to burdens already determined between T1 and L and which were enforceable against his, T2's, own property – his cattle and belongings. Whatever immediate lord T2 chose, there would be similar burdens created by superior tenures. In the technical language of the period, the services which a tenant owed to his own lord were intrinsec, *i.e.* inside the bargain between them and voluntarily agreed. The obligations of the superior tenure were forinsec, *i.e.* applied by law. They appeared to be law of a general kind, like public law today, even though their origin was simply the agreement between L and T1. The relativity of tenure meant that the distinction found today between public and private law did not really exist in the medieval period.

Of equal importance historically, as we shall see, was the fact that the lord paramount was incapable of determining the content of the obligations between his own tenant and any sub-tenant to whom his tenant subinfeudated. L had no power to determine the content of the bargain between T1 and T2 even though this bargain could adversely affect L, by, for example, reducing T1's ability to perform his services to L. These obligations constituted a powerful limitation on the freedom of feudal lords themselves to control the economic relations of society.

2. Substitution

This form became possible in the early 13th century. The grantee replaced the grantor as tenant of the grantor's lord. He would owe the same services to the lord as the grantor had done, since the layer of tenure was the same. Until the Statute *Quia Emptores*, 1290 one disadvantage was that the consent of the grantor's lord was needed to the substitution.

65 It may be noticed that this involves a form of reification even under feudal relations. Reification has a long history.

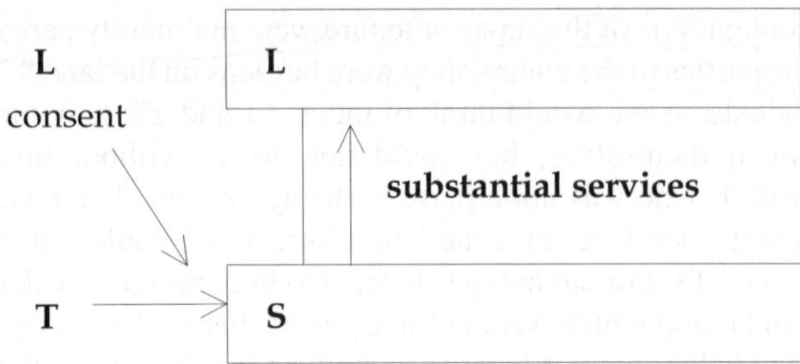

3. Mortmain

Mortmain was not really a single type of alienation or conveyance, but simply meant a grant in favour of a perpetual body such as a monastery or other ecclesiastical institution. The name mortmain was from the Norman French *morte main*, meaning dead hand. Let us say that L has granted land to T by subinfeudation. T then decides to grant part of the land to an abbey in frankalmoin tenure by further subinfeudation. The services of frankalmoin are of no economic value. If an escheat[66] occurs of T's tenure, then L will lose whatever valuable services could have been obtained from the part subinfeudated to the abbey. Furthermore, since the abbey was a perpetual body feudal incidents such as relief or aid did not arise. Mortmain tended to deprive the lords and the King of revenue. It undermined feudal economic relations. Moreover, the medieval church acquired a great deal of land. As it grew in economic wealth so it grew in political importance and came to be seen as a threat to the King's political dominance.

Mortmain was a threat to feudal political relations. However, it was open to another objection of a different kind. If land passed into the dead hand of a perpetual body, particularly an ecclesiastical one, it was unlikely ever to come on the market again. The land was withdrawn from the economic sphere of the market altogether. Mortmain was thus also objectionable from a market or capitalist point of view. Strong action was taken by the Statute of Mortmain, 1279. Under the statute, if a tenant attempted to grant his or her tenement or part of it to a perpetual body or person the tenure came to an end.

At this time the King still asserted the power to grant exemptions from the operation of the law to individuals. Hence the King granted licences to bodies to acquire land in mortmain despite the statute.[67] Granting licences in mortmain not only extended his patronage; it provided an additional source of

66 See pages 53–54.

67 There are examples of the Statute being enforced in Ireland. In 1300 and again in 1349 the Prior of Louth was summoned to answer for procuring land contrary to the Statute and without a licence: Archdall, *Monasticon Hibernicum* p.482.

income as well. It became accepted by the courts that the King had such a power.

Statutes regulating mortmain were passed from time to time and it was only in the this century that it was eventually abolished. This can probably be explained by the fact, as we have argued, that mortmain was seen as a threat to the expansion of the market in land and therefore to capitalism. There was in any case little point in requiring limited companies to obtain a licence in mortmain from the Crown before purchasing land, because, unlike ecclesiastical bodies, if they were successful then the land was being developed, or producing a profit, and if they were not, they could be wound up and the land sold off. Mortmain legislation was finally repealed in the Republic by the Mortmain (Repeal of Enactments) Act, 1954.[68]

K. Ending of the Bond of Tenure

A layer of tenure could be destroyed or come to an end in a number of ways, some of which have already been noted.

1. Escheat

This has already been dealt with above.

2. Forfeiture for Treason

This has already been dealt with above.

3. Disavowal

If a tenant denied the title of his lord in legal proceedings the tenure was destroyed.

4. Surrender

The tenant could surrender the land to his lord if, for example, the services were too onerous.

5. Mortmain

We have seen that if a tenant made a grant in favour of a perpetual body without a licence from the Crown, the tenure came to an end by virtue of the Statute of Mortmain, 1279.

68 Similarly in Northern Ireland by the Mortmain (Repeals) Act, 1960.

6. Gift of Frankalmoin

If land granted in frankalmoin was granted away by the donee that would defeat the purpose of the gift and be something like a fraud on the donor. It was a gift to charity and if the church did not want the land, then it was thought that it should go back to the donor or his family. The Statute of Westminster II, 1285 gave the donor's heirs a right of action to recover it.

7. Failure to Perform Services

Originally the only remedy of the lord if the tenant failed to perform services was to levy a distress on the land. However, the tenant could render the remedy valueless by arranging in advance that there would be no distrainable goods, or none of any value, on the land. The Statute of Gloucester, 1278 and the Statute of Westminster II, 1285 cc 21 and 41 provided that if the tenant ceased to do services for two years and arranged that there should be no distrainable chattels on the land, or prevented the lord having access to them, the lord had action to recover possession. Apart from the statutory provision the lord had no right to terminate the tenure unless there was an express forfeiture clause in the grant.

8. Eminent Domain?

In the United States the courts developed the doctrine of *eminent domain* which allows public and in some cases even private bodies to acquire land compulsorily for public purposes on payment of compensation. The supposed origin of this doctrine in Anglo-Irish feudal law is, however, without any foundation.[69] The doctrine found its way into the law of the United States from the law of New Spain.[70] One might note that the doctrine gave more extensive or despotic power to the monarchy in New Spain than was accorded to the Crown by the common law.

---

69 Some United States cases attribute the doctrine to feudal tenure: *e.g. New York City Housing Authority v. Muller* (1935) 155 Misc 681, 279 NYS 299, Supreme Court, Special Term, New York County ("The right of eminent domain is a remnant of the ancient law of feudal tenure"). But other judgments are historically more accurate: *United States v. Carmack* (1946) 329 US 230, 67 S Ct 252; (1946) US Lexis 2996, 91 L Ed 209, US Supreme Court ("No one doubts the existence in the State governments of the right of eminent domain, – a right distinct from and paramount to the right of ultimate ownership. It grows out of the necessities of their being, not out of the tenure by which lands are held. It may be exercised, though the lands are not held by grant from the government, either mediately or immediately, and independent of the consideration whether they would escheat to the government in case of a failure of heirs").

70 See *United States v. Castillero* (1862) 67 US 17, 2 Black 17, 17 L Ed 360, US Supreme Court ; *Doe d Clark v. Braden* (1850) 57 US 635, 14 L Ed 1090, US Supreme Court.

L. The Decline of Tenure

1. Effect of Subinfeudation on the Incidents

Some of the lord's incidents were unaffected by subinfeudation: suit of court, aids, relief, homage, fealty and wardship of the body. But others were affected. The incident of marriage, for example, was made less valuable since its value was related to the value of the land still held in demesne by the tenant. The effect on other incidents is considered below. The decline in the value of incidents eventually led to the decline of the feudal system.[71]

a) Wardship of the Tenement

If the tenant had subinfeudated some or all of his land, then when a wardship occurred, the lord would step into the shoes of the tenant and would be entitled only to such services as the tenant had reserved on the grant of the tenure with the tenant paravail.

b) Escheat

In the case of escheat, the same was true, except that the lord stepped permanently into the shoes of the former tenant.

2. Sale of Land

During the feudal period a new economic relationship developed. Land was used to produce products primarily for sale on the market. One of the earliest such products was wool. Tracts of land came to be valued for the amount of money they produced from the sale of wool and other commodities. Land came to have a money value itself. Freehold tenants wanted to sell land and realise this money value. How could they do it? Substitution was the obvious method, but it had disadvantages:

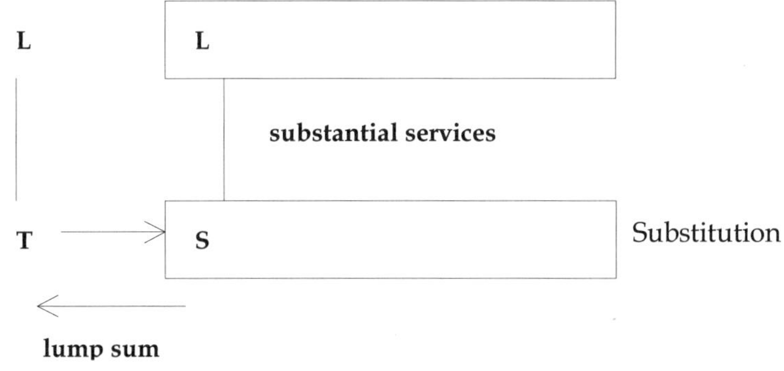

71 J.M.W. Bean, *The Decline of English Feudalism, 1215–1540*. (Manchester: Manchester University Press, 1968).

If S paid T a lump sum for the land he would have to take over the services due under the tenure to L. Also, L's consent was required to the transaction between T and S. T and S were not free to contract between themselves. Also, if T sold part of the land to S, he, T, remained liable for all the services due on the tenure unless he could get L to agree to apportion them between T and S.

Subinfeudation, the typically feudal form was, paradoxically, more attractive as a vehicle for sale. By the 13th century lords had lost control over subinfeudations. The buyer and seller were free to make their own bargain.

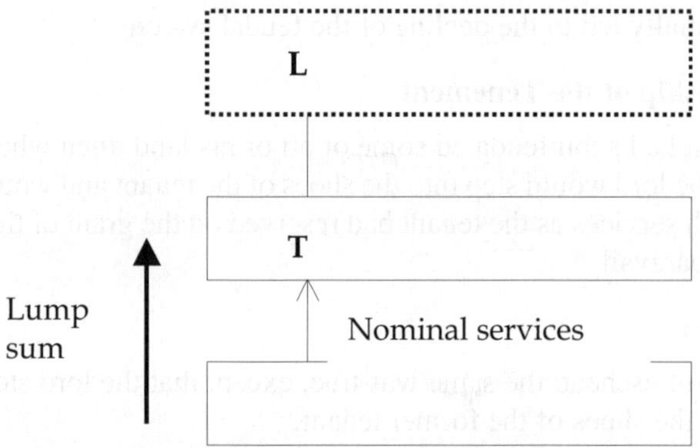

S would agree to pay T a nominal rent such as a peppercorn each year or a rose at midsummer. Nominal services caused problems for L. Legally he was still entitled to the same services from T as before, but T might be less able to pay them. More serious was the effect on incidents. If a wardship occurred, L dropped down into the position of T but only became entitled legally to nominal services from S. S could keep all the profits of the land and give L merely a peppercorn.

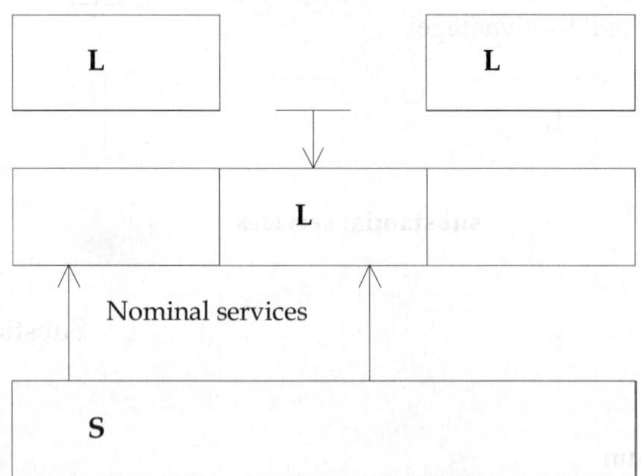

Even more serious was the effect on escheat. If T died without heirs, L becomes entitled only to nominal services from S, but in this case, permanently.

Sale of land was undermining the feudal system, depriving lords of their feudal income. Yet the situation was complicated by the fact that while some lords were losing income, others wanted to engage in sale to raise lump sums. Insofar as mesne lords were lords of a lower tenure, they were against sale by their tenants, but in so far as they were tenant they wished to be able to sell. Only the King, who was a lord but never a tenant, stood to lose but not gain. Magna Carta of 1217[72] prohibited tenants from alienating so much land that the part retained would be not be enough to supply the services due to the lord, but the measure seems to have been ineffective. The contradictions within the feudal system were resolved by a radical compromise, the Statute *Quia Emptores*, 1290.[73] So radical were the effects of the statute on the theory of land law that its effects can still be detected today.

3. Quia Emptores, 1290

The statute provided that:

1. Subinfeudation for a fee simple estate was prohibited in future.[74]
2. Substitution was to be the only method of granting land in fee simple and would no longer require the lord's consent.
3. If a tenant sold part of the tenement then the feudal services were to be apportioned between the two parts. Each party would be liable to distress by L only to the extent of the proportion of the services due from that part.
4. The Statute did not bind the Crown.[75] The Crown could and did create new tenures. It did so in the settlement of Ireland in the Tudor and Stuart periods.

---

72 18 John c.39. An Irish version of the Great Charter, *Magna Carta Hiberniæ* was promulgated in Ireland: see Richardson, "Magna Carta Hiberniæ" (1942) 3 IHS 31; *Hamilton v. The Marquess of Donegall* (1795) 3 Ridg PC 267; *Moore v. Attorney-General* [1934] IR 44; Wylie, *Cases* p.5; *Little v. Cooper* [1937] IR 1; *Foyle and Bann Fisheries Ltd v. Attorney-General* (1949) 83 ILTR 29.

73 Called after the first words of the statute: 'Because the purchasers of lands…'. See Plucknett, *Edward I* pp.102–109; Sutherland, *Novel Disseisin* pp. 95–96.

74 *Re Holliday* [1922] 2 Ch D 698.

75 *Abbot of Barking's Case* YB 10 Hen VII f 23a, 27 Hen VIII f 26 pl 5b; Verschoyle *v.* Perkins (1847) 13 Ir Eq R 72.

a) Quia Emptores in Ireland

(1) Application

An early Irish statute in 1293 declared that if tenants in chief alienated without licence from the king their lands were to escheat, but such tenants in march lands, *i.e.* on the border of the Pale, were permitted to subinfeudate for the purpose of defence.[76] This seems clearly to have been an adaptation for Ireland of *Quia Emptores*.[77] It is also an early example of exceptions to *Quia Emptores* being allowed in Ireland, a point we shall return to later. There are also references to the statute in pleadings in the period 1295 to 1303.[78] The statute has been applied by the courts in Ireland in modern times.[79]

(2) Exceptional Grants in Ireland

In Ireland, mostly dating from the Plantation period, the Crown granted land to freehold tenants purporting at the same time to give them a power to subinfeudate further *non obstante* (notwithstanding) *Quia Emptores*. In other words the Crown purported to grant them an exemption from the statute, an exercise of the dispensing power exercised by medieval kings. The tenants could thus create a new layer of tenure in fee simple and probably could still do so today, where the grants survive. These *non obstante* grants, as they are known, reserved a rent to the Crown, the Crown rent being known in Ireland as a quit rent.[80] These grants are considered in more detail in the chapter on fee farm grants.[81]

b) The Effect of the Statute on Tenure

In the long term the statute meant a decline in tenure and so also contributed to the decline of the feudal system itself. Every time an escheat occurred a layer of tenure was destroyed and it could not be replaced. Mesne lordships became

---

76 21 Edw. I, s.2; E. St. Ir. p.192; Hand p.162.

77 Donaldson (1952) p.80.

78 In a case before the justiciar in 1302 the king's serjeant pleaded successfully "the statute by which it is enacted that no one may alien a tenement in fee, to hold of the feoffor, or of any others, than the chief lords of the fee": Donaldson (1952); Hand p.162; Cal. Just. Rolls Ir. 1295–1303 p.384; and see *ibid.* pp. 383–5, Hand p.51.

79 *Verschoyle v. Perkins* (1847) 13 Ir Eq R 72; *Corporation of Dublin v. Herbert* (1862) 12 Ir CLR 502, *Delacherois v. Delacherois* (1864) 11 HLC 62, 11 ER 1254; *Chute v. Busteed* (1864) 14 Ir CLR 115 Exch at p.127 per Pigot CB.

80 *Esdaile v. Stephenson* (1835) 1 Ll & G t P 122; *Tuthill v. Rogers* (1844) 6 Ir Eq R 439, 68 RR 223; *Allen v. Linehan* (1860) 9 Ir CLR 291. By the 19th century the courts tended to regard quit rents as a type of tax or charge rather than as a rent service. The Landed Estates Court had power to redeem quit rents: Macnevin *Landed Estates Court* p.12.

81 See Chapter 7 Fee farm grants: Feudal Tenure.

rarer in course of time.[82] The feudal pyramid shrank. Eventually, almost everyone would become a tenant in chief.[83]

Some historians have seen evidence of a free market in land in England at a much earlier period than in most European countries.[84] It might be easy to draw the further conclusion, that the English possessed at an early stage a sense of individualism conducive to entrepreneurship and capitalism. It may well be true that considerable buying and selling was going on in the middle ages, but lawyers may ask what it was that was being sold. The common law never took the view that what was sold was land, as opposed to rights or interests in land. Villeins may have sold strips to each other, but in the three field system they possessed a right which lasted at most for two years and even then it was held at the mercy of the lord. Even freeholders owed services of tenure and suffered from disabilities unthinkable in a truly market economy, such as the inability to prevent lords paramount levying a distress on their land to recover debts which they did not owe. In the long term *Quia Emptores* led to the decline of tenure and assisted in the decline of feudalism, but only in the long term. Its immediate purpose and probably its short term effect may well have been to discourage sale of land since, by requiring compliance with the legal form of substitution, it also required that the purchaser continue to pay the services of tenure owed by the former tenant. So long as these remained substantial purchasers of land remained in a worse position than if they had taken by subinfeudation before the statute.

c) The Effects on Real Property Today

Some effects of the statute can still be detected in the law of real property today:

82 Thus, when escheats occurred, they usually did so for the benefit of the Crown: see *Lysaght v. McGrath* (1882) 11 LR Ir 142, CA.

83 *Quia Emptores*, 1290 allowed alienation by substitution without the consent of the lord of the tenure, but the statute did not bind the Crown and implied that, as most freeholders came to hold directly of the Crown, they would require consent to a substitution. However, a statute of 1327 gave tenants in chief the right of free alienation (1 Edw III st 2 cc 12, 13 (Eng) (1327).

84 See Macfarlane, *English Individualism.*

(1) Lesser estates

Since the act only applies to subinfeudations in fee simple, a grant of an estate less than a fee simple[85] may[86] still create tenure today, and so (i) could reserve a rent to the grantor without creating a separate rentcharge, and (ii) can impose freehold covenants binding between successors to the grantor and those who inherit the estate. The point has, however, little practical significance:[87]

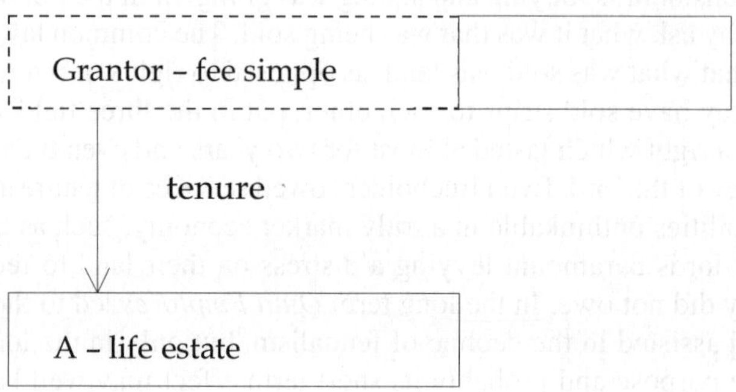

(2) Fees Simple

Since the statute still applies to fee simple estates, a grant of a fee simple today cannot create freehold tenure between grantor and grantee and so could not, for example, reserve a rent to the grantor without creating a separate rentcharge. Such a rent (*i.e.* not being a separate rentcharge could only exist as a rent service, *i.e.* a service of tenure, and no such service can be created after 1290. Land subject to *non obstante* grants is an exception. Furthermore, in Ireland hybrid grants within Deasy's Act, 1860 create leasehold tenure in respect of a fee simple estate and a leasehold rent can be reserved on such a grant.

---

85 *i.e.* a fee tail or life estate, including estates pur autre vie and, in the past, leases for lives renewable forever. The grant of the this last interest would, however, no longer take effect as such by virtue of the Renewable Leaseholds Conversion Act, 1849. See Chapter 9 Life Estates.

86 In *Delacherois v. Delacherois* (1864) 11 HLC 62, 11 ER 1254 it was held that, where a grant could take effect as a substitution or as a subinfeudation, an intention would have to be shown that it take effect as a subinfeudation. The case was, however, dealing with a grant in fee simple which was argued to be a *non obstante* fee farm grant. See also Chapter 7 Fee Farm Grants.

87 It has little practical importance (a) because grants of freehold estates less than a fee simple are now unusual if not rare, and (b) because where such estates are created they are usually granted to members of the grantor's own family and the grantor does not retain a rent, which would be one of the indications of tenure. The indication of tenure would be that the rent is a rent service, *i.e.* a service of the tenure, and so need not be created by a rentcharge which is a separate property interest.

4. Reversion and Tenure After 1290

After the statute the fallacy gained ground in England[88] that reversion and tenure were in some essential way connected, so that tenure could not exist without a reversion. No similar view developed in Ireland because exceptions to *Quia Emptores*, 1290 existed. The English view was a purely reifying concept – it was not the solution to a practical problem. It was thought to "follow" from the rules. It was true, of course, that after the statute in England one could not create tenure without at the same time creating a reversion. The statute did not prevent subinfeudation for grants of estates less than a fee simple and on the grant of such an estate one necessarily also created a reversion. But before the statute one could certainly create tenure without a reversion: that is exactly what happened when a subinfeudation in fee simple occurred. There was no reversion on a fee simple, before or after the statute, only an escheat.

The fallacy had little significance in relation to freehold itself, but when leaseholds were developed by the courts similar ideas found their way into concepts of leasehold estates in England. It gave rise to the idea that a sublease could not be created for the entire term of the head lease: no reversion, so no tenure. The statute was applied by analogy, as it were, to leaseholds. This fallacy caused a controversy between the English and Irish courts in the 18th and early 19th centuries.[89]

88 See for example Williams, *Real Property* p.370:

> "The doctrine that rent service, being incident to the reversion, always follows such reversion, formerly gave rise to the unpleasant consequence of the rent being sometimes lost when the reversion was destroyed."

Rent service was a service of tenure. There was no such thing as an "incident of the reversion." To refer to it as an "incident" is in any case confusing because "incident" had a technical meaning in relation to tenure. On the following page Williams says that "rent service is an incident [sic] of tenure," and so apparently uses tenure and reversion interchangeably.

89 See Chapter 19 Landlord and Tenant.

Tenure and Reversion in Irish and English Land Law

Ireland	England
Freehold	**Freehold**
1. Before Quia Emptores	*1. Before Quia Emptores*
Tenure without reversion, on subinfeudation in fee simple.	Same
2. After Quia Emptores	*2. After Quia Emptores*
Statutory exception to *Quia Emptores*; feudal fee farm grants. Still examples of tenure without reversion.	No subinfeudation in fee simple. Subinfeudation for life estate, estate tail possible, but then reversion also. Therefore no tenure without reversion:
Leasehold	**Leasehold**
1. Before the Union of 1801	No tenure without reversion:
Irish cases: Tenure without reversion: may sublet for whole term of lease.	grant for full term is an assignment, not a subletting.
2. Between Union & Deasy's Act, 1860	
British appeals: no tenure without reversion.	
3. After Deasy's Act, 1860	
Section 3 restores per-Union position: Tenure without reversion.	

5. The Abolition of Military Tenures

The decline of the economic power of the feudal lords meant also that the political power was increasingly concentrated at the apex of the pyramid. It led to the emergence of an absolutist monarchy under the Tudors and the early Stuarts.[90]

On the other hand, the rising economic power of non-feudal classes – the bankers, financiers and small landowners who invested their rent as capital – was not reflected in political power. The absolutist monarchy acted in ways that were not conducive to free trade and investment. It claimed the right to grant monopolies over trade in certain goods or services and its arbitrary exercise of power increased the risks faced by those contemplating investment in trade.

One of the functions of the 17th century Revolution in England was to destroy this arbitrary power, the remnant of feudalism and replace it by a form of government more conducive to the development of capitalism. It was anti-feudal in character, at least antagonistic to the remnants of feudal relationships that remained. To Cromwell, the law of real property was "a tortuous and ungodly jumble."[91] The opportunity was taken to abolish many of the features of feudal tenure.

The first step was taken in Ireland in 1641 by a resolution of the Irish Parliament, to be followed five years later in England by an ordinance of the Long Parliament in 1646.[92] This was later enacted as a statute of the Commonwealth in 1656.[93] The Restoration parliament of Charles II did not recognise the statutes of the Commonwealth and so re-enacted the legislation, in Ireland[94] as the Tenures Abolition Act, 1662.[95]

a) Knight Service

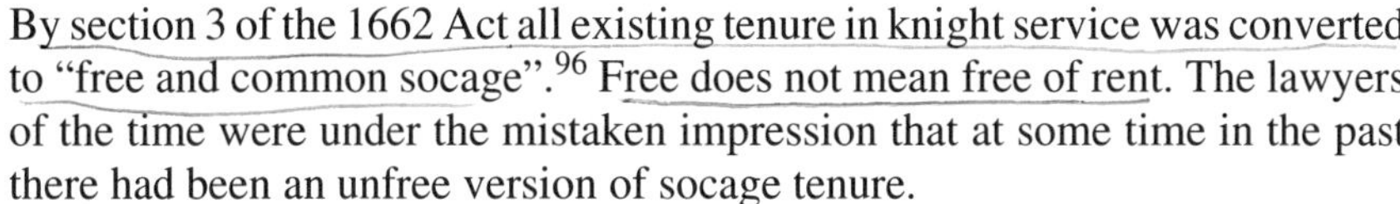

By section 3 of the 1662 Act all existing tenure in knight service was converted to "free and common socage".[96] Free does not mean free of rent. The lawyers of the time were under the mistaken impression that at some time in the past there had been an unfree version of socage tenure.

90 See Anderson, *Absolutist State* 113–142; Moore, *Dictatorship and Democracy* Chapter 1.

91 Megarry & Wade, *Real Property* p.1.

92 Ordinance for removing the Court of Wards, 24 February 1645/6, Firth and Rait *Acts and Ordinances of the Interregnum 1642–1660*, London, HMSO, 1911, vol. 1, p.833.

93 An Act for taking away the Court of Wards and Liveries, 27 November 1656, *ibid.* vol. 2, p.1043.

94 In England as the Tenures Abolition Act, 1660.

95 See Short Titles Act, 1962.

96 *Inchquin v. Burnell* (1795) 3 Ridg PC 425; *Verschoyle v. Perkins* (1847) 13 Ir Eq R 72, at p.77.

b) New Tenures

The Crown was prohibited from creating new tenures except in free and common socage. Here again, it seems that free does not imply free of rent and so the statute did not prevent the Crown from reserving a rent on the grant of a freehold tenure.[97]

c) Serjeanty

The 1662 Act did not abolish serjeanty, in fact the honorary services were expressly preserved by section 11.[98] The Act did, however, abolish most of the incidents.

d) Frankalmoin

The 1662 Act did not abolish frankalmoin and examples of it may still exist as to some land held by the Church of Ireland.[99]

e) Socage

The 1662 Act did not abolish the services of socage, which was a money rent by this time. Nor did it prevent the Crown reserving a rent when creating a new tenure in socage. Statutes in Ireland at the time of the Stuart settlements provided for the granting of freehold at rents.[100]

6. The Decline of Incidents

a) Homage

Homage was abolished by the 1662 Act as to all tenures. The military incident had ceased to be appropriate.

---

97 See *Stuart v. Easton* (1898) 170 US 383, 42 L Ed 1078, 18 S Ct 650, US Supreme Court, 170 US at 391, 42 L Ed at 1081, 18 S Ct at 653:

> "King Charles II, in granting the Province of Pennsylvania to William Penn and his heirs, gave it to be held in free and common socage...[at an] annual quitrent of a red rose being merely a feudal acknowledgment of tenure... [1082] by the Revolution and acts of the assembly of Pennsylvania subsequently passed, declaring all lands within the Commonwealth to be held by a title purely allodial."

98 There are still examples of serjeanties held in chief in England.

99 Frankalmoin may not have been abolished in England: The Administration of Estates Act, 1925 repealed s.7 of the English Act, 1660 which had merely declared that nothing in s.1 should affect frankalmoin. Section 1 abolished knight service, which did not affect frankalmoin in any case.

100 Settlement of Ireland Act, 1665, 17 & 18 Chas II c.2 repealed in NI by the Property (Northern Ireland) Order 1978 (SI 459, NI 4); RI – Statute Law Revision (Pre-Union Irish Statutes) Act, 1962.

b) Fealty

Fealty was expressly saved by the 1662 Act but has become obsolete in practice.

c) Suit of Court

This incident tended to be commuted to money payments from the 13th century onwards. It was preserved by the 1662 Act but has become obsolete. Manorial courts had become defunct by the end of the 19th century.[101] They had become defunct before that in most cases.[102]

d) Aids

Aids were abolished for all tenures by the 1662 Act. They had come to be of little value, having been fixed in amount in 1275 for mesne lords,[103] and in 1350 for tenants in chief.[104]

e) Reliefs

In most cases they had been fixed and inflation had reduced them to worthless amounts. The effect of the Statute of Wills (Ireland), 1634 was that no relief was payable if the land was left by will but continued to be payable on intestate succession. The 1662 Act preserved reliefs. They can still exist in theory but are obsolete in practice.

f) Wardship

Wardship in England was an incident of the military tenures and so the effect of the 1662 Act was to abolish it there since the statute converted knight service to socage and abolished the incidents of serjeanty. In so far as wardship

---

101 Copyhold Act, 1841, 4 & 5 Vict. c.35 (lords of manors, stewards, may hold manorial courts although no copyholders present), repealed in England by Copyhold Act, 1894, 57, 58 Vict. c.46. The 1894 Act did not apply to Ireland. Manorial courts were abolished in Ireland by the Manor Courts Abolition (Ireland) Act, 1859 and their jurisdiction transferred to petty sessions, but some manorial incidents were preserved. See also 25 Geo III c.44, 1785; 27 Geo III c.22, 1787; 36 Geo III c.25 ss. 15, 47, 1795; 44 Geo III c.90, (UK, 1804). "Manorial courts in England only lost their legal jurisdiction by the Administration of Justice Act, 1977 s.23 and Sch. 4. Copyhold tenure does not appear to have been abolished in Ireland. In England most of the incidents of copyhold were abolished by the Law of Property Act, 1922 s.128, although some, such as rights of the lord to markets and fairs, were preserved indefinitely, and so the tenure itself was not abolished": Megarry & Wade, *Real Property* p.37.

102 *Boyd v. Magee* (1849) 13 Ir LR 435; *Costelloe v. Hooks* (1848) 11 Ir CLR 294; *Herbert v. Maclean* (1862) 12 Ir Ch R 84.

103 3 Edw I st 1 c.36.

104 25 Edw III st 5 c.11.

applied in Ireland to socage tenure the incident could still exist here but it is obsolete in practice.

g) Escheat

Escheat was not abolished by the 1662 Act.

(1) For Felony

The Corruption of Blood Act, 1814[105] reduced the scope of escheat for felony to murder and petit treason. Escheat for felony was abolished by the Forfeiture Act, 1870[106] section 1.

The 1870 Act did not abolish escheat for outlawry.[107] It was abolished in Northern Ireland by the Criminal Procedure Act (Northern Ireland), 1951 section 2. The Forfeiture Act, 1870 was repealed in the Republic by the Criminal Law Act, 1997, and the law of felony assimilated to that of misdemeanour.[108]

(2) For Want of Heirs

Escheat for want of heirs was not abolished until the Succession Act, 1965 s11(3) which reads:

> "11.–(3) Escheat to the State and escheat to a mesne lord for want of heirs are hereby abolished."

Under section 73(1) of the 1965 Act if any person dies in the Republic possessed of land held for an estate in fee simple[109] intestate and without other intestate successors under Part VI of the Succession Act, 1965 the property passes to the State as ultimate intestate successor. Where a person dies in similar circumstances possessed of an absolute interest in personal property the same provision takes effect.

What happens in theory to a fee simple in such circumstances is open to question. On the one hand it could be argued that it remains a fee simple, in which case after 1 January 1967 in the Republic a fee simple never comes to an end. On the other hand, it does not seem consonant with theory to regard the State as holding a fee simple, for the State should hold by absolute ownership. Under the State Property Act, 1954 the Minister of Finance can waive the right

---

105 54 Geo III c.145, repealed SLRA, 1960.

106 The Act was the result of a change in public opinion brought about, in part at least, by Charles Dicken's novel *Great Expectations*. See also The Forfeiture Act, 1870 (Adaptation) Order, 1929 SR & O No. 29 of 1929, Statute of Limitations, 1957 s.48 (disability). *Talbot v. Jevers* [1917] 2 Ch. 363.

107 Forfeiture Act, 1870, s.1.

108 ss. 3, 16 & Sch.

109 *Fawcett v. Hall* (1833) Alc & Nap 248, at 253 (escheat an incident [*sic*] of the fee simple estate and not of other estates).

of the State in favour of any person he thinks fit.[110]

(3) Residual Forms of Escheat

(a) Land Registered Under 1891 Act

As regards agricultural land bought out under the Land Purchase Acts and compulsorily registered under the Local Registration of Title Act, 1891, all escheats were abolished in that year, since such land was to devolve as personal property.

Personal property, including leaseholds,[111] passed to the State as *bona vacantia* if no one else was entitled. As regards personal property owned by real persons, the doctrine of *bona vacantia* was replaced by the principle of the State taking as ultimate intestate successor under section 73(1) of the 1965 Act. The position of limited companies in such cases is discussed below. *Bona vacantia, i.e.* ownerless goods belonged to the Crown at common law as a royal prerogative. The right, where it survives, is assumed to adhere to the State in the Republic, probably under some Constitutional principle similar to that announced in *Webb v. Ireland.*[112] This could be challenged by the same argument as was used in *Webb v. Ireland,*[113] that the prerogative did not survive into the 1937 Constitution, but it would probably be dealt with in the same way by the Supreme Court, *i.e.* that the common law doctrine survives not as stemming from a prerogative of the Crown, but as part of the sovereign rights of the People vested in the State.

(b) Companies

In the past an escheat occurred where land was vested in fee simple in a limited company and the company was wound up before the fee simple became vested in any other party.[114] As regards land registered under the Local Registration of Title Act, 1891 that principle was replaced by *bona vacantia*. Other land continued to be governed by escheat. Section 28(2)(a) of the State Property Act, 1954 now provides that all land vested in or held in trust for a body corporate "immediately before its dissolution", other than land held by the body corporate on trust for another person, vests in the State. "Body corporate", however, would not include unincorporated bodies such as clubs, friendly societies or voluntary associations.[115]

110 Section 26.

111 *Re Sir Thomas Spencer Wells* [1933] Ch 29.

112 *Webb v. Ireland and Attorney General* [1988] IR 353, [1988] ILRM 565.

113 *ibid.*

114 *Re Strathblaine Estates Ltd* [1948] Ch. 228.

115 The property may revert to the grantor: *Hastings Corporation v. Letton* [1908] 1 KB at p.384; Co Litt 13b; but this may have been a characteristic of frankalmoin tenure: see Challis, *Real Property* p.467.

The case of *Re Kavanagh and Cantwell*[116] concerned the situation where the company was a trustee before it was dissolved. Mr and Mrs Silk were buying a house on mortgage. The fee simple was vested in the mortgage company by virtue of the mortgage. The mortgage company got into difficulties and a liquidator of the mortgage company was appointed. He agreed to transfer the mortgage debt and the mortgaged property to the purchasing company. The purchasing company paid the price of the mortgage property and also acquired the right to sue for the mortgage. The mortgage debt was transferred, but the liquidator failed to transfer the fee simple to the purchasing company before the mortgagee company was dissolved. The mortgagors had paid off the instalments of the mortgage. Thinking that they owned the house, they entered into an agreement to sell it to the applicants. The issue was whether they had any title to the property. Costello J held that immediately before the mortgage company was dissolved the position was that it held the fee simple on trust for the purchasing company. The applicants then became, and were at the time of the action, entitled to the benefit of that trust.

The Attorney General, on behalf of the State, made no claim to the property.[117] That being so, the judge held that the only remaining problem was that there were no trustees to hold the fee simple and in those circumstances the court had power under the Trustee Act, 1893, section 26[118] to vest the land in any such person in any such manner and for any estate as it may direct. The judge made an order vesting the land in the applicants.

h) Forfeiture

Forfeiture for treason was abolished by the Forfeiture Act, 1870.[119]

M. Freehold Tenure in Ireland Today

1. Land held of the State?

It is probable that freehold land is still held of"the State and that theoretically it is held in free and common socage by virtue of the Tenures Abolition Act, 1662. Freehold is really the modern term for free and common socage. The interest of the State is sometimes called a radical title. The issue is largely theoretical and the radical title gives the State few if any rights, since (a) there is no theory of eminent domain and (b) if the State wishes to acquire land it must do so by using the legislation on compulsory purchase. Furthermore, escheat to the State has been replaced with the concept of the State as ultimate intestate

116 Unreported, High Court, Costello J, 23 November 1984.

117 The report states "as *bona vacantia.*"

118 See also the Trustee Act, 1893, Amendment, Act, 1894.

119 ss. 1, 3.

successor. It could be argued that the Constitution of 1937 has replaced the radical title based on tenure and that it is inconsistent with a Republic in which individuals are citizens, rather than subjects of a monarch, but so far the point has not been argued in this jurisdiction. Also, feudal fee farm grants appear to be an example of freehold tenure existing between an individual and the State, whatever may be the case as to other land. In the United States, which has a similar form of government, the legislatures in some states passed statutes after the Revolution declaring land within the state to be allodial, *i.e.* without a lord, and not held in tenure and in others the courts made a similar declaration.[120] Since no such statute has been passed in the Republic and since also the Act of 1662 has not been repealed, it would seem that tenure still exists in the Republic. In Northern Ireland the theory is still that freehold land is held of the Crown.

2. Private Grants less than in Fee Simple

We have seen that a grant of land by a private person for less than a fee simple estate, *i.e.* for a life estate or fee tail, can still create freehold tenure. A rent can therefore be reserved which is a feudal rent service. The grantor has the right of distress at common law without any express provision in the grant, because it is an incident of the tenure.[121]

3. Feudal Fee Farm Grants

These are the grants *non obstante Quia Emptores* which have been dealt with above. The grants contain a power in the tenant to subinfeudate, thereby creating a mesne lordship. Many were created in the plantation of Ulster. It is not known how many, if any, still exist in the Republic.

4. Mesne Lordships

Mesne lordships, other than those arising under *non obstante* grants, can only exist if they were created before *Quia Emptores*, 1290.

120 *Stuart v. Easton* (1898) 170 US 383, 42 L Ed 1078, 18 S Ct 650, U S Supreme Court, 170 US at 391, 42 L Ed at 1081, 18 S Ct at 653: see footnote 97. *Waltz v. Security Trust & Savings Bank* (1925) 197 Cal 263, 240 p.19, Supreme Court of California (full court):

> "In the case of *Wallace v. Harmstead*, 44 Pa. St. 492, may be found an exhaustive treatment of the general subject of tenures, wherein it is held, even as affecting lands in Pennsylvania, that the tenure is allodial and not feudal; and in the early case of *Matthews v. Ward* 10 Gill & J. (Md. 1839) 443, it is laid down (syllabus) that: After the Revolution, lands in this state Maryland became allodial, subject to no tenure, nor to any services incident thereto..."

121 Such rents may be outside the ground rents legislation but might be redeemable under other legislation. See Chapter 20, Statutory Control and Enlargement of Tenancies: Ground Rents, and Chapter 7 Fee Farm Grants.

5. State Land

The traditional view is that the doctrine of estates does not apply to the State as landowner, *i.e.* if the State holds land directly it holds it as absolute owner. There is little significance in the point today. Where land is registered the owner is registered as full owner without mention of a fee simple, whether the owner is a private person or an official. Also, State land is usually vested in the relevant Minister.

6. Grants by the State

The traditional doctrine would also hold that where the State grants land it does so by subinfeudation. The State can thus create new fees simple and may reserve a rent service on doing so.

7. State Rents

State rents (quit rents) may survive on freehold land. The State was not bound by *Quia Emptores,* 1290, and the Tenures Abolition Act, 1662 allowed the State to create new layers of tenure in free and common socage. State rents may exist in any land, not merely that subject to *non obstante* fee farm grants.

8. Old Tenures

We have seen that frankalmoin and serjeanty tenures survive in theory.

9. Incidents

Some incidents, such as relief and fealty, as we have seen, may survive. Fealty might be open to Constitutional challenge today as infringing the guarantee of equality in Article 40.1. Reliefs would be more difficult to attack. It might be argued that they are an unjust attack on the property rights under Article 40.3.2, but this would not be easy to sustain given the common law origin of property rights. According to the social or popular concept of property, reliefs seem to be encroachments on the property rights of an owner of land, but as far as the law is concerned there are many rights of feudal origin, including the concept of a fee simple estate, and furthermore the common law does not draw a distinct line between ownership on the one hand and rights less than ownership on the other.

CHAPTER 4

EQUITY

"A Chancery Judge once had the kindness to inform me. . . that the Court of Chancery. . . was almost immaculate."

Dickens, *Bleak House* (Preface 1853).

"By force and virtue of the statute for transferring of uses into possession."

Stern, *Tristram Shandy* (1759. i. xv).

A. Introduction

The common law had many rigidities of procedure which, in a sense, had been necessary in their time but in the course of centuries and with changes in society came to be seen as deficiencies. The forms of action were not only defined legal rights but also excluded from the King's courts those who were not freeholders. Originally this exclusion extended to the mass of the population, who were villeins. Their only recourse was to the court of their own lord and since their dispute might well be against their lord, their chance of obtaining justice was limited. Legal notions based on equality of status were foreign to a society in which the law enforced unequal status. There was no concept of equality before the law, or, as this instance shows, of the notion that a person should not be a judge in his or her own cause. Even for freeholders, the common law had many shortcomings. The forms of action were highly technical and one could easily fail for lack of some formality. Wills of real property were not recognised. The only recourse was to appeal to the King as the fountain of justice. In the reigns of Edward II and Edward III many petitions were presented to the King. After the time of Edward III they were regularly referred to the Chancellor, one of the King's ministers. The Chancellor was often a cleric. For this reason the jurisdiction of his department, the Chancery was often exercised on moral grounds, taking into account the conscience of the plaintiff or defendant. In the time of Elizabeth I the post was secularised and the Chancellor became the Keeper of the Queen's conscience. At this time there were no reports of cases decided by the Chancellor, probably because they wished to retain a wide discretion and precedent would tend eventually to confine it, which is indeed what happened to equity when reports came to be published of equity decisions. No reports of the decisions of Cardinal Wolsey or Sir Thomas More survive. Wolsey was the last of the medieval ecclesiastical chancellors and more the first of the modern lawyers. Under Lord Ellesmere (1596–1617) and particularly Lord Nottingham (1673–82) equity developed into a distinct body of principles, aided by the recording of equity decisions.

If the courts of law gave a judgment which equity thought inequitable, it issued its own special remedy, the common injunction, to prevent the person who had succeeded at common law from enforcing the judgment they had obtained. This of course created a conflict between the common law courts and the Chancellor which came to a head in 1615 in the case of *Glanvill v. Courteney*[1], a case on a bond.[2] Sir Edward Coke (1552–1634), Chief Justice of the King's Bench, gave judgment for the plaintiff. Ellesmere, the Chancellor, gave judgment for the defendant. James VI & I, after consulting advisers, including Sir Francis Bacon, decided in favour of equity.[3]

The Irish Chancery began in 1232 when Henry III granted the English Chancellor, Ralph Neville, bishop of Chichester, the Chancery of Ireland for life.[4] Neville nominated a deputy to execute the office in his place and it is likely therefore that the Irish Chancery was in fact established by Neville's deputy, Geoffrey de Turville. From Neville's death in 1244 his deputy, Robert Luttrell, continued as Chancellor of Ireland and from then on the office had a continuous independent existence.[5]

In Ireland the equity jurisdiction of the Court of Exchequer (the equity side of Exchequer) may have been somewhat more important than in England.[6] The jurisdiction was abolished by the Exchequer Equitable Jurisdiction (Ireland) Act, 1850.[7] But the expertise in equity of the Exchequer barons was not entirely lost because in the previous year the Incumbered Estates Court had been established and it was provided that one of the three Commissioners of Incumbered Estates had to be a baron of the Exchequer.[8]

---

1 (1615) 2 Bulst 302, 80 ER 1139. The report is of the proceedings at common law before Sir Edward Coke. One might note that the conflict between law and equity in Shakespeare's *Merchant of Venice* concerned a bond.

2 As has been pointed out, the conflict between law and equity features in Shakespeare's *Merchant of Venice*. The central theme is the conflict between strict adherence to bargains on the one hand and justice and mercy on the other.

3 This was probably the last occasion on which the royal prerogative of justice was exercised by the Crown personally. See *R v. Foster* [1985] 1 QB 115, [1984] 2 All ER 679, [1984] 3 WLR 401.

4 Otway-Ruthven, *Medieval Ireland* p.154 *et seq.*

5 *ibid.*, p.154.

6 Otway-Ruthven, *Medieval Ireland* p.154–55; Hand, *English Law in Ireland 1290 - 1324* pp.99–103.

7 The last case in equity to come before the court was *Massy v. O'Dell* (1860) 9 Ir Ch. R 441. It was later transferred to the Court of Chancery.

8 By 12 & 13 Vict. c.77.

The role of equity was frequently, but not exclusively, to make the legal system more attuned to a society based on the market as a mechanism for the production and distribution of wealth. The common law still suffered from having procedures developed for a feudal society.

B. New Procedure

A feature of the Chancery was that it acted against persons. An action in Chancery was begun by subpoena, a summons to the defendant to appear on pain (sub poena) of forfeiture of a sum of money if the defendant failed to appear.

C. New Remedies

At common law if A was dispossessed by B then A could recover possession of the land by one of the forms of action. But in the case of personal property the common law generally only provided the remedy of damages. Equity granted specific performance of contracts. It ordered the promissor to carry out his or her promise, not just pay damages for breach of contract as the common law courts did. It issued injunctions to order a person to desist from a course of action or to do something. At common law, if a person proved their case they were entitled to a remedy even if they had not acted entirely honourably themselves. Equitable remedies were and still are discretionary.[9]

In modern times new equitable remedies have been developed. The Mareva injunction[10] is used to restrain dealing with bank accounts and other assets and so to prevent a person disposing of their assets before a trial can take place. Anton Piller orders[11] prevent the destruction of evidence by authorising the plaintiff with his or her solicitor to enter the defendant's premises to inspect and if necessary take away documents or other items specified in the order.

D. New Rights

Equity developed uses and later trusts: equitable estates in the beneficial interest of property corresponding to legal estates. It also developed the equity of

9 *Doran v. Carroll* (1861) 11 Ir Ch. R 379 (plaintiff entitled to at least nominal damages at law for breach of a covenant not to commit waste, but no action in equity unless intention to commit waste shown).

10 *Mareva Compania Naviera SA v. International Bulk Carriers SA* [1975] 2 Ll Rep 509; *Nippon Yusen Kaisha v. Karageorgis* [1975] 1 WLR 1093; *Re John Horgan Livestock Limited, O'Mahony v. Horgan* [1996] 1 ILRM 161, Supreme Court; Delaney (1996) p.415 *et seq.*

11 *Anton Piller K G v. Manufacturing Processes Ltd* [1976] Ch 55. Delaney (1996) p.426 *et seq.*

redemption in mortgages to protect mortgagors of property. The courts of equity in Ireland in the eighteenth century invented the equity to renew leases for lives renewable forever which made such interests practically equivalent to fee simple estates. Irish courts also devised the doctrine of graft. A person who was acting in a fiduciary capacity and not for their own benefit and who acquires more property because of their position may not take the benefit for themselves. Equity today is often used to intervene in situations in which it would be unjust for the holder of a common law title to take the benefits, or all the benefits, of ownership. Proprietary and promissory estoppel[12] are examples of new principles developing out of this intervention, as are the principles relating to the acquisition by a spouse of an equity in the matrimonial home when the legal estate is vested in the other spouse. The constructive trust is a doctrine which has developed, and continues to develop, in this context.[13]

E. Uses

1. The Rise of the Use

a) The General Form

When a grantor conveyed the legal estate by a feoffment to a feoffee to hold it for uses which the grantor declared, the Chancellor did not refuse to recognise that there had been a change in the legal title. Equity, as the maxim states, follows the law (*i.e.* the common law). Equity recognised that the feoffee was now the person who could, if required, make a conveyance of the legal title. The Chancellor nevertheless forced the feoffee as holder of the legal title to use the land for the benefit of the *cestui que use*, the person whom equity considered to be so entitled. Equity would not permit the feoffee to accept the grant and then take advantage of the failure of the common law courts to recognise the uses. The following diagram shows the general form of the use:

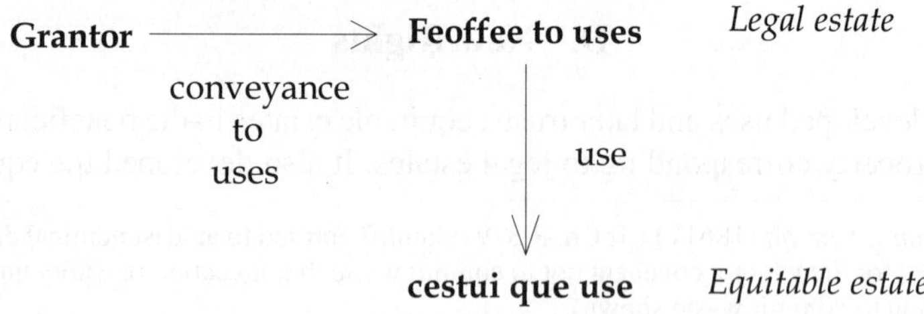

12 See Chapter 18 Licences, Estoppel and Constructive Trusts.

13 *ibid.*

b) Wills

It was not possible to leave land by will at common law. On the tenant's death the land went to the heir or heirs as determined by the rules of descent. At the beginning of the sixteenth century uses began to be developed as a device to avoid the common law rules of descent and such devices were recognised by the Chancellor.[14] The settlor, a person who creates successive interests in property, conveyed the land to the feoffee to the use (a) that the feoffee should hold it to the use of the grantor until the grantor's death (hence, the grantor gave himself or herself an equitable life estate), and then (b) that on the grantor's death to the use that the feoffee should convey the legal estate to X, the person to whom the grantor wished to leave the land.

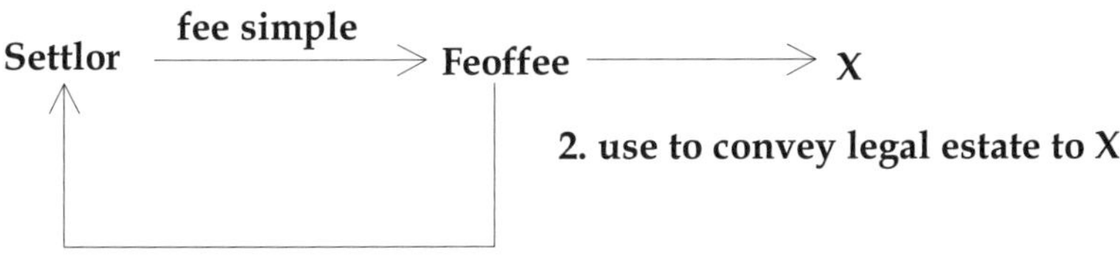

The device had another effect: when the settlor died, he or she did not die seized of the legal estate, and so no relief was payable, nor would wardships occur. By the time of the Tudors mesne lordships were becoming less common and so reliefs were often payable directly to the Crown as lord of the tenure. It was thus the Crown which stood to lose the reliefs and wardships.[15]

Since the device had the effect of avoiding reliefs, this early form of will still had a purpose even if X was the eldest son of the settlor *i.e.* the person who would inherit the land under the rules of descent by primogeniture.

One more development was needed to perfect the device. What if X died before the settlor, or the settlor changed his or her mind as to who should inherit the land? Use No. 2 had to be revocable by the settlor during his life. This final legal refinement was achieved in *Duke of Buckingham's Case*[16] which held that the uses were revocable.

c) Conveyance to Self, or Self and Another

At common law A could not convey seisin to himself. It was a strict, technical rule. But why should anyone wish to convey seisin to themselves in any case? Suppose H was getting married. He wanted to put the land in the joint names of

14 Barton, "The Medieval Use" (1965) 81 LQR 562 at p.570.

15 *Re Lord Dacre of the South* (1535) YB 27 Hen VIII Pasch f 7 pl 22; Baker & Milsom, *Sources* p.105.

16 (1504) YB 20 Hen VII pl 20.

himself and his wife.[17] The common law rule prevented H from making a feoffment in favour of himself and his wife, W, as joint tenants. If you could not convey the common law estate to yourself, it followed, so the common law courts held, that you could not convey to yourself and someone else jointly. Again, the use provided a way avoiding this awkward rule which the common law courts felt unable to change. H conveyed the fee simple to feoffees to the use of himself and his wife:

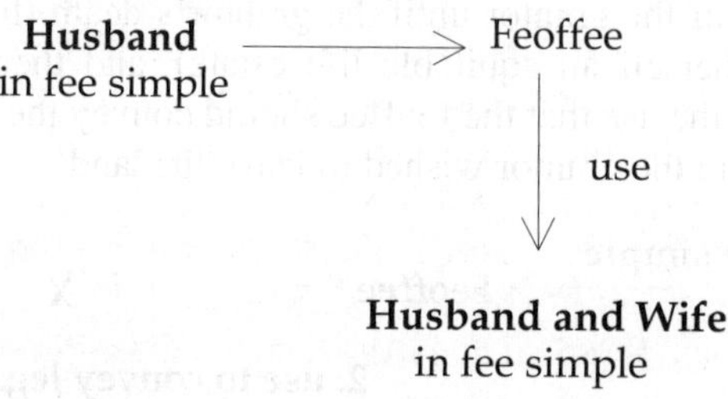

d) Settlements

The common law rule against conveying seisin to yourself also interfered with another transaction involving landowners: the settlement. From about the 16th to the 19th centuries landowners were constantly devising ways of keeping their land within the family and of preventing some future improvident heir from selling the estate. We shall see later how this was done and how legislation ultimately defeated such interests which had come to be one of the causes of agricultural decline, particularly in Ireland. But for the moment we may note that settlements depended on creating successive interests in land. If landowner X was to give himself a life estate, then a fee tail to his eldest son, how was he to do this? The common law courts would not recognise a deed in which X, who had a fee simple and therefore seisin, purported to convey a life estate to himself.[18] Again, uses could be used to achieve a settlement. X could convey the fee simple to a feoffee to the use that the feoffee should hold it for X for life, X's son in tail, and so on.

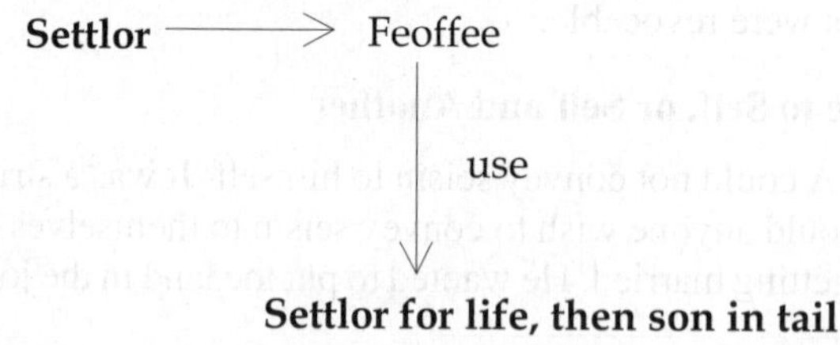

17 Barton, (1965) at p.566. See footnote 14.

18 See now s.50 Conveyancing Act, 1881.

If the uses were to convey corresponding legal estates to X and his son, a legal settlement could be created.

e) Implied and Resulting Uses

Apart from recognising these devices, equity developed its own rules about the effect of conveyances in order to do equity, *i.e.* to prevent anyone taking the benefit of land where it might not be the intention of the conveyor. Equity nevertheless made assumptions about the intention of those who entered into transactions and these assumptions often reflected the ideas of the rising age of capitalism. Equity in general assumed that individuals acted in their own self-interest in the absence of proof they had acted in some altruistic way. A leading example is the feoffment without consideration.

(1) Feoffment Without Consideration

If a person executed a feoffment in favour of another and no mention was made of any consideration, *i.e.* payment, in the document, or none actually paid,[19] then equity presumed that the grantee held the legal estate in the land to the use of the grantor:[20]

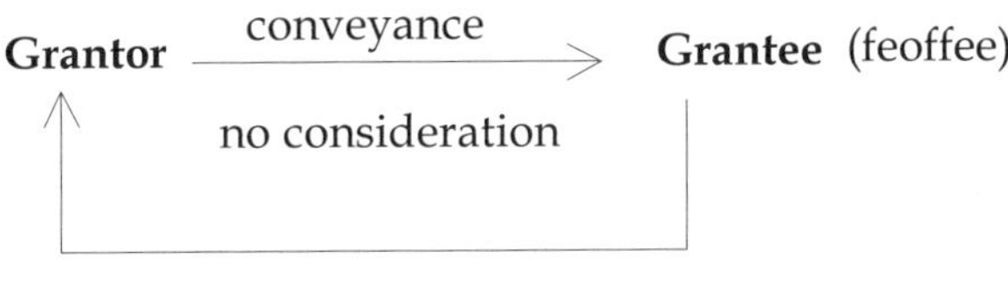

implied use

Consideration for this purpose included good consideration, *i.e.* natural love and affection.[21] There are two inter-connected explanations of this attitude of equity to a feoffment without consideration. First, grantors who made feoffments as devices to avoid feudal incidents would normally convey to feoffees without consideration, although they would normally declare the uses expressly. By implying a use where none was declared, equity assumed that the deed was a device rather than a genuine conveyance of the beneficial interest, and it made the device effective by enforcing the use. It assisted in the avoidance of feudal incidents, helping to hasten the decline of feudal legal relations. On a more general level, equity adopted the attitude that a conveyance was not intended to be a gift unless it was proved to be so. In other words it assumed that grantors acted out of their own self-interest and not altruistically in

19 Sanders, *Uses* 1: 68.

20 *Lord Camoy's Case* (1410). Baker, *English Legal History* puts the development as early as 1465, Plucknett, *Concise History* p.97, during the time Edward IV.

21 See footnote 41 below.

making conveyances. Such an attitude is more typical of an economy based on a market in which individuals appear as sellers of commodities and who part with their own only if they obtain its price.

Equity had its own definition of consideration distinct from the common law. In this context, equity recognised natural love and affection between near relatives as good consideration.[22]

(2) Vendor and Purchaser (Bargain and Sale)

Equity also intervened to regulate the position between a vendor of land and a purchaser after a contract of sale had been entered into and before the conveyance was executed, *i.e.* where A had bargained and sold the land to B. The vendor, who still held the legal estate, was considered in equity to hold it, for some purposes at least, to the use of the purchaser.

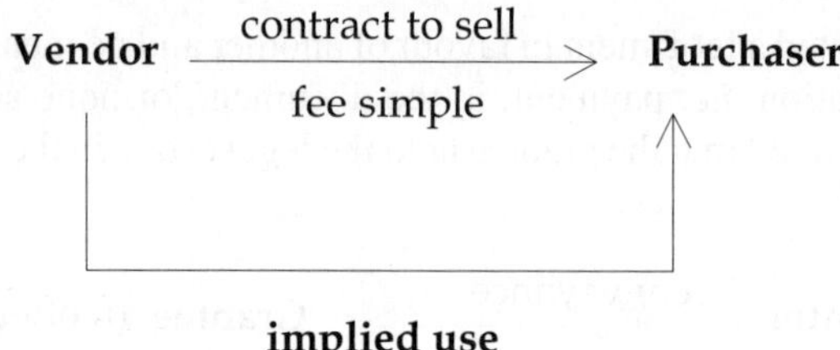

(3) Resulting Uses

Suppose G grants land:

> *to F in fee simple to the use of A for life.*

What happens when A dies? F still has the legal fee simple estate. It will last as long as his heirs survive. But the grantor has not said what is to happen to the beneficial interest after A's death. Equity assumes, unless there is some contrary intent, that F is not to take any benefit. There is a resulting use in favour of G. Equity assumes that G did not intend to make a gift of the remainder of the fee simple to F but intended to retain the benefit herself:

22 See below Voluntary Conveyances.

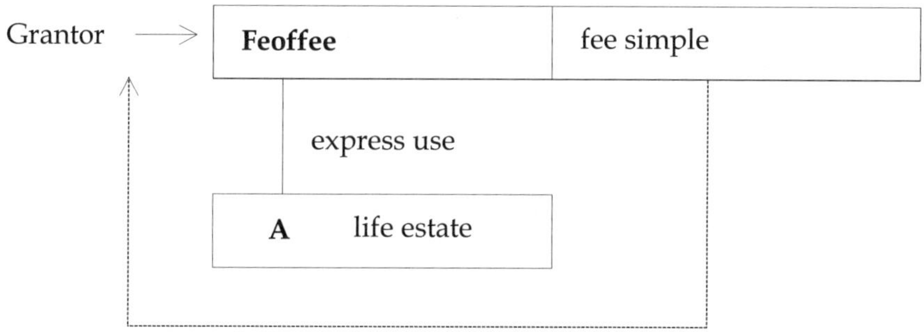

resulting use

f) Cestui could not have a Greater Estate than the Feoffee

A situation that in a way was the opposite of the resulting use was as follows:

to F for life to the use of A and his heirs.

In this instance the estate given to F is shorter than that which, supposed under the grant, is to go to the cestui. The Chancellor solved the problem by holding that the cestui could not have a greater interest than that given to the feoffee.[23] In the example, despite the words of the grant A has only an estate for the life of F, *i.e.* an *estate pur autre vie*. A reversion in fee simple remains in the grantor following on F's life estate.

2. Development of Recognition of Use

At first the Chancellor enforced the use against the feoffee named in the deed. That would not, however, be enough to protect the interest of the cestui. Suppose the feoffee died. His or her heir inherited the legal estate. In 1482[24] the Chancellor enforced the use against the heir. The heir had paid nothing for it, and so did not lose anything. In 1466[25] a purchaser from the feoffee was held bound by the use if he had express notice. In such a case the Chancellor held that the conscience of the purchaser was affected. This was the beginning of the equitable doctrine of notice which is discussed in more detail below.

3. The Problem of Uses

Uses were a problem for the King. The decline of mesne lordships meant that by the time of the Tudors most landowners held directly from the Crown. Reliefs and other feudal incidents were paid to the King as lord of the tenure and

23 *Re Ottley's Estate* [1910] 1 IR 1, per Wylie J at 11; Sanders, *Uses* vol. 1 p.113; Cro Car 231

24 YB 22 Edw IV Pasch f 4 pl 18; Simpson, *Land Law* (1st ed.) p.169.

25 YB 5 Edw IV Mich, f 7 pl 16; Simpson, *Land Law* (1st ed.) p.169.

uses, by avoiding feudal incidents, reduced the royal revenue. Moreover, Henry VIII wanted to increase his income by making new grants in tenure with incidents of real value attached to them. This policy has been called fiscal feudalism because it was an attempt to re-establish some of the feudal forms of landholding but only for the purpose of raising money.

Henry VIII wanted to solve the problem of uses, as he saw it. The difficulty was that many large landowners had conveyed the legal fee simple in their land to nominees, often lawyers, to hold to their, *i.e.* the landowners', use. If Henry VIII had induced Parliament to pass a statute which said that uses were ineffective or void the result would have been a social revolution: the lawyers would have been left with the legal estate for their own benefit and the landowners would no longer be landowners. Clearly, this was not a solution. Henry VIII's lawyers therefore proposed an alternative solution. If a legal estate is conveyed to A to hold to the use of X, the new statute would give X the legal estate and A would have nothing. Uses would not be abolished but executed. Thus if Z conveys the legal estate to A in fee simple to the use of X in fee simple, the words "to the use of X in fee simple" are not ineffective: on the contrary, X is to have an estate at law equivalent to the estate which he or she would previously have had in equity. This was the basis of the Statute of Uses, 1535. A slightly adapted version was introduced in Ireland in 1634.[26] We shall now turn to considering its effects in detail, since an understanding of the Statute is still essential in the understanding of Irish land law.

4. Statute of Uses, 1634

Section 1 of the Statute reads:

> "Where any person or persons stand to be seized, or at any time hereafter shall happen to be seized, of any honours, castles, mannors, lands, tenements, rents, services, reversions, remainders, or other hereditaments, to the use, confidence, or trust of any other person or persons, or any body politique, by reason of any bargaine, sale, feoffment, fine, recovery, covenant, contract, agreement, will or otherwise, by any manner or means whatsoever it be, that in every such case, all and every such person and persons, and bodies politique, that have, or hereafter shall have any such use, confidence or trust, in fee simple, fee tayle, for terme of life or years, or otherwise; or any use, confidence or trust, in remainder or reverter, shall from henceforth stand and be seized, deemed, and adjudged in lawfull seizin, estate, and possession, of and in the same honours. . .[*etc.*] to all intents, constructions and purposes in the law, of and in such like estate, as they had or shall have, in use, trust or confidence . . .

The Statute therefore applies, in short, where a person or persons are seized to the use, confidence or trust of another person or persons or body politic. The effect of the Statute is that the person or persons or body politic that had the benefit of the use shall be seized, *i.e.* have legal estates, in the property for the

26 The text can be found in Wylie, *Cases* at p.67.

same estates as they had under the use. In other words, instead of estates which were only recognised in equity, they will have estates at law.

a) Uses Executed, Not Abolished

It cannot be emphasised too much that the Statute does not abolish uses. It does not render meaningless words in a deed which refer to uses, but rather gives to them a new meaning. One must also remember that the Statute did not simply apply to deeds existing at the date the Statute was passed, but continues to affect the operation of deeds made at the present time (" . . . or at any time hereafter . . . "). Where such limitations are contained in deeds one must therefore consider what effect the deed would have had before the Statute, and then consider whether the Statute has the effect of executing the uses or not.

b) No Transfer of the Estate from the Feoffee.

The Statute does not transfer the estate of the feoffee to the *cestui que use.* Rather, it converts the estate of the *cestui que use* from an equitable estate to a corresponding legal estate. This difference can be seen in the following limitation:

to X and his heirs to the use of B for life.

The Statute executes the use giving B a legal life estate, it does not transfer X's legal fee simple to B. In one case, however, it may appear that there is a transfer, but this is not really so. In the limitation:

to A for life to the use of B and her heirs

an attempt has been made to give the *cestui que use* a greater estate than the feoffee. We have seen that before the Statute equity did not recognise that this could be done. Despite the words of the deed, B only had an equitable estate for the life of A. The Statute converts this into a legal estate for the life of A.

c) Seized

The Statute applies only if a person is seized to the use, confidence, or trust of another person. It therefore only applies if the feoffee has a freehold estate. Let us consider the effect of the following limitation before the Statute:

to A and her heirs to the use of B for 10 years.

A is seized of a freehold estate to the use of B. B has an equitable leasehold interest. Considering now the effect of the Statute on the limitation, it is clear that A is seized to the use of B. The Statute therefore executes this use and B has a legal lease for 10 years. A has nothing. At the end of 10 years the resulting use arises. A is now seized of the freehold estate for the benefit of the grantor. The Statute executes this use, giving the legal freehold to the grantor. The entire legal interest is disposed of. A has nothing, B has a legal lease from the grantor for 10 years, the grantor being his landlord for this time, and then the grantor has the remainder of the legal interest. One should notice that the effect of the Statute is that A, the feoffee, is left with nothing at all. After the Statute a feoffee is a mere name on the face of the deed if the use is executed.

If we take another limitation:

to A for 10 years to the use of B for 10 years

it can be seen that the Statute does not apply to the limitation at all because A is not seized to the use of B. A has only a leasehold estate. The use is not executed, and A holds the legal leasehold interest to the use of B who has an equitable leasehold estate.

It was further held that the grantor must first be seised of the property before the grant to uses could take effect, *i.e.* the property must be in existence before the grant was made.[27] It was thought that otherwise there would be no seisin to vest in the feoffee. The problem did not arise in relation to land itself but affected incorporeal hereditaments such as easements. A new easement could therefore not be granted in a feoffment to uses.[28] This pedantic rule was not reformed until the Conveyancing Act, 1881 provided by section 62 that a conveyance to the use that a person shall have an easement, right, liberty or privilege operates to vest the right in the grantee.

The Statute also dealt with another kind of incorporeal hereditament, the rentcharge. Section 4 of the Statute provides that a rentcharge can be created by a grant to uses and the *cestui que use* of the rentcharge is deemed to be seised of it on execution of the conveyance. The section also conferred a statutory right of distress which otherwise would have to be expressly reserved.[29]

d) Use, Confidence or Trust

The operation of the Statute does not depend on what words are used to describe the use. The question is whether in substance a use has been created to which the Statute applies, whatever are the words used to describe it.

e) "...of any other person..."

The Statute does not apply if a person is seized to their own use, so in the limitation:

to A and his heirs to the use of A for life, remainder to the use of B and his heirs

27 *Yelverton v. Yelverton* (1595) Cro Eliz 401, Moor 342, 78 ER 646. Sanders, *Uses* vol. 1, p.111–12.

28 *ibid.*.

29 See Chapter 22 Incorporeal Hereditaments: Rentcharges.

the use in favour of A for life is not executed and A has an equitable life estate, whereas the use of the remainder to B is executed and B takes a legal fee simple. In the limitation:

> *to A and B and their heirs to the use of A and his heirs*

the Statute has been held to apply, because although A is seized to his own use, B is seized to the use of A and that is sufficient to invoke the operation of the Statute.

f) The Doctrine of Scintilla Juris

This highly artificial doctrine was used at one time to explain the working of the Statute and although it is now obsolete, it is useful to describe it in order to gain an understanding of how lawyers thought about the operation of the Statute.

We have seen that in order that a use be executed by the Statute of Uses it was necessary that some person be seized to the use of the *cestui que use*. In the analytical minds of some lawyers this created a problem in relation to future uses. Suppose land was conveyed

> *to A and her heirs to the use of B for life, remainder to the use of C and his heirs.*

As far as the first use is concerned, A is seized to the use of B. The Statute executes the use, making B the legal life tenant. It follows that the seisin is now vested in B. Then B dies. How can it be, some lawyers asked, that the second use is executed? Who was seised to the use of C on the death of B? It cannot be A, because the Statute took the seisin from her and gave it to B. It cannot be B, because B is dead.[30]

A solution to this problem was found in the metaphysical doctrine of *scintilla juris*. Real property lawyers adopted the view that even after the execution of the first use by the Statute, a *scintilla juris*, a spark of title, remained in A, on which the Statute could operate.[31] When B died the seisin momentarily returned to A. A was then seised to the use of C during this moment of time. The Statute then applied and executed the use to C. The *scintilla juris*, was also

30 It should be noted that in the example, the remainder to C is vested. In the view of some lawyers there was no problem in such a case. They considered that A could be regarded as seised, as soon as the limitation took effect, not only to the immediate use of B, but also to the future use of C: the use in favour of C could then be regarded as executed at once, though not in possession until B's death. In the view of these lawyers the problem only arose only if the remainder to C was contingent, as for example if it said remainder to C and his heirs if C survive B. In this case there could be no question of A being seised to the use of C before the contingency occurred, and by the time it was clear that C had survived B, the problem would arise as to who held to the use of C.

31 *Brent's Case* (1575) 3 Dy 339b at 340b, 73 ER 766, per Dyer CJ and Manwood J. Megarry and Wade, (4th ed.) 188 n.27; *Bishop of Oxford v. Leighton* (1700) 2 Vern 376, 23 ER 837.

sometimes called a possibility of seisin. It was, in effect, a type of contingent future interest, and, since it lasted only an infinitely small period of time, it could be said to be the smallest legal interest it was possible to have in real property.

This ingenious answer seemed to have solved the problem, but it was still argued that in one instance it did not.[32] If, at B's death, *A* had already died without heirs and intestate, it was argued that there would be no one seised to the use of C. This does not seem such a serious problem as was thought, because in such a case there would have been an escheat of the legal title and the Crown would hold to the use of C. The objection was nevertheless taken seriously by Lord St Leonards and he introduced a bill which became the Law of Property Amendment Act, 1860.[33] It abolished the doctrine of *scintilla juris*, and provided that in future uses were to take effect in due course one after the other.

g) Implied and Resulting Uses.

We have already seen that the Statute applies to implied and resulting uses as well as to express ones. Thus, if land was granted:

to F in fee simple to the use of A for life

we have seen that on the death of A a resulting use arose in favour of the grantor. After the Statute, the use to A would be executed, giving A a legal life estate, and on A's death the resulting use would be executed giving the fee simple back to the grantor. Further examples of the application of the Statute to implied uses will be seen in due course.

h) Implied, Resulting, and Constructive Trusts

Distinct from the previous case is that of implied, resulting or constructive trusts. In the following example:

Unto and to the use of T and U in fee simple to the use of A for life

T and U are trustees and there is an express trust in favour of A. A trust is, broadly, a use which is not executed by the Statute. The words of limitation used to produce this result are discussed below. The remainder of the beneficial interest is not disposed of and equity today raises a resulting, or implied, trust in favour of the grantor. It could be objected that this resulting trust must be a single use – it does not matter what word you use to describe it – and should be executed by the Statute, so that implied, resulting or constructive trusts should not be possible after the Statute. Under section 5 of the Statute of Frauds, 1695 such trusts are not, however, executed by the Statute.[34] There are

32 *Chudleigh's Case* (1595) 1 Co Rep 113b at 132b, 76 ER 261, 270.

33 Section 7.

34 Sanders, *Uses* 1:211; *Lamplugh v. Lamplugh* (1709) 1 P Wms 112, 24 ER 316.

therefore still distinct situations in which uses are implied or result, and which are executed, and in which trusts are implied or result or are constructed, and are not executed.

i) Corporations

Before the Statute equity had not developed remedies which could be used against a corporation or body politic as they were then called. Its main remedy, if its orders were not complied with, was imprisonment for contempt, and corporations could not be imprisoned. The words of the Statute were therefore carefully chosen. The Statute does not apply where a corporation is seized to the use of another person.[35] In the following limitation the use is not executed:

to Acme Ltd to the use of B and his heirs.

At the time the Statute was enacted the use would not have been enforced either, but today remedies have been developed by which a modern trust may be enforced against a corporation. There was no problem, even then, however, in a corporation being a *cestui que use*, and if so, the Statute applied, so that:

to A and her heirs to the use of Acme Ltd

gave Acme Ltd the legal fee simple.

j) Active Uses

The main purpose of the Statute, as has been seen, was to deal with uses which were used as devices to avoid effects that would otherwise apply at common law. The lawyers at the time argued that the Statute should only be applied to such uses and not to uses similar to what we today would call trusts, *i.e.* uses where the feoffees had active duties to perform and were not just a passive holders of the legal estate. The judges upheld this view.

This issue arose in Ireland in modern times in the case of *Re Sergie*.[36] The mortgagors, who had a freehold fee simple estate, had mortgaged their property by conveying a leasehold term of 10,000 years to the mortgagees as security for the repayment of the loan, a usual form of mortgage. This left a freehold reversion vested in them, since in the eyes of the law a leasehold interest is a lesser form of interest to a freehold. The mortgage gave to the mortgagees a power of sale if the loan was not repaid. Clearly a purchaser would be somewhat more willing to buy the whole freehold interest rather than a lease and so the mortgage also contained a covenant that the mortgagors would stand seised of the freehold reversion in trust for any purchaser. The mortgage repayments were not made in accordance with the terms of the mortgage and the mortgagees, a bank, exercised their power of sale. They sold the 10,000 year term to Sergie. Sergie died and left a will disposing of his property. The

35 Plucknett, *Concise History* p.581.

36 [1954] NI 1, Wylie, *Cases* p.70.

dispute was as to the assessment of estate duty and this issue turned on the question as to whether the use, which it was, although described as a trust, was executed by the Statute or not. If it was, then Sergie had the 10,000 year term plus the legal reversion which would have merged with the term, giving Sergie the whole freehold interest. If the use had not been executed, then Sergie would have the legal term plus the equitable reversion, the legal title in the reversion remaining with the mortgagors. The Northern Ireland Court of Appeal held that the use was an active one and was not executed by the Statute:[37]

	Legal fee simple in reversion
Covenant to stand seised	Active use
10,000 leasehold term	Equitable fee simple

5. Statute of Wills (Ireland), 1634

We have seen that uses were used to make what amounted to a will in equity and that this device caused a loss to the Royal revenue. It was therefore the declared purpose of the English Statute of Uses, 1535 to abolish the power to make a will by this method and therefore to abolish the power to make wills generally, since this was the only effective method. This effect of the Statute caused a popular outcry and the demonstrations known as the Pilgrimage of Grace, 1539. The King compromised. The Statute of Wills, 1540 granted the power to make wills of all land held in fee simple by socage tenure and 2/3rds of all land held in fee simple by knight service. But it also provided that the devisee was to be liable for feudal incidents as if he or she were the heir. The decline in such incidents had the natural effect of increasing freedom of testation and the Tenures Abolition Act had the effect of completing this freedom by converting land held in knight service to socage.

The Statute of Wills (Ireland), 1634 was passed in the same year as the Irish Statute of Uses which therefore never had any effect in relation to wills in Ireland, although it curiously contained the same preamble as the English Act.

37 Since Sergie was entitled to the entire beneficial interest in the land he was entitled to call for the outstanding legal fee simple under the principle of *Saunders v. Vautier* (1841) Cr & Ph 240, (1841) 4 Beav 115, 49 ER 282, [1835–42] All ER Reprint 58; see below "Bare Trusts."

6. Effects of The Statute of Uses Today

The Statute of Uses still has many effects on the law of real property in Ireland today. These are principally:

a) words necessary to create a trust;

b) voluntary conveyances;

c) conveyances under the Statute;

d) conveyance to self or self and another;

e) legal powers of appointment and sale;

f) reservation of newly-created easements;

g) legal executory interests; and

h) active uses.

We shall deal with the first four of these in the following sections. As to the remainder, (e) is dealt with in Chapter 13 on powers, (f) is dealt with in Chapter 22 on easements, (g) is dealt with in Chapter 10 on future interests and (h) has already been discussed.

a) Words Necessary to Create a Trust

We have seen that before the Statute uses were used by landowners to avoid feudal incidents payable to the lord and that since mesne lordships tended to disappear after *Quia Emptores*, the lord was often the King who procured the Statute to recover his revenue. The Statute, by executing most uses, would effectively have prevented the creation of equitable interests in land. These were much too useful to landowners for them to accept this readily and they set their lawyers the task of finding ways of avoiding the Statute. The first method attempted was to convey land to a feoffee to the use of someone else and then to create a second use, often referred to as a trust to distinguish it from the first one, to take effect in favour of the intended beneficiary. So the limitation would be in the form:

> *to A [the feoffee] and his heirs to the use of B and his heirs in trust for C and his heirs [or for life. . . etc.]*

The use of the word trust instead of use would not in itself have the effect of avoiding the Statute, because the Statute expressly applied to a use, confidence or trust, but the hope was that the courts might hold the second use to be effective. The first response of the courts, in *Jane Tyrell's Case*[38] in 1557, was to hold that the device did not avoid the Statute. The court held that the Statute executed the first use, giving B the legal estate, but they also held that it was

38 (1557) 2 Dy 155a, 73 ER 336.

still the case, as it had been before the Statute, that a use upon a use was void, and so C got nothing.

In the course of the next seventy years the attitude of the courts underwent a change. This seems a considerable time, but it must be remembered that one of the principal benefits of uses, the ability to create wills, had been conceded by the Statute of Wills. The first case which changed the position is thought to be *Sambach v. Daston* (or Dalston) in 1635.[39] In that case it was held (a) that a use upon a use was valid, reversing *Tyrell's Case*, and (b) that it was not executed by the Statute. There was little logic in this position, but it suited the purpose of avoiding the Statute. After *Sambach*, therefore, all that had to be done to avoid the effect of the Statute was to insert a use to exhaust the effect of the Statute and then insert the second use or trust:

to A . . . to the use of B . . . in trust for C . . .

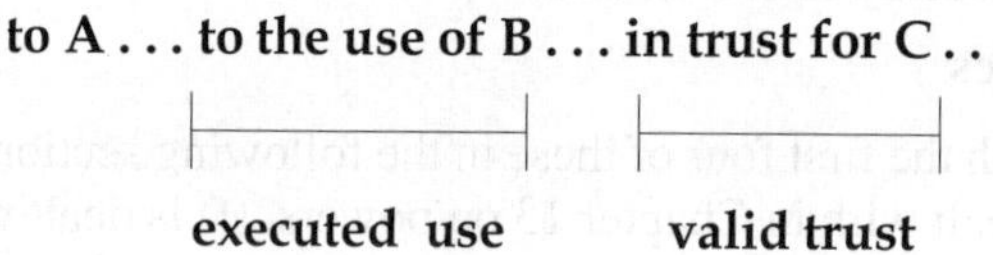

The first use was executed, giving B the legal estate as trustee, while the second use took effect, giving C the equitable estate.

One technical disadvantage of this form was that B, the trustee, obtained the legal estate by virtue of the Statute, *i.e.* by operation of law, and not by the deed. A more refined method overcame this disadvantage:

to B . . . to the use of B . . . in trust for C . . .

The Statute did not execute the first use as B was seised to his own use, so that B obtained the legal estate by the initial words of the limitation.[40] The courts were prepared to treat the words "to the use of B" as superfluous, in the sense that it did not give B anything more, and held the use upon a use valid as before, giving C the equitable estate:

to B . . . to the use of B . . . in trust for C . .

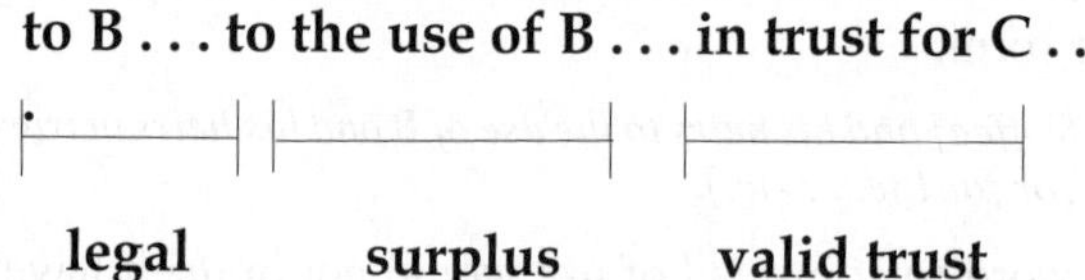

Later the formula was shortened to:

Unto and to the use of B . . . in trust for C . . .

39 (1635) 163 Toth 188, 21 ER 164, and sub nom *Morris v. Darston* in (1635) Nels 30, 21 ER 78, per Lord Keeper Coventry.

40 *Doe d Lloyd v. Passingham* (1827) 6 B & C 305, 108 ER 465.

Since the Statute of Uses, 1634 is still in force in Ireland, this is still the formula used to create a trust in this jurisdiction. If the trust is an active one, then it would not be necessary to use it and one could use the formula:

to B . . . in trust for C . . .

but lawyers prefer to be on the safe side and normally employ the use upon the use. A trust, from the point of view of the method of its creation, can be defined as a use which is not executed by the Statute of Uses.

b) Voluntary Conveyances

A voluntary conveyance of an estate is one in which there is no consideration paid or promised and no express disposal of the beneficial interest. Nevertheless what constitutes consideration depends on the context in which the transaction is considered: there is no definition of voluntary conveyance which is universally true.

If a grantor executes a deed granting land "to X and his heirs" without any mention of payment by X or who is to have the beneficial interest, the conveyance is voluntary. Equity generally presumes, as before, that the conveyance was not intended to be a gift and so implies a use back to the grantor.

The presumption can be rebutted by evidence that the beneficial interest is to be conferred on the grantee. Thus, if the deed states that it was executed in favour of X in consideration of natural love and affection, such consideration is for this purpose sufficient, since it rebuts the presumption that X is not to take the benefit. If the donor and donee are closely related by blood or marriage equity presumes natural love and affection is the consideration.[41]

The presumption of advancement may arise in some relationships.[42] If X is the son of the grantor, the father and son relationship raises the presumption of advancement. As Viscount Fitzgibbon, LC put it in *Redington v. Redington*:[43]

> "If before the statute of uses a man made a feoffment to a stranger without consideration, the use resulted to the feoffor. But if he made a feoffment to his son, the use did not result, because the consideration of blood did fix and settle the use in the son."[44]

The court of equity took account of the duty which a father owed to provide for his children, a duty they saw as arising from natural law, and so equity here presumed that the conveyance was in fulfilment of that obligation.

Where the presumption of resulting use is raised but not rebutted, a use is implied back to the grantor, as before.[45] Since the Statute executes implied

41 *Ellis v. Nimmo* (1835) Ll & G t Sug 333; *Re Luby's Estate* (1909) 43 ILTR 141.

42 See Chapter 17 Presumption of Advancement.

43 (1794) 3 Ridg PC 106.

44 (1794) 3 Ridg PC 106 at 177.

45 See above Feoffment without Consideration.

uses as well as express ones, the result, after the Statute, is that the use is executed, giving the grantor the legal estate back again.[46] The whole conveyance is ineffective:

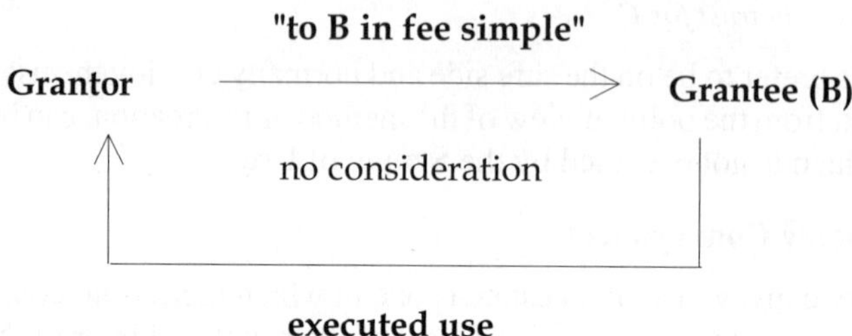

Hence, in order to make a conveyance without consideration effective in Ireland today the ordinary words of limitation cannot be used. Words have to be inserted to indicate that the grantee is to have the beneficial interest. The usual form of words of limitation in such a case is, then:

Unto and to the use of X and his [or her] heirs.[47]

The words "to the use of" indicate that X is to take both the legal estate and the beneficial interest in the land. Since there is an express use in favour of the grantee there is no implied use back to the grantor for the Statute to execute. The express use is not executed because X is seised of the legal estate to his own use.

c) New Forms of Conveyance

These are now usually referred to as the old forms of conveyance, but they were new to the law at the time of the Statute of Uses. The Statute made possible alternative forms of conveyance to the feoffment and they survive in theory if not in practice.

(1) Bargain and Sale

Under the law of uses we have seen that when X enters in to a contract to convey

46 Sanders, *Uses* 1:106; *Armstrong v. Wolsey* (1755) 2 Wils KB 19, 19 Doug 26, 95 ER 662; *Beckwith's Case* (1589) 2 Co Rep 56, 58, 76 ER 541; *Read v. Errington* (1591) Cro Eliz 321, 78 ER 571.

47 *Savill v. Bethell* [1902] 2 Ch D 523. And see *Doe d Lloyd v. Passingham* (1827) 6 B & C 305, 108 ER 465; *Orme's Case* (1872) LR 8 CP 281. Challis, *Real Property* p.389.

an estate to Y supported by consideration,[48] equity regarded X as holding the land to the use of Y. He had bargained and sold the land to Y. At common law he or she had bargained it, *i.e.* entered into a contract to sell it, but had not sold, it *i.e.* had not executed a common law conveyance. Equity, however, treated Y for some purposes as already the owner of the land. X held the legal estate to the use of Y.

The effect of the Statute of Uses would have been to execute the use, giving Y the legal estate without anything more needing to be done. It would have created a new kind of conveyance and one that was secret. It would not require the entry and public ceremony of a feoffment. At this time secret conveyances were regarded with suspicion, since, at least as far as large landowners were concerned, land transactions still had political implications. This effect was realised at the last moment by the draughtsmen of the Statute and in the same session of Parliament the Statute of Enrolments, 1535 was passed. When the Irish Statute was enacted it was incorporated into the Act as section 17. It provided that no bargain and sale of freeholds would be effective unless it was indented in writing, sealed and enrolled in the King's Court [High Court in Dublin today] within six months. Thus, a bargain and sale of freehold still requires a public act.[49] In theory it could still be done, but few solicitors would want to do so because at the time of entering into a contract the title to the land has not been investigated. Contracts for the sale of land today, which are not enrolled, therefore give rise to a kind of trust which is the equivalent of the old implied use.[50]

(2) Lease and Release

Before the Statute of Uses a form of conveyance was invented to avoid some of the disadvantages of the feoffment. The grantor first granted a lease, usually for one year, to the grantee. Then he or she released the freehold reversion to the grantee. A deed of release was used since the interest conveyed was a future interest and a feoffment could only be used to convey seisin. The lease merged with the freehold reversion, giving the grantee the full fee simple:

48 At the time the doctrine was developed it is not clear whether a promise to pay was a sufficient consideration, or whether actual payment had to be proved. Also, it was not enough at first for any consideration, *i.e.* of any amount, to be given. It had to represent the full value of the land: *Case of Sutton's Hospital* (1612) 10 Co Rep 1a. The law did not at first leave it to the market to determine price. Later, with the expansion of the market economy, the law retreated from its former role. Any amount would be a sufficient consideration for the purpose of raising a use in favour of the purchaser: *Barker v. Keate* (1680) 2 Vent 35, 86 ER 293.

49 But it does not require entry: *Dwyer v. Rich* (1869) IR 4 CL 424 at p.436, affirmed on appeal (1872) IR 6 CL 144.

50 Irish cases suggest that this trust only arises if part of the purchase money is paid: *Tempany v. Hynes* [1976] IR 101; See the first edition of this work, appendix A, for a discussion of this doctrine.

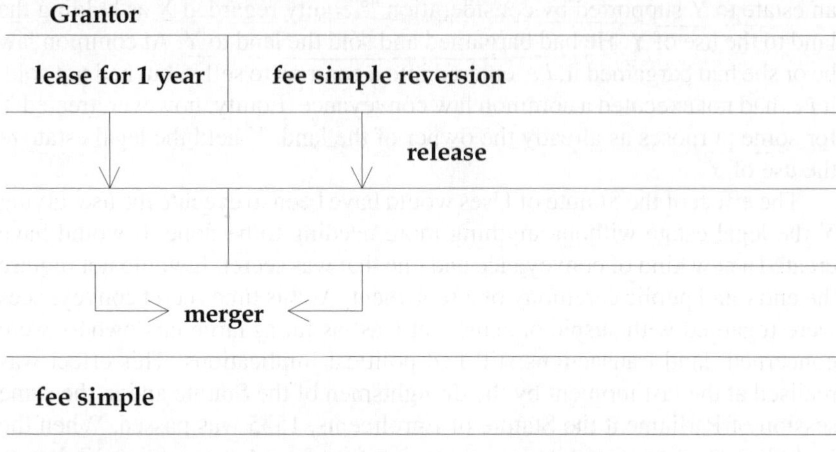

The whole transaction was known as a lease and release.

Although it avoided the necessity of a public ceremony of livery of seisin, the lease and release still had one disadvantage. The law of leaseholds, developed by analogy to freehold tenure, required an actual entry on the land as well as a document before the intended lessee was recognised as having a lease. Until the lessee entered he or she only had an *interesse termini*, an interest in the term.[51] The grantee would have to enter some time after the lease and before the release. Strictly speaking, the holder of a freehold reversion expectant on a lease had seisin, but the law had relieved such a person from the need to execute a feoffment.

(3) Bargain and Sale, Lease and Release Combined.

The bargain and sale, lease and release was a device, after the Statute, to avoid the need to enrol a bargain and sale and also to allow a secret conveyance to take place.[52] The loophole in the Act was that the requirement of enrolment applied only to freeholds. Lawyers soon saw that a bargain and sale of a leasehold would be executed by the Act without enrolment and they used this as the basis of a new conveyance. The procedure was as follows:

1. The grantor bargained and sold a lease, usually for a year, to the grantee. This raises a use in favour of the grantee in the lease.

51 See Chapter 19 Landlord and Tenant.

52 It was said to have been invented by Serjeant Francis Moore for Lord Norris: Williams, *Real Property* p.215.

2. The Statute executed the use without enrolment. The grantee now had a legal lease. Further, it was held that the execution of the use by the Statute dispensed with the need for entry to give effect to the lease.
3. The grantor then executed a release of the freehold reversion.

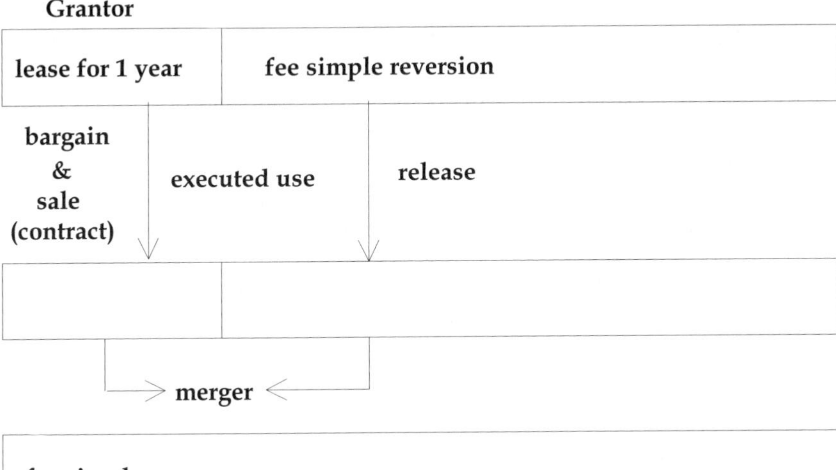

Two deeds were executed, the lease being dated the day before the release, although both were usually made on the same day.[53] This new form of conveyance is significant in the development of legal ideas because it marks a point at which the ownership of land becomes detached from the concept of possession. This method of conveyance was used generally until the Conveyance by Release Act, 1841 provided, rather illogically, that in future a release alone would be sufficient to pass the legal freehold in the land. This form of conveyance continued to be used until the enactment of the Real Property Act, 1845.[54]

(4) Covenant to Stand Seised

Before the Statute of Uses an owner of land might enter into a covenant, *i.e.* a contract under seal, to stand seised of the land in favour of someone else. In other words, instead of conveying the legal estate to a feoffee to hold to the use of X, the grantor simply declared that he held the legal estate himself to the use of X.

Before the Statute a seal was enough at common law to make a contract enforceable, even without consideration, but this was of no importance here be-

53 Williams, *Real Property* p.217.

54 See below.

cause the common law did not recognise a use in any case. Equity, on the other hand, was not impressed with bare formalities. It would not enforce the use unless something more than a wax seal was proved. There had to be consideration in equity. Equity recognised "natural love and affection" as consideration sufficient to enforce a covenant to stand seised, provided the parties were in fact near relations.[55]

Equity developed the doctrine further by recognising certain transactions as covenants to stand seized even though they were not expressed to be such. For example, if X covenanted with his son, Y, to grant land to Y on his forthcoming marriage, but never did so, equity would treat the covenant as one by which X stood seized of the land to the use of Y.[56] Furthermore, a feoffment without livery of seisin, which was ineffective at common law might be treated in equity as a covenant to stand seised if the parties were near relations.[57]

The effect of the Statute of Uses was to execute the use, conveying the legal estate to the relation. Although this was a new form of conveyance created by the Statute it is of limited use because it is only effective if the parties are near relatives.

(5) The Real Property Act, 1845

Section 2 of the Real Property Act, 1845 finally did away with the need for the bargain and sale and the release, by providing that "all corporeal hereditaments lie in grant" *i.e.* that a simple deed of conveyance is sufficient to grant freehold estates in land. But it did not abolish the old forms. It did, however, provide that after 1845 the feoffment with livery of seisin is void unless evidenced by deed – the old ceremony is not enough by itself.

d) Conveyance to Self, or to Self and Another

At common law freehold could not be conveyed to oneself or to oneself and another party, because the feoffment involved transfer of seisin. The common law adopted the strict rule that if a person was already seised they could not transfer it to themselves. Lawyers used the Statute of Uses to avoid this. This was, and still is, necessary, for example, where a tenant in tail disentails in his or her own favour. The tenant in tail has a statutory power under the Fines and Recoveries (Ireland) Act, 1834 to make a conveyance in fee simple. That is how the act of disentailing takes place. But the common law rule forbids the tenant in tail making the conveyance in his or her own favour. Instead, it must be made to a feoffee:

55 *Sharrington v. Strotton* (1565) 1 Plow 298, 75 ER 454.

56 *Maguire v. Scully* (1862) 12 Ir Ch. R 153.

57 *Shove v. Pincke* (1793) 5 TR 124, 310, 101 ER 72, 174; *Habergham v. Vincent* (1790) 2 Ves Jun 204, 226, 34 ER 678, 735, 776.

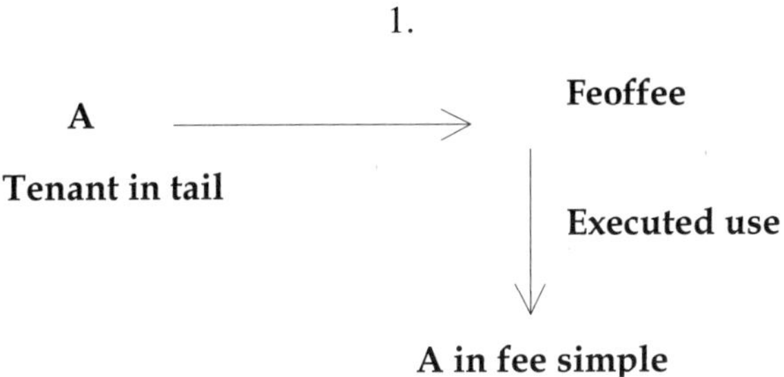

If A wished to convey his fee simple to himself and his wife he also had to convey to a feoffee:

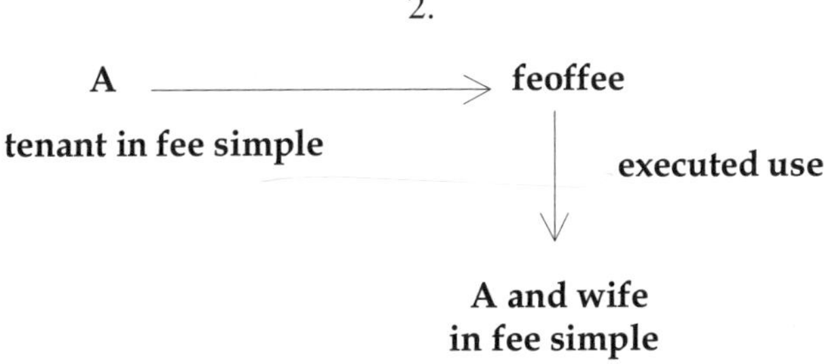

The Conveyancing Act, 1881 section 50 now provides that:

> "Freehold land may be conveyed by a person to himself jointly with another person, or conveyed by a husband to his wife, and by a wife to her husband, alone or jointly with another person."[58]

It may be noted that the section does not include the situation where a person conveys to himself or herself alone.[59] Oddly, the Act did not affect this situation and so the conveyance under the Statute is still necessary where a tenant in tail executes a disentailing assurance in favour of himself or herself.[60] The Act makes a conveyance to a feoffee unnecessary in 2 above, but not 1.

e) Express Reservation of an Easement

This is dealt with in Chapter 22 under easements.

58 See Property (NI) Order 1978 s.10.

59 The law in Northern Ireland does allow this: Property (Northern Ireland) Order 1978 s.10(2), except for leaseholds and fee farm grants.

60 *Re Ottley's Estate* [1910] 1 IR 1. The Married Women's Status Act, 1957 does not affect s.50.

f) Future Interests

The Statute of Uses gave rise to new types of future interests which did not have to conform to the feudal common law remainder rules. This topic is dealt with in Chapter 10 on future interests.

g) Legal Powers of Appointment and Sale

This topic is dealt with in Chapter 13 on powers.

F. Formalities

1. Creation

Section 4 of the Statute of Frauds, 1695 requires any "declarations or creations" of "trusts or confidences" of lands or hereditaments to be in writing and signed by the party able to make them. The word "confidence" recalls the words of the Statute of Uses, 1634 and appears to mean that the section applies regardless of what word is used to refer to the trust. Section 5 exempts implied and constructive trusts.

The phrase "trust or confidence" probably does not include the declaration or creation of other equitable interests. A purchaser's equity is created by implication of equity, and so need not itself be in writing, although in this instance it will necessarily arise only if there is an enforceable contract. Section 2 of the Statute of Frauds, 1695 requires a note or memorandum in writing for the contract to be enforceable, with part performance as an alternative.

2. Assignment

Section 6 requires "grants and assignments" of "any trust or confidence" to be in writing. Thus, any subsequent assignment of the beneficial interest under a trust requires writing. There is, however, no requirement of writing for the assignment of equities not falling within the phrase "trust or confidence", such as a purchaser's equity.

G. Merger of Law and Equity

1. The Problems of Separate Jurisdictions

It has already been mentioned that law and equity had reached a form of accommodation in the 17th century, but they remained separate systems. If a litigant wanted damages, then he or she had to go to one of the common law courts. Damages was the main remedy except for actions over land, where the real actions gave the remedy of recovery of the land, but they were attended by great technicality in pleading. If you wanted an injunction to stop somebody doing something or to order them to do it, or wanted specific performance of a contract, you had to go to the court of Chancery. There were many delays and inconveniences. In *Knight v. Marquess of Waterford*[61] the original bill was filed in the Court of Exchequer, which then had jurisdiction in equity, in 1830. It took 14 years to reach the House of Lords on appeal[62] and they decided that the suit should have been started in the common law courts. The plaintiff had to start all over again.[63] Equity regarded itself as supplementary to the common law and so if a remedy existed at common law the courts of equity refused to intervene and merely referred the party to the common law courts.[64]

In Ireland the Court of Chancery began to modify this rule and to allow actions to be brought where a common law remedy existed but was useless or difficult to obtain.[65] Differences in jurisdiction still caused problems. Courts of equity still had sometimes to consider granting injunctions to prevent actions at law.[66] Courts of equity had no jurisdiction to award damages[67] until the Chancery Amendment Act, 1858 (Lord Cairns' Act), which is still in force in Ireland, conferred jurisdiction to award damages "in addition to or in substitution for" specific performance or an injunction.[68]

---

61 (1844) 11 Cl & Fin 653, 8 ER 1250, HL.

62 (1835) 160 ER 296, (1839) 160 ER 1013, (1839) 160 ER 1148, (1846) 153 ER 913.

63 The case is only outdone by *Morgan v. Lord Clarendon* which was begun in 1808 and 16 years later was still in its interlocutory stages. The costs amounted to £3,700.

64 *e.g. McCarthy v. Barry* (1860) 9 Ir Ch R 377.

65 *Brady v. Fitzgerald* (1850) 12 Ir Eq R 273. Brady LC allowed an action on a rentcharge to succeed on this ground. He refused to follow the previous Master of the Rolls in *Cremen v. Hawkes* (1845) 8 Ir Eq R 153 (affirmed by Sugden LC at 503). The Brady case was criticised by the Master of the Rolls in *McCarthy v. Barry* (1860) 9 Ir Ch R 377 although he recognised that he was bound by the Lord Chancellor's decision.

66 *e.g. Mountcashell (Earl) v. O'Neill (Viscount)* [1855] 3 Ir Ch R 455 *Johnson v. Young* (1876) IR 10 Eq 403, V-C.

67 *Clinan v. Cooke* (1802) 1 Sch & Lef 22 at 25, 9 RR 3 (no power to grant damages for non-performance of an agreement).

68 The Act was repealed in England by the Statute Law Revision and Civil Procedure Act, 1883, although the 1883 statute provided that the jurisdiction should survive repeal of the Act. The 1883 statute did not extend to Ireland where the Act is still in force: see s.2; *Leeds Industrial Cooperative Society Ltd v. Slack* (1924) AC 851; and "Jessel" in Simpson, *Biographical Dictionary; Crabb v. Arun DC (No 2)* (1977) 121 SJ 86, per Lord Denning MR. Common law damages are not discretionary and are only awarded for past wrongs, whereas Lord Carns' Act damages are, like other equitable remedies, discretionary. They may also be awarded in respect of future wrongs as an injunction would have been, asssuming that the majority opinion in *Leeds Industrial Cooperative Society Ltd v. Slack* (1924) AC 851 is the law in Ireland. However, there are serious problems with this approach: see *Jaggard v. Sawyer* [1995] 2 All ER 189, [1995] 1 WLR 269, [1995] 13 EG 132, [1995] 1 EGLR 146. Jolowicz, "Damages in Equity – A Study of Lord Cairns' Act" [1975] CLJ 224. Spry, *Equitable Remedies* (1971) p.541.

Delays caused by the procedural division of jurisdiction were compounded by delays caused by the inadequacy of the resources allocated to equity jurisdiction at a time when business had greatly increased with the Industrial Revolution and the many changes it brought about. Until the early 19th century only one judge sat in the Court of Chancery and that was the Lord Chancellor. In 1801 the Master of the Rolls, formerly an administrative official in Ireland, was made a judge with equity jurisdiction.[69] In 1856 the Court of Appeal in Chancery was established and a Lord Justice of Appeal appointed to it who sat with the Lord Chancellor, but this did nothing to relieve the load of first instance proceedings. Some improvement came in 1867 when a Vice Chancellor with the same jurisdiction as the Lord Chancellor was created.[70] The Lord Chancellor had not been entirely alone as there were other courts having equity jurisdiction in Ireland. The Court of Exchequer had its equity side but this jurisdiction as we have seen, was transferred to the Court of Chancery in 1850.[71] As well as the Court of Probate[72] there was the Incumbered Estates Court, set up in 1849[73] to deal with the sale and title of landed estates burdened by debt. It had been intended as a temporary measure, but the court was replaced in 1858 by the permanent Landed Estates Court.[74] Nevertheless, it might take years before a will came before the court to be construed and in the meantime some or all of those entitled under it had died, themselves leaving wills, and so cases snowballed into vast complex disputes. *Jennens v. Lord Beauchamp*,[75] the case on which Dickens based the fictional *Jarndyce v. Jarndyce* in Bleak House, was archetypal. William Jennens, a miser, died in the 1780s possessed of a huge fortune. The original will was still being litigated in 1915.[76]

In addition to the delays in Chancery there was also an element of uncertainty in having to choose between three courts of common law, a circumstance which was not necessarily a matter for regret by practitioners, as Serjeant Sullivan, the last of the serjeants at law and a practitioner at the Irish Bar, well remembered:

> "Forty years ago in my old country the legal world was in a state of transition. The Judicature Act had just got into swing and although four Courts still opened in the hall beside the Liffey they were soon to be fused into one . . . The

Eastwood v. Lever (1863) 4 De G J & S 114; *Crabb v. Arun DC (No. 2)* (1977) 121 SJ 86, per Lord Denning MR; *Attorney General for New South Wales v. Quinn* (1990) 170 CLR 1, (1990) 64 ALJR 327; *Carson v. John Fairfax & Sons Ltd* (1993) 67 ALJR 634.

69 By 41 Geo III c.25.

70 30 & 31 Vict. c.44.

71 Exchequer Equitable Jurisdiction (Ireland) Act, 1850.

72 20 & 21 Vict. c.79.

73 By 12 & 13 Vict. c.77. Section 15 conferred full equity jurisdiction.

74 By 21 & 22 Vict. c.72.

75 (1810) 1 Phill Ecc 155, 161 ER 946.

76 *The Dickensian,* vol. 9 No. 2.

> Court of Chancery stood by itself, but it was thought in those days that you had your choice of the three Common Law Courts in which to have your case tried. If you had some merit on your side but thought that the law was against you, you issued your writ in the Queen's Bench, which was presided over by Mickey Morris, as he was invariably called although he was a lord, because Mickey had a good deal of common sense, a great deal of humanity, but his ideas of jurisprudence were peculiarly his own. On the other hand, if you were strongly of the opinion that however iniquitous your client was, he had the law on his side, you issued your writ in the Court of Exchequer, presided over by Christopher Palles, the greatest judge before whom I have ever appeared. Christopher Palles decided according to what he believed to be the law, and would pay no attention to any other consideration that might be advanced before him. On the other hand there was a third course: if you had neither law nor merits you went to the Court of Common Pleas, which in that day was presided over by Chief Justice May, before whom no case was certain and no case was hopeless."[77]

The Judicature Act, which will be discussed shortly, did not abolish this uncertainty, but removed from plaintiffs and their lawyers the ability to manipulate it to their own advantage.

2. Supreme Court of Judicature (Ireland) Act, 1877

Similar legislation was passed in England in 1873–75. The Irish Act, like its English counterpart, created a single High court in which both law and equity would be administered.  For convenience the court sat in divisions corresponding to the types of disputes dealt with by the old courts, but all divisions had identical jurisdiction.[78] On some points law and equity had adopted different rules, leading to awkward and absurd conflicts within what was supposed to be a single legal system. An Irish example is provided by *Johnson v. Midland Great Western Railway*[79] in which a judge in equity found that a litigant was entitled to have a certain fund treated as a guaranteed fund, despite the fact that the Chief Justice in a common law court had held the same fund not to be a guaranteed fund.[80] Section 28 provides for the resolution of conflicts between law and equity on some specific points.[81] Subsection 11 contains a general provision:

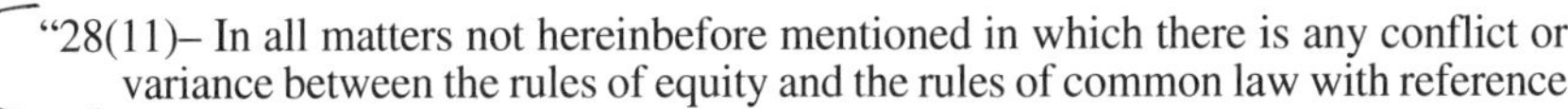

> "28(11)– In all matters not hereinbefore mentioned in which there is any conflict or variance between the rules of equity and the rules of common law with reference

77 Serjeant Sullivan, QC, "The Last Forty Years of the Irish Bar" (1927) 3 Camb L J, reprinted in Blom-Cooper (1965) p.7.

78 *Barber v. Houston* (1886) 18 LR Ir 475, CA (equity prevailed even in the common law divisions of the court).

79 (1857) 5 Ir Ch R 264.

80 See also *Talbot v. Cody* (1876) IR 10 Eq 138 (joint deposit receipts by husband and wife).

81 *e.g. Feehan v. Mandeville* (1891) 28 LR Ir 90, QB. Section 25 of English Supreme Court of Judicature Act, 1873.

> to the same subject matter, the rules of equity shall prevail."[82]

The first major case on the subsection was *Walsh v. Lonsdale*.[83] L agreed in writing not under seal to grant a seven year lease of a mill to W. One of the terms of the written lease was that one year's rent was to be paid in advance. After eighteen months L demanded the rent in advance. W refused. He said he would pay quarterly. L then distrained for the rent. W sued him for wrongful distress.

It was clear that the written document was not a valid lease because it was at that time required to be by deed: if not, it was void at law.[84] Before the Judicature Act there were two different approaches where a document was not valid as a lease. At common law if a person went into possession of land and paid rent on a basis referable to a year, e.g. quarterly, he or she held the land on a common law tenancy from year to year holding on the terms of the written document not inconsistent with such a tenancy.[85] Equity, on the other hand, held that a written document not valid as a lease could be treated as an agreement to grant a lease, *i.e.* a contract, and if it was a contract of which equity would grant specific performance, then equity "would regard as done that which ought to be done" and would treat the parties as if there already was a lease in equity.[86]

W's argument, based on the common law, was that he was a tenant from year to year at common law, that the provision for one year's rent in advance was inconsistent with such a tenancy and so must be struck out. Therefore, L's distress was unlawful. L's argument, based on equity, was that the agreement created a lease in equity and so all the terms in the written document were binding on the parties, including the provision for one year's rent in advance. Therefore the distress was lawful.

The court held in favour of L. There was a conflict between the rules of law and the rules of equity on the same issue and the rules of equity now prevailed. In the words of Jessel MR:

---

82 *Barber v. Houston* (1886) 18 LR Ir 475, CA. Equity prevailed over the common law in one other instance. Attorneys, who practised before the common law courts, became known as solicitors, the name by which their counterparts practising before the courts of equity were known.

83 (1882) 21 Ch D 9.

84 The applicable provisions were the English Statute of Frauds, 1677 and the Real Property Act, 1845. In *Parker v. Taswell* (1858) 2 De G & J 559, 44 ER1106 it was held that void at law did not mean void for all purposes.

85 *Fahy v. O'Donnell* (1869) IR 4 CL 332; *McCreesh v. McGeogh* (1872) IR 7 CL 236 (tenant under agreement could maintain trespass against landlord).

86 *Parker v. Taswell* (1858) 2 De G & J 559, 573, 44 ER 1106 at 1111f per Lord Chelmsford LC.

> "There are not two estates as there were formerly, one estate at common law by reason of the payment of rent from year to year, and an estate in equity under the agreement. There is only one court and the equity rules prevail in it."[87]

It should be noticed that there is a shift in ideas here, not merely a random difference of rules or procedure. The common law rule expressed the concepts of a pre-market society, a society in which commodity relations were not the dominant relation. The common law applied tests to determine what type of interest the parties had created and then supplied the contents of each available type of interest. The parties could not change these terms by agreement. By the latter part of the nineteenth century the common law had made one concession, however, in recognising the importance of the agreement between the parties. It recognised such of the terms of the written agreement as were not inconsistent with the tenancy imposed by the common law. In equity, on the other hand, agreement was fundamental. Equity in this respect expresses in a clear and uncompromising way the concepts of a market or capitalist society. Equity left the parties to make their own bargain and confined itself to examining what had been agreed and then to giving effect to it.

3. The Merger of Law and Equity.

Clearly for many purposes legal and equitable rights remain distinct after the Judicature Act. There are still distinct legal and equitable estates: the Act did not abolish trusts. There are still distinctions between legal and equitable remedies, principally that equitable remedies are discretionary. There is even still some distinction in jurisdiction in the Republic, since it appears that the District Court, although it has civil jurisdiction, has only a limited jurisdiction to grant equitable remedies.[88]

The discretion in the granting of equitable remedies has to some extent been reduced to recognisable rules, but that does not affect the point that a claimant may be disentitled from obtaining an equitable remedy on grounds which would not have a similar effect on a legal remedy.

At the same time it is clear that law and equity are no longer as distinct in some respects as they were before the Judicature Act. For example, an injunction may now be granted to give effect to a legal right.[89] There may also have developed some areas in which it is impossible to say whether the rules are legal or equitable, such as the law relating to rent review clauses in leases.[90]

87 (1882) 21 Ch D 9 at 14f.

88 Courts of Justice Act, 1924 s.77 as amended by Courts of Justice Act, 1936 ss. 52, 94; Local Government Act, 1946, s.48, Sch. 3; Courts Act, 1971. The civil jurisdiction is limited to "contract, breach of contract, tort. . .[with exceptions] and claims for damages unconnected with contract. . .[with monetary limit]".

89 *Corporation of Cork v. Rooney* (1881) 7 LR Ir 191, V-C.

90 *United Scientific Holdings v. Burnley BC* [1978] AC 904; *Hynes v. Independent Newspapers* [1980] IR 204 at 218 per Kenny J; *Ely Ltd v. ICR Ltd* unreported, High Court,

H. The Nature of Equitable Interests

So far we have looked at formal aspects of equitable interests. But do they differ from legal interests in quality? Are they definite claims to definite property at all?

1. Definite Property

In general, if T holds property in trust for B, B, the beneficiary cannot direct T how to go about his duties, he cannot tell him to buy or to sell a whole or part of the trust property. The trustee can use his own discretion and need not even consult the beneficiaries. They may only sue the trustee if he acts in breach of trust, *i.e.* contrary to the terms of the trust or to the standards of conduct laid down by the courts of equity.

But is B the real owner of the property? Let us say that income from the trust, such as dividends or rent, is received by the trustee. Is each sum of money the property of the beneficiary, subject only to the trustees right to deduct expenses, or has the beneficiary only an of account against the trustee to account for the balance? The courts have held that for this purpose the beneficiary owns each sum of money[91] and so is liable to pay income tax on the gross amount, before the trustee deducts expenses.[92] On the other hand, where a trustee has granted a lease of trust property it has been held that the trustee, and not the beneficiary, is entitled to distrain for the rent.[93] For this purpose the trustee was held to be the owner of the trust property.

Someone entitled as a potential beneficiary under a discretionary trust, who therefore only has a contingent interest in the property, has nevertheless been held to be entitled to bring an action to prevent dissipation of the fund[94] or to remedies appropriate to monitor the administration of the fund and its investments.[95] Even though they might never receive any of the property, if the trust fund is disspiated, they will lose even the possibility of receiving any, and that possibility is their property interest.

McWilliam J, 3 April 1979.

91 *Baker v. Archer-Shee* [1927] AC 844.

92 If the beneficiary is entitled under a settlement executed in Ireland to securities held abroad, the test of the proper law is applied to the foreign securities and liability to tax is not determined by the fact that the settlement was made in Ireland: *Re Knox* (1963) IR 263, judgment of the Supreme Court at 286.

93 *Schalit v. Joseph Nadler Ltd* [1933] 2 KB 79. One explanation of this is that distress was a common law remedy before the Judicature Act and this may be another example of the survival of the distinction between common law and equitable remedies.

94 *Jacob v. Revenue Commissioners*, unreported, High Court, 6 July 1983. See Chapter 10 Future Interests: contingent interests.

95 *Chaine-Nickson v. The Bank of Ireland* [1976] IR 393. See Chapter 10 Future Interests: contingent interests.

a) Definite Right

In the case of common law rights, once you establish them you are entitled to a remedy, even if it is nominal damages. In equity you are not so entitled because all equitable remedies are discretionary. So even if X proves he is entitled to an equitable interest X will not get a remedy if he has acted inequitably, *i.e.* dishonestly in some way. He who comes to equity must come with clean hands.[96]

b) Enforceability

Against whom can a person entitled to an equity enforce it? It has been said that legal rights are rights *in rem, i.e.* rights to a thing, whereas equitable rights are rights *in personam, i.e.* rights against persons. Legal rights are available against everybody, but equitable rights are available only against a limited class of people. This is misleading. All rights to property are really rights against persons. Even in the case of common law rights we have seen that there is relativity of title in land rights, so that the holder of a legal title to land may be able to defend it against most people, but not all. Like most misleading statements there is some truth in it. Equitable rights are enforceable against a more limited class of people than legal rights.

2. Common Law Rights

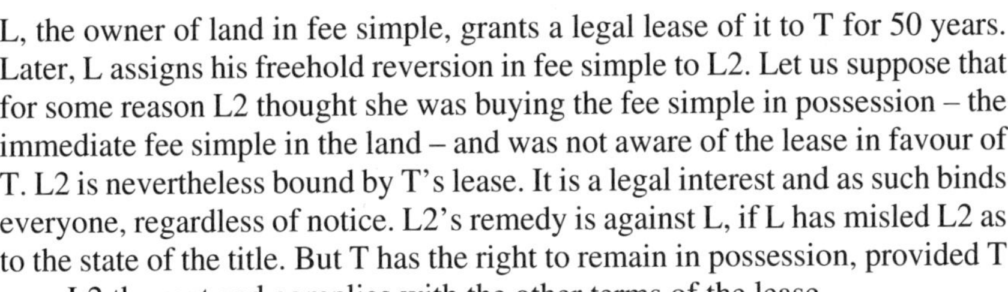

L, the owner of land in fee simple, grants a legal lease of it to T for 50 years. Later, L assigns his freehold reversion in fee simple to L2. Let us suppose that for some reason L2 thought she was buying the fee simple in possession – the immediate fee simple in the land – and was not aware of the lease in favour of T. L2 is nevertheless bound by T's lease. It is a legal interest and as such binds everyone, regardless of notice. L2's remedy is against L, if L has misled L2 as to the state of the title. But T has the right to remain in possession, provided T pays L2 the rent and complies with the other terms of the lease.

96 See *Re French's Estate* (1887) 21 LR Ir 283. See below.

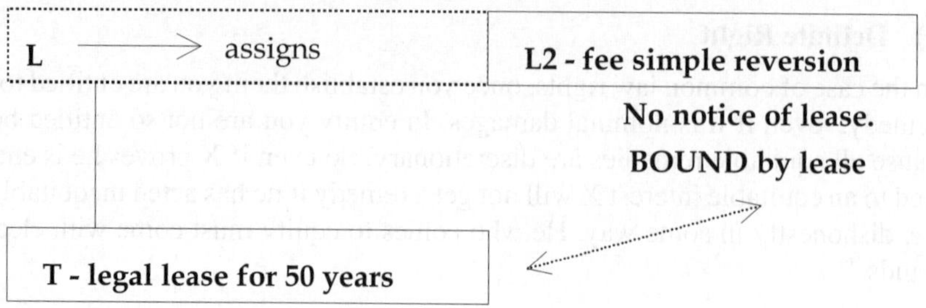

The assignee is bound. It matters not whether the assignee has notice of the prior legal right or not.[97] As between two legal interests, the first in time prevails.

3. Equitable Rights

When courts began to recognise equitable interests, they at first gave only a personal action against the trustee if he or she misused the property. But suppose the trustee sold the legal title to someone else? Courts of equity decided that they would not interfere with the alienability of legal estates. To do so would certainly have placed a restriction on the operation of the market and it may be that in developing this principle equity was again showing its preference for market relations.

Equity follows the law in the maxim of equity. It does not deny that the trustee as owner of the legal estate has the right to transfer it. What it does do is to say that the person who takes the legal estate from the trustee, is under some circumstances, bound by the equity. But when was such a person to be bound? Equity produced a compromise. It would enforce the equitable interests against everyone except a bona fide purchaser of the legal estate without notice of the equity, or anyone taking from such a person. This has been called the "Polar Star Rule" of equity, the guiding principle of all equitable interests:

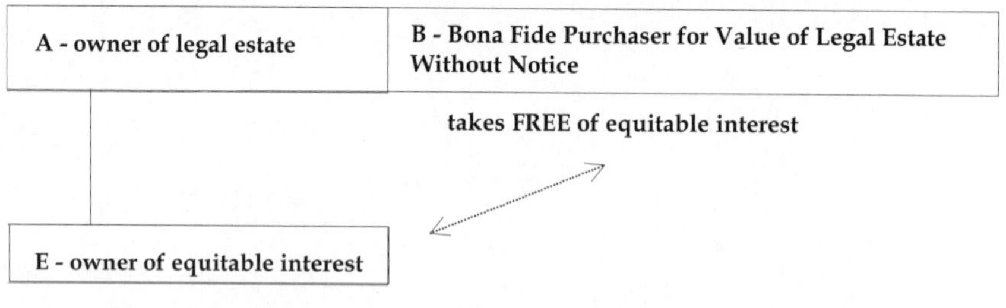

97 *Corry v. Cremorne* (1862) 12 Ir Ch R 136; *Finch v. Shaw* (1854) 19 Beav 500, 52 ER 445 per Sir John Romilly (notice no defence to action to enforce legal right to dower).

Although the compromise which equity adopted may have favoured the free market dealings in legal estates, this is not to say that it was so regarded at the time, or even, perhaps, that the courts of equity were aware that this was the consequence. At that time the courts had a different explanation of what they did. The early Chancellors were prominent members of the Church. They said that the legal owner was bound if his or her conscience was affected, and his or her conscience was affected if he or she knew of the equitable interest at the time they bought the legal estate. They were legally bound because they were morally bound to give effect to the equitable interest.

At first sight this might seem an adequate explanation, until one takes account of the other elements of the doctrine. It was not so that anyone who took without notice took free of the equity. They only did so if, in addition to the legal estate, they had given value for it. In this situation there were two innocent persons: on the one hand, the person entitled to the equity and on the other, the purchaser in the market who had given value for the legal estate. The courts favoured the purchaser in the market, the buyer of the commodity. The compromise therefore favoured the development of the market economy, or to put it another way, favoured the person who was actually or potentially a capitalist.

The courts expressed the rule as to the priority of the two interests in a maxim: "where the equities are equal the law prevails." Equity is not used here in the sense of equitable interests but in the sense of moral claims. As between two innocent parties, the legal estate prevails.

a) The Bona Fide Purchaser

The plea of bona fide purchaser of the legal estate for value without notice is a single plea and the burden of proof is on the person who asserts the plea to prove every element of it.[98] The purchaser cannot assert purchase for value of the legal estate and then leave it to the other side to prove notice.

(1) Bona Fide

This requirement means that the purchaser must act in good faith according to equitable principles. Equitable remedies are discretionary and any lack of honesty will disentitle the claimant to relief.

(2) Purchaser

Purchaser traditionally has had a special meaning in the law of real property. It denotes a person who takes other than by operation of law, *i.e.* by some act of a party or parties. Thus someone who takes under a will is a purchaser, but a person who takes on intestacy is not. The word in this technical sense does not imply that value has been paid.

98 *Heneghan v. Davitt* (1933) IR 325.

A case that illustrates this aspect of the doctrine is *Re Nisbett and Pott's Contract*.[99] The land in question was originally owned by X. A restrictive covenant, which is a type of equitable interest in land, restricted the use of the land to the benefit of an adjoining plot. X was dispossessed by a squatter. The limitation period expired which meant that the title of X was extinguished. The squatter sold the land to the present vendor who entered into a contract to sell it to the present purchaser. The purchaser discovered the existence of the restrictive covenant and claimed that the vendor had not shown a title free of such interests as he had contracted to do. The question was therefore whether the vendor held the land subject to the equitable interest. The court held that the squatter did hold the land subject to the restrictive covenant. He was not a purchaser as he had acquired his interest by operation of law.[100]

(3) For Value

The purchaser also has to give value for the legal estate. Thus someone who takes under a will is a purchaser in the technical sense of real property, *i.e.* takes the interest otherwise than by operation of law, but does not pay value and so will not take free of equitable interests. Here again equity shows that it favours the operation of a free market. It is not any "purchaser" who takes free of equities, but a purchaser in the real economic sense of one who buys in the market. As between two innocent parties, equity favours the one who pays money for the property as a commodity and not the owner of an equitable interest who may have come by it gratuitously under a trust.

The fact that this rule expresses a fundamental compromise favouring the market is also shown by the definition of value in this context. It includes money or money's worth, *i.e.* land, services, *etc.*, and also includes the satisfaction of an existing debt,[101] but it does not include "natural love and affection" which equity recognises as consideration in other contexts.[102]

(4) Of the Legal Estate

In order to take the property free of an equitable estate or interest the purchaser must have the legal estate. The only qualification on this is if the interest which is first in time is a lesser type of equity known as mere equity which is discussed below.[103]

---

99 [1906] 1 Ch. 386.

100 The vendor was bound because he had not investigated the title back for the full statutory period: see below "Without notice: length of title."

101 The satisfaction of an existing debt is not consideration at common law: *Foakes v. Beer* (1884) 9 App Cas 605, [1881-5] All ER Reprint 106.

102 Such as consideration sufficient to support a covenant to stand seized. See above.

103 See page 131.

(5) Without Notice:

(a) Doctrine of Notice

(i) Actual, Imputed, Constructive

There are three kinds of notice: actual, imputed and constructive.[104]

Actual notice is actual knowledge of facts, however acquired, although one need not listen to mere rumours.[105]

Imputed notice means that the notice of a legal representative, actual or constructive, is imputed to the client.

Constructive notice occurs if the person has actual notice that the property is affected in some way by another interest and fails to make inquires as to the nature of the other interest, when such inquiries would have revealed what it was, or a person deliberately abstains from making inquiries in order to avoid actual notice, or omits by carelessness or any other reason to make an inquiry which a purchaser acting on proper legal advice ought to make and which would have revealed the interest. The doctrine was given statutory form by section 3 of the Conveyancing Act, 1882:[106]

> "3–(1) A purchaser shall not be prejudicially affected by notice of any instrument, fact, or thing unless –
>
> (i) it is within his own knowledge, or would have come to his knowledge if such inquiries and inspections had been made as ought reasonably to have been made by him; or
>
> (ii) in the same transaction with respect to which a question of notice to the purchaser arises, it has come to the knowledge of his counsel, as such, or of his solicitor, or other agent, as such, if such inquiries and inspections had been made as ought reasonably to have been made by the solicitor or other agent.
>
> (2) This section shall not exempt a purchaser from any liability under, or any obligation to perform or observe, any covenant, condition, provision, or restriction contained in any instrument under which his title is derived, mediately or immediately; and such liability or obligation may be enforced in the same manner and to the same extent as if this section had not been enacted."

In *Northern Bank v. Henry*[107] a husband took an assignment of a lease in a house, but used money belonging to his wife in paying for it. The husband and wife lived for a time in the family home, but the husband later left. The wife started proceedings in the High Court seeking a declaration that the husband held the legal title to the house on trust for her. On the same day as the action was begun the husband mortgaged the lease to the plaintiff bank, conveying a

---

104 *Bank of Ireland Finance Ltd v. Rockfield Ltd* [1979] IR 21 at 29, Supreme Court.

105 *Waldron v. Jacob & Millie* (1870) IR 5 Eq 131; *Aldritt v. Maconchy* (1906) 1 Ch D 333.

106 See also Family Home Protection Act, 1976 s.3(7).

107 [1981] IR 7.

sublease to them as security for the loan. The bank searched the Registry of Deeds, but did not ask who was in occupation, nor did they inquire about any pending proceedings.

The Supreme Court held that the bank had constructive notice of the wife's equitable interest in the house. Henchy J, in a notable judgment, expressed the view that section 3 "gave statutory stress to the existing judicial insistence that constructive notice could be found only when the lack of knowledge was due to such careless inactivity as would not be expected in the circumstances from a reasonable man." He went on to draw a distinction between the conduct of prudent person in business and that of a reasonable person who is the subject of the legal test.

> "The default of a reasonable man is to be distinguished from the default of a prudent man. The prudence of the worldly wise may justifiably persuade a purchaser that it would be unbusinesslike to stop and look more deeply into certain aspects of the title. But the reasonable man, in the eyes of the law, will be expected to look beyond the impact of his decisions on his own affairs, and to consider whether they may unfairly and prejudicially affect his "neighbour," in the sense in which that word has been given juristic currency by Lord Atkin in *Donoghue v. Stevenson* (1932) AC 562."

Thus the judge refused to reduce the test of notice to the morality of a person acting in pursuit of his or her own economic self-interest.[108] Although the reasonableness test enlarges the scope of inquiries a purchaser should make, Blayney J has pointed out in an analogous situation[109] that there are difficulties in regarding it as a duty owed to the owner of the equity. If the purchaser fails to make the necessary inquiries it is the purchaser who loses, because he or she is then bound by the equity.

In *Bank of Ireland Finance Ltd v. Rockfield Ltd*[110] the Supreme Court approved of a line of authority to the effect that constructive notice should not be applied to purely commercial transactions, *i.e.* where both parties are engaged in a commercial undertaking. Kenny J quoted Lindley J in *Manchester Trust v. Furness*[111]:

> "... as regards the extension of the equitable doctrines of constructive notice to commercial transactions, the Courts have always set their faces resolutely against it. The equitable doctrines of constructive notice are common enough in dealing with land and estates, with which the Court is familiar; but there have

108 Where a third party, such as a bank, seeks consent of a spouse to a mortgage or charge of a family home under s.3 of the Family Home Protection Act, 1976 there is an analogous doctrine of notice, but in *Bank of Ireland v. Smyth* [1996] 1 ILRM 24 the Supreme Court held that the third party does not owe a duty to the non-conveying spouse. See Chapter 17 Family Property.

109 *Bank of Ireland v. Smyth* [1996] 1 ILRM 24. The case involved the Family Home Protection Act, 1976. See Chapter 17.

110 [1979] IR 21 at 29.

111 (1895) 2 QB 539 at p.545.

> been repeated protests against the introduction into commercial transactions of anything like an extension of those doctrines, and the protest is founded on perfect good sense. In dealing with estates in land title is everything, and it can be leisurely investigated; in commercial transactions possession is everything, and there is no time to investigate title; and if we were to extend the doctrine of constructive notice to commercial transactions we should be doing infinite mischief and paralyzing the trade of the country."[112]

(ii) Length of Title

At common law, if the contract did not specify the length of title to be shown by the vendor, *i.e.* it was an open contract, the title was to be investigated back for 60 years. If a good root of title was not encountered at that point, then the investigation continued until one was found. Now the Vendor and Purchaser Act, 1874 provides[113] that in unregistered conveyancing a purchaser must accept a good root of title at least 40 years old.[114] The purchaser may agree in the contract to investigate the title for a shorter period. Can the purchaser, by doing this, avoid notice of interests he would have discovered if he had investigated title back for the full 40 years? Whatever the position was before the Conveyancing Act, 1882, the courts have made it clear now that under subsection (2) he or she cannot do so.[115] It would be unfair for a vendor and purchaser, by agreeing between themselves to accept a shorter period, to prejudice the rights of a third party entitled to an equity.

In *Re Nisbett and Pott's Contract*[116] the vendor, who claimed through the squatter, would also be bound by the restrictive covenant unless he could prove the plea of bona fide purchaser. He failed to do so because he had not investigated the title back for the full statutory period. Had he done so he would have discovered the restrictive covenant. He therefore had constructive notice of the covenant.

(iii) Rights of Persons in Occupation

Normally a purchaser should inquire as to whether anyone is in occupation of the premises for they will have constructive notice of their rights if they do not.[117] We have already seen that this principle was applied in *Northern Bank v. Henry*.[118]

112 The passage was approved by Lopes and Rigby JJ. It was also cited with approval by Scrutton LJ in the Court of Appeal in *Greer v. Downs Supply Co* (1927) 2 KB 28.

113 Section 1.

114 See Wylie, *Conveyancing* para. 13.54, 13.60.

115 *Somers v. Weir* [1979] IR 94 at 108 per Henchy J; *Northern Bank v. Henry* [1981] IR 1. And see Wylie, *Conveyancing* para. 13.60. *Re Cox and Neve* [1891] 2 Ch. 109; *Re Nisbet and Pott's Contract* [1905] 1 Ch. 391, [1906] 1 Ch. 386.

116 [1906] 1 Ch. 386.

117 *Hamilton v. Lyster* (1844) 7 Ir Eq R 560; *Hunt v. Luck* [1902] 1 Ch. 428.

118 [1981] IR 7.

(b) Priority between Equitable Interests

If the bona fide purchaser only has an equitable estate then prima facie the equities are equal *i.e.* there are two estates of equal status and the first in time prevails, just as is the case with two legal estates. However, it is not the case that in equity the only question is as to the status of the interests. Since equitable remedies are discretionary the holder of the equitable interest which is first in time may lose priority over a later equity of equal rank because they have not acted equitably themselves.[119] Thus even though equity A and equity B both rank as equitable estates – equitable life estates, for example – and equity A is prior in time, the holder of equity A may lose priority over equity B if he or she has acted fraudulently or otherwise inequitably in the particular circumstances of the case.

There is one exception to the principle that in general priority between equitable interests is determined by the rule that the first in time prevails. There is an inferior type of equity known as a mere equity. A mere equity can be defeated by the later bona fide purchaser of an equitable estate (or interest, the words are used interchangeably) taken for value and without notice of the mere equity. This subject is pursued below.

(6) Or A Person Taking From Such a Purchaser

Successors in title to a bona fide purchaser for value of the legal estate without notice will also take free of the equity, even if they have notice of it themselves, provided they are bona fide.[120] An exception is the case of a fraudulent purchaser. We shall first illustrate the rule and then attempt to explain what policy or principle lies behind it.

In *Re Stewart's Estate*[121] an application was made in 1852 in the Incumbered Estates Court for the sale of an estate which had been settled on H for life and with remainder to his eldest son J in tail. A number of creditors, of which L was one, had previously registered judgment mortgages against the estate. These affected at that time only the life estate vested in H under the settlement. One year later H and J barred the entail on the land and conveyed the fee simple by deed to trustees on trust to sell the land in order to pay off creditors. Under the deed, any land remaining unsold, and any surplus proceeds of sale, were resettled on H and J. J was also given a power to charge the land. Part of the land was later sold in the Landed Estates Court, but since some creditors, including L, declared themselves satisfied that the remaining land would be sufficient to secure their debts, they agreed not to require immediate repayment. Six years after the sale, J exercised his power to charge. He ob-

119 *Re Ffrench's Estate* (1887) 21 LR Ir 283. See below.

120 *Salsbury v. Bagott* (1677) 2 Sw 603, 36 ER 745 at 747; *Mertins v. Jolliffe* (1756) Amb 311; 27 ER 211 per Lord Hardwicke at 212.

121 (1893) 31 LR Ir 405, Monroe J.

tained an advance of money from D. D was trustee of a fund and the money advanced was part of the trust fund. A, the solicitor who had acted many years before in the application for sale of the land in the Incumbered Estates Court, was also solicitor for one of the beneficiaries entitled to the trust fund in the hands of D. A, in order to avoid any impropriety, insisted that another solicitor act in the matter of the mortgage loan advanced by D to J. This was done. Later, D assigned the benefit of the mortgage to A for valuable consideration. A receiver was later appointed over the land. In the present proceedings L claimed priority over A. It was clear that he could not succeed on the basis of his judgment mortgage alone, because that only affected the life estate formerly vested in H. Nevertheless, his counsel perceptively, and successfully, argued that the agreement, by L and the other creditors not to insist on immediate payment on being satisfied as to the security of the remaining land, in itself constituted an equitable mortgage affecting the fee simple. The further question was whether this equitable interest was binding on A. As far as D was concerned, the court was satisfied that he was a bona fide purchaser of a legal interest without notice of the equity.

Monroe J held that notice could not be imputed to D through A because A could not be considered to be D's solicitor in the matter of the mortgage.[122] As far as A was concerned, he was a purchaser for value of a legal interest, but the court held that he also took free of the equity. Although he had actual notice that L had an interest in the land, he was bona fide because it had not occurred to him, as indeed it had not occurred to anyone until counsel in the present proceedings had suggested it, that L had an equitable mortgage over the land. Therefore, since D took free of the equity as a bona fide purchaser without notice, A also took free, despite his notice, as a bona fide purchaser from such a person as D. In the words of Monroe J:[123]

> "A purchaser with notice from a purchaser without notice is protected if the transaction be *bona fide*, the only exception being the case of a trustee buying back trust property which he has sold[124]; or that of a fraudulent person, who has acquired property by fraud, saying he has sold it to a *bona fide* purchaser without notice, and has got it back again."

This aspect of the bona fide purchaser doctrine does not seem particularly equitable. On the contrary, it seems that equity is acquiescing in conduct which falls short of the high standards it expects elsewhere. A possible explanation is that equity's concern with the conscience of individuals is superficial. At a deeper level equity is concerned with the efficient working of a market economy

122 Even if he had been, notice had not come to him in the same transaction as required by the Conveyancing Act, 1882 s.3.

123 *Re Stewart's Estate* (1893) 31 LR Ir 405 per Monroe J at 415 and see *Wilkes v. Spooner* [1911] 2 KB 473; *Re Stapleford Colliery Co (Barrow's Case)* 14 Ch D 432 per Jessel MR at 455.

124 See also *Kennedy v. Daly* (1803) 1 Sch. & Lef 355, per Lord Redesdale at p.379.

and in particular to maintain the commodity form of property interests. The rules and principles of equity seek to ensure that property interests may move freely from seller to buyer. Rules are then justified in moral or religious terms but their real concern is with economic efficiency.

These points can be illustrated by the case of *Wilkes v. Spooner*.[125] X was a lessee of two butchers shops on opposite sides of the same street. He rented No. 170 from landlord B, and No. 137 on the other side of the street from landlord A. X assigned his lease in 170 to the plaintiff. He entered into a covenant with the plaintiff to the effect that No. 137, which he retained, was to be used in future as a pork butchers only. This was to the advantage of the business at No. 170 because it would reduce the competition. X covenanted for himself and his assignees. The effect of this was that the covenant was not simply a contract binding between X and the plaintiff, but a property interest recognised in equity and known as a restrictive covenant. X later surrendered his lease in No. 137 to landlord A. Landlord A was held to be a purchaser for value of a legal estate, the lease, without notice of the equitable restrictive covenant, and so took the interest in No. 137 free of the covenant. In other words, the plaintiff could not force landlord A, if he carried on business at No. 137, to operate it as a pork butchers only. Landlord A then granted a new lease of 137 to X's son, who did have notice of the covenant. X's son then started trading as a general butcher.

The plaintiff sued to enforce the covenant. He did not succeed. The court was concerned with the position of landlord A. He had paid for the lease of No. 137 on the basis that the premises could be used as a general butcher, *i.e.* the value of the business without the restrictive covenant. As a buyer of a commodity he should be able to sell the same commodity and recover its value. If he could only do so by finding someone who, like himself, had no notice of the equity, his freedom to sell would be curtailed. Moreover, the owner of the equity could advertise it and so make it virtually impossible for the bona fide purchaser to recover the value of the commodity he had bought. Such is the attitude of the court: it sees the real issue as preserving the freedom of alienation of property. It might, however, be objected that the plaintiff has a similar kind of commodity interest, but which points to the opposite conclusion. He paid a higher price for No. 170 because it had the advantage, as he thought, of the restrictive covenant. He will not be able to recover that value unless the covenant is enforced.

125 [1911] 2 KB 473. And see *Re Stewart's Estate* (1893) 31 LR Ir 405, Monroe J.

b) Mere Equities

Mere Equities are usually rights to equitable relief, such as the right to have a document rectified for mistake[126] or to have a transaction set aside for fraud[127] or undue influence.[128] They are a lesser kind of equitable interest in that they are more easily defeated than equitable estates. A mere equity can be defeated by a bona fide purchaser for value of a legal or equitable estate without notice of the equity:

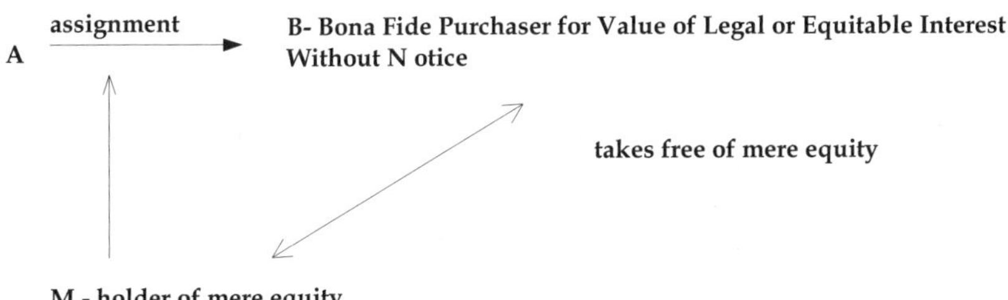

In *Allied Irish Bank v. Glynn*[129] a father was the registered owner of a piece of land. He executed a transfer of the land in favour of his son. The son later mortgaged the land by an equitable mortgage in favour of the Bank. The equitable mortgage ranked as an equitable estate. In the first set of proceedings, the Circuit Court held that the son had exerted undue influence on the father to transfer the land to him. This meant that the father had a right in equity to set aside the transaction. The plaintiff Bank brought the present action in the High Court claiming a declaration that they had a valid mortgage not affected by the equity in the father. This submission was upheld. The father's right to set aside the transfer was a mere equity which must yield to the equitable mortgage, even though the mortgage was later in time. The Bank were bona fide purchasers of an equitable estate without notice of the mere equity:

126 *Re Ottley's Estate* [1910] 1 IR 1; *Maguire v. Conway* [1950] IR 44, High Court; *Smith v. Jones* [1954] 1 WLR 1089, [1954] 2 All ER 823.

127 *Allied Irish Bank v. Glynn* [1973] IR 188; *Ernest v. Vivian* (1863) 33 LJ Ch. 513.

128 *Kelly v. Thewles* (1854) 2 Ir Ch R 510 at p.541; *Allied Irish Bank v. Glynn* [1973] IR 188.

129 [1973] IR 188.

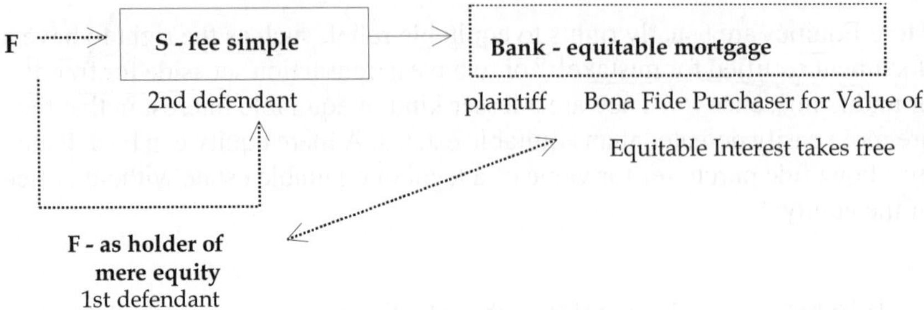

The father would still have a remedy against the son to recover the fee simple, but would hold it subject to the Bank's mortgage. He would also have a remedy against the son for money paid to the Bank in respect of the mortgage.

c) Undue Influence

One example of a mere equity that has been mentioned is the right to have a document set aside for undue inlfuence. Blackburne LC in *Kelly v. Thewles,*[130] speaking of wills, gave elegant expression to the doctrine when he said that:

> "...in no case has the doctrine [of undue influence] been applied or acted on, in which the evidence did not establish the ascendancy and dominion of the controlling power, and its actual exercise, by the constraint and coercion of an enfeebled, exhausted or subjugated intellect."[131]

In *inter vivos* dispositions certain relationships, such as parent and child[132], uncle and nephew,[133] guardian and ward,[134] doctor and patient,[135] solicitor and client,[136] trustee and beneficiary[137] and religious adviser and lay person[138] give rise to a presumption of undue influence.[139] Other relationships may give rise to the presumption.[140] The burden of proof is upon the benefited party to

130 (1854) 2 Ir Ch. R 510.

131 *ibid.* at p.541.

132 *Carroll v. Carroll* [1998] ILRM 218 at 229; *Gregg v. Kidd* [1956] IR 183; *Wallace v. Wallace* (1842) 2 Dru & War 452, 59 RR 766.

133 *Carroll v. Carroll* [1998] ILRM 218 at 229; *Gregg v. Kidd* [1956] IR 183.

134 *Mulhallen v. Marum* (1843) 3 Dru & War 317; *O'Connor v. Foley* [1906] 1 IR 20.

135 *Gregg v. Kidd* [1956] IR 183; *Ahearne v. Hogan* (1844) Dru t Sug 310.

136 *Gregg v. Kidd* [1956] IR 183; *Taafe v. Merrick* (1931) 65 ILTR 36.

137 *Provincial Bank of Ireland v. McKeever* [1941] IR 471.

138 *Gregg v. Kidd* [1956] IR 183; *Whyte v. Meade* (1840) 2 Ir Eq R 420.

139 There is no presumption in wills, as between testator and beneficiary: see Chapter 26 Succession.

140 *Carroll v. Carroll* [1998] ILRM 218; *Gregg v. Kidd* [1956] IR 183 per Budd J; *R (Proctor) v. Hutton (No. 2)* [1978] NI 139, per Lowry LCJ.

prove that there was no such influence brought to bear on the donor. Where no such relationship exists the onus is on the party alleging undue influence to prove it.[141]

In *Bank of Nova Scotia v. Hogan*[142] the property concerned in the case, St Rita's, belonged to the wife. The bank had a mortgage over the husband's property. In return for releasing it, the bank agreed to take a mortgage over St Rita's and the wife created it by depositing the title deeds with the bank. She had been advised by a firm of solicitors, who had acted for the husband in the purchase of his properties, that she was under no obligation to create the mortgage over St Rita's and that if she did, the bank would have the right to sell it in the event of a default by the husband. The husband later defaulted and when the bank sought to enforce its security over St Rita's, the wife claimed undue influence. The Supreme Court held on the facts that there was no evidence of undue influence either by the husband or by the solicitors. The court also expressed the view that a spouse is not entitled to the same amount of protection from the doctrine of undue influence in relation to placing a burden on his or her own property, as a spouse giving consent under the 1976 Act to a dealing by the other spouse with a family home vested in that spouse.[143]

d) Escheat

We have seen that the courts of equity did not generally follow purely feudal aspects of the common law: equity was a modernising influence. Equity did not apply the common law of escheat to equitable estates, even if it would have been possible to do so.

In *Burgess v. Wheate*[144] it was held that if A and B held the legal estate as trustees for C in fee simple and C died intestate and without heirs, the beneficial interest did not escheat to the Crown. The trustees were held to be entitled beneficially to the land. The case was correct as to legal history: the courts of equity did apply feudal concepts like escheat to the new, post-feudal equitable interests. But the case had undesirable practical consequences. If a beneficiary died intestate with no obvious heirs the trustees might be less than enthusiastic about tracing possible claimants since it was they who stood to gain if none were found.

---

141 *Carroll v. Carroll* [1998] ILRM 218.

142 [1997] 1 ILRM 407, Murphy J (O'Flaherty and Blayney JJ concurring); distinguishing *Bank of Ireland v. Smyth* [1996] 1 ILRM 24; see below, Consent.

143 Contrast *Bank of Ireland v. Smyth* [1996] 1 ILRM 24, Chapter 17 Family Property.

144 (1757–9) 1 Eden 128, 176, 28 ER 652. *Cox v. Parker* (1856) 22 Beav 168, 52 ER 1072; *Taylor v. Haygarth* (1844) 14 Sim 8, 16, 60 ER 259; *Beale v. Symonds* (1853) 16 Beav 406, 51 ER 835; *Craig v. Leslie* (1818) 16 US 563; 4 L Ed 460, US Supreme Court; *The Late Corporation of the Church of Jesus Christ of Latter-Day Saints v. United States* (1890) 136 US 1, 10 S Ct 792, 34 L Ed 478.

The Intestates Estates Act, 1884 section 4 provided that in future equitable estates should escheat as if they were legal estates. Hence, in such a case, the trustees would have held the legal estate on trust for the Crown.[145] The Act applied to Ireland[146] but was repealed by the Succession Act, 1965. Section 11(3) of the Succession Act, 1965 abolished escheat to the State and section 73(1) of the same Act provides that in default of any person taking the estate of an intestate, the State takes as "ultimate intestate successor." The position would therefore seem to be that in such a case the trustees hold on trust for the State.

4. The Personal and Proprietary Remedies

a) General

It is sometimes said, though less often now than it used to be, that equity acted *in personam* whereas the common law acted *in rem.*[147] This is true in a some senses, but untrue in others. It is true that if a person disobeys an equitable order of court he or she may be imprisoned for contempt, which does not automatically follow in the case of common law orders. Common law orders usually meant an award of damages and so the person's property could be sold before they need be punished or coerced by imprisonment. It is also true, as we have seen that whereas common law rights in property are available against all persons, equitable rights are available only against a restricted class. However, both are more accurately seen as rights against people. Property is essentially a relationship between people, and therefore mediated by moral and political values, rather than a thing or a relationship to a thing. In this sense there are, accurately, no rights *in rem* at all.

A further important proof that equity is just as proprietary as the common law lies in the fact that there are both proprietary and personal remedies in equity. The doctrine of the bona fide purchaser for value of the legal estate without notice, and his or her successors, *i.e.* the Polar Star Rule, defines the scope of the proprietary remedy. Such a bona fide purchaser is beyond the reach of the proprietary remedy, but this does not mean that everyone within the scope of the Polar Star Rule is personally liable to make good any loss even if they no longer have the property. Someone who takes the property with notice of the equity certainly is so liable: their notice makes them a constructive trustee. However, someone who is liable under the rule but who is wholly innocent, as, for example, someone who takes without notice but without value, is only liable to restore the property if they still have it.[148] They are not personally liable

145 *Re Lowe's Will Trusts* [1973] 2 All ER 1136, [1973] 1 WLR 882.

146 Section 9.

147 For example, Maitland, *Equity.*

148 *Re Diplock* [1948] Ch 465 at 477–479.

to make good deficiencies in the trust property or other losses to the beneficiaries.

On the other hand, the proprietary remedy may not be available because the property has been dissipated, or has been mixed with other property. In this case the person may be within the scope of the Polar Star Rule in that they received the property at some stage, with notice, but they no longer have it. In other cases, a person may never have received the property or an interest in it, but were a party to or assisted in a fraudulent design. In either case the personal remedy is available and they will be personally liable as constructive trustees.[149]

b) Tracing

Finally, equity developed the concept of tracing property in a more effective way than the common law concept of following. Equity would allow the proprietary remedy even if the trust property had been changed into another form, *e.g.* from money into land or vice versa. Equity in this sense is more proprietorial than the common law. The common law tended to regard property as a thing, or things, in the feudal sense, as objects with different and incomparable physical attributes. Equity, by contrast, tends to view property as commodities, as things in movement in a market, as exchange values. In relation to tracing equity approaches this concept, but does not fully realise it, because it has to maintain some distinction between trust property and other property of individuals. So the remedy is lost if the trust property becomes mixed inextricably with other property.

In *Re Ffrench's Estate*[150] the Irish Court of Appeal started a line of cases which suggested that in some circumstances the beneficiaries' interest under a trust in Ireland is reduced to little more than a mere equity.[151] In that case a tenant for life under a money fund had induced the trustees to advance the whole of the fund to him in breach of trust. He then used the money to buy land and then used the land as security for an equitable mortgage from a third party, telling the third party that there were no prior equitable interests affecting the land. The contest was between the other, innocent, beneficiaries under the trust and the later equitable mortgagee. Prima facie the equities being equal the first in

149 *Adair v. Shaw* (1803) 1 Sch & Lef 243 per Lord Redesdale LC at 262; *Alleyne v. Darcy* (1856) 4 Ir Ch. R 199; *Barnes v. Addy* (1874) LR 9 Ch. App 244; *Belmont Finance Corpn Ltd v. Williams Furniture Ltd* [1979] Ch. 250; *Selangor United Rubber Estates Ltd v. Craddock (No. 3)* [1968] 1 WLR 1555, per Ungoed-Thomas J at 1582, [1968] 2 All ER 1073; *Karak Rubber Co Ltd v. Burden* [1972] 1 All ER 1210.

150 (1887) 21 LR Ir 283. The case is discussed in more detail in the 1st edition of this work.

151 See Delaney, "Equitable Interests and Mere Equities" (1957) 21 The Conveyancer 195; Bell, *Modern Law of Personal Property in England and Ireland*, 1989, pp.155, 468–69 and 520; Keane, *Equity*, paras. 5.05, 20.10; Wylie, *Irish land Law (*3rd ed.) para. 3.077.

time, the beneficiaries, should have prevailed, but the court decided that the later equitable mortgage took priority. The judges gave a number of different reasons for their decision, but two of them were controversial. Porter MR held that because the trust property had been changed from money into land, so that the beneficiaries had to rely on the remedy of tracing, their right was defeated by the later bona fide purchaser for value of an equitable interest (the equitable mortgage) without notice of the trust.[152] In other words, a beneficiary's interest under a trust in Ireland would amount to a mere equity if the beneficiary had to rely on the remedy of tracing. Since this reason is put forward by only one judge it cannot strictly be the *ratio decidendi* of the case. The other two judges, Fitzgibbon LJ[153] and Barry LJ[154] among other reasons, held that beneficiaries under a trust lost priority to the later equitable interest whenever a third party was put at risk due to misconduct by the trustees, even if the beneficiaries under the trust were themselves innocent, although Fitzgibbon suggests it is otherwise if the trustees conduct amounted to fraud, which was not the case there.[155] This second proposition would virtually reduce the beneficiaries' interest under a trust in Ireland to a mere equity in almost all cases, because, if the beneficiaries were innocent, an innocent third party would usually be put at risk precisely because of a breach of trust by the trustees. It has been pointed out[156] that the decision in *Re Ffrench* was inconsistent with the decision of the British House of Lords in *Shropshire Union Railways & Canal Co v. The Queen*[157], which was not cited to the court and which at the time was binding upon it.

Re Ffrench was followed in a number of cases[158] before 1922 by Irish courts who considered themselves bound by it, and in *Scott v. Scott*[159], a decision of the Court of Appeal of the Irish Free State. In *Allied Irish Bank Ltd v. Glynn*[160] Kenny J described the issue of tracing as a "difficult and controversial

152 *Re Ffrench's Estate* (1887) 21 LR Ir 283 at 312.

153 *ibid.* at 319:

> "I think that where *cestuis que trustent* are represented by trustees, and are acting, or must claim, through trustees in whom the legal estate is or ought to be vested, and where innocent and independent third parties have been misled or defrauded by the conduct, or through the laches, of those trustees, such *cestuis que trustent* cannot be better off, in equity, than if they had been sui juris and had themselves acted as their trustees did."

154 *ibid.* at p.336–37.

155 *ibid.* at p.319.

156 *Scott v. Scott* [1924] 1 IR 141; Keane, *Equity* paras. 5.05, 20.10.

157 (1875) LR 7 HL 496. See also *Cave v. Cave* (1880) 15 Ch. D 639, Fry J.

158 *Bank of Ireland v. Cogry Flax* (1900) 1 LR 219; *Bourke v. Lee* [1904] 1 IR 280; *Re Bobbett's Estate* [1904] 1 IR 461.

159 [1924] 1 IR 141.

160 [1973] IR 188.

problem"[161]. Neither *Re Ffrench* nor the *Shropshire Union* case would be binding on the Supreme Court today. It would therefore have to address the issue of principle. It certainly seems wrong to suggest, as Porter MR did, that the misconduct of the trustees must be held to bind even innocent beneficiaries "whose remedy, if any, would be against the trustees and their estates"[162], as if their principal remedy were *in personam*. Even apart from tracing, which is a proprietary remedy *par excellence*, the Polar Star rule lays down the scope of the main proprietary remedy. There were narrower grounds for holding that the equities were not equal in *Re Ffrench*, namely that even the beneficiaries who were innocent of fraud were guilty of laches, whereas the equitable mortgagee had done everything possible to secure his title.[163]

5. Bare Trusts

There are instances where a trust exists but the beneficial interest is a fee simple vested in a single adult beneficiary, or in a number of adult co-owners who are in agreement about how to dispose of the property. For example a deed grants land:

> *Unto and to the use of F and G in fee simple in trust for A in fee simple; (A is of full age)*

or a testator grants land in her will:

> *Unto and to the use of F and G in fee simple in trust for A for life, remainder to the children of A alive at her death in fee simple.*

A has died and the land is now vested in a number of children of A, all of whom are of full age. The following diagram illustrates the basic position:

161 *ibid.* at p.193.

162 *Re Ffrench's Estate* (1887) 21 LR Ir 283 at 311.

163 *Re Ffrench's Estate* (1887) 21 LR Ir 283 at 311 per Porter MR:

> "even as regards the *cestuis que trustent*, there is nothing before use to show that they, one and all, have not lain by with full knowledge of their rights, and allowed the lands to be dealt with by Mr Ffrench." FitzGibbon LJ at 321: "The other *cestuis que trustent* under the settlement of 1825 have done nothing to assert their claim down to the present time." Barry LJ at 337: "But are the *cestuis que trustent* themselves guilty of no laches? Judging from the dates the respondents were adult very many years ago, but it is not until 1880 that they take any step to assert the equitable claim they now put forward."

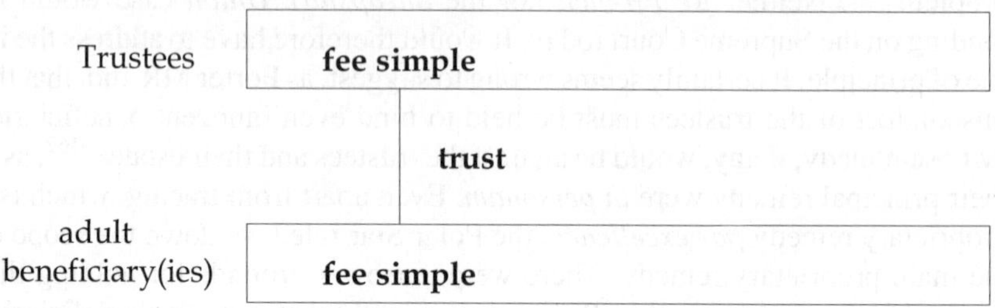

In these circumstances an English court in *Saunders v. Vautier*[164] took the view that equity would not intervene to enforce the terms of the trust if the beneficiaries did not wish it to continue, even if the intention of the grantor was that it should continue. Equity, in the court's view, intervenes to protect beneficiaries and if they do not require its protection, equity would not insist on enforcing the grantor's wishes. The beneficiaries can require the trustees to convey the legal fee simple to them and can sue the trustees for an order if they refuse. The same situation has been held to occur if A, an adult, has a life estate plus a general power of appointment by will.[165] In a general power, A can appoint to herself[166] and so such a limitation gives her the whole interest.

It is possible to detect in this rule a market-oriented value.[167] The notion is that the law will not intervene to enforce the grantor's wishes if they conflict with those of adult individuals. An adult human being is assumed to be autonomous and the best judge of his or her own interests. The holder or holders of the absolute equitable interest are the owners of the property in equity and they can do as they wish with it. The grantor has relinquished any right to control the property by the grant of it in their favour.

Despite the apparent aptness of this rule in the context of a capitalist economy, a court in Massachusetts decided differently. In *Clafin v. Clafin*[168] the court held that such beneficiaries could only demand the legal estate if that did not frustrate the purposes of the grantor who created the trust. Most jurisdictions

164 [1835–42] All ER Rep 58, (1841) Cr & Ph 240, (1841) 4 Beav 115; See Alexander (1985); *Wharton v. Masterman* [1895] AC 186 (charities); *Napier v. Light* 236 EG 273, CA; *Re Holt's Settlement* [1969] 1 Ch. 100, [1968] 1 All ER 470, [1968] 2 WLR 653; *Re Clore, decd* [1982] Fam 113, [1982] 2 WLR 314; *Re Myers Will Trusts* unreported, CA (Transcript: Lexis) 12 April 1983.

165 *Re Johnston* (1964) 48 DLR (2d) 573, Nemetz J.

166 See Chapter 13 Powers.

167 See Alexander (1985).

168 (1889) 149 Mass. 19, 20 N.E. 454.

in the United States follow *Clafin*,[169] although some prefer *Saunders*. *Saunders* has been followed in Canada[170] and New Zealand.[171] The reason for the choice of the rule in *Clafin* may lie in the fact that trusts in the United States tended to be of personal property where there was less of a problem of alienability than in the case of trusts of land, which tended to be the concern of the courts in England. On the few occasions when the point has arisen in Ireland the courts have followed *Saunders*.[172]

169 See Alexander (1985); *Brine v. Paine, Webber, Jackson & Curtis Inc* (1984) 745 F 2d 100, US CA 1st Circ; *Shelton v. King* (1912) 229 US 90, 33 S Ct 686, 57 L Ed 1086; *De Ladson v. Crawford* 93 Conn 402, 106 A 326; *Evans v. Rankin* (1931) 329 Mo 411, 44 SW 2d 644; *Carpenter v. Suffolk Franklin Savings Bank* 362 Mass at 777, 291 NE 2d at 614; *First Wisconsin Trust Co v. Hamburger*, 185 Wis 270, 201 NW 267, 37 ALR 1413, and cases there collected; *Crumlish v. Delaware Trust Co* 29 Del Ch. 503, 46 A 2d 888, Supreme Court of Delaware; Gray, *Rule against Perpetuities* (4th ed.), Sec 121.2 *etc.*

170 *Re Saracini* (1987) 39 DLR 4th 436, Ontario High Court, of Justice, and cases there cited.

171 *Re Chambers, deceased* [1971] NZLR 703, Supreme Court, Auckland, and cases cited.

172 *Brennan v. Brennan* [1894] 1 IR 69, per Chatterton V-C.

Reg. of Deeds (Irl) Act 1707.

CHAPTER 5

REGISTRATION OF DOCUMENTS

We have seen that the registration of specific types of deeds had been introduced in Ireland with section 17 of the Irish Statute of Uses, 1634 requiring bargains and sales of land to be registered if they were to be effective as conveyances. The Fines and Recoveries Act, 1834 requires disentailing deeds to be registered if they are to be effective. In contrast to these specific provisions is the general registry of documents set up under the Registration of Deeds (Ireland) Act, 1707.[1] This Act is still in force in the Republic[2] and is the basic Act governing the system of documents registration although it has been amended several times.[3]

The registration of documents system and registration of title are not mutually exclusive in relation to the same land as is sometimes supposed. If the title to an estate or interest in land is registered under the Registration of Title Act, 1964 the registry of documents system ceases to apply to that estate or interest but it does not cease to apply to estates or interests in the land not registered under the 1964 Act.[4]

A. Registrable Documents

The Irish legislation applies not only to deeds, *i.e.* documents under seal, but also to "any instrument affecting land".[5] A memorandum accompanying the

1 6 Anne c.2 (Ir). See also Madden, *Registration of Deeds;* Maguire, *Registration of Deeds.*

2 In Northern Ireland the Acts have been replaced by the Registration of Deeds Act (Northern Ireland), 1970.

3 Registration of Deeds Acts, 1709, 1721 and 1785; Registry of Deeds (Amendment) (Ireland) Acts, 1822, 1832 (s.36 repealed by SLRA, 1983 RI, s.35 repealed in part 10/1964 s.4 RI) and 1864; Land Transfer (Ireland) Act, 1848; Judgment Mortgage (Ireland) Acts, 1850 and 1858. See Short Titles Act, 1962. See also the Registry of Deeds (Ireland) Act, 1832 (Adaptation) Order, 1956, SI 281 of 1956 ("Minister for Justice" replaces "Treasury"), Housing Act, 1988 s.18(6).

4 Registration of Title Act, 1964 s.116; see Local Registration of Title Act, 1891 s.19. The first Act in Ireland providing for the registration of titles, the Record of Title (Ireland) Act, 1865 s.16 provided for the removal of all land the title to which was registered from the registration of documents system, but this was unnecessary and inconvenient.

5 Section 4. *Bushell v. Bushell* (1803) 1 Sch & Lef 92, 9 RR 21; *Forbes v. Deniston* (1722) 4 Bro PC 189, 2 Bro PC 425, 2 ER 129.

deposit of title deeds, which creates an equitable mortgage, is a document for this purpose.[6] "Instrument affecting land" also includes judgments, decrees and orders of court affecting land. Pending land actions may be registered in the Registry of Deeds or, as is more usual, as *lites pendentes* in the High Court.

Registration of documents is not compulsory in the sense that there is no criminal penalty for failure to register. There are, however, two forms of civil penalty for failure to register. Some documents are ineffective without registration while others are not ineffective on their own but will lose priority as against a later registered document.

1. Documents Ineffective Without Registration

The following documents must be registered or they are ineffective:

a) a judgment mortgage;[7]

b) a bankruptcy vesting certificate of adjudication; and

c) drainage and improvement charging orders.[8]

2. Documents Losing Priority Without Registration

In the case of other documents registration is compulsory only in the sense that they will, in accordance with section 5 of the 1707 Act, lose priority as against a later registered document. As between a document which is capable of being registered but is unregistered and a later registered document, the normal rule as to legal interests, that the first in time prevails, is replaced by the principle that the first to be registered prevails. The question of priorities is pursued below.

B. Exempted Documents

1. Wills

Wills were registrable under the 1707 Act but were excluded from the provisions as to priority between registered and unregistered documents. It may be that it was thought that the existing methods of revoking wills should not be replaced by the principle of registration. Whatever the reason, there was nothing to be gained by registering wills and it was rarely done. The provisions for registration were repealed by the Succession Act, 1965 section 8 and the second

6 *Rennick v. Armstrong* (1829) 1 Hud & Br 727.

7 Judgment Mortgage (Ireland) Act, 1850 ss. 6-8.

8 Maguire p.31.

Schedule.[9]

2. Leases Not Exceeding 21 Years

Leases for a term not exceeding 21 years, where actual possession is in accordance with the lease are not registrable.[10]

C. The Memorial

A Memorial summarising the effect of the deed dealing with the land and containing the date on which it was executed[11] is prepared and is registered. Section 6 of the 1707 Act provides that (a) the deed or other conveyance of the land has to be properly executed, (b) a memorial has to be presented signed and sealed by one of the grantors or grantees, (c) the execution of the memorial has to be attested by two witnesses, one of whom must also have been a witness to the original deed or conveyance, and (d) the latter witness also has to swear an affidavit attesting to the signing and sealing of the memorial, the execution of the deed or conveyance and the day and time of the delivery of the memorial to the Registrar.

In *Rennick v. Armstrong*[12] the Irish Court of King's Bench held that section 6 requires that the witness making the affidavit must also attest the execution of the deed or conveyance by the grantor. The same case also held that attestation of execution by the grantee alone made the registration void. The decision has been criticised[13] and Sugden appears to have withdrawn his earlier support of it.[14] It was not followed by the Court of Appeal in England in relation to a similar provision.[15]

The memorial must by statute contain the following information:

a) the date of the document and when it was executed;[16]

---

9 They have also been repealed in Northern Ireland: Registration of Deeds (Amendment) Act (NI), 1967, s.2.

10 1707 Act s.14; *Fury v. Smith* (1829) 1 Hud & Br 735; *Fleming v. Neville* (1830) Hayes 23.

11 *Re Monsell* (1857) 5 Ir Ch R 529.

12 (1819) 1 Hud & Br 727; followed in *Re Stevens* (1875) IR 10 Eq 282 and *Re Hurley* [1894] 1 IR 488 which were bound to do so.

13 *Report of the Royal Commission on the Law Relating to the Registration of Deeds* (1879) p.30.

14 Sugden, *Vendors and Purchasers* (11th ed.) p.970 expressed the same view as the court in *Rennick v. Armstrong* (1829) 1 Hud & Br 727 but later editions omit the point: Madden p.60.

15 *R v. Registrar of Deeds for County of Middlesex* (1881) 21 QBD 555.

16 *Re Monsell* (1857) 5 Ir Ch. R 529.

b) the names, addresses, occupations or descriptions of the parties and witnesses to the document as stated in the document; and[17]

c) the land affected by the document and the description of it as in the document, with in addition the county and barony or town, *etc.*[18]

The Registrar must check that the document is properly witnessed, must compare the document with the memorial and must ensure that the statutory requirements have been satisfied.[19]

D. The Register

Documents lodged for registration must have a certificate endorsed on them, stating the date and time of registration and signed by the Registrar or his deputy.[20] It must give a reference to the book and page number where it is to be found in the register. The requirement of stating the time of registration means that, in the Registration of Deeds system, two deeds registered on the same day take priority according to the time of day on which they were registered.

E. Searches

Searches are conducted of the Register to see what interests affect the land. If a search is not conducted the person taking an interest in the land may be affected in any case under the rules discussed below.

1. Hand Searches

These are searches undertaken by the applicant personally. The applicant may make notes from the Register. Liability for the accuracy of the notes lies, of course, with the applicant.

2. Common Searches

These are searches conducted by one official of the Registry and, although they are initialled by the Registrar, their accuracy is not warranted.

---

17 *Re Jennings* (1858) 8 Ir Ch. R 421.

18 Registry of Deeds (Ireland) Act, 1832 s.29 (memorial to specify county and barony, or town or county of a city and the parish or town and parish where the land lies).

19 Registry of Deeds (Ireland) Act, 1832 s.29.

20 1707 Act s.7.

3. Negative Searches

These searches are conducted by two officials of the Registry and a certificate is issued warranting that no memorials are registered other than those mentioned in the applicant's requisition applying for the search and other than those abstracted in the certificate. The Registrar is liable, whether of not he or she has signed the certificate, and an Assistant Registrar is liable if he or she has signed it, to a party aggrieved or injured by "fraud, collusion or neglect".[21]

Negative searches were instituted by the 1721[22] Act but are now governed by the 1832 Act.[23]

F. The Effect on Priority Between Deeds

1. Registered v. Registered

This shows the main principle of the Act, which is that priority between registered deeds is governed by their respective dates of registration. The deed that is registered earlier takes priority over a deed that is registered later. There is no difference in such a case between legal and equitable estates.[24] For example, a deed creating an equitable interest is registered. Later, a deed conveying the legal estate is registered. The person taking the conveyance of the legal estate takes it subject to the equity, whether he or she had notice of the equity or not. The later purchaser could have examined the register. The principle of notice is replaced in this instance by the principle of registration.

2. Unregistered v. Unregistered

Here the registration system has no application. Unregistered principles apply. If the first deed is a legal lease of land, and the second is a conveyance of the landlord's reversion, the lease binds the purchaser of the reversion regardless of notice as a legal interest. If the earlier transaction is an equitable mortgage and the later transaction is a sale of the legal fee simple, the later purchaser is bound unless he or she can prove the plea of bona fide purchaser for value without notice.

---

21 Registry of Deeds (Ireland) Act, 1832 s.26.

22 Registration of Deeds (Amendment) Act (Ircland), 1721, 8 Geo I c.15 s.2, repealed in part by 25 Geo III c.47, itself repealed by SLRA 1879. Madden, *Registration of Deeds* p.241.

23 Registry of Deeds (Amendment) (Ireland) Act, 1832 ss. 22–27.

24 *Eyre v. Dolphin* (1813) 2 Ball & B 290 at p.300, 12 RR 94 .

3. Unregistrable v. Registered

If a transaction is not reduced to writing there is nothing that can be registered and the registration system has no effect.[25] An example is an equitable mortgage created by deposit of the title deeds without any memorandum in writing. If there is a memorandum then the mortgage is registrable.[26] It would be unfair to give priority to a later registered deed when the other party could not have protected their interest by registration. In the words of the Lord Chief Baron in *O'Connor v. Stephens*:[27]

> It is but imputing common sense to the Legislature to hold that, when they framed the Registry Act, they could not have intended so far to repeal the Statute of Frauds as to enact that a registered deed should, by reason of its registry, acquire priority over another deed, which it was impossible by any diligence to register under the Act.

Thus, priority between the equitable mortgage and a later registered instrument is not governed by the Registration Acts, but by general equitable principles. Such a mortgage would be defeated therefore only by a later purchaser for value of a legal estate without notice, actual or constructive, of the earlier equity.[28]

4. Registrable but Unregistered v. Registered

This was intended also to show another aspect of the principle behind the Act. Section 5 of the 1707 Act provides that the registered document takes priority even if it is later. In other words, the holder of a deed who can register it, but fails to do so, runs the risk of losing priority to a deed which has been registered.[29]

---

25 *Re Stephens* (1876) IR 10 Eq 282, L E Ct; *Cleary v. Fitzgerald* (1880) 5 LR Ir 351, V-C, (1881) 7 LR Ir 229, CA; *Re Burke's Estate* (1882) 9 LR Ir 24, Court of Appeal; *Re Ffrench's Estate* [1887] 21LR Ir 283 at 305 per Porter MR; *Re Stevenson's Estate* [1902] 1 IR 23.

26 *Re Stephens* (1876) IR 10 Eq 282, L E Ct; *Rennick v. Armstrong* (1829) 1 Hud & Br 727.

27 (1862) 13 Ir CLR 63 at 68 cited by Lord O'Hagan LC in *Reilly v. Garnett* (1872) IR 7 Eq 1.

28 *Re Stephens* (1876) IR 10 Eq 282, Landed Estates Court, suggests that the owner of a registered mortgage would take subject to an earlier unregistrable equitable mortgage only if he or she had express notice of it. Since registration principles do not apply, the correct position should be that any form of notice would bind the owner of a legal estate acquired for value. *Re Burke's Estate* (1882) 9 LR Ir 24, CA, suggests that an unregistrable equitable mortgage takes priority over a later registered deed – apparently regardless of whether it dealt with a legal or equitable right – even if the owner of the registered deed had no notice at all of the unregistered right. Again, the owner of the later legal right obtained for value and without any form of notice should take free.

29 *Re McDonagh's Estate* (1879) 3 LR Ir 408, Land Js. *Cleary v. Fitzgerald* (1880) 5 LR Ir 351, V-C, (1881) 7 LR Ir 229, CA, see review of legislation by Deasy LJ at 250-255.

Someone who claims an interest under a document that is not registered cannot claim priority over a later registered document. There is no distinction in this between legal and equitable interests.[30] Thus, if a person obtains a document conferring an equitable interest and registers it, a later purchaser of a legal interest in the same land cannot make the plea of bona fide purchaser for value without notice. There are two qualifications to this general rule.

a) Actual Notice

This bare principle if unqualified would express a robust if extreme form of individualism favoured by those who believe that the market should be the sole mechanism for distributing property rights. Each person must look out for his or her own interests, and need have no regard to the interests of others if those others are capable of looking after themselves and fail to do so. Nevertheless, the courts found it difficult to accept such a self-centred view of morality. Two situations were distinguished on moral grounds.

(a) In the first, A knows that B is entitled to some interest in land under a registrable but unregistered deed. A obtains a similar or conflicting interest in the same land by deed and then registers it, with the intention of gaining priority over B.

(b) In the second situation A acquires an interest in land under a deed without knowledge at the time of its execution that B, under a prior deed, ad obtained a similar or conflicting interest. Having become aware of B's deed, A seeks to protect himself by registering his deed.

In the first situation the courts considered that A was guilty of fraud,[31] in the second that it was a legitimate exercise of self-interest. In the second case A was not bound by B's right after he had registered his own:

> ". . . I hold it to be undoubted law that a vendee whose equitable title has become complete before notice of a prior unregistered equity, but who afterwards obtains such notice, is perfectly free to protect himself by registration, as it is familiar learning that he may do by getting in the legal estate. To purchase and register after notice of a prior title is fraud. But if the purchase has been completed (though only equitably so) before notice, it is no fraud at all for that purchaser, when he afterwards hears of the impending danger, to grasp at the *tabula in naufragio* [plank in the shipwreck] which is afforded him by the Registry Act."[32]

---

30 *Drew v. Norbury (Lord)* (1846) 9 Ir Eq R 171.

31 *Bushell v. Bushell* (1806) 1 Sch & Lef 92, 9 RR 21, 100; *Blades v. Blades* 1 Eq Cas Abr 358, 21 ER 1100 (English Yorkshire Registry).

32 Per Christian LJ in *Reilly v. Garnett* (1872) IR 7 Eq 1 at 25.

> In a series of cases beginning in the 18th century with *Forbes v. Deniston*[33] the courts took the view that A's conscience was only affected if he had actual notice of the prior unregistered right, at the time he took the conveyance or had imputed to him the actual notice of his legal representative.[34] Constructive notice is not enough.[35] The moral difference between the first and the second situation, it can be argued, is that in the second situation the purchaser, having innocently entered into the conveyance, is now at risk of losing his purchase money, or putting it in jeopardy and was unable to avoid getting into this position. In the first situation the purchaser did not have to proceed with his conveyance if he had notice beforehand of a prior transaction. This rule is well established in the case law and probably too deeply imbedded to be altered by changes in moral attitudes.

Nevertheless, in the definition of actual notice itself there may be evidence of a judicial shift in recent times towards a more self-centred approach, although the evidence is slight. The earlier attitude was still evident in *Workingmen's Benefit Society v. Higgins*[36] decided in 1947, in which it was suggested that gross negligence by a purchaser in not discovering the existence of an earlier unregistered instrument would fix the purchaser with notice and defeat the registered instrument. In *Re Fuller and Co Ltd*[37] the High court held that it is irrelevant that the holder of a registered deed has knowledge of facts from which knowledge of an unregistered instrument can be inferred. The court characterised this as constructive notice. This is questionable. If a person possesses knowledge of facts which are sufficient to make an ordinary person suspect that there might be some unregistered document and the existence of the document would be discovered by making further inquiries, that is clearly constructive notice and would not affect the result. If, on the other hand, a person has knowledge of facts from which the existence of an unregistered deed can be inferred with logical certainty, then knowledge of the deed is not a matter of making further enquiries, but of mental deduction. This would seem to be more accurately characterised as actual notice. *Re Fuller* restricts actual notice to an extent, which tends to undermine the earlier decisions.

---

33 (1722) 4 Bro PC 189, (1722) 2 Bro PC 425, 2 ER 129; *Delacour v. Freeman* (1854) 2 Ir Ch R 633; *Montgomery v. McEvoy* (1857) 5 Ir Ch. R 126; *Clarke v. Armstrong* (1861) 10 Ir Ch R 263; *Re Flood's Estate* (1863) Ir Ch. R 312; *Agra Bank v. Barry* (1874) LR 7 HL 135; *Re Fuller* [1982] IR 161, HC.

34 If a solicitor actually knows of an unregistered deed, then that actual notice is imputed to the client. The client is bound even if an independent solicitor, exercising reasonable diligence, might not have discovered the unregistered deed: *Re Rorke's Estate* (1864) 14 Ir Ch R 442 at 446, Ch App; *Marjoribanks v. Hovenden* (1843) 6 Ir Eq R 238; *Espin v. Pemberton* (1859) 3 De G & J 547, 44 ER 1380 per Lord Chelmsford at p.554.

35 *Reilly v. Garnett* (1872) IR 7 Eq 1, per Christian LJ at p.24:

> "This, however, is but *constructive* notice, and, therefore, though it takes away the protection of the legal estate, it is of no avail against the Registry Act, for which nothing but *actual* notice will do."

36 [1945] Ir Jur Rep 38.

37 [1982] IR 161.

It may be that in the 1980s the courts leant more to the individualistic, and less altruistic, value that a person should look after their own interests and that if they fail to do so the party who has done so by registering their deed does not owe a moral duty towards them. The question is whether the courts should give effect to this ideology or should maintain a more altruistic standard of behaviour, a standard which denies that it is legitimate for a person consciously to take advantage of the failings of others to protect their own interests.[38]

It can be argued that an alternative approach to the moral argument is the economic one. This sees the problem as one of the distribution of risk in the market. One economic view is that a transferee who has actual notice of an earlier unregistered transaction can avoid the risk of loss (if the rule is that the earlier one takes priority) by not entering into their own transaction and therefore does not require the protection of the court. The role of the law on this view is to set a framework in which the market can operate efficiently by reducing only those risks which operators in the market cannot rationally avoid by themselves. It reduces risks that cannot be calculated or avoided, not those that can. This is an economic explanation of the result in *Forbes v. Deniston*.[39] Another economic view might be that the market operates most efficiently if those who operate within it can pursue profit exclusive of all other considerations and need not be deterred from entering into transactions, and so forgoing the advantage of them, by having to take into account the interests of others who have shown themselves inefficient at protecting their own interests. The law in this area appears to have held to the first view. One might also point out that the exclusion of all considerations except self-interest necessarily involves an ethical choice, and so the economic view, although it emphasises the effect of a choice of rule, is not in reality devoid of moral implications.

b) Volunteers

If the owner of the registered document has not given consideration in the transaction to which the document relates, then he or she is bound by an earlier unregistered deed regardless of notice. In the words of Christian LJ in *Reilly v. Garnett*[40]:

> "An unregistered title or right is binding upon the grantor himself, and upon all who claim under him as volunteers. His heir or devisee is bound by everything which bound the ancestor or testator, registered or unregistered, known or unknown."

This reproduces the result in the equitable doctrine of notice in which a donee or intestate successor, since they were not purchasers for value, took subject to

38 A similar problem arises in registration of title. See below Chapter 24 Registration of Title.

39 (1722) 4 Bro PC 189, (1722) 2 Bro PC 425, 2 ER 129.

40 (1872) IR 7 Eq 1 at 27; *Eyre v. McDowell* (1861) 9 HLC 619 at 620, 11 ER 871.

equities affecting the donor *etc.*, regardless of notice. Here again equity intervened to protect the purchaser in a market who had advanced and risked money.

CHAPTER 6

FEE SIMPLE

"Here's the lord of the soil come to seize me for a stray, for entering his fee-simple without leave."

– Shakespeare, *King Henry The Sixth, Part 2*
Act IV Scene X.

A. Heritability

Probably the first estate recognised by the common law, at least up to the end of the 12th century, was the life estate. During this period it follows that on the death of a freehold tenant, no one had the right to inherit the land. An indication of this was that until the end of the 12th century reliefs were of considerable value. On the one hand a feudal lord wanted to choose the person who would become the next tenant. On the other hand, the tenants wanted to pass the land on to their children and possibly to have some discretion as to which son it was going to be. The resolution of the contradiction was primogeniture. The tenants at least won the right to pass the land on to their children, while the lord at least knew who was going to be the next tenant. The right had been tacitly acknowledged in the Coronation Charter of Henry I in 1100, which provide that only reasonable reliefs were to be levied. Inheritance was recognised as a right by Henry II in the Assize of Northampton, 1176. This was, in effect, the origin of the fee simple estate. After 1176 the heir had a right, not merely a custom, to succeed.

A century later *Quia Emptores*, 1290 permitted freehold tenants to substitute without the lord's consent and so effectively permitted the sale of freehold land. It was held at about this time that if A held land in fee simple and then sold to B in fee simple, the land would pass to B's heirs on B's death. By selling the land, A had disinherited his heirs. It has also been seen that the combined effect of the Statute of Wills, 1634 and the Tenures Abolition Act, 1662 was to give freedom to the fee simple owner to devise land by will. Similarly, then, if A held land in fee simple and left it by will to B, who was not his heir, the land would pass to B's heir on his death, unless B in turn left it to someone else or sold it during his life. This meant another change had occurred. A's heirs no longer had a right to inherit the land, because A could disinherit them. A's heirs are said to have a mere *spes successionis i.e.* a hope of inheriting.

B. Heirs

Heirs at common law meant those persons determined by the old rules of descent (primogeniture). As to the fee simple, they have been abolished by section 11(1) of the Succession Act, 1965 and replaced by new rules which apply to personal property as well. In order to distinguish between heirs as determined by the old common law rules and those who take under the Succession Act, 1965, we shall refer to the latter as intestate successors.

C. The Right to Inherit Today

The Succession Act, 1965 section 111 provides that if a testator leaves a spouse and no children, the spouse has a right to half the estate (*i.e.* the property the testator left when he or she died). If the testator leaves a spouse and children the right of the spouse is to one third. This legal right overrides any devise in the will and so reintroduces a limitation on freedom of testation. Yet it is not a return to the past. No private individual is given the right to determine who is to take the testator's property. It may be seen as an expression of social policy, *i.e.* that persons who can be provided for by their families should not be a burden on the welfare state.

D. The Right to Alienate

Grantors of interests in land frequently wish to impose conditions on the persons to whom the grantee may alienate the land. In the case of fees simple, whether ordinary, *i.e.* without reservation of a rent of any kind, or by fee farm, the courts have in turn impose restrictions on the kind and extent of such conditions. It should also be remembered that there are other restrictions on the conditions that a grantor can impose which do not apply only to fee simple estates. These are dealt with in a separate section.[1]

1. Ordinary Fees Simple

Ever since *Quia Emptores*, 1290 it has been the policy of the law that restrictions cannot be imposed on the freedom of the holder of a fee simple estate to alienate it, whether those restrictions arise by custom, or by the grantor attempting to impose them in the grant.[2] A special feature of Irish land law is the extent to which this principle of alienability is compromised by statutory restrictions on fee simple and these will be considered below.

---

1 See below Modified Fees.

2 *Troy v. Kirk* (1832) Al & Nap 326, 1 L Rec NS 49; *Penny v. Gardner* (1833) Al & Nap 345; *Re Quin* (1858) 8 Ir Ch. R 578, CA; *Re McNaul's Estate* (1902) 1 IR 114.

a) Custom

In the English case of *Merttens v. Hill*[3] it was argued that restrictions arose by custom. The defendant bought a fee simple in the Manor of Rothley, Leicestershire in which freehold tenants held in the tenure of ancient demesne, *i.e.* it had belonged to the Saxon Crown before 1066. The lord of the manor claimed as a custom of the tenure that he was entitled to levy a fine on any purchaser who bought land within the manor and who was a foreigner, *i.e.* came from outside the manor. It was held that even if the custom existed, it was void as contrary to *Quia Emptores*, 1290. It is unlikely that similar customs survive in Ireland.

b) Grants

(1) General

An example of the general rule being applied in Ireland is to be found in *Re Lunham*.[4] The grant contained a proviso that the grantee was not to subdivide[5] the land into more than four lots without the consent in writing of the grantor, his heirs and assigns. Flanagan J in the Landed Estates Court held the proviso void as repugnant to the fee simple estate.[6]

More recent cases have reiterated the general rule against restrictions. In *Byrne v. Byrne*[7] a testator left land in his will to his nephew subject to the condition that "in the event of my nephew. . . attempting to sell the said farms. . . or in anyway parting with the possession of them I revoke the bequest of the said farms to him and in that event I leave them to the next heir on the same condition. . . as it was my intention that my said nephew, should work and keep my said farms and that they should remain the property of one of my kin". Budd J held the condition void as repugnant to the power of alienation. The judge found the English cases conflicting and that the Irish authorities were against such conditions.

On the other hand, in *Fitzsimons v. Fitzsimons*[8] a testator had transferred a farm to one of his sons during his, the testator's, lifetime and in his will he left additional property to the son on condition that the son should be beneficial owner of the farm which the testator had given to him in his lifetime. Keane J

---

3 [1901] 1 Ch. 842.

4 (1871) IR 5 Eq 170. The grant was in fee farm, but by rentcharge and so the fee simple was an ordinary one. See Chapter 7 Fee Farm Grants.

5 This could occur as a result of a sale, and so affect alienation, but would also occur without sale. The court does not distinguish between these effects.

6 *Re Cockerill* [1929] 2 Ch. 131 (condition that if the land was to be sold the holder of the fee simple should give an option to the governors of a school to buy at a price which proved to be half the market value. The condition was held void).

7 (1953) 87 ILTR 183, High Court.

8 [1993] ILRM 478.

held that the condition did not restrict the alienability of the farm, nor was it repugnant to the estate granted. If, however, the son sold any part of the farm, he would forfeit the legacy under the will.

Here again we find an example of reification: of presenting property as a thing which possesses inherent qualities. This disguises the fact that judges are implementing a policy in favour of the free market. The falsity of reification is demonstrated in the following sections dealing with fee simple subject to special statutory schemes. Such schemes interfere with or replace the market mechanism as a means of distributing property in pursuit of social goals such as the protection of vulnerable groups in society or, in the case of the Land Purchase Acts in the past, the creation of a new class of proprietors. Restrictions on alienation in such special fees simple are, by contrast, generally held not to be repugnant to the nature of the special fee simple. In other words, to the extent that judges maintained this position, they were upholding the policy behind the special statutory scheme.

In the case of ordinary fees simple the law is less clear when an attempt is made to restrict the alienation of the land to a particular class.

An attempt to restrict alienation to one named person only is certainly void.[9] On the other hand, a condition which restricts alienation to everyone except a named person may well be valid.[10] Between these two extremes the issue is whether a condition which restricts alienation to a particular group such as a family, or which permits alienation to all except a particular group, is valid or not.

Whatever the position in other jurisdictions, in Ireland conditions which restrict alienation to a particular group are invalid in principle.[11] The Irish case of *Billing v. Welsh*[12] held, *inter alia,* that a covenant prohibiting alienation except to a certain specified and limited class, and reserving a penal rent for breach of that covenant, is repugnant to the nature of an estate in fee simple. O'Brien J in that case said:

> "The general principles upon which covenants against alienation contained in a deed granting lands in fee simple are held to be void as being repugnant to the

9 *Re McDonnell's Will* [1965] IR 354, High Court, Budd J; *Attwater v. Attwater* (1853) 18 Beav 330, 52 ER 131.

10 Co Litt 361.

11 The main authority in favour of upholding such conditions is the English case of *Re Macleay* (1875) LR 20 Eq 186 which held that a restriction to sell only to members of the holders family, on the ground that it was a large and increasing class. But this case has been criticised in England and has not been followed in Ireland. *Doe d Gill v. Pearson* (1805) 6 East 173, 102 ER 1253 (condition confining sale to sisters or their children upheld). *Attwater v. Attwater* (1853) 18 Beav 330, 52 ER 131, where the restriction was "never to sell [the land] out of the family; but, if sold at all, it must be to one of his brothers hereafter named." Lord Romilly MR held that this restriction was inoperative. See also *Re Rosher* (1884) 26 Ch D 814.

12 (1871) IR 6 CL 88.

> estate granted by that deed, are laid down in several passages of Sheppard's Touchstone Vol. 1, pp.129 and 130 (Preston's Edition). In p.129, it is stated that no condition or limitation, whether by act executed, limitation or use, or devise, that contains in it matter repugnant to the estate is good. It is true (as stated in pp.129 and 130) that if a feoffment or other conveyance be made of land, upon condition that the feoffee or grantee should not alien to certain persons, such condition would be good; but the author adds that if the condition be that the feoffee or grantee should not alien the thing granted to any person whatsoever . . . such a condition is void . . . as repugnant to the nature of the estate."[13]

In *Crofts v. Beamish*[14] land was granted to brothers with the provision that if any of the brothers died under the age of 30 his portion was to go to the other brothers. The Irish Court of Appeal did not think that it was a condition subsequent but held that, if it had been, it would have been repugnant to the power of alienation and void.[15] More recently in *Re McDonnell's Will*[16] the testator directed that his freehold should not be sold or assigned to any person "who is not a member or a descendant of a member of my family." Budd J held that the restriction was repugnant to the fee simple and void.

Conditions which seek to permit alienation to all except a selected group restrict alienation to a lesser extent and may not be objectionable on that ground, although one case found another reason for striking down such a condition. In *Re Dunne*[17] the Irish High Court had to consider a will which left freehold land subject to a condition that it was not to be transferred to "any member of the Meredith families of O'Moore's Forest, Mountmellick." O'Hanlon J held that the condition was void both for uncertainty and as against public policy in that it tended to perpetuate old family resentments and antagonisms. Referring to the judgment of O'Brien J in *Billing v. Welsh*[18] quoted above, he went on:

> "That statement of the law would appear to support the validity of what was done by the testator in the present case. I would have reservations, however, about the consistency with public policy of incorporating conditions in the grant or devise of freehold property, the obvious purpose of which is to perpetuate old resentments and antagonisms and bind the grantee or devisee to bear them in mind and give effect to them when contemplating any further disposition of the property. This is particularly so when, as in the present case, the grantor or testator seeks to bind by the condition imposed, not merely the grantee or devisee but his or her successors and assigns as well-apparently for all time in the future.[19]

---

13 *ibid.* at p.101.

14 (1905) 2 IR 349; Wylie, *Cases* p.144.

15 The court in *Re Brown* [1954] Ch. 39 arrived at a similar result, on the ground that brothers was a limited and diminishing class.

16 [1965] IR 354, High Court, Budd J.

17 [1988] IR 155.

18 (1871) IR 6 CL 88.

19 [1988] IR 155 at 156–57.

Kinship or family solidarity is a detectable policy in land law, but often it is only given expression where it does not conflict with the efficient working of a market economy. In this case the two policies coincide. Both family solidarity and freedom of alienation point to striking down such conditions.

Conditions in fees simple which attempt to exclude sale to a particular race have been held void in the United States on the ground of public policy as an unacceptable restriction on the power of alienation.[20] This is therefore an objection to such conditions quite apart from the violation of a constitutional right to equality before the law or to equal treatment. Such grounds are considered below.

(2) Gifts to Charity

It is said that the general rule against restrictions on alienation does not apply to gifts to charities, so that the grant of a fee simple to a charity may contain a condition preventing the charity alienating the land.[21] This was held in two New Zealand cases, *Caldwell v. Fleming*[22] and *Re Clark*[23], which cited English authorities. Those cases were followed in the Chancery Division of the High Court in Northern Ireland in *Re Richardson*[24] by Murray J although without close analysis.[25] While it is settled that the rule against inalienability does not apply to charities[26] the exception is generally considered in the context of personal property.[27] For these reasons, the issue as to whether restrictions can be applied in the grant of a fee simple to a charity cannot be regarded as settled in this jurisdiction.

2. Statutory Schemes

a) Land Purchase Acts

The Land Purchase legislation was a response, beginning in the nineteenth century, to the agricultural distress in Ireland and to the reaction on the part of the rural population to the conditions under which they led their lives. This reaction had found its expression in the eighteenth century in such movements as

---

20 *Wayt v. Patee* (1928) 205 Cal 46; *Title Guarantee & Trust Co v. Garrott* 42 Cal App 152. See Modified Fees.

21 Coughlan, "Restraint on the Alienation of Fee Simples – A Repugnant Policy?" (1990) 12 DULJ 147 at 152–3.

22 [1927] NZLR 145.

23 [1961] NZLR 635.

24 [1988] 3 NIJB 35.

25 See Coughlan op cit footnote 21.

26 See Chapter 10 Future Interests.

27 *Chamberlayne v. Brockett* (1872) 8 Ch App 206 at 211 per Lord Selbourne LC; Megarry & Wade, *Real Property* (4th ed.) p.271.

the Whiteboys[28] and in the nineteenth century culminated in the Land League of Charles Stewart Parnell. A new word, "boycott," was added to the English language by one tactic adopted by tenants in their struggle against landlords. Absentee landlords had often extracted rents on their agricultural tenants which the tenants were unable to pay out of the meagre income from their farms, leading to increasing impoverishment of the rural population. Absentee landlords had little interest in their tenants other than as a source of income and their response to non-payment of rent was often to seek the eviction of the tenant. Insecurity was thus added to poverty as a source of discontent.

A significant step in the legislation was taken by Gladstone's administration by passing the Land Law (Ireland) Act, 1881. This gave security of tenure to agricultural tenants and also empowered the Irish Land Commission, set up by the Act, to lend money to tenants for the purpose of buying the fee simple in their farms.

This policy was continued in later years and after the creation of the Irish Free State in 1922 was carried a significant step further in the Land Act, 1923. The 1923 Act provided for the compulsory acquisition of tenanted land and its State-assisted sale to the tenants.

The purpose of the legislation was liberal in the sense that it sought to deal with social discontent by removing its causes rather than by oppressive force. On the other hand, it also sought in the process to produce, in the words of O'Byrne J, a "peasant proprietorship of a certain standard"[29] which would be

28 So called because they wore white shirts. They engaged in boycotts, violence and threats of violence, against landlords and against tenants who would not support them. A series of statutes, known collectively as the Whiteboy Acts, were passed to deal with their activities. These were the statutes of the Irish parliament: Tumultuous Risings Act, 1775, 15 & 16 Geo III c.21 (Ir); 27 Geo III, c.15 (Ir) (1787) (known as the Riot Act); 40 Geo III, c.96 (1800) and the statute of the Union parliament, the Tumultuous Risings (Ireland) Act, 1831 (1 & 2 Wm IV, c.44). Some sections of these acts remain in force to this day. In *The State (O'Connor) v. Governor of Mountjoy Prison* [1963] IR 112, 1 Frewen 524, Supreme Court, the accused had been charged and convicted under s.3 of the 1831 Act. This makes it an offence to write letters to a person threatening violence. The Supreme Court upheld the constitutionality of the section. The accused argued that the Act was repugnant to the Constitution as involving political or religious discrimination. The Supreme Court rejected this. The court noted that the preamble and s.15 of the 1775 Act did display prejudice or involve discrimination against Catholics, but s.15 had been repealed in 1831. The remaining sections did not discriminate on religious grounds and the court found that a law proscribing threatening letters should properly find a place in any criminal code.

29 *Foley v. Irish Land Commission* [1952] IR 118, at p.153; the point is in fact made by counsel for the Attorney General:

> The object of the Land Purchase Code, of which the Land Act, 1946, forms part, is to create a peasant proprietorship in the lands. The Land Act, 1923, under which the appellant became entitled to the allotment, provides that prior to the allotment the Land Commission must be satisfied that the intended purchaser is competent to work the land and that he intends to do so and not to sell, let or assign it, and, when the Land

both socially stable and politically conservative. A peasantry tends to be conservative because it is a landowning class. It would thus be a class which would resist even more radical change aimed at a redistribution of wealth affecting more than the politically and socially bankrupt absentee landlords. According to Marx, the State is the creation of social classes. In this instance the social class is a creation of the State and the State achieved its purpose through law. We therefore find an unfamiliar legal régime in property law: the State, instead of merely setting the conditions for the free operation of the market or acting as guarantor of the commodity form of land, intervenes directly to create a social class and to maintain it. Thus, it was one of the purposes of the detailed legislation to ensure that the fee simple conveyed would be used for the intended purpose. Such fee simple were therefore subjected to special régime quite different from that applying to the ordinary fee simple, which had become the expression of the free market form of property.

Under section 2 of the Land Act, 1946 the Irish Land Commission[30] was empowered to issue a notice to a freeholder to whom the fee simple has been conveyed under the Acts, to reside continuously on the land to the satisfaction of the Commission. In *Foley v. The Irish Land Commission*[31] it was held by the Supreme Court that section 2 of the Land Act, 1946, is not repugnant to the provisions of the Constitution, that the imposition of the condition as to residence in section 2(i) of the Land Act, 1946 is not an abolition of the rights of private ownership within the meaning of Art 43.1.2° of the Constitution, but a delimitation of these rights "with a view to reconciling their exercise with the exigencies of the common good" and in accordance with the principles of social justice, within the meaning of Art 43.2 of the Constitution. The court noted that the Land Purchase Acts, of which the Act of 1946 forms part, constitute an important branch of Irish social legislation, noting the words of O'Byrne J delivering the judgment of the court in *Foley v. Irish Land Commission.*[32] Thus the object of the legislation was not only to give secure residence to those who cultivated the land, but also to prevent a re-emergence of rural landlordism.

Both of these policy aims justified, or were expressed legally, in conditions as to residence.

> Commission build a dwelling-house on the lands it is their intention that the allottee should live in the dwelling-house.

The phrase is cited by Walsh J delivering the judgment of the court in *Dreher v. Irish Land Commission* [1984] ILRM 94.

30 See now Irish Land Commission (Dissolution) Act, 1992, s.4.

31 [1952] IR 118, (1952) 86 ILTR 44. Supreme Court (Maguire CJ, Murnaghan, O'Byrne, Lavery, and Kingsmill Moore JJ).

32 [1952] IR 118, at p.153, see footnote ; cited by Walsh J delivering the judgment of the court in *Dreher v. Irish Land Commission* [1984] ILRM 94; also cited in *Re Soden* [1985] ILRM 685, Supreme Court.

b) Labourers' Acts

A statutory restriction on alienation applying to fees simple can be found in Ireland under the Labourers' Acts.[33] The purpose of these Acts was to provide an equivalent to the land purchase scheme but applying to houses occupied by agricultural labourers. The labourers purchased the fee simple under a scheme providing for repayment of the purchase price by an annuity. During the period of repayment a statutory covenant restricts alienation "otherwise than by operation of law or by sale with consent of" the local authority.[34] An alienation without consent causes a forfeiture. Thus the fee simple can pass on intestacy but a devise in a will contravenes the covenant,[35] although legislation makes an exception for certain persons in possession at the death of the labourer, such as a widow or children. Subletting has been held to be an alienation and therefore if made without consent contravenes the covenant.[36]

c) Housing Acts

Dwellings sold by a housing authority[37] may be made subject to special conditions,[38] which include a condition not to mortgage, charge or alienate the dwelling "otherwise than by devise[39] or operation of law" without the consent of the housing authority,[40] and subject to conditions as to residence.[41]

3. Fee Farm Grants

The question of restrictions on the alienability of fee farm grants is dealt with in detail in Chapter 7. In summary, the position is that where the rent under a fee farm grant arises by a rentcharge the fee simple is an ordinary fee simple and conditions restricting alienation have to satisfy the tests set out above.[42] Conversion fee farm grants, however, are on a different footing and restrictions on alienation contained in the leases from which they were converted survive

---

33 Some provisions of the Labourers Act, 1936 remain in force. See Housing Act, 1966 1st Sch. *Westmeath County Council v. Claffey* [1952] IR 1, Supreme Court; *Rogers v. Louth County Council* [1981] IR 265, Sup Ct; *Attorney General (Annaly) v. Guardians of Ballymallon Union* (1888) 21 LR Ir 534.

34 Labourers' Act, 1936, s.17(2).

35 *Cork County Council v. O'Shea* [1947] IR 369, (1947) 81 ILTR 24.

36 *Westmeath County Council v. Claffey* [1952] IR 1, Supreme Court.

37 Housing Act, 1966, s.90 as replaced by the Housing (Miscellaneous Provisions) Act, 1992 s.26.

38 *ibid.* s.89.

39 This word may have been inserted to avoid the problem referred to above under the Labourers' Acts.

40 *ibid.* s.89(c).

41 *ibid.* s.89(b).

42 *Re Lunham* (1871) IR 5 Eq 170.

conversion and are valid as restrictions on the fee simple.[43] This is said to be because the fee simple is a special statutory fee simple. There is doubt as to whether similar restrictions can be imposed in a Deasy's Act grant.[44] Restrictions in leasehold fee farm grants are also in principle subject to the statutory controls now contained in section 66 of the Landlord and Tenant (Amendment) Act, 1980 which provides that conditions in leases which seek to prohibit alienation or to prohibit it without the landlord's consent take effect as conditions not to alienate without the landlord's consent which cannot be unreasonably withheld.

E. Words of Limitation

The following discussion refers to the words used to convey ordinary fees simple. The position as to fee farm grants in Ireland is dealt with in the chapter dealing with those interests.

1. History

At common law in order to pass or create a fee simple estate in land the correct words of limitation had to be used. To pass the fee simple a grant had to be made to the grantee and his/her heirs. Nothing else would do. No account was taken of the intention of the maker of the document. It was a ritualistic formula characteristic of early legal systems. In the late eighteenth century and early years of the nineteenth century, which saw the rise of industrial capitalism, it became apparent that there existed a conflict within the legal system between two competing views both of which were derived from the needs of the new economic system itself and which were concerned about the nature of changes it made necessary in legal rules as to property.

On the one hand, if individual capitalists were to be able to buy land as a means of production, land must be able to be freely bought and sold. On this view, the need to use a strict formula to pass a fee simple estate constituted a restriction on this desired free alienability.[45] In addition, industrial capitalism favoured the view that individual capitalists should be left to themselves to develop the economy by entering contracts together as free as possible from the interference of state institutions. The role of law is then simply to give effect to the intentions of the parties to such transactions rather than, in interpreting them, to impose rules which have other functions.

On the other hand, if purchasers of land were to be sure of the titles which they thus acquired, it was necessary for them to be sure that the vendors them-

43 *Re McNaul's Estate* [1902] 1 IR 114.

44 See Chapter 7 Fee Farm Grants.

45 Atiyah, *Freedom of Contract* p.122–123 suggests ideological reasons also.

selves had a good title to convey to them. Max Weber saw the connection between the rise of commerce and a demand for legal certainty:

> "bourgeois interests. . . had to demand an unambiguous and clear legal system that would be free of administrative arbitrariness as well as of irrational disturbance by concrete privileges, that would also offer firm guarantees of the legally binding character of contracts, and that, in consequence of all these features, would function in a calculable way."[46]

In unregistered conveyancing, which then prevailed, a rule that no title would pass unless a strict formula was adhered to would favour this certainty required by purchasers. If no special formula was required it might not be possible to know whether a title had passed under a deed unless one went through the expense of court proceedings.

The chief proponent of the liberal view, that no special words should be required, was Lord Mansfield, expressed in his judgment in *Loveacres d Mudge v. Blight*[47] and in an Irish case, *Hogan d Wallis v. Jackson*.[48] Opposed to this view and in favour of strict words was Fearne, author of a famous work on contingent remainders.[49] "Surely" he wrote, "it is better that the intentions of twenty testators every week should fail of effect, than those rules should be departed from upon which the general security of titles and quiet enjoyment of property so essentially depend."

The rules that operate in Ireland today show a compromise between these two views. The liberal view has prevailed so far in wills, while the strict formulas are still required in the case of an *inter vivos* deed if the fee simple is to pass. There is some reason for making such a distinction. The maker of an *inter vivos* deed can remedy his mistake: a testator is in no position to do so.

2. Conveyances Inter Vivos

a) At Common Law

(1) Natural Persons

In the early common law, down to the end of the 12th century, a person who held a fee simple could not alienate it without the consent of his or her heirs. In other words, the heirs had a real interest in the property. The relationship of kinship was treated as more important than the relationship of the market, but this changed in the course of time and it came to be accepted that the tenant in fee simple could sell the land without the consent of the heirs. This meant that after this change had taken place, if a grant was made:

to A and his heirs

46 Rheinstein, *Max Weber on Law in Economy and Society* p.267.

47 (1775) 1 Cowp 352, 98 ER 1125.

48 (1775) 98 ER 1096.

49 Fearne, *Contingent Remainders* (1772).

the words "to A" were "words of purchase" giving A an interests in the property , but that the words "and his heirs" were only "words of limitation" which did not give the heirs an interest in the property. They served merely to indicate the duration of the estate given to A. This is still so today.

It also came to be accepted that if A, during his life, makes a grant to B of his fee simple then B holds the land for himself and his heirs. A can make a grant "to B and heirs" and again, only the words "to B" are words of purchase. The words "and his heirs" are again words of limitation. This further change meant that the fee simple became likely to endure for a long period. Even if A had in fact no heirs, so that the fee simple would come to an end, he could still, in his lifetime, make a grant to B in fee simple and it could pass to B's heirs.

In the course of time the common law formula became rigidified so that only that form of words and no other would pass the fee simple. The person to take the estate had to be named, followed by the phrase "and his/her heirs." Nothing else would do. Thus, even if the intention was clearly to grant a fee simple, if the words used were "to A for ever" or "to A and her relatives" or "to A and his issue" or even, until altered by statute,[50] "to A in fee simple", A only acquired a life estate.

Thus, in *Re Adam's Estate*[51] a settlement granted land "to the use and behoof of the 2nd, 3rd, 4th, 5th, 6th, and of every other the son and sons of A" with a gift over if they died without issue, the court held that although the intention was to grant a fee simple to the sons of A, they only took life estates. In *Re Coleman's Estate*[52] C, who owned a house in fee simple, agreed with H to allow H to occupy the house, C covenanting for "herself, her heirs, executors and assigns" and H covenanting for his "executors, administrators and assigns." It was held that H took only a life estate despite the fact that the court accepted that the intention was to grant H an indefinite right. The word heirs had not been used in relation to H.

(2) Corporations

One must first distinguish between a corporation aggregate and a corporation sole. Both terms are somewhat illogical, as a corporation in law is a single artificial person which is distinct from the real persons who act on its behalf.

A corporation aggregate is a corporate body on whose behalf a number of persons act together, *e.g.* a limited company.

A corporation sole is an office occupied by a single person and recognised as such by common law or statute, as for example, in the past, a bishop or priest of an established church. Clergy of the Church of Ireland ceased to be corpora-

50 See below.

51 [1965] IR 57.

52 [1907] 1 IR 488.

tions sole on the disestablishment of that church in 1869.[53] Clergy of the Roman Catholic church were corporations sole at common law, since that was the recognised church when the common law was formed, but that status did not survive the Reformation and the Penal Laws. It seems unlikely that the status has revived since 1937. Corporations sole today would include ministers of the government, the President of the High Court,[54] the Chief Justice, and a Lord Mayor.

At common law a conveyance to a corporation aggregate in its corporate name, *e.g.*

to Acme Ltd

gives it a fee simple without the need for words of limitation, for the reason that such a body cannot hold land for a fee tail estate since it does not have heirs of the body nor may it hold land for a life estate. This is not entirely logical as it could be argued on that basis that since it does not have heirs it could not hold land in fee simple, but this would mean that it could not hold land at all and so logic gives way to practical necessity. It does, however, mean that the fee simple has a different meaning when held by a corporation aggregate. It is then an estate which will endure so long as it or its successors endure and will only come to an end if a corporation is wound up without the fee simple becoming vested in a successor before that happens. This at least was the position in the past when an escheat would then occur or the land would become *bona vacantia.*[55] This situation has already been considered in Chapter 3 on tenure.

A conveyance to a corporation sole, if it is to convey the fee simple to the office, must use words of limitation in the form:

to the Minister of X and his successors.

A conveyance to the minister and his heirs would give him a fee simple in his private capacity.[56] A gift to a person and his successors, if not a corporation sole, gives a life estate.[57]

53 Irish Church Act, 1869 s.13 repealed SLR(2)A 1893.

54 Succession Act, 1965 s.13.

55 Nevertheless, courts tried to avoid this result if possible: *Re Strathblaine Estates* (1948) Ch 228.

56 In *Gibson v. Representative Church Body* (1882) 9 LR Ir 1, V-C, there was a bequest to the R chapel on trust to pay the income to the person who was the chaplain at the testator's death for life and then to his successors. It was held that the intention was to benefit chaplains for the time being and not the person who filled the office at her death personally, so that when that person retired the income ceased to be payable to him and became payable to his successor.

57 *White v. Baylor* (1846) 10 Ir Eq R 53.

b) Statute

The position as to conveyances *inter vivos* has been changed by the Conveyancing Act, 1881 section 51 of which now provides an alternative expression "to and his/her heirs". The words in fee simple may now be used. The alternative is construed just as strictly as the older one. Thus, "to A in fee" will only give a life estate. To this must be added the qualification that there is jurisdiction in equity to rectify documents in order to give effect to the intention of the parties, and, even under the guise of construction, courts have been prepared to read in fee to mean in fee simple.[58]

c) In Equity

The question here is whether the same words of limitation are needed in the grant of a trust as they are in the conveyance of a fee simple at common law. In the example:

unto and to the use of T and U and his heirs in trust for A for ever..

the legal fee simple is clearly vested in the trustees, but has the equitable fee simple vested in the beneficiary, A, by the informal words for ever?

In *Meyler v. Meyler*[59] it was suggested that the same words of limitation are required in equity as at common law,[60] but in *Re Houston*[61] where land was conveyed to trustees on trust for a number of persons as tenants in common without words specifying what estate they were to take, the court held that they took fees simple, and indicated that in such a case the court looks at the intention of the settlor. In *Jameson v. McGovern*[62] the court approved of the distinction in

58 *Re Ottley's Estate* [1910] 1 IR 1, a case of a disentailing assurance under the Fines and Recoveries (Ireland) Act, 1834. Section 45 of the Act excludes the jurisdiction of equity to rectify, but, the court held, not the common law jurisdiction of construction. There was also evidence that the mistake in that case was a copying error, since in fee simple was used later in the same deed. Also, the policy of the Act, which s.45 reflected, was to make a single deed and that alone effective to disentail. The evidence of intention did not come from outside the deed and so, in the court's view, satisfied this policy. In *Re Ethel & Mitchell & Butler's Contract* [1901] 1 Ch 945, a case on a reconveyance on mortgage, Joyce J refused the same construction possibly because there was no evidence that the mistake there was other than a mistake of law. In *Re Ford & Ferguson's Contract* [1906] 1 IR 607 in which an interpretation clause in the deed stated that "grantee" should include the "grantee, his heirs and assigns." There were no words of limitation used in the habendum. It was held that the fee simple did not pass. And see *Annesley v. Annesley* (1893) 31 LR Ir 457, V-C.

59 (1883) 11 LR Ir 522; *Re Courtney* [1981] NI 58.

60 Also *Barron v. Barron* (1859) 8 Ir Ch R 366, although in that case the interest was a lease for lives. A grant of it in a marriage settlement to trustees on trust for ever to the issue male of the marriage passed only life estates, and not a quasi fee, to the sons of the marriage.

61 [1909] 1 IR 319.

62 [1934] IR 758.

Re Bostock's Settlement[63] between formal words, which are construed formally, and informal words which are given the effect intended. In the case itself a fee simple was held to pass without words on limitation. *Savage v. Nolan*[64] came to a similar result. Both cases involved marriage settlements.

3. Registered Land

The Registration of Title Act, 1964 section 123 provides that no words of limitation are necessary in a transfer of registered land. This is consistent with the position that the estate in registered land is transferred when the entry is made on the register and not when the transfer is executed. Registration of a person as full owner will vest the fee simple in that person and if this is done the fact that the transfer itself said merely to A will not affect the vesting of the fee simple.

4. Wills

The principle in wills has long been to give effect to the wishes of the testator as far as possible. This particularly important when it is remembered that if a mistake has been made it too late by the time the will takes effect for the testator to remedy it. Before 1838 it was only necessary to show an intention to pass a fee simple for it to pass under the will, so that: "to A for ever"[65] or "to A absolutely"[66] would be enough to pass the fee simple, but "to A" would not pass more than a life estate unless there was something else in the will to show that a fee simple was intended.

The Wills Act, 1837 altered the presumption so that fee simple would pass unless the contrary intention was shown.[67] This made it even easier for a fee simple to pass.[68] This was consistent with a policy in favour of a market economy in that it meant that it was more likely than before that the land would be held for a fee simple in the hands of the person entitled under the will.

This policy position has been repeated in section 94 of the Republic's Succession Act, 1965 which replaced the Wills Act, 1837. Section 94 states that:

---

63 [1921] 2 Ch. 469. But see *Re Harte's Settlement* (1947) 81 ILTR 78, Dixon J.

64 Unreported, High Court, Costello J, 20 July 1978; Wylie, *Cases* p.112.

65 *Doe d Dacre v. Roper* (1809) 11 East 518, 103 ER 1104.

66 *Hogan d Wallis v. Jackson* (1775) 1 Cowp 299, 98 ER 1096 (Ir), "all my worldly substance" to X. The fee simple passed to X. But "to A and his heirs" might only pass a fee tail, if such was the intention: *Idle v. Cook* (1699) 2 Ld Raym 1144, 92 ER 257, 2 Salk 620, 91 ER 525, 11 Mod 57, 88 ER 883.

67 Section 28. The section applied to existing fees simple, not to estates created *de novo* such as on the creation of a new rentcharge: *Nichols v. Hawkes* (1853) 10 Hare 342, M & W 795, 68 ER 958; *Re Hutchin's Estate* (1887) 19 LR Ir 215, Monroe J. Thus a new rentcharge created in a will for ever did not grant it for a fee simple estate.

68 *Fowler v. Lightburne* (1861) 11 Ir Ch R 495.

> "94.–Where real estate is devised to a person (including a trustee or executor) without any words of limitation, the devise shall be construed to pass the whole estate or interest which the testator had power to dispose of by will in the real estate, unless a contrary intention appears from the will".

Thus, the words "to A" are now sufficient to pass the fee simple or the whole of whatever interest the testator has in the property, unless a contrary intention is shown.[69] Section 94 is in almost identical terms to section 28 of the Wills Act, 1937 which it replaces and so it would appear that, like the former section, it only applies to existing interests. If a new fee simple in real property is to be created by the testator, words of limitation must be used. Of course, a testator cannot create a new fee simple in land itself, but can create a new rentcharge[70] or easement in fee simple.

F. The Rule in Shelley's Case

The rule in *Shelley's Case*[71] states that:

> when an estate of freehold[72] is given to person and under the same disposition an estate is limited in remainder either mediately or immediately to his or her heirs or to the heirs of his or her body, then the words "heirs" or "heirs of his/her body" are words of limitation and not words of purchase.[73]

This is a correct statement of the rule as to deeds *inter vivos*, but now requires modification in relation to wills, as will be seen later. The result of applying the rule may be to create either a fee simple or a fee tail, depending on the words used in the instrument.

1. A Rule of Law

It seems that originally the rule was a rule of law and that, where the grounds existed for its application, it applied regardless of the grantor's intention. In the case of *inter vivos* gifts of legal estates this is still said to be the case, although there are some indications that the judges have narrowed the grounds to which

69 See *Re Ball* [1933] NI 173 (A gift to "my brother JB or his heir" held to confer a fee simple. The word heirs had been originally written, but the final "s" crossed through.)

70 See footnote 67.

71 (1581) 1 Co Rep 88b, 76 ER 199 at 206, 3 Dy 373b, 73 ER 838. See Challis, *Real Property* p.154. 'Legislative Attacks Upon the Rule in Shelley's Case' (1932) 45 Harv L Rev 571 (discussion and history on how different states in the USA have abolished the rule). *Society National Bank v. Jacobson* (1990) 560 NE 2d 217 (Ohio); Comment: Hoover (1991) 17 Dayton L Rev 253.

72 The rule has no application to personal property: *Atkinson v. L'Estrange* (1885) 15 LR Ir 340, V-C.

73 (1581) 1 Co Rep 104a; *Van Grutten v. Foxwell* [1897] AC 658, Eng HL and see *Mandeville v. Carrick (Lord)* (1795) 3 Ridg PC 352, Irish HL, per Yelverton CB at 369.

the rule applies. In the case of equitable gifts and gifts in wills it is questionable whether the rule is still applied irrespective of the grantor's intention.[74] This issue is related to the question of the policy behind the rule and this will be dealt with in a later section.

2. Legal Estates Inter Vivos

In the limitation:

> *to A for life, remainder to A's heirs*

it would seem that A obtains a life estate and then the remainder gives some interest to A's heirs, but, under the rule, the words A's heirs are not words of purchase giving an interest to the heirs, but words of limitation describing what interest is given to *A*. A therefore takes a life estate and a fee simple by the remainder. These merge to give A a fee simple in possession:

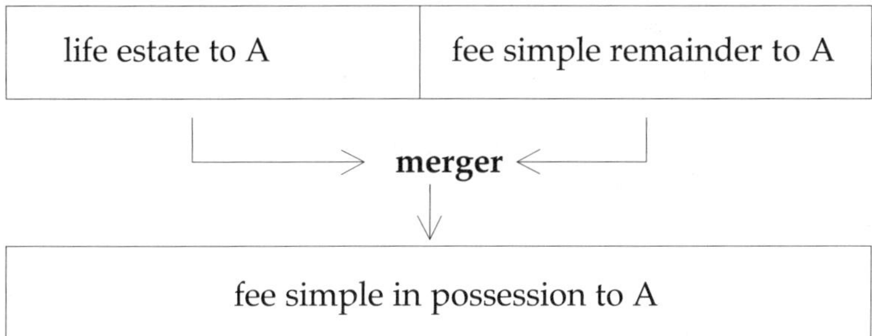

The result is the same as if the limitation had been "to A and his/her heirs."

a) Same Person

For the rule to apply the estate in the remainder clause must be in favour of the heirs of the person to whom the previous freehold estate was given. If the limitation was instead:

> *to A for life, remainder to B's heirs.*

then *Shelley's Case* would not apply. The word "heirs" in the remainder clause is therefore a word of purchase and its effect is explained below.[75]

---

74 See *Whitelaw v. Whitelaw* (1880) 5 LR Ir 120. ("no evidence of intention to justify the application of Shelley's Case").

75 See below Heirs as a Word of Purchase.

b) Informal Words

It should be noticed that in order that the rule apply, the words in the remainder clause must be capable of functioning as words of limitation in relation to A, so that in an *inter vivos* deed the word heirs must be used. If the limitation is:

> *to A for life, remainder to A's issue*

informal words have been used in the remainder clause. They cannot give a fee simple to A. The rule in *Shelley's Case* does not apply and therefore the words are words of purchase, giving interests to A's issue. Since no words of limitation have been used in relation to them, they will take joint life estates.

c) Intermediate Remainders

If the rule had been applied without regard to intermediate remainders occurring between the life estate and the remainder to the heirs of the life tenant, great care would have been needed in drafting settlements or they would simply have resulted in a fee simple or a fee tail. For that reason the rule applies whether the remainder to the heirs is mediate or immediate *i.e.* whether it follows at once or after intermediate remainders. The rule could have made settlements of land ineffective by destroying intermediate remainders, but it was held that although the rule applies, a vested remainder created by the same conveyance prevents merger of the two estates. In the limitation:

> *to A for life, remainder to B for life, remainder to the heirs of A [or to A's heirs]*[76]

the rule applies in that A not only has a life estate but also the remainder in fee simple as well, *i.e.* the words "heirs of A" are words of limitation in relation to A, not words of purchase giving an interest to the heirs. But the vested life estate to B prevents the two estates merging to give a fee simple to A in possession. When the life estate ends, merger then takes place. Where the remainder is contingent, merger takes place initially, but if the remainder vests the two estates will open up again, letting in the remainder. In the limitation:

> *to A for life, remainder to A's eldest son in tail, remainder to the heirs of A (A has no son)*

A has a fee simple in possession at once, while A's son remains unborn, but as soon as the son is born there is merger in reverse. The fee simple in possession divides into the two estates, like the Red Sea parting for Moses, and A has both a life estate in possession and a fee simple in remainder, allowing the son's vested remainder to fall into place.[77]

---

76 *Shannon v. Good* (1885) 15 LR Ir 300, CA (remainder to the issue).

77 *Lewis Bowle's Case* (1615) 11 Co. Rep. 79b, 77 ER 1252; *Archer's Case* (1698) 1 Co. Rep. 66b, 76 ER 139, 146. Holdsworth 7 HEL 110. As to trustees to preserve contingent remainders, see *Rochford v. Fitzmaurice* (1842) 4 Ir Eq R 348.

d) Heir in the Singular

If the word heir is used in the singular, as in the limitation:

> *to G for life, remainder to G's heir,*

the position is the same as if some informal word, such as issue, had been used. Heir does not accord with the strict rule as a word of limitation and so must function as a word of purchase. The use of the word heir as a word of purchase is considered below.

e) Superadded Words

If the limitation were:

> *to A for life, remainder to A's heirs and their heirs*

the difficulty arises as to whether it attracts the rule in *Shelley's Case* or whether it is a case of heirs used as a word of purchase. Such a limitation *inter vivos* would provide a test of whether the rule is still a rule of law to be applied regardless of the intention of the grantor, or whether it can yield to an intention expressed in the superadded phrase which indicates that the grantor intended the heirs to take by purchase. There appears to be no authority on the point in *inter vivos* conveyances. The question of superadded words has arisen in relation to wills, and in that context it is treated as a matter of discovering the intention of the testator.[78]

3. Wills

The rule has become modified in relation to wills since the Wills Act, 1837[79] and now section 94 of the Succession Act, 1965 no longer require words of limitation to confer a fee simple by will. The whole interest of the testator in the property passes unless there is a contrary intention in the will. Thus, the Rule in *Shelley's Case* can apply even if the word heirs is not used. The effect of the reform has therefore been to extend the scope of *Shelley's Case*, although it is not clear whether this was intended or not.

If the testator intended the words to refer to the whole succession of heirs as a class, then the rule applies and the words in the remainder clause are treated as words of limitation.[80]

If, on the other hand, the words are intended to refer to a specific person or persons (*personae designatae*) then the rule does not apply and the persons

---

78 See below.

79 For a case on a will before the Wills Act, 1837 see *Rotheram v. Rotheram* (1884) 13 LR Ir 429, V-C, 442, CA.

80 *Re Keane's Estate* [1903] 1 IR 215.

take by purchase.[81]

So, for example, if the words in the will are:

to A for life, remainder to his issue

the question to be decided by the court in each case, taking the will as a whole, is whether the testator intended only the first generation, as individuals, to take interests, or whether the testator intended the word issue to refer to future generations, in other words, to mean the same thing as heirs. In the former case they take by purchase and since no words of limitation have then been used in relation to them, they take a fee simple jointly. If the latter is the case, then A takes a fee simple.[82]

Even if the word heirs is used this is not necessarily decisive. It is still open to the court to find that the testator intended to refer only to the first generation as individuals, so that the children take by purchase.[83]

The formal position is then that the courts treat the question of intention as relating solely to the issue of whether specific persons, or the heirs collectively, however described, are referred to. If the heirs collectively are intended to benefit by the remainder, *Shelley's Case* applies regardless of whether the result so obtained was intended by the testator.[84] For example, if the limitation is "to A for life, remainder to A's issue," it may well be that the intention was that A should take a life estate and that A's children should take a fee simple at his death, the next generations benefiting by inheritance, but once it is shown that the intention is to benefit collectively all those who would in the course of devolution inherit his property the rule applied and A takes a fee simple.

The formal position notably expresses a compromise between a rule of law applied to produce some result dictated by social policy and a rule of construction aimed at giving effect to the testator's intent. This, however, is the formal position and it may be questioned whether courts in fact keep the two issues entirely separate, so that in practice the intention of the testator may have entirely displaced the rule in wills.

a) Heir in the Singular

If the word heir is used in the singular, *i.e.*:

81 *Whitelaw v. Whitelaw* (1880) 5 LR Ir 120, MR. (The addition of the phrase "living at my death" to "issue" including children or remoter issue pointed to the intention being to benefit specific persons); *Van Grutten v. Foxwell* [1897] AC 658, Eng HL.

82 *Shannon v. Good* (1885) 15 LR Ir 300, CA (intermediate estates tail prevented merger); *Kavanagh v. Morland* (1853) Kay 16, 69 ER 7; *Montgomery v. Montgomery* (1845) 3 Jo & La T 47, 81 ER 740, 72 RR 17.

83 *Crozier v. Crozier* (1843) 5 Ir Eq R 419, 61 RR 77; *Phillips v. Phillips* (1847) 10 Ir Eq R 519, where the devise was to S for life, remainder to trustees to preserve, etc., and after S's death to the use of the heirs male of S in such shares and proportions as S should appoint.

84 Megarry & Wade, *Real Property* (4th ed.) p.64.

to A for life, remainder to his heir...

then the conclusion is more readily drawn that a specific person is intended and *Shelley's Case* does not apply.

In *Gilbourne v. Gilbourne*[85] the testator left freehold land of which he was the registered owner to his nephews P and W "as joint tenants so that the same shall pass to the heir at law of the survivor of them". Kenny J held that *Shelley's Case* did not apply. "Heir at law" was intended to refer to a specific person, namely, the person who should turn out to be the heir at law of the survivor. That as it turned out was the plaintiff, the heir of P. The judge found that this was indicated both by the use of heir in the singular and by the phrase "so that the same shall pass" which implied words of purchase.

b) Superadded Words

If further words are used in a will after the word heir then *Shelley's Case* will be unlikely to apply. For example, in the limitation:

to A for life, remainder to A's heir and his heirs

the superadded words indicate that the word heir is intended to function as a word of purchase.[86]

4. Equitable Estates Inter Vivos

Although there is some conflict in the authorities, it seems that equity does not require the same strict words of limitation as are required in a deed at common law and that equity will seek to discover what estate was intended to be granted. Thus, in the limitation:

Unto and to the use of F and G and their heirs in trust for A for life, remainder in trust for A's heirs for ever

equity will apply a similar rule to that applicable to wills. If the intention is to refer to a specific persons, they take by purchase.[87] If, on the other hand, the intention is to refer to the whole class of intestate successors, the rule will apply.

5. The Policy of the Rule

There are at least two possible explanations of the rule in terms of policy. One is a feudal explanation and the other is an explanation in terms of the effect on the operation of a market economy.

The rule may be of feudal origin and have as its object the preservation of the lord's feudal incident of relief. If a grant was made "to A and his heirs" or

85 Unreported, High Court, Kenny J, 9 July 1975; Wylie, *Cases* p.129.

86 Note that in *inter vivos* deeds heir cannot function as a word of limitation in any case.

87 *Brennan v. Fitzmaurice* (1840) 2 Ir Eq R 113 at 122.

"to A and the heirs of her body" then when A died the heirs or heirs of the body would have taken the land under the rules of descent. The incident of relief would have become payable before they could succeed to the tenancy. On this view, the typical limitation which is the subject of *Shelley's Case* was an attempt to avoid the feudal incident by giving the estate to A's heir or the heir of the body by purchase and not by descent. The rule prevented this result and so protected the income of feudal lords.[88] On this view the rule is clearly an anachronism.

On the other hand, the rule has the effect of making land more freely alienable and so promotes a market economy. The result of the rule is that A gets a fee simple, which can freely be bought and sold, or a fee tail which today can be barred and so he or she can so obtain a fee simple. The whole interest in the land is thus immediately alienable. If the rule did not apply, and the heirs took by purchase, then A would only have a life estate and the land would cease to be marketable for a considerable period. As a justification for the rule this reason is now greatly diminished in significance by the provisions of the Settled Land Acts, 1882–1890 which give power to a life tenant to convey a fee simple, but it may explain why the rule survived for so long in so many jurisdictions.

Originally the rule was a rule of law, *i.e.* if the limitation was in the form which attracted the rule, it applied regardless of whether it expressed the intention of the grantor or not. This shows that the rule was intended to impose a general policy which might not coincide with the intention of the grantor, or, if the feudal explanation is correct, would always defeat the intention. The modern tendency, realised in wills and perhaps present even in its application to *inter vivos* deeds, is paradoxically to treat the rule as a guide to interpretation, as an aid to discovering the intention of the grantor. Since it was never designed for this purpose, that is merely a way of rendering the rule inoperative without breaking the convention of legal discourse that judges do not abolish rules, or make law.

6. Avoiding the Rule

One method of making sure that the rule does not apply is to employ the device of a use. Thus in the following limitation:

88 See Yelverton CB in *Mandeville v. Lord Carrick* (1795) 3 Ridg PC 366 at 369: "...It was originally founded in the principles of the feudal law, to prevent conveyances in fraud of the tenure; because if by such a limitation the issue could take an estate tail in remainder, as purchasers, it would at any time be in the power of the ancestor to defeat the contingent remainder to his issue and thus acquire a dominion over the estate. Or if he did not defeat the remainder, to transmit the remainder to his issue exonerated from the duties to which the lord was entitled from his tenant coming in by descent..."

to F and G and their heirs to the use of A for 100 years if he shall so long live, then to the use of the heirs of A in fee simple

the heirs of A do not have a remainder at common law because it is not supported by a prior estate of freehold.[89] A's interest is leasehold. *Shelley's Case* does not apply.[90]

G. Heirs As A Word of Purchase

So far we have seen that the word heirs is treated as a word of limitation. Section 15(1) of the Succession Act, 1965[91] provides that the word heir or heirs used as words of limitation are to be given the same meaning in instruments and deeds taking effect after the Act came into force as they had before the Act. This confirms that a grant "to A and her heirs" will still confer a fee simple on A. Since the words ". . . and her heirs" function as words of limitation they do not describe a class of persons and no rules are required to define such a class. There are, however, situations in which the courts have recognised that the word heir or heirs may function as words of purchase. In the following examples:

to A's heir and her [or his] heirs

to the heir of A and her [or his] heirs

it is clear that the words "and her heirs" are words of limitation, but "A's heir," or "the heir of A," is intended to identify the person who is to take an interest.

The Succession Act, 1965 section 15(2) now provides that:

> "15(2).–The word heir or heirs used as a word of purchase in any enactment, deed or instrument passed or executed before the commencement of this Act [*i.e.* 1st January 1967], shall bear the same meaning as if this Act had not been passed."

As to instruments executed after the Act, section 15(3) provides:

> "15(3).–The word heir or heirs, used as a word of purchase in any enactment, deed or instrument passed or executed after the commencement of this Act, shall, unless the contrary intention appears, be construed to mean the person or persons, other than a creditor, who would be beneficially entitled under Part VI to the estate of the ancestor if the ancestor had died intestate."[92]

89 See the common law remainder rules, below.

90 *Atkinson v. L'Estrange* (1885) 15 LR Ir 340, V-C.

91 The section is copied from the Local Registration of Title (Ireland) Act, 1891 section 89.

92 The wording of the section is curious. The section does not expressly refer to wills although it is to wills that it chiefly applies. The reason appears to be that the the change was first introduced by section 114 of the Registration of Title Act, 1964 in relation to registered land and the Succession Act, 1965 repeats the words of that section. The Registration of Title Act is not, of course, solely concerned with wills and for that reason only refers to deeds. More oddly, section 15 retains the dichotomy between deeds

The effect of these provisions is as follows.

1. Before 1967

Before the Act was passed the law was, both as to wills and as to *inter vivos* deeds, that, to take the above example, if A were dead at the time the limitation took effect, then the heir, determined according to the old rules of descent, took the interest. The words of purchase "to A's heir" took effect and the words of limitation, "and her [or his] heirs," indicated that the interest was a fee simple. On the other hand, if A were alive when the limitation took effect, then the gift to the heir was void. This was because of the common law rule *nemo est heres viventis*: a living person has no heir.[93] He or she might have an heir apparent, *i.e.* someone who would be A's heir if he survived A, such as (under the old rules of descent) A's eldest son, or an heir presumptive, *i.e.* someone who would be A's heir if they both outlived A and were not displaced by someone with a better claim, as, for example, A's daughter, if she at present were his only child. But A had no finally determined heir while he was alive. If A had an eldest son he would be the heir apparent, but he might die before his father and might never be the heir.

Even at common law there was at least one apparent exception to the general rule. If a gift were in the form:

> *to A for life, remainder to A's heir and his heirs [or for life, etc.]*

then, even if A were alive, the remainder was held valid.[94] By the time the remainder took effect in possession A would be dead.[95] Also, it has been held that if the limitation is under the Statute of Uses, 1634 in the form:

> *to F and G [feoffees] in fee simple to the use of the heirs of A [in fee simple, or for life, etc.]*

---

executed before or after the Act comes into force, whereas the general rule as to wills, contained in section 89 of the Succession Act, is that a will takes effect on the death of the testator.

93 Co Litt 8.

94 *Re Beaupré's Trusts* (1888) 21 LR Ir 397, CA. If the gift is "to A for life, remainder to B's heir in fee simple" the remainder should be valid if at A's death B is also dead. *Gilbourne v. Gilbourne,* unreported, High Court, Kenny J, 9 July 1975; Wylie, *Cases* p.129. In the latter case the person whose heir was referred to was dead by the time the case got to court, which the court evidently thought sufficient.

95 In *Re Midleton's Will Trusts* (1969) 1 Ch 600 Stamp J in the English High court refused to recognise that a gift to the person who should become A's heir on A's death gave a contingent interest, making the distinction that a gift to "B, who shall be A's heir" would give such an interest if B did in fact become A's heir. But it is suggested that this is incorrect, since an interest can be contingent because the person to take it is unacertained. See also *Gilbourne v. Gilbourne,* unreported, High Court, 9 July 1975. *Shelley's Case* would not apply in the above example in an *inter vivos* deed because heir is used in the singular.

then, even if A is alive, the gift is valid as a future interest (*i.e.* a springing use) which will vest in possession when A dies, if such an intention can be spelled out of the deed.[96] It could not be valid as a common law limitation as it would be a springing interest.

2. From 1967

It is probable that the only change which it was intended that section 15(3) should make is as to the definition of heir. If A is dead the gift takes effect in favour of those persons who "would be beneficially entitled. . . to the estate of the ancestor if the ancestor had died intestate." The words may even render the gift effective if A died leaving a will, since they are phrased hypothetically. If A is alive the gift is probably still void, subject to the above exceptions. On the other hand it could be argued that the conditional tense allows a court, even if A is still alive, to assume hypothetically that A died intestate immediately before the execution of the instrument.

H. Modified Fees

Estates can be made subject to conditions which may bring them to an end before they would normally do so, or which have to be satisfied before they can arise. The word conditions is used in inverted commas because, as we shall see, the law makes a technical distinction between conditional interests and determinable interests, and so conditions should be reserved for the former type of interest. We use modified to cover both types and determining event as the equivalent of condition when discussing determinable interests. In theory any estate can be made conditional or determinable, but when such modified estates occur they are more usually fee simple and so we shall only deal with the law in relation to such modified fees.[97]

1. Conditions Precedent and Subsequent

A preliminary issue which courts often have to decide is whether the condition is a condition precedent or a condition subsequent. If it is a condition precedent the estate will not vest until the condition is fulfilled. Such estates are therefore future interests and are dealt with in a later chapter. Suffice it to say here that they could not exist at common law, but became possible, as springing interests

96 *Harris v. Barnes* (1768) 4 Burr 2157, 98 ER 125; *Scattergood v. Edge* (1699) 1 Salk 229, 91 ER 203 (sub nom *Scatterwood v. Edge*) cited in *Crozier v. Crozier* (1843) 5 Ir Eq R 419, 3 Dru & War 364, 61 RR 77.

97 See Powell, "Determinable Fees" (1923) 23 Colum L R 207. For a discussion of the law in Ireland relating to modified estates generally, including life estates, see Lyall, "Human Rights and Conditional and Determinable Interests in Freeholds" (1987) *Irish Jurist* 250.

under the Statute of Uses and the Statute of Wills. If the condition is a condition subsequent the estate vests at once but will be divested if the condition occurs. The law was neatly summarised by Lord Lowry LCJ in the Northern Ireland case of *Re Porter*:[98]

> "Whether the condition is precedent or subsequent to the vesting of the interest given depends on the intention of the testator as gathered from the words used. It has been stated that there are no technical words to distinguish a condition precedent from a condition subsequent and that, where it is doubtful whether a condition is precedent or subsequent, the court leans towards a construction which will hold it to be a condition subsequent, for that construction will lead to the early vesting of the gift and there is a presumption in favour of early vesting. A void condition precedent will prevent the gift from vesting, but a void condition subsequent will cause the donee to take free from the condition. The setting of a time limit for performance may show a condition to be precedent: *In re Doherty* [1950] NI 83; but, where a specific time is mentioned for the performance of the condition but not for the vesting of the estate or interest, the condition, it is said, will in general be subsequent: *Walker v. Walker* (1860) 2 De GF & J 255; 45 ER 619. It has further been suggested that, if the condition is capable of being performed *instanter*, it will probably be precedent, whereas, if time is requisite for its performance, it is more likely to be subsequent. If the nature of the interest is such as to allow time for the performance of the act before the interest can be enjoyed, it is generally precedent, whereas, if it is reasonable to suppose that the interest must vest in possession before the donee can be expected to comply with the condition, it will be subsequent. See Williams on Wills, 3rd ed., Ch. 40, pp 266–267 and cases there cited; also Theobald, 13th ed., paragraph 1564, and Jarman, 8th ed., pp. 1458–1465".

It may also be pointed out that whether a condition is precedent or subsequent may depend on the situation of the person referred to and the knowledge of the grantor of that situation. Take, for example, a condition which specifies that X should reside at a certain house. If X does not at the time of the disposition reside there the condition is precedent, at least if that fact is known to the grantor for then that must be the grantor's intention. If he resides there already then it is a condition subsequent. As the judge points out the general principle is to hold the condition a condition subsequent so that the property vest at once: the presumption favours the early vesting of property.[99] This can be seen as market-specific principle. A market or capitalist economy is likely to work more efficiently if property interests are vested and so free to be bought and sold on the market rather than suspended until some event or condition occurs, for in the meantime they will be effectively inalienable. Thus the rule is not really a rule of interpretation, but a rule of social policy to be imposed unless deliberately excluded by the testator.

---

98 [1975] NI 157, 160, cited with approval by Carswell J in *Morgan v. McCaughey* unreported, NI Ch. D, 8 September 1986 (Transcript: Lexis).

99 The point is applied in *Re McDonnell' Will* [1965] IR 354, High Court, Budd J, citing *Re Greenwood* [1903] 1 Ch 749.

Conditions subsequent which would operate to defeat a vested estate are construed strictly,[100] and so the Supreme Court has held that a condition as to marriage which it held unobjectionable in itself was not severable from a condition as to residence with which it was combined and which the court held void for uncertainty, so that the composite condition failed as a whole.[101]

2. Modified Fees at Common Law

In the past a distinction was drawn by judges between a condition and a determining event. The reason for this distinction will not be clear until we have dealt with the common law remainder rules. Suffice it to say that those rules, although still in force in Ireland, are mainly feudal in character and the distinction between conditional and determinable interests arose out of a judicial attempt to avoid the effect of one of those rules. It is a matter of construction whether a deed gives rise to a determinable or a conditional interest. The effect of many decisions on many deeds is that words suggesting a natural continuation up to a point, such as while, during, as long as, until, indicate a determinable fee, whereas words suggesting an artificial interruption or cutting short of an interest that would otherwise continue, such as provided that, on condition that, but if, if it happen that, create a conditional interest:

Determinable	Conditional
while	provided that
during	on condition that
as long as	but if
unitl	if it happen that

The distinction, according to the textbooks, is purely linguistic, although it cannot be stated with complete confidence that judges always attach the same meaning to those expressions. We shall see later, in the chapter on future interests, that this highly artificial distinction was adopted in order to avoid one of the feudal common law remainder rules and so is not simply abstract reasoning, but is one minor step in adapting the system of land law from feudalism to capitalism.

It is not possible fully to understand conditional and determinable interests in property without a knowledge of the rule against perpetuities and its effects on such interests. We therefore have to anticipate here the later discussion of

100 *Re Coghlan Deceased* [1963] IR 246 at 249, (1964) 98 ILTR 134 (Kingsmill Moore and O Dalaigh JJ, Maguire CJ dissenting); *Clavering v. Ellison* (1859) 7 HL Cas 707.

101 *ibid.*

the perpetuity rule. Readers may wish to ignore the discussion of perpetuities in the following sections and return to it after studying future interests in detail.

a) Conditional Fees

(1) Effects

A conditional fee, unlike a determinable interest, does not end automatically if the event occurs. When the event specified in the condition occurs the grantor can exercise a *right of entry for condition broken.*[102] At common law this was the only interest it was possible to have after a conditional fee. The grantor could not, in the same document, create a conditional fee simple and then provide that if the event occurred the land was to pass to some third party.[103] Thus, in the limitation:

> *to D in fee simple, but if he becomes an accountant, [over to E in fee simple]*

the gift to E is void. There is a conditional fee in favour of D and a right of entry for condition broken in the grantor if the event occurs. Until it occurs there could be said to be a possibility of a right of entry in the grantor. In the case law the phrase right of entry is used rather loosely to mean both the possibility and the right that becomes immediate if the event occurs.[104] If the event occurs the grantor recovers the fee simple.

The courts have treated the condition as separable from the estate it qualifies. If the condition itself is objectionable on grounds of public policy or as infringing constitutional rights, then it will be struck out, leaving the grantee with a fee simple absolute. Thus in the limitation:

> *to A in fee simple provided she remains unmarried*

the condition is void as infringing the right to marry,[105] but it can be severed from the rest of the limitation so that A obtains the fee simple free of the condition. This contrasts with determinable interests in which the determining event is regarded as part of the estate it qualifies.

(2) Right of Entry

(a) Perpetuity

It is settled in Ireland that rights of entry for condition broken at common law

---

102 Goldstein, "Rights of Entry and Possibilities of Reverter as Devices to Restrict the Use of Land" (1940) 54 HLR 248.

103 Co Litt 143a; *Doctor & Student* Dial 2 c.20, 21; Sanders, *Uses* 1 p.144. The reason was that it would be a remainder after a fee simple: see Chapter 10 Future Interests: Common Law Remainders.

104 See Lord Brougham in *Cole v. Sewell* (1848) 2 HLC 185 at 231, 9 ER 1062.

105 See below Restrictions on Marriage.

are not subject to the perpetuity rule.[106] The limitation

to M in fee simple on condition the land be used as a school

would create a valid conditional fee with a right of entry in the grantor, which would pass like a fee simple to the grantor's successors. If the land ceases to be used for agriculture the person then entitled to the right of entry would have 12 years under the Statute of Limitations to assert their right.

(b) Alienability

At common law rights of entry for condition broken were heritable, *i.e.* they passed to the heirs on intestacy, but could not be assigned or released.[107] The Wills Act, 1837 first made them devisable by will, and this Act has been replaced by the Succession Act, 1965 sections 10 and 76. It would seem that rights of entry remain inalienable *inter vivos* in Ireland.[108]

b) Determinable Fees

(1) Effects

The determinable fee[109] is a fee simple which will end automatically on the happening of a specified event which may never happen.[110] If the event is one

106 *Walsh v. Wightman* [1927] NI 1. The case was decided before statutory reform in Northern Ireland. The Perpetuities Act (Northern Ireland), 1966, section 13(1) provides that a right of entry in respect of a fee simple for condition broken shall not be exerciseable after the perpetuity period. Section 13(3) provides that a possibility of reverter under a determinable fee or a possibility of resulting trust shall cease to exist at the end of the perpetuity period and that the fee or interest in question shall cease to be determinable. *Walsh v. Wightman* is consistent with *Attorney General v. Cummins* in the Republic: See footnote 114 and the accompanying text.

107 *Orr v. Stevenson* (1843) 5 Ir LR 2, per Pennefather B. They were a mere possibility: *Denham v. Dormer* 2 And 84, 123 ER 558.

108 The Real Property Act, 1845, which is in force in the Republic, by section 6 makes rights of entry alienable *inter vivos*, but specifically refers to rights of entry "in England." It reads:

> "...a contingent, an executory, and a future interest, and a possibility coupled with an interest, in any tenements or hereditaments of any tenure... also a right of entry, whether immediate or future, and whether vested or contingent, into or upon any tenements or hereditaments in England, of any tenure, may be disposed of by deed..."

Also, in *Hunt v. Remnant* (1854) 9 Exch 635 at 640 Pollock CB says that the phrase does not refer to rights of entry for condition broken. Section 6 was amended in the Republic by the Married Women's Status Act, 1957 section 19 but the amendment does not affect the words referred to.

109 Powell, "Determinable Fees" (1923) 23 Colum L R 207.

110 The grantor or successors in title may have to bring an action to establish that the grantee's estate has come to an end, but there is still a contrast with conditional fees here because a determinable fee will come to an end when the event occurred whereas a conditional fee will be come to an end when the action to enforce the right of entry succeeds.

which, by its nature, must happen, then the interest is not a determinable fee, but something else. For example:

to A in fee simple until B dies

gives A an *estate pur autre vie*, while

to C and his heirs for 25 years

gives C a lease for 25 years. An example of a determinable fee would be:

to B and his heirs until he qualifies as an accountant.

At common law, if the determining event occurs, the land reverts automatically to the grantor. The grantor has a possibility of reverter. Indeed, this is the only interest that can exist after a determinable fee at common law. At common law the grantor cannot, in the same deed, create a determinable fee and then provide that if the event occurs the land is to pass to someone else. The grantor cannot create a gift over to a third party after a determinable fee. So in the limitation:

to X and his heirs until he becomes an accountant, [then to Y and his heirs]

the gift to Y is void. The common law does not allow a remainder after a fee simple, even a determinable one.[111] The grantor retains a possibility of reverter. If X becomes an accountant, then the land reverts to the grantor, or if he or she is dead, to whoever has become entitled to his or her interest. A possibility of reverter thus passes on intestacy in the same way as a fee simple, to the heirs of the grantor, or now in the Republic, to the intestate successors under the Succession Act, 1965. If X dies without becoming an accountant then the event can no longer occur and the fee simple becomes absolute. This will be the case whatever the event.

By contrast with a conditional fee, the determining event is regarded at common law as an integral part of the estate which it qualifies, so that if it fails, the whole limitation fails.[112] If the determining event is contrary to public policy, or infringes constitutional rights, the whole determinable interest is void. So the limitation:

to A in fee simple until she marries

is prima facie void as in total restraint of marriage and A gets nothing.[113]

111 The common law remainder rules are discussed later.

112 This common law position is now modified by section 51(2) of the Settled Land Act, 1882. An determining event which would or might prevent a tenant for life under the Act from exercising the powers under the Act is severed from the estate and the tenant for life continues to enjoy the estate free of the restriction: *Re Ames* (1893) 2 Ch. 479.

113 See below Restrictions on Marriage.

(2) Possibility of Reverter

(a) Perpetuity

It has been held in Ireland that the perpetuity rule does not apply to possibilities of reverter.[114] Thus the following limitation:

> *to X and his heirs so long as the land shall be used for agriculture*

creates a determinable fee followed by a valid possibility of reverter in the grantor. If the land ceases to be used for agriculture the land reverts to the grantor or those who have by then become entitled to the grantor's right of reverter. Again, they have 12 years in which to assert it.

(b) Alienability

At common law a possibility of reverter could not be transferred by the grantor: it could only descend as on an intestacy to the heir-at-law. Today, it is probably the case that a possibility of reverter can be left by will. The Succession Act, 1965 by section 10 provides that all the real and personal property of a person shall on his or her death, devolve on his personal representatives. Section 76 provides that a person by his will may dispose of all property to which he is beneficially entitled to at his death and which on his death devolves on his personal representatives.[115] It is not clear whether possibilities of reverter may be alienated *inter vivos* in Ireland.[116]

c) Summary

The main differences between conditional and determinable fees may be summarised as follows:

---

114 *Attorney General v. Cummins* [1906] IR 406. Quit rents were granted in fee simple until the recipient or his heirs were paid a lump sum. Palles CB held that the rule against perpetuities did not apply to possibilities of reverter at common law. Palles was known for his strict adherence to the historical reason behind rules and he pointed out that the common law had recognised possibilities of reverter long before the development of the rule against perpetuities. There is in any case a logical problem about subjecting possibilities of reverter to the perpetuity rule which will not have escaped the notice of the observant, and that is that if they were so subjected it would also render void determinable interests themselves. See Lyall, "Human Rights and Conditional and Determinable Interests in Freeholds" (1987) Irish Jurist 250 at 255.

115 Note that the case of *Pemberton v. Barnes* [1899] 1 Ch. 544 held that a possibility of reverter on a determinable fee in copyholds was within the Wills Act, 1837.

116 Section 6 of the Real Property Act, 1845 provides: "...a possibility coupled with an interest, in any tenements or hereditaments of any tenure... may be disposed of by deed..." A possibility of reverter may come within the phrase "possibility coupled with an interest," the interest being the determinable fee simple. See footnote 108.

Conditional	Determinable
1. Words suggesting premature cutting short.	1. Words suggesting natural continuation.
2. Followed by right of entry.	2. Followed by possibility of reverter.
3. Does not terminate automatically.	3. Terminates automatically.
4. Condition separable from estate.	4. Event part of limitation.

3. Modified Fees Under the Statute of Uses

a) Legal Executory Gifts Over

We have seen that at common law the only interest that could exist after a conditional fee is a right of entry for condition broken in the grantor. It is not possible at common law to create a gift over, *i.e.* an interest contained in the deed to take effect in favour of some third party if the event occurs. It is nevertheless possible to do so under the Statute of Uses, 1634[117] or in a will after the Statute of Wills (Ireland), 1634.

A limitation:

> *to F and his heirs to the use of X and his heirs, but if X fails to pay the grantor £2000 within one year, then to Y and his heirs*

gives X a conditional fee followed by an executory interest to Y.[118] Y's interest can be described as an executed shifting use which will take effect in possession on the specified event. It therefore became possible, by using such a formula, to create gifts over after a conditional interest.[119] Although it is possible by using these words to create a gift over, since it is an executory interest it must comply with the perpetuity rule. In the example just given the condition was one which complied with the rule. But in the following limitation:

> *to F and her heirs to the use of K and his heirs, but if the land ceases to be used as a school, [then to L and his heirs]*

the condition on which the shifting interest is to vest does not comply with the perpetuity rule. Hence, the gift over is void. The grantor retains an executory right of entry.[120]

117 1535 in England (27 Hen VIII c.10), 1634 in Ireland (10 Chas I sess 2 c.1).

118 Sanders, *Uses* 1 p.144.

119 *Tisdall v. Tisdall* (1840) 2 Ir CL 41.

120 This interest is not subject to the perpetuity rule in Ireland: *Walsh v. Wightman* [1927] NI 1. This result is consistent with the position at common law and under trusts. See

A similar position arises as to determinable interests taking effect as executed uses. It is possible to create gifts over after them, provided they comply with the perpetuity rule. So that:

> *to F and his heirs to the use of A and his heirs until he becomes an accountant, then over to B and his heirs*[121]

creates a use which is immediately executed by the Statute, giving A a legal fee simple which will determine on his becoming an accountant and B will then have a fee simple, by way of a shifting use.[122] In the example just given the event is one which in any case must occur within the perpetuity period because it is limited to A's life. But in the following limitation:

> *to F and his heirs to the use of O and her heirs so long as the land is used for agriculture, [then to P and her heirs]*

the gift over to P is void for perpetuity.[123] There is a determinable fee in O followed by what may be called an executory possibility in the grantor.[124]

b) Future Trusts

(1) Gifts Over

Gifts over after determinable or conditional equitable estates can be created as equitable interests, provided they comply with the perpetuity rule. So a gift:

> *unto and to the use of T and U and their heirs in trust for A in fee simple until she qualifies as a accountant, then in trust for B and her heirs*

gives a valid equitable determinable fee to A followed by a gift over in fee simple to B. The gift over must vest, if at all, within the life of A.

---

text accompanying footnote 127.

121 A grant by M "to E and his heirs until M pays £800 to E" is valid at common law. It creates, in effect, a mortgage. The fee simple returns automatically to M when he pays the debt. The disadvantage of this limitation as a mortgage was that it could not easily be discovered who had the fee simple, *i.e.* whether M had paid the debt or not. Hence, the later form is to require an express reassignment of the estate. And see Holdsworth HEL Vol. 7 p.122, a limitation by X "unto F and G and their heirs to the use of W and his heirs till A pays £40 to W, then to the use A and his heirs" is valid: Brooke's Abridgement.

122 See *City of Klamath Falls v. Bell* (1972) 7 Ore App 330, 490 P.2d 515 discussed below in "the Modern Rule against Perpetuities: Gifts Over"; *Re Davey* [1915] 1 Ch. 837; 84 LJ Ch. 505 113 LT 60. It is this type of interest that is referred to in the Settled Land Act, 1882 in s.58(1)(ii) as a "conveyance in fee simple subject to an executory limitation, gift or disposition over". Since such an interest is possible by way of shifting use, it also creates an element of succession sufficient to bring it within the Settled Land Acts.

123 *City of Klamath Falls v. Bell* (1972) 7 Ore App 330, footnote 122.

124 In Northern Ireland the possibility ceases to exist at the end of the perpetuity period. See footnote 106.

The following gift:

> *unto and to the use of T and U and their heirs in trust for P and his heirs, but if he becomes a accountant, then in trust for Q and his heirs*

gives a valid equitable conditional fee to P followed by a gift over to Q. The event is bound to occur within the life of P and so satisfies the perpetuity rule.

If the event on which the gift over is limited to take effect is void for perpetuity,[125] then the gift over is void and there will instead be a possibility of resulting trust, which is discussed in the next section.

(2) Possibilities of Resulting Trust.

In the following example:

> *unto and to the use of T and U and their heirs in trust for R and his heirs, but if the land ceases to be used for agriculture, [then over to S and her heirs]*

the gift over to S is void for perpetuity. The better view would seem to be that the gift over being void, there remains a resulting trust[126] in the grantor which is not subject to the perpetuity rule.[127] In the Northern Ireland case of *Walsh v. Wightman,*[128] the court upheld Palles' view that a right of entry at common law was not void for perpetuity and went on to decide that the same applied even if a similar interest occurred under a trust. This is sensible, as it preserves a consistency in the rules, and gives effect to the intention of the donor. The same would no doubt apply if the event were phrased as a determining event:

> *unto and to the use of T and U and their heirs in trust for R and his heirs, so long as the land is used for agriculture, [then over to X in fee simple]*

The gift over to X is void for perpetuity. R gets a determinable fee in equity which comes to an end if the land ceases to used for agriculture. The trustees then hold the land on trust for the grantor, or whoever is by then entitled to the

---

125 Where a determining event in a determinable interest is void for public policy the entire gift is void since the event forms part of the limitation of the interest.

126 Equity does not appear to distinguish between a right of entry and a possibility of reverter.

127 In *Re Cooper's Conveyance Trusts* [1956] 1 WLR 1096, a conveyance was made to trustees in fee simple on trust for an orphan girls' home, and on failure of that trust, then in trust for persons mentioned elsewhere in the deed. It was held that the gift over was void for perpetuity, but there was a valid resulting trust in favour of the grantor's estate.
The American case of *Commerce Union Bank v. Warren County* (1986) 707 SW 2d 854 (Tennessee) recently came to the same conclusion. A testator had left land on trust as a county home and the court held that once the county ceased to operate it as a home the land reverted to the heirs of the deceased, also holding that the possibility of reverter as they termed it was not subject to the perpetuity rule.

128 [1927] NI 1.

grantor's property. There is thus a possibility of resulting trust. This is not subject to the perpetuity rule.[129]

4. Invalidity of Determining Events or Conditions

a) Introduction

Determining events or conditions (which we shall henceforth refer to as restrictions) may be held void as contrary to public policy or constitutional rights. Today these events or conditions more often occur in equitable limitations under trusts. Where they occur in limitations drafted as common law interests the formal distinction between determinable and conditional limitations has been held significant because in a determinable limitation if the determining event is void for any reason, then the whole interest which was intended to be conveyed will be held void.[130] This result appears to be simply a logical consequence of the attempt by common law judges to avoid the common law remainder rules, specifically the rule that a remainder must not cut short a prior estate. In order to do this the judges had to draw a highly artificial distinction between conditions and determining events, the latter being seen as an integral part of the prior estate and not something which cut it short before its time. But the solution to one problem created a new problem when the issue of objectionable determining events arises. Courts have been reluctant to hold determining clauses void on the ground of public policy because, if they were true to logic, the only result would be that if the determining event is struck out, the prior estate of which it is an integral part will also have to go. Thus, the person who would in a sense be the victim of unlawful discrimination would, as a result of the court's striking down the forfeiting event, be deprived of any benefit at all under the gift.

It is suggested that such an unfortunate result need not be a consequence if the courts were to hold that the words in the limitation were not decisive. Thus the phrase "so long as" would not necessarily indicate a determinable interest unless it was intended to create such an interest. The old distinction between determinable and conditional interests was, or became, purely a matter of form. But it can be argued that there is a matter of substance in the distinction which the forms should express. One kind of gift is one which attempts to provide for a person until an event occurs, the idea of the property-giver being that he has only so much property to distribute and must therefore distribute it where it will be of greatest use, bearing in mind the needs of others for whom he wishes to provide. This notion involves the idea that where the recipient's needs decline to a point where provision may come from another quarter, or where they are exceeded by the need to provide for some other person for

129 See footnote 127.

130 Contrast the situation where a gift over after an executory determinable interest is void for perpetuity. See footnote 125.

whom the donor also feels a responsibility to benefit, the property owner will arrange matters so that the property interest terminates and the property may be applied elsewhere. It implies something that will naturally last for so long as a particular purpose is to be met and then come to an end. This is the essence of a determinable interest.

The other type of interest is where the property owner confers property on another but, without considering the needs of that person, but rather considering his or her own preferences. He or she attempts to satisfy that preference by providing that the interest given shall end if some event occurs. In other words, a conditional interest can be seen as less altruistic than a determinable interest. This is the essence of a conditional interest: a premature cutting short, a penalty, a forfeiture. Where the event specified contravened constitutional rights, such as the right to marry, or involved an unconstitutional discrimination, it would also be more readily found to be a conditional and not a determinable interest. The condition could be struck out, leaving the donee with the complete interest.

b) Relief Against Forfeiture

There is a general jurisdiction in equity to grant relief against forfeiture arising by reason of a condition subsequent. However, the normal rule is that no relief will be granted if there is a gift over in the event of the condition occurring.[131] To relieve the holder of the conditional interest in such a case would also be to deprive the person entitled to the gift over of their interest. Since the one is divested and the other invested with the property on the event occurring the only question in such a case is whether the event has occurred or not.

c) Restrictions on Alienability

Conditions which seek to prevent or restrict alienation by a fee simple owner are likely to be held void as contrary to the policy of the law, stemming from the Statute *Quia Emptores*, 1290. These have already been dealt with above.[132]

---

131 *Morgan v. McCaughey* unreported, NI Ch D 8 September 1986 (Transcript: Lexis) Carswell J:

> "Nor is the court able to grant relief, when there is a gift over on failure to perform the condition. It has jurisdiction to grant relief against breach of condition, when it is equitable for it to take such a course; *Simpson v. Vickers* (1807) 14 Ves Jun 341, 33 ER 552; and see *In re Porter* [1975] NI 157, 162-3. If it were open to me to do so, I should have been very ready to grant relief in the circumstances of this case. It is established, however, that relief cannot be granted where there is a gift over, and for these purposes a direction that a gift should fall into residue is treated as a gift over: see *Lloyd v. Branton* (1817) 3 Mer 108, 36 ER 42."

132 See above, The Right to Alienate.

d) Restrictions on Occupation or Ownership.

Some forms of attempted restrictions on ownership or occupation by racial groups may be challengeable under the general rule as to the free alienability of fees simple without necessarily raising a constitutional issue. Thus, racial restrictions on sale are restictions on alienability[133] and have been dealt with above. Attempts to restrict occupation or ownership by particular racial, religious or other social groups are also challengeable on constitutional grounds. In jurisdictions such as the United States they have often taken the form of restrictive covenants. Attempts in this form are discussed in the chapter on such covenants. In this jurisdiction the history of discrimination involving property rights has been rather different. In the past it largely concerned religious issues, either attempting to prevent the practice of a particular religion, usually the Catholic faith, or marriage to Catholics. It also tended to take the form of forfeiture of property rights by way of determinable or conditional interests.

e) Restrictions on Residence

Conditions which seek to make residence a condition precedent or subsequent may be impugned on a number of grounds.

In *Morgan v. McCaughey*[134] such a condition was struck down on the ground that, in the case at hand, it would cause a child to live separately from its parents. The testator left property on trust for his sister for life with remainder after her death to his grandnephew Nathaniel, "provided he comes to live in the said property after my death and continues to reside therein with my said sister... until the death of my said sister". Nathaniel was to have no legal or equitable right to reside on the property "otherwise than as licensee of [my sister] . . . who may at any time revoke the said licence at her will and pleasure". Nathaniel was 15 years old at the time of the testator's death. He offered to go and live with the testator's sister but she declined the offer. Nathaniel occasionally stayed at the house with his mother at weekends. In 1972 the sister engaged a paid companion, on medical advice, and this arrangement lasted until her death. There was no ill will between the parties and Nathanial continued to visit the sister until her death, but the effect was that, while Nathaniel had done everything he could to comply with the condition, the sister's preference to arrange her own affairs prevented him from living in the house.

The judge first held that the condition was a single one and was subsequent. The remainder would vest in interest in Nathaniel immediately and under the will he was to be divested if he ceased to continue to reside, although the judge noted that it had not been argued that he should necessarily continue to reside until the sister's death. The judge then held that the condition, whether valid or

133 *Wayt v. Patee* (1928) 205 Cal 46; *Title Guarantee & Trust Co v. Garrott* 42 Cal App 152.

134 Unreported, NI Ch. D, 8 September 1986, (Transcript: Lexis) Carswell J.

not, had not been performed. Nathaniel had done his best to perform it, but the testator had given his sister the power to frustrate the performance of the condition and she had done so. The judge further held that a condition which tended to lead to the separation of a child from its parents was void as contrary to public policy.[135] Nathaniel therefore took the estate free of the condition.[136] In the Republic the protection afforded to the family by the Constitution would probably be sufficient reason to hold such a condition void.[137]

In *Re Fitzgibbon, deceased*[138] the testator left a farm to his grandnephew "provided he lives and works on the land" with a gift over to his niece on breach of the condition. Carroll J held that where there was a doubt as to whether a condition in a will was a condition precedent or subsequent, the court would apply the presumption in favour of early vesting and treat it prima facie as subsequent. The judge further held, however, that the condition was void for uncertainty, citing *Re Hennessy deceased*[139] in which Budd J had held a condition "to farm it and carry on same as he thinks best" as subsequent and as void for uncertainty. On the other hand, Gavan Duffy J in *Re Callaghan*[140] held that although a condition precedent that a devisee "arranges within... three months of my death to take over possession and permanently reside" on a farm was void for uncertainty, the further condition precedent that he "actually takes up his residence within six months" was valid as sufficiently definite.

Conditions as to residence may also fall foul of the Settled Land Act, 1882 where land comes within the Act.[141] Section 51 prohibits any attempt to restrict the statutory powers.[142]

f) Name and Arms Clauses

Property is sometimes given in family settlements subject to the condition that the person entitled shall use the name and coat of arms of some particular individual, usually the testator or settlor. Such conditions may be precedent or subsequent, or both. In theory they could also create determinable interests. It is a matter of interpretation for the court to decide which type of interest has been created.

---

135 *Re Boulter* [1922] 1 Ch. 75. And see *Re Sandbrook* [1912] 2 Ch. 471; *Re Piper* [1946] 2 All ER 503 (condition causing forfeiture if children went to live with their father, held void).

136 *Re Elliott* [1952] Ch. 217, [1952] 1 All ER 145; *Re Piper* [1946] 2 All ER 503.

137 Article 41.

138 [1993] IR 520.

139 (1963) 98 ILTR 39.

140 [1937] IR 84.

141 *i.e.* where there is an executory gift over. See Chapter 14 Settlements of Land.

142 *Re Fitzgerald* [1902] 1 IR 162; *Atkins v. Atkins* [1976-77] ILRM 62, Kenny J; *Re Thompson* (1888) 21 LR Ir 109, MR. It is a difficult question as to what effect section 51 would have on limitations framed as determinable interests.

In *Re de Vere's Will Trusts*,[143] for example, the clause specified that the person was to "take use and bear and continue to use and bear" the name specified in all documents which he should sign and to "use and continue to use" the arms of de Vere. This was phrased as both precedent and subsequent, as the court recognised. If the condition is capable of being construed as both precedent and subsequent, the facts existing at the time the condition takes effect become relevant. If the person specified is already using the name and arms at that time, then the condition precedent has already been satisfied and only the condition subsequent is in issue. If the person has not yet adopted them, the condition precedent is in issue.

As will be seen, name and arms clauses have frequently been held void for uncertainty. If the condition is subsequent and is held void for uncertainty, the vested estate becomes absolute. If, on the other hand, the condition were phrased as a determinable interest the whole interest would be void. If the condition is held to be precedent and were held void for uncertainty the property interest would be void since there would be no valid events on which it could come into existence.

Name and arms clauses have not been treated sympathetically by the judiciary in the Republic since 1922. In *Re Montgomery*[144] the clause in issue was a condition subsequent, and so the court was concerned with a condition which was to apply when a person ceased to use the name and arms specified. The High Court held such a clause void for uncertainty, not on the ground that the acts or omissions were in themselves uncertain, which the court declined to hold, but on the ground that it was uncertain as to when the acts or omissions might occur.

In *Re de Vere's Will Trusts*[145] the court was concerned with that part of the disposition which created a condition subsequent terminating the property interest. Budd J held the condition void for uncertainty. The English Court of Appeal in *Re Neeld*[146] had used the *de minimis* principle to overlook mistakes or forgetfulness or temporary lapses in use. In *Kearns v. Manresa Estates Ltd*[147] Kenny J held a clause in defeasance to be void for uncertainty. The judge was critical of *Re Neeld*. How many lapses would bring the principle into operation? How many would mean that it no longer applied? Must they be intentional or unintentional? He went on:

> "None of the judgments in *Re Neeld* deal with the question as to how the Court is to decide that at any given moment of time (and that, as Mr Justice Fry

143 [1961] IR 224.

144 (1955) 89 ILTR 62.

145 [1961] IR 224.

146 [1962] Ch. 643.

147 Unreported, High Court, Kenny J, 25 July 1975, Wylie, *Cases* p.148.

> pointed out,[148] is the critical question) a person has disused or discontinued to use the surname which he is obliged to assume."

Conditions requiring the use of a name as a condition precedent may cause less difficulty. One can adopt a name by deed poll, and although one can also adopt a name by repute, the condition in de Vere was limited to the use of the name in documents. In such a case it could be argued that a single instance of the person using the name in a document would satisfy the condition precedent.

Arms may obtained by a grant from the Chief Herald of Ireland and possibly can only be adopted legally in this way.[149] In addition, the children of a person entitled to bear arms may adopt a version of them with a suitable difference.[150] In *Bevan v. Mahon-Hagan*,[151] a case before the adoption of the present Constitution, it was held that a surname may be adopted voluntarily,[152] but the Court of Appeal did not agree as to whether or in what circumstances a person had the right to bear arms other than, at that time, under a Royal licence issued by the Ulster King of Arms.[153] Porter MR held that it was possible to assume arms, Fitzgibbon LJ held that one could not bear arms without a grant and Barry LJ found that the right of a person to bear arms otherwise than under a grant from the Crown was so obscure that he could not express an opinion on

---

148 *Re Exmouth* (1883) 23 Ch. D 158. See Wylie, *Land Law* para. 4.053.

149 Lyall, "Irish Heraldic Jurisdiction" (1993) 10 *Coat of Arms (n.s.)* 134-42; (1994) 10 *Coat of Arms (n.s.)* 179-87, 238-44, 266-75; National Cultural Institutions Act, 1997 ss. 12–13.

150 Where arms exist and are borne by the head of a family, junior or collateral members of the family may bear a version of the arms altered in some way to distinguish them from the head of the family. Arms may be associated with a name, but there are no family arms, nor is a person with the same surname entitled to use the undifferentiated arms. Arms pertain to individuals and were used to distinguish one individual from another when wearing armour, particularly in jousts. Thus, the arms of de Vere are properly those of the head of the main branch of the de Vere family.

151 (1891) 27 LR Ir 399, V-C, (1893) 31 LR Ir 342, CA.

152 See also *Doe d Luscombe v. Yates* (1822) 5 B & Ald 544, 106 ER 1289. The case concerned a testator by the name of Luscombe who left property in his will on condition that any beneficiary who did not bear the name of Luscombe should adopt it by Act of Parliament as a condition precedent. John Luscombe Manning changed his name to John Manning Luscombe, but not by Act of Parliament, and claimed the property. The court held him entitled to it. The condition only applied to persons whose surname was not Luscombe, and John Manning Luscombe had validly adopted the surname. It could have been argued that the condition referred to someone whose name was not Luscombe at the time of the testator's death, when the condition came into effect, but to restrict it in that way would not achieve a more just result because it would only exclude those who had not heard about the condition in the will before that time. Those who knew of it before the testator's death could still change their name and qualify.

153 Ulster King of Arms' heraldic authority, despite the title, extended throughout Ireland. Lyall, "Irish Heraldic Jurisdiction" (1993) 10 *Coat of Arms (n.s.)* 134 (Pt 1), (1994) 10 Coat of Arms 179 (Pt 2).

it.[154] The court held that the Crown could grant a coat of arms to a minor, and so a condition to adopt the name and arms of X before attaining the age of majority was capable of being performed.[155]

g) Restrictions on Marriage

(1) Total Restraints

It has long been held that a condition or determining event involving a total restriction on marriage would be void on grounds of public policy, so that a limitation:

to A in fee simple until she marries

is prima facie void and would only be upheld if the court were convinced that the intention was not to induce her not to marry, but to provide for her until marriage. Courts appear more likely to come to this conclusion in the case of a determinable interest, in order to save the gift. If they held the determining event invalid the intended donee would get nothing. This a clear example of the way in which the conditional/determinable distinction distorts the treatment of human rights issues. Thus in *Re Robson*[156] the High Court of Northern Ireland held a gift of property to A "whilst remaining unmarried" to be a valid determinable interest in spite of the suggestion of the words that a restraint was intended.

In *Re King's Trusts*[157] an annuity was given to each of five children of the testator's brother for their lives "or until any of them shall marry," the annuity to cease on their death or marriage. There was no gift over on the event occurring. The court held the proviso was "a limitation and not a condition subsequent or defeasance", *i.e.* it was a determinable interest and so the proviso was part of the words of limitation, but that as such it was valid and the claimant had forfeited the annuity on marriage. On the other hand, a condition, since it is not part of the limitation of the estate, can be severed from the estate. Hence, if the condition is void the effect of striking out the condition is to leave the estate

154 In England the Court of Chivalry, which had not sat for the previous 200 years, held in *Manchester Corpn v. Manchester Palace of Varieties Ltd* [1955] P 133, [1955] 1 All ER 387, [1955] 2 WLR 440, 53 LGR 269, 119 JP 191, that the display of the Corporation's arms in a theatre by the theatre company was not an infringement of any right, because arms were widely used for decoration or embellishment without complaint, but to use the arms on the theatre company's seal could be restrained by the court because the seal was used to authenticate documents. The court also held that the right to bear arms was not recognized by the ordinary courts and so only the Court of Chivalry had jurisdiction.

155 See judgment of the Vice Chancellor, (1891) 27 LR Ir 399.

156 [1940] Ir Jur Rep 72.

157 [1892] 29 LR Ir 401.

freed from it and the donor has a fee simple absolute.[158] So in the limitation:

to A and her heirs provided she remains unmarried

the condition is void as against public policy unless, which seems unlikely, the court construes it as not intended to restrain marriage. A has a fee simple absolute. Hence the courts are less inhibited in finding a condition to be contrary to public policy since to do so will not adversely affect the donee.[159] A more just result might be obtained if, as has been suggested, the nature of the restraint determined the issue of whether it was a conditional or determinable interest, rather than the mere form of words.

(2) Partial Restraints

The cases before the present Constitution took the view that a partial restraint was not necessarily void on that account, but would be so only if it restrained marriage to an extent which conflicted with public policy. In the Irish House of Lords case of *Keily v. Monck*[160] real property was devised to the testator's daughters subject to the proviso that should any of them marry someone who was not, at the time of the marriage, seized of a freehold estate of the clear yearly value of £500 sterling over and above every charge and incumbrance, then the legacy to such a daughter was to be forfeited. The proviso would only have been satisfied by a very wealthy man indeed. John Fitzgibbon, Lord Clare LC held that it would amount virtually to a total restraint on marriage, and was void. The judge's indignation was aroused by the thought that it would have excluded all members of the legal profession at the time, and the growing mercantile classes. The judge's remarks are interesting in that they provide some evidence that the judiciary was more sympathetic to these professional and capitalist classes at the time than to the landed aristocracy:

> "The case reported in Eq. abr.[161] is that a condition in restraint of marriage excluding a particular profession is void. How many particular professions are naturally excluded by that condition? What man of the profession of the law has set out with a clear unincumbered real estate of £500 a year, or has acquired such an estate for years after entering the profession? . . . It will in effect exclude ninety-nine men in one hundred of every profession, whether civil, military, or ecclesiastical. It in effect excludes nearly every mercantile man in the kingdom. . . In a word, the condition which this weak old man would impose upon his daughters. . . does, to my judgment, clearly and unquestionably lead to a total prohibition of their marriage, and as such ought to be condemned in ev-

158 *Kiely v. Monck* (1795) 3 Ridg PC 205 per Lord Clare LC at 261: "But with respect to conditions subsequent the law is clearly settled. that if they are illegal the condition is rejected and the estate vests absolutely."

159 See *McConnell v. Beattie* (1904) 38 ILTR 133.

160 (1795) 3 Ridg PC 205.

161 *Jarvis v. Duke* (1681) 1 Vern 20, 2 Eq Abr 110, 21 ER 918.

ery Court of Justice."[162]

The judge's indignation was selective. It was aroused by the thought that he himself and those like him would be discriminated against by the provisions of the will, but apparently impervious to the consideration that the vast majority of Irish people at the time, being Catholics, were excluded from the very body in which the judge took his seat.

In *Greene v. Kirkwood*[163] at the end of the 19th century a court took a different view on a condition that gave rise to a forfeiture in the event of a daughter marrying a man "beneath her in life, that is to say, below her in social position". The court upheld the validity of the condition. Distinctions of social rank may still have been widely accepted in 1895, or at least by the judges, but today such a condition would almost certainly fail for lack of certainty. The court cited with approval *Duggan v. Kelly*[164] which upheld a condition not to marry a "Papist," *Perrin v. Lyon*[165], in which it was not to marry a Scotchman,[166] and *Jenner v. Turner*[167], where the condition prohibited marriage to a person who had been a domestic servant.

In *Duggan v. Kelly*[168] the testator left a number of devises and bequests to his wife, sons and daughters among which were sums to his second daughter Anne and his youngest daughter Mary to be paid when they reached 21, provided they married with the consent of the executors of the will. The will also provided in relation to all the children that should any of them "at any time hereafter intermarry with a Papist, or person professing the Roman Catholic religion or Popish religion, or a reputed Papist" the gifts were to be revoked, the child concerned was to receive the sum of one shilling and their share was to be distributed equally among the "survivors," as the testator put it. The question was whether the testator's daughter Mary had forfeited her interest by marrying a Catholic. The Master of the Rolls held the condition against marrying a Catholic to be legal and to extend to the whole life of the legatees, because it specified "at any time". On appeal the validity of the condition was upheld, but the restrictions as to consent and as to not marrying a Catholic were held to apply only during a minority, so that if a child attained 21 she would be paid her legacy and could then marry whom she chose. Richards B felt constrained to this interpretation because if it were otherwise it would be possible for a daughter to marry a Protestant with consent while under age, have chil-

162 (1795) 3 Ridg PC 205.

163 [1895] 1 IR 130.

164 (1847) 10 Ir Eq R 295.

165 (1808) 9 East 170.

166 Against whom there was considerable prejudice in the 18th century due to the Jacobite rebellions.

167 (1879) 16 Ch D 188.

168 (1847) 10 Ir Eq R 295, 473.

dren who were Protestants and then for her husband to die and for her to then marry, after coming of age, a Catholic. This would then cause a forfeiture of her interest which would not then pass by the normal course of devolution to her children, who were Protestants. The judge took the view that such a result could not have been intended by the testator. Similarly-worded clauses must have been quite common and the case had the effect of limiting their scope considerably. Apart from this case it would seem that the only restriction definitely disapproved of by the judges before the adoption of the present Constitution was an attempt to prevent someone marrying a person of a particular profession, particularly the legal profession.[169]

(3) The Constitutional Right to Marry

The old cases contain an inherent notion of a right to marry. Nevertheless, such a right, if it exists, must today be located in the Constitution expressly or impliedly and the old cases will no longer be of authority insofar as they limit the right or permit discrimination against individuals to an extent that would now be found unjustifiable under the Constitution. There is no doubt that the Constitution accords to marriage a particularly important place as an institution. Article 41.3.1 states that "the State pledges itself to guard with special care the institution of Marriage, on which the Family is founded and to protect it against attack". Article 41.3.2, uniquely in Europe, prohibits the legislature from enacting a law providing for the dissolution of marriage. The Constitution does not expressly provide for a right to marry, as opposed to rights flowing from the protection of the institution of marriage itself, but such a right has been established in a line of authority beginning with Kenny J in *Ryan v. Attorney General*[170] who held it to be an unenumerated right stemming from Article 40.3.1. and he repeated this view in *MacAuley v. Minister for Posts and Telegraphs*.[171] This dictum was also cited in *McGee v. Attorney General* by Budd J[172] and by Griffin J in the Supreme Court.[173] In the same case Fitzgerald CJ said:

> "The right to marry and the intimate relations between husband and wife are fundamental rights which have existed in most, if not all, civilised countries for many centuries. These rights were not conferred by the Constitution in this country in 1937. The Constitution goes no further than to guarantee to defend and vindicate and protect those rights from attack".

169 *Keily v. Monck* (1795) 3 Ridg PC 205 per Lord Clare LC at 229.

170 [1965] IR 294, at 313.

171 High Court, [1966] IR 345, at 357.

172 [1974] IR 284 at p.322.

173 [1974] IR 284, at 333:

> " Mr Justice Kenny instanced the right to bodily integrity and the right to marry. It seems to me that the right of married persons to establish a home and bring up children is inherent in the right to marry."

The implication behind the Chief Justice's statement is that the fact that the right to marry is not expressly stated in the Constitution does not detract from its existence, but on the contrary it was taken to be so fundamental as not to require statement at all.[174] In addition to domestic law the European Convention on Human Rights by Article 12 expressly binds the high contracting parties to respect the right to marry.[175] It is clear, then, that the right to marry exists and, given the indications that the courts regard it as in the nature of a natural right, is worthy of extensive protection.

In view of this constitutional basis of the right to marry in the Republic that any attempt whatever to influence the choice of a marriage partner infringes the constitutional right. It might either be that all such purported restrictions are void, or the courts might adopt a distinction between state action and private action, so that such a restriction would merely be unenforceable. In the case of a determinable interest, if the determining event were held void as encroaching on the right to marry, the donee would receive nothing at all, and the latter course, that of holding the forfeiture merely unenforceable might avoid this result.

Unfortunately, the first case that might have taken the opportunity to review this area of the law after 1937 did not really approach the problem from the perspective of human rights derived from the Constitution. In *Re McKenna*[176] a testator who had left a fund to trustees to apply the income of the fund to his daughter until she became 21 or married before that time, and afterwards to her for life, provided that if she should marry a Roman Catholic she should forfeit the interest and the property should go instead to her issue. Gavan Duffy P declined to hold that the test was void for uncertainty, which was the main issue argued in the case. He cited Lord Parker in *Re Sandbrook*[177] to the effect that "conditions subsequent, in order to defeat vested estates, or

174 Kenny J's statement has also been cited with approval, or without dissent, by Costello J in *Murray v. Attorney General*, [1985] IR 532, [1985] ILRM 542; by McCarthy J in *Norris v. Attorney General*, Supreme Court [1984] IR 36, at p.97; Barrington J in *RSJ v. JSJ* [1982] ILRM 263 at 264; by Finlay P in *State (KM and RD) v. Minister for Foreign Affairs* [1979] IR 73 at p.80. and by the same judge in *State* (C) *v. Frawley* [1976] IR 365 at p.374. The High Court, in *Somjee v. Minister for Justice and Attorney General* [1981] ILRM 324 assumed such a right to exist.

175 Article 12 reads: "Men and women of marriageable age have the right to marry and found a family, according to the national laws governing the exercise of this right"; and see *Johnston v. Ireland* (1987) 9 EHRR 203 European Court of Human Rights, (non-availability of divorce not a violation of the right to marry); *Reed v. United Kingdom* (1987) 9 EHRR 56 European Court of Human Rights, (right to marry does not extend to transsexuals); *Springer v. United Kingdom* (1983) 5 EHRR 141. European Commission of Human Rights. *Hamer v. United Kingdom* (1982) 4 EHRR 139 European Commission of Human Rights. (extends to prisoners in jail.)

176 [1947] IR 277.

177 [1912] 2 Ch 474 at 477.

cause a forfeiture, must be such that from the moment of their creation the court can say with reasonable certainty in what events the forfeiture will occur". The test in the case before him was only as to whether an individual was a Catholic or not and he was of the view that it did not involve any theological test, but was a matter of applying the words as understood by ordinary people, and cited Lord Greene, MR in *Re Samuel*[178] to the effect that the words must describe the intention with sufficient distinctness to enable practical action to be based upon them, that if that test was met, then the difficulty of proving by evidence that a person was or was not an adherent of the relevant faith did not in itself mean that the test was too vague, and that the best evidence of whether a person was of a particular faith was their own testimony in court. The latter test is significant in one respect, in that it indicates that the courts, although they may not have articulated it in that way, have produced a test which adopts a principle that the individuals freedom to choose a religion is to be respected and have rejected the notion that a person could be found to be a Catholic or Protestant if they themselves deny the epithet. Where the test itself involves the assessment of the degree of adherence to a faith, however, it may fail for uncertainty. In the later case of *Re Burke's Estate*[179] Gavan Duffy himself held a condition void for uncertainty in that it purported to give rise to a forfeiture if the recipient of the property ceased to practice the Roman Catholic religion.[180]

h) Ethnic or Sectarian Restrictions

Some forfeiture clauses which may at first sight appear to fall into one or other or both of the previous categories may, when analysed, involved a form of discrimination which goes beyond an attempt to impose a particular form of ideology on another person. Such was the condition in *Re Knox*,[181] a case decided before the present Constitution was in force. The condition was that if the testator's son should marry he should

> ". . . marry a Protestant wife, the daughter of Protestant parents, and who have always been Protestants."

The issue of uncertainty was not argued before the court. The judgment of the Irish Court of Appeal was delivered by Naish J who said:

> "Conditions of this kind, requiring a legatee or devisee to marry persons of a particular religious denomination, and forfeiting their interest if they did not, have been repeatedly held valid, and it is now too late to question their validity".[182]

178 [1942] Ch 1 at p.13.

179 [1951] IR 216, (1950) 84 ILTR 70 High Court. See also *Re Waring's Will Trusts* [1985] NI 105 at 111E per Hutton J.

180 See below the text accompanying footnote 197.

181 (1889) 23 LR Ir 542.

182 *ibid.* at 544.

The problem with this judgment is that the clause did not in fact require a person to marry a person of a particular religious denomination. It went beyond that to require that his or her parents should also have been of that religious denomination and even that they should have been so from birth. This involves a fundamentally different form of test. The test is not concerned with the beliefs or faith of the intended spouse at all but with factors which can only be described as sectarian in character. The court in *Knox* failed to perceive this distinction and this failure means that the reason given by the court does not in logic support the conclusion, *i.e.* even if it were the case that clauses requiring a devisee to marry "persons of a particular denomination" were still valid, it would not follow that a clause in the form before the court in *Knox* would be valid. The intended spouse in this example cannot satisfy the test by changing their religion or by any other means, even supposing that to be a tolerable imposition on a person. It is the same as if someone had given property to another subject to being forfeited if they marry a black person or someone selected on some other racial criterion.

A similar issue would arise if a grant of land was made subject to a proviso that it should not be sold to or occupied by persons belonging to a particular ethnic group. These issues bring into play the guarantee of equality before the law contained in Article 40.1.[183] The main authority on the issue is the statement of Walsh J in *Quinn's Supermarket Ltd. v. Attorney General*[184] where, in a judgment approved of by Ó Dálaigh CJ, Budd, FitzGerald and Kenny JJ, he said

> ". . . this provision is not a guarantee of absolute equality for all citizens in all circumstances but it is a guarantee of equality as human persons and (as the Irish text of the Constitution makes quite clear) is a guarantee related to their dignity as human beings and a guarantee against any inequalities grounded upon an assumption, or indeed a belief, that some individual or individuals or classes of individuals, by reason of their human attributes or their ethnic or racial, social or religious background, are to be treated as the inferior or superior of other individuals in the community. This list does not pretend to be complete; but it is merely intended to illustrate the view that this guarantee refers to human persons for what they are in themselves rather than to any lawful activities, trades or pursuits which they may engage in or follow".

This dictum has been applied in a number of subsequent decisions.[185] But they have all been concerned with challenges to legislation or to subsidiary legisla-

183 Article 40.1 reads:

> "All citizens shall, as human persons, be held equal before the law. This shall not be held to mean that the State shall not in its enactments have due regard to differences of capacity, physical and moral, and of social function".

184 1972] IR 1 at 11, Supreme Court.

185 *Madigan v. Attorney General* [1986] ILRM 136, Supreme Court; *McHugh v. Commissioner of the Garda Siochana* [1985] ILRM 606, High Court; *Tormey v. Attorney General and Ireland* [1984] ILRM 657, High Court; *Brennan v. Attorney General* [1984] ILRM 355, Supreme Court.

tion.[186] Would it be true to say that Article 40.1 is confined only to State action, and if so what form of state action? On the one hand, since it is a guarantee of equality before the law and law is enforced only by state action, the qualification is in a sense self-evident. The real issue is as to what is meant by state action.

In the United States the Fourteenth Amendment to the Constitution, which guarantees equal treatment before the law, is confined expressly to "state action," which refers to actions by the individual states which make up the Union. Even so, such action has been held to include judicial action as well as legislative measures, so that the courts of a state were held, in *Barrows v. Jackson*[187] to be precluded from enforcing racially discriminatory covenants at law and, in *Shelley v. Kraemer*[188], in equity. The covenant in *Barrows* purported to restrict the occupation of premises by black persons. There was no question of a restriction on sale to black persons as it had long been the law in California[189] that such restrictions were void as repugnant to the fee simple estate. In *Shelley* the court took the view that private agreements which discriminated on racial grounds were not in themselves illegal, but that if the court were to enforce them the discrimination would cease to be a private choice and would become a choice of the court. To do so would be to make available the full coercive power of the state to deny blacks, on grounds of colour, the enjoyment of premises which they were willing and financially able to acquire. Thus *Shelley* rejected the so-called neutral principles approach to constitutional interpretation

186 In *East Donegal Cooperative v. Attorney General* [1970] IR 317; 104 ILTR 81 the Supreme Court per Walsh J. considered the question in relation to subordinate legislation made under the Livestock Marts Act, 1967 which purported to enable the minister to grant exemptions from the provisions of the act in certain cases. The Court said:

> "The constitutional right of the Oireachtas in its legislation to take account of difference of social function and difference of capacity, physical and moral, does not extend to delegating that power to members of the executive, to the exclusion of the Oireachtas, in order to decide as between individuals... which of them shall be exempted from the application of the Act..."

Kelly, *The Irish Constitution* (2nd ed.) p.448 says that this means that the court was confining the whole section to primary legislation and criticises this interpretation. However, the second sentence of Art. 40.1 is a qualification on what precedes it and the court seems to have been indicating that the minister was not therefore empowered to make distinctions based on differences of capacity. This can surely only mean that the minister was bound by the first part of Art. 40.1, namely by the guarantee of equality. If he was not, then there was nothing to prevent him making such distinctions. Nevertheless, this would seem to be a some what unrealistic distinction.

187 (1953) 346 US 249; 97 L Ed 1586; 73 S Ct 1031.

188 (1948) 334 US 1; 92 L Ed 1161; 68 S Ct 836; 3 ALR 2d 441.

189 *Wayt v. Patee* (1928) 205 Cal 46, 269 P 660; *Title Guarantee & Trust Co. v. Garrott* 42 Cal App 152, 183 P 470.

promoted by conservatives in the United States[190] under which the enforcement by the courts of private agreements, regardless of their content, whether it be racist, sectarian or otherwise, and regardless of the effect on the human rights of third parties, is seen as neutral. Both *Barrows* and *Shelley* concerned restrictive covenants rather than conditional or determinable interests.

However, two later cases came before the Supreme Court which did concern such interests and both arose out of the same will. Senator Bacon of Georgia left land in his will to the city of Macon, Georgia, to be used for a park for white persons only. The city operated it for some time as a segregated park but later opened it for use by all citizens. The managers of the park sought to have the city removed as trustee, since it, as a public body, could not legally operate a segregated park. The managers claimed that if the title were to be vested in them, they could then operate it as a segregated park. The Supreme Court held in *Evans v. Newton*[191] that the public character of the park rendered it subject to the Fourteenth Amendment whoever held the title. The trustees of the Bacon estate then applied for a declaration that, the trust having been held to be unenforceable, the land should revert to the testator's heirs. The majority in the Supreme Court[192] upheld this view, with dissenting judgments by Douglas and Brennan JJ. The majority took the view that the Georgia Supreme Court was empowered to construe the will only so as to give effect to the testator's intent and that the trust having been held unenforceable, the only jurisdiction under the Georgia cy près statutes to vary the terms of the trust was to conform as closely to this intent as possible. In doing so they were entitled to take the view, which they had, that the wish to segregate on racial grounds was an inseparable part of the testator's intent, holding that the land reverted to the heirs. Douglas J, dissenting, expressed the view, *inter alia,* that, as there was no express provision for reverter to the heirs, the construction adopted by the Georgia Supreme Court did as much violence to the testator's intent as returning the land to the heirs. He also pointed out that the testator had left "all remainders and reversions" arising under his will to the city. The question of perpetuity was not entered into, but Douglas J took the point that such a provision, effective or not, was a valid guide to the testator's intent. The majority did not accept that their ruling involved the courts lending their power to enforce an unconstitutional discrimination, apparently on the ground that it had not been proved that the Georgia judges had been motivated by racial prejudice in coming to their decision. This indicates that the majority were adopting the neutral principles[193] approach and also shows up the weak point in that theory. Once it is conceded

190 See Bork, *The Tempting of America* pp. 78, 147-48, on *Shelley:* p.151 and Bork, *Neutral Principles and Some First Amendment Problems* (1971) 47 Ind LJ 1. See also Chapter 8 Fee tail: Constitutionality.

191 382 US 296, 15 L Ed 2d 373.

192 *Evans v. Abney* (1970) 396 US 435, 90 S Ct 628, 1970 US Lexis 3133, 24 L Ed.

193 See footnote 190.

that a private choice ceases to be simply a matter of private choice once the state lends its power to the transaction by enforcing it by law, the neutral principles thesis collapses. Again, once that point is conceded, then it is irrelevant what the motives of the judges were. The question is as to whether the law can then be said to be acting consistently with the commitment to equality and to be vindicating the rights of all citizens, not merely those confined within the bounds of a property transaction.

In Ireland, O'Hanlon J's decision in *Re Dunne*[194] rejected the basis of the neutral principles approach in that it recognised that social consequences could result from a restriction entered into between individuals. O'Hanlon J indeed went further than the United States cases in declaring such a restriction to be illegal in itself, not merely unenforceable.

i) Religious Restrictions

Restrictions on the freedom of religion may occur independently of marriage. Such tests may sometimes be held void for uncertainty. Since a definite interest in property is to pass to someone or to remain vested in the present owner on the happening of an event, or the presence or absence of some quality, the courts will refuse to uphold the validity of such a test if it cannot definitely be stated when the event has occurred or when the quality is present or absent. On the other hand, one suspects that the test of certainty has been used, particularly in jurisdictions without a constitutional bill of rights, to dispose of cases in which the substantive issue is one of discrimination on religious or racial grounds.

The Northern Court of Appeal in *McCausland v. Young*[195] held that the term Roman Catholic was not void for uncertainty,[196] but Gavan Duffy P in *Re Burke's Estate*[197] held that the phrase "cease to practice the Roman Catholic religion" was void on this ground. The law itself is to some degree uncertain here, for the extent to which a person practices or does not practice a religion would seem to have some bearing on whether they can be described, or would describe themselves, as adhering to it. Furthermore, religion and national or cultural identity are not always distinct attributes, so that a person who does not practice the Jewish religion may nevertheless still regard themselves as being Jews in the sense of a national identity.

Courts in the Republic have not yet had to decide whether an interest given to a person on condition that it is to be forfeited if they themselves become a Catholic (or a Protestant or a Jew, *etc.*) is void as discriminating on religious

---

194 [1988] IR 155. See above The Right to Alienate.

195 [1949] NI 49, consisting of only two judges.

196 And see *Blathwayt v. Cawley (Lord)* (1976) [1976] A.C. 397; [1975] 3 All ER 625; [1975] 3 WLR 684, HL.

197 [1951] IR 216, (1950) 84 ILTR 70 High Court.

grounds.[198] The court in the first case after the 1937 Constitution did examine the question of constitutional rights, but only on the issue of the freedom of parents to educate their children. In *Re Burke's Estate*[199] a testator by her will left the residue of her property upon trust after conversion and re-investment to pay and use the income for the purpose of maintaining, educating in Ireland and bringing up as a Roman Catholic one, GQ, an infant, and directed (a) that the selection of a Roman Catholic school to be attended by GQ should be in the absolute discretion of the trustees and (b) that upon GQ leaving school and taking up a position the income should be paid to him until he attained the age of twenty-five years and that thereafter the residue should be paid to him absolutely. The testator further provided that if at any time GQ should leave Ireland without the consent of the trustees for any period exceeding six months or should cease to practise the Roman Catholic religion he should forfeit all benefit under the will. GQ had lived in England for about three years prior to the death of the testator and had since continued to live in that country. Gavan Duffy P held that the direction in the will that the selection of a school should be in the absolute discretion of the trustees was inoperative and must be ignored since it tended to override the parental authority and right and duty of education declared by Article 42 of the Constitution. He further held that, GQ having lived outside Ireland since before the testator's death, the condition against GQ leaving Ireland without the consent of the trustees for any period exceeding six months could not be applied and was void and unenforceable. On the religious test he held that the provision for forfeiture if GQ should cease to practice the Roman Catholic religion was void for uncertainty. Immediately on the death of the testator GQ took a vested interest and on attaining 21 years of age GQ would be entitled to have transferred to him the funds representing the residuary estate.

The same issue arose in the case of *Re Blake*.[200] A legacy was given to trustees to apply the income to maintain the children of the grantor's daughter "provided they should be brought up in the Roman Catholic faith." Dixon J. in the High Court held that the condition was unconstitutional as it infringed the right of a parent to provide for the education of their children.

198 In *Re Vaughan* [1925] IR 67 a testator who died in 1923 devised and bequeathed all his freehold and leasehold estate to trustees in trust for his wife for life and after her death for such persons as she should by deed or will appoint. By a codicil he provided that in the case that any person who might come into possession of the property should "profess to be, or become a Roman Catholic, or marry a Roman Catholic" the bequest to him or her was to be "absolutely void." It was held that the gift in the will of a life estate followed by a general power of appointment gave the wife an absolute interest which had already vested before the codicil and therefore the attempt to impose a condition subsequent in the codicil was ineffective. The decision did not deal with the issue of public policy or human rights.

199 [1951] IR 216, (1950) 84 ILTR 70 High Court.

200 [1955] IR 89.

In *McCausland v. Young*[201] a deed of resettlement, executed by father and son, conferred a life estate on a father and a life estate on his son with further remainders to his son's children. The deed provided that if a tenant for life or a person entitled in remainder became, or professed to be, a Roman Catholic then the interest was to be forfeited. The Court of Appeal for Northern Ireland consisting unfortunately, as it turned out, of only two judges, held: (1) that the term Roman Catholic was not void for uncertainty: (2) that where the choice of religion may involve a forfeiture the court will not hold the beneficiary to have made a binding choice until he or she is of age, so such a condition did not interfere with the parent's right to determine the religious education of the child: (3) that the forfeiture clause was not brought to the attention of the son who executed the deed in ignorance of in and without professional advice. Since the father was in a fiduciary relationship to the son and the clause was of such an unusual and drastic character the court held the son entitled to a right to rectify the deed for undue influence, and (4) that if the son had by a series of unequivocal acts shown a determination to abandon his claim, he would lose his right to rectify. The judges disagreed as to whether he had done so. Since there were only two judges this meant that the High Court decision stood and it was that the son had abandoned his right. The appeal was a waste of time and money.

More recently the English House of Lords in *Blathwayt v. Cawley (Lord)*[202] held there was no public policy prohibiting religious discrimination by a testator in framing the provisions of a will. In that case a testator had made a gift by will to a person on the condition that the property was to forfeited if the donee of the gift became a Roman Catholic.[203] Lord Wilberforce, while conceding that conditions which discriminated on religious grounds "are, or at least are becoming, inconsistent with standards now widely accepted," did not feel able to introduce a rule against them, both on the narrow ground that the particular will before him had been before the courts on previous occasions and had not been impugned on that ground, but also because such a rule would interfere with testamentary freedom, which he therefore impliedly treated as having a superior value.[204]

Lord Cross recognised that

> ". . . it is true that it is widely thought nowadays that it is wrong for a government to treat some of its citizens less favourably than others because of differences in their religious beliefs" but went on to say that "it does not follow from that that it is against public policy for an adherent of one religion to distinguish in disposing of his property between adherents of his faith and those of another". If it were, he thought that it would amount to saying that, although it is in order for a a person to have a mild preference for one religion as opposed to

201 [1949] NI 49.

202 [1976] AC 397; [1975] 3 All ER 625; [1975] 3 WLR 684.

203 *ibid.* [1976] AC 397.

204 [1976] AC 397 at p.426.

> another, it would be "disreputable for him to be convinced of the importance of holding true religious beliefs and of the fact that his religious beliefs are the true ones".

It is submitted, however, that the issue was not one of the strength or weakness of the testator's adherence to his or her own religious beliefs. A court could, with consistency, uphold the right of a person to his or her strongly-held beliefs and yet at the same time deny that a person is justified in using their property as a means of inducing another person to give up his or her faith, or to gain a convert to the property owner's preferred religion. Had either of these two cases occurred in the Republic the court would have been bound to consider the issue as a conflict between competing freedoms: the freedom of the property owner to make such dispositions as he or she may choose, and the freedom of the donee to practice his or her religion free of interference. It is submitted that it does not involve a conflict between the freedom of religion of both parties, because the freedom of the donor to practice his or her religion would be unaffected even if they were restrained from imposing such conditions in gifts of property. Moreover, it can be cogently argued that a condition which attempts to induce the donee to put his or her own financial interest before moral or religious belief is in itself an invasion of the donee's freedom of religious belief and should be held void for that reason.

Given that religious freedom is a right worthy of protection, it is justifiable for the courts, while not favouring one version of religious ideology as against another, to define the boundaries of religious freedom between citizens by laying down a negative test of integrity in relation to such decisions, that it to say, that the court will not lend its power to enforce conditions which would have the effect of introducing ulterior and non-religious considerations into what is properly a matter of religious conviction.

CHAPTER 7

FEE FARM GRANTS

"How now! A kiss in fee farm!"

– Shakespeare, *Troilus and Cressida* Act III Scene 2.

A. Introduction

A fee farm grant is a fee simple held subject to the payment of a rent by the grantee and his or her successors in title to the grantor and his or her successors in title.[1] Fee farm grants are a peculiar feature of the Irish law of real property.[2] There are three major types in Ireland:

1) Feudal Tenure
2) Leasehold tenure (hybrid)
   a) Conversion Grants:
      i) from Bishop's Leases
      ii) from College Leases
      iii) under Renewable Leasehold Conversion Act, 1849
      iv) under Landlord and Tenant Act, 1980 section 7
   b) Deasy's Act Grants
3) No tenure at all – rentcharge fee farm grants

B. Feudal Tenure

a) Origins

Before *Quia Emptores,* 1290 a private person who had a fee simple could make a grant by subinfeudation in fee simple and if it was at an economic rent it was called a fee farm grant. After 1290 only the Crown could make such a grant, because *Quia Emptores* did not bind the Crown. This type of fee farm grant is more common in Northern Ireland than in the Republic having been frequently created in the Ulster Plantation Settlement. Land was granted by the Crown to a grantee in fee simple often in return for a chief rent, or quit rent as it is known

1 *Browning v. Beston* (1553) Plowd 131 at 132a, 75 ER 202.

2 In some parts of England rentcharges are commonly reserved on a grant in fee simple, which is one kind of fee farm rent, and the only kind in England: Megarry & Wade, *Real Property* pp. 138, 800.

in Ireland. After 1662 the Crown could still create fee farm grants provided the tenure was free and common socage.

What was more questionable was that some grants by the Crown in Ireland contained a licence giving the grantees themselves the power to subinfeudate further "*non obstante Quia Emptores*", *i.e.* notwithstanding *Quia Emptores*, 1290. These grants seem to have been part of the plantation policy of creating a landowning class dependent on the Crown, and they occurred in the South[3] as well as the North. Since *Quia Emptores* expressly prohibited subinfeudation in fee simple by private persons, the *non obstante* clause was an exercise of the dispensing power, *i.e.* the prerogative power exercised by the medieval kings to exempt individuals from the operation of statutes.[4] By the 16th and 17th centuries it came to be seen as inconsistent with emerging democratic constitutional principles. In England James II asserted the dispensing power, possibly as a means of exempting Catholics from the penal laws, and this, as well as the fact that the power had come to be seen as inconsistent with the supremacy of parliament, contributed to his being deposed in 1688.[5] The power itself was declared illegal in England by the Bill of Rights of 1689. In Ireland, however, no Bill of Rights was enacted[6] and it was therefore arguable that the dispensing power still existed here even after 1688. At any rate, James's Stuart predecessors had purported to exercise the power in Ireland in the preceding decades and a compliant Irish Parliament had confirmed the grants.[7] Some feudal fee-farm grants survive today, although they are few in number. The validity of such titles was recognised in the 19th century.[8]

The following diagram shows the situation that obtained after such a grant and further subinfeudation by the grantee:

3 Cal St Pap Ir, 1633–47, p.4, 12 March 1633 (Brittas); Cal St Pap IR, 1663–65, vol. 2, p.353, 17 January 1664 (manor of Roscommon); Cal St Pap IR, 1663–65, vol. 2, p.438, 28 September 1664 (manor of Mount Kennedy, Wicklow, in 'free and common socage' with power to alienate 'in fee or for lives *non obstante* the statute *Quia Emptores*').

4 See above, licences in mortmain, *i.e.* exemptions granted by the king from the Statute of Mortmain.

5 See Kelly, *Western Legal Theory* p.220.

6 W.N. Osborough, 'The Failure to Enact an Irish Bill of Rights: A Gap in Irish Constitutional History' (1998) 33 *Irish Jurist* 392-416.

7 Settlement of Ireland Acts, 1634 (10 Chas I c.3; 10 Chas I sess 3 cc. 2, 3); 1639 (15 Chas I sess 2 c.6), 1665 (17 & 18 Chas II c.2); 1695 (7 Wm III c.3). The 1634 statute 10 Chas I sess 3 c.2 s.1 includes among defects: '…lack or omission of sufficient and special *non obstantes* of particular statutes', not conceding any doubt as to the *non obstante* clauses themselves. *Non obstante* grants continued to be made after 1634: see footnote 3. The Settlement of Ireland Acts were repealed in the Republic by the Statute Law Revision (Pre-Union Irish Statutes) Act, 1962.

8 *Verschoyle v. Perkins* (1847) 13 Ir Eq R 72; *Delacherois v. Delacherois* (1864) 11 HLC 62, 11 ER 1254.

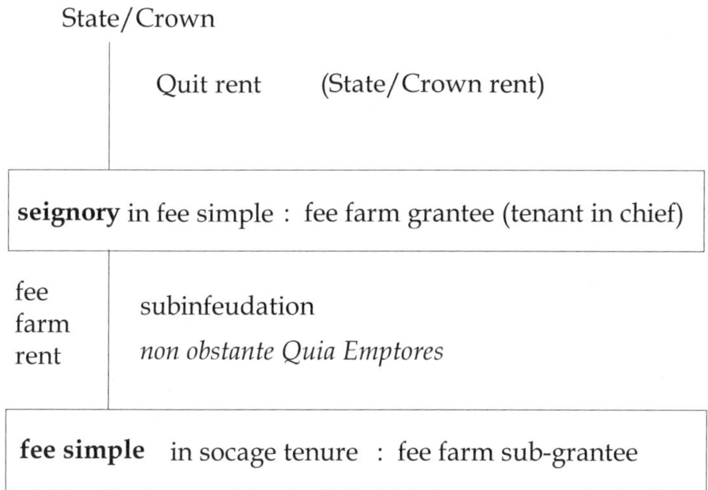

Hence there are two types of feudal fee farm grant: (a) the original grant from the Crown to the grantee in fee simple at a quit rent, and (b) the subinfeudation by the grantee in exercise of the *non obstante* power, which is a sub-grant in fee simple reserving a rent payable to the grantee by the sub-grantee.

The interest of the grantor is not a reversion. There can be no reversion on a fee simple.[9] The grantor has a seignory in fee simple. Freehold tenure exists between him or her and the grantee and the service of the tenure is a rent. The grantor has as one of the rights under the tenure a right of distress for rent at common law. Previously he also had the incident of escheat. Since the Wills (Ireland) Act, 1634 that incident could be defeated by a will made by the tenant. The Succession Act, 1965 section 11 abolished escheat to the State and to a mesne lord for want of heirs. Therefore, if the heirs of the sub-grantee die out the estate will pass to the State as ultimate intestate successor. The State would then become liable to pay the fee farm rent to the grantee, *i.e.* the tenant in chief. In the Republic this would create an odd situation: the tenant in chief would hold of the State and the State in turn would be in the position of the sub-grantee holding from the tenant in chief. The State Property Act, 1954[10] provides that in such a case the Minister for Finance may disclaim the interest and vest it in the grantor or his or her successors. It also provides that the rent shall thereupon cease. Since in the case of feudal fee farm grants the grantor is the tenant in chief these provisions would appear to result in the destruction of the sub-grant. However, the tenant in chief could challenge the destruction of

9 *ibid.*

10 Section 32.

the rent on constitutional grounds and claim still to be entitled to the rent from the State.

Even where the grantor holds by such a title the courts have leaned against construing the grant as a subinfeudation where another interpretation is possible. *Delacherois v. Delacherois*[11] concerned a grant by Charles I of estates in free and common socage with a licence to grant in fee simple notwithstanding *Quia Emptores*. In 1721 the holders of the grant granted a part of the estate in fee simple subject to a rent and reserved an express power of distress. A successor to the holder of the original grant made a will devising the entire estate. The gift was only valid if the grantor had retained some interest having made the grant in fee simple. It was held:

(a) That the grant of a part of the estates, if it were to be take effect by subinfeudation, would have to show an express intention to do so.

(b) The reservation of an express power of distress ousted the intention to subinfeudate and the grant was an outright sale of the part of the estates, reserving only a rentcharge.

(c) Hence, at the time of the will the successor of the holder of the whole estate had no interest left in the part granted and so no right in such land passed under the will.

b) Characteristics

(1) Words of Limitation

Words of limitation would have to be used unless one of the old forms of conveyance are used. The fee farm rent is a rent service, carrying with it a common law right of distress. Early English and Irish statutes may apply to the power. One Irish statute that does so expressly is the Fee Farm Rents (Ireland) Act, 1851.[12]

(2) Forfeiture

Under the principle of feudal tenure a denial by the tenant of the lord's title forfeits the tenant's interest. There will be forfeiture for non-payment of rent either if the agreement to pay rent is a condition of the grant or if there is an express clause for forfeiture. The grantee has a right of relief against forfeiture in equity.

(3) Covenants

As to covenants in the grant, the law as to their enforcement is obscure, since it depends on the extent to which covenants run in feudal freehold tenure. In the-

11 (1864) 11 HLC 62, 11 ER 1254.

12 It provides that a person entitled to the rent has all the remedies provided for by the Renewable Leasehold Conversion Act, 1849 except ejectment.

ory it would seem that all covenants which are not purely personal will run at law both as to the benefit and burden, *i.e.* both parties as between whom tenure exists can both sue and be sued on the covenant.

(4) Redemption

The fee farm rents may be redeemed by various statutes.

The Chief Rents Redemption (Ireland) Act, 1864 seems clearly to apply, but redemption may be by agreement only.

There is a controversy as to whether the Redemption of Rent (Ireland) Act, 1891 applies to a feudal fee farm grant. The Act only applies to agricultural land and most fee farm grants over such land would not have survived the land purchase schemes which provided themselves for redemption, and so the issue is probably of little importance.

As to the Landlord and Tenant (Ground Rents)(No. 2) Act, 1978, lease under the Act includes a fee farm grant. If the grant complies with the conditions in the Act in sections 9 and 10, which restrict the operation of the Act to occupational, building and proprietary leases, then it would seem that the holder of an existing fee farm grant has the right to a fee simple under the Act. It could be argued against this that the holder already has a fee simple under the fee farm grant, but on the other hand the legislation is intended to recognise the holder of an interest coming within the conditions in the two sections as the substantial owner of the premises and therefore to allow him or her to acquire a fee simple free of rent. Since, however, the 1967 Act, which the No. 2 Act of 1978 modifies, defines fee simple as not including the interest of a person holding under a fee farm grant, the grantee can only exercise the power if they are willing to redeem any other rents affecting the fee simple, *i.e.* where superior fee farm interests exist, by earlier subinfeudations, the fee farm grantee in demesne will have to redeem those also in order to acquire the fee simple under the Act.

C. Leasehold Tenure

Another kind of fee farm grant occurs when the grant of a fee simple estate also creates the modern relationship of landlord and tenant. Such has been held to occur in Ireland under various statutes.

1. Conversion Grants

a) Origins

All these arise from the statutory conversion of leases. There are four types:

(1) Church Temporalities Act, 1833

These arise by conversion of Bishop's Leases. Irish statutes limited the power of bishops to grant leases of land belonging to the Church of Ireland. Bishops thereafter took to granting leases with a covenant to renew subject to payment of a fine.[13] Hence, they were virtually perpetual interests. This Act gave the tenants power to buy the fee simple subject to the fee farm rent. The Irish Church Act, 1869, which disestablished the Church of Ireland, prohibited any more conversion grants after 1 January 1873. This is therefore a closed category. They must have been created between 1833 and 1874. Most would have been redeemed under the Land Purchase Acts and the Redemption of Rent (Ireland) Act, 1891.

(2) Trinity College Dublin Leasing & Perpetuity Act, 1851

These are converted College Leases. Various statutes limited the power of Trinity College Dublin to grant leases. The College avoided these provisions by granting renewable leases that were virtually perpetual interests. Section 3 of the Act allowed tenants to demand a grant of a fee simple at a rent, providing the tenant applied within four years of the passing of the Act. This is therefore another category of fee farm grants which is closed.

(3) Renewable Leasehold Conversion Act, 1849

This statute and the Renewable Leasehold Conversion (Ireland) Act, 1868 are, together, the main source of conversion fee farm grants.

In the 18th and 19th centuries landowners granted leases for lives[14], *i.e.* estates *pur autre vie,* at a rent with covenants for renewal of the lives upon payment of a sum of money called a fine. Again, these were virtually perpetual interests especially as the courts in Ireland recognised that the tenant had an equity to renew, called the old equity of the country, even after all the lives had died.[15] The right was confirmed by the Tenantry Act, 1779 section 1. As to such leases existing on 1 August 1849 the Renewable Leasehold Conversion Act, 1849 gave lessees the right to a fee farm grant[16] from the lessor. The rent was to be recoverable by leasehold remedies including ejectment.[17] Where the power was exercised, it has been assumed that the effect of the Act was to convert the pre-existing freehold tenure into leasehold tenure. Although the tenure

---

13 *e.g. Haig v. Homan* (1841) 8 Cl & F, 8 ER 319; *Lanauze v. Malone* (1855) 3 Ir Ch. R 354.

14 See Chapter 9 Life Estates.

15 *ibid.*.

16 Provided the lessor had a fee simple himself. If the lessor had only a life estate, a grant in fee farm did not bind the remaindermen or reversioners: *Brereton v. Twohey* (1859) 8 Ir CLR 190.

17 Section 20.

of leases for lives had always been freehold, since they were estates *pur autre vie*, the judges in Ireland had nevertheless treated the tenure in such cases, *i.e.* as to the running of covenants, *etc.*, as identical to leasehold tenure.[18] The tenure was leasehold in all but name, and it is assumed that the Act made it leasehold by name.

Section 37 provides that leases for lives made after 1 August 1849 operate automatically as fee farm grants under the provisions of the Act.[19]

The Act also applies to leases for years with a covenant for renewal.[20]

(4) Landlord and Tenant (Amendment) Act, 1980 section 74.

Leases granted prior to 1 August 1849 and not converted under the power contained in the 1849 Act and still subsisting in 1980 were converted into a fee simple by this section. The fee simple is to be a graft on the previous interest. The rights and equities affecting the lease for lives continue to affect the fee simple. The section therefore seems to have created a new category of fee farm grants. Wylie[21] argues that the rent no longer applies because the definition of fee simple incorporated in the Act excludes a fee farm rent. However, what follows the words fee simple, *i.e.* the graft provision, appear to oust that interpretation. It would also be anomalous if a person were to be in a better position as a result of not exercising the power under the 1849 Act than they would be if it had been exercised. Also, abolition of the rent without compensation is open to constitutional challenge and an interpretation that is constitutional is to be preferred to one that is not.[22]

It is open to question whether the effect of section 74 was to convert the freehold tenure which applied to such leases into leasehold tenure. As we have noted above, the judges in Ireland treated the tenure in leases for lives as leasehold in all but name, but it could be argued that the tenure has not been converted to leasehold and that Deasy's Act, for example, does not apply. The provisions of the Renewable Leasehold Conversion Act, 1849 would not seem to apply to such grants since they are not converted by the Act. These points should be borne in mind in considering the following characteristics.

18 See Chapter 9 Life Estates:Leases for lives renewable forever.

19 See *Gun-Cunningham v. Byrne* (1892) 30 LR Ir 384, Land Commission.

20 *Re Gore* (1859) 8 Ir Ch R 589.

21 Wylie, *Irish Land Law* para. 4.081.

22 It was the intention of the government in introducing the bill to preserve the rent: see *Dáil Debates,* 26 February 1980 col. 514.

b) Characteristics

(1) Words of Limitation

Re Johnston's Estate[23] held that in the case of a purported grant of a lease for lives after 1 August 1849, the fee farm grant was created under the statute and no words of limitation were required to create the fee simple. On the face of it, the deed creates a lease for lives, but because of the Act, takes effect as a fee farm grant.

(2) Rent

Sections 20 and 21 of the Renewable Leasehold Conversion Act, 1849 provide that the rent is recoverable by the same remedies as for a leasehold rent and in addition include a special statutory remedy of ejectment for non-payment. As will be seen from the next section, it is arguable that this remedy is no longer available where the fee farm grant constitutes a ground rent within the ground rent legislation. The sections do not apply to a conversion grant under section 74 of the 1980 Act.

(3) Forfeiture

The statutory remedy of ejectment made express clauses for forfeiture unnecessary. It is arguable that this remedy is no longer available as to grants in respect of dwelling houses where the fee farm grant comes within the definition of a ground rent under the Landlord and Tenant (Ground Rents)(No. 2) Act, 1978, so that the tenant has the right to acquire the unincumbered fee simple. The argument is as follows. Section 52 of Deasy's Act provides for a statutory remedy of ejectment for non-payment of rent in the case of Deasy's Act grants (and other landlord and tenant relationships). Section 27 of the No. 2 Act of 1978 provides that section 52 shall not apply where a person has a right to acquire the fee simple in a dwellinghouse within the Act. The reason for section 27 is clear: it would be inappropriate to give such a radical remedy to the person entitled to the rent where the tenant is in a position to acquire the fee simple free of the rent. The Act does not specifically take account of the similar situation of conversion fee farm grants where the owner of the rent has a similar remedy under sections 20 and 21 of the 1849 Act, but it would be equally inappropriate for such a remedy to be given where the fee farm grantee has the right to acquire the fee simple in a dwelling house free of the rent.

Section 14 of the Conveyancing Act, 1881,[24] governing forfeiture covenants, does not apply to covenants to pay rent.

---

23 [1911] 1 IR 215.

24 As amended by s.2 and s.5 of the Conveyancing Act, 1892.

(4) *Covenants*

What effect do covenants in the original lease have after the conversion of the estate into a fee simple? A particular problem here are covenants that purport to restrict the alienation by the tenant, either by sale, assignment, or subletting. These are not uncommon in a lease, but in the case of a fee simple they have been held inconsistent with the statute *Quia Emptores*, 1290 and the policy of the law of which it was an early expression, that a fee simple be a freely marketable commodity.[25]

In *Re McNaul's Estate*[26] a covenant in the original lease for lives provided that the tenant was to pay an increased rent if he alienated without the lessor's consent to someone other than the child or grandchild of the lessor. The Irish Court of Appeal held (1) that it was doubtful if such a condition would be valid in an ordinary conveyance in fee simple, but (2) that it was valid in a fee farm grant by conversion under the 1849 Act. They expressly overruled the earlier case of *Billing v. Welch*.[27] In that case it had been held that if a covenant would be void in a grant of an ordinary fee simple, it should also be void in a grant under the 1849 Act. The court in *Re McNaul's Estate*[28] took the view that a fee simple by conversion was a special statutory fee simple and that the common law rules did not apply.

This seems an unsatisfactory result. The real issue is whether fees simple should be subjected to a leasehold régime, in the sense of rent and covenants restricting alienability. In some cases this is arguably justified where the fee simple is granted in pursuit of some social policy, such as under the Labourers' Acts,[29] where the holder is granted an interest considerably greater than they previously held in the land, on the basis that they belong to a category of people who are disadvantaged economically. The fees simple under the 1849 Act, however, were conferred on people who already had an interest which was virtually perpetual. The same arguments apply to the fee simple under section 74 of the 1980 Act.

If such restrictions do apply, then in principle so should the statutory control over such conditions which are now contained in section 66 of the Landlord and Tenant (Amendment) Act, 1980. These apply to tenements as defined by section 5 of the Act, *i.e.* land mostly covered in buildings where there is a lease and it had not been granted for temporary convenience only. Lease in the Act includes a fee farm grant. Section 66 provides that a covenant seeking ab-

25 Sometimes reified into the form that such a condition is repugnant to the nature of a freehold estate.

26 [1902] 1 IR 114.

27 (1871) IR 6 CL 88; and impliedly *Re Quin* (1859) 8 Ir Ch. R 578.

28 [1902] 1 IR 114.

29 See for example *Westmeath County Council v. Claffey* [1952] IR 1, Supreme Court, on the fee simple under the Labourers' Acts. See also Chapter 6 Fee Simple.

solutely to prohibit alienation takes effect as a covenant not to alienate without the landlord's consent. Where there is a covenant, expressly or under the statute, not to alienate without the landlord's consent, the section provides that consent shall not be unreasonably withheld.[30]

(5) Redemption

There is no authority as to the application of the Chief Rents Redemption (Ireland) Act, 1864, but the Act is no longer important.

The Redemption of Rent (Ireland) Act, 1891 applies to conversion fee farm grants over agricultural land.[31] The statute was part of the land purchase legislation and aimed to remove incumbrances on the fee simple.

In the Landlord and Tenant (Ground Rents)(No. 2) Act, 1978 lease includes a fee farm grant and so the Act applies if the conditions in sections 9 and 10 of the Act are complied with. Urban tenants can redeem under this Act if they redeem all superior rents.

2. Deasy's Act Grants

a) Origin

This is the largest group of fee farm grants existing in Ireland today, mainly because they can still be created by act of parties.

Section 3 of the Landlord and Tenant (Amendment) Act, 1860 (Deasy's Act) provides that the relationship of landlord and tenant is founded on contract, express or implied, and not upon tenure or service and "shall be deemed to subsist in all cases in which there shall be an agreement by one party to hold land from or under another in consideration of any rent". Section 4 speaks of lease or contracts "whereby the relation of landlord and tenant is intended to be created for any freehold estate or interest..." Irish courts have held this to mean that the relationship can exist even where the estate granted is freehold.[32] In *Chute v. Busteed*[33] it was held that sections 3 and 4 allowed fee farm grants to be created in this way.[34] In Ireland a person can therefore grant a fee simple reserving a rent without creating a separate rentcharge. Hence, in a Deasy's Act grant the estate is freehold but the tenure (if one should still use the term in

30 Landlord and Tenant (Amendment) Act, 1980, s.3.

31 *Hamilton v. Casey* [1894] 2 IR 224 (grants under Church Temporalities Act, 1833). *Gormill v. Lyne* (1894) 28 ILTR 44 (Trinity College Dublin Act, 1851). *Longtry v. Sheridan* (1896) 30 ILTR; *Gun-Cunningham v. Byrne* (1892) 30 LR Ir 384, Land Commission (grant under 1849 Act).

32 *Stevelly v. Murphy* (1840) 2 Ir Eq R 448 (grant of fee simple at a rent before Deasy's Act could not create landlord and tenant relationship).

33 (1865) 16 Ir CLR 222.

34 It was also held that the Act was not retrospective, and so such grants could only be created from 1 January 1861 onwards.

view of section 3), is leasehold. Such a grant must indicate an express intention to create the relationship of landlord and tenant.

In *Irish Land Commission v. Holmes*[35] it was held that in such a grant the grantor does not retain any reversion: there can be no reversion after a fee simple. There is simply a statutory right to recover the fee simple if the covenants are broken. The fee simple is a conditional one, the sanction being the statutory right rather than a right of entry.

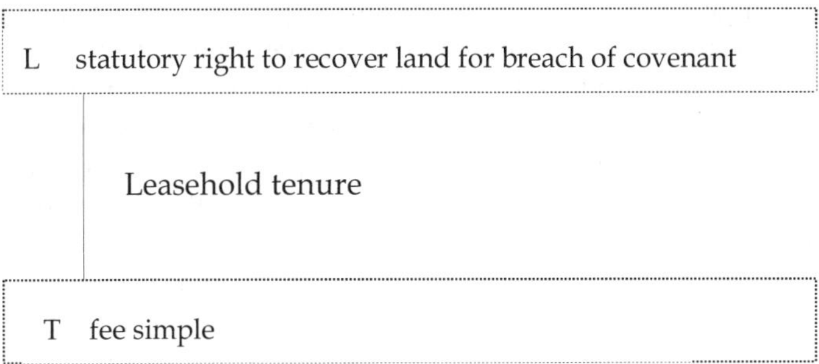

In view of sections 3 and 4 of Deasy's Act, 1860 there seem no reason why a Deasy's Act grantee should not make a Deasy's Act sub-grant, creating a further layer of leasehold tenure and retaining a statutory right to recover the fee simple.

b) Characteristics

(1) Words of Limitation

One view[36] is that section 3 of Deasy's Act, 1860 abolishes the requirement of words of limitation in the creation of a grant taking effect under the statute. On this view the creation of landlord and tenant relations is, under section 3, founded upon contract and so one must look to the agreement of the parties to see how long the relation is to subsist. If this is so then "to A forever" would create a Deasy's Act grant. "To A" would not, as there must be a contractual intention to create a grant of the type coming within the Act. Even if this view is correct it would only refer to the creation of a new Deasy's Act grant, not to the assignment of an existing one since an assignment does not fall within section 3.[37] In *Twaddle v. Murphy*[38] a deed, which was confused to say the least, granted and demised land:

35 (1898) 32 ILTR 85.

36 Cherry, (3rd ed.) p.5 note (c) citing *Twaddle v. Murphy* and dictum of Palles CB in *Hodges v. Clarke* (1883) 17 ILTR 82 at 84: "When we are obliged to determine for what period a tenant holds, we are bound to look to the agreement of the parties."

37 *Re Courtney* [1981] NI 58.

38 (1881) 8 LR Ir 123.

> *to A and B, their heirs and assigns, for the lives of C,D and E, or for 999 years, or for ever, which ever should last the longest.*

It was held that this created a fee farm grant. The fee simple absorbed the lesser estates.

Although Cherry[39] cites the case in favour of the view that words of limitation are not required to create a Deasy's Act grant, the word heirs was used and so words of limitation had in fact been employed. Alternatively there is authority for the view that formal words are still required.[40] An original fee farm grant under Deasy's Act does not create a new fee simple: it conveys the existing one while grafting onto it the relation of landlord and tenant. No private individual after *Quia Emptores* can create a new fee simple, with the exception in Ireland of *non obstante* fee farm grants, and Deasy's Act created no new exception.[41] Section 4 of Deasy's Act speaks of creating the relationship of landlord and tenant "for any freehold estate or interest" and could therefore be taken to assume that such estates are to be conveyed as before the Act. The Conveyancing Act, 1881, section 51, passed after Deasy's Act, introduced "in fee simple" as an alternative to the common law formula, and in so doing assumed that the common law words were still required before the Act. The 1881 Act did not contain any special exceptions for Deasy's Act grants. The standard words used by practitioners in Ireland today to create a Deasy's Act grant are:

> *to A, his [or her] heirs and assigns for ever.*

This is probably taken from *Twaddle v. Murphy*, with the twaddle removed.

(2) Rent

The landlord has the usual remedies: an action for debt and distress. Section 52 of Deasy's Act provides a statutory action for ejectment, thus dispensing with the requirement at common law that there should be a forfeiture clause in the lease to confer such a right.

This position is now modified where the rent reserved on a Deasy's Act grant qualifies as a ground rent within the Landlord and Tenant (Ground Rents) (No. 2) Act, 1978. Section 27 of the Act provides that section 52 of Deasy's Act no longer applies to dwelling houses where a person "is entitled to acquire the fee simple".[42] If a person entitled to a Deasy's Act grant is so entitled, then it would follow that section 52 no longer applies. The 1978 Act de-

39 See footnote 36 above.

40 *Re Ford & Ferguson's Contract* [1906] 1 IR 607 ("unto and to the use of the grantee for ever" held insufficient to pass the fee simple on a new grant under Deasy's Act).

41 *Irish Land Commission v. Holmes* (1898) 32 ILTR 85. There can be no reversion on a fee simple and the grantor does not retain a seignory under Deasy's Act: the grantor's fee simple passes to the grantee subject to conditions which may lead to its return.

42 See Redemption below.

fines lease to include a fee farm grant (section 3) so that a person with such an interest prima facie could enlarge it into a fee simple free of the covenants except for those preserved by section 28. A person with a Deasy's Act grant already has a fee simple vested in them, and so it could be argued that the Act cannot confer such a right upon them. However, the policy of the 1978 Act is that the tenant under the grant is the substantial owner of the property and so should not only be entitled to the fee simple free of rent, but also that a mere holder of a ground rent should not be able to disturb the possession of such an owner.

(3) Forfeiture

There may be an express clause for forfeiture in the lease, in which case the landlord need not rely on the statutory remedy in section 52. As to forfeiture for breach of covenants other than rent, they are now governed by section 14 of the Conveyancing Act, 1881, which places restrictions on their enforcement.

(4) Covenants

Deasy's Act implies certain covenants into leases and the provisions apply to grants in fee farm coming within the Act. Section 41 implies a covenant by the landlord for good title and quiet enjoyment. Section 42 implies a covenant by the tenant to pay the rent, taxes and do repairs. By sections 12 and 13 successors in title to the landlord and tenant are bound by the covenants.

One issue is whether section 66 of the Landlord and Tenant (Amendment) Act, 1980 applies to such grants. If so it would seem impliedly to approve of restraints on the alienability of a fee simple estate, subject to the provisions of the section as to consent to alienation not being unreasonably withheld. The freehold argument is that such restraints are contrary to *Quia Emptores*, 1290 unless the restraint has a minimal effect on alienability. On this view, one should first look to see whether the restraint would have been valid if it had been contained in a grant of an ordinary fee simple. If so, it is valid in a grant in Deasy's Act but is subject to the control of section 66. The leasehold argument is that Deasy's Act grants should be treated in the same way as conversion grants and the fee simple regarded as a special statutory fee simple to which can be appended restraints which are valid in an ordinary lease. To this it could be objected that Deasy's Act does not create the fee simple, which passes under the deed, but merely allows leasehold tenure to be created at the same time. One arguable advantage of the Deasy's Act grant is that it provides a technical means of ensuring that the benefit and burden of either restrictive or positive covenants affecting the use of the land can be made to pass to successors in title of the original grantor and grantee. This freedom has now been restricted by the ground rents legislation.

(5) Redemption

The Chief Rents Redemption (Ireland) Act, 1864 seems to apply.

The Redemption of Rent (Ireland) Act, 1891 applies to Deasy's Act grants of agricultural land.[43] The Act was part of the land purchase legislation and as such aimed to remove incumbrances on the fee simple such as fee farm rents.

The Landlord and Tenant (Ground Rents)(No. 2) Act, 1978 seems to apply, provided the grant comes within the conditions laid down in sections 9 and 10 of the Act.

D. Rentcharge Fee Farm Grants

a) Introduction

An interest in the nature of a fee farm grant is created if a grantor grants a fee simple estate and at the same time creates a rentcharge in their own favour burdening the land of the grantee. No tenure is created, either freehold or leasehold. The grantor could just as easily have created a rentcharge in favour of a third party, and may do so in addition to the rentcharge in his own favour.

b) Characteristics

(1) Words of Limitation

Words of Limitation are the same as for a grant *inter vivos* of an ordinary fee simple, since that is what the fee simple is. Words of limitation are not required in a will, under section 94 of the Succession Act, 1965. For the rentcharge, words of limitation must be used even in a will if the grantor of the land, or any third party, is to have a rentcharge in fee simple. Section 94 of the Succession Act, 1965 does not apply to a newly created rentcharge.

(2) Rent

There is an action for debt at common law by the pernor of the profits, *i.e.* the person entitled to the profits of the rentcharge, against the terre tenant, *i.e.* the freeholder for the time being entitled in possession to the land the subject of the rentcharge.[44] As there is no tenure, the rent is a rent seck and so there is no right of distress unless reserved in the grant.

Under the Fee Farm Rents (Ireland) Act, 1851 the owner of the rentcharge has all the rights of a landlord under a lease except ejectment. Section 44 of the Conveyancing Act, 1881 also provides remedies for the recovery of rentcharges, a duplication so far as Ireland is concerned.

---

43 Section 14(b) of the Land Law (Ireland) Act, 1896.

44 *Swift v. Kelly* (1889) 24 LR Ir 107, QB, 478, CA.

(3) Forfeiture

There is only a right to re-entry for non-payment of the rent if such a right is expressly inserted in the deed. The rule against perpetuities does not apply in the Republic to a right of re-entry at common law.[45]

Since there is no tenure, statutory provisions applying to forfeiture of a tenancy do not apply. Thus, unlike conversion grants under the Renewable Leasehold Conversion Act, 1849 and Deasy's Act, there is no special statutory remedy of ejectment in this type of fee farm grant, which makes it specially important for practitioners to establish which kind of grant they are dealing with.

(4) Covenants

Any restraints in the deed granting the fee simple will be judged on the same basis as any other ordinary fee simple and so will be void if they restrict alienation to any substantial extent. In *Re Lunham's Estate*[46] a grant of a fee simple reserving a rentcharge to the grantor provided that the land was not to be subdivided into more than four lots without the consent of the grantor. The restriction was held void as repugnant to the fee simple estate.

(5) Redemption

The Chief Rents Redemption (Ireland) Act, 1864 seems to apply to rentcharge fee farm grants, but, as noted above, it is of little use since redemption is by application to the court and is voluntary.

The Redemption of Rent (Ireland) Act, 1891 does not apply because there is no landlord and tenant relationship.[47]

The Landlord and Tenant (Ground Rents) (No. 2) Act, 1978 seems to apply. It does not distinguish between different kinds of fee farm grant.

In addition to the above, under section 5 of the Conveyancing Act, 1881 the owner of land subject to an incumbrance, which includes a rentcharge, may sell the land free of it by obtaining the permission of the court to lodging a sum of money in court , the sum being sufficient to provide an income, after investment in government securities, to pay the annual amount.[48]

45 *i.e.* which is neither equitable nor taking effect as a legal executory interest.

46 (1871) IR 5 Eq 170.

47 *Christie v. Peacocke* (1892) 30 LR Ir 646, Land Commission.

48 *Re McGuiness's Contract* (1901) 35 ILTR 65.

CHAPTER 8

FEE TAIL

"Oh! my dear," cried his wife, "I cannot bear to hear that mentioned. Pray do not talk of that odious man. I do think it is the hardest thing in the world, that your estate should be entailed away from your own children; and I am sure that if I had been you, I should have tried long ago to do something or other about it.

Jane and Elizabeth attempted to explain to her the nature of an entail. They had often attempted it before, but it was a subject on which Mrs Bennett was beyond the reach of reason; and she continued to rail bitterly against the cruelty of settling an estate away from a family of five daughters, in favour of a man whom nobody cared anything about."

– Jane Austen, *Pride and Prejudice.*[1]

A. History

In the feudal period many freehold tenants wanted to ensure that their land remained within their own immediate family: they wanted an estate which their descendants could not sell or otherwise alienate. In a sense this demand contradicted another demand: the right to alienate freely. But both were aspects of a more general demand by tenants: to control land free of the lord's interference. Tenants wanted the flexibility to buy and or sell or to retain land in the family at their own discretion. After *Quia Emptores*, 1290 the fee simple no longer satisfied the demand to have an inalienable estate, since it then became fully alienable by substitution by any tenant of the land for the time being.

A common form of gift in the 13th century was the *maritagium*. This was a gift of land on marriage, usually by a father on the marriage of his daughter. Land would be conveyed to the daughter or her husband "and the heirs of their bodies." The courts had to decide what effect such a gift had in law. By the 13th century they adopted the view that the phrase "heirs of their bodies" imposed a condition that issue should be born. Before issue were born the donee merely had a life estate. Once issue were born to the husband and wife, the donee, whichever one of them it was, took a fee simple, but still subject to a condition that issue should continue, so that if the issue died out the estate would revert to the donor. There was both a condition precedent and a condition subsequent. In the meantime, however, the donee was free to alienate the

1 See Treitel, (1984).

land, just as in the case of an ordinary fee simple.[2] This interpretation was not popular with landowners because it frustrated their intention that the land should remain within the new family. They did not want the holder of the land for the time being to have the power of alienation. The landowners achieved what they wanted by the Statute *De Donis,* 1285 which is discussed in the next section. The statute created the fee tail estate.

B. De Donis, 1285

The statute *De Donis Conditionalibus,* 1285 (Of conditional gifts) or as it is often called, *De Donis*, provides[3] that a grant "to X and the heirs of his body" or a similarly phrased grant should take effect according to the intention of the donor expressed in the terms of the gift (*forma doni*).[4]

The estate has several distinctive features. First, it passes only to the descendants of the grantee, unlike the fee simple which passes, in the absence of children, to parents or even cousins of the intestate. Secondly, a fee tail is not alienable by the person who holds it, either *inter vivos* or by will. So long as a fee tail remains unbarred[5] the heirs of the body have the right to inherit it.[6]

The tenants probably would have preferred the estate to pass to their heirs general, but that would have created an estate which would have lasted much longer potentially and therefore would have meant that much land could be withdrawn from the market. The limitation to heirs of the body was therefore probably a concession that they had to make. An estate which only passes to the descendants of a named person will not last as long as a fee simple. For this reason, the fee tail is regarded as a lesser estate than the fee simple.

C. Types of Fee Tail

The descent of a fee tail can be limited to a particular kind of descendants. A grant

> *to T and the heirs male of his [or her] body*

creates a fee tail male. It descends only to male descendants of T. A grant

> *to K and the heirs female of her [or his] body*

---

2 *Nevill's Case* (1605) 7 Co Rep 33a, 77 ER 460 at 35. The estate resembled what would now be termed a base fee (see below).

3 Originally applied by writ (Berry 1907 p.47, 105–77), confirmed by 13 Edw II c.2 (Ir), 1319 and Poynings' Act, 1495.

4 Baker, *English Legal History* p.232.

5 See below for barring the entail.

6 Decided after the statute by *Helton v. Brampton* (1344).

gives a fee tail female. A fee tail can also be limited to the descendants of a person by a particular spouse:

to Q and the heirs of her body by her husband R

creates a fee tail special.

A fee tail special may give rise to a peculiar interest in property. Suppose there is no issue of the marriage and then R dies? There is no possibility that the fee tail will continue after Q's death. She is known as a tenant in tail after possibility of issue extinct or a tenant in tail after possibility for short. Such a tenant is more like a life tenant. For this reason tenants in tail after possibility cannot bar the entail.[7]

Combinations of the above types of fee tail may also be created. For example:

to X and the heirs female of her body by her husband Y

would create a fee tail special female.

In Ireland it has been held that these are not the only possibilities. In *Re Elliot*[8] the grant was:

to TE and the heirs of his body, excluding his eldest son.

It was held to be a valid fee tail special. The eldest son was excluded from inheriting the entail. It has also been held[9], in a case concerning a will, that a fee tail may be limited, as a single limitation, to A and the heirs male of his or her body and on failure of such issue, to the heirs male of the body of B, an ancestor of A and as to whom A is the heir male. Both these results are consistent with the intent of the statute *De Donis*, namely, that the gift should take effect according to its tenor.

The Status of Children Act, 1987 sections 3 and 27 provide that references to relationships between persons in dispositions of property made after 14 December 1987, "including a disposition creating an entailed estate", include non-marital as well as marital children unless a contrary intention is shown.[10] Thus, a grant after that date "to X and the heirs of his body" would create an entail which would pass to non-marital children.[11] On the other hand a grant:

---

7 Fines and Recoveries (Ireland) Act, 1834 s.15. They cannot even bar it partially to produce a base fee.

8 [1916] 1 IR 30.

9 *Re Mountgarret* [1919] 2 Ch. 294 (Irish estates of Viscount Mountgarret).

10 The latter qualification is in s.3.

11 The old rules of descent were retained for entails by the Succession Act, 1965 s.11 (see below Descent), but are now modified by the Status of Children Act, 1987, so that, in the case of a fee tail general, subject to constitutional challenge, the eldest male child, whether marital or non-marital, would take the entail to the exclusion of younger males and to females, whether marital or non-marital.

to X and the marital heirs of his body

would now create a fee tail special. In so far as the Act allows discrimination against non-marital children it is open to challenge on constitutional grounds.

D. Tenure

If A, who has a fee simple, creates a fee tail in favour of B then in theory the tenure in Ireland may be either freehold or leasehold. It can be freehold because *Quia Emptores*, 1290 only prohibited subinfeudation for a fee simple estate. It can be leasehold because section 4 of Deasy's Act, 1860 allows the relationship of landlord and tenant to be created "for any freehold estate or interest." The point is of little practical importance because (a) fees tail are now rare and (b) when they are created they are created in favour of family members and it is unlikely that covenants to pay rent or to perform other obligations would be inserted in the grant.

E. Descent

The descent of an entail is always traced from the original donee.[12] This again follows from the wording of the statute *De Donis*, to the effect that the issue of the donee take according to the words of the grant. Section 11(1) of the Succession Act, 1965 specifically preserves the old rules of descent as to entails, so that primogeniture still applies. These rules have now been modified, as to dispositions made after the date of the Act, by the Status of Children Act, 1987 to include non-marital children.[13] The following example illustrates both points. A donor gives an entail "to X and the heirs male of his body". X has three sons, A, B, and C. B is a non-marital child of X. X dies. The land passes to A alone, by primogeniture. A dies without issue. The entail does not come to an end, because the grant was not to the heirs male of the body of *A*, of whom there are none, but to the heirs male of the body of *X*. The land therefore passes to B. On B's death the land will go to his eldest son, if he has one. If B dies without male descendants, or if they die out, the land passes to C.

F. Constitutionality

The validity of fees tail male and female is now open to challenge on the ground that it breaches the constitutional guarantee in Article 40.1 of equality between citizens as human persons. The challenge might be to the statute *De Donis*, 1285 which permitted these forms to be created or, more cogently, to

12 *Doe d Gregory v. Wichelo* (1799) 8 TR 211, 101 ER 1350, Challis 244.

13 See Types of Fee Tail above.

section 11(1) of the Succession Act, 1965 which preserves the old rules of descent which discriminate in favour of males against females and elder children against younger children.[14]

One argument in favour of the validity of estates which discriminate on the ground of gender is that, since both a fee tail male and a fee tail female are possible, the requirement of equality is satisfied. This argument depends upon the proposition that discrimination in favour of one group in society, in this case males, can be legitimised by proof that it is also possible to discriminate against the opposite group.

There are at least two objections to this argument. First, even if one were to accept the cancelling out proposition, it could be argued that the requirement of equality is only satisfied on proof that the patterns of discrimination actually do balance in practice. In this instance, such a balance is not in fact achieved because fees tail male were, and to the extent that such interests still exist, still are, far more common than fees tail female. Indeed the latter are extremely rare. Secondly, a general balancing argument of this kind does not meet the specific case. If X is excluded from inheriting under a specific entail because she is female it is not particularly cogent to point out that other persons, having no connection with her, are excluded by other entails on the ground that they are male.

A constitutional theory which seeks to avoid the above objections is known as the neutral principles[15] approach and is favoured by conservatives in the United States. This asserts that the role of the law is simply to provide forms, such as contracts or estates in land, which can be used by individuals to express property and power relationships. The law is not concerned with the use to which its forms are put. The law is not concerned with redressing factual inequality: it provides the forms and the market, or free enterprise, or human nature, decides who ends up with more of the earth's resources. Followers of this view maintain, for example, that the law can enforce covenants in conveyances which purport to restrict the occupation of land to members of a particular race and yet they deny that the law is thereby enforcing racial discrimination. They maintain that the law is still neutral.

Against this it can be argued that the State, in recognising the legal effectiveness of certain forms and granting remedies to enforce them, is conferring power on individuals which they would not otherwise possess. By granting remedies in such cases the law is putting itself on the side of the enforcing

---

14 It is arguable that *De Donis* allows a donor to create a fee tail special by using heirs to mean the intestate successors of the donee in accordance with the Succession Act, 1965 but confined to descendants only, but that does not remove the objection to section 11(1).

15 See Bork, *The Tempting of America* pp. 78, 147–48, 151 and Bork, "Neutral Principles and Some First Amendment Problems" (1971) 47 Ind LJ 1. See also Chapter 6 Fee Simple.

party. Where the covenant, or other form, is discriminatory, it is putting itself on the side of the discriminator. Furthermore, courts frequently hold ordinary citizens responsible for the consequences of their acts, even if the consequence was not the motive for the act. A principle of criminal law is that a person is taken to intend the natural and probable consequences of their own acts. The courts impose duties of care and apply tests of foreseeability in negligence. It arguably lacks integrity for the courts to deny any responsibility for the consequences of their own actions, however foreseeable they may be. Moreover, judges have not taken the view in other contexts that the law is neutral. Unconscionable bargains are unenforceable, the concept of foreseeability in negligence attributes liability on the basis of anticipated consequences. The list of instances in which individuals are held responsible for the foreseeable consequences of their acts is a long one. It includes notice in equity, priority in registration of title and documents. The adoption of a consistent neutral principles approach would require radical alteration of large bodies of the law. It would not be a return to basic principles, but would require a wholesale recasting or rejection of basic principles. It is interesting, then, to question why in this particular area the common law should limit its role to providing alternative forms and turned a blind eye to their social effects.

These points have not been litigated in the Republic up to this time. Kelly[16], while pointing out that Article 40.1 is primarily addressed to the State, also recognises that the obligation on the State to vindicate the rights of persons whose personal rights are infringed implies that Article 40.1 cannot be limited to state action. Entails male have occurred in cases, but their constitutionality has not been contested.[17] It also not entirely clear what would be the effect of holding such entails unconstitutional. If it were simply the restriction to males or to females which would be objectionable, the restriction could possibly be struck out, leaving the limitations as fees tail general. However, the old rules of descent also discriminate on grounds of age.

G. Escheat and Forfeiture

If an escheat for felony occurred as to land held in fee tail, the escheat only affected the estate during the life of the felon.[18] This was probably so for a num-

16 Kelly, (3rd ed.) 716–17.

17 *Bellew v. Bellew* [1982] IR 447 at 454; *Bank of Ireland v. Goulding* unreported, Supreme Court, 14 November 1975.

18 G.E. Cokayne, *The Complete Peerage* (London, 1926) p.448, note c. Lord Barry of Santry (born 1710) was tried by the Irish House of Lords and convicted of the murder of Laughlin Murphy, a footman whom he had stabbed in a fit of passion in August 1738. He was condemned to death on 27 April 1739 and also attainted. His estates escheated. The effect of attainder on his peerage, however, was only that it was suspended for his own life. The peerage descended in the same way as an entail and under

ber of reasons. For one thing, the Statute *De Donis*, 1285 required the land to descend according to the words of the gift, *i.e.* to the descendants of the original donee. For another, unlike the heirs of a fee simple, the heirs in tail had more than a mere *spes successionis*: they had a right to inherit which therefore remained unaffected by the escheat. Similar results seem to have followed in the case of a forfeiture for treason. Both escheat for felony and forfeiture for treason have now been abolished.[19]

H. Words of Limitation

1. Inter vivos

a) At Common Law

At common law the words of limitation required are the word heirs plus words of procreation, *i.e.* the phrase heirs of the body is not essential, but one must use the word heirs and also something to indicate that the class of heirs are to be restricted to descendants only.

> *to Y and the heirs from her proceeding. . .*

or

> *to D and the heirs of her flesh. . .*

create a valid entail, but

> *to A and her issue. . .*

does not. Nor does "to A and her children." In spite of this clear rule the judges were sometimes prepared to construe other words as meaning heirs plus words of procreation, at least if the word "heirs" was present, so that where in a marriage settlement the limitation was to the husband and wife for life, remainder to the first son of the marriage and his heirs, with further remainder to the second, third and other sons of the marriage and their heirs, the word "heirs" could be construed as implying words of procreation since the context showed that the first and later sons were intended to take fees tail.[20] Here again, rule sceptics may question whether there really is any rule as to specifying words of procreation. The use of the word heirs is probably mandatory.

---

the statute *De Donis* as interpreted, the escheat did not affect the heirs. He obtained a pardon in June 1740 and so survived his attainder. His estates were restored but not his title.

19 See above Chapter 3 Tenure.

20 *Re Smith's Estate* (1891) 27 LR Ir 121, Land Js, following *Doe d Litteldale v. Smeddle* (1818) 2 B & Ald 126, 106 ER 313.

b) Statute

Section 51 of the Conveyancing Act, 1881 provides an alternative formula as words of limitation: "to A in tail" or "in tail male" or "in tail female" *etc.* but presumably "to A in fee tail" would also be allowed.

c) In Equity

It is not clear whether strict words of limitation must be used in creating equitable estates in tail in *inter vivos* deeds. It may be that today they must be used. The trend of statute law has been to make the creation of such estates more difficult by requiring strict words, as in the Succession Act discussed below, and judicial opinion may reflect this trend of policy.

2. By Will

a) Before 1967

Before 1967 any words showing an intention to create an entail were sufficient to do so in a will.

> *To A and his issue*[21]

or

> *and his descendants*

gave a fee tail general, while:

> *to A and his heirs male*

gave a fee tail male, the court construing the limitations as intended to restrict the heirs to those of the body.[22] In fact the court could construe "to the sons of A" as giving them successive fees tail where earlier in the will other property had been so given to them.[23]

If the words were "to A and his children" a special rule applied, called the Rule in *Wild's Case* which is discussed below.

b) Succession Act, 1965

The modern policy is to make it more difficult to create this old-fashioned estate, and so the Succession Act, 1965 section 95(1) provides that an estate tail, of whatever kind, can only be created[24] in a will by the use of the same words

21 *Kavanagh v. Moreland* (1853) Kay 16, 69 ER 7.

22 *Wood v. Ingersole* (1610) 1 Bulst 61at 63, 80 ER 763 ; *Baker v. Wall* (1697) 1 Ld Raym 185, 91 ER 1019.

23 *Studdart v. Von Steiglitz* (1889) 23 LR Ir 564, V-C.

24 Note the use of the word "created". An existing fee tail cannot be disposed of by will.

of limitation as are required *inter vivos*.[25] If those words are not used then section 95(2) of the Succession Act, 1965 provides that:

> "95(2)–Words of limitation in a will in respect of real estate which do not create a fee simple or an estate tail have the same effect as words used in a deed in respect of personal property."

If a phrase such as "to A and his issue" is used in a will, then it will not, by virtue of section 95(2) create an entail, because personalty cannot be entailed in the Republic. Any expression will pass a fee simple unless there is a contrary intention. The use of issue might be a contrary intention, but the alternative is a life estate, and the expression seems definitely contrary to that. The limitation would probably give a fee simple to A, or jointly to A and any issue alive at the testator's death.

It is clear that under section 95 the expression:

> *to A and his heirs male*

can no longer create a fee tail. It seems likely that the word male would be ignored as superfluous and the limitation would then confer a fee simple.

3. The Rule in Wild's Case

a) Wills

Formerly the Rule in *Wild's Case*[26] applied when a testator made a gift of realty[27] in his or her will:

> *to A and his [her] children.*

The effect depended on the facts existing at the time the will was made. If at that time A had no children, then, since there were no children to take by purchase,[28] the words "and his children" were treated as words of limitation and A took an estate tail, even if by the time the testator died, children had been born to A.[29] A could, of course, subsequently defeat the expectations of the children

25 An existing entail cannot be devised by will, but there is nothing to prevent the creation of a new entail by a will.

26 (1599) 6 Co Rep 16b, 77 ER 277.

27 It did not apply to personalty: Heron v. Stokes (1842) 4 Ir Eq R 286.

28 *Clifford v. Koe* (1881) 5 AC 447, HL, affirming Irish CA and QB. See footnote 30. The House of Lords reaffirmed the rule and held (1) that children in its primary meaning referred to the first generation only, (2) that this meaning was displaced by *Wild's Case*, which was a rule of construction, but (3) it should not be departed from in cases where it applied.

29 See O'Brien J in *Clifford v. Brooke* (1877) IR 10 CL 179 at 185-6 affirmed at (1878) 2 LR Ir 184, CA and (1880) 6 LR Ir 439, sub nom *Clifford v. Koe* (1881) 5 AC 447, HL:

> "According to the doctrine laid down in *Wild's Case* it may be stated as a general rule, that if by a will made before the Wills Act of 1837, lands were devised to A and his children, and if he had no children at the date of the will, such devise would give him

by barring the entail. The rule applied also if the first-mentioned person was given a power of appointment, so that a gift "to M and to any child or children she might have as she should appoint" would also give M an estate tail, if there were no children.[30]

If at the time the will was made, A had children, the original rule was that A took jointly with all his children living at the testator's death. *i.e.* "and his children" were then treated as words of purchase.[31] Children born between the date when the will was made and the testator's death were allowed to participate in the gift.

The rule was not a product of feudal policy and probably always had the purpose of expressing the presumed intent of the testator. If A had no children at the time the testator was drawing up his will, the only way any future children could benefit was through A.

But the rule always yielded to evidence of a contrary express intention. Irish courts by the mid-19th century showed a tendency to depart from the rigidity of the old rule, at least in the latter case, and to pay regard to the testator's intention, so that even a slight indication that a joint estate was not intended would lead them to give A a life estate with remainder to the children of A born in the testator's lifetime.[32]

The Succession Act, 1965 abolished the Rule in *Wild's Case* by two provisions. First, section 95 requires strict words of limitation in a will in order to create a fee tail and so after 1967 the phrase "and his/her children" can never function as words of limitation. Secondly, section 89 provides that wills take effect on the death of the testator. They "speak from death".[33]

Hence, if A has children at the testator's death, he or she takes jointly with the children. The estate will be a fee simple unless a contrary intention is shown.

If A has no children at the testator's death, A takes a fee simple unless a contrary intention is shown.

---

prima facie an estate tail."

See also *Re Moyle's Estate* (1878) 1 LR Ir 155; *Seale v. Barter* (1801) 2 B & p.485, 126 ER 1398; *Doe d Davy v. Burnsall* (1794) 6 TR 30, 1 B & P 215, 101 ER 419; *Phillips v. Phillips* (1847) 10 Ir Eq R 520.

30 But otherwise if the limitation were followed by a gift to the children on default of appointment: *Re Moyle's Estate* (1878) 1 LR Ir 155; *Doe d Davy v. Burnell* (1794) 6 TR 30, 1 B & P 215, 101 ER 419.

31 *Hayes v. Ward* (1788) 2 Ridg PC 85.

32 *Scott v. Scott* (1861) 11 Ir Ch. R 114.

33 Section 89: "Every will, shall, with reference to the estate comprised in the will and every devise or bequest contained in it, be construed to speak and take effect as if it had been executed immediately before the death of the testator". The 1837 Act, s.24 had adopted this principle as a general rule, but the Rule in *Wild's Case* was preserved as an exception.

b) Inter vivos

If the phrase "to A and his/her children" were used *inter vivos*, *Wild's Case* did not apply. The words could never create a fee tail because the word heirs had not been used. If A has children at the date of the deed, A takes jointly with them. Since "and his children" are words of purchase, there are no words of limitation and so A and his children take joint life estates.

4. The Rule in Shelley's Case

a) Legal Estates Inter vivos

The rule here has a similar application as in the case of fee simple estates, except that here the word heirs is used with words of procreation.

In the limitation:

> *to A for life, remainder to the heirs of her body [or from him proceeding, or of her flesh, etc.].*

the words in the remainder clause, *i.e.* heirs plus the words of procreation, are, under the rule, treated as words of limitation defining the estate given to A. Thus, A has a life estate under the first gift, a fee tail in remainder under the remainder clause and the two then merge to give A a fee tail in possession. The effect of the limitation is the same as if it had said "to A and the heirs of her body".

b) Wills

The old rule here was similar to the rule in wills applied in the case of words producing a fee simple. The rule could apply even where informal words had been used and in such a case it was a matter of construction whether the testator meant the same as heirs plus words of procreation, in which case the rule applied, or whether the testator was referring to specific persons, in which case they took by purchase and the first devisee took only a life estate.[34]
Section 95 of the Succession Act, 1965 now requires the same words of limitation to be used in a will as are used in an *inter vivos* deed if a fee tail is to be produced. It is therefore clear that informal words can no longer function as words of limitation. *Shelley's Case* can only apply to produce a fee tail if strict words

34 *Mandeville v. Lord Carrick* (1795) 3 Ridg PC 366, Ir HL ("to EM for life only, remainder to the lawful issue male [of EM] and the lawful issue male of such heirs, the eldest of such sons always to be preferred..." On failure of such issue the estate was to go to Lord Carrick in tail male. On the testator's death in 1788 EM purported to bar the entail by suffering a recovery. EM died two years later leaving a wife and daughter, the latter being the heir at law of EM. Lord Carrick then claimed the land. The Irish House of Lords, upholding the King's Bench, held that EM took a life estate only and that therefore Lord Carrick was entitled, the estates in tail male having failed. *Sandes v. Cooke* (1888) 21 LR Ir 445, MR, 460, CA.

have been used, *i.e.* heirs plus words of procreation. The question arises as to the effect today in a will of a limitation using informal words, such as:

to A for life, remainder to his issue [or descendants].

It may be the case that the question today would be whether the testator really meant heirs, in which case *Shelley* applies to give A a fee simple, or whether he or she meant to refer to specific persons, in which case the rule does not apply and A gets a life estate and the issue or descendants take jointly by purchase. Since no words of limitation have been used in relation to them, they would take a fee simple unless there is a contrary intent to be gathered from the will.

c) Equitable Estates Inter Vivos

In the case of equitable estates *inter vivos* there is no similar provision to that contained in section 95 of the Succession Act, 1965 as to wills. Since the general approach of equity is to look at the intention it is probably the case that a similar rule applies to that which applied in wills before the Succession Act.[35]

I. Power to Lease

Tenants in tail, having only an interest in the premises for their own life, were in the same position as regards creating leases as were tenants for life. Any lease they granted would come to an end at their death.[36] They could not create leases which would bind either the issue in tail after their death or those entitled in remainder or reversion after the end of the fee tail.

A statute of Charles I gave a general power to create leases for 3 lives or 41 years binding on the issue in tail.[37] The leases were not binding on those entitled in remainder or reversion.[38] Leases in excess of the statutory power were not void: the issue in tail could confirm them.[39] This seems to have been the origin of leases for lives and years in Ireland. Other statutes gave powers for special purposes[40] and the policy was continued by the Fines and Recoveries (Ireland) Act, 1834.[41] Today, the tenant in tail has the same powers of leasing under the Settled Land Acts, 1882–1890 as tenants for life under the Acts.[42]

35 *Brennan v. Fitzmaurice* (1840) 2 Ir Eq R 113 at 122.

36 *Homan v. Skelton* (1861) 11 Ir Ch R 75 (quasi-tail).

37 10 Chas I sess 3, c. (Ir), 1634.

38 8 Co 34; Co Lit 44a; Cro Eliz 602; Smythe 5–6.

39 *Earl of Bedford's Case* (1587) 7 Co Rep 7b, 77 ER 421.

40 For places of worship, schools, corn mills, prisons, mining, bog reclamation: Wylie, *Irish Land Law* para. 1.36.

41 Section 19.

42 Section 58(1)(i).

J. Barring the Entail

"Why may not that be the skull of a lawyer? Where be his quiddities now, his quillets, his cases, his tenures, and his tricks?. . . This fellow might be in his time a great buyer of land with his statutes, his recognisances, his fines, his double vouchers,[43] *his recoveries: is this the fine of his fines, and the recovery of his recoveries to have his fine pate full of fine dirt? Will his vouchers vouch him no more of his purchases and double ones too, than the length and breadth of a pair of indentures?"*

– Shakespeare, *Hamlet* Act 5 Scene 1.

With the development of the market in land the courts began to look favourably on attempts by tenants in tail to change the estate into a fee simple. They did this by devious means – by allowing fictional actions to take place in court whereby this result was produced. It should be remembered that the heirs of the body, or issue in tail as they were sometimes called, *i.e.* the tenant in tail's descendants, have a right to inherit the entail. They do not have a mere *spes successionis* as the heirs of a fee simple owner do. It was therefore necessary to bar, *i.e.* to destroy, this right. Furthermore, there would necessarily be a reversion or a remainder after the fee tail, or possibly both, and in order to obtain a fee simple it would also be necessary to bar the right of those entitled to such estates.

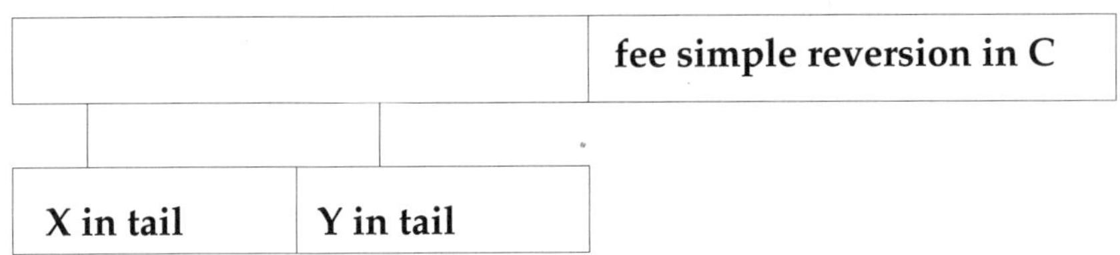

Thus, in the diagram, if X is to bar his entail successfully and obtain a fee simple, he must bar not only the right of the heirs in tail, *i.e.* his own descendants, but also the right of Y and Y's descendants, who are entitled in remainder, and the right of C who is entitled to the ultimate reversion in fee simple.

Taltarum's Case, decided in 1472[44], shows that the courts had by that time invented a method of barring entails by a collusive action known as a common recovery.[45] If another kind of action, called a fine, was brought instead, the issue in tail were barred but not remaindermen or reversioners.[46] This created a type of estate called a base fee. This will be discussed shortly. The obvious

43 See footnote 46.

44 YB 12 Edw IV, Mich, fo 14b, pl 16, fo 19a, pl 25; 13 Edw IV, Mich fo 1a, pl 1.

45 For a description of the common recovery with double voucher, see the first edition of this book p.224 n.41; or Simpson, *Land Law* pp. 35–7.

46 *Hume v. Burton* (1785) 1 Ridg P C 204 at 207.

question is "why would anyone want to levy a fine instead of the common recovery"?In fact, not everyone could suffer a recovery. It was only available to tenants in tail whose interests were vested, and if they were not vested in possession, it required the consent of the tenant in possession.[47] The Fines and Recoveries (Ireland) Act, 1834[48] simplified the procedure for barring the entail. It is recognised as a masterpiece of conservative drafting, in that it abolished all the old forms while retaining the distinction in their effects within a new scheme.

1. Fines and Recoveries (Ireland) Act, 1834

The Act abolished fines and recoveries and replaced them by a single deed, called a disentailing assurance. Entails are to be barred by this deed alone.[49] Since it is an *inter vivos* conveyance, entails cannot be barred by will.[50] This remains the case in Ireland[51] The Act thus greatly reduced the cost of disentailing. The deed must be enrolled in the High Court within 6 months.[52] It also provides that there is to be a person called the protector of the settlement. The protector is the person entitled to the first freehold estate, or lease determinable on life, created by the settlement.[53] The Act also allows the grantor to appoint not more than three persons who together will act as special protector and they can be anyone.[54] The consent of the protector is necessary if a fee simple is to result. The statute thus preserves the distinction between a tenant in tail in possession and in remainder which used to exist under the old actions while abolishing fines and common recoveries themselves.

G, the father of A, creates settlement. B is the son of A:

---

47 Megarry & Wade, *Real Property* p.89.

48 The Act was drafted by Peter Brodie: see Anderson, *Lawyers and the Making of English Land Law 1832–1940* (Oxford: Clarendon Press, 1992).

49 See *Re Ottley's Estate* [1910] 1 IR 1, interpreting section 45 of the Fines & Recoveries (Ireland) Act, 1834. Evidence of the intention of the parties to explain a mistake is inadmissible under s.45 if it is extrinsic to the deed, but in that case the evidence came from within the deed itself. The parties used the phrase "in fee simple" later in the deed.

50 *Campbell v. Sandys* (1806) 1 Sch & Lef 281 at 295, 9 RR 33, per Lord Redesdale LC. Entails could not be barred by will before the Act, since the procedure involved the fictitious action of a common recovery, brought, necessarily, by a living person.

51 Entails were made barrable by will in England by section 176 of the Law of Property Act, 1925.

52 Fines and Recoveries (Ireland) Act, 1834 s.39. The section also provides that a disentailment by bargain and sale is valid despite not being enrolled under the Statute of Uses, 1634 s.17 if it is enrolled under the 1834 Act.

53 Section 19; *Re Dudson's Settlement* (1878) 8 Ch D 628; *Re Blandy Jenkins' Estate* (1917) 1 Ch 46. He or she remains the protector even if they part with their estate. Williams, *Real Property* (23rd ed.) 107.

54 Section 30; except an alien.

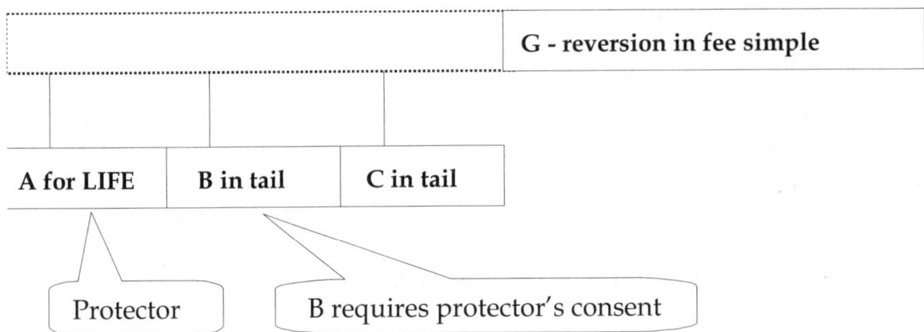

A is the protector. If B wants to disentail so as to produce a fee simple he must get A's consent. If he executes a disentailing assurance without A's consent, only a base fee is produced, which only bars the right of B's issue in tail (descendants) to inherit the entail, but not C or the grantor.[55] If A consents, B obtains a fee simple but still subject to A's life estate unless A also releases the life estate. Usually in such a situation A will do this because it will be part of a resettlement of the land in which A, who would normally be the father of B, will join with B to produce a complete fee simple which they will then re-settle, *i.e.* split up again into successive estates. Take the above example, but assume that A has died. When A died the protectorship came to an end. B is now a tenant in tail in possession. If B wants to disentail all he has to do is to execute a disentailing assurance and a fee simple will result.

If the grant had only created a fee tail:

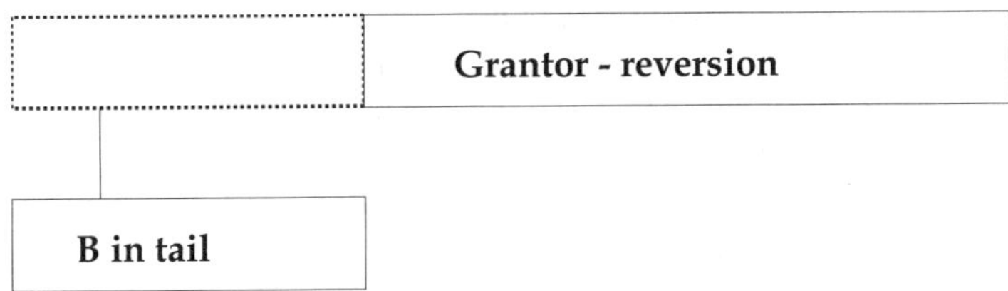

then a protectorship has never existed and again, B can disentail so as to produce a fee simple without anyone's consent. The invention of the protector cleverly reproduced the results of the old actions.[56] In the old actions it was

55 For an explanation of the base fee estate, see below.

56 A disentailing assurance does differ in at least one respect from the fine or recovery which it replaces. If T, a life tenant with power to lease, joins with U who is entitled in tail in remainder, and they disentail in favour of T for life with remainder to U in fee simple, T's power of leasing is not destroyed by the disentailing deed: *O'Fay v. Burke* (1859) 8 Ir Ch R 225, per Smith MR.

necessary, if a fee simple was to be produced, to obtain the consent of the person seised of the land.[57]

Whether a protectorship exists or not, the tenant in tail does not require the consent of the remaindermen or the reversioner. The effect of the Fines and Recoveries (Ireland) Act, 1834, as was the case with the old actions it replaced, is simply to destroy the remainders and reversion without any compensation. Disentailing costs the tenant in tail nothing – except the cost of the deed.

2. Constitutionality of the Fines and Recoveries (Ireland) Act, 1834

It could be argued in the Republic that insofar as the barring of an entail under the Act destroys remainders or reversions without compensation, it is unconstitutional. The point has not yet arisen. Against the view that the Act is unconstitutional it could be argued that remainders and reversions after a fee tail are in a different position to other remainders and reversions. The right to bar an entail has been recognised for centuries, through fines and recoveries, and has become one of the rights of a tenant in tail. In reified terms, it is one of the characteristics of the estate, and therefore it is also one of the characteristics of remainders and reversions after such an estate that they may be defeated.

3. Tenant in Tail in Possession

Today a tenant in tail in possession *i.e.* where there are no prior estates, has the extensive powers of a tenant for life under section 58(1) of the Settled Land Act, 1882. This includes a statutory power to sell the fee simple. However, if he or she were to exercise that power, the proceeds of sale would be invested and the tenant in tail is only entitled to the income for life. The interests of the remaindermen and reversioners are not destroyed but only overreached *i.e.* turned into interests in the consideration from the sale. A tenant in tail in possession would therefore almost always be much better off by disentailing under the 1834 Act instead. The powers in the Settled Land Acts may be useful for other things, however.

K. Base Fee

1. Characteristics

As the Fines and Recoveries (Ireland) Act, 1834 defines it,[58] a base fee is "that estate in fee simple into which an estate tail is converted where the issue in tail

57 It was only they who could create the warranty on which the actions depended. The Act replaces seisin with the protector. It is brilliantly imaginative in its technical means and utterly conservative in its effect.

58 Fines and Recoveries (Ireland) Act, 1834 s.1.

are barred, but persons claiming estates by way of remainder or otherwise [*i.e.* in reversion] are not". In principle, however, there is no reason why a base fee could not be created deliberately by a limitation, in which case it would be in the form:

> *to A and her heirs for as long as B has heirs of his body.*[59]

It is a type of determinable fee simple.[60] The heirs of B's body have no property interest. Their lives measure the estate given to A. In fact, since the estate in essence is a fee simple, A's heirs have no interest either, but, unlike the heirs of B's body, do have a *spes successionis*.
A base fee is a type of fee simple in that:

1. it is alienable, *i.e.* it can be sold or left by will; and
2. it passes on intestacy to the general heirs (now the intestate successors under the Succession Act, 1965) of the holder for the time being.

But it is unlike an ordinary fee simple in that:

3. it only continues to exist as long as the heirs of the body of the original tenant in tail exist.

For example, land is held by A for life, remainder to B in tail, remainder to C in fee simple. A is the protector under the Fines and Recoveries (Ireland) Act, 1834. B bars the entail without A's consent. B therefore obtains a base fee only. Let us assume that A has died. The situation is then as follows:

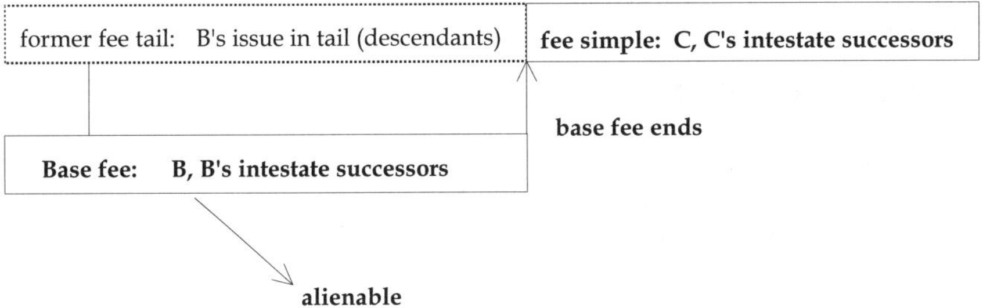

B has barred the right of the heirs in tail to inherit, the heirs in tail being the descendants of B. But he has not barred the estate in remainder, the fee simple vested in C. Thus the estate now held by B will come to an end when B's descendants die out. Before the entail was barred the heirs in tail had the right to inherit the estate, but now their lives are merely measures of the duration of the

59 *Idle v. Cooke* (1699) 2 Ld Raym 1144 1148, 92 ER 257, 1 P Wms 70, 2 Salk 620, 91 ER 525, Holt 164, 11 Mod 57, 88 ER 883.

60 Powell, "Determinable Fees" (1923) 23 Colum L R 207.

estate vested in B, or whoever then holds it. If that happens then C, or if C is dead, then C's testate or intestate successors, or the person to whom C has conveyed his future interest, will become entitled to the land in fee simple. In the meantime B can sell his base fee *inter vivos* to X or leave it by will to Y: a base fee is an alienable estate. If B sells it to X, X will have an estate which will come to an end when B's heirs in tail die out, and if X leaves it by will to Y, it will also end on that event. C, etc, will then become entitled in fee simple. If B does neither of these things then the base fee will pass on his death to his intestate successors under the Succession Act, 1965. They will similarly only hold it until B's heirs in tail die out. To take a further example:

to A for life, remainder to B in tail male, remainder to C in fee simple

B has a daughter, D, and a son S. S is married, with no children. S also has a successful business and does not need the property. B wants D to have the fee simple. A, the protector, does not consent. B executes a disentailing assurance in favour of D. D gets a base fee. D has a daughter, GD, and a son, GS. D dies. Under the Succession Act, 1965 they inherit their mother's property jointly. S dies. The base fee comes to an end. S was the person who would have inherited the fee tail if it had not been barred. C becomes entitled to the land. The same would occur if S died leaving only daughters, since this was a fee tail male.

2. Voidable Base Fee

A technical defect in disentailing, such as failure to enrol the deed, gives rise to a base fee voidable by the heirs in tail.[61] The heirs in tail may put an end to the base fee by entering the land, or by action.

3. Enlargement of a Base Fee

The examples we have just considered did not take into account the power to enlarge a base fee into a fee simple. We shall now deal with the circumstances in which this can be done. A base fee can be enlarged into a fee simple in a number of ways.

1. It can only be enlarged by a new disentailing assurance with the consent of the protector, or after the protectorship has ceased.
2. It can only be enlarged by a new disentailing assurance by the former tenant in tail or the person who would have been the heir in tail if it had not been barred, who is not necessarily the same person as the holder of the base fee. The holder of the base fee cannot enlarge it by executing a new disentailing assurance unless he or she is also the former tenant in tail or would have been the tenant in tail if the entail had not been

61 *Re St George's Estate* (1879) 3 LR Ir 277; *Witham v. Notley* [1913] 2 IR 281, Wylie, *Cases* p.170.

barred.[62]

3. The holder of the base fee can enlarge it:

   a) by buying out the remaindermen and reversioner. This is expensive, but the consent of the protector is not required.[63] If there is still a protector, then that means there is still a prior life estate and unless the holder of the base fee also buys out this interest, he or she will not acquire a fee simple in possession; and

   b) under the Statute of Limitations, 1957 section 19,[64] by the person entitled to possession by virtue of the disentailing assurance remaining in possession for 12 years after the tenant in tail would have been able to effect a complete bar.[65] The section bars the right of those entitled in remainder or reversion.

In *Re Domvile*[66] it was held, in relation to section 6 of the Real Property Limitation Act, 1874 which was replaced in identical terms by section 19, that a base fee could not be enlarged by a former tenant in tail remaining in possession after executing a disentailing assurance, because his or her possession was not by virtue of the disentailing assurance but by virtue of the settlement creating the fee tail. The possession of such a person was not a new possession under the disentailing assurance.[67]

---

62 *Bankes v. Small* (1887) 36 Ch D 716.

63 Because it does not involve a disentailing assurance. The 1834 Act requires the consent of the protector to a disposition as aforesaid, *i.e.* a disentailing assurance. The 1834 Act provides that if the holder of the base fee buys out the reversioner and/or remaindermen the base fee is thereby enlarged into a fee simple absolute.

64 Formerly under the Real Property Limitation Act, 1874 s.6. There is some authority that the latter section did not apply to bar issue in tail where the deed itself was ineffective to bar the issue in tail, as in the case of a voidable base fee. *Morgan v. Morgan* (1870) LR 10 Eq 99; *Penny v. Allen* (1857) 7 De G, M & G 426, 44 ER 160 per Cranworth LC. In the case of an effective base fee section 19 bars the remainders after 12 years although the deed itself did not bar them. It is not clear why, on the other hand, the statute should not bar the issue in tail where a deed does not itself bar their right. The position may be different under section 19 of the 1957 Act.

65 The original tenant in tail would not necessarily have been able to effect a complete bar by a new disentailing assurance, as where B, the tenant in tail, dies before the protector, A. The section appears to mean that if A then dies during the lifetime of B's son, the period runs from then, because from that point onwards (the complete bar point) S, who would have been the tenant in tail, would have been able to effect a complete bar and can indeed still do so. If B's daughter D, to whom B has left the base fee, or her successors, remain in possession, the period of possession is 12 years from the complete bar point.

66 [1952] IR 37.

67 It seems unlikely that this principle, being based upon possession, would extend to someone who was entitled to inherit the fee tail under the settlement, but who was never in possession under the settlement as tenant in tail, *i.e.* the holder of a base fee who was also an heir of the body of the donee in tail, but who inherited the base fee.

In the above example, if B bars in his own favour without A's consent and gets a base fee, then, according to *Re Domvile,*[68] B cannot enlarge by remaining in possession for 12 years. B can enlarge by a new disentailing assurance if A, the protector, changes his mind and consents, or if A dies. Suppose B dies without executing a new disentailing assurance. B had a son, S and a daughter, D. S and D inherit the base fee jointly, since it devolves as a fee simple. S and D can enlarge it into a true fee simple by remaining in possession under section 19. S alone can enlarge it by a new disentailing assurance, because he alone would have inherited the fee tail had it remained a fee tail.

It would seem that during the 12 years there is nothing that the remaindermen or reversioners can do to prevent the base fee becoming enlarged in the course of time.[69] This places them in a curious position, but the policy behind the provision is clear. If time began to run against their interests only when they fell into possession, this might not be for many years, even centuries. It would be impossible for purchasers of the land to know if such a defect in the title existed. There might be a remainder expectant on a base fee created perhaps 150 years ago which has not been time-barred because it has not yet fallen into possession. Almost any title would be subject to such a defect and so the framers of the Act took the opportunity of removing it.[70]

To take an example to illustrate the working of these rules:

to A for life, remainder to B in tail male, remainder to C in fee simple

B has a daughter D and a son S. B wants D to have the land. A is alive and does not consent to a disentailment. B executes a disentailing assurance in favour of D. D gets a base fee. The heirs in tail have been barred, *i.e.* that legal category of persons is no longer entitled to inherit, and so there is no longer any restriction to males. But can the base fee vested in D be enlarged so as to give her the fee simple?

On the above facts it can be enlarged in the following circumstances:

1. if A is still alive: B persuades A to consent, or D buys out C's remainder;
2. if A dies: the protectorship has come to an end. In these circumstances B can execute a new disentailing assurance in favour of D. D gets a fee simple;
3. if A dies and then B dies without executing a new assurance, the only person who can enlarge D's base fee by executing a new assurance is S, the person who would have inherited the fee tail had it not been barred. There is nothing to stop S charging money for exercising this right; and

68 [1952] IR 37.

69 Sugden, *New Statutes* p.89.

70 See Chapter 1 Introduction.

4. in any case, provided D is in possession under the base fee, by D remaining in possession for 12 years.

In 3 above, it is open to question whether the right to enlarge a base fee is itself an alienable right. S, in the example, is apparently accorded the right because he would have inherited the entail. This points to the right not being alienable since the entail itself was not. If S does not consent, D can enlarge the base fee herself by remaining in possession for 12 years. However, if S has no male descendants the base fee would come to an end if S died before the 12 years expire.

CHAPTER 9

LIFE ESTATES

"I think he'd become your tenant, for the whole of your share, at a rent of five-hundred a year; and maybe he'd give you three hundred pounds for the furniture and stock, and things about the place. If so you should give him a laise of three lives."

– Anthony Trollope, *The Kellys and the O'Kellys* Chapter 20.

A. Introduction

The life estate may have been the earliest estate recognised at common law. If this is correct, then grants of land were originally grants for the life of the recipient. When the fee simple and the fee tail became recognised, the life estate took on a new role. By the 13th and 14th centuries most life estates were not created by grant, but arose by operation of law: they were imposed on the parties.

Originally at common law when a woman married, all her property came to her husband. The ideology was that the husband and wife were in law one person. This reflected the religious notion that marriage was a union of two people. One might add, sceptically, that the one person was, in effect, the husband. The woman's legal personality was almost entirely subsumed within that of the husband. All effective powers of dealing with the property were vested in the husband. But the husband only retained the powers while the marriage lasted. When one of the partners to the marriage died, life estates were used to provide for the surviving partner.

B. Dower

This was the name of the life estate given to the widow in one third of her husband's land which he held for estates of inheritance (*i.e.* fee simple, fee tail), provided her children could inherit them.[1] If the husband held land in fee tail special, inheritable only by the offspring of himself and a previous wife, then his widow did not have dower in that land.

Originally the widow had the right of dower over land the husband had sold or granted away during the marriage. The person who owned it on the husband's death had to allow the widow to occupy it or retain the rents *etc.* for the

1 *Re Duignan* [1894] 1 IR 138, MR.

rest of her life. This may have protected widows but it was a severe restriction on the marketability of land. The Dower Act, 1833 abolished this aspect of dower.

Dower itself was abolished by the Succession Act, 1965 section 11(2). The Act replaced it with the provision for the widow's legal right to a share of the deceased's estate.[2]

C. Curtesy

Curtesy was the life estate which the widower had in all the land of his deceased wife which she held for an estate of inheritance, and provided his children could inherit. The estate also only arose if his wife had borne him living children. The common law made a connection between the birth of children and property rights, as if the two were interchangeable equivalents. The wife's property was only diminished by the widower's right if the wife had conferred upon him the benefit of an heir. This rule did not have a rational basis, but the general connection between children and land arose from the social context of a landed aristocracy concerned with the preservation of their estates over generations.

Curtesy was abolished by the Succession Act, 1965 section 11(2). The Succession Act, 1965 entitles the spouse of a deceased person to a legal share of their estate and does not discriminate, as the old law did, between male and female spouses.

D. Alienability

A characteristic of the estate, however created, is that the only interest a tenant can convey is an *estate pur autre vie* [for other life] *i.e.* an estate for the life of another. If A conveys his life estate to B, B gets an estate for the life of A. A is the called the *cestui que vie,*[3] Law French for the one who lives. A is a kind of human egg-timer. His life is used to measure the length of B's estate. A does not retain any interest in the land. Any other grant by A is not void, but voidable, like grants by a tenant in tail. Unlike the fee tail, however, those entitled in remainder or reversion when the life comes to an end can seek immediate possession of the land. Forfeiture in this way is a deterrent to such grants.[4]

The real, unreified, reason why, in the above example, B only obtains an estate for the life of A is easy to see: if it were otherwise, so that B obtained an estate for

2 Part IX.

3 Pronounced "settee kuh vee." The plural is correctly "ceux que vie" but often rendered as "cestuis que vie."

4 Statute of Gloucester, 1278 c.7 laid this down as to dower. Courts subsequently, within 10 years of the statute, extended the rule to all life estates.

her own life, then the land could be kept away from the original grantor of the life estate for generations even though the intent was to make a grant for one life only. This effect would be increased if, for example, B kept the estate until she became elderly and then conveyed it to C who was a young person, and C then did likewise. The estate could be passed from hand to hand virtually indefinitely. Fee simple owners would be reluctant to create life estates at all.

E. Power to Lease

At common law life tenant was able to grant leases, but any lease granted came to an end when the tenant died, regardless of the length of the term granted by the lease. One explanation for this was that a leasehold interest was regarded as essentially inferior to a freehold and dependent upon it. This is a reifying explanation, based upon an assumed essential nature of property interests. A more realistic explanation, based on considering the relationship between the parties, is that it was regarded as unjust if a tenant for life could unilaterally postpone the interests of remaindermen or reversioners by granting a lease. This limitation nevertheless hindered the development of landed estates and, eventually, power to grant leases that would bind the remaindermen or reversioner was conferred by statute.[5]

F. Escheat and Forfeiture

If escheat for felony or forfeiture for treason occurred and the person convicted of felony or treason held the land for life, the life estate came to an end and the next person entitled to possession took the land as if the life tenant were dead. It was not a true case of escheat or forfeiture, because it did not bring that layer of tenure to an end. Both were abolished by the Forfeiture Act, 1870, section 1.

G. Waste

The life estate was of a limited nature and the life tenant might be tempted to exploit the property without regard to the interest of the remaindermen and so cause damage that might still be apparent when they came into possession of their interests. In order to protect the remaindermen, therefore, the common law developed the doctrine of waste. This defined the types of alterations to the property for which the life tenant was to be answerable to those entitled in remainder or reversion.

5 At first private acts of parliament had to be obtained: *Herbert v. Madden* (1858) 6 Ir CLR 28. The power is now governed by the Settled land Acts, 1882–1890. See Chapter 14 Settlements of Land.

1. Ameliorating Waste

This is an act which actually improves the property and therefore at first sight there seems to be no problem about such waste. But operations which improve the value of property may be destructive to the environment, such as ploughing up old meadows or pastures. In *Murphy v. Daly*[6] it was held that pasture which has been in grass for 20 years or more is ancient pasture and it is waste to plough it up. This may be regarded as an example of the common law protecting the environment at the expense of the short-term interest of the tenant for life.

Since the leading Irish case of *Doherty v. Allman*[7], it is clear that the courts will not restrain a tenant for life from causing ameliorating waste. This indicates a shift of judicial opinion at the end of the 19th century in favour of industrial development at the expense of the environment. Today, most forms of such development come within the sphere of planning law and environmental issues are resolved in that context.

2. Permissive Waste

This a failure to do what ought to be done to preserve the value of the property, such as a failure to repair. The common law does not impose liability for permissive waste and a tenant for life is only liable if the settlement itself expressly imposes liability.

3. Voluntary Waste

Voluntary waste is doing something positive which reduces the value of the property so that the reduction affects the reversion or the remainders, *i.e.* it will still be apparent when the interest of the person next entitled falls into possession, for example opening and working mines, felling timber. At common law timber comprises oak, ash and elm.[8] A tenant for life is liable for voluntary waste unless the settlement exempts him or her expressly. If it does so then the tenant for life is said to be unimpeachable of waste.

---

6 (1860) 13 Ir CLR 239.

7 (1878) 3 AC 709, (1878) 1 LR Ir 249, HL, affirming IR 10 Eq 460, CA in Chancery.

8 See footnote 13.

a) Estovers

At common law *estovers*[9], the Norman French name for a number of rights recognised by Anglo-Saxon law, are an exception to waste. Tenants have the right to cut suitable wood for the purpose repairing the house occupied by the tenant or burning as fuel in it (housebote and firebote), or fences and ditches (haybote), or making and repairing farm implements (ploughbote and cartbote).[10] A tenant who cuts live wood where dead wood is suitable would therefore be liable for waste.[11] In Irish common law it includes the right to cut turf for fuel in the house where the land includes turf bog.[12] The right is now subject to limits imposed by the Forestry Acts and planning legislation.

b) Irish Timber Acts

In Ireland the doctrine of waste in relation to timber was altered by the Irish Timber Acts,[13] a series of statutes aimed at encouraging the growing of timber and replanting of forests in Ireland. The replanting was to replace the ancient forests which had been depleted over the centuries by, among other causes, the felling of hardwoods such as oak to build the wooden ships of the navy.

Tenants for life or lives could register trees planted by them. The registration was by affidavit lodged with the clerk of the peace of the county. They then became entitled to cut and sell the same trees.[14] Until cut down, the trees remained part of the land and passed with it.[15] The right was withdrawn as to tenants under leases in 1791[16] but the Act exempted tenants under leases for lives renewable forever.[17]

---

9 From L. *stuffare*, to furnish. Baker, *Law French* "estover".

10 Co Litt 41b.

11 Cheshire, *Real Property* (15th ed.) p.271.

12 *Howley v. Jebb* (1859) 8 Ir CLR 435; *Jones v. Meany* [1941] Ir Jur Rep 50.

13 Timber Acts (Ireland): 1698, 10 Wm III c.12 (Ir); 1705, 4 Anne c.9 (Ir); 1710, 9 Anne c.5 (Ir); 1721, 8 Geo I c.8 (Ir). Land Improvement Acts (Ireland): 1735, 9 Geo II c.7 (Ir); 1765, 5 Geo III c.17 (Ir); 1767, 7 Geo III c.20 (Ir); 1776, 15 & 16 Geo III c.26 (Ir); 1784, 23 & 24 Geo III c.39 (Ir); 9 Geo IV c.53 (Ir) s.1; SLR (Ir) A, 1879. See *Kirkpatrick v. Naper* (1945) 79 ILTR 49; *Standish v. Murphy* (1854) 2 Ir Ch R 264. The 1776 Act did not enlarge the common law definition of timber which comprises oak, ash and elm: *Kirkpatrick and Maunsell v. Naper* (1944) 79 ILTR 49.

14 *Mountcashel v. O'Neill* (1857) 5 HLC 937; *Pentland v. Somerville* (1851) 2 Ir Ch. R 289.

15 *Alexander v. Godley* (1857) 6 Ir CLR 445; *Galway v. Baker* (1840) 7 Cl & F 379, 7 ER 1114.

16 By 31 Geo III c.40 (Ir).

17 See below.

4. Equitable Waste

This is "that which a prudent man would not do in the management of his own property," *e.g.* acts of wanton destruction such as cutting down ornamental timber,[18] stripping lead of a roof and selling it. A tenant for life is liable for equitable waste unless the settlement or other document expressly exempts him from equitable waste. If it merely says he or she is to be unimpeachable of waste or some such phrase that will not be enough to render the tenant for life unimpeachable for equitable waste. Equity intervenes here to restrain a person who was expressly made not liable for voluntary waste abusing that privilege. It is interesting to notice that it does not interfere with acts which will develop the estate economically in a rational way.

H. Emblements

Where a tenant has a term which is uncertain as to its duration, such as a life estate or a term of years determinable on an uncertain event during the period, a particular problem arises and that is that the tenancy may come to an end unexpectedly and, in the case of agricultural land, while crops are still standing on the land. In the case of a tenancy for life the personal representatives, or, in the case of an estate pur autre vie, the tenant, have a right to emblements, *i.e.* the right to enter the land after the tenancy has come to an end in order to remove the crops sown during the tenancy.[19] It only applies to cultivated crops.[20]

I. Estate pur autre vie

A lesser form of life estate was the estate pur autre vie, *i.e.* for the life of a person other than the holder of the estate. An estate pur autre vie normally arises by grant. This can occur in two ways.

1. If A has an estate for her own life, or an entail after possibility[21] and makes a grant of it to B, B obtains an estate pur autre vie, namely, for the life of A. A is the cestui que vie. Or,
2. P has a fee simple and makes a grant "to Q for the life of X."

---

18 *De la Bedoyere v. Nugent* (1890) 25 LR Ir 143, MR.

19 *Short v. Atkinson* (1834) H & J 682; *O'Connell v. O'Callaghan* (1841) L & T 157; de Moleyns, Chapter 26.

20 *Flanagan v. Seaver* (1858) 9 Ir Ch R 230.

21 Challis 357, Megarry & Wade, *Real Property* p.100.

1. Escheat, Forfeiture

Felony or treason had a similar effect as in the case of the life estate. It was as if the tenant pur autre vie had died.

2. Waste

A tenant pur autre vie is generally liable for waste in the same way as a life tenant.[22]

3. Rules of Occupancy

We have seen that if A holds land for his own life and makes a grant of it to B, B then holds the land for the life of A. The question arises as to what happens if B dies before A. There is still something left of the estate, but who gets it? An estate pur autre vie is a lesser kind of life estate and as life estates were not estates of inheritance, *i.e.* not inheritable, the common law did not regard estates pur autre vie as inheritable either. Special rules were developed to provide for devolution in such a cases.

a) General Occupancy

If G granted land:

> *to B for the life of A*

without mentioning B's heirs, then whoever first took possession of the land at B's death was entitled to hold it until A died. The common law took the view that the remnant of the estate belonged by right to no one, and so the first person to take possession of it could keep it.[23] That was called general occupancy. In practice it was usually the heir who took possession.

b) Special Occupancy

If G granted the land:

> *to B and her heirs for the life of A*

or

> *to have and to hold to B and his [her] heirs, during the life of X [or the lives of X, Y and Z, etc.] [or the lives of the cestui(s) que vie hereafter described, etc.]*[24]

22 Differences in the case of tenants under leases for lives renewable forever, in regard to the Irish Timber Acts, are noted below in dealing with those interests.

23 *McClintock v. Irvine* (1861) 10 Ir Ch R 480.

24 *ibid.* at 485.

then it was the heir of B who was entitled on B's death, under the rule of special occupancy. The person who was B's heir did not strictly take as heir, but as special occupant.[25] The common law did not regard the heir of B as entitled strictly by the rules of inheritance, *i.e.* by descent, because an *estate pur autre vie*, being a species of life estate, was not an estate of inheritance. This is the reified explanation. The practical explanation was that, if the heir had been regarded as taking by descent, feudal incidents such as relief would have been payable. This would have been rather onerous since the new tenant's interest could end before his own death, and so such tenants were excused the obligation to pay a relief.

c) Next of Kin

If G granted land:

to B and his next of kin during the life of A . . .

then the next of kin were entitled to take possession on B's death, as with personal property.[26]

d) Abolition of Occupancy

The rules made sense in the context of a feudal system with its incidents of tenure. With the decline of feudalism the rules became an anachronism. The Statute of Frauds, 1695[27] made the following changes:

(1) A tenant pur autre vie was given the right to leave the residue by will. This evidently applied to estates pur autre vie whether general or special occupancy applied.

(2) Where the tenant did not do so, and there was no special occupant, the estate devolved upon the tenant's personal representatives on trust[28] for the next of kin, so that it was distributable as personal property.

(3) Whether it passed to the heir or the personal representative, it was made subject to the payment of the deceased's debts.

---

25 If a tenant pur autre vie died and the estate was subject to special occupancy, but no special occupant existed, then something like an escheat occurred. The Wills Act, 1937 s.6 provided that in such a case the executor or administrator of the deceased's property took the interest: *Plunket v. Reilly* (1854) 2 Ir Ch R 585.

26 *Campbell v. Sandys* (1806) 1 Sch & Lef 281, 9 RR 33. There was some conflict in the authorities as to the position if the grant was "to X and his executors". The better view is probably that executors could not take as special occupants, and that only heirs could do so. The English Statute of Frauds, 1677, 29 Chas II c.3 s.12 assumes so. See *Campbell v. Sandys* (1806) 1 Sch & Lef 281 at 289 where the authorities are reviewed, and *Croker v. Brady* (1879) 4 LR Ir 653, CA.

27 Section 9. See the English Statute of Frauds, 1677, s.12.

28 The trust was a creation of a later statues in 1740 and 1837: see Challis, 362. *Witter v. Witter* (1730) 3 P Wms 99, 24 ER 985.

General occupancy is not expressly abolished by the 1695 Act, but it has been assumed[29] that provision (2) above is not limited to estates pur autre vie subject to special occupancy, but where there was no special occupant in fact, but that it applied in addition to cases where there was no special occupant because the estate was subject to general occupancy. If this interpretation is correct, then no general occupancy could arise in Ireland after 1695.[30]

Special occupancy was abolished by the Succession Act, 1965, section 11(1). The interest of the deceased tenant in such a case will now devolve like any other property, by will or on intestacy. Under the Succession Act, 1965 if the tenant dies intestate the residue of the estate passes to intestate successors determined in accordance with Part VI of the Act.[31]

4. Alienability Inter Vivos

Although a tenant pur autre vie could not dispose of any interests in the estate by will until the above reforms, there was never any question that they could dispose of their interest *inter vivos.* Like a life tenant, a tenant pur autre vie can only grant an estate pur autre vie with the same cestui que vie as determined the length of his or her own estate. If A grants his life estate to B, B holds the land for the life of A. If B grants her estate to C, C also holds it for the life of A.

The position of the tenant pur autre vie is now radically altered by the Settled Land Acts, 1882–1890.

It is to be assumed that a tenant pur autre vie can convey during his or her lifetime, as a future interest, whatever interest might survive his or her death. It would be in the nature of a contingent interest, *i.e.* contingent upon the cestui que vie surviving the tenant.

J. Leases for Lives Renewable Forever

A lease for lives renewable forever (or perpetually renewable)[32] was a species of estate pur autre vie, the difference being that there were commonly three

29 See, for example, Megarry & Wade, *Real Property* p.102.

30 Similar words appeared in section 6 of the Wills Act 1837 which provided that: "if no disposition by will shall be made of any *estate pur autre vie* of a freehold nature… and in case there shall be no special occupant… it shall go to the executor or administrator of the party that had the estate thereof by virtue of the grant". See *Re Murray* [1916] IR 302; *Plunket v. Reilly* (1854) 2 Ir Ch. R 585. Similar words also appear in section 9 of Deasy's Act 1860 which make it clear that the personal representative holds the estate on trust for the next of kin. See also *Mcdermott v. Balfe* (1868) IR 2 Eq 440; *Cornwall v. Saurin* (1886) 17 LR Ir 595.

31 Succession Act, 1965 s.66.

32 It was matter of construction whether the right to renew was perpetual. In *Sheppard v. Doolan* (1842) 3 Dru & War 1 "renewable forever" in the habendum of the deed was held enough.

cestuis que vie and the grant contained a clause providing that when any of the cestuis died they could be replaced with another life on payment of a fine, *i.e.* a lump sum to the grantor. The typical form of grant is: "to X for the lives of A, B and C" with a covenant[33] to renew the lives of the cestuis que vie, A, B and C. As with other estates pur autre vie, A, B and C have no property interest in the land and their lives serve simply to measure the duration of the estate.

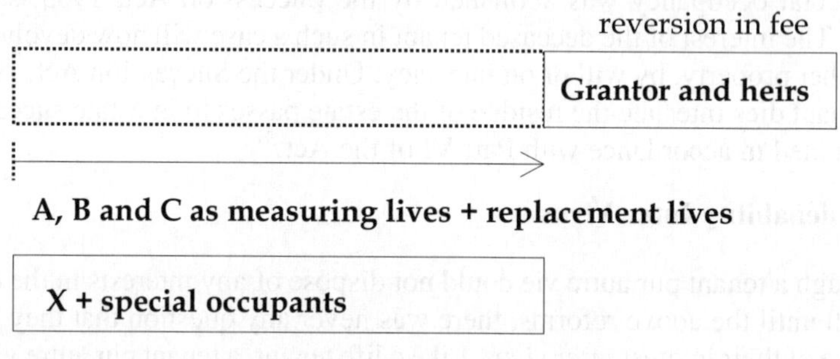

lease for lives renewable forever

The interest is called a lease because the tenant pays a rent and it is a commercial, *i.e.* a commodity relationship rather than a family one. But the estate is freehold and not leasehold. At common law this would have implied that the tenure was freehold. Freehold tenure could still be created by such a grant after *Quia Emptores*, 1290 because the statute only prohibited subinfeudation for a fee simple estate.[34] Since there was freehold tenure, a rent and other covenants could be attached. The law as to the running of the benefit and burden of covenants in the grant would be governed by the law of freehold tenure. By the 18th century this law had become extremely obscure. Thus, even before Deasy's Act allowed the modern landlord and tenant relationship to be grafted onto virtually any estate, the courts in Ireland treated the covenants as governed by the more familiar rules of leasehold tenure.[35] The cases are not explicit as to whether they considered the tenure actually to be the modern form of leasehold tenure, in which case the lease for lives renewable was the original hybrid interest in Ireland, or merely that they assumed the rules as to the running of covenants in freehold tenure to be identical to those in leasehold tenure. The latter is more consistent in principle, but it appears to have mattered little in practice.

33 A separate covenant was not necessary: *Chambers v. Gaussen* (1844) 2 Jo & Lat 99, and see footnote 32.

34 One of the reasons for the use of leases for lives renewable forever may have been that it effectively avoided *Quia Emptores*, 1290. This is further discussed below.

35 *Peacock v. O'Grady* (1849) 13 Ir CLR 292.

The grantor retained a reversion in fee simple which would pass to his or her heir at law or could be assigned.[36] This interest was known as the reversion in fee and the holder of it the reversioner in fee.

The tenant of a lease for lives could assign or sublet the interest. This topic is dealt with below.

1. History

The origin of leases for lives renewable forever is obscure. Sugden[37] was of the view that the tenure was introduced as a means of conveying land to Catholics at a time when the Penal Laws were in force, but, as Smythe points out[38] the earliest examples of such leases pre-date the first Penal Law,[39] and so this cannot be correct. The tenure might incidentally have avoided one provision of the Penal laws, namely that prohibiting Catholics from inheriting from Protestant relatives. The prohibition may have applied only to inheritance in the true sense, *i.e.* through the laws of descent. Lease for lives devolved, as other estates pur autre vie, by the rules of occupancy. It would also have avoided the "Gavelkind Act"[40] under which on the death of a Catholic land held in fee simple or fee tail was to be divided among the sons of the landowner unless the eldest son was, or thereupon became, a Protestant.[41] The law was aimed at reducing the size and therefore the influence of Catholic landed estates. The estate may therefore have been used to avoid this, although this does not explain its origin.

In *Boyle v. Lysaght*[42] it is said that the tenure may have originated in Northern Ireland but that in the South it had been introduced by the second Duke of Ormonde who procured a private Act of Parliament[43] enabling him to make such grants of his estate, which he did in favour of Protestant tenants. The motive was apparently both to pay off the landlord's debts and to encourage the planted tenants to improve the land. An additional motive is thought to be that,

36 *Long v. Long* (1860) 10 Ir Ch R 406, (1861) 11 Ir Ch. R 252.

37 Sugden arguendo in *Attorney General v. Hungerford* (1834) 2 Cl & Fin 371, 6 ER 1189.

38 Smythe, *The Law of Landlord and Tenant in Ireland* Dublin 1842 pp. 229-232.

39 The first Penal Law affecting landed property was 2 Anne c.6 (Ir), 1703. The lease in *Boyle v. Lysaght* (1787) 1 Ridg PC 384 dated from 1660; in *Nangle v. Smith* 1 West 184, 1 Law Rec 3rd ser, Eq 119, from 1672; in *Brown v. Tighe* (1834) 8 Bligh N S 272 from 1663; in *Inchquin v. Burnell* (1795) 3 Ridg PC 376 from 1668; in *Ross (Earl) v. Worsop* (1740) 1 Bro PC 281, 1 ER 568 from 1682. A note in pencil in the author's copy of Smythe reads "*Earl of Arran v. Quigley – 1609.*"

40 Actually section 10 of 2 Anne c.6 (Ir).

41 *ibid.* s.12. See *Redington v. Redington* (1794) 3 Ridg PC 201.

42 (1787) 1 Ridg PC 384 at 402.

43 8 & 9 Wm III c.5, 1697 (Eng) (private).

at a time when the vote was confined to Protestant freeholders and there was no secret ballot, the landowners, by granting freehold estates, thus conferred the right to vote on small Protestant tenants and at the same time secured to themselves considerable political influence.

Whatever the political motives, the tenure certainly seems to have been designed to avoid the effect of *Quia Emptores*, 1290. That statute had prohibited subinfeudation for a fee simple estate. Lease for lives renewable forever nevertheless conferred on tenants a freehold interest of possibly perpetual duration while at the same time providing landlords with an income from the rent and the renewal fines. It thus created a form of tenure analogous to subinfeudation in fee simple. It achieved a dependent form of freehold tenure reserving benefits of real economic value to the landlord while not falling foul of the letter of the statute. It was a suitable form of property for plantations or colonies of English and Scottish small farmers. It created a structure with freeholders at the bottom, who had potentially perpetual interests, giving them both an incentive to develop the land and a sense of permanence in their new home, but at the same time it was a hierarchical structure with the freeholders still to some extent dependent on the favourable opinion of the larger landowners who in turn owed allegiance to the British Crown. It was form of property which incorporated notions of dependence, permanence and authority, all of which were elements in a planned settler colony. This may be contrasted with the forms of tenure in unplanned colonies, such as North America and South Africa, where the remoteness of central authority contributed to more independent forms of tenure.

To the many ironies of Irish history there should now be added the consideration that a form of property, which began life as a form of dependent tenure for plantation settlers, came to be used as a device by which Catholic landowners avoided aspects of the Penal Laws.

2. Presumption of Death

One problem with leases for lives was that it might be uncertain whether one or more of the cestuis que vie were still alive. The Life Estates Act, 1695[44] was passed by the Irish parliament to deal with the problem. The normal legal presumption is in favour of life.[45] The statute reverses this presumption where it is shown, by the lessor or a reversioner, that a cestui que vie of a lease for lives or other life estate has been "absent or beyond the seas" for seven years or more

44 7 Wm III c.8 (Ir); Short Titles Act, 1962. It was based on the English Cestui que Vie Act, 1665 18 & 19 Chas II c.11. The English Act was followed by c.1the Cestui que Vie Act, 1707, 6 Anne c.72, , 6 Anne c.18 in Ruffhead, but no equivalent Irish statute was passed. See Smythe, pp. 576–581.

45 Wigmore, *Evidence in Trials at Common Law*, 1981, vol. 9, § 2531. And See *Chard v. Chard* [1955] P 259, [1955] 3 All E R 721, [1955] 3 W L R 954, per Sachs J.

with no proof that they are still alive. The statute and its English counterpart are credited with having given rise, by analogy, to the general presumption of death after a similar period in the law of evidence.[46]

In so far as the statute applied to leases for lives renewable forever, the effect of applying the Act was to entitle the tenant to renew on payment of a fine. In the case of an estate pur autre vie where the lives are not renewable, or not renewable perpetually, then the effect of applying the Act, if there is only one life, or if there is only one remaining life, is to bring the estate to an end and entitle the grantor to recover the land. If the tenant is ejected from the land under the Act and then the absentee cestui que vie later turns up alive, section 3 of the Act provides that the tenant can re-enter the land and has an action for loss of profits against the lessor or reversioner who brought ejectment.[47]

3. The Equity to Renew

One of the first[48] cases to hold that, in addition to the contractual or common law right to renew, there was an equity to renew the lives was *Sweet v. Anderson.*[49] A lease was made to Arthur Anderson for the lives of his nephew, "Black Jack" Anderson, and another, with a covenant to renew the lives on payment of a fine within 12 months of the death of the life concerned.

Arthur, the grantee, died in 1714 leaving his interest by will to the respondent. The respondent applied for a renewal. It was refused. Black Jack had not been heard of since 1697. The appellant argued that he must be presumed dead, by statute,[50] after seven years. Since no fine had been paid within 12 months, there was no longer any right to renew. In 1718 the case came before the Irish Court of Exchequer. Chief Baron Gilbert noted that Black Jack had been absent for 21 years. He came up with a novel solution. Since Jack would be presumed dead after seven years, the respondent could have his renewal if he paid three fines, *i.e.* one fine for every seven years. These became known as

46 Smythe 576-581; *Doe d George v. Jesson* (1805) 6 East 80, 85, 102 ER 1217; *Doe d Lloyd v. Deakin* (1821) 4 B & Ald 433, 106 ER 995. See also *In bonis Cooke* (1870) IR 5 Eq 240 (if lost at sea must prove he embarked on vessel and was believed to have been aboard when lost); *Re Webb's Estate* (1871) IR 5 Eq 235, Ch Ap; *Pennefather v. Pennefather* (1871) IR 6 Eq 171, V-CV-C (son, tenant in tail in remainder, emigrated in 1858 and never heard of again. Father died the same year. Presumption that son survived father); *In bonis Atkinson* (1873) IR 7 Eq 219.

47 *Hurly v. Hanrahan* (1867) IR 1 CL 700, QB; *Caruth v. Northland* (1831) Hayes 233 per Joy CB (otherwise if the tenant voluntarily surrendered under belief that the cestui que vie was dead).

48 See Lord Lifford LC in *Bateman v. Murray*, (1779) 1 Ridg PC 187 at 196: "Lord Chief Baron Gilbert only invented the mode of making satisfaction for lapse of time by the rule he adopted respecting septennial fines".

49 (1772) 2 Bro PC 256, affirmed 430, 1 ER 927. The case was heard in 1722.

50 7 Wm III c.8 (Ir). See Presumption of Death.

septennial fines. The decision, which temporarily[51] made Gilbert CB the most popular Englishman in Ireland, at least among tenants, was upheld on appeal to the British House of Lords in 1722.[52] The case also asserted the proposition, though may not have invented it,[53] that the equity overrode any negative covenant in the lease requiring renewal within a given period of time.[54]

Thereafter it became common for the courts in Ireland to renew the lives in almost all cases. Purchasers, relying on these authorities, began to buy land in Ireland under titles which were only an equity to renew[55] and to treat them as perpetual freehold interests in the nature of fees simple, by settling and mortgaging them.[56] Then towards the end of the century Lord Mansfield in *Kane v. Hamilton*[57] and Lord Thurlow in *Bateman v. Murray*,[58] both cases before the British House of Lords on appeal from Ireland, refused to recognise that the Irish equity was as extensive as the Irish courts had held it to be. In particular they held that it did not permit a renewal after indefinite delay contrary to limiting clauses in the lease itself, apart from cases of fraud or accident, against which even the English courts would give relief.[59] The Irish Parliament responded in 1780 by passing the Tenantry Act, 1779[60] which recognised the Irish equity and gave it statutory form. The provisions of the Act are discussed below.

---

51 He became unpopular again by following the British House of Lords in preference to the Irish House in *Annesley v. Sherlock* (1718) 21 Journals of the House of Lords [Great Britain] 55, reversing *Sherlock v. Annesley* (1716) 2 Journals of the House of Lords [Ireland] 541. See footnote 62.

52 (1772) 2 Bro PC 256; 1 ER 927.

53 See footnote 48.

54 See also *Ross (Earl) v. Worsop* (1740) 1 Bro PC 281, 1 ER 568; *Pendred v. Griffith* (1744) 1 Bro PC 314, 1 ER 590 (lordship of Baltinglas: no renewal if tenant conceals death of cestui). See also cases in Ireland after *Sweet* cited in *Bateman v. Murray*, (1779) 1 Ridg PC 187 at 193: *O'Hara v. Burke*, unreported Exchequer, Hilary 1756, per Bowes LCB; *Shore v. Darnley*, unreported Exchequer, 1766.

55 See footnote 69.

56 See footnote 71.

57 (1784) 1 Ridg PC 180 at 185.

58 (1779) 1 Ridg PC 187 at 201.

59 Per Lord Thurlow at (1779) 1 Ridg PC 201:

> "... when the lessee has lost his legal right, he must prove some fraud on the part of the lessor, by which he was debarred the exercise of his right, or some accident or misfortune on his own part which he could not prevent, by means whereof he was disabled from applying at the stated times for a renewal according to the terms of his lease."

Notice the change in Thurlow's statement of the law after the Tenantry Act: see footnote 76.

60 19 & 20 Geo III c.30 (Ir). The title is given by the Short Titles Act, 1962. It should have been called the Tenantry Act, 1780. The bill was before the Irish House of Lords in August 1780 and received the royal assent on 7 September 1780.

A number of cases came before the courts in Ireland between the reversal on appeal in *Bateman v. Murray* and the passing of the Tenantry Act. *Freeman v. Boyle*[61] was before the Lord Chancellor, Lifford, in June 1780 and he refused the renewal, following the British House of Lords in *Bateman v. Murray*. The Tenantry Act came into force in September 1780 and *Freeman v. Boyle* reached the Irish House of Lords, to whom jurisdiction had been restored in 1782.[62] The Irish House promptly reaffirmed the Irish equity to renew on payment of septennial fines.[63] The Irish Lords in a number of cases reaffirmed that the equity was an extensive one indeed. In *McGrath v. Lord Muskerry*[64] the court held that equity would grant a renewal even after all the lives had died out.[65] In *O'Neil v. Jones*[66] the covenant expressly providing that the right to renew was to expire six months after the death of the life for which renewal sought. The court held that a renewal would be granted even after the six months had expired.[67] The Irish courts held, then, that the equity overrode any

61 (1780) 2 Ridg PC 69, 76.

62 There had been some confusion as to the court of ultimate resort in Ireland. In *Annesley v. Sherlock* (1717–1720) appeals were taken from the Irish Court of Exchequer to both the British ((1718) 21 Journals of the House of Lords [GB] 55) and the Irish House of Lords ((1716) 2 Journals of the House of Lords [Ireland] 541). See M.S. Flaherty, "The Empire Strikes Back: *Annesley v. Sherlock* and the Triumph of Imperial Parliamentary Supremacy" (1987) 87 Columbia L Rev 593. They gave conflicting judgments and neither would retract their decision. The statute 6 Geo I c.5, 1719 (The Declaratory Act) declared that the Irish House had no appellate jurisdiction. Appeals then went to the British House of Lords. In 1782 the Act 22 Geo III c.53 (The Repealing Act) repealed the 1719 statute, but did not expressly confer jurisdiction on the Irish House. Shortly afterwards 23 Geo III c.28 excluded the jurisdiction of the English courts from Irish appeals, but still did not expressly confer appellate jurisdiction on the Irish House of Lords which nevertheless assumed it and continued to exercise it until the Act of Union came into effect on 1 January 1801. The article referred to unfortunately gives the impression that the Irish House of Lords did not hear any appeals after *Annesley v. Sherlock*. See further Lyall, 'The Irish House of Lords as a Judicial Body 1783–1800.' (1993–95) 28–30 *Irish Jurist* 314–360.

63 (1787) I Ridg PC 384 at 405, per Lord Lifford LC.

64 (1787) 1 Ridg PC 501.

65 See also *Harrison v. Sir Thomas Prendergast*, unreported 16 May 1754, cited by counsel for the plaintiff in *Bateman v. Murray* (1785) 1 Ridg PC 187 at 191, (a renewal was decreed by the court of Exchequer after all the lives had died); *O'Hara v. Bourke* unreported 1756, Exchequer, Hilary Term, per Bowes CB, cited in *Bateman v. Murray* (1785) 1 Ridg PC 187 at 193. The covenant provided that unless fines and rent were paid within a limited time, the landlord might ever after refuse a renewal. By 1749 all three lives had died. There was no excuse gives for the laches. The court ordered a renewal.

66 (1785) 1 Ridg PC 175.

67 Following *Carpenter v. Stewart*, unreported 15 February 1733, Exch cited in *Bateman v. Murray* (1785) 1 Ridg PC 187 at 193.

express term in the leases seeking to restrict the right to renew.[68] In that respect it had become comparable to the equity to redeem a mortgage.

Why did the judges go that far? Purchasers and tenants under such leases in Ireland had long been in the habit of treating them as equivalent to fees simple, possibly even before *Sweet v. Anderson*, and certainly afterwards. Land subject to such titles had been sold as if they were fees simple.[69] Tenants had mortgaged them and settled[70] them, creating jointures in favour of family members.[71] Mortgagees and those entitled to jointures would lose their interests if the lease was held to have terminated. The grant was in effect a perpetual interest and the equity produced that result. It recognised the perpetual nature of the tenant's interest. It may be, of course, that the judges acted on the reified view, that they saw it as a real and substantial reason.

The establishment of the equity would have had some social effects. If the tenure was originally the form in which Protestant settlers held their land, then the equity would give them greater independence from the political influence of the landowners. The equity to renew the lives had the effect of reducing the political influence of Protestant landowners, especially as it was held to exist despite express clauses seeking to limit it.[72] This may be explained historically as consistent with the emergence in the 17th and 18th centuries of a professional middle class, of which the judges were a part, and whose power reached its peak in the Constitution of 1782 and Grattan's Parliament and who were unsympathetic to the landowners' political influence. It is also true that before Catholics obtained the vote in 1793[73] the only political influence which might be exercised by Catholics was by Catholic landowners[74] over their Protestant freehold tenants. The equity would also tend to reduce that factor also.

---

68 In *Kirkwood v. Lord Tyrone*, unreported, cited by counsel in *Bateman v. Murray* (1785) Ridg PC 192 a renewal was decreed in equity after a recovery in ejectment at common law. This point was upheld by the British House of Lords after the Union in *Mountmorris (Earl) v. White* (1814) 2 Dow 459, 3 ER 931.

69 Counsel for plaintiffs in *Bateman v. Murray*, (1779) 1 Ridg PC 187 at 193.

70 See Quasi-settlements below.

71 Carleton as counsel in *Boyle v. Lysaght* argued in his pleadings that the lands were "security for creditors and a fund for family settlements – circumstances in the contemplation of the legislature at the enacting of that salutary law [*i.e.* the Tenantry Act, 1779]." "House of Lords Appeals" (Pleadings) 1787-90 Vol. 47, King's Inns.

72 *O'Neil v. Jones* (1788) 2 Ridg PC 69, 76.

73 By the Catholic Relief Act, 1793, 33 Geo III c.21 (Ir). Catholics, like other voters, had to be freeholders, but, unlike other voters, could not sit in parliament, hold senior positions in the executive or be judges or practice at the Bar.

74 Cullen "Catholics under the Penal Laws" (1986) 1 Eighteenth Century Ireland 23 suggests that the Penal Laws were not in fact enforced as rigorously as it was once thought. It also seems that legal loopholes in them were exploited.

4. The Tenantry Act, 1779

Section 1 of the act, which is still in force, recognises the old equity of the country and provides that tenants and their assigns have the right to renew the lease if they are prepared to pay arrears of rent and have not acted inequitably. The section is set out below. In accordance with the practice of the time, section 1 follows on from the preamble to the statute and begins after the phrase "be it. . . enacted. . . that. . .":

> "Whereas great parts of the lands in this kingdom are held under leases for lives with covenants for perpetual renewals upon payment of certain fines at the times therein respectively mentioned for each renewal. . . and whereas it has been for a long time a received opinion in this kingdom, to which some decisions in courts of equity and declarations of judges have given countenance, that courts of equity would in such cases relieve against lapse of time upon giving adequate compensation to the persons, to whom such fines were payable, or their representatives: and to the end that such interests may not be defeated by a mere neglect, where no fraud appears to have been intended, upon making full satisfaction to the lessors, or those deriving under them; *be it. . . enacted. . . that* courts of equity upon an adequate compensation being made shall relieve such tenants and their assigns against such lapse of time, if no circumstance of fraud be proved against such tenants or their assigns; unless it shall be proved to the satisfaction of such courts, that the landlords or lessors, or persons entitled to receive such fines, had demanded such fines from such tenants or their assigns, and that the same had been refused or neglected to be paid within reasonable time after such demand".

Section 1, begins, in the quotation above, after the word "enacted. . ." with the words "that courts of equity. . ." The section therefore only refers to such tenants and the landlords and the definition of these phrases is left to the words in the preamble. The preamble, if it is to be considered a definition of the scope of the Act, confines it to "leases for lives with covenants for perpetual renewals upon payment of certain fines. . ." but, despite these words, at least one case has held that the Act extends to perpetually renewable leases for years.[75] It may be that courts of equity in Ireland before the Act would have extended the old equity of the country to such cases.

The Act provides that, after the dropping of one or more lives, the landlord may demand that the tenant renew the lease. One must therefore now distinguish between the position before such a demand has been made and after.

a) Before Demand

Before the landlord makes such a demand, the correct position is that the doctrine of laches does not apply to the right. Delay on its own does not defeat it, although fraud and other inequitable conduct will. As Lord Thurlow put it after the Act was passed:

---

75 *McDermott v. Caldwell* (1877) IR 10 Eq 504, V-C.

> "Equity will relieve where there is mere lapse of time unaccounted for, without misconduct in the lessee, or where the lessor has lost his right by fraud in the lessor."[76]

Lord St Leonards also commented after the Act was passed:

> "Now, on the one hand, no advantage can be taken by the landlord of mere neglect; he must be active and put the tenant on his guard; and, on the other hand, the tenant cannot, after demand, evade his legal obligation to renew without delay, if he insist on his right of renewal; nor can he insist on that right at all, if his conduct in delaying the renewal amount to fraud."[77]

b) After Demand

Once the landlord makes a demand for renewal the tenant must renew within a reasonable time.[78] The effect of the demand is therefore to apply the equitable doctrine of laches from that point. The demand need not be made in any particular form: an oral request is enough.[79] Where there have been several demands, the first one brings the Statute into play.[80] What is a reasonable time depends on the circumstances of each case[81] but it should be no more than is necessary to give the tenant the opportunity of finding out when the cestuis que vie died, for calculating the fines due and preparing the new lease and tendering it for execution by the reversioner in fee.[82]

5. Succession

Since leases for lives renewable forever were estates pur autre vie, succession to them on the death of the tenant was governed by the law of occupancy. Suppose G, who had the fee simple, granted land to B "and her heirs" for a lease for lives renewable forever. When B died B's heir would take as special occu-

---

76 Quoted by Lord Redesdale LC in *Lennon v. Napper* (1802) 2 Sch & Lef 689 and Brady LC in *Roberts v. Mayne* (1859) 8 Ir Ch R 523. In that case the Court of Appeal in Chancery decided that the representatives of the original lessee were entitled to renew notwithstanding the many years that had passed since the death of the last cestui que vie.

77 Sugden, *House of Lords* p.569 cited by Brady LC in *Roberts v. Mayne* (1859) 8 Ir Ch R 523 at 536.

78 *Wood v. Know* (1855) 3 Ir Ch R 109.

79 *Jackson v. Saunders* (1806) 1 Sch & Lef 443, 2 Dow 437, (1814) 3 ER 923; *Ex parte Peyton* (1888) 21 LR Ir 371, MR.

80 *Mountmorris (Earl) v. White* (1814) 2 Dow 459, 3 ER 931.

81 *Jackson v. Saunders* (1806) 1 Sch & Lef 443, 2 Dow 437, (1814) 3 ER 923; *Dyott v. Viscount Massareene* (1874) IR 9 Eq 149 (4½ months total delay reasonable); *Mountmorris (Earl) v. White* (1814) 2 Dow 459, 3 ER 931 (8 years too long).

82 *Freeman v. Marquis of Waterford* (1795) 1 Sch & Lef 454 (note), Ch, per Lord Clare LC.

pant.[83] Section 9 of the Statute of Frauds, 1695 gave B the right to leave her interest in the remainder of the estate by will.

6. Position of a Person holding under an Equity to Renew

Where the former tenant remains in possession paying rent, what is the nature of the right under which he or she holds? Assuming that there is a right to renew in equity, it is arguable that, until actual renewal, equity would "regard as done that which ought to be done", as was argued in *O'Neil v. Jones*[84], so that the former common law tenant is a subsisting tenant for lives in equity. This position is reinforced, if anything, by the fact that the right to renew is statutory under the 1779 Act.

Suppose A was a tenant under a lease for lives renewable forever granted to her "and her heirs" and the lease then terminated leaving A with a right to renew in equity. A then died, leaving B as her heir at common law. B, as special occupant, would become the tenant in equity and therefore be entitled to renew lease, subject to the 1779 statute.[85] An equity to renew may be assigned and any assignee becomes entitled to the renewal.[86] Special occupancy was abolished in the Republic by section 11 of the Succession Act, 1965. Real and personal property now vests in the personal representatives of the deceased who hold for those entitled by will or on intestacy to the property.

---

83 *Stewart v. Lord Blaney* (1790) 2 Ridg PC 204 at 206.

84 (1785) 1 Ridg PC 175 at 178. The point was made by counsel for the successful respondent: "...and equity will consider that as done, which had been agreed to be done, and therefore that the respondent ought to be considered as having a subsisting title". The Irish House of Lords ordered a renewal without giving reasons (p.178) as was then customary. Counsel for the respondent included Fitzgibbon, later Lord Chancellor, and Carleton, later to become a judge of the Irish House of Lords. See also *Walsh v. Lonsdale* (1882) 21 Ch D 9.

85 Section 1 of the Tenantry Act 1779 refers to "tenants and their assigns". A person who took as special occupant becomes the tenant, either at law or in cquity. They do not hold as special occupant, but as tenant. Special occupancy is merely the title by which they become tenant.

86 The Tenantry Act, 1779 section 1 refers to assigns and in *O'Neil v. Jones* (1785) 1 Ridg PC 175 the successful respondent was purchaser for value of the person entitled to the equity. Before the Judicature Act a person entitled to a lease for lives renewable who remained in possession of land and paid rent would have a common law estate, a tenancy from year to year.

7. Covenants

It was common to insert a covenant against alienation or parting with possession without the consent of the reversioner and to insert a condition terminating the estate on the event of alienation without the required consent. This would confer a right of entry on the reversioner in addition to the nominal reversion.[87]

8. Waste

Tenants for life or lives were liable for waste from an early period.[88] In Ireland before the Union it seems that tenants under leases for lives renewable forever were not held liable for waste by Irish courts, or only in exceptional circumstances.[89] This was consistent with the view in Ireland that they were perpetual interests. After the Union the English view, that such tenants were liable for waste, prevailed until Deasy's Act, 1860. Section 25 of Deasy's Act, 1860 makes lessees of perpetually renewable leases unimpeachable of waste other than fraudulent or malicious waste.[90]

It has been seen that the Irish Timber Acts permitted tenants for life to register trees which they had planted themselves and allowed them to fell these registered trees.[91] A statute of 1765,[92] one of the Irish Timber Acts, made tenants for lives renewable forever unimpeachable of waste as to any trees planted by them after the Act, any covenant in a grant notwithstanding.[93] They were also exempted when the general right under the Irish Timber Acts to fell registered trees was abolished in 1791.[94]

9. Assignment and Subletting

There was some controversy in the 19th century and probably before, as to what constituted a subletting, *i.e.* a subinfeudation, of a lease for lives renewable forever, as opposed to an outright assignment. Judicial opinion seemed

87 *Scott v. Redmond* (1881) 8 LR Ir 112.

88 Statute of Gloucester, 1278, 6 Edw 1 c.5.

89 Smythe, *Landlord and Tenant in Ireland* p.243, 728. *Hunt v. Browne* (1827) 1 Sausse & Sc 178, 5 Law Rec NS 30.

90 The phrase is not defined by the Act.

91 See above Waste.

92 5 Geo III c.17 (Ir.) s.1. *Pentland v. Somerville* (1852) 2 Ir Ch R 289; *Ex parte Armstrong* (1857) 8 Ir Ch R 30; *Moore's Estate* (1902) 36 ILTR 14.

93 *Pentland v. Somerville* (1852) 2 Ir Ch R 280. Such a covenant would not be carried over in a fee farm grant under the Renewable Leasehold Conversion Act, 1849 since a fee simple owner is not liable for waste: *Ex parte Armstrong* (1859) 8 Ir Ch R 30; *Re Moore's Estate* (1902) 36 ILTR 14.

94 By 31 Geo III c.40 (Ir).

settled that if A held for the lives of X, Y and Z, renewable, and made a grant in favour of B for different lives, also renewable, since this could not be an assignment, it was a subletting, so that A could reserve a rent service on the grant.[95] This was probably also the case if some of the lives were the same and some were different.[96] The position was less clear if A made a grant for the same, renewable lives.[97] In this case it was possible to interpret it as an assignment, but it could also be argued that it was a subletting, *i.e.* a subinfeudation. A did not retain a reversion, but the Irish courts had never taken the view that a reversion was necessary to create tenure.[98] Also, *Quia Emptores*, 1290 did not prohibit subinfeudation on a grant for renewable lives.

K. The Conversion of Leases for Lives

1. Grants After 1 August 1849

Section 37 of the Renewable Leasehold Conversion Act, 1849 provides that a grant of "every lease of lands in Ireland for one or more life or lives, with or without a term of years determinable upon one or more life or lives, or for years absolute, with a covenant or agreement for perpetual renewal" granted after 1 August 1849 shall operate automatically to create a fee farm grant.[99] The estate is a fee simple and the old rent is preserved. This is, of course, provided the grantor was capable of granting a fee simple.

2. Grants Subsisting on 1 August 1849

a) Power Exercisable by Tenant

Where land in Ireland was held on 1 August 1849 under a lease in perpetuity section 1 of the Renewable Leasehold Conversion Act, 1849 gives a power to the tenant[100] to demand the grant in fee farm from the grantor of the lease whether or not the date for renewal has arrived.[101] The tenant thus acquires a

95 *Church v. Dalton* (1847) 9 Ir CLR 355; *Kent v. Stoney* (1859) 8 Ir Ch R 249, (1860) 9 Ir Ch R 249.

96 *Lord Clanmorris v. Bourke* (1849) 13 Ir CLR 305.

97 *Roberts v. Mayne* (1859) 8 Ir Ch. R 523; *Tobin v. Redmond* (1861) 11 Ir Ch R 445.

98 See Chapter 19 Landlord and Tenant: Reversion. Before *Quia Emptores*, 1290 a subinfeudation in fee simple produced tenure without a reversion and in Ireland the existence of *non obstante* grants meant that in those cases the same could still occur after 1290.

99 See also the Renewable Leaseholds Conversion (Ireland)

100 Where there are co-owners they all have to concur: *Betty v. Humphreys* (1872) IR 9 Eq 332.

101 In *Morris v. Morris* (1872) IR 6 CL 73, IR 7 CL 295 it was held by a majority of the Court of Exchequer Chamber that the grant destroyed any quasi-entail. See also *Betty v. Humphreys* (1872) IR 9 Eq 332.

fee simple estate subject to the rent. The power applies where the lease for lives was originally granted before the operative date but was renewed after 1849 under the covenant for renewal.[102] If the power was exercised the tenant obtained a fee farm grant. The holder of the reversion in fee simple was not entitled to compensation unless a special loss is incurred.[103] This is now open to constitutional challenge on the ground that it arguably amounts to an unjust attack on property rights.

One question is whether the section applies to land held on 1 August 1849 under an equity to renew, *i.e.* where the lives had died before that date.

If an equity to renew amounts to an equitable lease,[104] then the section applies and the person entitled, in addition to the right to demand a renewal of the contractual lease, had a right under the 1849 Act to demand a fee farm grant, which would normally be preferable.

If lease in perpetuity refers only to the contractual lease, then the person entitled to the equity had no immediate right to a fee farm grant under the 1849 Act, although they would still have had their right to renew under the Tenantry Act. If they renewed after 1849, and before 1980 in the Republic, then it would seem that the renewal itself would operate automatically as a fee farm grant under the 1849 Act. If they did not, and the equity still existed in 1980, it would have been converted by the 1980 Act.[105]

b) Landlord and Tenant (Amendment) Act, 1980 section 74

As to leases for lives renewable forever subsisting on 1 August 1849, there remained in theory, and probably in practice also, a category of interests which had not been converted to fee farm grants. Either the person would have a lease as to which the lives had been renewed since 1849, or it might be that all the lives had expired, in which case the tenant would be holding under an equity to renew under section 1 of the Tenantry Act, 1779.

The Landlord and Tenant (Amendment) Act, 1980 section 74 provides that a person entitled to "an interest in land the title to which interest originated under a lease for lives renewable forever which was created prior to[106] the 1st day of August 1849 and was not converted into a fee farm grant" under the 1849 Act "shall from the commencement of this Act hold the land for an estate in fee simple". The fee simple "... shall be deemed to be a graft upon the previous interest and shall be subject to any rights or equities arising from its being such graft". This appears to mean that the covenants in the original lease still have

102 *Ex parte Barlow* (1854) 2 Ir Ch R 272.

103 Section 5 of the 1849 Act; and see *Re Lawless* (1856) 4 Ir Ch R 230; *Thackwell v. Jenkins* (1856) 4 Ir Ch R 243.

104 See above page 261.

105 See next section.

106 This would appear to exclude inadvertently leases created on 1 August 1849.

effect, including the covenant to pay rent and, if included, covenants restricting alienation or parting with possession.[107] It seems unfortunate that another category of fee simple with leasehold characteristics has been created in the Republic, but the drafters of the 1980 Act may have felt constrained by Art 40.3.2° of the Constitution protecting property rights against unjust attack.

In effect, section 74 has created a new kind of fee farm grant by conversion. In theory this may be a fee farm grant with freehold tenure, although the point is probably purely theoretical.[108] The 1980 Act does not expressly convert the tenure from freehold to leasehold.

Wylie in the second edition of his book[109] points out that the 1980 Act incorporates definitions in earlier statutes under which fee simple does not include a fee farm grant and so argues that the rent has been abolished. If this is correct, then a person who had exercised the power under the 1849 Act would be in a worse position than someone who had not done so, because the former would still have to pay a rent while the latter would not. Furthermore, the abolition of the rent without compensation is open to constitutional challenge as an unjust attack on property rights, and one would expect a court, where there is doubt, to favour the interpretation which is consistent with the Constitution. More technically, even if fee simple on its own does not include a fee farm grant, the fee simple referred to in the section is said be a graft, and subject to existing rights or equities, one of which is the rent.

The section seems designed to apply not only to leases for lives still running in 1980,[110] *i.e.* a lease as to which the lives had been renewed, but also to equities to renew. Such equities are still governed by the Tenantry Act, 1779. The expression "interest in land the title to which originated under a lease for lives renewable forever. . ." seems wide enough to include such interests.[111] In such a case the further issue arises as to whether the landlord had made a demand for renewal under the Tenantry Act prior to 1980 or not. If he or she had made a demand, then if a reasonable time had elapsed before 1980 without renewal, the interest had ceased to exist before 1980. If a demand had not been made, or it had been made, but a reasonable time had not elapsed before 1980,

107 Such would be subject to statutory control under s.66 of the 1980 Act: see Chapter 19 Landlord and Tenant.

108 See page 211.

109 Wylie, *Irish Land Law* para. 4.082

110 *e.g.* the lease in *Re Supatone (Eire) Ltd* [1973] ILTR 105, concerning Rathfarnham Golf Club, which had originally been granted in 1738 but the current lease was dated 1938. See also *Clancy v. Whelan and Considine* (1958) 92 ILTR 39, High Court on Circuit, at Ennis, which concerned a lease dating from 1793.

111 Even if it is not, the tenant holding under such an interest could renew, if the Tenantry Act, 1779 is satisfied, and then, since it is a lease first made before 1 August 1849, exercise the power to acquire a fee farm grant.

the equity to renew still existed in 1980 and section 74 converted it to a fee farm grant.

3. Northern Ireland

Perpetually renewable leases in Northern Ireland under the Property (Northern Ireland) Order 1997[112] are not capable of being created at law or in equity after 10 January 2000.[113] Where before that date such a lease was subsisting is converted into a fee simple subject to a fee farm rent.[114] Conditions in the lease prohibiting or restricting assignment, sub-demise or parting with possession, or any other provisions repugnant to a fee simple no longer apply[115], and so the fee simple is to be distinct from those by conversion under the 1849 Act[116] and the position in the Republic. The lease is subsisting so long as the rent is still being paid, and is not in arrear, whether or not the lease had been renewed or the fine due on renewal has been paid.[117] This clearly includes an equity to renew.

L. Quasi-Entails

A lease for lives renewable forever was a virtually perpetual interest and it came to be recognised by the courts that it could be entailed just like a fee simple estate. Such an entail was not a real entail because it was not created out of a real fee simple. It was known as an estate in quasi-tail, or a quasi-entail. Suppose G has a fee simple and grants land "to X and his heirs for the lives of A, B, and C" with a covenant for perpetual renewal. G retains the reversion in fee. X makes a grant, *inter vivos* or by will, in favour of "Y (his son) and the heirs of his body". Y has a quasi-entail in the lease for lives. X now holds a "reversion for lives". The land passes to Y and after his death to his descendants so long as A, B, and C survive, and those lives can be renewed.

112 (SI 1179, NI 8) Article 36. The order applies not only to leases for lives, as the Republic's 1980 Act, but also to renewable leases for years, with or without a life or lives.

113 *ibid.* Article 1(2). Property (1997 Order) (Commencement No. 1) Order (Northern Ireland) 1997 (SR 1997/328); Property (1997 Order) (Commencement No. 2) Order (Northern Ireland) 1999 (SR 1999/461); Land Law Working Group, *Final Report* (HMSO 1990) Vol. 1, paras. 1.6.6–19.

114 Article 36(4) and Sch. 2.

115 Schedule 2 para. 1(2).

116 See Chapter 7 Fee Farm Grants.

117 Article 36(9).

1. Barring

a) Method

Quasi-entails could be barred by any *inter vivos* disposition.[118] The Fines and Recoveries (Ireland) Act, 1834 did not apply.[119] Nevertheless, the courts did hold, by analogy to the statute, that if the quasi-entail preceded by a quasi-life estate, the tenant in quasi-tail required the consent of the quasi-life tenant to bar successfully.[120] If the tenant in quasi-tail did not obtain the consent of this quasi-protector the result was a quasi-base fee. Apart from this, quasi-entails could be barred by any act which vested a new interest in a person, *e.g.* a sale of the lease for lives,[121] or a renewal of the lives, by the tenant in quasi-tail[122] or, after 1849, a deed vesting a fee farm grant in the tenant in quasi-tail under Renewable Leasehold Conversion Act, 1849.[123]

Quasi-entails could not be barred by will.[124] They were treated as true entails in this respect.[125]

---

118 *Allen v. Allen* (1842) 4 Ir Eq R 472, 2 Dr & War 307, 59 RR 696.

119 *Allen v. Allen* (1842) 4 Ir Eq R 472, 2 Dr & War 307, 59 RR 696; *Walsh v. Studdart* (1872) IR 7 CL 482, Exch Ch affirming (1870) IR 5 CL 478 (quasi-entail barred by grant of power of sale over whole fee in joint deed by quasi-tenant for life and tenant in quasi-tail in remainder); *Lynch v. Nelson* (1870) IR 5 Eq 192; *Morris v. Morris* (1872) IR 7 CL 295, Exch Ch affirming (1872) IR 7 CL 73; (a fee farm grant under Renewable Leasehold Conversion Act, 1849 in favour of tenant in quasi-tail bars the quasi-tail and all remainders); *Blackhall v. Gibson* (1878) 2 LR Ir 49; *Batteste v. Maunsell* (1876) IR 10 Eq 314 at 337; *Re Carew's Estate* (1887) 19 LR Ir 483; *Norton v. Frecker* (1737) 1 Atk 524, 26 ER 330, per Lord Hardwicke:

> "Any heirs depending on such an estate tail are entirely in the power of the first taker in tail, and may be destroyed by any conveyance, or even by articles, in Equity."

120 *Allen v. Allen* (1842) 4 Ir Eq R 472, 2 Dr & War 307, 59 RR 696; *Edwards v. Champion* (1853) 3 De G M & G 202, 43 ER 80; Furlong, *Landlord and Tenant* p.247.

121 It seems that after the Renewable Leasehold Conversion Act, 1849 a contract of sale of the fee simple by a tenant in quasi-tail would show a good title, on the ground that it would bar the quasi-entail: *McClenaghan v. Bankhead* (1874) IR 8 CL 195, Exch. This, however, assumes that the tenant in quasi-tail would obtain, and was bound to obtain, a fee farm grant from the reversion in fee before the conveyance.

122 *Re McNeale* (1858) 7 Ir Ch R 388; *Baker v. Bayley* (1691) 2 Vern 225, 23 ER 746 (quasi-entails not within *De Donis*); *Betty v. Humphreys* (1872) IR 9 Eq 332; and see *Leake v. Leake* (1843) 5 Ir Eq R 361; *Steele v. Mitchell* (1841) 3 Ir Eq R 1; *Crozier v. Crozier* (1843) 5 Ir Eq R 415, 61 RR 77.

123 *Morris v. Morris* (1872) IR 7 CL 295, Ex Ch affirming (1872) IR 7 CL 73.

124 *Campbell v. Sandys* (1802) 9 RR 33, 1 Sch & Lef 281 per Lord Redesdale LC at 294; *Lessee of Hopkins v. Ramage* (1826) Bat 365; *Dillon v. Dillon* (1808) 1 B & B 77-95; *Allen v. Allen* (1842) 4 Ir Eq R 472, 2 Dr & War 307, 59 RR 696, per Sugden LC.

125 *McClenaghan v. Bankhead* (1874) IR 8 CL 195, Exch ; *Morris v. Morris* (1872) IR 7 CL 295, Ex Ch affirming (1872) IR 7 CL 73.

b) Effect

In the example taken above, if Y barred the quasi-entail he became the tenant under the lease for lives, *i.e.* he barred his descendants and X, the holder of the reversion for lives. The reversion in fee was not barred. The reason for this is explained in the next section.

2. Quasi-Settlements

The following diagram illustrates the complicated situation that could arise:

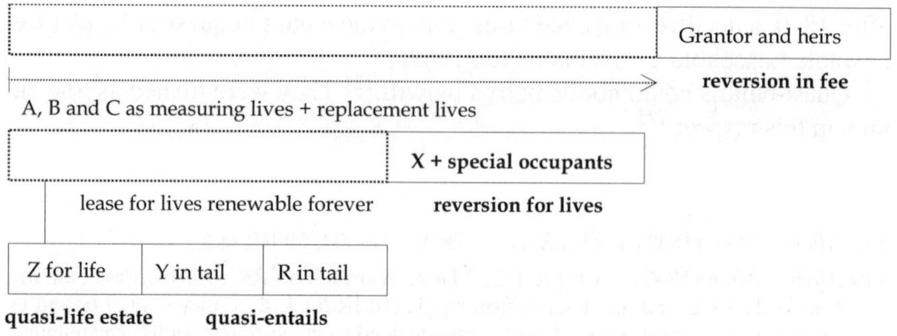

G, the owner in fee simple, has made a grant to X for the lives of A, B and C renewable forever. X has made a grant of the lease for lives "to Z for life, remainder to Y and the heirs of his body, remainder to R and the heirs of her body". Z has a quasi-life estate and Y has a quasi-entail in remainder. R has a further quasi-entail in remainder. Consider Y's position. Y needed the concurrence of the prior life tenant, Z, if he was to bar R's remainder and X and the special occupants of X. If Y failed to get Z's agreement Y would only bar his own issue in quasi-tail.[126] He would thus have a quasi-base fee. After Z's death, or with his concurrence, Y could bar the remainder. If Y barred the quasi-entail this resulted in Y becoming the tenant for lives. The ultimate reversion in fee remained unaffected. The explanation of this is that if Y, by barring the quasi-entail, could bar the reversion in fee then he could destroy G's entitlement to the rent and fines. In the case of a true fee tail the holder of the reversion in fee would have no such valuable interest. A lease for lives renewable forever, on the other hand, was a commercial interest and the reversion in fee upon it gave the grantor economically valuable rights to rent and fines. It no doubt seemed unreasonable that a tenant in quasi-tail could destroy such valuable rights. Furthermore, if barring a quasi-entail were to have such an effect,

126 *Allen v. Allen* (1842) 4 Ir Eq R 472, 2 Dr & War 307, 59 RR 696; *Edwards v. Champion* (1853) 3 De G M & G 202, 43 ER 80; Furlong, *Landlord and Tenant* p.247.

then all a tenant for lives renewable would have had to do to get the whole fee simple would have been to entail the lease in his or her own favour and then bar it.[127]

The courts did not appear to distinguish between the tenant in quasi-tail and the person entitled to lease for lives in reversion (*i.e.* X or X's special occupant). This was probably because they would usually be the same person. It was quite usual for the tenant for lives to create quasi-entail in favour of his own son in his will. Let us assume that X had left the lease for lives in his will to his son, Y "and the heirs of his body". Y is the donee in quasi-tail, but also X's heir general. Thus, while the quasi-entail existed, if one of the cestuis que vie of the lease for lives died, Y can apply for a renewal. Strictly this is because Y is entitled to the reversion for lives, rather than as quasi-tenant in tail, but the distinction is not always made clear. It was also Y who could demand a fee farm grant under the 1849 Act, due to the definition of "owner of the lease" in the Act.[128]

M. Quasi-Fee

A quasi-fee, *i.e.* a quasi-fee simple, arose if a person who held a lease for lives renewable forever granted it to someone else "and his [or her] heirs".[129] Words of limitation were not necessary to create a quasi-fee and it would arise if some other expression were used which indicated an intention that the entire interest of the tenant for lives should pass.[130] It would seem that the only effect of the expression "quasi-fee" was to indicate that the interest was subject to special occupancy at a time when special occupancy still existed.

---

127 Moreover, if a tenant for lives had been able to do this then the Renewable Leasehold Conversion Act, 1849 would have been unnecessary.

128 Section 35 of the Renewable Leaseholds Conversion Act, 1849 defines the "owner of the lease" for the purposes of the Act as including a "person entitled at law or in equity to a lease. . . in perpetuity for the whole estate. . . or for any derivative estate in tail, or quasi in tail, for life or lives or for a term of years absolute. . . "

129 See *Wall v. Byrne* (1845) 2 Jo & La T 118, 69 RR 253; *Doe d Lewis v. Lewis* (1842) 9 M & W 662, 152 ER 280; *Re English* (1854) 2 Ir CLR 284; *Keefe v. Kirby* (1858) 6 Ir CLR 591; *Fetherstone v. Mitchell* (1848) 11 Ir Eq R 35; *Barron v. Barron* (1859) 8 Ir Ch R 366 at 372: "an estate quasi in fee or an estate quasi in tail male. . . " *Courtney v. Parker* (1866) 16 Ir Ch R 320; *Croker v. Brady* (1879) 4 LR Ir 653 at 660.

130 In *McClintock v. Irvine* (1861) 10 Ir Ch R 480 a lease for lives renewable was conveyed "for all the estate" of the tenant to trustees as trustees for JWB "for his use and benefit and no other" and this was held to vest an equitable quasi-fee in JWB.

N. Leases for Lives Not Perpetually Renewable

1. Leases for Lives

These can still be granted in theory, although they are unlikely to occur in practice. Section 37 of the Renewable Leasehold Conversion Act, 1849 which automatically converts future grants of perpetual leases into grants in fee farm, specifically applies only to leases for lives "with a covenant or agreement for perpetual renewal". In theory these interests can be of two kinds:

(i) lease for lives not renewable at all; and

(ii) lease for lives renewable, but not perpetually, *i.e.* leases for lives renewable on a fixed number of occasions. There appears nothing in theory to prevent the creation of a lease for lives renewable on a large but finite number of occasions, such as a 100 times. The courts would probably interpret such grants, if for a large number of renewals, as amounting to a clause for perpetual renewal.

In Northern Ireland, leases for lives at a rent or in consideration of a fine cannot be created at law or in equity after 10 January 2000[131] and subsisting leases are converted to a term of 90 years determinable after the dropping of the last or only life.[132]

2. Leases for Lives and Years

This is an estate pur autre vie but there is annexed to it a leasehold term of years, usually between 30 and 99 years.[133] This rather curious type of hybrid interest may have had its origin in a statute of Charles I which allowed tenants in tail to create leases for a maximum of three lives or 41 years which would bind the issue in tail after their death.[134] There are two kinds:

1) Concurrent

A lease for lives and years is said to be concurrent where the term of years begins at the date of the grant and runs concurrently with the lives. While the freehold estate continues the term of years is suspended and the estate is free-

131 Property (Northern Ireland) Order 1997, (SI 1179, NI 8) Article 37(1)(a), 37(2); Property (1997 Order) (Commencment No. 2) Order (Northern Ireland) 1999 (SR 1999/461).

132 Property (Northern Ireland) Order 1997, (SI 1179, NI 8) Art. 37(4) & Sch. 3.

133 *e.g. Maultby v. Maultby* (1854) Ir Ch R 32.

134 10 Chas I sess 3 c.6 (Ir), 1634. It was held on earlier statutes that the leases would not bind remaindermen or reversioners: Co Litt 44a; 8 Co 34; *Keen v. Cope* (1597) Cro Eliz 602, 78 ER 845; Smythe, 5–6. See Chapter 8 Fee Tail.

hold.[135] When the last of the lives die, the estate becomes a leasehold for the remainder of the term. The tenure also becomes leasehold and would be governed by Deasy's Act, 1860. If the term expires while at least one of the lives survives, then the estate continues to be freehold. In theory the tenure should also be freehold.

2) Consecutive

In this case the term of years is to start on the death of the survivor of the lives.[136] The estate is freehold while the lives survive and then becomes leasehold. In theory the tenure should also be freehold while the lives survive, and then become leasehold when they die.

If granted after Deasy's Act, the Act itself allows the creation of the modern landlord and tenant relationship even while the estate is freehold.

a) Northern Ireland

In Northern Ireland, leases for lives with a concurrent or reversionary term of years cannot be created at law or in equity after 10 January 2000[137] and subsisting leases are converted.[138] Where a concurrent term exceeds 90 years, the lease is converted to the concurrent term absolutely, where it is 90 years or less, to a term of 90 years determinable on the dropping of the last or only life or after the determination of the concurrent term. Where the term is reversionary, the lease is converted to a term of 90 years plus the period of the reversionary term.

---

135 *Jones v. Duggan* (1841) 4 Ir LR 91; *Midland Railway v. Craig* (1852) 13 Ir CLR 1. This was apparently the opinion of lawyers at the beginning of the 19th century. In 1802 the attorney of the 2nd Marquess of Donegall wrote:

> "... It is the wish of the family to create as many freeholds as they can, and therefore I shall make all the future building leases for three lives or 99 years concurrent. . ." (Malcomson, *John Foster* p.284–5).

136 *Long v. Rankin,* reported by Sugden, *A Treatise of the Law of Property as administered by the House of Lords* (1849) Appendix Case No. 2 p.481; *Fitzgerald v. Vicars* (1839) 2 Dru & War 298, 56 RR 235.

137 Property (Northern Ireland) Order 1997, (SI 1179, NI 8) Art. 36(1)(b); Property (1997 Order) (Commencment No. 2) Order (Northern Ireland) 1999 (SR 1999/461). Note that Art. 36, unlike Art. 37, is not limited to leases at a rent or in consideration of a fine.

138 Property (Northern Ireland) Order 1997, (SI 1179, NI 8) Art. 36 & Sch. 3.

O. Leases for Lives and Years Perpetually Renewable

In the past lease were sometimes granted for lives and years with a clause for renewal.[139] If a lease for lives and years contains a covenant for perpetual renewal then the 1849 Act would apply. If granted before 1 August 1849, as a lease in perpetuity, the tenant has a power to require a grant in fee farm. If granted after that date the grant would operate automatically under section 37 of the Act 1849 as a fee farm grant.

P. Leases Determinable on Life

A grant to A "for 50 years [or any other number of years] so long as X shall live" creates a purely leasehold estate determinable on the event specified. The event need not be the ending of a life and X's life does not create an *estate pur autre vie* in addition to the leasehold term. The interest cannot endure beyond the term of years and will end before that if the specified life dies during the term.

The Irish House of Lords in *Boyle v. Lysaght*[140] held that a renewable lease for years determinable on life came within the Tenantry Act, 1779, and further that this was so even if the clause in the deed was not expressly perpetual, provided the parties intended that the lease be perpetually renewable.[141]

Under section 58(1)(iv) of the Settled Land Act, 1882 the tenant of a lease determinable on life has the powers of a tenant for life under the Acts.

In Northern Ireland, leases at a rent or in consideration of a fine for a term determinable with a life or the marriage of a specified person cannot be created at law or in equity after 10 January 2000[142].

Q. Leases for Years Renewable

A perpetually renewable lease for years falls within the 1849 Act. Being purely leasehold, these interests are dealt with in Chapter 19 on landlord and tenant.

---

139 *Gorman v. King-Harman* [1894] 2 IR 238, Land Commission (lease for 3 lives or 31 years with a covenant to renew for one life and a concurrent term of 21 years. Held not to be a "lease" within the Land Law (Ireland) Act, 1881 s.1).

140 (1787) 1 Ridg PC 401–407.

141 The lease in the case was for 99 years determinable on life with a covenant which the court held was intended to be perpetual.

142 Property (Northern Ireland) Order 1997, (SI 1179, NI 8) Article 37(1)(d), 37(2); Property (1997 Order) (Commencment No. 2) Order (Northern Ireland) 1999 (SR 1999/461).

CHAPTER 10

FUTURE INTERESTS

A. Vested or Contingent

Interests in land may be (a) vested in possession, (b) vested in interest, or (c) contingent. If they fall either within (b) or (c) they are future interests. Vested in possession means the present right to present enjoyment, not a future interest. In possession does not imply physical possession necessarily, but rather the immediate freehold interest. The land may be let under a lease, but the immediate freehold estate is still said to be vested in possession. Vested used by itself, however, usually means vested in interest. To give an example before further definition:

> *to A for life, remainder to B in fee simple at the age of 21.*
> (B is under 21 at the date of the gift).

A's interest is vested in possession. B's interest is contingent - on his becoming 21. If B becomes 21 in A's lifetime, his interest is said to be vested in interest. Assuming B has become 21 in A's lifetime, when A dies B's interest falls into possession, or becomes vested in possession.[1]

To take another example:

> *to A for life, remainder to the first child of A in fee simple.*
> (A has no child at the time of the gift).

Here, the interest is contingent because the person who is to take it is not ascertained. Hence, it can be said that an interest is vested in interest if:

1) the person or persons who are to take it are ascertained; and
2) the only thing that prevents it taking effect in possession is the existence of the prior estate.

If either of these conditions is not satisfied, the interest is contingent.[2] In the first example above, B's fee simple was prevented from vesting in possession not only by A's prior life estate but by the fact that he is under 21.

A distinction between contingent and vested in interest which occurs more frequently in relation to personal property and which also depends upon the type of limitation created, is that where an interest is vested the person so enti-

1 *Bank of Ireland v. Conmee,* unreported, High Court, McWilliam J, 8 December 1978.

2 This definition is accurate in relation to common law remainders, but modified in relation to the perpetuity rule as it affects 'springing' and 'shifting' executory interests and similar interests under trusts. See below p.310.

tled will be entitled to the income of the property before it vests in possession, unless it is expressly granted to someone else, whereas in the case of a contingent interest, they are not.

This definition of contingent is not, however, natural in the sense of being logically the only definition possible, given the system of estates. It developed historically and grew out of the common law remainder rules, as the second of the two tests indicates. This point will be appreciated better when the common law remainder rules have been dealt with and so students may wish to return to this chapter at a later stage and read it again. It also means that the definition may need to be modified when dealing with the full range of future interests.[3]

The fact that an interest is contingent does not mean that the person, if he or she is ascertained, has no right at all. If it is under a trust he or she has the present right to prevent the trustees from dissipating the fund. In *Jacob v. Revenue Commissioners*[4] trustees held a discretionary trust of money. The trustees were to accumulate the income until the beneficiary became 33, then to pay the income to her. But they also had a power to appoint the capital to her. She was held to have the right to prevent them dissipating the fund.[5] The holder of a contingent interest, legal or equitable, would also have an action of waste against the holder of the prior estate in possession.[6]

Where a trust gives to the trustees a discretion to appoint property among a class of persons, each member of the class has a contingent interest in the trust property: contingent in this case upon the trustees exercising their discretion in favour of that member.

In *Chaine-Nickson v. The Bank of Ireland*[7] it was held that such a potential beneficiary had the right, at his or her own expense, to copies of the trust accounts and profit and loss accounts of a company in which trust funds had been invested. He also had the right to be informed as to who was in possession of land held by the trustees and as to outgoings of the land paid by trustees out of trust moneys. These are specific remedies in support of a contingent property interest in preventing dissipation of the trust fund.

An interest can be contingent even if the event on which it depends is bound to occur:

to A for life, remainder to B in fee simple on the death of C.

While A, B, and C are alive, B's interest is contingent. Nevertheless, although this is the traditional position it may no longer be the case at least where reve-

3 See 'Modern Rule Against Perpetuities: Contingent and Vested.

4 Unreported, High Court, McWilliam J, 6 July 1983.

5 See also *Love v. Love* (1881) 7 LR Ir 306, V-C.

6 *Simpson v. Simpson* (1879) 3 LR Ir 308, V-C (equitable tenant in tail).

7 [1976] IR 393; and see *Moore v. McGlynn* [1894] 1 IR 74; *Moran v. Moran* [1910] 1 IR 346; Re Dunne, deceased, unreported, Supreme Court, 26 November 1997.

nue statutes are concerned.[8]

An interest may be vested although there is no certainty of it ever falling into possession. In the limitation:

to A for life, remainder to B for life.

while A and B are alive, B's interest is vested even if A is ten years old and B is 90. Personal characteristics are irrelevant.

An interest may be vested although the size of the interest has not been finally ascertained.[9] This occurs in the case of a class gift:

to A for life, remainder to such of B's children as attain 21 in fee simple.

When a child of B becomes 21 in A's lifetime their interest becomes vested despite the fact that it is liable to be reduced in size if and when later children become 21.[10] But children under 21 have only a contingent interest.[11]

An interest can be vested although it is subject to a condition subsequent. In the above example, a child who becomes 21 has a vested interest although it is liable to be partially divested later if other children become 21.[12] Vested conditional interests are also an example of this rule. On the other hand, if an interest is subject to a condition precedent it is necessarily contingent. Nevertheless, an interest may appear to contain a condition precedent, but be held not to do so. For example, in the limitation:

to A for life, but if A die, remainder to B in fee simple

B has a vested fee simple. The phrase "but if A die" adds no contingency which was not inherent in the natural determination of A's life estate.

B. Assignability

In the limitation:

to A for life, remainder to B in fee simple at the age of 21

---

8 See the English case of *IRC v. Trustees of Sir John Aird's Settlement* [1983] 3 All ER 481, [1984] 1 Ch. 382, [1984] 2 WLR 178, CA. Where tax is involved some taxpayers attempt to take advantage of the tax position as to discretionary trusts by creating contingencies that are bound to occur, and within a short period. The Newspaper-Franco Scheme was one of these devices.

9 Note this point is true in relation to the common law remainder rules, and for the purpose of paying the income of a fund to those entitled to vested interests, but in the modern rule against perpetuities, an interest is not vested unless its size is also ascertained. See Chapter 12 Class Gifts.

10 *Re Lechmere* (1881) 18 Ch D 524.

11 *Rhodes v. Whitehead* (1865) 2 Dr & Sm 532, 62 ER 722. Megarry & Wade, *Real Property* p.176.

12 Again, this is not so for the purpose of applying the perpetuity rule.

if B dies under 21 in A's lifetime then there is no interest which survives B's death. The contingency can no longer occur. Hence, even if B had made a will before she died leaving her contingent fee simple to X, at the time of her death there is no fee simple left, not even a contingent one. But it is possible that a person could have a contingent interest which remains contingent at her death. This will occur if the contingency is not one which is to be satisfied by the donee. For reasons which will become clear later, it is not easy to find an example of this in a common law limitation, but it is quite possible in an executory limitation or under a trust. For example in the limitation:

> *Unto and to the use of T and U in fee simple in trust for A for life, remainder to B in fee simple when C marries*

if B dies before A, and C is still unmarried at that time, the fee simple is still contingent. Those entitled to B's estate will inherit the contingent fee simple. If C then marries in A's lifetime, the fee simple will vest in interest at that time, and when A dies it will vest in possession.[13]

At common law contingent remainders and legal executory interests were held to give no present interest but only a possibility of acquiring one and so they could not be left by will or otherwise alienated.[14] Thus, in the above example, B was held to have no interest capable of passing to her heirs even if the contingency could still occur after her death. The growth of the ideology of the market and, with it, the idea that any form of property should be freely alienable led to this principle being extended to future interests. The Statute of Wills, 1634[15] was interpreted liberally to mean that future interests could be left by will, and this was confirmed by the Wills Act, 1837. The provision was repealed and replaced in the Republic by the Succession Act, 1965 sections 10 and 76. The Real Property Act, 1845 section 6 made future interests alienable *inter vivos* in England, but it is doubtful whether it had the same effect in Ireland.[16]

C. Types of Future Interests

Future interests may be of the following kinds:

---

13 If, in the example, C is still unmarried when A dies, the property would vest in the grantor by resulting trust until the contingency occurs.

14 Challis p.76.

15 1540 in England.

16 Section 6 provides: "...a contingent, an executory, and a future interest, and a possibility coupled with an interest, in any tenements or hereditaments of any tenure... also a right of entry, whether immediate or future, and whether vested or contingent, into or upon any tenements or hereditaments in England, of any tenure, may be disposed of by deed...". If the phrase "in England" refers to the whole phrase after "right of entry" then the section would not apply to rights of entry in Ireland.

1. reversions;
2. future estates other than reversions:
   a) common law remainders;
   b) legal executory interests; and
   c) future trusts.
3. possibilities of reverter at common law;
4. rights of entry for condition broken at common law;
5. executory interests corresponding to 3 and 4; and
6. equitable interests corresponding to 3 and 4.

Interests of types 3 to 6 have already been dealt with and the rest of this chapter is concerned with types 1 and 2.

D. Reversions and Remainders

A reversion arises when the grantor fails to dispose of the whole of his interest by a grant, as when A, the holder of a fee simple, makes a grant to B for life. A retains the reversion if fee simple.

A remainder is part of the grantor's estate which is granted away and is that part which is postponed to an estate granted in possession at the same time.

It follows from this that a reversion arises by operation of law, whereas a remainder arises by a grant. A reversion is always vested in the grantor, although he or she may alienate it later, whereas a remainder is vested in someone other than the grantor. There can only be one true reversion,[17] whereas there may be several remainders. Reversions are necessarily vested,[18] whereas remainders may be vested or contingent.

E. Common Law Remainders

Remainders at common law are still governed by old common law rules which are now, in terms of policy, obsolete. They derived from the concern, in the main, that there should be no abeyance of seisin. Only freeholds had seisin and so the principle meant that there must at all times be an identifiable freehold tenant. This was in the interests of the feudal lords who had to have an identifiable tenant from whom they could demand the services of the tenure and against whom they could proceed by distress if the services were not paid.

17 When a quasi-settlement has been created out of a lease for lives renewable forever there is both a reversion in fee and a reversion for lives, but the latter is only a quasi-reversion.

18 *Rae v. Joyce* (1892) 29 LR Ir 500 per Walker C at 509.

Needless to say, this principle is entirely obsolete and the rules no longer perform any valid function, but they are so deeply embedded in the law that judges have not felt able to get rid of them. The rules are as follows:

1. A remainder is void unless it is supported by a prior estate of freehold created by the same instrument

E.g.

to A and his heirs when he becomes 21

the estate is void at law.

E.g.

to A and his heirs after my death

the estate is also void. At common law you cannot create a springing interest, *i.e.* an interest which is to arise in future without any preceding estate created at the same time. The rule derives from the old feoffment with livery of seisin at common law. We have already noted that the feudal law confused ownership, in the sense of title, with legal possession, or seisin. The feoffment, which transferred title, was in theory a transfer of seisin to the land, and therefore divested the holder of seisin and at the same time vested it in a new holder. Given this theory, it was inconceivable that the seisin should be divested from the holder without immediately being vested in someone else.[19]

2. A remainder is void if it cuts short a prior estate of freehold

A remainder must follow on the natural determination of the prior estate and not defeat it. At common law you cannot create a shifting interest.

The origin of this rule is again feudal and probably reflected the demand of feudal lords that they should know who was their tenant at any given time. If the tenancy could shift to some other tenant on the happening of an event other than the death of the previous tenant, then the feudal lord might not be able to discover if this had occurred.

The rule means that in the limitation:

to A for life, on condition she does not marry C, then to B and his heirs

B's fee simple is void. If the condition itself is not void as against constitutional rights or public policy, then the grantor retains a right of entry which he

---

19 By the 16th century, when feudalism had declined, and conveyances had been developed which did not depend on seisin, attempts were made by the judges to depart from the strict feudal rule. Originally the prior estate had to be freehold, but in *Boraston's Case* (1587) 3 Co Rep 16 at 19a, 76 ER 664, it was held that in the limitation: "to A for 21 years, then to B and his heirs" since the prior estate was leasehold, it did not prevent the freehold vesting in possession: Challis 129.

can enforce to terminate A's estate if the event occurs.[20] If the condition is void as against constitutional rights, then A has an absolute life estate. The grantor retains a reversion which falls into possession on A's death.

At some time in the past the rule was modified so that if, instead of a condition, the limitation is drafted to create a determinable interest, the remainder is valid:

to A for life or until she marries C, then to B and his heirs.

The prior life estate is determinable. It is regarded as ending naturally on the happening of two events: A's death or her marrying C. The judges took the view that the remainder does not cut short the prior estate, and so is valid. This is probably the origin of the distinction between conditional and determinable interests, *i.e.* it was invented at the end of the feudal period by the common law courts as a means of avoiding this old rule. One might notice that it is only effective if the prior estate is a life estate or a fee tail. As will be seen in the next rule, it was not possible to have a remainder after a fee simple, even a determinable one.

Since the determining event was regarded as being part of the limitation of the estate, *i.e.* an inseparable part of the estate granted, if the event is held to be void as against public policy, or as against constitutional rights in the Republic, the grant of the estate is void.[21] However, the result of this rule has been that judges have been inhibited from finding that such estates offend against such rights, since the effect of doing so is that the intended recipient takes nothing at all.

Judges have little discretion, at least according to the formal rules, in deciding whether a limitation creates a conditional or determinable interest, since the law laid down long ago which words create a determinable interest and which create a conditional one.

3. Any remainder after a Fee Simple is void

The reifying explanation of this rule is that the fee simple estate is the largest estate known to the common law and therefore, having granted it, the grantor has nothing left to give. The practical explanation lies again in the interest of the feudal lords. If a fee simple came to an end because the tenant died without heirs, the lord recovered the land by escheat. If a further estate could be limited

---

20 According to Challis if the right of entry is not exercised, the remainder revives on A's death and can take effect. The result might, however, depend on the wording of the gift. If the limitation was "to A for life but if she marries C, then to B and his heirs," the intention seems clearly to be that B should take only if A marries C and not otherwise, so that when A dies, if the right of entry has not been exercised, the reversion is in the grantor.

21 *Re Moore* (1888) 39 Ch D 116 (determinable interest in personalty).

to take effect after the first fee simple, the lord would lose this right. Hence, in the limitation:

> *to A and his heirs, remainder to B and his heirs*

the remainder to B is void at common law.[22] The rule also applies to both conditional and determinable interests. Thus in the limitation:

> *to A in fee simple until the land cease to be used for agriculture, remainder to B in fee simple*

the remainder to B is void. The grantor retains a possibility of reverter. The application of the rule in this case shows the falsity of the reifying explanation, since if the rule applies where less than a fee simple absolute is first granted, the explanation of it can hardly be that the grantor has disposed of his or her whole interest.

The rule does not prevent the creation of alternative limitations, *i.e.* a fee simple limited to arise on the failure of the contingency which was to give rise to the first fee simple:

> *to A for life, remainder to his eldest daughter, if any, in fee simple, remainder to B in fee simple.*
> (A has no daughter at the date of the gift.)

If A never has a daughter, then the first fee simple will not take effect and the fee simple to B may take effect as an alternative. It is not a remainder after the first fee simple, because one or the other may take effect, but not both.

4. A remainder is void (a) unless it is limited so that it is capable of vesting during the prior estate or at the moment it comes to an end, and (b) unless it does in fact do so

This is the rule that has given rise to the most discussion and problems. It is derived directly from the concern of feudal lords that there should not be an abeyance of seisin. When an estate comes to an end, at common law the next estate must take effect immediately. If not, there would be a gap in the seisin, that is to say there would be no freehold tenant for a period until the next estate took effect. This would run directly counter to the interests of feudal lords who would be deprived of the services of the tenure during such a gap.

If it is clear from the start that there will be a gap in the seisin, then the remainder is void from the beginning, as contrary to 4(a). So in the limitation:

> *to A for life, remainder to B and her heirs if O survives A by one month*

22 *Duke of Norfolk's Case* (1681) 3 Chan Cas 1, 22 ER 931; *United States v. 31,600 Acres of Land in Richland County SC, et al* (1942) CA 391, 47 F Supp 21, District Court, ED South Carolina, Columbia Division. Such a remainder may be valid under the Statute of Uses, 1634.

the remainder to B is void. It is clear from the beginning that if the remainder takes effect there will be a gap in the seisin. But a limitation may be phrased so that there might or might not be a gap in the seisin depending on the facts existing when the prior estate comes to an end. For example:

> *1. to A for life, remainder to his first child to attain 21 in fee simple;*

or

> *2. to A for life, remainder to B in fee simple if he marries.*

In the first example there will only be a gap in the seisin if, at A's death, there is no child aged 21:

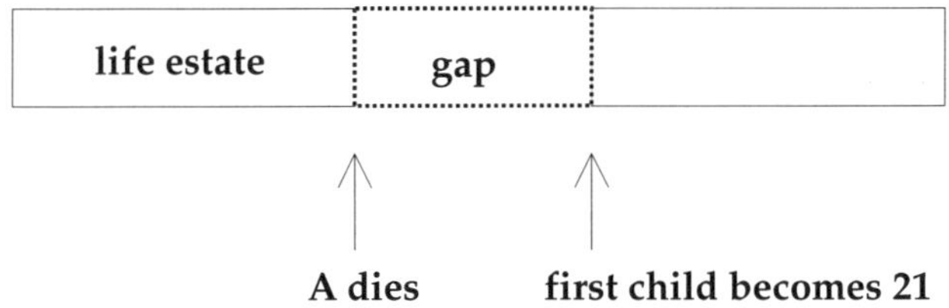

In the second example there will only be a gap if B is unmarried at A's death. In the such a case the common law rule allows you to wait and see. The remainder is only void if, as matters turn out, a gap actually occurs. The remainder becomes void at that point. In the first example one can wait until A's death. If at that point there is no child aged 21 the remainder is void. If there is, then the remainder is valid. In the second example one waits to the same point. If B is unmarried at A's death the remainder is void, if he has married by then, it is valid.

A special case of this rule arose at common law where there was a gift to a class, *i.e.* to a number of people who fall within a description:

> *to A for life, remainder to his children and their heirs when the children attain the age of 21.*

The class here is children of A. Thus, each child is supposed to get a fee simple when it becomes 21. But suppose at A's death some of the children are 21 and others are still under that age? Does the whole remainder fail so that even those who are 21 get nothing? This was considered to harsh a result even for the common law judges. They developed a special rule called the Rule in *Festing v. Allen*.[23] The effect of this is that those children who have attained 21 by the time of A's death take fees simple but those are still under 21 take nothing. Their remainders fail under Rule 4. Thus, even though it was a class gift, the courts treated the children as if they each had separate remainders.

---

23 *Festing v. Allen* (1843) 12 M & W 279, (1844) 5 Hare 573, 67 ER 1038; *Brackenbury v. Gibbons* (1876) 2 Ch D 417; *Cunliffe v. Brancker* (1876) 3 Ch D 393.

F. Legal Executory Interests

1. Inter Vivos

Before the Statute of Uses, 1634 equity recognised future estates in equity and it did not require them to comply with the common law remainder rules. Equity saw that the rules were based on feudal policy which, at the time equity developed, was obsolescent. So before the Statute:

> *to X and Y in fee simple to the use of A in fee simple at the age of 21*
> (A is under 21)

would give A a future contingent fee simple in equity although there was no prior estate. Before A became 21 there would be a resulting use to the grantor. The effect of the Statute is to execute the uses and to give A the same estate at law as he previously had in the use. A has a future legal estate in fee simple. The resulting use in favour of the grantor is also executed, giving her the legal fee simple until A becomes 21. X and Y, as feoffees, take nothing at all:

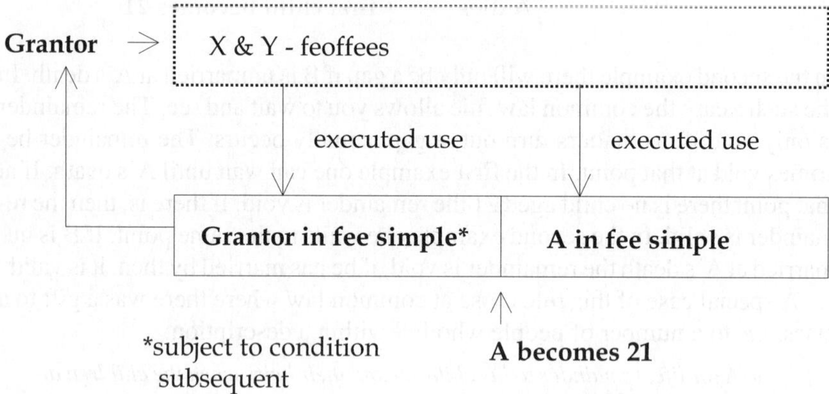

You can therefore create a legal springing interest, which was not possible before the Statute, provided you insert a use. Thus the Statute gave rise to a new class of future interests and they are known as legal executory interests. The above example is a springing interest in the sense that the effect of the deed is to create an interest in A which is to spring up in future. It also became possible to create legal shifting interests after the Statute. In the limitation:

> *to X and Y and their heirs to the use of A and his heirs until B marries, then to B and her heirs*

a legal fee simple is given to A which is to shift to B on the stated event.

2. Wills

The Statute of Wills, 1634[24] permitted testators to make wills at their free will and pleasure. The courts interpreted this as meaning that the statute allowed testators to create legal estates in wills which would not have been valid as common law remainders.[25] This wide interpretation was probably also a result of the change in judicial attitudes at the time which was generally against the now obsolete feudal policy of the common law. Thus, even if no use was inserted, the courts treated limitations as if one had been. Shifting and springing interests could be created in wills even more easily than *inter vivos*. A limitation:

> *to A and his heirs when he becomes 21*

in a will would create a springing devise. Similarly, a limitation :

> *to A and his heirs until B marries, then to B in fee simple*

would create a shifting devise.[26] These future legal estates were known collectively as executory devises.[27] Due to changes in the law of succession, which will be discussed shortly, they are now obsolete.

G. The Rule in Purefoy *v.* Rogers

It might be thought from what has been said that grantors could always avoid the common law rules by inserting a use, or even without this in the case of wills. However there is one exception to their ability to do so and this is the Rule in *Purefoy v. Rogers*.[28] This is where the limitation is subject to rule 4(b) discussed above, *i.e.* the wait-and-see rule.

---

24 1540 in England.

25 *Pells v. Brown* (1620) Cro Jac 590, 79 ER 504 held executory devises not to be destructible. Note that *Ferguson v. Ferguson* (1885) 17 LR Ir 552, MR, (appeal on other issues at p.567, CA) is authority in Ireland for the position that executory devises were subject to *Purefoy*, or, in other words, did not escape the common law remainder rule merely because such limitations were contained in wills.

26 *Ingham v. Ingham* (1876) IR 11 Eq 101, R.

27 *Sealy v. Stawell* (1875) IR 9 Eq 499. The first case of an executory devise was probably the *Duke of Norfolk's Case* (1681) 3 Chan Cas 1, 2 Swanst 454, 22 ER 931, 949. See argument of counsel, Hodgson and Napier of the Irish Bar, in *Dungannon (Lord) v. Smith* (1845) 12 Cl & F 546, 8 ER 1523

28 (1671) 2 Wms Saun 380, 85 ER 1181. The courts in the US State of Georgia recognize this rule: *Glore v. Scroggins* (1906) 124 Ga 922, 53 SE 690. *In the Matter of McLoughlin* (1975) 507 F 2d 177; 3 Collier Bankr Cas (MB) 318, United States Court of Appeals, Fifth Circuit, Coleman, Circuit Judge. So also have the courts in Canada, in the second case with unfortunate results: *Hiltze v. Langille* (1959) 18 DLR (2d) 464; *Re Crow* (1984) 12 DLR (4th) 415.

Stated generally, the rule is that no limitation can take effect as a legal executory interest (or in the past, an executory devise) if it is capable of taking effect as a common law remainder. If, when it is made, it is so capable, then it must be treated as such even if, having waited to see what happens, it turns out to be void. The word capable shows that it is the wait-and-see rule that is referred to. For example, a limitation:

to A for life, remainder to B and her heirs when she marries

complies with common law rules 1,2,3 and 4(a). It is supported by a prior estate, the remainder will not cut short the prior estate, it does not involve a fee simple after a fee simple and, as to rule 4(a), it is capable of taking effect immediately at the end of the life estate. But, under rule 4(b), it may not in fact do so. B may be unmarried at A's death. Under rule 4(b) one has to wait until A's death. If B is then married, the remainder takes effect. If not, it is void. Grantors did not like this uncertainty and wished to avoid it. The Statute of Uses (and formerly the Statute of Wills) seemed to provide a means by which this could be done, so that the remainder could take effect even if B did not marry until after A's death. It would seem that all that the grantor had to do, in an *inter vivos* deed, was to insert the words "to X and Y and their heirs to the use of. . ." at the beginning. But the case of *Purefoy v. Rogers*[29] held that this could not be done. Even if a use were inserted[30], the wait-and-see rule still applied. We can now restate the rule in this form: the common law wait-and-see rule cannot be avoided by inserting a use.

One should also note that *Purefoy* only applies where it is uncertain whether there is to be a gap or not at the time the instrument takes effect. If it is clear from the beginning that there will be a gap, the limitation is not capable of taking effect as a common law remainder and *Purefoy* does not apply. It will be valid as a legal executory interest, provided it complies with the perpetuity rule. So in the limitation:

to X and Y and their heirs to the use of A for life, remainder to C in fee simple if Q survives A by one month.

the contingent interest to C can only occur, if at all, after A's death. It is certain from the beginning that there will be a gap between A's death and C's remainder. It is not a case of wait-and-see. *Purefoy v. Rogers* has no application, and the remainder to C is valid as a legal executory interest.

It is difficult to explain the rule in Purefoy on any policy ground, since it can quite easily be avoided. A gap can be inserted deliberately in order to avoid

29 (1671) 2 Wms Saun 380, 84 ER 1181.

30 Formerly, in the case of wills, it might have been thought that it could be treated as an executory devise even without an express use (see below), but the rule in *Purefoy* prevented this also.

Purefoy, as in the limitation last mentioned. The rule could also be avoided by creating a lease for years determinable on life instead of the life estate:

> *to F and his heirs to the use of A for 99 years or until A dies, remainder to A's eldest son at 21 and his heirs.*

The limitation breaks Rule 1 because the remainder is not supported by a prior freehold estate.[31] However, there remained the problem of deeds which failed to employ such devices.

H. Destruction of Contingent Remainders

We have seen that a contingent remainder could be destroyed because the contingent remainder had not vested by the time the prior estate came to an end. This was known as natural destruction. However, contingent remainders could be destroyed artificially, *i.e.* by a deliberate act of the owner of the prior estate which brought it to an end while the remainder was still contingent. There were various acts which could have this result. For example, in the limitation:

> *to A for life, remainder to his eldest son for life, remainder to B and his heirs.*
> (A has no son)

A could destroy the contingent remainder in favour of his eldest son by a surrender of his life estate to B. There was no one to take the remainder to the eldest son at once, and so it failed, thus depriving any future son of A of an interest in the property. It could also occur, in the above example, if B conveyed his estate to A. The vested remainder merged with A's life estate, giving A the fee simple in possession and again destroying the contingent remainder. Artificial destruction defeated the intention of the grantor and various Acts in the 19th century abolished this form of destruction. The Real Property Act, 1845, for example, operated so that if A surrendered his life estate to B before the birth of a son, the contingent remainder was no longer destroyed. B took an estate *pur autre vie*, for the life of A. If there was a son of A alive at A's death, the remainder in his favour took effect. If there was no son, B took the fee simple.

There remained, however, the problem of natural destruction. The Contingent Remainders Act, 1877 attempted, with partial success, to deal with this problem and is discussed in the next section.

---

31 Radcliffe, *Real Property* 1933 p.219. See also *Re Lechmere* (1881) 18 Ch D 524 and the first edition of this work.

I. Contingent Remainders Act, 1877

1. The Need for the Act

There remained the problem that if grantors or their lawyers created a common law remainder, or did not use the words required to avoid *Purefoy,* the remainder could still be void at the end of the prior estate. This occurred in England in the case of *Cunliffe v. Brancker*[32] in 1876. The testator left property in his will to A and B, *inter alia,* to the use of JC for life with remainder to all the children of JC and his wife SC who should be living at the death of the survivor of them. The testator died in 1817. JC died in 1871 and his wife SC survived him. She died two years later and several children survived her.

Jessel MR and the English Court of Appeal held that the limitations, including the limitation to the children, were certainly intended to be legal estates, *i.e.* executory devises, and as such failed at the death of JC for lack of a prior estate to support them.[33] As a result of the case the Contingent Remainders Act, 1877 was passed.

2. The Act

The Act is not the most clearly drafted of statutes. Its effect can also not be fully understood without an understanding of the rule against perpetuities and so here again students may wish to return to this section after studying that rule. Section 1 of the Act provides that:

> "Every contingent remainder. . . which would have been valid as a springing or shifting use or executory devise or other limitation had it not had a sufficient estate to support it as a contingent remainder, shall, in the event of the particular estate determining before the contingent remainder vests, be capable of taking effect in all respects as if the contingent remainder had originally been created as a springing or shifting use or executory devise or other executory limitation."

As to limitations which before the Act fell within the rule in *Purefoy v. Rogers*, the Act means that they may now take effect as executory limitations if, like all executory interests, they comply with the perpetuity rule. Take, for example, the following limitation:

> *to X and Y in fee simple to the use of A for life, remainder to his eldest son in fee simple at the age of 21.*
> (A has no son aged 21.)

It is uncertain whether A will have a son who is 21 years of age at A's death. Therefore, under *Purefoy*, even though a use had been inserted the gift to the

32 (1876) 3 Ch D 393.

33 If JC had died in the lifetime of the testator and the testator had died after 1837 then a different result would have occurred. At the time the will took effect at the death of the testator the limitation would have been a springing devise and valid as such.

son still had to comply with Rule 4: one had to wait-and-see until A's death. If there was no son aged 21 the gift would fail. There might be a son aged 19, but that was to no avail. The gift would still fail.

Under the Contingent Remainders Act, 1877 the gift to the son can take effect provided it complies with the perpetuity rule. It does so in the example: it is bound to vest, if at all, within 21 years of the death of A, who is the life in being. Therefore, since it is valid as an executory interest it can take effect as such even if the son is under 21 at A's death. To put it more crudely, the future interest can take effect even if there may be a gap, because the gap will not be too long:

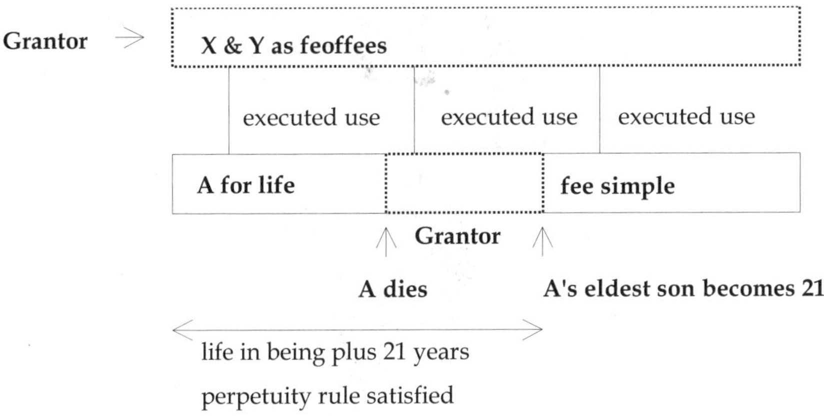

Although there may be a gap between A dying and A's eldest son becoming 21, the future fee simple is valid. The gap is in fact filled by a resulting executed use in favour of the grantor.

On the other hand, if a future gift is void for perpetuity, then it cannot take effect under the Act as an executory interest, but, and this also must be grasped, this does not prevent it being treated as a contingent remainder at common law, and so one can still wait-and-see until the end of the prior estate. Thus in the limitation:

> *to X in fee simple to the use of A for life, remainder to A's first grandson to marry in fee simple*

if A has no married grandson, then there may not be one for a remote time in the future. The rule against perpetuities is not satisfied. The limitation cannot take advantage of the Contingent Remainders Act, 1877, but it can still take effect, under *Purefoy v. Rogers*, as a common law remainder under Rule 4, the wait-and-see rule. If, as matters turn out, there is a married grandson of A at A's death, the remainder is valid.

3. Scope of the Act

a) Interests Outside Purefoy

The Act itself expressly applies to "every contingent remainder. . . which would have been valid as a springing or shifting use or executory devise. . . had it not had a sufficient estate to support it as a contingent remainder". The problem is that if contingent remainder is used in its strict sense then no contingent remainder could be valid if it had no prior estate to support it, and so it is difficult to see how the Act could have any application at all! It seems that "would have been" was intended to mean ". . . but for the rule in *Purefoy*", but the Act does not expressly say so. It has been generally accepted, however, that the Act applies to interests which, before the Act, were contingent remainders because of the operation of the Rule in *Purefoy v. Rogers*, *i.e. inter vivos* interests falling within Rule 4(b) of the common law remainder rules where a use had been inserted, or similar interests in wills even where a use had not been inserted.

One problem remains. Does the Act apply to an *inter vivos* contingent remainder if the contingent interest could be valid as an executory interest because it satisfies the perpetuity rule, although no use has been inserted? For example, the following limitation, if contained in an *inter vivos* deed, was clearly a common law remainder before the 1877 Act because no use had been inserted:

> *to A for life, remainder to his eldest son and his heirs at the age of 21.*

It was a clear example of a common law remainder subject to Rule 4 - the wait-and-see rule. If the son had not attained 21 by the time the A died, the remainder failed. Does it still fail? The son is bound to become 21, if at all, within the perpetuity period (*i.e.* a life in being, A, plus 21 years) and so if the limitation could be treated as an executory interest the son could still take even though he was still under 21 when A dies. It could be argued that the Act can only apply if the limitation would have been valid, as it stands, as an executory interest, *i.e.* that it not only complied with the perpetuity rule but also, in the case of *inter vivos* interests, a use had been inserted in it.

This is a possible literal reading of the Act, but it would have created, at the time it was passed, a highly artificial distinction between a limitation in a will which was a contingent remainder because of *Purefoy*, and an identical limitation *inter vivos*. The limitation just discussed is an example. Before the Act, if contained in a will, it would have been treated, by virtue of *Purefoy*, as being subject to Rule 4. One would still have to wait-and-see. The Act clearly applied to it. It would be valid as a springing devise because (a) by virtue of the Statute of Wills it could be treated as if it had contained a use, and (b) it satisfied the perpetuity rule. No other condition had to be satisfied. But would the identical limitation be within the Act if contained in an *inter vivos* deed? There was no use inserted and nothing before the Act to allow one to treat it as if one had been.

There is no direct authority on the point. Some[34] but not all[35] real property lawyers have taken the conservative view that the Act applies only to such interests as were treated as contingent remainders because of *Purefoy*. The present writer finds it difficult to accept that if the point arose today the statute would be given such a restricted meaning, thereby defeating a limitation to which there is no objection in substance. "Would have been valid" could also mean ". . . if a use had been inserted and but for Purefoy. . .".

b) Class Gifts

Another, and similar, problem arises as to the application of the Act to class gifts. In the case of *Brackenbury v. Gibbons,*[36] decided just before the 1877 Act came into force, a testator devised land:

> "To my daughter HN for life, and after her decease, in case she has no child, to the child or children of my daughter EG who either before or after her death should attain the age of 21, or die under that age, leaving issue living at my or her or our death, in fee simple as tenants in common."

HN died without issue and at her death two children of EG had attained the age of 21. None died under the age of 21 leaving issue, but others attained the age of 21 after HN's death. Hall V-C held that the two children of EG who had attained the age of 21 at HN's death took to the exclusion of those who did not do so until later. The limitation was subject to *Purefoy v. Rogers* at that time[37] and so had to be treated as a contingent remainder if it could take effect as such under the wait-and-see rule. The judge therefore applied the Rule in *Festing v. Allen.*[38] The result was that a discrimination was made between the daughters of EG for reasons which would be impossible to justify on common sense. In commenting on the case and the effect of the 1877 Act, Joshua Williams, the noted property lawyer and author of the standard work on the subject at the time, expressed the view that the Act had failed to mitigate such cases.[39] The prior estate had not, in the words of the Act, determined before the contingent remainder vested, since it was held to vest in the two daughters of EG who had

---

34 Wylie, *Irish Land Law* para. 5.029; for Joshua Williams see footnote 39.

35 See Hargreaves, *Land Law* p.117; and Megarry, *Manual (*3rd ed.) p.144: '... if the point ever arises, the court is likely to construe the Act generously, and hold that it applied to any legal remainder requiring its help'.

36 (1876) LR 2 Ch D 417.

37 Limitations in wills are not now so treated. See below.

38 *Festing v. Allen* (1843) 12 M & W 279, (1844) 5 Hare 573, 67 ER 1038.

39 See J Williams, *The Seisin of the Freehold.* Appendix B (cautiously adopts the narrower interpretation); G Sweet [1878] Sol Jour (in favour of the wider interpretation). *Symes v. Symes* [1896] 1 Ch. 272 appears to adopt the wide interpretation. See also *Re Wrightson* [1904] 2 Ch 95.

already attained 21. On the other hand it can be argued that the effect of *Festing v. Allen* is to divide a single class into two parts, the purpose being in the case itself to save at least one part. This being so it can be argued that the remainder did not vest in the two daughters who became 21 after HN's death because the prior estate determined before they were ready to do so, and so the Act may apply to save their interests.

J. Equitable Interests

The common law remainder rules have no application to future equitable interests. Neither, therefore, does the rule in *Purefoy v. Rogers*, or the Contingent Remainders Act, 1877. Equitable interests have to comply with the perpetuity rule and cannot in any circumstances take effect as legal remainders.

Equity never applied the common law remainder rules to equitable interests. The reason normally given for this is that there is no transgression of the feudal rules: the legal estate is held by trustees in fee simple and so no abeyance of seisin can occur.[40] *Purefoy* does not apply because it only applies where there is an executed use. The 1877 Act does not apply because it can only apply to interests which can take effect in some circumstances as legal estates.

For this purpose limitations created by a mortgagor who has mortgaged the fee simple subject to a condition for reconveyance are equitable limitations. The mortgagor retains an equity of redemption and limitations carved out of it take effect in equity. This point was decided in the Irish case of *Ferguson v. Ferguson*,[41] a case which highlighted the artificiality of distinctions in this area. The testator held some lands in fee simple, some under leases for lives renewable forever and some estates subject to mortgages by conveyance of the fee simple in which the testator therefore retained only an equity of redemption. He devised all of his land to his eldest son, if any, who should attain 21 or marry, and, failing such son, in equal shares to such of his daughters who should attain 21 or marry, for their lives. Failing all sons and daughters who should attain 21 or marry, he left it to his sisters in equal shares for their lives, with remainder, as to their respective shares, to their eldest sons who should attain 21 or marry. The testator died without issue. His four sisters survived him, two of whom died leaving sons under 21 and unmarried. The will had come into effect before the Contingent Remainders Act, 1877 was enacted.

The Irish Master of the Rolls held that the common law rule of destructibility did not apply to the equitable interest under the mortgaged lands, nor did it apply to interests created out of leases for lives, which, however much they might resemble traditional common law remainders, were merely interests

40 *Astley v. Micklethwaite* (1880) 15 Ch D 59.

41 (1885) 17 LR Ir 552, MR, appeal on other issues at p.567, CA.

created out of an *estate pur autre vie*. As to the land held in fee simple, however, he held that the remainders failed under the common law rule. The life estates to the daughters had come to an end before the remainders to their son were able to vest in possession. There was a gap in the seisin.[42] The rule against perpetuities applies to future trusts and so they must satisfy it or be void *ab initio*. Thus a limitation

> *unto and to the use of T and U and their heirs in trust for A for life, remainder in trust for such of A's grandchildren who marry and their heirs*

creates only an equitable life estate in A. The remainder is void for perpetuity. The trustees hold the estate after A's death on a resulting trust for the grantor. It cannot be treated as a common law remainder and so subject to the wait-and-see rule because it is not a legal interest of any kind.

Equitable interests are therefore at a disadvantage in this respect over legal estates. They only have one way of being valid and that is to comply with the perpetuity rule. One of the few reasons in favour of retaining the highly complex rules as to future interests in relation to legal estates in Ireland is that if they cannot comply with the perpetuity rule, they can, if they are of the Rule 4 type, take effect as common law remainders, if, after waiting-to-see, there is no gap.

K. Leases for Lives

It has been seen that *Ferguson v. Ferguson*[43] decided that limitations created out of leases for lives renewable forever were not subject to destructibility: they are legal interests but they are not true common law remainders.

It may be that blind logic had less to do with the result in *Ferguson v. Ferguson*[44] than the thought that the result had the effect of reducing the scope of an increasingly meaningless rule. The exception of equitable interests and interests under leases for lives renewable forever greatly reduced the scope of destructibility of contingent remainders in Ireland, but while it mitigated the harshness of outmoded rules, the artificiality of the distinctions which were introduced to achieve this only added to the sense of injustice in those cases which still fell under its shadow.

---

42 He could not hold that the remainders were vested until divested by failure to fulfil the conditions, since the conditions affected not merely the time of enjoyment but the description of the person who was to take. Nor was there, as in *Edwards v. Hammond* (1684) 3 Lev 132, 83 ER 614, a gift over on the same contingency. For a discussion of the latter case, see also *McGredy v. CIR.* [1951] NI 155; *Re Murphy* [1964] IR 308, 311–313.

43 (1885) 17 LR Ir 552, MR, (appeal on other issues at p.567, CA).

44 *ibid.*

L. Future Interests in Wills

In the past, when a person died intestate his or her real property vested automatically in the heir-at-law. If a person died leaving a will the real property vested automatically in the devisee. If legal estates had been created by the will, they took effect as such and at once. There were many reasons why this could lead to inconvenience and so the law was reformed so that the legal estate in a deceased person's land now vests initially in the personal representatives, *i.e.* the executors where there is a will or the administrators of the estate appointed on intestacy. This change was brought about in the Republic by the Administration of Estates Act, 1959 section 6, now replaced by the Succession Act, 1965 section 10.

The effect is that the personal representatives hold the legal estate in trust for the persons entitled to the estates created by the testator in the will. When they administer the estate and distribute the property they will confer legal estates on those entitled. It is clear from what has been said that some interests which are valid as equitable interests may be invalid as legal estates. When the personal representatives vest legal estates in those entitled, should the interests then be judged as legal estates, even though that may mean they then become void? In *Re Robson*[45] an English court[46] took the view that it did not. If the interests were valid initially their becoming legal estates did not make them void. To take an example, if a testator leaves land in his will:

> *to A for life, remainder to his eldest son in fee simple at the age of 21*

despite the fact that the words create no trust, section 10 of the Succession Act, 1965 causes the whole fee simple to vest in the executors who hold it in trust for A for life and in trust to give effect to the remainder. As an equitable estate the future interest is valid. It need only comply with the perpetuity rule and it does so. But the executors will later confer a legal life estate on A. If A survives the testator, there is no problem. The remainder is supported by a prior estate and the limitation is subject to the wait-and-see rule. Furthermore, since the remainder satisfies the perpetuity rule, it can take effect under the Contingent Remainders Act, 1877 even if there is no son aged 21 at A's death. But suppose that A dies before the testator. The remainder is no longer supported by a prior estate when the limitation takes effect. It is valid as an equitable interest, because a springing interest is possible in equity. But does it become void when the executors later come to vest legal estates in those entitled, because a springing interest is not possible at common law? According to *Re Robson*, this does not render it invalid. It may take effect if and when the eldest son reaches 21. One way of explaining the result is to say that at A's death if there is no son of

45 [1916] 1 Ch 116. See also *Re Freme* [1891] 3 Ch 167. The opposite result was reached in Canada in *Re Crow* (1984) 12 DLR (4th) 415.

46 A Canadian court a different view in *Re Crow* (1984) 12 DLR (4th) 415.

the required age, the legal estate continues in the executors and so there is no abeyance of seisin. In any case, the result is satisfactory because there is no reason in policy why an interest which is initially valid should later become void because of an outdated rule.

The opposite problem could also arise. Some interests which are void as equitable interests are valid, or may be valid, as common law remainders. These are interests which would break the perpetuity rule if treated as equitable interests, but which may turn out to be valid as common law remainders under the wait-and-see rule. If the testator leaves land:

> *to A for life, remainder to his grandchildren when they marry in fee simple*
> (A has no grandchildren)

it can be argued that since it now vests in the executors at the testator's death, the future interest is void *ab initio* for perpetuity. Supposing, when A dies, there is in fact a married grandchild, can it take the remainder? It has satisfied the wait-and-see rule. But once having been void, can it now revive? It is difficult in logic to see how it can be, but this is a point that remains to be decided.

M. Rule in Edwards *v.* Hammond

In determining whether an interest was vested or contingent, a special rule at common law, known as the Rule in *Edwards v. Hammond*[47], applied to wills. The rule was to the effect that:

> "where property, real or personal, is given in a will to a person on his or her attaining a certain age and a gift over is given on the event of that person not attaining the age, the primary gift is construed as vested and not contingent, but liable to be divested if the person fails to attain the age."

For example, in the limitations:

> *to A in fee simple when he becomes 21, but if he dies under that age, to B in fee simple*
>
> *to X for life, remainder to A in fee simple when he becomes 21, but if he dies under that age, to B in fee simple*

---

47 *Edwards v. Hammond* (1684) 3 Lev 132, 1 B & P (NR) 324n, 83 ER 614, 49 Digest (Repl) 968. *Bromfield v. Crowder* (1805) 1 Bos & P (NR) 313, 127 ER 483; *Doe d Willis v. Martin*, [1775-1802] All ER Rep 343, (1790) 4 Term Rep 39, 100 ER 882, 37 Digest (Repl) 342, 859; *Finch v. Lane* (1870) LR 10 Eq 501; *Re Kilpatrick's Policies Trusts* [1965] 2 All ER 673, [1966] Ch 730, [1965] 2 WLR 1346, affirmed CA, [1966] 2 All ER 149, [1966] Ch at p.747, [1966] 2 WLR at p.1360; *Phipps v. Ackers*, (1842) 9 Cl & Fin 583, 8 ER 539; *Re Young's Settlement Trusts* [1959] 2 All ER 74, [1959] 1 WLR 457; *Re Penton's Settlements* [1968] 1 All ER 36, [1968] 1 WLR 248; *Brotherton v. Inland Revenue Commissioners* [1978] 2 All ER 267, [1978] 1 WLR 610, [1978] STC 201, 52 Tax Cas 137, [1977] TR 317 Court of Appeal Civil Division.

the fee simple to A is vested, subject to being divested on A's failure to reach 21. The rule probably originated as a way of preventing common law limitations failing under the contingent remainder rules, as it would do in the example. If it were not for the rule, the gift to A would, in the first example, be an attempt to create a springing interest and would be void. In the second example, if A was under 21 at X's death, the remainder would fail under the wait-and-see rule. However, by the 19th century the courts had extended the rule beyond common law limitations to personal property[48] and to equitable interests.[49] The modern explanation of the rule is that the grantor intends to dispose of the property either to A or to B, so that anything not taken by B should be taken by A.[50] In the case of a trust, if A's interest were treated as contingent, then A would not be entitled to the income before attaining the age and if B's interest were also treated as contingent, neither would B, so that the income would not be disposed of at all, would fall into residue and either go to a residuary legatee or on a partial intestacy, which was probably not what the testator intended.

The rule was examined by Kenny J in *Re Murphy's Estate*.[51] The testator in the case devised his freehold farm:

> in trust for his wife for her life and after her death in trust "for my son" S "absolutely provided he has attained the age of twenty-five and in the event of my said son" S "predeceasing my said wife or dying before reaching the said age of twenty-five years then in trust for my son" M "provided he attains the said age of twenty-five years".

The will contained a residuary clause. The testator died in 1935. His widow died in 1937. S attained 25 years in 1956. The issues were (a) did S take a vested estate on the death of the testator's widow in 1937, or on his attaining 25 in 1956? and (b) who was entitled to the income arising from the farm between the two dates?

Kenny J commented on the rule:

> "The reasoning on which the rule was based is plainly fallacious when there is a residuary clause as it is then probable that the testator intended that the income of the property devised on condition should form part of the residuary estate un-

---

48 *Re Heath* (1936) Ch. 259.

49 *Phipps v. Ackers* (1842) 9 Cl & F 583, 8 ER 539.

50 In *Phipps v. Ackers* (1842) 9 Cl & F 583, 8 ER 539 the opinions in the House of Lords were given after the advice of eleven Common Law judges had been heard. The Judges advised that the earlier cases went on the principle:

> "that the subsequent gift over in the event of the devisee dying under 21, sufficiently shows the meaning of the testator to have been that the first devisee should take whatever interest the party claiming under the devise over is not entitled to, which of course gives him the immediate interest, subject only to the chance of its being divested on a future contingency."

51 [1964] IR 308 at 311, 313; *McGredy v. CIR* [1951] NI 155; *Ferguson v. Ferguson* (1885) 17 LR Ir 552.

> til attainment of the specified age. The rule did not have its origin in the reasoning which was subsequently developed in its defence but in the common law doctrine that the seisin and the legal estate in freehold lands had to have an owner so that the subsequent estate which was contingent would not be destroyed by not having a particular estate to support it."

In other words, the true origin of the rule lay in the application of the Rule in *Purefoy v. Rogers* to wills.[52] The judge went on to hold that, whatever may have been the case in the past, the rule was now merely one of construction. It may possibly be useful in some cases, but it is arguable that it no longer serves any real purpose. *Purefoy* no longer applies to wills, and one wonders why the rule survived the change in the law.[53]

On the facts the judge held that the property passed to S in 1956, when he attained the age of 25. He further held that the income of the farm between the two dates was held by the trustees on the trusts declared by the residuary clause of the will. The judge noted that the limitation before him not only made the gift to S dependent on his attaining 25, but also made the gift over to M subject to a similar age qualification. The judge held this to be an additional factor in holding that both interests were contingent, a decision which he found was consistent with precedent. Nevertheless, it would seem that today it is always a matter of construction and there is no fixed rule of law in such a case.

N. Possibilities of Reverter and of Resulting Trust

These interests have been described already in the chapter on the fee simple under conditional and determinable interests. The only aspect of them which needs fuller treatment is the rule against perpetuities. The interests are exceptions to the application of the rule and that aspect is dealt with in Chapter 11 on rules against remoteness.

O. Rights of Entry for Condition Broken

Palles CB in *Attorney General v. Cummins*[54] held, *obiter,* that a right of entry for condition broken following a conditional fee is not subject to the perpetuity rule. Similar interests created by executory interests or trusts also seem to be immune from the perpetuity rule in the Republic. These interests are also dealt with later as exceptions to the perpetuity rule.

---

52 See above Chapter 10 Future Interests.

53 It might also be noticed that it should only apply, given its history, if the gift at the specified age is preceded by a prior estate, as it was in *Murphy* and in *Edwards v. Hammond* itself, *i.e.* where the common law wait-and-see rule applied.

54 [1906] 1 IR 406.

P. Gifts Over

1. After a Conditional or Determinable Estate

We have seen that the only kind of gift over one could create at common law was a remainder after a determinable life estate. The following limitation:

to A for life or until she becomes a solicitor, then to B and his heirs

creates a determinable life estate and a valid gift over.

A purported gift over after a conditional life estate is void as cutting short the prior estate, while a purported gift over to follow a determinable or conditional fee is void because it breaks the rule against remainders after a fee simple.[55] Gifts over to following determinable and conditional fees[56] can be created only under executed uses or as equitable interests, and only if they comply, as all such interests must, with the perpetuity rule. They are dealt with later in Chapter 11 in the context of the perpetuity rule.[57]

2. After a Fee Simple Absolute

One question that might arise in relation to the effect of the Statute of Uses is whether it allows a gift over after a fee simple absolute. If the following words were contained in a deed:

to A and his heirs, remainder to B and his heirs

the effect would be that A would take a fee simple absolute, but the remainder to B would be void. The limitation is phrased as a common law interest - there is no mention of a uses or trust - and the gift to B falls foul of the common law rule that prohibits remainders after a fee simple. Is it possible to avoid the common law rule by inserting a use so that the limitation takes effect under the Statute of Uses? In other words, if the limitation were phrased:

to F and his heirs to the use of A and his heirs, remainder to the use of B and his heirs

would the insertion of the use permit the gift over to B to take effect? A rational approach would be to say that it can, unless the reason for the common law rule is a principle or policy that still should be applied. The reason often given for the common law rule is that the fee simple is the largest interest that it is possible to have in real property, so that the grantor, in conferring a fee simple on A has disposed of his entire interest and has nothing left to give to B. The result is supposed to be a logical conclusion drawn from some metaphysical quality inherent in the fee simple estate. This is a mystification, a false representation of

55 *Attorney General v. Cummins* [1906] 1 IR 406 at 410 per Palles CB.

56 Or after a conditional life estate.

57 See page 324.

a result which had nothing to do with metaphysics and a great deal to do with the class struggle within feudal society. The real reason was that such a limitation ran counter to the economic interests of feudal lords. If A died without heirs A's lord would have the benefit of the escheat that would then occur. If, however, an estate in fee simple could be limited to take effect upon the happening of that event, the lord would be deprived of benefits that would accrue to him under the escheat. Since this reason is now obsolete it does not constitute an objection to the limitation.

There is, however, a more direct answer provided by section 73(1) of the Succession Act, 1965, which provides that in default of any person taking the estate of an intestate, the State takes the estate as ultimate intestate successor. In other words, A's estate will never come to an end, for if he, or his assigns, die without heirs the estate passes to the State. Section 73 means that after 1 January 1967, the date on which the Succession Act, 1965 came into force, a fee simple absolute never comes to an end. There is one possible qualification to this. Section 73(2) provides that the Minister of Finance may waive the right of the State in favour of such person and on such terms as he thinks proper. Presumably, in the case of such a limitation, the State might wish to waive its right in favour of B. It is arguable that such a waiver would bring the first fee simple to an end and vests in B the fee simple in remainder.

Q. Reform of the Law of Future Interests

The scheme of future interests in Ireland is unnecessarily complex. The present scheme is set out in Appendix A. The complexity is partly due to the retention of the common law remainder rules which pursue an obsolete feudal policy. The complexity is compounded by the survival of the rule in *Purefoy v. Rogers*, which is pointless, and the limited reform of it by the 1877 Act.

A number of options are open to legislators contemplating a reform of future interests. One would be to adopt the approach of the English 1925 reforms contained in the Law of Property Act, 1925. That is to restrict legal estates to two kinds, one freehold and one leasehold, the freehold being a fee simple absolute and the leasehold a term of years absolute, both of which would have to be defined by statute. The idea is that only a fee simple absolute, *i.e.* not being subject to conditions or to determining events, could exist as a legal estate, all other forms being transformed into equitable interests under a trust. This has the effect of simplifying future interests because all such interests would be future trusts and so subject only to the perpetuity rule. The old rule against perpetuities (the rule in *Whitby v. Mitchell*) could also be repealed as no longer necessary. Since future interests could no longer exist as legal estates, the common law remainder rules, *Purefoy* and the Contingent Remainders Act, 1877 would no longer apply. This scheme has a lot to be said for it in terms of simplification and little to be said against it. One point against it might be that it would mean that a legal life estate could no longer be granted and this might be seen as an undue restriction on freedom to dispose of property, but in Ireland the right of residence, if retained as a legal interest, or even as a third form of legal estate, might well provide an acceptable alternative way of providing family members with a secure life interest in property, secure because it could not be defeated as easily as an equitable interest. Consequential changes would have to be made to the perpetuity rule itself, however, for example, to bring conditions subsequent and determining events within its scope.

Another, less radical alternative scheme, would be to allow the creation of legal future interests but repeal the common law remainder rules, the Statute of Uses, the Rule in *Purefoy* and the Contingent Remainders Act and therefore produce a single category of legal future interests subject only to the perpetuity rule, with similar consequential changes to that rule as in the first option.[58] This would produce a scheme similar to that operated in many states in the United States, which recognise the same general scheme of legal future interests as in Ireland, but treat future interests as legal executory interests if it is necessary to their validity, even if they do not contain an express use.[59] One objection to this might be that it would allow too many uncertainties as to the passing of legal estates from one proprietor to another, as for example, if a springing interests were created, and would interfere with the efficient operation of a free market in land. On the other hand, this does not seem to be seen as a major obstacle in the United States whose political system certainly favours the market mechanism. This is partly because future interests are now rarely created in any case, which is also an argument for making no change at all. The remaining argument in favour of change is that it would relieve the tedium of most law students who have to grapple with a complex and increasingly unnecessary subject.

58 It would also be necessary to provide by statute that, if a gap occurred, the interest in the meantime would vest in the grantor, since no common law rule ever applied to produce this effect.

59 Simes, *Future Interests* pp. 25–28; Powell, *Real Property,* 1998, 3:20.05

CHAPTER 11

RULES AGAINST REMOTENESS

"Any construction that would violate the rule against perpetuities cannot be adopted, it is true; but the law does not search for a perpetuity in a will, though it abhors it, when obvious, as nature abhors a vacuum."

– Lord Brougham in *Dungannon v. Smith* (1845–6) 12 Cl & Fin 546 at 551–2, 8 ER 1523 at 1526.

A. The Old Rule Against Perpetuities

This rule, although sometimes known as the Rule in *Whitby v. Mitchell*[1] after a 19th century case which restated the rule, or the rule against double possibilities,[2] is of considerable age and probably developed in the early 17th century at the time that entails became barrable.[3]

1. Application

The rule applies to legal remainders and to legal executory interests and future trusts if the last two mentioned resemble legal remainders,[4] but not to shifting or springing uses or trusts. It thus differs in scope from the modern rule against perpetuities which does not apply, in this jurisdiction, to legal remainders. The rule remains in force in the Republic, although it has been abolished in Northern Ireland.[5]

2. The Rule

The rule is that:

1 (1890) 44 Ch D 85. See also Holdsworth HEL VII p.209; C Sweet, "The Rule in *Whitby v. Mitchell*" 25 LQR 385; P Bordwell "Alienability and Perpetuities", IV, 25 Iowa LR 1; Morris and Leach, *Perpetuities* Chapter 10; Simpson, *History* p.216.

2 Per Cotton and Lindley LJJ in *Whitby v. Mitchell* (1890) 44 Ch D 85. The rule does not prohibit double possibilities as such, as we shall see, but only gifts to unborn issue after gifts to unborn issue.

3 Simpson, *History* p.215 states that this position was reached by 1614 in *Mary Portington's Case* (1614) 10 Co Rep 35b, 77 ER 976. *Re Rosher* (1884) 26 Ch D 801 at 812, per Pearson J.

4 *Re Nash* [1910] 1 Ch 1.

5 Section 15 of Perpetuities Act (Northern Ireland), 1966.

> If an interest in real property is given to an unborn person, then any further grant to his or her issue, however described, is void together with all subsequent limitations.

For example:

> *to X for life, remainder to his son for life, remainder to that son's son for life...(etc.).*
> (X has no son.)

The second remainder in favour of the grandson of X is void together with all subsequent remainders. Another example is provided by *Bank of Ireland v. Goulding*[6] in which a limitation in a will was in the form:

> *to my grandson (B) for life, remainder to his eldest son for life, provided he is born within 21 years of my death,*[7] *but if he is not, then to him absolutely, and in case of failure of male issue of such [great-grandson], remainder to the second or other of my grandsons for life. . .*

B was living at the testator's death. The gift to B's eldest son, a great-grandson of the testator, was valid, but the gift on failure of male issue of that great-grandson was void as contrary to the rule.[8] The original reason for the rule dates back to the time when entails became barrable. This meant that landowners were no longer able to keep land within their families by means of the entail. Their lawyers therefore attempted a new method: they tried to create a succession of contingent life estates to each generation of the family in a form similar to the limitation above. This was known as a perpetual freehold. If successful, this new device would have achieved the same result as an unbarrable entail, and so the courts reacted by creating the rule.

In *Bevan v. White*[9] the limitation was:

> *to A for life, remainder to his first and every other son in succession for life, and in default to B for life, remainder to his first and every other son in succession for life. . .*

It was held to give rise to a valid series of life estates. There was no gift to unborn issue of unborn issue. All the sons mentioned were the sons of A or B, both of whom were in existence. For the rule to apply it is not sufficient that there be a gift to an unborn issue of an unborn person. There must first be a gift to an unborn person followed by another gift to that unborn person's issue. For example, in the limitation:

---

6 Unreported, Supreme Court, 14 November 1975. Griffin J, Henchy and Budd JJ concurring, O'Higgins CJ and Walsh J dissenting, judgments by Griffin and O'Higgins only.

7 The drafter of the deed evidently thought that it was necessary to limit the gift in this way, although a limitation to 21 years from the death of B would have been sufficient.

8 The majority held that the cy pres doctrine could not be applied as the gift concerned was one of personalty. See below.

9 (1845) 7 Ir Eq R 473.

> *unto and to the use of T and U and their heirs in trust for A for life, remainder in trust in fee simple for the first-born grandson of A born within 21 years of A's death.*
> (A has no son.)

The rule does not invalidate the remainder to the first-born grandson. The rule only applies if there is grant of a property interest to unborn issue, followed by a grant of a property interest to their issue. In the above example no remainder is given to the first-born grandson's parent, *i.e.* A's unborn son.

There seems little reason to retain the rule. The basic "perpetual freehold" limitation would be void after the first remainder under the modern perpetuity rule, as there is no certainty that X's grandson will be born within 21 years of any living person's death, including X. In addition, a limitation may be valid under the modern rule against perpetuity, but be void under the old rule. For example, if, in the preceding limitation, an interest is given to A's unborn son:

> *unto and to the use of T and U and their heirs in trust for A for life, remainder in trust for A's son for life, remainder in trust in fee simple for the first-born grandson of A born within 21 years of A's death*
> (A has no son)

the limitation is void under the old rule, but would be valid if only the modern rule applied, since the contingency on which the second remainder is to vest is expressly limited to the perpetuity period. A's first-born grandson may be born more than 21 years after A's death, but if so it will not have the effect of causing a contingent interest to vest. Since the modern rule is generally regarded today, by those who regard it as necessary at all, as the only means required to control contingent interests, the result in the above limitation would be regarded as irrational.

3. Cy Pres

The cy pres doctrine[10] which is also found in relation to charitable trusts, was developed by the courts to mitigate the harshness of the Rule in *Whitby v. Mitchell*. It allows the court a limited jurisdiction to rewrite the limitation so as to conform to the rule while carrying out the intentions of the grantor as far as the law allows. Where, for example, the limitation is in the form:

> *to A for life, remainder to the first son of A for life, remainder in tail male to the first and every other son of such son and their issue male successively, [with remainders over if A should die without male issue of his body]*
> (A has no sons)

the remainders to the sons of A's sons are void. The court may redraft the limitation as a grant to A for life with remainder to his sons successively in tail

10 Law French meaning near to it, and pronounced "see pray" or "sigh pray".

male.[11] The redrafted limitation must give interests only to those persons who would have been entitled under the original limitation.[12]

The doctrine applies also to the perpetual freehold limitation which was an attempt to create an unbarrable entail, as for example:

> *to A for life, remainder to his eldest son for life, remainder to that son's first and other sons successively for life. . .*[13]
> (A has no sons)

the remainder to the unborn son's unborn son is void, together with subsequent remainders, but the cy pres doctrine allows the court to give A's eldest son a fee tail.[14] But in the limitation:

> *to A for life, remainder to his eldest son in tail male, remainder to that son's eldest son in tail male*

without any further limitations to the other sons of A's son, then the doctrine was not applied, because to give an estate tail to A's son would let in the younger sons of A's son whom the testator did not intend to benefit.[15] The doctrine also means in effect that life estates are replaced by a fee tail. It is probably for this reason that it was held in *Bank of Ireland v. Goulding*[16] that the doctrine does not apply to dispositions of personal property.[17] Personal property cannot be entailed in Ireland, nor could it in England before 1925.[18]

4. Wills

It could be argued that section 94 of the Succession Act, 1965, which requires the same words of limitation in wills to create a fee tail as are required *inter vivos*, has abolished the cy pres doctrine in the case of wills. Against this it

---

11 *Peyton v. Lambert* (1858) 8 Ir LR 485. It may be noticed that the first remainder is valid, but is necessarily affected by the application of the cy pres doctrine.

12 *ibid.* per O'Brien J.

13 *East v. Twyford* (1853) 4 HLC 517, 10 ER 564; *Parfitt v. Hember* (1867) LR 4 Eq 443.

14 *ibid.*.

15 *Re Rising* [1904] 1 Ch. 533; *Re Mortimer* [1905] 2 Ch. 502.

16 Unreported, Supreme Court, 14 November 1975. Griffin J, Henchy and Budd JJ concurring, O'Higgins CJ and Walsh J dissenting, judgments by Griffin and O'Higgins only.

17 Unreported, Supreme Court, 14 November 1975, following *Routledge v. Dorril* (1794) 2 Ves Jun 357 at p.365 per Arden MR, 30 ER 671, not following the English case of *Mackworth v. Hinxman* (1836) 2 Keen 658, 48 ER 782. In the latter case the doctrine was applied to personalty, the court holding that the quasi-entail gave the recipient an absolute interest. It could be argued, in favour of the Goulding approach, that only a fee tail would reflect the intention of the donor to keep land in the family, but the fact that entails are barrable rather destoys the force of that argument.

18 The statute *De Donis* applies only to "tenements". Personalty was made entailable in England by the Law of Property Act, 1925 s.130.

could also be argued that a doctrine which allows the court to rewrite the limitation also allows it to supply what is not present in the will, namely, correct words of limitation creating a fee tail.

B. The Modern Rule Against Perpetuities

"Lives plus one and twenty years
The learned fathers thought
Should be the time for vesting
Or the gift would come to naught

As many lives as are ascertained
Without undue delay
For you light the candles all at once
as Twisden used to say[19]

This was to keep the land well oiled
And free to come and go
For a dead man's hand must idle be
And his mind works awful slow.

– Written by a student of Barton Leach[20]

1. Introduction

If land is subject to a contingent interest then the marketability of the land is reduced. If the interest is contingent because the person entitled to it is not ascertained, then the whole fee simple cannot be sold. The persons entitled to the various estates cannot join together to sell the fee simple because the owner of the contingent estate is unknown. In the case of legal contingent remainders this situation cannot continue for long because the common law rules have the gratuitously beneficial effect, so far as marketability is concerned, of limiting the period during which interests can remain contingent. For example, in the *inter vivos* limitation:

to A for life, remainder to his eldest grandchild in fee simple at the age of 21

---

19 See footnote 20.

20 Barton Leach (1952). The reference to Sir Thomas Twisden (1602-1683) [DNB], a judge of the King's Bench at the time of Charles II, comes from a line in *Scattergood v. Edge* (1699) 1 Salk 229, 91 ER 203 (sub nom *Scatterwood v. Edge* 2 Eq Ca Abr 337, 22 ER 287 by counsel (Powell): "... for let the lives be never so many, there must be a survivor and so it is but the length of that life (for Twisden used to say, the candles were all lighted at once)." Barton Leach admits he was fond of quoting the saying. One might, however, point out that, since there was no wait-and-see in the perpetuity rule at common law, the saying is more appropriate as to the determination of the time of distribution.

the wait-and-see rule ensures that the contingent interest will either vest at A's death or be void. The basis of the rule was a feudal policy against an abeyance of seisin, but it had the by-product of reaching a result which favoured marketability. When, however, equity, before the Statute of Uses, 1634, recognised contingent interests in uses, it did not subject them to the old feudal common law rules. It was therefore necessary to develop a new rule which would directly control the vesting of such contingent interests. In the limitation:

> *unto and to the use of T and U in fee simple in trust for A for life, remainder to his eldest grandchild in fee simple at the age of 21*

if A has no grandson at the date the instrument takes effect, then the fee simple cannot be sold, because the owner of the contingent interest is unknown and there is no one to join with A to sell the fee simple in possession. A contradiction exists, therefore, even within a system of land law which rejects outmoded feudal rules. The contradiction is between the freedom of owners of individual property in land to do what they will with it and an ideological position which favours the efficiency of a capitalist economy in which land is a commodity which can be bought and sold and which supports the mechanism of this economy in redistributing land ownership towards those with money to invest and away from owners of impoverished or inefficiently-run estates. This position also stresses freedom: the freedom of those with money to be able to use the market mechanism. The modern rule against perpetuities is a compromise, typically, between these contradictory freedoms. The basis of the rule was laid down by Lord Nottingham in *Duke of Norfolk's Case*[21] at the end of the 17th century.

The rule against perpetuities applies to equitable interests and to legal executory interests under the Statute of Uses, 1634,[22] since the latter are, as it were, converted equitable interests. It also applies to contingent interests in personal property.

2. The Perpetuity Period

The rule is to the effect that:

> a contingent interest in property is valid only if it is certain from the beginning to vest, if it vests at all, within the period of a life or lives in being when the instrument takes effect and 21 years thereafter. If there are no such lives, the period is 21 years.

An good example of the application of the rule is the case of *Smithwick v.*

21 (1681) 3 Chan Cas 1, 2 Swanst 454, 22 ER 931, 949; Plucknett, *Concise History* p.563–5; Siegal "John Chipman Gray, Legal Formalism and the Transformation of Perpetuities Law" (1982) 36 Miami L R 439.

22 *Abbiss v. Burney* (1880) 17 Ch D 211.

Hayden.[23] A somewhat eccentric testator by the name of John Hayden had no children of his own, but had a sister and a friend, Edward Fleming. The testator left all his property to trustees to pay the income to his sister for life, then after her death to Edward Fleming, and after Edward Fleming's death to "any female niece or relative" of Edward Fleming who should marry "a person by the name of John Hayden who should reside in Tipperary", where the testator's ancestors apparently came from, and who should be "born and reared a Roman Catholic". Any person by the name of John Hayden would do, provided he satisfied the other tests. Hayden is a Tipperary name and no doubt the testator believed that such a person might be related to him. However, it might be hundreds of years before a female relative married a person of that name, even though they might have had some incentive to do so. What defeated the gift was the consideration that there was no certainty that if a female relative of Fleming ever did marry a John Hayden from Tipperary she would do so within the period.

a) Points to note

(i) No Wait-And-See

The common law perpetuity rule is not a wait-and-see rule.[24] One cannot wait to see if the contingency does in fact occur within the period. The limitation is void if it is possible that it may not do so. So, in *Smithwick v. Hayden*[25] one could not wait to see if a female relative of Edward Fleming married a man called John Hayden within 21 years of the testator's death. The gift was void because the event was not certain to happen within the period.

The reason for this approach was no doubt to maintain the character of the rule as one which a lawyer could apply to a limitation at the time the instrument took effect and be able to say at that time whether it was valid or void. However, the courts applied the logic of no wait-and-see to the extent of holding that even if, by the time the limitation came before a court, the contingency had occurred within the period, that had to be ignored so that the limitation would still be void if , at the time the instrument containing the limitation took effect, there was no certainty that events would occur in this way.[26] This aspect of the rule has been much criticised as leading to absurdity and attempts at reform, such as the Northern Ireland statute[27], often introduce a wait-and-see principle.

---

23 (1887) 19 LR Ir 490, CA.

24 *Exham v. Beamish* [1939] IR 336.

25 (1887) 19 LR Ir 490, CA.

26 *Exham v. Beamish* [1939] IR 336. It was clear at the time of the case, 1939, that William and Anne Thompson had not in fact had more children after the date of the *inter vivos* deed, *i.e.* 1865. Gavan Duffy J held that that did not save the gift.

27 Perpetuities Act (Northern Ireland), 1966.

(ii) Contingent and Vested

For the purpose of the rule against perpetuities interests are vested (in interest) if (i) the person to take is ascertained, (ii) there is no unfulfilled condition precedent and (iii) in the case of a class gift, the size of each share is ascertained.

Where there is a prior estate,[28] the perpetuity rule only requires it to be certain that contingent interests shall vest in interest within the period. It is immaterial that they may vest in possession outside the period.[29] So in the limitation:

> *Unto and to the use of T and U in fee simple in trust for A for life, remainder in trust for her children for their joint lives, remainder in trust for B in fee simple*
> (A has no children)

the ultimate trust to B is valid. Although it will not vest in possession until after the perpetuity period if A's children survive her for more than 21 years, it is a vested interest from the beginning.

Where there is no prior indefeasible estate, as in the case of executory springing or shifting interests, or similar interests under trusts, or an easement to arise in future,[30] most texts say that the perpetuity rule requires it to be certain that such contingent interests shall vest in possession[31] within the period. Vesting in interest and vesting in possession in any case coincide in this instance. It could still be said that the rule is concerned with vesting in interest: it is just that vesting in interest occurs at the same time as vesting in possession in this type of interest.

(iii) Applies to Contingent Interests Only

The rule, as has been stated, controls the vesting in interest of contingent interests.[32] It has no application to the duration of vested interests. If it had, then all fee simple estates would be void.

The fact that a contingent interest may never vest at all is immaterial. Many contingencies are of the kind that may never occur at all. In the limitation:

> *[a trust] to A in fee simple, but if B marries C, in trust for B in fee simple*

B may never marry C, but the contingent fee simple to B is valid, because it is absolutely certain from the beginning that if B does marry C, she must do so in her own lifetime and B is a life in being. If B dies without marrying C, then it

---

28 It will be recalled that the rule against perpetuities does not apply in Ireland to contingent remainders at common law. It applies to equitable interests and legal executory interests, either of which may or may not have an estate prior to the future interest.

29 *Craig v. Stacey* (1794) Ir Term Rep 249.

30 *Dunn v. Blackdown Properties Ltd* [1961] Ch. 433.

31 Morris and Leach, *The Rule Against Perpetuities* p.1.

32 *Stevens Mineral Company v. State of Michigan* (1987) 164 Mich App 692, 418 NW 2d 130, 98 Oil & Gas Rep 316, Court of Appeals of Michigan.

becomes clear at that point that the contingent interest cannot vest, but the gift is not void for *perpetuity* and so not void from the beginning.[33]

(iv) The Effect of Life Estates and Fees Simple

It may be that the nature of the contingent estate is relevant in applying the rule. In the limitation:

> *a rent [in trust] to B for life when coal is mined on the land*

Coal mining may not begin, if it ever does, until a remote time in the future. Since, however, the estate given to B is for life, if the contingency is to cause the contingent life estate to vest, it will only do so within B's lifetime, and so the interest is valid. The rule against perpetuities does not apply to any contingency, but only to contingencies causing the vesting of contingent interests in property. So, on the other hand:

> *a rent [in trust] to B in fee simple when coal is mined on the land*[34]

is invalid because if coal mining has not begun by B's death the contingent fee simple would be inherited by B's successors and could vest in interest in them at any time coal mining began thereafter, which could be beyond the period.

So in *Re Edwards*[35] the testator left realty by will to his two sons as tenants in common in fee simple with a direction in a codicil to his sons and their heirs to make to each of his daughters for life "and afterwards to and amongst the children of each and their heirs" certain payments out of the coal under a certain farm when worked or let. The coal was not worked or let in the testator's lifetime. Lord Macnaughten in the British House of Lords held that the codicil, insofar as it related to the children of his daughters, was intended to create future limitations which were to impose burdens on land at some future and indefinite time on a contingency which might or might not happen but which, if it did, would impose burdens on the owners for the time being of the land which they could not get rid of without the consent of the persons entitled to the limitations. The limitations in favour of the testator's grandchildren were therefore void for perpetuity. The limitations in favour of the daughters were, of course, perfectly valid although dependent upon the same contingency. The daughters were lives in being and the interests were bound to vest, if at all, during their lives since they had been given life estates.

---

33 *i.e.* at common law the validity is judged at the beginning.

34 *Kennedy v. Kennedy* [1914] AC 215 (when a house ceases to be maintained as a dwelling).

35 [1909] AC 275.

b) Lives in being

(i) Express or Implied

The measuring lives are either those expressly mentioned in the instrument or those of persons referred to by implication. For example, a gift in a will:

> *to my grandchildren who shall reach the age of 21 in fee simple*

is a valid gift. All the grandchildren of the testator must be born in the lives of their parents, the testator's children. The testator's children are lives in being by implication:

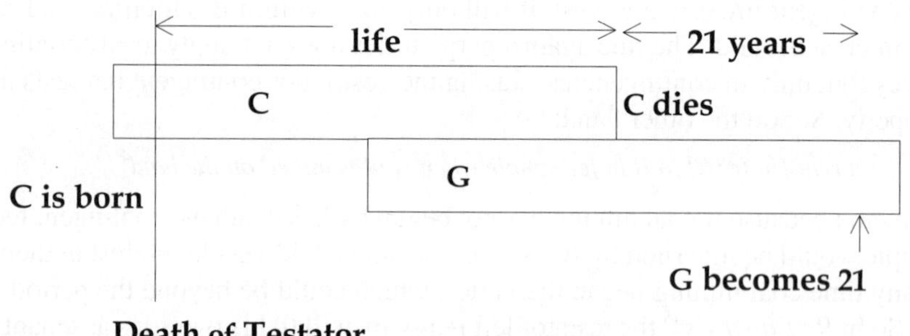

They are, as a class, lives in being for the purpose of the rule because none of them can be born after the testator's death (allowing for any period of gestation). Some may have died before the testator, of course, and it may be objected that such children are not lives in being at the testator's death. This is true, but it only illustrates that lives in being has a somewhat artificial sense in the rule against perpetuities. It is used in contradistinction to future, not past, lives. Children of the testator might have predeceased him or her, but their children must take within the period anyway. The point is that no more children can be born of the testator in future. The class of children is a closed class. Two other limitations also illustrate the point. In a deed *inter vivos*:

> *to my grandchildren who shall reach the age of 21 in fee simple*

the contingent interest is void. Since the limitation is in an *inter vivos* deed the grantor may have more children after the date the instrument comes into effect and so it is possible that a grandchild who becomes 21 may be the child of a child of the grantor born after the date of the instrument. The possibility renders the gift void:

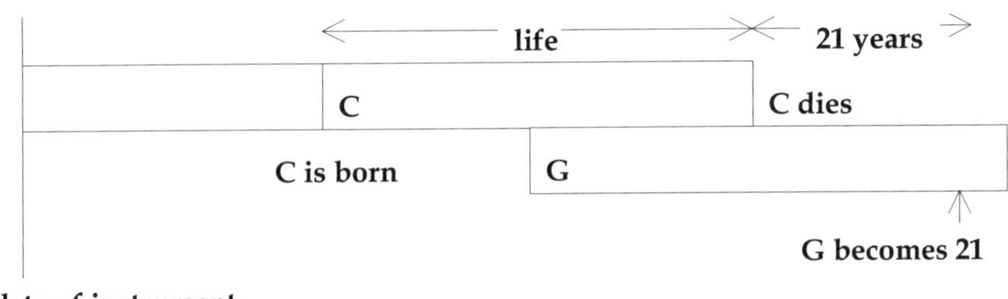

C is a child of the grantor born after the date of the instrument. G is a child of C and a grandson of the grantor. G must become 21 not later than 21 years after C's death, but C is not a life in being. Hence, the grantor's children, as a class, are not lives in being at the date if the instrument. Again, the following limitation in a will:

> *to the grandchildren of A at 21 in fee simple*

is void if A is alive at the testator's death. A may have more children after the date the will takes effect, and again there is the possibility that such a child might have a child, a grandchild of the testator, who might become 21, and if they do, that will be beyond the period. If A has died before the testator, the gift is valid. A's children are lives in being by implication.

It is not necessary that persons who are lives in being for the purpose of the perpetuity rule should take interests under the limitation. Persons who are lives in being by implication are a case in point.

(ii) Human Lives

Lives in being must be human lives. In *Re Kelly*[36] there was a bequest of a sum of money out of which £4 a year was to be spent "on the support of my dogs" and this was followed by a contingent gift over to charity of any balance remaining "on the death of my last dog". The contingent gift as it was drafted could only be upheld if one could take the life of the surviving dog as a life in being for the purpose of the perpetuity rule. Meredith J held, in an elegant judgment, that this was not permissible:

> "The court does not enter into the question of a dog's expectation of life. In point of fact, neighbours' dogs and cats are unpleasantly long-lived. . . Anyway, the maximum period is exceeded by the lives of specified butterflies and twenty-one years thereafter. And, even, according to my decision. . . – and, I confess, it displays this weakness on being pressed to a logical conclusion – the expiration of the life of a single butterfly, even without the twenty-one years, would be too remote, despite all the world of poetry that may be thereby de-

36 [1932] IR 255.

stroyed."[37]

Accordingly, the contingent gift of the balance of the fund was void for remoteness and the fell into residue.[38]

The preference for human lives is not based upon any moral or religious distinction between the value of human as against other forms of life. It is motivated purely by the consideration that if the lives of animals or plants were to be allowed the rule would be rendered completely pointless. Conveyancers would simply insert an express clause limiting the contingency to the lives of a class of particularly long lived species of plant or animal life, such as giant tortoises or of California Redwood trees.[39]

(iii) Lives at common law are Lives which Validate the Gift

Lives in being at common law, to be accurate, are lives which validate the gift.[40] If the gift is void, there are no lives in being. In other words, the question is whether, at the date the instrument takes effect, it can be said that the contingency must occur, if it does so at all, not later than 21 years from the death of lives in existence at the date the gift took effect. If there is such a person or persons, the gift is valid and those persons are lives in being for the purpose of the rule. If there is no such person or persons, there are no lives in being. The gift may still be valid, however, if limited to the 21 year period. A gift may be valid without lives in being, but if it is void, there are none.

---

37 *ibid.*

38 As to the vested gift of the fund, the rule against perpetuities did not apply, but the rule against inalienability, which has the same perpetuity period, (discussed below) did do so. The vested fund would be void if inalienable for longer than the perpetuity period. In applying that rule the judge felt able to uphold the vested gift as valid under the rule for each year the dogs lived up to a maximum of 21 years. See below: the rule against inalienability. In view of this it is difficult to see why the judge did not also rewrite the contingent gift which could have taken effect on the same contingency and so have been made valid for perpetuity. This would have been open the objection that it introduced a cy pres rule into the perpetuity doctrine, which is contrary to case law, but the judge's treatment of the vested gift is open the same objection.

39 The age of California Redwoods is well known, but in fact the *Guinness Book of Records* (1993) states that certain creosote bushes (*larrea tridentata*) in the Arizona desert are the longest-lived known organisms, one being estimated to be 11,700 years old. The longest-lived tree is the bristlecone pine (*pinus longaeva*), the oldest recorded specimen of which reached 5,100 years, although the life expectancy of the giant Sequoia (*sequoiadendron giganteum*) has been estimated at 6,000 years. In the animal kingdom giant turtles may reach about 150 years or more. Of mammals, *homo sapiens* is the longest lived and so there would have been no real harm in confining lives for the purpose of the rule to mammals.

40 This is not so under the Northern Ireland Act or the English Perpetuities and Accumulations Act, 1964 because of the wait-and-see element. Under that legislation it is possible to have lives for the purpose of wait-and-see which do not necessarily therefore validate the gift.

This also means that at common law lives in being necessarily have some causal connection to the contingency.[41] Reform statutes, such as that in Northern Ireland, which introduce a wait-and-see rule, have to change this definition and specify those persons who may be considered lives in being during the period of wait-and-see. During that period there are statutory lives in being although it has not become clear whether the gift is valid or not.

c) Express Limitation of Gifts to the Perpetuity Period

A contingency that would otherwise be void may be saved by expressly limiting it to the perpetuity period by reference to a life or class of lives. In *Re Villar*[42] a testator who died in 1926 made a contingent gift in favour of:

> all my descendants who shall be living 21 years after the death of the survivor of all the lineal descendants of Queen Victoria living at my death.

It was held to be a valid gift. Any number of lives could be chosen so long as they are not so numerous as to be completely unascertainable. But the court did not go so far as to say that an attempt to ascertain the class membership would actually have to be made. The case has been criticised on the ground that the particular limitation in the case does not satisfy the test laid down. It was probably impossible to ascertain, even in the equivocal sense used by the court, whether the Grand Duchess Anastasia had survived.[43]

After the case the clause became known as a "Royal lives clause", but there is of course no need for the lives to be those of royalty, a fact of some relevance in a Republic. Royal lives were probably chosen because it was assumed, without much basis in fact as it turned out, that they would all be well-known and well-documented. Any class of lives satisfying the test can be chosen, such as, probably, the lives of all babies whose births are reported in a given newspaper the day before the testator's death, or whose births were registered in Dublin on a given day.[44]

It should be noted that from the point of view of perpetuity the question in *Re Villar* was not "How can you tell when the point has arrived which is 21 years after the death of the last survivor". The perpetuity rule at common law is not a "wait-and-see" rule. The question was: "Could you 'reasonably' have ascertained who the members of the class were in 1926". It was a problem of class definition. Since the court decided that the class could be reasonably as-

41 Apart, that is, from a royal lives clause. See below.

42 (1929) 1 Ch. 243.

43 See Peter Kurth, *Anastasia: The Life of Anna Anderson* (Fontana, 1985). The author produced circumstantial evidence to the effect that that Anna Anderson was indeed Anastasia, but DNA tests in 1994 disproved her claim.

44 *Re Moore* [1901] 1 Ch 936 went too far. A gift of capital to take effect at the "end of a period of twenty-one years from the death of the last survivor of all the persons who shall be living at my death" was held void.

certained at that time, the gift satisfied the perpetuity rule and was valid. Of course, having decided that it was a valid gift, quite a separate problem would arise in the future and that is the problem of deciding whether the time had come to distribute the property. This problem does involve wait-and-see, but it does not concern the perpetuity rule. It is a problem of distribution. Here also, it would not be expected that all the members of the class should be traced and their deaths recorded. After a period of perhaps one hundred years a presumption would arise that they had all died. The court in *Re Villar* did not address that issue because it was clear that the time of distribution had not arrived, and it may still not have done so.

d) No Valid Lives

If there are no valid lives in being the perpetuity period is 21 years.[45] The 21 year period, with or without lives, is a period in gross *i.e.* unrelated to the minority of any person.[46] It has not therefore been affected by the reduction of the age of majority to 18 years.[47]

e) Gestation

There are actually two rules as to periods of gestation. These rules are as follows:

1. a child *actually* in the womb (*en ventre sa mere*)[48] when the gift takes effect is counted as a life in being for the purpose of the rule; and[49]
2. the *possibility* that anyone in future may have a child in the womb at the time of their death does not invalidate the gift.[50]

The following limitation illustrates both points. T gives property in his will:

---

45 *Palmer v. Holford* (1828) 4 Russ 403, 38 ER 857.

46 *ibid.*; *Re Kelly* [1932] IR 255.

47 *Re Hooper* [1932] 1 Ch. 38; Age of Majority Act, 1985.

48 Sperm banks have made the birth of children medically possible long after the death of the biological father, through artificial insemination. Such children would be posthumous but not literally *en ventre sa mere* at the time of the father's death. Courts in this jurisdiction have not considered such a possibility for the purpose of the rule. See Sappideen, "Life After Death – Sperm Banks, Wills and Perpetuities"(1979) 53 Aust LJ 31; Frozen embryos are conceived but still not *en ventre sa mere*, *i.e.* they are not in the womb. A student of Barton Leach wittily suggested the phrase "*en ventre sa frigidaire*": Leach, "Perpetuities in the Atomic age: the Sperm Bank and the Fertile Decedent" (1962) 48 ABAJ 942 at 943 n.3.

49 *Doe d Clarke v. Clarke* (1795) 2 H Bl 399; *Elliot v. Joicey* [1935] AC 209; *Re Brown* [1933] NZLR 114; whether or not the child benefits: Morris and Leach, *The Rule Against Perpetuities* p.65; *Re Wilmer's Trusts* [1903] 2 Ch. 411, CA.

50 Under the common law rule, without wait-and-see, it is a mere possibility. With wait-and-see, as in Northern Ireland, the period is extended by the period of gestation.

to my children for their lives, remainder to my grandchildren who shall reach the age of 21 in fee simple.

At T's death T has one child living, C1, and one child in the womb, C2. If C2 were not a life in being the gift would be void. But C2 is a life in being for the purpose of the perpetuity rule (rule 1 above). The children of C2 may take at 21.[51]

There is a factual possibility that either C1 or C2 may die leaving a child in the womb. If this were taken to mean that such a child, which is a grandchild of T, would become 21 more than 21 years after the death of its parent, a life in being, the gift to the grandchildren would be void.[52] But the possibility can be discounted under rule (2) above. The gift to the grandchildren is valid. If such a child is born, it may take.[53]

On the other hand, a period of nine months cannot be added expressly by a donor to a period of a life plus 21 years. A period of gestation cannot, in other words, be in gross.

f) The Surviving Spouse or Unborn Widow/Widower Trap

This a common mistake made in drafting limitations. For example:

[a trust] to A [unmarried] for life, remainder to any husband she may marry for life, remainder to the children of the marriage alive at the death of the survivor of A and her husband in fee simple.[54]

The remainder to the children is void. It is possible that A may marry someone who was not alive at the date the instrument took effect, and so is not a life in being. If he survives A for more than 21 years the contingent interest to the children of the marriage will vest outside the period. This possibility renders the remainder to the children void:

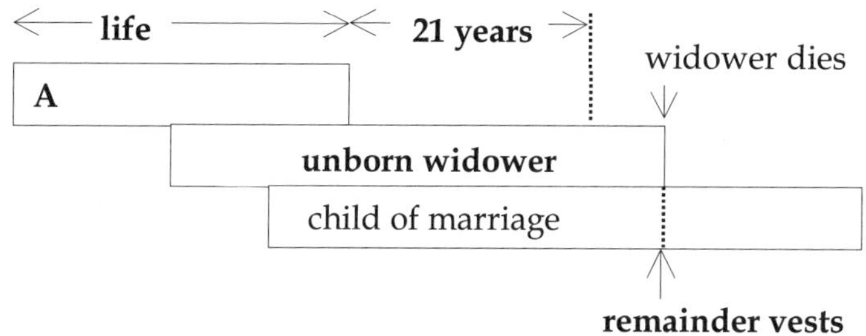

51 Morris and Leach, *The Rule Against Perpetuities* p.65.

52 See Chapter 12 Class Gifts. The possibility that one member of the class may take outside the period is sufficient at common law to invalidate the gift to the whole class: *Leake v. Robinson* (1817) 2 Mer 363, 35 ER 979.

53 Morris and Leach, *The Rule Against Perpetuities* p.65.

54 *Re Frost* (1889) 43 Ch D 246.

A mistake has been made in drafting the limitation. The mistake was to insert the words "alive at the death of the survivor of A and her husband." Even without those words, the gift would not vest in possession until that point, but the words have the effect of postponing the vesting in interest until the death of the survivor of A and her husband. There is no reason why vesting in interest should be postponed to that point. If the words had been omitted the interest would vest in interest not later than the death of A, a life in being, and the gift would be valid. Similarly:

> *[a trust] to B for life, remainder to his widow, if any, for life, remainder to B's children then alive.*

B is 45 years old and is married with grown children. But his wife may die, he may marry again and so his widow may not be his present wife. His second wife may not be a life in being at the date of the instrument and may survive him by more than 21 years. Of course, it is most unlikely that B would marry someone 45 years younger than himself, but it is possibilities, however slight, not probabilities, that matter.[55] The remainder to the children is void. A similar mistake has been made here. It is the insertion of the words then alive. They again postpone the vesting in interest of the contingent remainder to the end of the widow's life. Had they been omitted the interest would have been valid.[56]

g) The Presumption of Fertility

In *Jee v. Audley*[57] an English court took the view that in considering possibilities, the common law refused to recognise that a person was too old or too young to have children.

This is contrary to common sense and has been attacked as so absurd as bringing the law into disrepute. It did have some justification, however, and that was what von Ihering called formal realisability. That is, it attempted to preserve the logical precision of the rule so that a lawyer looking at a limitation could advise with certainty as to its validity or invalidity without the need for expensive litigation. If evidence on the point were admissible, such as age or more direct medical evidence, then no such certain advice could be given, quite apart from the distress that such evidence might cause in some cases. One might also consider that the medical evidence available in the 18th century was, apart from age, virtually non-existent.

The cost of such logical certainty was the absurdity produced in some cases, especially when combined with the no wait-and-see rule. These cases were ridiculed by Barton Leach who referred to them as the "Fertile Octoge-

55 It is possible that a court in Ireland would discount an absurd possibility: see *Exham v. Beamish* [1939] IR 336, discussed below.

56 See *Re Garnham* [1916] 2 Ch 413.

57 (1787) 1 Cox Eq Cas 324, 29 ER 1186.

narian" and "Precocious Toddler" cases.[58]

In *Re Dawson*[59] a testator set up a trust "for D for life, then to her children attaining 21 and to such grandchildren attaining 21 born of children dying under 21". The court held (1) that the gift after the life estate was a gift to a single composite class consisting of children and grandchildren, (2) applying the case of *Leake v. Robinson*,[60] that if any member of the class could take a vested interest outside the perpetuity period the gift to the whole class would fail and (3) in law it was possible for D to have a child in future who would not therefore be a life in being and for that child to die under 21 leaving a child, a grandchild of D, who might thus attain 21 outside the period. Hence, the whole remainder after the life estate was void. The fact was, however, that D was a woman of 66 and she had three daughters, all of whom had attained 21.

In *Re Gaite*[61] a gift in a will was:

> *to G's grandchildren living at the testator's death, or born within five years of the testator's death, as should attain 21. . .*

If one ignores physical impossibilities, G could have a child within five years of the testator's death, and who would not therefore be a life in being, and who, still within five years of the testator's death, itself have a child who might therefore become 21 outside the period. It would necessarily become 21, if at all, not more than 26 years after the testator's death, but that would also exceed the 21 year period. The English court managed to avoid the conclusion that the gift to the grandchildren was void by taking the view that grandchildren referred to legitimate grandchildren and that since it was not possible for a child under five to have a legitimate child, one could take into account the legal impossibility and hold the gift valid. This method of upholding the gift, however, suffered from the disadvantage that it legitimised discrimination against issue born to parents who were not married.

The courts in the Republic have refused to apply the rule in *Jee v. Audley*, replacing it instead with a presumption in favour of fertility. In *Exham v. Beamish*[62] the case concerned an *inter vivos* settlement made in 1865 by William Thompson. Under the settlement land was to be vested in trustees for the lives of the settlors, William Thompson and his wife Anne, and then for the grandchildren of the settlors at the age of 21. In 1865 the settlors had four children. If grandchildren were confined to the children of the four existing children of the settlors, then the trust would not have contravened the perpetuity rule, since all the grandchildren would necessarily have become 21 within the period as their parents were lives in being at the date of the settlement. But

58 (1938) 51 HLR 1329; (1952) 65 HLR 721; (1952) 68 LQR 35 at 44.

59 (1888) 39 Ch D 155. See also *Ward v. Van der Loff* [1924] AC 653.

60 (1817) 2 Mer 363, 35 ER 979.

61 [1949] 1 All ER 459.

62 [1939] IR 336.

Rule Against Perpetuities

Exham v Beamish [1939] IR 336

Inter vivos: "... to [the settlors] for life...then to Edith and Fanny for life...then to the grandchildren of the settlors at 21..."

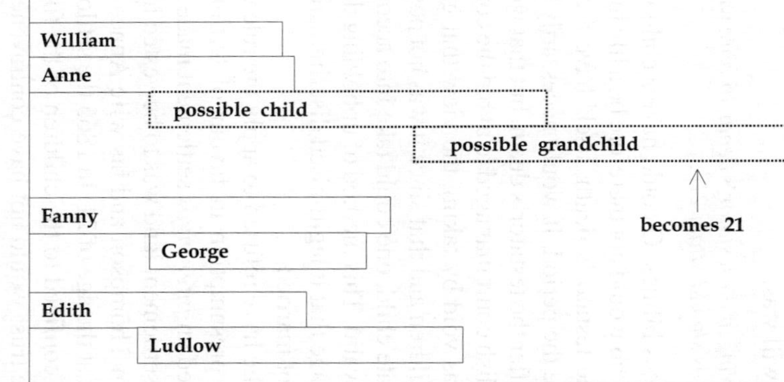

1. If the class "grandchildren" were restricted to the grandchildren of Fanny and Edith, they must all become 21 within the period, since their parents are lives in being.
2. It was argued that since the conveyance was *inter vivos* the possibility that William and Anne might have another child must be taken account of, however absurd (*Jee* v *Audley*). Such a child could become 21 outside the period, i.e. more than 21 years after the death of lives in being at the date of the instrument, since its own parents would not be lives in being at that date, i.e. 1865.
3. Gavan-Duffy, however, rejects the Rule in *Jee* v *Audley.* In Ireland it is presumed that any person may have a child, but if it would be absurd according to modern medical science to assume that they could have another child, the possibility can be discounted. Case adjourned for medical evidence re Anne Thompson in 1865, i.e. age.
4. Anne Thompson was in fact 46 years old in 1865 (see text, "The Modern Rule Against Perpetuities: The Presumption of Fertility").

since it was an *inter vivos* deed the possibility existed, if the rule in *Jee v. Audley* were applied, that the settlors might have another child, who would not be a life in being, who itself might have a child, a grandchild of the settlors, who might therefore become 21 outside the period.[63] The only way the gift to the grandchildren could have been saved was by deciding that the settlors could not have had more children in 1865, and on the face of it *Jee v. Audley* prevented this.

Gavan Duffy J accepted that the no-wait-and-see rule applied in Ireland, but declined to follow *Jee v. Audley*. He held instead that if modern medical science would regard as absurd the possibility that a given person could have a child, then the court is not required to regard it as possible. The effect of Exham is to replace the rule that any living person can have a child with a presumption to that effect, rebuttable by evidence which shows not that it is merely improbable, but absurd to make such a supposition.

The hearing in Exham was adjourned, the judge indicating that he was prepared to hear evidence as to the possibility of further children being born to the settlors in 1865. It is interesting to note that historical evidence shows that Anne Thompson was in fact 46 years old in 1865.[64] It seems unlikely that the presumption would have been rebutted by that evidence alone since it is not absurd to presume that a woman of 46 may have another child.

Gavan Duffy's decision in *Exham v. Beamish* may accurately be described as a *tour-de-force*. It is bold and self-confident in its rejection of an absurd rule and sensible in its framing of an alternative approach. Nevertheless, when one attempts to unravel the absurdities of the perpetuity rule at common law it is not easy to justify stopping at any particular point. The judge, for example, accepted that the law in this jurisdiction did not allow wait-and-see in the common law perpetuity rule. It was possible, and not actual, events which had to be taken into account and the possibilities which existed must be those at the date

63 The class-closing rule would not have saved the gift in the circumstances of the case. If there had been a grandchild of the settlors aged 21 at the date of the settlement, the class would close at the end of the life estates, including grandchildren then alive who would therefore necessarily qualify within the period. Since the class would have been bound to close in this way (taking into account *Kimberley v. Tew* (1843) 5 Ir Eq R 389) the perpetuity rule would have been satisfied. But there was no such grandchild.

64 In L.G. Pine, ed, *Burke's Genealogical and Heraldic History of the Landed Gentry of Ireland* (4th ed.; London: Burke's Peerage Ltd., 1958). See also Burke's *Irish Family Records* (London, 1976) p.94. Anne Thompson appears under the entry "Beamish, formerly of Mountbeamish", as Anne Jane Margaret, daughter of William Beamish. Her birthdate is given as 1819. Her daughter Edith Anne married North Ludlow Axel Beamish, her first cousin. The entry shows their children, Ludlow Hamilton (the defendant in the case and the only surviving grandchild of the settlors at the death of the life tenant, Fanny) Harold Delacour, Edith Anne, who died aged two, and Ethel Hulda Frances. I am grateful to Dr Paul Brand for reference to this source.

of the settlement.[65] But does this not also lead to the absurdity of inquiring into the ability of someone over 70 years before to have a child, when it was known by the time the case came to court that she had not done so?

h) Administrative Contingencies

This occurs where a contingent gift is made to take effect on the happening of an event of an administrative kind.

In *Re Wood*[66] the testator owned some gravel pits and wanted them to be operated until exhausted, at which time the land was to be sold and the proceeds distributed to his issue. Evidence showed that at the normal rate of working the pits were expected to last another four years. In fact, they lasted six years. The court held that the actual period was irrelevant, as there was no wait-and-see. Nor was the expected duration. They held that as there were no lives in being by reference to whom the contingency was limited and so the period was 21 years. They held there was nothing necessarily to confine the life of the pits to this period either, and so the gift was void for remoteness. Professor Barton Leach termed this case "the Magic Gravel Pit."

Another example is *Re Lord Stratheden and Campbell*[67] in which an annuity was given to "the Central London Rangers on the appointment of the next colonel-in-chief". The gift was held void, as the event could have occurred at any time in the future. This might be called "The Case of the Leaderless Regiment".

Other examples of void gifts under the rule would be:

> a bequest of royalties payable out of land in favour of the testator's grandchildren and their heirs when coal under the land should be mined or let,[68]
>
> an absolute interest "after the termination of the present war with Germany",[69]
>
> when an unborn person, ascertainable within the perpetuity period, takes the testator's surname,[70]
>
> upon "the realisation of my foreign estate,"[71]
>
> a covenant to convey to a management company the fee simple in the land and

65 It had been so decided by O'Loghlen MR in *Smith v. Dungannon* (1841) Fl & K 638, 4 Ir Eq R 343, upheld in the House of Lords sub nom *Dungannon (Lord) v. Smith* (1845) 12 Cl & F 546, 8 ER 1523.

66 [1894] 3 Ch D 381.

67 [1894] 3 Ch 265; See *Re Petrie* [1962] Ch 355.

68 *Re Edwards* [1909] AC 275, discussed above.

69 *Re Engels* [1943] 1 All ER 506.

70 *Re Fry* [1945] Ch. 348 at 352, [1945] 2 All ER 205 at 206.

71 *Re Jones* [1950] 2 All ER 239.

common areas when the last flat in a block of flats is sold.[72]

In each case these would be absolute interests, in the case of land, the fee simple, and not life estates to a living person. It would seem from the above cases that the English courts adopted a rule by analogy to *Jee v. Audley*, to the effect that an administrative event may occur, in law, at any time in the future unless expressly confined to the perpetuity period, however absurd such an assumption would be from a scientific or even common sense point of view. If so, then such an analogy must be affected in the Republic by the decision in *Exham v. Beamish*. It seems, therefore, that in this jurisdiction if such an assumption would be absurd according to modern scientific knowledge then it can be discounted. In cases similar to the Leaderless Regiment the question is not one of science so much as common sense and so the test would probably be extended to include it.

3. Cy Pres

It has been seen in the section on the Rule in *Whitby v. Mitchell* that the courts have applied the cy pres doctrine in limited circumstances to rewrite a limitation which offended against the rule in order to produce one that did not. The rule in *Whitby v. Mitchell,* including cy pres, still applies in Ireland to limitations which are not subject to the perpetuity rule, such as common law remainders, but the *Whitby v. Mitchell* rule also applies to limitations creating trusts in wills,[73] which are also subject to the perpetuity rule. In such situations the application of cy pres as part of the *Whitby v. Mitchell* rule to save the gift will also have the effect of preventing the limitation from being void for perpetuity under the modern rule. For example, in the limitation

> *to A for life, remainder to the first son of A [unborn] for life, remainder to the first and every other son of such son in tail male*

the remainders after the first son of A are prima facie void as offending against the Rule in *Whitby v. Mitchell*, and void under the modern rule against perpetuities. Nevertheless, one can apply the cy pres doctrine as part of the *Whitby v. Mitchell* rule and rewrite the limitation. The effect of this is to give a fee tail to the first son of A. But the effect of doing so is that the limitation is no longer void for perpetuity under the modern rule. In other words, there are cases now in this jurisdiction in which cy pres is applied and the effect is to save a gift otherwise void for perpetuity, although, admittedly, not as part of the perpetuity rule itself. There is nevertheless a case for saying that the cy pres doctrine

72 Such covenants have been inserted in sale of flats.

73 It was applied to an executory trust in a will in *Humberston v. Humberston* (1716) 1 P Wms 332, 24 ER 412, and to a testamentary trust in *Parfitt v. Hember* (1867) LR 4 Eq 443 and *Hopkins v. Hopkins* (1738) 1 Atk 581, 26 ER 365.

should not be artificially confined to such limitations and for holding that cy pres may also be applied where the modern rule alone is in issue.

There is also a general policy argument in favour of a cy pres rule in the modern rule. Where the choice is between a disposition that will be entirely void and one which is valid and as near as possible to the intention of the donor it is arguably sensible to redraft the gift. Simes[74] gives the example of a gift by a testator to his grandchildren at the age of 30. As it stands the gift is void. Would it not be preferable, Simes asks, to rewrite it as a gift to his grandchildren at the age of 21? If the testator had been given the choice, at the time the will was made, of leaving the gift as it was, in which case it would be ineffective, and rewriting it as a gift to his grandchildren at the age of 30, he would almost certainly have agreed to the change.

English courts have declined to give the doctrine such an extended application in the modern rule, but some United States jurisdictions have done so. In other cases, however, the court may be faced with a number of possible ways of rewriting the limitation and it may not be clear that the testator would prefer one of them to others.[75] They will also often involve discriminating between members of the same family, and courts are understandably reluctant to undertake such a course. In such a case a fairer result may be obtained in the case of wills, especially where the children or grandchildren of the testator are concerned, by holding the gift void and leaving the distribution to the rules of intestacy.

4. Succession Act, 1965 s.117

It maybe that section 117 of the Succession Act, 1965 gives a limited jurisdiction to remake bequests which are void for perpetuity. The jurisdiction will only apply, of course, to bequests to the testator's children. If the void gift is the only provision for the children, or, without it, there would be only inadequate provision, they might consider applying under section 117 for provision to be made out of the estate on the ground that the testator had failed in his moral duty to make proper provision for them. Their success would depend upon the court interpreting section 117 to mean that a failure could occur for technical reasons, such as, in this case, failure to take account of the perpetuity rule.[76]

5. Gifts Over

It has been seen that gifts over, *i.e.* interests created in the grant and vested in someone other than the grantor, can only be created after determinable and

74 Simes, (1955) p.67.

75 See Maudsley, *Perpetuities*.

76 I am grateful to John O'Dowd for this suggestion.

conditional fees either by executed uses or as equitable interests under trusts. Such interests, to be valid, must comply with the perpetuity rule. Thus the limitation:

> *unto and to the use of T and U and their heirs in trust for A in fee simple until she qualifies as a solicitor, then in trust for B and her heirs*

creates a valid determinable equitable fee simple followed by valid gift over to B on the happening of the event. The event must occur, if at all, in the lifetime of A.

In *City of Klamath Falls v. Bell*[77] a corporation conveyed land in 1925 to the city of Klamath Falls, Oregon in the United States for use as the site for a city library. In 1969 the city ended the use of the site as a library and the question was whether the land passed back to the successors of the corporation or remained with the city. The original deed provided that if the land ceased to be used for a library the fee simple was to go to two named individuals.

The Court of Appeals of Oregon held that the limitation created a determinable fee and since there was a gift over it was intended to create an executory interest. Courts in the United States are prepared to interpret deeds in this way even if they do not expressly include a use. However, the gift over was subject to the rule against perpetuities and was void. A possibility of reverter remained in the grantor corporation. Thus, to refer to the example previously given in relation to possibilities of reverter:

> *to F and his heirs to the use of O and her heirs so long as the land is used for agriculture, [then over to P and her heirs]*

the words in square brackets create no valid interest. The gift over is void for perpetuity, leaving an executory possibility in the grantor.

6. Subsequent Gifts

The general rule is that the perpetuity rule must be applied to each gift separately. There are four situations where a gift follows a void gift.

a) Subsequent Vested Gifts

Any vested interest falls outside the rule and so is valid, *e.g.*:

> *[in trust] to A for life, remainder in trust for life to the first child of A to marry, remainder in trust for B in fee simple.*

A is alive and has no children, or no married child.[78] The first child to marry may not be a life in being and may not marry within 21 years of A's death. The

77 (1972) 7 Ore App 330. See also *Smith v. Bedell* (1932) 349 Ill 523, 182 NE 622, Supreme Court of Illinois; *Williams v. Watt* (1983) 668 P 2d 620, 80 Oil & Gas Rep 162, Supreme Court of Wyoming.

78 Even if A has a child, if it is unmarried then it may not be the first to marry.

first remainder is therefore void. But the second remainder is vested from the beginning. Whether or not A has a child who marries, the fee simple will vest in possession after the prior estate, or estates are exhausted, either in B or, if B is then dead, in whoever inherits the fee simple from B.

b) Contingent and Independent Gifts

Even if the subsequent gift is contingent, if the contingency must occur, if at all, within the perpetuity period, and it is independent of the void gift, the subsequent gift is valid. So, in a limitation in a will:

> *to A for life, remainder for life to the first child of A to marry, remainder to B in fee simple at 21*

A is alive and has no married child. The first remainder is void. But the second remainder is valid. B's fee simple is contingent on his becoming 21. This must happen, if at all, within his own life and he is a life in being. The contingency is independent of the contingency on which the first remainder depends.[79] It may be, however, that this is not in itself the conclusive argument leading courts to uphold the second remainder, but rather that, in the absence of evidence to the contrary, the logical independence of the contingency indicates that the donor intended the second remainder to take effect whether or not the contingency in the first remainder occurred. This point will perhaps be clearer after considering the next section.

c) Contingent but Dependant Gifts

In this case the subsequent gift, although not in itself void for perpetuity is held to be void because of the invalidity of the prior gift. For example:

> *[a trust] to A for life, remainder in trust for life to the first child of A to marry, but if there is no such child, remainder in trust for B for life.*

A has no married child. The first remainder is void. The second remainder does not offend against the perpetuity rule because it must vest, if at all, in the lifetime of B, because B is given a life estate. But courts have nevertheless held the second remainder void. The reason has nothing to do with the perpetuity rule. Courts have taken the view that the phrase "but if there is no such child", or a similar phrase in such a limitation, indicate that the intention of the donor was that the second remainder was only to take effect if the first contingency did not factually occur. It is further assumed that the donor would not intend the second remainder to take effect simply because the first remainder was void because of a rule of law.[80] Even remainders which seem clearly vested have been struck down on this ground.[81] It may also be noted that if the remainder to

79 See *Re Hay* [1932] NI 215; Wylie, *Cases* p.275; *Re Coleman* [1936] Ch. 528.

80 *Proctor v. Bishop of Bath & Wells* (1794) 2 Hy Bl 358, 126 ER 594.

81 *Re Backhouse* [1921] 2 Ch. 51.

B in the above limitation had been of a fee simple, the remainder would be void for a different reason, namely that it offended against the perpetuity rule. It could vest in a successor in title to B's contingent fee simple beyond the period, because a child of A could marry more than 21 years after A's death, or B's death, or all of A's children might die unmarried.[82]

d) Alternative Contingencies

In the previous case, where the remainder to B is of a fee simple dependent on the contingency that there is "no such child", it can be seen on logical analysis that there are in fact two contingencies implicit in what appears to be one: that A has no married child. The contingencies are:

i) that A has no child at all, or

ii) that A has children, but they all die unmarried.

The first contingency is valid for perpetuity, for it will occur if at all not later than A's death. The second contingency, however, is void, because it will only occur, if at all, when all A's children have died unmarried. If both of these contingencies are expressed in the gift, courts have adopted the rule that, even under the common law perpetuity rule, one may wait and see which contingency occurs first. If the void one occurs, the remainder is void, but if the valid contingency occurs, the remainder may take effect. So if the limitation had been worded as follows:

> *[a trust] to A for life, remainder in trust for life to the first child of A to marry, but if A has no children, or if A has no married child, remainder in trust for B in fee simple*

one can wait to see which contingency occurs. If A dies without leaving children, the remainder to B takes effect. But if A dies leaving children who are unmarried, the void contingency has occurred and the remainder to B is void. It should be noted that one cannot wait to see whether the void contingency in fact occurs within the perpetuity period, *i.e.* in this example one cannot wait to see whether any of A's children marry within 21 years of A's death. One can only wait to see which of the two contingencies occur, not to see whether a contingency in fact occurs within the period. It is not, therefore, a true wait and see rule.[83]

In the United States case of *Springfield Safe Deposit v. Ireland*[84] a testator died in 1891. His will directed that his estate was to be distributed during January 1922 to B's then living children and to the issue of deceased children, if B was then dead, or if B was then living, distribution was to be made during the first January after B's death. B died in 1928 and was survived by his son, C.

82 *Re Hubbard* [1963] Ch. 275.

83 *Re Curryer's Will Trusts* [1938] Ch. 952.

84 (1929) 268 Mass 62, 64 ALR 1071.

The gift was held valid. The first contingency, that distribution was to be made in January 1922, was void for perpetuity because the period was a fixed number of years in excess of the 21 year period. But the alternative contingency was valid because it consisted of the life of B, a person alive at the testator's death, plus a period of up to one year.

There seems to be no valid reason why one should be permitted to see which contingency occurs only if both contingencies are expressed in the gift. The two contingencies are logically inherent in such a gift.

7. Exceptions to Perpetuity Rule

a) Gift from One Charity to Another

Gifts to charities are subject, in general, to the perpetuity rule in the same way as other gifts, in that a contingent gift to a charity must be certain to vest within the period or be void. There is, however, one exceptional case and that is where a gift to one charity is followed by a contingent gift in favour of a second charity to take effect on a contingency which may occur outside the period. The contingent gift to the second charity is valid. This exception is in fact a device allowed by the courts to enable a non-charitable purpose trust to take effect which would otherwise be void because of the rule against inalienability.[85] A gift to Charity A so long as it maintains a tomb, or maintains animals with a gift over to Charity B if the tomb is not kept in repair is valid. This device need no longer be used in the Republic in the case of tombs, due to a special statutory provision in relation to non-charitable purpose trusts[86] but could be used to provide for maintenance of animals, for example.[87]

b) Possibilities of Reverter

It has been seen that the only interest it was possible to have by a conveyance at common law after a determinable fee was a possibility of reverter.

In *Attorney General v. Cummins*[88] Palles CB held that such interests are not subject to the perpetuity rule.[89] Thus the following limitation:

to A and her heirs until the land ceases to be used as a school

creates a valid determinable fee with a possibility of reverter in the grantor. Palles' judgment is based essentially on the historical point that the perpetuity rule was an invention of equity, which had not subjected its own future interest to the old feudal remainder rules of the common law but which consequently

85 See below.

86 See below.

87 See below Rule against Inalienability: Non-Charitable Purpose Trusts.

88 [1906] IR 406.

89 In the case itself quit rents were granted in fee simple until the recipient or his heirs were paid a lump sum.

needed to place some limit on the remoteness of vesting of contingent interests.[90]

After the Statute of Uses there came into being a new type of legal estate, the legal executory interest, to which the perpetuity rule applied, but interests at common law had never been subject to the perpetuity rule. As to common law remainders there had been no need to apply the perpetuity rule, because Rule 4 had the incidental effect of placing a limit on the remoteness of vesting. However, there is no similar common law limit in relation to possibilities of reverter. Technically speaking they may be said to be vested from the beginning in the same way as reversions, but from a practical point of view they create the problem that a fee simple may end at some time in the remote future and it is then difficult to discover who is entitled to the land at that point. Legally it will be those who have inherited the original grantor's possibility, which has now become a fee simple, but it may not be known who they are. True, it is for those entitled to it to claim their right and if they fail to do so the occupier will bar their title under the Statute of Limitations, 1957 after 12 years' adverse possession.[91] But the problem of the occupier is that his possession is now uncertain and his title possibly worthless.

The problem of such interests is compounded by the fact that the better view is probably that the perpetuity rule does not apply even if a similar interest is contained in a conveyance to uses, *i.e.* an executory possibility, as in:

> *to F and G in fee simple to the use of A in fee simple until the land ceases to be used as a school.*

The executory possibility in the grantor is valid. If the land ceases to be used as a school there is a resulting use for the grantor which is executed, giving the grantor, or his or her successors, the fee simple.

Nor does it matter if a similar limitation takes effect as an equitable interest under a trust, which is discussed in the next section.

---

90 [1906] 1 IR 406, Palles CB at 409:

> "Thus the rule as to perpetuities became a Common Law doctrine applicable to springing and shifting uses, and executory and other limitations of property, which could not be created by a Common Law conveyance, and which could only take effect under the Statute of Uses. If I am right in this, the doctrine must be inapplicable to estates created by Common Law conveyances, and especially to estates which reverted to donors on the performance of conditions which determine estates..."

91 *Re Rowhook Mission Hall, Horsham*; *Re Ladypool Road Old National School, Birmingham* [1984] 3 All ER 179, [1984] 3 WLR 710, (100 LQR 528). The second case concerned a determinable interest. The court held that the determining event had occurred, vesting the fee simple absolute in the revertee absolutely. The trustees possession had from then on been adverse and had resulted in them acquiring title (p.187 a to g, p.188 to f and p.192 f g, post); *Re Clayton's Deed Poll* [1979] 2 All ER 1133 not followed.

c) Possibilities of Resulting Trust

In the Northern Ireland case of *Walsh v. Wightman*[92] the court held that a possibility of resulting trust was not subject to the perpetuity rule.[93] Thus a gift:

> *unto and to the use of X and Y in fee simple in trust for the B school so long as the land is used as a school*

creates a valid equitable determinable fee and a possibility of resulting trust in the grantor. One reason why the courts have treated such interests as exception to the perpetuity rule is probably consistency: that it would be artificial to insist on the distinction between common law and executory or equitable interests. But a more cogent one is that it follows from the perpetuity rule itself. The rule against perpetuities applies only to contingent interests and not to vested ones. It has no application to events that bring estates to an end, but only to those that prescribe when a estates are to begin. In the limitation:

> *unto and to the use of X and Y in fee simple in trust for O in fee simple so long as the land is used for agriculture*

if the possibility of resulting trust in favour of the grantor were void for perpetuity then in whom would the land vest? The only solution would be to hold the determinable interest itself void, but this is unsatisfactory because the perpetuity rule was never intended to invalidate vested interests.[94]

One case that has been criticised is *Re Chardon*.[95] This English case apparently decided that although a gift over in a will was void for perpetuity, the land could then fall into residue and so benefit the residuary legatee, even beyond the perpetuity period. The criticism stems from the view that a gift of residue in a will is really a gift over, and so should be void if contrary to the perpetuity rule. The policy point behind this view is that although it may be a concession to recognise that possibilities of reverter and rights of entry are not subject to the perpetuity rule, the anomalous exception should not be extended. To do so is to increase the kinds of interests in land that may take effect at some

---

92 [1927] NI 1.

93 The same rule operates in the United States. See *Commerce Union Bank v. Warren County* (1986) 707 SW 2d 854 (Tennessee). A house was held on trust by the county for use as a home for the elderly. It was held that when the county ceased to operate it as a home it reverted to the heirs of the deceased and that the possibility of reverter was not subject to the perpetuity rule.

94 An English court in *Hopper v. Corporation of Liverpool* (1944) 88 Sol J 213 thought it had found a way of avoiding this logical problem by holding that in the above example O takes an absolute fee simple. The cost of such an approach is that the court effectively redrafts the gift and in so doing confers a interest on the donee which the grantor never intended to confer. It also violates the long-accepted rule that the determining event is part of the determinable limitation and not severable from it.

95 [1928] Ch. 464.

time in the remote future. Such interests cause problems in tracing the persons entitled and makes the land difficult to sell if they cannot be found.

Recent English cases may indicate a greater willingness on the part of courts to hold, in the case of possibilities of resulting trust, that trustees hold adversely to those entitled on reverter when the determining event occurs and the effect of this is to cure the defect in the trustee's title after the 12 year limitation period.[96]

d) Rights of Entry for Condition Broken

Palles CB in *Attorney General v. Cummins*[97] held *obiter* that rights of entry for condition broken following a conditional fee were not subject to the perpetuity rule. It would seem that the same would apply to similar interests created by executed uses or under trusts.

e) Legal Contingent Remainders

Remoteness of vesting of contingent remainders at common law is governed by the Old Rule against perpetuities, and by the common law remainder rules. The modern rule against perpetuities was only developed after the emergence of equitable future interests and executory interests. Palles CB's views on this were accepted in *Walsh v. Wightman*[98] by the Northern Ireland Court of Appeal. It was also the view expressed in *Cole v. Sewell*,[99] an Irish case that went to the British House of Lords, by Sugden LC and Lord Brougham.[100] It is therefore the case that a limitation:

> *to A for life, remainder to his eldest child in fee simple at the age of 25*

creates a valid remainder in favour of an eldest child provided there is such a child aged 25 at A's death. It may be noticed that a similar limitation would be void *ab initio* if contained in a grant to uses or a trust because, in this example, the age specified is greater than 21.

f) Contractual Rights

The rule against perpetuities only applies to contingent interests in property and so has no application to rights of a purely contractual character. It does not therefore apply if original contracting parties are suing each other. This is not a true exception, because the rule does not apply even in principle, but it is convenient to deal with the point here.

---

96 *Re Rowhook Mission Hall, Horsham, Re Ladypool Road Old National School, Birmingham* [1984] 3 All ER 179, [1984] 3 WLR 710, (100 LQR 528).

97 [1906] 1 IR 406.

98 [1927] NI 1.

99 (1843) 4 Dru & War 1 esp 28, 6 Ir Eq R 66, 65 RR 668 .

100 (1848) 2 HLC 186 esp 230-5, 9 ER 1062 at 1079–1081.

In *Jameson v. Squire*[101] a lease for three years contained what was expressed to be an option to purchase but in fact gave the tenant the right to a sublease for the rest of the landlord's reversion, less one day, at a rent. At the end of the three years the tenant remained in occupation and became a tenant from year to year. The tenant then purported to exercise the option. The Supreme Court held he was entitled to do so. The case had been argued for the tenant on the ground that the rule against perpetuities did not apply because, it was argued, the option was in reality an option to renew a lease and such an option is an exception to the rule.[102] However, Maguire CJ recognised in his judgment that Murnaghan J had pointed out that there was a better reason why the tenant could succeed: the rule against perpetuities was not involved at all, because the issue was between original contracting parties.[103] The option remained exercisable so long as the original parties remained landlord and tenant.

If rights arising under a contract were limited to the lives of the contracting parties, the exception would be of little significance. In law, however, the personal representatives of a deceased person can sue or be sued on contracts entered into by the deceased person. Thus if a right is properly a contractual one it may take a provision out of the scope of the rule against perpetuities in a dispute arising many years after the death of one or more of the original contracting parties. In *Walsh v. Secretary of State for India*[104] Lord Clive, in 1770, gave a pension fund to the East India Company. The company entered into a covenant to repay the sum to Lord Clive, his executors, administrators, and assigns if at any time in the future the company should cease to employ military force in India. In 1858, because of reforms introduced after the Indian Mutiny, the event occurred. It was held that Lord Clive's estate could sue the company in contract and recover the money.

The exception as to contract has been extended in one respect. At common law the benefit of a contract is assignable to a third party, so that the third party acquires the right to sue the original contracting party in contract. Such a right is not subject to the perpetuity rule. But the assignment itself has been treated as proprietary so that it must be certain to take effect within the period. If a contracting party or assignee of the benefit seeks to enforce the right against a third party, then that is the exercise of a proprietary right and it will fail unless its exercise is limited to the period.[105] Even if a contract creates an interest in land its

101 [1948] IR 155, Supreme Court.

102 See below.

103 *South Eastern Railway v. Associated Portland Cement Manufacturers* (1900) Ltd [1910] 1 Ch. 12, Cozens – Hardy MR at p.28 : "I have listened with some amazement to the contention that the rule of perpetuities applies where the action is brought, not against an assign of the covenantor, but against the covenantor himself, . . ."

104 (1863) 10 HLC 367, 11 ER 1068.

105 *Jameson v. Squire* [1948] IR 153, 155; *Re Tyrrell's Estate* [1907] 1 IR 292; *London & South Western Railway v. Gomm* (1882) 20 Ch. D 562.

enforceability between the contracting parties is unaffected by the perpetuity rule.[106]

g) Rights in Leases

(i) *Options*

(a) Contract or Property?

Options to purchase interests in property may be purely contractual in nature, in which case they are not subject to the perpetuity rule, or they may be in the nature of property rights. Some options may only exist as contractual rights, since they do not concern land. The general rule is that options to purchase interests in property are subject to the perpetuity rule since they are themselves property interests. To the extent, therefore, that a given option is a property right, it is subject to the perpetuity rule and will be void if it is exercisable outside the perpetuity period. So, if A and B enter into an option giving B or his heirs or assigns the right, as against A and his heirs or assigns, to buy Gortbane currently owned by A, as between A and B the option is contractual in nature and the rule does not apply. It is still contractual if B assigns the benefit to C and C sues A. But if A assigns his interest to D and D is then sued by B or by C, they will fail unless the exercise of the option was limited to the perpetuity period.

(b) Options to Renew Leases

The major exception to the foregoing principle allowed at common law are options to renew leases. Such options are not subject to the rule against perpetuities, so that if a lease contains an option to renew the term, the option being exercisable at any time during the term, then the option is valid however long the term may be.[107] There has some doubt as to whether this is an exception to the rule, or whether the right to renew is regarded as an incident of the lessee's present interest.[108]

A right to renew a lease for lives renewable forever, whether under a covenant or from the equity to renew, was never regarded in Ireland as being void

---

106 *Woodall v. Clifton* [1905] 2 Ch. 257 judgment of Warrington J; *Hutton v. Watling* [1948] Ch. 26; *Griffith v. Pelton* [1958] Ch. 205, [1957] 3 All ER 75, [1957] 3 WLR 522 (CA).

107 *Re Tyrrell's Estate* [1907] 1 IR 292 at 298; *Re Garde Browne* [1911] 1 IR 205 at 210; Morris & Leach, *Perpetuities* pp. 223-27.

108 Morris & Leach, *Perpetuities* p.223.

for perpetuity,[109] probably on the ground that it was part of the lessee's interest, which was akin to a fee simple.

The equitable right to renew could be exercised at any time in the future, even after all the lives had died out, provided section 1 of the Tenantry Act, 1779 was complied with.[110] It did not fall within the mischief of the rule since it could be exercised, and could be released, by the lessee for the time being.[111]

A right to create a lease in future, which is not a renewal of an existing lease, but the creation of a new type of lease, is subject to the rule and its exercise must be limited to the perpetuity period.[112]

(c) Options to purchase

These are dealt with below.

(ii) Other Rights in Leases

It is common for lease to contain a forfeiture clause providing that the landlord and successors in title may re-enter and forfeit the lease if the tenant commits breaches of the covenants or conditions in the lease. Such a right of re-entry, although it gives rise to a contingent property interest, is not subject to the perpetuity rule and may be exercised at any time during the lease.[113] It is regarded as incident to the relationship between landlord and tenant.

h) Options to Purchase

The exception, as to options to renew leases, does not apply to options, contained in leases or otherwise, to purchase the fee simple or the landlord's reversion. The exercise of options to purchase must be limited to the period,[114] unless of course an original contracting party seeks to enforce it against another original contracting party.[115]

It follows that an option to purchase the fee simple contained in a lease and exercisable during the term is valid if the term does not exceed 21 years, or if the term is longer than that, if expressly limited to 21 years, or the survivor of a

109 *Ross (Earl) v. Worsop* (1740) 1 Bro PC 281, 1 ER 568; *Sweet v. Anderson* (1772) 2 Bro PC 256, 22 ER 180; and see *Bridges v. Hitchcock* (1715) Bro P C 6; *Pollock v. Booth* (1874) IR 9 Eq 229.

110 See Chapter 9 Life Estates.

111 *Pollock v. Booth* (1874) IR 9 Eq 229 per Sullivan MR at 244–245.

112 In *Redington v. Browne* (1893) 32 LR Ir 347, Land Commission, an agreement to grant a reversionary lease for lives with a covenant for perpetual renewal, to take affect after a lease for lives or 99 years, was held void where the lives in the future lease were to be specified at a later date. The interest was held contingent and so might vest beyond the perpetuity period, since the current lease might outlast the lives plus 21 years.

113 *Re Tyrrell's Estate* [1907] 1 IR 292 at 298; *Re Garde Browne* [1911] 1 IR 205.

114 *Jameson v. Squire* [1948] IR 153, Maguire CJ at p.160.

115 See footnote 103 above.

number of lives plus 21 years. If the lease is void for any reason, an option to purchase may be held to be independent, but if so, its exercise will have to be limited to the perpetuity period independently of the term of the void lease.[116]

An exception to the application of the perpetuity rule to options to purchase has been created in the case of shared ownership leases by the Housing (Miscellaneous Provisions) Act, 1992 section 2(2). A shared ownership lease[117] is a scheme in which the lease provides for the lessee to buy out the reversion of the landlord over a period and is suitable for the purchase of local authority housing, *etc.* The problem was that the repayment period had to be limited to 21 years, or lives plus 21 years. The section exempts such options to purchase from the perpetuity rule.

i) Right of Entry to Enforce a Rentcharge

Grants of rentcharges often included express rights of entry and distress to enforce the rent. There was weighty opinion in favour of the view that such rights of entry did not offend the rule, as being part of the property interest of the owner of the rentcharge.[118] Section 44 of the Conveyancing Act, 1881 implies such rights in grants of rentcharges.[119]

Some grants, however, gave the holder of the rentcharge the power to grant a term of years to trustees on trust to raise the money to pay off arrears. Since the term was a contingent interest in property, the power was void unless the exercise of it is limited to the perpetuity period. Section 44 of the 1881 Act implies a statutory power to create a term, but, as with the other powers, only where such a power might have been validly conferred by the grant. There was some doubt as to whether the section validated such a term.

Section 6(1) of the Conveyancing Act, 1911 provides, in case of doubt, that the perpetuity rule is not to apply to the statutory powers and remedies implied by section 44 of the 1881 Act nor to the same or like powers or remedies expressed in grants. In Ireland, rights of entry for condition broken have been held not subject to the rule in any case,[120] but there may be remedies for the enforcement of rentcharges not included in section 44 and section 6.

---

116 *Tiernan v. Feely* [1949] IR 381 per Davitt J; *Jameson v. Squire* [1948] IR 153.

117 Defined for the purposes of the Act by section 2(1) as a lease: (a) granted for a term of more than 20 years but less than 100 years, (b) granted on payment to the lessor of a sum of money being not less than 25 per cent and not more than 75 per cent of the market value of the house, and (c) which provides for the right of the lessee to purchase, in one or more transactions, the interest of the lessor...

118 See Williams, *Real Property* p.472 text and note (h); Wolstenholme, p.118.

119 Conveyancing Act, 1881 s.44(1).

120 See above text at footnote 97 and footnote 92.

In Northern Ireland section 6(1) was repealed and replaced in order to remove these doubts.[121] It may also be noted that while the Northern Ireland legislation has applied the perpetuity rule to rights of entry for condition broken generally,[122] but not where they are remedies to enforce a rentcharge.[123]

j) Right to Redeem a Rentcharge

In *Switzer & Co v. Rochford*[124] Sir Andrew Porter held that an express right to redeem a rentcharge and exercisable beyond the perpetuity period, was not subject to the rule against perpetuities. The rentcharge was in the form of a term of 500 years, or so long as the sum of £300 (the redemption price) should not be paid by the grantor, his personal representatives and assigns. The rentcharge was enforceable by a right of re-entry. The judge held that it was created by a common law conveyance, not involving a use or trust, and as such was not subject to the perpetuity rule, apparently by analogy to Palles CB's judgment in *Attorney General v. Cummins.*[125] *Switzer* was not followed in *Re Tyrell's Estate*[126] in which the rentcharge was equitable, but the court was clearly unhappy with the distinction and unconvinced by *Switzer*. The rentcharge in *Re Tyrell's Estate* was subject to a proviso that the terre tenants, instead of paying the rentcharge, could at any time pay instead the interest on a number of bonds, and the latter was a contingent interest and technically within the rule, although seemingly it would not restrict the alienability of the bonds, so it was not within the mischief of the perpetuity rule. The notion that the right to redeem the rentcharge in *Switzer* is subject to the perpetuity rule rests on the notion that it was an option to purchase the rentcharge,[127] whereas in reality it was power to destroy it.[128] A right to reduce a rentcharge to a peppercorn on payment of a fine has been held not to be subject to the perpetuity rule.[129] There seems every reason to exempt rights to redeem rentcharges from the rule.[130]

---

121 Perpetuities Act (NI), 1966 s.12(1).

122 *ibid.* s.13(1).

123 *ibid.* s.12(1).

124 [1906] 1 IR 399.

125 See footnote 97 and *Re Tyrell's Estate* [1907] 1 IR 292, Walker C at 297.

126 [1907] 1 IR 292; and see *Re Donoughmore's Estate* [1911] 1 IR 211; *Re Ramadge's Estate* [1919] 1 IR 205.

127 *Re Tyrell's Estate* [1907] 1 IR 292 Fitzgibbon LJ at 301.

128 *Switzer & Co v. Rochford* [1906] 1 IR 399. On payment of the purchase price the rentcharge was to become void.

129 *Re Tyrell's Estate* [1907] 1 IR 292 at Fitzgibbon LJ at 299; *Re Garde Browne* [1911] 1 IR 205.

130 Law Reform Commission LRC 30–1989 para. 20.

k) Mortgagor's Right of Redemption

A mortgagor's right to redeem the mortgage is valid even though it may be exercised beyond the perpetuity period, namely at any time during the fee simple or term conveyed to the mortgagee.[131]

l) Contingent Interests after Entails

If an entail is followed by a contingent interest, in fee simple or in tail, then the interest may not vest for many generations. As a common law remainder it will have to comply with Rule 4 – the wait-and-see rule. If it is a legal executory interest or an equitable interest then it is not subject to the common law rules, and if it were made subject to the perpetuity rule then it would always be void, since an entail is not certain from the beginning to end not more than 21 years from the death of the first tenant in tail. The courts therefore devised a special rule for such interests. Such a contingent interest is valid if it is certain from the beginning to vest during or immediately on the termination of the fee tail.[132] Contingent interests which are bound to vest in this way would be destroyed if the entail were barred and so from a policy point of view do not come within the mischief of the perpetuity rule.[133] So in the limitation:

> *Unto and to the use of X and Y and their heirs in trust for A in tail, remainder in fee simple jointly to such of B's issue alive when the entail ends*

or,

> *[a trust] to A in tail, and if A should have no child who attains 27 years, to B in fee simple*[134]

the contingent fee simple is in each case valid. But where the limitation is:

> *Unto and to the use of T and U and their heirs in trust for P in tail, remainder in trust in fee simple for the first child of Q to marry*
> (Q has no children.)

---

131 *Knightsbridge Estates Trust Ltd v. Byrne* [1939] Ch. 441 at 463, [1940] AC 613.

132 *Nicholls v. Sheffield* (1787) 2 Bro CC 215, 29 ER 121; *Craig v. Stacey* Ir Term Rep 249; *Bandon v. Moreland* [1910] 1 IR 220 at 226.

133 Co Lit 47b; *Cole v. Sewell* (1843) 4 Dru & War 1, 6 Ir Eq R 66, 65 RR 668; *Cochrane v. Cochrane* (1882) 11 LR Ir 361, per Chatterton V-C at 368:

> "The [perpetuity] rule is general in its application, but is subject to the exception that, if the limitation or the trust be posterior to a limitation in tail, it will be valid, as in that case the barring of the estate tail sweeps away all subsequent limitations and trusts."

As can be seen this is not an entirely accurate statement of the exception. *Hare v. Burges* (1857) 4 K & J 45, 70 ER 19; *Sadleir v. Biggs* (1859) 4 HLC 435, 10 ER 53 (sub nom *Sadlier v. Biggs*).

134 Goodeve, *Real Property* p.287.

the contingent fee simple is void. The rule is unlike the common law rule in that there is no wait-and-see, but it also unlike the rule against perpetuities in that the normal perpetuity period does not apply.

C. Reform of The Rule Against Perpetuities

The strictness of the common law rule has led to reforms in a number of jurisdictions. In the Republic the main options open to reformers are to rely on case law development by the judges, to enact statutory cy pres, or to enact a statute similar to the Perpetuities Act (Northern Ireland), 1966 which is based on the wait-and-see principle.

1. Case Law

It has been seen that Gavan Duffy J in *Exham v. Beamish*[135] was prepared to modify one aspect of the common law rule, namely the rule in *Jee v. Audley.*[136] The judge in that case nevertheless declined to introduce a wait-and-see rule or modify the rule in *Leake v. Robinson*[137] as to class gifts, which would be difficult to modify without a wait-and-see principle. Judges feel constrained by case law method from introducing such radical reforms. Some states in the United States have introduced a principle of *cy pres* without statutory authority.[138]

2. Statutory Cy Pres

One option is to enact legislation giving power to courts to apply a cy pres doctrine where the existing law renders a gift void for perpetuity. This has been done in nine states of the United States.[139]

3. Perpetuities Act (Northern Ireland), 1966

The reform Act in Northern Ireland[140] in 1966 (hereinafter the Act) made changes in the law intended to mitigate the absurdities or inconveniences of the common law rule. This book is primarily concerned with the law in the Re-

135 [1939] IR 336.

136 (1787) 1 Cox Eq Cas 324, 29 ER 1186.

137 (1817) 2 Mer 363, 35 ER 979.

138 Four states, *i.e.* Hawaii, Mississippi, New Hampshire and West Virginia, have introduced cy pres through case law: Cunningham, *The Law of Property* p.152. New Hampshire also introduced wait-and-see by case law: *ibid.* and see *Re Clayton J Richardson Trust* (1993) 634 A 2d 1005, Supreme Court of New Hampshire (Lexis).

139 *i.e.* California, Idaho, Kentucky, Missouri, Ohio, Oklahoma, Texas, Vermont and Washington: Cunningham, *The Law of Property* p.152.

140 The law in England was reformed by the Perpetuities and Accumulations Act, 1964.

public to which the Act does not apply, but since the perpetuity rule is an area in need of reform in the Republic it is therefore worthwhile to examine the provisions of the Act.

a) Express 80-year Period

Section 1 of the Act allows the donor to specify a period of up to 80 years as the express perpetuity period within which the vesting of contingent interests is to take effect. This means that it is no longer necessary to resort to a Royal Lives Clause in Northern Ireland.

It should be noted that specifying a period under section 1 has the effect of validating the gift under the common law rule. It is not necessary to wait-and-see if the gift is valid for the purpose of the perpetuity rule. Given that the gift is valid, it is still necessary, as it always was, to wait and see for the purpose of distribution of the property. Under section 10(3) an option for valuable consideration to acquire an interest in land, other than an option within section 10(1), is subject to a 21 year perpetuity period and section 1 does not apply. Section 10(1) applies to options to acquire the reversion on a lease. Options under the Act are dealt with below.

b) Wait-and-See

The Act introduces, by section 3, a general principle of wait-and-see. As has been seen, at common law a disposition was in general void if it might possibly vest outside the period. Under section 3 of the Act this is no longer so in Northern Ireland. If it is clear from the beginning that the interest must vest, if at all, outside the period, there is clearly no scope for wait-and-see. But if it may or may not vest outside the period, section 3 applies. One can then wait until it becomes clear that the interest cannot vest within the period. Only then does it become void. Take, for example, the following limitation in a will:

> *to the first child of A to become a doctor in fee simple.*
> (A has no child who is currently a doctor.)

At common law it is void *ab initio*. A might have a child after the testator's death and that child might be the first of A's children to become a doctor and might do so beyond the period. There is no certainty that it would do so within 21 years of A's death, or within 21 years of the death of anyone alive at the testator's death.

Under section 3 of the Act one may now wait to see if A's first child to become a doctor does so within 21 years of A's death. If so, the gift then vests. But if one arrives at the point 21 years after A's death and at that time no child of A has by then become a doctor, the gift fails at that point.

This is the general rule. Other mitigating rules for specific problems or interests are contained in section 3, 4 and 5. But an important principle of the provisions is that the wait-and-see rule is to be applied before resorting to such other devices.[141] This is in order to ensure that the result produced by the Act differs as little as possible from that intended by the donor. Before going into the specific provisions in detail we can illustrate this general point by the following limitation in a will:

> *to the first son of Q to attain the age of 25 in fee simple.*
> (Q is alive at the testator's children and has no son aged 25.)

At common law Q might have a child after the testator's death, who would not therefore be a life in being itself, and who might become 25 years of age more than 21 years after Q's death – if Q died while the child was less than four years old. But if the age specified had been 21 or less the gift would have been valid.

The problem is that an age greater than 21 has been specified. Under section 4 of the Act one may reduce the age to whatever age nearest to the one specified will have the effect of validating the gift, but one may only do so after waiting to see. One must allow the gift to take effect according to the testator's wishes if possible. The intention of the testator was to give property to someone aged 25, not 21. One therefore waits to see if a son of Q becomes 25 within 21 years of Q's death. If so, the gift is valid in favour of that son. If, 21 years after Q's death, there is still no son aged 25 one may then reduce the age to the extent necessary to produce a valid gift. If there was at that point a son aged 23, one can reduce the age to 23 so that the son takes the property. It should be noted that if wait-and-see were not applied before resorting to age reduction, a different son might take the gift. For example, suppose Q had a son Y who became 21 but then died under 25, within 21 years of Q's death, leaving a brother Z who then later attains 25 but still within 21 years of Q's death. If one applied age reduction first and reduced the age to 21 at the beginning, Y's estate would have taken the property. But if, as is the case under the Act, one waits to see first, then Z will get the property, on attaining 25.

c) Lives in Being

It has been seen that at common law lives in being are those which validate the gift. If the gift is void, there are, logically, no lives in being. If the wait-and-see principle is introduced, then this definition of lives in being becomes inadequate. During the period of wait-and-see the gift is neither valid nor void. For the duration of whose life, then, does one wait? Section 3(5) of the Act contains a definition of lives in being for the purpose of wait-and-see. They in-

141 Section 3 merely says that "apart from the provisions of this section and sections 4 and 5, a disposition would be void..." which seems to imply that those provisions should be applied first, but section 4, on age reduction, applies where "it is apparent at the time the disposition is made or becomes apparent at a subsequent time..." The latter words indicate that wait-and-see is to be applied first. Section 5, on the surviving spouse trap, applies where the time of death of the survivor of a person alive at the testator's death and their spouse "has no arrived at the end of the perpetuity period...", which also indicates that wait-and-see is to be applied first.

clude the donor and the donee, and, in the latter case, include any members or potential members of a class. In the case of special powers of appointment they include the donee of the power and the object or class of objects of the power. They also include a person having a child or grandchild who comes within the definition of donees of dispositions or of donees or objects of a special power, or who would come within the definition if subsequently born, or a person whose grandchild, if subsequently born, would take a vested interest under the disposition. It also includes any person on the failure or determination of whose prior interest the disposition is limited, mediately or immediately, to take effect, or a person whose child or grandchild is such a person.

d) Presumption of Fertility

The Act modifies the Rule in *Jee v. Audley*[142] in section 2 by providing that it is presumed that male can have a child at the age of 14 or over and a female at the age of 12 and over but not over the age of 55. In the case of a living person evidence may be given to show that he or she will not be able to have a child at the time in question. The expression having a child includes having a child by adoption, legitimation or other means,[143] except that the provision as to rebuttal by evidence does not apply in such cases. Whether a person could or could not adopt a child requires the exercise of discretion and could not yield a definite answer in such an artificial context.

e) Age Reduction

In the Republic a limitation may be void for perpetuity because an age over 21 has been specified, unless the courts are prepared in future to modify the rules by introducing some form of cy pres.[144] Where such a situation occurs in Northern Ireland and this is "apparent at the time the disposition is made or becomes apparent at a subsequent time" section 4 of the Act allows the age to be reduced to an age nearest to the age specified which would, if specified instead, prevent the disposition from being void. The phrase or becomes apparent indicates that the wait-and-see principle introduced by the Act is to be applied first. If this results in the disposition being validated, then there is no

142 (1787) 1 Cox Eq Cas 324, 29 ER 1186.

143 NI Act, s.2(4).

144 This case was dealt with in England by s.163 of the Law of Property Act, 1925. This provision subsituted 21 for the age specified. As will be seen below, this mechanical approach may go further than necessary to save gifts and may also lead to a different person obtaining an interest than the one whose age was closest to 21. The Northern Ireland Act follows the same solution as the English Perpetuities and Accumulations Act, 1964. Difficult problems have arisen under the English Act due to the repeal of section 163 being included in section 4 of that Act. See Megarry's, *Manual* (6th ed.) p.212–4.

need to invoke section 4. Take, for example, the following limitation contained in a will:

> *to the first son of X to attain 30 years. . .*
> (X dies after the testator and is survived by a son, Y, aged 10.)

If any person is to meet the description in the will it must be Y, and Y will do so, if at all, within 21 years of the death of his father, X, the life in being. We wait-and-see until X dies, and doing so has validated the gift. But wait-and-see may be of no help. If X dies leaving a child, Z, aged five, then it will be 25 years before the contingency can occur, *i.e.* before Z can attain the age of 30 and claim the gift and this is beyond the period. The section allows the age specified to be reduced to 25 years.

f) Class Reduction

The Act abolishes the common law rule that a gift to a class cannot be partly good and partly bad. Section 4(4) provides that:

> "Where. . . it is apparent at the time the disposition is made or becomes apparent at a subsequent time that, apart from this subsection, the inclusion of any persons, being potential members of a class or unborn persons who at birth would become members or potential members of the class, would cause the disposition to be treated as void for remoteness, those persons shall, unless their inclusion would exhaust the class, thenceforth be deemed for all purposes of the disposition to be excluded from the class".

The section therefore serves to confirm that wait-and-see applies to class gifts. In a class gift one applies wait-and-see first and if actual members qualify within the period one can exclude potential members.

g) Age and Class Reduction Combined

It has been seen that the wait-and-see provisions of section 3 are applied first, that is if a limitation would be void apart from the provisions of this section and sections 4 and 5. Section 4 concerns age and class reduction and so one ignores these provisions in deciding whether there is scope for section 3 to apply. One must therefore apply the wait-and-see provision before resorting to age or class reduction. It is also clear from section 4(3) that one applies age reduction before class reduction, because that section applies "where the inclusion of any persons, being potential members of a class. . . prevents the foregoing provisions of this section from operating to save a disposition from being void for remoteness". To take an example, the following limitation in a will:

> *to such of A's children as attain 25 and such children as attain 25 of any children of A who may die under 25.*
> (A is alive at the testator's death.)

The gift would, apart from section 3, 4 and 5, be void. But even if the age is reduced to 21 the class is a composite class and would still be void because A, who is still alive, could have a child born after the testator's death who is not therefore a life in being, that child could die under 21 leaving a child who could therefore qualify beyond the period. Under the Act one can therefore exclude the children of those children of A who die under 21. Although this saves the gift it is not an ideal solution since not all such members need be excluded. If one is to rewrite the gift, which is what the statute does, then it would be closer to the testator's original gift to include children attaining 21 of those children of A who die under 21 but who are in being at the testator's death.

h) Abolition of Old Rule Against Perpetuities

The Act, by section 15, abolishes the old rule against perpetuities, or the rule in *Whitby v. Mitchell* as it is also known. The Act refers to it as the double possibility rule. It has already been noted that the retention of the rule in the Republic is unnecessary and in some cases is objectionable, since it may invalidate limitations which are valid under the modern rule against perpetuities.

i) Legal Remainders

Section 14 of the Act provides that the rule against perpetuities "shall not be inapplicable" to limitations merely because they create contingent remainders. The negative formulation was probably chosen because of the doubts as to which class or classes of contingent remainders are subject to the rule after the Contingent Remainders Act, 1877. That doubt now exists as to limitations *inter vivos* and not containing a use which are of the Rule 4 type and which therefore before 1877 could only exist as common law remainders. The effect of the Northern Ireland Act is that all limitations which create contingent remainders are subject to the rule. This seems unnecessary as the one point in favour of the law as it stood before the Act, and still stands in the Republic, is that a remainder of the Rule 4 type which breaks the perpetuity rule can still take effect if it can do so immediately upon the determination of the preceding estate.

j) The Surviving Spouse Limitation.

Section 5 of the Act provides:

> "5.– Where a disposition is limited by reference to the time of death of the survivor of a person in being at the commencement of the perpetuity period and any spouse of that person, and that time has not arrived at the end of the perpetuity period, the disposition shall be treated for all purposes, where to do so would save it from being void for remoteness, as if it had instead been limited by reference to the time immediately before the end of that period".

What this appears to mean is that in the typical surviving spouse limitation:

> *[a trust] to H for life, remainder for life to any wife he may marry, remainder in fee simple to the children of the marriage alive at the death of the survivor of H and his wife*

one waits first to see if H marries someone who was alive at the time the disposition was made. If so, then the remainder to the children of the marriage is valid because it must vest within the period. If H marries someone who was not alive at the time the disposition was made, then one can wait to see if that spouse survives H. If they do not, then the gift to the children is valid, again because it must vest within the period. If they do, then one can continue to wait up to a point 21 years after the death of H, which is the end of the perpetuity period under the Act. If the surviving spouse dies during that period the remainder is valid because it has vested within the period. These results follow from the general wait-and-see provision. Section 5 only addresses what is to happen at the end of the perpetuity period. What section 5 requires is that if, 21 years after the death of H, the unborn spouse is still alive, one can take the remainder as having vested in the children of the marriage at that point.

k) Options

Section 10 of the Act exempts from the operation of the rule options in leases to acquire for valuable consideration an interest reversionary (whether directly or indirectly) on any lease if –

(i) the option is exercisable only by the lessee or his or her successors in title; and

(ii) it ceases to be exercisable at or before the expiration of one year after the end of the lease.

Section 10(2) applies the section to an agreement for a lease as well as a lease. The phrase would include an equitable lease within the *Walsh v. Lonsdale*[145] principle.

Section 11 makes it clear that the rule does not apply to options as purely contractual rights.

l) Powers of Appointment

Section 7 of the Act provides that powers of appointment shall be treated as special powers unless the instrument creating the power is expressed (i) to be exercisable by one person only and (ii) it could at all times during its currency when that person is of full age and capacity be exercised by him or her so as immediately to transfer to him or herself the whole of the interest governed by the power without the consent of any other person.

D. The Rule Against Inalienability

A confusing aspect of the laws against remoteness is that there is a rule which appears similar to the modern rule against perpetuities and which has the same

145 (1882) 21 Ch D 9.

period as a test and is even sometimes referred to also as the rule against perpetuities but which is quite distinct. The rule against inalienability, as it is now generally called, applies to vested gifts and controls how long the subject matter can remain inalienable. Whether there is a single general overall rule against inalienability is open to question, because the alienability of property is controlled in a number of contexts by different specific rules. As we shall see the rule which is today referred to as the rule against inalienability arises in the context of non-charitable purpose trusts. In order to see why this is so, it is necessary to examine how alienability is dealt with in other property contexts.

1. The Control of Alienability

Since the Statute *Quia Emptores*, 1290 there has been a basic principle that property should not be rendered inalienable by a disposition by a fee simple owner. As to legal estates, the principle is realised by various rules which have essentially the same result.

As to fee simple estates, *Quia Emptores*, 1290 provides that the freehold tenant has the power of free alienation and the courts have struck down attempts to limit the power to any extensive degree. The types of clause struck down have generally been those which attempt to restrict alienation in terms of the description of people to whom the land can be sold or not sold, but a condition which attempted to prevent any alienation for a given period would also be void on this ground.

Fee tail estates have long been barrable so as to produce an alienable estate, and so there was no need to give expression to the principle of alienability in any other rules. Life estates can be alienated to an extent consistent with the tenants original interest by creating an estate pur autre vie. The Settled Land Acts, 1882–1890 now give most limited owners the power to sell the fee simple estate. Therefore, as to legal estates, it can be said that the specific rule as to inalienability dealt with here does not apply because the principle of alienability is satisfied by other rules.

2. The Rule

The rule requires that the trust fund in the hands of trustees should not be rendered inalienable in their hands for an infinite period. The fact that the assets represented by the fund, *e.g.* stocks and shares, may be bought and sold by the trustees does not satisfy the rule, which is concerned with the trust property itself. The trust fund itself will be rendered inalienable if there is a direction to employ the income from the fund for a given purpose for an infinite period, and so such a direction is void.[146] Thus, a trust in which the income is to be used to provide a cup for the best yachtsman in a sailing club is void if not lim-

146 *Boyle v. Boyle* (1877) IR 11 Eq 433.

ited to the period.[147] A trust to provide a prize for students in an educational establishment on the other hand would fall within the exception to the rule in favour of charitable trusts being for educational purposes.[148]

3. The Period of Inalienability

The rule incorporates a period of the same extent as that in the modern perpetuity rule, namely a life or lives in being plus 21 years. This may be called the period of inalienability. It is often confused with the perpetuity period and indeed the latter term is sometimes used to refer to it. However, the rule against perpetuity applies to contingent interests and determines the period within which they must vest in interest, whereas the rule against inalienability applies to vested interests and determines the period within which they may remain inalienable.

4. Charitable Trusts

One exception to the rule is charitable trusts. The income from the fund may be used by the trustees for the charitable purpose for an infinite period without rendering the trust void. In policy terms this may be said to be the case because the definition of charity incorporates public benefit and the benefit to the public resulting from the charitable purpose outweighs the disadvantage of removal of property from the market.

5. Non-Charitable Trusts

Non-charitable trusts are subject to the rule. Where there are human beneficiaries it would be rare for the rule to be invoked, because today the Settled Land Acts ensure that a "tenant for life" or person having the powers of a tenant for life, which includes nearly all cases where there is a trust of land, where their interest is in possession, may alienate the fee simple in the land. A bare trust, *i.e.* a trust not involving successive interests, where the beneficiaries are of full age, is outside the Settled Land Acts, but there is no problem of inalienability in such a case. The rule in *Saunders v. Vautier*[149] ensures that beneficiaries who are absolutely entitled can put an end to the trust at any time and have the legal estate conveyed to them. A condition which attempted to exclude the rule would be not be enforced. The rule is therefore usually invoked in non-charitable trusts where there are no human beneficiaries, the so-called purpose trusts.

---

147 *Re Nottage* [1895] 2 Ch. 649.

148 The fact that the trust fund, as opposed to assets in which it is invested (which will be alienable under the Settled Land Acts or as trustee investments) will have to be retained to give effect to the beneficial interests does not in itself invalidate the trust: *Re Gage* [1898] 1 Ch. 506.

149 (1841) Cr & Ph 240, 41 ER 482; see Chapter 4 Equity.

In *Re Fossit's Estate*[150] the testator left one third of his residuary estate to the Orange Institution of Ireland "for the upkeep of the Orange Hall, 10 Rutland Square, Dublin." It was held void as contrary to the rule.

The question is often one of interpretation. In *Re Byrne*[151] the gift was "for the absolute use and benefit of the Jesuit Order of Ireland." It was held valid, on the ground that the members of the order could dispose of the fund at any time.[152] Gifts have also been upheld on the ground that they are to the members that make up the institution at the date of the gift rather than to the institution, and so been held valid. If the gift includes future members it would be void unless limited to the period, or, as in the *Byrne* case the members for the time being were empowered to alienate it at their discretion.

Many trusts that fell foul of the rule were gifts to trustees for the purpose of maintaining a tomb. The courts came to the aid of such trusts by upholding a gift to charity A with a proviso that the fund should shift to charity B if charity A failed to maintain the testator's tomb.[153] They interpreted the condition as not imposing a trust to maintain the tomb, but a bare condition. They also held that the contingent gift over to charity B did not infringe the perpetuity rule as it fell within an exception in favour of gifts over from one charity to another. This artful device need not be used in all cases in the Republic as the legislature has provided by section 50 of the Charities Act, 1960 that a gift for the indefinite upkeep of a tomb is valid if the income is not over £60 per year or the capital is not over £1,000. There is no similar exception for trusts for the upkeep of animals, and so the device would still have to be used in such a case, or the gift limited to a 21 year period.

In *Re Kelly*[154] there was a bequest of a fund out of which £4 a year was to be spent "on the support of my dogs". Meredith J held that for the purpose of the inalienability rule the lives must be human lives. In the absence of such lives the period was 21 years, as in the case of the perpetuity rule. The question then was whether there was anything to limit the duration of the vested gift to 21 years. Meredith J refused to accept that the lives of dogs could be taken for this purpose. This should have rendered the gift of the fund void for inalienability, because there was nothing else by which to limit the gift to the 21 year period. The judge nevertheless felt able to uphold the gift as valid for each year the dogs lived up to a maximum of 21 years. This may have been in accordance with common sense, but seems open to the objection that it introduced both a

150 [1934] IR 504.

151 [1935] IR 782.

152 See also *Re Keogh's Estate* [1945] IR 13.

153 *Re Tyler* [1891] 3 Ch. 252.

154 [1932] IR 255. See above under Rule Against Perpetuities.

cy pres doctrine, and a possibly also a wait-and-see rule,[155] into the rule against inalienability, neither of which had been recognised before in this jurisdiction.[156]

6. Cy pres

The case law in Ireland and England does not support the view that there is a cy pres jurisdiction in the rule against inalienability, with the exception of *Re Kelly*[157] itself. Meredith J did not refer to the doctrine by name but an alternative way of looking at the case, *i.e.* apart from its being wrong, is to regard it as a precedent for cy pres in the inalienability rule.

E. The Rule Against Accumulations

There is certainly a rule at common law which controls accumulations of income from land or from a fund consisting of personal property such as money or stocks and shares. However, the nature of the rule is open to question. Some writers regard the supposed rule as similar to the rule against inalienability in that it applies to vested interests, in this case the vested fund, and limits its duration.[158] Stated in this way, the rule lays down that a direction to trustees to accumulate funds is void if the accumulation may endure beyond a period identical to the period of inalienability. It is certainly the case that charitable trusts are an exception. They may accumulate funds for the charitable purpose indefinitely. It has already been noted that a similar exception for charities exists in the rule against inalienability.

In fact one may question whether the supposed rule against accumulations is anything more than an example of the application of the rule against inalienability. It is true that land out of which income is produced may remain alienable during the period of accumulation, as where the land is held in fee simple subject to a rentcharge and the income from the rentcharge is to be accumulated. But in such a case the rentcharge itself is the property out of which the income is produced and it would remain inalienable during the accumulation. Other writers and judges, on the other hand, treat the supposed rule as controlling the

155 Because the number of years is not ascertainable unless you take into account when the surviving dog dies.

156 It also makes it more difficult to appreciate why the judge also struck down the contingent gift over to charity, under the rule against perpetuities, since it depended on the same contingency. See above.

157 [1932] IR 255. See above.

158 Megarry & Wade, *Real Property* p.271: "The principle at common law was that accumulations of income could validly be directed only for so long as property might validly be rendered inalienable".

vesting of the contingent gift of the accumulated fund. Chatterton VC, for example, in *Smith v. Cuninghame*[159] stated it as follows:

> "The rule as to trusts for accumulation is the same as that as to executory devises, namely, that they are held void for remoteness if they do not necessarily vest in interest within a life or lives in being, and twenty-one years afterwards, and one or two periods of gestation, if such gestation should exist in fact".[160]

Stated in this way a contingent gift of an accumulated fund is void if it may not vest in interest within the perpetuity period. If this is the correct formulation, then it is nothing more than an application of the perpetuity rule.

There is one remaining issue here and that is whether the gift of the accumulated fund is always necessarily contingent, as for example where it is to be accumulated for a period in excess of 21 years and then given to a named person. If such a gift is not contingent, but was still invalid, that would indicate the existence of a distinct accumulations rule. According to Morris and Leach the gift of the fund is always contingent because it depends on the accumulation having taken place.[161] If so, then the supposed rule against accumulations is, as applied to the gift of the fund, identical to the perpetuity rule.

The better view is that the supposed rule against accumulations at common law is an example of the application (a) of the rule against inalienability to the capital fund, or the property which is the source of the income, and (b) of the rule against perpetuities to the contingent gift of the accumulated fund. It is fortunate, from a logical point of view, that they do both apply because this avoids an otherwise awkward result. The perpetuity rule makes a contingent gift of an accumulated fund void if it might vest beyond the period. In such a case the accumulation itself would also necessarily be void. But the perpetuity rule is not supposed to affect vested interests.[162] But fortunately the vested gift is also void under the separate rule against inalienability, and so the extension of the perpetuity rule beyond its proper sphere is obscured.

In England there is indeed a separate rule against accumulations but it has its origin in the Accumulations Act, 1800.[163] The purpose of the Act was to cut down drastically the period during which income could be accumulated in a

---

159 (1884) 13 LR Ir 480.

160 Morris and Leach, p.302 seem unable to make up their mind on the matter:

> "An accumulation infringes the rule against perpetuites if it may last longer than the perpetuity period and the right to enjoy the income is contingent on the accumulation having taken place: or (to put it differently)[!] if the persons entitled to the accumulated fund may not be ascertained within the period.

161 See footnote 160.

162 Notice the similarity between this situation and the case of possibilites of reverter. The logical problem is avoided there by the fact that such interests are exempted from the rule against perpetuites.

163 The English law is now contained in the Law of Property Act, 1925 ss. 164–166 and the Perpetuities and Accumulations Act, 1964 s.13.

fund and it was a result of the famous case of *Thellusson v. Woodford.*[164] The testator in that case, Mr Thelluson, directed in his will that the income from all his property was to be accumulated during the lives of his sons, grandsons and great-grandchildren living at his death, and that on the death of the survivor the accumulated fund should be divided among specified descendants. Since the period of accumulation was limited to lives in being the court upheld the validity of the direction under the supposed common law rule. This caused an outcry and demands in Parliament for reform. It was felt to be grossly unfair that a testator could deprive his immediate descendants of all benefit from his fortune, and confer a vast fortune on remoter and as yet unascertained descendants, in order to satisfy a desire that his own remote posterity should become prominent in society, from a motive of what might be described as posthumous greed.

The Act of 1800 therefore sought to cut down the period in which accumulations should take place.[165] The 1800 Act was passed in England just before the Union and so never applied to Ireland, but the Accumulations Act, 1892 was, curiously, applied to Ireland. This appears to be due to ignorance of the Irish law. This Act applies only to directions for the sole purpose[166] of purchasing land[167] and contained in wills where the testator dies after 27 June 1892.[168] In such a case only the fourth period specified in the 1800 Act may be selected, namely the minority or respective minorities only of any person or persons who under the limitations of the instrument directing accumulation would for the time being, if of full age, be entitled to the income directed to be accumulated. Under this period it is possible to have successive minorities since it is possible also to accumulate during the minorities of persons unborn at the date of the gift.[169] For example, T devises the residue of his property to trustees on trust for his grandchildren born before or after his death. He directs that they should accumulate the income of their shares during their minorities and then use the fund to purchase land for the grandchild concerned. At T's death there is one grandchild, G1, who is under age. The income of the whole fund is accumulated during her minority, and if she is still the only grandchild when she comes of age, the whole accumulated fund,[170] or land bought with it,

164 (1799) 4 Ves Jun 227, 31 ER 117, (1805) 11 Ves Jun 112, 32 ER 1030.

165 The period was to be the life of the settlor or grantor, or 21 years from the death of such person or testator, or the minorities of persons living or in the womb at the death of the grantor, *etc.*, or the minorities of person who under the limitation would be entitled, if of full age, to the accumulated fund. See Megarry & Wade, *Real Property* 272–3.

166 *Re Knapp* [1929] 1 Ch. 341.

167 The restriction does not apply to capital money held under the Settled Land Act, 1882.

168 *Re Baroness Llanover (No. 2)* [1903] 2 Ch. 330.

169 *Re Cattell* [1914] 1 Ch. 177.

170 Since after-born grandchildren are to be included it is not known when the first grandchild qualifies for an interest vested in possession what the total number of shares will

will go to her. But if, even after she has come of age, another grandchild, G2, is born – since after-born grandchildren are specified – that grandchild will become entitled to half the entire estate. G1 will be divested of half the property. The income of G2's share will b accumulated during G2's minority. This process could continue until no more grandchildren can be born, *i.e.* until the death of the last of T's children.

be. Hence, the whole fund must be distributed to that grandchild, subject to divesting if more members of the class qualify.

CHAPTER 12

CLASS GIFTS

Probably the most complex rules in property law developed about class gifts, *i.e.* gifts to persons by reference to a description.

A. The Class-Closing Rules

The class-closing rules were developed to define the membership of a class in the absence of a precise definition by the donor. Class gifts can exist in any of the three types of future interests we have dealt with: common law remainders, legal executory interests and future trusts, gifts in wills now being considered as part of the latter category. Common law remainders have their own class-closing rules which are a consequence simply of the common law remainder rules applied to class gifts. We dealt with the most important of these, the Rule in *Festing v. Allen*[1], in the chapter on future interests. However, we shall not deal here with class gifts as common law remainders nor as legal executory interests. Such interests occur today only in *inter vivos* deeds[2] and class gifts in *inter vivos* deeds other than those taking effect as trusts are now rare. The whole range of class gifts in the Republic is also dealt with elsewhere.[3] We shall therefore deal here only with class gifts in wills and in *inter vivos* trusts. We have seen that future interests in wills and future equitable estates must comply with the perpetuity rule. Where there is a future estate in favour of a class one therefore has to apply the perpetuity rule, but in doing so the class-closing rules have to taken into account because the effect of doing so is often to render valid an estate that otherwise would be void for perpetuity. After considering the meaning of class and the modern class-closing rules we shall then take the same examples and apply the rule against perpetuities to them, taking into account the class-closing rules. Finally, although this subject may appear to be far removed from any actual social conditions or values, in reality it is not entirely detached, as we shall see later in the chapter. Although any sophisticated legal system needs to have class-closing rules to define what a testator means by such expressions as my children or the children of X, not all societies will produce the same rules.

1 *Festing v. Allen* (1843) 12 M & W 279, (1844) 5 Hare 573, 67 ER 1038.

2 Since executory devises are no longer possible. See Chapter 10 Future Interests.

3 See Lyall, "Class-Closing Rules and Future Interests in Freehold: Law and Political Economy" (1985) 20 Irish Jurist 66.

B. The Meaning of Class

A class gift[4] is a gift or limitation in favour, not of an individual, but of a number of persons by some form of description. So, for example a limitation "to A" is an individual gift to the person called A, whereas a gift to "my children" is a class gift to such persons who answer the description of being children of the donor. An obligation on trustees to employ the trust funds for the benefit of some members of a class at the trustees' discretion, *i.e.* a discretionary trust, is not a gift to a class.[5]

It is a matter of construction, which a court may have to consider first, as to whether a gift is to a class or to an individual, or individuals. In *Re Ramadge*[6] the gift was to "my four cousins, A, B, C and D". The issue was whether it created a class gift or a gift to four designated persons. The testator had more than four cousins at the date of death. When the will was made the four named cousins had a factor in common in that they were the only cousins on the Ramadge side of the family. Three other Ramadge cousins were born later. Lowry J decided that it was not a class gift but a gift to the four designated cousins. He held that naming them pointed to that result, although it was not conclusive in itself. Two of the four named belonged to the same stirpes and so the will itself made for an uneven division between persons in the same relation to the testatrix. If the testator had in any case discriminated between the named cousins then it was reasonable to suppose that she did indeed intend to include those cousins and to exclude all other cousins. If the gift is held to be a class gift then the question often arises as to which persons are included in the description and which do not. The class-closing rules were designed to resolve this issue.

C. The Modern Class-Closing Rules

Whenever there is a gift to a class, such as to the children of A, quite apart from any question of perpetuity there is, assuming the gift to be valid, the question of who is included in the gift. Does it mean the children of A born at the time when the testator was writing the will? Or born by the time of the testator's death? Or whenever born, *i.e.* even after the testator's death? The modern class-closing rules were developed by the judges to solve these problems. They apply to executory limitations and limitations under trusts. Unfortunately the law is complicated in Ireland by the survival of legal remainders at common law. There is a separate set of class-closing rules which apply to them

---

4 Casner, "Class Gifts Other Than to 'Heirs' or 'Next of Kin': Increase in the Class Membership "(1937) 51 HLR 254; Morris, "The Rule Against Perpetuities and the Rule in Andrews v. Partington" (1954) 70 LQR 61; Sherrin, (1972); Lyall, (1985).

5 *Re Davoren's Estate* [1994] 2 ILRM 276.

6 [1969] NI 71.

which are not based, even notionally, on the presumed intent of the testator, but simply follow as a consequence of applying the common law remainder rules to class gifts. These will be considered later. As to executory interests and trusts, the rules will be applied twice. First, they will be applied in determining the validity of the gift for the purpose of the perpetuity rule. The class-closing rules were not invented with the perpetuity rule in mind, but their effect is sometimes to save a gift which otherwise would be void. Secondly, if the gift is valid, they will be applied in actually distributing the property.

1. Policies: The Market versus Family Solidarity

The rules are, as we have seen, usually described by the judges as rules of construction, as rules to supply a result when the intention of the donor is not expressed. They therefore are said to yield to a contrary expressed intention.[7] Their validity is often said to be based upon the principle of presumed or implied intent. This asserts that the role of the courts is limited in this instance to discovering what the donor would have done if he or she had thought about it. One is entitled, however, to question whether or not the courts are, under the guise of finding the presumed intent, actually applying social policies. One may detect that judges are willing, or unwilling, to find an intention contrary to the rules and so to depart from the rules. To the extent that social policies are embodied in the rules, this is a way of detecting shifts towards or away from such policies.[8]

---

7 *Re Bleckly* (1951) Ch. 740, 749.

8 In *Williamson v. Williamson* [1974] NI 92 there was an *inter vivos* trust for the children of the settlor equally who should attain 25 in the lifetime of the settlor or within 21 years of the settlor's death. The reference to 21 years was made to avoid a breach of the perpetuity rule. The Rule in *Andrews v. Partington* was not applied. In England some recent cases display a critical attitude on the part of the judges to the rules. See Sherrin, (1972) Ch. 5 p.144. Nevertheless, not all cases in which the rules have been found not to apply can be explained in terms of social policy. In *Re Kebty-Fletcher's Will Trusts* [1969] 1 Ch 339, for example, the rule was to said have no application where the gift was to children following a life interest to their parent because the class would close at the parent's death in any case. In *Re Harker's Will Trusts* [1969] 1 WLR 1124 the rule was held not to apply to close the class at the termination of a life estate where the life tenant had released his interest and so terminated it before the point contemplated by the testator. Accordingly the class closed at the life tenant's death, which is when it would have done had the limitation taken its natural course and the rule been applied. It is doubtful in view of this and similar cases, therefore, whether the criticism of the judges really carries through to the results in the sense of a greater willingness to find that the donor intended to exclude the rules. See also Sherrin, (1972) Chapter 6 p.182 *et seq*. Certainly a willingness to depart from the rules is discernible when the result would not render the gift void for perpetuity. *Re Clifford's Settlement Trusts* [1980] 2 WLR 749 has recently emphasised that words excluding the rule must not merely point to its exclusion, but be "inescapably incompatible with its application".

Two main social policies seem to be at work. First, the rules generally have the effect of closing the class at the earliest possible moment, which is when a member of the class becomes entitled to an interest vested in possession.[9] This ensures that a person entitled to consume or to deal with property is able to do so from the moment that right arises. This can also be seen as an expression in terms of individual rights of an economic system in which rights in land are distributed by the market mechanism. In this sense the rules developed by the courts are such as to promote the efficient working of a market economy, and they are at the expense of more communal values which support the cohesion of the family or other social unit by seeking to include as many of its members in a class gift.

A second and often conflicting concern detectable in the rules is not to discriminate between members of the same kinship group in the distribution of the property. This favours the communal values of the cohesion of the kinship group. As will be seen from the detailed working out of the rules, the policy of maintaining the kinship unit is usually carried into effect only if it will not hinder the policy in favour of the early vesting of property, which is therefore the dominant policy. This in itself indicates that the rules contain an inherent bias in favour of the market, rather than kinship solidarity, as a means of distributing property. This point will be examined in more detail after considering the application of the rules to the four basic types of gift discussed below.

2. The Rule in Andrews *v.* Partington

The basic modern rule is known as the general rule in *Andrews* v *Partington*[10] or sometimes simply as "the Rule in *Andrews v. Partington*. The case itself applies to a specific situation which will be dealt with later. The general rule contains two distinct propositions. First, it holds that the time of distribution, *i.e.* the time when the property should be distributed, in any class gift is the point at which the first member of the class qualifies for an interest in possession (note, not in interest only) for it is at this point that a person becomes entitled to consume or deal with the property.[11] The second part of the Rule holds that the class closes at the time of distribution. The operation of the rules can best be illustrated by taking examples of the four most common kinds of class gifts.

9 *Donoghoe v. Mooney* (1891) 27 LR Ir 26, at 34 per Porter MR; *Re Smith* (1862) 2 J & H 594 at 601 per Page-Wood V-C, 70 ER 1196, 1198.

10 (1791) 3 Bro CC 401, 29 ER 408, 610, 2 Cox 223, 30 ER 103.

11 See footnote 9. *Re Smith* (1862) 2 J & H 594 at 601, 70 ER 1196 at 1198 per Page Wood V-C:

> "As long as a fund is in hand, the general rule is that new members of the class may be let in. The time when the money is distributable is the time for ascertaining the class, after which no more can be let in. Children born after the fund becomes divisible are not entitled to share".

D. The Four Basic Types of Class Gift

The word heirs used as a word of purchase is really a special type of class gift, and has already been considered on its own. Words such as issue may give rise to special problems of interpretation. We shall confine the words used here to children or grandchildren.

1. Simple Class Gift.

An example would be, in a will:

to the grandchildren of X in fee simple.

If there are grandchildren of X when the instrument takes effect[12] the class closes then. It includes grandchildren born up to that time[13] and still in existence.[14] It excludes later-born grandchildren.[15] This particular application of the general principle is known as the Rule in *Viner v. Francis.*[16]

If there are no grandchildren of X at the date the instrument takes effect then the time of distribution has not arrived. It will do so when the first grandchild is born. In this case if that were done, then the class would consist of only one person, which is presumably not what the donor intended. The courts therefore have preferred to hold that the class remains open and all later-born grandchildren are included.[17] A distribution may be made to the first to qualify, subject to divestment later, but this suffers from the disadvantage that the recipient may have spent or dissipated the property. Alternatively, distribution can be postponed until the maximum membership becomes known which will be when the class can no longer physically increase. In the latter instance the distribution is indefeasible. The disadvantage of this is that it postpones the enjoyment of the property by those who have already qualified for an indefinite period.

---

12 In the case of a deed *inter vivos* this is when it is executed. In the case of a will it is now when the testator dies: Succession Act, 1965 s.89.

13 This is not universally followed. In *Shaw v. McMahon* (1821) 4 Dru & War 431, 65 RR 724, Sugden decided otherwise where the testator had disinherited one of his children. See also *Re Finnerty* [1970] IR 221.

14 This has now been altered where the class consists of the children or remoter issue of the testator: Succession Act, 1965 s.98; and see Chapter 26 Succession: Lapse.

15 *Warren v. Johnson* (1673) 2 Rep Ch. 69, 21 ER 619; *Heathe v. Heathe* (1740) 2 Atk 121, 26 ER 476; *Sprackling v. Ranier* (1761) Dick 344, 21 ER 302; *Singleton v. Gilbert* (1784) 1 Cox 68, 29 ER 1066; *Hill v. Chapman* (1791) 1 Ves 405, 30 ER 408; *Davidson v. Dallas* (1808) 14 Ves 576, 33 ER 642; contra *Cook v. Cook* (1706) 2 Vern 545, 23 ER 952.

16 (1789) 2 Cox 190; 50 ER 88; *Re Manners* [1955] 3 All ER 83.

17 *Weld v. Bradbury* (1715) 2 Vern 705, 23 ER 1058; *Shepherd v. Ingram* (1764) Amb 448, 27 ER 296; Casner (1937) 270 n.31.

An Irish court in *Re Pilkington*[18] found a third and perhaps the most sensible solution. The capital can be withheld until the class can no longer increase, or until an expressly-postponed time of distribution arrives, and in the meantime only the income from their respective shares is paid to those qualified.

12. Class Gift at a Prescribed Age or Other Event

An example would be, in a will:

> *...to the grandchildren of X at 21 in fee simple*[19]

The general rule of construction closes the class when the first grandchild obtains an interest vested in possession, in this case, when it reaches 21.[20] The class would then include, of course, only the grandchild first to become 21. However, it seems unfair to exclude other grandchildren born before the class closes but still under the age specified, and so the courts have modified the general rule to include them as potential members, who will take when and if they reach the specified age.[21] Grandchildren born after the first grandchild becomes 21 are excluded.[22] In policy terms, this compromises the efficient market principle in favour of kinship solidarity. But the maximum size of the class is certain and so an initial distribution can be made to each as they qualify, shares being reserved for those who may do so later. If they die under the age, then their shares can then be distributed among those already qualified, reserving shares for those still under the age. It follows that there are four possible situations. If there is a grandchild or grandchildren of X and they are all of the required age at the date the instrument takes effect, the class closes then.[23] If there is a grandchild or grandchildren when the instrument takes effect, but it or they are under 21, the class closes when the first becomes 21 and will include potential members at that point, including grandchildren born after the instrument took effect but before the time of distribution. If there were no grandchildren at the time the instrument took effect, the class closes when the

---

18 (1892) 29 LR Ir 370; see Morris, (1954) p.64; *Re Manners* [1955] 1 WLR 1096 at p.1101.

19 It is assumed, so that the limitation may be valid for perpetuity, that X is dead at the date the will takes effect.

20 *Gilbert v. Boorman* (1805) 11 Ves Jun 238, 8 RR 137, 32 ER 1079.

21 *Gilmore v. Severn* (1785) 1 Bro CC 582, 28 ER 1310 (bequest of personalty); *Andrews v. Partington* (1791) 2 Cox 223, 30 ER 103, 3 Bro CC 60, 401, 29 ER 408, 610 (bequest of personalty); *Re Knapp's Settlement* [1885] Ch. 91; Casner (1937) at p.287 n 92. *Re Poe* [1942] IR 535.

22 *Crone v. O'Dell* (1811) 1 Ball & B 449; *Ellison v. Airey* (1748) 1 Ves Sen 111, 27 ER 924; *Devisme v. Mello* (1782) 1 Bro CC 537, 28 ER 1285.

23 *Picken v. Mathews* (1878) 10 Ch D 264; Casner (1937) at p.291 n 105. *Re Poe* [1942] IR 535.

first subsequently-born grandchild becomes 21[24] and includes potential members. This last point is not universally acknowledged, as, according to at least one authority, the class remains open.[25] If there are grandchildren when the instrument takes effect and some of them are under 21 while others are over that age, the class closes at once and includes the grandchildren still under age as potential members.

3. Class Gift after a Prior Estate

An example would be, in a will:

> *...to A for life, remainder to the grandchildren of B in fee simple.*

The general rule of construction would close the class when the first grandchild becomes entitled to an interest in possession. In this example, this will happen when the prior estate ends or when the first grandchild of B is born, whichever is the later.[26]

The first possible situation is that, by the time A dies, grandchildren of B have already been born, so that there are class members at the termination of the prior estate. In this case, under the general rule of construction the class closes at this point, the time of distribution. Persons coming into existence afterwards are excluded.[27] Persons born before are included.[28] Suppose that, during A's life, grandchildren of B were born, but that they died before A? Should they be included in the class? Both logic and a policy that favours the unity of kinship groups indicate that they should be. In order to obtain a vested interest, all the grandchildren have to do in this example is to be born and this they have done. Their vested interests survive for the benefit of their estates and fall into possession at A's death. This is the effect of the decision in *Kimberley v. Tew*.[29] Logic here supports policy. In the ordinary course of de

24 *Re Bleckly* [1951] Ch 740 at 749 per Evershed MR Casner (1937) 292 n 107; *Prescott v. Long* (1795) 2 Ves Sen 690, 30 ER 845; *Andrews v. Partington* (1791) 2 Cox 223, 30 ER 103, 3 Bro CC 60, 401, 29 ER 408, 610.

25 *Armitage v. Williams* (1859) 27 Beav 346, 54 ER 135. See the Kentucky rule mentioned by Casner (1937) at p.292 n.107. But also see Casner (1937) at p.293 n.110, 111.

26 *Finch v. Hollingsworth* (1855) 21 Beav 112, 52 ER 801, *Reid v. Swann* [1911] 1 IR 405, 410 and Sherrin (1972) 603, 615; *Re Gun* [1915] 1 IR 42.

27 *Ayton v. Ayton* (1787) 1 Cox Eq 327, 29 ER 1188; *Baldwin v. Rogers* (1853) 3 De G M & G 649, 43 ER 255.

28 *Devisme v. Mello* (1782) 1 Bro CC 537, 28 ER 1285; *Pulsford v. Hunter* (1792) 3 Bro CC 416, 29 ER 618; *Crone v. O'Dell* (1811) 1 B & B 449; *Holland v. Wood* (1871) LR 11 Eq 91; Morris, (1954) at p.67. If the time of distribution is postponed until after the expiration of a period of years the rule is the same, *i.e.* the class closes at the expiration of the period: *McKay v. McKay* [1900] 1 IR 213, *Valentine v. Fitzsimons* [1894] 1 IR 93.

29 (1843) 5 Ir Eq R 389, per Sir Edward Sugden; *Re Dennis' Trusts* (1858) 6 Ir Ch R 422.

volution the property of grandchildren would pass to their own children in the course of time. As to the children of grandchildren who died before A, it would not unfair to deprive them of the prospect of inheriting a share in the property under the present gift merely because they were unfortunate enough to be born of parents who died in A's lifetime.[30] Kinship solidarity prevails here, but not at the expense of the early distribution of property, for the extra members may be included without postponing the time of distribution.[31]

The second situation is that at A's death there are no members of the class in existence – nor are there shares of those who predeceased A. In this case the general rule of construction would close the class when the first grandchild of B is born, for, until then, the time of distribution has not arrived. However, to close the class at that point in this example would leave only one member of the class – the first to be born. Courts have preferred to allow the class to remain open to give effect to the presumed intent of the donor – to benefit a class rather than an arbitrarily chosen individual.[32] Here again, a policy in favour of kinship solidarity is evident. As the maximum membership is unknown, the preferred solution is to distribute all the property to the first to qualify subject to later divesting when later members are born.[33] The alternative would be to postpone distribution to the point when the class could no longer increase which would deprive all members except the last of their property for an indefinite period of time. The preferred solution can then be seen as paying regard to the general principle in that it favours vesting whenever a member obtains an interest in possession.

---

30 See also English case of *Re Chartres* [1927] 1 Ch. 466.

31 In *Northern Bank Ltd v. Allen* unreported, High Court, Gannon J, 18th July 1979, the testator left a fund to his three children for limited estates with power of appointment. It was provided that if the children died without issue and without exercising the power of appointment, which happened, the fund was to go, on the death of his last surviving child without issue, to his brothers and sisters living at the death of the last surviving child and to their respective issue. Issue was held to include descendants of any degree. Only issue living at the death of the last surviving child were entitled to share, so that a descendant who died in the lifetime of the last surviving child was excluded. Nevertheless, in such a case its own children or descendants would, if living, presumably be entitled as coming within the description of issue and so there would be no discrimination between the offspring of descendants of the same degree.

32 *Chapman v. Blissett* (1735) Cas t Talb 145, 25 ER 708; *Wyndham v. Wyndham* (1789) 3 Bro CC 58, 29 ER 407; *Re Chartres* [1927] 1 Ch. 466, 471-472, per Astbury J; *Re Bleckly* [1951] Ch 740, per Evershed MR at 749, per Jenkins L J at 755; contra, *Godfrey v. Davis* (1801) 6 Ves Jun 43, 31 ER 929. Morris, (1954) suggests that in the latter case there perhaps was a contrary intention.

33 *Chapman v. Blissett* (1735) Cas t Talb 145, 25 ER 708; *Wyndham v. Wyndham* (1790) 3 Bro CC 58, 29 ER 407; *Hutchison v. Jones* (1817) 2 Madd 124, 56 ER 281; Casner, (1937) at p.281.

4. Class Gift at a Prescribed Age or Other Event after a Prior Estate

An example would be, in a will:

to A for life, remainder to the grandchildren of B at 21 in fee simple.

In this example[34] the general rule of construction would close the class when the first grandchild of B becomes entitled to an interest in possession. This cannot occur while A is alive, for even if a grandchild of B becomes 21 during A's life, its interest will be vested in interest but not in possession. The class will close when the first of B's grandchildren to become 21 reaches that age, or when the life estate comes to an end, whichever is the later of those two events.[35] In this instance the general principle is applied in all the four possible situations, taking into account potential members when required.

The first situation is where at A's death there is a grandchild or grandchildren and it or they are 21. The time of distribution has arrived and the class closes, excluding later-born grandchildren.[36] The principle in *Kimberley v. Tew*[37] applies here, so that if a grandchild had reached 21 and then died before A, its vested interest would survive for the benefit of its estate, and so the class would close at A's death.

The second situation is where there is no grandchild at all at A's death. The time of distribution has not yet arrived and so the class will remain open until the first grandchild to reach 21 does so. The class closes then, excluding later-born grandchildren, but including any potential members at that point *i.e.* grandchildren under 21 when the first grandchild reaches that age. This may include grandchildren of B born after A's death, and therefore after the time of distribution contemplated by the donor, but before the time of distribution under the rules.[38] As the maximum membership is fixed, an indefeasible distribution can be made to the first grandchild of a proportionate share, and to later members when they qualify. The shares of potential members who die under

34 It is assumed, so that the limitation may be valid for perpetuity, that B is dead at the date the instrument takes effect.

35 *Kevern v. Williams* (1832) 5 Sim 171, 58 ER 301; *Re Canney's Trusts* (1910) 101 LTR (ns) 905; *Re Chartres* [1927] 1 Ch. 466. When the first member reaches the age, that being the later event: *Bartlett v. Hollister* (1757) Amb 334, 27 ER 224; *Re Emmet's Estate* (1880) 13 Ch D 484. *Caldbeck v. Caldbeck* [1911] 1 IR 144.

36 *Murray v. Murray* (1847) 3 ICR 120; *Crone v. O'Dell* (1811) 1 Ball & B 449.

37 (1843) 5 Ir Eq R 389; *Re Chartres* [1927] 1 Ch. 466.

38 This is not to say that the donor's intention is disregarded in this case, but merely that it could not be put into effect in the events that turned out. Theoretically the class could be closed as soon as any grandchild is born, *i.e.* there would only be one member of the class and that one would only be a potential member. This would represent the donor's intent even less than the preferred solution.

21 are distributed among those already qualified.[39]

Thirdly, there may be grandchildren at A's death, but they are all under 21. The time of distribution has therefore not arrived and the class remains open until the first one to attain 21 does so. Grandchildren born after this point are excluded, but potential members are included, and this may also include grandchildren born after A's death but still under 21 when the first grandchild under 21 reaches that age.

Finally, there may be grandchildren of B at A's death, some of whom are 21 and some of whom are still under that age. The modern rule closes the class at A's death as the time of distribution has arrived, and includes potential members then alive. Later-born grandchildren are excluded. As the maximum membership of the class is fixed, an indefeasible distribution can be made in favour of those grandchildren who have reached 21, reserving shares for potential members. They will take them when they qualify, or if they die under 21, their shares will be distributed among the already qualified members.[40]

E. Policy Revisited: The Explanation of The Rules

Casner's view was that the class-closing rules functioned simply to express the unexpressed intentions of the donor:

> "Whether the exclusion of some persons who come within the primary meaning if the class description is sound or not depends on the extent to which this effectuates the probable intention of the average transferor".[41]

Not only did he regard this as the function of the inclusive aspect of the rules, *i.e.* the inclusion of persons within the primary meaning of the gift up to the time of distribution, but also of its exclusionary aspect, the general exclusion of persons within the primary meaning who qualify after the time of distribution:

> "In the formulation of the general rule of construction the courts have decided that the average transferor, familiar with all the problems, would probably intend that when all conditions precedent to the interest of a class member are performed and when all prior interests are ended, the class member should receive a share in possession which is not defeasible by the birth of more class members. This can only be done if all persons who are born after the period of distribution are excluded from any share in the gift".[42]

---

39 It may be noted here that such a situation could only occur in the case of future trusts or interests in wills if B were dead, or incapable of having children (*Exham v. Beamish*) at the date the instrument took effect, for otherwise the gift after the life estate would be void for perpetuity.

40 It may be noted in anticipation of the discussion that follows that this will satisfy the perpetuity rule, as potential members will either qualify, or die and increase the size of existing members shares, within 21 years of the death of A, the point where the class closes.

41 Casner, (1937) p.264.

42 *ibid.* p.263.

Questions which are therefore essentially ones of social policy are represented as questions about the state of mind, indeed of a fictionally contrived state of mind, of the donor. Yet there is another person whose interests the courts mentions. That is a person who has become entitled as a member of a class to a property interest in possession. It is often said that such a person should not have to wait for others to qualify before obtaining their property. A property owner should be free to dispose of their property from the moment they have become entitled to it. It is not necessarily the case that this is the intent of the donor. It is a value on its own account in a society which places a high value on the right to property, particularly private property. One can therefore question whether the only directing policy behind the rules is a search for the donor's intent. Where that is not made clear the illusory search for an unexpressed intention is often a cloak for the pursuit of a social value in favour of those who are entitled to property interests to exercise the full rights of ownership. However, there is a social cost in placing such a high value on private property and that is that kinship solidarity is sacrificed. Where the two policies do not directly conflict then there is no problem, but where the two policies point to different results kinship solidarity may be sacrificed. If we examine the results of the rules applied the four main types of class gift it can be seen that this has in fact happened. The following table shows the results obtained and their effect in terms of policy.

Political Economy of the Class-Closing Rules				
CLASS MEMBER:	1. Beneficiary first entitled.	2. Potential Member.	3. Later-born.	4. Died in Tenant for life's lifetime.
CLAIM:	Vested interest			Vested interest
	Right to deal with property	Kinship Solidarity	Kinship Solidarity	Kinship Solidarity of offspring
POLITICAL ECONOMY:	Kinship negative	Kinship positive	Kinship positive	Kinship positive
	Market positive	Market neutral	Market negative	Market positive
LEGAL RESULT:	Recognised	Recognised	Not recognised	Recognised

1. Claims

At the top, the table shows that the courts tend to treat all other considerations as a part of the search for the donor's intent. In fact there are basically four types of individuals who may be affected by the rules:

(a) the beneficiary who is the first to qualify for an interest in possession;

(b) the potential members of a class, in certain types of gift;

(c) later-born members who are not in existence at the time of distribution; and

(d) where the class gift is preceded by a life estate, members of the class who have qualified but died before the life estate comes to an end.

The claim of the first-qualified beneficiary is based on having a vested interest in property. He or she can claim that they should be assured of their full property rights at this point. The Rule in *Andrews v. Partington*[43] achieves this aim.

The fourth party indicated in the table, the qualified but deceased member, also has a claim, albeit posthumous, of the same type. He or she had a vested interest and so it can be claimed that once vested it should follow the rules as to devolution of property generally, either by will or intestacy, and should be unaffected by the death of the property owner occurring after the point at which the interest vested. The real claim that is present here is therefore not that of the qualified but deceased member, who is dead, but of that members' children, who, if their parent is excluded, will be excluded from benefit by inheritance, while their cousins born of parents who were still alive at the date of distribution will receive their share.

If one looks at the two remaining parties, the potential member and the unborn member, neither can claim a vested right to property. Their claim is based purely on kinship solidarity: that they should not be discriminated against as against other members of the same family as this would be likely to give rise to resentment. In the case of the member unborn at the time of distribution, the claim is of the same type. The expression used by the donor seems to include them, according to the ordinary use of language and so their possible resentment will be directed not against the donor for leaving them out, but against other members of the class.

2. Results

If one turns to considering the results of legal decisions on the position of each party, it can be seen that the conflicts at different points between market efficiency and kinship solidarity are resolved in the following way. The claim of the beneficiary first entitled is market-positive because, if recognised, it would mean that the property is distributed at the earliest possible moment. The prop-

43 (1791) 3 Bro CC 401, 29 ER 408, 610.

erty will therefore enter the market as a commodity at the earliest possible moment. On the other hand, it is kinship-negative. It is inimical to kinship solidarity, because in order to make a distribution it is necessary to fix the maximum number of shares and this can only be done if later-born members of the class, *i.e.* kin members, are excluded. Thus the two policies are directly opposed.

The Rule in *Andrews v. Partington*,[44] chooses in favour of the market at the expense of kinship solidarity. It holds that the time of distribution is the point at which the first beneficiary obtains an interest vested in possession. Where the class gift is of a kind that admits of potential members, their claim to a share on the basis of kinship solidarity is stronger than that of possible later-born members since they are actually in existence at the time of distribution and their feelings of resentment are likely to be real and not merely a contingent possibility. At the same time, their claim is market-neutral in the sense that, even if they are included in the class, a distribution can still be made to those already qualified, since the maximum membership will be known and the shares of the potential members will be held back until they qualify, or distributed among qualified members if they do not.

It can be argued that the inclusion of potential members is not really market-neutral because if they are excluded all the property could be distributed immediately, instead of only part of it, but the result at least in part achieves alienability. Perhaps it is better to see it as a compromise between kinship solidarity, which is fully realised, and a pro-market value which is partly achieved. In the case of the later-born, their inclusion would certainly satisfy the demand for kinship solidarity. But the inclusion of such members would be totally contrary to market alienability since no indefeasible distribution could be made in favour of already-qualified members, since the maximum membership would remain unknown. The alternative is a defeasible distribution but this has all the disadvantages already discussed. The law here chooses to exclude the later-born and so chooses in favour of the market. As to qualified members who have died in the lifetime of a tenant for life, their claim is market-positive because they have already qualified for a vested interest. At the same time, to uphold it would also promote kinship solidarity because it would mean that their own kin would not be excluded from benefit while their cousins, born of parents still alive at end of the life interest, would be included. In this instance, then, both the policy in favour of kinship solidarity and in favour of the market coincide and favour the inclusion of the deceased member. This is in fact the solution adopted by the courts. Nevertheless, there is still an indication here that the market principle is dominant. The kinship solidarity of the offspring is not given consistent recognition by the rules where a member qualifies and dies before the time of distribution, because, in relation to the same limitation,

44 *ibid.*

those born after the time of distribution – the later-born – would still be excluded, raising the possibility not only of their resentment, but also that of their offspring vis-à-vis the offspring of included members. One can therefore come to the following conclusions based on all four of these results in the case law:

a) where recognising the claim would undermine kinship solidarity, but would favour the market, the market prevails;
b) where the kinship value is positive and the effect on the market is neutral, the kinship value is effective;
c) where the kinship value is positive but the market value is negative, the market value prevails; and
d) where the kinship value is positive and the effect on the market is also positive, the claim is recognised, and both are given effect to.

In other words, the market always wins. In a capitalist society this is not in itself a surprising result but it may give the lie to ideological claims that the law is concerned to protect the integrity of the family. In reality it does so only where the efficient operation of the market economy is not impaired.

This is not to say that the results summarised in the table are the only possible solutions to the problem of class gifts on the basis of a capitalist economy. They may, of course, be the only solutions that produce the most efficient working of the market, but that is a different matter. To return to the point at issue, there are obviously competing political ideologies within the society. The view that sees the market model as the only, or the dominant, criterion may be characterised as a conservative model. It is in fact the kind of conservative model associated with the governments of some Western democracies in recent years and variously characterised as Thatcherism or Reaganomics, *etc.* Other models, characterised as liberal or social democratic, would emphasise social responsibility as a dominant aim to which the efficient functioning of the market must take second place. Religious ideology might also favour the solidarity of the family over the efficiency of the market. Indeed, there are versions of conservative opinion which stress the solidarity of the family and which might be prepared to accept a limit on market efficiency in this area as a price to pay to achieve that goal, although they tend to confine family to the nuclear family based upon marriage, a tendency shared by those who advocate a religious approach. One conclusion that may be drawn from the history of case law is, however, that the rules developed by the judges since the end of the 18th century represent a fairly consistent choice in favour of the efficient functioning of the conservative model in preference to others and so also represent, in the broad sense, a political choice in favour of free market values as having a higher priority than kinship solidarity.

F. Class Gifts and the Perpetuity Rule

The perpetuity rule applies to class gifts in a special way. The basic principle is that to be valid for perpetuity it must be certain at the testator's death that all members of the class will take interests within the period. If it is possible for any member to qualify for an interest outside the period, the gift to the whole class fails. The rule can be traced back to the English case of *Leake v. Robinson*.[45] It has been criticised by Leach and others, but has been followed consistently. His criticism will be considered shortly. The principle can also be stated another way, and that is to say that for the purpose of the perpetuity rule a member of a class cannot be said to have a vested interest unless the size of his or her share is ascertainable within the period. It can only be ascertainable if the number of members in the class – not merely the minimum or maximum – will be known within the period. Hence if it is possible for any member to qualify beyond the period then the gift is void and none can take vested interests. Although the principle can be stated in this way, it is artificial to do so. The special definition of vested is simply a consequence of applying to class gifts the no-wait-and-see rule in the common law rule against perpetuities. For example a gift in a will is "to the children of A at the age of 25". A is alive at the testator's death and has no children. It may be that if we could wait and see, all of A's children will become 25 within 21 years of A's death. But the possibility that one may not is enough to defeat the gift. We cannot wait to see if some qualify within the period and confine the class to them.[46] The only point to be made here is that this is logically consistent with the common law rule and is only unreasonable or not to the extent that the common law rule is unreasonable or not.

G. Wills

We have seen that today class gifts in wills are to be treated, for the purpose of determining their validity, as future trusts.[47] One is not therefore concerned with the common law remainder rules, *Purefoy v. Rogers*[48] or the Contingent Remainders Act, 1877. They do have to comply with the rule against perpetuities and in applying it one has to take into account the class-closing rules since they may have the effect of saving a gift that would otherwise be void. One also has to remember that a will today takes effect at the testator's death. One

45 (1817) 2 Mer 363, 35 ER 979; and see Barton Leach, "The Rule Against Perpetuities and Gifts to Classes" (1938) 51 HLR 1338.

46 Note that this is possible now under the Northern Ireland legislation.

47 See Chapter 10 Future Interests; G. C. Cheshire, "The Case of *Re Robson*" (1920) 6 Conv 44.

48 See Chapter 10 Future Interests.

has to remember that the no-wait-and-see rule in the common law perpetuity rule means in this context that an event occurring after the testator's death cannot be taken into account, even if its effect would be to close the class in such a way that, as events turn out, all members do in fact take interests within the period.

1. Simple Class Gift

An example would be:

> *to the grandchildren of X.*

If, at the testator's death, X is dead, then the gift is valid. Even if there are no grandchildren of X at the testator's death, so that the class remains open, X's children are lives in being by implication and all grandchildren must come into existence - and so take vested interests - during their lives (*i.e.* of X's children). The gift is valid without the help of the class-closing rule.

If, at the testator's death, X is alive, then the gift is prima facie too remote because X may have a child after the testator's death who may have a child, a grandchild of X, more than 21 years after the death of any person alive at the testator's death.[49] This result is qualified by the dictum in *Exham v. Beamish*[50] as to the possibility of introducing evidence as to X's ability to have more children. But if there are any grandchildren of X in existence at the testator's death, the class closes then and later grandchildren are excluded. All members of the class take vested interests at once, and the gift is valid.

2. Class Gift at a Prescribed Age or Other Event

An example is

> *to the grandchildren of X at 21...*

If X is dead at the testator's death, then the gift is valid. X's children are lives in being by implication.

If X is alive at the testator's death, then the gift is prima facie too remote because X may have a child after the testator's death who is not therefore a life in being, who may have a child (a grandchild of X) who may become 21 more than 21 years after the death of any person alive at the testator's death. Again this is subject to *Exham v. Beamish*.[51]

If there is a grandchild of X already 21 at the testator's death, the class closes then and excludes later-born grandchildren. Although the class will include, as potential members, grandchildren alive at the testator's death but still

---

49 *Shepherd v. Ingram* (1764) Amb 448, 27 ER 296.

50 [1939] IR 336. The case is discussed in Chapter 11 under the modern rule against perpetuities.

51 *ibid.*

under 21, they are themselves lives in being. Thus they will either become 21 and take vested interests within the period, or die under 21 and increase the size of the shares of those already qualified, still within the period. The gift is valid. In this instance the testator could have specified any age, even one greater than 21, and the gift would be valid - provided a grandchild of that age existed at the testator's death, *vide Picken v. Mathews.*[52]

If there is a grandchild at the testator's death, but who is under 21, this is insufficient to save the gift. It has not yet obtained a vested interest and there is no certainty that it ever will. The class does not therefore close at the testator's death, and would remain open to include later-born grandchildren. X could have a child after the testator's death who could itself have a child (a grandchild of X) who would be a member of the class and become 21 more than 21 years after the death of any person alive at the testator's death. Hence the gift is void.

3. Class Gift after a Life Interest

An example is:

> *to A for life, then to the grandchildren of B in fee simple...*

If B is dead at the testator's death, the gift is valid, because B's children are lives in being by implication. As soon as the grandchildren of B are born they obtain vested interests and they must be born in the lifetime of B's children, their parents.

If B is alive at the testator's death, the gift is prima facie too remote, because B may have a child after the testator's death who is not therefore a life in being, who may have a child (a grandchild of B) more than 21 years after the death of persons alive at the testator's death. Again, this is subject to *Exham v. Beamish*[53] as to medical evidence relating to B.

---

52 (1878) 10 Ch D 264. It is necessary for the grandchild to be of the age specified to save the gift if the maximum size of the class is not fixed. If it is fixed, then even if there are only grandchildren under the age specified, the gift would seem to be valid. For example, there is a gift "to the grandchildren of F at 25..." At the testator's death F is dead and so are F's children. There are two grandchildren of F, G aged 2 and H aged five. The gift is valid as to both. No more grandchildren can come into existence and so both G and H are lives in being and must satisfy the condition within the period. It is true that the class gift is not grandchildren but grandchildren aged 25. Nevertheless, although G and H are not fully-qualified members of the class they are fully-qualified lives in being. The definition of lives in being for the purpose of the perpetuity rule is not the same thing as the definition of a class for the purpose of the class-closing rules. The reason why both G and H can take is that, for the purpose of determining lives in being for the perpetuity rule, they belong to a class, namely "grandchildren," expressly mentioned in the gift and that class is closed so that all members of it are lives in being for the purpose of the rule.

53 [1939] IR 336.

But if there are grandchildren of B alive at the testator's death, the class is bound to close at A's death. Grandchildren of B born after that date will be excluded. The class will therefore include only grandchildren of B born not later than A's death. The gift is therefore valid in this case.

It may be objected that a grandchild of B alive at the testator's death may not survive until A dies, but since in order to obtain a vested interest in this limitation it is only necessary to be born, it has acquired such an interest and this will survive for the benefit of its estate and cause the class to close at A's death, as in *Kimberley v. Tew*.[54] The vested interest must fall into possession at A's death whether the grandchild itself survives to that point or not. The certainty required by the perpetuity rule is satisfied, and the gift is valid.

If there are no grandchildren of B at the testator's death, the class is not certain to close at A's death and the gift is void - because the class may remain open and so could include a grandchild of B born more than 21 years after the death of A. Even if a grandchild of B were born after the testator's death and before that of A, so that the class would otherwise close at A's death, this is not certain to happen at the testator's death and you cannot wait and see.

4. Class Gift at a Prescribed Age or other Event after a Life Estate

An example is a limitation in a will:

to A for life, remainder to the grandchildren of B at 21 in fee simple...

If B is dead at the testator's death, the gift to his grandchildren is valid. This is so even if there is no grandchild aged 21 at the testator's death so that the class remains open at that point. B's children are lives in being by implication. The grandchildren take vested interests when they become 21 which can be no later than 21 years after the death of their own parents, who are lives in being.

If B is alive at the testator's death, the gift is prima facie too remote. B may have another child after the testator's death who is not therefore a life in being and who may itself have a child (a grandchild of B) who may become 21 more than 21 years after the death of any person living at the testator's death. Again, this is subject to *Exham v. Beamish*.[55]

But if there is a grandchild of B aged *21* at the testator's death, the gift is valid. The class is bound to close at A's death and will exclude grandchildren born after that date. Grandchildren alive at that date but under 21 must become 21 not later than 21 years after that date, the death of A, who is a life in being. Even if the grandchild of B aged 21 at the testator's death dies before A, it has obtained a vested share which survives for the benefit of its estate and which will fall into possession at A's death, closing the class, as in *Kimberley v.*

54 (1843) 5 Ir Eq R 389; *Re Chartres* [1927] 1 Ch. 466.

55 [1939] IR 336.

Tew.[56]

If there is a grandchild of B alive at the testator's death but under 21, this is insufficient to save the gift, since it has not yet obtained a vested interest and may die under 21 and so never obtain one. If so, the class will remain open at A's death and could include a grandchild of B born after that time who could therefore become 21 more than 21 years after that point, *i.e.* the death of a life in being, and whose parent would not be a life in being either, because it was a child of B, born after the testator's death. Again, this is subject to *Exham v. Beamish*.[57]

H. Future Trusts

Future trusts *inter vivos* do not present any special problems for the present purpose since the rules applicable to them are the same as those applying to wills. The only additional element from the point of view of the perpetuity rule is that since the donor is still alive, the possibility that he or she may have another child is one which, depending on the nature of the gift, is a circumstance which may render it void. Thus a gift:

to my grandchildren

is valid if contained in a will because the testator's children are lives in being by implication, *i.e.* they are a closed class, so that any grandchildren will take interests, by being born, at some time during the span of lives in being.

If, however, the same gift is contained in an *inter vivos* deed the possibility that the grantor of the deed may have another child is one which may render the gift invalid. We say may here because, as we have seen, the law in Ireland allows evidence of the grantor's ability to have further children to be introduced. There is a presumption, which such evidence may rebut, that a person living at the date the instrument takes effect may have another child. That possibility, if not rebutted, will render the gift void because the grantor's children are not a closed class and so a further possible child may be born after the date of the instrument and the child of such a child, *i.e.* a grandchild of the testator, may be born during its life which is not necessarily within the perpetuity period, since it is not a life in being. This was the situation that arose in the case of *Exham* v *Beamish*,[58] which is discussed above, with the exception that the gift was to grandchildren reaching the age of 21. It will be recalled that a family settlement provided, *inter alia*, for land to be vested in trustees for the lives of the settlors, William Thompson and his wife Anne, and then for the grandchildren of the settlors at the age of 21. In 1865 when the settlement was made the sett-

56 (1843) 5 Ir Eq R 389.

57 [1939] IR 336.

58 *ibid.*

lors had four children Charles, Quintin, Edith and Fanny. If grandchildren were confined to the children of the four existing children of the settlor's, then the trust would not have contravened the perpetuity rule, since all the grandchildren would necessarily have become 21 within the period as their parents were lives in being at the date of the settlement. But since it was an *inter vivos* deed the possibility existed, if the rule in *Jee v. Audley*[59] were applied, that the settlors might have another child, who would not be a life in being, who itself might have a child, a grandchild of the settlors, who might therefore become 21 outside the period.

In this case the class-closing rule would not have saved the gift. If there had been a grandchild of the settlors aged 21 at the date of the settlement, the gift would have been valid, because the class would then have been certain to close at the end of the life estates, and would include grandchildren then alive who would therefore qualify not more than 21 years after that point, *i.e.* within the period. But there was no such grandchild. The only way the gift to the grandchildren could be saved was by deciding that the settlors could not have had more grandchildren in 1865. Gavan Duffy J, it will be recalled, refused to apply the English rule in *Jee v. Audley*[60], holding instead that there was a presumption in favour of a person living at a given date being able to have further children, but that this could rebutted by evidence that on available scientific evidence it would be absurd to presume so.[61]

59 (1787) 1 Cox Eq Cas 324, 29 ER 1186.

60 *ibid.*.

61 [1939] IR 336, at p.350.

CHAPTER 13

POWERS

A power is an authority given to a person so that the person concerned may determine the legal relations affecting him or herself, or between him or herself and other persons, or between other persons.[1] Thus, A may be given by a will the power to appoint the testator's property among a class of persons at A's discretion and the class may or may not include A herself.

A. Classification

Powers may be classified in a number of different ways. Legal results will follow from a power being classified in one way rather than another.

1. Collateral, In Gross and Appurtenant

Powers simply collateral are those where the donee of the power is not given any estate or interest in the property. Powers simply collateral could not be released at common law.[2] Section 52 of the Conveyancing Act, 1881 now allows them to be. Powers in gross are those in which the donee does have an interest in the property but the exercise of the power cannot affect that interest, as in the following limitation in a will:

> *to A for life and after his death to his children for such interests as he may appoint.*

Powers appurtenant, or appendant are those in which the donee has an interest and which can be affected by the exercise of the power, as in this limitation in a will:

> *to X to appoint by deed or will to her children.*

---

1 See also Cheshire, *Real Property* (13th ed.) p.267: ". . . a power may be defined as an authority given by one person called the donor to another person called the donee entitling the latter to deal with or dispose of realty or personalty, either absolutely or partially and either for his own benefit or for the benefit of others, and whether or not he is already beneficially interested in the subject-matter before he exercises the authority".

2 *Re Dunne's Trusts* (1878) 1 LR Ir 516, MR. See below.

2. Common Law and Equitable Powers

Even before the Statute of Wills (Ireland), 1634 gave power generally to leave land by will, the common law recognised that land held in burgage tenure could be devised. Customs also existed in certain boroughs allowing land within the borough to be devised. In such cases the common law also recognised that a testator could give power to the executors to sell the land even though the testator had not devised it to them. Such powers today take effect subject to any specific devise in the will. The common law recognised powers of sale and powers of attorney but not powers of appointment. Such powers were developed by equity and can now exist as legal powers as a result of the Statute of Uses, 1634.

3. General and Special Powers

These are different types of powers of appointment and so are discussed below in the section dealing with such powers.

B. Powers of Sale

A testator may give executors a power to sell his or her land after the testator's death. The executors in such a case have power to vest the freehold estate in a purchaser although they do not have the estate themselves. In the past real property would pass automatically to the heir-at-law on the death of a testator. Until exercise of the power the estate remained vested in the heir.[3] Statutory powers of sale have been a part of the reform of property law, particularly in order to make land more freely available for sale on the market. Examples are the power of a tenant for life to sell the fee simple under the Settled Land Acts and the power of a tenant in tail to disentail under the Fines and Recoveries (Ireland) Act, 1834, which includes a power to convey a fee simple to a purchaser or to feoffees to his or her own use.

C. Powers of Appointment

1. History

Equity recognised powers of appointment since before the Statute of Uses, 1634. Such powers could only affect the equitable interests in land. After the Statute of Uses, 1634 powers of appointment created by a use executed by the Statute are legal powers affecting the legal estate. For example:

3 Megarry & Wade, *Real Property* pp. 461–2.

> *to X and his heirs to the use of A for life, remainder to such uses as A shall appoint, and in default of and until appointment, to the use of the children of A in fee simple in equal shares.*

The use is executed. A has a legal life estate, and there is a vested legal estate in the children of A, who are expressly entitled in default of appointment, subject to being divested[4] by a proper exercise by A of her power. Equitable powers can still be created by a use not executed by the Statute:

> *unto and to the use of T and his heirs in trust for A for life, remainder as A shall by will [or 'by deed' or 'by deed or will'] appoint.*

A can dispose of the equitable fee simple in remainder.

2. General and Special Powers

Powers of appointment may be general or special.

a) General Powers

Where the donee, *i.e.* the person to whom the power is given, can confer interests in property to which the power relates on anyone including himself or herself the power is a general power.[5] In the limitation:

> *to A and his heirs to such uses as B may by deed or will appoint and in default of and until appointment to the use of C and his heirs*

B has a power. B is not required to appoint among a specified class and so may appoint to himself, *i.e.* it is a general power. C takes a vested estate subject to divesting by B. Clearly, a general power is akin to ownership of the fee simple. Hence, general powers form part of a deceased's estate at his or her death vesting in the personal representative of the deceased when the power was exercised by will.[6]

b) Special Powers

If the donee of the power may not appoint to himself or herself then the power is special. Such a donee will have a power to appoint among a class of persons, the objects of the power, or to one person. The essential difference between special and general powers is that the donee of a general power may appoint to himself or herself, for it is this feature that makes a general power akin to ownership in fee simple. It follows that a power to appoint to anyone in the world except oneself is a special power. If the donee of a general power exercises it in favour of X, then it is a gift from the donee to X, for the donee has given away

4 *Re Earl of Kingston's Estate* (1880) 5 LR Ir 169.

5 Sugden, *Powers* p.104. *Bishop of Oxford v. Leighton* (1700) 2 Vern 376, 23 ER 837.

6 Section 10(4) of the Succession Act 1965; It is also therefore available for a claim under s.117 of the Succession Act, 1965: *Reidy v. McGreevy* unreported, High Court, Barron J, 19 March 1993.

his or her own property, whereas if the donee of a special power exercises it in favour of X, it is a gift from the donor of the power.

3. Creation

For a power to be valid a test of certainty must be satisfied. There must be criteria in the grant which are sufficiently clear so that it can be said in relation to any claimant that they come within the power or not. It is not required, however, that a complete list of all the objects be capable of being drawn up.[7] In *In the Estate of Bayley*[8] the Supreme Court held that the phrase my Irish relatives satisfied the test.

4. Entitlement in Default

If there is no express gift in default of appointment the objects of the power are impliedly entitled.[9] Moreover, equality is equity and they are entitled equally.[10] If the power is to appoint the whole interest of the estate subject to the power, then the gift in default, whether express or implied, cannot be less than that which might have been appointed by the exercise of the power.[11]

5. Exercise

Consider again the example given previously:

> *to A and his heirs to such uses as B may by deed or will appoint and in default and until appointment to the use of C and his heirs.*

Suppose that B exercises the power by deed. If B appoints the land:

> *to the use of D and her heirs*

B has created a simple use which is therefore executed by the Statute of Uses. The exercise of the power is read with the original limitation, so that it is as if that limitation had been:

> *to A and his heirs to the use of D and her heirs.*

D has a vested legal estate in fee simple. A, as a mere feoffee, takes no interest. C's estate comes to an end: it is divested by the exercise of the power. On the other hand, if B appointed:

> *to D and her heirs to the use of E and his heirs*

---

7 *Brown v. Gregg* [1945] IR 224; *Re Parker's Will* [1966] IR 309.

8 [1945] IR 224.

9 *Sinnott v. Walsh* (1880) 5 LR Ir 27, App. And see *Mill v. Mill* (1877) IR 11 Eq 158.

10 *Doyley v. Attorney General* 4 Vin Abr 485 pl 16, 2 Eq Cas Abr 194, 22 ER 167; *Sinnott v. Walsh* (1880) 5 LR Ir 27, App.

11 *Crozier v. Crozier* (1843) 3 Dru & War 353, 373, 5 Ir Eq R 415, 540, 61 RR 65, 77.

B has created a use upon a use. It is as if the original limitation had read:

to A and his heirs to the use of D and her heirs to the use of E and his heirs.

The first use is executed as before, but the second use, *i.e.* the use upon a use, is not executed by the Statute of Uses. D takes the legal estate and E has an equitable estate. D is a trustee and E the beneficiary under the trust.

a) Formalities: Defective Execution

Such formalities as are required by the donor[12] and general law must be complied with. If the donee fails to do so the exercise of the power is said to be defective. By section 12 of the Law of Property Amendment Act, 1859 a non-testamentary power must be executed in the presence of and attested by two or more witnesses. Testamentary powers must comply with the formalities for wills. The Leases Acts, 1849 and 1850 validate leases in Ireland which, when they were made, exceeded the terms of the powers under which they were made.[13]

b) Excessive Execution

An excessive execution of a power is one which exceeds the terms of the power of appointment, as where a donee attempts to appoint to person who are not objects of the power. Excessive executions may not be wholly void. Where possible courts try to save the valid part and discard the invalid. Where the donee exercises the power in favour of some objects and some non-objects, the courts will uphold the exercise of the power as to the objects.[14]

c) Illusory Appointments

Equity made a distinction between what it termed exclusive powers, in which the intention of the donor was that some of the objects might not take anything at all, and non-exclusive powers, where the intention was that each object should obtain something. In the latter case, if the donee appointed a purely token amount to one or more objects, the courts of equity set it aside as an illusory appointment, *i.e.* an appointment creating the illusion that the power had been complied with, while in substance it had not.[15] The doctrine proved difficult to apply in practice and led to the passing of the Illusory Appointments Act, 1830[16] which provided that the appointment of a nominal amount was not

---

12 *Reid v. Thompson* (1854) 2 Ir Ch R 26 (settlement required exercise to be in writing, sealed and delivered in the presence of two witnesses).

13 Wylie, *Irish Land Law* para. 11.17.

14 *Crozier v. Crozier* (1843) 3 Dru & War 373, 5 Ir Eq R 540, 61 RR 65, 77; *Re Shekleton's Trusts* [1945] IR 115.

15 *Gibson v. Kinven* (1682) 1 Vern 66, 23 ER 315 per Lord Nottingham.

16 It applied to Ireland and England.

to be invalid unless the terms of the power expressly provided otherwise. Then the Powers of Appointment Act, 1874 provided that every power of appointment is to be construed as an exclusive power so that the donee may make no appointment at all to one or more objects, unless the terms of the power expressly provides otherwise. Farwell, the author of *A Concise Treatise on Powers*, commented that "The Act of 1830 enabled an appointor to cut off any object of the power with a shilling: the Act of 1874 enables him to cut off the shilling also".[17]

d) Fraud on a Power

The doctrine applies to special powers only. The basic principle is that persons entitled in default of an appointment have vested interests until the exercise of the power divests them of those interests. An appointment for improper motives is therefore a fraud on those entitled in default of appointment.[18]

(i) Prior Agreement

Unless the donee is a person entitled in default of appointment, the appointment is fraudulent if it is made under an agreement between the donee and the appointee whereby a person other than an object of the power (such as the donee) is to benefit.[19]

(ii) Intention Only

Even if there is no agreement, if the predominant intention is that a non-object (who is not entitled in default either) is to benefit, then there is a fraud.

(iii) Benefit to Appointer

An appointment to the benefit of the donee (*i.e.* the appointer) is fraudulent, unless the donee is entitled in default.[20]

Thus in *Duggan v. Duggan*[21] the tenant for life, a mother, had power to appoint to her children. She had incurred debts although for the benefit of the family and for the upkeep of the farm which was the family home. She appointed the fund to the children on condition that they bought her life estate and paid the price out of the appointed fund. The Irish Court of Appeal held that the appointment was a fraud on the persons entitled in default. The primary purpose and only certain effect was to confer a personal benefit on the

17 Farwell, *Powers* (2nd ed.) p.374, (3rd ed.) p.427 cited in Snell, *Equity* (28th ed.) p.553 n.1.

18 *Heron v. Stokes* (1842) 4 Ir Eq R 285.

19 *Hutchins v. Hutchins* (1877) IR 10 Eq 453.

20 *ibid.*.

21 (1880) 7 LR Ir 152, Lord O'Hagan, LC.

mother by discharging her debts. Retention of the farm might benefit the children also, but that was not the immediate purpose.

In *Kiely v. Kiely*[22] the owner of the power exercised it in favour of his own child who was dying of tuberculosis, so that the parent would inherit the property. The court set aside the appointment.

(iv) Acquiescence

If all the objects of the power agree or confirm the exercise of the power then they cannot later challenge it on the ground of fraud unless there is undue influence.[23]

(v) Release

The doctrine of fraud on a power does not apply to the release of a power by the donee, *i.e.* a deed by which the donee relinquishes the power. A release of the power benefits the persons entitled in default and so cannot be a fraud. It is a not a fraud on the objects of the power because the donee owes no duty to them to exercise it. A power is unlike a trust in this respect.

(vi) Revocation

The doctrine of fraud on a power does not apply to a revocation of an appointment by the donee. The donee has no duty to the appointees deprived by the revocation. The donee is free to make another appointment.

(vii) The Effect of Fraud

The fraud affects the whole appointment. Nevertheless, the donee is free to make a new appointment. The fraud does not disqualify the donee from making further appointments[24] but the burden of proof shifts to those asserting the validity of the new appointment to show that it is proper.[25] Fraud has a different effect at common law and in equity. At common law a fraudulent appointment of a legal interest is only voidable by the aggrieved party, and so is valid until avoided. A fraudulent appointment of equitable interests is void *ab initio*.[26]

A bona fide purchaser (from an appointee) for value of the legal estate without notice of the fraud takes free of it and obtains a good title.[27] Notice in

22 (1843) 5 Ir Eq R 442.

23 *Skelton v. Flanagan* (1867) IR 1 Eq 362 at p.369. Presumably persons entitled in default are in the same position.

24 *Hutchins v. Hutchins* (1877) IR 10 Eq 453.

25 *ibid.*

26 *Cloutte v. Storey* [1911] 1 Ch 18.

27 *Hamilton v. Kirwan* (1845) 2 J & L 393, 8 Ir Eq R 278, 69 RR 322; *McQueen v. Farquhar* (1805) 11 Ves 467, 32 ER 1168; Farwell, *Powers* p.429.

this instance must be actual, not constructive, if it is to affect the purchaser.[28] Equity recognises that a legal estate obtained for value prevails where there are two innocent parties. A bona fide purchaser (from the appointee) for value of an equitable interest without notice of the fraud still obtains no title. Where the equities are equal, the first in time prevails. However, if there is anything in the conduct of those defrauded to alter the "balance" of equity, the scales will tip towards the later equity.

D. Powers of Appointment and the Rule Against Perpetuities

The rule against perpetuities applies in a special way to powers of appointment. A distinction must be made between the power itself and an appointment made under the power.

1. General Powers

In the case of general powers, since the donee can appoint in his or her own favour he or she is virtually in the position of an owner of the property which is the subject of the power. If the power is vested in the donee it is as if the property itself is vested in the donee, and in such a case there is no perpetuity. The property is not fettered by an outstanding contingent interest, even though the power in theory remains unexercised. It may be objected that the donee of the power may not in fact exercise it in favour of himself and exercise it instead in favour of the third party, but then it is as if an owner of the property had decided to make a gift of it to another person. Such a possibility exists in relation to any property, but that does not restrict the owner's control over it - it is merely an example of the owner's control.

The rule at common law then is that the rule against perpetuities only applies to general powers of appointment if the power itself is not vested in the donee, *i.e.* only if the power is contingent.[29] If a contingent power is defined in such a way that it may not vest in the donee until after the perpetuity period, it is void *ab initio*.

As far as appointments are concerned, it does not have to be certain that an appointment must be made within the period. This follows from what has already been said. The only requirement is that if the appointment itself creates a contingent interest in the property, the contingent interest must be certain to vest within the period, the period being measured from the date of the appointment creating the interest. In other words, an appointment will be valid unless a contingent interest created by it may vest in the object beyond the period. The

28 *McQueen v. Farquhar* (1805) 11 Ves 467, 32 ER 1168; *Skelton v. Flanagan* (1867) IR 1 Eq 362; Farwell, *Powers* p.429.

29 *Stuart v. Babington* (1891) 27 LR Ir 551, V-C.

rule against perpetuities applies here in the same way as to a direct gift by the owner of property.

2. Special Powers

In the case of special powers of appointment, since the donee cannot appoint in his or her own favour, the situation is not analogous to a fee simple vested in an owner. While the power remains unexercised the fee simple is not vested in a person with power to alienate it. The persons entitled in default of appointment have vested interests, but they are liable to be divested if the power is exercised. For this reason the rule against perpetuities applies both to the power itself and to any appointment made under it.

a) The Power Itself

As to the power itself, it will be void under the rule if it is so phrased that an appointment may be made under it outside the period, which is calculated from the date of the instrument creating the power.

It follows from this that, insofar as the power itself is concerned, not only must the donee be ascertained within the period, but it must also be certain that the donee will exercise the power within the period. However, the fact that an appointment could be made within the period but could be invalid because it could create contingent interests which could vest beyond the period does not invalidate the power itself.

b) Appointments Under the Power

In so far as the appointment is concerned, it is also subject to the rule and for this purpose also the period is calculated not from the date of the appointment but from the date of the instrument creating the power. This in itself involves an element of wait-and-see, because, as we have already seen, the fact that an appointment could possibly be made within the period but creating interests that might not vest within the period, does not invalidate the power and therefore it does not invalidate any appointment under it. Provided the power itself is valid, one can wait to see what appointment is actually made before judging its validity. Since the perpetuity period is calculated from the date of the instrument creating the power, lives in being are determined at this point.

Thus, in *D'Abbadie v. Bezoin*[30] A had a power under the will of B to appoint lands to such children as she might have. She appointed the lands by her will to her eldest son for life, remainder on his death to his eldest son, living at his death, in fee simple. The limitation following the life estate was held void for remoteness. A's eldest son was not a life in being at the time B's will came into effect.

---

30 (1870) IR 5 Eq 205.

In *Re Hancock's Trusts*[31] a marriage settlement gave land to H for life, then after his death to such of the issue of the marriage as H might by deed or will appoint and in default to the issue equally. H appointed by will to his six children living at the date of the will and to the survivor of them, and on the death of the survivor, to such of his grandchildren as being males attained 21 years, or being female attained 21 years or married under that age. The Court of Appeal held the appointment by will to be void for remoteness. The appointment would have been valid if one could treat their parents, the testator's children, as lives in being, and if the relevant point for determining this were the testator's death, one could do so as testator's children are a closed class. However, the point at which to apply the rule was the date of the instrument creating the power, and that point was the date of the marriage settlement.

Although lives in being are determined at this point, case law made a concession, somewhat inconsistently, as to other facts relevant to the issue of validity. Such facts are not restricted to those known at the date of the instrument creating the power. Facts known at the date of the appointment itself can be taken into account. The reason given for this is that since the period is to be calculated from the date of the instrument creating the power this means that the appointment is read as if it had been made at the date the power was created.[32] In view of this it would also seem consistent to allow a fiction whereby the facts existing at the date of the exercise of the power were read as if they existed at the date of the creation of the power. For example the following disposition is made in 1950:

> *to A for life, remainder to such of her children as he shall appoint.*

The power itself is valid. Since A is given a life estate she must exercise the power, if at all, within her own life and she is a life in being. In 1960 A exercises the power in favour of her son, S provided he reaches 25. S is not yet 25. If S was unborn in 1950 at the date of the power then a strict application of the rule would make the appointment void since a gift to an unborn son at the age of 25 would not be certain to vest within 21 years of A's death. But if S is already at least 5 years old in 1960 then he is bound to reach 25, if he does so at all, within 21 years of A's death. The appointment can be read as if we knew in 1950 that this would occur, and so the appointment is valid. This seems to be an example of judges allowing a partial exception to the no wait-and-see principle to avoid the harshness of the common law rule against perpetuities.

---

31 (1889) 23 LR Ir 34, V-C, 42, CA.

32 *Long v. Blackhall* (1797) 7 TR 100 at 102, 101 ER 875; *Crompe v. Barrow* (1799) 4 Ves Jun 681, 31 ER 351; *Williamson v. Farwell* (1887) 35 Ch D 133.

CHAPTER 14

SETTLEMENTS OF LAND

"What between the duties expected of one during one's lifetime and the duties exacted from one after one's death, land has ceased to be either a profit or a pleasure. It gives one position and prevents one keeping it up. That is all that can be said about land."

– Oscar Wilde, *The Importance of Being Ernest* Act 2, Lady Bracknell.

A. History

The rise of settlements of land reflected the wish of landowners to keep their landed estates within their own[1] families for generation after generation. However, the history of settled land can only be understood if one also recognises that at the same time and running parallel with this concern was a contrary policy, sometimes expressed judicially and sometimes by the legislature, which reflected the existence of a market in land for production, a policy which sought to prevent land being removed from the market for an indefinite period.

At the earliest period of the common law, before the statute *Quia Emptores*, 1290, settlements played little part. Although the extent to which, during this period, land held in fee simple could be sold without the lord's consent is a matter of controversy, it seems that this was a factor militating against such land passing out of the families of freeholders. At the higher levels, the existence of strong local feudal dynasties and the weakness of the market economy meant the relative stability of land ownership within feudal families. Nevertheless, even in the early period the development of a money economy and trade tended to undermine the feudal structure in ways that have been discussed earlier. The fee simple, especially after *Quia Emptores*, 1290 allowed alienation without the lord's consent, was becoming a less secure form in which to express retention of land in the family. The passing of the statute *De Donis* marked a victory for the feudal lords in that it established the fee tail as an inalienable estate and so was apt to express the interest of landowners in retaining land in their family and keeping it from the market. In the succeeding centuries, however, the rise of capitalism saw the emergence of financial and commercial classes who possessed money and often wished to buy landed estates. This may be partly explained by cultural factors such as the wish of the

1 *Re Tuthill* [1907] 1 IR 305 per Meredith J.

newly-rich to acquire the superior social status still paradoxically accorded to the declining landowning classes. But there were also economic factors. Capital operating in the sphere of circulation of commodities, merchant capital, was now beginning to enter the process of production itself, and this included the sphere of agricultural production. Thus the retention of land within landowning families was not necessarily in conflict with the expansion of capitalism. The acquisition of landed estates by former merchants and financiers was part of the process by which this expansion came about.[2]

The increasing social influence of the commercial and financial classes had its effect on the legal system and produced as a result, at an early period, the development of fines and recoveries as a means whereby the previously inalienable entail could be barred to produce a fee simple, thus transforming the landed estates into commodities available to be sold to those with the money to buy them. But these landed estates also represented new forms of capital investment. These had to be carefully nurtured if they were to expand and grow. They could not be left to survive by themselves in the harsh winds of a totally free market. In this essentially privately-owned form of capital, spendthrift and improvident heirs might attempt to break the settlement and dispose of the land or use it as security to borrow money from moneylenders. Thus a degree of protectionism should exist, protecting the new investment from the free play of the market. At the same time, a contradictory requirement was that land should not be removed form the market altogether or the process could not continue. The task for the legal system was to find a new resolution of these conflicting social forces. The compromise between the need to provide a legal means of retaining estates within families and the need to ensure that land would still be a commodity on the market was found in the settlement and the rule against perpetuities which lay at its heart.

B. Development of Methods of Settlement

An early method of settling land[3] was for a landowner to make the following disposition when his son married:

> *to [the settlor] for life, remainder to [his son] in tail.*

This was not very effective. When the father died the son could bar the entail and obtain the fee simple. An alternative was to make a grant on the son's marriage:

> *to [the settlor] for life, remainder to [his son] for life, remainder to [his son's eldest son – unborn] in tail.*

---

2 See M.R. Chesterman, "Family Settlements on Trust: Landowners and the Rising Bourgeoisie" in G.R. Rubin and D. Sugarman eds, *Law Economy & Society*.

3 See Pollock, *The Land Laws*.

This involved a new kind of interest, the contingent remainder, and of course the device only became possible when the courts recognised such an interest. Even after contingent remainders came to be recognised they had a more precarious existence than vested estates. After the settlor died the son, because he then had seisin, could execute a feoffment in fee simple. This feudal conveyance was accorded an almost mystical power by the common law. The son, in executing the conveyance, was committing a wrong, a tort on the remaindermen and the reversioner, but despite that a feoffment in fee simple passed the fee simple to the purchaser, or to the son if he used the device of a conveyance to a feoffee to his own use. This could be challenged, but in the case of the contingent interest there was no one to challenge it. The contingent remainder was destroyed. Thus, if the father died before the son himself had a son, the settlement was vulnerable.

Other attempted methods of settlement which would have created a perpetual series of estates and which would have removed the land permanently from the market were struck down by the courts: successive life estates to the son, an unborn grandson, and then to the unborn great-grandson fell foul of what has become known as the Rule in *Whitby v. Mitchell*, which had its origin in *Chudleigh's Case*.[4] The Statute of Uses, 1634 provided the opportunity of creating more flexible settlements by employing legal executory interests and legal powers of appointment created by executed uses.

The weakness of the settlement still lay in the destructibility of contingent remainders. In the 17th century conveyancers[5] invented the device known as trustees to preserve contingent remainders. The settlement would be in the following form:

> *to [the settlor] for life, remainder to A [his son] for life, remainder, if A's life estate is destroyed, to X & Y for the life of A on trust to preserve contingent remainders, remainder to A's eldest son in tail. . .[etc.].*

It was thought that, if the son's life estate were destroyed, the land would pass to the trustees for the rest of A's life and so the contingent remainder to A's eldest son would be preserved. But doubts remained as to whether the device was effective. It could plausibly be argued that the remainder to the trustees was itself only contingent, *i.e.* on A destroying his life estate, and so could also be destroyed by a tortious conveyance.

The courts came to the rescue in *Duncomb v. Duncomb*[6] and held, by ignoring the older definition of the word, the remainder to the trustees to be vested.

4 (1595) 1 Co Rep 113b, 138, 76 ER 261, 270.

5 The invention of the device is variously attributed to Sir Orlando Bridgman or to Sir Jeffrey Palmer.

6 (1695) 3 Lev 437, 83 ER 770. It was not finally settled until *Smith d Dormer v. Packhurst* (1740) 3 Atk 135, 26 ER 881, and see Lord Hardwicke in *Garth v. Cotton* (1753) 1 Ves Sen 546, 3 Atk 751, 27 ER 1182. *Lemon v. Mark* [1899] 1 IR 445.

The final development was the passing of the Real Property Act, 1845 which, by section 8, provided that if a prior estate was destroyed by surrender, forfeiture or merger that would not prevent the contingent remainder taking effect. It was now legally possible to remove land from the market until the point in time when the father was dead, the son had died and the grandson had attained his majority, since the grandson on coming of age could bar the entail, provided his father were dead, and produce a fee simple. Barring the entail in this way destroyed all subsequent remainders and the reversion.[7]

C. Pin Money, Jointures & Portions

It was usual for settlements to make provision for various payments to members of the family charged on the land. An annual sum would be provided for the wife of the settlor or tenant for life during their joint lives as pin money to provide the wife with an independent income for her expenses. After the tenant for life's death the settlement would also provide for the widow or widows by periodic payments, called jointures, also secured by rentcharges. The younger members of the family would be provided for by lump sums, called portions. Since these were not annual sums they could not be secured by rentcharges. Instead, the settlement created long terms of years, typically 1,000 years, vested in trustees. The trustees could raise the lump sums by sale[8] or mortgage[9] of the terms, which, since they were granted without impeachment of waste and without rent, were attractive. When the money was paid the term of years became a satisfied term under the Satisfied Terms Act, 1845[10] and ceased automatically. This statute was passed to overcome problems[11] which had previously existed as to when such terms came to an end. A more modern and less cumbersome device was to create a trust to raise the portions by creating a legal mortgage if required.

D. Resettlement

Although the maximum period for which land could be removed from the market was that stated above, there were economic factors which meant that land was often removed for generations. In the example above, when the grandson

7 See Chapter 8 Fee Tail.

8 Sale of a lease of the whole land would, of course, deprive the tenant for life of possession and so this was usually used as a last resort, or a lease of part of the estate was sold.

9 *Kelly v. Lord Bellew* (1707) 4 Bro PC 495, 2 ER 338; *Townend v. O'Callaghan* (1856) 4 Ir Ch R 511.

10 8 & 9 Vict. c.112. In England the Act was replaced by s.5 of the Law of Property Act, 1925.

11 These are now of historical interest only.

came of age he might well wish to have a sizeable income. In return for an annuity charged on the land his father might induce him to join with him in barring the entail so as to produce a fee simple and then to execute a new settlement under which he and his father would take life estates with a contingent entail to the grandson's unborn son. The land was thus tied up for another generation.

E. The Problem with Settlements

The existence of legal settlements and the method of resettlement in particular meant that landed estates were unable to respond to economic and social change. The Napoleonic wars were followed by agricultural depression and this was particularly acute in Ireland. The legal restrictions gave rise to three particular problems.

1. Alienability

The process of settlement and resettlement meant that the person entitled in possession to the land normally only had a life estate. He or she could not sell the fee simple. The most the life tenant could do was to sell the life estate, but an estate pur autre vie was not attractive to buyers. The life tenant's ability to create leases that would survive his or her death was limited.[12]

2. Management

The management of the estate was hampered by the difficulty of raising money. The life tenant could only mortgage his own life estate which again was not worth as much for security as the fee simple. Furthermore, unless he was made unimpeachable of waste by the settlement, the tenant for life was impeachable for voluntary waste and so could not cut timber or open mines. In other words the legal settlement prevented new capitalist forms of investment in the settled land.

3. Indebtedness

The existence of portions and jointures often meant that the estate was already burdened with debts and even these had not been incurred from productive investment in improving the economic efficiency of the land, but simply to provide an income to individuals. The capitalist system, however, provided a way of providing such an income through stocks and shares which did not hamper agricultural development. Some settlements gave the tenant for life power to appoint or sell the fee simple during his life, and if he did so the other interests

12 See Smythe, *Landlord & Tenant*.

under the settlement were to be overreached, *i.e.* they would become corresponding interests in the purchase money raised by sale of the land and would no longer affect the title. The tenant for life was normally also given power to create leases which would be effective even if he should die during their term. Twenty-one years was a usual period for agricultural leases and 90 years for building leases. But not all settlements were so drafted as settlors and their lawyers were often cautious about giving powers to the tenant for life which he might use to dissipate the estate.

Where such problems had led to impoverished and run down estates, the only solution at first was to procure a private act of parliament, which was an expensive procedure. The long term solution was for parliament to intervene by giving all tenants for life greater control over the estate. Because the problem was particularly acute in Ireland the earliest legislation was applied here, starting with the Mining Leases Act, 1723.[13]

With the coming of the Industrial Revolution the pressure for capital to expand into agriculture increased and also the need to acquire land for industrial purposes. Moreover, the new industrial capitalists now had increasing political power whereby to influence the making of laws. The Incumbered Estates Acts of 1848 and 1849 allowed settled land to be sold by a special court set up by the acts, the Incumbered Estates Court. The instrument of sale was executed by the court.

The next stage in the development of the legislation was to allow the tenant for life to sell the land with the consent of the court and this was done by the Settled Estates Acts, 1856 and 1876, replaced by a single act in 1877. Other transactions normally required the consent of the other persons entitled under the settlement – the remaindermen or reversioner. This proved to be the weakness of the Act. The other persons entitled to the settled land often wanted to retain it in the family even if the estate and the farms on the estate would be more efficiently run by a buyer with capital to develop them.

The final stage was to give the tenant for life full powers of dealing with the land without the consent of the court or of the other persons entitled under the settlement. This was achieved by the Settled Land Acts, 1882–1890. These acts did not, however, repeal the Settled Estates Act, 1877 which remains in force in Ireland. The 1877 Act does contain one power not found in the Settled Land Acts. By section 16 of the Settled Estates Act, 1877 the court is given power to order sale of the settled land even if none of the parties to the settlement, including the tenant for life, wish to do so.[14]

13 10 Geo I c.5.

14 The same Act and the same power was held to survive in Nigeria: *Taylor v. Kingsway Stores* [1962] 2 All NLR 154.

F. Settled Land and Shelley's Case

A badly drafted settlement can fall foul of the Rule in *Shelley's Case* and fail to create successive interests. In *Finch v. Foley*[15] there was a devise

> *to A and his first and other sons successively in remainder one after another according to their respective seniorities in tail male.*

It was held that *Shelley's Case* applied, so that A received a fee tail male. The limitation was no more than a description of the class of heirs who would take if A had a fee tail male.[16] Under the rule then applicable, since it was in a will and the word heirs plus words of procreation had not been used, the question was whether the expression used was intended to bear a similar meaning to heirs, in which case *Shelley* would apply, or whether the expression was intended to identify individuals, in which case they would take by purchase.

On the other hand, in *Mandeville v. Lord Carrick*[17] the limitation was:

> *to EM for life, remainder to his lawful issue male and lawful male heirs of such heirs, the eldest always of such sons of EM to be preferred to the youngest according to their seniority in age.*

It was held that EM took only a life estate, with remainders to the first and other sons successively in tail male. *Shelley's Case* did not apply. The court here took the view, on the basis of the old rule, that the testator intended to identify individuals, although there seems little difference between this limitation and the one in *Finch*. It may be that courts in the 18th century were more apt to find the existence of a settlement than is the case today.

If the courts today were to consider the same limitation as in *Finch* they would be unlikely to come to reach the same result. Under section 95 of the Succession Act, 1965 a fee tail can only be created in a will after the Act by the use of the same words of limitation as are required in a deed *inter vivos*. The words "first and other sons" clearly cannot function as words of limitation. Moreover, the phrase "in tail male" would probably be taken to be "superadded words" of limitation which on some authority excludes *Shelley's Case*.[18]

G. The Settled Land Acts, 1882–1890

The basic principle behind the Settled Land Acts is to vest in the person whose interest under the settlement is in possession full powers to deal with the land including the right to convey the fee simple, even though, in the latter case, the

15 [1949] Ir Jur Rep 30.

16 Since descent in a fee tail is traced from the original donee.

17 (1795) 3 Ridg PC 352, Ir HL.

18 See Chapter 6 Fee Simple.

fee simple is not vested in that person. Where the settlement is created by legal remainders or legal executory interests the fee simple is divided up into the various successive interests. Where it is created by a trust, it will be vested in the trustees. Having given such extensive powers to someone who normally has only a life estate, the rest of the Acts are concerned mainly to protect the interests of the other persons entitled under the settlement.

There are basically four problems inherent in such a statutory scheme with which the acts attempt to deal:

1. the limited owner to whom the powers are given may abuse them. Since he or she is not entitled to keep all the proceeds of a sale, there is no real interest in obtaining the best price for the land. Also, the limited owner might try to abscond with the purchase money;
2. a purchaser must be able to tell whether the land is settled land and whether the person who purports to exercise the statutory powers has them vested in him;
3. the interests of the other persons entitled under the settlement must be cleared off the title so that the purchaser can acquire the unincumbered fee simple; and
4. a purchaser must be protected if he acts in accordance with the provisions of the act.

H. The Definition of Settled Land

There are three broadly defined cases where land comes within the Acts:

1. where there are successive interests, legal or equitable: section 2(1) 1882 Act;
2. where land is held by an infant, *i.e.* a minor: section 59 of the 1882 Act; and
3. where there is a trust for sale of the land and the beneficial interests are to be held for successive interests: section 2(1) and section 63 of the 1882 Act.

The first two are cases where there is a problem of alienability, in 1. because there is no one who can dispose of the fee simple, and in 2. because although a minor can make a conveyance of the fee simple he or she can repudiate it on coming of age. The third case is anomalous. The whole question of trusts for sale is unsatisfactory under the 1882 Act as we shall see.

1. Successive Interests

The definition of a settlement is contained in section 2(1) of the Settled Land Act, 1882:

> "2.(1) Any deed, will, agreement for a settlement, or other agreement, covenant to surrender, copy of court roll, Act of Parliament, or other instrument, or any number of instruments. . . under or by virtue of which instrument or instruments any land, or any estate or interest in land, stands for the time being limited to or in trust for any persons by way of succession, creates or is for the purposes of this Act a settlement. . ."

Section 2(2) amplifies the definition by providing further that:

> "2.(2) An estate or interest in remainder or reversion not disposed of by a settlement, and reverting to the settlor or descending to the testator's heir, is for the purpose of this Act an estate or interest coming to the settlor or heir under or by virtue of the settlement."

It is clear from this phrase that the Act applies whether the successive interests are legal (limited to. . .) or equitable (. . . or in trust for. . .).

a) Successive Legal Estates

Where the interests are legal the future interests will either be common law remainders or legal executory interests.[19] Where the settlement is created in this way the land is said to be held or limited in strict settlement. The phrase also implies that the settlement contains provisions as to jointures, portions and charges which the landed classes usually inserted into such deeds.

The successive legal estates were commonly in the form of legal executory interests since they allowed greater flexibility than common law remainders, and allowed the creation of legal powers of appointment and sale. In such a case the legal fee simple is, as it were, split up among those entitled to the interests under the settlement. There are no trustees holding the whole fee simple, but it was common to appoint trustees of the settlement who were trustees of certain powers under the settlement and also were necessary in the past as a device to preserve contingent remainders.[20]

Where the settlement created legal executory interests the trustees of the settlement would usually be the persons named in the deed as feoffees to uses. As feoffees they had no functions at all, since the uses were executed, but the same persons would be given the special powers under the settlement.

b) Successive Equitable Estates

In this case, which is less common, the legal fee simple is vested in trustees and the those entitled under the settlement have equitable interests. This is sometimes referred to as a "holding trust," to distinguish it from a trust for sale which is discussed below.

19 Or, as has been seen, legal powers of appointment.

20 See below.

c) Instrument

It would seem from the definition in section 2(1) that a disposition of land, in order to come within section 2(1) must be contained in an instrument, *i.e.* it must be in writing. Section 2(1), after the list "deed, will. . ." *etc.* gives the general term ". . . or other instrument. . . " and the later phrase "under or by virtue of which instrument or instruments. . . " confirms this view.

However, it is not necessary that all the estates which make up the succession of interests must be contained in or granted by the instrument. Section 2(2) expressly states that a reversion not disposed of by the instrument is sufficient to make up the element of succession in order to bring the land within the Act. Thus the following dispositions come within the Act:

to X for life, remainder to his eldest son in tail, remainder to Z in fee simple

to F and G in fee simple to the use of A in tail female, remainder to B in fee simple

Unto and to the use of T and U in fee simple in trust for P for life, remainder to Q in fee simple

because each disposition creates a succession of estates. In the first two instances they are legal, in the third instance, equitable. But so also would the following:

to X in tail

or

to A for life

because the element of succession is created by the grant of the estate in the deed together with the reversion vested in the grantor and left undisposed of by the grant.

The requirement of an instrument is important in relation to dispositions of land which create successive equitable interests. Such a succession can arise through the doctrines of implied, resulting and constructive trusts and other equitable doctrines that give rise to interests, usually equitable, in land. In the following limitation:

Unto and to the use of T and U in fee simple in trust for A for life

only part of the beneficial interest is disposed of, *i.e.* the life estate to A. The rest of the beneficial fee simple is held by T and U on a resulting trust for the grantor. Such an instrument clearly creates a succession of interests and although a resulting trust is not specifically mentioned by section 2(2) the land is presumably settled land.

On the other hand, if the instrument conveys land "to X in fee simple" but circumstances arise in which equity would regard X as holding the legal estate on trust for Y for life, or for any estate less than a fee simple, under the doctrine of constructive trust or proprietary estoppel, it is questionable whether the situation falls within the Settled Land Acts, at least where the circumstances which give rise to the doctrines are an oral arrangement or conduct. So if X agrees orally with W that W may occupy the land rent free for the rest of her life, and a court decides that this creates an equitable life estate in W, it seems that the land is not settled land.[21] The element of succession has not arisen by virtue of the instrument nor by the instrument failing to dispose of part of the interest. It has arisen by the operation of the jurisdiction of equity on the factual situation. This seems to be confirmed by the wording of section 2(2) which refers to an instrument, *etc.*, "under or by virtue of which instrument. . . any land, or any estate or interest in land, stands for the time being limited to or in trust for any persons by way of succession". In other words, settlement includes cases where land is held in trust for successive equitable estates, but only where the trust itself can be said to be under or by virtue of an instrument. On the other hand, in the above example, if X agreed in writing it could be argued that the written agreement constitutes the instrument for the purposes of section 2 and the land is settled land.[22]

d) Are All Successive Interests within the Acts?

Apart from the preceding section of the text, if section 2 of the 1882 Act is taken literally it would mean that virtually all cases where there is an element of succession would fall within the Acts. However, as we shall see when considering the definition of person having the powers of a tenant for life under section 58 of the Act of 1882, that definition is more specific and narrower than the definition of settlement within section 2. This may mean one of two things. It may mean, in cases in which there is a succession of interests within section 2, but which are excluded by the specific provisions of section 58, that the land is settled land falling within the Acts, but that there is no one with the powers of a tenant for life within section 58. Such a situation would be anomalous because it would make the land difficult or impossible to deal with while that state of affairs continued. Or it may mean that those cases which are excluded by section 58 are not settled land at all and fall outside the Acts altogether.

Judicial and academic opinion is not entirely consistent on the point. As will be seen later, it does appear that there are cases in which the land is settled land but there is no tenant for life.

21 In *National Bank Ltd v. Keegan* [1931] IR 344, 66 ILTR 101 a written agreement was held by the Supreme Court to have created a life estate, but the court did not consider whether the situation came within the Settled Land Acts. The situation has been considered by the courts in England: see *Bannister v. Bannister* [1948] 2 All ER 133; *Binions v. Evans* [1972] Ch 359 where however the statutory provisions differ.

22 See preceding footnote.

On the other hand, there are other instances, such as common law determinable and conditional interests, which may not only fall outside section 58 but outside the Acts altogether. These problems are best dealt with by considering the definition of person having the powers of a tenant for life under section 58:

> "58.–(1) Each person as follows shall, when the estate or interest of each of them is in possession, have the powers of a tenant for life under this Act, as if each of them were tenant for life as defined in this Act . . ."

Section 58(2) goes on to state that "in every such case, the provisions of this Act, referring to a tenant for life, either as conferring powers on him or otherwise, and to a settlement, and to settled land, shall extend to each of the persons aforesaid . . . and to the land . . .". Thus, where a person falls within section 58(1), not only do they have the powers of a tenant for life, but the land is settled land: this would seem to be inevitable. But it does not necessarily follow that if a person is excluded from section 58(1) that the land is also outside the Act.

In some cases it apparently is, in other case not. One general point may be made and that is that the policy of the Act was to reach the case of family settlements, but not forms of holding land entered into for commercial reasons. Commercial forms are usually distinguished by the fact that rent is payable by the owner of the interest, whereas this would be uncommon between family members.

It will be seen that section 58(1) does exclude certain cases where rent is paid and in view of the policy such cases were also presumably intended to fall outside the Acts altogether.

(1) Life Estates

Section 2(5) contains the definition of a tenant for life for the purpose of the Act as "the person who is for the time being . . . beneficially entitled to possession of settled land for his life . . .". It seems that to fall within this section the grantee must be given the right to physical possession of the land or to the receipt of rents and profits.[23] This necessarily implies that the right must be in possession as opposed to in remainder, or vested in interest, or contingent only, as the general words of section 58 in any case require.[24] A legal or equitable tenant for life would fall within this definition.[25] But the question is always whether the instrument grants a life estate. A right to occupy the property

---

23 Wolstenhome, p.369. Note that this is not required under section 58 which merely says "in possession" not "to possession".

24 *Re Strangways* (1885) 34 Ch D 423.

25 "Unto and to the use of AB in fee simple in trust for C for life" gives C the right to physical possession: *Re Jones* (1884) 26 Ch D 736 at 742.

"rent- free for life or as long as he pleases" does so[26] but not a right "to reside rent free in any one of the testator's houses at X".[27] Section 58(1) on the other hand covers cases where a person is entitled for life falling short of the definition in section 2(5). For this reason the section only requires that their interest be in possession, rather than entitling them to possession, or to the rent and profits, of the land. The definitions in section 58 are evidently intended to include some cases not covered by section 2, as in subsection (vi):

> "(vi) A tenant for his own or any other life, or for years determinable on life, whose estate is liable to cease in any event during that life, whether by expiration of the estate, or by conditional limitation, or otherwise, or to be defeated by an executory limitation, gift, or disposition over, or is subject to a trust for accumulation of income for payment of debts or other purpose . . ."

Thus life tenants whose estates are determinable or conditional, and whether there is a gift over or merely a reversion, would fall within this section although they may not come within the strict words of section 2(5).

One question here is whether a life tenant paying a rent would fall within the section and whether such a case would be settled land at all. Such a situation would be rare, since commercial interests would normally have been leases for lives other than that of the grantee. What authority there is suggests that such a person would not be within the section despite the absence of express exclusion,[28] and possibly the land would not be within the Acts at all. It may be noticed that section 58(1)(iv) excludes tenants for years determinable on life where they hold under a lease at a rent.

(2) Estates Pur Autre Vie

Estates pur autre vie create a succession of interests and so on the face of it the land will be settled land within section 2. However, section 58(1)(v) excludes from the definition of persons having the powers of a tenant for life, tenants pur autre vie where there is a rent.

> "(v) A tenant for the life of another, not holding merely under a lease at a rent. . ."[29]

---

26 *Re Eastman's Settled Estates* (1898) 68 L J Ch. 122; *Re Carne's Settled Estates* [1899] 1 Ch. 324.

27 *Re Bond* (1904) 48 Sol J 192.

28 In *Re Drew's Settled Estate* (1911) D No. 377 a testator during his lifetime had granted a house by deed to A for life at a rent of £1 subject to lessee's covenants and a proviso for re-entry. By will he then devised the land after A's death to B for life. Eady J in chambers, 3 April 1911, held that A did not have the powers of a tenant for life under section 58. The decision is open to the criticism that the deed was essentially one of gift and the rent nominal. But a court might be reluctant to enter into the question of the adequacy of the rent.

29 *Re Mundy and Roper* (1899) 1 Ch. 298.

Here again, the intention was to reach such estates when they occurred in family settlements, but not where they occurred as commercial, *i.e.* commodity, relationships.

Leases for lives renewable forever at commercial rents were a common form of commercial holding in Ireland and so the tenant is not included within the definition of person having the powers of a tenant for life under section 58 of the Act. Even though there is an element of succession within section 2, and a reversion under section 2(2), it has long been assumed that the intention behind section 58(1)(v) was to exclude such interests from the operation of the Acts. By 1882 such tenants would have had the power to demand a fee farm grant from the lessor and so did not require the powers.

(3) Estate Plus Power of Appointment

An instrument which grants a life estate followed by a power of appointment creates a succession of interests because the remainder after the life estate is vested in those entitled in default of appointment until a valid exercise of the power divests them and vests it in an object of the power. Thus, in *Re Bective Estate,*[30] R devised land to his wife for life, with remainder as she should by will appoint. It was held that the land was settled land within the Act.

(4) Rights of Residence

Wills in Ireland sometimes confer on a person the right to reside on land for their life with other associated rights.[31] Such interests have been held in Ireland to give rise to a distinct interest in land known as a right of residence. It binds third parties but it is doubtful if it can be transferred by the holder of it to any other person, and to that extent is personal.[32] It would entirely defeat the purpose of such an interest if the holder had the powers of a tenant for life under the Settled Land Acts and the better view would seem to be that it does not fall within them. However, the right exists in two forms, a general right and a special right, the latter conferring a right over part of a property. While the general right has been held not to fall within the Settled Land Acts, 1882-90,[33] the position of the special right is less clear.

(5) Fees Tail

Tenants in tail whose estate is in possession[34] have the powers of a tenant for life within the Acts:

30 (1891) 27 LR Ir 364, MR.

31 See "Rights of residence" in Chapter 18 Licences, Estoppel and Constructive Trusts.

32 See *National Bank Ltd v. Keegan* [1931] IR 344, 66 ILTR 101; *Kelaghan v. Daly* [1913] 2 IR 328; *Re Shanahan* [1919] 1 IR 131.

33 *Lahiffe v. Hecker,* unreported, High Court, Lynch J, 28 April 1994.

34 See section 58(1) above.

> "58.–(1)(i) A tenant in tail, including a tenant in tail who is by Act of Parliament restrained from barring or defeating his estate tail. . . but not including such a tenant in tail where the land in respect whereof he is so restrained was purchased with money provided by Parliament in consideration of public services."[35]

A tenant in tail whose interest is in possession would clearly prefer in most conceivable cases to bar the entail rather than exercise his or her powers under the Settled Land Acts.

This subsection includes cases where the entail by statute may not be barred. These were generally entails conferred by statute on military commanders, *etc.* It is unlikely that entails made unbarrable under an express grant by Parliament exist in the Republic. It may be noticed, however, that subsection (vii) includes:

> "(vii) a tenant in tail after possibility of issue extinct"

whose entail is unbarrable under the Fines and Recoveries (Ireland) Act, 1834. Such a tenant has the powers of a tenant for life under the Act. This is not surprising as their interest resembles a life estate.

(6) Base Fees

A person entitled to a base fee in possession[36] may sell the fee simple under the Acts.

> "58.–(1)(iii) A person entitled to a base fee, although the reversion is in the [Crown], and so that the exercise by him of his powers under this Act shall bind the [Crown]".

In the 19th century there were apparently many instances of base fees in Ireland in which the reversion lay at that time in the British Crown, evidently as a result of old Crown grants in fee tail being barred by the tenants in tail. As the Crown was not bound by the disentailment, the reversion remained. If such reversions still exist, they are vested in the State. The above provision gives the holder of the base fee power to overreach the reversion by the exercise of his powers under the Act.

The opening words of section 58 make it clear that only the holder of a base fee in possession has the powers of a tenant for life under the Acts. Thus, if land is limited "to A for life, remainder to B in tail", and B bars the entail without the consent of the protector, A, B obtains a base fee, but, since it is not in possession, B cannot exercise the powers under the Acts. It is A, the tenant for life, who has the powers.

---

35 This would include estates such as those granted to the Duke of Wellington and Admiral Lord Nelson by Parliament, but not land provided by the Crown with the sanction of Parliament, such as the Duke of Marlborough's estate: see *Re Duke of Marlborough's Parliamentary Estates* (1891) 8 TLR 179; *Re Duke of Marlborough's Blenheim Estates* (1892) 8 TLR 582.

36 Section 58(1) above.

(7) Conditional and Determinable Fees

Where there is a gift over the person entitled such interests is within section 58(1):

> "(ii) A tenant in fee simple, with an executory limitation, gift, or disposition over, on failure of his issue, or in any other event".

It has already been seen that at common law the grant of a fee simple, even conditional or determinable, could not be followed in the deed by a remainder in favour of another person. But such a limitation is possible either under an executed use:

> *to F and G to the use to A in fee simple until X returns from America, then, on that event occurring, over to B in fee simple*

or under a trust:

> *unto and to the use of T and U in fee simple in trust for A in fee simple on condition that if X becomes a solicitor, on trust for B in fee simple.*

The person entitled under such executory interests and trusts is within section 58, if there is no gift over, he or she does not. Thus, where the interest is a determinable or conditional fee at common law, followed by possibility of reverter or right of re-entry vested in the grantor, the person entitled to the fee does not fall within section 8. Thus the following limitations do not fall within section 58(1)(ii):

> *to S in fee simple until the land ceases to be used for agriculture; (determinable fee plus possibility of reverter)*
>
> *to S in fee simple provided X does not become a solicitor.* (conditional fee plus right of entry)

Even corresponding interests under executed uses or trusts would not fall within the section either, since no gift over is created:

> *Unto and to the use of T and U in fee simple in trust for S in fee simple so long as the land is used as a school.* (equitable determinable fee plus resulting trust to grantor)

It is clear that in none of these cases does S have the powers of a tenant for life under the Act. But do such interests come within the Act at all? Although there is an element of succession, and hence a problem of alienability, it can be argued that they do not fall within section 2(1) as the land is not "limited to. . . persons by way of succession" as the possibility of reverter or right of entry is not limited, *i.e.* contained in the deed. As for section 2(2), that only refers to reversions and remainders and the predominant opinion of land lawyers is that possibilities of reverter and rights of entry are not to be so classified. If this is correct it would have the unfortunate effect that possibilities of reverter, rights of entry for condition broken and similar interests existing as resulting trusts could not be overreached . No one would be able to sell the absolute fee simple.

The problem is all the more unfortunate when it is remembered that such interests in Ireland are not subject to the rule against perpetuities and the contingency could remain outstanding for a long period, as in the last example.

One special form of this type of limitation may be mentioned. We have seen that in the limitation:

> *To A for life, remainder to his eldest son [unborn] in tail, remainder to B in fee simple.*

When the eldest son became 21 he could join with his father, the protector of the settlement, and bar the entail, thus destroying the ultimate remainder to B and producing a fee simple estate that could be readily sold. Since his interest had been destroyed, B's consent to the sale was not required. But essentially the same interests could be conferred if the limitation was drafted as follows:

> *to F and G in fee simple to the use of A in fee simple, and if he die without issue living at his death, to B in fee simple.*

This limitation had the added advantage, as far as the settlor was concerned, that it rendered the land more difficult to alienate. Before A's death the condition was still not void despite the birth of A's son, because it depended on facts present at A's death. Until then, B still had a contingent interest, and so the land could not be sold without his joining in the conveyance.

This device was rendered ineffective by section 10 of the Conveyancing Act, 1882 which provides that the condition shall become void as soon as any living issue of A reaches the age of 21. As a result of section 58(1)(ii) of the Settled Land Act, 1882, while the condition remains valid, A has the powers of a tenant for life under the Act and can sell the fee simple absolute, overreaching B's remainder. As soon as issue of A reaches the age of 21 the condition becomes void and A has a fee simple free of any other interest. The land will also cease to be settled land at that point as there is no succession of interests under section 2. The restriction in section 10 of the Conveyancing Act, 1882 has been extended in the Republic, in so far as it applies to wills, to any property, not only land, and the condition becomes void as soon as issue is born to A, without the requirement of reaching the age of 21.[37]

As to conditions requiring the donee to reside in a house, the condition will be rendered void under section 51 of the Act.[38] If the gift to the donee is of a life estate, the land clearly remains settled land. If the gift is of a fee simple subject to the condition, the better view would seem to be that the condition having been made void by section 51, the land at once ceases to be settled land at all, but an English court in *Re Richardson*[39] took the view, somewhat artificially, that section 51 only rendered the condition void in so far as it attempted

---

37 Succession Act, 1965 ss. 96, 100.

38 See below.

39 [1904] 2 Ch. 777.

to restrict the powers under the Act, that the land remained settled land, but that the donee was entitled to the entire proceeds of sale.

(8) Lease for Lives and Years

These interests would seem to be excluded from section 58(1)(vi).

2. Land Held by a Minor

If land is held by a minor, or by a minor as a co-owner with an adult,[40] even for a fee simple estate, then the land comes within the Act under section 59, provided the minor is "in his own right seised of or entitled in possession to land".[41]

Under section 59 the minor is deemed to be the tenant for life, but section 60 provides that in such a case the powers of the tenant for life may be exercised on the infant's behalf by the trustees of the settlement.

In *Re Conroy's Trusts*[42] the court, by a gloss on the act, read the section as requiring the trustees to act in such a case. Alternatively, on an application by the minor the court may appoint an adult to act on the minor's behalf,[43] provided the adult is not a co-owner with the infant,[44] for in the latter case the interest of the adult co-owner might conflict with those of the minor.

3. Trusts for Sale.

An anomaly of the Settled Land Acts is that trusts for sale are specifically deemed to be settled land by section 63 where the beneficial interests are successive. It would have been wiser to exclude them, since no problem of alienability arises under a trust for sale. In the case of a trust for sale there is a special definition of tenant for life under section 63. This will be dealt with under the section on trusts for sale.[45]

I. Interests Outside the Acts

Apart from the doubtful cases just considered, there are other cases which are clearly outside the provisions of the Acts.

---

40 *Re Greenville's Estate* (1882) 11 LR Ir 138 (land held by partners descended to minor on death of one partner).

41 Section 59; *Re Scally* (1952) 86 ILTR 171.

42 [1938] Ir Jur Rep 26.

43 *Re McClintock, an infant* (1891) 27 LR Ir 462, V-C.

44 *Re Greenville's Estate* (1882) 11 LR Ir 138, V-C.

45 See below.

a) Fee Simple Subject to Family Charges

This situation may arise when land which was once subject to a strict settlement has become vested in a person in fee simple, but family charges, *i.e.* jointures or rentcharges , still remain.

In *Re Bective Estate*[46] R left land in his will to his wife for life with remainder as she should appoint. She appointed it to a relative in fee simple. The judge suggested that the land remained settled land because it was subject to family charges.

In *Re Blake's Settled Estates*[47] a tenant in tail executed a disentailing deed the effect of which was to vest the fee simple in him subject only to family charges outstanding under the settlement. The Supreme Court held, not following *Re Bective*, that the existence of family charges did not make the land settled land. They did not create any successive interests.

The mere fact that a person derives title to the fee simple under an original deed of settlement does not in itself mean that there is still a settlement. Section 2(1) provides that land only comes within the section if it is for the time being limited to or in trust for persons by way of succession.

Although the incumbrances cannot be cleared off the title by a sale under the Settled Land Acts, under section 5 of the Conveyancing Act, 1881 the owner of land subject to an incumbrance, which includes a jointure or rentcharge, may sell the land free of it by obtaining the permission of the court to lodging a sum of money in court, the sum being sufficient to provide an income, after investment in government securities, to pay the annual amount.

b) Fee Farm Grants

Since the estate under a fee farm grant is a fee simple there is no element of succession and so the land is not settled land under section 2. There is no express provision in section 58 giving the holder of a fee farm grant the powers under the Act, and so such an interest does not fall within the Acts. The fee farm rent cannot therefore be overreached on a sale under the Acts. The rent may however be redeemed under the various statutes dealing with this topic[48] or under section 5 of the Conveyancing Act, 1881 discussed in the previous section.

c) Bare Trusts

Where both the legal estate and the beneficial interest are held in fee simple there is no succession of interests and so the land is not settled land[49] unless the beneficiary is a minor. This situation may occur because the land was so limited

46 (1891) 27 LR Ir 364.

47 [1932] IR 637.

48 See Chapter 7 Fee Farm Grants.

49 *Re British Land and Allen's Contract* (1900) 44 SJ 593.

from the beginning, or it may arise in the course of time under a limitation which originally created a settlement. In the limitation:

> *Unto and to the use of T and U in fee simple in trust for X for life, remainder to Y in tail, remainder to Z in fee simple*

if X has died and the heirs of the body of Y have died out, the land is held by T and U in fee simple in trust for Z. Z is in the special position of a beneficiary under a bare trust and, under the principle of *Saunders v. Vautier*,[50] may call for the legal fee simple.[51]

d) Life Estates or Estates Pur Autre Vie at a Rent

These have been considered already.

e) Conditional and Determinable Fees with no Gift Over

These have also been considered.

J. No Tenant for Life

There appear to be certain cases where, although the land is settled land under section 2 subsection (1) and (2) in the sense that the land is limited to persons by way of succession, there is no tenant for life under section 2(5) nor any person having the powers of a tenant for life under section 58 nor a person deemed to be a tenant for life under section 63.

1. Cases

a) Discretionary Trust

In *Re Horne's Settled Estate*[52] property was devised on trust for sale subject to a direction that it was not to be sold for 21 years after the testator's death. In the meantime the income was to be applied in the same way as the proceeds of sale, namely, to be invested and held in trust for the testator's sons at the age of 25 or daughters at 25 or when they married if they did so under that age. Until the children satisfied those conditions the income was to be applied to the education or maintenance of any child at the discretion of the trustees. Any unapplied surplus was to be accumulated. The English Court of Appeal held that there was no trust for sale during the 21 year period. There was a holding trust, but the interests of the beneficiaries were contingent pending their fulfilment of the conditions. They did not fall within section 2(5) as being entitled to the possession of land, nor did they fall within section 58(1)(ix) as persons "en-

50 (1841) Cr & Ph 240, (1841) 4 Beav 115, [1835-42] All ER Reprint 58.

51 See Chapter 4 Equity.

52 (1888) 39 Ch D 84.

titled to the income of land under a trust. . . during his own or any other life. . ." since they were not entitled to anything. If they all died under 25 the accumulated income would go to the heir-at-law of the testator, but that might not happen, so the heir could not be said to be entitled to the income either.

b) Direction to Accumulate.

A similar problem was held to arise if, instead of discretionary trust, there is a direction to accumulate the income, or it is to go to residue, until a contingency is fulfilled. In *Re Astor*[53] residuary legatees were held not to have any interest in the land. Nor were they entitled to income during their lives, but only to the money as part of the residue.

c) No Person Entitled to the Whole Income.

A third case where there is no person having the powers of a tenant for life was held to have arisen in *Re Frewen*[54] where a person was entitled only to part of the income and not to the whole.

2. Effect

If there is no tenant for life or person having the powers of a tenant for life, then the land cannot be sold unless:

(a) the settlement confers an express power of sale on the trustees of the settlement, or

(b) there is a trust for sale in which case the trustees of the settlement may sell without the consent of other persons,[55]

or

(c) an application is made to the court under section 16 of the Settled Estates Act, 1877.[56]

K. The Tenant for Life

The solution to the problem of alienability was to confer, as we have seen, extensive powers on the tenant for life. This contained an inherent danger. The tenant for life might be tempted to abuse his powers to the detriment of the remaindermen. The Act therefore contains mechanisms by why this can be avoided.

---

53 [1922] 1 Ch. 364.

54 [1926] Ch. 580.

55 *Re Earle & Webster's Contract* (1883) 24 Ch D 144.

56 See above.

1. Sale

Under section 4 the land must be sold by private treaty or auction at the best price reasonably obtainable. Exchange or partition must be for the best consideration in land or money reasonably obtainable. The tenant for life may not buy the land by private treaty, but may bid at the auction. The power of sale in Ireland includes the power to create a fee farm grant.[57]

It should be remembered that the powers under the act do not derogate from other powers which a tenant for life may have in other capacities, so that if the person having the powers of a tenant for life under the Act is in fact a tenant in tail he may bar the entail and obtain the fee simple free of charge.

2. Power to Lease

A tenant for life has a general power to create leases up to 35 years under section 65(10).[58] Building leases can be created for up to 99 years under section 6.[59] Mining leases can be created for up to 60 years under section 6.

Under section 45 a tenant for life when intending to exercise his or her powers under the Acts of sale, exchange, partition, leasing, mortgaging *etc.*, must give at least one month's notice to the trustees for the purposes of the Acts if the dispositions are to bind those entitled in remainder.[60] If there are no trustees for the purposes of the Acts then application must be made to the court to appoint them.[61]

3. Power to Mortgage

One of the problems with settlements is that the land may become burdened with debt. It was not therefore the policy of the Acts to grant extensive powers of mortgaging to the tenant for life. Unless the settlement otherwise provided, the tenant for life could, apart from the Acts, only mortgage his own estate, usually a life estate. The money so raised could be used at the tenant for life's

---

57 *Re Braithwaite's Settled Estate* [1922] 1 IR 71.

58 In England the maximum was 21 years, but the special provision for Ireland was to bring the Act into conformity with the powers of limited owners under the Land Law (Ireland) Act, 1881 section 25. See also the earlier Landed Property (Ireland) Improvement Act, 1860 s.25; *Re Casey's Estate* (1878) 1 LR Ir 481. The general power was extended by s.43 of the Landlord and Tenant Act, 1931 to 99 years where required under the Act, but the 1931 Act was repealed by the Landlord and Tenant (Amendment) Act, 1980.

59 This was extended to 150 years for urban land by the Landlord and Tenant Act, 1931 s.62, but that extension was abolished as to dwellings by the Landlord and Tenant (Ground Rents) Act, 1978 and the whole of the 1931 Act was repealed by the 1980 Act.

60 *Hughes v. Fanagan* (1891) 30 LR Ir 111; *Re Naper* (1952) 86 ILTR 106, High Court. And see Notice below.

61 *ibid.*; and *Marlborough (Duke) v. Sartoris* (1886) 32 Ch D 616, per Chitty J at 623.

discretion since it was a mortgage of his own interest in the land. Section 18 of the 1882 Act confers power on the tenant for life to create mortgages binding the remainders for the purpose of equality of exchange of land or partition of it. The tenant for life may convey the fee simple or a term of years as security and so the mortgage will bind those entitled in remainder under the settlement. On the other hand, the money so raised is to be treated as capital money, *i.e.* it must, under section 22, be paid to the trustees of the settlement and applied by them. Section 11 of the 1890 Act extended these powers to mortgage in order to pay off incumbrances.

4. Improvements

Section 25 of the Act authorises the expenditure of capital money for the purpose of effecting improvements, including the purchase of other land.

5. Qualifications

a) Mansion House

The 1882 Act made few concessions to the sentimental attachment of landed families to their ancestral estates. The Act of 1890 introduced such a concession by limiting the power of the tenant for life or person having such powers to dispose of the mansion house and ornamental garden that such estates frequently included. Section 10 of the 1890 Act provides that the mansion house and ornamental garden cannot be sold without the consent of the trustees of the settlement under the Acts or of the court.

The weakness of this provision was revealed by *Re Marquess of Ailesbury's Settled Estates*[62] in which the tenant for life applied to the court for consent. Had the court refused, the tenant for life could have sold the estate without the house and garden without the necessity for any consent. The court in granting consent took this into account and the fact that, had they refused, the estate might have remained unsold. This would have reduced the efficiency of the entire estate, given that the proposed purchaser was in a position to invest considerable sums in improvements to the agriculture of the tenant farms on the estate. The court held that this latter factor was a legitimate consideration to be taken into account in granting consent to the sale of the whole estate. The case therefore also indicates that the judges were more concerned with the efficient economic running of the estate and the tenant farms rather than the sentimental attachments of the landed aristocracy.

b) Heirlooms

The 1882 did contain one concession to the landed interest. Section 37 provides that heirlooms cannot be sold without an order of the court.

---

62 [1892] AC 356.

6. The Position of the Tenant for Life

a) Exercise of the Powers

Section 53 provides that a tenant for life in exercising any power under the Act must have regard to the interests of all parties entitled under the settlement and in relation to the exercise of the powers is deemed to be a trustee for those parties. On the other hand, sections 50 and 51 invalidate any attempt by the settlor to restrain the exercise of the powers. These sections are considered in more detail below. The courts have interpreted this to mean that the tenant for life may make the decision whether or not to sell or otherwise deal with the property in his or her own interests and will not be restrained merely because his motive is selfish, such as to pay off his debts or to provide a more comfortable existence for himself.

In *Wheelwright v. Walker*[63] the tenant for life was over 70 years of age. He had one daughter and she and her husband (whose concurrence was required under the law as it then stood) contracted to sell her reversion to the plaintiff. The Settled Land Act came into operation three years later, and shortly after the tenant for life advertised the estate for sale under the powers in the Act. The plaintiff brought an action for an injunction to restrain the tenant for life from selling. The motive of the tenant for life in selling was that the house was too large for his needs and, if were to be sold, the proceeds of sale on investment would provide him with enough money to provide a smaller residence and, in addition, there would be capital money left over which, after investment, would increase his income. The court held that it had no power to interfere with the tenant for life's power of sale provided the Act was complied with. Pearson J expressed the position as follows:

> "So far as I can see, there is no restriction whatever in the Act on the power of a tenant for life to sell. There is nothing that I can see in the Act to enable the Court to restrain him from selling, whether he desires to sell because he is in debt and wishes to increase his income; or whether, without being in debt, he thinks he can increase his income; or whether he desires to sell from some unwillingness to take the trouble involved in the management of landed property; or whether he acts from worse motives, as from mere caprice or whim, or because he is desirous of doing that which he knows would be very disagreeable to those who expect to succeed him at his death. There is not, so far as I can see, any power either in the Court or in the trustees to interfere with his power of sale."

In other words, to this extent the tenant for life may act as any other owner of a commodity for sale on the market. Nor will he be restrained merely because what he wishes to do is contrary to the feelings of sentimental attachment felt by other members of the family to an ancestral home, especially if a sale would be in the interest of tenants on the estate and the more efficient working of the

63 (1883) 23 Ch D 752.

land as an economic unit.[64] As will be seen in the section below on mortgaging powers, special limitations apply in that case because they may be used to further burden the estate and reduce its economic viability. Protection for the beneficiaries is provided for by the sections dealing with the payment of purchase money dealt with below.

In the event, the plaintiff in *Wheelwright* offered to buy the house for £7,500.[65] The tenant for life was unwilling to sell to him and there was evidence that he intended to sell at a lower price to another person. On the reversioner's undertaking not to withdraw the offer, the court restrained the tenant for life from selling, other than at a public auction, without communicating any other offer to the plaintiff-reversioner and allowed the latter two days to make an advance on the purchase price.

In *Middlemas v. Stevens*[66] the defendant was entitled under the will of her deceased husband to the use, rent free, of a certain house so long as during her widowhood she personally resided in the house. She wished to marry again and did not wish to give up residence in the house. She therefore proposed to exercise the leasing powers as tenant for life under the Act in favour of her husband and to grant him a 21 year lease.[67] The plaintiffs, who were entitled in remainder, objected to the lease and brought an action to restrain her from exercising the power. Joyce J in a short judgment in the English Chancery Division held that it would not be a bona fide exercise of the powers and found in favour of the plaintiff. It is suggested that the case is wrongly decided. The tenant for life had the power to grant the lease under the Act and the fact that the exercise would be contrary to the wishes of the settlor was irrelevant: the exercise of many of the powers under the Act will be contrary to the wishes of the settlor. The policy of the Act is to override those wishes where they conflict with those of the tenant for life.

b) No Restriction on the Statutory Powers

Sections 50 and 51 of the 1882 Act secure the policy of freeing the land so that it can enter the market by providing that no restrictions of any kind may be placed on the powers of the tenant for life under the Acts.

Section 50 provides that the powers cannot be assigned or released by the tenant for life and this is so even if he or she alienates their estate in the land.[68]

64 *Re Marquess of Ailesbury's Settled Estates* [1892] AC 356.

65 *Wheelwright v. Walker (No. 2)* (1883) 31 Weekly Reporter 912.

66 [1901] Ch D 574.

67 The maximum in England. In Ireland the maximum is 35 years under section 65.

68 But see *Re Bruen's Estate* [1911] 1 IR 76 in which Wylie J held on a limitation in the form "to A for life, remainder to B for life, remainder to C in tail..." that an assignment by A of his life estate to B, which caused a merger, made the statutory powers exercisable by B. The court left open the question as to whether the powers could still be exercised by A.

A contract by a tenant for life not to exercise the powers is void.[69] Section 51 renders void any attempt by a settlor to insert into a settlement any restriction on the powers of the tenant for life, whether directly or by way of an inducement not to exercise them.

In *Re Fitzgerald*[70] a testator gave AB the use of her house at 29 Merrion Square, Dublin for life as a residence, subject to a proviso that if AB ceased to use it as a residence it should go to the residue of the testator's estate. She also gave AB the income from £10,000 for life so long as she lived in the house. AB later wished to exercise the powers under the Settled Land Acts and to leave the house, as her health made it difficult to continue to live there. Porter MR held that the proviso was void and further that AB would not lose the income on the £10,000. He commented that the policy of the Acts was to make settled land absolutely disposable by sale so that there should not be any land not capable of changing hands. In *Atkins v. Atkins*[71] Kenny J held that a condition to use a house as a principal residence was void for the same reason.[72]

In *Re Richardson*[73] a devise was made to C in fee simple on condition that she resided at a specified house and provided a home there for E, with a gift over on failure to comply with the condition. It was held that C had the powers of a tenant for life and that the condition was void under section 51 insofar as it prevented the exercise of the powers. This meant that C was then a fee simple owner and entitled to the proceeds of sale absolutely.

c) Grant of Greater Powers

There is nothing to prevent a settlor conferring additional powers on the tenant for life,[74] provided they do not conflict with the provisions of the Acts, so that, for example, the settlor, having granted a life estate, cannot exempt the life tenant from the provisions requiring that the proceeds of sale must be paid to the trustees of the settlement.[75]

d) Notice

A tenant for life must normally give notice to the trustees of the settlement.[76] By section 5(1) of the 1884 Act, it may be notice of a general intention.[77]

---

69 Section 50(2).

70 [1902] 1 IR 162.

71 [1976–77] ILRM 62.

72 And see *Re Thompson* (1888) 21 LR Ir 109, MR.

73 [1904] 2 Ch. 777; *Re Haynes* (1887) 37 Ch D 306.

74 Section 57(1).

75 *Re the Estate of Kenny, Deceased; Roberts and Others v. Kenny*, unreported, High Court, Geoghegan J, 10 March 1998.

76 Section 45.

77 *Re Naper* (1952) 86 ILTR 106, High Court.

e) Power to Give Directions

Another important power of the tenant for life is to give directions to the trustees of the settlement as to how the capital money arising from the exercise of powers under the Acts is to be invested. This is an important distinction between the position of the tenant for life under the Acts and a beneficiary under an ordinary trust, for in such a trust the trustees do not generally have to accept directions from the beneficiaries.[78]

L. Trustees of the Settlement

A distinction must be made between trustees of the land, *i.e.* those who have the legal estate vested in them, and trustees of the settlement. Only if the settlement is created by successive equitable estates will the legal fee simple in the land be vested in trustees. In such a case it would be usual for them also to be trustees of the settlement for the purposes of the Acts. If, however, the settlement is created by successive legal estates, there will be no trustees of the land, but there will still have to be trustees of the settlement within the meaning of the Settled Land Acts. They will be trustees of certain powers under the Acts and may also have powers vested in them by the settlement. Where, as was often the case, the settlement was created by uses executed by the Statute of Uses, 1634, they will usually be the persons named as feoffees in the settlement. As a result of the execution of the uses they will have no interests in the land but may have powers vested in them.

The settlement may confer on the trustees of the settlement powers such as a power to sell the settled land but under section 56 of the 1882 Act they cannot exercise such powers without the consent of the tenant for life. This is consistent with the policy of the Acts in concentrating the powers of ownership in the tenant for life.

1. Who are the Trustees of the Settlement?

There are now four tests to define the persons who are the trustees of the settlement under the Settled Land Acts. Applied in order, they are:

a) the persons who, under the settlement, are trustees with power of sale of the settled land or power to consent of the exercise of the power of sale;[79]

if there are no such persons, then they are:

b) persons declared by the settlement to be trustees of the settlement for

78 Section 22(1).

79 Section 2(8) Settled Land Act, 1882.

the purposes of the Act;[80]

as a result of the case of *Wheelwright v. Walker*[81] two additional tests were added by the Act of 1890, section 16:

c) persons who, under the settlement are trustees with power or trust for sale of other land in the settlement, or power to consent to the exercise of such a power; and

if there is none, then:

d) the persons under the settlement with a future trust or power of sale or with power to consent to such a power.

If there are still no persons who qualify, then the tenant for life or any other person with an interest in the settlement can apply to the court under section 38 of the 1882 Act for trustees to be appointed. They must do so before a sale *etc.*, as the purchase money must be paid to the trustees.

Under section 39(1) capital money must be paid to two trustees unless the settlement authorises otherwise. In the case of a settlement by will there is now no need to go to court as section 50(30) of the Succession Act, 1965 provides that the personal representatives proving the will shall for all purposes be deemed trustees of the settlement until trustees are appointed.

2. Powers of the Trustees of the Settlement

We have already seen that although the trustees of the settlement may have apparently important powers conferred on them by the settlement, they cannot exercise such powers of sale or leasing without the consent of the tenant for life. As Porter MR pointed out in *Hughes v. Fanagan*[82] the main role of the trustees is to protect the interests of those entitled in remainder. The powers are as follows.

a) Notice

It has already been seen that the tenant for life must give notice of intention to exercise the powers under the Acts to the trustees of the settlement,[83] but this power was cut down by the section 5 of the 1884 Act to the extent that the notice may be of a general intention in this regard. It is not entirely clear whether this general intention must be a general intention to sell, or a general intention to partition, *etc.*, or whether a general intention to exercise the powers, without specifying which powers, is sufficient. However, the tenant for life must in any

80 Section 2(8).

81 [1883] 23 Ch D 752.

82 (1891) 30 LR Ir 111.

83 Section 45 1882 Act.

case supply the trustees, as required, with particulars of sales, leases *etc.*[84]

The 1890 Act, by section 7, provides that notice is unnecessary before granting a lease for 21 years at the best rent reasonably obtainable. This appears to ignore the fact that the maximum length of a lease which a tenant for life in Ireland may grant so as to bind the remaindermen is not 21 but 35 years.[85] It should also be noted that under section 45(3) of the 1882 Act a purchaser in good faith of settled land dealing with the tenant for life is not concerned to inquire whether notice has been given to the trustees. However, in *Hughes v. Fanagan*[86] it was held that this did not avail a purchaser who actually knew that there were no trustees.[87]

b) Mansion House

It has also already been noted that the 1890 Act made a concession to the sentiment of aristocratic landowning families by requiring the consent of the trustees or of the court to a sale of the principal mansion house or the ornamental garden on an estate.[88]

c) Capital Money

Capital money arising under the act must be paid to the trustees of the settlement or into court.[89] This is one of the principal protections of the remaindermen and other persons having an interest in the settlement, since it prevents a dishonest tenant for life absconding with the money. The trustees then invest it at the direction of the tenant for life. The tenant for life, in giving directions, must have regard to the interests of the other persons entitled under the settlement under section 53 as the trustee of his powers and the court, on application by the trustees, may restrain an unwise investment.[90]

(1) Rent

Rent arising under a lease made by the tenant for life is not capital money but belongs to the tenant for life[91] but in the case of a mining lease, since mining diminishes the capital value of the land and so will affect the value of the remainders, in the case of such a lease a proportion of the rent is retained as capital money.[92]

84 Section 5(2) of 1884 Act.

85 Under section 65(10) of the 1882 Act.

86 (1891) 30 LR Ir 111.

87 There were no trustees for the purposes of the Settled Land Acts in *Hughes* at the time.

88 Section 10 Settled Land Act, 1890.

89 Section 22 of 1882 Act.

90 *Re Hunt's Settled Estates* [1905] 2 Ch. 418.

91 *Re Wix* [1916] 1 Ch. 279.

92 Section 11 of 1882 Act.

(2) Improvements

Capital money may be expended on improvements to the land. Section 25 of the 1882 Act contains a list of such authorised improvements, which include drainage, embankments to prevent flooding from the sea or rivers, houses for employees of the estate, offices and outbuildings, saw mills and other mills, roads and reservoirs, *etc.* The Act of 1890 section 13 added a number of items to the list, including bridges and alterations to the buildings including the principal mansion house. The latter provision is of some practical significance as it is often the mansion house that needs modernisation or repair. The section nevertheless contains limits on such expenditure. Section 13(ii) sanctions expenditure for alterations or additions to buildings, but only such as are reasonably necessary or proper to enable the buildings to be let. Section 13(iii) allows expenditure on buildings in substitution for those compulsorily acquired by a local authority, but only to the extent of the compensation received. Section 13(iv) allows for the rebuilding of the principal mansion house, but provided the sum involved does not exceed half the annual rental of the settled land. Where greater expenditure is needed an application would therefore have to be made to the court to sanction the additional expenditure as salvage. This jurisdiction is discussed below.

In *Re O'Farrell's Settled Estates*[93] the original estate house was sold and a smaller and more convenient one purchased by the trustees. It needed money spent on it to modernise it, including plumbing, electrical installations and kitchen fittings. Dixon J in the High Court held that the plumbing qualified as an improvement under section 25 and that the rest of the expenditure could be justifiably met out of capital money as falling within section 21(vii) which authorises the trustees to invest in the purchase of land. If the trustees had bought a house which had already been modernised it would have cost an additional amount which would clearly have been authorised under the section, and no meaningful distinction could be made between this and the facts of the case.

(3) Salvage

Finally, where an expenditure is not specifically authorised the court has an inherent jurisdiction to sanction the use of capital money as salvage, *i.e.* a payment out of capital money to avoid an imminent loss to the estate.[94] This applies where the property would otherwise be damaged.[95] It does not seem that this jurisdiction only applies where the settlement is created under a trust.

93 [1951] IR 387.

94 *Neill v. Neill* [1904] IR 513; *De Vere v. Perceval and Cole* (1845) Ir Jur Rep 9, per Gavan Duffy J.

95 *Re Johnson's Settlement* [1944] IR 529.

Re Lisnavagh Estate[96] concerned the Lisnavagh Estate, in County Carlow. The tenant for life of the settled estate applied to the Court for authorisation to be given to the trustees to raise and to expend capital moneys in demolishing a wing, constituting about one half of the mansion house and in reconstructing the remainder. There was no electric light in the house and the acetylene plant lighting some of the rooms was worn out. The rooms were large, with high ceilings. It was impossible to heat the house adequately, it was too large for the tenant for life and his family. The tenant for life, William McClintock, Baron Rathdonnell, nevertheless wanted to continue to live on the estate on which his family had resided for about three hundred years. Section 13 of the 1890 Act only sanctioned expenditure up to half the annual rental of the land which would be insufficient for the scheme. The court allowed the extra expenditure of capital money as salvage.

Dixon J referred to *Neill v. Neill*[97] in which the court sanctioned a large mortgage in order to preserve the property, an Australian sheep farm. He continued:

> "There, a mortgage was authorised to prevent loss or deterioration in a sheep farm and the expenditure was allowed on the principle that there was a danger of serious loss to the estate. That consideration applies here. Also, there, there was a risk that what was sanctioned would prove to be thrown away, while that risk does not exist here. Here what is expended will not only prevent a loss but will enhance the value of the estate as a whole."

The salvage principle has been used to sanction expenditure on repairs[98] and, as in *Re Lisnavagh,* partial demolition[99] "so as to make the mansion house, as it exists at present, more suited to modern requirements and the size and value of the estate to which it is now attached".[100]

d) Borrowing Money

The trustees may be given express power to borrow money. In *Re O'Reilly*[101] it was held by the High Court that such a power may be implied in some instances. In that case a settlement created by trust vested wide powers in the trustees as to the management of a family farming business. The settlement referred to the trustees powers "as if beneficially entitled to the land". Kenny J held that this was enough to imply a power to borrow.

---

96 [1952] IR 296.

97 [1904] 1 IR 513.

98 *Re Johnson's Settlement* [1944] IR 529.

99 *Re Dunham Massey Settled Estates* 22 TLR 595; *Re Windham's Settled Estate* [1912] 2 Ch. 75. In the latter the rebuilding was due to the unhealthy and ruinous condition of the old house, and for the purpose of making it habitable. The erection of complete new wings was sanctioned.

100 *Re Walker's Settled Estate* [1894] 1 Ch. 190, per North J at p.192.

101 (1975) 109 ILTR 121.

M. Overreaching Effect of Sale

One of the principal aims of the Settled Land Acts was to ensure that the land could be sold so that the purchaser would obtain a fee simple freed of the interests under the settlement. This is achieved by the process of overreaching those interests, *i.e.* they are transformed on sale from being interests in the land to being interests in the purchase money. The Act of 1882 does this in two provisions:

a) The purchaser is protected by providing that a deed executed under the Act is effectual to pass the land conveyed. . . discharged from all the limitations, powers and provisions of the settlement.[102]

Excepted from this are leases, easements *etc.* created by the tenant for life and also interests "having priority to the settlement". If, for example, a fee farm grant had been settled, the fee farm rent, since it pre-dated the deed of settlement, would not be overreached on sale and the purchaser will take the fee simple still subject to it.

b) The interests of the beneficiaries are protected by providing that for all purposes capital money from the sale is to be considered as land and is to be held for the same interests successively and in the same way as the land would have been held.[103]

This creates a fiction of non-conversion in relation to the purchase money, so that, in the eyes of the law, it remains land. This means it can be held for the same estates as the actual land was before the sale. Thus, if there are fees tail under the settlement they continue to exist in relation to the purchase money despite the fact that personal property cannot normally be entailed.

N. Compound Settlements

The definition in section 2(1) of the 1882 Act makes it clear that a settlement exists where successive interests result from any number of instruments. Where there is more than one instrument this is usually the result of resettlements having occurred. Let us say that deed No. 1 give A a life estate with a remainder to his son in tail subject to charges in favour of other members of the family. When A's son attains his majority he bars the entail with A's consent and they resettle the fee simple, by deed No. 2, on A for life, with remainder to A's son for life and remainders over. For the purposes of the acts there are now three settlements:

a) the settlement arising from deed No. 1;

b) the settlement arising from deed No. 2; and

102 Section 20(2) of the 1882 Act.

103 Section 22(5) of 1882 Act.

c) the compound settlement, arising from both deeds, which is a distinct entity.[104]

The problem with compound settlements is that it may not be possible to overreach all the interests under the settlements or that all the powers conferred by them may not be capable of being exercised. In the example given above, the position of A is as follows:

1. He or she can act as tenant for life under the original settlement and can overreach the family charges and other interests under that settlement, provided there are trustees of that settlement to receive the purchase money. He or she can also overreach the rights of those entitled under the resettlement since it is only interests having priority to the settlement under which the tenant for life is acting which are exempted from the overreaching effect.[105]

The statutory powers of the tenant for life under the original settlement still exist despite the destruction of the original life estate since section 50(1) expressly provides that they continue even if the tenant for life parts with his estate. The disadvantage of the tenant for life acting under the original settlement is that he or she cannot exercise any additional powers conferred by the resettlement.

2. He or she can act as tenant for life under the resettlement and exercise any additional powers conferred by it, but by so doing the interests, such as family charges existing under the original settlement, cannot be overreached because they have priority to the resettlement.[106]

In the example above the effect of the resettlement, on the face of it, is to destroy A's life estate and then immediately to replace it with another. There is some doubt as to the effect of inserting a restoration clause in the settlement which states that the life estate under the resettlement is in restoration and confirmation of the original life estate. It was at first held in England that the clause did not preserve the original life estate but did replace it by a new one, but further that it did allow the tenant for life under the resettlement to exercise powers conferred in the original settlement.[107] But a later House of Lords case[108] held that the original life estate did continue. This again is an example

104 *Re Earl of Pembroke & Thompson's Contract* [1932] IR 493; *e Blake's Settled Estates* [1932] IR 637, Wylie, *Cases* p.406; *Re Meade's Settled Estates* [1897] 1 IR 121; *Lord Annaly's Settled Estates* (1896) 30 ILTR 45; *Re Domvile & Callwell's Contract* [1908] 1 IR 475; *Re Mundy & Roper* [1899] 1 Ch. 275.

105 *Lord Wimbourne & Browne's Contract* [1904] 1 Ch. 537. The power to overreach subsequent interests does not extend indefinitely into the future, of course. When a fee simple is conveyed under the statutory powers the land ceases to be settled land and the tenant for life ceases to be such.

106 *Re Meade's Settlement Estates* [1897] 1 IR 121.

107 *Re Constable's Settled Estates* [1919] 1 Ch. 178.

108 *Parr v. Attorney General* [1926] AC 239.

of reifying property concepts. The important point is that it seems to be clear that such a clause enables the tenant for life under the resettlement to overreach interests contained in the original settlement.

3. He or she can act as tenant for life of the compound settlement.

This avoids the disadvantages of both (a) and (b) above, so that interests under both settlements can be overreached and powers conferred by either settlement can be exercised, but this can only be done if there are trustees of the compound settlement. It is questionable whether merely appointing the same persons as trustees of the resettlement is sufficient.

It is probably ineffective for the deed of resettlement expressly to appoint trustees of the compound settlement[109] unless the settlors control the entire estate. In such cases the tenant for life will have to go to the expense of applying to the court to appoint them or accept the disadvantages of (a) or (b).[110]

O. Trusts for Sale

The definition of settlement in section 2(1) on the face of it would have included trusts for sale of land where there were successive interests, since it refers to land "limited. . . in trust for any persons by way of succession". While the 1882 Act was in the process of being enacted an amendment, now contained in section 63, was introduced to make it clear that trusts for sale of land were indeed to be within the scope of the Act. It was in fact quite unnecessary to subject trusts for sale of land to the provisions of the Act since there is no problem of alienability. Their inclusion has generally been regarded as a mistake in policy and has led to an unnecessarily complex position.

Section 63 of the Act provides that:

> "63(1) Any land, or any estate or interest in land, which under . . . any deed, will, agreement . . . act of parliament , or other instrument or any number of instruments . . . is subject to a trust or direction for sale . . and for the application or disposal of the money to arise from the sale, or the income of that money, or the income of the land until sale, or any part of that money or income, for the benefit of any person for his life, or any other limited period, or for the benefit of two or more persons concurrently for any limited period, and whether absolutely, or subject to a trust for accumulation of income . . . or to any other restriction, shall be deemed to be settled land . . .".

In other words, the section applies to trusts for sale only where the beneficial interest is for a limited period, whether the income belongs to the beneficiary absolutely or is subject to some restriction. Where there is a trust for sale of land not for a limited period, *i.e.* the beneficiaries have a fee simple, but they

109 *Re Spencer's Settled Estates* [1903] 1 Ch. 75.

110 *Re Hayes Settled Estates* [1907] 1 IR 88.

are minors, or where one of the beneficiaries is a minor,[111] it would seem that the land will be settled land, but by virtue of section 59, not section 63. Where there is a trust for sale of land for beneficiaries all of whom are of full age and they have a fee simple, the land is a bare trust for sale and outside the Acts.[112]

Section 63 also contains a special definition of tenant for life where there is a trust for sale within the Act. It is the person, or persons, "for the time being beneficially entitled to the income of the land until sale".

The effect of the section was to give control of the land not to the trustees for sale but to the tenant for life. This was unnecessary as the trustees had power in any case to sell and to confer on the purchaser a fee simple freed from the other interests under the trust. In equity, since there was an obligation to sell, the doctrine of conversion meant that the interests under the trust were, by a fiction, regarded as already being interests in money even before sale and so were overreached when the sale took place.

The 1884 Act attempted to reform the position. Section 6 provides that the trustees for sale can exercise their powers without the consent of the tenant for life, thus reversing section 56 of the 1882 Act in relation to trusts for sale, and by section 7 of the 1884 Act the tenant for life cannot exercise his or her powers under the Acts without leave of the court.

The result is that the trustees have full power of sale unless the tenant for life has obtained such an order under section 7. However, they have no power of leasing or mortgaging or other powers, other than sale, unless the trust for sale expressly or impliedly conferred these on them.[113] The tenant for life is not entitled to an order, but must satisfy the court that the contemplated sale would benefit all parties.[114]

These provisions were invoked in *Re Naper*.[115] The plaintiff was entitled for life to the income from certain freehold property devised to trustees in trust for sale. The trust conferred wide powers of management upon the trustees until sale. In earlier proceedings, *Kirkpatrick and Maunsell v. Naper,*[116] Gavan Duffy J ordered that a sum of money, being the portion of the proceeds of sale of trees sold for cutting on the deceased's estate attributable to non-timber trees, be paid to the plaintiff, and that the balance of the purchase money be paid to the trustees to be held by them as capital. It was further ordered that the plaintiff be given leave to exercise the powers of a tenant for life in relation to leases and surrenders of leases under sections 6, 7 and 13 of the Settled Land Act, 1882.

---

111 *Re Greenville* (1882) 11 LR Ir 138.

112 *Re Earle and Webster's Contract* (1883) 24 Ch D 144, 290.

113 *Re Bellinger* [1898] 22 Ch. 534.

114 *Re Tuthill* [1907] 1 IR 305 per Meredith J.

115 (1952) 86 ILTR 106, High Court.

116 (1944) 79 ILTR 49.

In the present proceedings Dixon J held that the Court, in the exercise of its judicial discretion, was entitled, upon the plaintiff giving proper undertakings for the protection of the estate and the trustees, to let the plaintiff into possession of the settled land, and that the plaintiff was thereupon entitled to exercise all the powers conferred by the Acts on a tenant for life, provided only that she should not be entitled to exercise the power of sale or exchange without the consent of the trustees. The judge commented:

> "It is proper to give her these powers, but where the testator has directed that the trustees shall have the power of sale, the qualification should be that the plaintiff be given all the powers of the tenant for life under the Settled Land Acts, save that the power of sale and exchange may be exercised by her only with the consent of the trustees".

P. The Need for Reform

Before the 19th century legislation the strict settlement was the normal method employed to keep land in a family by restricting the power of alienation. The trust for sale, on the other hand, was a suitable form where the land was to be sold. The effect of the 19th century legislation is that the roles are effectively reversed. The Settled Land Acts allow the tenant for life under the Acts to dispose of the fee simple in accordance with the legislation. On the other hand, in the case of a trust for sale within section 63, the trustees are not given the full powers of management under the Acts. This creates a paradox and makes it difficult for lawyers to explain the law to lay clients. A possible solution is to remove trusts for sale from the operation of the Settled Land Acts altogether, or, as has recently been done in England, to create a single statutory régime of trusts of land.[117] In Ireland, however, successive estates may still exist as legal estates, not under a trust, and so the latter reform would have to be part of a more radical reform whereby successive estates could in future only exist under a trust.

117 See the Trusts of Land and Appointment of Trustees Act, 1996.

CHAPTER 15

THE IRISH LAND PURCHASE ACTS

"Partiality, one-sidedness, and partisanship, as between classes, were not nice things in themselves, but they were the very life and essence of the statute which they were considering. Its avowed purpose and policy were to take large masses of the land value of Ireland away from the landlord class and hand it over to the tenant class... He was not saying that it was wrong, or that it was right; he was merely stating that it was the fact. There might be social mischiefs or social crises so grave as to require that those things to which the lawyers were in the habit of paying, perhaps, a superstitious reverence – namely, the sacredness of property and the inviolability of contracts, should give way to the exigencies of a great public policy; and the present might be an occasion of that kind. He could not tell. He was no judge of high politics."

– Lord Justice Christian in *Shearman v. Kelly* (1878) 12 ILTSJ 98 at 99.

A. General Effect of the Acts

The Irish Land Commission was created by the Land Law (Ireland) Act, 1881 enacted during Gladstone's administration. It was the means of resolving the Land Question, *i.e.* the chronic agricultural unrest caused by the Irish land tenure system, if it can be called that, whose main features were:

1) absentee landlords who had little or no interest in their Irish estates other than collecting rent;
2) tenants with little or no security of tenure and little incentive or ability to improve the land;
3) a system of tenure which required tenants to make all improvements, including the erection of their own cottages, but which held the landlord entitled to them at the end of the tenancy or on eviction;
4) the eviction of tenants unable to pay rent, resulting in their total destitution;
5) the attempt to replace evicted tenants with landless people from the local community, resulting in great bitterness on the part of the dispossessed and imposing a cruel dilemma on those offered the chance to replace them; and

6) the reaction of agricultural tenants to their situation which took various forms, from the Whiteboys of the 18th century to the boycotts, Land War and Land League of the 19th century.

The 1881 Act, which replaced the less effective Act of 1870[1], was based on the policy of the three F's , as they were known: fixity of tenure, fair rents and free sale.[2] The Act gave security of tenure to tenants, provided a means of fixing fair rents and gave tenants the right to assign their tenancies without the landlord's consent. These measures were denounced by some at the time as an expropriation of the landlords' property rights.[3] Landlords who wished to do so could, as an alternative, sell the fee simple to the tenant. The Act established the Irish Land Commission as an intermediary, providing an advance for the purchase of the land and recovering the loan from the erstwhile tenant by an annuity charged on the land. The Land Commission was also given power to acquire land by agreement for resale to tenants. Later Acts replaced the system of advances with a system of payment by land stock and later land bonds.[4] Compulsory purchase of holdings was introduced by the Evicted Tenants Act, 1907 for the purpose of providing land for evicted tenants. The Land Act, 1923, the first land purchase Act enacted by the newly-independent government, introduced compulsory land purchase in the Republic on a general basis for the first time and the Land Act, 1933 continued the process by extending the compulsory powers of the Land Commission and removing many of the restrictions which had previously applied to acquisition.

The Irish Land Commission, having operated for over 100 years, had completed its work by 1992 and the Irish Land Commission (Dissolution) Act, 1992 provided for its abolition.[5] Although it was passed by the Oireachtas it has not as yet been brought into force by order.[6] The Act provides that the powers of the Land Commission to acquire land, except for the purposes of exchange of holdings, and to resume holdings, parcels or tenancies, are to be abolished.[7] Other powers are to be transferred to the Minister for Agriculture and Food.[8]

1 The Landlord and Tenant (Ireland) Act, 1870.

2 For an account of the Land Purchase Acts and their economic effects, see Kolbert and O'Brien, *Land Reform*.

3 See Hogan, "Arrows Too Sharply Pointed: the relations of Lord Justice Christian and Lord O'Hagan, 1868–1874" in J. F. McEldowney & Paul O'Higgins, *The Common Law Tradition: Essays in Irish Legal History* (Dublin, Irish Academic Press, 1990).

4 See Kolbert and O'Brien for a concise modern description of the Acts and their economic effects.

5 s.4.

6 See *O'Cleirigh v. Minister for Agriculture, Food and Forestry* [1998] 2 ILRM 263, Supreme Court.

7 *ibid.*, s.2(2).

8 *ibid.*, s.4.

The Irish Land Purchase Acts represented probably the most extensive system of acquisition of land in Europe carried out by legal means. Their social effects were immense. Their technical legal effect on titles was also profound, more radical in many ways than that of the Settled Land Acts.

From a technical point of view the Land Purchase Acts had an overreaching effect similar in some ways to the Settled Land Acts, 1892-90, and so they remain important from a conveyancing point of view. The following points should be noted:

1. Like the Settled Land Acts

They apply to most instances of where land is held for freehold interests other than an unencumbered fee simple estate.

The effect of a sale is to overreach other interests in the land, termed superior interests in the Land Purchase Acts, such as future freehold estates or landlords' reversions, *i.e.* to convert them into interests in the purchase money, and to convey to the purchaser, the former tenant farmer, a fee simple estate free of these interests.

2. Unlike the Settled Land Acts

The Land Purchase Acts vested the powers in the Irish Land Commission, not in a tenant for life or any other private individual.

The operation of the powers in relation to any given piece of land was a once-and-for-all exercise. Under the Settled Land Acts, the powers may be invoked more than once in relation to a given piece of land, namely, at any time it is the subject of a settlement.

Overreaching under the Land Purchase Acts was more radical than under the Settled Land Acts. Under the Settled Land Acts interests "having priority to the settlement" are not overreached, whereas under the Land Purchase Acts virtually all interests affecting the land, except easements and an important category of sporting rights , were overreached. A sale under the Land Purchase Acts thus has the effect of curing defects in the title to the fee simple. This is considered in more detail below.

A vesting deed executed by the Irish Land Commission is a good root of title since it is one of the best proofs of title in fee simple. It is proof that superior interests affecting the title were cleared off the title at the time of the vesting deed. A conveyance in fee simple under the Settled Land Acts is proof that other interests under the settlement were cleared off the title but it does not clear off interests having priority to the settlement.

The effects of the Land Purchase Acts are now almost entirely spent.[9]

---

9 See footnote 5.

B. Overreaching Effect

The Land Law (Ireland) Act, 1896 section 31 provided for the overreaching of superior interests when the fee simple was vested by the Land Commission in a purchaser[10]:

> "31. (1) Where any land has been sold under the Land Purchase Acts. . . or where land is sold by the Land Judge to the tenant thereof, and an advance under the Land Purchase Acts is made for the purpose of such sale, or where a lessor or grantor has signified his consent to the redemption of a rent under the Redemption of Rent (Ireland) Act, 1891, the sale of such land. . . or the redemption. . . shall be made discharged from all superior interests as defined by this section, or from any of them, and in every such case the land shall be vested accordingly in the purchaser in fee simple, and such superior interests, or the value thereof, shall become a lien upon, and be redeemed or satisfied out of, the purchase money of such land."
>
> (2) [Vesting order is subject to such exceptions and reservations as specified in the order.]

Section 16 of the Irish Land Act, 1903 provided that, when the Land Commission agreed to purchase land, the Land Commission could vest the land in itself prior to sale in certain cases and in such a case the section provides for overreaching to take effect when the fee simple vested in the Land Commission rather than when it vested in a purchaser:

> 16. (1) The Land Commission may, where they agree to purchase any land, make a vesting order which shall be effectual to vest in the Commission the fee simple of the land purchased, subject–
>
> (a) to any public rights affecting the land;
>
> (b) to any sporting rights[11] reserved by the vendor;
>
> (c) to any maintenance charge under the Public Works Acts; and
>
> (d) to any interests of the tenants on the land, or of persons having claims upon those interests, and to any easements, rights and appurtenances mentioned in section thirty-four of the Act of 1896; [see below] but save as aforesaid and subject to the provisions of this Act with respect to minerals, discharged from the claims of all persons who are interested in the land, whether in respect of *superior* or *intervening* interests or incumbrances or *otherwise*, and all such claims shall, as from the date of the vesting order, cease as against the land and attach to the purchase money, in like manner as immediately before the date of the order they attached to the land.

A holding vested in a purchaser was still to be subject, as the section says, to "easements, rights and appurtenances; and any privilege previously in fact enjoyed, whether by permission of the landlord or otherwise. . ." under section 34 of the 1896 Act, and to certain sporting rights, which are considered below.

---

10 Replacing Landlord and Tenant (Ireland) Act, 1870 s.35. See also Irish Land Act, 1903 s.98 and Irish Land Act, 1909 s.23(5).

11 See below for sporting rights.

1. Superior Interests

The Land Law (Ireland) Act, 1896 contained a wide definition of the superior interests overreached by a vesting order:

> "31.–(8) The expression "superior interest" shall include any rent, rentcharge, annuity, fees, duties, services, payable to or to be rendered in respect of the land sold to any person, [including the Crown] and any estates, exceptions, reservations, covenants, conditions, or agreements, contained in any fee-farm grant, or other conveyance in fee, or lease, under which such land is held, and, if such land is held under a lease for lives or years renewable forever, or for a term of years of which not less than 60 are unexpired at the date of the sale, shall include any reversion or estate expectant on the determination of such lease or expiration of such term, and notwithstanding that such reversion or estate may be vested in the [State]."

Superior interest also includes any reversion expectant on the determination of an estate tail or a base fee, whether or not vested formerly in the crown.[12]

The more radical effect of overreaching under the Land Purchase Acts can be seen here, in that it actually cures defects in the title to the fee simple. If the title purchased and conveyed to a former tenant was really a base fee, the section nevertheless has the effect of overreaching it and therefore, in effect, converting the base fee into a full fee simple. This gets rid of one of the possible defects in a title which would not be entirely cured by the Statute of Limitations, 1957.[13]

It may be noticed that the definition does not include a reversion expectant on a life estate, but section 31(7) of the 1896 Act provides that where the superior interest is settled land within the Settled Land Acts, the person who is tenant for life or has the powers of tenant for life of the interest has the power to consent to the sale being made discharged from such interest. Section 16 of the 1903 Act (above) applies not only to superior interests but to the claims of "all persons who are interested in the land". This section replaces the earlier provision contained in the Landlord and Tenant (Ireland) Act, 1870 section 35.

This section is extended by the Congested Districts Board (Ireland) Act, 1899 section 2 to cases where the land is sold by the Congested Districts Board.

Superior interests vesting in Land Commission under the Land Act, 1923 are converted to personalty for the purpose of determining their destination or of the redemption money.[14]

12 Irish Land Act, 1903 section 98(2), State Property Act 1954 section 21.

13 See Chapter 25 Adverse Possession.

14 Land Act, 1931, s.32(2).

2. Intervening Interests

The Land Commission had power to vest the fee simple in a subtenant rather than the tenant. The policy of the acts was generally to vest the fee simple in the person substantially occupying the land and farming it and where there was a subtenancy the subtenant was likely to be that person. The provisions are in the Irish Land Act, 1903:

> "15(1) In the case of the sale of an estate the Land Commission may, if they think fit, declare that any person who, as a subtenant, is in the exclusive occupation of a parcel of land comprised in the estate shall be deemed the tenant of that parcel, and the parcel shall be deemed to be a holding.
>
> (2) The Land Commission shall in such case redeem the interests (in this Part of this Act referred to as "intervening interests") intervening between the owner of the estate and the person in such exclusive occupation as aforesaid, at a price which [in default of agreement] shall be fixed by the Land Commission and the redemption money shall be paid out of the purchase money of the estate. . . provided that, if the Land Commission are of opinion that any intervening interest is of no appreciable value, they shall by order declare that interest to be extinguished."

3. Sporting Rights

Many sporting rights of the vendor were exempted from the overreaching effect of the Acts and so remained vested in the former owners.[15]

4. Resumption of Holding

Where the Land Commission resumed a holding[16] there is a separate overreaching provision in section 12 of the Land Act, 1953, but sporting rights were further preserved from the effect of that section[17] where they were vested in someone other than the tenant.

C. Registration of Vesting Orders

Registration of vesting orders was provided for by section 16(3), *i.e.* for registration under the 1891 Act. The section was replaced by the Land Act, 1931 section 31 (as full owner), which was repealed by the Registration of Title Act, 1964 section 5. Vesting orders now come within the compulsory registration provision of section 23 of the 1964 Act ("where the land has been, or is deemed to have been, at any time sold and conveyed to or vested in any person under any of the provisions of the Land Purchase Acts"), and section 26 provides that

15 See Chapter 22.

16 See Land Act, 1939 s.54; Land Act, 1953 s.18; Land Act, 1965 s.14.

17 s.12(6).

where land has been so sold, conveyed or vested before 1 January 1892, the person appearing to the Land Commission to be in possession shall be registered as the owner.

D. Land Purchase Annuities

The original form of land purchase was that the Land Commission paid the landowner the purchase price of the land as an advance and then recovered the money over a period of time from the former tenant and successors in title by attaching to the land a land purchase annuity. Under section 20 of the Land Law (Ireland) Act, 1887 such an annuity has priority over all existing and future estates, interests and incumbrances created either by the landlord or the tenant with the exception of a quit rent, other charges incident to the tenure, other charges for public money, and, where the land is subject to a fee farm rent or a lease reserving a rent, to such a rent. The annuity is an incorporeal hereditament separate from and paramount to the estate of the owner.[18]

18 See also *Re Parkinson* [1898] 1 IR 390.

CHAPTER 16

CO-OWNERSHIP

A. Introduction

Interests in land may be held by more than one person at the same time, which implies some form of co-ownership. The common law recognised four forms of co-ownership: joint tenancy, tenancy in common, coparcenary and tenancy by entireties. Coparcenary is now rare and tenancy by entireties is practically obsolete.

B. Joint Tenancy

The characteristics of joint tenancy are the principle of survivorship and the four unities.

1. Survivorship (*Jus Accrescendi*)

a) General

The basic principle is that when one joint tenant dies his or her interest in the land ceases and the surviving joint tenants hold the property among themselves. If the death of a joint tenant leaves only one remaining owner, then co-ownership ceases and the sole survivor holds the estate alone. It follows from this that the principle of survivorship takes precedence over a gift of his or her interest by a joint tenant by will.[1] The Succession Act, 1965 section 4(c) confirms this by providing that:

> "4(c) – the estate or interest of a deceased person under a joint tenancy where any tenant survives the deceased person shall be deemed to be an estate or interest ceasing on his death".

If land is held in fee simple by A and B as joint tenants and A leaves his interest by will to X, then the result depends on whether A survives B or not. If A survives B, then A has become sole owner and the gift in the will can take effect. If A dies before B, then at A's death, when the will takes effect, A has ceased to have any interest in the land and the gift in his will fails.[2] There is nothing to

1 Co Litt 185b.

2 The result is not produced by pure logic, because it may be noticed that the event on which rule of survivorship and the will depend is the same, *i.e.* the death of A, and in logic they take effect simultaneously.

prevent a joint tenant disposing of his or her interest *inter vivos*, the effect being to sever the joint tenancy as between the conveying tenant and the other joint tenants.[3]

The principle of survivorship developed in the feudal period possibly because the class of feudal lords wished to ensure that the tenements held from them did not become divided up among an ever-increasing number of tenants. If that had been allowed to occur the enforcement of feudal services would have become more difficult. It also corresponded with social relations between family members who would be likely to want the property on their death to be held by remaining family members. The rule has survived to the present day because it has come to perform a different requirement. It is a convenient mode of holding for trustees. When one trustee dies the property vests automatically in the remaining trustees without the necessity of a deed vesting it in them.

The principle of survivorship is the main reason why the interest of a joint tenant is not spoken of by lawyers as an undivided share as is the case with a tenancy in common. But this conceptual distinction is rather artificial. If A, B and C hold land in joint tenancy, A has something which she can sell to a third party, X. If A does sell her interest this has the effect of creating a tenancy in common between X on the one hand and B and C on the other. X has a one third share as tenant in common. So A really had something in the nature of an inchoate one third share for this purpose. Equally, if A, B and C had decided to sell the land, A would have been entitled to one third of the proceeds.[4]

b) Simultaneous Death

One special problem that arises on the death of joint tenants is that of *commorientes* (those dying together), *i.e.* when two or more joint tenants all die in the same accident or catastrophe. Those claiming the estates of the various joint tenants could only succeed by showing that the one from whom they claimed had survived the others. Usually this could not be done due to lack of evidence. In such a case the common law treated the heirs of the deceased joint tenants as themselves holding on joint tenancy. The Succession Act, 1965 section 5 now provides that:

> "5.– Where, after the commencement of this Act, two or more persons have died in circumstances rendering it uncertain which of them survived the other or others, then, for the purposes of the distribution of the estate of any of them, they shall all be deemed to have died simultaneously".[5]

---

3 See "Severance of a Joint Tenancy" below.

4 *Re Wilks* [1891] 3 Ch. 59. In the absence of an intention to sever, the money is held on joint tenancy until divided: *Byrne v. Byrne*, unreported, High Court, McWilliam J, 18 January; *Re Hayes' Estate* [1920] 1 IR 207

5 Apparently taken from the German Civil Code, Art. 20, as amended in 1951. Also see the Swiss Civil Code, Art. 32 and McGuire p.10.

The effect of this would seem to be that none of those who hold the property can take by survivorship. It is now the personal representatives of the deceased who hold the property on trust for the persons entitled under the will or on intestacy.[6] It may be the case that while the personal representatives hold the legal estate as joint tenants, the equitable interest is held by those entitled to it as tenants in common, so that simultaneous death causes a severance in equity.

c) Unlawful Killing

An exception to the survivorship rule occurs as a result of the rule that a wrongdoer may not benefit from his or her wrong.[7] If one joint tenant kills another in order to benefit by survivorship, or possibly even where there is no such motive but the killing is unlawful, then a rule of forfeiture operates and deprives the joint tenant of the benefit of survivorship.[8] It is not, however, clear in this jurisdiction whether this operates so as to prevent the legal title vesting in the surviving joint tenant, or, which is the solution favoured by the English courts,[9] that the legal estate vests in the killer by survivorship but that he or she holds it on a constructive trust. The latter solution is seen as an application of the unjust enrichment principle in equity.

It is also open to question whether the killer is merely deprived of the benefit flowing from the wrong, or whether his or her own interest is forfeit as well, which is arguably going beyond the principle involved. If A and B are joint tenants and A kills B, then survivorship does not operate to vest the property in A as sole beneficial owner. But should it vest instead solely in those entitled to B's estate, which would impose the additional penalty of depriving A of his or her original interest as joint tenant? A's original interest as joint tenant was not attributable to the wrong. An alternative is that A continues to hold in co-ownership with those entitled to B's estate, either in joint tenancy or that the joint tenancy is severed, producing a tenancy in common between A and B's estate.

The problem of unlawful killing also arises in succession, where it is now governed by section 120 of the Succession Act, 1965.[10]

---

6 Succession Act, 1965 s.10.

7 Note: "Disposition of Property held in Joint Tenancy When One Co-tenant Causes the Death of the Other" (1957) 41 Minn L Rev 639; Ague, "Homicide – Effect on Wrongdoer's Inheritance, Intestate and Survivorship Rights," (1953) 7 Miami LQ 524. *Riggs v. Palmer* (1889) 115 NY 506; 22 NE 188, Court of Appeals of New York; *Cleaver v. Mutual Reserve Fund Life Association* [1892] 1 QB 147, CA (Eng); *Re Crippen's Estate* [1911] P 108, [1911–13] All ER Reprint 207.

8 *Oleff v. Hodapp* (1935) 129 Ohio 432; *Re K (deceased)* [1986] 1 Ch 180, [1985] 2 All ER 833, [1985] 3 WLR 202, [1985] FLR 79, [1986] Fam Law 19, CA (civil). *Re H (deceased)* unreported, Ch D, 19 June 1987 (Transcript: Lexis).

9 *Cleaver v. Mutual Reserve Fund Life Association* [1892] 1 QB 147, CA (Eng); In England after 1925 there can be no severance of the legal title.

10 See Chapter 26 Succession: Failure of Benefit: Lapse.

2. The Four Unities

In order that a joint tenancy can exist there must be the four unities. These are the unities of possession, interest, title and time.

d) Possession

This unity is a characteristic shared by all forms of co-ownership. Each co-owner is entitled to possession of the whole premises. A co-owner who evicts another co-owner from the premises is therefore liable in trespass.[11] Acts which destroy the enjoyment of the property in common can amount to ouster.[12] At common law a co-owner who had not been ousted had no action against another co-owner, so that if the property had been rented out in his absence he had no action to recover his part of the rent if it had been retained by the other co-owner. The Administration of Justice Act, 1707[13] gives a co-owner the right to sue for an account against a co-owner who received more than his share of rent or profit.

There are problems with the unity of possession which do not seem to have been resolved by caselaw, probably because the concept depends upon co-owners resolving disputes between themselves. If each co-owner has the right to possession the whole premises, can one have no exclusive right to a bedroom? Can one not exclude the others from the bathroom while the one is actually using it, without being liable for trespass?

In *Lahiffe v. Hecker*[14] Lynch J had to grapple with some of these problems in a fact situation complicated by an attempt to give one of the joint tenants an additional right of residence.[15] The testator left a house to his three daughters, A, B, and C and son, D, as joint tenants, subject to a right of residence in C "until she marries". A, B and D were married. The parties subsequently severed the joint tenancy by an assent, which vested the house in them as tenants in common in equal shares. Lynch J held that, while C was not entitled to exclude the other tenants in common from possession, they, on the other hand, could not exercise their right to possession so to overcrowd the property that it would render C's right of residence ineffective. C, while "not legally entitled to the exclusive use of any particular part of the house" would be entitled to choose

11 Cheshire, (13th ed.) 209; *Beaumont v. Kinsella* (1859) 8 Ir CLR 291. In Wylie, *Irish Land Law* para, 7.07 "such an action" seems to refer only to account. See now section 3 of the Housing (Miscellaneous Provisions) Act, 1997 under which a tenant of a housing authority who is a joint tenant may obtain an exclusion order against another joint tenant. Barring orders made under section 3 of the Domestic Violence Act, 1996 would also seem to apply to joint tenants.

12 *Beaumont v. Kinsella* (1859) 8 Ir CLR 291.

13 6 Anne c.10 (Ir); *Dawson v. Baxter* (1887) 19 LR Ir 103, V-C.

14 Unreported, High Court, Lynch J, 28 April 1994.

15 On rights of residence see Chapter 18.

one of the three bedrooms in the house for her exclusive use, "to enable her properly to enjoy her general right of residence in the house". He further held that the right of residence did not inhibit the discretion of the court to order a sale on an application under the Partition Acts.[16] The judge also held that on sale C would be entitled to an additional fractional share in respect of her right of residence. One might note that the intention of the testator may well have been to ensure C's right to possession rather than to give her an extra share of money. It seems unfortunate that the courts have been unwilling, with at least one exception[17], to give effect to this intention behind rights of residence and to hold that they may be overreached.

e) Interest

Every joint tenant must have an identical interest in the land. If one co-owner has a freehold interest and another a leasehold interest they do not hold as joint tenants. Moreover, they must have the same estates, *e.g.* both fees simple, or both life estates. The unity of interest is not affected if one joint tenant has an additional interest in the land created at the same time (or possibly before) the joint tenancy:

> *to X and Y for life, remainder to X in fee simple.*

X and Y still have a joint tenancy for their joint lives.[18]

f) Title

Joint tenants must take by the same title, *e.g.* the same deed, or will or the same act of adverse possession.[19] If A conveys land to B and C jointly and then C sells his interest to D, B and D are not joint tenants. B's title derives from the conveyance by A, D's from the conveyance by C. It should be noted here that it is a common situation in rural Ireland for members of a family to remain in possession of land after the death of the owner without the estate being administered. In such a case the members of the family who remain acquire by adverse possession the interests of those who are absent. They acquire them as joint tenants so that, as between those who remain, the principle of survivorship applies.[20] It may be that the courts here support the notion not

---

16 See below.

17 *Johnston v. Horace* [1993] ILRM 594, per Lavan J. See Chapter 18.

18 Contrast subsequent acquisition of an interest by a joint tenant: See Severance of a Joint tenancy below.

19 *Maher v. Maher* [1987] ILRM 582, High Court, Circuit App; *Gleeson v. Feehan* [1997] ILRM 522.

20 *Maher v. Maher* [1987] ILRM 582; *Gleeson v. Feehan* [1997] ILRM 522. They also acquire their own prospective shares as joint tenants: Succession Act, 1965 s.125, reversing *Smith v. Savage* (1906) 1IR 469, 48 ILTR 41; *Gleeson v. Feehan* [1997] ILRM 522.

only that those who have left should be excluded, but also that those who remain constitute a new family unit as to which survivorship rightly applies.

g) Time

(1) General

Joint tenants must also take vested interests at the same time. If land is granted at common law:

to A for life, remainder to the heirs of B and C

and B and C die in A's lifetime, the heirs of B and C are tenants in common. The class of heirs of a person are ascertained when that person dies[21] and so although the heirs of B and of C take by the same title, their interests vested at different times. The common law principle is not satisfied by the interests vesting in possession at the same time.

(2) Legal Executory Interests and Trusts

There is now an important exception to the unity of time and that is where the limitation creates an executory interest or a trust. Such interests often arose in family settlements. Equity before the Statute of Uses, and afterwards the common law courts in relation to executed uses, were less stringent than the common law once was. The explanation seems to be that joint tenancy is a more appropriate form in the case of limitations to members of the same family.

In *O'Hea v. Slattery*[22] a settlement was made of tenancies from year to year (and personal chattels) to trustees on trust for the settlor until his intended marriage and then on trust for the settlor, his wife and the children of the present marriage and that of his previous marriage. The court held that the intention was that the settlor, his wife and the children should hold as co-owners. Furthermore they held as joint tenants. Later-born children would take interests when they were born, existing joint tenants being divested of their interests to the extent necessary to provide such interests. Unity of time was not required.[23]

21 See Chapter 6 Fee simple: Heirs used as a Word of Purchase.

22 [1895] 1 IR 7.

23 A similar exception existed in the past in relation to executory devises, so that in a limitation in a will "to A for life, remainder to her children in fee simple" the children took as joint tenants although their interests vested in interest at different times. It is suggested that the exception now applies to all gifts in wills, either because they take effect initially as equitable interests, the legal estate vesting in the personal representatives, See Chapter 10 Future Interests.

C. Tenancy in Common

1. No Survivorship

The principle of survivorship does not apply to tenancies in common. When one tenant in common dies his or her interest passes to the devisee or legatee under their will or to the persons entitled on intestacy. For this reason land held on tenancy in common is said to be held in undivided shares. Each tenant has a claim to a share in the property which will not be destroyed by their death.

2. Unity of Possession

The only unity that need be present for a tenant in common to exist is the unity of possession.

D. The Problem of Legal Tenancies in Common

Legal tenancies in common potentially create a problem of alienability in Irish land law because they allow the possibility of dividing the legal title into many separate shares. Suppose a legal tenancy in common was originally vested in A, B and C in equal shares. Suppose that A, B and C have now died. A left his share by will to D, E and F. B died intestate leaving children G and H. C also died intestate leaving children I, J, K and L. D, E and F now have one ninth of the legal interest each. G and H both have one sixth. I, J, K and L each have one twelfth. All these people will have to join together to convey the whole fee simple in the land, since they must all be parties to the deed. Underhill,[24] who investigated the law of property in England before the 1925 legislation, found a case of a house the title to which had become divided among 17 people, each entitled to one seventieth or multiples of that fraction. This had resulted from two relatively simple wills.[25] A reform of the law in this area might make it impossible in future to create a legal tenancy in common and also make it impossible to sever a legal joint tenancy so as to produce one.

---

24 Sir Arthur Underhill in Fourth Report, 1919 p.30. Cited in Cheshire, *Real Property* (9th ed.) pp. 307–8, (13th ed.) 218.

25 A man had devised the house by will to his wife for life, remainder to his children in fee simple. He had ten children, one of whom died in the widow's lifetime leaving seven children and a widow and a similar will.

E. Creation of Joint Tenancy and Tenancy in Common

1. At law

At common law there is a presumption in favour of a joint tenancy rather than a tenancy in common. Thus if land is conveyed:

to A and B in fee simple

prima facie they hold the legal title as joint tenants. This rule is a survival of the feudal policy referred to above. It might also be noticed that the common law prefers to regard the relationship as a non-market one – in the feudal period co-tenants were presumed by the law to be family members as between whom survivorship was appropriate. In fact co-tenants in the feudal period would probably be members of the same family or kin group, and so the presumption also corresponded with social reality. The common law presumption is rebutted by:

a) Lack of One of the Four Unities

If one of the four unities is absent there can be no joint tenancy, although, as we have seen, exceptions to the unity of time are allowed.

b) Words of Severance

Certain words used in a limitation have been held to rebut the presumption of a joint tenancy and to indicate that a tenancy in common is intended. Words such as: "in equal shares," "share and share alike,"[26] "equally"[27] "between" "among" and "respectively"[28] suggest an undivided share rather than the interest of a joint tenant.

2. In Equity

Equity tends to favour a tenancy in common rather than a joint tenancy: equity leans against survivorship. Equity reveals here again its preference for commodity relationships in which survivorship would be inappropriate. There is, however, no general presumption in equity. There are instead a number of situations in which equity intervenes and presumes a tenancy in common. There are other situations in which equity does not intervene.

In situations where equity intervenes the single legal owner or the legal joint tenants will hold the legal title on trust for the beneficiaries as tenants in common. Thus, if A, B, and C hold the legal title as joint tenants in circum-

26 *Hayes v. Ward* (1788) 2 Ridg PC 85.

27 *Lewen v. Dodd* (1595) Cro Eliz 443; *Lewen v. Cox* (1599) Cro Eliz 695.

28 *Flemming v. Fleming* (1857) 5 Ir Ch R 129. But *Re Newsom's Trusts* (1878) 1 LR IR 373 ("sole and separate use of herself and her daughters" in a will held to give joint tenancy).

stances in which equity would infer a tenancy in common, they will hold the legal title as trustees for themselves as tenants in common in equity. Survivorship operates as to the legal title but not as to the beneficial interest. Thus if C dies, the legal title is held by A and B alone, since they are the surviving joint tenants. But C's beneficial interest will pass to whoever becomes entitled to his estate on his death.

a) Multiple Title

(1) Equal Contribution

If two or more people hold the legal title to property as joint tenants, and the purchase money is provided by them in equal shares, then equity presumes that there is nothing to displace the common law position and the parties hold the beneficial interest as well as the legal title as joint tenants.

The presumption can be rebutted by evidence of an actual intention to the contrary. In *O'Connell v. Harrison*[29] there was such evidence. A number of shares were purchased and put in the joint names of two sisters, MW and EW. There was no evidence as to the proportion in which the purchase price was provided, although the judge was prepared to assume that it was in equal shares. EW became of unsound mind and MW was appointed her legal committee. MW died not long after and was survived by EW, who died two years after her sister. The personal representative of EW claimed that the shares were held in joint tenancy and that EW's estate was entitled to them by survivorship. Kennedy CJ held that the sisters held the shares as tenants in common in equity. There were three pieces of evidence which pointed to this conclusion. The sisters had inherited a business and some other shares from their father and had later executed a deed declaring that these were held as beneficial tenants in common. They had themselves bought other shares which, although taken in their joint names, were declared by deed to be held as tenants in common. Finally, MW, while she was the committee of EW, had declared that EW was entitled to half the shares and asked that they be applied to her maintenance.

(2) Unequal Contribution

If the legal title is in the name of more than one person as joint tenants but the purchase money is provided by them in unequal shares, equity presumes that the person who provided the greater share did not intend to make a gift of the excess amount to the other party or parties, and therefore that they hold the legal title on trust for themselves as tenants in common. Thus, if A and B buy property and A provides £6,000 and B provides £4,000, then if they were to be beneficial joint tenants, if the joint tenancy were to be put to an end by partition, each would receive half the proceeds. A would, by his initial contribution,

29 [1927] IR 330.

have made a gift to B of a proportion of the property initially represented by £1,000. The presumption in equity, however, is that A did not intend to make a gift to B and so they hold the joint tenancy in trust for themselves as tenants in common in proportion to the amounts contributed.[30] Equity shows its commodity-oriented aspect here. The relationship that it assumes is one in which the parties seek to maximise their own advantage and so only part with something in order to obtain a corresponding benefit.

b) Single Title

It may be that, although the legal title is held by one person only, more than one person has contributed to the purchase of the property. Equity presumes that the holder of the legal title holds it on trust for himself or herself and the other party as tenants in common in equity. Equity presumes that the party who contributed but who does not hold the legal estate did not intend to make a gift of the money to the titleholder, but intended to acquire some interest in the property.

In the English case of *Bull v. Bull*[31] the plaintiff and his mother bought a house to be a home for themselves. The son provided most of the purchase money and the conveyance was taken in his name alone. The court held that the mother did not intend to make a gift of the money to him. The son later married and it was agreed that the mother should occupy two rooms in the house and the son and his wife the rest of the house. Differences of opinion arose between the mother and her daughter-in-law and the son gave his mother notice to quit. When she refused to leave, he sued her for possession. Denning LJ in the English Court of Appeal held that the provision by the mother of part of the purchase price had made her a tenant in common with the son in equity. As such she was entitled to remain in possession concurrently with the son. Although this conclusion had the effect of securing the mother's possession, it ignored the fact that the agreement entered into on the son's marriage gave her possession of only two rooms in the house. Ignoring the fact did have the advantage of avoiding the awkward conclusion, which would seem to be inevitable, that the agreement had caused a partition in equity.

In *Jones v. Jones*[32] a father bought a house near his own home for his son. The son moved into the house with his wife and family, having given up a job in a different town in order to do so. The son gave his father money equal to a quarter of the price of the house. The son understood from his father that the house was to be his. The father then died and the house vested in the plaintiff

30 *Lake v. Gibson* (1729) 1 Eq Ca Abr 290, 291.

31 [1955] 1 QB 234, [1955] 1 All ER 253, [1955] 2 WLR 78, 164 EG 660, [1954] EGD 136, (Denning, Hodson and Parker, LJJ).

32 [1977] 2 All ER 231, [1977] 1 WLR 438, 33 P&CR 147, 242 EG 371, [1977] EGD 793, (Lord Denning MR, Roskill and Lawton LJJ)

who was the son's stepmother. The English Court of Appeal held that the son was a tenant in common and could not be evicted. In the reported proceedings the step-mother sued for rent, but it was held that, as with joint tenants, one tenant in common could not claim rent from another unless the claimant had been ousted from possession.[33]

c) Mortgage Loans.

In the past it was not uncommon for private persons to invest money by advancing it on the security of a mortgage. If two or more people lent money on the mortgage of property, whether in equal or unequal shares, then even if the legal interest which they took in the property mortgaged to them was a joint tenancy, equity presumed a beneficial tenancy in common. Since it was a commercial transaction the assumption was readily made that survivorship was not an appropriate principle to apply.

d) Partnership

Since partnership is a commercial relationship then, even if the legal estate in property vested in partners is a joint tenancy, equity presumes that partnership assets are held as between the partners themselves[34] in a tenancy in common.

Reilly v. Walsh[35] is an instance of the presumption being rebutted. In that case a partnership was carried on by two brothers. One of the brothers became insane and took little part in the business from then on. He was later discharged from hospital as cured and left a will in which he purported to leave his share of the assets to the plaintiff. It was held that the assets were held beneficially as joint tenants and so the gift in the will was defeated by survivorship. The result was due in part to the fact that the deceased brother had taken little part in the business and to the augmentation of the assets. It may also have been because the partners were also brothers.

e) Other Situations

The above situations are not exhaustive of the instances in which equity will intervene to find a tenancy in common.

In *Twigg v. Twigg*[36] the testator directed trustees to sell the residue of his estate and to hold the money on trust for his nephews and nieces. He then strongly recommended, without imposing a trust to that effect, that the nephews and nieces should expend the money on the education of their children. Some of the beneficiaries were unmarried. It was held that the money was held

---

33 The facts were held also to have given rise to a claim under the doctrine of proprietary estoppel and that the step-mother was bound by the claim.

34 *Hayden v. Carroll* (1796) 3 Ridg P C 545 per Lord Carlton at 620.

35 (1849) 11 Ir Eq R 22.

36 [1933] IR 65.

in tenancy in common in equal shares. The testator could not be taken to have intended that the unmarried beneficiaries should contribute out of a joint fund for the education of the married beneficiaries' children.

In *L'Estrange v. L'Estrange*[37] the testator devised the residue of his estate to trustees for six of his children with power to advance such sums for the education and advance in life of the children as the trustees thought fit. Lord Ashbourne LC held that the power of advancement was inconsistent with a joint tenancy. It showed that they were treated as having different needs and so were intended to take separate interests. The children were held to be tenants in common of the residue.

In *Malayan Credit Ltd v. Jack Chia MPH Ltd*[38] two businessmen took a lease of the seventh floor in an office block in Singapore. There was no lump sum to be paid, but they agreed to divide the rent and the floor space in the same unequal proportions. The Privy Council held that they were tenants in common in equity.

f) Presumption of Advancement

In some situations the normal presumption is replaced by the presumption of advancement. This applies in certain relationships in which equity recognises that one person owes an obligation to provide for another, such as a father for a son[39] or a grandfather for a grandson.[40] If, for example, a father and son both contribute to the purchase of property the title to which is put in the son's name, the presumption is that the father made an advancement, *i.e.* a gift, to the son and the father does not obtain a beneficial interest in equity.

The presumption of advancement used to apply between husband and wife, in that a husband was regarded as being under an obligation to provide for his wife, but the increasing recognition of equality of the sexes has lead the courts to reduce the strength of the presumption of advancement in the case of married couples.[41]

---

37 [1902] 1 IR 467.

38 [1986] 1 All ER 711, Privy Council.

39 *Redington v. Redington* (1794) 3 Ridg P C 201, Ir HL; *Scroope v. Scroope* (1663) 1 Chan Cas 27, 22 ER 677, per Lord Clarendon; *Grey (Lord) v. Grey (Lady)* (1666) 1 Chan Cas 296, Finch 338, 22 ER 809, per Lord Nottingham; *Elliot v. Elliot* (1677) 2 Chan Cas 231, 22 ER 920.

40 *Ebrand v. Duncer* (1680) 2 Chan Cas 26, 22 ER 829; *Stileman v. Ashdown* (1737) 2 Atk 477, 26 ER 688, per Lord Hardwicke; *Taylor v. Taylor* (1737) 1 Atk 386, 26 ER 247.

41 *RF v. MF,* unreported, Supreme Court, 24 October 1985, Henchy J nem diss. *Heavey v. Heavey* (1977) 111 ILTR 1, High Court; *McGill v. S* [1979] IR 283; *Parkes v. Parkes* [1980] ILRM 137, High Court; *Pettit v. Pettit* [1970] AC 777, [1969] 2 All ER 385, [1969] 2 WLR 966, 20 P& CR 991, 211 EG 829, [1969] EGD 764, House of Lords, and see Chapter 17 Family Property.

In *RF v. MF*[42] Henchy J treated it as still applying to some degree where the wife adopts the traditional role of homemaker, but as weak and easily rebutted when both parties go out to work and provide for the family out of their own income. There is said to be no presumption that a wife owes an obligation to provide for her husband.[43]

g) Express Declaration of Trust

A question that sometimes arises is whether an express declaration by the parties as to their respective beneficial interests is conclusive. One view derives from a political attitude which supports the idea that the market mechanism should operate as free from state intervention or interference as possible.

This view asserts that parties are the best judges of their own interests. They are also assumed to be equal in their economic strength, and so it is also assumed that the agreement is a free one. Thus, on these assumptions, the role of equity is limited to spelling out the intentions of the parties only where they have not made them clear.

This being the case, any express declaration by the parties as to their intentions is treated as conclusive and renders the intervention of equity unnecessary.[44] An alternative approach is based upon a political attitude to the market which regards it as producing injustice in that it does not satisfy human needs unless the subjects have the means to pay for the goods to satisfy them. This approach is prepared to question the assumptions of the free market approach and in particular to question whether the terms of the agreement represent the interests of both parties, or merely those of the stronger.[45] Irish courts, where the issue has arisen, have tended to find that an express declaration ousts the inference of a tenancy in common in equity, but without stating categorically that it is conclusive.[46]

F. Severance of Joint Tenancy

Severance of a joint tenancy does not put an end to the co-ownership but converts the joint tenancy to a tenancy in common. Essentially, therefore, it means that survivorship ceases to apply. Logically, since it is possible to have a tenancy in common with all the four unities, severance does not necessarily require the

42 Unreported, Supreme Court, 24 October 1985, Henchy J nem diss.

43 *Containercare v. Wycherley* [1982] IR 143, per Carroll J at p.152.

44 This approach is seen in the English case of *Goodman v. Gallant* [1986] 1 All ER 311.

45 In *Bedson v. Bedson* [1965] 3 All ER 307 Denning and two other judges held that such a declaration was not necessarily conclusive and were prepared to scrutinise it to see if represented the real interests of the parties.

46 See *W v. W* [1981] ILRM 202; *Containercare Ltd v. Wycherley* [1982] IR 143, Carroll J at p.147.

destruction of one of the four unities, but for severance to take effect at law, *i.e.* to sever the legal title, the common law does require some objective transaction which has this effect. On the other hand, since it is not possible for a joint tenancy to continue if one of the four unities is absent, destruction of any one of them, at law or in equity, will cause a severance. There are two exceptions to this, however. Since the unity of possession is essential both to a joint tenancy and to a tenancy in common, destruction of this unity will put an end to the co-ownership altogether. This is known as partition and is dealt with later. The unity of time is a pre-condition. Either it is present at the beginning or it is not. Severance, where it is caused by the destruction of one of the unities, therefore concerns the unities of interest and of title.

1. Severance at Law

In order to cause a severance the common law required some transaction which destroys one of the unities, in effect, as we have seen, the unity of interest or the unity of title. Mere intention of the parties, whether mutual or unilateral, is not enough. There are possibly two reasons why the common law took this view. First, early legal systems tend to the notion that it is external acts that are significant, rather than subjective states of mind. Secondly, we have already seen that the feudal common law favoured joint tenancies over tenancies in common and was not disposed therefore to make it easy to put an end to a joint tenancy.

a) Subsequent Acquisition of Another Interest

First, one should notice that the fact that an interest is given to a number of persons as joint tenants and at the same time an additional interest is given to one of them, that does not prevent the joint tenancy taking effect as such.[47]

If a legal joint tenant acquires an additional interest in the property at a later time it destroys the unity of interest and produces a severance.[48] So if the original limitation was:

> *to X and Y for life, remainder to Z in fee simple*

and Z conveys his interest to X, the joint tenancy between X and Y is severed.[49] Y retains a half share as tenant in common for life. X's life interest merges with the fee simple and so he has a half share in fee simple as tenant in common with Y during Y's life. When Y dies, X or his estate has the fee simple in sole ownership, as Y's interest has come to an end. If X dies first, then the

47 Although it may exacerbate problems raised by the unity of possession: see *Lahiffe v. Hecker*, unreported, High Court, Lynch J, 28 April 199, above, where the point was assumed.

48 *Connolly v. Connolly* (1866) 17 Ir Ch R 208; *Flynn v. Flynn* [1930] IR 337.

49 *Wiscot's Case* (1599) 2 Co Rep 60b.

person entitled to his estate holds the fee simple as tenant in common with Y during Y's life, and when Y dies, as sole owner.

Such was the primitive concern of the feudal common law with form rather than substance, that the effect of a transaction depended on technical distinctions between different forms of deed, such as a conveyance and a release, the latter being the correct deed to use in transferring interests between joint tenants. So in the limitation:

to X, Y and Z in fee simple

if X releases his interest to Y, it operates only between X and Y. It causes a severance in relation to X's interest only. Y holds a one third share as tenant in common, representing X's interest. Z and Y hold the other two thirds as joint tenants:

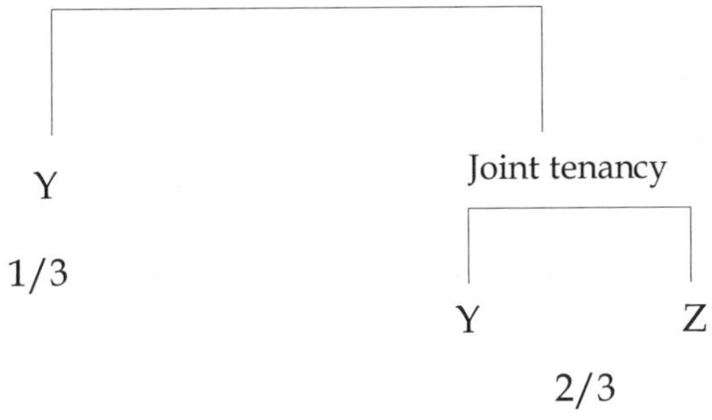

If Y dies before Z, Z takes the whole two thirds by survivorship, but the other one third remains part of Y's estate. In the limitation:

to X for life, remainder to Y and Z in fee simple

if X surrenders her estate to Y, the surrender has the effect of destroying X's interest rather than conveying it. There is no severance between Y and Z.[50] In theory Y has not acquired any additional estate. Hence the fee simple takes effect in possession in favour of Y and Z as joint tenants. Z benefits, although not a party to the deed. If, on the other hand, X conveys her interest to Y, Y has obtained an additional interest and this causes a severance between Y and Z.[51] It would seem that the effect is that the fee simple vests in possession at once, both as to Y and to Z, since there is no prior estate to postpone either interest, but that Y and Z take as tenants in common. This distinction follows from the purely technical distinction between the effect of a surrender and a conveyance.

50 Co Litt 192a.

51 Co Litt 183a, 192a.

b) Alienation by One Joint Tenant to a Third Party

Alienation by one joint tenant of his or her interest to a third party destroys unity of title and causes a severance.[52] So, if land is conveyed "to A, B, and C in fee simple" and A later sells to X, X is a tenant in common as to one third in relation to B and C and they are tenants in common as to two-thirds in relation to X, but B and C are still joint tenants in relation to each other.[53] Thus, if X dies, her interest passes to those entitled to her estate, but if B dies then C takes the two-thirds by survivorship from him. The explanation of these rules seems to be that sale introduces a market or commodity relationship into what was otherwise an extra-market relation and the law reflects this by severance. It does not, however, affect the relationship between the original joint tenants.

Other forms of alienation, such as a lease or mortgage, have the same effect, since they give a right to possession, but not a mere incumbrance, such as a rentcharge.[54]

c) Unilateral Dealing

It follows from the previous method that a joint tenant could bring about a severance vis-à-vis the others by conveying his interest to feoffees to hold to the use of himself. Suppose A, B and C hold land in fee simple as joint tenants. A conveys to F in fee simple to hold to the use of A in fee simple. The Statute of Uses would execute the use, giving A back his interest, but this time as a tenant in common as the conveyance would have caused a severance.

d) Act of a Third Party under Statutory Powers

There are instances in which an individual may be given power under statute to effect a transfer of an interest in property belonging to another person. Where that other person is a joint tenant it would follow that the exercise of such a power will cause a severance.

Such a situation arose in *Containercare v. Wycherley*.[55] A married couple bought a house as joint tenants. The husband got into debt and the creditor, having sued him and obtained judgment, secured the judgment debt by a judgment mortgage under the Judgment Mortgage (Ireland) Act, 1850. The effect of registering the affidavit under section 6 of the Act was, as the court held, to transfer the debtor's interest to the creditor as security, and so it caused a sever-

52 Co Litt 185a; *Re Gilburn*, unreported, High Court, Kenny J, 9 July 1975 at p.2.

53 Co Litt 189; Bacon's Abridgment, title Joint Tenants: "If there be three joint tenants and one aliens his part, the other two are joint tenants of their parts that remain, and hold them in common with the alienee". See also *Stephen v. Beall et Ux* (1874) 89 US 329, 22 L Ed 786.

54 Litt 286.

55 [1982] IR 143. See also *Murray v. Diamond* [1982] ILRM 113; *McIlroy v. Edgar* (1881) 7 LR Ir 521.

ance of the joint tenancy.[56] The court also held that this effect was not prevented by section 3 of the Family Home Protection Act, 1976 since that section only prevented conveyances by a spouse without the consent of the other spouse. The conveyance here was not effected by a spouse, but by a third party.

2. Severance in Equity

A characteristic of equity which has already been noted is that, in contrast to the concern of the common law for objective formalities, it paid greater regard to the subjective intentions of the parties to a transaction, having come into being at a time when commodity relations were coming to dominate economic activity. While, therefore, equity recognised the methods of severance at common law as also giving rise to a severance of the beneficial interest, it regarded the common law methods as inadequate in providing for all the cases where the equitable interest should be regarded as severed.

Page-Wood V-C in *Williams v. Hensman*[57] stated three ways in which severance could occur in equity and this has become a classic formulation of the position:

> "A joint-tenancy may be severed in three ways: in the first place, an act of any one of the persons interested operating upon his own share may create a severance as to that share... Secondly, a joint-tenancy may be severed by mutual agreement. And, in the third place, there may be a severance by any course of dealing sufficient to intimate that the interests of all were mutually treated as constituting a tenancy in common. When the severance depends on an inference of this kind without any express act of severance, it will not suffice to rely on an intention, with respect to the particular share, declared only behind the backs of the other persons interested. You must find in this class of cases a course of dealing by which the shares of all the parties to the contest have been effected, as happened in the cases of *Wilson v. Bell* (1843) 5 Ir Eq R 501[58] and *Jackson v. Jackson* (1804) 9 Ves 591".[59]

It may be noted that the first method is the same as at common law, the other two are peculiar to equity.

a) Mutual Agreement

In the English case of *Burgess v. Rawnsley*[60] it was held that an agreement between the parties by which one agreed to convey an interest in the property to another need not be enforceable as a contract in order to sever the joint tenancy in equity. It was not therefore necessary that it should be evidenced in writing under the Statute of Frauds or accompanied by an act of part performance. The

56 The point had been decided in *McIlroy v. Edgar* (1881) 7 LR Ir 521.

57 (1861) 1 J & H 546 at p.557, 70 ER 862 at 867.

58 See below.

59 *Jackson v. Jackson* (1804) 9 Ves Jun 591, 32 ER 732, 36 Digest (Repl) 540, 1006.

60 [1975] 1 Ch. 429.

significance of the agreement was what it showed as to the intention of the parties, not whether one could have enforced it on the other. Mr H, a widower, had the tenancy of a house. The owner offered to sell the freehold to Mr H. Mr H had come to be on friendly terms with Mrs R, a widow. They had met at a scripture rally and Mrs R felt sorry for him. His appearance was dishevelled and he was 'picking up fag ends'. Mr H wanted to marry Mrs R and had evidently persuaded himself that she also wanted to marry him. He once expressed his romantic feelings towards her by presenting her with a rose wrapped in a newspaper. Mrs R never had such an intention. Mr H suggested to Mrs R that they buy the house together. She agreed, but only because she intended to occupy the upstairs flat while Mr H occupied the lower one. Mr H told his solicitor to put the conveyance in the joint names of himself and Mrs R, because of his belief that they were to be married. Mrs R contributed half the purchase price. Mrs R refused to marry Mr H as a result of which he refused to allow her to move into the house. This was evidently his way of expressing his disappointment at her refusal. They remained otherwise on friendly terms. Subsequently Mr H agreed orally with Mrs R to buy her interest in the house for £750. Mrs R later changed her mind, saying that she wanted £1000. The matter rested there until Mr H died. The house was then sold and the plaintiff, Mr H's daughter, claimed that, as Mr H's administrator, she was entitled to a half share in the house. Mrs R claimed that the house remained held on a joint tenancy at Mr H's death and that she had become entitled to the whole interest by survivorship. The English Court of Appeal held that the oral agreement, which had never been completed and was unenforceable since it did not satisfy the Statute of Frauds, nevertheless had the effect of severing the joint tenancy prior to Mr H's death. The plaintiff's claim therefore succeeded. The agreement established that the parties no longer intended their interest to be a joint tenancy. The fact that the agreement was later repudiated did not affect the matter.

b) Course of Dealing

The phrase course of dealing includes not only negotiations falling short of an agreement but also the way in which the property in question has been dealt with by those concerned.

Wilson v. Bell[61] concerned the residue of personal estate left by a testator. The residuary legatees had dealt with the property in various transactions, including a marriage settlement and a will, is if it were held in tenancy in common. The Irish Court of Exchequer held that the property had been severed in equity. Lefroy B said:

> "...if the acts and dealings of the parties in respect of the joint tenancy *indicate an intention* to treat it as property held in common and not jointly, the court

61 (1843) 5 Ir Eq R 501.

will, from those acts and dealings, infer an agreement to sever the joint tenancy".[62]

In *Re Wallis' Trusts*[63] the testator gave property to his sons in equal shares and also appointed them residuary legatees. It was held that they held the property as residuary legatees in joint tenancy, since there were no words of severance as to the residue, but the fact that dividends arising from the residue had been paid to the sons as residuary legatees in equal shares, and after their deaths to the personal representatives of each, was a course of dealing from which a subsequent severance of the joint tenancy could be inferred. The solution is not without problems. A course of dealing implies more than one transaction, but the court seems to have meant that the first of such payments to the sons during their joint lives caused the severance. If it were otherwise another problem would arise: at what point in a series of transactions does the severance occur?

It is a matter of doubt as to how far short of an actual agreement a course of negotiations may be in order still to effect a severance in equity. In *Burgess v. Rawnsley*[64] Sir John Pennycuick considered that an offer by one joint tenant to another followed by a counter-offer by the other would not be sufficient, whereas the other judges did not specifically adopt this view. An offer followed by a counter-offer is, in any case, typical of negotiations. But must the negotiations have arrived at the point whereby some agreement has been reached and if so, about what?

It is suggested that what is required in such a case is not so much explicit agreement about severance, which is unlikely to occur, but evidence that the relations between the parties have changed from one in which each would be content for the property to pass to the other on the death of one party to one in which this is no longer the case. [65]

c) Unilateral Notice

Another controversial point in this area in the Republic is whether a unilateral notice given by one joint tenant to the others is sufficient to sever the joint tenancy. The English Law of Property Act, 1925 specifically provided by section 36(2) that a unilateral notice in writing by one joint tenant to the others was to be sufficient. In *Burgess v. Rawnsley* Pennycuick referred to it as a new method which had not existed before, but Lord Denning MR maintained that the section was merely declaratory of the previous law. Page-Wood V-C's statement in *Williams v. Hensman* is somewhat equivocal on the point, when

62 *ibid.* at p.507.

63 (1889) 23 LR Ir 460, MR.

64 [1975] 1 Ch. 429.

65 But see *Gore v. Carpenter* (1990) 60 P & CR 456 (course of dealing not alone enough: must be mutual intention).

he says that in the case of severance inferred without an express act, an intention "declared only behind the backs of the other persons interested" would not be enough. Lefroy B in *Wilson v. Bell* in speaking of the same situation, still talks of an "agreement to sever".[66]

In the absence of a statutory change, it is suggested that it is open to judges to distinguish at least between cases where the joint tenancy was created by the present parties, in which case, since the joint tenancy arose by their mutual agreement it might not be justifiable for one to go back on their agreement, and cases in which the joint tenancy arose by the act of someone other than the present party who wishes to sever, in which case a social value in favour of the freedom of the individual would produce the result that if a party does not wish to maintain the principle of survivorship as against the other parties, he or she should have the right to sever unilaterally. If such a judicial reform, or re-interpretation, were introduced, there would seem no basis for requiring the severance to be in writing.

Another argument in favour of such a reform is that, as we have seen, a joint tenant can unilaterally sever at law by a conveyance to uses and, in view of the undesirability of legal tenancies in common, a joint tenant should not be forced to adopt such a drastic method.

d) Contract by One Joint Tenant

At common law if a joint tenant enters into a contract to sell with a third party that does not in itself produce a change in the interests themselves. But in equity, under the doctrine of *Tempany v. Hynes,*[67] part payment of the purchase price by the purchaser would give rise to an equitable interest in the property in the purchaser's favour. This would cause a severance in equity.

e) Contract by All Joint Tenants

In *Byrne v. Byrne*[68] All the joint tenants entered into a contract of sale together. One joint tenant then died. A conveyance was executed after his death. The question was whether the contract had severed the joint tenancy prior to his death. The High Court held that it had not as there was no intention to sever. In such a case, even if an equity arises in favour of the purchaser, it is not one that affects the interest of one joint tenant in a distinct way to that of the others. The only other issue which may arise is as to whether the contract itself was evidence of a mutual intention to sever.[69]

66 (1843) 5 Ir Eq R 501.

67 [1976] IR 101, Supreme Court.

68 Unreported, High Court, McWilliam J, 18 January 1980.

69 See also *Re Hayes' Estate* [1920] 1 IR 207.

f) Simultaneous Death

It has been seen that it is arguable that the simultaneous death of joint tenants may cause a severance in equity, rather than at law, as to the interests of those who take under the will or on intestacy.[70]

G. Coparcenary

Before the Succession Act, 1965 came into force the rules of intestacy were still based on primogeniture, so that where there were males of equal degree to the intestate, the eldest took to the exclusion of the others. If, however, there were no males, then females inherited, but they did so jointly as coparceners.

The old rules of descent were replaced in the 1965 Act by a new scheme, but the Act expressly retained the old rules in the case of estates tail. Coparcenary can still occur today if a tenant in tail dies without barring the entail[71] leaving female descendants entitled to inherit the fee tail. It follows that the estate would have to be a fee tail general or a fee tail female.

If the estate is a fee tail general it does not necessarily follow that the coparceners would be female. Suppose T, the original donee in tail general, has three daughters, D1, D2 and D3. D1 predeceases her father, T, leaving sons GS1 and GS2. On T's death the entail descends to his daughters as coparceners. Under the old rules the principle of representation means that the issue of a deceased person represent the deceased person, and so the son[72] GS1 takes with D2 and D3 as coparceners.

1. No Survivorship

Like a tenancy in common, there is no right of survivorship in coparcenary.[73] The interest of each coparcener passes under her will or on intestacy.

2. Unities

The four unities are not required, but are usually present since coparceners take by operation of law on descent. Nevertheless, if there are three daughters, A, B and C who are coparceners and C dies leaving a son and a daughter, the son[74] is a coparcener with A and B although the son takes by a different title and at a

---

70 See page 425.

71 Which can only be done by an *inter vivos* deed, namely, a disentailing assurance under the Fines and Recoveries Act, 1834. See Chapter 8 FeeTail.

72 Among males, primogeniture applies.

73 *Re Matson* [1897] 2 Ch. 509.

74 The old rules apply since the estate is a fee tail: Succession Act, 1965 s.11.

different time.[75] If C had two daughters, C's share would be split between them and they would take with A and B as coparceners although they take lesser interests in the property than A or B.

3. Operation of Law

Coparcenary arises by operation of law. If there are three original coparceners, A, B and C, and C sells her interest to X, X holds as tenant in common with A and B who remain coparceners as between themselves.[76] Also, if F who has a fee simple conveys it "to the heirs of O", O being dead[77] and leaving daughters, the effect is to create a joint tenancy and not coparcenary, on the ground that coparcenary is only created by operation of law.[78] However, what if there are three coparceners, A, B and C and C leaves her share by will to Y? It would seem that Y also holds as tenant in common with A and B who again continue to hold as coparceners between themselves.[79]

4. Undivided Shares

Coparceners hold in undivided shares, like a tenancy in common. The share may pass on intestacy or be alienated *inter vivos* or by will. In the latter case, as we have seen, the effect is that the recipient takes as tenant in common, the remaining coparceners continuing to hold as coparceners between themselves.

5. Ending of Coparcenary

Coparcenary may be terminated by the same methods as joint tenancy and tenancy in common.

H. Tenancy by Entireties

At common law a conveyance to A and B which would, if they were not married to each other, create a joint tenancy, would instead, if A and B were married to each other, create a tenancy by entireties as between themselves.[80] If O conveys "to A, B and C in fee simple" and A and B are married at the date of the conveyance, A and B held in tenancy by entireties between themselves but C held as joint tenant, *i.e.* in relation to C, A and B were joint tenants, but were

75 Challis, pp. 375–6.

76 Co Litt 175a.

77 See Chapter 6 Fee simple: Heirs as a Word of Purchase.

78 *Owen v. Gibbons* [1902] 1 Ch. 636.

79 Co Litt 175a.

80 *Crofton v. Bunbury* (1854) 2 Ir Ch R 465; *Re Tyrell* [1894] 1 IR 267, V-C; *Kennedy v. Ryan* [1938] IR 620 at 625; see Wylie, *Cases* p.372.

tenants by entireties as between each other.[81] An express statement that they were to take as joint tenants had no effect. The law thus imposed the legal form regardless on the intention of the donor. This clearly indicates that the rules were imposing a policy to which was ascribed a higher value than the intention of donors, and that policy appears to have been the subjection of wives to the authority of their husbands.

1. Complete Unity

At common law husband and wife were regarded as a single person, albeit that the powers of management were vested in the husband. But if H and W are married and held by entireties and one of them died, the survivor took the whole but not by the principle of survivorship, as in joint tenancy, but by virtue of the original limitation, so the law held. This is not to say that it was a matter of the intention of the limitation, for as we have seen, an express limitation to them both as joint tenants would not override tenancy by entireties.

2. Unseverable

Tenancy by entireties, unlike joint tenancy, was not severable. Neither husband nor the wife could sell without the concurrence of the other in the conveyance.[82]

3. No Undivided Shares

Tenants by entireties, like joint tenants, did not hold by undivided shares. The principle of unity was maintained to the extent of holding that the husband was entitled to the whole of the rents or profits during the joint lives of the spouses.[83]

4. Abolition

The effect of the Married Women's Property Act, 1882 was generally held to be that it prevented the creation of new tenancies by entireties after 1882.[84] The Act provided for the wife's separate estate, which she could control and dispose of, apart from her husband. The courts extended this by interpretation, in the light of the policy behind the Act, to mean that in future conveyances to husbands and wives would take effect as joint tenancies.

---

81 *Back v. Andrew* (1690) 2 Vern 120, 23 ER 687.

82 *Crofton v. Bunbury* (1854) 2 Ir Ch R 465.

83 *Re Tyrell* [1894] 1 IR 267.

84 *Kennedy v. Ryan* [1938] IR 620; Wylie, *Cases* p.372; Challis, pp.378-9; *Thornley v. Thornley* [1893] 2 Ch. 229.

I. Ending of Co-Ownership

The relationship of both joint tenancy and tenancy in common may be ended so that the result is separate ownership vested in the former co-owners.

1. Partition and Sale

Partition is the legal division of the property so that each co-owner occupies and owns a separate part of the property. Partition ends the unity of possession and therefore puts an end to co-ownership.

At common law co-owners could put an end to their relationship by agreement in such a manner as they might agree, by partition , or by sale to a third party and division of the proceeds. But one joint tenant or tenant in common could not force a partition on the others at common law. Only co-parceners could do so because their co-ownership is "cast upon them by the act of the law, and not by their own agreement".[85] One joint tenant or tenant in common could sell their own interest, but this would be likely to be less valuable than a share of the proceeds from selling the entire property to a purchaser and also less attractive to purchasers.

More significantly, one joint tenant or tenant in common could not force a sale of the property on another such tenant against their will. This had the result of withdrawing such land from the market, but the common law was more concerned to protect the right to possession of land by those who wished to retain it than to advance the cause of the market economy.

An act of 1542[86] allowed one party to force a legal partition of the property. Since this was usually inconvenient, it probably had the indirect effect of making reluctant joint tenants and tenants in common agree to a sale and indeed some of the instances of absurd partitions may be instances of the courts deliberately using the Act indirectly to force a sale.[87] The Act itself expressly conferred jurisdiction on the common law courts, but courts of equity soon asserted that they possessed a similar jurisdiction. It seems that the equitable jurisdiction to partition survived until the Judicature Act and, since after that date it can be exercised in any court, the Act of 1542 had become obsolete. The Act of 1542 was therefore repealed in the Republic by the Statute Law Revision (Pre-Union Irish Statutes) Act, 1962.[88]

---

85 Williams, *Real Property* (23rd ed.) 243, 244.

86 33 Hen VIII c.10 (Ir). The equivalent English Act is 32 Hen VIII c.32, 1540 (Eng).

87 *Turner v. Morgan* (1803) 8 Ves Jun 143, 32 ER 307, per Lord Eldon LC (owner of two thirds given all the chimneys and fireplaces and the only stairs); *Lewis v. Maddocks* (1803) 8 Ves Jun 150 at 157, 32 ER 310, 313.

88 *O'D v. O'D* unreported, High Court, Murphy J, 18 November 1983; *FF v. CF* [1987] ILRM 1, High Court, (Circuit Appeal) Barr J.

It was only by the Partition Acts, 1868 and 1876 that the court was given power to order sale of the property on application by one of the parties. One moot point is whether the statutes give a co-owner the right to a sale in lieu of partition, so that if the court refuses to order partition it must then order sale, or whether the court has jurisdiction to refuse both, in which case a co-owner has no absolute right to either. This point has now become of considerable importance in property disputes between husband and wife. The issue is whether a spouse, usually the husband, who is also a co-owner, or a judgment mortgagee of unregistered land,[89] can demand sale and so deprive the wife, and possibly children also, of continued possession of the house, or whether, on the other hand, the court has a discretion to refuse both partition and sale.

Earlier authorities such as Story[90] tended to adopt the former view, holding that the equitable jurisdiction copied the one conferred by the 1542 Act, that it thus gave a right to partition, and that the Partition Acts had modified this only to the extent of giving a right to sale in the alternative. On this view, the applicant under the Partition Acts has a right either to partition or to sale. The court must grant one or the other. An alternative view is that all equitable remedies are discretionary and, at least since 1962 when the 1542 Act was repealed in the Republic, all partition has been discretionary and so the statutory alternative of sale is also discretionary.

Whatever the true historical position may have been, recent cases in the Republic show that the courts here, at least where the parties are husband and wife, assert a discretion to refuse sale even if no partition has been ordered. In *O'Neill v. O'Neill*[91] the judgment recites that a wife with a beneficial share in the house had tried and failed on two occasions to obtain an order for sale in lieu of partition. Where a wife with an equity is left in possession of a family home and more so where there are children of the marriage, the benefit to the wife and children of remaining in the family home may be felt to outweigh the inconvenience to the husband or to a judgment mortgagee of being unable to sell the premises.

The court in *O'D v. O'D*[92] held that if the property is a family home within the Family Home Protection Act, 1976 that may be a valid reason to refuse the order. In *AL v. JL*[93] it was held that where the property is a family home a sale cannot be ordered unless the other spouse consents or the court can dispense with consent under section 4 of the 1976 Act. However, both these cases seem

89 Where the land is registered a judgment mortgage does not have the effect of transferring the debtor's interest to the creditor and so the creditior does not have the remedies of a co-owner. See Registration of Title.

90 Story, *Equity Jurisdiction.*

91 Unreported, High Court, Barron J, 6 October 1989.

92 Unreported, High Court, Murphy J, 18 November 1983.

93 Unreported, High Court, Finlay P, 27 February 1984. The case is also dealt with later: see Chapter 17 Family Property: Family Home Protection Act: Partititon Acts.

inconsistent with the reasoning of the Supreme Court in *Nestor v. Murphy*[94] in so far as they are based on the premise that the Family Home Protection Act, 1976 applies where the legal title is vested in both spouses.[95]

In *First National Building Society v. Ring*[96] Denham J held that the jurisdiction under the Partition Acts is wholly discretionary. The wife was a joint owner of the family home, the title to which was registered, and had also contributed to its purchase. There were three children of the marriage, two of whom were still at school. The husband had become indebted to the plaintiff building society which had sued and obtained judgment against him for approximately £158,000 and had subsequently registered a judgment mortgage against the husband's interest. The judgment states that the wife was not personally indebted to the plaintiff nor had they obtained any judgment against her. The judge also expressed the view that if the property were to be sold the disruption to family life would be enormous and detrimental. The plaintiffs sued for a declaration that the judgment mortgage was well charged against the property and for an order for sale in lieu of partition. The wife, as second defendant, joined the action solely to defend her interest in the family home. She opposed the order for sale sought by the plaintiff. The property was also subject to a prior mortgage vested in the Allied Irish Bank plc, on which there was owing about £20,000. Allied Irish had obtained an earlier judgment mortgage against the husband's interest but had taken no further steps to enforce it. The house was estimated to be worth somewhere between £40,000 and £80,000. In these circumstances the judge refused to grant the order for sale, but granted leave to re-enter the proceedings after an inquiry as to the interests in the property, the feasibility of sale and as to whether there was any possibility of the wife buying the husband's share.

The judge held, applying *Containercare v. Wycherley,*[97] that the wife had no veto over the registration of the judgment mortgage. The further question was what rights the judgment mortgage gave the plaintiffs. On this she held, following *O'D v. O'D,*[98] that the fact that the property was a family home within the meaning of the Family Home Protection Act, 1976 was a valid reason, within section 4 of the Partition Act, 1868, to refuse an order for sale. Again, this seems inconsistent with the decision in *Nestor v. Murphy*. Denham J did not go on to address directly the nature of the jurisdiction under the Partition Acts, 1868 and 1876, but rather assumed that the court could refuse both partition and sale:

94 [1979] IR 326.

95 See Chapter 17 Family Property: Family Home Protection Act: Partititon Acts.

96 [1992] 1 IR 375.

97 [1982] IR 143. See also *Murray v. Diamond* [1982] ILRM 113 *McIlroy v. Edgar* (1881) 7 LR Ir 521.

98 Unreported, High Court, Murphy J, 18 November 1983.

> "The second defendant who is a co-owner and who is an innocent party and has no judgment registered against her would undoubtedly suffer a significant sacrifice if her property, part of the family home, were sold now. In these circumstances it does not appear appropriate now to order partition or sale in lieu of partition".

The Family Law Act, 1995 section 36(1) now provides that a husband or wife may apply to the court in a summary manner to determine any question between them as to the title to or possession of any property. The court may make such order as it thinks proper, including an order for sale or partition of the property.[99]

Where an application is made under the Partition Acts, 1868 and 1876 for partition of agricultural land the discretion is subject to the power of the Minister mentioned in the next section.

2. Subdivision of Agricultural Land

In Ireland agricultural land was often subdivided among family members and eventually the uneconomic units so produced reduced the productiveness of the land. Under the Land Act, 1965 section 12 no agricultural land in the Republic may be subdivided without the consent in writing of the Minister.[100]

3. Partition of Commonage

It has been seen that commonage, *i.e.* pasture rights held in common, is a traditional form of land holding akin to a separate form of tenure. It can also be regarded as a form of co-ownership, although it has not been dealt with as such since it is not really part of the common law categories.

In some areas where land purchase was not carried out commonage remained. Section 24 of the Land Act, 1939 provides that where some, but not all, owners of land held in commonage wish to partition it they may apply, formerly to the Irish Land Commission, now to the Minister[101] for the compulsory partition of the holding. The Minister[102] may then prepare a scheme for partition of the land. After objections have been invited and heard, the Minister may then approve, modify or cancel the scheme. Appeal lies to the High Court.[103]

---

99 *ibid.* s.36(2)(a).

100 Irish Land Commission (Dissolution) Act, 1992, s.4, formerly of the Irish Land Commission. *H v. O* [1978] IR 194.

101 Irish Land Commission (Dissolution) Act, 1992, s.4. The Act is to be brought into force by order, but the order has not yet been made, although functions have been transferred. But see the consent procedure provided for in SR 13 of 77, 8 December 1977: *AIB v. O'Neill and Kidd,* unreported, High Court, Laffoy J, 13 December 1995.

102 *ibid.*.

103 Irish Land Commission (Dissolution) Act, 1992, s.3. The Act is to be brought into force by order, but the order has not yet been made.

In *Re Commonage at Glennamaddoo*[104] Carroll J held that the interests of those who wanted partition, those who wanted to continue in commonage, and the objectors to the original scheme of total partition could be accommodated by a new scheme. The new scheme partitioned only sufficient land to satisfy those who wanted partition, leaving a commonage area for those who wanted to continue the common rights. The new scheme would also allow public access to the land, which would meet one of the objections made to the original plan.

4. Union in a Sole Tenant

Tenancy in common and joint tenancy may also be terminated by one party buying out interests of the others, or in the case of joint tenancy, by survivorship resulting in a sole survivor.

104 [1992] 1 IR 297.

CHAPTER 17

FAMILY PROPERTY

A. Matrimonial Home: The Equity Acquired by Contributions

The Family Law Act, 1995 section 36(1) provides that either spouse may apply to the court in a summary manner to "determine any question arising between them as to the title to or possession of any property".[1] The court is the Circuit Court, known for this purpose as the Circuit Family Court, or the High Court.[2] The court may make such order, with respect to the property in dispute and as to costs, as the court thinks proper, including an order for sale or partition of the property.[3] Hence, the statute gave to the courts a discretion in recasting property interests where the parties are married. The similar provision in section 12 of the Married Women's Status Act, 1957, which the present provision replaced,[4] was interpreted by the courts as conferring on them power to resolve disputes according to existing principles of law and equity, extended where they deemed necessary. Significantly the court did not use the previous section to confer property rights to the matrimonial home on the homemaker wife.

Where the conveyance of the matrimonial home is in the name of one spouse alone the question may arise as to whether the other spouse has acquired a part of the beneficial interest by contributions to the purchase price. The contributions may be direct, or indirect in that the spouse has undertaken expenses which the other spouse would otherwise have had to bear. It is more usual for the conveyance to be in the name of the husband alone than in the name of the wife, but the principles discussed below may be applied to either spouse. It was thought for a time that there might be an exception in the case of domestic work by a wife. Barr J in the High Court in *BL v. ML*[5] found that a wife's claim to an equity in that case was based upon Article 41 of the Constitution which is exclusively concerned with the place of women in the home.

1 The Act replaced 12 of the Married Women's Status Act, 1957 and came into force on 1 August 1996; *JD v. DD*, unreported, High Court, McGuinness J, 14 May 1997.

2 Family Law Act, 1995 s.38. Litigation as to property of higher rateable value may be transferred to the High Court.

3 *ibid.* s.36(2)(a).

4 See footnote 1.

5 [1992] 2 IR 77; [1989] ILRM 528.

However, the decision was reversed on appeal to the Supreme Court.[6]

It may also be that the legal title to the house is in their joint names, but that their respective contributions are not in equal proportions. Equity in such a case presumes that the beneficial interest is held in a tenancy in common, the shares being in proportion to their respective contributions.

1. Direct Contributions

Where a spouse contributes directly to the purchase of the house, by paying part of a lump sum, or more usually, contributing to the mortgage repayments, the general approach is to hold that the spouse in whose name the house is held holds the legal title on trust for them both as tenants in common in equity, the proportional shares being the same as the proportions in which the actual contributions to the purchase price are made.[7]

In *HD v. JD*[8] the family house had been purchased in the husband's sole name. The wife's earnings were paid into a family pool out of which the mortgage payments were made. At one stage the husband had bought a pub and the wife took a major part in running it. She did the work without pay. It was held that both forms of contribution gave her an equity in the house.

2. Indirect Contributions

a) Conflict in the Early Cases

Considerably greater problems are posed by what are argued are indirect contributions to the purchase of the house and the problem here is to define when a payment that has been made can be linked in some way with the purchase of the house. Another main issue was whether there had to be some agreement between husband and wife that expenses undertaken by her were to give her an equity in the house. The adoption of such a test would, of course, mean that wives would not be able to prove such an agreement very often. In a domestic situation the parties usually do not work out an express understanding of their rights as they would in a business transaction. Originally in Ireland there seems to have been a divergence of views in the High Court as to the basis of liability and two lines of cases developed.

The first line of cases took the view that indirect contributions by a wife did give rise to an equity in her favour without any evidence of express agreement. This line can be traced to the dictum of Lord Reid in the English House of

6 [1992] 2 IR 77; sub nom *L v. L* [1992] ILRM 115. The case is discussed in detail below: see page 463.

7 *C v. C* [1976] IR 254, High Court, Kenny J, the same case as *Conway v. Conway* [1977] 111 ILTR 183.

8 Unreported, High Court, 31 July 1981, Finlay P.

Lords case of *Gissing v. Gissing.*[9] The dictum was taken up by Lord Denning in a line of cases in the English Court of Appeal.[10] This approach was also adopted in the Republic in *FG v. PG.*[11] In that case the wife contributed money to a joint account. No money from the pool was used to pay off the mortgage. Finlay P nevertheless held that the wife was entitled to a share of the equity. The payments into the pool were indirect contributions relieving the husband of expenses he would otherwise have had to bear. There are also *dicta* of Kenny J in *Heavey v. Heavey*[12] to the effect that it is unrealistic to look for an agreement as between husband and wife where each has made contributions. The same judge in *C v. C*[13] does not distinguish between direct and indirect contributions. He said it was futile to try to infer an agreement where the wife has made payments or undertaken expenses.

The other line of cases can be traced to the judgment of the majority in the English House of Lords in *Gissing.*[14] In that case the house was in the husband's sole name. There had been no direct contributions by the wife but she paid for household items and the cost of laying the lawn. She went out to work and paid for her own clothes and those of the son. All the judges agreed that she did not have an equity in the house, but the majority so held on the ground that an indirect contribution was not enough in itself to raise a trust. There had to be an agreement or arrangement to that effect.

In the Republic, some cases in the High Court followed the majority in *Gissing*. In *MG v. RD*[15] the house was in the husband's sole name. The wife continued to work as an air hostess after the marriage as she had done before. She had a separate bank account. The husband had suggested several times that they operate a joint account, but she refused. The husband made the mortgage repayments. The wife bought food and household items, and a car which they both used. There was no evidence of any express agreement between them. Keane J held that the wife did not have an equity in the house. *R v. R*[16] also held that an agreement was necessary.[17]

---

9 [1971] AC 886.

10 *Falconer v. Falconer* [1970] 3 All ER 499; *Hargrave v. Newton* [1971] 3 All ER 866; *Hazell v. Hazell* [1972] 11 All ER 923 at 926; *Kowalczuk v. Kowalczuk* [1973] 2 All ER 101.

11 [1982] 2 ILRM 155, High Court, Finlay P.

12 (1977) 111 ILTR 1.

13 [1976] IR 254, High Court, sub nom *Conway v. Conway* [1977] 111 ILTR 183.

14 [1971] AC 886.

15 Unreported, High Court, Keane J, 28 April 1981.

16 Unreported, High Court, McMahon J, 12 January 1979.

17 See also *CMCB v. SB*, unreported, High Court, Barron J, 17 May 1983. Barron J held that the wife's contributions gave her an equity because intention that they should do so.

The Northern Ireland Court of Appeal in *McFarlane v. McFarlane*[18] also followed the majority in *Gissing* to the effect that an agreement or arrangement is necessary although recently the position has been attenuated by the Northern Ireland High Court finding an equity on the basis of a tacit understanding or where the parties took it for granted that they both owned the house.[19]

In *W v. W*[20] the husband bought a farm subject to mortgages. Both spouses applied their savings to stocking and improving the farm. The wife claimed that her contributions increased the income of the farm and effectively contributed to paying off the mortgages. Finlay P accepted that contributions to a general family fund made during a period when mortgages were being paid off by the husband could not be distinguished in principle from direct contributions to mortgage instalments. He held that the wife's contributions during the period when the mortgages were being redeemed gave her an equity amounting to 50 per cent. He stated principles which were generally approved in the Supreme Court in *McC v. McC,* considered below.

b) McC v. McC

The conflict in the High Court has now been resolved by the Supreme Court in *McC v. McC.*[21] The husband and wife in that case lived in Dublin. The husband was employed by an insurance company and in the course of time the company transferred him to Cork. That meant selling the family home, which he did. It realised £5,000 and after paying off the mortgage there was £1,800 left over. It was agreed that, since the wife had contributed one third of the purchase price of the house, she was entitled to one third of that sum, *i.e.* £600. She agreed to allow her husband to use the money in connection with buying the new home in Cork. His employers, the insurance company, provided a 100 per cent mortgage, so the husband did not have to spend any part of the money on the purchasing the house. The mortgage instalments were deducted from his salary. He spent the £1,800 left over from the sale of the Dublin house on furniture and other fittings for the house in Cork. In the High Court Costello J held that the wife was entitled to one third of the furniture and fittings. A single judgment was delivered in the Supreme Court by Henchy J without dissent. Referring to the judgment of Kenny J in *C v. C,*[22] Henchy J said that since then it had become judicially accepted that:

> "Where the matrimonial home has been purchased in the name of the husband, and the wife has, either directly or indirectly, made contributions towards the

18 [1972] NI 59 at 78.

19 *Northern Bank Ltd v. Beattie,* unreported, NI Ch D, Murray J, (Transcript: Lexis) (no date in original source).

20 [1981] ILRM 202, Finlay P.

21 [1986] ILRM 1, Supreme Court, Henchy J, nem diss.

22 [1976] IR 254 High Court, sub nom *Conway v. Conway.* [1977] 111 ILTR 183.

> purchase price or towards the discharge of mortgage instalments the husband will be held to be a trustee for the wife of a share in the house roughly corresponding with the proportion of the purchase money represented by the wife's total contribution. Such a trust will be inferred when the wife's contribution is of such a size and kind as will justify the conclusion that the acquisition of the house was achieved by the joint efforts of the spouses.
>
> When the wife's contribution has been indirect (such as by contributing, by means of her earnings to a general family fund) the court will, in the absence of any express or implied agreement to the contrary, infer a trust in favour of the wife, on the ground that she has to that extent relieved the husband of the financial burden he incurred in purchasing the house".[23]

In the present case the £600 due to the wife was not used in purchasing the new house in Cork because of the 100 per cent mortgage. The court therefore found that the wife had failed on the facts to prove that she had made indirect contributions. There was apparently no suggestion that the wife had contributed to household expenses and so there were no indirect contributions in that form. The payment for the furniture was not considered an indirect contribution, even though it relieved the husband of expenses which he would otherwise have to bear, presumably because the wife did obtain something in return for it, namely, ownership of the furniture. To treat her expenditure as an indirect contribution to the purchase of the house would be to count it twice. This illustrates that the kind of contributions which are held indirect contributions to the acquisition of the house are those which do not give any immediate interest in other property.

Henchy J's assertion that it had become judicially accepted that contributions to the purchase of a house give rise to an equity in the absence of an agreement to the contrary is intriguing. He can hardly have been referring to the High Court bench, since the cases there were conflicting. The phrase seems carefully chosen to indicate that the Supreme Court judges had decided that this was the correct approach. The fact that there was no dissenting judgment must strengthen this view. Viewed restrictively, the judge's formulation could be said to be *obiter* since the wife was not found to have made contributions to the purchase of the house on the facts, but there is really no distinction to be drawn between *obiter dictum* and *ratio decidendi* in the final appeal court, since the court is evidently indicating what it would decide if such were the facts.

In the wider context of equity, *McC v. McC*[24] marks a milestone in that it recognises that the social and legal context itself, in this case the institution of marriage, and not any particular conduct by the parties involved, gives rise to an equity unless it can be proved to be unjust in the particular case. Given the social context, the courts have held as a matter of principle that it would be inequitable for indirect contributions not to give rise to an equity. This is therefore,

23 [1986] ILRM 1 at p.2.

24 [1986] ILRM 1, Supreme Court, Henchy J, nem diss.

arguably, an example of the principle of unjust enrichment so long resisted by the English courts.

c) Later Cases

Some cases immediately after *McC v. McC*[25] in the High Court show that the High court was slow to realise the significance of the case.

In *CR v. DR*[26] the husband qualified as a vet. He had a drinking problem. He lost his job and the accommodation which went with it. His drinking affected his work. His father was also a vet, but was old and his practice had declined to almost nothing. The husband and wife went to live near the father and took over what was left of the practice. The wife helped out with the practice, covering up for the husband when he was drunk. The wife's father guaranteed a bank loan and that enabled them to buy the family home which was put in the husband's sole name. The husband paid off the loan and paid for furnishing and redecorating. Apart from helping with the practice the wife looked after cows on a small piece of land. She took the milk to a local creamery and exchanged it for butter. The husband joined Alcoholics Anonymous and gave up alcohol. Then the wife took up with another man. Judgment was reserved and in the meantime the Supreme Court delivered judgment in *McC v. McC*.[27] Lynch J, in refusing the wife an equity in the house, held that there was no evidence that the wife's contributions in working on the farm or helping her husband in the practice relieved him of expenses which he would have been unable to bear. It is questionable whether the court applied the correct test. The Supreme Court in *McC v. McC*[28] did not lay down that the husband must have been unable to bear the cost on his own, but merely that the wife's contribution "to that extent relieved the husband of the financial burden he incurred in purchasing the house".[29] Again, according to Henchy J, the test is whether the property was acquired through "the joint efforts of the spouses".[30]

---

25 *ibid.*

26 Unreported, High Court, Lynch J, 5 April 1984.

27 [1986] ILRM 1, Supreme Court, Henchy J, nem diss.

28 *ibid.*

29 See also *R v. R*, unreported, High Court, McMahon J, 12 January 1979; *MB v. EB*, unreported, High Court, Barrington J, 19 February 1980. Both these cases treat the test as being whether the payments by the wife relieved the husband of expenses he would otherwise have had to bear.

30 See also *B v. B*, unreported, High Court, MacKenzie J, 22 April 1986 which appears to be wrongly decided. The judge held that the wife's indirect contributions did not give rise to an equity unless there was evidence that the spouses intended that the legal relations should be altered, following Keane J in *MG v. RD*, unreported, High Court, 28 April 1981 and Finlay P in *W v. W* [1981] ILRM 202, cases which had been overruled by *McC v. McC*. A similar objection could be raised against the judgment of Barron J in the High Court in *EN v. RN* [1990] 1 IR 383.

3. Improvements

W *v.* W[31], a High Court decision before McC *v.* McC, Finlay P proposed a distinction between, on the one hand, contributions to the acquisition of property by the other spouse and, on the other, contributions to the improvement of property which had already been acquired in the name of the other spouse, either by immediate payment or by paying off mortgages. In the case of improvements the judge considered that the spouse who was not the legal owner would have no claim to an equity "unless she established by evidence that from the circumstances surrounding the making of it she was led to believe (or of course that it was specifically agreed) that she would be recompensed for it". It is suggested that such a distinction may not reach a fair result in all cases, especially where the contribution is to the physical extension of the property, in money or in kind, or arguably to its total value, and which is therefore a contribution to acquiring a part of the property or a proportion of the value of the completed whole. Also, the phrase "led to believe" suggests that principles of proprietary estoppel are likely to be applied in such a case in future.

The judge further took the view that "even where such a right to recompense is established either by an express agreement or by circumstances in which the wife making the contribution was led to such belief it is a right to recompense in monies only and cannot and does not constitute a right to claim an equitable share in the estate of the property concerned". It is questionable whether this will stand the test of time. Where agreement is concerned it would surely be a matter of interpreting what the parties had agreed between themselves, and as to expectations, that may raise an equity and it is then matter for the court in each case to decide in what form the equity should be satisfied.

In *NAD v. TD*[32], a case between married partners after McC *v.* McC, Barron J followed W *v.* W in treating contributions to improvements as in a separate category. In that case the husband bought a vacant site and built a house on it using his own labour and supervising hired labour. The wife sought a declaration as to the ownership of the first house. She claimed she had supported the family on her income while the husband was building the house and had paid sums in cash while the building was in progress. Barron J cited *McC v. McC*[33] for the proposition that indirect contributions to the acquisition of the property give rise to the presumption of an equity. He then went on essentially to follow W *v.* W as to improvements. He held that the sums in cash were direct contributions to the purchase of the house, but discounted the expenditure by the wife in maintaining the family, even though he found that if she had not done so it would have cost the husband an extra £500. He discounted these payments

31 [1981] ILRM 202 at p.204–05, cited in *CD v. WD and Barclays Bank plc,* unreported, High Court 5 February 1997, McGuinness J.

32 [1985] ILRM 153, 10 May 1984.

33 [1986] ILRM 1, Supreme Court, Henchy J, nem diss.

because he found no evidence of conduct on the part of the husband leading the wife to believe she would have an interest or a right to compensation. The wife therefore failed on the facts.

On the question of improvements the judge cited Finlay P in *W v. W*[34] and the same judge in *Heavey v. Heavey*[35] although Kenny J in the latter case drew no distinction between purchase or improvements as Barron J acknowledged. The distinction is not found in *McC v. McC*.[36] McWilliam J in *Power v. Conroy*[37] did not seek to discount that part of the claim which was based upon improvements.

Contributions to the purchase price of property have long been recognised as a case of the intervention of equity and a source of equitable interests quite apart from marital situations. Improvements to property, on the other hand, have generally only been recognised in the context of proprietary estoppel. Nevertheless, given the special definition of "indirect contributions" as laid down by *McC v. McC*[38] a clear distinction between acquisition and improvement may not survive that case where the total value of the property at the end of a period is attributable to the joint efforts of both spouses. Furthermore, as to contributions made after the price of the property has been paid, either as a lump sum or by paying off a mortgage, the wife may rely on proprietary estoppel. Under that doctrine it would seem to be sufficient to prove that the husband acquiesced or stood by while the wife spent money in the belief that she would acquire some interest or an increased interest in the house.[39]

4. Express Declarations

The principle expounded by Henchy J in *McC v. McC*[40] is subject to agreements or arrangements to the contrary, and so the parties retain the right to exclude the presumption of equity. Such a situation occurred in *GK v. EK*.[41] In that case the wife had made direct contributions to the purchase of the house in the form both of down payments and mortgage repayments. Both were considerably larger than those of the husband. The conveyance of the house was nevertheless taken in their joint names. O'Hanlon J held that the parties intended the house to be in their joint ownership with equal rights to the beneficial interest, but his view was not based on the mere fact that the property was put in

34 [1981] ILRM 202.

35 (1977) 111 ILTR 1.

36 [1986] ILRM 1, Supreme Court, Henchy J nem diss.

37 Unreported, High Court, McWilliam J 22 February 1980.

38 [1986] ILRM 1, Supreme Court, Henchy J, nem diss.

39 See Chapter 18 Licences, Proprietary Estoppel and Constructive Trusts.

40 [1986] ILRM 1, Supreme Court, Henchy J, nem diss.

41 Unreported, High Court, O'Hanlon J, 6 November 1985.

their joint names, but also on evidence given by the wife that they intended equal beneficial ownership.

5. Domestic Work of the Wife

a) Case Law

In *C v. C*[42] Kenny J expressed the view that the domestic work of a wife in the home did not count as an indirect contribution to the acquisition of the matrimonial home:

> "When the matrimonial home is purchased in the name of the husband, either before or after marriage, the wife does not as wife become entitled to any share in its ownership either because she occupies the status of wife or because she carries out household duties".[43]

If this were to be so the law would encompass a great anomaly. The wife who goes out to work and is thus able to contribute financially to the acquisition of the home is rewarded by a property interest in it, whereas the wife who adopts the traditional role and stays at home would obtain no financial security by so doing. Yet such a position does not arise by chance. Law in a society dominated by the economic phenomenon of the market finds it easy to ascribe property rights on the basis of the expenditure of money and leans naturally against the notion that an expenditure of money is a gift: in market no one parts with cash unless he or she obtains some tangible asset in return. This is the assumption of the law. Indeed there may be something in the nature of law itself that makes it easier to translate value in terms of the market into value in property rights, rather than to translate the more intangible and indeterminate obligations of family and kinship into property interests.[44]

In *BL v. ML*[45] Barr J in the High Court found that a wife had acquired a 50 per cent interest in the equity in the house through her contributions to the running of the home and family. The husband had bought a substantial house in need of repair and land which he later developed into a successful farming business. The wife contributed some labour to the running of the farm, although this was not great in amount. She also played an important part in refurbishing and redecorating the dwelling-house which in its restored state was of considerable value and described by the judge as "now an outstanding example

---

42 [1976] IR 254, High Court, sub nom *Conway v. Conway* [1977] 111 ILTR 183.

43 [1976] IR 254 at 257.

44 See in this context the difficulties involved in erecting the deserted wife's equity. Lord Denning MR in the English Court of Appeal had attempted to create such an equity in a series of cases, but it was struck down by the House of Lords, among other reasons because it would be terminable on divorce and the court found it difficult to accept that a property interest in land should terminate on such an event.

45 [1992] 2 IR 77, [1989] ILRM 528, Supreme Court, judgment reported sub nom *L v. L* [1992] ILRM 115.

of an 18th century manor house". The wife played a "crucial role" in designing the restoration scheme and in carrying out a large part of the papering and internal painting involved. She was also "a devoted homemaker and mother". The husband had used the premises to advise foreigners who were considering buying property in Ireland and the wife had contributed labour while they stayed on the premises. The husband had from time to time subjected the wife to physical violence and although there had been reconciliations at various times the husband's behaviour led to the present proceedings in which the wife also, successfully, sought judicial separation.

The judge set out his conclusion applying the existing principles of equity:

> "Reviewed in the light of the formidable line of judicial authority on this topic since 1976, the conclusion is inescapable that the wife is not entitled to a beneficial interest in the family home or farm because she has made no contribution in money or money's worth, directly or indirectly, towards the acquisition of either property".[46]

As to the wife's work in the business, the judge concluded that the wife had not contributed significantly to the work of the farm or the business such that it could be said that she had relieved the husband wholly or in part of the financial burden of acquiring the house. Despite this position the judge felt that there was a different line of reasoning which led instead to the conclusion that the wife was entitled to an equity in the home. Article 41.1 of the Constitution declares that the State "recognises the family as the natural primary and fundamental unit group of Society" and in subsection 2 it "guarantees to protect the Family in its constitution and authority, as the necessary basis of social order and as indispensable to the welfare of the Nation and the State". Article 41.2 provides that:

> "2.1° In particular, the State recognises that by her life within the home, woman gives to the State a support without which the common good cannot be achieved.
>
> 2° The State shall, therefore, endeavour to ensure that mothers shall not be obliged by economic necessity to engage in labour to the neglect of their duties in the home".[47]

Applying the Article to the case before him, the judge went on:

> "It is also in harmony with that philosophy to regard marriage as an equal partnership in which a woman who elects to adopt the full-time role of wife and mother in the home may be obliged to make a sacrifice, both economic and emotional, in doing so. In return for that voluntary sacrifice, which the Constitution recognises as being in the interest of the common good, she should receive some reasonable economic security within the marriage. That concept can be achieved, at least in part, by recognising that as her role as full-time wife and mother precludes her from contributing, directly or indirectly, in money or

46 Cited in the judgment of Finlay CJ in the Supreme Court [1992] 2 IR 102 at 103.

47 See judicial comment on the Article in *De Burca and Anderson v. AG* [1976] IR 385 per O'Higgins, CJ, and Walsh J; *W v. Somers* [1981] IR 126 per McCarthy J.

> money's worth from independent employment or avocation towards the acquisition by the husband of the family home and contents, her work as home maker and in caring for the family should be taken into account in calculating her contribution towards that acquisition - particularly, as such work is of real monetary value".[48]

The size of the share in the beneficial interest thus acquired should depend on the "nature, quality and duration" of the wife's domestic work. The judge felt that such a wife's share of the beneficial interest, bearing in mind that marriage was an "equal partnership" should not exceed 50 per cent unless there were exceptional circumstances. He also considered that since her interest was based upon her position as wife and mother that it was confined to the home itself and did not extend to other property owned by the husband, such as, in this case, the farm.

One inconsistency which may be noted at this point, and which is by no means confined to Barr J, is that the contribution of the homemaker wife is discounted on the ground that it is not in "money or money's worth" and yet as Barr J to his credit notably recognises, it is a contribution of "real monetary value".

Barrington J in *H v. H*[49] followed Barr's judgment but other judges in the High Court declined to follow *BL v. ML*,[50] namely Barron J in *EN v. RN*[51], whose view was subsequently upheld in the Supreme Court,[52] and Lardner J in *JF v. BF*.[53] Lardner J in the latter case expressed the view that Article 41 was not intended to confer property rights or to confer a specific jurisdiction on the court to determine property disputes in accordance with its principles. In the judge's view any change in the law should be left to the legislature.

After these judgments were delivered the appeal in *BL v. ML*[54] was decided by the Supreme Court. Finlay CJ, McCarthy, O'Flaherty and Egan JJ, Hederman J concurring, allowed the appellant's appeal. All the judges appeared to have accepted the inconsistency and unfairness which exists between the position of a wife who contributes financially and the wife who performs unpaid domestic work. They also agreed (a) that existing precedent precluded them from finding that a homemaker wife acquired an equity in the home and (b) that it was inappropriate to use Article 41 to supply the defect in the law.

---

48 [1992] 2 IR 77 at 98-99.

49 *Ex tempore* judgment, High Court, Barrington J 20 June 1989.

50 [1992] 2 IR 77, [1989] ILRM 528, Supreme Court, reported sub nom *L v. L* [1992] ILRM 115.

51 *EN v. RN* [1990] 1 IR 383, High Court, Barron J, Supreme Court [1992] 2 IR 116, sub nom N *v.* N & C [1992] ILRM 127.

52 *EN v. RN* [1992] 2 IR 116, sub nom *N v. N & C* [1992] ILRM 127.

53 Unreported, High Court, Lardner J, 21 December 1988.

54 [1992] 2 IR 77; sub nom *L v. L* [1992] ILRM 115, High Court, [1989] ILRM 528.

> "After careful consideration and with a reluctance arising from the desirable objective which the principle outlined in the judgment of Barr J would achieve, I conclude that to identify this right in the circumstances set out in this case is not to develop any known principle of the common law, but is rather to identify a brand new right and to secure it to the plaintiff. Unless that is something clearly and unambiguously warranted by the Constitution or made necessary for the protection of either a specified or unspecified right under it, it must constitute legislation and be a usurpation by the courts of the function of the legislature".[55]

More specifically the Chief Justice found that:

> "Neither Article 41.1.1° or 2° purports to create any particular right within the family, or to grant to any individual member of the family rights, whether of property or otherwise, against other members of the family, but rather deals with the protection of the family from external forces.
>
> I accept the contention made that the judiciary is one of the organs of the State and that, therefore, the obligation taken by the State to endeavour to ensure that mothers shall not be obliged by economic necessity to engage in labour outside the home to the neglect of their duties is an obligation imposed on the judiciary as well as on the legislature and the executive.
>
> There is, however, I am satisfied, no warrant for interpreting that duty on the judiciary as granting to it jurisdiction to award to a wife and mother any particular interest in the family home, where that would be unrelated to the question of her being obliged by economic necessity to engage in labour to the neglect of her duties".[56]

The judge found the Article 41 would be relevant in assessing the alimony or maintenance payable by a husband to a wife and mother and a court may act on the duty "by refusing to have any regard to a capacity of the wife to earn herself, if she was in addition to a wife a mother also, and if the obligation so to earn could lead to the neglect of her duties in the home".

McCarthy J agreed that precedent was against the acquisition of an equity by a homemaker wife:

> "In *C v. C* [1976] IR 254, there does not appear to have been any reference to Article 41 and Kenny J held the wife/mother entitled to a share in proportion to the amount of the contribution she had made towards the purchase or the repayment of the mortgage. So also in *McC v. McC* [1986] ILRM 1 the decision is entirely related to monetary contribution, whether direct by way of payment towards purchase or repayment of the mortgage, or indirect by contribution into the family pool. This is a true development of the law in a common law framework. That common law, like all statute law, must conform to or not be inconsistent with the Constitution.[57]

He also found that to use Article 41 would be create new anomalies. Article 41.2.2 refers not to women in general but to mothers. To found property rights upon it would be to introduce a discrimination on grounds of gender:

---

55 [1992] 2 IR 102 at 107 per Finlay CJ.

56 *ibid.* at 108.

57 *ibid.* at 110.

"It would be making a quantum leap in constitutional law to hold that by her life within the home the mother acquires a beneficial interest in it. This would be in recognition of the support that the mother gives by her life within the home in carrying out her constitutional role as a mother. No complementary role is accorded a father, although such a role reversal is, nowadays, by no means uncommon".[58]

Egan J referred to subsection 1:

> "I do not think that subsection 1 contains anything which imposes a positive obligation. It voices a 'recognition' and, in my opinion, is really a prelude to explain the positive obligation in the following subsection which provides that the State shall, therefore, endeavour *etc.* The obligation imposed by the subsection has nothing to do with the family home so far as the ownership thereof is concerned".[59]

As to present state of the law regarding equities acquired by wives the judge concluded:

> "Present case law is based on long-standing equitable principles as a result of which trusts are implied in favour of a contributing spouse. These principles have been extended to their permissible limit".[60]

The equitable principles of which the judge speaks may be long-standing but they have not been unchanging. As *McC v. McC* illustrates, and as the judge in that case recognises, they have been extended. The permissible limits have, therefore, also been set by the judges themselves.

The judicial reluctance to continue the development of equity in this direction has now probably been offset to some extent by the Family Law Act, 1995 which is discussed below.[61] Nevertheless, the 1995 Act does not address the vulnerability of a homemaker wife to third parties.

b) Comment

The decision in the Supreme Court in *BL v. ML*[62] has two aspects: (a) the use of precedent and the state of the existing equity gained by contributions and (b) the rejection of Article 41 as a means of repairing a perceived defect in the law.

(1) Precedent

On the first point, it is open to question whether the domestic work of a wife had been so decisively dealt with by precedent as the court appeared to think. The only clear statement positively rejecting the homemaker equity was by

58 *ibid.* at 111.

59 *ibid.* at 115.

60 *ibid.*

61 See below page 474.

62 [1992] 2 IR 102.

one judge in the High Court, namely Kenny J in *C v. C*[63], a decision which was not binding upon the Supreme Court. Such an important point should not have been considered as settled by anything less than a full bench of the Supreme Court and it is difficult to see why the judges of the Supreme Court treated the statement by a single judge with such deference. McCarthy J cited *McC v. McC*,[64] commenting that "the decision is entirely related to monetary contribution", but it could equally be seen as not excluding contributions in money's worth. In fact, Henchy J in delivering the judgment of the court in that case refers to indirect contributions and adds "such as by contributing, by means of her earnings to a general family fund". In other words, contributions in money are given as an example of indirect contributions, not as the only case. As to the rest of the case law on indirect contributions, it is marked more by an extreme reluctance to find an equity on the facts in any circumstances, rather than by any explicit statements on homemaker wives. Yet there are examples, as will be seen below, of judges accepting that unpaid work by a wife in a family business can give rise to an equity. Why not, then, unpaid domestic work which is part of a joint undertaking?

(2) Article 41

As to Article 41, there were some arguments in favour of Barr J's approach:

1) judges had failed to extend the general principles of equity to homemaker wives;
2) it would overcome the anomaly of working wives being better protected than wives adopting what, in terms of the Constitution as it stands, is the "preferred role";
3) while it may not be appropriate to use Article 41 to place women in an inferior position to men, it could be acceptable to use it to achieve equality, or avoid inequality; and
4) the Constitution is the fundamental law of the State and its provisions must therefore be presumed to have some legal effect and not to be mere expressions of moral principle or aspiration.

While it might seem to offer an escape route for judges who had painted themselves into a corner, the Supreme Court was on firmer ground when pointing out the problems of using it as a basis for property rights. Some of these problems are as follows:

1) unlike existing rules as to property in the domestic sphere, Article 41 applies only to wives and not to husbands. A married couple may jointly decide to reverse the traditional roles and the use of Article 41 arguably interferes in matters which are the concern of the married partners, either as such or simply as adult human beings, and fails to

63 [1976] IR 254, High Court, sub nom *Conway v. Conway* [1977] 111 ILTR 183.

64 [1986] ILRM 1.

respect their decision. It is also of no avail to husbands who through necessity, such as disability, stay at home and carry out domestic work while the wife adopts the role of bread-winner;

2) the second section of Article 41 refers specifically to *mothers*, not to women in general. To qualify for a property interest a wife would also have to bear children. There seems little sense in such a distinction. The domestic work of a homemaker wife is no doubt greater where there are children, but this is a matter of degree and while it would affect the size of a property right, it is difficult to see why it should disqualify a childless wife altogether;

3) Article 41 is of no use in dealing with domestic situations in which the parties are not married, whether or not they have any sexual relationship, and courts have to do justice in these situations also; and

4) the whole concept of a constitutionally preferred role for women is open to question and is regarded by many as offensive. Many women today aspire to the same economic and intellectual challenges and rewards as men. Women played little or no role in drafting Article 41. There is no corresponding constitutionally-preferred role for men and this conflicts with the assertion of equality in Article 40. The Constitution should be seen as providing a framework of rights within which individuals may freely choose their own mode of life.

6. Work in Spouse's Business

In *HD v. JD*[65] a wife's work in the husband's public house was held by Finlay P to be a contribution entitling her to an equity in the matrimonial home. Other judges have been less willing to recognise such work as giving rise to an equity in the wife. The authority of these cases is affected adversely by the fact that many different reasons have been given by the judges for the result, and none of them are particularly convincing.

We have seen that Barr J in *BL v. ML*[66] drew a distinction between work in the home, which he felt to be specially protected by Article 41, and work on the farm which he necessarily discounted as not protected by Article 41. He maintained this distinction in *CM v. TM*,[67] this time on the ground that the claim was outside the scope of section 12 of the Married Women's Status Act, 1957 because the section related to the title to property and the wife's claim was properly only one to remuneration. The wife apparently claimed compensation which the judge interpreted as a claim to a money sum. He seems to have regarded this as alternative to a property interest in the *business* and therefore to have discounted the claim as one to a interest in the matrimonial home. This

65 Unreported, High Court, Finlay P, 31 July 1981.

66 [1992] 2 IR 77.

67 Unreported, High Court, Barr J, 30 November 1989.

appears to be inconsistent with the reasoning of Finlay P in *HD v. JD*.[68]

In *CR v. DR*[69] Lynch J discounted the work of the wife in helping in the husband's business and on the family farm, the judge holding that it was not related to the acquisition of the property.[70] One of the implications of *McC v. McC*[71] is that work of the type contributed by the wife in *CR v. DR*[72] cannot be so readily discounted in future. Since no agreement is required there need be nothing to link the wife's contribution and the acquisition of the house other than the circumstance that her spouse was in fact thereby relieved to some extent of the expense of acquiring it and whether or not he or she could have borne the extra expense without that relief. The High Court decision in *B v. B*[73] appears to be *per incuriam* on the point, and Lynch J in *CR v. DR*[74] appears to have misinterpreted Henchy J in *McC v. McC*.[75] The Supreme Court more recently in *EN v. RN*[76] took into account the indirect contribution of a wife to the repayment of a mortgage used to convert the house into rented flats. The wife managed the rented flats and the rental income was used to pay off the mortgage.

B. Presumption of Advancement

This is an equitable principle which is based on the notion that where one party is under an obligation to provide financially for another then if the person who is under the obligation transfers property to the other it is presumed to be in discharge of the obligation and so the transferor will not retain any interest by trust or use in the property. It used to be the case that a husband was regarded as being under the obligation of providing for his wife and the presumption would apply in such a case. This position is clearly based upon assumptions about the social role of parties to a marriage, and specifically on the assumption that it is the husband who has the role of being the breadwinner, the party who has a job and a career, while the wife is seen as performing the role of remaining at home and doing domestic work. Today these assumptions can no longer be as readily made in the past and many married women also seek to fulfil themselves in a paid job or career. Not surprisingly, therefore, the courts

68 Unreported, High Court, Finlay P, 31 July 1981.

69 Unreported, High Court, Lynch J, 5 April 1984, see above.

70 See also *Grant v. Edwards* [1986] 2 All ER 426, in which domestic work of a *de facto* wife was apparently taken into account.

71 [1986] ILRM 1, Supreme Court, Henchy J nem diss.

72 Unreported, High Court, Lynch J, 5 April 1984, see above.

73 High Court, MacKenzie J, 22 April 1986.

74 Unreported, High Court, Lynch J, 5 April 1984, see above.

75 [1986] ILRM 1, Supreme Court, Henchy J, nem diss.

76 *EN v. RN* [1992] 2 IR 116, Supreme Court.

have had to examine the application of the presumption of advancement to marriage in a sceptical light.[77]

In *W v. W*[78] Finlay P suggested *obiter* that the presumption still applied. His statement was *obiter* because in that case the house was in the husband's name. He said that where property is in the wife's sole name and the husband contributes there is a rebuttable presumption that it was an advancement and gives the husband no interest in the house.

In *CC v. SC*[79] the husband and wife operated a joint account in the bank and this account had been used to pay for the matrimonial home. McMahon J held that in the absence of evidence to rebut the presumption they were beneficial as well as legal joint owners. Even if the husband had in fact put more into the account than the wife, the additional amount was presumed to be an advancement. They were not, therefore, tenants in common in proportion to their contributions. Hence they were also beneficial joint tenants of a house bought with the fund.

In *JC v. JHC*[80] the house was paid for by the husband but conveyed to the husband and wife as joint tenants. Keane J held that the husband and wife were beneficial joint tenants. The presumption of advancement had not been rebutted. On the contrary, the evidence was that the husband intended to make a gift to the wife and that she should have the property if he predeceased her. The judge noted that the English House of Lords in *Pettit v. Pettit*[81] had said that the presumption was inappropriate today between husband and wife and although it still applied it would be rebutted by comparatively slight evidence. But here, the evidence supported it. The changing social context of the presumption of advancement was memorably described by Lord Diplock in *Pettit v. Pettit*:

> "The consensus of judicial opinion which gave rise to the presumptions of advancement and resulting trust in transactions between husband and wife is to be found in cases relating to the propertied classes of the 19th century and the first quarter of the twentieth century among whom marriage settlements were common, and it was unusual for the wife to contribute by her earnings to the family income. It was not until after World War II that the courts were required to consider the proprietary rights in family assets of a different social class. The advent of legal aid, the wider employment of married women in industry, commerce and the professions and the emergence of a property-owning, particularly a real-property-mortgaged-to-a-building-society-owning, democracy has compelled the courts to direct their attention to this during the last 20 years.

77 See *RF v. MF*, unreported, Supreme Court, Henchy J nem diss, 24 October 1985. *Parkes v. Parkes*, [1980] ILRM 137, High Court. *M v. M* (1980) 114 ILTR 46, High Court; See also *Lynch v. Burke* [1990] 1 IR 1, unreported, Supreme Court, 7 November 1995, O'Flahery J, nem. diss.

78 [1981] ILRM 202.

79 Unreported, High Court, McMahon J, 2 July 1982.

80 Unreported, High Court, Keane J, 4 August 1982.

81 [1970] AC 777.

> It would, in my view, be an abuse of the legal technique for ascertaining or imputing intention to apply to transactions between the post-war generation of married couples presumptions which are based on inferences of fact which an earlier generation of judges drew as to the most likely intentions of earlier generations of spouses belonging to the propertied classes of a different social era".[82]

The Supreme Court in *RF v. MF*[83] further qualified the circumstances in which the presumption operates. The husband in that case bought a house and put it in the joint names of himself and his wife. He did so at the suggestion of his wife and in order to revive their relationship which was under some strain. The wife then refused to move into the new house and continued to live in their original family home. She nevertheless claimed that she was entitled to a half share because it was jointly owned. Henchy J held that:

> "The equitable doctrine of advancement, as applied to transactions between husband and wife, has the effect that when a husband (*at least where the circumstances show that he is to be expected to provide for his wife*) buys property and has it conveyed to his wife and himself jointly, there is a presumption that the wife's paper title gives her a beneficial estate or interest in the property. Unless the presumption is rebutted by evidence showing a contrary intention on the part of the husband at the time of the transaction, he will be deemed to have entered into the transaction for the purpose of conferring a beneficial estate or interest on the wife. That estate or interest is treated in law as an advancement, that is to say, a material benefit in anticipation of the performance by the husband of his duty to provide for the wife".[*emphasis supplied*][84]

The words in italics indicate a narrowing of the test. In the past all husbands were expected to provide for their wives. The duty flowed from the marital relationship itself. The court in *RF v. MF*[85] is redefining the test so that it now only applies to certain husbands, and probably only where the wife has no means of providing for herself.

Henchy J goes on to state that the presumption is rebuttable by the husband showing by "acts or statements before or around the transaction" that a beneficial interest was not intended to be conveyed in the circumstances relied on. The judge went on to say that the authorities show that subsequent acts or statements are admissible as evidence against the party making them but not in his or her favour. Subsequent acts or statements by the wife are admissible in evidence to rebut the presumption. Quite what circumstances the judge had in mind are not clear, but it is hardly more than common sense to suggest that where the wife remains in the home performing domestic work and the husband

82 [1970] AC 777, [1969] 2 All ER 385, [1969] 2 WLR 966, 20 P& CR 991, 211 EG 829, [1969] EGD 764, HL.

83 Unreported, Supreme Court, Henchy J, nem diss, 24 October 1985. See also *Lynch v. Burke* [1990] 1 IR 1, High Court, unreported, Supreme Court, 7 November 1995; *Parkes v. Parkes*, [1980] ILRM 137, High Court.

84 Unreported, Supreme Court, 24 October 1985 at p.6.

85 Unreported, Supreme Court Henchy J, nem diss, 24 October 1985.

is the breadwinner, that is a circumstance in which the husband may be expected to provide materially for the wife, and that therefore the presumption will continue to apply more strongly in such a case than where the wife has a career of her own and the parties are, in economic terms, on a more equal footing.

C. People Living Together

Questions also arise as to direct and indirect contributions to the acquisition of property where two people are living together who are not married to each other.

In *McGill v. Snodgrass*[86] the plaintiff and defendant met in 1963 while living in Munich. The plaintiff was married and living with his wife and daughter. The defendant, an American, was separated from her husband. The plaintiff left his wife and daughter and set up home with the defendant in her house. They had holidays in Ireland together. In 1967 the plaintiff bought a house and was registered as owner. The defendant moved in. The plaintiff then sought to evict the defendant. The defendant claimed a beneficial interest with the plaintiff based on indirect contributions to the purchase price. The defendant had spent £1,000 and had worked on the house.

Gannon J declined to hold that she had obtained any interest, on the ground that there was no evidence of an agreement before the purchase of the house that her contributions should give her an interest, nor was there anything to connect the contributions, all of which were made after the payment of the purchase price, with the purchase itself. The judge said that:

> ". . . in the case of two persons who are not spouses, evidence of consensus derived from words or conduct and intended to have legal consequences would support a trust expressed or implied or constructive. . .".[87]

But he did not think that the mere fact of their living together was sufficient to create a trust.

However, there is authority in the Republic for the opposite view, that an agreement or arrangement is not required in such a case. In *Power v. Conroy*[88] the defendant was a married man with five children. The plaintiff was at all material times a single woman. The plaintiff and defendant began living together and so continued for about five years. For the first three and a half years they lived in rented accommodation in various parts of Dublin. Most of the time the plaintiff was employed. They had a child and in 1975 they decided to buy a house. The purchase was taken in the name of the defendant alone. The plaintiff gave up work before the birth of the child. At the time of the purchase

86 Reported sub nom *McGill v. S* [1979] IR 283, High Court.

87 [1979] IR 283 at 289.

88 [1980] ILRM 31, High Court, McWilliam J.

the plaintiff had some savings and contributed £1,000 by way of deposit on the house. Later she paid another £1,000 to pay the builders who were pressing for their money. The defendant obtained a loan of 90 per cent of the purchase price and spent a further £1,000 on furnishings. Repayments were made by the defendant. There were considerable arrears due. There was no agreement or discussion as to how the house was to be owned. Both contributed to the upkeep of the household.

McWilliam J held that one had to see what sums were paid by the parties towards the acquisition of the house and in doing so one should take into account such contributions to the household expenses by either party as enabled the other party to make payments towards the purchase price. Having done so, the house would be held on trust by the defendant in proportion to the shares. On the facts of the case before him he found it impossible to make an accurate estimate, but put the plaintiff's contribution at 55 per cent. The defendant therefore held the house as to 11/20th on trust for the plaintiff. The case is remarkable in that the judge did not treat the situation as in any way different to that of a married couple and did not treat the absence of an agreement or arrangement as material. Such a view would also seem to be more consistent with the decision of the Supreme Court on married partners in *McC v. McC*.[89]

One English case has treated labour expended on a house as giving rise to an equity through a constructive trust. In *Cooke v. Head*[90] the defendant man and the plaintiff woman planned to build a bungalow in which they would live. The woman's work on the house consisted of demolishing a building, removing rubble, using a cement mixer and painting. They both saved as much money as they could each week from their earnings. They pooled these savings and used the money to pay off the mortgage. When the bungalow was near completion they separated. The defendant lived in it alone and continued to pay the mortgage. The plaintiff claimed a declaration that the house was owned jointly by them. The Court of Appeal assessed her interest as one third. Lord Denning MR expressed the view that:

> "... whenever two parties by their joint efforts acquired property to be used for their joint benefit, the courts may impose or impute a constructive or resulting trust".[91]

Lord Denning said that the constructive trust doctrine applied "to husband and wife, to engaged couples, and to a man and mistress, and maybe to other relationships too." The beneficial interest was not to be determined according to the parties separate contributions but the value of the equity was to be determined at the time the parties separated and then divided between them as the circumstances merited. Karminski and Orr JJ concurred.

89 [1986] ILRM 1, Supreme Court, Henchy J, nem diss.

90 [1972] 1 WLR 518.

91 [1972] 1 WLR 518 at 520.

The English case of *Pascoe v. Turner*[92], dealing with a *de facto* marriage, treated the facts as coming within the doctrine of proprietary estoppel. P, a wealthy man, had told T, a widow with whom he had lived for some years, that the house in which they lived and which he had bought, would be hers together with everything in it. T spent money on repairs and improvements and furniture in reliance on this assurance, to the knowledge of P. The Court of Appeal held that the assurance and the reliance upon it raised an equity which would only be satisfied by P transferring the fee simple to T. The facts of such cases seem to exert a pressure towards adopting different doctrinal approaches to the solution. In *Pascoe* the facts certainly were highly suggestive of proprietary estoppel and were so treated by the court. But where no assurances or acts of reliance upon them are present judges have tended to look to the constructive trust principle instead. Yet, if the approach in *Power v. Conroy*[93] and *Cooke v. Head*[94] is adopted it would seem to make reference to proprietary estoppel unnecessary. The implication of trust arises from the situation in which the parties have placed themselves and not upon any specific assurances. If the constructive trust arises, similarly to the case of married partners, in the absence of agreement or understandings to the contrary, this excludes the need to resort to estoppel. The overlap in decisions on proprietary estoppel and constructive trusts in these cases may indicate that judges find proprietary estoppel a more satisfactory basis where the facts justify such an inference, but where they do not, the constructive trust provides a concept of next, if not last, resort.[95]

D. A Right to Possession?

Where the legal title to a matrimonial home is in the name of the husband but the wife has an equity and is in occupation of the house, the question frequently arises as to whether she has a right to retain possession. The husband may still be in possession with the wife, or he may have left and a third party, often a judgment mortgagee, may have an equitable interest vested in it. Generally speaking a beneficiary under a trust only has possession of the land with the consent and at the discretion of the trustees, since possession is a right at common law primarily vested in the common law owner. On the other hand it is clear that one co-owner has no right to evict the other,[96] Where the husband

92 [1979] 1 WLR 431; 2 All ER 945. See Chapter 18 Licences, Estoppel and Constructive Trusts for a fuller discussion of this case.

93 [1980] ILRM 31, High Court, McWilliam J.

94 [1972] 1 WLR 518.

95 The English case of *Grant v. Edwards* [1986] 2 All ER 426 seems to express this uncertainty in attempting to straddle both concepts.

96 Cheshire, (13th ed.) 209; *Beaumont v. Kinsella* (1859) 8 Ir CLR 291.

holds the legal estate on trust for himself and the wife as co-owners in equity, the courts would seem to have had a choice as to whether they regard the husband as a trustee or as a co-owner in relation to the wife. In fact, they have generally chosen to regard him as a co-owner for this purpose and unable unilaterally to evict the wife. The only other recourse is to partition or sale in lieu of partition.

Courts in the Republic have also taken the view that the court has a discretion whether or not to order sale in lieu of partition, *i.e.* that it may refuse both.[97]

E. Engaged Couples

The Family Law Act, 1981[98] introduced certain changes in the law as to engaged couples. Section 3 provides that where two people have agreed to marry one another and any property is given as a wedding gift to either or both of them by any other person, it is presumed, in the absence of evidence to the contrary, that the property is given to both of them as joint owners and subject to the condition that it will be returned at the request of the donor or his personal representative if the marriage does not take place "for whatever reason". There is one obvious difficulty in interpreting this section. It creates a presumption of joint ownership where property is given to "either or both" of the parties to the engagement, subject to evidence to the contrary, and yet if property was given to one of them, rather than both jointly, that in itself would seem to constitute evidence that it was not intended that they be joint tenants.

Section 4 deals with gifts from one engaged person to another. It is presumed, subject to evidence to the contrary, that gifts are subject to the condition that they will be returned at the request of the donor or his or her personal representative if the marriage does not take place for any reason other than the death of the donor. Section 3 applies to any property and therefore includes land and buildings attached to land. Section 4 does not include the phrase any property and so it could be argued that the omission is deliberate and that the section only refers to personal property, such as engagement rings, which is commonly the type of gifts given by one engaged person to another. On the other hand, land is not excluded, and gift is apt to include it. If land is within the section then there would seem to be some overlap with the provisions of section 5. Section 5 is a general provision applying where the agreement to marry is terminated. It says that the rules relating to the rights of spouses relating to

97 *O'D v. O'D* unreported, High Court, Murphy J, 18 November 1983; *AL v. JL* unreported, High Court, Finlay P, 27 February 1984; *FF v. CF* [1987] ILRM 1; *O'Neill v. O'Neill* unreported, High Court, Barron J, 6 October 1989; *First National Building Society v. Ring* [1992] 1 IR 375. See Chapter 16 Co-Ownership: Partition.

98 As amended by Family Law Act, 1995 s.48.

property in which either or both of them has or have a beneficial interest shall apply to any property in which either or both of the parties to the agreement had a beneficial interest while the agreement was in force in the same way as they apply to property in which spouses have a beneficial interest.[99] This provision clearly seems to apply to engaged couples the law as to direct and indirect contributions by one spouse to the acquisition of property held in the name of the other spouse. Thus, where a house is being purchased on mortgage by one party to an engagement, the other may acquire an equitable interest in it as tenant in common by contributions. Unlike gifts given to the couple by a third party, there is no presumption of joint tenancy in equity. The contributions may be included in a later assessment after the marriage has taken place, and even if the engagement is called off, a claim to an equity would still be possible, since there is no equivalent provision in this section to the conditions presumed in sections 3 and 4.

F. The Effect of Domestic Violence

Barring orders made under section 3 of the Domestic Violence Act, 1996[100] have the effect of suspending the right to possession of one party to a marriage to the family home and where that party has a property interest in it, they suspend the right to possession. Barring orders may also now be made where the parties are not married, provided they have lived together for six months in a nine month period before the application.[101] A parent may also apply for barring order against a child of full age who is not a dependent person in relation to the parent.[102] Where the applicant is not married to the respondent, or is the parent, no barring can be made if the respondent has a legal or beneficial interest in the house and the applicant either has an interest less than that of the respondent.[103]

A tenant of a housing authority may apply under section 3 of the Housing (Miscellaneous Provisions) Act, 1997 for an exclusion order in respect of the house let to the tenant excluding a person from the house on the ground of anti-social behaviour, which includes the possession of drugs or threatening or violent behaviour.

---

99 Family Law Act, 1995 s.48 declares that s.5 of the 1981 Act does not apply to rights of spouses under the Succession Act, 1965, the Family Home Protection Act, 1976, the Judicial Separation and Family Law Reform Act, 1989 or the Family Law Act, 1995.

100 Replacing section 2 of the Family Home (Protection of Spouses and Children) Act, 1981.

101 Domestic Violence Act, 1996 s.3(1)(b).

102 *ibid.*, s.3(1)(c).

103 *ibid.*, s.3(4).

Domestic violence may have other effects also. In *Dennis v. McDonald*[104] a mistress contributed to the acquisition of a house in which she and her partner lived. She was forced to quit because of the man's violence. It was held that they were tenants in common in equity, that the man had ousted her from possession, and since a tenant in common is not entitled to exclusive possession as against a co-tenant he had to pay her rent. Had she left voluntarily he would not have had to pay her rent.

G. Judicial Separation

The Family Law Act, 1995[105] which replaced[106] the property provisions in the Judicial Separation and Family Law Reform Act, 1989[107] (the 1989 Act) provides for various orders affecting property to be made on the grant of a decree of judicial separation.[108]

1. Property Adjustment Orders

Section 9 of the 1995 Act[109] gives the court jurisdiction, when granting a decree of judicial separation to make a property adjustment order. The order may include, an order that a spouse shall transfer to the other spouse, to any dependent child of the family or another person for the benefit of the child, property belonging to the first-mentioned spouse, either in possession or reversion. Property may also be settled[110] for the benefit of the other spouse or for the benefit of dependent members of the family, and a settlement may be varied.[111]

Section 16 specifies factors which the court shall take into account in making property adjustment and other orders, including contributions both financially and "by looking after the home or caring for the family". The court is

104 [1982] 1 All ER 590.

105 It came into force on 1 August 1996.

106 See *JD v. DD* unreported, High Court, 14 May 1997, McGuinness J.

107 *TF v. Ireland, the Attorney General and MF* [1995] 2 ILRM 321, Supreme Court (upheld constitutionality).

108 *O'D v. O'D* [1998] 1 ILRM 543, Supreme Court (where applicant granted a divorce a mensa et thoro, *i.e.* judicial separation, under s.13 of the Matrimonial Causes Act, 1870 or had entered into a separation agreement before 1989 Act, could not obtain ancillary reliefs under 1989 Act).

109 Replacing s.15 of the 1989 Act. The new section omits the phrase "or at any time thereafter" in s.15(1) of the 1989 Act, but contains no equivalent of s.15(2) of the 1989 Act which provided that the court could consider whether to make an order "on one occasion only" unless a spouse had concealed information.

110 1995 Act, s.9(1)(b).

111 *ibid.* s.9(1) (c) and (d).

therefore empowered, in making property adjustment orders, to take into account the contribution of a homemaker,[112] which they have declined to do in assessing an equity acquired by contributions to the purchase of the house.[113]Section 9 uses the word may and so the court is not obliged to make a property adjustment order, but if does so it is required to take into account the factors set out in section 16.

There is some evidence that the courts are using the powers conferred by the 1989 and 1995 Acts although it is not yet clear that they are doing so in a way which makes good the defects in the previous law. In *JC v. CC*[114] Barr J awarded a 50 per cent share in a family home to a wife who had made direct contributions and ordered the husband to continue making the annual mortgage and insurance payments in respect of the property. In *VS v. RS*[115] Lynch J granted a declaration that the family home vested in the husband and wife as tenants in common in equal shares without a review of contributions by the wife.

In *AS v. GS and Allied Irish Banks plc*[116] a wife instituted proceedings against her husband seeking, *inter alia,* a property adjustment order. The husband had become indebted to the bank which, in the meantime, had obtained judgment against him. The bank, which had actual notice of the proceedings instituted by the wife, sought to register a judgment mortgage against the property in priority to any property adjustment order the wife might obtain in those proceedings. Geoghegan J held that the wife's claim to the order was itself a *lis pendens* binding on a purchaser or mortgagee of the property if the *lis pendens* was registered under the Judgments (Ireland) Act 1844, or, under section 10 of the Act, if the purchaser or mortgagee had actual notice of the proceedings. Hence, it was already too late for the bank to gain priority over any order that might be made.

2. Order for Sale

On granting a decree of judicial separation the court may also make an order for sale of the family home[117] subject to such conditions as the court may specify.

112 In other jurisdictions recognising divorce, "homemaker" contributions may give rise to an entitlement to a share of the beneficial interest in property: *LaRue v. LaRue* (1983) 172 W Va 158, 304 S E 2d 312, 41 A L R 4th 445 the Supreme Court of Appeals of West Virginia, overruling an earlier case, *Patterson v. Patterson* (1981) 167 W Va 1, 277 S E 2d 709.

113 In *BL v. ML* [1992] 2 IR 77 Finlay CJ noted that the 1989 Act, had it applied to the facts, would have given statutory power to do what the court believed it did not have power to do in equity.

114 Unreported, High Court, Barr J, 15 November 1991.

115 Unreported, High Court, Lynch J, 10 June 1991.

116 [1994] 1 IR 407, [1994] 2 ILRM 68.

117 1995 Act s.10.

Where the court makes a lump sum order, secured periodic payments order or a property adjustment order it may also order a sale of property vested in, or in which a beneficial interest is vested in, either or both of the spouses.[118]

3. Right to Occupy

On an application for judicial separation the court may make an order conferring on one spouse "for life[119] or for such other period (definite or contingent) as the court may specify the right to occupy the family home to the exclusion of the other spouse".[120]

H. Family Law (Divorce) Act, 1996

Divorce was introduced into the Republic by the amendment to Article 41.3.2° of the Constitution which now provides that a court may grant divorce where spouses have lived apart for four out of the previous five years, and where there is no reasonable prospect of reconciliation and where proper provision is made for the spouses and children and any other person prescribed by law. Any further conditions may also be prescribed by law.

The Family Law (Divorce) Act, 1996 provides that on granting a decree of divorce the court may make a property adjustment order,[121] which, like such an order made on judicial separation, may provide for the transfer of property belonging to one spouse to the other or a dependent member of the family, or its settlement. The court may also confer a right to occupy the family home, for life or other period (definite or contingent) on a spouse[122] or for the sale of the family home.[123]

I. Family Home Protection Act, 1976

The purpose of the Family Home Protection Act, 1976 is to protect a spouse who does not have the legal title to the matrimonial home vested in them, against being deprived of their security in the home through the other spouse conveying or creating other interests in the home, such as a mortgage, to a third party. It seeks to give this protection to the non-conveying spouse whether or

118 1995 Act s.15.

119 Section 10(1)(a)(i). *JC v. CC* unreported, High Court, Barr J, 15 November 1991 (right of residence for life).

120 Presumably the right is binding on third parties, although the last phrase is somewhat ambiguous.

121 Section 14(1).

122 1996 Act s.15(1)(a).

123 *ibid.*

not that spouse has a beneficial interest in the matrimonial home. The means it adopts is to require the consent of the non-conveying spouse to a conveyance executed by the other spouse. Section 3 of the Act provides that:

> "3.–(1) Where a spouse, without the prior consent in writing of the other spouse, purports to convey any interest in the family home to any person except the other spouse, then, subject to subsections (2) and (3) and section 4, the purported conveyance shall be void".

Subsection (2) provides that subsection (1) shall not apply to a conveyance if it is made by a spouse in pursuance of an enforceable agreement made before the marriage of the spouses. Subsection (3) is discussed in detail below, but basically provides that a conveyance shall not be rendered void under subsection (1) if it is made to a purchaser for full value. Full value means such value as amounts or approximates to the value of that for which it is given.[124]

Section 4 provides that a court may dispense with the consent of a spouse if it is unreasonably withheld. As can be seen from the provisions, the protection of the family home is not absolute in the case of lack of consent to a conveyance. The provisions represent a compromise between protecting the family home, or rather, the security of tenure in the family home of the spouse and children, on the one hand, and protecting innocent purchasers of property on the other. The policy of protecting the family home is balanced against the protection of the commercial market in land.

1. The Meaning of Conveyance

Section 1(1) of the Act defines conveyance as including:

> "a mortgage[125], lease, assent, transfer, disclaimer, release and any other disposition of property otherwise than by a will or a donatio mortis causa and also includes an enforceable agreement (whether conditional or unconditional) to make any such conveyance, and convey shall be construed accordingly".

The section makes it clear that the Act applies to contracts as well as conveyances. Most conveyances of land are carried out in two stages: a contract to convey a title followed by the actual conveyance of the title. The section does not require two consents, one for the contract and one for the conveyance. In *Kyne v. Tiernan*[126] the wife consented to the contract. Then the husband and wife agreed to separate. The wife then refused to sign a consent contained in the deed of conveyance. McWilliam J held that the wife's consent to the contract was a consent to the entire transaction.

---

124 Section 3(5). And see *Bank of Ireland v. Carroll*, unreported, High Court, Hamilton P, 10 September 1986.

125 Including an equitable mortgage by deposit of title deeds: *Bank of Ireland v. Purcell* [1990] ILRM 106, Supreme Court; see below, Interest.

126 *Kyne v. Tiernan*, unreported, High Court, McWilliam J, 15 July 1980; see also *Lloyd v. Sullivan*, unreported, High Court, McWilliam J, 6 March 1981.

Consent is required for mortgages, but in *National Irish Bank Ltd v. Graham*[127] the Supreme Court held that where a conveyance and a mortgage are, in reality, part of a single transaction, consent to the conveyance operates as consent to the mortgage also. The court held that different consideration would apply where land was acquired under a conveyance and was then, within a short time, subsequently mortgaged so as to provide the purchase price which up to then had been supplied by means of a bridging loan.[128]

The statute applies to disclaimers or releases, so that where the family home was vested in a company and the husband merely had a licence to occupy, any release of his licence would be a conveyance and would be void without consent.[129]

2. Family Home

Section 2(1) defines"family home" as meaning:

> "primarily, a dwelling in which a married couple ordinarily reside. The expression comprises, in addition, a dwelling in which a spouse whose protection is in issue ordinarily resides or, if that spouse has left the other spouse, ordinarily resided before leaving".

In *LB v. HB*[130] the argument was made that the section did not apply unless the married couple were residing in the house at the relevant time as husband and wife, *i.e.* that they were having regular sexual intercourse. The judge rejected this interpretation. It was enough if they both resided on the premises. It might also be noted that the 1976 Act is often invoked when the relationship between the parties has deteriorated.

The definition does not depend on ownership: even if the title to a house is vested in a company,[131] a trust, or in someone other than one of the spouses, it can still be a family home under the Act. The statute cannot be avoided by putting a family home in the name of a company.

The definition does depend on residence, and an intention to reside is not enough. If a spouse enters into a contract to buy a house, which the spouses intend to be their future home, the mere fact that they intend to reside there, or that the purchasing spouse acquires a purchaser's equity by virtue of the con-

127 [1994] 2 ILRM 109, Supreme Court (Finlay CJ, Egan and Blayney JJ concurring); see also *Kyne v. Tiernan*, unreported, High Court, McWilliam J, 15 July 1980; *Lloyd v. Sullivan* High Court, McWilliam J, 6 March 1981.

128 [1994] 2 ILRM 109, per Finlay CJ at 114.

129 *Walpoles Ltd v. Jay,* unreported, High Court, McWilliam J, 20 November 1980. The case is discussed in Lyall, "The Family Home Protection Act, 1976 and Conveyances Other Than by Spouses " (1984) 6 DULJ (ns) 158.

130 [1980] ILRM 257.

131 *Walpoles Ltd v. Jay,* unreported, High Court, McWilliam J, 20 November 1980.

tract, does not confer rights on the non-purchasing spouse under the Act.[132] She only acquires such rights when she takes up residence.

The land comprised in a conveyance may consist of a family home together with other land, such as a farm, which is not part of the family home in the normal sense of that phrase. Before 1996 the issue arose in a number of cases in which no valid consent was held to have been given to a such a conveyance as to whether the court could notionally sever the land and uphold the transaction in relation to the land not forming part of the family home.[133] Section 2(2) of the Family Home Protection Act 1976 has now been amended by section 54 of the Family Law Act 1995 as follows:

> "In subsection (1), 'dwelling', means any building or part of a building occupied as a separate dwelling and includes any garden or other land usually occupied with the dwelling, being land that is subsidiary and ancillary to it, is required for amenity or convenience and is not being used or developed primarily for commercial purposes, and includes a structure that is not permanently attached to the ground and a vehicle, or vessel, whether mobile or not, occupied as a separate dwelling".

3. Consent Required at Common Law or in Equity

In *Nestor v. Murphy*[134] the Supreme Court held that section 3 of the Act does not require a separate consent of a spouse to a conveyance if the spouse's consent is in any case essential to that conveyance. The defendants were husband and wife. They were entitled as joint tenants to a lease of the dwelling house which was a family home under the Act. The defendants executed a contract under which they agreed to transfer the house to the plaintiff. They failed to complete the sale and the plaintiff applied to the High court for an order of specific performance. The defendants argued that the contract was void because the wife had not consented to it in writing before it was entered into.[135] Henchy J, delivering the judgment of the court, said that what has been called "a sche-

132 *National Irish Bank Ltd v. Graham* [1994] 2 ILRM 109, Supreme Court.

133 *Hamilton v. Hamilton & Dunne* [1982] IR 466, Supreme Court (Costello J at 490). The High Court ordered a severance in *Bank of Ireland v. Slevin* unreported Circuit Appeal, Johnson J, 16 February 1989, a case cited by Blayney J in the Supreme Court in *Bank of Ireland v. Smyth* [1996] 1 ILRM 241, Blayney J nem. diss. Blayney J left the point open. In *Allied Irish Banks plc v. O'Neill,* unreported, High Court, 13 December 1995, Laffoy J had to consider an equitable charge over registered land. The charge was created by deposit of the land certificate, and there was no document describing the land subject to the charge. The judge interpreted Blayney J's remarks in *Smyth* as not precluding her from deciding that the equitable charge applied only to the land other than the family home and adjourned the proceedings to hear submissions as to where the dividing line should be drawn.

134 [1979] IR 326.

135 It might be pointed out that if the defendants' argument were correct it would follow that in such a case the consent of the husband would also be required, since, in relation to the conveying wife, he would be the 'other spouse' referred to by s.3.

matic or teleological approach" must be adopted in interpreting Section 3(1) of the 1976 Act:[136]

> "This means that Section 3, subsection (1), must be given a construction which does not overstep the limits of the operative range that must be ascribed to it, having regard to the legislative scheme as expressed in the Family Home Protection Act of 1976 as a whole. Therefore, the words of Section 3, subsection (1), must be given no wider meaning than is necessary to effectuate the right of avoidance given when the non-participating spouse has not consented in advance in writing to the alienation of any interest in the family home".

It was held that the wife's consent was not required under the Act because they were legal joint tenants and therefore any conveyance or contract would be ineffective without her participation.

A close reading of subsection (1) supports Henchy J's view. It refers to a spouse who conveys – conveys includes contracts – and opposes to it the expression the other spouse, who, impliedly, is not conveying. Where both spouses must convey it is therefore arguable that there is no "other spouse" within the meaning of the section. This would exclude spouses who are legal co-owners from the scope of the 1976 Act.

If the legal title is vested in spouse H alone and spouse W has an equitable interest in the family home, W's equitable interest cannot be conveyed without her consent because it is she who would have to convey it.

If the legal title is vested in H alone and W has an equitable interest, W's consent would still be required to a conveyance by H of the legal title, since, in relation to that conveyance, W is the non-conveying spouse. It is the policy of the Act that the legal title should not pass to a third party without the consent of the non-conveying spouse.

If the legal title is vested in H alone and W has an equitable interest, W's consent would be necessary to give X, a mortgagee of H's interest, priority over W's equity, assuming the mortgage is created after the equity, because W's consent is required under the Act to the creation of the mortgage between H and X.

4. Interest

Section 3 applies to the conveyance of any interest in the family home. Interest is defined by the Act as meaning "any estate, right, title or other interest, legal or equitable".[137]

In *Bank of Ireland v. Purcell*[138] the plaintiff held an equitable charge over the defendant's lands by virtue of the deposit of title deeds to secure present

136 *Nestor v. Murphy*, (1979) IR 326 at page 329. See also *AIB v. O'Neill and Kidd*, unreported, High Court, Laffoy J, 13 December 1995.

137 Section 1(1).

138 [1990] ILRM 106, Supreme Court; [1988] ILRM 480, High Court Barron J.

and future advances. The lands included the family home, within the meaning of the 1976 Act, of the defendant and his wife, but the deposit was made before the 1976 Act came into force. Further advances were made to the defendant on security of the deposit after the Act came into force but no consents to these advances were obtained from the defendant's wife. Barron J granted a declaration that no security was created in favour of the plaintiff over the family home in respect of advances made after the date on which the Act came into force. All the advances made after the 1976 Act came into force required the consent of the defendant's wife since, although the bank obtained an estate in the lands, the word interest in the 1976 Act is defined more widely than a reference to an estate and the fact that an estate had been conveyed need not prevent a subsequent transaction from conveying an interest in the lands. The judge referred to Kenny J's definition of an equitable mortgage in *Allied Irish Bank v. Glynn*[139]and continued:

> "Each time there is a further advance the amount which is being charged on the lands is altered and accordingly the interest of the mortgagor in those lands is altered. I have no doubt that future further advances are the conveyance of an interest in the lands for the purposes of s.3 of the Act".[140]

The *ratio* was upheld in the Supreme Court.[141]

5. Prior

The consent must be prior consent in that it must be given before the conveyance purports to take effect. In the case of a deed that point is the delivery of the deed.[142] In the case of registered land, it is the time of entry on the register.

In the case of a deposit of title deeds or a land certificate creating an equitable mortgage, the time is not necessarily the time when the title deeds or land certificate are left with the intending mortgagee. In *Bank of Ireland v. Hanrahan*[143] the defendants had deposited the land certificate of their farm with the plaintiff bank as security for a loan. The husband had gone to the bank with the certificate. The Bank then told him that the consent of his wife was required under the 1976 Act. He left the certificate with the Bank, saying he would return later that day with his wife. He duly returned with his wife who then executed a consent form. O'Hanlon J held that the requirements of the Act as to a prior consent by the wife to the equitable deposit had been complied

139 [1973] IR 188 at 191.

140 *Bank of Ireland v. Purcell* [1988] ILRM 480 at 482.

141 *ibid.* [1990] ILRM 106.

142 *AD v. DD and Irish Nationwide Building Society,* unreported, High Court, McWilliam J, 8 June 1983.

143 Unreported, High Court, O'Hanlon J, 10 February 1987; see also *Bank of Ireland v. Smyth* [1993] 2 IR 109, [1993] ILRM 790, High Court, [1996] 1 ILRM 241, Supreme Court.

with. There was a tacit agreement that the Bank held the certificate as mere custodians in the period before the wife executed her consent, and that the character in which they held the certificate changed once she executed it to that of equitable mortgagee. While the distinction between the two different types of possession provides a sophisticated rationale, it can nevertheless be objected, that the reasoning leads only to the conclusion that the execution of the consent and the change in the nature of the bank's possession coincided in point of time, whereas the Act requires the consent to precede the possession as mortgagee. It must be assumed that there is a fictional fraction of a second in time, between the moment of execution of the consent and the change in the character of possession.

6. Consent

It seems that the court may scrutinise the reality of consent by a wife with particular care. The onus is on the third party to ensure that the consent of the non-conveying spouse is a real one.[144]

In *Bank of Ireland v. Smyth*[145] the wife had signed a deed of charge in favour of the plaintiff over registered land owned by her husband. The land consisted of a farm and included the family home. The family home had been built with the aid of a loan secured by a mortgage on the farm. At the time she signed the consent to the present mortgage the wife believed, incorrectly, that this circumstance meant that the present bank would have no right to obtain possession of the family home. The wife argued, *inter alia,* that her consent was invalid since she did not have a proper understanding of what she was signing. Geoghegan J agreed with this submission and held the charge void on the ground that the plaintiff had failed to take reasonable steps to ensure that the wife understood the nature and effect of the charge or, alternatively, to advise her to obtain independent advice. The judge described married women as a protected class because of the probability of influence by their husbands and the probability of reliance on their husbands.

The Supreme Court, in a single judgment by Blayney J, upheld the decision, but on somewhat narrower grounds. The judge noted that the purpose of the Family Home Protection Act, 1976 was not merely to protect the non-conveying spouse, but to protect the family. The consent must be fully informed. The onus was on the bank to prove a valid consent had been given.[146] As they

144 *Bank of Ireland v. Smyth,* [1996] 1 ILRM 241, Supreme Court.

145 [1993] 2 IR 109, [1993] ILRM 790, High Court, [1996] 1 ILRM 241, Supreme Court. See also *Barclay's Bank v. O'Brien* [1992] 4 All ER 983, where the court was also scrutinising the reality of consent given by a married woman to a charge by her husband.

146 Contrast undue influence in equity, where the party alleging it generally has to prove it: see *Bank of Nova Scotia v. Hogan* [1997] 1 ILRM 407, Supreme Court. The court assumed, without deciding, that the relationship of husband and wife did not itself raise a

had not discharged this onus, the consent was invalid and the charge was void. The bank should have made inquiries of the wife to discover the state of her knowledge as to the effect of the proposed charge. Since they had failed to do so, they had constructive notice of what they would have discovered and therefore that her apparent consent was unreal.

The judge also held that the bank should have advised the wife to obtain independent advice, but rejected the notion that this stemmed from a duty owed by the bank to the wife. It was in the bank's own interest to ensure that a real consent had been obtained, because if they did not, the consequence was that the charge was void.[147]

Consent by a wife, or the circumstances surrounding it, may also operate to prevent a third party obtaining constructive notice, in the equitable sense, of a spouse's equity obtained by contributions or otherwise. In *Hibernian Life Association Limited v. Gibbs*[148] the defendant, the husband, was assignee of a lease in the house subject to a first mortgage. The husband later entered into a second mortgage with the plaintiff. In relation to that transaction the husband and the wife made a statutory declaration which declared that they were married and that the husband was the owner of the house. The mortgage was in the ordinary standard form. It recited that the leasehold property which was being mortgaged was vested in the borrower, that is the husband, for the residue of the term granted and that the defendant as beneficial owner demised to the plaintiffs the house for the mortgage term, but subject to the first mortgage. The wife executed a consent to the mortgage under the Family Home Protection Act, 1976. The husband defaulted in the repayments under the second mortgage and the plaintiffs obtained an order declaring the second mortgage to be well-charged. In 1989 the wife instituted proceedings against her husband under the provisions of the Married Women's Status Act, 1957 claiming a beneficial interest in the premises. McKenzie J in the High Court held that the wife was beneficially interested to 100 per cent in the property. The wife then applied to discharge the well-charging order. The husband was joined as a second defendant in the proceedings. The plaintiff then sought a declaration that any interest which the wife enjoyed in the premises was held subject to the prior rights of the plaintiffs under its mortgage. The plaintiffs claimed they were purchasers for value without notice of the wife's interest in the lands. The defendants argued that the plaintiff had constructive notice. Costello J did not agree. Initially a joint loan to husband and wife was contemplated but when it was found that that the husband alone was the lessee it was decided, without any demur on the part of husband or wife, that the loan should be made to the

presumption of undue influence in favour of the wife.

147 Contrast the position in equity, where a third party who has constructive notice takes a title, but subject to the equity.

148 Unreported, High Court, Costello J, 23 July 1993.

husband alone. The wife had thus consented to a loan to the husband alone on the basis that he alone held the beneficial interest.

7. Right of Veto, not a Property Right

The Act does not confer any property right on the spouse.[149] It is merely a statutory right of veto.[150] The right of veto is not, therefore, one of the unregistered rights referred to by section 74(1) of the Registration of Title Act, 1964 subject to which a judgment mortgage takes effect on registration, because that phrase refers to property rights only.[151]

A spouse may have acquired a share of the beneficial interest through contributions, direct or indirect, to the acquisition of the house, but that is an entirely distinct issue. A spouse who has acquired such an equitable interest will have both proprietary rights in the home and, in addition, rights under the 1976 Act. A spouse who has not acquired an equity will still be able to rely on their rights under the 1976 Act.

Although the right of a spouse under the Act does not rank itself as a positive property right, it may create a defect in title with which third parties need be concerned. Yet the line between this necessary result of the statutory provisions and the personal nature of the right in some contexts needs to be carefully drawn. In *Bank of Ireland v. Carroll*[152] G conveyed a house to C and C was registered as owner. On the same day he mortgaged it to the bank. G's wife had consented orally to the conveyance, but not in writing as required by the Act. C was made bankrupt. The Official Assignee sought to establish that the conveyance was void for lack of consent. Hamilton P held, citing *Nestor v. Murphy*[153], that the basic purpose of the Act is to protect the home by giving a right of avoidance to the spouse who was not a party to the conveyance and ". . . this means that section 3 must be given a construction that does not overstep the limits of the operative range that must be ascribed to it. . .". The section must be given no wider meaning than "necessary to effectuate the right of avoidance. . .". This, the judge felt, meant that only the wife could impugn the transaction, and she did not wish to do so here.

Although the point taken by the judge disposed of the issue before the court, it must still be the case that an intending purchaser may object to a title proffered by a vendor in the case of a family home on the ground that the non-conveying spouse has not consented to the transaction, or has only con-

149 In the High Court in *Bank of Ireland v. Smyth* [1993] 2 IR 109, [1993] ILRM 790 the judge referred to the right of veto as "quasi-proprietary", but this language was not repeated in the Supreme Court: unreported Supreme Court, 15 November 1995.

150 *Guckian v. Brennan* [1981] IR 478.

151 *Murray v. Diamond* [1982] ILRM 113.

152 Unreported, High Court, Hamilton P, 10 September 1986.

153 [1979] IR 326 per Henchy J.

sented orally, and that consequently no title can pass. Lack of consent is a fatal flaw in the title.

8. Registered Land

Under section 72(1)(j) of the Registration of Title Act, 1964 the rights of persons in actual occupation of the land bind a transferee of registered land even though they do not appear on the register. The right of veto under the 1976 Act is not, however, an interest within the section. It refers to property rights only.[154] A spouse may, however, make an entry in the Register (and the Registry of Deeds) under section 12 of the 1976 Act noting the power of veto under section 3 of the Act.

In *Murray v. Diamond*[155] it was held, following *Tempany v. Hynes*[156] that the effect of a judgment mortgage is similar to a voluntary conveyance in that the effect of registering it is to charge the interest of the judgment debtor, subject, under section 71(4) of the Registration of Title Act, 1964, to all unregistered rights subject to which the judgment debtor held the interest. But the court went on to hold that rights under section 71(4) refers to property and does not include the spouse's statutory right of veto under the Family Home Protection Act. The spouse's right of veto under the Act is not protected against creditors of the other spouse if they obtain a judgment mortgage.[157]

9. Mortgages

a) General

Section 7(1) of the Family Home Protection Act, 1976 provides:

> "Where a mortgagee or lessor of the family home brings an action against a spouse in which he claims possession or sale of the home by virtue of the mortgage or lease in relation to the non-payment by that spouse of sums due thereunder, and it appears to the court –
>
> (a) that the other spouse is capable of paying to the mortgagee or lessor the arrears (other than arrears of principal or interest or rent that do not constitute part of the periodical payments due under the mortgage or lease) of money due under the mortgage or lease within a reasonable time, and future periodical payments falling due under the mortgage or lease, and that the other spouse desires to pay such arrears and periodical payments; and
>
> (b) that it would in all the circumstances, having regard to the terms of the mortgage or lease, the interests of the mortgagee or lessor and the respective interests of the spouses, be just and equitable to do so, the court may

154 *Murray v. Diamond* [1982] ILRM 113.

155 *ibid.*.

156 [1976] IR 101.

157 See also the section below on the position of mortgages under the 1976 Act.

> adjourn the proceedings for such period and on such terms as appear to the court to be just and equitable".

Although in general mortgagees have power at common law to go into possession of the mortgaged property, it was held in *McCormack v. Irish Civil Service Building Society*[158] by Blayney J that this is not necessarily so in relation to a family home. By providing for the adjournment of proceedings claiming possession of a family home in certain circumstances, sections 7 and 8 of the Family Home Protection Act, 1976 may imply, the judge held, that a mortgagee of a family home may not enter into possession of the premises without first commencing legal proceedings, even where it has express authority to enter under a clause in the mortgage, since for it to do so might circumvent the provisions of the Act.

b) Judgment Mortgages

If one spouse gets into debt the creditor may wish to register a judgment mortgage against that spouse's property.

There are two questions which have arisen: (a) Does the Family Home Protection Act, 1976 prevent the registration of a judgment mortgage without the consent of the other spouse? (b) What effect, once registered, does a judgment mortgage have, particularly bearing in mind any property rights which the other spouse has acquired in the home?

The first question was answered in *Containercare (Ireland) Ltd v. Wycherley*.[159] The defendants, who were husband and wife, lived in a house which had been demised to them jointly for a term of years. In 1974 they assured the house to a building society by a mortgage which secured the repayment to the society of the principal sum which had been advanced to the defendants by the society. Until December, 1977, the first defendant paid all the instalments of principal and interest becoming due under the mortgage of 1974, and thereafter those instalments were paid by the second defendant. The house was a family home for the purposes of section 3 of the Act of 1976. Having recovered judgment against the first defendant for a liquidated sum, the plaintiff registered an affidavit in the Registry of Deeds on the 1 March, 1979 (describing the judgment and claiming that the first defendant had an estate in the house) for the purpose of converting the judgment into a judgment mortgage in accordance with the Judgment Mortgage (Ireland) Act, 1850.

The plaintiff issued a summons in the High Court and claimed a declaration that its judgment was well charged on the interest of the first defendant in the house, an order for sale, and ancillary relief. At the hearing of the summons the second defendant submitted that no estate in the house had vested in the plaintiff

158 *Ex tempore*, Irish Times Law Reports, 17 April 1989, (Lexis: Transcript) High Court.
159 [1982] IR 143.

pursuant to section 7 of the Judgment Mortgage (Ireland) Act, 1850 since she had not consented to a disposition of any such estate.

Carroll J held, first, that the estate of a judgment debtor in premises which are a family home within the meaning of section 3(1) may be vested in the judgment creditor notwithstanding the absence of consent by the other spouse because a judgment mortgage takes effect under section 7 of the 1850 Act by operation of law. It is not a conveyance by a spouse within section 3 of the 1976 Act. Secondly, she held that the proceedings could not be adjourned under section 7 of the 1976 Act (allowing the non-conveying spouse to pay off the mortgage) because section 7 referred only to mortgages repayable by instalments and a judgment mortgage was not so repayable. The judge also held that the registration of the judgment mortgage had the effect of severing the joint tenancy[160] of the defendants in the premises and that from then on the plaintiff and the second defendant held the premises as tenants in common in equal shares subject to the equities of redemption. She further held that by reason of the mortgage payments made by her to the first mortgagee after the creation of the tenancy in common, the second defendant was entitled in equity to claim an increase in her share of the tenancy in common equal to the increase in the value of the equity of redemption resulting from those mortgage payments.

These findings seemed to reveal a flaw in the Family Home Protection Act, 1976. A spouse who does not have a legal interest in the family home is powerless to prevent a judgment creditor of the legal owner/spouse from registering a judgment mortgage.

From this it might also seem to follow that the judgment creditor thereby acquires and may exercise the remedies of a mortgagee including sale of the premises. But this is not necessarily the case. It is one of the reasons for the decision in *Containercare* that consent of a spouse under the 1976 Act is not required for the registration of a judgment mortgage. From this it cannot be assumed that the judgment mortgagee thereby obtains a remedy enforceable against a spouse's equity. That would be contrary to the decision in *Tempany v. Hynes*[161] in which the Supreme Court held that a judgment mortgage is a transaction without valuable consideration and, as such, is subject to all the equities which bound the judgment mortgagor. Where the non-debtor spouse has an equity it therefore takes priority over the judgment mortgage. It is submitted that it is then for the court to decide how that equity is to be satisfied. It may be that in some cases the just result would be to order sale. In other cases the circumstances may require that the non-debtor spouse should remain in possession. The court has a discretion.

160 The title being unregistered. In registered land the registration of a judgment mortgage does not vest the judgment debtor's interest in the judgment mortgagee.

161 [1976] IR 101.

In *Curran v. Curran*,[162] the plaintiff wife claimed the whole or an undivided share of the house of which the husband was registered as full owner. The wife had paid off part of the mortgage debt by direct contributions. The husband had got into debt in the course of his business with the plaintiff company and had agreed that the debt would be secured by a legal charge over the house. None was ever executed or registered. These facts in themselves would give rise to an equitable mortgage, but the company chose instead to sue on the debt and registered a judgement mortgage.

McWilliam J held that when the wife paid off the mortgage the husband then held the property in trust for them both as tenants in common in equity in equal shares. He held that the shares were equal because they had mutually agreed to put the legal title in their joint names, although they had never in fact done so. Nevertheless, the intention to do so was enough in equity to constitute conclusive evidence of their intention as to how the beneficial interests were to be held. Nothing appeared on the register as to this equity. Secondly, the judge held that the effect of *Tempany v. Hynes*[163] was that a judgment mortgage is not a charge on land created for valuable consideration within section 68(3) of the Registration of Title Act, 1964, and so, under section 71(4)(c) of the same Act, it was subject to all the unregistered rights subject to which the judgment debtor held the registered land at the time of the registration of the judgment mortgage. This clearly included the wife's equity in the house.

Thus, the wife's interest takes priority in these circumstances whether or not she is in actual occupation of the land. If she is, then under section 72(1)(j) even a transferee for value would be bound, assuming at any rate that the Irish courts would take the view that such an equity came within the section.

In *Curran* the company had brought the action to have the sum awarded in their judgment declared well charged on the interest of the husband. It might have been argued that this could have been done without affecting the wife's interest, in that the value in monetary terms of her interest would not be affected. The fact that the court did not take this view indicates that they considered that the wife's interest did not consist only of a financial interest. In other words, the judgment necessarily rests on the holding that the wife was entitled, by virtue of her equity, to possession of the premises, and that if the judgment mortgage was declared well charged on the husband's interest it would necessarily have put that element of her interest in jeopardy. Had the judgment mortgagees been able to enforce their rights, they could have applied for an order for sale, indeed that was also part of their claim in the case.

A court would have a discretion whether or not to grant such an order. This

162 Unreported, High Court, McWilliam J, 10 March 1981.

163 [1976] IR 101.

was reaffirmed in *O'D v.O'D*[164] and the cases are reviewed in *Re Whitwell's Estate*.[165]

10. Notice

a) The Effect of Notice under the Act

Under section 3(3)(a) of the 1976 Act a purchaser for full value takes a good title despite lack of consent by the non-conveying spouse. Purchaser is defined by section 3(6) as a purchaser in good faith.[166]

In *Somers v. Weir*[167] it was held that the expression in good faith imports a doctrine of notice into section 3 and in *Allied Irish Banks plc v. Finnegan*[168] the Supreme Court held that the plaintiff purchaser in that case had to establish that it did not have any actual or constructive notice of the possible invalidity of the consent The doctrine is not identical with but is analogous to the doctrine of notice in equity. It is also quite different in its effect. In equity a bona fide purchaser without notice of a legal estate will take the legal title free of the equity. A purchaser with notice of the equity will nevertheless still obtain the legal title by the conveyance, but will take it subject to the equity. The intervention of equity does prevent the passing of the common law title. Under the Family Home Protection Act, by contrast, the question of notice determines whether the purchaser acquires any title at all. A purchaser who takes without notice of the non-conveying spouses rights under the Act takes a good title. A purchaser *with* notice takes no title at all: the purported conveyance rendered void by section 3.

b) Constructive Notice

A purchaser of a house today will have to inquire of the vendor whether it is a family home within the Act. If the answer is that it is, then the purchaser will require the vendor to obtain the consent of the non-disposing spouse under section 3, or if that cannot be obtained, then the vendor must apply to the court under section 4 for an order dispensing with the consent on the ground that it is being unreasonably withheld. Section 4 will be considered later.

What is the position of the purchaser if the conveying spouse denies that the house is a family home? Can the purchaser rely on that? Can he or she accept

164 Unreported, High Court, 18 November 1983. See also *First National Building Society v. Ring* [1992] 1 IR 375 and Chapter 16 Co-Ownership.

165 (1887) 19 L R Ir 45 (fall in the value of the land not a good reason to refuse); *Pemberton v. Barnes* (1871) LR 6 Ch App 685 (nor is the wish to retain a large family estate); *Wilkinson v. Jobberns* (1873) LR 16 Eq 14 (nor is great personal inconvenience).

166 The sub-section is reproduced in Third Parties below.

167 [1979] IR 94.

168 *Allied Irish Banks plc v. Finnegan* [1996] 1 ILRM 401, Supreme Court (Blayney J; Hamilton CJ and O'Flaherty J concurring).

the plain statement itself? Or should the purchaser obtain a statutory declaration setting out the facts which if true, would make it a correct answer? Is even that enough? Or can the purchaser insist on a second declaration corroborating the first?

In *Reynolds v. Waters*[169] in answer to the purchaser's inquiry the vendor replied that it was not a family home and, after a further inquiry from the purchaser as to the facts, informed him that he was separated from his wife who had deserted him before he took up residence in the house which he was now selling. He said that he and his wife were now divorced and that his wife had never lived in the house. A draft statutory declaration was included. The purchaser asked for the consent in writing of the wife or a joint declaration with reasons attached. The vendor refused and then applied to the High Court for a declaration that the wife's consent was not required. It was granted. The sale was eventually closed. The question now was as to whether the purchaser was liable to pay interest on the money from the date when the vendor replied. He would be so liable if he should have accepted a statutory declaration on that basis. It was held that:

1. the purchaser's solicitor had been too cautious. There was no general principle that a prudent purchaser should not accept the uncorroborated statutory declaration of a vendor merely because the vendor had a financial interest in the transaction;
2. if the statement later turned out to be incorrect due to fraud or carelessness then the purchaser is said to have acquired the property in good faith and, if for full value, the conveyance is then valid under s3(3)(a); and[170]
3. the court suggested that it might be otherwise if the purchaser's solicitors had reason to doubt the truth of the statement.

If the decision of the High Court is correct then it secures the position of purchasers but leaves wives vulnerable to unscrupulous husbands. To say that, if the husband commits a fraud, the purchaser is unaffected by notice is little comfort to the wife. It is unclear why the loss in those circumstances should fall on the wife. The court seems more concerned to reduce the risk to purchasers, rather than to protect the wives whom it was the avowed aim of the legislation to protect. If the wife is in actual occupation of the house does that in itself put a purchaser on notice? In other words, is the doctrine of *Hamilton v. Lyster*[171] imported into section 3? That of course would not protect the wife in all circumstances because a house can still be a family home even though not

169 [1982] ILRM 335.

170 See *Stephenson v. Royce* (1856) 5 Ir Ch R 401; *Jones v. Smith* (1843) 1 Phil 244, 41 ER 624.

171 (1844) 7 Ir Eq R 560; *Hunt v. Luck* [1902] 1 Ch. 428. Wylie, *Irish Land Law* para. 20.12.

occupied by the wife at the relevant time.[172] Furthermore, in *Reynolds* there was a statement of the facts on which the husband's assertion was based. But is the purchaser fixed with notice if he or she asks if it is a family home and the vendor executes a statutory declaration simply saying that it is not?

In *Somers v. Weir*[173] the defendant wife lived in a house in Dublin with her husband. The husband had a lease of the premises. The wife claimed that she had helped to buy the lease. In 1973 she was, she said, compelled to leave the house and moved into a council house with the children for some time. In 1976 the husband entered into a contract to sell the house to the plaintiff, Mrs Somers. The plaintiff's solicitor asked for the defendant's written consent. The husband's solicitor replied that she had left the house some years ago and was no longer relying on it as a family home, that the husband was abroad, and that the defendant's address was unknown. When the husband returned to Dublin he made a statutory declaration to the effect that the defendant had not relied on the house as a family home since they had separated. He also stated that by virtue of their separation agreement she had no interest in the house. The separation agreement, which was not produced, did not mention the house. The plaintiff, relying on the declaration, paid the balance of the purchase money and the husband assigned the lease to her (the plaintiff). In 1977 the plaintiff decided to sell the house.

Defendant (W) - H ⟶ Plaintiff ⟶ New Purchaser
Mrs Somers

The new purchaser negotiated a mortgage with a building society. The plaintiff's solicitors in order to satisfy the building society, traced the whereabouts of the defendant wife and asked her to consent to the original sale by the husband. She refused. The plaintiff, Mrs Somers, sought an order in the High Court dispensing with the defendant's consent under section 4 of the Act, on the ground that she was withholding her consent unreasonably. Doyle J granted the order.

The Supreme Court (Henchy, Griffin, and Park JJ) held, first, that the court had no jurisdiction under section 4 to dispense with consent after the conveyance (from the husband to the plaintiff) had been executed. Secondly, they held that, nevertheless, the plaintiff had constructive notice both of the defendant's prima facie valid claim to a proprietary interest in the premises in equity and of her statutory right to refuse consent.

As to the proprietary interest, Henchy J noted that the wife claimed that she had paid a deposit on the lease and had pooled her wages with those of her hus-

172 See above, Family Home.

173 [1979] IR 94.

band. The plaintiff's solicitor knew of the existence of a separation agreement and should have obtained a copy of it. The plaintiff had gone to the Free Legal Advice Centre (FLAC) where the agreement was drawn up and the plaintiff's solicitor was told that a copy could not be supplied because the centre was closed for the holidays. The court held that he should not have accepted the excuse. Had he seen the agreement he would have seen that there was no reference to a claim by the wife and that would have put him on notice.

It seems that a purchaser in these circumstances gets notice in either event. They get notice if there is a reference to a claim or if there is not. What the court may mean is that knowledge that the vendor is married but separated gives notice that the other spouse may be claiming an equity, in which case there is no need to examine the separation agreement because knowledge of its existence alone is enough to put the party on notice. Alternatively the court thought that the statutory declaration itself in referring even negatively to a claim, put him on notice.

As to the defendant's statutory right to refuse consent under the Family Home Protection Act section 3(3)(a) the statute allows a conveyance to escape being void under that section if it is made to a purchaser for full value and purchaser is defined by section 3(6) as a person who acquires property in good faith. The Supreme Court decided that this imports a doctrine of notice. They were also led to this conclusion because subsection 7 specifically refers to section 3 of the Conveyancing Act, 1882 which gives statutory form to the equitable doctrine of notice and extends it to some extent.[174] It was held that the conveyance was void. The plaintiff had failed to discharge the onus, which fell on her under section 3(4), of proving that the conveyance was valid.

The Supreme Court in *Bank of Ireland v. Smyth*[175] recently held that the consent under section 3 of the Act must be an informed consent and that consequently a bank obtained constructive notice of a wife's lack of understanding that a mortgage was intended to give the bank the right to sell the family home.

c) Registration

The only real protection of a spouse is provided by section 12 of the Act which says that a spouse may register in the Registry of Deeds Acts or the Registration of Title Act, 1964 a notice stating that she is married to a person being a person having an interest in such property or land. However, it is doubtful if many spouses are aware of, or use, the section.

---

174 On notice see also *Northern Bank v. Henry* [1981] IR 1.

175 [1993] 2 IR 109, [1993] ILRM 790, High Court, [1996] 1 ILRM 241, Supreme Court, see above.

11. Third Parties

A question of considerable importance is the effect of the 1976 Act on dealings with a family home.[176] Section 3(1), as we have seen, provides that where a spouse without the prior consent in writing of the other spouse, purports to convey any interest in the family home to any person except the other spouse, then "subject to subsections (2) and (3) and section 4, the purported conveyance shall be void". Section 3 continues:

> "(2) Subsection 1 does not apply to a conveyance if it is made by a spouse in pursuance of an enforceable agreement made before the marriage of the spouses.
>
> (3) No conveyance shall be void by reason only of subsection (1) –
>
> (a) if it is made to a purchaser for full value,
>
> (b) if it is made, by a person other than the spouse making the purported conveyance referred to in subsection (1), to a purchaser for value, or
>
> (c) if its validity depends on the validity of a conveyance in respect of which any of the conditions mentioned in subsection (2) or paragraph (a) or (b) is satisfied.
>
> (4) If any question arises in any proceedings as to whether a conveyance is valid by reason of subsection (2) or (3), the burden of proving that validity shall be on the person alleging it.
>
> (5) In subsection (3), "full value" means such value as amounts or approximates to the value of that for which it is given.
>
> (6) In this section "purchaser" means a grantee, lessee, assignee, mortgagee, chargeant or other person who in good faith acquires an estate or interest in property".

a) Initial Transaction

The phrase initial transaction is not one found in the Act but what I mean by it is the first actual or purported transaction dealing with the legal title to a house or flat, *etc.* after it has become a family home within the meaning of the Act. The initial transaction may be made by a spouse or by some other person. It will be made by some other person if the legal title to the home is vested in someone other than the spouses, as, for example, if it is vested in a company.

If the initial transaction is, properly, made by someone other than a spouse,

176 See Lyall, "The Family Home Protection Act, 1976 and Conveyances Other Than by Spouses "(1984) 6 DULJ (ns) 158.

then it cannot be rendered void by section 3. Section 3 only applies to conveyances by spouses. This is a loophole in the Act.[177]

X (a non-spouse) ⟶ P1
family home VALID

If the initial transaction is made by a spouse, then it is void if made without the prior consent in writing of the other spouse, unless, within section 3(3)(a) it is made to a purchaser for full value, in good faith[178] and without notice.[179] In which case such a purchaser will take a good title.

b) Subsequent Transaction

(1) The Prima Facie Position

If the conveyance is a subsequent transaction, *i.e.* transaction following an initial transaction dealing with a family home, then the import of section 3 is that if the initial transaction is void under the Act, then any subsequent transaction is prima facie void. The prima facie position will then be displaced if it falls within one of the exceptions set out in subsections 3(3)(b) and (c). When subsection 3(3) says "No conveyance shall be void by reason only of subsection (1)–", *etc.*, it must be taken not only to refer to initial transactions expressly made void by subsection 3(1), but also to incorporate the principle that a transaction which follows a transaction void under 3(1) is also void – prima facie. This principle may be regarded either as implied in 3(1) or an application of the *nemo dat quod non habet* rule,[180] *i.e.* that a person who has no title cannot confer it on another. This, it must be said, is nowhere expressly stated in section 3, although it is assumed, I would argue, by section 3(3)(b).. It is an unfortunate aspect of the drafting of the Act that this is not stated explicitly, but the assumption appears sound as a matter of law independent of the 1976 Act and to be the only one which would give any meaning to 3(3)(b).

If a family home is owned by a spouse, H, who purports to transfer it to P1, but without obtaining the consent of W, the other spouse, the transaction to P1 is prima facie void. This is the position taking into account section 3(1), the prima facie position as to initial transactions. If P1 then purports to convey the

177 *Containercare (Ireland) Ltd v. Wycherley* [1982] IR 143, High Court, Carroll J; *Walpoles v. Jay,* unreported, High Court, McWilliam J, 20 November 1980; Lyall (1984).

178 Section 3(6) defines purchaser as a person who in good faith acquires an estate or interest in property.

179 *Somers v. Weir* [1979] IR 94.

180 In the law of sale of goods, although there are many exceptions to it, so that the exceptions are now in reality the rule, the *nemo dat* principle is still the prima facie position.

house to P2, that transaction is also prima facie void under general principles of law. If P1 had no title, he has nothing to transfer to P2.[181]

H →	P1 →	P2
	void for lack of consent of other spouse	prima facie void as it follows a prima facie void transaction. (not stated in section 3)

To see if the prima facie position is displaced one must look at section 3(3). There are logically four possible situations.

(2) P1 has notice, P2 does not

What is the position of P2 who, we shall assume here, does not have notice of these matters? This is the subject matter of section 3(3)(b). There is a problem with interpreting section 3(3)(b). It is that section 3 begins by saying that 'no transaction shall be void by reason only of subsection (1)...' and then subsection 3(3)(b) refers to a transaction by a person other than a spouse. But 3(1) only makes void certain transactions by spouses, *i.e.* it does not make a transaction by a person other than a spouse void in any case. It is therefore arguable that if subsection 3(3)(b) is to have any meaning at all, the phrase 'void by reason only of subsection (1)', in relation to subsection 3(3)(b), must assume that a consequential effect of subsection 3(1) is not only to make void without consent an initial transaction, but also, prima facie, to make void a subsequent transaction by a person other than a spouse.

The conveyance is made "by a person (P1) other than the spouse making the purported conveyance referred to in subsection (1)". It refers to where there has been a purported conveyance by a spouse, followed by a conveyance by a non-spouse. In this instance the conveyance is valid if made in favour of a purchaser for value. . . (P2). The prima facie position is displaced.

McWilliam J pointed out in *Walpoles v. Jay*,[182] that section 3(1) does not appear to make any subsequent transactions void. Nevertheless, as I argue here, subsection 3(3)(b) only makes sense if section 3(1) is taken to imply that subsequent transaction would be prima facie void if the initial transaction is made void by subsection 3(1).

181 This, as careful observers will note, is a reifying explanation. Our point is that it is the principle which seems to have been in the minds of the draftsmen of the Act.

182 Unreported, High Court, McWilliam J, 20 November 1980.

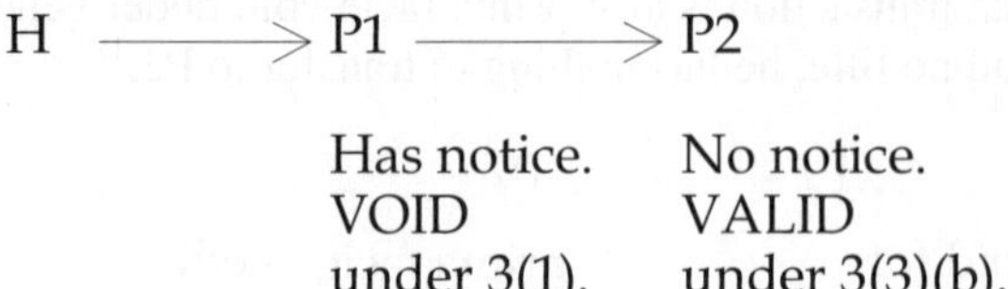

It may also be noticed that while subsection 3(3)(a) speaks of purchaser for full value, 3(3)(b) only uses the phrase purchaser for value. The only apparent reason for this difference is that subsection (a) refers to an initial transaction when the price paid to the spouse can be compared at least approximately to the price for which the house was bought, while subsection (b) refers to subsequent transactions which may occur long after the original purchase of the family home and therefore it would be unrealistic to require a comparison to be made.

This situation raises a conveyancing problem: how does P2 acquire a title if P1 did not have one? There is a break in the chain of title deeds because the conveyance to P1 was void, even though the conveyance from P1 to P2 is valid. There are circumstances in the law of real property where a person acquires a title from a person who did not have one to give. Many of the reforms of the law have been brought about by this means: disentailment under the Fines and Recoveries (Ireland) Act, 1834 a conveyance by a tenant for life under the Settled Land Acts, and tortious feoffments at common law until the Real Property Act, 1845. But in all those cases it could be seen from the type of document that it had this effect.

This situation also raises another interesting question. If P1 makes a profit on the transaction, can he keep it? P2 will be quite content with matters as they are - he has paid the purchase price and has a good title. The conveying spouse, H, has the money from the void sale to P1. He is quite content also. The aggrieved party is the non-conveying spouse. Does she have an action against P1 to recover the profit? Or against H? Could H claim the profit? The non-conveying spouse would seem to have an action against the conveying spouse under section 5(2) of the 1976 Act on the a basis that the spouse "has deprived the applicant spouse or a dependent child of the family of his residence in the family home by conduct that resulted in the loss of any interest therein or rendered it unsuitable for habitation as a family home". The conveying spouse's conduct in conveying to P1 did have the effect of depriving the other spouse or a child of their residence because, as a result of the further conveyance to P2, P2 obtained a title good against them.

(3) Both P1 and P2 have notice

In this case P2 does not gain a good title.

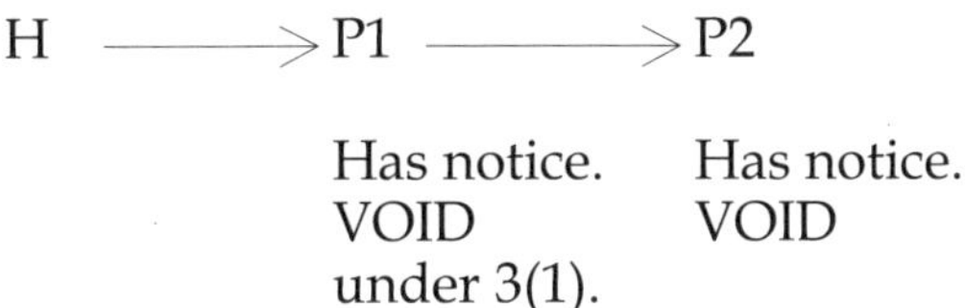

This may be called the *Somers v. Weir*[183] situation since it occurred in that case. The position appears to be that P2's conveyance is void because of the unstated assumption of section 3(1) that a conveyance that follows a prima facie void conveyance is also prima facie void, and further that P2's conveyance does not fall within any of the exceptions, which are stated in section 3(3), to the assumed position. P2's conveyance is not valid under 3(3)(a) because he is not a purchaser for full value without notice. Nor does section 3(3)(b) apply because P2 is not a purchaser for value in good faith and without notice. Nor can he take advantage of 3(3)(c). It would only apply if P1's conveyance were valid under 3(2) or 3(3)(a) or 3(3)(b). We shall assume that section 3(2) is not satisfied. It may be said of P2's conveyance that its validity depends on the validity of P1's conveyance in prima facie terms, but P1's conveyance does not satisfy 3(3)(a) because it is not made to a purchaser for full value without notice and it does not satisfy 3(3)(b) because it is not made to a purchaser for value without notice.

(4) Neither P1 nor P2 has Notice

In this case P2 obtains a good title under section 3(3)(c).

H	——> P1	——> P2
	No notice. VALID under s3(3)(a)	No notice. VALID under s3(3)(c)

This seems to be the situation contemplated by section 3(3)(c). Since P2's conveyance is a subsequent transaction its validity depends, prima facie, on the validity of P1's conveyance and P1's conveyance is valid because it satisfies paragraph (a), being made to a purchaser for full value without notice, P1.

On the other hand, if one assumes, as we argue that one must, that section 3 assumes that a subsequent conveyance which follows a prima facie void conveyance by a spouse is also prima facie void, then one can arrive at the same conclusion under 3(3)(a). P2's conveyance is not made void under subsection

183 [1979] IR 94.

(1) because, as section 3(3)(a) provides, it is made to a purchaser for full value, P2. However, one should avoid this route because it requires one to show that, regardless of P1's position, P2 acquired for full value.

(5) P1 has No Notice, P2 has Notice

In this case P2's position also falls within section 3(3)(c), but despite having notice here, P2 obtains a good title.

H ⟶	P1 ⟶	P2
	No notice. VALID under s3(3)(a)	Notice. VALID under s3(3)(c)

This may be termed the *Re Stewart's Estate*[184] or *Wilkes v. Spooner*[185] situation since it is analogous to those cases. P1, who does not have notice that the house is a family home, conveys to P2 who does have notice. The somewhat surprising result is that P2 obtains a good title despite the fact that he has notice. This also falls within section 3(3)(c). P2's conveyance depends for its validity on that of P1, on the assumption of the prima facie situation, *i.e.* that if P1's conveyance is prima facie void, then so is P2's. Subsection 3(3)(c) specifies that it will nevertheless be valid if conditions (a) or (b) in subsection (3) are satisfied by P1's conveyance. P1's conveyance does satisfy (a) because he is a purchaser for full value without notice.

This seems to be an odd result, but the reason for it may be similar to the rationale of *Wilkes v. Spooner*.[186] When P1 bought the land without notice of the wife's rights, he presumably paid the market price for the property. In capitalist society courts try to ensure that an innocent buyer on the market can at least sell the commodity he or she has bought. In the case of land the commodity consists of a number of rights defined by the law of property. If P1 could only sell the same title he had acquired by finding a buyer who also, like himself, did not have notice, the wife could prevent this happening by advertising her right, or in this case, by registering it under section 12 of the 1976 Act.

Where two innocent parties, in the sense of not having notice, are concerned, the law has to make a choice between them. That choice will also be informed by the social policies that each one in a sense represents or personifies. To favour the buyer on the market is to favour the efficient working of the mar-

184 *Re Stewart's Estate* (1893) 31 LR Ir 405, Monroe J at 415. *Re Stapleford Colliery Co (Barrow's Case)* 14 Ch Div 432 per Jessel MR.

185 [1911] 2 KB 473.

186 *ibid.*

ket as a mechanism for distributing wealth and to deny the validity of other considerations. To favour the non-property-owning wife is to reject the market as the sole mechanism and to assert that society, through the law, has a responsibility to protect those who cannot defend their interests through that mechanism. The law in this case has evidently chosen the free market approach.

12. Conduct Depriving the Spouse of an Interest

Section 5 of the 1976 Act provides that:

> "5.– (1) Where it appears to the court, on the application of a spouse, that the other spouse is engaging in such conduct as may lead to the loss of any interest in the family home or may render it unsuitable for habitation as a family home with the intention of depriving the applicant spouse or a dependent child of the family of his [or her] residence in the family home, the court may make such order as it considers proper, directed to the other spouse or to any other person, for the protection of the family home in the interest of the applicant spouse or such child.
>
> (2) Where it appears to the court, on the application of a spouse, that the other has deprived the applicant spouse or a dependent child of the family of his [or her] residence in the family home by conduct that resulted [in the loss of any interest *etc.*. .] . . . the court may order the other spouse or any other person to pay the applicant spouse such amount as the court considers proper to compensate the applicant spouse and any such child for their loss or make such other order. . . as may appear. . . just and equitable".

a) Future and Past Conduct

Subsection (1) contemplates that the conduct referred to has not yet resulted in the loss of an interest but may do so in future. It permits any order to be made, and not merely compensation as in subsection (2), so that it could order the transfer of an interest in the land to be made. Furthermore, such an order can be directed not only against the other spouse but against any third party who might have acquired an interest in the family home. Subsection (2), on the other hand, is in the past tense. It refers to conduct which has already had the effect of depriving the spouse of his or her residence in the family home by causing the loss of an interest in it or rendering it unsuitable as a family home. But the difference is not merely as to the future or past tense. The conduct in subsection (1) is conduct which may either (a) lead to a loss of any interest, or (b) render it unsuitable as a family home. It need not affect, or be likely to affect, residence. Residence in subsection (1) is relevant to intention, not to conduct. The conduct in subsection (2), on the other hand, is conduct which is relevant to residence.

It might also be noted that subsection (1) does not require that the conduct may lead to a loss of an interest vested in the other spouse. Conduct by spouse A which may lead to the loss of an interest vested in spouse A is within the section. Thus if spouse A, who has a beneficial interest in the house, gets into debt, and this results in creditor X obtaining a judgment mortgage against A's interest, that may be conduct within the section. Strictly speaking, therefore, conduct which has already led to the loss of an interest in the family home, such as indebtedness, which has resulted in the registration of a judgment mortgage, but which has not yet resulted in loss of residence is neither within subsection (1) nor subsection (2). If the section had been applied literally this would be a major loophole in the Act, since the issue of one spouse's indebtedness and its effect upon the residence of the other spouse usually comes before the court at precisely this point. But it does not seem that the courts have been so strict in their application of the words of the section. They seem to have taken the view that where an interest has been lost, as by a judgment mortgage, but residence has not yet been affected, the other spouse can apply under subsection (1), while, if residence has already been lost, that still does not preclude a spouse bringing an action under subsection (1) if the reason for the loss of residence was attributable to the other spouse, as where the applicant spouse had been driven from the home by the violence of the other spouse.[187] Thus, on this aspect of the section, the judges have adopted a liberal interpretation.

b) Intention to Deprive

Subsection (1) specifically provides that the conduct must be accompanied by an intention of depriving the spouse of his or her residence in the family home. Subsection (2) does not require intention at all.

The cases interpreting intention in subsection (1) have taken a restrictive view of it, requiring a subjective test of intention. This, it must be said, is usually to the advantage of husbands, since it is more usual for wives to apply under the section than husbands.

In *ED v. FD*[188] a husband left wife and children and went to live in London to work as a television journalist. He spent extravagantly on fast cars, holidays in expensive hotels and other luxuries and entertained lavishly. He failed to make maintenance payments in accordance with an interlocutory maintenance order, although he had recently made some attempt to do so. The wife brought proceedings to commit him for contempt of court and to fix future maintenance payments. She also asked for an order under section 5 transferring the family home into her name. The defendant had substantial debts in Ireland. Ejectment proceedings had been instituted by the mortgagees[189] of his family home. Costello J held that the discretion under section 5 was very wide, but that it could only be exercised where the court was satisfied that the spouse was

187 See McWilliam J in *AD v. DD & Irish Nationwide Building Society* unreported, High Court, McWilliam J, 8 June 1983. The judge noted the print, but did not have to decide it on the facts.

188 Unreported, High Court, 23 October 1980.

189 The judgment says "mortgagors".

acting with the intention of depriving the applicant spouse or a dependent child of the family of his or her residence in the family home. The court noted that the defendant had certainly acted in a most improvident way but there was no evidence that he had the necessary intention to deprive the wife of an interest. No order was made for committal. Leave was given to renew the application under section 5, but in the meantime an order was made under section 11 of the Guardianship of Infants Act, 1964, which contains wide powers for the protection of infants' welfare, requiring him to enter into negotiations with his creditors and the revenue commissioners with a view to reducing his debts.

In *DC v. AC*[190] the family home was purchased in the joint names of the husband and wife. It was purchased by a mortgage, a gift from the wife's father and a loan from the husband's father. Both parties were described as young and immature when they married, although the wife had become rather more mature through looking after the two children of the marriage. She had supported the children on her earnings after the husband left home. He had used some violence towards the wife and although the court in the present proceedings considered it was partly due to frustration, a barring order was granted.[191]

The husband had also run up some debts. Only two mortgage payments were made. The building society obtained an order for possession in other proceedings, but delayed execution of it pending the outcome of the present proceedings. In the earlier proceedings the father had offered to repay all the arrears and future mortgage instalments, provided the house was transferred to the wife, his daughter, with a clear title. Carroll J held that conduct includes inactivity as well as activity, so that the husband's failure to pay the mortgage instalments was conduct such as might lead to the loss of an interest in the family home, but the judge refused an order under the section transferring the family home to the wife on the ground that it would divest the husband of his share of the equity of redemption at a time when he had considerable debts.

The judge went on to indicate the terms of the order she would make if the house were to be sold. First, £4,000 would be distributed to the wife in respect of her contribution (*i.e.* her father's gift). The husband contributed nothing and so was not entitled to any sum under this head. Secondly, the wife would receive such a sum as would represent any proportionate increase in the value of the house attributable to her contribution, so that if the value of the house had doubled, the wife would receive another £4,000. Thirdly, any balance remaining was at common law the joint property of the husband and wife, since the legal title to the house was in their joint names, but since the wife would have to find accommodation for herself and the children and maintain them, she would be allowed [in equity?] at her option, to withdraw sufficient from the balance to repay debts in her name, their joint names and to repay the husband's fa-

190 [1981] ILRM 357, Carroll J.

191 Under the Family Law (Maintenance of Spouses and Children) Act, 1976.

ther's loan. Fourthly, any balance then remaining would be used, at the husband's option, to pay off his debts. Fifthly, if there was still a balance remaining, it would be divided between the wife and the husband. Carroll J felt that as the wife's father had offered to pay off the arrears of the mortgage the wife might, with her father's help, be able to put down a deposit on a smaller house.

The reason given by the judge in *DC v. AC* for refusing an order under section 5, standing on its own, seems to be excessively restrictive. It will usually be the case that the conduct which has put the existing property interests in the house in jeopardy is the husband getting into debt. It is probable, however, that the judge meant that debt was a sufficient reason for refusal in the absence of the intention to deprive the other spouse of an interest. It also seems probable that other factors influenced the refusal, namely the need to reimburse the husband's father and the fact that the wife could manage with a smaller house.

In *CP v. DP*[192] the defendant husband was an architect and, although not professionally qualified, had a reasonably successful business in partnership with another person. A recession in the building industry affected the business adversely. Arguments took place between the partners and the partnership was dissolved. In order to secure an overdraft with the bank the husband had deposited the title deeds of the family home with the bank. The wife did not know of this transaction. The husband had other debts also. The plaintiff wife alleged that the defendant's conduct was such as could lead to the loss of the family home with the intention of depriving the wife and dependent children of their residence in it. It was also claimed that in those circumstances section 5(1) of the Act gave the court a discretionary power to direct the husband to transfer the entire legal and beneficial ownership in the family home to the plaintiff wife. It was submitted that the word intention in the section should be construed so as not to be equivalent to notice, but rather with the intention which could be imputed to any person as to the natural and probable consequences of their conduct. This would clearly be a less stringent test.

Finlay P held first that the mortgage was void without the wife's consent, but that this was a theoretical point because the decision in *Containercare (Ireland) Ltd v. Wycherley*[193] meant that the bank could still sue the husband for the money due as a debt and obtain a judgment mortgage. This they could then register against the husband's interest in the property without the wife's consent. The judge appeared to assume that it would follow that the wife could not then resist an action by the bank for possession. This was no doubt because on the facts of the case there was no claim by the wife for an equity in the

192 [1983] ILRM 380, High Court.

193 [1982] IR 143, High Court, Carroll J.

house.[194]

He then went on to say that before a court could impute, in section 5, the intention which can arise from the natural and probable consequences of an act or omission, there must first be an element of deliberate conduct involved. The evidence did not sustain the assertion that there was sufficient premeditation as was required to constitute "intention" in section 5. He therefore refused to countenance a test which would have made it easier for, generally, wives to establish conduct within section 5. The judge argued that this result followed from the wording of the subsections. He noted that subsection (1) refers to intention whereas subsection (2) does not use the word at all. If intention could be inferred from consequences alone, he reasoned, then the distinction would be unnecessary. There is some force in this argument, even if one takes into account the fact that the consequences in subsection (1) have not occurred, and are therefore speculative, while in subsection (2) they are actual. Finlay P in *CP v. DP*[195] found on the facts that there was insufficient evidence to support the element of deliberateness of the conduct.

In *S v. S*[196] the court came to a similar conclusion, finding that the loss of an interest would have been a natural and probable consequence on the facts, but declined to find that section 5 had been satisfied. In that case the wife sought an order transferring the home into her name. The home had been purchased in the joint names of the husband and the wife. The husband incurred debts. A creditor approached the wife and told her that the home would have to be sold. This was the first she knew of the husband's debts. The husband then disappeared. The court dismissed the wife's claim, finding that the husband's conduct was improvident and possibly dishonest but did not disclose an outright intention of depriving the wife and children of their residence.

The cases in which section 5 has been held to be satisfied do not, unfortunately, provide any consistent guide as to evidence of deliberate intention. In *CMCB v. SB*[197] The parties had married in England and bought a house there. They were both employed at the time and the house was purchased through their joint efforts, both wife and husband contributing to a lump sum which partly paid for the house, the rest being raised by borrowing. In 1970 the parties returned to Ireland. The house in England was sold and part of the surplus left over after paying off the loan was used to buy the house in Ireland, although the conveyance of this house was taken in the name of the husband.

Barron J in the High Court held that the wife was entitled to an equitable interest in the house. The parties separated in 1982 and from then on the husband's

194 The registration of a judgment mortgage would not affect a prior unregistrable equity. See above and Chapter 5 Registration of Deeds.

195 [1983] ILRM 380, High Court.

196 [1983] ILRM 387.

197 Unreported, High Court, Barron J, 17 May 1983.

financial position went from bad to worse. He had a hamburger stall which caught fire on more than one occasion. He failed to make maintenance payments to the wife. He said that he had plant and machinery stored in the garage next to the house and tried to get access to it despite a barring order which had been granted against him. The wife was supported partly by her own job and by payments to her by the husband's sister, but these were not made on the husband's behalf. The judge held that the terms of the section had been satisfied, but made no order under it as he had not been asked to do so.

In *GP v. IP*[198] the husband obtained an order under section 4 of the 1976 Act dispensing with the wife's consent to a disposition of the family home on the basis that he needed to raise money on mortgage to start his own business. The order specified that he was to use the money to discharge a debt he owed to a bank and to keep the wife's solicitors informed as to repayments of the mortgage debt. He did neither, nor did he start a business. This was held to be conduct sufficient to satisfy section 5. The court ordered the husband to transfer his interest in the house to the wife, not to raise loans and added a declaration that until the conveyance was executed by the husband the wife was deemed to be beneficial owner subject only to the mortgage. In *D v. D*[199] the court also found the intention proved and ordered the family home to be transferred into the wife's name.

It is difficult to see how the intention was proved in these cases while it had failed in earlier ones. The one factor that stands out in *CMCB v. SB*[200] and *GP v. IP*[201] is that the husband had either misled the court or had violated its orders. A realistic approach to the case law suggests that this factor is likely to overcome the general reluctance of the judges to find the necessary intention in section 5.

13. Nature of the Order

Another difference between subsection (1) and subsection (2) of section 5 is that under subsection (1) the court may make "such order as it considers proper, directed to the other spouse or to any other person" for the protection of the family home, whereas under subsection (2) the court may order the other spouse or any other person "to pay the applicant spouse such amount as the court considers proper to compensate the applicant spouse and any such child for their loss or make such other order. . . as may appear. . . just and equitable". Thus subsection (2) allows the award of compensation whereas subsection (1) does not contemplate such an award. One reason for the difference is no doubt

198 Unreported, High Court, O'Hanlon J, 19 October 1984.

199 Unreported, High Court, Costello J, 16 December 1981. The case is only noted in *S v. S* [1983] ILRM 387.

200 Unreported, High Court, Barron J, 17 May 1983.

201 Unreported, High Court, O'Hanlon J, 19 October 1984.

that subsection (1) refers to conduct that has not yet resulted in a loss of an interest in the home and so no interest will have become vested in a third party. On the other hand, where subsection (2) is invoked, this may already have occurred. If the third party is one who, under section 3, obtains a good title, it would create a conflict in the Act if section 5 were to sanction an order transferring an interest from such a party back to an applicant spouse. Compensation is therefore a more appropriate remedy. It has already been seen that section 5 is drafted in wide enough terms to permit an order directed to an owner/spouse to transfer his or her interest in the family home to the other spouse.[202]

The section has been held not to require an absolute transfer of the interest of the errant spouse in favour of the claimant spouse or children. In *O'Neill v. O'Neill*[203] both the partners to a marriage had beneficial interests in the family home. The wife left and went to live with another man. The husband and two children of the marriage continued to live in the house. The wife borrowed money from a bank to buy furniture and when she became unable to pay the instalments on the loan, she sought to obtain an order of sale in lieu of partition. This was refused. The bank obtained judgment against her for the amount due and registered a judgment mortgage against her interest in the family home. Barron J found that she had put the residence of the husband and children at risk by not making efforts to pay off the judgment mortgage. He ordered her beneficial interest to be transferred to trustees until such time as she discharged the judgment mortgage.[204] The judge felt that a court would be unlikely to order a sale of the property until the children were grown up.

14. Minor Spouses

In *Lloyd v. Sullivan*[205] the defendant entered into a contract to sell a farm to the plaintiff. The defendant's wife consented to the sale. She was under age at the time. The plaintiff brought an action under the Vendor and Purchaser Act, 1874 claiming a declaration that good title had not been shown. It was held that the same principles apply under the Family Home Protection Act, 1976 as in the law of contract. The minor was dealing with a valuable right and agreeing to surrender it without consideration. If the transaction was not shown to be to

202 *GP v. IP*, unreported, High Court, O'Hanlon J, 19 October 1984. *D v. D*, unreported, Costello J, 16 December 1981. The latter case is noted in *S v. S* [1983] ILRM 387. See the preceding section.

203 Unreported, High Court, Barron J, 6 October 1989.

204 Assuming the title to the house to be unregistered, the effect of registration of the affidavit would be to transfer the interest of the judgment mortgagor to the mortgagee, leaving the wife with a type of equity of redemption expectant upon the discharge of the mortgage. It was presumably this interest which was ordered to be vested in trustees.

205 Unreported, High Court, McWilliam J, 6 March 1981.

her advantage, she would be entitled to repudiate it on coming of age.[206] In the meantime a good title had been shown.

As result of the case section 10 of the Family Law Act, 1981 was passed. It provides that consent under Family Home Protection Act "shall not be invalid by reason only that the spouse is under age". This formulation still leaves a doubt. *Lloyd* did not hold that the consent was invalid by reason only of the spouse being under age. The case held that the consent of a minor is valid unless and until avoided on coming of age. If it is invalid it is so because (a) being under age at the time of consent, he or she had the power to repudiate it on coming of age, and (b) on coming of age he or she did repudiated it.

15. The Partition Acts and The Family Home Protection Act, 1976

One spouse/joint tenant can bring an action for partition or sale against the other under the Partition Acts 1868 and 1876,[207] but the courts have a discretion whether to grant such an order or not.[208]

In *AL v. JL*[209] the parties bought a house before they were married. W was under the age of majority at time of marriage. Both contributed to the purchase. They had agreed that the house should be put into their joint names, but their solicitor told them that W could not take a conveyance in her name as she was under age. This was incorrect.[210] Nevertheless, because of the advice given the deed was put in the husband's name alone. When the wife came of age they went back to the solicitor to have a new deed executed putting the house in their joint names, but, on learning the cost, they decided against doing so. Later, their relationship broke down and the wife left the house. The husband remained in possession. The issue arose as to the interests existing in the house. The court held that the wife had a half share[211] in equity, their intention being to hold the property jointly. In view of this manifest intention the court felt that it was unnecessary to go into the question of contributions. The court further held that the husband could not succeed in a claim for partition and sale under the Partition Acts, 1868-76 unless the other spouse consented or the

206 Irish case on infant contracts: *Allen v. Allen* (1842) 4 Ir Eq R 472, 2 Dru & War 307, 338, 346, 59 RR 696.

207 See Chapter 16 Co-Ownership.

208 *ibid.*

209 Unreported, High Court, Finlay P, 27 February 1984.

210 A minor may hold an interest in land although in such case the land is settled land within the Settled Land Acts, 1882-90: see Chapter 14 Settlements of Land and Trusts for Sale. In such a case the trustees of the settlement exercise the powers of a tenant for life under the Acts.

211 In other words, she was entitled to half the proceeds if the land were sold. Strictly speaking a joint tenant does not have an undivided share, because of the principle of survivorship: see Chapter 16 Co-ownership.

court could dispense with her consent under section 4 of the Family Home Protection Act, 1976.

Where the owning spouse is bankrupt, section 61 subsections (4) and (5) of the Bankruptcy Act 1988 provide that a family home cannot be sold without the prior sanction of the court. The court has power to order postponement of the sale of the family home and may have regard to the interests of the spouse and dependants of the bankrupt as well as the interests of the creditors.[212]

J. Reform

The Matrimonial Home Bill, 1993 was an attempt to redress the anomaly of the homemaker wife, whose work was not recognised by the courts as a contribution giving her an equity in the matrimonial home. The Bill proposed to vest a joint tenancy in equity in the matrimonial home and household effects in both spouses regardless of the state of the legal title. After being passed by both Houses of the Oireachtas it was referred by the President under Article 26 of the Constitution to the Supreme Court to determine whether it was constitutional. The Bill was held to be unconstitutional.[213] The Bill provided, in Clause 6, for the court to set aside the joint tenancy on an application by a spouse who did not benefit from it. The Supreme Court, however, took the view that the imposition of a joint tenancy in equity interfered to an unjustified degree with the relationship between husband and wife and Clause 6 did not avoid this result, and indeed may even have aggravated it, by requiring one of the parties to seek redress in the courts.

212 *Rubotham (Official Assignee) v. Duddy,* unreported, High Court, Shanley J, 1 May 1996 (sale postponed 10 years); *Rubotham (Official Assignee) v. Young,* unreported, The High Court, McCracken J, 23 May 1995.

213 *Re Matrimonial Home Bill, 1993* [1994] 1 ILRM 241.

CHAPTER 18

LICENCES, ESTOPPEL AND CONSTRUCTIVE TRUSTS

A. Introduction

The topic of licences is at the present time one of the most difficult and confusing areas of property law. There are a number of reasons for this. For one thing, judges have resorted to the concept of the licence in a number of widely differing factual situations in order to solve quite different problems. In the commercial sphere, oil companies have sought to use the concept of the licences in defining the relations between them and operators of their petrol stations and landlords of residential premises have also sought to use the concept. This has often been, in both cases, in order to avoid the effects of legislation restricting the rent which can be charged in leases and tenancies. In this area the cases are therefore concerned with the extent to which, if at all, judges were prepared to countenance this evasion of the Rent Acts, or to recognise genuine arrangements which fell outside them if such existed.

The concept of the licence has also been employed in a quite different area, namely, domestic relationships. Here the issues are very different, and the picture is again complicated by the fact that judges have often resorted to other concepts in order to resolve the problems which arise, concepts such as proprietary estoppel and the constructive trust. It is therefore appropriate to deal with these three concepts in the same chapter.

B. Licences

A licence, at its simplest, is a permission given by an owner of an interest in land to another person to enter his land, which entry would otherwise be a trespass. The definition given by Vaughan CJ in *Thomas v. Sorrell* in 1674[1] is frequently quoted as the classic formulation:

> "A dispensation or licence properly passeth no interest nor alters or transfers property in any thing, but only makes an action lawful, which without it had been unlawful".[2]

1 (1674) Vaugh 330, 124 ER 1098.

2 (1674) 124 ER 1098 at 1109.

But it should not be forgotten that this is merely the definition at common law before the Judicature Act and therefore excludes all consideration of equitable principles. Insofar as this definition denies that licences affect third parties it must now be heavily qualified, as we shall see.

1. Bare Licence

A licence may be bare, *i.e.* not supported by consideration, or not intended to give rise to legal relations, such as an invitation to dinner. The law of contract does not, therefore, provide any remedy to prevent its being revoked or to make its breach liable to damages. Apart from contract, however, courts have been prepared to hold that a licence cannot be revoked so as to leave the licensee with no opportunity to avoid committing a trespass, so that even a gratuitous licence granted by A to allow B to cross A's field cannot be revoked while B is still part of the way across.[3] Expenditure in reliance on a licence can render it irrevocable[4] or possibly only revocable if the licensor can put the party in the position they were in before the licence was entered into.[5] Some such situations may today be indistinguishable from proprietary estoppel giving rise to an enforceable licence, but at least one Irish case has held such licences to be irrevocable at common law.[6] Since proprietary estoppel is now capable of giving rise to legal interests,[7] the distinction is of little importance.

2. Licence Coupled with an Interest

When an interest such as a profit *à prendre* is granted, for example the right to extract minerals from land, or to hunt or fish on it, a licence to enter and remain in the land for the purpose of giving effect to the rights granted is normally granted at the same time. It has long been recognised that such a licence is irrevocable while the property right to which it attached continues in being.

In *Woods v. Donnelly*[8] an agreement provided that the defendant was to have the right to "draw sand and gravel. . . as long as he requires it". It was also specified that "James Donnelly only. . . is hereby authorised" and that he was to make full, prompt payment for the sand and gravel each month. The Northern Ireland court held, *inter alia,* that the licence was not revocable except in accordance with the contract. It held that the agreement was a licence coupled with an interest, namely a profit à prendre, which together were valid for the

3 *McDonald v. Bord na gCon* [1965] IR 217, High Court.

4 *Armstrong v. Sheppard & Short Ltd* [1959] 2 All ER 651, [1959] 2 QB 384; *Blood v. Keller* (1861) 11 Ir CLR 124.

5 *Blood v. Keller* (1861) 11 Ir CLR 124.

6 *ibid.*

7 See below.

8 [1982] NI 257.

life of the defendant, so that they could not be revoked during that life. But the right was expressly limited to the defendant and so would not pass to his personal representatives after his death.

3. Contractual Licences

The history of contractual licences is one made tortuous by procedural fallacies as well as by the generally well-founded reluctance of most judges to allow individuals to create burdens that would affect future owners of land at will and without restraint of any kind. We shall deal with these formative themes separately.

a) Contracting Parties

It has never been in doubt that A can make a contract with B whereby A gives B the right to enter and remain on A's land for a certain period. What has given rise to confusion in the past are the circumstances in which such an arrangement ceases to be a matter of contract and becomes a property right.

In *Wood v. Leadbitter*,[9] a case at common law before the Judicature Acts, the Court of Exchequer asserted that the right to remain on land for a period, in order not to be revocable at the will of the licensor, had to be coupled with a property interest known to the common law, such as an easement or profit à prendre, or a freehold or leasehold estate. It was thought to follow from this that, in the absence of such an interest, although it might be a breach of contract for A to revoke a contractual licence, the court could not prevent the revocation, so that B could not even succeed in tort if he or she were removed from the land by force. In addition, the court even doubted that B would be entitled to damages for breach of contract[10] unless there was an express term in the contract to that effect, for all that the licensor had bought for his or her money was a right which was inherently revocable. It was thus an assumption in *Wood v. Leadbitter* that the licence was distinct from the contract and had the inherent quality of revocability. This reified concept of the licence was to be rejected later in *Winter Garden Theatre (London) Ltd v. Millennium Productions Ltd*.[11] Yet this absurd position was a result of the lack of equitable remedies in a common law court before the Judicature Act. A common law court could not prevent the licensor revoking the licence in the sense of granting an injunction, because it had no jurisdiction to grant such a remedy. This led the court to explain this result, produced by procedure, in substantive terms. A licence, it rea-

9 (1845) 13 M & W 838, [184–60] All ER Rep 190, 153 ER 351; *Atkinson v. King* (1878) 2 LR Ir 320.

10 *Hurst v. Picture Theatres Ltd* [1915] 1 KB 1 per Buckley LJ.

11 [1948] AC 173, [1947] 2 All ER 331, 177 LT 349, 63 TLR 529, [1947] WN 233, House of Lords; in the Court of Appeal sub nom *Millennium Productions Ltd v. Winter Garden Theatre (London) Ltd* [1946] 1 All ER 678, [1946] WN 151. See below.

soned, could be revoked by the licensor because it was not a property interest. They reified the problem and saw a licence as an inherently revocable thing. This led the court further to deny even remedies which it did possess, such as damages for tort or even damages for breach of contract.

At least one court in Ireland doubted if licences were revocable at common law in all circumstances. In *Blood v. Keller*,[12] a case in the Court of Exchequer before the Judicature Act, a river ran through the land of the plaintiff and that of the defendant. The defendant erected a weir across the river which raised the water level above its natural height. He did this in order to supply water to a mill which he erected on the land. This led to the plaintiff's land being flooded by the river. The plaintiff sued for damages. The defendant pleaded in defence that he had sought and obtained the plaintiff's permission before erecting the weir. He had proceeded to erect the mill in reliance on this licence. Fitzgerald B expressed the view that:

> ". . . a parol licence given to do an act on the licensees own land, which would, *prima facie*, be lawful independently of the licence, but which might from the circumstances, be attended with injuries consequent to the licensor, cannot be countermanded, if the act be done and accepted and expense incurred on the part of the licensee. . .".[13]

The judge went on to say that this was at least so unless the licensor was prepared to put the licensee in the position he or she was in before the license was granted.[14] It might be argued, in view of *Blood*, that *Wood v. Leadbitter* was never good law in Ireland, but the authority of *Blood* is weakened by the fact that it was not a typical licence. It was not a licence to occupy land. Nor did the defendant need a licence to erect a weir on his own land. It was a permission to do something which might in future lead to damage to the plaintiff's land, and was a waiver of a future cause of action.

The absurdity of *Wood* was exposed in *Hurst v. Picture Theatres Ltd*,[15] a case after the Judicature Act. The plaintiff paid for a ticket at a cinema to see a film. The ticket was in the form of a metal token which he gave up to the usherette at the door of the auditorium. While the performance was still continuing he was accused of not having paid the entrance fee. In spite of his protests he was forcibly evicted from the cinema by a porter. There was obviously no

12 (1861) 11 Ir CLR 124.

13 *ibid.* at p.130.

14 The apparently reasonable proposition, that expenditure in reliance could render a licence irrevocable, had been doubted in the earlier case of *Smith v. Earl of Howth* (1861) 10 Ir CLR 125. Monohan CJ (at p.129) found it a "startling proposition" that a small amount of money spent could convert a revocable right into an "irrevocable estate".

15 [1915] 1 KB 1, CA. *Wood* was followed in preference to *Hurst* by the High Court of Australia in *Cowell v. Rosehill Racecourse Co Ltd* (1937) 56 CLR 605, although the action in the Australian court is said to be "at common law" and so the court may have found itself in the same position as the court in *Wood*.

point in suing for an injunction to prevent revocation of the licence, since the performance had already ended before any such remedy would have been available and the token was for that particular performance. It has been pointed out that in the case of such a short-term licence one would need to have a judge sitting in the next seat. But the court accepted in principle that such a remedy could be obtained in suitable circumstances. The plaintiff sued instead for assault and false imprisonment and was awarded £150 damages. Had he sued for breach of contract the only damages would have been the price of the ticket, sixpence. The English Court of Appeal held that there was an implied term of the contract that the licence would not be revoked until the performance was over. His right to remain in the theatre was founded on contract and did not involve the grant of a property right. It was also pointed out that, even before the Judicature Act, a court of equity would grant an injunction to prevent the revocation of a licence in breach of contract.[16]

Wood v. Leadbitter had also given rise to the notion that a licence was in some way a separate entity from the contract which gave rise to it, a proposition laid to rest by the later case of *Winter Garden Theatre (London) Ltd v. Millennium Productions Ltd.*[17] The real distinction between a contractual and proprietary interest is that proprietary interests affect third parties. An irrevocable contract whereby A allows B onto his land, even if enforced by specific performance or injunction, remains a purely contractual right so long as it is only enforceable by B against A.

In the *Winter Garden* case itself[18] the theatre company granted a licence to Millennium of the theatre for the production of plays, concerts and ballets. The licence was for an initial period of six months with an option to renew for another six months at a higher rent. At the end of the second period there was a further option to renew at a rent of £300 a week. The licensees were to give the licensors one month's notice to terminate the licence but there was no provision expressly allowing the licensors to terminate the licence after the second option had been exercised. The licensees duly exercised both options and some time later the theatre company purported to terminate the licence. Lord Greene MR in the Court of Appeal held that the terms of the licence were identical with the terms of the contract that created it. He held that there was no term al-

16 *Frogley v. Lovelace (Earl)* (1859) John 333, 70 ER 450. See also Scarman LJ in *Chandler v. Kerley* [1978] 2 All ER 942 at 945, discussed below.

17 [1948] AC 173, [1947] 2 All ER 331, 177 LT 349, 63 TLR 529, [1947] WN 233, House of Lords; in the Court of Appeal sub nom *Millennium Productions Ltd v. Winter Garden Theatre (London) Ltd* [1946] 1 All ER 678, [1946] WN 151 per Greene MR. Reversed by the House of Lords on other grounds.

18 In the Court of Appeal sub nom *Millennium Productions Ltd v. Winter Garden Theatre (London) Ltd* [1946] 1 All ER 678, [1946] WN 151 per Greene MR, reversed on other grounds by the House of Lords [1948] AC 173, [1947] 2 All ER 331, 177 LT 349, 63 TLR 529, [1947] WN 233.

lowing the licensors to terminate the licence. He also held that the grant of an irrevocable licence implied a negative obligation not to terminate the licence and an injunction could be granted to enforce this obligation and so to restrain the breach of contract. The House of Lords reversed the Court of Appeal on the interpretation of the contract holding that it was not intended to be perpetual and that the licensors could terminate it on reasonable notice after the second option had been exercised.

Megarry J in *London Borough of Hounslow v. Twickenham Garden Developments Ltd*[19] held that merely because a contract could not be enforced by specific performance - as where it was a contract for personal services - that the court would then grant the licensor an injunction to evict the licensee. To do so would be to assist a breach of contract. In *Hurst* the court held *obiter* that even if specific performance could not be granted, the court would not be precluded from granting an injunction to the licensee to prevent the licensor revoking the licence in breach of contract.

Both in *Hurst* and in *Hounslow* the theory of the implied term was used to render the licence irrevocable. A weakness of the theory is that implied terms yield to express terms. It might be argued that all the licensor has to do is to insert an express term reserving the right to revoke the licence even before the performance or the operations, *etc.*, are complete. However, a contracting party cannot rely on an exemption clause to justify a fundamental breach of contract.[20]

In *Woods v. Donnelly*[21] the agreement was found, in the alternative, to constitute a contractual licence, but the case was between the original contracting parties and did not involve a property issue.

In *Gale v. First National Building Society*,[22] a proprietor of registered land registered a charge as a burden against the land in order to secure the repayment of a loan. The charge contained a term whereby the chargor agreed that if he defaulted in the repayments the chargee had the right to enter the land. A default occurred and the chargee entered the land. Costello J refused an injunction to prevent the chargee continuing in possession, holding that the charge created a contractual licence.

b) Third Parties

Although *Hurst* and the *Winter Garden* cases made it clear that the full range of contractual remedies was available after the Judicature Act to enforce a contractual licence between the contracting parties, they did not resolve the question

19 [1971] Ch. 233, [1970] 3 All ER 326, [1970] 3 WLR 538, 69 LGR 109, 7 Build LR 81, 215 EG 303, [1970] EGD 515.

20 *Alexander v. Railway Executive* [1951] 2 KB 882.

21 [1982] NI 257.

22 [1985] IR 609, [1987] ILRM 30, High Court.

of the effect if any that such rights had on third parties. The cases in England on this issue fall into three broad categories depending on which of three propositions they support. The three propositions are:

(a) that a contractual licence creates no interest in land and so is not binding on third parties at all;

(b) that a contractual licence is binding on third parties who take with notice of it, so that it is creates in effect an equitable interest; and

(c) that a contractual licence is not binding on third parties even with notice of it, without more, but there are circumstances in which a constructive trust may be imposed upon a third party.

(1) The No Interest Cases

A number of cases have held that contractual licences do not bind third parties even if they have notice of the licence.

Daly v. Edwardes[23] was concerned with front of house rights in a theatre, *i.e.* the right to operate the bars and other refreshment rooms in the front part of a theatre. In 1894 Edwardes granted to Daly a lease of two theatres for a term of years. The lease contained a covenant by the lessee not to part with any estate or interest in the premises. Daly subsequently granted to Warr "the free and exclusive licence or right to the use of the refreshment rooms and bars in the theatre together with the free right of access thereto". The lessor claimed that this was a breach of the covenant against disposing of any estate or interest in the premises. The claim failed. The court held that Warr took no estate or interest in land, but merely a licence to provide refreshments. The case went to the House of Lords as *Edwardes v. Barrington*[24] and the decision of the Court of Appeal was affirmed.

In *King v. David Allen and Sons (Billposting) Ltd*[25] King owned premises in Dublin. David Allen had for many years, under an agreement between the predecessors of King and David Allen, enjoyed the right to exhibit posters on the wall of the premises. King wished to let the premises to a third party. David Allen had no objection provided the rights were preserved. In July 1913 King and David Allen agreed that David Allen should have exclusive permission to fix posters to the flank wall of a cinema which it was proposed to build on the site. In August 1913 King agreed with F, a trustee for a company to be formed, that a lease should be granted to the company. King was to assign to F, as a trustee for the company, his interest in the July 1913 agreement, and F agreed that the company would accept the lease and ratify the July 1913 agreement. The company, when formed, duly did so. The cinema was built. The July 1913

23 (1900) 83 LT 548. See also *Frank Warr & Co Ltd v. London County Council* [1904] 1 KB 713.

24 (1901) 85 LT 650.

25 [1916] 2 AC 54.

agreement was not referred to in the lease and King did not assign his interest under that agreement to the company. David Allen attempted to post advertisements on the flank wall but the company, despite opposition from King (a director), prevented it. David Allen then sued King. They alleged that he was in breach of the July agreement by putting it out of his power to perform it. The company was not a party to the action but the effect of the licence *vis-à-vis* the company was in issue because King would not have been liable to David Allen in damages had the licence been binding on the company, which had notice of it. The claim succeeded. The House of Lords regarded the contract as creating nothing more than a personal obligation. Hence, the company was not bound to give effect to it in the absence of a contractual term in the lease or elsewhere. King had therefore put it out of his power to comply with the licence.

In *Clore v. Theatrical Properties Ltd*[26] the agreement, which referred to the parties as lessor and lessee, provided that the lessor granted "the free and exclusive use of all the refreshment rooms" to the lessee. The definition clause provided that the terms lessor and lessee should include their executors, administrators and assigns. The assignee of the lessor sought to prevent an assignee of the lessee from exercising any of the rights under the agreement. It was held that the agreement was not a lease but a licence, and was not binding upon a third party. Lord Wright MR said: "I do not think that a personal covenant as in the present case can be binding on a third party with notice. . .".[27]

(2) Contractual Licence as an Equitable Interest

In Errington v. Errington and Woods[28] the plaintiff's husband bought a house through a building society for his son and daughter-in-law, the first defendant, taking the conveyance in his own name, but agreeing that so long as they kept up the repayment of the instalments on the mortgage they could occupy the house, and that when the mortgage was finally paid off the property would be theirs. The father died and left the house by will to the plaintiff. At about the same time the first defendant's husband left her and she continued in occupation with her sister, the second defendant. The plaintiff sued for possession claiming that the first defendant and her husband were in occupation under a bare licence revocable at will. The defendants argued that if they were tenants at will the claim was barred by the Limitation Act, 1939, or, alternatively, that they were occupying the premises as tenants at a rent represented by the instalments paid to the building society and were protected by the Rent Acts. The county court judge agreed with the first proposition and held the claim statute barred. The case seems to have been argued and decided in the county court on common law alone, as if equity did not exist. In the Court of Appeal Lord Den-

26 [1936] 3 All ER 483.

27 *ibid.* at p.491.

28 [1952] 1 KB 290, [1952] 1 All ER 149.

ning MR took the bold step of asserting that contractual licences were a species of equitable interest. Referring to the effect of the Judicature Acts in merging common law and equitable jurisdictions, the judge went on:

> "This infusion of equity means that contractual licences now have a force and validity of their own and cannot be revoked in breach of the contract. Neither the licensor *nor anyone who claims through him* can disregard the contract except a purchaser for value without notice".[29]

Denning restated this view in later cases, particularly the ill-fated "deserted wife's licence" cases and variously described the interest as "a licence coupled with an equity"[30] and an "equitable licence".[31]

The argument of Denning in *Errington* is faulty. From the premise that a contracting party may be restrained from revoking the licence, established in the *Hurst* and *Winter Garden* cases, the judge sought to derive the conclusion that third parties can also be prevented from revoking it. This does not follow. Thus, the phrase "nor anyone who claims through him" is a *non sequitur*. Nor does the judge cite any relevant authority for the view. Nor does it seem that the proposition would lead to a just result in all cases falling within its wide ambit. This is in substance a more serious objection than even the lack of precedent in favour of Denning's view. The decision in *Errington* was no doubt a just one on the facts, but it could have been decided on a number of narrower grounds, [32]namely:

(a) the agreement created a purchaser's equity binding on the widow, who had notice of it;

29 [1952] 1 KB 290 at 299.

30 *Inwards v. Baker* [1965] 2 QB 29, [1965] 1 All ER 446, [1965] 2 WLR 212, 193 EG 245, Lord Denning MR: "It is quite plain from those authorities [*i.e. Dillwyn v. Llewelyn* [1861–73] All ER Rep 384; *Ramsden v. Dyson* (1866) LR 1 HL 129, *Plimmer v. Wellington Corporation* (1884) 9 AC 699] that if the owner of land requests another, or indeed allows another, to expend money on the land under an expectation created or encouraged by the landlord that he will be able to remain there, that raises an equity in the licensee such as to entitle him to stay. He has a licence coupled with an equity". *National Provincial Bank v. Hastings Car Mart* [1964] Ch. 665, [1964] 1 All ER 688, [1964] 2 WLR 751, 189 EG 511, CA judgment, [1964] 1 All ER at 695 per Lord Denning MR: "The wife has no tenancy. She has no legal estate or equitable interest in the land. All that she has is a licence. But not a bare licence. She has a licence coupled with an equity. I mean an 'equity' as distinguished from an equitable interest". See also the appeal in the House of Lords sub nom *National Provincial Bank v. Ainsworth* [1965] AC 1175, [1965] 2 All ER 472. See also *Bendall v. McWhirter* [1952] 2 QB 466.

31 *Hardwick v. Johnson* [1978] 1 WLR 683 at 688.

32 As the court in *Ashburn Anstalt v. Arnold* [1989] Ch. 1, [1988] 2 WLR 706, [1988] 23 EG 128 pointed out. See below.

(b) it could be supported on the ground of proprietary estoppel.[33] The daughter-in-law acted in reliance on the representation and the representation was binding on the widow as privy to the representor. The facts are similar to *Re Basham*[34] and *Smyth v. Halpin*[35] except that the father promised to transfer the property by an *inter vivos* transaction;

(c) the payment of instalments, as contributions to the purchase price, gave rise to a constructive trust in proportion to the contributions; and

(d) Lord Wilberforce in *National Provincial Bank v. Ainsworth*[36] suggests that the case can be explained on the basis of contract alone, the widow being bound in her capacity as personal representative of her husband.

Several cases since have pointed out that *Errington* cannot be reconciled with earlier decisions, in particular the House of Lords in *King v. David Allen and Sons Billposting Ltd*[37] and the Court of Appeal in *Clore v. Theatrical Properties Ltd*[38] neither of which were cited to the court. The former case is of greater persuasive authority in this jurisdiction, since it was an appeal from Ireland. But the authority of *King* has been considerably weakened by *dicta* in the House of Lords in *National Provincial Bank v. Ainsworth*.[39] In that case the House of Lords rejected the attempt by Lord Denning MR to establish the doctrine of the "deserted wife's equity", that is, a licence arising specifically in favour of wives left in occupation of a matrimonial home after being deserted by their husbands and independent of any contributions they might have made to the acquisition of the house. While the court refused to categorise a wife in occupation of a matrimonial home as a licensee, contractual or otherwise, the judgments notably did not endorse the statement of Russell LJ in the Court of Appeal to the effect that a contractual licensee had no enforceable rights against a third party who took for value with actual notice of the licence. Lord Upjohn, referring to *Errington*, said:

> "... the licensees were in exclusive occupation upon the terms of paying off the mortgage instalments... This, I would have thought would have given the spouses an interest in the land, in accordance with the well-known line of authority starting with *Webb v. Paternoster* (1619) Pop 151, valid against all except a purchaser for value without notice".[40]

33 See Hargreaves, (1953) 69 LQR 466.

34 [1986] 1 WLR 1498.

35 [1997] ILRM 38.

36 [1965] AC 1175.

37 [1916] 2 AC 54, HL(I).

38 [1936] 3 All ER 483.

39 [1965] AC 1175.

40 *ibid.* at p.1239. In *Webb v. Paternoster* (1619) Pop 151, 79 ER 1250 the licensee may have bought hay as a standing crop with liberty to stack it on the land as so amounted to a licence coupled with an interest, as Baron Alderson commented in *Wood v.*

Lord Wilberforce also left the issue open:

> "... even if one accepts the leap from the wife as licensee to other (*e.g.*, contractual) licensees, one has not reached a solution, for the legal position of contractual licensees, as regards 'purchasers,' is very far from clear. The Court of Appeal has attempted to reach a generalisation by which licences, or at least licences coupled with occupation, are binding upon 'purchasers' but I note that the members of that court are not wholly agreed as to this doctrine. No doubt the time will come when this whole subject will have to be reviewed; this is not the occasion for it and I think that it would be undesirable now to say anything which might impede the development of this branch of the law".[41]

(3) An Equity or a Constructive Trust?

The first case to give serious consideration to the connection between contractual licences and constructive trusts was *Binions v. Evans*.[42] The defendant's husband had been an agricultural worker on an estate and lived in a cottage owner by the estate. He paid no rent or rates. When the husband died his widow, the defendant, was 73 years old. The owners of the estate entered into a written agreement with the widow which said that, in order to provide "a temporary home" for her "but not otherwise", the owners agreed to permit her "to reside in and occupy" the cottage "as tenant at will of them free of rent " for the remainder of her life "or until determined as hereinafter provided". Clause 2 provided that the agreement could be terminated by the defendant giving notice in writing. By Clause 3 the defendant agreed to keep the cottage and garden in repair, to occupy the cottage personally as a residence and not to assign or sublet and on ceasing to live there to give vacant possession to the owners of the estate. Later, the owners entered into an agreement to sell the cottage to the plaintiffs. The agreement stated that the sale was subject to the tenancy of the cottage in favour of the defendant, Mrs Evans. The plaintiffs paid a lower price than they would have done if the cottage had been sold with vacant possession.

The Court of Appeal held unanimously that Mrs Evans was protected, but they disagreed as to the reasons. The agreement itself was far from clear. On the one hand it referred to Mrs Evans as a tenant at will and to the arrangement as temporary; on the other hand it said that she could remain in the cottage for the rest of her life and, while it provided for her to terminate her occupation by giving notice, it made no provision for the owners of the estate to terminate the arrangement. Megaw and Stephenson LJJ held that the agreement created a life estate and further that Mrs Evans was a tenant for life within the English Settled Land Act, 1925. Megaw LJ held in the alternative that knowingly to induce a breach of contract was in itself a tort, a point we shall return to in a later section. Lord Denning MR held, alone, that the agreement constituted a con-

Leadbitter (1845) 13 M & W 838, 153 ER 351.

41 *ibid.* at p.1251.

42 [1972] 1 Ch. 359.

tractual licence. In the early part of his judgment Lord Denning referred to a licence to occupy premises for life as an equitable interest in land, which implies that it would in all circumstances be binding on third parties with notice. Nevertheless, his formulation at the end of the judgment mentioned particular factors present in the case in addition to notice as reasons why the plaintiffs were bound by the licence. He also introduced the concept of a constructive trust intervening between the licence and the conclusion that the third party was bound:

> "When the landlords sold the cottage to a purchaser "subject to" her rights under the agreement, the purchaser took the cottage on a constructive trust to permit the defendant to reside there during her life, or as long as she might desire. The courts will not allow the purchaser to go back on that trust".[43]

Earlier in his judgment Denning suggested that the constructive trust doctrine implies some conduct on the third party which makes it inequitable for him or her to take the property free of the licence:

> "This imposing of a constructive trust is entirely in accord with the precepts of equity. As Cardozo J once put it: 'A constructive trust is the formula through which the conscience of equity finds expression'; see *Beatty v. Guggenheim Exploration Co* (1919) 225 NY 380 at 385, or, as Lord Diplock put it quite recently in *Gissing v. Gissing* [1970] 2 All ER 780 at 790, [1971] AC 886 at 905, a constructive trust is created 'whenever the trustee has so conducted himself that it would be inequitable to allow him to deny to the *cestui que trust* a beneficial interest in the land acquired'".[44]

The conduct which Lord Denning saw in *Binions* as founding the constructive trust was the express undertaking by the plaintiff that the sale was subject to Mrs Evans' occupation. He distinguished *King v. David Allen* and *Clore* on the ground that there was no such undertaking in those cases. Nevertheless, having introduced the constructive trust concept Lord Denning then went on to eliminate the difference between a contractual licence plus a constructive trust and a contractual licence as an equitable interest in itself. Even if the plaintiff did not take expressly subject to the rights of the licensee, he may do so impliedly, the judge said. If the licensee is in actual occupation of the land then the third party would have constructive notice of the licensee's rights.[45] However, as Russell LJ pointed out in the Court of Appeal in *National Provincial Bank v. Hastings Car Mart*,[46] actual occupation, whether in registered or unregistered land, does not create new rights: it is merely a form of notice. Equity presumed that a purchaser had notice of the rights of persons who are in actual occupation, and in

43 *ibid.* at p.369.

44 *ibid.* at p.368.

45 *Hamilton v. Lyster* (1844) 7 Ir Eq R 560; *Hunt v. Luck* [1902] 1 Ch 428. *Hodgson v. Marks* [1971] Ch. 892, [1971] 2 All ER 684.

46 [1965] Ch. 665 at 696-697.

registered title a purchaser is bound by such rights without registration.[47] Lord Denning is therefore, in effect, restating his position in *Errington* that notice alone is sufficient to bind a purchasers of land subject to contractual licences, or notice plus actual occupation by the licensee. Perhaps it is that Denning realises that to construct a contractual licence into an equitable interest would not in all cases meet the demands of justice and imposes the requirement of actual occupation as a test of the kinds of licence that are to be protected. Yet there is no reason why the fact that the licensee is in occupation should always point to the third party being bound in equity: the licensee might have somewhere else to live, occupation under the licence might have been granted for commercial purposes and alternative premises might be easy to find. The circumstance in *Binions* which made it inequitable for the purchaser to deny the licensees rights was not simply that they had notice of the contract but that they had expressly taken the land subject to the contract and also had paid a lower price for the land than they would otherwise have done.

These issues were more recently explored by the English Court of Appeal in *Ashburn Anstalt v. Arnold*[48] which sought to resolve them by returning to the earlier notion of equity acting on the conscience of the third party.

(4) The Conscience of the Third Party

In *Ashburn Anstalt v. Arnold*[49] the second defendant entered into an agreement in 1973 to sell its leasehold interest in shop premises which formed part of the registered land. The agreement provided by clause 5 that from the date of completion the vendor would be at liberty to remain on the premises as licensee until a given date without payment of rent and from that date the vendor would be entitled to remain on the premises but could be required by the purchaser to give up possession on not less than one quarter's notice. In 1985 the plaintiff purchased, subject to the 1973 agreement, the freehold of the premises where the defendants carried on business. The judge dismissed the plaintiff's claim for possession and held that the 1973 agreement created a licence entitling the defendants to possession.

It was held in the English Court of Appeal by Fox LJ (Neill and Bingham LJJ concurring) that the 1973 agreement gave the second defendant exclusive possession of the premises for a certain term and thus created a tenancy notwithstanding the description of it as a licence in the 1973 agreement. This holding was, however, subsequently held to be incorrect by the House of Lords in *Prudential Assurance Co Ltd v. London Residuary Body*.[50] The court went

47 In the Republic by s.72(1)(j) of the Registration of Title Act, 1964.

48 [1989] Ch. 1, [1988] 2 WLR 706, [1988] 23 EG 128. See below.

49 [1989] Ch. 1, [1988] 2 WLR 706, [1988] 23 EG 128.

50 [1992] 2 AC 386, [1992] 3 All ER 504, [1992] 3 WLR 279, 64 P & CR 193, [1992] 36 EG 129. See below, Chapter 19 Landlord and Tenant.

on to hold, in the alternative, that if they were wrong and no tenancy had been created, the agreement would constitute a contractual licence. In that case the court held (a) that a contractual licence would not, without more, be binding on a third party even though they took with notice of it, but (b) that appropriate facts might give rise to a constructive trust. The court therefore held that the proprietary remedy did not apply, but the personal one would do so if facts were proved to give rise to it. As to (a), the court was unable to reconcile the approach of the House of Lords in *King,* or the two "front-of-house" cases, with the submission, on behalf of Arnold & Co, that a mere contractual licence is an interest in land binding on a purchaser with notice. The court considered itself bound by *King*. As to (b), the court held that it would not impose a constructive trust unless it was satisfied that the conscience of the owner of the land had been affected so that it would be inequitable to allow the owner to deny the claimant an interest. They then held that the available evidence in the present case was insufficient to infer a constructive trust.[51] Unlike the court in *Binions v. Evans,*[52] the present court did not accept that purchase of the land subject to the contractual licence was sufficient in itself, on the evidence, to bind the purchasers to give effect to the contract. There was no evidence that the plaintiffs had paid a lower price for the land.

The judge also cited *Lyus v. Prowsa Developments*[53] as an instance of the conscience of a third party being affected. In that case the vendor company were developing a housing estate. They had borrowed money from a bank and had given the bank a legal charge over the estate to secure the loan. The plaintiffs contracted to buy a plot in the estate. The vendor company was to build a house on the plot which would then be occupied by the plaintiffs. The plaintiffs paid a deposit to the company, but it later became insolvent before the house was built. The bank was under no liability, in the law of contract, to complete the plaintiffs' contract. The bank, as mortgagee, then sold the land to the first defendant. By the contract of sale it was provided that the land was sold subject to and with the benefit of the plaintiffs' contract. Subsequently the first defendant contracted to sell the plot to the second defendant. The contract provided that the land was sold subject to the plaintiffs' contract so far, if at all, as it might be enforceable against the first defendant. The first defendant's solicitors also wrote to the bank giving an assurance that their client would take reasonable steps to make sure the interests of contractual purchasers were dealt with to their satisfaction. The house was duly completed. The plaintiffs sought a declaration that their contract was binding on the defendants and an order for specific performance. The action succeeded. Fox LJ in *Ashburn* commented:

51 [1988] 2 WLR 706 at 719F, 725G-H, 728H, 729D, 730B.

52 [1972] 1 Ch. 359.

53 [1982] 1 WLR 1044, [1982] 2 All ER 953, 44 P & CR 213.

> "This again seems to us to be a case where a constructive trust could justifiably be imposed. The bank were selling as mortgagees under a charge prior in date to the contract. They were therefore not bound by the contract and on any view could give a title which was free from it. There was, therefore, no point in making the conveyance subject to the contract unless the parties intended the purchaser to give effect to the contract".

While *Ashburn* identified instances of factors, in addition to notice, which would cause a third party to be bound by the licence, it is less successful in explaining what would seem to be a just result in *Binions*. It is not clear why the conscience of a third party who expressly agrees to take the land subject to the licence, as in *Binions*, should remain unaffected without some additional factor being present.

In support of the proposition that a contractual licence is not binding on a third party through notice alone, Fox LJ made the point that, by analogy, a restrictive covenant is similarly not binding on a third party by notice alone.[54] This is true, but only because the plaintiff must show that he or she has land, or rather, an interest in land, capable of being benefited. In the case of a licence this would seem to beg the question, because the issue is precisely whether or not the licence is binding on the third party.

(5) The Tort of Interfering with Contractual Rights

Magaw LJ in *Binions v. Evans*[55] reached the same result as Denning by another route. He pointed out that there is a tort of interfering with contractual rights.[56] The plaintiffs took the purchase of the land with knowledge of the contract between the widow and the owners of the estate and so if they disregarded it they would be committing the tort. The widow could therefore restrain them from doing so. This is an ingenious argument and unobjectionable on the face of it, but has not been used since, perhaps because there is a problem here which judges feel must be articulated and resolved in terms of property rights. The most recent attempt has been in the English case of *Ashburn Anstalt v. Arnold*[57] which is discussed in the next section.

4. Domestic Arrangements

The concept of licence has frequently been invoked in order to characterise domestic arrangements when it is clear that the parties did not consider what legal rights would exist or did not consider what rights would exist in the circum-

---

54 *LCC v. Allen* [1914] 3 KB 642 and see also *London & South Western Railway v. Gomm* (1882) 20 Ch D 562 at 583, Jessel MR. *Power Supermarkets Ltd v. Crumlin Investments Ltd* unreported, High Court, Costello J, 22nd June 1981.

55 [1972] 1 Ch. 359 at p.371.

56 The line of authority stems from *Lumley v. Gye* (1853) 2 Bl & Bl, 118 ER 749; McMahon & Binchy, *Torts* p.560.

57 [1989] Ch. 1, [1988] 2 WLR 706, [1988] 23 EG 128.

stances which subsequently arose. Courts have sometimes found difficulty is such cases in defining when such a licence may be terminated or revoked.

In *Tanner v. Tanner*[58] a young mother of twins gave up a tenancy protected under the English Rent Acts in order to move into a house bought by the father of the children. When he later evicted her the English Court of Appeal awarded her compensation for the loss of her contractual licence. In the view of Lord Denning MR the house had been "provided for her as a house for herself and the twins for the foreseeable future".[59] Having given up the protected tenancy she had acquired a contractual tenancy to "have accommodation in the house for herself and the children so long as they were of school age and the accommodation was reasonably required for her and the children". The factors which led the court to recognise a licence of such extensive duration seem to have been (a) the fact that the mother had given up a protected tenancy, and (b) the moral obligation which they considered the father to be under to provide for his own children.

The relevance of the latter point is reinforced if one contrasts the result in another English Court of Appeal decision, *Chandler v. Kerley*.[60] The defendant and her ex-husband conveyed the former matrimonial home to Mr C who was the lover of the defendant. They had advertised the house for sale at about £14,000 but were unable to find a buyer. Mr C agreed to buy it for £10,000, which was probably below the market price, and the defendant was to remain in occupation as were the children of the marriage. Although Mrs K had an equal share in the beneficial interest with her ex-husband, she agreed to accept £1,000 while her ex-husband retained £1,800 of the proceeds remaining after paying off a mortgage. Mr C had thus acquired a house below market value and the vendor's wife and children into the bargain. The latter part of the bargain proved to be of limited value to him and within six weeks of the purchase Mr C ended his relationship with the defendant and brought an action for possession. The English Court of Appeal showed some sympathy for Mr C in his predicament. They held the defendant entitled to a contractual licence terminable on reasonable notice which they fixed at 12 months. The court refused to accept that the defendant had a licence for life and, by contrast to *Tanner v. Tanner*[61] did not hold that the licence should last until the children were grown up. Lord Scarman thought it "wrong... to infer, in the absence of an express promise, that the plaintiff was assuming the burden of housing another man's wife and children indefinitely, and long after his relationship with them had ended".

58 [1975] 1 WLR 1346.

59 [1975] 1 WLR 1346 at 1350B.

60 [1978] 1 WLR 693. [1979] Conv 184 (J. M. Masson).

61 [1975] 1 WLR 1346.

If one compares this result to that in *Tanner* it seems to exhibit a patriarchal bias in a male judiciary: a male may be expected to support his own children but should not be expected to support those of another male. The responsibilities of marriage were not in issue in either case. The results therefore indicate the values of the judges purely in the context of sexual roles.

One can also question whether it was right for Lord Scarman in *Chandler* to reject the notion of estoppel. Mrs K had asked Mr C after the sale of the house what would happen if their relationship broke down and he had assured her that he "could not put her out". Mrs K had also accepted less than half her share of the proceeds of sale from her husband on the basis that she was to remain in possession. Arguably, therefore, there was both the raising of an expectation and detrimental reliance in *Chandler*.

C. Rights of Residence

1. Nature of the Right

A right of residence is a right peculiar to Irish land law and consists of a personal right to occupy a house or a room or rooms in a house and often includes also the right of support or maintenance out of the profits of the land, by provision of food, fuel or other products.[62] Nevertheless the nature of the right is still in some doubt as the case law is somewhat vague and inconclusive on the subject.

a) Special and General Rights

Kennedy CJ in the Supreme Court in *National Bank v. Keegan*[63] described the right as follows:

> "The residential rights, which are so commonly given in farm holdings in this country, especially by way of testamentary provision for testator's widows, also frequently by the reservations to parents of rights in settlements made on the marriage of sons, are of two types, namely, the type which is a general right of residence charged on the holding usually coupled with a charge of maintenance; and the type which is a particular right of residence created by reserving or giving the right to the exclusive use during life of a specified room or rooms in the dwelling-house on the holding. The general right of residence charged on a holding is a right capable of being valued in moneys numbered at an annual sum, and of being represented by an annuity or money charge".[64]

The judge went on to hold that the instrument in the present case created the special type of interest and further held that it amounted to a life estate, apparently

62 Harvey, "Irish Rights of Residence – The Anatomy of a Hermaphrodite" 21 NILQ 389–424 at 391.

63 [1931] IR 344, 347.

64 *ibid.* at p.354.

in the specified part of the land. If this distinction between a general and a special right of residence is correct, then the two forms are really quite different. The special right would then not be a distinct interest in land at all, but merely a method of granting a life estate.

In *Lahiffe v. Hecker*[65] Lynch J held that the holder of a right of residence in a house was entitled to choose one of the three bedrooms in the house for her exclusive use, "to enable her properly to enjoy her general right of residence in the house". The judge nevertheless treated it as a general right in that he held that it was not a life estate, did not confer the powers of a tenant for life under the Settled Land Acts, 1882-90 on C, and did not inhibit the power of the court to order a sale.[66]

b) Rights of Maintenance

The right or charge of maintenance has often taken eccentric forms. Among the things to be provided have been "the grass of a donkey wet and dry on the said lands and stabling therefor",[67] "a quart of new milk daily, one quart of sour milk daily, two eggs daily, a pound of butter weekly, 10 horse rails of turf annually to be cut saved and delivered by my son, ten pecks of good table potatoes yearly"[68] *etc.*.

It would come naturally to someone living in the largely subsistence economy of rural Ireland to express an amount needed to maintain a person in use values: *i.e.* in actual produce with its useful qualities, rather than in exchange value, *i.e.* money. The advantage of use value as an expression is that it need not be index-linked: a pound of butter remains a pound of butter no matter what happens to prices. But in other cases the right of maintenance was subordinate to the right of residence and there is a dominant intent to give the donee the right to reside on that particular piece of land, usually for the rest of his or her life. This may be particularly so where the donee is elderly and has already lived in the house for many years. The intention is to secure their residence in a familiar house and to give effect to their evident reluctance to move.

It may be noticed that Kennedy CJ in *National Bank v. Keegan*[69] suggests that a right of maintenance is only granted with a general right of residence and not a special one. This is far from being established.

---

65 Unreported, High Court, Lynch J, 28 April 1994.

66 See below.

67 Harvey, op cit footnote 62 at p.391.

68 *ibid.* at p.391.

69 [1931] IR 344, 347.

c) Money Charge or Right to Reside?

The implication of the judgment of Kennedy CJ in *National Bank v. Keegan*[70] is that the special type, unlike the general right, is not a money charge on the land but amounts to a life estate.

The view that there is some distinction between the general and special right is now backed by statutory authority since it has found its way into the Statute of Limitations, 1957 which provides in section 40:

> "40.– An action in respect of a right in the nature of a lien for money's worth in or over land for a limited period not exceeding life, such as a right of support or a right of residence, not being an exclusive right of residence in or on a specified part of the land, shall not be brought after the expiration of twelve years from the date on which the right of action accrued".

If the special right of residence is in effect a life estate it would give rise to some awkward, even absurd, results and ones which would not accord with the intention of the donor. If the grant is contained in an instrument it falls within the Settled Land Acts 1882–1890 and it confers on the recipient the powers under the Acts including the power to convey the fee simple. The life estate itself would be overreached by a sale by the donee under the Acts: it would be converted into a life interest in the capital produced in the unlikely event of a sale. If, as appears to be the case, the life estate is only over the specified room or rooms in the house, then the donee would have the right to sell the fee simple in those rooms separately from the rest of the house.

Some grants of rights of residence specify that it is to be a charge while others do not. It is not clear whether these different formulations express two different forms of the right or not. Some judicial statements, such as Kennedy CJ in *National Bank v. Keegan*[71] just quoted, suggest that a general right of residence is a mere charge, while a particular or special right of residence is not. There is also authority for the view that the court has a discretion whether to convert the right to reside in the house into a money charge, or interpret it to be one *ab initio*. Johnson J in the High Court in *National Bank v. Keegan*[72] considered a voluntary promise in writing to grant to the defendant "during her life the exclusive use of the drawingroom and the bedroom. . . with fuel and support and maintenance" of property in County Westmeath. The judge said:

70 *ibid.*

71 *ibid.*

72 *ibid.*

> "It is well settled that a general right of residence and support in a house or upon a farm does not amount to an estate in the land, but is a mere charge in the nature of an annuity upon the premises in respect of which it exists and when it becomes necessary to sell such property a Court of Equity has power and authority to ascertain the value of such charge, so that the purchaser may get the property discharged from the burden. This was decided in the case of *Kelaghan v. Daly*[73] and later and more authoritatively in *In re Shanahan*".[74]

Before turning to these cases we shall consider *Ryan v. Ryan*[75] which appears to be the first Irish case on the right. The testator's will contained the statement: "I also order that my beloved wife shall have her diet and lodging in this my house... as long as the lease of it will last, provided she will wish to remain in it with my aforesaid nephew Patrick Ryan . . .". The widow at first lived in the house with the nephew but then left when he married. She later wished to return to the house and when the nephew refused to allow her to do so, she sued for the benefit under the will. Brady LC held that:

> "I think the plaintiff is entitled to relief. I read this devise as at least creating an obligation. Whether it creates a trust or not is not material. There are cases where a mere obligation attached to property makes the holder a trustee, and others where it has been held not to do so, but without reference to any such question, it is plain that this is an obligation such as this Court will enforce... it would be very difficult to lay down a rule as to the quantity of diet the legatee should have, or the room in the house which she should get; but it is perfectly plain she is entitled to have some diet or lodging, and there is no insuperable difficulty in enforcing that right. . . . probably the best course will be to decree the plaintiff entitled in the words of the will, and leave her then to work out that declaration if she is dissatisfied with the way in which it is obeyed. . .". (The case was referred to the Master.)[76]

In *Kelaghan v. Daly*[77] a farm was assigned to Catherine Kelaghan's son in consideration of natural love and affection and included a covenant by the son, his executor, administrators or assigns "to clothe, support maintain and keep the said Catherine Kelaghan and her daughter Lizzie during their joint lives and the life of the survivor of them in a manner suitable to their condition in life ; and will permit... them to use, occupy and enjoy the dwellinghouse on the said farm in the same manner as they now occupy and enjoy the same". The property was then mortgaged and sold by the mortgagees subject to "all rights which may now be vested in Lizzie Kelaghan", Catherine Kelaghan having died. The covenant therefore created what Kennedy CJ would call a general right of residence. Boyd J held there was a lien on the land binding on the purchaser since he "had express notice of the rights of the plaintiff". This suggests that the lien was equitable. The judge then went on to note that:

73 [1913] 2 IR 328.

74 [1919] 1 1 IR 131.

75 (1848) 12 Ir Eq R 226.

76 *ibid.* at p.228.

77 [1913] 2 IR 328.

> "It has been admitted on the argument before me that the covenant, so far as relates to the occupation of the said house, affects land, and that the vendor's lien in respect thereof is operative; but it has been contended that the rest of the covenant is merely personal and does not run with the lands".[78]

The judge apparently did not consider whether the right created a life estate in the mother and daughter. This may have been an oversight, or the argument may not have been made, but it seems this error may be the basis of the supposed distinction in the later case law, especially evident in *National Bank v. Keegan,*[79] between the special right, which is in effect a life estate, and the general right which is said to be a mere charge. Secondly it is highly questionable whether the right can be captured by the concept of a vendor's lien. Those who took the benefit of the lien were not the mortgagee-vendors but the mother and daughter.

The court in *Re Shanahan*[80] also decided that the general right created a charge on the land. If the right is a charge on the land, then under section 5 of the Conveyancing Act, 1881 the owner of land subject to an incumbrance, which includes a rentcharge, may sell the land free of it by obtaining the permission of the court to lodge a sum of money in court, the sum being sufficient to provide an income, after investment in government securities, to pay the annual amount.[81] If this is correct, then the general right does not secure the donee's occupation on the land.

In *Leonard v. Leonard*[82] the court found that a right of residence created an implied trust. An ante-nuptial settlement contained a covenant to "support, maintain and clothe and keep in a suitable and proper manner in his house on the said farm [TL] and his wife and family ...". Holmes J found that the covenant was not merely personal but created a trust. More recently judges have shown a reluctance to infer a trust where words in a will do not expressly impose a trust but merely a wish or desire as to the use of the property in the hands of the donee, *i.e.* where precatory words are used.[83]

More recently the High Court in *Johnston v. Horace*[84] treated a general right of residence as giving an actual right to occupy. Since the case involved registered land it is discussed in the next section.

---

78 *ibid.* at p.330.

79 [1931] IR 344, 347.

80 [1919] 1 IR 131.

81 *Re McGuiness's Contract* (1901) 35 ILTR 65.

82 (1910) 44 ILTR 155; *Gallagher v. Ferris* (1881) 7 LR Ir 489; *Re Butler* (1925) 59 ILTR 166.

83 Wylie, *Irish Land Law* para 9.016; *Lefroy v. Flood* (1854) 4 Ir Ch R 1; *McAlinden v. McAlinden* (1877) IR 11 Eq 219; *Bradshaw v. Bradshaw* [1908] 1 IR 288; *Berryman v. Berryman* [1913] 1 IR 21; *Re Blackwood* [1953] NI 32.

84 [1993] ILRM 594, discussed below.

2. Registered Land

Section 81 of the Registration of Title Act, 1964 states that:

> "81.–A right of residence in or on registered land, whether a general right of residence on the land or an exclusive right of residence in or on part of the land, shall be deemed to be personal to the person beneficially entitled thereto and to be a right in the nature of a lien for money's worth in or over the land and shall not operate to create any equitable estate in the land".

The declaration that a right of residence is personal to the holder presumably means that it is not alienable. The further declaration that it is "in the nature of a lien for money's worth" is not entirely clear, but a lien in general is a right to possession until money is paid. The sentence might imply that the right can be bought off, but the courts have rather sought to discover the intention of the testator. The second part of the sentence may indicate that the purpose of the section was to avoid the awkward consequences, already mentioned, of a life estate.

In *Johnston v. Horace*[85] Lavan J had to consider a right of residence created over registered land. The judge took the view that the role of the court is to find the intention of the testator and if that was to secure the occupation of the donee, the court will give effect to it. The testator, PK, had appointed his daughter, BH, sole executor and beneficiary of his estate subject to a right of residence in favour of his son Edward, who had since died, his other daughter, TJ, who was the plaintiff in the case, and her daughter, the second plaintiff. The latter was struck out of the action before trial. The defendant was the son of BH and had inherited the property on her death, subject to the right of residence. The plaintiff alleged that after the death of Edward the defendant began a campaign of bullying and oppressive behaviour towards her. This eventually lead to her leaving the house against her will and moving in to live with her daughter. It seems that this was the probably the object which the defendant wished to achieve. Lavan J held that the right was a general one, giving the plaintiff the right to share with the others the use and occupation of the premises and although she had the personal use of one bedroom in a three bedroom cottage she had not been granted any exclusive right. The judge valued the right at a one third interest in the cottage. However, the testator had not intended to create a mere charge:

> "I view any conduct which, in this era of homelessness, puts a person out of their home as being reprehensible. . . The provision by the deceased might appear modest. It was not. It made provision for one of the most basic requirements that any human being yearns to attain. That is a roof over their heads for life, and a security that same would be available until the end of their days – that is a right of residence for life".[86]

85 [1993] ILRM 594; Coughlan, "Enforcing Rights of Residence" (1993) ILT 168.

86 [1993] ILRM 594 at 600.

The judge held that it would not be appropriate to make a monetary award in respect of the right:

> "I consider the suggestion of valuing the right of residence unreal. Where I have to value same, I take the view that it would have to be on an actuarial basis, having regard to the defendant's conduct and his ability to pay. In addition, I take the view that a secured right of residence would otherwise become an unsecured right with no certainty that periodic payments would or could be made".[87]

The judge went on the hold that although a right of residence could be voluntarily abandoned expressly or by efflux of time, the plaintiff had not abandoned the right as she had left the premises under duress. The court would require strong cogent evidence from a party seeking to defeat the right while it remained a burden on the register. The judge granted the plaintiff injunctions restraining the defendant from preventing the plaintiff exercising her right to residence and ordering the defendant to supply a key to the cottage. He also awarded £7,500 damages for interference to the right of residence to date.

The judgment in *Johnston v. Horace*[88] may indicate a growing willingness to use the discretion of court, mentioned in earlier cases, even in the case of a general right of residence, to secure the occupation of the donee.

3. Reform

There appears to be a need in land law for a form of right which confers on the recipient, usually an elderly member of a family, a right to reside in a house for the rest of their life, or until incapacity requires other arrangements, which is personal to the recipient in the sense that he or she cannot alienate it, but which is secure against third parties. The uncertainty of the rights conferred by a right of residence in Ireland mean that it does not fulfil that requirement. Licences, on the other hand, may be insecure against third a parties, while life estates, if created in writing, fall within the Settled Land Acts, 1892–90 and confer more extensive rights than intended, namely, the right to sell the fee simple. The legislature should therefore consider creating a statutory form of right which could be conferred in such cases. There is no doubt a concern that such a right should not withdraw land from the market for an unduly long time, but that could be met by restricting it in some way, perhaps by providing that it could only be conferred on recipients above a certain age.

87 *ibid.* at p.601.

88 [1993] ILRM 594.

D. Proprietary Estoppel

1. Introduction

Proprietary estoppel, or estoppel by reliance has become an important way in which rights in land may be acquired in equity. From its origins as an equity recognised in a number of limited situations it has developed into a more general principle whose limits are still to be explored.

a) Origins

The modern doctrine of estoppel has its origins in three strands of case law. These three strands are:

1. equitable extensions to the rules as to improvements to land by tenants;
2. exceptions to the rule that equity would not perfect an imperfect gift; and
3. the circumstances in which a licence to occupy land may become irrevocable.

(1) Improvements by Tenants

At the end of the 18th century John Fitzgibbon, the Earl of Clare LC, giving judgment in the Irish House of Lords in *Kenney v. Browne*,[89] stated the position in equity as regards someone who makes improvements to property believing it to belong to them or believing that they will receive a property interest in future, such as new lease to take effect on the termination of a present lease:

> "As to the equity arising from lasting and valuable improvements, I do not consider a man, who is conscious of a defect in his title and with that conviction in his mind expends a sum of money in improvements, as entitled in any sort to avail himself of it. If the person really entitled to the estate will encourage the possessor of it to expend his money in improvements, or if he will look on and suffer such an expenditure, without apprising the party of his intention to dispute his title, and will afterwards endeavour to avail himself of such fraud; upon the ground of fraud the jurisdiction of a Court of Equity will clearly attach upon the case. But does it follow from thence, that if a man has acquired an estate by rank and abominable fraud, and shall afterwards expend his money in improving the estate, that therefore he shall retain it in his hands against the lawful proprietor? If such a rule should prevail, it will certainly fully justify a proposition, which I once heard stated at the bar of the Court of Chancery, that the common equity of this country was, to improve the right owner out of the possession of his estate".[90]

---

89 (1796) 3 Ridg PC 462, Ir HL.

90 (1796) 3 Ridg PC 462, at 518. For a discussion of estoppels in the 18th century see *Hume v. Burton* (1785) 1 Ridg PC 247.

Lord Yelverton in the same case stated the principle in similar terms:

> "Improvements are also relied upon; but I know of no case where they have assisted a man in a defence of this kind, except where a party having the deeds or title in his pocket, and knowing they would avoid the tenants interest, stands by, sees the improvements going on, encourages them, and then seeks to recover possession of the land, with those improvements upon it".[91]

One may notice that even at this early stage Fitzgibbon perceives the distinction between active encouragement by the legal owner and looking on while the non-owner acts under a mistaken belief that he or she has an interest in the land. Yelverton also mentions both aspects, but does not really treat them as distinct from one another. In *Ramsden v. Dyson*[92] Lord Kingsdown spoke of two situations:

> "If a man, under a verbal agreement for a certain interest in land, or, what amounts to the same thing, under an expectation created or encouraged by the landlord, that he shall have a certain interest, takes possession of such land, with the consent of the landlord, and upon the faith of such promise or expectation, with the knowledge of the landlord, and without objection by him, lays out money upon the land, a court of equity will compel the landlord to give effect to such promise or expectation . . .".[93]

> "If, on the other hand, a tenant, being in possession of land, and knowing the nature and extent of his interest, lays out money upon it in the hope and expectation of an extended term or an allowance for expenditure, then, if such hope or expectation has not been created or encouraged by the landlord, the tenant has no claim which any court of law or equity can enforce".[94]

At common law buildings erected on land by a tenant became the property of the landlord at the end of the lease. By the 19th century the common law had itself developed exceptions to this rule, including a category of tenants fixtures. Lord Kingsdown's statement, in the context of its own time, was a statement of the circumstances in which courts of equity would make an exception to the general principle.

Logically it is clear, both from Lord Kingsdown's speech and that of Fitzgibbon, that the exceptional cases were not confined to cases in which A, who has a tenancy, makes improvements to the land in the belief, encouraged by the landlord, that he, A, would obtain a new lease to take effect at the end of the present one. It would equally apply where the improver had no original interest

---

91 *Kenney v. Browne* (1796) 3 Ridg PC at 529–30.

92 (1866) LR 1 HL 129; See also *Sheridan v. Barrett* (1879) 4 LR Ir 223.

93 In *Flood v. O'Gorman* (1856) 4 Ir CLR 578 such a situation occurred. The defendant went into occupation after the plaintiff agreed to grant him a lease for years. The defendant spent money on the land and was then sued at law for use and occupation. A lease was never granted. The defendant had been in occupation for six years. His plea of the promise and expenditure was held to be no defence. But this was a court of common law, not equity.

94 (1866) LR 1 HL 170, 171.

at all but mistakenly believed a tenancy to exist, or that he or she was to be granted a tenancy, or was to be granted any other kind of interest in land and where the owner of the land encouraged the belief, or stood by and said nothing, knowing that the belief had no foundation.

(2) *Imperfect Gifts*

The case of an imperfect gift arose in the English House of Lords in *Dillwyn v. Llewellyn.*[95] A father gave possession of land which he owned to his son. Both of them signed a memorandum which evidenced an intention that the land should be given to the son for the purpose of providing him with a dwelling house. The son then proceeded to build the house, at great expense. Lord Westbury LC recognised the general principle that equity will not perfect an imperfect gift. Thus if A promises to convey land to B, and the promise is unsupported by consideration or there is neither a memorandum under the Statute of Frauds nor part performance in equity, and A does not execute the conveyance, a court of equity will not force A to do so. The judge held, nevertheless, that there were circumstances in which the court would make an exception to this general principle. The additional element on the facts was that the son had incurred substantial expenditure in reliance on the father's assurance, and this gave the son a "right or ground of claim" independent of the original gift.[96] The court held that the intention was that the father would convey the fee simple in the land to the son and this they ordered him to do.

(3) *Licences*

A third origin of proprietary estoppel can be traced to cases on licences. Common law courts had refused to restrain a breach of contract where a licence to enter land was revoked contrary to the agreement between the parties.[97] Common law courts had no remedy of injunction, but they even declined to award damages for assault in removing the licensee.[98] As early as 1861 an Irish common law court in *Blood v. Keller*[99] had held that a licence could become irrevo-

---

95 (1862) 4 De G F & J 517, 45 ER 1285.

96 (1862) 45 ER 1285 at 1286. Lord Westbury's judgment is written in the language of contract: he speaks of "the subsequent expenditure by the son, with the approbation of the father" supplying "valuable consideration originally wanting" and the son's right was to call upon the donor to "perform that contract and complete the imperfect donation", etc, but clearly the basis of the claim could not literally be reduced to contract, even a unilateral one, without making nonsense of contract law. The expenditure by the son was not valuable consideration for the father's promise because the father would receive no benefit from it, since he was to convey the fee simple to the son.

97 See Licences above.

98 For a discussion of the falsity of this distinction see Licences above.

99 (1861) 11 Ir CLR 124; and see *Armstrong v. Sheppard & Short Ltd* [1959] 2 All ER 651, [1959] 2 QB 384.

cable once the licensee had expended money in reliance on the assurance contained in the licence, or possibly only revocable if the licensor could put the party in the position they were in before the licence was entered into, but since it was a common law court it could not articulate the principle in equitable terms.

b) The Development of the Modern Doctrine

(1) From Promissory to Proprietary Estoppel

In *Central London Property Trust v. High Trees House Ltd*[100] a property company had entered into a lease of High Trees House[101] with the tenant. During the Second World War the company indicated that it would not insist on the full rent payable under the lease while the war continued. The tenant paid the reduced rent while the war continued. After the war was over the landlord company then demanded the back rent which they claimed was due under the lease. Denning J (later to become Lord Denning MR) held that they were estopped in equity from doing so. It is clear from the judgment that the judge held that the tenant had relied on the assurance so that they would have suffered a detriment if they had been liable to pay the arrears under the lease. Although there was earlier authority[102] for a new branch of estoppel known as promissory estoppel the case gave it general recognition. Nevertheless, the new doctrine was thought to have its dangers, since it recognised that promises could be binding other than by the law of contract and this might threaten to undermine the law of contract itself.[103] It was therefore thought that the principle of promissory estoppel was "a shield and not a sword." It was available as a defence to an action to enforce a contract, but did not found an independent cause of action.

Dillwyn v. Llewelyn[104] and *Ramsden v. Dyson*[105] and the principle which underlay them had largely been forgotten until the case of *Inwards v. Baker.*[106] In that case a father allowed his son to build a bungalow on the father's land.

100 [1947] KB 130, [1956] 1 All ER 256; and see now *Brikom Investments Ltd v. Carr* [1979] QB 467 at 482f.

101 The premises, a block of flats, is situated near Stockwell Underground station in London.

102 *Hughes v. Metropolitan Railway Co* (1877) 2 App Cas 439.

103 Promissory estoppel had been recognised in the United States as a sword supplying a lack of consideration: *Restatement on Contracts,* 2d 90, but it was pointed out in *Waltons Stores (Interstate) Ltd v. Maher* (1987) 164 CLR 387 (see below) by the judges in the High Court of Australia that consideration in the United States is based on a narrower bargain theory not found in Australia or England.

104 (1862) 4 De G F & J 517, 45 ER 1285.

105 [1866] LR 1 HL 129 at p.141.

106 [1965] 2 QB 29. See R.H. Maudsley (1965) 81 LQR 183.

The son went into occupation of the bungalow and remained there in the belief, which the father had encouraged, that he would be able to remain there for the rest of his life. The father died without having granted the son any interest in the property or making any contract to do so and did not leave the property to his son in his will. The trustees under the will attempted to evict the son, but the court refused to allow them to do so. They held that the expenditure by the son had entitled him to an equity in the land in the form of a licence.[107] Lord Denning MR said:

> "If the owner of land requests another, or indeed allows another, to expend money on the land under an expectation created or encouraged by the landlord that he will be able to remain there, that raises an equity in the licensee such as to entitle him to stay. . . . All that is necessary is that the licensee should, at the request or with the encouragement of the landlord, have spent the money in the expectation of being allowed to stay there".[108]

The view which developed after *Inwards v. Baker* in England was that promissory estoppel was a doctrine of contract law which provided a defence to an action to enforce a contractual right: it was a shield and not a sword. Proprietary estoppel, on the other hand, was a cause of action which gave rise to property interests: proprietary estoppel was a sword and not merely a shield.[109]

In *Crabb v. Arun District Council*[110] the plaintiff sold part of his land without reserving a right of way for the retained part because he had been led to believe by a representative of the district council that they would allow him to construct and use an alternative access over their land. The plaintiff constructed and used the alternative access and the district council then tried to prevent him from so doing. Lord Denning MR said that if a person:

> "by his words or conduct, so behaves as to lead another to believe that he will not insist on his strict legal rights – knowing or intending that the other will act on that belief – and he does so act, that again will raise an equity in favour of the other; and it is for a court of equity to say in what way the equity may be satisfied".[111]

---

107 The case also apears to have decided that the licence bound not only the father and his personal representatives but also successors in title except bona fide purchasers for value of the legal estate without notice. This is now doubtful in view of the decision in *Ashburn Anstalt v. Arnold* [1989] Ch. 1, [1988] 2 WLR 706, [1988] 23 EG 128 which held, as an alternative *ratio*, that a contractual licence is not binding on third parties in the absence of a contructive trust binding the third party. This, however, is a problem as to the nature of licences and not as to the nature of the equity which gives rise to them.

108 *ibid.* at pp. 36–37; and see Danckwerts LJ at p.38.

109 *Dillwyn v. Llewelyn* (1862) 4 De G F & J 517, 45 ER 1285; *Pascoe v. Turner* [1979] 1 WLR 431 at 436.

110 [1976] Ch. 179.

111 *ibid.* at p.188.

Scarman LJ in the same case,[112] accepted the formulation of Lord Kingsdown in *Ramsden v. Dyson,*[113] referred with approval to the judgment of Fry J in *Willmott v. Barber*[114] and deprecated the distinction between proprietary and promissory estoppel and stated that equity would interfere if:

> "it would be unconscionable and unjust to allow the defendants to set up their undoubted rights against the claim being made by the plaintiff".[115]

A strong example of proprietary estoppel as a sword was *Pascoe v. Turner.*[116] A businessman, P, lived with T, a widow living on an invalidity pension. P bought a house and they moved in, living as husband and wife. Seven years later P started an affair with another woman. T stayed in the house. P told her the house and everything in it was hers. In reliance, T spent money on repairs and improvements and furniture, to the knowledge of P. P moved out in the same year in which he started the affair with the other woman. Three years later he told her to leave.

The Court of Appeal, not presided over by Lord Denning MR on this occasion, held that the assurance he gave to her and her reliance on them raised an equity in her favour. It was for the court to decide how that equity could best be satisfied. The court considered conferring a licence on T, but felt that would not allow her to raise money for other improvements which might be necessary. They held that the equity could only be satisfied here by the conveyance of the fee simple to her. The court also commented on the ruthlessness with which P had sought to avoid his obligations and to evict his erstwhile companion from the house,[117] and held that the transfer of the fee simple was necessary to protect her against this ruthlessness in the future.

Academic criticism of the decision tended to the view that the court conferred on the widow a greater interest than her contributions justified.[118] But against this it can be argued that the decision of the court was not based upon the monetary contributions so much as on the unfulfilled promise to convey the house to the widow. The case may therefore belong rather to the perfecting an imperfect gift class of case than to the type of case in which the court is recompensing a person for an outlay of money. This is consistent with the language of the court which spoke of "compelling the plaintiff to give effect to his promise and her expectations".[119] It is also consistent with Lord Kingsdown's

112 *ibid.* at p.194.

113 [1866] LR 1 HL 129, 170.

114 (1880) 15 Ch D 96.

115 [1976] Ch. 179 at p.195.

116 [1979] 1 WLR 431, [1979] 2 All ER 945. See above.

117 [1979] 1 WLR at 438f per Cumming-Bruce LJ.

118 See B. Sufrin (1979) 42 MLR 574.

119 [1979] 1 WLR 431 at p.439B. A rule-sceptic might also stress that P was a relatively wealthy man, while T had only limited financial resources.

statement of the principle in *Ramsden v. Dyson* when he said that "a court of equity will compel the landlord to give effect to such promise or expectation".

(2) Towards a General Principle

Doubts were beginning to appear as to whether the distinction between promissory estoppel and proprietary estoppel could be maintained. In *Holiday Inns Inc v. Broadhead*[120] Robert Goff J summarised the position as follows:

> "the authorities clearly establish that there is a head of equity under which relief will be given where the owner of property seeks to take an unconscionable advantage of another by allowing or encouraging him to spend money, whether or not on the owner's property, in the belief, known to the owner, that the person expending the money will enjoy some right or benefit over the owner's property which the owner then denies him. . . . The authorities also establish . . . that this relief can be granted although the agreement or understanding between the parties was not sufficiently certain to be enforceable as a contract, and that the court has a wide, albeit of course judicial, discretion to what extent relief should be given and what form it should take".[121]

In *Taylors Fashions Ltd v. Liverpool Victoria Trustees Co Ltd*[122] Oliver J reviewed all the authorities and in a statement which he repeated in the Court of Appeal in *Habib Bank Ltd v. Habib Bank AG Zurich*[123] concluded:

> "the more recent cases indicate, in my judgment, that the application of the *Ramsden v. Dyson*, LR 1 HL principle – whether you call it proprietary estoppel, estoppel by acquiescence or estoppel by encouragement is really immaterial – requires a very much broader approach which is directed rather at ascertaining whether, in particular individual circumstances, it would be unconscionable for a party to be permitted to deny that which, knowingly, or unknowingly, he has allowed or encouraged another to assume to his detriment than to inquiring whether the circumstances can be fitted within the confines of some preconceived formula serving as a universal yardstick for every form of unconscionable behaviour".[124]

In *Re Basham*,[125] discussed below, an English court was prepared to enforce an unperformed promise to make a will where the party to whom the promise had been made had acted in reliance on it. It is also clear from *Dillwyn*

120 (1974) 232 EG 951.

121 (1974) 232 EG 951 at p.1087. See also *Taylor Fashions Ltd v. Liverpool Victoria Trustees* [1981] 2 WLR 576 at 589, [1981] 1 All ER 897 at 915; *Shaw v. Applegate* [1977] 1 WLR 970, [1978] 1 All ER 123; *Habib Bank Ltd v. Habib Bank AG Zurich* [1981] 1 WLR 1265 at 1285, [1981] 2 All ER 650 at 666; *Amalgamated Investment & Property Co Ltd v. Texas Commerce International Bank Ltd* [1982] QB 84, 122 Lord Denning MR; *Attorney-General of Hong Kong v. Humphreys Estate (Queen's Gardens) Ltd* [1987] AC 114; *JT Developments Ltd v. Quinn* (1990) 62 P & CR 33 Court of Appeal (Civil Division).

122 (Note) [1982] QB 133.

123 [1981] 1 WLR 1265, 1285.

124 [1982] QB 133 at p.151.

125 [1986] 1 WLR 1498.

v. Llewelyn[126] and other authorities that a court in similar circumstances will perfect an imperfect *inter vivos* gift. If estoppel can perfect an imperfect gift, can it also perfect an imperfect contract? There was ample authority for the view that it would do so where the parties were already landlord and tenant and the landlord had encouraged the tenant to believe that a new lease would be granted at the end of the present one and there was detrimental reliance by the tenant.[127] In *JT Developments v. Quinn*[128] Ralph Gibson LJ rejected a distinction in this context:

> "One distinction between promissory and proprietary or equitable estoppel, hich has been regarded as established, is that a promissory estoppel cannot create any new cause of action where none existed before: see Halsbury's Laws of England: *Combe* v *Combe*. In this case, it is common ground that the defendants have asserted a right in equity by agreement or estoppel to a new lease of their shop and have not merely denied the plaintiffs' right to possession. It is clear that, by whatever name it is called, the defendants have set out to prove such an equity as gives rise to that cause of action. The defendants, in short, rely upon the principle, expounded and illustrated in the authorities considered by Lord Templeman in *Attorney-General of Hong Kong v. Humphreys Estate (Queen's Gardens) Ltd*[129] upon which a litigant, who is led to believe he will be granted an interest in land, and who acts to his detriment in that belief, is enabled to obtain that interest".[130]

It was now possible to argue that where parties were negotiating to create a property interest, promissory estoppel was no longer a mere defence and that equity would confer rights where the law of contract had failed for some reason. In the landlord and tenant situation there was already an existing legal relationship between the parties. Yet it did not seem that this could found a valid distinction. Where the elements of the equity were present it was no less unconscionable for the party creating the expectation to resile from it.

In *Waltons Stores (Interstate) Ltd v. Maher*[131] the High Court of Australia considered a case where there was no prior lease, but parties were negotiating to enter into one. The owners of a developed site proposed to demolish existing buildings and erect a new one suitable for a supermarket. The owners proposed certain amendments to the draft lease and were told verbally by the company's solicitors that the amendments were acceptable. The company returned an amended, but unexecuted, copy of the lease. The owners executed the lease

---

126 (1862) 4 De G F & J 517, 45 ER 1285.

127 *Kenney v. Browne* (1796) 3 Ridg PC 462, at 518, Ir HL; *Taylors Fashions Ltd v. Liverpool Victoria Trustees Co Ltd* (Note) [1982] QB 133. See *Haughan v. Rutledge* [1988] IR 295, Blayney J, below.

128 (1990) 62 P & CR 33, Court of Appeal (Civil Division).

129 [1987] 1 AC 114, [1987] 2 All ER 387, [1987] 2 WLR 343, Privy Council.

130 (1990) 62 P & CR 33 at p.45.

131 (1987) 164 CLR 387, High Court of Australia. See also *Commonwealth v. Verwayen* (1990) 170 CLR 394, High Court of Australia.

and returned it to the company by way of exchange. The company, which had become aware that the demolition was proceeding, then told the owners that they did not wish to proceed with the lease. The owners sued in the Supreme Court of New South Wales for a declaration that there was a valid and enforceable agreement for a lease, an order for specific performance and alternatively damages in lieu. The New South Wales court gave judgment for the owners for damages in lieu of specific performance. The company's appeal to the New South Wales Court of Appeal was dismissed.[132]

The company appealed to the High Court of Australia which dismissed the appeal. Brennan J reformulated the doctrine of estoppel, which he did not characterise as promissory or proprietary:

> "In my opinion, to establish an equitable estoppel, it is necessary for a plaintiff to prove that (1) the plaintiff assumed that a particular legal relationship then existed between the plaintiff and the defendant or expected that a particular legal relationship would exist between them and, in the latter case, that the defendant would not be free to withdraw from the expected legal relationship; (2) the defendant has induced the plaintiff to adopt that assumption or expectation; (3) the plaintiff acts or abstains from acting in reliance on the assumption or expectation; (4) the defendant knew or intended him to do so; (5) the plaintiff's action or inaction will occasion detriment if the assumption or expectation is not fulfilled; and (6) the defendant has failed to act to avoid that detriment whether by fulfilling the assumption or expectation or otherwise. For the purposes of the second element, a defendant who has not actively induced the plaintiff to adopt an assumption or expectation will nevertheless be held to have done so if the assumption or expectation can be fulfilled only by a transfer of the defendant's property, a diminution of his rights or an increase in his obligations and he, knowing that the plaintiff's reliance on the assumption or expectation may cause detriment to the plaintiff if it is not fulfilled, fails to deny to the plaintiff the correctness of the assumption or expectation on which the plaintiff is conducting his affairs".[133]

The High Court of Australia upheld the award by the lower court of damages for the "concluded agreement by way of exchange" which the judge found to exist between the parties and so was not called upon to order the execution of the lease. In these circumstances the word proprietary may indeed not have been appropriate. But the judgments indicate that there is no reason in principle why a conveyance should not have been ordered in appropriate circumstances and the members of the court agreed that the equivalent of the Statute of Frauds in force in New South Wales would not have been a bar to doing so.[134]

---

132 (1986) 5 NSWLR 407.

133 *ibid.* pp. 428–429.

134 Brennan J held that section 54A of the Conveyancing Act, 1919 (NSW) did not preclude the enforcement of the agreement on the ground that equitable estoppel does not create a contract to which the section applies, even where the equity is satisfied by treating the defendant as though a contract had been made; Deane J so held on the ground that estoppel precluding the denial of a valid and enforceable agreement ex-

In the later case of *Commonwealth v. Verwayen*[135] Brennan J stated the doctrine in the context of unfulfilled promises:

> "Equitable estoppel or, as I prefer to call it, an equity arising by estoppel precludes a person who, by a promise, has induced another party to rely on the promise and thereby to act to his detriment from resiling from the promise without avoiding the detriment: *Waltons Stores (Interstate) Ltd* v *Maher* (1988) 164 CLR 387 at p 427".[136]

Where estoppel arises in the context of property rights there is another argument against it operating in a purely negative way: if the person in whom the expectation was raised cannot enforce it by action, then if the other party manages to get back into possession the expectation will be defeated.

c) Modern Irish Cases

An early Irish authority on proprietary estoppel is *Cullen v. Cullen*.[137] The plaintiff (the father) lived with his family on premises that comprised the family residence, the business premises and some other land. His son, M, had joined him in the business after leaving school. At one point the plaintiff had given money to M to buy land of his own and this he had done. The father began to show signs mental problems and, in an attempt to avoid being committed to a mental hospital, agreed to transfer the business and house to his wife (the wife) in return for her promise not to have him committed. About the same time his wife won a portable house in a competition. She gave this house to her son, M. M began to prepare a site for it on his own land, but the wife suggested to his father that M should erect the house on the land where the family house and business was situated. The father that as he was transferring the place to her she could do as she wished. M therefore erected the house on the land near the family business. Later, the father decided to resume control of his affairs and told M to remove his house. He brought the present action claiming, *inter alia,* an injunction to restrain the defendant from trespassing on the property. M counterclaimed that he was entitled to the house and the land on which it stood.

Kenny J held that plaintiff had granted a licence (either to the wife, or to the son through the wife) and that he had revoked it. The judge awarded a lump sum of damages to the plaintiff against M for trespass. However, he went on to

tends to preclude the assertion of unenforceability of the assumed agreement, so that the estoppel outflanked section 54A; Gaudron J so held on the ground that the fact that the company was estopped from denying that exchange had taken place involved an assumption that the agreement was duly executed by the company; and by Mason CJ and Wilson J for the reasons given by the other members of the Court.

135 (1990) 170 CLR 394, High Court of Australia.

136 *ibid.* at p.422.

137 [1962] IR 268, High Court, Kenny J. See also *McMahon v. Kerry C C* [1981] ILRM 419, below.

hold that the plaintiff was estopped from asserting his title against M. He could therefore not succeed in his claim to an injunction against M. The judge declined to hold that M could require the plaintiff to execute a conveyance of the site of his house. The existing authorities, he considered, recognised estoppel as a shield but not as a sword: they allowed M to resist a claim for an injunction, but did not allow the court to order the plaintiff to convey the land to M. He nevertheless suggested that if the son remained in possession for 12 years, which the father could do nothing to prevent, the son could then register his title with the Land Registry. The judge also rejected the idea that the wife had acquired an equity giving her a proprietary interest in the land. She had used her money in running the business but monetary compensation would be an adequate remedy.

The case should clearly now be considered in the context of its time. In 1962 there was no judicial consensus in favour of the view that proprietary estoppel was a distinct doctrine from promissory estoppel. *Dillwyn v. Llewelyn*[138] and *Ramsden v. Dyson*[139] remained forgotten. It is clear that Kenny J thought that he was applying a principle derived from the *High Trees* case. He felt bound to treat the estoppel as a shield and not a sword. The judgment nevertheless amounted to awarding the fee simple to the son, but conferred only a possessory title rather than a documentary one. It is arguably not a good policy to increase the number of possessory titles if the intention, and the result, was to confer a fee simple. In the meantime, before the limitation period ran out, the effect of the judgment was that the son, as a trespasser, still had a fee simple as regards anyone except his father.[140] But if the father managed to retake possession of the land by stealth before the 12 years had expired, the son could not recover his possession. This illustrates the inappropriateness of the shield and not a sword shibboleth when dealing with property interests. The estoppel should bar a resort to self help as well as bar an action in court.

The solution found by the judge also seems unsatisfactory in that the plaintiff could revoke the licence but was left without an adequate remedy. He was unable to evict the son by an equitable remedy and the judge seems to have ignored the point that trespass is a continuing tort which should have allowed the father to bring successive actions until the son left. It is also unclear why the judge held that the plaintiff was estopped from enforcing his title against M, but was not estopped from revoking the licence in the first place.

The suggestion of Kenny J that the son would acquire title under the Statute of Limitations after 12 years depends upon the possession of a licensee becoming adverse once the licence is revoked. Some doubt was cast on this in the

138 (1862) 4 De G F & J 517, 45 ER 1285.

139 (1866) LR 1 HL 129; See also *Sheridan v. Barrett* (1879) 4 LR Ir 223.

140 See Chapter 1 Introduction.

High Court in *Bellew v. Bellew*[141] but the *ratio decidendi* of the Supreme Court was that when a licence was revoked, or otherwise came to an end, the former licensee was from then on in adverse possession, and the licensee in that case was held to have acquired title under those circumstances.[142]

The shield but not a sword approach of *Cullen* has unfortunately been followed more recently in *McMahon v. Kerry C C.*[143] In 1964 the plaintiffs acquired a plot of land for the purpose of building a secondary school. The defendants, a local authority, had assented to this. Later the plaintiffs decided that it would not be feasible to build a school and abandoned their plan. They did not visit the site again until 1968 and discovered that employees of the defendant local authority were preparing to build on it. Upon complaint being made the work ceased. The plaintiffs never fenced or marked off the site. Beginning in 1972, the local authority built two houses on the site. In 1973, the plaintiffs discovered this situation and after some delay began proceedings to recover possession of the site. In the same year the local authority put tenants in the two houses. The plaintiffs claimed possession of the site and the houses. The local authority submitted that the court should exercise its equitable jurisdiction and refuse an order for possession in the circumstances. The judge quoted the passage in *Ramsden v. Dyson*[144] as to circumstances in which a person mistakenly erects buildings on land belonging to another:

> "If a stranger begins to build on my land supposing it to be his own and I perceiving his mistake abstain from setting him right and leave him to persevere in his error a Court of Equity will not allow me afterwards to assert my title to the land on which he had expended money on the supposition that the land was his own. It considers that when I saw the mistake into which he had fallen it was my duty to be active and to state my adverse title and that it would be dishonest in me to remain wilfully passive on such an occasion in order afterwards to profit by the mistake which I might have prevented.
>
> But it will be observed that to raise such an equity two things are required first that the person expending the money suppose himself to be building on his own land; and secondly, that the real owner at the time of the expenditure knows that the land belongs to him and not to the person expending the money in the belief that he is the owner. For if a stranger builds on my land knowing it to be mine, there is no principle of equity which would prevent my claiming the land with the benefit of all the expenditure made on it. There would be nothing in my conduct,

---

141 [1982] IR 447, McWilliam J:

> "I was also referred to *Hughes v. Griffin* ((1969) 1 WLR 23) and *Heslop v. Burns* ((1974) 1 WLR 1241) which establish that a person in occupation by permission, or as a licensee, cannot acquire title and that, where a person is allowed into occupation, the court will be slow to assume that a tenancy at will has been created and will normally assume that there has been a licence to occupy".

142 *Bellew v. Bellew* [1982] IR 447 at 454 per Griffin J.

143 [1981] ILRM 419, Finlay P.

144 (1866) LR 1 HL 129 at 140–41 per Lord Cranworth LC; See also *Sheridan v. Barrett* (1879) 4 LR Ir 223.

active or passive, making it inequitable in me to assert my legal rights".[145]

Finlay P admitted that the case before him fell into neither of the categories contained in the passage quoted. There was no question of the plaintiffs remaining wilfully passive when the defendants began to build on their land since he was satisfied on the evidence that the plaintiffs did not know of such building until December when they immediately made a complaint to the County Council. The judge went on to consider what, in his view, was "the real underlying principle" of the quoted statement in *Ramsden v. Dyson*[146]:

> "It is an enunciation of a principle of equity solely referable to the conduct of the plaintiff. If it were then it could not apply to this case and unless some other principle prevented the assertion by the plaintiff of his right to possession of the lands together with the value of these two houses on them he must succeed. Undoubtedly the first proposition dealing with the person who remains wilfully passive whilst another builds on his land is referable to the conduct of the plaintiff equity preventing him in effect from profiting by a conscious wrong. The very last sentence in the passage which I have quoted, would seem to suggest that the second category falls also into a consideration of the conduct of the plaintiff where the judgment states: 'There would be nothing in my conduct active or passive making it inequitable in me to assert my legal rights'.
>
> The example, however, of the case where the person may recover his land with the value of the building made by a stranger on it clearly provides 'if the stranger builds on my land knowing it to be mine'. It seems to me that the principles of equity stated in this passage depend not exclusively on the action or inaction of the plaintiff or on the state of his knowledge but have regard also to the action of the defendant.
>
> In the first case where the defendant is protected it is of course essential that he was innocent and in the second case where he is deprived of the buildings he has made it seems to be an essential constituent that he put them on the land of another knowing that it was the land of another and therefore either acting fraudulently or at least with knowledge of the risk he was running.
>
> If a court applying equitable principles is truly to act as a court of conscience then it seems to me unavoidable that it should consider not only conduct on the part of the plaintiff with particular regard to whether it is wrong or wilful but also conduct on the part of the defendant and further more the consequences and the justice of the consequences both from the point of view of the plaintiff and of the defendant".[147]

This passage indicates how close the judge came to detaching the principle from conduct on the part of the owner, and therefore how close he came to basing the decision on a theory of unjust enrichment. The judge then went on to list the factors which led him to conclude that it would be unjust to allow the plaintiffs to recover possession of the land. They were:

(1) the plaintiffs secured possession of the site for the express purpose of building a school, which purpose was never realised;

145 See also *East India Company v. Vincent* (1740) 2 Atk 83 at 84, 26 ER 451.

146 (1866) LR 1 HL 129; See also *Sheridan v. Barrett* (1879) 4 LR Ir 223.

147 [1981] ILRM 419 at 421.

(2) the plaintiffs never secured the site nor did they keep it under surveillance;

(3) there was no intrinsic value in the site so far as the plaintiffs were concerned;

(4) the defendants' mistake was excusable;

(5) if given possession the plaintiffs would realise a large profit without having expended any effort or money; and

(6) the houses were now in the occupation of needy persons.

The combination of these factors persuaded the judge that it would be unconscionable and unjust for the plaintiffs to recover possession. He held they were nevertheless entitled to the market value of the site, without the houses, and to damages. Citing *Cullen v. Cullen,*[148] the judge said that at the expiration of 12 years the defendants could apply to have themselves registered as owners of the plot. Thus he still appears to have taken the view that to order a transfer of the fee simple would go beyond the jurisdiction of the court.

If the plaintiffs had recovered possession of the land and title to the houses, they would have received a considerable benefit at public expense, but it is less easy to explain the decision in terms of legal principle. It was not, as the judge recognised, a case of mistake in which the owner, aware of the mistake and wilfully refrained from intervening until the houses had been built. As soon as they were aware of the situation the plaintiffs took action. The judge described the conduct of the defendant local authority as excusable even though they were well-placed to know the true position since they had approved the proposed use of the site and, as a local authority, had ready access to the relevant plans of the site. The judge emphasised the conduct of the plaintiffs and the fact that they had not kept the site under surveillance. The law does indeed provide that an owner may lose his or her rights by failing to pursue them, but that is only after the limitation period has expired, and here it had not done so. It is difficult to see why a mere lack of surveillance, in the absence of the requisite period of adverse possession, should lead to a loss of ownership. The case appears to stand for a new proposition, *i.e.* that in the mistake type of case an equity will be raised if an owner can be said to have contributed to the mistake by negligence in failing to demarcate the plot or failing to inspect it. Thus actual knowledge of a mistake is extended to something like constructive knowledge. It remains to be seen if later courts will extend proprietary estoppel in this way. A usual formulation of the doctrine today is to speak of encouragement of a belief or expectation. Can it really be said that the plaintiffs encouraged the mistaken belief of the local authority? A more justifiable solution might have been have been to leave it to the local authority to acquire the site by compulsory purchase. Had it done so, it is arguable that the plaintiffs might have been

148 [1962] IR 268, High Court, Kenny J.

estopped from claiming as compensation more than the value of the land before the buildings were erected.

More recently the Irish High Court has been more willing to accept proprietary estoppel as a sword. In *Haughan v. Rutledge*[149] the plaintiffs claimed that the defendant had encouraged them to believe that they would be granted a 20 year lease of the defendant's land on which to establish a horse racing track. Blayney J found there was no foundation for their belief, nor had the defendant done anything to create such an expectation. The plaintiff had merely been let into occupation on a trial basis for one year. The judge nevertheless cited with approval the often-quoted formulation of Lord Kingsdown in *Ramsden v. Dyson* and also the four conditions stated in the 28th edition of Snell's *Principles of Equity*[150] which he described as correct statement of the law and which were not disputed by counsel for the defendant. The four conditions are: (a) detriment, (b) expectation or belief, (c) encouragement, and (d) there must be no bar to the equity. He found that the claim failed to satisfy the second and third conditions. They could not have believed they were to obtain a 20 year lease since there had been no agreement for such a lease. They had also argued that even if no definite interest had been agreed, so that the matter had been left vague, they nevertheless believed that they would obtain some interest. Blayney J rejected this because none of them had testified to any belief other than that they were to get a lease for 20 years. Neither had the plaintiff encouraged any such belief. The judge quoted Lord Cranworth LC in *Ramsden v. Dyson*[151] to the effect that:

> "It follows as a corollary from these rules, or, perhaps it would be more accurate to say that it forms part of them, that if my tenant builds on land which he hold under me, he does not thereby, in the absence of special circumstances, acquire any right to prevent me taking possession of the lands and buildings when the tenancy has determined.
>
> He knew the extent of his interest, and it was his folly to expend money upon a title which he knew would or might soon come to an end".[152]

The judge said that in his view that statement of the law applied in the present case. The judge found no special circumstances in the case. The difficulty here is that if the more extensive work in making a permanent track was to be regarded as compensation for past use of the land, then there was no need to consider whether it was performed in expectation of an interest in the land in future. On the other hand, if it cannot be explained in this way it becomes difficult to resist the conclusion that some expectation was created since the landowner had agreed to the revision of the term. It was also possible that any

149 [1988] IR 295, Blayney J.

150 Snell (1982) at p.558.

151 (1866) LR 1 HL 129.

152 *ibid.* at p.141.

letting would have been void under section 12 of the Land Act, 1965.[153] Blayney J did not consider that this would put the party expending money in any better position. "If the landlord is entitled to possession on the termination of the tenancy", he commented, "he must equally be entitled to possession when it is discovered that there never was a tenancy at all". This would also seem to come within the fourth of Snell's conditions: if the section made void a tenancy it would also probably make void an interest which would otherwise arise by proprietary estoppel.

In *Re JR, a Ward of Court*[154] JR, who suffered from mental illness, was made a ward of court and a committee appointed of his person and estate. He later entered a mental hospital for treatment. While there he formed a relationship with the respondent, a female temporary patient in the hospital. JR invited her to go and live with him in his house and told her that he would look after her and that she would be sure of a home for the rest of her life. The respondent moved into JR's house. The judge had no evidence before him of where she was living at the time she was admitted to the hospital and met JR, but held that the court was entitled to assume she had a house or flat which she had given up in order to move in with JR. In 1988 JR made a will leaving all his property to the respondent. He handed the will to her saying "it is not my house now: it's our house and eventually it will be your house". The couple lived in the house for another two years. JR, who was then 71 years old, was readmitted to hospital as his mental health had deteriorated and it was found that he would need institutional care for the rest of his life. The respondent continued to live in the house which had fallen into an advanced state of disrepair. The committee of JR sought an order for sale of the house to pay for medical and other expenses. The respondent claimed she had an interest in the premises due to representations made by JR.

Costello J in the High Court held that the respondent had established an estoppel as she had acted to her detriment on JR's representations at the time he invited her to stay in his house. The judge found, citing *Maharaj v. Chand*[155] that the detriment consisted of her leaving her existing home on the faith of the assurance that she would have another in its place. The judge found that the respondent had an equity in the house on the basis that it would be inequitable for JR to deny that she had a right to live in his house rent free for as long as she wished. It was then for the court to decide how that equity was to be satisfied. The judge found that it would be unreasonable to authorise the use of JR's meagre resources to put the house in good repair, which he estimated would cost about £34,000. The judge ordered that the house be sold provided

153 This forbids subdivision of agricultural land without the consent of the Minister (formerly the Irish Land Commission).

154 [1993] ILRM 657.

155 [1986] AC 898.

that another dwelling suitable to the respondent's needs be purchased in JR's name in which the respondent would be free to live as long as she wished.

In coming to his decision the judge found that the respondent did not acquire a distinct interest by virtue of the representations made by JR in 1988 and the fact of his handing her his will because (a) the respondent had not acted on them to her detriment and (b) JR had not intended to give her expressly an immediate beneficial interest because had he done so he would have transferred the house to her or to them both jointly. He intended only that she should have "a right to reside in the house during his life" and secondly, ownership of it after his death. The respondent had nevertheless acquired an equity by "promissory estoppel" at the time she moved in.[156] In arriving at this decision the judge distinguished between promissory and proprietary estoppel. Speaking of promissory estoppel he said:

> "If the subject matter of the representation is land, no right or interest in the land results from this estoppel – a personal right is vested in the representee which will preclude the representor from enforcing a title to the land. A proprietary estoppel is different in a number of ways. When it relates to land it may result in the creation of rights in or over land".[157]

The judge cited *Re Basham*[158] and *Greasley v. Cook*[159] as examples of the latter. The judge clearly considered the case before him to be one of promissory estoppel. This seems to be because he considered that the remedy he awarded created a personal licence and not a property interest. In fact there is nothing in the judgment to indicate that there was any other difference in the judge's view between the two doctrines, in which case there is little difference at all. No third parties were involved and so a property interest was probably not necessary to secure the respondent's position until JR's death, when she would in any case acquire one under the will. However, she had acquired by the estoppel something in the nature of a personal licence which, on the *Ashburn* principle, could give rise to a constructive trust binding on third parties during JR's life.

The case is novel in that it decides that the personal licence is available not only against the property originally occupied in response to the representation, but attaches to property to be acquired later by the representor and this was no doubt an appropriate remedy on the facts. However, merely because the judge decided that the minimum equity necessary on the facts of the case was a personal licence should not have led to the estoppel being classified as promissory.[160] It would be more flexible to regard the estoppel as raising an equity of an indeterminate kind and the issue of how it is to be satisfied on the facts to

156 [1993] ILRM 657.

157 *ibid.* at 663.

158 [1986] 1 WLR 1498.

159 [1980] 1 WLR 1306. See below.

160 It may be noted that the case widens the definition of promissory estoppel since there was no prior contractual relationship between the parties.

determine whether a personal licence would be sufficient or some interest of a proprietary nature binding on third parties. It is also not easy to see why JR's statement in 1988 that "it is not my house now: it's our house" was not a declaration of trust. The ghost of *Cullen* may still have been evident.

In *Reidy v. McGreevy*[161] the plaintiff stayed at home and worked his father's lands between 1962 and 1969, and again for approximately a year, prior to his father's death. He claimed that on both occasions he did so as the result of promises by his father that if he did so, he, *i.e.* the father, would exercise a special power of appointment vested in him in favour of the plaintiff. The father died leaving his own property to his widow, the mother of the plaintiff, and exercised the power of appointment in favour of his widow and his three daughters. The plaintiff claimed, *inter alia,* that the committee of the widow and the daughters held the property which was the subject of the power of appointment on trust for him. In the present proceedings the issue was, *inter alia,* whether the claim was statute barred. Barron J referred to the decision in *Re JR* and continued:

> "Where it would be unconscionable to disregard a promise such as that alleged here, the Court will declare the existence of a constructive trust. The question which arises here is whether such a claim is one available against the promisor and so capable of being barred after the lapse of two years from the date of his death".

Barron J therefore seems to have regarded *Re JR* as an example of a constructive trust, even though, as we have seen, the judge in the case itself referred to it as promissory estoppel. Barron J continued:

> "The nature and extent of the claim is dependent upon the facts. What may be unconscionable upon one set of facts may not be upon another set. So, depending upon the facts, the Plaintiff may be entitled to an estate in the property; to a charge over it; or to nothing. But whatever the facts, the claim could not be maintained until the death of the testator because it could not have been ascertained until then that he had failed to honour his promise. Of course, if he had repudiated his promise during his life-time, this would have given rise to a cause of action at that stage. That, however, is not the case here".

In other words, since the breach of the promise alleged in the case consisted of the failure to exercise the power in the plaintiff's favour, that had not ocurred until the testator's death and was not barred. The *obiter dictum* is also an interesting one, since it asserts that liability may arise in estoppel, or constructive trust, if a promise or expectation, which has been relied upon, is departed from by an anticipatory breach.

In *Smyth v. Halpin*[162] Geoghegan J in the Irish High Court went further than previous Irish cases in giving effect to the doctrine of proprietary estoppel. The father, who owned a house and farm, made a will in which he

161 Unreported, High Court, Barron J, 19 March 1993.

162 [1997] ILRM 38.

had left the property to his wife for life with remainder to the plaintiff, his son, subject to the rights of his two daughters who were each to be entitled to chose a half-acre pot on which to build a house. The plaintiff became engaged to be married and asked his father for some land on which to build a house. The father replied that 'this place is yours after you mother's day – what would you be doing with two places?'. The father then suggested that the plaintiff build an extension to the family home. It was designed by an architect who took into account that the plaintiff would eventually own the whole house. The site on which the extension was to be built was conveyed to the plaintiff so that he could use it as security to for a loan to finance the extension. The extension was built. In a later will the father left the land to his wife for life with remainder to plaintiff absolutely, and the house to his wife for life with remainder to one of the plaintiff's sisters absolutely. The father died. The plaintiff sought a declaration that he was entitled to the remainder interest in the house after the life estate. Geoghegan J, citing *Dillwyn v. Llewelyn*[163] and *Pascoe v. Turner*[164] granted the declaration and ordered the execution of a conveyance transferring the remainder to the plaintiff. The case is important in that it held in Ireland (a) that the equity raised may require the conveyance of the legal fee simple, and (b) that the doctrine may displace a will.[165]

While there appears to be a lack of consensus among the judges in Ireland as to the recognition of proprietary estoppel, it can be argued that even those judges who have characterised cases before them as examples of promissory estoppel, in pursuing their intuitive feel for the just result, have in fact gone beyond estoppel as a mere defence. Kenny J in *Cullen*, while rejecting the notion that the wife had acquired a proprietary interest in the land, nevertheless took the view that she was entitled to monetary compensation for the work done in running the business. This is surely going beyond estoppel as a mere defence. It entitled her to a remedy, and therefore was a cause of action. Costello J in *JR* surely went further than holding that the respondent could only use the estoppel to defend her present possession. It gave her an equity to a new possession in a new house to be purchased, admittedly out of JR's funds and in his name, but suitable for her needs.

In *McCarron v. McCarron*[166] the Supreme Court took a step nearer a full recognition of the principle. The plaintiff in that case helped the deceased with the management and operation of his farms over a period of 16 years, since the deceased had an accident which limited his mobility. The plaintiff's late father was a first cousin of the deceased. The plaintiff claimed that the deceased had entered into a contract with him to remunerate him for the work he did on the

163 (1862) 4 De G F & J 517, 45 ER 1285.

164 [1979] 1 WLR 431, [1979] 2 All ER 945. See below.

165 In *Re Basham* [1986] 1 WLR 1498, below, the promisor died intestate.

166 Unreported, Supreme Court, 13 February 1997, (Hamilton CJ, Keane, Murphy JJ).

farm by leaving the farm to him by will, or that the farm, and sought specific performance of it. In the alternative he claimed he was entitled to the farm by proprietary estoppel. The defendant did not plead the absence of any note or memorandum in writing as required by the Statute of Frauds, 1695. Little discussion took place between the plaintiff and the deceased as to the form of remuneration. On one occasion the deceased had asked whether he, the plaintiff, was wondering about some compensation for his work and the plaintiff replied "I suppose I will not be forgotten" to which the deceased responded: "Well, you will be a rich man after my day". At a later date the deceased said that he would soon have to take to a wheelchair and that he wanted the plaintiff to look after him and that he and the plaintiff's father would draw up "some class of an agreement". The plaintiff replied: "I will not put you out of house or home, George" and the deceased replied: "Right, we will leave it at that". The trial judge held that the contract had been proved and the action succeeded on that basis. Murphy J in the Supreme Court commented:

> "What is noticeable from the transcript and in particular the evidence of the Plaintiff was that natural courtesy (which John Millington Synge associated with the west of Ireland) which often results in an unwillingness to pursue discussion to a logical and perhaps harshly expressed commercial conclusion. In other parts of Ireland the concept of a person working long hours over a period of four years before any discussion takes place in relation to remuneration or reward might be unthinkable... I would merely conclude that in some, particularly rural areas, a meeting of minds can be achieved without as detailed discussion as might be necessary elsewhere".

He found that such nuances should be left to the trial judge. The Supreme Court therefore upheld High Court order for specific performance and did not have to decide the issue of proprietary estoppel. Murphy J nevertheless commented:

> "If successfully invoked this doctrine would permit the Plaintiff to claim in equity an estate in the lands of the Deceased irrespective of any testamentary disposition by the latter".

He then went on to cite *Plimmer v. Wellington Corporation*[167] and continued:

> "In principle I see no reason why the doctrine should be confined to the expenditure of money or the erection of premises on the lands of another. In a suitable case it may well be argued that a plaintiff suffers as severe a loss or detriment by providing his own labours or services in relation to the lands of another and accordingly should equally qualify for recognition in equity. In practice, however, it might be difficult to determine the extent of the estate or interest in land for which a plaintiff might qualify as a result of his personal efforts. Perhaps a claim of that nature would be adequately compensated by a charge or lien on the lands for a sum equivalent to reasonable remuneration for the services rendered".

We shall now consider some individual aspects of the doctrine.

167 [1884] 9 AC 699.

2. Elements

a) Detriment

Some judges have treated the requirement of detriment in proprietary estoppel as if it were the same as detriment in the doctrine of consideration in the law of contract, *i.e.* as if it required some actual expenditure of money, or money's worth, the value of which would be lost if no corresponding benefit were received.[168] This restricted sense of detriment, however, fails to address the different basis of proprietary estoppel and has proved inadequate to reach the number of situations in which the estoppel requires a remedy.

Several cases indicate that more recently judges have preferred to use the term prejudice[169] or change of position[170] to detriment. Dixon J in the High Court of Australia in *Grundt v. Great Boulder Property Gold Mines Ltd*[171] expressed it as follows:

> "... the real detriment or harm from which the law seeks to give protection is that which would flow from the change of position if the assumption were deserted that led to it. So long as the assumption is adhered to, the party who altered his situation upon the faith of it cannot complain. His complaint is that when afterwards the other party makes a different state of affairs the basis of an assertion of right against him then, if it is allowed, his own original change of position will operate as detriment".[172]

Brennan J in *Waltons Stores (Interstate) Ltd v. Maher*[173] also used detriment in the same sense when he defined the doctrine as applying where the party relying on the expectation "would suffer detriment if the assumption were not adhered to". In the contract sense any expenditure of money can be said to be a detriment, because it is a sufficient consideration. This detriment is then compensated for by the other party performing, or promising to perform, their part of the bargain. In the situations in which proprietary estoppel has been held to apply, on the other hand, there may be no detriment in the contract sense at all, but a detriment would occur if the other party were allowed to enforce their legal rights because the relior would then be worse off than if they had not relied on the assurance.

---

168 *Ramsden v. Dyson* (1866) LR 1 HL 129 at 170; *Willmott v. Barber* 1880) 15 Ch D 96 at 105f, see the second of Fry J's five tests of estoppel.

169 *Watts v. Story* [1983] CAT 319, (Transcript: Lexis), Slade J.

170 *E R Ives Investments Ltd v. High* [1967] 2 QB 379 at 405 F per Winn LJ; *Re Basham, dec'd* [1986] 1 WLR 1498 at 1504 D; *Bhimji v. Salih* unreported, Court of Appeal, 4 February 1981 (Lexis) per Brightman LJ; *Grundt v. Great Boulder Pty Gold Mines Ltd* (1937) 59 CLR 641 at 674.

171 (1937) 59 CLR 641.

172 *ibid.* at p.674.

173 (1987) 164 CLR 387, High Court of Australia.

These points were brought into focus in *Greasley v. Cook*.[174] The defendant, C, claimed a declaration that she had the right to occupy a house rent-free for life. She had come to live in the house at the age of 16 as a live-in maid. The owner was a widower with four children. At first she was paid a weekly wage, but after eight years she began a relationship with K, one of the sons of the owner. For the next 30 years she looked after various members of the family, including a mentally handicapped daughter of the owner. She received no wages during this long period. C gave evidence that she had not asked for payment because she had been encouraged by members of the family, including one of the present plaintiffs, to believe that she could look upon the house as her home for the rest of her life. When both the owner and K died other family members brought the present proceedings to evict her. The county court judge refused to find proprietary estoppel on the ground that she had not expended money on the property. This decision was reversed by the Court of Appeal. Lord Denning MR held that expenditure was not essential for estoppel:

> "It is sufficient if the party, to whom the assurance is given, acts on the faith of it – in such circumstances that it would be unjust and inequitable for the party making the assurance to go back on it. . . it can be seen that the assurances [given by K and his brother] – leading her to believe that she would be allowed to stay in the house as long as she wished – raised an equity in her favour. There is no need for her to prove that she acted on the faith of those assurances. It is to be presumed that she did so. There is no need for her to prove that she acted to her detriment or to her prejudice. Suffice it that she stayed on in the house – looking after [K and the daughter] – when otherwise she might have left and got a job elsewhere. The equity having thus been raised in her favour, it is for the courts of equity to decide in what way that equity should be satisfied. In this case it should be by allowing her to stay on in the house as long as she wishes".[175]

However satisfactory the result in *Greasley*, the treatment of the issue of conduct and detriment is less convincing. The judge appears to create a presumption in favour of both when, in the sense used by the judge, neither were present. The defendant did not act" in reliance on the expectation of residential security. She did nothing. Yet that was precisely the behaviour which such an expectation was likely to produce. She was, to use the cliché, lulled into a sense of false security. Had she not been under the impression that she would have been able to stay in the house for the rest of her life she might have made some financial provision for her accommodation after retirement. She might have revived her claim to be paid wages. The detriment therefore consisted of the circumstance that if the court did not give her a remedy she would have been worse off than if the expectation had not been created. But a proper analysis would show that this is what detriment amounts to in proprietary estoppel in general. It is not an immediate detriment suffered while the factual situation is

174 [1980] 1 WLR 1306.

175 [1980] 1 WLR 1306 at 1311f.

developing, but one that would only arise if the party creating the expectation is allowed to depart from it. The detriment in *Greasley* was the same as in any other case involving the doctrine. It was the reliance which was negative.

This is not to say that there is no problem of proof in cases of negative reliance. What a person might do, or might have done, or been forced to do, cannot be proved in the same way as what they did in fact do. But a court can still be persuaded that a person desisted from conduct, of even failed to consider it at all, because of assurances they had been given. It should also be noted that the editor of Snell in formulating the first of the conditions specified that the person claiming "must have incurred expenditure or otherwise have prejudiced himself or acted to his detriment".[176]

It may also be the case that in the mistake type of case, where the conduct on the part of the property owner is of a negative or inactive kind, reliance in the form of expenditure of money may be required to raise the equity. It is, after all, difficult to imagine circumstances in which an equity would be raised by a person acquiescing in another doing nothing. But this is arguably still a question of reliance. In such a case the reliance is that of the mistaken party relying on their own mistaken view of their rights, a reliance fortified by the knowing failure of the property owner to correct it.

If this is so, a further question arises as to the necessary elements in prejudice. Does it imply an element of irrevocability? In *Greasley* it was too late for the old lady to make provision for accommodation by the time she was given notice to quit. That was why it would be inequitable to deny her a remedy. There is one suggestion in the Irish authorities that irrevocability may be an element in the conduct of the relior. In *Cullen* Kenny J found that there was no equity in favour of the mother because she could readily reimburse herself for the money she had spent in running the business. Nevertheless, it may simply depend on what a court sees as necessary to satisfy the equity. It may be that in some cases even though the relior could be compensated or could recover their position in other ways, the equity would not be satisfied short of a property interest.

b) Reliance

Proprietary estoppel is often formulated in terms of reliance on an assurance to the detriment of the relior. Reliance has thus been sometimes treated as a separate element in the doctrine to detriment. We have argued here that problems which have been perceived as one of detriment may really be problems of reliance. It is the act of reliance, or failure to act induced by reliance on the assurance, which gives rise to the equity. A party relies on an assurance or a mistaken impression of their rights when they alter their position on the faith of the assurance or impression emanating from the other party, or desist from

176 See above, footnote 150.

some course of action which they would otherwise have undertaken in the absence of such an assurance or impression and this action or lack of it means that they would be worse off than if no such assurance or impression had been created or encouraged.

c) Expectation or Belief

The doctrine of proprietary estoppel has frequently been invoked when the estoppee has acted in some way to induce an expectation or belief in the other party that they are to have, or do have, some property interest.[177] We have seen that in *McMahon v. Kerry County Council*[178] there was no element of wilful knowledge of a mistaken belief in the owner of the land. If the case is to be explained in terms of what it decided about the conduct of the owner of the land then it can only be justified by accepting that negligence in discovering that a mistake has been made is sufficient to deprive an owner of his or her land. It stands for the proposition that the price of ownership is eternal vigilance.

3. Third Parties

The estoppel, or perhaps more accurately the equity raised by the estoppel, binds not only the original estoppee whose conduct gave rise to it, but also third parties who would be bound in equity, namely all those except a bona fide purchaser of the legal estate without notice of the equity.

In *Re Basham*[179] the plaintiff lived at her step-father's house since she was 15 until her marriage. She helped her mother and step-father run the step-father's business. She was never paid for this but understood that she would inherit the deceased's property when he died. The deceased purchased a tenanted cottage with money provided largely by the plaintiff's mother. When the mother died the deceased moved into the cottage which had become vacant. He told the plaintiff that the cottage was hers. The plaintiff and her family lived near the deceased and the plaintiff's husband provided food for him, kept the garden in order and helped the plaintiff with work about the house. The plaintiff bought carpets for it and laid them herself and regularly prepared meals for him. She was told by the deceased that she would lose nothing by doing those acts for him. A few days before his death the deceased indicated that he wanted to make a will leaving money to the plaintiff's son and that she was to have his house. The deceased died intestate and the plaintiff claimed a declaration against the administrators of his estate, that she was absolutely and beneficially entitled to the house and other property. The English Chancery Division held that she was entitled to the declaration.

177 For the position in estoppel by representation see *Doran v. Thompson* [1978] IR 223.

178 [1981] ILRM 419.

179 [1986] 1 WLR 1498.

The point that the equity raised by the estoppel binds the personal representatives of the estoppee had already been decided by *Inwards v. Baker*,[180] but the implications of *Re Basham,*[181] rather than what it actually decided, are intriguing. The cases make it clear that although the doctrine raises an equity the equity may in some circumstances only be satisfied by the conferment of a legal estate. This was the case in *Pascoe v. Turner*,[182] in which the man was ordered to convey the legal fee simple to the widow. In that case no third party was involved. In *Re Basham*[183] a third party was involved, but one who would have been bound in equity in any case. Nevertheless, the situation could arise in which the third party involved was not someone who would be bound in equity, but only if the interest conferred was a legal estate, *i.e.* a purchaser of the legal estate without notice. Would a court order such a party to convey the legal estate to the relior in order to satisfy the equity? If, in *Pascoe v. Turner*,[184] the man had conveyed the legal estate to a third party and the third party had tried to evict the widow, would the widow have succeeded?

In *Re Sharpe (A Bankrupt)*[185] these issues were brought into focus. J was an elderly woman. She had contributed much of the purchase price of a lease in a shop and maisonette bought by her nephew, S. In order to increase her contribution, J had sold her existing home and had moved into the maisonette with S and his wife on the understanding that she would be able to remain there for as long as she wished. S later became bankrupt. J, acting on her solicitor's advice, then obtained a promissory note from S for £15,700. S's trustee in bankruptcy contracted to sell the lease to a purchaser, P, with vacant possession. When S's trustee in bankruptcy sought vacant possession, J argued that she had an interest in the premises. Browne-Wilkinson J declined to hold that she had an equitable interest by way of what he termed a resulting trust, and held that the money contributed by her was primarily intended to be a loan. He took the promissory note to be evidence of this. She had "something less than an aliquot share of the equity in the premises" which was the right to remain in occupation until the loan was repaid. Referring to *Ramsden v. Dyson,*[186] he went on:

> "Recent authorities have extended this doctrine and, in my judgment, it is now established that, if the parties have proceeded on a common assumption that the plaintiff is to enjoy a right to reside in a particular property and in reliance on that assumption the plaintiff has expended money or otherwise acted to his detriment, the defendant will not be allowed to go back on that common assump-

---

180 [1965] 2 QB 29. Or was it the licence which bound them? See above.

181 [1986] 1 WLR 1498.

182 [1979] 1 WLR 431, [1979] 2 All ER 945. See above.

183 [1986] 1 WLR 1498.

184 [1979] 1 WLR 431, [1979] 2 All ER 945. See above.

185 [1980] 1 WLR 219. See G. Woodman, (1980) 96 LQR 336; J. Martin, [1980] Conv 207.

186 (1866) LR 1 HL 129 at p.141.

> tion and the court will imply an irrevocable licence or trust which will give effect to that common assumption."[187]

He held that the right, "whether it be called a contractual licence or an equitable licence or an interest under a constructive trust", was binding not only upon S but also upon a S's trustee in bankruptcy, who was essentially in the same position as S. This was sufficient to dispose of the issue before the court, but the judge was clearly concerned as to whether the right would be binding on P. He observed that P would not necessarily be bound by it "as a purchaser without express notice" and that he might take priority over it if he sued for specific performance of the contract. The judge clearly did not find this satisfactory, since if it were to occur J's right would be at an end and she would be left with only the right to sue S who was, in any case, bankrupt. The judge said that he found this area of the law "very confused and difficult to fit in with established equitable principles". He expressed the hope that the whole question would soon receive full consideration in the Court of Appeal, so that, "in order to do justice to the many thousands of people who never come into court at all but who wish to know with certainty what their proprietary rights are, the extent to which these irrevocable licences bind third parties may be defined with certainty".

Re Sharpe illustrates the problems which arise in this area of the law where the doctrines of proprietary estoppel, constructive trust and, at least in this case, contractual licence, overlap. Was the issue in *Re Sharpe* as to the circumstances in which:

(a) a contractual licence binds third parties? or

(b) a third party is bound as constructive trustee? or

(c) the equity raised by proprietary estoppel binds third parties?

The judge seems far from clear. The doctrines are liable to intersect and become confused where, as in this case, the result of applying proprietary estoppel is to find that the equity so created should be satisfied by a licence, especially if it is termed, oddly, a contractual licence.[188] The problem was compounded by the judge apparently holding that the equity raised by proprietary estoppel can only be satisfied by a licence or a trust. The issue will have to be disentangled from the quite separate issue of the extent to which a contractual or occupational licence can be binding on third parties. It has been seen that in *Ashburn Anstalt v. Arnold*[189] Fox LJ in the English Court of Appeal suggested, as an alternative *ratio*, that a contractual licence is not binding on third parties

187 [1980] 1 WLR 219 at 223.

188 The equity arising under proprietary estoppel may be satisfied by a licence, but it is hardly contractual. If there was a contract it would not be necessary to invoke proprietary estoppel.

189 [1989] Ch. 1, [1988] 2 WLR 706, [1988] 23 EG 128.

in the absence of a constructive trust. But the court arrived at this conclusion having already held that a contractual licence was not an equitable interest in itself. Hence, a third party was not bound merely by notice of it. However, the equity raised by proprietary estoppel is not to be confused with the further interest which an owner may be required to convey as a result of it, whether by way of licence or fee simple or something else. The equity raised by proprietary estoppel is, it is submitted, an equitable interest and as such should bind third parties with notice of it. It will, of course, be necessary to decide what degree of knowledge or constructive knowledge the third party must have in order that the test of notice is satisfied. It is suggested tentatively that it should be a knowledge of all the elements which gave rise to the proprietary estoppel, unless the relior is in occupation, in which case that fact should put the third party on notice.

E. Constructive Trusts

There are a number of instances of the constructive trust, some based upon older and some on newer and expanding doctrinal categories. Constructive trusts can be categorised as arising:

(1) In Ireland, where there is no existing trust but there is an existing fiduciary relationship. In Ireland there is a general principle to the effect that no one in a fiduciary position may benefit from it. This is known as the doctrine of graft. It not only applies to trustees but to other fiduciary relationships as well. This means that it does not only apply, strictly, where there is an existing trust.[190] The doctrine applies to executors,[191] administrators,[192] guardians of minors,[193] committees of mental patients,[194] limited owners, *i.e.* persons having less than a fee simple estate,[195] agents,[196] tenants in common,[197] mortgagees,[198] and solicitors.[199] Perhaps for this reason it has always been seen in Ireland

---

190 Wylie, *Irish Land Law* paras. 9.063-9.067.

191 *McCracken v. McClelland* [1877] IR 11 Eq 172; *Re Egan* [1906] 1 IR 320.

192 *Gabbett v. Lawder* (1883) 11 LR Ir 295.

193 *Quinton v. Frith* (1868) IR 2 Eq 494.

194 *Smythe v. Byrne* [1914] 11 IR 53.

195 *O'Brien v. Egan* (1880) 5 LR Ir 633; *Robinson v. Crosse & Blackwell Ltd* [1940] IR 56; *O'Donnell v. Grogan* [1941] IR 557. The terminology is used in the Land Purchase Acts.

196 *Patten v. Hamilton* [1911] 1 IR 46.

197 *Hunter v. Allen* [1907] 1 IR 212.

198 *Nesbitt v. Tredennick* (1808) 1 Ba & B 29, 12 RR 1.

199 *Lawless v. Mansfield* (1841) Dru & War 557; *Atkins v. Delmege* (1847) 12 Ir Eq R 1.

as an example of the constructive trust.[200] In England the doctrine is not known by the name of graft and is simply part of the doctrine of constructive trusts.[201] The leading English case is *Keech v. Sandford*.[202] It is questionable whether there are any significant differences between the Irish and English doctrines, although the doctrine in Ireland has found expression in statute law for specific purposes.[203]

(2) Where there is an existing trust and:

(a) a trustee, or trustees, convey the legal title to a third party, equity will treat the third party as holding the property on trust unless the third party can make the plea of bona fide purchaser for value of the legal estate without notice of the equity. This we have called the proprietary remedy against third parties, or

(b) if a third party has not actually received the trust property, or has received it but has subsequently parted with it, equity will hold the third party personally liable as a constructive trustee if he or she has been a party to a fraudulent use of trust property or has knowingly interfered with it in other ways inconsistent with the trust. This we have called the personal remedy against third parties. In both these instances there is an existing trust, which for the sake of clarity we shall for the moment assume is an express trust. The more controversial question is as to when a court will find there to be a trust even though there is no express trust to begin with.

(3) Where there is no existing trust but the court finds something in

(a) the conduct of a party, or

(b) in the circumstances

which makes it inequitable for the party concerned to be immune from liability or to retain a benefit from property. This a large and expanding category.

---

200 See Chatterton V-C in *Gabbett v. Lawder* (1883) 11 LR Ir 295 at 299; Wylie, *Cases* p.385.

201 Underhill and Hayton, (14th ed.) Chapter 7 Article 33 pp. 301–325.

202 (1726) Sel Cas Ch 61, Cas t King 61, 25 ER 223, 2 Eq Cas Abr 741, 22 ER 629.

203 The Land Law (Ireland) Act, 1887 s.14(3) provides that any tenant has power to enter into an agreement for purchase of the holding and any interest conveyed to the tenant under such an agreement is "shall be deemed to be a graft on the previous interest of the tenant" in the holding. See also now the Landlord and Tenant (Amendment) Act, 1980 s.74 which applies to a person entitled to an interest in land "the title to which interest originated under a lease for lives renewable forever which was created prior to the 1st day of August 1849 and was not converted into a fee farm grant". Section 74 provides that such a person "shall from the commencement of this Act hold the land for an estate in fee simple" and that "the said estate shall be deemed to be a graft upon the previous interest". See Chapter 9 Life Estates. Under Section 39 of Landlord and Tenant (Amendment) Act, 1980 a reversionary lease is a graft on the previous lease. See Chapter 20 Statutory Control and Enlargement of Tenancies.

An orthodox view of common law jurisdictions is to the effect that type 3(a) has long been recognised in North America while the English courts have tended to limit the constructive trust to 3(b). In the North American model the constructive trust is seen as a general remedial device, rather than an institution. It is a solution which judges impose on situations which are impossible to categorise, rather than a concept which can be seen to arise on the basis of some special set of facts common to the instances in which the trust has been found to exist. The North American model imposes a constructive trust wherever it would be unjust for the holder of the legal title to property to take all its benefits: it is a theory of unjust enrichment, a separate head of liability, distinct from contract or tort, but just as important. As Cardozo J put it:

> "When property has been acquired in such circumstances that the holder of the legal title may not in good conscience retain the beneficial interest, equity converts him into a trustee".[204]

The English model on the other hand is said to fall short of a general theory of unjust enrichment. Where there is no existing trust an English court will find a constructive trust where the legal owner of property has created an expectation that the other party will have some interest in the property and where the other party has acted to his or her detriment in reliance on that expectation. How real these limitations of conduct, reliance, and detriment are remains to be seen. At this point the doctrine of constructive trust overlaps with the doctrine of proprietary estoppel and licences.

In Ireland the category 3(a) can be seen as a development of the doctrine of graft in that there is an existing relationship between the parties, not in itself a trust, which has the character of making it inequitable for one party to benefit from money or property contributed by another. Finally, an existing trust in (1) and (2) above should be understood to include not only an express trust, but all other types of trust including a constructive trust, so that if a trust is found under head (3) above, the principles in (1) and (2) will apply to it also.

In fact the North American versus the English approaches are not as distinct, or as easily distinguished as the description suggests. First, the institution/remedy distinction is not particularly helpful, since it is difficult to avoid the conclusion that even if the constructive trust is not extended beyond cases of reliance it has a remedial character in such cases since the parties did not expressly or impliedly create a trust themselves. Secondly, there has been a tendency in the English case law recently in the direction of using the constructive trust as a general remedy in cases which cannot be defined in terms of reliance, or only by artificial reasoning. On the other hand, English courts have treated an owner as a constructive trustee on the basis of events or circumstances which have occurred after the owner has acquired the legal estate, *e.g.* the reliance cases, a situation not covered by Cardozo's classic statement of the

---

204 *Beatty v. Guggenheim Exploration Co* (1919) 225 NY 380 at 386.

American model. It is in this latter type of situation that the concept of the constructive trust more usually overlaps with the concept of licence. The starting point of the more general approach in England is the judgment of Lord Diplock in the House of Lords in *Gissing v. Gissing*[205]:

> "A resulting, implied or constructive trust - and it is unnecessary for present purposes to distinguish between these three classes of trust - is created by a transaction between the trustee and the *cestui que trust* in connection with the acquisition by the trustee of a legal estate in land, whenever the trustee has so conducted himself that it would be inequitable to allow him to deny to the *cestui que trust* a beneficial interest in the land acquired. . . ".[206]

This is a general statement of principle resembling Cardozo's formula, although the reference to conduct is more limiting. Both statements, it may be noticed, confine the principle to situations in which the person who is later held to be a trustee is in the process of acquiring an interest in land. Nevertheless, referring more specifically to the case before him, the judge went on to formulate a more limited rule. A person, he said:

> ". . . will be held so to have conducted himself if by his words or conduct he has induced the *cestui que trust* to act to his own detriment in the reasonable belief that by so acting he was acquiring a beneficial interest in the land".[207]

The specific case before the court concerned indirect financial contributions by a wife to the discharge of a mortgage on the matrimonial home, the legal title to which was vested in the husband alone. The wife had paid for items of general household expenditure over a period of 25 years, so enabling the husband to devote his income to paying the mortgage instalments. The majority of the court, Lord Diplock included, found that the wife had failed to produce evidence of the kind such as would be required by the narrow rule stated above. There would have to be some evidence, if not of an agreement between them, then at least that they had consciously contemplated the legal consequences of their respective contributions in relation to the house, and this evidence was lacking. There was no evidence of special facts connecting the wife's payments with the acquisition of the house.

The decision in *Gissing v. Gissing* is open to the criticism that it failed to deal justly with the wife's claim. It is also arguable that this failure is caused by imposing an unrealistic test on the facts. Persons sharing a house in a degree of intimacy do not calculate precisely the advantage they will obtain from some monetary detriment. But it has been pointed out that this does not mean that their dealings are entire altruistic or without any thought of return.[208]

---

205 [1971] AC 886.

206 [1971] AC 886 at 905.

207 *ibid.*

208 Gray & Symes, (1981) p.472-473; W.J. Goode, "The Resistance of Family Forces to Industrialisation" in Eekelaar & Katz (1980), xiv.

Each expenditure may not be gauged against an expected benefit soon to be obtained. Reciprocity is not sought immediately but rather over a whole series of transactions and over many years. But the very intimacy of the relationships involved ensures that these assumptions remain unexpressed and unspoken. Neither party expects to make all the sacrifices while the other takes all the benefits. If such is the case, then the relationship is one which is likely to break down over time. If it does not, then it is because one party has accepted an inherently inferior position. On this issue the law necessarily has to take a position. The court in *Gissing*, while no doubt correctly rejecting the notion that parties to such a relationship operate on the immediate *quid pro quo* found in market transactions, assumed that no reciprocity was to be expected in the more subtle domestic sense either.

Since *Gissing* English law has developed beyond the narrow rule in (3) above and in the hands of Lord Denning the constructive trust may have become more extensive than the American model.

In *Cook v. Head*[209] Lord Denning MR stated the equitable treatment of domestic situations in these terms:

> "... whenever parties by their joint efforts acquire property to be used for their joint benefit, the courts may impose or imputed a constructive or resulting trust".[210]

Lord Denning considered that the constructive trust doctrine applied generally to domestic situations, not merely to husband and wife. In *Cook* itself a woman who had contributed labour and financial savings to the building of a house in which she and a man planned to live was awarded a one third beneficial interest in it. Karminski and Orr JJ concurred.

In *Eves v. Eves*[211] the Court of Appeal awarded a one quarter interest in the beneficial interest in a house to a *de facto* wife. Lord Denning said that "a few years ago" the court would not have provided a remedy, but that "things have altered now". He traced the new departure to Lord Diplock's judgment in *Gissing*:

> "Equity is not past the age of child bearing.[212] One of her latest progeny is a constructive trust of a new model. Lord Diplock brought it into the world and we have nourished it".[213]

---

209 [1972] 1 WLR 518.

210 *ibid.* at p.520.

211 [1975] 1 WLR 1338.

212 In *National Provincial Bank v. Ainsworth* [1965] AC 1175, [1965] 2 All ER 472, the House of Lords rejected the notion, fostered by Lord Denning, that there was such a thing as a deserted wife's equity to remain in the matrimonial home. In his judgment Lord Hodson dismissed the notion with the words: "Equity may not be past the age of child-bearing, but an infant of the kind suggested would lack form or shape".

213 [1975] 1 WLR 1338 at p.1341.

The judge referred to Diplock's general statement but almost ignored the limitation Diplock placed upon it, but it would certainly be disingenuous to claim that Lord Diplock had no intention of stating the principle of the constructive trust any more widely than had been done before, or that his words could not reasonably bear that meaning.

In *Hussey v. Palmer*[214] Denning had stated the principle even more expansively. He expressed the view that a constructive trust is imposed by law whenever justice and good conscience require it:

> "It is a liberal process, founded upon large principles of equity to be applied in cases where the legal owner cannot conscientiously keep the property for himself alone, but ought to allow another to have the property or the benefit of it or a share in it. The trust may arise at the outset when the property is acquired, or later on, as the circumstances may require".[215]

In the case itself a mother-in-law had paid for the construction of an extra bedroom in a house which belonged to her son-in-law. It was to provide a home for her in her old age. She later moved out after disagreements with the son-in-law. Lord Denning held it "entirely against conscience" that the son-in-law should keep the whole interest in the enlarged house.

In Ireland the Supreme Court has not adopted the narrow view of the majority in *Gissing* in the specific context of marital contributions.[216] Instead, in *McC v. McC*[217] it has asserted that indirect contributions of a wife give her a share of the equitable interest in the house in the absence of an agreement or arrangement to the contrary. Thus it has treated the domestic situation of the parties itself, rather than any specific conduct on their part, as determining property rights.

How far this new approach will extend beyond marriage to other relationships remains to be seen. Authority before the *McC v. McC* decision was equivocal. Gannon J in *McGill v. Snodgrass*[218] required words or conduct to give rise to a constructive trust, while McWilliam J in *Power v. Conroy*[219] recognised indirect contributions as giving a share in the beneficial interest without more. It must be assumed that Supreme Court's adoption of the principle in *McC* makes it more likely that McWilliam's approach to non-marital situations will be followed in future.

One argument against the constructive trust as a general remedial device is

214 [1972] 1 WLR 1286.

215 *ibid.* at p.1290.

216 In England the further development of the trust concept in this area was cut short by legislative reform.

217 [1986] ILRM 1, Supreme Court, Henchy J, nem diss.

218 Reported sub nom *McGill v. S* [1979] IR 283, High Court.

219 Unreported, High Court, McWilliam J, 22nd February 1980.

that entirely innocent third parties may be prejudiced by it. As Gray[220] points out, someone who is held to be a beneficiary of an equitable interest automatically obtains priority over the unsecured creditors of the constructive trustee if the latter becomes insolvent. However, one must remember that the court retains a discretion whether to find such a trust or not and if substantial injustice would be done by doing so they may decline to find one. Furthermore, the conflict is often between two innocent parties: the original beneficiary and the third party taking the property. In such a case there may be nothing to distinguish the parties in individual moral terms. Where one is a deserted wife or an elderly resident in a house and the other is a financial institution, can, or should, the court avoid such considerations as the fact that the financial institution can recoup its loss through the market, while the private individual is less able to bear the loss, or, on the other hand, favouring the financial institution through some concern that a market in which the risks and costs of financial institutions are reduced is in some way a public benefit or a matter of public policy?

220 Gray & Symes, *Real Property* at p.482.

CHAPTER 19

LANDLORD AND TENANT

"The manufacture of a five-pronged implement for manual digging results in a fork even if the manufacturer, unfamiliar with the English language, insists that he intended to make, and has made, a spade."

– Lord Templeman in Street v. Mountford [1985] 1 AC 809 at 819.

"Cecily. ... When I see a spade I call it a spade.
Gwendolen. (Satirically.) I am glad to say that I have never seen a spade. It is obvious that our social spheres have been widely different."

– *Oscar Wilde*, The Importance of Being Earnest, Second Act.

A. The Relationship in Ireland

The basis of landlord and tenant relations was fundamentally affected by the Landlord and Tenant Law (Amendment) Act (Ireland), 1860, commonly known as Deasy's Act after the Attorney General who introduced it. It was a conservative measure aimed at increasing the power of landlords over their tenants and it remains something of an anomaly not only in the curiosity of its provisions but in the fact of its being retained on the statute book at all. The most radical section of Deasy's Act is section 3 which defines the relationship of landlord and tenant in Ireland. It provides that:

> "3.–The relationship of landlord and tenant shall be deemed to be founded on the express or implied contract of the parties and not upon tenure or service, and a reversion shall not be necessary to such relation, which shall be deemed to subsist in all cases in which there shall be an agreement by one party to hold land from or under another in consideration of any rent".

The section on its face would seem to have the effect of reducing all tenancies to mere contracts rather than property interests, but this has not been literally applied in all its logical consequences and probably was never intended to be. The Act itself, for example, provides for the running of covenants between successors to the original contracting parties, assuming that some interest is created by the contract which can be alienated in the first place. If the agreement was only a contract and nothing more this would not be the case. It is therefore necessary to examine each aspect of the landlord and tenant relationship to see how it has been affected by the Act.

B. Interesse Termini

At common law a tenant had no estate until he or she entered the land. Until actual entry the tenant had merely an *interesse termini*, an interest in the term and a right of entry.[1] The absence of an estate caused problems for tenants who had not entered under the lease.[2] It is arguable that section 3 abolishes this common law doctrine since it provides that the relationship of landlord and tenant arises as soon as the contract is formed.

C. Reversion

One effect of section 3 is that a reversion need not be retained on the grant of a leasehold interest in order that the relationship of landlord and tenant be created. The notion that a reversion has to be retained on the grant of a leasehold term if it is to be a sublease and not an assignment of the landlord's interest, is in fact a misconception having its origin in freehold tenure and will need to be explained.

We have seen that the statute *Quia Emptores*, 1290 prohibited subinfeudation in fee simple after the date of the Act.[3] This meant that if, after the statute, a grantor who had a fee simple made a grant to B in fee simple that grant was a substitution and did not create a relationship of tenure between the grantor and grantee. At the same time, the grantor retained no reversion. If, however, an estate less than a fee simple were granted, it could still occur by subinfeudation and, indeed, still can. In such a case the grantor would also retain a reversion.

In England this coincidence of no reversion/no tenure, reversion/tenure gave rise in the course of time to the misconception that the retention of a reversion had always been necessary to create tenure. This misconception gained ground because in England there were no exceptions to *Quia Emptores*. In Ireland it was otherwise, as we have seen. The case of fee farm grants *non obstante Quia Emptores* provided an instance of a fee simple estate being granted after the Statute which also, despite the lack of a reversion, created a tenure and in this instance a freehold tenure. In England when leaseholds began to be recognised many of the rules that were applied to them were, again as we have seen, derived from the law of freehold tenures. However, the law of freehold tenures was the law as it was understood at that time and it therefore incorporated the misconception that to create tenure the grantor had to retain a

---

1 The doctrine was abolished in England, as to all leases, whether made before or after 1925, by the Law of Property Act, 1925 s.149(1), (2).

2 Merger could not occur: *Doe d Rawlings v. Walker* (1826) 5 B & C 111, 108 ER 41 nor could the tenant surrender to a reversioner: *ibid.* at 5 B & C 122.

3 See Chapter 3 Tenure.

reversion. It therefore became part of the common law relating to leaseholds that the grantor had to retain a reversion on the term, whether a freehold reversion or a leasehold reversion if he himself had only a leasehold.

In Ireland, on the other hand, since the misconception had never taken root in relation to freeholds, it was never applied to leaseholds. It had long been the practice in Ireland, therefore, for absentee landlords to grant terms of years to their agents in Ireland and for the agents to grant the entire term to an agricultural tenant while intending that to be a sublease so that the agent would be in the position of a landlord and hence be able to impose the remedies available to a landlord. This remained the position until the Union.

After the Union the Irish Court of Exchequer Chamber upheld the Irish practice in *Pluck v. Digges*.[4] However, when the appeal went to the British House of Lords they reversed the Irish court,[5] apparently regarding the Irish practice as heretical. The House of Lords decision was followed in Ireland by the King's Bench[6] and Chancery[7] but it was not greeted with universal approval. The Court of Exchequer in one case was prepared to confine *Pluck* to the remedy of distress at common law and allowed an action in ejectment despite the absence of a reversion.[8]

The effect of the House of Lords decision would have been to leave the Irish land agents without the remedies available to a landlord and although this may not have greatly concerned the English judges, it caused some concern among the landed class in Ireland and probably in response to representations from that quarter, section 3 of Deasy's Act restored the position as to leases and tenancies under the Act. After the Act the case of *Gordon v. Phelan*[9] confirmed that section 3 had restored the position.[10] Nevertheless, section 3 of Deasy's Act, 1860 only recognises the relation of landlord and tenant for the purposes of the Act where a rent is reserved, and so leasehold terms where no

4 (1828) 2 Hud & Br 1.

5 (1832) 5 Bligh NS 31, 5 ER 219; 2 Dow & Cl 180, 6 ER 695.

6 *Lessee of Fawcett v. Hall* (1833) Al & Nap 248, Bushe CJ accepted that the principle of *Pluck* applied to ejectment and to replevin.

7 *Cremen v. Hawkes* (1846) 8 Ir Eq R 153, affirmed on appeal at 503, a case of a lessee for years who leased for his own term reserving a rent.

8 *Lessee of Walsh v. Feely* (1835) 1 Jones 413, following *Lessee of Coyne v. Smith* (1826) Batty 90, n. The former case involved a holder of an estate pur autre vie who demised it for the life of the same cestui que vie, reserving a rent.

9 (1881) 15 ILTR 70.

10 By holding that a landlord retained the common law right of distress for rent although he had retained no reversion. Section 51 of Deasy's Act gives a statutory right of distress more limited than the common law right. It arises only after one year's rent is in arrear. It seems to have been intended to replace the common law right, but *Gordon v. Phelan* also had the effect of holding that it did not do so: see also *Mennons v. Burke* (1890) 26 LR Ir 193, Exchequer.

rent is reserved would seem to be governed by the law as it stood immediately before Deasy's Act, *i.e.* a reversion would still be required on a sub-grant.[11]

D. Concurrent Leases

At common law landlord L having granted a lease to A can still grant a lease to take effect at the same time to B. This is known as a lease of the reversion or a concurrent lease. The effect in terms of tenure is to insert B between L and A, making B the new landlord of A and the new tenant of L.[12] It operates as a disposition by the landlord of his or her reversion.[13] Hence, the purpose is to confer on B the position of landlord and not to disturb the possession of A.

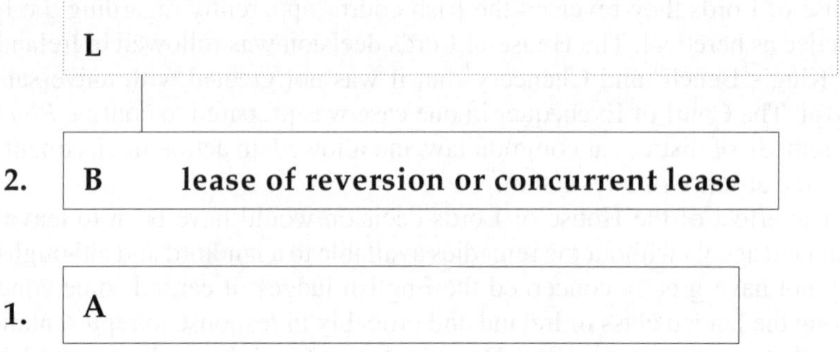

Hence L can no longer give notice to quit to A.[14] There is authority at common law for the proposition that B's concurrent lease may be of the same duration[15]

11 See below for mortgage terms.

12 *McKeague v. Hutchinson* (1884) 18 ILTR 70; *Beamish v. Crowley* (1885) 16 LR Ir 279 at 290.

13 *Neale v. Mackenzie* (1836) 1 M & W 747, 150 ER 635, per Lord Denman CJ. But note the older cases say that the concurrent lease had to be by deed and the first tenant had to attorn, *i.e.* accept the grantee as landlord: *Neale v. Mackenzie* (1836) 1 M & W 747, 150 ER 635, per Lord Denman CJ. In *Jones v. Wrotham Park Settled Estates* [1980] AC 74, [1979] 1 All ER 286, [1979] 2 WLR 13, HL, an attempt was made, unsuccessfully, to use a concurrent lease as a means to prevent the original tenant from acquiring the landlord's reversion.

14 *Wordsley Brewery Co v. Halford* (1903) 90 LT 89.

15 *Burton v. Barclay* (1831) 7 Bing 745 at 746, 131 ER 288 at 293, citing *Hughes v. Robotham* (1593) Poph 30, 79 ER 1150 at 1151 per Popham CJ and Fenner J. The power to create concurrent leases, even where possession is granted, was expressly preserved in England by the Law of Property Act, 1925 s.149(5). Megarry & Wade, *Real Property* p.649.

as the original lease to A and some authority for the view that it may even be shorter.[16] B may collect rent from A and enforce the covenants in A's lease.[17] In such a case there would be tenure between A and B although B did not have a reversion in the sense of a longer estate than A. This is not consistent with the general rule followed in England, that a reversion is necessary for tenure, a principle which we have argued is a misconception, but it is consistent with the view held in Ireland before Deasy's Act.

It is unusual for concurrent leases to occur in leases granting the right to occupy, but such leases do occur in successive mortgages by demise and sub-demise. In such terms a rent is not normally reserved, since it is not intended that the mortgagee should pay rent to the mortgagor. Where the granting landlord has the freehold then on the grant of a lease he or she will always retain a reversion since a freehold estate is notionally greater than leasehold. But where the landlord only has a leasehold it may be questioned whether he or she must retain a reversion on the original lease if they are later to grant a concurrent lease. The better view in Ireland as to mortgage terms is that, since no rent is reserved, they fall outside section 3 of Deasy's Act, therefore the law immediately before Deasy's Act applies. It is the normal practice for the landlord/mortgagor to retain a reversion on the original demise although, in view of what has been said above, it is doubtful if this is necessary.[18] Thus the first mortgage term might be for 99 years less 10 days, and the second mortgage term for 99 years less nine days:

16 *Neale v. Mackenzie* (1836) 1 M & W 747, 150 ER 635, per Lord Denman CJ; *Watt v. Maydewell* (1628) Hut 105, 123 ER 1132; *Re Moore & Hulm's Contract* [1912] 2 Ch 105 (mortgage terms, second one the same length as first, second held valid). Megarry & Wade *Real Property* p.649.

17 *Burton v. Barclay* (1831) 7 Bing 745 at 746, 131 ER 288 at 293.

18 Section 80 of the Landlord and Tenant (Amendment) Act, 1980 refers to the "normal reversion" where a lessee mortgages by sub-demise. A reversion is necessary to ensure that the Satisfied Terms Act, 1845 applies. See Chapter 23 Mortgages.

E. Exclusive Occupation

The right to exclusive occupation means the general right to exclude all others from the premises, including the landlord. The right of exclusive occupation is an essential of a lease or tenancy.[19] The issue as to whether the right exists often arises today in the context of deciding whether an agreement is a tenancy or a licence. This topic is dealt with below. The right of exclusive occupation may still exist even if the agreement includes terms which give the landlord or his or her agents the right to enter the premises from time to time for specific purposes, such as to inspect equipment or repairs. Indeed the view has been expressed that the existence of such terms may positively indicate that exclusive possession has been granted since the grant of a right to the landlord to enter for specific purposes implies that in general the landlord has no right to do so.[20]

F. Subletting

There is no provision in Deasy's Act expressly authorising subletting, apparently because subletting creates a new contract between the sub-landlord and the sub-tenant and is governed by the Act like any other lease. Subletting does not require the consent of the head-landlord unless the lease contains a provision to that effect.[21]

G. Lease or Licence?

1. A Question of Substance, Not Form

Land may be a commodity under capitalism, but unlike most other commodities, its supply is necessarily limited. Ownership of it confers a monopoly control over a scarce resource. Landlords have often used this power to extract terms in leases and tenancies which would be more beneficial to them than they could extract in the case of a free market in which the supply of a commodity can be increased to reach the demand. The existence of democratic institutions has led to a demand by the more numerous part of the population who are tenants or who sympathise with tenants for the State to intervene to reduce the monopoly power of those whose income is derived from rent. The re-

19 See below Lease or Licence?

20 Per Griffin J in *Irish Shell v. Costello (No. 1)* [1981] ILRM 66, Supreme Court.

21 If the subletting is made with the landlord's consent s.19 of Deasy's Act provides that the receipt of the sub-landlord for the rent paid by the sub-tenant is a full discharge of the latter as against the head-landlord. However, if the sub-landlord is in arrear with his rent to the head-landlord, the head-landlord can give notice under s.20 to the sub-tenant to pay rent or part of it directly to him.

sulting statutes were phrased so as to apply to leases or tenancies. Landlords tried to evade the Acts by calling tenancies or leases licences instead. The question has therefore come before the courts as to whether these devices to avoid the rent control acts would be recognised or not. If the terminology used were to be taken at face value, the landlords would virtually have restored their monopoly position despite the aims of democratic legislatures. The courts have generally chosen not to accept the terms used by the parties, but scrutinise the agreements and to create their own tests to determine whether a tenancy or licence has been created. In *Irish Shell v. Costello (No. 1)*[22] the Supreme Court adopted this position and held that an agreement under which an oil company allowed the other party to occupy a service station[23] was in law a tenancy although it was described in the agreement itself as a licence. Griffin J cited Lord Denning, MR in *Shell-Mex v. Manchester Garages*,[24] to the effect that:

> "Although a document may be described as a licence it does not necessarily follow that, merely on that account, it is to be regarded as amounting only to a licence in law. Whether the transaction is a licence or a tenancy does not depend on the label which is put on it. It depends on the nature of the transaction itself: see *Addiscombe Garden Estates Ltd* v *Crabbe* ([1958] 1 QB 513). Broadly speaking, we have to see whether it is a personal privilege given to a person (in which case it is a licence), or whether it grants an interest in land (in which case it is a tenancy).
>
> At one time it used to be thought that exclusive possession was a decisive factor. But that is not so. It depends on broader considerations altogether. Primarily on whether it is personal in its nature or not".

Griffin J applied these tests to the facts before him:

> "Looked at in this way, what do the 'licensees' get? The premises were intended by the parties for use, and were in fact used, by the defendants as a lock-up garage. They were, according to the evidence, visited approximately once per month only by a representative of the plaintiffs. The defendants carried on what might be called a full garage business there, providing their own mechanics and an apprentice in the workshop, and petrol pump attendants for the sale of petrol on the forecourt. The petrol pumps were kept locked and the plaintiffs or their representatives had no keys to them. It was thought necessary to include clause 4(e) in relation to permitting the plaintiffs to inspect the equipment; to do so they would of course have to enter the premises. If they had a right to do so, this clause would seem to be completely unnecessary. Further, the omission from the Agreements with the defendants of (a) clause 4(x), *i.e.* the covenant not to interfere with the possession and user of the premises by the plaintiffs, and of (b) the proviso in clause 8 that nothing in the Agreement should be deemed to confer on the defendants the right to exclusive possession, shows that it was intended that the defendants should have the right to occupy

22 [1981] ILRM 66, Supreme Court; followed in *National Maternity Hospital v. McGouran*, unreported, High Court, Morris J, 3 November 1993.

23 The Friarsland Service Station, Roebuck Road, Dublin 4. The station has since been rebuilt.

24 [1971] 1 WLR 612 at 615. *ibid.* per Buckley LJ at 618; *Gatien Motor Co v. Continental Oil* [1979] IR 406.

> the premises and that this was intended to be a right to exclusive occupation and possession. . .".

The judge went on to find that the payments in the agreement which ostensibly were for the hire of equipment were in fact rent and their being described otherwise did not prevent them being so.[25]

Some of the uncertainty that now exists in this area is illustrated by *Irish Shell v. Costello (No. 2)*.[26] The No. 2 case concerned the nature of the relationship between the parties after the 1974 agreement had been terminated. O'Higgins in the majority cited Scarman LJ in *Heslop v. Burns*[27] and found that it was a tenancy at will which had been terminated by the letter of 5 November 1974 and that since that time the defendants were trespassers. Henchy J, also in the majority, held that had the defendants stayed on and paid a monthly rent they would have been monthly tenants, but the payment was said to be a licence fee and not rent and had been accepted as such. They were tentative interim payments pending negotiations. This rebutted the presumption at common law of a monthly tenancy. The judge concluded therefore that they were licensees after the end of the 1974 agreement. This licence had expired on 12 November 1974 after which they had become trespassers.[28] McCarthy J dissenting found that they were monthly tenants and that the tenancy still continued.

In *Bellew v. Bellew*[29] the concept of a licence was preferred in a case between family members. Barmeath Castle, Dunlear, Co Louth had been in the possession of the Bellew family for many centuries. Until 1953 the fee simple was vested in the then Lord Bellew (the uncle) who lived in London and had no children. He asked the first defendant (the father) who was his brother to live in the castle. The father moved into the castle together with his wife. The uncle gave the father what was referred to as a yearly tenancy of the castle but not of the adjoining farmland. In 1949 the plaintiff (the son) joined him and brought his wife and family including his own son (the grandson), the second defendant. The plaintiff looked after the farm. In 1953 the uncle conveyed the fee simple of the whole estate to the son, subject to the yearly tenancy of the castle vested in the father. The son later settled the land in trust for himself for life with remainder to his son, the grandson, in tail male. The settlement was necessarily subject to the father's yearly tenancy of the castle. After a marital disagreement the son left the castle in 1961 and never returned. Negotiations took

25 [1981] ILRM 66 at p.70–71.

26 [1984] IR 511, Supreme Court.

27 [1974] 3 All ER 406, [1974] 1 WLR 1241, 233 EG 263, [1975] EGD 293.

28 The two judges in the majority nevertheless disagreed about the assessment of mesne profits. O'Higgins CJ held it should be at a rate of £1,500 per year from 5 November, Henchy J held that it should be the same rate but from the 12 November. Presumably this left a majority vote in favour of that rate from the 12 November.

29 [1982] IR 447, [1983] 3 ILRM 128.

place between solicitors acting for the son and his father to arrange for the maintenance of the son's family and for the running of the farm. The negotiations broke down in 1963 and were not resumed. While they were going on the son authorised the father to farm the lands pending further negotiations. The father did so and was assisted by the grandson. The father thus continued in occupation of the castle and the farm without accounting to the son for the profits and without acknowledging his title. After the death of the uncle, the father and the son's wife made a lease in favour of the grandson of the lands for 21 years. The son learned of the lease and, in 1978, brought the present proceedings claiming a declaration that he was tenant for life of the lands and that the father and the grandson had no interest in them.

The Supreme Court unanimously held that the son's title to the lands had been extinguished by adverse possession. The majority (Griffin and Hederman JJ) held that the exclusive occupation of the lands by the father had begun under a licence from the plaintiff son, that the licence expired upon the termination of the negotiations and that adverse possession by the father had begun from the termination of the licence.

O'Higgins CJ, in the minority on the point, held that the father originally was a tenant at will of the son. He held further that under section 17 of the Statute of Limitation, 1957, a tenancy at will is deemed to terminate one year after it begins, that in accordance with s.17(1)(b) the right of action of a person entitled to land subject to a tenancy at will accrues when the tenancy terminates, and that consequently the father had been in adverse possession for the required 12 years, extinguishing the son's title. In rejecting the tenancy at will concept Griffin J, representing the majority, referred to *Shell Mex v. Manchester Garages Ltd*, to *Gatien Motors v. Continental Oil Ltd*[30] and to Scarman LJ in *Heslop v. Burns*.[31] Licences were more appropriate, he felt, in matters of family arrangement, in Scarman's phrase.

2. Exclusive Occupation

While the absence of exclusive occupation means that the agreement is not a tenancy, the fact that the right is granted will not resolve the issue of whether a particular agreement constitutes a lease or a licence.

In the past judges were apt to say that the presence of exclusive occupation negatived a licence. In *Lynes v. Snaith*[32] Lawrence J said:

> "As to the first question, I think it is clear that she was a tenant at will and not a licensee; for the admissions state that she was in exclusive possession – a fact which is wholly inconsistent with her having been a mere licensee".

30 [1979] IR 406, Supreme Court. See below.

31 [1974] 3 All ER 406, [1974] 1 WLR 1241, 233 EG 263, [1975] EGD 293.

32 [1899] 1 QB 486, [1895-9] All ER Reprint 997.

The courts have since departed from this position and no longer hold exclusive possession to be decisive. Scarman LJ in *Heslop* commented:[33]

> "Today, however, a very different approach appears to be adopted by the courts; and one can see it is the first sentence of the headnote in *Cobb v. Lane*[34] to which Roskill LJ referred: 'The fact of the exclusive occupation of property for an indefinite period is no longer inconsistent with the occupier being a licensee and not a tenant at will.'".

a) Intention of the parties or policy?

It is now clear that, whatever was the case in the past, the courts no longer pursue the vexed question of the intention of the parties in deciding whether an agreement is a lease or a licence, since the reason for the intervention of parliament was that landlords inserted provisions intended to avoid the legislation and intending tenants had no choice but to accept them if they wished to obtain accommodation.

b) Commercial Agreements

The modern attitude is to permit the devise of a licence to avoid statutory control at least where the parties are, in the view of the court, on equal terms.

In *Gatien Motor Co Ltd v. Continental Oil*[35] the occupier of premises would have been entitled, after three years occupation as a tenant, to a new tenancy of the premises. In order to prevent the occupier acquiring this right the grantor inserted a term which made the occupier a caretaker for a two-week period immediately preceding the expiry of the three years. The Supreme Court held that a caretaker agreement was not a tenancy despite the fact that it also conferred the right of exclusive possession on the caretaker. It may be that the court considered that the parties had contracted on an equal footing and the grantee had acted in their own interests in contracting out of their rights. In *Irish Shell v. Costello (No. 1)*[36] the Supreme Court held, an agreement to be a tenancy, to the tenant's advantage, despite its description as a licence, in a commercial context, namely, an agreement between an oil company and the operator of a service station, in which the station operator is generally considered to be at a disadvantage.

---

33 [1974] 3 All ER 406, [1974] 1 WLR 1241, 233 EG 263, [1975] EGD 293.

34 [1952] 1 All ER at 1199.

35 [1979] IR 406, Supreme Court.

36 [1981] ILRM 66, Supreme Court; followed in *National Maternity Hospital v. McGouran*, unreported, High Court, Morris J, 3 November 1993.

c) Residential Agreements

In *Street v. Mountford*[37] the English House of Lords shifted the emphasis back to exclusive possession as indicating a tenancy rather than a licence where residential accommodation is concerned. In that case the landlord granted the appellant the right to occupy a furnished room under a written agreement which stated that the appellant had the right to occupy the room "at a licence fee of £37 per week", that "this personal licence is not assignable", that the "licence may be terminated by 14 days written notice" and that the appellant understood and accepted that "a licence in the above form does not and is not intended to give me a tenancy protected under the Rent Acts". The appellant had exclusive possession of the room. Some months after signing the agreement the appellant applied to have a fair rent registered in respect of the room. The landlord then applied to the county court for a declaration that the appellant occupied the room under a licence and not a tenancy.

The county court judge held that the appellant was a tenant entitled to the protection of the Rent Acts, but on the landlord's appeal the Court of Appeal held that the occupier was a mere licensee since, notwithstanding the fact of exclusive possession, the agreement bore all the hallmarks of a licence and the parties had in fact only intended to create a licence.

The judgment of the House of Lords was delivered by Lord Templeman. He held that where the occupier of residential accommodation had been granted exclusive possession of the accommodation for a fixed or periodic term at a stated rent, the interest was presumed to be a tenancy and not a licence. The presumption could be rebutted by proving special circumstances which negatived a tenancy, for example where from the outset there was no intention to create legal relations or where the possession was granted pursuant to a contract of employment. The intention of the parties, as manifested in the agreement, that they only intended to create a licence (and expressed the agreement to be a licence) and that they agreed not to be bound by the Rent Acts was irrelevant. In the memorable words of the judge: "The manufacture of a five-pronged implement for manual digging results in a fork even if the manufacturer, unfamiliar with the English language, insists that he intended to make and has made a spade".[38] Accordingly, since the effect of the agreement between the appellant and the landlord was to grant the appellant exclusive possession for a fixed term at a stated rent, and no circumstances existed to negative the presumption of a tenancy, it was clear that the appellant was a tenant. The appeal was therefore allowed.[39]

---

37 [1985] 1 AC 809, [1985] 2 All ER 289, [1985] 2 WLR 877, 50 P & CR 258, 274 EG 821, [1985] 1 EGLR 128, [1985] Conv 328, [1986] Conv 39.

38 [1985] 1 AC 809 at 819.

39 [1985] 2 All ER 289, p.290 g to j, p.292 g, p.293 j to p.294 c and g to j, p.295 a and j to p.296 b g h, p.297 a, p.299 a b g h and p.300 b to e and h j, post). *Dicta* of Denning LJ in

AG Securities v. Vaughan[40] and *Antoniades v. Villiers*[41] two appeals heard together, the English House of Lords refined and qualified the principles in *Street v. Mountford*. In the first appeal, the occupants of a four-bedroom flat had entered into separate agreements at different times and for different monthly payments. The agreements, which expressly were called licences, granted the exclusive right to use the flat in common with three other occupants who had or might from time to time be granted the similar right. The landlords claimed a declaration in the county court that the four occupants were licensees and not tenants of the flat. The judge granted the declaration. On appeal by three of the occupants, the Court of Appeal, by a majority, held that they were jointly tenants of the flat. The House of Lords in allowing the appeal, held that the agreements did not grant exclusive occupation to any of the occupants principally because the agreements included a clause whereby if any one of them terminated his or her agreement the remaining occupants were obliged to find a replacement flat-mate and if they failed to do so the owner could require them to accept someone of his choice. The House of Lords also held that they could not be joint tenants of a tenancy since they has signed agreements at different times and so the four unities were not present.

In the second appeal two occupants of a one-bedroom flat and who lived as man and wife had signed separate agreements; also called licences, at the insistence of the landlord. The agreements included a clauses which purported to give the landlord the right to grant other occupants the right to live in the flat and also gave himself the right to move into and share the flat with the two original occupants. The landlord, who represented himself, said that he had inserted the latter provision so that, if his own house burned down or was otherwise destroyed, he would have somewhere to live. The judges found that neither cause was intended to be implemented and was only inserted to avoid the Rent Acts. The court held that the two agreements should be construed as a single document and that the occupants were tenants with exclusive occupation.

Errington v. Errington [1952] 1 All ER at 154-155, of Denning LJ in *Facchini v. Bryson* [1952] 1 TLR at 1389–1390 and *Addiscombe Garden Estates Ltd v. Crabbe* [1957] 3 All ER 563 applied. *Abbeyfield (Harpenden) Society Ltd v. Woods* [1968] 1 All ER 352 distinguished. Dictum of Lord Denning MR in *Marchant v. Charters* [1977] 3 All ER at 992 disapproved. Dictum of Windeyer J in *Radaich v. Smith* (1959) 101 CLR at 222 adopted. *Murray Bull & Co Ltd v. Murray* [1952] 2 All ER 1079; *Aldrington Garages Ltd v. Fielder* (1978) 37 P & CR 461; *Somma v. Hazelhurst* [1978] 2 All ER 1011 and *Sturolson & Co v. Weniz* (1984) 272 EG 326 overruled.

40 [1990] AC 417, [1988] 3 All ER 1058, [1988] 3 WLR 1205, 10.

41 *ibid.*

3. Rent

If no rent is reserved does this mean that the agreement is not a lease? It would seem that while rent is a requirement of a landlord and tenant relationship within section 3 of Deasy's Act, 1860, if no rent is reserved the relationship may still exist, but is not governed by the Act. The main argument in favour of this interpretation is that if this were not so then mortgage terms, in mortgages created by devise, could not exist as legal estates. However, the interpretation does lead to one inconsistency in the interpretation of section 4. As will be seen below, the courts have taken the view that a lease required by section 4 to be created in writing, but which is made orally, can exist as an equitable lease under the doctrine of *Walsh v. Lonsdale,*[42] provided it is enforceable as a contract. Thus the courts have held that such a lease, lacking one of the requirements of Deasy's Act, can exist apart from the statute, but only in equity. The courts have not taken the view that such leases can exist at law but are not governed by the provisions of the Act. The existence or otherwise of rent does not resolve the issue of whether an agreement is a licence or a lease.

In *Gatien Motor Co Ltd v. Continental Oil*[43] Kenny J held that the caretaker agreement was not a tenancy and gave among a number of reasons the fact that that no rent was paid, citing section 3 of Deasy's Act, 1860. Had rent been decisive no other reasons would have been required, but the judge mentioned a number of other factors, including the surrounding circumstances.[44] Kenny J, dissenting in *Irish Shell v. Costello (No. 1)*[45], suggested that rent was a requirement of a lease in Ireland, but the majority did not decide the point. They found that the periodic payments were rent, even though disguised as periodic payments for hire of equipment.

In *Bellew v. Bellew*[46] the majority in the Supreme court held that a licence had been granted by the plaintiff to the father. The majority held the case was one of family arrangement, quoting Scarman in *Heslop v. Burns.*[47] No rent had been reserved but the court did not decide it on that ground. Section 3 of Deasy's Act does not repeal section 3 of Real Property Act, 1845 so far as it relates to leases. The 1845 Act requires leases which previously had to be in writing to be by deed. Thus, if there are leasehold terms outside Deasy's Act, they would have to be created by deed.

42 (1882) 21 Ch D 9. See below.

43 [1979] IR 406, Supreme Court.

44 In the earlier case of *Davies v. Hilliard* (1967) 101 ILTR 50 an agreement was held to be a caretaker agreement even though exclusive possession was granted and the caretaker paid sums termed rent.

45 [1981] ILRM 66.

46 [1982] IR 447; [1983] ILRM 128.

47 [1974] 3 All ER 406, [1974] 1 WLR 1241, 233 EG 263, [1975] EGD 293.

H. Time Certain

The main distinction between leaseholds and freeholds at common law is that leaseholds are for a time certain, *i.e.* for a definite time, either in years months weeks, days *etc.*[48] Thus a lease granted for the duration of the war has been held void.[49]

The law has recently been reviewed in England by the House of Lords in *Prudential Assurance Co Ltd v. London Residuary Body.*[50] In that case a purported lease to last until the land is required for road widening was held void in itself as creating uncertain term, but since the grantee had gone into possession and paid rent referable to a year, the court held that should be interpreted as a tenancy from year to year terminable by notice. Lord Templeman reviewed the law in these words:

> ". . . I consider that the principle in *Lace v. Chantler* [1944] 1 All ER 305, [1944] KB 368 reaffirming 500 years of judicial acceptance of the requirement that a term must be certain applies to all leases and tenancy agreements. A tenancy from year to year is saved from being uncertain because each party has power by notice to determine at the end of any year. The term continues until determined as if both parties made a new agreement at the end of each year for a new term for the ensuing year. A power for nobody to determine or for one party only to be able to determine is inconsistent with the concept of a term from year to year: see *Doe d Warner v. Browne* (1807) 8 East 165, 103 ER 305 and *Cheshire Lines Committee v. Lewis* & Co (1880) 50 LJQB 121. . .

---

48 2 Bl Com p.143:

> "Every estate which must expire at a period certain and prefixed, by whatever words created, is an estate for years. And therefore this estate is frequently called a term, terminus, because its duration or continuance is bounded, limited and determined: for every such estate must have a certain beginning, and certain end".

See also *Say v. Smith* (1530) 1 Plowd 269, 75 ER 410 per Anthony Brown J at 1 Plowd 272, 75 ER 415:

> "Every contract sufficient to make a lease for years ought to have certainty in three limitations, viz. in the commencement of the term, in the continuance of it, and in the end of it: so that all these ought to be known at the commencement of the lease, and words in a lease, which don't make this appear, are but babble...And these three are in effect but one matter, shewing the certainty of the time for which the lessee shall have the land, and if any of these fail, it is not a good lease, for then there wants certainty."

49 *Lace v. Chantler* (1944) KB 368. An attempt had been made in *Great Northern Railway v. Arnold* (1916) 33 TLR 114 in the First World War to to make an exception in the case of leases granted for the duration of the war.

50 [1992] 2 AC 386, [1992] 3 All ER 504, [1992] 3 WLR 279, 64 P & CR 193, [1992] 36 EG 129.

> A lease can be made for five years subject to the tenant's right to determine if the war ends before the expiry of five years. A lease can be made from year to year subject to a fetter on the right of the landlord to determine the lease before the expiry of five years unless the war ends. Both leases are valid because they create a determinable certain term of five years. A lease might purport to be made for the duration of the war subject to the tenant's right to determine before the end of the war. A lease might be made from year to year subject to a fetter on the right of the landlord to determine the lease before the war ends. Both leases would be invalid because each purported to create an uncertain term. A term must either be certain or uncertain. It cannot be partly certain because the tenant can determine it at any time and partly uncertain because the landlord cannot determine it for an uncertain period. If the landlord does not grant and the tenant does not take a certain term the grant does not create a lease".[51]

The judge held two previous decisions of the English Court of Appeal to be wrongly decided on the point, namely *Charles Clay & Sons Ltd v. British Railways Board*[52] and *Ashburn Anstalt v. Arnold.*[53] Of *Ashburn* the judge said:

> "That case, if it was [*sic*] correct, would make it unnecessary for a lease to be of a certain duration. In an agreement for the sale of land the vendor reserved the right to remain at the property after completion as licensee and to trade therefrom without payment of rent – 'save that it can be required by Matlodge Ltd [the purchaser] to give possession on not less than one quarter's notice in writing upon Matlodge certifying that it is ready at the expiration of such notice forthwith to proceed with the development of the property and the neighbouring property involving *inter alia* the demolition of the property.'
>
> . . . The Court of Appeal held that the term was not uncertain because the vendor could either give a quarter's notice or vacate the property without giving notice. But of course the same could be said of the situation in *Lace* v *Chandler* [1944] 1 All ER 305, [1944] KB 368. The cumulative result of the two Court of Appeal authorities, *Charles Clay & Sons Ltd* v *British Railways Board* [1971] 1 All ER 1007, [1971] Ch 725 and *Ashburn's* case, would therefore destroy the need for any term to be certain. . .
>
> In my opinion both those cases were wrongly decided. A grant for an uncertain term does not create a lease. A grant for an uncertain term which takes the form of a yearly tenancy which cannot be determined by the landlord does not create a lease".[54]

The majority concurred with Lord Templeman.

The principle on which the decision is based appears to be that, in the case of periodic tenancies, if the right of either party to determine the tenancy is suspended, the maximum period of suspension must be certain at the time the ten-

51 [1992] 2 AC 386 at 394–95.

52 [1971] 1 All ER 1007, [1971] Ch. 725. In *Clay* the lease was for a period of six months, to continue from half year to half year until determined on three month's notice, subject to a proviso that the landlords should not exercise that right unless they required the premises for a specified undertaking.

53 [1988] 2 All ER 147, [1989] Ch. 1. The court held the agreement a tenancy although it was to continue until the grantors required the site for road widening. The case is discussed in Chapter 18 under Licences.

54 [1992] 2 AC 386 at 395.

ancy is created. Hence, a suspension for a period of five years unless an uncertain event occurs in the meantime is valid, but a suspension until an uncertain event occurs, without a term, is void. So also is a provision which prevents either party from terminating the tenancy at any time.

It might be thought to follow from the judgment that a periodic tenancy may be created with a provision which suspends the right of a party to terminate it for the first 500 years, or 1,000 years. The last quotation, however, suggests that another test is implied: that the power to determine by notice must not effectively be taken away.

In Ireland the common law has been displaced by Deasy's Act, 1860. Section 3 of that Act which, as we have seen, provides that the relation of landlord and tenant "shall be deemed to exist in all cases where there is an agreement by one party to hold land from another in consideration of any rent". It has already been noted that the courts in Ireland have held that this allows the relation of landlord and tenant to be created in Ireland where the estate granted is freehold, such as a fee simple. Freehold estates are not definite periods of time and so the question arises as to whether a landlord and tenant relation can be created in Ireland for an indefinite period of time which is not a freehold estate, such as "for the duration of the Rugby World Cup competition" or "until the land ceases to be used as a school", *etc.* Some light is shed on this by section 4 of Deasy's Act, 1860.[55] Section 4 requires leases or tenancies to be in writing if they are to create the legal[56] relation of landlord and tenant "for any freehold estate or interest, or for any definite period of time not being from year to year or any lesser period. . .". This contemplates two types of lease, *i.e.*

(a) one granted for a freehold estate, and
(b) one granted for a definite period of time or successive definite periods, *i.e.* periodic tenancies.

In addition, hybrid interests granted for a combination of (a) and (b) may also exist, such as leases for lives and years. It seems clear that leases for successive definite periods, such as tenancies from week to week or year to year come within the Act but can be made orally. However, the implication of section 4 is that there is no third category of leases for indefinite periods not being freehold estates. It has to be admitted that section 3 does not expressly require a lease or tenancy to be for a certain period and in fact the provision of the section that landlord and tenant relationships depend upon the contract of the parties could be taken as a contrary indication. Whether or not a wholly uncertain period is possible, the sections clearly allow a lease to be created for a determinable life estate, such "to A for life or until the war ends".

55 See below Formalities.

56 Oral grants may nevertheless create equitable leases: see below Agreements for a Lease: *Walsh v. Lonsdale*.

As to leases falling outside the Act, such as where no rent is reserved,[57] they will be governed by the common law and will have to be for definite periods of time or successive definite periods.

Section 3 also implies that the grant of estates less than a fee simple may also give rise to the modern landlord and tenant relationship, but a rent would have to be reserved. The grant of estates less than a fee simple and not at a rent may give rise to freehold tenure but they would not be governed by Deasy's Act.[58]

I. Periodic Tenancies

The common law recognised that tenancies could be created for successive definite periods, as from week to week, month to month, year to year, *etc.* In such periodic tenancies each period is automatically renewed and the tenancy is therefore terminable by notice. The periods of notice were laid down by the common law and have been modified by statute.[59]

The requirement of time certain can only be said to be satisfied in that at the end of each period the tenancy is renewed for another certain period unless terminated by notice.[60]

J. Tenancy at Will

A tenancy at will is an ancient common law concept to categorise situations which did not easily fall within any other category of property right. Nevertheless, the tenancy at will itself does not easily fall within the category of tenancies since it is not for a definite period and must be considered as an exception to that test. Tenancies at will are without rent by definition, for if rent is payable weekly, or monthly, *etc.*, the relation is not a tenancy at will but a weekly or monthly tenancy. In view of section 3 of Deasy's Act it would therefore seem to follow that such tenancies are outside the statute. Tenancy at will is a concept that has declined in importance.[61]

---

57 Or arguably a lease for a greater term than from year to year "or any lesser period" but which is created orally, but the cases take the view that they cannot exist as legal leases outside the Act, only as equitable leases.

58 See Chapter 3 Tenure.

59 See below Notice to Quit.

60 *Prudential Assurance Co Ltd v. London Residuary Body* [1992] 2 AC 386, [1992] 3 All ER 504, [1992] 3 WLR 279, 64 P & CR 193, [1992] 36 EG 129. See above.

61 *Binions v. Evans* [1972] Ch 359.

Lord Scarman in *Heslop v. Burns*[62] suggests that the concept of licence now performs the function that used to be covered by tenancies at will. In *Bellew v. Bellew*[63] the majority in the Supreme Court preferred the concept of licence to that of tenancy at will where it was a matter of a family arrangement.

Section 17 of the Statute of Limitations, 1957 provides that a tenancy at will is deemed to end one year after it begins unless previously determined. The possession of the tenant then becomes adverse to that of the landlord, and time begins to run against him.[64] This rule was first adopted in 1833.[65] The rule favours the development of land, perhaps reflecting the ideas of a time shortly after the beginning of the Industrial Revolution.[66]

K. Tenancy at Sufferance

This is the interest that arises if a tenant continues in possession at the end of a lease or tenancy without continuing to pay rent and without the landlord's consent or dissent. The position is full of anomalies and was classified by the common law with common law tenancies although it has little in common with leaseholds. A tenant at sufferance differs from a trespasser in that the original entry is lawful and from a tenant at will in that occupation is without the landlord's consent. Tenants at sufferance are not liable to pay rent, but compensation for the use of the land. Exclusive possession continues until the landlord terminates the tenancy. Thus the landlord cannot sue other trespassers until he or she terminates the tenancy at sufferance.

Before 1833 a tenant for years who held over after the termination of the tenancy and without paying rent was not in adverse possession against the landlord or those claiming under him. The former tenant's possession was deemed to be possession by the landlord.[67] One of the aims of the Real Property Limitation Act, 1833 was to do away with these cases of deemed possession and replace it by the test of actual possession. Time would then begin to run from the moment that a right of action to oust the possession accrued to some other party. A tenant at sufferance after 1833 is in adverse possession and the landlord has 12 years from the expiry of the previous tenancy within which to bring an action for possession.[68]

62 [1974] 3 All ER 406, [1974] 1 WLR 1241, 233 EG 263, [1975] EGD 293.

63 [1982] IR 447.

64 See O'Higgins CJ dissenting in *Bellew v. Bellew* [1982] IR 447.

65 Real Property Limitation Act, 1833 s.7.

66 See George Eliot's, *Middlemarch*.

67 See above Adverse Possession. *Howard v. Sherwood* (1832) Al & Nap 217.

68 Real Property Limitation Act, 1833 s.5, Statute of Limitations, 1957 s.15. The rule is implied from the general provisions of the sections which provide that the right of action shall accrue to the owner of an estate in reversion when it falls into possession,

Under section 5 of Deasy's Act the landlord has the option to treat the tenant holding over as a tenant from year to year where the original lease was in writing and it was for a term. The yearly tenancy is at the old rent and subject to such of the terms of the old tenancy as may be applicable.

L. Perpetually Renewable Leases for Years

A lease for years containing a clause providing for the renewal of the term, including the clause for renewal, is a perpetually renewable lease. In *McDermott v. Caldwell*[69] a lease was granted of O'Connell Street[70] for 50 years from 1754 with a clause for renewal for further terms of 31 years during a total term of 1000 years. It was held to be within the Tenantry Act, 1779. Thus there is an equity to renew the term under section 1 of that Act even after the previous term has expired. The preamble to the Act expressly refers only to leases for lives with covenants for perpetual renewal, but perpetually renewable leases for years may well have been within the scope of the old equity applied by courts of equity in Ireland before the Act. *McDermott v. Caldwell*[71] itself concerned a lease which was not even strictly perpetual, since the renewals were limited to a total term of 1,000 years. The application of the Act to such leases might give rise to a difficult question of interpretation: if 1,000 years is regarded as perpetuity, what of 500 years? Or 300?

Perpetually renewable leases for years clearly fall within the Renewable Leaseholds Conversion Act, 1849.[72] Section 1 of the Act refers only to a lease in perpetuity but section 38 provides that the phrase:

> "... shall be taken to apply to all cases where any hereditaments have been or shall be, ... demised, leased, or granted, for one or more lives, with or without a term of years, or for years determinable upon one or more life or lives, *or for years absolute*, with a covenant or agreement ... for the perpetual renewal of such lease or contract".[emphasis supplied]

---

subject to other provisions. Section 17 of the Statute of Limitations, 1957 does not apply to a tenancy at sufferance since a tenant at sufferance is in adverse possession *ab initio*.

69 (1877) IR 10 Eq 504, V-C.

70 Then called Drogheda Street.

71 (1877) IR 10 Eq 504, V-C.

72 *Re Gore* (1859) 8 Ir Ch R 589. The lease in this case was created out of a lease for lives renewable and the term was to be renewed with the lives, but the same would seem to apply to an normally renewable term.

1. Granted After 1 August 1849

Thus, if granted after 1 August 1849, the purported grant of a lease in perpetuity operates automatically as a grant in fee farm subject to the covenants in the lease with the exception of the covenant for renewal.[73]

It is open to question whether a lease in the terms of the one in *McDermott v. Caldwell*[74] would fall within the 1849 Act. It is certainly not perpetual in a literal sense. If not, then if created today it would take effect according to its terms and the tenant could take advantage of the right to renew under the Tenantry Act, 1779 after the expiry of a term.

2. Subsisting on 1 August 1849

If the lease in perpetuity was subsisting on 1 August 1849, the 1849 Act vests in the tenant a power to demand a grant in fee farm.[75] Section 74 of the Landlord and Tenant (Amendment) Act, 1980 does not apply to perpetually renewable leases for years, since the statute expressly refers only to leases for lives. Thus, where land was held under a perpetually renewable lease for years on 1 August 1849, and the power under the 1849 Act has not been exercised, the power still exists and may still be exercised.

Since such pre-1849 leases also come within the Tenantry Act, 1779, the tenant has an equity to renew the lease even after a term has expired. The tenant therefore has a choice: either to renew the term under the 1779 Act or to exercise the power under the 1849 Act to demand a fee farm grant.

3. Northern Ireland

Under the Property (Northern Ireland) Order 1997[76] perpetually renewable leases for years are not capable of being created at law or in equity in Northern Ireland after 10 January 2000.[77] Subsisting[78] leases are converted into a fee simple subject to a fee farm rent.[79]

---

73 Section 37.

74 (1877) IR 10 Eq 504, V-C.

75 Section 1.

76 (SI 1179, NI 8).

77 *ibid.* Article 36(1)(c), Article 1(2), Property (1997 Order) (Commencement No. 2) Order (Northern Ireland) 1999 (SR 1999/461). Land Law Working Group *Final Report* (HMSO 1990) Vol. 1, paras. 1.6.6–19.

78 A lease is subsisting for the purposes of the Article if rent is still being paid and is not in arrear, whether or not the lease itself has been renewed: Article 36(9).

79 Article 36(4) and Schedule 2.

M. Time-Share Leases

A new form of lease has appeared in recent years designed to provided holiday accommodation. The typical time-share lease[80] will grant the right to occupy a holiday flat or house for one or two weeks at the same time each year for a specified number of years. Judges have been in some doubt as to how to treat such leases.[81] An obvious question here is whether, in order to fall within the phrase definite period in section 4 of Deasy's Act, the term has to be a continuous one. If so, then time-share leases would fall outside the Act.

In *An Application of O'Sullivan, Folio 27742 Co Cork*[82] D'Arcy J had to consider a lease granted under a holiday time-share scheme which granted "week No 25 in each year" for a term of 1100 years. The applicant applied for registration of the lease as a burden under section 69(1)(g) of the Registration of Title Act, 1964. The section refers to "any lease where the term granted is for a life or lives, or is determinable on a life or lives, or exceeds twenty-one years, or where the term is for any less estate or interest but the occupation is not in accordance with the lease".[83] The Registrar refused registration and an appeal was taken to the court. D'Arcy J upheld the Registrar's decision. He interpreted the phrase "twenty-one years" to imply a continuous term of 21 years. This, he felt, was the ordinary meaning of the words. The judge expressed the view that the court could not make new law, it could only apply existing law. New law was a matter for the Oireachtas.

The decision is unfortunate. The total term of 1,100 years was no doubt chosen because 1,100 weeks divided by 52 equals just over 21 years. It is obviously desirable that those who buy such leases should have the protection of the registration Act. Fitzgerald[84] suggests that any amending legislation should classify such interests as section 72 burdens under the 1964 Act so that a note of their existence could then be entered on the register under section 72(3). This assumes that time-share leases are not within section 72 already. It is however open to question as to whether it follows from D'Arcy J's judgment that a time-share term is not within section 72(1)(i) as a tenancy "created for any term not exceeding twenty-one years or for any less estate or interest, in

80 See Edmonds, 1984.

81 In the English case of *Cottage Holiday Associates v. Customs & Excise* [1983] 1 QB 735, [1983] 2 WLR 861. Wolff J had to consider a lease granting the right to occupy for 1 week per year for 80 years at a peppercorn rent and substantial management fees. The issue was whether it was a lease "exceeding 21 years" for the purposes of a tax statute – the English Finance Act, 1972. The judge held that it was a lease for 80 weeks and so did not fall within the provision.

82 Unreported, High Court, D'Arcy J, 24 March 1983.

83 If it is in accordance with the lease and the term exceeds 21 years then the lease is a registrable interest under section 27(c) and see section 3 leasehold interest.

84 Fitzgerald, *Land Registry Practice* p.252.

cases where there is an occupation under such tenancies". The section the judge was considering certainly also includes the phrase "any less estate or interest" but the judge's mind seem to have been directed towards the length of the term rather than any other issue. It is also arguable that there is occupation under the tenancy, namely during the occupational week.

A more intriguing question is whether a time-share is within section 72(1)(j) as the right of a person in "actual occupation of the land or in receipt of the rents and profits thereof, save where, upon enquiry made of such person, the rights are not disclosed". Such interests are binding even without registration. Is the tenant in actual occupation? He or she certainly is during the occupational week, but not for the rest of the year. Rights of persons in actual occupation are included within section 72 for the reason that their existence is relatively easy for a purchaser to discover, and as the subsection itself provides, they only bind after an inquiry is made if they are disclosed. If a lease grants "week 25 in each year" to a tenant and a prospective purchaser of the registered title inspects the land in week 25 he or she may well find the holiday makers in residence. But if they inspect it during any other week in the year they will not. But another tenant might be in occupation in that week. Would this be sufficient to bind the purchaser not only as to the tenancy granted for that week, but also put him on notice that there is a time-share scheme in operation and so also that other leases exist? In unregistered land the doctrine of notice may act in this way, but the doctrine of notice has been replaced in the case of registered land by the provisions of the Act.

N. Formalities

1. Certain Leases To Be in Writing

Deasy's Act, 1860 section 4 lays down the formalities of a lease if it is to fall within the provisions of the Act:

> "4.– Every lease[85] or contract with respect to lands whereby the relation of landlord and tenant is intended to be created for any freehold estate or interest, or for any definite period of time not being from year to year or any lesser period, shall be by deed executed or note in writing signed by the landlord or his agent thereunto lawfully authorized in writing".

---

85 Section 4 may apply to leases or terms without a rent which do not otherwise fall within Deasy's Act, 1860. The alternative view, that such terms fall outside Deasy's Act, 1860 altogether, because they are outside s.3, would mean that no formalities apply to them, since Deasy's Act, 1860 repealed the Real Property Act, 1845, which required a deed, except as to feoffments, exchanges and partitions. If no formalities were required, it was then also follow that there would be no scope for *Walsh v. Lonsdale* in relation to such terms.

2. Agreements for a Lease: Walsh *v.* Lonsdale

Equitable tenancies may arise through the doctrine of *Walsh v. Lonsdale*.[86] In that case the parties failed to create a legal lease through failure to comply with the necessary formalities. It was held that equity would treat the failed lease as an agreement to create a lease, provided the formalities required for contracts was complied with. Furthermore, provided that it was a contract which equity could enforce by specific performance, equity would treat "that as done which ought to be done" and would treat it as already a lease in equity. The principle applies in Ireland, and so it is necessary to identify in this jurisdiction the situations in which a lease may fail to be a legal lease because of lack of formalities, but where the agreement complies with the formalities required of a contract to create an interest in land.

These situations occur where an agreement fails to be a valid legal lease because it fails to comply with the formalities for a grant, under section 4 of Deasy's Act but still satisfies the requirements of a contract under section 2 of the Statute of Frauds (Ireland), 1695[87] or of part performance in equity. Section 2 of the Statute of Frauds reads:

> "2.–. . .no action shall be brought whereby to charge.. any person. . . upon any contract or sale of lands, tenements, or hereditaments, or any interest in or concerning them. . . unless the agreement upon which such action shall be brought, or some memorandum or note thereof, shall be in writing, and signed by the party to be charged therewith, or some other person thereunto by him lawfully authorized".

The courts of equity in the past considered that the Statute required a certain kind of evidence, namely the note or memorandum, but that they could, in order to avoid fraud, accept an alternative form of evidence and this gave rise to the doctrine of part performance. Part performance of a contract for the sale of land will make it enforceable in the same way as if a memorandum existed.

The following are therefore the cases which fall to be considered.

a) Tenancy from Year to Year or Any Lesser Period.

This type of agreement is outside section 4 and there are no formalities that apply, so that it can be made orally and still operate as a legal lease. There is no scope for the application of *Walsh v. Lonsdale*.[88] It should be noted that the assignment of such a tenancy must be in writing under section 9 of Deasy's Act, 1860.

---

86 (1882) 21 Ch D 9. See Chapter 4 Equity.

87 *Walsh v. Lonsdale* (1882) 21 Ch D 9. See Sheridan, "Walsh *v.* Lonsdale in Ireland" (1952) 9 NILQ 190.

88 (1882) 21 Ch D 9.

What if the lease is for one year? In *Wright v. Tracey*[89] the Irish Court of Exchequer had to decide whether a term of one year was "less than a tenancy from year to year" for the purpose of section 62(2) of the Landlord and Tenant (Ireland) Act, 1870. By a majority of four to three they held that it was not. A tenancy from year to year was essentially for one year certain renewed automatically. This suggests that a tenancy for one year certain is included in the first part of the phrase "tenancy from year to year or any lesser period" and so is outside section 4 of Deasy's Act and can be made orally.[90]

b) Term Greater than from Year to Year

The doctrine of *Walsh v. Lonsdale*[91] will apply where the agreement is for a term greater than from year to year in the following situations, *i.e.* where the agreement falls within the terms of section 4 but does not comply with it, and yet does comply with section 2 of the Statute of Frauds, 1695:

(1) Where the agreement is in writing signed by the landlord's orally authorised agent.

It fails as a lease under section 4 of Deasy's Act because the landlord's agent was not authorised in writing. Under section 2 of the Statute of Frauds the agreement, to be enforceable, must be signed by "the party to be charged". The tenant can sue the landlord in any case, since it has been signed by the landlord's agent.[92]

(2) Where the agreement is in writing signed by the tenant.

In this case it is enforceable only by the landlord.

(3) Where the agreement is in writing signed by the landlord's orally authorised agent and by the tenant.

There could also be a combination of 1. and 2. above in which the agreement is in writing signed by the landlord's orally authorised agent and by the tenant. In such a case the agreement is enforceable both by the landlord and by the tenant since both parties to be charged have signed the memorandum under the Statute of Frauds.

(4) Where the agreement is oral, but written evidence of it exists or comes into existence later.

The agreement is enforceable against the party or parties by whom or by whose agent the written evidence is signed.

---

89 (1874) IR 8 CL 478, Ex Ch.

90 See also *Brew v. Conole* (1875) IR 9 CL 151; *McGrath v. Travers* [1948] IR 122.

91 (1882) 21 Ch D 9.

92 *McAusland v. Murphy* (1881) 9 LR Ir 9.

In *Craig v. Elliot*[93] the defendant landlord entered into a verbal agreement with the plaintiff to grant the plaintiff a lease of a house for a term of years. The draft lease was sent by the plaintiff's solicitors to the defendant's solicitors. The defendant's solicitors signed the draft on behalf of their client and returned the draft lease. The defendant later wrote to the plaintiff complaining that the draft lease had not been engrossed, and later refused to carry out the agreement. The plaintiff sued for specific performance of the agreement. It was held that the letter signed by the defendant - the party to be charged - contained a sufficient reference to the draft lease to connect them together to form the memorandum required by the Statute of Frauds.

In *Babington v. O'Connor*[94] the intending tenant executed the draft. The landlord had not done so, but it was he who sued the tenant under a covenant in the draft to pay rent in advance. The defendant tenant had gone into possession and paid rent. The landlord was held entitled to the rent in advance. The court did not refer to *Walsh v. Lonsdale* although the facts are almost the same. The tenant was holding as a tenant in equity bound by the covenants in the agreement.

(5) The agreement is oral, but is subsequently partly performed.

Babington v. O'Connor could also be seen as an example of this situation since there was clearly part performance in that case. It used to be said that the act of part performance had to be unequivocally referable to the contract. In *Steadman v. Steadman*[95] the British House of Lords reviewed the law on part performance and modified it somewhat: the acts relied on did not have to refer to specific terms. Also, contrary to what was previously the case, they held that payment of money can be an act of part performance.[96]

In *Sweeney v. Denis*[97] a tenant was in possession under an existing lease which was due to end. He entered into an agreement for a new lease at an increased rent. He remained in occupation, paying the old rent. It was held not to amount to part performance as he was not doing anything which he had not done before.

There is one possible further case where the doctrine of *Walsh v. Lonsdale* may apply:

(6) Future Lease

This situation arises where an agreement conforms to section 4 of Deasy's Act but it is for a lease to begin at a future date. *Walsh v. Lonsdale* could then apply

93 (1885) 15 LR Ir 257.

94 (1887) 20 LR Ir 246.

95 [1976] 2 All ER 977.

96 Wallace (1974) 24 NILQ 453.

97 (1883) 17 ILTR 76.

if it could be said that the agreement did not create a lease to begin in future (*i.e.* a future interest) but created only a contract to grant a lease in future to take effect at the date specified. If the doctrine applied there would be a lease in equity immediately, to take effect at the future date, but no legal lease.

There seem to be two difficulties in the way of coming to this conclusion. The first is that it is not clear whether it is possible in Ireland to have an agreement to create a lease in future which does not immediate give rise to a lease, albeit a future legal lease. Section 3 of Deasy's Act appears to lay down that a lease is no more than a contract and a contract is a lease.

The second difficulty is the familiar one at common law, namely that a contract to grant a lease in future would be a contract to enter into a contract, and it has long been doubted whether the law recognises such a contract. What is it a contract to do? To negotiate in good faith?[98] In the case of contracts for leases these problems may be less than in other cases. If the parties agree on the duration and the rent the law implies other terms. In *Union v. McDermott*[99] an agreement for a weekly tenancy to begin in future was held not to be a mere agreement to make a letting in future. It was a legal tenancy to take effect in future, but the court said that it held this on the facts of the case and did not purport to lay down a general rule.

Finally, an agreement may comply neither with section 4 of Deasy's Act nor with the Statute of Frauds. Where the doctrine of equity cannot apply, it would seem that a common law tenancy at will may result. In *Ward v. Ryan*[100] an oral agreement purporting to grant a term of years was held to create a tenancy at will.

3. Is an Agreement for a Lease as Good as a Lease?

Where the doctrine of *Walsh v. Lonsdale* applies, it is sometimes said that "an agreement for a lease is as good as a lease". This is misleading because a lease in equity suffers from the following defects as compared to a legal lease:

a) Remedies Discretionary

The doctrine gives rise only to a lease in equity, and so depends on the discretionary remedy of specific performance. If for some reason that remedy cannot be granted the doctrine cannot apply.[101] Where, for example, the grant of the lease was subject to a condition precedent which remains unperformed by the

98 *May & Butcher v. King* [1934] 2 KB 17 (contract to contract is a nullity). Sheridan, (1952) 9 NILQ 190 says that if this is so one cannot enter into a contract to create a lease in future. One can only enter into a legal lease to take effect at a future date.

99 (1921) 55 ILTR 194.

100 (1875) IR 9 CL 54 at 55, on appeal IR 10 CL 17, Exch Ch, Whiteside CJ at p.20.

101 *Kingswood Estates v. Anderson* [1963] 2 QB 169.

proposed tenant and has not been waived by the landlord, there is no lease in equity.[102]

b) Not a Conveyance.

Statutory provisions that apply to conveyances do not apply to an equitable lease under the doctrine, so, for example, section 6 of the Conveyancing Act, 1881 would not apply to equitable leases arising under the doctrine.[103]

c) Prior Equities

Equitable tenants cannot plead purchase of a legal estate without notice in order to take free of prior equities. The situation can still arise under the Registry of Deeds system where the prior equity in not registrable because it is not created by deed as in the case, for example, of equitable mortgages by deposit. In relation to such interests the equitable doctrine of notice still applies. A similar situation can also arise in registered land.

d) Liable to be Defeated

Like all equitable interests, equitable tenancies are liable to be defeated by a later purchaser of the legal estate without notice of them. In the case of registered title an equitable tenant in actual occupation may be protected as having a section 72 interest. If not in actual occupation the tenancy would need to be protected by an entry on the register as a minor interest.

e) Outside Deasy's Act?

The requirements of section 4 of Deasy's Act are necessary if, as the Act says, "the relation of landlord and tenant" is to be created. This presumably means for the purposes of the Act. If so, then on the face of it leases in equity within the *Walsh v. Lonsdale* principle are valid but not governed by Deasy's Act. An alternative view is that the equitable doctrine treats such agreements as if specific performance had been granted in which case they would notionally comply.

O. Implied Tenancies

1. Under Section 5 of Deasy's Act

Implied tenancies may arise under section 5 of Deasy's Act:

> "5.–In case any tenant or his representative, after the expiration or determination of the term agreed upon in any lease or instrument in writing, shall continue in

102 *Cornish v. Brook Green Laundry Ltd* [1959] 1 QB 394, [1959] 1 All ER 373, [1959] 2 WLR 215, 173 EG 307, [1959] EGD 116.

103 *Borman v. Griffith* [1930] 1 Ch. 493 at 497f.

> possession for more than one month after demand for possession by the landlord or his agent, such continuance shall, at the discretion of the landlord, be deemed to constitute a new holding of the lands from year to year, subject to the former rent and to such of the agreements contained in the lease or instrument as may be applicable to the new holding".

In *O'Keefe v. Walsh*[104] O'Keefe was a tenant for life. He created a tenancy from year to year in favour of the defendant. Then he died. For 15 months the defendant remained in occupation. He assumed that the plaintiff who was entitled in remainder after O'Keefe, did not want to alter the arrangement. He offered rent and it was refused. The question was whether the defendant was entitled to notice to quit, *i.e.* had the tenancy continued after the death of the tenant for life? It could only have done so if it had been adopted by the remaindermen and it was held on appeal that there was insufficient evidence that they had done so.

Section 5 presupposes a previous term which has expired and therefore deals with holding over by an existing tenant. Nevertheless, it is clear that section 5 is not exhaustive of the situations in which courts in Ireland may find implied tenancies, and the next section deals with these.

2. Outside Section 5

Tenancies under the doctrine of *Walsh v. Lonsdale*[105] are valid apart from the section[106] although it is arguable that they are not really implied but rather result from equity providing a remedy to avoid an otherwise unfair result.

The courts have also held there to be an implied tenancy even though there was a prior valid term which had expired but the situation did not fall within section 5. In *Phoenix Picture Palace Ltd v. Capitol & Allied Trustees Ltd*[107] there was a lease for three years of the cinema at a weekly rent with an option to renew for another two years. The three years came to an end. The tenants did not exercise their option, but continued in possession paying a weekly rent. During the three year term by agreement between the parties, rent had been paid in quarterly instalments of 13 times the weekly rent. After the three years were up, the tenants paid rent weekly. The court held that there was only a weekly and not a yearly tenancy. Even if section 5 were wide enough to include the present case, its application was excluded by the circumstance that the section only provided for the landlord to treat the tenant as a yearly tenant.

One should notice that under section 40 of the Landlord and Tenant (Amendment) Act, 1980 a tenant entitled to a reversionary lease to begin at the end of his or her present tenancy is entitled to remain in possession and under

---

104 (1880) 8 LR Ir 184, (1881) 8 LR Ir 184, App.

105 (1882) 21 Ch D 9. See above.

106 *Kennan v. Murphy* (1880) 8 LR Ir 285.

107 [1951] Ir Jur Rep 55.

sections 27 and 28 so also is a person entitled under statute to the fee simple or to a new lease *i.e.* long term residents of residential or business premises who have made substantial improvements. What interest do they have in the meantime? In *Cooke v. Dillon*[108] a tenant was entitled to a new tenancy. He remained in possession and paid rent as he had done before, which was on a monthly basis. The court refused to imply a tenancy from year to year. He was held to be a monthly tenant.

P. Tenancies by Estoppel

Tenancies can also arise through the operation of the doctrine of estoppel.[109] As between the parties to an agreement an estoppel is no more than a matter of evidence or procedure, but it requires more than that to extend the binding effect to third parties. Various attempts have been made to do so. The doctrine of feeding the estoppel is of common law origin and produces the result that the tenancy is a legal estate. The doctrine of proprietary estoppel produces an equity which may nevertheless only be satisfied by the vesting of a legal estate in the relior. The general characteristics of that doctrine are discussed in Chapter 18.

1. Original Parties

If A, who has no interest in a piece of land, purports to grant a lease in it to B, then each is estopped, as against the other, from denying that the relationship of landlord and tenant exists between them.

In *Keenan v. Walsh*[110] K executed a mortgage on his house. Afterwards he sublet two rooms in the house to Walsh. The tenant was not satisfied with the rent and brought an action under the then Rent Restrictions Act, 1946. The mortgage contained a clause prohibiting subletting without the consent of the mortgagees.[111] It was held that the tenancy, even though contrary to the mortgage, was valid between the parties. It was a tenancy by estoppel that neither party could dispute.

2. Feeding the Estoppel

The common law held that if A, who had no estate, purported to grant a tenancy to B, then if A later acquired an estate in the land granted, the tenancy

108 (1959) 93 ILTR 48.

109 *Sturgeon v. Wingfield* (1846) 15 M & W 224, 15 LJ Ex 212, 153 ER 831; *Gowrie Park Utility Society Ltd v. Fitzgerald* [1963] IR 436.

110 (1951) 85 ILTR 86.

111 The lease was not within powers conferred by the Conveyancing Acts.

which had operated by estoppel between A and B became a full legal estate.[112] Later cases referred to the estoppel as being fed by the legal estate.

One of the earliest cases in which an estoppel was held to bind a third party is the Irish case of *Jones v. Kearney*.[113] In that case it was said that if a person who has not got an estate enters into a contract in respect of it, then if he or she afterwards acquire the estate, it will be bound by the contract. That was a case of a contract but in *Church v. Dalton*[114] A, a tenant at will of B, purported to grant a lease to C. B later obtained a lease from A. It was held that the grant from B to A operated retrospectively, turning the estoppel created between A and C into an estate at law.[115]

In *Universal Permanent Building Society v. Cooke*[116] a purchaser entered into a contract to buy a shop with a flat over it. Before the legal estate was conveyed to her she let the flat to her sister. The sister went into possession and paid rent. The premises were then conveyed to the purchaser in fee simple. The next day she mortgaged the premises to the building society. Three years later the mortgagor went into default. The building society claimed they were entitled to vacant possession *i.e.* not subject to the tenancy. It was held that in the absence of evidence that the conveyance and mortgage were all one transaction, there was an interval of time during which the mortgagor was the owner of the fee simple not subject to the mortgage and as a result the tenancy by estoppel of the sister was fed by the legal estate giving her a legal tenancy before the mortgage was executed and which therefore bound the mortgagee.

In *Woolwich Equitable Building Society v. Marshall*[117] it was held that even when the conveyance and the mortgage are executed on the same day there was a presumption that the conveyance was executed first, as it should be, and the estoppel was still fed.[118] In *Abbey National Building Society v.*

112 *Webb v. Austin* (1844) 7 Man & G 701, 135 ER 282; *Sturgeon v. Wingfield* (1846) 15 M & W 224, 153 ER 831; *Church v. Dalton* (1847) 9 Ir CLR 355. Co Litt 47b.

113 (1841) 4 Ir Eq R 82.

114 (1847) 9 Ir CLR 355.

115 See also *Eyre v. Sadleir* (1865) 15 Ir Ch R 1 (S was to take the conveyance of an estate sold by the Incumbered Estates Court. Before the conveyance was executed in his favour, S executed a conveyance in favour of W, using forged documents as proof of his title. The Incumbered Estates Court then executed the conveyance in favour of S. It was held that the conveyance by the court vested the land in W); *Sexton v. McGrath* (1872) IR 6 Eq 381 (A had agreed to purchase land from the Landed Estates Court. Before the conveyance was executed in his favour A purported to grant a lease to B. The conveyance to A was then executed, but it made no reference to the lease. It was held that the conveyance to A was nevertheless subject to B's lease, the court noting that the lease was effective not only in equity, but also at law as a lease by estoppel); *Ward v. Ryan* (1875) IR 10 CL 17.

116 [1952] Ch. 95.

117 [1952] Ch. 1.

118 See also *Church of England Building Society v. Piskor* [1954] Ch. 553.

Cann[119] a considerable restriction was placed on the doctrine by the English House of Lords in holding that it was inequitable for a person to claim a tenancy by estoppel where they knew at the time of the conveyance that a mortgage was to be entered into by the grantor and that the building society would not grant it if there were tenancies in existence. In *First National Bank plc v. Thompson*[120] the English Court of Appeal held that the doctrine did not depend on a representation by the grantor, but on the common law principle that a grantor could not deny his or her own title.[121]

3. Proprietary Estoppel

The decision in *Haughan v. Rutledge*[122] has been discussed in Chapter 18.[123] In that case the plaintiffs claimed a lease based on proprietary estoppel and Blayney J accepted the principle, although he found that it had not been established on the facts in the case. The judge cited a passage from Snell's *Principles of Equity*[124] setting out the test of proprietary estoppel and he described this as a "correct statement of the law".

In *Law v. Murphy*[125] a claim to a tenancy by estoppel failed on another ground. A licence had been granted to remove gravel. The owner of the land offered the licensee a lease. It was held that there was an insufficient memorandum for the Statute of Frauds because there was no reference to the area to be leased or to the term. McWilliam J held that there could be no lease by estoppel because the licensee had suffered no detriment. They merely continued excavating on the land, which they had previously been doing under the licence.

Q. Assignment and Subletting

As to the tenant, the question as to whether they have an estate is largely meaningless in view of Deasy's Act. The attributes of the leasehold relationship in this respect are governed by the statute, not by the common law. Section 9 of Deasy's Act provides that the estate or interest of any tenant in any lands under any lease or contract of tenancy shall be assignable by deed or instrument in writing signed by the assignor or his agent lawfully authorised in writing, or by

119 [1991] 1 AC 56, [1990] 1 All ER 1085, [1990] 2 WLR 832, 60 P & CR 278, 22 HLR 360, HL.

120 [1996] Ch. 231, [1996] 1 All ER 140, 2 WLR 293.

121 *ibid.* per Millet LJ; *Goodtitle d Edwards v. Bailey* (1777) 2 Cowp 597, [1775] All ER Rep 554.

122 Unreported, High Court, Blayney J, 19 January 1988.

123 See page 546.

124 Snell, (1982) at p.558.

125 Unreported, High Court, McWilliam J, 12 April 1978.

devise or bequest (*i.e.* a will) or by operation of law, and not otherwise. And not otherwise indicates that if the assignment is in writing it must be signed by the assignor or his agent lawfully authorised in writing. Thus, in *McIlherron v. McIlherron*[126] it was held that an oral agreement to assign followed by an actual change of possession is not enough without the landlord's consent to effect an assignment by operation of law.

Section 9 also applies to tenancies that can be created orally under section 4 of Deasy's Act, *i.e.* tenancies "from year to year or any lesser period". The death of the tenant causes an assignment by operation of law.[127] Section 11 provides that the assignee is subject to all the agreements in respect of assignment or subletting to the same extent as the assignor.

1. The Running of Covenants at Common Law

a) Assignees of the Tenant

In 1583 in *Spencer's Case*[128] it was held that an assignee of the tenant could enforce against the landlord an express covenant in the lease conferring a benefit on the tenant provided the covenant "touched and concerned the land", *i.e.* was for the benefit of the land and did not confer a purely personal benefit on the tenant.[129] The benefit of such a covenant "ran with the land" *i.e.* passed to the person in possession of the land under the lease. *Spencer's Case* also held that the burden of covenants touching and concerning the land ran with the land. Thus, if the original lease contained a covenant binding the tenant to keep a wall in repair, assignees of the original tenant could be sued by the landlord if they failed to repair the wall.

b) Assignees of the Reversion

At common law an assignee of the reversion, *i.e.* an assignee of the landlord's interest, could sue on covenants implied in the relationship of landlord and tenant by the general law, such as the covenant by the tenant to pay rent, but had no right to enforce express covenants in the lease entered into between the original parties.[130] At the dissolution of the monasteries the grantees of monastic lands wished to enforce covenants in leases entered into by the monasteries with their tenants and so the Grantees of Reversions Act, 1540 was passed to

126 (1892) 27 ILTR 62; and see Lawson J in *Bourke v. Bourke* (1874) IR 8 CL 221 at 223.

127 *Wallis v. Wallis* (1883) 12 LR Ir 63.

128 (1583) 5 Co Rep 16.

129 *Mayor of Congleton v. Pattison* (1808) 10 East 130 at 135, 103 ER 725 at 727: "[it] affected the nature, quality, or value of the thing demised, independently of collateral circumstances; or if it affected the mode of enjoying it".

130 Cheshire, *Real Property* (15th ed.), p.450.

enable them to do so. [131]It also made them liable to be sued on express covenants by the tenants. A similar Act was passed in Ireland in 1634.[132] The statutes were regarded as having changed the law to allow all grantees of reversions to sue and be sued on express covenants which touched and concerned the land.[133]

The relationship between assignees of the original landlord and assignees of the original tenant came to be called privity of estate.[134] Between the original landlord and the original tenant there was privity of contract, and all covenants were binding within the limits of the law. Between assignees of the original parties there was privity of estate and those covenants were binding which touched and concerned the land:

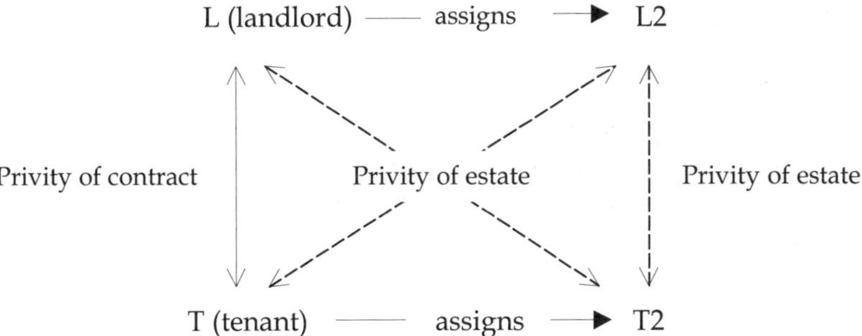

2. Touching and Concerning: Examples

The following are examples from the case law of covenants which have been held to touch and concern the land:

131 32 Hen VIII c.34, 1540.

132 10 Chas I sess 2 c.4 (Ir), 1634, repealed by Deasy's Act, 1860 s.104 & sch.

133 Cheshire, *Real Property* (15th ed.), pp. 450–52.

134 *Berney v. Moore* (1791) 2 Ridg PC 310.

By the lessor	By the lessee
To supply the premises with pure water.[135]	To pay rent.[136]
Not to build on adjoining land.[137]	To repair the property or fixtures on it.[138]
To renew the lease.[139]	To insure against fire.[140]
Not to determine a periodic tenancy during its first three years.[141]	To use as a private dwelling house only.[142]
	To pay a sum of money towards redecorating on quitting.[143]

3. The Running of Covenants under Statute

a) Benefit and Burden of Covenants

Sections 12 and 13 replace the common law concept of privity of estate[144] by providing that the benefit and burden of covenants and agreements contained or implied in leases or tenancies are enforceable by or against successors to the landlord and tenant.

135 *Jourdain v. Wilson* (1831) 4 B & Ald 266.

136 *Parker v. Webb* (1693) 3 Salk 5, 91 ER 656.

137 *Ricketts v. Enfield Churchwardens* [1909] 1 Ch. 544.

138 *Matures v. Westwood* (1598) Cro Eliz 599, 78 ER 842; *Williams v. Earle* (1868) LR 3 QB 739 at 751f.

139 *Chandos (Duchess) v. Brownlow* (1791) 2 Ridg PC 383 at 409; Lyne, *Leases for Lives* p.123; Shepp Touch 161. Every assignee can take advantage of it and every person who comes lawfully by the term: Lyne p.123; *Hyde v. Skinner* 2 P W 196.

140 *Vernon v. Smith* (1821) 5 B & Ald 1, 106 ER 1094 at 1096ff.

141 *Breams Property Investment Co Ltd v. Stroulger* [1948] 2 KB 1.

142 *Wilkinson v. Rogers* (1864) 2 De GJ & S 62, 46 ER 298 at 300f.

143 *Boyer v. Warbey* [1953] 1 QB 234.

144 See footnote 132.

The sections do not include the common law qualification that the covenants only bind successors if they touch and concern the land. But the court in *Lyle v. Smith*[145] placed a similar qualification on the sections. Madden J[146] and Gibson J[147] held that "covenants not capable of vicarious performance" do not bind, nor would "collateral agreements", but that covenants which touch and concern[148] the land will bind under Deasy's Act. In so holding they were overruling the earlier case of *Borrowes v. Delaney.*[149] *Lyle v. Smith* therefore confirms that Deasy's Act does not consistently treat the parties to leases as fictionally in the same position as the original contracting parties.

b) Liability Under Covenants

The sections in Deasy's Act do change one common law rule: at common law if the landlord only assigned a part of the reversion, the assignee of the part could not sue on the covenants. In *Liddy v. Kennedy*[150] it was said by Lord Hatherley that Deasy's Act was intended to remove technical difficulties that stood in the way of justice. The House of Lords, affirming the Irish Court of Exchequer Chamber and the Common Pleas, held that section 12 abolished the common law rule so that where a landlord constituted himself and another the landlord, then both together had the benefit of the covenants.

Section 16 of Deasy's Act provides that the assigning tenant is released from future liability on the covenants when he or she assigns the lease with the landlord's consent. At common law the original tenant would remain liable on the covenants even after assigning the lease unless he or she had contracted with the landlord only to be liable while he or she retained an interest in the land. It was a matter of privity of contract and parties could contract to be liable to whatever extent they had agreed. Deasy's Act alters this so that the tenant's liability ends with their parting with the interest in the land, and so in this respect the Act, far from treating leases like contracts, removes the position of the original parties from the realm of contract and links liability with ownership of a property interest.

Section 14 of Deasy's Act provides that the assignee of a tenancy is liable only in respect of breaches of covenant that occurred while he or she was a tenant, *i.e.* while there is what at common law would be called privity of estate. Here the Act merely declares what was the position at common law. Between an assignee and the landlord, whether the original landlord or a new one, there was no privity of contract, and therefore the assignee of the tenant was only liable to

145 [1909] 2 IR 58, 43 ILTR 255.

146 [1909] 2 IR 58 at p.78, 43 ILTR 255.

147 [1909] 2 IR 58 at p.77.

148 [1909] 2 IR 58 per Madden Jat p.79.

149 (1889) 24 LR Ir at 503 at 517.

150 (1871) LR 5 HL 134.

the extent that there was privity of estate. But notice that under section 14 the assignee only ceases to be liable on assigning his interest if he gives written notice to the landlord. Also, he can only take the benefit of the covenants while he is assignee, so that if the covenant was broken before he became tenant he cannot sue for the breach at that time.[151]

c) Waiver

Sections 18 and 43 of Deasy's Act provide that no act of a landlord is a waiver of a breach of covenant, unless the landlord signifies agreement in writing.[152] Section 22 of Deasy's Act provides that agreement by a landlord to a particular subletting is not a general waiver of the covenant, as it would be at common law.[153]

d) Payment for Consent

Section 3 of the Conveyancing Act, 1892 provides that no fine (lump sum) or similar sum is to be payable for the landlord's consent unless the lease provides for it. Is there any qualification on that express provision? If the lease provided for an excessive sum, then it may be that it would amount to an unreasonable withholding of consent for the landlord to demand it.

e) Covenants Restricting Assignment or Subletting

In other areas of property law we can see that there is a conflict between two objectives or policies both of which derive from the relations of a society based on the market. One is that people should be free to make their own bargains without intervention by the State. This has an ideological aspect, in that it may be assumed or asserted that the freedom exists regardless the factual position of the parties. Without factual equality there can be no freedom in the market, a point which those who advocate the market as a mechanism of distribution often ignore. The other objective is that interests in land should be freely marketable like other commodities. If a lease contains terms which absolutely prohibit assignment, the land is rendered unmarketable during the continuance of the lease. Alternatively, the covenant may give the landlord the right to refuse consent to an assignment or subletting, which may both be the result of the fact that the landlord was able to insist on the term being included through his unequal economic position and also confer on the landlord a power to restrict in his own interests, the marketability of the leasehold interest.

---

151 *Doyle v. Hart* 4 LR Ir at 467 per Palles CB.

152 *O'Toole v. Lyons* [1948] IR 115 (acceptance of rent).

153 Section 22 duplicates in Ireland ss. 1, 2 of the Law of Property (Amendment) Act, 1859 and s.6 of the Law of Property (Amendment) Act, 1860 which are to the same effect.

Statutory controls were contained originally in Deasy's Act[154] but are now[155] replaced in the Republic by sections 66 of the Landlord and Tenant (Amendment) Act, 1980.[156] Section 66(1) of the Landlord and Tenant (Amendment) Act, 1980 applies to covenants in leases of tenements before or after the commencement of the Act which absolutely prohibit or restrict alienation of the tenement either generally or in a particular way.[157] It provides that they shall take effect as covenants against alienation without the landlord's consent. Section 5 of the Act defines tenement in such a way as to include land mostly covered by buildings, and not just residential land.

Section 66(2) applies to three situations of which the first two are by far the most common, *i.e.*:

(a) leases containing covenants not to alienate without the landlord's consent;

(b) leases containing covenants not to alienate at all which, by virtue of section 66(1) take effect as covenants not to alienate without the landlord's consent; and

(c) leases or agreements for leases made between 1st June 1826 and 1st May 1832[158] and which (by the 1826 Act) are for less than 99 years and contain no reference to subletting. This was the result of the Landlord and Tenant (Ireland) Act, 1826[159] which was repealed with saving by section 104 & Schedule B of Deasy's Act, 1860. The 1826 Act rendered void any subletting made without the landlord's consent.[160]

Section 66(2) provides that in the above cases there is implied a proviso, notwithstanding any express provision to the contrary, that the consent shall not be withheld unreasonably. If the landlord could not reasonably have refused consent then an assignment or subletting is with consent for this purpose whether an application was made for consent and was refused or whether it was not sought at all.[161] Such as assignment is valid and effective.

154 Sections 10, 18. Before Deasy's Act there was a statutory control of subletting in the Subletting Act, *i.e.* the Landlord and Tenant (Ireland) Act, 1826, 7 Geo IV c.29 (see below). See *Robinson v. Wakefield* (1892) 30 LR Ir 547, CA.

155 Previously by s.56 of the Landlord & Tenant Act, 1931.

156 The section did not, oddly, repeal ss. 10 & 18. Sections 10 & 18 Deasy's Act were not repealed until 1967 by Landlord and Tenant (Ground Rents) Act, 1967 s.35.

157 34 NILQ 56.

158 The 1826 Act was repealed by 2 & 3 Wm IV c.17 but only as to leases after 1 May 1832

159 7 Geo IV c.29.

160 *Penney v. Gardner* (1833) Al & N 345; *Meares v. Redmond* (1879) 4 LR Ir 533, affirmed on appeal, not reported.

161 Note under (c) above the 1826 Act does make a subletting void: *Meares v. Redmond* (1879) 4 LR Ir 533.

(1) Effect of Lack of Consent

There is some question as to whether section 66 makes an assignment or subletting without consent void. It seems to follow from what has been said that an assignment without consent means an assignment or subletting where it would not be unreasonable for the landlord to refuse consent and either has in fact refused consent to an application or no application was made.

At common law an assignment or subletting without consent did not prevent the passing of an estate, although the landlord could forfeit the lease where the covenant was made a condition of the lease, or, if the lease was subject to a proviso for re-entry for breach of covenant, re-enter and put an end to the lease. In *UDC of Tralee v. McSweeney*[162] a lessee sublet part of the premises without the landlord's consent. The lessee later tried to recover the premises. The sub-lessee applied to the landlord for consent to the sub-lease, and the landlord did so. The lessee obtained an order for possession in the High Court. The Supreme Court upheld the judgment. The sublease was inoperative until the consent of the landlord was obtained, but became operative after that[163] so that all previous acts of the parties had the effect they would have had if the consent had been obtained at the time of execution of the sublease.[164] This, however, included the notice to quit given by the lessee to the sub-lessee, which would have been valid in accordance with the sub-lease. An assignment or subletting made without consent is ineffective unless and until it is subsequently ratified by the landlord, the ratification retrospectively validating earlier acts, provided that any retrospective action does not prejudice innocent third parties.[165]

(2) Conacre

Conacre agreements were considered by the courts before Deasy's Act not to constitute sub-leasing and therefore did not fall within covenants prohibiting

162 [1954] IR 233.

163 *Scott v. Redmond* (1880) 6 LR Ir 374, Exchequer, (1881) 8 LR Ir 112, App (lease for lives – ratification by infant reversioner effective provided no intervening transactions to interfere with it.) following *Davis v. Davis* (1827) 4 Ir LR 353; *Tobin v. Cleary* (1872) IR 7 CL 17 at 22.

164 This essentially follows earlier cases on s.10: Monaghan CJ so held in *Butler v. Smith* [1864] 16 Ir CLR 213 and Shannon J in *Whyte v. Sheehan* (1943) Ir Jur R 38, in which he said he need not refer to authorities on the point, but could be revived by ratification: *Scott v. Redmond* (1881) 8 LR Ir 112, App. See also *Manning v. Saul* (1890) 25 LR Ir 640, QB, 651 n, CA.

165 *Scott v. Redmond* (1880) 6 LR Ir 374, Ex, (1881) 8 LR Ir 112; *Davis v. Davis* (1827) 4 Ir LR 353; *Tobin v. Cleary* (1872) IR 7 CL 17 at 22.

subleasing without the lessor's consent.[166] Indeed they were also held not to amount to parting with possession or ceasing to occupy in express covenants.[167] Section 2 of the Land Act, 1946,[168] which prohibits the subletting of land sold under the Land Purchase Acts, specifically excludes conacre and agistment.

f) Covenants Restricting User

Many leases contain covenants restricting user of the premises, for example, to that of a dwelling house, or not for trade or business or not to sell alcohol. Section 67 of the Landlord and Tenant (Amendment) Act, 1980 modifies these in a similar way to covenants as to assignment and subletting, so that a covenant absolutely prohibiting alteration of user shall have effect as if it were a covenant prohibiting a change of user without the landlord's consent, and the consent shall not be unreasonably withheld.

g) The Test of Reasonableness

What is unreasonable in relation to withholding consent to an assignment or subletting has been the subject of considerable case law and some general categories of considerations have emerged.

(1) General Commercial Considerations

In *Rice v. Dublin Corporation,*[169] a case involving similar provisions in the Landlord and Tenant Act, 1931,[170] the Supreme Court held that the onus is on the tenant to prove a refusal is unreasonable, apparently on the general principle that the person who asserts must prove.[171] A plaintiff tenant would have to establish at least a prima facie case of unreasonableness. The court went on to hold that the onus was not shifted even if the landlord originally gave no reason for the refusal at all. It was open to a landlord to state the reason at the trial of the action. This could, however, put a tenant at a disadvantage. If no reasons are given at the trial stage then the refusal must be unreasonable, otherwise the statutory provisions would be nullified.

In *Rice v. Dublin Corporation* the tenant was the plaintiff. If a landlord sues to enforce a covenant against a tenant who has changed the user without apply-

166 *Dease v. O'Reilly* (1845) 8 Ir LR 52; *Booth v. McManus* (1863) 12 Ir CLR 418.

167 *Booth v. McManus* (1863) 12 Ir CLR 418 (conacre agreement to grow oats and to cut the crop).

168 Formerly the Land Law (Ireland) Act, 1881 s.2.

169 [1947] IR 425.

170 Section 57.

171 *White v. Carlisle Trust* [1976-77] ILRM 311; *Egan Film Service v. McNamara* (1952) 86 ILTR 189. *Shanley v. Ward* (1913) 29 TLR 714; *Pimms Ltd v. Tallow Chandlers in the City of London* [1964] 2 All ER 145 at 147, [1964] 2 QB 547 at 564.

ing for consent, is the onus then on the landlord, as plaintiff, to establish not only the existence of the covenant, but also that, in accordance with the statutory provisions, that had an application been made by the tenant it would have been reasonable to refuse it? The assumption in the judgments in *Rice* seems to be that it is not. If this is so then it is for the tenant to plead the statute and make a prima facie case.[172]

A criticism of *Rice* is that is has the effect of putting tenants in a less favourable position than landlords for no apparent reason. The legislation was intended to prevent landlords from acting on arbitrary or capricious grounds and probably also now on discriminatory grounds. There seems no good reason why the onus should always be on the tenant in every case to establish unreasonableness rather than for the landlord to establish that his or her act was reasonable. Such a position may in some instances be incompatible with the guarantee of equality before the law contained in Article 40.1. It is true that that article has been generally held not to affect commercial relations, since is refers to equality as human persons but it is not necessarily the case that landlord and tenant relationships always fall into the commercial category.

In *White v. Carlisle Trust*[173] McWilliam J held that a landlord was acting arbitrarily if he refused consent solely on the ground of the effect which a change of user would have on other tenants. It was argued by them that a change of user from a hatter's to a confectionery shop would compete with their trade as confectioners.

McWilliam J did in fact consider whether the change would affect them or not, but concluded that no effect could be shown, as the shops of the other tenants were in central Dublin and although they were near the applicant's shop there was no demonstrable effect. The judge however went on to hold that a detriment to one of the landlord's other tenants would not be a reasonable ground for refusal of consent without showing some consequential effect on the landlord's own financial position.

In *Green Property v. Shalaine Modes*[174] it was held that a lessor can legitimately consider his or her own financial interests in refusing consent. This was also held to be a valid ground in *Crowe Ltd v. Dublin Port & Docks Ltd*[175] in relation to subletting.

Green Property v. Shalaine concerned a shopping centre containing more than one toy shop. The premises in dispute, plots 45 and 46, had originally been used as a hardware store in accordance with a term in the lease. The lessee's interest was assigned to the defendant, Shalaine Modes, with the consent

172 In *Green Property v. Shalaine Modes*, unreported, High Court, McWilliam J, 20 November 1978, discussed below, the lessor was the plaintiff but did not raise the issue of reasonableness as such.

173 [1976–77] ILRM 311, High Court, McWilliam J.

174 Unreported, High Court, McWilliam J, 20 November 1978.

175 [1962] IR 194.

of the plaintiff but without a specific application for consent to a change of user. Shalaine Modes traded as a boutique selling women's clothes without the specific consent of the lessor but also without objection by the lessor.

In 1977, before Christmas of that year, the premises were sublet to B who had a toy shop elsewhere in the centre and who used the windows of 45 and 46 to display toys. B was the tenant of the premises next door, plot 47. Again, the lessor did not object to the change of user and no application was made by B for consent. In a subsequent year plots 45 and 46 were sublet to C to sell toys in the weeks before Christmas. B then objected to the landlord.

McWilliam J in the High Court upheld the right of the landlord to enforce the covenant. He considered that the lessor in the case of a shopping centre has a legitimate interest in maintaining a tenant mix, *i.e.* a variety of different shops, in order to attract customers. The lessor's own interest in this was that the more attractive the shopping centre, the higher the rents the lessor could charge for tenancies in the centre. This would seem to be the distinction between *Shalaine* and *White*, and also to constitute shopping centres as a special legal regime in the sense that this factor is not present in other situations, such as that in *White* itself. It would seem that the one thing a landlord must not be is altruistic. It could be argued that the effect of such cases as *White* and *Shalaine* is that tenants cannot take advantage of the supposedly random factor that they have the same lessor as against a tenant who wishes to change the user of his or her premises in a way which will compete with their business. Tenants of separate landlords could not restrain what would be normal market competition by a change of user in a nearby shop, in the absence of restrictive covenants and it is arguable that tenants should be in no better position because they happen to have the same landlord. Their remedy, if any, must lie in their bargain with their own landlord. In the shopping centre context it is possible that they may bargain for a term in their lease to control or specify the number of other businesses in the shopping centre which may compete directly with theirs. In the absence of this the court in *Shalaine* appeared unwilling to interfere in what are commercial decisions.

The court in *Shalaine* notably refused to apply any form of estoppel. It had been argued on the basis of *Shaw v. Applegate*[176] that the failure of the lessor to object in the past had created an expectation that he would not object on this occasion. The court did not, however, accept that a failure to enforce a covenant in one year could reasonably raise an expectation that it would not be invoked in a subsequent year, any more than the grant of permission in one year would constitute a general waiver of the covenant as to the future. Nor would consent to a change of user in one year constitute a general waiver of the term

176 [1978] 1 All ER 123. See also *Attorney General v. Guardian Newspapers* [1990] AC 109, [1988] 3 All ER 545, [1989] 3 WLR 776, HL; *Westland Savings Bank v. Hancock* [1987] 2 NZLR 21, High Court, Christchurch, NZ; *British Leyland Motor Corp & Others v. TI Silencers Ltd*, unreported, Ch D (Lexis), 17 October 1984.

for future years, binding the landlord to consent if a similar application were made in a subsequent year. It was simply left to the lessor's discretion. This is not to say, of course, that a court in the Republic may not apply concepts of acquiescence such as were raised in *Shaw v. Applegate*.

In *OHS Ltd v. Green Property Co Ltd*[177] a plot in the Northside Shopping Centre in Dublin was used as a fruit and vegetable store. The defendant's interest in the plot was assigned to the plaintiff subject to a covenant that the plot should continue to be used as a fruit and vegetable store. After a supermarket was opened in the centre the plaintiff found it increasingly difficult to make its business pay. It found a building society which was willing to take over the site and applied to the defendant for permission to change the user. The defendant refused on the ground that a building society was dead frontage. By this the defendant meant that it had been shown that potential customers of the shopping centres were not attracted to by commercial premises of that kind, although they might make use of them once they were there. In the High Court the defendant also argued that the Northside shopping centre already had a higher proportion of dead frontage than other centres in Dublin and that they had refused in order to avoid an excessive amount of such frontage. The plaintiff conceded that this was a valid reason, but argued as to the weight to be attached to it. Lynch J allowed the appeal and held that the defendant had acted reasonably on "valid estate management grounds".[178]

In the English case of *International Drilling Fluids Ltd v. Louisville Investments (Uxbridge) Ltd*[179] it was held that although in general a lessor was only bound to consider his or her own relevant interests when deciding whether to refuse consent to an assignment of a lease, it was nevertheless unreasonable for a landlord not to consider the detriment which would be suffered by the tenant who applied for a change of user if consent were to be refused and if that detriment would be extreme and disproportionate in relation to the benefit gained by the landlord.[180]

(2) Competition

The provisions of sections 66 and 67 of the Landlord and Tenant (Amendment) Act, 1980 and the case law on them are now subject in the Republic to

---

177 See also *Wanze Properties v. Mastertron Ltd* [1986] IR 39, [1986] ILRM 451, High Court (Chinese take-away).

178 [1992] ILRM 746.

179 [1985] 1 Ch. 513, [1986] 1 All ER 321, [1986] 2 WLR 581, 51 P & CR 187, [1986] 1 EGLR 39, CA.

180 See also *Ponderosa International Development Inc v. Pengap Securities (Bristol) Ltd*, 277 EG 1252, [1986] 1 EGLR 66, Ch D. The case distinguishes *International Drilling Fluids* on the ground that the landlords in the present case were willing to consent to a subletting and so there was no recognisable detriment to the tenants.

the Competition Act, 1991.[181] A tenant whose landlord refuses consent on the ground that the proposed user would not provide a sufficiently attractive mixture of shops could appeal to the Competition Authority under the Act on the ground that these are incompatible with the aim of free competition which is the policy of the Act. A landlord whose tenant took this course of action might argue that competition should be judged as between shopping centres and not merely within them.

(3) Human Rights

Rights under both the Constitution and the European Convention on Human Rights may be involved in the application of section 67. In the notorious case of *Schlegel v. Corcoran*[182] Gavan Duffy J held that it was reasonable for a landlady to refuse consent to an assignment because the assignee was Jewish and she was, in her own estimation at least, a Christian. The judge also unfortunately made some derogatory remarks in the course of his judgment. First, a distinction must be made between the constitutional issue raised and the specific statutory test. It may be that a ground would satisfy the statutory test as reasonable but violate constitutional rights. It could also be the case that a ground does not violate constitutional rights, but fails to satisfy the statutory test of reasonableness. As to the statutory test, McWilliam J in the High Court has taken the view that reasonable is opposed to arbitrary and capricious. A refusal on the ground of race or religion arguably falls within the latter category. As to Constitutional rights, Article 40.1 guarantees the equality of citizens as human persons. The case law supports the view that this introduces a distinction between discrimination on grounds of human attributes, which is proscribed, and discrimination on some ground not related to a persons human qualities, such as economic or commercial grounds, which is not. It may also be the case that there is a private area where the Article does not protect even against discrimination on human qualities.

(4) Conditions in Lease

To what extent are conditions in the lease relevant? If a landlord has not imposed a certain condition in the lease, is it then unreasonable of him or her to use that reason to refuse consent under a covenant? One would think not unreasonable, since, if it were otherwise, all the possible reasons would have to be given in advance. But one case held it relevant. In *Boland v. Dublin Corporation*[183] the landlord was a local authority. It let a house under the Housing (Ireland) Act, 1919 but had not required its maintenance as accommodation for members of the working classes. They refused to consent to an assignment to a

181 See also Competition (Amendment) Act, 1996.

182 [1942] IR 19.

183 [1946] IR 88.

person on the ground that he was not working class. It was held to be unreasonable.

h) Covenants as to Commercial User: The Restraint of Trade Doctrine

If the premises are used for business purposes and the lease contains a restriction on user then the common law doctrine of restraint of trade may be invoked. If the doctrine applies, then the restrictions are void if they are not reasonable. If the doctrine does not apply, then there is no test of reasonableness.

The general rule is that if A has an interest in a piece of land called Gortduff and the interest is not subject to any covenant restricting trade and then A enters into a contract or lease of the premises whereby his or her freedom of trade is restricted, the restraint of trade doctrine applies and the restriction is only valid if it satisfies a test of reasonableness. On the other hand, if A has no interest in Gortduff, but then enters into a lease of the land containing a covenant restricting freedom to trade, the common law doctrine does not apply and there is no test of reasonableness. In the latter case there was no prior freedom to trade which was diminished by the covenant.

The question of when the doctrine applied arose in *Irish Shell v. Elm Motors*[184] The lease contained a common form of covenant. A garage operator agreed that during the lease he would buy only the oil company's products. The plaintiff oil company bought a plot of land in Limerick. Some years later the defendants who had been trading as garage proprietors bought a plot of land immediately adjoining the plaintiff's land. They were given to understand that they would not obtain planning permission to develop the site as a petrol station. The defendants then asked the plaintiffs to lease them their plot and allow them to incorporate it into a combined site of a proposed new garage. The plaintiffs agreed. The defendants then obtained planning permission to develop the whole site as a petrol station. A lease was granted and it contained a covenant whereby the defendants agreed both as to their own plot and that of the demised premises that the defendants would only buy the petroleum products of the plaintiff oil company. Disagreements arose, the defendants claiming that the oil company showed little interest in the business or its development. The defendants then notified the plaintiffs that they did not consider themselves any longer bound by the covenants. The plaintiffs sued for an injunction.

The Supreme Court continued the injunction granted by the High Court and held that the extensive review of the law of restraint of trade by the judge was unnecessary in an interlocutory application. The court held that there was a fair case to be made and that the balance of convenience lay in favour of granting the interlocutory injunction.

184 [1984] ILRM 200 Supreme Court at 220.

The issue of restraint of trade was dealt with in the High Court by Costello J. It is, despite the strictures of the Supreme Court, a useful exposition of the law on the subject. He referred to two English cases, *Esso Petroleum v. Harper's Garage Ltd*[185] and *Cleveland Petroleum Ltd v. Dartstone Ltd*[186] and a Privy Council decision on appeal from Australia, *Amoco Australia Property Ltd v. Rocca Bros Motor Engineering.*[187] He held:

1) That the effect of those decisions, which he agreed with in principle, was that the doctrine of restraint of trade only applies where a person who previously had unfettered freedom of trade enters into a contract or covenant whereby he or she restricts that freedom. In other words, it does not apply where a person buys or leases a plot of land already subject to a restriction because in that case they have not given up a freedom which they previously enjoyed.
2) In the present case he held that the principle was not limited to covenants as to user of the land – the covenant was to use the land as a petrol station. It also applied to covenants restricting trading activity as such, *e.g.* to buy only the plaintiff's products.
3) The present covenant could be regarded as positive or negative, but it made no difference. A positive covenant might be more onerous but it did not mean that the restraint of trade doctrine would necessarily apply to it.
4) He noted that the covenant applied not only to the land the defendant leased from the plaintiffs but also to his own land which he had owned free of the restriction, but he considered that they could not have traded as a garage on the land without obtaining planning permission and they had not obtained it without the additional lease from the plaintiffs of the adjoining land, so in effect he had not held his own land with freedom to trade. Hence he was not giving up an unfettered freedom to trade in relation to it.

Thus the restraint of trade doctrine applied neither to the leased land nor to his own land.

Does the existence of planning legislation mean that no one has freedom to trade on their own land any more until and unless they have obtained planning permission, so that the restraint of trade doctrine has effectively been abrogated? It seems not. In *Irish Shell v. Elm Motors*[188] planning permission would probably have been refused without the additional plot and so it was possible to say that the defendants had no prior freedom to trade, but it might be otherwise if permission would possibly, or probably have been obtained. McCarthy J in the Supreme Court did refer to two factors that might influence the out-

185 [1968] AC 269, HL.

186 [1969] 1 WLR 116, CA.

187 [1975] AC 562.

188 [1984] ILRM 200 Supreme Court at 220.

come of the case on the substantive issue. One was that although it was unlikely that the defendants would have obtained planning permission on their own plot alone, that situation might change. The other was that although the covenant in the lease was to build the station on the demised premises and on his own, in fact it was built on defendant's land only. In other words, the scheme to include the leased land in the new application for planning permission looked like a mere device.

In the *Amoco Case*[189] the proprietor of the land built a service station on the land and then leased it to the Oil Company which then subleased it back to him. The High Court of Australia held that the covenants were subject to the restraint of trade doctrine and were unreasonable. Costello J in *Irish Shell v. Elm Motors*[190] agreed with the application of the doctrine in such a situation. The lease-back arrangement was a device to evade the doctrine and would not succeed in this jurisdiction. The courts would look at the substance of the transaction, which was that a proprietor who had previously enjoyed a freedom to trade had given it up.

The principle here seems to be that the law protects the original free owner, but does not seek to confer a freedom on someone who had not acquired it for themselves through the market, or inheritance, *etc.* The law takes the view that someone who had not previously enjoyed freedom of trade in relation to the land has a free choice: they may reject the lease with the restriction if they wish. What characterises this as ideology in support of the market mechanism is that the fact of freedom is asserted without a test of whether it is actually present. Could an intending petrol station operator obtain a lease of another petrol station free of the restriction?

Costello J dealt with a number of objections to the doctrine, in particular those raised by Heydon:[191]

1) It would lead to gross anomalies. For example, X owns two shops. He sells or leases one to A. A and X mutually covenant that neither shop should be used as a butcher's shop. Restraint of trade doctrine would apply to X's obligations, because he accepted a restraint on a freedom he previously enjoyed, but not to A's, because he had no previous freedom to trade in relation to the shop he bought. So A may not be able to enforce X's obligations while X could enforce A's obligations. Absurd. But Heydon himself says that A might invoke the principle of *Halsall v. Brizell*[192] *i.e.* that X could not take advantage of a deed unless he was prepared to submit to its obligations.

189 *Amoco Australia Property Ltd v. Rocca Bros Motor Engineering* [1975] AC 562.

190 [1984] ILRM 200 Supreme Court at 220.

191 Heydon, *The Restraint of Trade Doctrine*.

192 [1957] Ch. 169. The case is discussed in Chapter 21 Covenants between Freeholders.

2) That the restraint of trade doctrine is undesirable because it could easily be avoided by sale with lease-back. Costello J took the view that the courts would not accept the device.

3) That if positive covenants are exempt it could impose onerous obligations on the covenantor. Costello J rejected this. It is not a reason that vitiates the exemption of these covenants from the principle.

i) Covenants of Repair

Section 65 of the Landlord and Tenant (Amendment) Act, 1980 applies where a tenancy includes an agreement by the tenant to put or keep the premises in repair at the end of the tenancy. Damages for breach of the covenant are not the cost of repair. Section 65(2) provides that the damages shall not exceed the amount by which the value of the reversion in the tenement is diminished.[193] Except where the want of repair is due to wilful damage or waste, no damages are recoverable for breach if it is shown that:

(a) in regard to the age and condition of the premises its repair is physically impossible; or

(b) in regard to the age, condition, character, and the situation of the tenancy its repair would involve expenditure which is excessive in proportion to the value of the tenement; or

(c) in regard to the character and situation of the tenement the tenement could not when so repaired be profitably used or could not be used unless it was rebuilt reconstructed or structurally altered to a substantial extent.

In *Trustees of St Catherine's Parish, Dublin v. Alkin*[194] the plaintiff claimed damages for breach of a repairing covenant in a lease for 100 years which expired in 1981. The lease was of a number of houses. One of them had been demolished and as a result the flank wall of the next house had been exposed to the weather causing it to decay. The front wall also had an incipient bulge which had become worse. Carroll J held that the damage caused by the exposure of the flank wall was not the lessee's responsibility. It was for the landlord to seal the exposed wall. But the lessee was responsible for allowing the bulge to become worse – that was permissive waste. On the measure of damages, Carroll J laid down the method of calculation to determine the amount by which the reversion is affected. This was:

1. Estimate the annual rental value in its unrepaired state and multiply it by the multiplier – 7 in this case.

193 Similar provisions had been contained in earlier legislation: s.55(b) of the Landlord and Tenant Act, 1931, *Gilligan v. Silke* [1960] IR 1 at 9, (1964) 98 ILTR 161, Supreme Court.

194 Unreported, High Court, Carroll J, 4 March 1982.

2. Estimate the annual rental value in its repaired state and multiply it by the multiplier – 7.5 here.
3. Take the difference between the two which is the amount by which the reversion is reduced.
4. Deduct the proportion of that sum for which the lessee is not responsible – 10 per cent deducted here.

The amount so calculated was less than the cost of the repairs, as section 65 intended.

R. Implied Covenants, Statutory Rights and Duties

1. By the Landlord

Section 41 of Deasy's Act implies two covenants on the part of the landlord.

a) Good Title

Section 41 implies a covenant that the landlord has a good title to grant the lease. This is not a very significant provision since if there is a written contract, such a term would usually be included, and if the tenancy is one that can be enforceable although oral, the common law implies such a term. However, it was held in *Leonard v. Taylor*[195] that it did extend the common law, as it also applied to landlord and tenant relationships under Deasy's Act which could not exist at common law.

b) Quiet Enjoyment

Section 41 implies a covenant that the lessee should have quiet and peaceable enjoyment of the premises without interruption by the landlord "or any person whatever" during the term and so long as the tenant performs his obligations. The tenant has another remedy which may overlap with this one in protecting quiet enjoyment and that is the tort of nuisance. In *O'Leary v. Islington LBC*[196] it was held that there was no implied term in a tenancy at common law obliging the landlord of A to sue to enforce the covenant of another tenant, B, binding B not to cause a nuisance. A can bring an action for nuisance against B. But Deasy's Act says "any person whatever", so it would seem that in Ireland the landlord would be liable on his or her covenant to A if another tenant, B, causes a nuisance.

195 (1872) IR 7 CL 207.

196 *The Times*, London, 5 May 1983.

c) Condition of the Premises

(1) At Common Law

At common law there was, by the 17th and 18th centuries at any rate, no implied term in a lease of land that the land was fit for any particular purpose at the time the lease began. If the lessor was to be liable for any defect in the premises it could only be by an express term. In relation to vacant land this rule made some sense, because it could be said that the lessor should not be liable in the absence of some specific agreement because land could be used for a number of purposes. Even so, the courts at this time were prepared to use their power to protect the economic interests of landowners, of agricultural land at any rate, and this can be seen in the rule that the absence of an implied term applied even to agricultural land where it was obvious that the land was to be used, for example, for pasture. So in *Sutton v. Temple*[197] a lessor was held not liable where the tenant's cows died of lead poisoning in a contaminated field. The immunity was also extended to tort. Landlords were held to be immune from liability to the tenant's guests or customers from damage caused due to the condition of the premises at the time the lease or tenancy came into effect. The law at the time was summarised by Erle CJ in *Robbins v. Jones*:[198]

> "A landlord who lets a house in a dangerous state is not liable to the tenant's customers or guests for accidents happening during the term: for, fraud apart, there is no law against letting a tumble-down house; and the tenant's remedy is upon his contract, if any".[199]

By the early 19th century the industrial revolution had led to a movement of population to the towns. The people who worked in the new factories and shops often lived in appalling conditions, conditions which the law did little to alleviate. In one case the courts took a small step towards decent housing standards by creating a new exception to the old immunity of landlords. In *Smith v. Marrable*[200] it was held that the immunity did not apply in the case of furnished accommodation. The distinction lacked any justification in principle, because although it could be said of furnished residential premises that they were evidently let with the intention that they should be occupied by human beings, it could also be said of unfurnished residential premises. Not for the first time the courts were prepared to adopt an artificial distinction in order to change the law as far as they could, consistent with their deference to precedent.

---

197 (1843) 12 M & W 52 at 65, 152 ER 1108 at 1113.

198 (1863) 15 CB NS 221.

199 Cited in the English House of Lords in *Cavalier v. Pope* [1906] AC 428, per Lord MacNaghten at p.430. See *McNerny v. London Borough of Lambeth* [1989] 19 EG 77, 21 HLR 188, Court of Appeal (Civil Division).

200 (1843) 11 M & W 5, 8f, 152 ER 693, 694.

The main principle was nevertheless reaffirmed by the English House of Lords in *Cavalier v. Pope*[201] as late as 1906. The decision in that case confirmed a number of earlier English decisions in the common law courts to the same effect, and by a decision of the Court of Appeal *Lane v. Cox.*[202]

The next development was the decision of the British House of Lords in *Donoghue v. Stevenson*[203] on appeal from the Scottish Court of Session. This laid down both a general theory of the law of negligence liability, the so-called neighbour principle, and also an area of manufacturers' liability. The neighbour principle proposed that a person should be liable in negligence if, at the time they were acting, it was foreseeable that some other category of persons would be detrimentally affected by their actions if they did not take care.

Since this principle would, without more, make a lessor who let defective premises liable to a tenant who was injured due to the defect, the question arose as to whether *Cavalier v. Pope*[204] had survived *Donoghue v. Stevenson.*[205] At the time *Donoghue* was decided the House of Lords did not consider itself free to depart from its own decisions, and so the court itself could not have intended to reverse *Cavalier* even if it wished to do so. However, the principle of manufacturer's liability in *Donoghue* provided another exception to the general rule of immunity. It was held that if the lessor was also a manufacturer, *i.e.* the builder of the house, or person who had financed the building, then manufacturers' liability prevailed over the immunity, and the lessor was liable.[206]

Thus, in England *Cavalier v. Pope*[207] began to resemble a sand castle facing the incoming tide. The sea had swept around it causing parts of it to collapse, leaving a mound still visible above the surrounding water but no longer possessing any discernible shape. It was nevertheless confirmed in *Rimmer v. Liverpool City Council*[208] that the immunity in *Cavalier* survived in England except for furnished dwellings and where the lessor was the builder.

The decision in *Cavalier v. Pope*[209] and the cases which preceded it are open today to the criticism that they placed landlords as a class in a more favourable position than other subjects of the law and so violated notions of equality, if not specifically in the form of the constitutional right to equality as

201 [1906] AC 428, per Lord MacNaghten at p.430.

202 [1897] 1 QB 415.

203 [1932] AC 562.

204 [1906] AC 428, per Lord MacNaghten at p.430.

205 [1932] AC 562.

206 *Anns v. Merton London Borough Council* [1978] AC 728, HL and *Rimmer v. Liverpool City Council* (1983) 12 HLR 23, CA.

207 [1906] AC 428, per Lord MacNaghten at p.430.

208 (1983) 12 HLR 23.

209 [1906] AC 428, per Lord MacNaghten at p.430.

human persons, then in a more general political sense stemming from the nature of a democratic state. It is difficult to justify it by showing that the immunity confers some benefit on society generally or some compensating benefit to tenants. It appears to be an example of the law directly favouring a particular social class and doing so because of the superior influence which that class enjoyed on the process of law-making.

The common law and English authorities were reviewed as to their application in the Republic in *Siney v. Dublin Corporation*[210] which is discussed in the section below.

(2) Siney v. Dublin Corporation

In *Siney v. Dublin Corporation*[211] the issue arose as to whether the immunity had been carried over into the law of the Republic. Mr Siney took a tenancy of a new flat from Dublin Corporation. After he moved in damp and fungus appeared due to insufficient ventilation and the condensation that resulted from it. The special factor in the relationship between landlord and tenant in this case was that the landlord was a local authority providing housing under the Housing Acts, whose aim was to provide low cost rented accommodation on terms that the private market was not able to provide. The Supreme Court held that these special circumstances created in law an implied warranty by the defendant in the tenancy agreement that the flat was fit for human habitation at the date of the letting. The court also held that the provisions of section 114 of the Act of 1966, now repealed,[212] did not apply to a housing authority and that, accordingly, the implied warranty was not excluded nor replaced by the more limited statutory warranty of fitness for human habitation created by section 114. The court also held the landlords liable in negligence, finding that defendant owed the plaintiff a duty to take reasonable care in the special circumstances of the tenancy to ensure that the flat was fit for human habitation at the date of the letting.[213] While O'Higgins CJ was prepared to hold that *Cavalier v. Pope*[214] was not part of the law of the Republic, Henchy J held that the special circumstances of the letting on the facts before him provided another exception to the rule in *Cavalier*. He preferred to leave the removal of whatever vestige remained of *Cavalier* to the Oireachtas. Kenny J concurred with the other to judges while expressing no view on these issues. There was thus a ma-

210 [1980] IR 400.

211 [1980] IR 400. For the position in Northern Ireland see *Gallagher v. N McDowell Ltd* [1961] NI 26, CA.

212 By Housing (Miscellaneous Provisions) Act, 1992 s.37 and Schedule.

213 *Donoghue v. Stevenson* [1932] AC 562; *Batty v. Metropolitan Realisations Ltd* [1978] QB 554 and *Anns v. Merton London Borough* [1978] AC 728 considered.

214 [1906] AC 428, per Lord MacNaghten at p.430.

jority in favour of Henchy's more limited *ratio decidendi*. O'Higgins CJ referred to the common law position as follows:

> "The immunity originated as an immunity enjoyed by vendors or lessors of land but seems to have been extended to vendors and lessors of buildings erected upon land and to defects in such buildings. It is not easy to see the basis in logic for the existence of such an immunity, particularly where the defect which causes the damage was known or could have been known to the lessor, were it not for his carelessness, and was not known and could not have been known to the tenant or to those whom he brought into the building or house pursuant to the letting. Because of this difficulty of finding a logical basis to justify a general immunity accorded to all vendors and all lessors in relation to defects in premises sold or let, it is not surprising to find in recent decisions certain clear exceptions being established".

In *Gallagher v. N McDowell Ltd*[215] the Court of Appeal in Northern Ireland refused to regard the immunity as being one which attached to realty. In that case the court held that the builders were liable for injury to the wife of the tenant of a house let by the Northern Ireland Trust; the wife's injury had been caused by a defect in the house. The judge then went on to quote from the judgment of Lord MacDermott LCJ in *Gallaher*:[216]

> "In my opinion, the cases since *Donoghue* v *Stevenson* [1932] AC 562 show that the land-owner's immunities, which I have described as settled before that decision, have not been disturbed by it. But the fact that these immunities arise in relation to defects and dangers on land does not mean that the law imposes no neighbourly duty of reasonable care as respects defects and dangers of that kind. The immunities attach to land-owners as such, and I do not think one is at liberty to jump from that to saying that the law of negligence in relation to what is dangerous draws a clear distinction between what are chattels and what, by attachment or otherwise, form part of the realty. Why should it? Such a distinction does not justify itself, and it is not required by the immunities I have mentioned when one is not dealing with land-owners as such".

O'Higgins CJ continued:

> "In that passage from his judgment, Lord MacDermott seems to assume a continuing immunity for land-owners, as such, from the rule in *Donoghue* v *Stevenson* [1932] AC 562 in respect of defects or dangers on their land. Such a view of the law is not consistent with the decisions of this Court in *Purtill* v *Athlone UDC* [1968] IR 205 and *McNamara* v *Electricity Supply Board* [1975] IR 1. In relation to their particular facts, those cases regarded the liability of the occupier of land (whether as owner or otherwise) in respect of defects or dangers found on the land as proper to be treated under the principles of *Donoghue v. Stevenson* [1932] AC 562".

Henchy J, for once finding himself in the unusual position of being more conservative than O'Higgins CJ, preferred to leave the matter to the legislature to resolve:

---

215 [1961] NI 26.

216 *ibid.*, at p.38.

> "It would be beyond the true scope of the essential circumstances of this case to decide whether there would be liability in negligence if the flat had not been provided under the Act. That broader question will be given a legislative solution if the proposals in the Law Reform Commission's Working Paper No. 1 are given effect by Parliament".

The point has already been made that Deasy's Act purported to put landlord and tenant relations in Ireland on the footing of contract. This could have provided a basis for the courts refusing to apply English cases such as *Cavalier v. Pope*[217] and assimilating instead the law of leaseholds to the law of contract and so reading into contracts of tenancy the same kind of implied terms as one would find in modern commercial contracts. The courts in the United States have adopted this approach and so have placed implied terms in leases on a more rational and defensible basis.

In *Coleman v. Dundalk UDC*[218] the Supreme Court held that the implied warranty in *Siney* applied to a lease for 99 years.

(3) Unfit Houses

Under section 66 of the Housing Act, 1966 a housing authority has power to issue a repair notice or a demolition order in extreme cases where houses are unfit for human habitation.[219]

(4) Health and Safety Legislation

Various Acts deal with health and safety for residential as well as commercial premises. They include the Public Health (Ireland) Act, 1878, the Factories Act, 1955, the Safety in Industry Act, 1980 and the Office Premises Act, 1958.[220]

d) Rented Houses

In addition to the general provisions already discussed, the Housing (Miscellaneous Provisions) Act, 1992 introduced a number of measures which taken together constitute a "Housing Code" for privately rented houses and are mainly aimed at strengthening the position of tenants.

(1) Notice to Quit

Section 16 of the 1992 Act provides that notice by a landlord or a tenant to the other to terminate the tenancy of a house let for rent or other valuable consideration is not valid unless it is in writing and is served not less than four weeks before the date on which it is to take effect. Exceptions are made for tied

217 [1906] AC 428, per Lord MacNaghten at p.430.

218 Unreported, Supreme Court, 17 July 1985.

219 See Chapter 28 Housing Law.

220 Wylie, *Landlord and Tenant* para. 15.06.

houses let in connection with employment, tenancies let for temporary convenience or necessity, and holiday lettings and other tenancies prescribed by the Minister.

(2) Rent Books

Section 17 of the 1992 Act and the Housing (Rent Books) Regulations, 1993[221] require landlords of rented houses to provide tenants with rent books. The landlord must acknowledge all rent and other payments by the tenant in the rent book. The rent book must also contain details of the landlord and of the tenancy, including the rent reserved, any advance payments or deposits, the terms of the tenancy and details of furnishings and appliances supplied by the landlord for the use of the tenant. The rent book must also contain a basic statement of information for the tenant which is set out in the Schedule to the Regulations.

(3) Housing Regulations

The Housing (Standards for Rented Houses) Regulations, 1993[222] are made under section 5 of the Housing Act, 1966 as amended by the 1992 Act.[223] They came into force on 1 January 1994 except as to houses let by housing authorities in which case they came into force on 1 January 1998.[224]

The Regulations impose standards on rented houses as to the structural condition, the condition of sinks, waterclosets, baths and showers, heating, cooking and food storage, the safety of gas and electricity installations, ventilation and lighting, common areas, stairways, basements and yards, *etc.* The Regulations apply to houses whether furnished or not.[225]

(4) Distress

Section 19 of the 1992 Act prohibits levying of the common law remedy of distress for any rent or rentcharge due in the case of premises let solely as a dwelling. Insofar as it applied to dwellings the remedy may in any case offend against Article 40.5 of the Constitution which provides that: "The dwelling of every citizen is inviolable and shall not be forcibly entered save in accordance

221 SI 146 of 1993.

222 SI 147 of 1993, replacing the Housing (Private Rented Dwellings) (Standards) Regulations, 1984, SI 337 of 1984.

223 Sections 18, 24 of the Housing (Miscellaneous Provisions) Act, 1992.

224 Previously, bye laws under s.70 of the Housing Act, 1966 applied. Section 37 of the Housing (Miscellaneous Provisions) Act, 1992 which repeals s.70 of the Housing Act, 1966 came into effect on the 1 January 1994: Housing (Miscellaneous Provisions) Act, 1992 (Commencement) Order, 1993, SI 145 of 1993.

225 The Regulations apply to houses, and Art 3 defines house as "a building used or suitable for use as a dwelling and any outoffice, yard, garden or other land appurtenant thereto or usually enjoyed therewith".

with law". Distress is law, but it is possible that Article 40.5 implies some degree of due process and that common law distress would fail to meet the test, since it is instituted unilaterally by the landlord.[226] It could also be argued that to justify forcible violation of a dwelling there would have to shown some serious danger to the public or at least something more than the mere wish to enforce an ordinary civil right by a private citizen which is already adequately protected by an action to recover the rent.

(5) Registration

Section 20 of the 1992 Act makes provision for the registration by landlords of tenancies with the housing authority in whose area the house is situated.[227] Certain lettings are exempt from registration, such as those for temporary convenience or necessity, holiday accommodation, lettings by housing authorities, to students by a recognised educational institution or other approved body, to close relatives of a landlord, or where the landlord is normally resident.[228]

2. By the Tenant

a) To Pay the Rent

(1) General

In the past the courts treated the tenant's obligation to pay rent as absolute. Thus, in the classic case of *Paradine v. Jane*,[229] a tenant who had been dispossessed by the forces of Prince Rupert during the English Civil War was held still liable to pay rent to the landlord for the period of dispossession. The rule was associated with the cases suggesting that the doctrine of frustration in contract law did not apply to leases, although this has recently been held not to be the case.[230] A tenant thus remained liable to pay rent even if the premises were destroyed by fire.[231] These rules probably indicate that judges in the past favoured the dominant landowning classes at the expense of tenants. In the

---

226 The Article has been considered in the criminal law context in *People v. O'Brien* [1965] IR 142; *DPP v. Corrigan,* unreported, High Court, Blayney J, 18 July 1986; *DPP v. Gafney,* unreported, Supreme Court, 23 February 1987; and see Forde, *Constitutional Law* p.542 *et seq*.

227 SI 30 of 1996, Housing (Registration of Rented Houses) Regulations, 1996, as am. SI 12 of 2000, Housing (Registration of Rented Houses) (Amendment) Regulations, 2000.

228 *ibid.*: SI of 1996 Art. 4, as substituted by SI 12 of 2000 Art. 2.

229 (1647) Aleyn 26, 27f, 82 ER 897, 898.

230 See below, Frustration.

231 *Balfour v. Weston* (1786) 1 TR 310, 312, 99 ER 1112, 1113.

United States, where landowners were less influential, the courts in the 19th century departed from these rules.[232]

Section 42 of Deasy's Act provides that the tenant and successors are obliged to pay the rent.

The tenant is now entitled to make certain deductions from rent. This is discussed in the next section.

(2) Deductions and Set-off

(a) **Common Law**

At common law the tenant originally had no right in general to deduct from the rent sums owed to him or her by the landlord. In *Corkerry v. Stack*[233] it was held that the common law rule by which the tenant is not relieved from paying the rent because the landlord defaults on his obligations applies in the Republic. In *Shipsey v. McGrath*[234] a tenant was sued for rent and successfully claimed the right to deduct sums spent by him on repairs, although the court apparently accepted this on the ground that the landlord had allowed him to make such deduction in the past. On the other hand it has been held that the landlord's covenant of quiet enjoyment only binds the landlord if the tenant performs his obligations.

There is some evidence that recently the courts have become more willing to depart from or whittle down these rules. It has been held in England that a tenant has the right to deduct from rent the amount he or she has spent on repairs which were the responsibility of the landlord.[235] At common law, if a landlord is liable to do repairs and the failure to do so causes a nuisance, the tenant can sue for damages[236] or an injunction.

(b) **Statute**

Section 48 of Deasy's Act, 1860 provides:

> "48.– All claims and demands by any landlord against his tenant in respect of rent shall be subject to deduction or set-off in respect of all just debts due by the landlord to the tenant".

Despite the apparently deliberate use of the word deduction in addition to the word set-off the 19th century case law held that the section only conferred a

---

232 *e.g. Graves v. Berdan* (1868) 26 NY 498.

233 (1948) 82 ILTR 60.

234 (1879) 31 ILTR 77.

235 *Lee Parker v. Izzet* [1971] 3 All ER 1099. *British Anzani (Felixtone) Ltd v. International Marine Management (UK) Ltd* [1979] 2 All ER 1063. Waite, "Disrepair and Set-off of Damages against Rent: the Implications of British Anzani" [1983] Conv 373.

236 *Byrne v. Martina Investments Ltd,* unreported, Circuit Appeal, High Court, 30 January 1984.

right by the tenant to set-off such debts in an action by the landlord to recover the rent, and did not provide a defence to an action for ejectment for non-payment of rent.[237] In other words, the tenant had no right to deduct sums at source.

More recently, and more specifically, the Landlord and Tenant (Amendment) Act, 1980 section 87 provides:

> "87.–(1) Where a landlord refuses or fails to execute repairs to a tenement which he is bound by covenant or otherwise by law to execute and has been called upon by the tenant to execute, and the tenant executes the repairs at his own expense, the tenant may set off the expenditure against any subsequent gale or gales of rent until it is recouped".

The section applies to tenements under the Act.

It is clear that in this section set off includes a right to deduct. This is reinforced by section 87(2) which provides that if the tenant validly sets off the amount of repairs against rent and provides the landlord with evidence that this has been done, the landlord is bound to give a receipt of the gale of rent as if the full rent "had been paid in money".

There are differences in procedure between: (a) a set off in an action by the landlord, (b) a counterclaim, and (c) a right to deduct . A set off is a defence. It means that the landlord's claim should be reduced in part or in whole in respect of the amount which the tenant can set off against it.[238] A counterclaim is an action independent of the landlord's action, so that a tenant can succeed on a counterclaim even if the landlord fails to prove his or her case. A right of deduction is the right on the part of the tenant to deduct sums of money from payments of rent, *i.e.* before any action arises.

The difference in normal legal language between a set-off and a right to deduct can be illustrated as follows. T is tenant of landlord L. L has failed to make repairs which he is bound to do under the lease. T does the repairs herself and deducts the sums from the rent, paying the balance. If L sues T for the full amount, T may answer that the full amount has been paid. Doing the repairs, paying the bill and tendering the evidence is an alternative way of paying the rent. The same would apply if, instead, L brings an action of ejectment for non-payment of rent. T can say she has paid it.

As to the cost of repairs which the landlord was bound to undertake, the tenant has a right to deduct at source under section 87. As to other just debts, there is merely a right of set off under section 48 of Deasy's Act, 1860.

b) To Give Up Peaceable Possession

The tenant is obliged to give up peaceable possession and leave the premises in good and substantial repair, subject to the tenant's right to remove fixtures and

237 *Cahill v. Kearney* (1868) IR 2 CL 498 at 500 per Monaghan CJ; *Dalton v. Barlow* (1867) 1 ILT 490; Wylie, Landlord and Tenant para. 12.10.

238 See *In the Matter of Irish Shipping Ltd* [1986] ILRM 518.

compensation for improvements under Part IV of the Landlord & Tenant (Amendment) Act, 1980.

c) Waste

At common law the tenant was liable, subject to agreement to the contrary, for permissive, voluntary, or equitable waste. In leasehold tenure the common law rules have been almost entirely replaced by the provisions of Deasy's Act.

Section 25 of Deasy's Act made fee farm grantees of Deasy's Act grants[239] made after 1 January 1861[240] and lessees under perpetually renewable leases for lives or years[241] impeachable only for fraudulent or malicious waste.

Under Section 26 of Deasy's Act tenants cannot open mines, quarries or cut trees[242] without the landlord's consent, unless the land was leased for that purpose. The tenant can cut turf, but not for profit.

S. Frustration

Section 40 of Deasy's Act provides that where there is no express covenant to repair the tenant may surrender leases on the destruction or making uninhabitable of the premises through fire or other inevitable accident due to no fault of the tenant. In other words, the risk of fire does not fall on the tenant. This reversed what was thought to be the common law rule that the doctrine of frustration did not apply to leases.[243] However, the English House of Lords has more recently held that the doctrine of frustration applies in principle to leases, although it may rarely be held do so on the facts.[244] It was held not to apply where the only means of access to a warehouse, leased for 10 years, was closed after five years of the lease had elapsed.[245] But it may apply where the land is physically destroyed, *e.g.* by being washed away by the sea, or by fire before the term begins, or, possibly, shortly after the term begins.

---

239 Fee farm grants by virtue of the Renewable Leasehold Conversion Act, 1849 are excluded.

240 The section does not apply to renewals after the Act of leases originally granted before the Act, since that would alter the terms originally agreed.

241 See "perpetual interest" s.1.

242 See also forestry and planning restrictions: Chapter 27.

243 But see now *National Carriers v. Panalpina (Northern) Ltd* [1981] AC 675, [1981] 1 All ER 161, House of Lords.

244 *ibid.*

245 *ibid.*

T. Fixtures

1. Common Law

In *Holland v. Hodgson*[246] Blackburn J, who delivered the unanimous judgment of the six judges of the Court of Exchequer Chamber said:

> "There is no doubt that the general maxim of the law is, that what is annexed to the land becomes part of the land; but it is very difficult, if not impossible, to say with precision what constitutes an annexation sufficient for this purpose. It is a question which must depend on the circumstances of each case, and mainly on two circumstances, as indicating the intention, viz, the degree of annexation and the object of the annexation.
>
> Perhaps the true rule is, that articles not otherwise attached to the land than by their own weight are not to be considered as part of the land, unless the circumstances are such as to show that they were intended to be part of the land, the onus of showing that they were so intended lying on those who assert that they have ceased to be chattels, and that, on the contrary, an article which is affixed to the land even slightly is to be considered as part of the land unless the circumstances are such as to show that it was intended all along to continue a chattel, the onus lying on those who contend that it is a chattel".[247]

In a Northern Ireland case, *Re the Companies (Consolidation) Act 1908 and Ross and Boal Ltd*[248] the Court of Appeal ruled that power-driven sewing machines placed on benches which were affixed to the floor by spikes or bolts, should not be regarded as fixtures as they were not permanently affixed to the benches in any way.
Andrews LJ said:[249]

> "Two matters must be considered. The first is the mode, the second is the object, of the annexation; and, as appears from the speech of Lord Macnaghten in *Leigh v. Taylor* [1902] AC 157, the trend of modern authority is undoubtedly to assign relatively less importance to the former than in earlier times".

A television aerial has been held to be a fixture both because of the substantial way they are fixed to the building and also because the purpose is to enhance the use of the building as a dwelling house.[250]

Originally, anything attached to the soil other than by gravity (*i.e.* its own weight) became part of the realty and belonged to the owner of the freehold. This was not merely a matter of definitions. Fixtures attached to the land at the tenants' expense were simply acquired free of charge by the landlords. It was a rule which favoured the landed class and reflected the views of the Physiocrats, a school of political cconomists who developed an economic theory

246 (1872) LR 7 CP 328.

247 At pp. 334-6.

248 [1924] 1 IR 129.

249 At p.176 of the report.

250 *Maye v. The Revenue Commissioners* [1986] ILRM 377, High Court, O'Hanlon J.

which supported the position of a progressive section of the landed class in the 18th century who were investing capital in agriculture. The Physiocrats asserted, surprisingly, that only agriculture produced economic value. Industry did not. They ascribed this unique ability of agriculture to the bounty of nature and to capital invested in drainage and other improvements by the landowners which improved the productivity of the land. Nature to the Physiocrats was thus not nature in its raw state, but the rationally ordered nature of the 18th century Enlightenment. According to the theory, landowners were both the guarantors of political stability and also the custodians of nature on behalf of the Almighty and for the benefit of society generally. The product of nature, according to the theory, therefore rightfully belonged to the landowners.

This economic theory fell into decline with the rise of trade and the industrial revolution and was the notion began to grow that the person who had invested either own labour or money in purchasing a commodity should be entitled to the monetary value of it. The courts began to recognise and develop categories of fixtures which tenants could sever and remove. Trade fixtures were probably the first to be recognised.[251] Today they would include such things as petrol pumps attached to tanks embedded in the ground,[252] or a shed used for the manufacture of concrete products and secured to the ground by bolts passing through holes in the bottom of the posts at each corner and through metal tags set in the floor.[253] The method of attachment is probably today merely evidence of the intention as to the use of the fixture and its relative permanence. The amount of damage that would be caused by removing the fixture is relevant.[254]

In the late 19th century the Irish Court of Appeal in *Cosby v. Shaw*[255] showed its indulgence for trade fixtures by exempting from a clause in a lease, which restricted the right of a tenant to remove fixtures, trade fixtures which had been introduced "as scientific improvements to fulfil functions previously performed by manual labour...". The courts were thus choosing a result which would favour the introduction of scientific inventions. Next, the courts recognised that ornamental and domestic fixtures may be removed by a tenant.[256] But the English courts never recognised that agricultural tenants had the right to remove fixtures, and this continuing refusal to develop the law in that direction may be taken as a concession to the landed class.

251 *Poole's Case* (1703) 1 Salk 368, 91 ER 320.

252 *Smith v. City Petroleum* [1940] 1 All ER 260.

253 *Webb v. Bevis* [1940] 1 All ER 247.

254 *Spyer v. Phillipson* [1931] 2 Ch. 183.

255 (1889) 23 LR Ir 181, CA.

256 *Spyer v. Phillipson* [1931] 2 Ch. 183.

In 1803 in *Elwes v. Maw*[257] a tenant farmer had built at his own expense a beast-house, a carpenter's shed, a fuel house, a wagon house and a fold-yard. He removed all of them at the end of the lease leaving the land in the same condition as at the beginning of the lease. He was held liable in damages. The court held that even if the sole purpose of annexation was to promote the use of the land by the tenant for agriculture, they could not be regarded as trade fixtures and they refused to create a new category. The decision upheld the expropriation of the labour, or capital, of improving tenants and failed to extend the new category of trade fixtures to agricultural tenants. The position was only remedied by the Landlord and Tenant Act, 1851 which gave agricultural tenants the right to remove fixtures, subject to the landlord's right to elect to buy them.

2. Deasy's Act s.17

Section 17 of Deasy's Act, 1860 partially codified this area of the law in Ireland by providing that:

> "Personal chattels, engines, and machinery, and buildings accessorial thereto, erected and affixed to the freehold by the tenant at his sole expense, for any purpose of trade, manufacture, or agriculture, or for ornament or for the domestic convenience of the tenant in his occupation of the demised premises, and so attached to the freehold that they can be removed without substantial damage to the freehold or to the fixture itself, and which shall not have been so erected or affixed in pursuance of any obligation or in violation of any agreement in that behalf, may be removed by the tenant, or his executors or administrators, during the tenancy, or when the tenancy determines by some uncertain event, and without the act or default of the tenant, within two calendar months... except so far as may be otherwise specially provided by the contract of tenancy; provided that the landlord shall be entitled to reasonable compensation for any damage occasioned to the premises by such removal".

Some points of difference with the common law position should be noticed. The section only applies where the fixture is attached at the tenant's sole expense. Damage to the fixture itself is relevant. It is unclear to what extent the common law still applies where the Act does not. It must do so to some extent since the Act does not itself define the terms used in the section and reference would probably be made to the case law if such words a affixed or domestic convenience.

257 (1802) 3 East 38, 102 ER 510.

U. Enforcement of Covenants

1. Original Parties

a) Action

As there is privity of contract between the original parties to the tenancy they may sue each other in contract for a breach of the covenants. In addition to this common law right, section 45 of Deasy's Act 1860 gives a statutory right to a landlord to sue for rent in arrear. Section 46 gives the right to a grantor of an interest in land, where no rent is specified, to sue for reasonable satisfaction for use and occupation. Under section 48 the tenant can set off in an action all just debts owed to him by the landlord.

b) Distress

The remedy of distress vested in landlords is another example in the law of landlord and tenant of rules imported by analogy to the old law of freehold tenure. At common law the landlord has the right, if the tenant fails to perform his obligations, to enter the premises and seize the chattels of the tenant and hold them as a pledge until the tenant performs his obligation.

Under the Distress for Rent Act, 1741, section 5, and the 1751 Act, section 5, the landlord can sell the goods after eight days if they are not redeemed by then. Section 51 of Deasy's Act provides that no distress for rent may be levied where the rent payment is overdue for more than one year before making the distress. There are many other restrictions on the remedy of distress.[258] It is odd that Deasy's Act assumes in section 51 that the remedy continued to exist at all after the Act in view of section 3 which states that the landlord and tenant relationship in Ireland does not depend any longer on tenure but on contract. The remedy of distress, as we have noted already, was applied to that relationship by analogy to freehold tenure and is therefore an incident of tenure.

We have already noted above that the remedy was always open to challenge in Ireland on the ground that it was unconstitutional as in violation of Article 40.5 of the Constitution. The Housing (Miscellaneous Provisions) Act, 1992 by section 19 now expressly prohibits distress to be levied for the rent, including rent due under a rentcharge, of "any premises let solely as a dwelling".[259]

c) Forfeiture

A tenancy may be forfeited by the failure of the tenant to comply with a covenant in the lease in which case the landlord has the right to terminate it by entry

258 Wylie, *Irish Land Law* para. 17.065.

259 See above.

or action.[260] This is dealt with in the section on the ending of the landlord and tenant relationship below.

d) Ejectment

Ejectment is the general term for an action by a landlord to recover possession of the premises let to a tenant. It takes various forms, but since, if successful, it results in the termination of the relationship of landlord and tenant the topic is more suitably dealt with as part of the substantive section dealing with that topic.

2. Successors in Title

Whether successors in title can enforce covenants in the original lease at all depends upon sections 12 and 13 of Deasy's Act. Since the basic principle of the Act, contained in section 3, was to place landlord and tenant relations in Ireland on the basis of contract rather than on tenure it was felt necessary to provide expressly that successors should be bound by covenants and able to enforce those for their own benefit. *Lyle v. Smith*[261] held that the sections meant that all covenants bound successors except those that were not capable of vicarious performance. The judge may have meant this simply to indicate a distinction between covenants which refer to the land and are for the benefit of it, which run with it as part of the property interest, and those which refer to some personal agreement between the original parties which were included in the lease but which are not for the benefit of the land. If that is so, then it is difficult to see any real distinction between the first category and the phrase touch and concern, which was the test before 1860. On the other hand, there are covenants which are capable of vicarious performance but which are still personal in the sense that they are not for the benefit of the land as such.

V. Ending of the Relationship of Landlord & Tenant

1. Expiry

Where the tenancy is for a fixed term the relationship of landlord and tenant will naturally come to an end when the term expires. Periodic tenancies, on the other hand, will continue indefinitely unless terminated by notice to quit. The same is true of tenancies at will. Special provision is made for their termination by expiry in the Statute of Limitations, 1957.

---

260 *Bank of Ireland v. Lady Lisa Ireland Ltd* [1992] 1 IR 404; *Serjeant v. Nash, Field & Co* [1903] 2 KB 304.

261 [1909] 2 IR 58; 43 ILTR 255.

a) Tenancy at Will

In the case of a tenancy at will section 17 of the Statute of Limitations, 1957 provides that it is deemed to terminate one year after it began.[262]

b) Periodic Tenancy in Writing

The same section deems a tenancy from year to year or for other successive periods "without a lease in writing" to terminate at the end of the first year or other period and a right of action accrues unless rent is paid subsequently.

In *Foreman v. Mowlds*[263] a written agreement was made in 1907 creating a tenancy from year to year. Since 1922 M and later his successors in title had remained in possession without paying rent. The question was as to whether M or his successors had acquired title by adverse possession. They could only have done so if the periodic tenancy had terminated at least 12 years before after which the possession had become adverse to the landlord's title. Barrington J found that the Statute of Limitations, 1957 gave no assistance to the question. He held that M's successors had good title because the tenancy had ended probably in 1922 when M had stopped paying rent.

In *Sauerzweig v. Feeney*[264] the parties entered into a weekly tenancy in writing. The tenant had not paid rent since 1950. In 1956 the tenant offered to pay rent but was dissuaded from doing so by the landlord's solicitor because the tenant was negotiating to buy the landlord's reversion. The landlord demanded rent on three occasions between 1977 and 1981. The tenant claimed he had acquired the landlord's title by adverse possession. The Supreme Court held that section 17 clearly did not apply to periodic tenancies in writing. *Foreman v. Mowlds* was not cited to the court but the doubt in that case has clearly been resolved. They also held that the tenancy had not been abandoned in view of the landlord's demands for rent. The tenancy did not end until the landlord served notice to quit in 1982. They held that the landlord had lost the right to rent due for more than six years under section 28 of the Statute. The rationale behind section 17 seems to be that where there is a lease in writing the parties may provide for the original period to be renewed for a maximum number of times, or for some other ultimate term, but if they do not do so the tenancy may be terminated by notice to quit in any case. If the parties do not choose to insert an express provision the legislature seems to have taken the view that it is not necessary for statute law to intervene. The appropriate remedy of the landlord where the tenancy has expired and the tenant has not vacated the premises is ejectment for overholding. Section 72 of Deasy's Act provides that any tenant who wilfully holds over is liable to pay double rent for the period of

262 See Chapter 25 Adverse Posession.

263 Unreported, High Court, 28 January 1985, extempore judgment by Barrington J, noted in McHugh (1985) 3 ILT 47.

264 [1986] IR 224.

overholding, but this is rarely claimed in practice.[265] Courts would be reluctant to hold that the overholding was wilful.

2. Non-Payment of Rent & Adverse Possession

If the tenant fails to pay rent then this may give rise to a forfeiture if there is an express clause. This topic therefore falls under the heading of forfeiture and is dealt with in the section below.

Another aspect which may be considered a separate method of termination is the extent to which failure to pay rent may render the tenant's possession adverse so that, if the landlord takes no action to claim a forfeiture, the tenant may in time extinguish the landlord's title. If a tenant holds over after the end of a lease for a fixed term, then he or she becomes a tenant at sufferance and in adverse possession.[266]

When a tenant under a periodic tenancy ceases to pay rent the case law holds that there is a presumption that the tenancy has come to an end and that the tenant is thereafter in adverse possession. In *Re Shanahan*[267] the Supreme Court held that non-payment of rent had merely barred claims to the rent due for more than six years and did not make the possession of the tenant adverse to the title of the landlord. The parties had, however, remained in a debtor/creditor relationship for 20 years and Ó Dálaigh CJ held that this relationship negated "any presumption of the determination of the tenancy that might otherwise arise from the non-payment of rent". The case was cited to the court in *Foreman v. Mowlds*[268] which distinguished it on the ground that there were no circumstances on the facts to negate the presumption that non-payment had rendered the tenant's possession adverse. This holding is an alternative *ratio decidendi* to the one overruled by *Sauerzweig v. Feeney*,[269] *i.e.* that the tenancy had determined under section 17. In *Sauerzweig* itself the court held that the tenancy had been determined by notice to quit and therefore, impliedly, not by adverse possession following from non-payment of rent, although there were grounds on which they could have held that the presumption was negated, namely the continued demands of the landlord. The court did not cite *Re Shanahan* nor *Foreman*. It is probably the case that the presumption survives *Sauerzweig*.

---

265 Section 76 Deasy's Act.

266 Since 1833: *Doe d Bennett v. Turner* (1840) 7 M & W 226, 151 ER 749; *Remon v. City of London Real Property Co Ltd* [1921] 1 KB 49; see Adverse Possession: tenant at suffrance.

267 Unreported, Supreme Court, 5 July 1968. Judgment of the court delivered by O'Dailaigh CJ nem. diss.

268 Unreported, High Court, 28 January 1985, extempore judgment by Barrington J, noted in McHugh (1985) 3 ILT 47.

269 [1986] IR 224.

Non-payment of rent over a long period may give rise to other presumptions, to the effect that the rent has been paid[270] or, in suitable cases, redeemed,[271] or the term enlarged[272] although the cases on these points may have to be reviewed in the light of *Re Shanahan* and *Sauerzweig*. In *Atkins v. Atkins*[273] it was held that where rent in a lease had remained unclaimed for a long period (40 years on the facts) the court could assume that it had been redeemed as a ground rent or under other applicable legislation.[274] The court refused to presume that the lease had been enlarged into a fee simple under section 65 of the Conveyancing Act, 1881, but where the lease fell within the terms of the section when rent ceased to be paid, or at some time during that period, there is authority for the view that such a presumption can be made.[275]

3. Notice to Quit

A lease may provide for the tenure to be terminated by notice on either side. When a tenancy is terminated by the landlord he or she is said to give the tenant notice to quit the premises. Since periodic tenancies will not terminate by expiry the common law provided that they may be terminated by notice after periods which it laid down.

In the case of a weekly tenancy the period was one week,[276] in the case of a monthly tenancy, one month. In the case of a yearly tenancy the period at common law was six months, but under the Notice to Quit (Ireland) Act, 1870[277] in Ireland in the case of agricultural or pastoral holdings[278] which, as a result of the Land Purchase legislation, are now rare, the period of notice is one year, unless there is an agreement to the contrary.[279] The year's notice must expire on any gale day of the calendar year in which the rent becomes due. The section also provides that the landlord, having given notice, may waive the right

270 *Courtney v. Parker* (1866) 16 Ir Ch R 320 per Smith MR at 338.

271 *Atkins v. Atkins* [1976-77] ILRM 62.

272 See Chapter 20 Statutory Control and Enlargement of Tenancies.

273 [1976–77] ILRM 62.

274 Citing *Lefroy v. Walsh* (1852) 1 Ir CLR 311. In *Lefroy* the tenant paid reduced rent for 30 years. The court held that there was evidence to go to the jury that the original tenancy had been surrendered and a new one granted. This was a common law court before the Judicature Act and it could not consider equitable principles. Today the same facts might be held to give rise to a promissory estoppel. The court distinguished *Fitzgerald v. Portarlington (Lord)* 1 Jones 431 in which there was evidence of an intention that the original tenancy should continue.

275 *Re Waugh* [1943] Ir Jur Rep 50; *Blaiberg v. Keeves* [1906] 2 Ch. 175.

276 *Harvey v. Copeland* (1892) 30 LR Ir 412, QB.

277 Section 1.

278 Section 5. It also applies to partly agricultural and partly pastoral holdings.

279 An exception is made where the tenant has been adjudged bankrupt or has made an agreement with his or her creditors.

by accepting rent after the period has expired. The section does not affect weekly or monthly tenancies or tenancies at will,[280] or yearly tenancies for other than agricultural or pastoral purposes. However, the Housing (Miscellaneous Provisions) Act, 1992 section 16 now provides that:

> "16.–(1) Subject to *subsections (2)* and *(3)*, a notice by a landlord or a tenant to the other of termination of the tenancy of a house let for rent or other valuable consideration shall not be valid unless it is in writing and is served not less than four weeks before the date on which it is to take effect".

House includes "any building or part of a building used or suitable for use as a dwelling and any outoffice, yard, garden or other land appurtenant thereto or usually enjoyed therewith". Subsection 2 provides that the section shall not apply:

(a) to the tenancy of a house let to a person in connection with any office, appointment or employment;

(b) to a tenancy let bona fide for temporary convenience or to meet a temporary necessity;

(c) to a holiday tenancy; and

(d) to such other classes of tenancies prescribed by the Minister for the Environment under the section.

Nothing prevents any provision in a contract or other rule of law prescribing a greater period of notice.[281]

The effect of section 16 of the 1992 Act on the common law periods appears to be to lengthen the period of notice required in the case of a tenancy of residential premises to one month where the period of notice would otherwise be less than one month, *i.e.* where the tenancy was for a period less than one month or was a periodic tenancy for periods less than one month.[282] Where such premises are let on a yearly basis, the common law period of six months still applies. Where the land is agricultural or pastoral, the one year period in the 1870 Act still applies unless, under the Act, there is agreement to the contrary. The section also appears to override an express term in a tenancy specifying any period of notice less than one month. It should be noted that section 16 applies to notice to terminate a tenancy by a landlord to a tenant as well as by a tenant to the landlord. An issue which may arise is whether a landlord or a tenant may waive his or her right to a month's notice.

The appropriate remedy of the landlord where a tenant continues in occupation after a notice to quit is ejectment for overholding.[283]

280 Section 2.

281 Housing (Miscellaneous Provisions) Act, 1992 s.16(3).

282 As noted above, the period of notice at common law in repsect of a monthly tenancy was already one month.

283 See page 627.

4. Surrender

Section 7 of Deasy's Act provides that a tenancy may be surrendered to the landlord by deed or writing signed by the tenant or his agent authorised in writing or by act or operation of law. Where a purported surrender does not comply with section 7 it may nevertheless operate as surrender by operation of law as the landlord or tenant may be estopped from pleading the absence of formalities.

5. Forfeiture

a) Express Clause

If the lease contains a proviso for re-entry on breach of condition or a forfeiture clause, *i.e.* a clause providing expressly that if the tenant does not comply with specified terms of the lease, the lease is to be forfeited, then either a right of entry, which may be enforced either by actual entry on the premises or by action, will be created in the event of the breach, or a forfeiture will occur, which may be enforced by action. However the clause is worded the tenancy will not determine automatically on the breach of the term: the lease is merely voidable at the landlord's option, for a tenant cannot rely on his own breach to terminate the tenancy.

In *Bank of Ireland v. Lady Lisa Ireland Ltd*[284] the plaintiff landlord had purported to determine a tenancy by serving on the tenant a notice of re-entry and forfeiture reciting that the rent due had not been paid. The defendant tenant contended that this was insufficient to determine the tenancy and this contention was upheld by O'Hanlon J in the High Court. There must either be an actual entry, or some act which sets in motion an action for possession based on a valid claim. The judge cited Collins MR in *Serjeant v. Nash, Field & Co*:[285]

> "There is a final determination of a tenancy under a lease when the lessor, by some final and positive act which cannot be retracted, treats a breach of covenant by the lessee as constituting a forfeiture...".

O'Hanlon J added that the ineffective notice ". . . need not be fatal to the plaintiff's case if the procedure followed thereafter was effective of itself to forfeit the lease and set in motion a valid claim for an order for possession". He held further that the present proceedings, which were for possession on the ground of non-payment of rent under section 52 of Deasy's Act, 1860, and which were by summary summons, were inappropriate where the landlord's claim was based on forfeiture.[286]

---

284 [1992] 1 IR 404.

285 [1903] 2 KB 304.

286 Citing *Keating v. Mulcahy* [1926] IR 214.

b) Condition Subsequent

If there is neither of these then it is a matter of interpretation whether the term which has been broken is a condition subsequent. If it is interpreted as a condition subsequent then the position is analogous to a conditional fee. It is as if the grantor had granted the land:

to A for N years, on condition that . . .

The breach of the condition will give rise to a right of re-entry at common law or a right of forfeiture in equity, subject to the jurisdiction of equity to grant relief against forfeiture. A right of entry is an old-fashioned remedy since it relies on self-help by the landlord and this makes it open to abuse. For this reason a number of restrictions on the exercise of a right have been developed by the law to prevent abuse by the landlord.

Where a right of entry exists section 14(1) of the Conveyancing Act, 1881 provides that the lessor must serve notice on the lessee before the right is exercised whether by actual entry or by action, the notice to specify the breach and require it to be remedied if possible.[287]

c) The Entry

A number of ancient statutes sought to prevent the use of force by the landlord in gaining entry to the land, but these have now been replaced by the Prohibition of Forcible Entry and Occupation Act, 1971. Section 2 makes it a criminal offence to use force to enter land or a vehicle unless the person entering (a) is the owner of the land or vehicle or (b) if he or she is not the owner, does not interfere with the use and enjoyment of the land or vehicle or (c) has a bona fide claim of right. Section 1 provides that owner in relation to land includes, *inter alia,* the lawful occupier, every person lawfully entitled to the immediate use and enjoyment of unoccupied land, and any person having "an estate or interest in land".[288] Section 1(5) provides that nothing in the Act shall be regarded as conferring on any person any right to entry or occupation of land which did not exist immediately before the Act. In *Dooley v. Attorney General*[289] the Supreme Court held, interpreting the statute as a whole, that a person having an estate or interest only qualifies as an owner within the Act if they have an immediate right to possession of the land and hence a right to enter it. "Owner" does not include a mortgagee or a reversioner unless they have such a right of entry.

---

287 Section 14 does not apply to non-payment of rent.

288 In *Sweeney v. Powerscourt Shopping Centre,* unreported, High Court, Carroll J, 6 June 1984, the defendants entered premises let to a tenant, after a notice under section 14 of the Conveyancing Act, 1881 had been issued, using a master key. Carroll J held that they had not violated the law in doing so as they had entered peacefully.

289 [1977] IR 205.

d) Relief against Forfeiture

It has long been held in Ireland that a tenant in this jurisdiction always has the right to invoke the jurisdiction of equity to grant relief against forfeiture of a lease.[290] If equity grants relief against the forfeiture then the common law right of entry cannot be enforced. At common law a forfeiture of a lease also destroyed all sub-leases, even though the sub-lessees were not in breach of their covenants.[291] This result seems to have been purely the effect of reifying the concept of estate. If the estate on which the sub-estates depended was destroyed, went the reasoning, so were the sub-estates. This illustrates the dangers of reification in that it ignored the reality of property as a set of relations between persons and ignored also therefore the rights and wrongs of the issue. A sub-tenant could, however, obtain relief in equity, in the case of the tenant being sued in ejectment for no-payment of rent, by paying the rent due.[292] Sections 4 and 5 of the Conveyancing Act, 1892 reformed the law by providing that a sub-lessee has a statutory right to apply to the court for relief. The court may order the term of the lease to be vested in the sub-tenant.

e) Forfeiture for Non-Payment of Rent

At common law a landlord could only bring ejectment for failure to pay rent where the lease contained an express clause for forfeiture in this event. The effect of the clause was to make the lease subject to a condition subsequent and the right to recover possession rested on the ending of the tenancy by the condition rather than on the failure to pay rent in itself.

In Ireland before Deasy's Act a number of Acts were passed which strengthened the legal position of landlords as against tenants by imposing terms in tenancies favourable to landlords. The Acts were known collectively as the Ejectment Code. The Ejectment Code "gradually removed every formality by which the old Common Law delayed and obstructed the forfeiture of the tenant 's estate".[293] Courts of equity could nevertheless grant relief to tenants against ejectment under the code.[294] Landlords were given the right to bring ejectment after one whole year's rent was in arrear, regardless of whether the tenancy contained a clause for forfeiture, but the provision only applied where there was a written agreement.[295] This created an anomaly, from the

290 Per Sugden LC in *Malone v. Geraghty* (1843) 5 Ir Eq R 549 citing the decision of the Irish House of Lords in *Berney v. Moore* (1791) (1791) 2 Ridg PC 310; *Breaden v. Fuller & Son* [1949] IR 290.

291 *Dowding v. Commissioner of Charitable Donations and Bequests* (1862) 12 Ir Ch R 361, Ch.

292 *Berney v. Moore* (1791) 2 Ridg PC 310.

293 Kolbert and O'Brien, *Land Reform in Ireland* p.31.

294 *Berney v. Moore* (1791) 2 Ridg PC 310.

295 5 Geo II c.4 s.1 (Ir); 25 Geo II c.13 s.2 (Ir).

landlord's point of view, as to tenancies from year to year, which were a common form of holding in agricultural tenancies. Such tenancies would only come within the statutory ejectment code if they were in writing, and many were not. In such a case the landlord could only determine the tenancy by notice to quit and he could lose two and a half year's rent.[296] A further statute[297] remedied this by extending statutory ejectment to landlords of holdings let orally for a low rent.

Deasy's Act replaced these provisions by an even more extensive one. Section 52 of Deasy's Act gives a statutory remedy of ejectment to a landlord where land is held under a fee farm grant, lease or other contract of tenancy or from year to year and whether by writing or otherwise. Thus despite the pretensions of the Act to base tenancies on the basis of contract, it failed to do so when this would mean taking rights away from landlords, and in this instance it actually extended them.

In *Chester v. Beary*[298] it was held that it need not be an unbroken year's rent. It is enough that the total amount of rent due is equal to that of a year's rent. Section 53 provides that a demand by the landlord is not required here before the action is brought. Under ground rent legislation[299] section 52 no longer applies where the tenant of a dwelling house has the right to acquire the fee simple, *i.e.* it no longer applies to a ground rent of a dwelling house as defined by statute. A tenant who has such a right is clearly in a different position to other tenants: the legal form here does not fit the social perception of them or their substantive rights. It would not be sensible to allow a landlord to evict a tenant who had the right to acquire the landlord's interest and therefore be put back in to possession within a short time. On the other hand a tenant who exercises his or her right to acquire the fee simple is required to pay arrears of rent before interest is vested in him or her.[300]

Under section 7 of the Family Home Protection Act, 1976 if a landlord brings an action under section 52 of Deasy's Act and the premises are occupied by a married couple and one spouse is the legal tenant in arrear then if it appears that the other spouse is able to pay the rent, the court can adjourn the proceedings.

The restrictions on forfeiture contained in the 1881 and 1892 Acts do not apply to a forfeiture or re-entry for non-payment of rent.[301] At common law the

296 Ritchie, *Irish Land Laws* p.41.

297 14 & 15 Vict. c.57 s.73.

298 (1852) 2 Ir CLR 120

299 Landlord and Tenant (Ground Rents) (No. 2) Act, 1978 s.27.

300 This requirement is contained in Form C, the form prescribed for the purposes of s.20 of the 1978 Act by the Minister under s.5 of the Act. See Fitzgerald (1989) pp. 260, 264.

301 Conveyancing Act, 1881 s.14(8).

landlord has to make a formal demand for rent unless the lease dispenses with this requirement. The tenant may apply in equity for relief against the forfeiture. Landlords often prefer to rely on section 52 of Deasy's Act. Previously section 14 of the Conveyancing Act, 1881 did not apply to a forfeiture under a covenant against assignment or subletting, but now it does so by virtue of section 35 of the Landlord and Tenant (Ground Rents) Act, 1967.

f) Denial of Title

The law of landlord and tenant also followed the old law of freehold tenure in holding that a denial by a tenant of the landlord's title gives rise to a forfeiture.[302] The title of the tenant derives from that of the landlord and so the landlord can claim that the tenant has in effect denied his own title.

In *O'Reilly v. Gleeson*[303] the Supreme Court held that a denial by a tenant of the landlord's title otherwise than in legal proceedings, *i.e.* by an act *in pais*, does not forfeit the lease. It may be that courts today are less inclined to treat the tenant as dependant or subservient to the landlord except in purely technical terms. To accept that a denial outside legal proceedings could cause a forfeiture would be to put the tenant in an invidious position as against the landlord in a social sense. The appropriate remedy of a landlord where a forfeiture has occurred is ejectment on title. This is also called simply an action for possession and is brought where the landlord alleges that a forfeiture has occurred. It will also be the appropriate form where the land is occupied by a person having no title valid against the proprietor, *i.e.* someone in adverse possession.

6. Satisfied Term

This applies to terms of years created under settlements to secure payment of portions. On payment of the money the term of years comes to an end.[304]

7. Enlargement

This topic is dealt with in the next chapter, on the Statutory Control of Tenancies.

---

302 *Foot v. Warren* (1861) 10 Ir CLR 1. It is said *obiter* in this case that a tenant can, however, claim that his landlord's title has come to an end, at least where the landlord proceeds under a statutory right to ejectment. See now s.52 of Deasy's Act.

303 [1975] IR 258.

304 Satisfied Terms Act, 1845, 8 & 9 Vict. c.112. See Settlements.

CHAPTER 20

STATUTORY CONTROL AND ENLARGEMENT OF TENANCIES

There are a number of legislative enactments which either control the terms on which tenancies and leases can be granted or which provide for the enlargement of leases and tenancies into a fee simple.

The provisions which control specific terms of tenancies, such as attempts to restrict alienability or subletting, have been dealt with in the chapter on landlord and tenant. This chapter concerns statutory provisions providing for continuation or extensions of the original term or its enlargement into a fee simple.

We shall also deal with provisions for compensation for improvements. The chapter is divided into sections according to the type of premises, *i.e.* general, business, residential, *etc.*, rather than conceptually according to extension of the term, enlargement into a fee simple *etc.*.

A. Conveyancing Act, 1881

Section 65 of the Conveyancing Act, 1881 provides for the enlargement of certain long leases into fees simple. The section applies to tenants holding under leases for 300 years or more with a term unexpired of 200 years "without any rent, or with merely a peppercorn rent or other rent having no money value".[1] The tenant of such a lease may execute a deed enlarging the lease into a fee simple.[2] The rent must be valueless in money and so if the rent consists of money at all, however small the amount, it would seem the lease may not be enlarged under the section.[3]

1. Covenants

The fee simple remains "subject to all the same trusts, powers, executory limitations over, rights, and equities, and to all the same covenants and provisions relating to user and enjoyment, and to all the same obligations of every kind, as

1 Section 65(1) and Conveyancing Act, 1882 s.11.

2 Section 65(2) and (3).

3 *Re Smith & Stott* (1885) 29 Ch D 1009 (A lease with a rent of 3 shillings, infrequently paid, is not within the section); *Blaiberg v. Keeves* [1906] 2 Ch. 175 (one shilling assumed to take lease out of the section; *Re Chapman & Hobbs* (1885) 29 Ch D 1007 (one silver penny).

the term would have been subject to if it had not been so enlarged".[4] This would seem to include the valueless rent, if any, and if so the enlarged fee simple would in theory be a fee farm grant. The section can be used as a device to attach covenants to a fee simple the burden or benefit of which would not otherwise run under the rules as to the running of covenants between freehold owners.[5] However, the section has now probably been affected by section 28 of the Landlord and Tenant (Ground Rents)(No. 2) Act, 1978 (the No. 2 Act of 1978) so that only certain types of covenants, namely those enhancing the amenities of the land, would survive enlargement.[6]

2. Constitutionality

Since the section does not provide for compensation it is challengeable in the Republic as an infringement on the property rights of those entitled to the reversion. A reversion on an unexpired term of 200 years and a valueless rent in the meantime is of minimal value to those alive today, and the terms of the section were probably drafted with this in mind, but the reversion could be of considerable value to their posterity. There is as yet no decision in the Republic on the constitutionality of the section.

B. Agricultural and Pastoral

1. Land Purchase Acts

The Land Purchase legislation provided for the transfer of the fee simple to the tenant farmers. The legislation is, however, no longer used and the work of the Irish Land Commission is completed.[7] The legislation is discussed in Chapter 15.

2. The Labourers Acts

These have been discussed in Chapter 6 on the fee simple.

---

4 Section 65(4).

5 *Re McNaul's Estate* [1902] 1 IR 114 held that covenants originally contained in a lease continued to affect the fee simple under the Renewable Leaseholds Conversion Act, 1849, even though they would have been invalid in the grant of an ordinary fee simple.

6 See below Ground Rents Legislation; Right to Acquire the Fee Simple.

7 See Irish Land Commission (Dissolution) Act, 1992, s.4. Remaining powers have been transferred to the Minister for Agriculture and Food.

C. Business Tenancies

1. History

The Town Tenants (Ireland) Act, 1906[8] gave two principal rights to business tenants in towns. First, it gave tenants of premises situated in towns or villages and used wholly or partly for business purposes a right to compensation for improvements on quitting the premises. Secondly, it gave tenants of premises wherever situated, but used wholly or substantially for business purposes, a right to compensation for loss of goodwill and removal expenses on disturbance without good cause.

The weakness of the Act was that landlords could avoid its effect if they offered the tenant an extension of the existing tenancy or a new tenancy on reasonable terms. Landlords could also avoid the Act by designing leases which did not fall within its provisions. The Act was therefore largely a failure. The 1906 Act was repealed and replaced in the Republic by the Landlord and Tenant Act, 1931[9] which was itself repealed and replaced by the Landlord and Tenant (Amendment) Act, 1980. The Act of 1931 was not confined to business premises and applied also to residential premises where there had been occupation over a long period, giving such tenants the right to compensation for improvements and the right to a new tenancy.[10] Such provisions have been replaced by similar provisions in the 1980 Act.

2. Landlord and Tenant (Amendment) Act, 1980.

a) Scope of the Act

The Act applies to tenements. A tenement is defined by section 5[11] as referring to land wholly or partly covered by buildings or a defined portion of a building and if the land is only partly covered by buildings, the portion not covered is subsidiary and ancillary to the buildings.[12] The land must be held by the occupier under a lease or other contract of tenancy express, implied or arising by statute. The tenancy must not be one made for the temporary convenience of the lessor or lessee, and if granted since 1931 the temporary convenience must be stated in the lease. Lease includes fee farm grant. The 1931 Act only applied

8 See Wylie, *Land Law* para. 18.04.

9 No. 55 of 1931.

10 See also the Landlord and Tenant (Reversionary Leases) Act, 1958 repealed by the Landlord and Tenant (Amendment) Act, 1980.

11 Replacing s.2 of the 1931 Act. The replacement incorporates the recommendations of the 1967 Landlord and Tenant Commission Report Pr No. 9685 para. 84 in abolishing the distinction between urban and non-urban land.

12 *Terry v. Stokes* [1993] 1 IR 204 (significant factor is not relative area or value but use made by tenant); *Dursley v. Watters* [1993] 1 IR 224; *Lynch v. Simmons* (1954) 88 ILTR 3.

to tenants in occupation of the premises[13] but this is no longer required by the 1980 Act. Section 3 of the 1980 Act extends business to include activities for providing "cultural, charitable, educational, social or sporting services" and also the public service and local authorities, health boards and harbour authorities carrying out their functions.[14] Section 4, on the other hand, in a new provision, restricts the operation of the Act by providing that it shall not bind a State authority in its capacity as lessor. This seems to put the State in an unnecessarily favourable position as against private lessors. If a private lessee of the State has made improvements to the premises there seems no reason why they should be deprived of the rights they would otherwise have under the Act, such as compensation for improvements attributable to them, merely because they have the misfortune to have the State as lessor. If the principle that a person should not benefit from expenditure which is not their own is a desirable one then it is no less desirable where the lessor is the State. The principle itself is desirable not simply as founded on a general moral principle but also as founded on a social policy favouring development: people are unlikely to expend labour, money or capital on making improvements if they are simply to make a present of them to the landlord. It is the same principle, probably more pro-capital than pro-labour, which lay behind the development of the law of fixtures. The same reasons would equally apply to the State and are even reinforced by the consideration that it would be particularly unprincipled for the State to exempt itself, since it is the State which promulgated the principle by enacting legislation. The practical, or, some would say, unprincipled objection might be made that the burden on public funds would be too great if many tenants, perhaps companies, suddenly claimed large sums as improvements, but in fact, as we shall see, the Act requires the tenants to submit improvements notices before the improvement is made and the question as to whether the improvement should be made can be referred to the court. The constitutionality of the section must be in doubt.

b) Compensation for Improvements

Under Part IV of the 1980 Act a tenant of a tenement is entitled to compensation from the lessor on quitting the tenement. Under section 45 improvement means an addition or alteration to the building including the installation of water, gas or electricity conduits but excludes redecoration or repair. The tenant is entitled on quitting the premises to compensation from the lessor for improvements made by the tenant or any predecessor in title which is suitable for the character of the building and which adds to its letting value.[15] Compensation does not apply, however, if the tenancy is terminated by surrender or by

---

13 Section 2 of 1931 Act.

14 See *Rice v. Dublin Corporation* [1947] IR 425; Wylie, *Cases* p.562.

15 Section 46 of 1980 Act.

non-payment of rent.[16] In the case of surrender, a lessor does not have to accept it and the parties can agree on the terms of a surrender. There is therefore no need to provide for compensation by statute. As to non-payment of rent, the statute, by excluding compensation for improvements in such a case, creates a new sanction for failure to pay the rent, but it can be questioned whether the forfeiture of improvements is appropriate. Even if a lessee has failed to pay rent, the moral principle behind the legislation, that a lessor should not gain from expenditure by the lessee, should still apply. It would be more appropriate for the rent owed to be deducted from the compensation, or vice versa, depending on which is greater than the other.

The amount of compensation is to be agreed between the parties or, in the absence of agreement, by the Circuit Court.[17] In the latter case it is to be assessed under section 47 as the capitalised value of the addition to the letting value of the tenement at the termination of the tenancy attributable to the improvements. Deductions are to be made in respect of benefits received by the tenant or predecessors such as reduction in the rent expressly or impliedly in consideration of the improvements.[18] Part IV of the Act contains new provisions to give greater flexibility in some cases. Under section 60 a lessor can obtain an order terminating an occupational tenancy where the buildings are obsolete or are in an obsolete area[19] in some circumstances. The lease must be for a term of which not less than three and not more than 25 years remain unexpired.[20] The lessee is not able to take advantage of the Act unless he or she submits an improvement notice under section 48. The notice must contain a statement of the works proposed and their estimated cost. If the development is one for which planning permission is required, a copy of the permission must be attached. The landlord then has a choice of three courses of action. He or she can:

(a) consent to the improvement, (referred to in the Act as an improvement consent); or

(b) undertake to execute the improvement themselves at an increased rent specified or to be fixed by the court (an improvement undertaking); or

(c) object to the improvement (an "improvement objection.")[21]

In the case of (a) the tenant has one year in which to execute the improve-

16 Section 46(1)(b).

17 Section 8 of 1980 Act.

18 Section 47(2).

19 1980 Act, s.60(1).

20 1980 Act, s.60(2).

21 1980 Act, s.48(2).

ment.[22] In the case of (b) the tenant can object to the increased rent and bring an action in the Circuit Court to determine the new rent or to deal with the matter as an improvement objection.[23] In the case of (c) the tenant can bring an action in the Circuit Court[24] or withdraw the notice.[25] An improvement objection can only be served on the ground that the tenant holds the tenement otherwise than under a lease for a term of which at least five years are unexpired and furthermore that the tenant would not be entitled to a new tenancy under section 17(2)(a). The principle here is that the lessor can only legitimately object on the ground that the tenant's interest is too slight to justify the improvement. Where the immediate landlord is a tenant of a superior landlord the improvement will affect the relation between the immediate landlord and the superior one. Section 48 provides that in such a case where the landlord on whom the notice is served holds from a superior landlord for a term of which less than 25 years is unexpired, or under a lease for life or lives in being either without a concurrent term or with one, if it for less than 25 years unexpired, or under a tenancy from year to year or a lesser tenancy, then the landlord has to serve notice on the superior landlord. In such a case the superior landlord can serve on the landlord and the tenant either an improvement consent or an improvement objection, but not an improvement undertaking. Where an improvement is carried out by the tenant then, under section 55, the landlord must issue, if asked, an improvement certificate certifying that the improvement has been made in accordance with the notice or order. This will assist the tenant in case the landlord or a successor challenges the improvement at a later time.

c) New Tenancies

Part II of the 1980 Act confers on tenants of certain tenements[26] the right to a new tenancy on satisfying certain conditions. Business tenants have the right to a new tenancy under section 13(1)(a) if they have been in continuous occupation of the premises for five years.[27] Sections 13(1)(b) and 13(1)(c), which are not confined to business premises, give the same right to tenants of other premises on proof of continuous occupation for 20 years, or of improvements such that the tenant would, but for the section, have the right to compensation under the Act and that not less than half the letting value of the premises is attributable to

22 1980 Act, s.50.

23 1980 Act, s.51.

24 1980 Act, s.52.

25 1980 Act, s.52(1)(a) and (2).

26 *Mason v. Leavy* [1952] IR 40, (1954) 88 ILTR 61 Supreme Court; *Hardiman v. Galway County Council* [1966] IR 124, (1967) 101 ILTR 110; *McEvoy v. Gilbeys of Ireland Ltd* (1962) 96 ILTR 143, Circuit Court; *The Commissioners of Public Works v. Kavanagh* [1962] IR 216, (1963) 97 ILTR 180, Supreme Court.

27 As am. Landlord and Tenant (Amendment) Act, 1994 s.3.

the improvement. Tenancies in the Custom House Docks Area used for financial services are exempt.[28]

(1) Controlled Business Premises

Part II of the 1980 Act also applies to business premises formerly controlled under the Rent Restrictions Act, 1946[29] and 1947. Although Part II is headed "Right to New Tenancy" the part does not operate in relation to these controlled premises in quite that way. Rather than a right to a new tenancy, the Act confers a new tenancy on the tenant in the same terms as the old one in the same way that most rent acts confer a statutory tenancy. Since in the present case the premises were formerly subject to a statutory tenancy, the effect of Part II of the 1980 Act is to confer a new statutory tenancy, but subject to a term that the landlord may terminate the tenancy on three month's notice to quit.[30]

(2) Break in Use

Under section 13(2) a temporary break in the use of a tenement can be disregarded if the court considers it reasonable to do so. The subsection expressly qualifies only section 13(1)(a), the section dealing with business premises. Where statutes give rights to tenants it is common for landlords to react by adopting devices to deprive the tenants of those rights. Avoidance of the Act is considered in the next section.

(3) Avoidance of the Act

In *Gatien Motor Co Ltd v. Continental Oil of Ireland Ltd*[31] the Supreme Court had to decide as to the validity of a device to avoid the Landlord and Tenant Act, 1931. The 1931 Act specified a qualifying period of three years but did not include a provision entitling the court to disregard a period during which the applicant was not in occupation as tenant. However, section 42 of the 1931 Act declared to be void any contract which purported directly or indirectly to prevent an applicant acquiring a right to a new tenancy. In *Gatien* the respondent landlord let a certain tenement to a tenant for three years from the 6 February 1970, and the tenant used the tenement for the purposes of his business during that period. Before the expiration of that term of years, the tenant sought a renewal of his tenancy from the respondent, but the latter was unwilling to grant a renewal unless the tenant surrendered possession of the tenement

28 Section 13(3), 13 (4) inserted by the Landlord and Tenant (Amendment) Act, 1989. The exemption originally applied for 5 years from the date of the Act (1 March 1989) but was extended to 10 years (SI 36 of 1994) and then 15 years (SI 52 of 1999).

29 Section 14.

30 Section 14(2).

31 [1979] IR 406; Wylie, *Cases* p.543.

for a week. The tenant was unwilling to vacate the premises for the week since he believed that it would damage the goodwill of his business. Eventually it was agreed that the tenant would remain in possession of the tenement from 6–12 February 1973, as a caretaker for the respondent, and not as a tenant, and without payment of rent. The respondent was to grant to the applicant company (formed by the tenant) a new tenancy for three years from the 12 February 1973. The tenant knew that the compromise was designed to prevent the acquisition of a statutory right to a new tenancy under the 1931 Act. The appropriate caretaker's agreement and new tenancy agreement were executed by the parties, and the applicant used the tenement for business purposes as tenant. On the expiration of the new tenancy on the 12 February 1976, the applicant company claimed to be entitled to a new tenancy under the Act of 1931 and contended that the tenant had been in possession of the tenement as a tenant from 6–12 February 1973, and that, accordingly, the tenement had been used by the tenant for the time being for a complete period of three years and three months immediately preceding the 12 February 1976.

The Circuit Court held the tenant to be entitled to a new tenancy. An appeal was taken to the High Court which stated a case for the opinion of the Supreme Court. It asked whether the caretaker's agreement had created a tenancy and, if not, whether that agreement was void under section 42 of the Act of 1931 on the ground that it indirectly deprived the applicant of a right to a new tenancy under that Act.

It was held by the Supreme Court (Griffin, Kenny and Parke JJ), that the answer to both questions was No. The judges accepted the caretaker agreement at face value even though that agreement had expressly conferred possession on the caretaker.[32] Griffin J laid stress on the fact that there was no rent payable during the period for which the caretaker's agreement was to run, and no rent was paid. One might also point out that there is another argument that runs almost exactly counter to this and that is that if the landlords had genuinely been employing the erstwhile tenant as a caretaker it is customary to pay such a person for their services, but the agreement made no mention of wages or salary and none was paid. Griffin J went on to consider the effect of section 42 of the 1931 Act. He held that, as no tenant of the tenement had acquired a right to obtain relief under the Act of 1931, the provisions of section 42 of the Act of 1931 did not apply. He justified this position in the following way:

> "Although it is not lawful to contract out of the Act of 1931, a distinction must be drawn between a provision which attempts to exclude the Act from a transaction to which it applies, and a transaction to which the Act has no application. Thus, in *Hardiman* v *Galway County Council* [1966] IR 124 this Court held that a covenant by a tenant not to claim compensation for disturbance offended against section 42 of the Act of 1931 and was void. In that case the term of the lease was 20 years and the tenant would clearly have been entitled to a new tenancy on the expiration of the lease... Although section 42 of the Act of 1931

32 *Shell-Mex v. Manchester Garages* [1971] 1 WLR 612 considered.

> avoids contracting out of the Act, it does not prevent the parties from so arranging matters that there is nothing to which the Act can apply. When the lease of 1970 expired, Coady was fully aware of the fact that he was not entitled to a new lease, and also that the respondents were not prepared to give him, or the company which he was in the process of forming, a new lease which would have the effect of giving the tenant rights under the Act of 1931 on its expiration... The agreement was not for the purpose of evading the Act of 1931 but of preventing the provisions of the Act from applying or, in other words, of arranging a lease which would be outside the scope of the Act. In my opinion, that is not in breach of section 42 of the Act of 1931".

This is curious reasoning: the judge says that the applicant knew that the landlords were not prepared to give him a lease which would qualify under the Act, as if the application of the Act were a matter of choice on the part of the landlord. If it were a matter of choice on the part of landlords whether the Acts applied or not, it becomes difficult to explain why the legislature considered the Acts necessary at all. Landlords do not require special statutory powers to grant a new tenancy to a tenant if they wish to do so. Kenny J agreed with the general trend of Griffin J's reasoning:

> "In my opinion s.42 operates to make void a contract which would deprive a tenant of a right which he has to obtain relief under the Act of 1931. He must have such a right before he can rely on the section to make void a contract which, directly or indirectly, deprives him of that right. The foundation of the section is that there is an existing right of a tenant to relief under the Act; if he has this, a contract which deprives him of it, whether directly or indirectly, is void. Section 42 of the Act of 1931 was considered by this Court in *Hardiman* v *Galway County Council* ((1966) IR 124) but the meaning of the terms "indirectly deprived" in the section did not arise for decision in that case. I confess that I do not understand what the parliamentary draftsman had in mind when he referred to "indirect" deprivation. How can a tenant be indirectly deprived of his right to obtain relief under the Act of 1931?".

The treatment of section 42 by the court amounts to sanctioning a device to avoid the Act and to render it almost useless except in relation to leases entered into before it took effect. It also requires an artificial reading of the section. The section states that a contract "by virtue of which a tenant would be directly or indirectly deprived of his right to obtain relief" under the Act "shall be void". The court reads it to mean that before one can be deprived of a right one must first have a right. This does, admittedly, make use of a mistake in the drafting of the section. The drafter of the section should have said "by virtue of which a tenant would. . . have been deprived of a right which, but for the contract, they would otherwise have obtained". A court more disposed to protect rights which the legislature had evidently intended to confer on tenants would no doubt have interpreted the section in that way. It might be objected that, in that case, it could be argued that even a lease for one year would be caught because, being for a term of less than three years, it prevented the tenant from obtaining a right under the Act which he or she would otherwise have acquired. However, courts are capable of developing rules to distinguish between devices which effectively prevent the tenant acquiring rights to possession for periods to which the Act is intended to apply and agreements which are genuinely for lesser periods. As to the facts of *Gatien* itself, the court indicated that they considered the tenant to be on an equal footing with the landlord and that he accepted the new terms after independent legal advice. This suggests perhaps that the court did not intend to lay down a rule that the Act could be avoided in all cases by caretaker agreements.

It does not seem that section 13(2) of the 1980 Act is sufficient to reverse the effect of *Gatien*. A caretaker agreement does not necessarily involve a break in use. Indeed, according to *Gatien*, it does not necessarily involve a break in possession. Section 85 of the 1980 Act now provides that any contract, whether made before or after the Act, which "provides that any provision of this Act shall not apply in relation to a person or that the application of any such provision shall be varied, modified or restricted in any way in relation to a person" shall be void. The wording is different from that in section 42 of the 1931 Act and is no doubt deliberately so. While it is still true that the agreement in *Gatien* did not expressly oust the provisions of the Act, the section indicates that it was the intention of the legislature that the provisions of the Act should not be avoided by agreement. Agreements may be induced by economic pressure and it seems that the Act is one instance of where the law takes account of this and does not consider such an agreement as expressing the free will of both parties. This might induce a court to take a different approach to such arrangements after the 1980 Act. Whether or not it would find that a caretaker agreement actually falls within section 85, as a provision whose sole purpose is to provide that the Act should not apply to a particular person, is difficult to say. To treat *Gatien* as purely making the point that the Act can only be availed of by tenants and not caretakers[33] ignores the real issues of economic and political policy which are inescapably part of the judges' decision. Where the demand for commercial premises exceeds the supply landlords will be in a position to demand the insertion of such agreements into leases and so deprive commercial tenants under the initial lease of a right which they would, but for the agreement, acquire under the Act. In upholding such agreements the judges in *Gatien* necessarily gave legal sanction to the *de facto* economic power of landlords over their commercial tenants and in so doing adjusted the power relationships between landlords and tenants in society. To pretend otherwise is to engage in ideological mystification.

In the previous section it was noted that section 85 of the Act renders void contracts which purport to exclude the operation of the Act. In *Bank of Ireland v. Fitzmaurice*[34] a lease provided that from 1983 until 1986 the rent on the premises would be increased by an amount calculated in relation to the Cost of

33 As Wylie, *Irish Land Law* para. 18.08 does.

34 [1989] ILRM 452, High Court.

Living Index published by the Central Statistics Office in the Republic of Ireland. From June 1986 until May 1988 the increase would be calculated in a similar fashion, save that after ascertaining the index-linked increase, that figure would be multiplied by four to arrive at the new rent for the period in question. The defendant asserted that the multiplier clause constituted a device to force him to surrender the tenancy and, as such, was in contravention of section 85 of the Landlord and Tenant (Amendment) Act, 1980 and was therefore void. He also alleged that certain representations had been made on behalf of the lessors prior to the execution of the lease to the effect that these clauses would not be enforced against him. It was claimed that the indexation clauses were incapable of operating since the cost of living index referred to in the lease has never been published by the Central Statistics Office. Lardner J held that by providing for a rent greatly in excess of that available in the open market, the plaintiff intended to exercise a compelling pressure on the defendant to surrender his tenancy in order to escape liability for the increased rent. By surrendering the lease, the defendant would exclude himself from any right to claim a new tenancy under section 17(1)(a)(iii) of the 1980 Act. The judge held that the multiplier clause was, in effect, a provision which restricted the application of the provisions of the 1980 Act to the defendant. He held the multiplier clauses void as contrary to section 85 of the 1980 Act. Thus the case is authority for the view that section 85 is contravened not simply by a provision which expressly purports to oust the application of the Act, but also by an agreement which has the effect of doing so. This impliedly casts doubt on the authority of *Gatien*.[35]

(4) Disentitlement

Under section 17(1) of the 1980 Act the tenant has no right to a new tenancy if the tenancy has been terminated:

(i) by ejectment for non-payment of rent, whether the action is so termed or not; or

(ii) by the landlord for breach of covenant by the tenant; or

(iii) by the tenant by surrender or otherwise; or

(iv) by the landlord by notice to quit with good and sufficient reason, or

(v) otherwise than by notice to quit and the landlord refused for good and sufficient reason to renew the lease, or would have had good and sufficient reason to refuse a renewal of the lease if he or she had been asked.

Good and sufficient reason means a reason based upon some action or conduct by the tenant and which in the opinion of the court is a good and sufficient reason

35 See also *Hardiman v. Galway County Council* [1966] IR 124.

for terminating or refusing to renew the lease.[36]

The Landlord and Tenant (Amendment) Act, 1994 allows tenants to renounce their right to a new tenancy by a bona fide written renunciation made before the tenancy begins.[37] The provision is limited to tenements let wholly and exclusively as an office and where the tenant has received independent legal advice.[38]

Under section 17(2) the tenant is not entitled to a new tenancy:

(i) if the landlord intends or has agreed to pull down and rebuild or reconstruct the buildings or part of them included in the tenement and has obtained planning permission to do so; or

(ii) if the landlord requires vacant possession in order to carry out a scheme of development and has planning permission to carry it out; or

(iii) if the landlord is a planning authority and the area is an obsolete area; or

(iv) the landlord is a local authority and will require possession within five years under a compulsory purchase order; or

(v) if for any reason the new tenancy would be inconsistent with good estate management. A good and sufficient reason within the section is one which is related to some conduct on the part of the tenant.[39]

(5) *Terms*

The terms of the new tenancy are to be fixed by agreement, but failing that, by the Circuit Court. Where the terms are fixed by the court section 23 lays down certain limits as to duration,[40] rent payable (not less than the landlord pays to his or her landlord and generally the gross rent less the allowance for improvements), and an allowance for improvements.

---

36 Section 17(1)(b).

37 1994 Act s.4, adding s.17(1)(a)(iiia).

38 *ibid.*

39 *ibid.*

40 35 years generally, 20 years for business premises: 1980 Act ss. 13, 23 as am. Landlord and Tenant (Amendment) Act, 1994 ss. 3, 5.

The gross rent[41] is to be the rent which a willing tenant not already in occupation and a willing landlord would agree upon with vacant possession and without regard to goodwill.[42] The letting value of other tenements of similar character in comparable areas may also be taken into account under the section. This is a new provision. The gross rent is also reduced by the allowance for improvements where it applies.[43] The court can also order the tenant to carry out specified repairs before the new tenancy takes effect.[44]

(6) Compensation for Disturbance

Where a tenant of business premises would have been entitled to a new tenancy but for section 17(2) being satisfied, *e.g.* the landlord wishes to rebuild the premises,[45] the tenant has a right to compensation for disturbance. The measure of compensation is the pecuniary loss, damage or expense which the tenants directly incurs or will directly incur by reason of quitting the premises.[46] The availability to a tenant of accommodation in other premises which are available for letting is a relevant factor in assessing compensation for disturbance under section 23 of the Landlord and Tenant Act 1931.[47]

(7) Notice

A claim by a tenant for relief under the 1980 Act must be preceded by service

41 For discussion of the meaning of the term under the 1931 Act, see *Farrell v. Caffrey* [1966] IR 170; *Byrne v. Loftus* [1978] IR 211, [1979] 113 ILTR 17, Supreme Court. See also *Olympia Productions Ltd v. Olympia Theatres Ltd* [1981] ILRM 424, High Court; *McGovern v. Governors and Guardians of Jervis St Hospital* [1981] ILRM 197, Supreme Court; *Gilsenan v. Foundary House Investments Ltd* [1980] ILRM 273, Supreme Court; *Caulfield v. DH Bourke & Son Ltd* [1980] ILRM 223, High Court (whether rent to fixed under 1931 Act or 1980 Act); *Rowan & Co Ltd v. Bank of Ireland* (1973) ILTR 91, High Court (amount of rent where no rent review clause); Overholding after original tenancy expires: *Eamon Andrews Productions Ltd v. Gaiety Theatre (Dublin) Ltd* unreported High Court (1976 No. 33), and see Supreme Court, [1973] IR 295; *Cook v. Dillon* (1959) 93 ILTR 48, Circuit Court.

42 Section 23(5).

43 Section 23(6).

44 Section 23(7).

45 See Disentitlement, above.

46 Section 58 (2).

47 *Aherne v. Southern Metropole Hotel Co Ltd* [1989] ILRM 693, Supreme Court. (Therefore, an offer to grant a new tenancy by agreement in premises formerly occupied or still occupied by a tenant would be a factor in the assessment of compensation, provided that the court was made aware of the precise terms on which that offer was made and was in a position to assess whether such terms were as favourable from the tenant's point of view as might be the terms to be fixed by a court had a new tenancy been granted).

of a notice of intention to claim relief.[48] The court has power to extend the time within which such a notice must be made "on such terms as it thinks proper".[49] The court must extend the time "unless satisfied that injustice would be caused" where the failure was due to "disability, mistake, absence from the State, inability to obtain information or any other reasonable cause". This has been interpreted to mean that where a reasonable cause exists the time should be extended unless a clear injustice would be caused.[50] The tenant may remain in occupation until the application has been dealt with.[51]

d) Right to Acquire the Fee Simple

In some circumstances the occupier of premises used for business purposes may be entitled to acquire the fee simple. The general powers are contained in Part II of the Landlord and Tenant (Ground Rents)(No. 2) Act, 1978 (the No. 2 Act of 1978). They are discussed below, for the sake of convenience, in the section on Residential and Occupational tenancies. Part II of the No. 2 Act of 1978 contains a special procedure by which owners of dwelling houses could acquire the fee simple and such provisions have no application, of course, to business premises. There are in addition some restrictions affecting the general powers which apply to business premises specifically[52] and one factor affecting the determination of the purchase price by arbitration which applies specifically to business premises.[53]

---

48 Section 20.

49 Section 83.

50 On the discretion under section 45 of the 1931 Act, see Wylie, para. 18.12; *Bridgeman v. Powell* [1973] IR 584; *Hayes v. Kilbride* [1963] IR 185; doubted by O'Higgins J in *Linders Garage Ltd v. Syme* [1975] IR 161; (court should extend time "unless a clear injustice would be caused"). *Grey Door Hotel ltd v. Pembroke Trust Ltd* unreported High Court Hamilton J 1976 (court can therefore decide case anew on its merits). *H Wigoder & Co Ltd v. Moran* [1977] IR 112 (applicants gave correct instructions to solicitor who through a mistake of law induced by wrong advice from a barrister failed to apply in time. Held by the Supreme Court that the court has a discretion to extend the time, at least (per Parke and Henchy JJ) where no injustice would be caused to the other party).

51 Section 28. It is not entirely clear whether a tenant may continue in occupation pending an application for extension of time within which to serve a notice of intention. Section 28 applies to an application "pending under this Part". Section 83 is not within that Part of the statute. Nevertheless the discretion under section 83 may be wide enough to order that a tenant remain in possession until the application itself is dealt with.

52 Section 16(2)(a) of the No. 2 Act of 1978.

53 Section 7(3)(d) of the 1984 Act.

D. Residential and Occupational Tenancies

1. Landlord and Tenant (Amendment) Act, 1980

a) New Tenancies

(1) General

It has already been mentioned that the right to a new tenancy is not confined to business premises. As to non-business premises section 13(1) specifies a period of 20 years of continuous occupation by the tenant or his predecessors in title.[54] The alternative basis for a claim is that the tenant has made improvements which would, apart from section 13, entitle the tenant to compensation for improvements and which amount to not less than half of the letting value.[55] Section 13(2), which provides that temporary breaks in the use of the premises does not, as we have already noted, apply to non-business premises.

(2) Controlled Dwellings

In the case of controlled dwellings, which were subject to a statutory tenancy immediately before the Rent Restrictions (Amendment) Act, 1967, they are now subject to a statutory tenancy on the same terms as the former statutory tenancy except that the landlord can terminate it on three month's notice to quit.[56]

b) Compensation for Improvements

It has already been seen that the provisions of Part IV of the 1980 Act apply to residential premises as well as business premises. They entitle a tenant to compensation for improvements carried out by the tenant which add to the letting value of the premises at the end of the tenancy. These provisions have already been discussed.[57]

2. Ground Rents Legislation

a) Ground Rent

Ground Rent has no common law definition but is generally understood to mean a rent which is charged in respect of the soil, or ground, itself. It is either, or both, (a) the rent charged on vacant land, or (b) the rent charged on land with buildings on it, but is then that part of the rent which is not attributable to the value of the buildings.[58] The statutory definition is complex due to its attempt

54 Section 13(1)(b).

55 Section 13(1)(c).

56 Section 15.

57 See above Business Tenancies: Compensation for Improvements.

58 See *Report on Ground Rents* Ground Rents Commission, Pr 7783 of 1964.

to include the various circumstances in which such a rent exists or arguably exists.

b) Ground Rents Acts

The main provisions are now contained in the Landlord and Tenant (Ground Rents) Act, 1967, the Landlord and Tenant (Ground Rents) Act, 1978 (the No. 1 Act of 1978) and the Landlord and Tenant (Ground Rents)(No. 2) Act, 1978 (the No. 2 Act of 1978). The two acts passed in 1978 are to be construed together as one Act.[59] Other relevant legislation, now repealed, is contained in the Landlord and Tenant Act, 1931 and the Landlord and Tenant (Reversionary Leases) Act, 1958.

c) History

The 1967 Act gave to certain persons the right to enlarge their leasehold interest into a fee simple. The No. 1 Act of 1978 attempted a more radical technical solution to ground rents by providing that leases which attempted to create ground rents should be void, thus making it impossible to create them. A purported tenant who had paid consideration for the void lease was to have the right to acquire the fee simple instead,[60] but this has the disadvantage that many purported grantees under void leases might continue in possession unaware of their right to obtain the fee simple and whose title would therefore consist only of a statutory right to the fee simple rather than the fee simple itself. The No. 2 Act amended the 1967 Act and the No. 1 Act of 1978 and contains a new definition of leases as to which the lessee would have the right to acquire the fee simple, *i.e.* the statutory definition of a ground rent.

d) Problem

Unfortunately the No. 2 Act of 1978 created a problem in that it appears to have removed the prohibition on the creation of ground rents in future, which may not have been the intention of the legislature.[61] Section 2 of the No. 1 Act of 1978 provided:

59 No. 2 Act of 1978 s.1(2). The effect of such a provision is that every part of each of the two Acts are to be construed as if they were contained in one Act, unless there is some manifest discrepancy making it necessary to hold that the later Act has modified something in the earlier Act: *Bank of Ireland v. Kavanagh*, unreported, High Court, Costello J, 19 June 1987 (Lexis); *Canada Southern Railway Co v. International Bridge Co* (1883) 8 App Cas 723.

60 No. 1 Act of 1978, s.2(4).

61 It is what the legislature did, not what it intended to do, as the decision in *Rowe v. Law* [1978] IR 55 demonstrates. O'Higgins CJ, who was a member of the Oireachtas when s.90 of the Succession Act, 1965 was passed, took the view that the intention of the legislature had been to change the common law to admit extrinsic evidence of wills even when the will was clear, but the majority took the view, that, even if this was the case, the words of s.90 do not have that effect.

> "2.–(1) Subject to subsection (2), a lease of land made after the passing of this Act shall be void if the lessee would, apart from this section, have the right under section 3 of the Act of 1967 to enlarge his interest into a fee simple and the permanent buildings are constructed for use wholly or principally as at dwelling.
>
> (2) Subsection (1) shall not apply where the lease is a reversionary lease under the Act of 1958".

The No. 2 Act of 1978, however, while it did not repeal section 2 of the No. 1 Act of 1978, repealed section 3 of the 1967 Act.[62] Part II of the No. 2 Act of 1978 contains a new definition of leases as to which the lessee has the right to acquire the fee simple, but there is nothing to connect that with section 2, and therefore no express provision that such leases granted after the No. 2 Act of 1978 are to be void. It is true that the No. 2 of 1978 provides in section 1(2) that "the collective citation, the Landlord and Tenant Acts, 1931 to 1978, shall include this Act and those Acts and this Act shall be construed together as one Act" but it would seem to be going beyond the bounds of statutory interpretation for a court to hold that the reference in section 2 of the No. 1 Act to section 3 of the Act of 1967 is to be read as if it said "Part II of the Landlord and Tenant (Ground Rents) (No. 2) Act, 1978" without an express provision to that effect, especially as it would render certain leases void.[63] Preventing the creation of certain types of leases is a restriction on the rights of ownership and it is persuasively arguable that the Constitution would surely require that to be done by express words. The No. 2 Act of 1978 could simply have substituted a new section 3 in the 1967 Act, which it did not, in any case, wholly repeal. Moreover, the repeal of section 3 of the 1967 Act does not leave section 2 of the No. 1 Act of 1978 without any meaning. It would still render void leases created after the No. 1 Act of 1978 which fell within the definition in the then section 3 but granted before the No. 2 Act of 1978 came into effect.

It may be noted here that if the prohibition does survive the No. 2 Act of 1978, by importing the definition of the right to acquire the fee simple in Part II into section 2 of the No. 1 Act, then the restrictions[64] on Part II would also be imported, so that, for example, a lease of a building divided into not less than four self-contained flats with the specified type of rent review clause would not be void if granted after the No. 2 Act of 1978 even if it otherwise fell within Part II.

If the effect of the No. 2 Act of 1978 is to remove the prohibition then the result would be as follows:

1) If a lease is granted after the No. 2 Act of 1978 to a person coming within the conditions laid down in Part II of the No. 2 Act of 1978,

---

62 Section 7(1) repealed s.3 except for ss. 5 which refers to rateable valuation certificates.

63 In fact, the definition s. of the No. 2 Act of 1978 provides on the contrary that "the Act of 1967 means the Landlord and Tenant (Ground Rents) Act, 1967".

64 See below.

then the lease is not void but the person has the right to enlarge it into a fee simple under the No. 2 Act of 1978.

2) If a lease was granted before the No. 1 Act and it came within the definition of ground rent in the 1967 Act the lease was valid and the tenant had the right to acquire the fee simple. If they had not exercised that right by the time the No. 2 Act of 1978 came into force, they retain the same rights, but the right to acquire the fee simple is now governed by Part II of the No. 2 Act of 1978 (by virtue of section 73 of the 1980 Act).

3) There is a residual category of leases, namely those granted after the No. 1 Act of 1978 came into force but before the No. 2 Act of 1978 came into force, *i.e.* between the 16 May and 28 June 1978. Where such a lease was granted to a person who would have been entitled to enlarge his or her lease into a fee simple under the 1967 Act the lease is void, but if the person has paid consideration for the void lease, they have a right to a conveyance of the fee simple.

e) Policy

The provisions which allow a tenant to acquire the fee simple (which certainly apply to leases within the definition granted up to the No. 1 Act of 1978) or a reversionary lease in the land apply where the situations outlined below exist. These situations are broadly described, because when we turn to the detail it will be seen that there are restrictions which apply, so that not everyone who falls into the broad descriptive categories outlined below will necessarily be entitled to the fee simple. Obviously few people would be interested in acquiring a reversionary lease if they could acquire the fee simple, but the difference is that there are fewer restrictions that apply to the acquisition of reversionary leases than apply to the acquisition of the fee simple. The three basic situations to which the provisions apply are:

1) where a lease is what used to be called a building lease or proprietary lease *i.e.* the buildings were erected at the expense of the lessee, then the old common law rule that fixtures belong to the landlord would not reflect the economic reality. Statutory provisions (below) providing compensation for improvements do not provide an adequate remedy in such cases. Economic development would therefore be discouraged. Legal relations should reflect economic ones, so that the person at whose expense the buildings were erected should have the fee simple;

2) where people have bought houses in housing estates, but instead of buying the fee simple they have been given a long lease. The developer or management company retaining a reversion, to ensure that covenants as to user *etc.* would be enforceable. This avoided problems that would have arisen if the covenants were freehold (the burden of positive covenants not running, *etc.*) But such arrangements also frequently involved the payment by house buyers of a ground rent *i.e.* a

rent to the developer/lessor. Since buyers had paid, or raised on mortgage, a sum that was little less than they would have paid for the freehold and regarded themselves as buying their own home they resented continuing to pay rent; and

3) where a tenant is not entitled to the fee simple, he or she may be entitled to a reversionary lease (see below). This is commonly the case where the letting is of business premises or a residential letting[65] "divided into not less than four separate and self-contained flats".

f) Right to Acquire the Fee Simple

The general right to acquire the fee simple is conferred by section 8 in Part II of the No. 2 Act of 1978. It certainly applies to leases falling within the definition granted up to the No. 1 Act of 1978. It is also applied retrospectively by the Landlord and Tenant (Amendment) Act, 1980 section 73 in order to preserve similar rights under the Act of 1967. The persons entitled to acquire the fee simple are listed in sections 9 to 16 of the No. 2 Act of 1978 and are discussed below.[66] The unrepealed sections of the 1967 Act continue to apply to such persons, so that, for example, a county registrar can determine disputes in regard to the acquisition of the fee simple.[67]

A person entitled to acquire the fee simple also has the right to acquire intermediate interests.[68] If a person does not have the right to acquire the fee simple, they have no right to acquire intermediate interests.[69] There is no right to acquire the fee simple in a lease in a horizontal layer above the ground.[70]

Part II of the No. 2 Act 1978 does not apply to a person holding a house under a shared ownership lease under the Housing (Miscellaneous Provisions) Act, 1992 since that is a separate scheme for acquiring the fee simple in a house from a housing authority.

Section 26 of the No. 2 Act of 1978 gives a tenant of a housing authority, other than a tenant under a shared ownership lease, the right to acquire the fee simple under the section.

(1) Business Premises

Although the problem of ground rents arose mainly, in social and political terms, in relation to residential premises, Part II of the No. 2 Act of 1978 is capable of applying to business premises also. Its application to them has been discussed briefly above in the section on business premises.

---

65 Section 16 of the No. 2 Act of 1978.

66 See Conditions.

67 *Heatons Wholesale Ltd v. McCormack* [1994] 2 ILRM 83.

68 Section 8 of No. 2 Act of 1978.

69 *Metropolitan Properties v. O'Brien* [1995] 2 ILRM 383.

70 *ibid.*, per O'Flaherty Jat 391. The judge held that the legislature did not contemplate the situation.

(2) Dwelling Houses

Since the main objection to ground rents arose in relation to dwelling houses, the No. 2 Act of 1978, in addition to general powers applying to the acquisition of the fee simple, contained a special scheme in Part III applicable only to dwelling houses.[71]

Under Part III of the No. 2 Act of 1978 the Registrar of Titles, upon application made to him or her by a lessee, can, if satisfied that the lessee is entitled to acquire the fee simple, and with or without the consent of the lessor, where the lessor is known, issue a vesting certificate under section 22 which has the effect of vesting the fee simple in the applicant. The registrar has to satisfy him or herself that the purchase price has been paid to the person entitled to the fee simple or deposited with the Registrar,[72] but can proceed to act as arbitrator if necessary.

(3) Conditions

Section 9 of the No. 2 Act of 1978 contains the conditions to be satisfied by a lease if the person entitled is to have the right to purchase the fee simple. All the following conditions in section 9 have to be fulfilled:

a) there are permanent buildings on the land and the portion of the land not covered by buildings is subsidiary to them (*i.e.* residential and office sites);

b) there are permanent Buildings are not an improvement within the Act. "Improvement" means (subsection 2) "Addition to or alteration of a building unless it is such as to alter its original identity"; and

c) the buildings were not in breach of covenant in the lease.

In addition, one of the alternative conditions in section 10 must be complied with:

1. the buildings were erected by the lessee or person entitled to the lessee's interest;
2. the lease is for a term of 50 years or over and the rent is less than the rateable valuation – and the permanent buildings were not erected by the lessor – it is presumed in this case that they are not unless the contrary is shown;
3. where the lease was granted by the lessor to the nominee (*i.e.* the buyer or tenant) of a builder to whom the land was demised for the purpose of erecting the buildings under an agreement between the lessor and

71 It was originally designed to run for five years from the date the No. 2 Act of 1978 came into force (1 August 1978): No. 2 Act of 1978, s.18. It was extended: Landlord and Tenant (Ground Rents)(Amendment) Act, 1983 s.1, Landlord And Tenant (Ground Rents) (Amendment) Act, 1984 s.2, but the restriction was later removed: Landlord and Tenant (Ground Rents) (Amendment) Act, 1987 s.1.

72 No. 2 Act of 1978, s.22(2).

the builder whereby the builder, after contracting to sell the buildings, would surrender his or her lease in consideration of the lessor granting a new lease to the builder's nominee;

4. where lease granted by the lessor to the nominee (*i.e.* the buyer or tenant) of the builder under an agreement between the lessor and the builder whereby, on the erection of the buildings by the builder, the lessor would grant a lease to the builders' nominees; (Same as 3, but the builder has no lease.)

5. that the lease was granted, either at the time of the expiration or surrender of a previous lease or subsequent to such expiration or surrender[73]:

   a) at a rent less than the rateable valuation of the property at the date of the grant of the lease; or

   b) to the person entitled to the lessee's interest under the previous lease, provided that the previous lease would have been a lease to which this part would have applied had this Act been in force and provided that it shall be presumed, until the contrary is proved, that the person to whom the lease was granted was so entitled. [*I.e.* it is a lease granted in renewal of a previous lease and the previous lease would have entitled the lessee of it to enlarge it into a fee simple had this Act been in force at the time];

6. the lease is a reversionary lease granted after 31 March 1931 to a person entitled to it under the 1931, 1958 [or 1980] Acts;[74]

7. the lease is:

   for a term of not less than 50 years made:

   a) partly in consideration of a sum of money other than rent paid by the lessee before the grant of the lease and this is deemed to include money paid in redemption of rent (whenever paid); or

   b) partly in consideration of the expenditure of a sum of money other than on decoration, by the lessee on the premises; or

   c) both a) and b)

   where the sum is not less than 15 times the yearly amount of the rent.

A lease for a term of not less than 50 years[75] shall be deemed to comply with condition 7 if:

a) it was granted partly in consideration of the lessee undertaking to carry out specified works on the premises;

b) the amount to be spent on the works was not specified;

c) the works were carried out by the lessee; and

---

73 Amended by s.71 of Landlord and Tenant (Amendment) Act, 1980.

74 Reference to 1980 Act added by 1980 Act s.30(2)(c).

75 Section 12 of the No. 2 Act of 1978.

d) the reasonable cost of the works alone or together with any fine or other payment mentioned in the condition is not less than 15 times the yearly rent or the greatest rent reserved, whichever is the lesser.

Condition 7 has been extended to cover leases for less than 50 years by the 1980 Act.[76] A person entitled to such a lease has the right to acquire the fee simple if, in addition to one of the above, all the following conditions are complied with:

a) it is a sub-lease under a (superior) lease to which Part II of the 1978 Act applies;

b) the land demised in the sub-lease is the whole or part of the land demised in the superior leasel;

c) the term equals or exceeds the lesser of the following periods: 20 years or two-thirds of the term of the superior lease, and in any case expires at the same time as or not more than 15 years before the expiration of the superior lease;
and the other requirements of Condition 7 are fulfilled. [*i.e.* 7(a) or 7(b) or 7(c).]

In *Walsh v. Registrar of Titles*[77] the premises consisted of a dwelling house, shop, offices, and a slaughter house store. The premises had been used for business purposes for some years. The registrar refused a vesting certificate on the ground that he was not satisfied that the buildings were constructed wholly or principally as a dwelling house. The Circuit Court held that the premises were deemed to be a dwelling house within the meaning of section 19. In *Eastern Health Board v. O'Beirne*[78] a lease granted in 1899 for 99 years contained a covenant that it should be used as a dispensary. At the time of the proceedings the lease was held by the Eastern Health Board who wished to enlarge it. The owner of the fee simple resisted the application. The Circuit Court upheld the decision of the Registrar that the buildings were not constructed wholly or principally as a dwelling house.

(4) Restrictions

The No. 2 Act of 1978 contains restrictions on the right to acquire a fee simple under the Act. A person declared under section 15(1)[79] of the Act of 1958 not to be entitled to a reversionary lease of the land under that Act and who is in possession of the land under a lease or tenancy, or by virtue of section 15(2), is

76 Landlord and Tenant (Amendment) Act, 1980 s.72 extends Condition 7 in s.10 and s.12 of the No. 2 Act of 1978.

77 Unreported Southern Circuit Court Rec No E 309/84, 24 October 1984.

78 Unreported Circuit Court, Wicklow No. 5/83, 17 April 1984

79 Continued by s.3(4)(a) of the 1967 Act, itself now repealed by the No. 2 Act of 1978, s.7.

not entitled to acquire the fee simple.[80] Section 15(1) of the 1958 Act applied where the lessor of such a person had a reversion of at least 15 years and intended to develop the property themselves. It should be noted that this case is not continued for the future under the No. 2 Act of 1978.[81] Section 15(1) of the 1958 Act is in almost identical terms to section 33(1) of the 1980 Act which continues the restriction in relation to reversionary leases. A person is not entitled to acquire the fee simple under section 8 as to the future if the lease is:

(a) used for business purposes or includes a building divided into not less than four self-contained flats with a rent review clause allowing the rent to be altered within 26 years of the beginning of the lease, not being a clause that allows for the alteration of the rent once only and within five years from the beginning or upon erection of buildings or upon breach of covenant in the lease, or[82]

(b) granted before the Act of 1967, for business purposes where the lessee is restricted to dealing in commodities supplied by the lessor [*e.g.* a solus agreement where the land is used as a garage, service station, *etc.*], or

(c) contains a covenant requiring the lessee to erect buildings on the land if and so long as the covenant has not been complied with.

Previously the section contained two other cases where a person would be disqualified:

(d) if the lease was made by the Commissioner of Irish Lights; or

(e) if the lease was made by a harbour authority within the Harbours Act, 1946.

It should also be noted that a person could formerly also be disqualified under section 4 of the No. 2 Act of 1978 because that Act did not bind a Minister of the Government or the Commissioners of Public Works or the Irish Land Commission. These cases were amended by the 1980 Act[83] so that, in the case of section 4 of the No. 2 Act of 1978, the disqualification applies if the appropriate State authority, or under section 16, the Minister of Transport, are satisfied that the acquisition of the fee simple would not be in the public interest.

(5) Purchase Price

The original sections providing for the determination of the purchase price of

---

80 Section 16(1).

81 Section 15 of the 1958 Act was continued by s.3(4)(a) of the 1967 Act, but this was then repealed by the No. 2 Act of 1978, s.7.

82 Amended by Landlord and Tenant (Amendment) Act, 1984 s.8: the right to acquire the fee simple is not to be excluded by reason only of a provision in a reversionary lease granted after the 1984 Act for review of the rent.

83 Section 70 Act of 1980.

the fee simple[84] were found to be unworkable by the Supreme Court in *Gilsenan v. Foundry House Investments Ltd.*[85] The purchase price, if determined by arbitration, was to be the open market value, *i.e.* the price agreed between a willing buyer and a willing seller. This would be determined with reference to various factors including the current rent and current interest yields on securities and the value of previous sales. In *Gilsenan* the Supreme Court held that in some instances the formula was unworkable because it was based upon the rent reserved on a reversionary lease for 99 years. The court held that such a lease would today certainly contain a rent review clause and this, combined with the uncertainties of the inflation rate over such a long period, made it impossible to apply the formula.[86] A new formula has therefore been introduced by section 7 of the Landlord and Tenant (Amendment) Act, 1984.

(6) Deasy's Act Grants

Lease in the No. 2 Act of 1978 is defined as including a fee farm grant[87] and so a new Deasy's Act Grant which complies with the conditions in Part II would appear to come within the provisions, although the tenant would already have a fee simple. Nevertheless there is good ground for believing that such an interest is enlargeable under the Act because the acquisition of a fee simple under the No. 2 Act has important effects on the covenants. Although the estate would remain the same, the interest of the tenant is enlarged in the sense that his or her rights of ownership are greater than before.

(7) Yearly Tenants

Provisions as to yearly tenants are contained in section 15 of the No. 2 Act of 1978 as amended by the Landlord and Tenant (Amendment) Act, 1984 section 9. This applies where the land is:

(a) mostly covered by buildings[88] which were not erected by the lessor;[89]

(b) is held under a yearly tenancy; and

(c) has been so held by the tenant or by predecessors in title for 25 years prior to the service of notice by the tenant of intention to acquire the

84 Originally contained in section 18 of the 1967 Act, replaced by s.17 of the No. 2 Act of 1978.

85 [1980] ILRM 273, Supreme Court.

86 In *Byrne v. Loftus* [1978] IR 211, [1979] 113 ILTR 17 the Supreme Court had adopted a formula for determining the gross rent under the 1931 Act for a new tenancy, but the same court in *Gilsenan* pointed out that in *Loftus* the formula was based on a much shorter 21 year period.

87 Section 3.

88 Section 15(1)(a).

89 Section 15(1)(d).

fee simple under section 4 of 1967 Act[90] and where the rent is less than the rateable value[91] and is not tied accommodation , *i.e.* dependant on a person continuing to hold a particular job.[92]

(8) Sporting Leases

The Landlord and Tenant (Amendment) Act, 1971 had as its object the extension of the rights to reversionary leases under the then 1958 Act[93] to clubs and societies using land for recreational purposes, such as tennis, football or athletic clubs, *etc.* The 1980 Act substituted for references in the 1971 Act to the Act of 1958 references to the 1980 Act. This had the effect of giving such clubs the right, in addition, to acquire the fee simple in their premises under the No. 2 Act of 1978.

One problem in relation to sports clubs was whether, in terms of the above conditions, the area of land not covered by buildings was subsidiary to the land covered by buildings, bearing in mind that the area used for sport, such as a golf course, was likely to be more extensive in area than the land covered by buildings, such as the club house. In *Fitzgerald and Others (Trustees of Castleknock Tennis Club) v. Corcoran*[94] the trustees of the Castleknock Tennis Club held the premises under lease for a term of 99 years from 1973, being a sporting lease within the meaning of the Landlord and Tenant (Amendment) Act, 1971, granted to them by the landlord by virtue of an order of the High Court. The trustees brought an application to enlarge their interest in the property to a fee simple under section 4 of the Landlord and Tenant (Ground Rents) Act, 1967. Lardner J in the High Court held that the words permanent buildings in the Act could not be construed as including a hard tennis court and car park, which were part of the premises and that the tennis courts could not be considered as being subsidiary or ancillary to the club house. The judge rejected the trustees' application to acquire a fee simple in the whole of the leased premises and raised the question, *inter alia,* for the opinion of the Supreme Court by way of consultative case stated, whether the club was entitled to invoke the provisions of section 14 of the Landlord and Tenant (Ground Rents) (No. 2) Act, 1978 so as to entitle it to acquire the fee simple in the club house and such ground as was subsidiary and ancillary thereto within the terms of the Act?

The Supreme Court (Finlay CJ, Griffin and O'Flaherty JJ concurring) held that the trustees were entitled to invoke section 14 of the 1978 Act so as to entitle them to acquire the fee simple interest in the club house and such ground as

90 Section 15(1)(c).

91 Section 15(1)(d).

92 Section 15(1)(g).

93 The Landlord and Tenant (Reversionary Leases) Act, 1958.

94 [1991] ILRM 545, Supreme Court.

was subsidiary and ancillary to it, the balance of the ground being deemed to be a vacant lease within the meaning of section 14(2) of the Act.

Finlay CJ (Griffin and O'Flaherty JJ concurring) quoted section 14 of the Act of 1978. That section reads as follows:

> "14 (1) Where a person holds land under a lease (in this section referred to as a partly-built lease) which would entitle him to acquire the fee simple but for the fact that the portion of the land which is not covered by the permanent buildings is not wholly subsidiary and ancillary to those buildings, the following provisions of this section shall have effect.
>
> (2) The partly-built lease shall, for the purpose of this Act, be deemed to comprise two separate leases as follows:
>
> (a) one lease (in this section referred to as the built-on lease) comprising that portion of the land demised by the partly-built lease which is covered by the permanent buildings, together with so much of the land as is subsidiary and ancillary to those buildings, and
>
> (b) the other lease (in this section referred to as the vacant lease) comprising the residue of the said land".

Referring to section 14(2) the judge continued:

> "The reference in that subsection to 'so much of the land as is subsidiary and ancillary' in subclause (a), and the reference to 'the residue of the land' in subclause (b) makes it abundantly clear that the true meaning of the words 'not wholly subsidiary and ancillary,' contained in s 14(1), must be referring to a portion of land held under a lease, some area of which is subsidiary and ancillary, and some area of which is not".

Finlay CJ concluded that the provisions of section 14 applied to sporting leases and therefore the fiction of a partly-built lease allowed the sporting lease to qualify within the conditions for the acquisition of the fee simple.

(9) The Effect on Covenants: Section 28

Section 28 of the No. 2 Act of 1978 provides as follows:

> "(1) Where a person having an interest in land acquires the fee simple in the land, all covenants subject to which he held the land, other than a covenant specified in subsection (2), shall thereupon cease to have effect and no new covenant shall be created in conveying the fee simple.
>
> (2) In the case of a covenant –
>
> (a) which protects or enhances the amenities of any land occupied by the immediate lessor of the grantee, or
>
> (b) which relates to the performance of a duty imposed by statute on any such person, or
>
> (c) which relates to a right of way over the acquired land or a right of drainage or other right necessary to secure or assist the development of other land,
>
> the covenant shall, notwithstanding anything contained in this Act, continue in full force and effect and shall be enforceable as follows:

(i) in the case of a covenant which does not relate to a right of way, right of drainage or other right aforesaid, by any such person or his personal representatives or successors in title, as if their acquisition had not occurred, and

(ii) in the case of a covenant which does so relate, by any person aggrieved by breach of the covenant".

(a) Scope of the Section

The section applies where a person having an interest in land acquires the fee simple in the land. The section does not say acquires the fee simple under this Act and so it can be argued that the section applies in all cases where a person who previously had an interest acquires the fee simple. This could include the following:

(1) enlargement under section 65 of the Conveyancing Act, 1881;

(2) a tenant acquiring the lessor's reversion by purchase from the lessor whether under an option in the lease or otherwise;

(3) acquisition under the Labourers Acts;

(4) acquisition by a tenant of a housing authority under section 26 of the No. 2 Act of 1978;

(5) acquisition under a shared ownership lease[95];

(6) any other case where a person having less than a fee simple in the land buys the fee simple, *e.g.* a tenant for life or person having any other interest under a settlement buys the fee simple under the Settled Land Acts, 1892–90.

(b) Third Party Covenants

One question that arises is whether, in view of the words all covenants, the section discharges restrictive covenants the benefit of which is vested not in the former landlord or former tenant, but in a third party under the doctrine of *Tulk v. Moxhay*.[96] We shall refer to such covenants as third party covenants. In *Whelan v. Cork Corporation*[97] Murphy J, upheld by the Supreme Court,[98] held that the section did discharge such covenants.

In *Whelan* the freehold owner of land in 1908 granted a lease for 99 years to a lessee. In 1948 the lessee was granted a further term from the year 2007 by a reversionary lease of the same land. In 1937 the lessee sublet part of the land, known as Instow, to a sublessee. The sublease contained a covenant binding the lessors not to build, erect or permit or suffer to be built or be erected on any

95 Housing (Miscellaneous Provisions) Act, 1992 s.2(2).

96 (1848) 2 Ph 774, 41 ER 1143. Pringle J in *Williams & Co Ltd v. LSD and Quinnsworth,* unreported High Court, 19 June 1970 at p.16. See Chapter 21 Covenants between Freeholders.

97 [1991] ILRM 19, High Court Murphy J. See also below p.706.

98 There was an unsuccessful appeal to the Supreme Court which gave an extempore judgment.

part of the lands which later became known as Riverside Cottage any building or erection of a greater height than 12 feet from the existing ground level. Lessors was defined in the lease to mean the persons for the time being entitled to receive rent under the lease. In 1989 the sublease of 1937 became vested in the plaintiffs by assignment. The assignment was expressly subject to covenants contained in the leases. In 1948 the lessee under the 1908 lease granted a second sublease of the land to a second sublessee. This part of the land became known as Riverside Cottage. The 1948 lease of Riverside Cottage contained a covenant, in similar terms to that contained in the 1937 sublease of Instow. In 1984 the second sublessee assigned his interest under the 1948 lease to the defendant, subject to the covenants. In 1989 the defendants also obtained the lessor's interest in Riverside Cottage under the leases of 1908 and 1948 and a few days later obtained a conveyance of the freehold in Riverside Cottage. The conveyance was subject to the intent that the leases should merge with and be extinguished in the freehold reversion. The defendants, Cork Corporation, began roadworks which involved the construction of a fly-over which would exceed 12 feet in height. The plaintiffs brought the present action for an injunction claiming that the roadworks would be in breach of the covenant in the 1937 sublease of Instow. The issue was whether the defendants were bound by the covenant.

The defendants argued that they were not lessors within the meaning of the 1937 lease and so not expressly bound by the covenant (*i.e.* in privity of estate), that they were not bound under the principle of *Tulk v. Moxhay* because they had no notice of the covenant and in any case when they exercised their right, which they had done, to obtain the fee simple to the Riverside Cottage land, the covenant had ceased to affect them by virtue of section 28 of the Landlord and Tenant (Ground Rents (No. 2) Act, 1978.

Murphy J held first that the defendants were lessors under the 1937 sublease if it were given an extended interpretation. That expression, he held, was intended to identify not simply the immediate lessors as such, but those persons who were also entitled to an interest in the Riverside land and able to burden it with a similar covenant. The judge went on to apply *Tulk v. Moxhay* and held that the defendants had constructive notice of the covenant at the time they acquired the fee simple in the Riverside land. They had acquired the fee simple in order to free themselves of the burden of covenants contained in the leases of the Riverside land and so it would have been reasonable to make inquiries as to whether any third parties might claim the benefit of other covenants. Thus, apart from section 28, the judge held that the covenant would have bound the defendants in equity. Despite these findings the judge then found that the covenant had ceased to bind the defendants when they acquired the fee simple under the 1978 Act. The judge found that the covenants which, with a "very limited number of exceptions", ceased to have effect under section 28 were not only those contained in the lease formerly held by the enlarging lessee, but also third party covenants. The judge did not decide, as a constitutional issue, whether this contravened Article 40.2 as an unjust attack on property rights since the Attorney-General did not appear to argue the issue.

The Supreme Court upheld Murphy J on the same terms in an extempore judgment. It is, however, difficult to see how the defendants were lessors of the Instow land in any sense at all. Not only were they never entitled to receive rent on the Instow land, they never acquired any interest in the Instow land at all. All they acquired was an interest in the Riverside land. Even if lessor in the 1937 lease of Instow is taken to mean someone who had, or later acquired, an interest in the 1908 or 1948 leases, those leases referred to the whole land and the interests acquired by the defendants in those leases related only to the Riverside land. Furthermore, if they were indeed lessors in a literal sense, then they would have been bound by the covenant in the 1937 lease under Deasy's Act, or in privity of estate, to use the common law expression.

It is open to question whether it was intended that section 28 should destroy not only covenants which were binding between the former lessor and the former tenant, but also third party covenants. The evident purpose of the section was to relieve the new fee simple from the burden of covenants contained in the original lease which might have been appropriate between landlord and tenant but which might unduly restrict a fee simple. But it goes far beyond this to say that the fees simple created under the No. 2 Act of 1978, which was concerned with enlarging leases into freeholds, should be freer of covenants than ordinary fees simple. The burden of covenants in equity under the doctrine of *Tulk v. Moxhay* has always affected fee simple estates. Under the section all covenants affecting the land except those in subsection 2 thereupon cease to have effect. It would seem that the only effect of subsection 2 is to preserve those covenants the burden of which ran with the land before the enlargement and this can only refer, as far as third parties are concerned, to restrictive, *i.e.* negative, covenants.

After *Whelan* it seems that in relation to third parties section 28 exempts very few covenants from the generally destructive effect of the section. It therefore follows that the section provides some scope for use as a means of destroying restrictive covenants. It should also be noted that section 28(4) amends the Registration of Title Act, 1964 section 72 by adding, to the list of interests which bind a purchaser of registered land without registration, covenants preserved by section 28. It seems unfortunate that the Act did not instead require such covenants to be noted on the register at the time the fee simple is granted under the Act. Most interests coming within section 72 are of the kind which could be discovered, although not without difficulty in some cases, by inspecting the land itself, but one could hardly expect to do so in the case of section 28 covenants unless, perhaps, they relate to a right of way and there is a visible path on the land.

(c) Constitutionality of section 28

The issue of constitutionality was left unresolved by *Whelan*. It was argued in the case that if the section rendered ineffective covenants which had previously affected the land under *Tulk v. Moxhay*, then it would be unconstitutional, given the absence of compensation, and that a court, faced with a choice between alternative interpretations, one of which would render the section unconstitutional and one which would not, should, in accordance with the decision in *East Donegal Co-operative Livestock Marts Ltd v. Attorney-General*,[99] choose the constitutional interpretation. That decision also recognised, however, that where words were clear and unambiguous, the court should give effect to them even if that rendered a statute void as being unconstitutional. Murphy J considered that the words were clear and unambiguous so that there was no real choice to be made:

> "It is difficult to escape the wide net cast by the words 'all covenants' subject to which the land was held and any argument that the comprehensive expression should be limited to the relationship between the lessee and those entitled to the superior interests would be inconsistent with the subsequent provisions of the section which provide that certain covenants which do not cease to have effect may be enforced 'by any person aggrieved by breach of the covenant'. The Oireachtas clearly recognised that the covenants which were ceasing to have effect (subject to a very limited number of exceptions) included covenants for the benefit of a wide range of covenantees and not only the lessor or owner of a superior interest. In my view the Oireachtas has shown a clear and unambiguous intention to eliminate a wide range of covenants, including those for the benefit of third parties, where the fee simple is acquired under the provisions of the 1978 Act. This does not necessarily render the section unconstitutional. Indeed it would be impossible to reach such a conclusion without the benefit of hearing argument from the Attorney General to the contrary".[100]

In reaching this conclusion the judge did not consider that the literal meaning was necessarily unconstitutional:

> "It is impossible to anticipate all of the arguments which might be raised by the Attorney General on a constitutional issue less still to adjudicate upon them in advance of a plenary hearing. It is sufficient for the purposes of this case to say that I am not convinced that a literal interpretation of section 28 of the 1978 Act would necessarily render that section in conflict with the Constitution. In any event it seems to me that the words used are so clear and unambiguous that they do not admit of the interpretation which the plaintiffs seek to place on them".[101]

It could certainly be argued in future that section 28 is unconstitutional, in so far as it affects covenants which are property interests, as an unjust attack on such interests under Article 40.3.2°. of the Constitution. The effect of *Tulk v. Moxhay* itself is that restrictive covenants are not merely contracts but a species

99 [1970] IR 317.

100 *Whelan v. Cork Corporation* [1991] ILRM 19 at p.27-28.

101 *ibid.* at p.28.

of equitable property interest, and the section deprives third parties of the ability to enforce such covenants and provides no compensation for the loss.

3. Reversionary Leases

The grounds are the same as for enlargement, but there are fewer restrictions that apply to persons entitled to a reversionary lease than there are to enlargement.

The topic is now dealt with by Part III of the Landlord and Tenant (Amendment) Act, 1980 as amended by the Landlord and Tenant (Amendment) Act, 1984 sections 3 and 4.

a) Right to Reversionary Lease.

The right to a reversionary lease, *i.e.* a lease to take effect immediately after the determination of the current lease, is now contained in section 30 of the 1980 Act. Sections 9, 10 to 12, and 14 of the No. 2 Act of 1978 apply and the conditions in them must be complied with.[102]

b) Restrictions.

It should be noted that the restrictions in section 16 of the No. 2 Act of 1978[103] do not apply to reversionary leases. The applicable restrictions are contained in section 33 of the 1980 Act. A person is not entitled where an interested party proves:

a) that they have an interest in reversion that is either a freehold or is for a term of not less than 15 years; and

b) (i) that they intend or have agreed to pull down and rebuild and have planning permission;

(ii) that they need vacant possession to carry out a scheme of development; or

(iii) that the grant of a reversionary lease would not be consistent with good estate management;[104] or

(v) a planning authority shows that the land is in an obsolete area in the development plan.[105]

Under section 33(3) a local authority may refuse a reversionary lease where it is in relation to business premises and the local authority will require possession

102 No. 2 Act of 1978 s.30(2).

103 See above.

104 Section 33(1).

105 Section 33(2).

within five years of existing lease for a purpose for which it could acquire the land compulsorily.

c) Damages

Section 33(5) provides that if the successful objector to the reversionary lease does not carry out the intention upon which the objection was based, the Court can award punitive damages.

d) Terms

The lease is for a term of 99 years.[106] The rent is not to be less than the rent under the previous lease and if fixed by the Court is one eighth of the gross rent as defined in section 36.

The rent can be reviewed by the Court under section 3 of the Landlord and Tenant (Amendment) Act, 1984. Previously it had been held in *Gilsenan v. Foundry House Investments Ltd*[107] that the existing provisions as to the determination of rent in reversionary leases were unworkable.

e) Reversionary Lease a Graft

Section 39 of 1980 Act provides that a reversionary lease shall be a graft on the previous lease for all purposes and is subject to the same rights and equities that affected the previous lease. The section applies to reversionary leases "whether granted on terms settled under this Part or negotiated between the parties". The words seem capable of applying to all reversionary leases, not merely those to which the tenant is entitled under the provisions of the Act.

E. Human Rights

The question may arise as to whether legislation that gives a right to acquire a freehold reversion to a tenant contravenes the right to property of the owner of the reversion. This question has been answered in the negative by the European Court of Human Rights in *James v. United Kingdom (The Duke of Westminster's Case)*[108] in which English leasehold enfranchisement legislation was upheld.

106 Section 34(2) of 1980 Act.

107 [1980] ILRM 273, Supreme Court.

108 Sub nom *James v. United Kingdom* (1986) 8 EHRR 123, Series A No. 98, Application No. 8795/79, 21 February 1986.

F. Rent Restriction

1. Introduction

The Housing (Private Rented Dwellings) Act, 1982, as amended,[109] provides for the control of rents and security of tenure in relation to certain tenancies. The Act is a successor to earlier legislation, in particular the Rent Restriction Acts, 1960 to 1981 and, although the 1982 Act repealed the earlier legislation, reference must still be made, by virtue of the 1982 Act, to the earlier legislation in order to determine whether or not a particular dwelling comes within the 1982 Act. Furthermore, certain dwellings were decontrolled under the earlier Acts and the 1982 Act also contains decontrolling provisions.

The occasion for the passing of the 1982 Act was the decision of the Supreme Court in two appeals heard together, *i.e. Blake v. Attorney-General* and *Madigan v. Attorney-General.*[110] The appeals held that provisions of the rent restriction legislation then in force were unconstitutional in that they were based on rent levels in 1941, or in some cases in 1914, that there was no provision for review of the rents and that the restrictions on the recovery of possession by the landlords unfairly restricted their property rights.

The law in this area is complicated and what follows is a summary of the main features.[111]

2. Definition of Controlled Dwellings

Section 8(1) of the Housing (Private Rented Dwellings) Act, 1982 provides that:

> "Subject to subsection (2), this Part applies to every dwelling which would, at the commencement[112] of this Act, be a controlled dwelling within the meaning of the Rent Restriction Acts, 1960 to 1981, if those Acts had full force and effect at such commencement, other than such a dwelling held at such commencement under a contract of tenancy for greater than from year to year during such period as it is so held".

109 Housing (Private Rented Dwellings) (Amendment) Act, 1983.

110 [1982] IR 117. The first Bill, the Housing (Private Rented Dwellings) Bill 1981 was referred by the President to the Supreme Court under Art. 26. In *Re The Housing (Private Rented Dwellings) Bill, 1981* [1983] IR 181, [1983] ILRM 246 the Supreme Court (O'Higgins CJ) held the Bill unconstitutional. The Bill provided for a five year period in which the landlords were to receive the market rent reduced by a percentage. It was held to be an unjust attack on property rights. A new Act was passed, the Housing (Private Rented Dwellings) Act 1982, and this time the President signed it without referring it to the Supreme Court.

111 A more detailed treatment is to be found in Wylie, *Landlord and Tenant* Ch. 29. See also de Blacam.

112 20 July 1982.

The provision therefore requires continued reference to the earlier legislation. The meaning of the obscure last phrase is considered under the heading "Let" below.

a) Dwellings

The 1982 Act applies only to a dwelling which is defined by section 2(1) of the Act as "a house let. . ., or part so let, of any house". One of the effects of the continued reference to the earlier legislation is that the 1982 Act applies to premises which are not exclusively residential, since such premises came within the earlier Acts, and so premises partly used for business purposes are a dwelling for the purposes of the 1982 Act.[113] There must be some residential use, however.[114] On the other hand, premises which are mainly used for business but which have been used temporarily for residence for a night or two have been held not to amount to a dwelling.[115]

In *Foley v. Galvin*[116] the Supreme Court held that residence need not be continuous for the Acts to apply and it is sufficient if there is occupation by a member of the tenant's family or a caretaker or a person "who, though not at the moment in actual occupation, does in fact require the dwelling-house for his own use".[117]

b) Let

The 1982 Act only applies if the dwelling is let, *i.e.* if the relation of landlord and tenant has been created or exists between the parties. This would include any such relation within Deasy's Act, 1860, which is necessarily at a rent.[118] It has been held that the Rent Restriction Acts did not apply to tenants at will.[119] However, section 3 of Deasy's Act provides that the relation of landlord and tenant "shall be deemed to subsist in all cases in which there shall be an agreement by one party to hold land from or under another in consideration of any rent" and so it is arguable that let in the 1982 Act is governed by that provision so that whenever those elements are present the premises are let. Apart from that, section 8(1) of the 1982 Act specifically excludes "such a dwelling held at such commencement [of the Act] under a contract of tenancy for greater than

113 *Mullane v. Brosnan* [1974] IR 222; *Foley v. Johnson* [1988] IR 7 (licensed premises with living accommodation above); *Walsh v. Coyne* [1958] IR 233 (ditto); *Hardwicke Ltd v. Byrne* [1963] IR 52 (dwelling accommodation plus cobbler's business).

114 Rent Restrictions Act, 1960 s.4.

115 *Bradley v. McGowan* [1951] IR 72.

116 [1932] IR 339.

117 Per Fitzgibbon J, *ibid.* at pp.361-362; *Walsh v. Coyne* [1958] IR 233.

118 Deasy's Act, 1860 s.3.

119 *Delany (Blanchardstown Mills Ltd) v. Jones* [1938] IR 826; *Irish Soldiers' and Sailors' Land Trust v. Donnelly* [1944] IR 464.

from year to year during such period as it is so held". It is not clear what the phrase "during such period as it is so held" is intended to mean. A fixed term tenancy seems clearly to be excluded from control, but the phrase suggests, as Wylie points out,[120] that this is so only in so far as a tenant holds under such a tenancy at the commencement of the Act, implying that it is otherwise if the same tenant continues in occupation after the end of the term on, for example, a monthly tenancy, at some time after the commencement of the Act. This would mean that a tenant who was not protected at the date of commencement of the Act would later become protected, but it is doubtful whether the Act was intended to have such an effect. The whole purpose of the Act was merely to continue control over dwellings already controlled. However, it is difficult to see what else it could possibly mean.

c) Separate

Section 2(1) of the 1982 Act requires the house or part of the house to be let as a separate dwelling. Prima facie this means that the tenant must have exclusive possession of the whole of the house, or part of the house, which constitutes the dwelling. Nevertheless the section goes on to say: "whether or not the tenant shares with any other persons any portion thereof or any accommodation, amenity or facility in connection therewith". While this allows certain types of shared accommodation to come within the control provided by the Act, the requirement of letting means that the tenant would have to have exclusive possession in some sense, otherwise there is no landlord and tenant relationship and therefore no control.[121]

d) Valuation Limits

The 1982 Act, as has already been pointed out, controls only dwellings controlled under the earlier legislation at the date the 1982 Act came into force. Since the control under that legislation[122] was based on valuation limits set in the past, the valuation limits under the 1982 Act are low and the number of dwellings coming under the control is consequently small. The limits are:

(1) In the county borough of Dublin and borough of Dun Laoghaire:

a house	£40
a separate and self-contained flat	£30
other dwelling	£60

---

120 Wylie, *Landlord and Tenant* para. 29.07.

121 Wylie, *Landlord and Tenant* para. 29.08.

122 Rent Restrictions Act, 1960 s.3(2)(a) as amended by the Rent Restrictions (Amendment) Act, 1967 s.2(1).

(2) Elsewhere:

a house £30

a separate and self-contained flat. £20

other dwelling £40

The figures represent the estimated annual income produced from rent. If the rateable valuation is increased above the limit for the dwelling in question, the dwelling remains controlled until the landlord recovers possession.[123] This is an important provision, because in most cases the most usual way in which the valuation increases is by the Rent Tribunal, discussed below, fixing a new rent for the property in question above that fixed in the past.

The limits set out above were introduced by the Rent Restrictions (Amendment) Act, 1967 and the effect was to decontrol many dwellings. The 1967 Act also decontrolled any house with a rateable value exceeding £10 of which a person being a bachelor or spinster over the age of 21 and under 65 became tenant.[124] Such property remains decontrolled under the 1982 Act. There is at least one case where property which had been decontrolled under earlier legislation is recontrolled by the 1982 Act, namely, where parts of dwelling houses had been let and the dwelling house itself had not been decontrolled.[125] Nevertheless, the 1982 Act only applies to tenants in possession at the date of the coming into force of the Act and the dwelling ceases to be controlled when that possession comes to an end. It is, in fact, tenants who are protected rather than dwellings as such. It follows that once the protected possession comes to an end so does control and it will not revive.

e) Land Other Than Site

A dwelling is not controlled if it is let with land "other than the site of the dwelling", and where the rateable valuation exceeds the lesser of:

(1) half the rateable valuation of the site including the building or buildings thereon; or

(2) (i) in the case of a dwelling situated in the county borough of Dublin or the borough of Dun Laoghaire, £10;

(ii) in any other case, £5.[126]

---

123 1960 Act s.3(4) as amended by the 1967 Act s.2(1), 1960 Act s.3(7) as amended by the 1967 Act s.2(5); Wylie, *Landlord and Tenant* para. 29.09.

124 1967 Act s.2(4). The provision could possibly be challenged on constitutional grounds as infringing the guarantee of equality as human persons.

125 *Donnelly v. O'Neill* [1935] IR 286; *Logan v. Donoghue* [1938] IR 427; Wylie, *Landlord and Tenant* para. 29.10.

126 Rent Restrictions Act, 1960 s.3(2)(h); *McGrane v. Wills* (1930) 65 ILTR 86; *Mason v. Leavy* [1952] IR 41; *O'Reilly v. Acres* [1974] IR 454.

Site means only the ground on which the dwelling and outhouses are built and not surrounding land.[127]

f) Date of Construction

A dwelling is not controlled if it was erected after, or was in the course of being erected, on 7 May 1941.[128] Erected includes the conversion of existing premises to a dwelling.[129]

g) Repossession By Landlord

It was noted under Valuation Limits above that if the rateable valuation is increased above the limit for the dwelling in question, the dwelling remains controlled until the landlord recovers possession. As to dwellings under the limits, repossession by the landlord after 8 June 1966 decontrols the dwelling.[130] The 1967 Act also decontrolled separate and self-contained flats not forming part of a building reconstructed by conversion into flats.[131] Possession means actual possession and not possession by a new tenant with the landlord's consent.[132] Under the 1982 Act a dwelling also is decontrolled when the right of the tenant to retain possession cease to subsist[133] and where a landlord recovers possession under section 16.[134]

h) Assignment, Subletting by Tenant

The 1982 Act ceases to apply if the tenant assign or sublets the tenancy.

i) Wholly Excluded Lettings

(1) Public Housing

Dwellings let or deemed to be let[135] under the Housing Act, 1966 are excluded from control.[136] The 1982 Act may nevertheless apply where the dwelling is owned by the State, *e.g.* the Commissioners for Public Works.[137]

---

127 *ibid.*, especially *O'Reilly v. Acres* [1974] IR 454 at 460.

128 Rent Restrictions Act, 1960 s.3(2)(b).

129 *Somers v. Huchinson* (1930) 64 ILTR 103; *Keeler v. Brangan* (1930) 64 ILTR 213; *McDonagh v. Mulholland* [1957] Ir Jur Rep 4.

130 Rent Restrictions Act, 1967 s.2(2).

131 *ibid.* s.2(3).

132 *Griffin v. Kennedy* (1965) 99 ILTR 199.

133 1982 Act s.8(3)(a).

134 1982 Act s.8(3)(c).

135 For example, housing provided under the Labourers Acts or the Housing for the Working Classes Acts.

136 Rent Restrictions Act, 1960 s.3(2)(c).

137 Wylie, *Landlord and Tenant* para. 29.13.

(2) Unfit Housing

The control provisions cannot be relied on where a housing authority takes action against an unfit house by means of a repair notice, a closing order or a demolition order.[138]

(3) Furnished Lettings

The Rent Restrictions Act, 1960 excluded from control furnished lettings and those where the rent included payment for services such as board, or heating, hot water, fuel electricity or other services unless the portion of the rent attributable to the dwelling alone was equal to or exceeded three quarters of the reserved rent.[139] The court must apportion the rent between payment for the dwelling and payment for the services.[140] An agreement between the parties apportioning the rent is not binding on the court.[141] The time for making the apportionment is the date when the issue is raised in court.[142] Services for the purpose of the Acts are those provided by the landlord, and not, for example, by another tenant.[143]

(4) Owner-Occupied Houses

The 1982 Act has no application to owner-occupied houses. The Rent Restrictions Acts were designed to protect tenants and so excluded such houses.[144]

(5) Separate Self-Contained Flats

A separate and self-contained flat in a building reconstructed by way of conversion into such flats after the coming into force of the Rent Restrictions Act, 1960 was also excluded from control.[145] Repair necessary to make the building once again fit for human habitation does not constituted reconstruction and so

138 Housing Act, 1966 s.66(17).

139 Rent Restrictions Act, 1960 s.3(2)(d).

140 *ibid.*; *Hanratty v. Hardy* [1947] Ir Jur Rep 42; *Parkinson v. O'Malley* [1940] IR 498.

141 *Parkinson v. O'Malley* [1940] IR 498.

142 *Fridberg v. Doyle* [1981] ILRM 370.

143 *Elkinson v. Cassidy* (1975) 110 ILTR 27.

144 Rent Restrictions Act, 1960 s.3(2)(e). For this purpose the Act defines owner as including a person holding under a long lease, *i.e.* "any estate or interest in a house except under a tenancy not being for more than twenty-one years": s.3(6). However, the 1982 Act excludes all fixed-term tenancies from control.

145 Rent Restrictions Act, 1960 s.3(2)(g); *Boyle v. Fitzsimons* [1926] IR 378; *Broadhead v. Knox* (1974) 109 ILTR 116.

such repair will not decontrol the flat.[146] Substantial refurbishment may not have this effect either.[147]

j) Partially Excluded Lettings

(1) Service Letting

The 1982 Act partially excludes from control, as did earlier legislation, dwellings let to a person "in connection with his continuance in any office, appointment or employment".[148] Such dwellings are only excluded from the those parts of the Act which entitle the tenant to retain possession and restrict the landlord's right of recovery. The Act does not prevent a tenant of such a dwelling from applying to have the terms of the tenancy determined. Such a right is, however, unlikely to be effective since the tenancy is not otherwise protected.

(2) Temporary Convenience Letting

The 1982 Act also partially excludes, as did earlier legislation, dwellings let "*bona fide* for the temporary convenience or to meet a temporary necessity of the landlord or the tenant".[149] Such dwellings again are only excluded from those parts of the Act which entitle the tenant to retain possession and which restrict the landlord's right to recovery. Again, the Act does not prevent the tenant applying to have the terms of the tenancy fixed, but without the other protections, the right is hardly significant.

3. Fixing the Terms of Tenancies

a) Rent Tribunal

In default of, or notwithstanding, agreement between landlord and tenant the terms of the tenancy are fixed by the Rent Tribunal,[150] established by the Housing (Private Rented Dwellings) (Amendment) Act, 1983. Under the 1982 Act the jurisdiction had been vested in the District Court.

The Rent Tribunal consists of a chairperson,[151] several vice-chairpersons and ordinary members whose period of office is not to exceed three years.[152]

---

146 *Gore-Grimes v. Foley* (1930) 64 ILTR 52. Wylie, *Landlord and Tenant* para. 29.19. As to partial conversion: *Connolly v. Gleeson* [1942] IR 68; *Downes v. Kennedy* (1976) 110 ILTR 25.

147 *Noyk v. O'Brien* (1941) 76 ILTR 66; *O'Sullivan v. Cullen* (1925) 29 ILTR 133.

148 1982 Act s.8(2)(a).

149 1982 Act s.8(2)(b).

150 Housing (Rent Tribunal) Regulations, 1983 (SI 222 of 1983); Wylie, *Landlord and Tenant* para. 29.27-29.30.

151 The Act uses the word chairman but the holders of the office have so far both been female, the first chairperson being Mary Laffoy SC (1983-88).

152 1983 Act s.2(2). Housing (Rent Tribunal) Regulations, 1983 (SI 222 of 1983).

Members are part-time. Some are lawyers, other have experience in valuation of property. The Tribunal sits in divisions usually consisting of the chairperson or one of the vice-chairpersons and two other members. Any party can appear in person or be represented.[153]

A landlord or tenant may apply to the Rent Tribunal to fix the terms of the tenancy notwithstanding any agreement already entered into between landlord and tenant.[154]

b) Fixing the Rent

The Rent Tribunal may fix the rent for the dwelling.[155] The statutory rent is defined by section 13 of the 1982 Act as the gross rent reduced by an amount in respect of improvements made by the tenant.[156] The gross rent is the rent which in the opinion of the Tribunal is a:

> ". . . just and proper rent having regard to the nature, character and location of the dwelling, the other terms of the tenancy, the means of the landlord and the tenant, the date of purchase of the dwelling by the landlord and the amount paid by him therefor, the length of the tenant's occupancy of the dwelling and the number and ages of the tenant's family residing in the dwelling".[157]

The gross rent is clearly not the same as the market rent since it may be fixed by reference to the criteria laid down in section 13. In *Quirke v. Folio Homes Ltd*[158] McCarthy J in the Supreme Court divided the criteria into three categories:

> "The criteria set out in the subsection fall into three categories, the first of them objective – the nature, character and location of the dwelling and the other terms of the tenancy; the second personal but potentially common to both sides and the third matters capable of exact detail and touching upon the second category".[159]

The judge went on to comment in a typically ironic but somewhat cryptic fashion:

> "Whilst there is much appeal in the philosophy - "From each according to his ability, to each according to his need, (Karl Marx - Criticism of the Gotha Programme) it is not an aid to statutory construction".

This was apparently intended as a rejection of the view that the relative means of the landlord and the tenant were always relevant, so that a disparity in their means would always entitle a poor tenant to a reduction of rent. In the judge's

153 *ibid.* art. 10(1)(b).

154 1983 Act s.5.

155 1982 Act s.13, as amended by the 1983 Act s.9(2).

156 1982 Act s.13(1).

157 1982 Act s.13(2).

158 [1988] ILRM 496.

159 *ibid.* p.499.

view the categories were not an automatic check list all of which had to be considered in every case. Although the factors in the first category were always relevant, those in categories 2 and 3 were not necessarily so and should be considered only when relevant. In the instant case the landlord company had stated before the Tribunal that its income was greater than that of the tenant. The Tribunal had refused the tenant's demand for information as to the means of the shareholders or directors of the landlord company. The Supreme Court held that the means of the landlord were only relevant when the landlord sought to counter a claim by the tenant to hardship by showing hardship to itself.

In *Dowd v. Pierce*[160] the dwelling was in a state of disrepair due to the landlord's failure to repair and this in turn had meant that the tenant was unable to effect internal repairs. Circuit Court held that the proper course of action was to adjourn the landlord's application to fix the rent until the landlord had carried out the repairs. If the landlord failed to do so, the housing authority could be informed that the dwelling was unfit for human habitation.[161] If the application had been made by the tenant a similar procedure would have been adopted.[162]

c) Rent Allowances

Since the rents of properties affected by the 1982 Act had been fixed at an unrealistically low level, the effect of the Act was to raise the rents of many of the properties by a substantial amount. Section 23 of the Act sought to offset any hardship on tenants arising from this by providing for tenants to claim rent allowances.[163]

d) Registration

Where a dwelling is controlled and a new rent is fixed, either by agreement or by the Rent Tribunal, the landlord is under a duty to inform the housing authority who are to enter the details in their register maintained under section 20 of the Housing (Miscellaneous Provisions) Act, 1992.[164] Registration is not required where the new rent is less than the previous one.

e) Rent Review

Where a rent has been fixed by the District Court under the 1982 Act or the Rent Tribunal under the 1983 Act, no new application can be made until the

160 [1984] ILRM 653.

161 See Chapter 28 Housing Law: Unfit Houses.

162 [1984] ILRM 653 at 655.

163 Social Welfare (Rent Allowance) Regulations, 1998 (SI 188 of 1998).

164 Housing (Private Rented Dwellings) Regulations, 1982 (SI 217 of 1982) art. 7 as substituted by Housing (Private Rented Dwellings) (Amendment) Regulations, 1983 (SI 286 of 1983) art. 4.

expiration of four years and nine months from the date when it was previously fixed.[165]

f) Appeals

The landlord or tenant may appeal to the High Court within three months of a decision of the Rent Tribunal, or such longer period as the court allows. Strictly speaking, the appeal is on a point of law, but some latitude is allowed and appeals on issues of mixed fact and law have been entertained.[166]

4. Recovery of Possession

One of the constitutional objections to the original legislation was that it unduly restricted the right of the landlord to recover possession. The 1982 Act therefore gives to the tenant a more restricted liberty to retain possession.

a) Tenant

Tenant for the purpose of the 1982 Act is the person:

(a) who would have been defined as being protected if the Rent Restrictions Acts, 1960 and 1967 had been in force at the date of coming into force of the 1982 Act;

(b) who was in possession at that date; and

(c) provided no order for possession had been made under the Rent Restrictions (Temporary Provisions) Act, 1981.[167]

Included in category (a) are, as a result of the earlier legislation, statutory tenants, *i.e.* tenants whose contractual tenancy had expired but whose security of possession was protected under the earlier Acts, the spouse or family member who had inherited the right to retain possession on the death of the protected tenant and in some circumstances an assignee of the protected tenant.[168]

The Supreme Court has held[169] that it is sufficient if there is occupation by a member of the tenant's family or a caretaker or a person "who, though not at the moment in actual occupation, does in fact require the dwelling-house for his own use".[170]

---

165 1983 Act s.5(3).

166 Wylie, *Landlord and Tenant* para. 29.36.

167 1982 Act s.7(1).

168 1960 Act ss. 31, 32; *Jordan v. O'Brien* [1960] IR 363; Wylie, *Landlord and Tenant* para. 29.39–29.43.

169 *Foley v. Galvin* [1932] IR 339.

170 Per Fitzgibbon J, *ibid.* at pp. 361–362; *Walsh v. Coyne* [1958] IR 233.

b) Order For Possession

Section 16(1) of the 1982 Act sets out the grounds on which the District Court may grant an order for possession, provided it considers it reasonable to do so.

(1) Specific Grounds

(2) Breach of Tenancy

The landlord may apply for an order for possession if the tenant fails to pay the rent or commits some other breach of the terms of the tenancy.[171] Where the amount due was small a court has declined to grant an immediate order on condition that the tenant pays the arrears.[172]

(3) Nuisance, etc.

Nuisance or annoyance to the landlord, his or her agent, or adjoining owners is a ground for possession, and so also is the use of the premises for "any immoral or illegal purpose" whether or not there has been a conviction arising out of the use.[173]

***(a)* Deterioration**

The landlord may seek possession if the condition of the dwelling deteriorates due to waste, neglect or default of the tenant or any person residing in the dwelling.[174]

***(b)* Required By Landlord**

The landlord may seek possession if he or she bona fide requires the dwelling:

a) for occupation as a residence for himself or any person bona fide residing or to reside with him, or her; or

b) for occupation as a residence for a person in the wholetime employment of the landlord; or

c) in the interests of good estate management.[175]

The landlord must pay into court such a sum as the court considers reasonable to meet the tenant's expenses in leaving the dwelling and a sum not exceeding three years' rent of alternative accommodation which is "reasonably suited to the residential and other needs of the tenant, his spouse and his family *bona*

---

171 Housing (Private Rented Dwellings) Act, 1982 s.16(1)(a).

172 *Boyle v. Fitzsimons* [1926] IR 378.

173 1982 Act s.16(1)(b).

174 1982 Act 16(1)(d).

175 *Hardwicke Ltd v. Byrne* [1963] IR 52; Wylie, *Landlord and Tenant* paras. 29.55, 30.35.

fide residing with him in the dwelling".[176] There is no express requirement under the new legislation that the accommodation should be available.[177]

(c) Scheme of Development

A landlord may also seek possession where he or she requires vacant possession in order to carry out a scheme of development[178] which includes the dwelling and has planning permission for the scheme.[179] The same requirement of paying money into court to cover the tenant's expenses and the rent of alternative accommodation applies as in the preceding section.

(4) Reasonableness

Even if the landlord establishes one or more of the above grounds the District Court may only grant an order for possession if it considers it reasonable to do so.[180] In exercising this discretion the court may consider the conduct of the landlord,[181] and also, where the ground is a breach of the tenancy by the tenant, if the landlord acquiesced in the breach the court may refuse the order.[182] Motive has also been found relevant, as where the landlord's real purpose is to replace the present tenant with a new one.[183]

---

176 1982 Act s.16(1).

177 Contrast the earlier 1960 Act s.29(1)(e)(ii), (f) and (g).

178 1982 Act s.16(4).

179 1982 Act s.16(1)(e).

180 1982 Act s.16(1).

181 1982 Act s.16(2).

182 *Fitzsimons v. Parker* [1949] Ir Jur Rep 59.

183 *Westport Harbour Commissioners v. McBride* [1931] LJ Ir 50.

CHAPTER 21

COVENANTS

A. Introduction

1. Terminology

a) Positive and Negative

Covenants, *i.e.* binding promises, may be positive covenants (covenants to do something) or negative (covenants to refrain from doing something). As we shall see, it is a basic principle that the burden of positive covenants does not run at law. The burden of negative covenants may run in equity, and so restrictive covenants, as they are called, are a special type of equitable interests in land. In Northern Ireland the rules of common law and equity have been replaced by a statutory scheme in which the burden of some kinds of positive covenants runs. This scheme is referred to at the end of the chapter.

b) Burden and Benefit

The question may arise as to whether the benefit or burden of a covenant passes to another party. If A covenants, *i.e.* promises, B that he, A, will only use the land he has purchased from B for residential purposes, then A has undertaken the burden, the disadvantage, of the covenant, and B has obtained the benefit of it. If B assigns the interest in the land she has retained to X, the question may arise as to whether the benefit of the covenant has passed to X, so that he can sue A to enforce it.

2. Types of Covenant

Covenants (*i.e.* promises contained in legal documents) may exist in three forms. First, they may be contractual terms. Secondly, they may be contained in leases or tenancies. Thirdly, they may exist between independent owners of separate plots of land. In order to see whether a given person is able to enforce a covenant against another party, or is bound to perform the covenant at the behest of another party, it is necessary to identify which of these three relationships exist and then to apply the appropriate rules. In resolving problems as to covenants three questions therefore have to be asked:

1. is there privity of contract? *i.e.* are the parties contracting parties? If the answer is yes then the extent to which the benefit or burden of the covenant can be enforced is governed by the law of contract, *i.e.* all

covenants will bind and be enforceable subject to illegality, the law relating to minors, *etc.*;

2. if the answer to 1 is "no", then is there tenure (privity of estate) either freehold or leasehold between the parties? If there is a leasehold relationship, then the extent to which covenants run is governed by Deasy's Act and the interpretation of it in *Lyle v. Smith*[1], *i.e.* covenants which affect the land as property will run for and against successors, but purely personal covenants will not. If there is freehold tenure between the parties, which would be rare, then the extent to which covenants run would be governed by the, now obscure, rules of the common law which broadly applied the test of whether the covenant touched and concerned the land and was not purely personal;
3. if the answer to 2 is "no", then the issue is as to the law of covenants between independent owners or, at least, between persons who are not mutually landlord and tenant. Such owners could themselves have either freehold or leasehold interests. It is this subject which is the main concern of this chapter.

B. Privity of Contract

Here the parties are the original contracting parties to the conveyance. The law of contract applies. The promisee can enforce the covenant against the promissor unless the promisee has assigned the benefit.

Who are contracting parties? At common law no one could claim a benefit under a contract unless they were named as parties to it. Section 5 of the Real Property Act, 1845 provides, as to deeds taking effect after 1 October 1845, that:

> "An immediate estate or interest in any tenements or hereditaments, and the benefit of a condition or covenant respecting any tenements or hereditaments, may be taken although the taker thereof be not named as a party to the same indenture".

Thus a person can take the benefit of a covenant although not named in it. The section is expressly limited to covenants respecting any tenements or hereditaments and Irish cases have taken this to imply that the section is limited to covenants affecting the land as property and does not extend to purely personal covenants.[2] *Beswick v. Beswick*[3] held on the corresponding section 56 of the English Law of Property Act, 1925, that the section did not fundamen-

1 (1909) 2 IR 58, 43 ILTR 255.

2 *Lloyd v. Byrne* (1888) 22 LR Ir 269; *Monroe v. Plunket* (1889) 23 ILTR 76; *Grant v. Edmondson* [1931] 1 Ch. 1.

3 [1968] AC 58, Eng HL, at 104–5.

tally affect the law of privity of contract.[4]

This appears to mean that if P covenants with V and the owners for the time being of certain adjacent plots, *e.g.* not to build on the land, then the owners of the plots at the time of the conveyance who are identifiable can enforce the benefit as parties to the contract, but anyone who bought one of the adjoining plots after the conveyance between V and P could not rely on those words. They would have to show the benefit had passed to them by one of the means discussed below.

Equally, V could not confer the right to enforce the benefit of the covenant on future successors in title to his own plot by covenanting for himself "and my heirs and assigns" and relying on the section. Such successors would have to rely upon one of the methods of passing the benefit discussed below, such as annexation or assignment. Covenanting for yourself and your heirs and assigns is not even sufficient in itself to show annexation and is in fact unnecessary in view of section 58 of the Conveyancing Act, 1881 by virtue of which it would be implied in any case.

In the past[5] it was assumed that if there is privity of contract a party may be able to sue even though they have no land capable of benefiting, a clear statement of promissory liability. But the law shows signs of moving away from promissory liability towards a property notion, so that where a covenant is for the benefit of land rather than being personal the original contracting party will not longer be liable after they have parted with the interest in the land, in the absence of evidence to the contrary.[6]

C. Privity of Estate

For some reason the textbooks on this subject usually use the phrase "privity of estate" in dealing with covenants for the more usual word tenure, although there appears to be no difference in meaning. In Ireland privity of estate, or tenure, can exist in two forms, freehold and leasehold.

---

4 Lord Upjohn (Lord Pearce concurring) held that s.56 was intended to abolish the old common law rule that, in an indenture *inter partes,* the covenantee must be named as a party to the indenture and take the benefit of an immediate grant or the benefit of a covenant. He further held that s.56(1) did not apply unless three conditions were satisfied, *i.e.* (i) the agreement must contain a contract or grant of the benefit, (ii) it must be under seal, the words "conveyance or other instrument" in s.56(1) being limited to documents under seal, and (iii) s.56(1) referred only to documents strictly *inter partes*: [1967] 3 WLR 932 at 1224, A and F, and 1216, E.

5 *LCC v. Allen* (1914) 3 KB 642.

6 *London & County Ltd v. Wilfred Sportsman Ltd* [1970] 2 All ER 600, concerning a covenant in a lease.

1. Freehold

There is a surviving example of freehold tenure in fee simple in Ireland, *i.e.* fee farm grants by feudal tenure *non obstante Quia Emptores*. Since, as we have seen, the statute *Quia Emptores*, 1290 only forbade subinfeudation in fee simple, a grant of an estate less than a fee simple could also create freehold tenure and contain covenants falling into this category. In Ireland, it was usual to include covenants in a grant of a lease for lives. Such covenants theoretically were governed by the rules as to covenants in freehold tenure but the law is now obscure and the judges seemed to have treated them as being governed by the same rules as leasehold covenants.[7] The law of covenants in freehold tenure is obscure, being feudal in nature[8] but probably it is to the effect that all freehold covenants touching and concerning the land will bind those as between whom freehold tenure exists.

2. Leasehold

Privity of estate has been dealt with earlier.[9] Deasy's Act replaces the concept of privity of estate at common law with sections 12 and 13. But it is still a convenient term to use. It should also be noted that such a relationship can exist in Ireland on the grant of a fee simple estate under Deasy's Act, 1860, *i.e.* a fee farm grant under the Act.

If L and T are the original contracting parties to a lease or tenancy, privity of contract exists between them. If T has assigned to T2, then privity of estate, but no privity of contract, exists between L and T2. If L has assigned his reversion but T has not assigned his interest, privity of estate would exist between L2 and T. If both L and T have assigned their interests, privity of estate would exist between L2 and T2.

D. Neither Privity of Contract nor of Estate

1. Description

The rest of this chapter is concerned with this situation. One has to remember that there are separate rules at common law and in equity, for equity here developed ways by which the benefit and burden can run even though it does not

---

7 See Landlord and Tenant. This is an interesting form of legal development: leasehold covenants were originally developed by analogy to covenants in freehold tenure. The law of freehold tenure became obsolete, and so when a form of freehold tenure re-emerged in Ireland the law was reinvented by analogy to leaseholds.

8 Law in this area is more developed in Scotland, because of the general survival in that jurisdiction of feudal grants. See Gordon, (1989).

9 See Chapter 19 Landlord and Tenant.

at common law. One also has to distinguish between the burden and the benefit of the covenant.

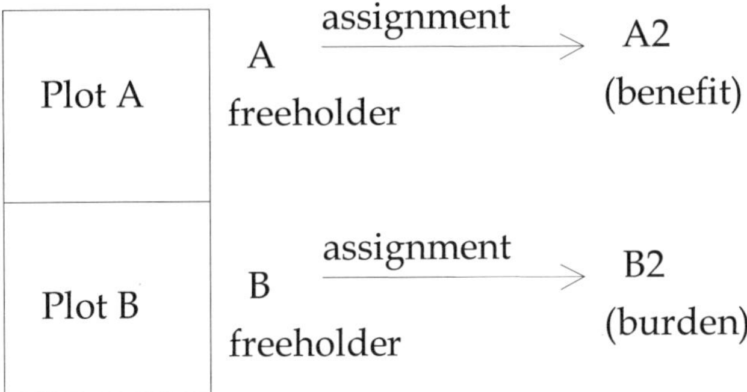

In this example B covenants with A to use plot B only for residential purposes. The burden of the covenant affects Plot B, *i.e.* it restricts the use of Plot B. The benefit accrues to Plot A, in that the use of Plot A is enhanced by the covenant. The situation in which a covenant affects the land of two independent owners usually arises when A, who originally owns Plot A and Plot B, sells off Plot B to B, retaining Plot A. In the case of a housing estate, A will be a developer who sells each plot in turn to the various house buyers. A2 can only enforce the covenant against B2 if the benefit of the covenant has passed to A2 and the burden has passed to B2.

There is another situation in which a party may seek to enforce a covenant against another party where there is neither privity of contract nor privity of estate and that is between head landlord and sub-tenant. If HL is the landlord of T and T has sub-let to ST, then neither privity of contract nor privity of estate exists between HL and ST.

2. The Historical Trend

The law relating to the running of covenants between independent owners shows a historical trend.

The old rules, particularly the common law rules, began by treating covenants as purely personal obligations, affecting only those parties who originally entered into them. In some cases the common law, more frequently equity, went beyond this stage and began to recognise covenants as property rights. As such they could bind successors to the original parties between whom there was no privity of contract. Finally, equity in some cases goes even beyond the recognition of covenants as private property rights and begins to recognise them as a form of planning law.

Thus, before modern planning legislation, the courts had developed covenants into a species of planning obligations as means of maintaining land for a particular use, usually residential. Private law may not be best adapted for functions which properly belong in the public domain and subject to public and democratic scrutiny, but the law of covenants can be seen as a response to a genuine social need. They may also function today to govern matters outside the normal planning rules or which are too detailed for public planning law to concern itself. For, example, when developers sell plots of land in a housing estate it is usual to include in the deed of conveyance a covenant on the part of the purchaser promising not to erect television aerials[10]. There is probably a public interest (in avoiding unsightly additions to buildings) sufficiently strong to bring the matter within the realm of planning law, but those immediately affected are the residents of the area and so it is dealt with by restrictive covenants in the deeds.

3. Burden

a) At Law

The general rule at common law is that the burden of freehold covenants does not pass at all. This is clearly a contractual principle. Privity of contract involves the notion that parties to a contract cannot impose liabilities on a third person who is not a party to the agreement.[11] The next stage in the development of the law was that devices were developed to avoid the rule. These are as follows.

(1) Chain of Covenants

A covenantor remains liable on the covenant to the covenantee even after parting with his or her interest in the land,[12] unless they contract otherwise. Thus if A promises B, for consideration or under seal, that no television aerial shall be

10 Such covenants leave the resident owner with a choice, if they wish to have television, of buying a satellite dish and paying the company for a card to use the satellite, or entering into similar arrangement with a cable television company. Satellite dishes may qualify as aerials, leaving no choice at all if there is only one cable company in the area, which is likely to be the case. Such covenants might be challengeable on the ground that they constitute, under Art. 40.3.2º of the Constitution, an unjust attack on property rights. Against this it could be argued that (a) the purchaser freely entered into the covenant and (b) that the covenants are justified in terms of Art. 43.2.2º by the exigencies of the common good in that they are aimed at preventing unsightly additions to buildings spoiling the appearance of the area. It might well be that such arguments in themselves would not justify such covenants without control over monopoly pricing to protect the property owner.

11 *Austerbury v. Corporation of Oldham* [1885] 29 Ch D 750.

12 *Belmont Securities Limited v. Crean,* unreported, High Court, O'Hanlon J, 17 June 1988.

erected on plot X, this promise will bind A even after A sells plot X to someone else unless A has been careful to qualify the promise by specifying that the promise is only to apply so long as A owns plot B. This follows from general principles of contract law. Hence one method of making the burden pass at law is for the covenantor to take an indemnity from P1 to indemnify her if she is sued by the covenantee. P1 does the same with P2:

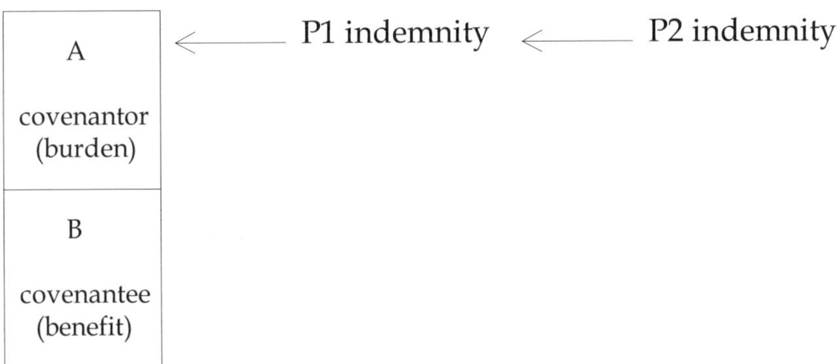

P1 similarly remains liable on his indemnity to the covenantor even after he has sold the land to P2. Thus, if P2 erects a television aerial on the land, the covenantee can sue the covenantor who in turn joins P1 in the action, pleading the indemnity, and P1 in turn joins P2 who will be liable on the indemnity entered into with P1. Thus P2 will be ultimately liable. The problem with this solution, however, is that if any person in the chain fails to insist on the new purchaser taking an indemnity, the burden fails to pass to the next purchaser.

(2) The Principle of Reciprocity

This principle was applied in the English case of *Halsall v. Brizell*.[13] It is to the effect that if a person takes the benefit of a corresponding covenant they must be subject to the burden of the covenant in issue. This refers to the moral principle that would condemn a person for insisting that some benefit is rightfully due to them from X while themselves refusing to confer the same benefit on Y who is in the same position in relation to them as they are to X.

In *Halsall v. Brizell* the vendor sold off a series of plots, to A, B and C in turn. The plots fronted onto a road which provided access to each of the plots:

13 [1957] Ch 169. It is known in England as the Rule in *Halsall v. Brizell*. See also *Tito v. Waddell (No. 2)* [1977] Ch. 106; E.P. Aughterson, [1985] Conv 12.

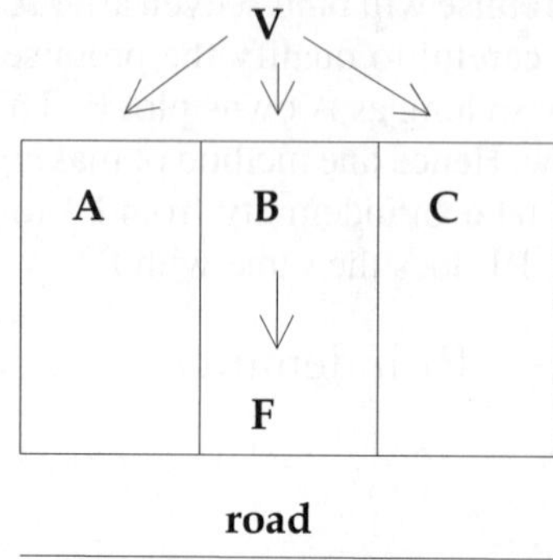

A, B and C covenanted to contribute to the cost of repair of the road. F purchased B's plot and later refused to contribute to the cost of repair of the road. F argued that the burden of the covenant had not passed to him.

Upjohn J in the English High Court held that if F wanted the benefit of the covenants entered into by A and C, he had to accept the burden of B's covenant. In this case it was clear that F would take the benefit of those covenants since he occupied a plot between plot A and plot C. But the judge admitted that there was a flaw in the doctrine. If F did not derive any benefit from the other covenants, or was willing to forego it, he would not be bound. Thus if F had bought a plot on the edge of the estate and either did not use, or undertook not to use, the road running past the other plots, the principle would not be sufficient to impose the burden on him.

(3) Right of Entry.

Another method is for the vendor to reserve a right of entry exercisable for condition broken, the condition being the performance of the covenants. Since a right of entry is an interest in land it could pass to his successors who could enforce it against the purchasers' successors.[14] One problem in some jurisdictions is that such a right is subject to the rule against perpetuities. This is so in England where there is the further disadvantage, from the point of view of the effectiveness of this device, that after 1925 such a right can only exist in equity and not at law. In Ireland, however, if created as a conditional fee at common law, a right of entry is both legal and, in the Republic, not subject to the perpetuity rule.[15] The better view is that it is not subject to the perpetuity rule even if

14 *Shiloh Spinners Ltd v. Harding* [1973] AC 691, [1973] 1 All ER 90, [1973] 2 WLR 28, 25 P & CR 48, 225 EG 1913, [1973] EGD 284, House of Lords.

15 *Walsh v. Wightman* [1927] NI 1. The case was decided before statutory reform in Northern Ireland. The Perpetuities Act (Northern Ireland), 1966, s.13(1) provides that a right of entry in respect of a fee simple for condition broken shall not be exerciseable after the perpetuity period.

created by executed use or as an equitable interest. It would seem that the device for this reason would be more useful in the Republic, except that if a forfeiture occurred equity might grant relief from it.

(4) Enlarged Leases

These instances of the burden of covenants passing at law to successors in title are the result of statutory reforms whose main purpose was to enlarge certain kinds of leases into fee simple estates. The statutes provide that certain covenants which were contained in the leases before enlargement continue to bind after the tenant's interest becomes a fee simple. They are therefore instances of where the burden of a covenant will bind all successors in title of the land at law, which really means regardless of notice, since the burden passes by express statutory provision. The statutes may also be used as a device by someone who wishes to attach the burden of covenants to land so that the burden will affect all successors in title to the land. The core of this device is deliberately to create a leasehold which, under statute, can be enlarged into a fee simple, and then the lessee will enlarge it, or to create a leasehold which is automatically enlarged, depending on the effect of the statute.

(a) Section 65 Conveyancing Act, 1881

The section applies to tenants holding under leases originally for 300 years or more with an unexpired term of not less than 200 years "without any rent, or with merely a peppercorn rent or other rent having no money value".[16] It applies to such leases whether the reversion is freehold or not, but does not apply to a term liable to be determined by re-entry for condition broken or a term created by sub-demise out of a term which could not itself be enlarged.[17] The tenant of such a lease may execute a deed enlarging the lease into a fee simple.[18]

There are considerable problems with using the section to attach covenants affecting the user of the land. First, the rent must be valueless in money and so if the rent consists of money at all, however small the amount, it would seem the lease may not be enlarged under the section.[19] This should not be a problem as to the term which is created in order to be enlarged, since it could be made for a valueless rent, but since the term out of which it is created must also qualify, if that term were for a valuable rent the section could not be used. Secondly, where third parties had the benefit of covenants the burden of which affected the demised land while it was a lease, the issue might arise as to whether the burden of them continues to bind after enlargement. For example, X sells Little Meadows to L. The conveyance contains a covenant whereby L

16 Section 65(1).

17 Conveyancing Act, 1882 s.11.

18 1881 Act, s.65(2) and (3).

19 *Re Smith & Stott* (1883) 29 Ch D 1009; *Blaiberg v. Keeves* [1906] 2 Ch 175; *Re Chapman & Hobbs* (1885) 29 Ch D 1007.

undertakes for himself and the owners for the time being of Little Meadows not to construct buildings above a certain height. L then grants a lease of part of Little Meadows to T. The lease qualifies under section 65 and L's real purpose is to enable T to obtain the fee simple, but also to attach a similar restrictive covenant so that it will bind not only T, but all successors in title of T. L wants to attach the covenant for the benefit of the part of Little Meadows retained. There is no privity of estate between X and T but T has notice of X's covenant and so T is bound by it under *Tulk v. Moxhay*.[20] If T enlarges the lease into a fee simple the covenant in the lease continues to bind T, and T's successors, and L can enforce it. But can X continue to enforce his covenant against T? If not, then the device has lost most of its attraction for L because X's only remedy would be to sue L and this would not be to L's advantage. Under the section the fee simple remains "subject to all the same trusts, powers, executory limitations over, rights, and equities, and to all the same covenants and provisions relating to user and enjoyment, and to all the same obligations of every kind, as the term would have been subject to if it had not been so enlarged".[21] On the face of it the words of the section are wide enough to continue the burden of such covenants.

Section 28 of the Landlord and Tenant (Ground Rents) (No. 2) Act, 1978 apparently applies whenever a person who has an interest in land acquires the fee simple. The general purpose of section 65 appears to be to continue in force all covenants which affected the land before enlargement, whereas the wording of section 28 is considerably more restrictive. The purpose of section 28 seems to be to reduce drastically the number of covenants affecting the land after the fee simple is acquired. Presumably section 28, being the later enactment, would prevail over the provisions as to covenants in section 65. Section 28 was considered in *Whelan v. Cork Corporation*[22] which is discussed in the section below.

(b) Landlord and Tenant (Ground Rents) (No. 2) Act, 1978

The Act applies to dwelling houses where a ground rent, as defined by the Act, is created and gives right to the tenant to acquire the fee simple. Section 28(1) provides that "all covenants subject to which [the former lessee] held the land", other than a covenant within subsection (2), shall cease to have effect and "no new covenant shall be created in conveying the fee simple". Subsection (2) of section 28 preserves covenants which protect or enhance the amenity of

20 (1848) 2 Ph 774, 41 ER 1143 at 1144f. The case concerned Leicester Square in London and upheld a covenant not to erect buildings on it. *Whelan v. Cork Corporation* [1991] ILRM 19, High Court Murphy J; *Williams & Co Ltd v. LSD and Quinnsworth,* unreported, High Court, Pringle J, 19 June 1970 at p.16; *Power Supermarkets Ltd v. Crumlin Investments Limited,* unreported, High Court, Costello J, 22 June 1981.

21 Section 65(4).

22 [1991] ILRM 19, High Court Murphy J.

the land occupied by the immediate lessor of the grantee, covenants which relate to the performance of a statutory duty by such a person, or which relate to a right of way over the acquired land or a right of drainage "or other right necessary to secure or assist the development of other land". A covenant which does not relate to a right of way, *etc.*, can be enforced by any such person or personal representatives or successors in title as if the acquisition of the fee simple had not occurred. Where it does so relate, it can be enforced by any person aggrieved by a breach of the covenant.

There are several problems with using the section to attach covenants to the freehold. First, the statutory definition of ground rent is complex[23] and care would have to be taken to ensure that the lease created for the purpose of being enlarged did qualify within the provisions. Secondly, the covenants would have to be of a type that would qualify within section 28(2). That subsection may be restrictively interpreted in view of the general purpose of the section which is to free the fee simple from covenants which previously affected the land. Thirdly, the section has been held to apply not only to covenants which previously bound because of privity of estate but also to those in favour of third parties which bound the land under the doctrine of *Tulk v. Moxhay*.[24] Such covenants, if they are within section 28(1), cease to have effect. This might constitute an objection, similar to that discussed under section 65 of the Conveyancing Act, 1881, to the use of the section as a device to attach covenants to the freehold. *Whelan v. Cork Corporation*[25] which decided the point is discussed below in the section on discharge of covenants.

(c) Deasy's Act Grant

A grant of a fee simple under Deasy's Act can also create leasehold tenure as a fee farm grant, if granted at a rent. Covenants contained in the grant would bind as leasehold covenants. This might seem a method of creating covenants restricting user of the land, or even positive covenants, the burden of which would affect successors in title of the servient tenement. Where the land concerned is a house plot, however, the rent would be likely to qualify as a ground rent and so the fee farm grantee would acquire a right to a fee simple under the No. 2 Act of 1978, which would presumably mean the right to a fee simple free of leasehold tenure. The effect in such a case would be to put the grantee in the same position as the last device and nothing would be gained by granting a fee farm grant originally rather than a ground rent lease.

---

23 See Ground Rents.

24 (1848) 2 Ph 774, 41 ER 1143 at 1144f; *Whelan v. Cork Corporation* [1991] ILRM 19, High Court Murphy J; *Williams & Co Ltd v. LSD and Quinnsworth,* unreported, High Court, Pringle J, 19 June 1970 at p.16; *Power Supermarkets Ltd v. Crumlin Investments Limited,* unreported, High Court, Costello J, 22 June 1981.

25 [1991] ILRM 19, High Court Murphy J.

(d) Renewable Leasehold Conversion Act, 1849

It has been seen that this Act gives a power to tenants under leases for lives renewable forever granted before the Act came into force (on 1 August 1849) the right to demand a grant in fee farm from the owner of the reversion on the lease in substitution for the lease. Under section 1 the fee farm grant is to be subject to the same covenants as affected the former lease for lives except for those covenants commuted under section 3 of the Act. Section 3 provides for the commutation of exceptions, reservations or rights under covenants annexed to the reversion which interfere with the proper cultivation of the land. The section empowers the grantee if he thinks fit to require that the exception, reservation or right under covenant cease wholly or partially. In such a case the grant is to be modified accordingly and compensation is provided for the owner of the reversion in the sense that the fee farm rent is to be increased by an amount equivalent to the value of the covenant, *etc.* The Act provides for the method for ascertaining the amount of the increase if the parties do not reach agreement. If the lessee does not think fit to commute a covenant then it remains in the fee farm grant even though it interferes with proper cultivation.[26]

Section 10 provides that, subject to section 3, all covenants by law implied on the part of landlord or tenant in a lease, and every covenant for the payment of rent, and every other covenant contained in pursuance of the Act in any such grant in substitution for a similar covenant in the lease where the last-mentioned covenant is of a kind the burden of which runs with the land at law shall run with the estate in fee simple into which the lease is converted.

It was held in *Re McNaul's Estate*[27] that these provisions clearly had the intent of preserving covenants which had previously been binding as between the lessee and the owner of the reversion on the lease for lives. The court held that the fee simple was a special statutory fee simple so that even covenants which would have been void in an ordinary fee simple, such as those restricting alienation, could be valid in a fee simple granted in substitution of a lease for lives under the 1849 Act.

It seems to follow from this that covenants in the original lease which restricted the use of the demised land continue to affect it after conversion, subject to the power contained in section 3 under which the grantee can insist on the commutation of covenants restricting the proper cultivation of the land.[28] These provisions apply primarily in relation to leases for lives renewable and granted before the Act came into force where the lessee exercises the power to demand a fee farm grant. Nevertheless, it has been seen that section 37 pro-

26 *Re McNaul's Estate* [1902] 1 IR 114, per Fitzgibbon LJ at 126.

27 [1902] 1 IR 114.

28 An interesting point is whether a covenant restricting use of the land to residential purposes is such a covenant. Residential plots can usually be cultivated, though only as a garden.

vides that attempts after the Act to create leases for lives renewable forever take effect as fee farm grants, and that section further provides that the other provisions of the Act shall apply. This suggests that the provisions as to covenants take effect in the same way, in that covenants contained in the purported lease continue to affect the fee simple to the same extent as already outlined. If so, then it would be possible to grant a purported lease for lives renewable forever, the grant containing restrictive covenants, or indeed any landlord and tenant covenants, and although the grant takes effect under the Act as a fee farm grant, the resulting fee simple would be subject to the covenants except in so far as the grantee chose to commute them under section 3.

b) In Equity

(1) Tulk v. Moxhay

In the leading case of *Tulk v. Moxhay*[29] it was held that the burden of a restrictive, *i.e.* negative, covenant binds the covenantor's land - the servient tenement – in equity. The principle was explained by Pringle J in *Williams & Co Ltd v. LSD and Quinnsworth*[30] in the following terms:-

> "The principle established in the well-known case of *Tulk v. Moxhay* (is) that a negative bargain, as for instance a covenant against a particular use of land retained on a sale or lease of part of an estate, may be enforced by any person entitled in equity to the benefit of that bargain against any person bound in equity by notice of it, either express or to be imputed at the time of acquisition of his title".

A restrictive covenant is therefore an equitable interest in land and like other equitable interests it binds all except a bona fide purchaser for value of the legal estate in the servient tenement without notice of the restrictive covenant. The registration of deeds system in Ireland means that it is unlikely that lack of notice could be shown.

The case of *Luker v. Dennis*[31] in the 19th century suggested that notice, actual or constructive, was sufficient in itself to bind successors to the servient land, but this was overruled in *London & South Western Railway v. Gomm.*[32] The case held that the person attempting to enforce the burden must show that they have an interest in land capable of being benefited. The basis of the rule is

29 (1848) 2 Ph 774, 41 ER 1143; 1 H & Tw 105, 47 ER 1345; 11 Beav 571,50 ER 937; *Whelan v. Cork Corporation* [1991] ILRM 19, High Court Murphy J; *Williams & Co Ltd v. LSD and Quinnsworth,* unreported, High Court, Pringle J, 19 June 1970 at p.16; *Power Supermarkets Ltd v. Crumlin Investments Limited,* unreported, High Court, Costello J, 22 June 1981.

30 Unreported, High Court, 19 June 1970 at 16 of the transcript, cited by Murphy J in *Whelan v. Cork Corporation* [1991] ILRM 19.

31 (1877) 7 Ch D 227.

32 (1882) 20 Ch D 562 at 583, Jessel MR. *Power Supermarkets Ltd v. Crumlin Investments Limited,* unreported, High Court, Costello J, 22 June 1981.

the preservation of the value of the covenantee's land – the land benefited by the covenant. A personal interest is not sufficient. In this respect restrictive covenants are like easements: they are enforced against one piece of land for the benefit of another piece of land. They do not exist in gross.

The principle that *Tulk v. Moxhay*[33] applies only to restrictive covenants, not to positive covenants, was confirmed in *Haywood v. Brunswick Permanent Building Society*.[34] Nevertheless, if a covenant has both positive and negative aspects the positive can be severed from the negative and the negative part enforced.[35] The test of whether a covenant is positive or negative is one of substance, not form, so that merely because a covenant is phrased negatively will mean that the burden of it will pass if it is in substance positive, so that a covenant "not to allow the building to fall into disrepair" is in essence a positive covenant to repair: positive because it requires expenditure of money to comply with it. A covenant "to use the premises for residential purposes only" is negative because it impliedly prohibits other uses, and arguably, does not involve expenditure exceeding other uses. This is not to say that expenditure of money is the only test: expenditure of labour is also sufficient. A covenant not to permit a path to become overgrown is positive because imposes a positive duty to clear the path, either through spending money to employ someone to do so, or by the owner of the servient tenement doing so through their own labour. The policy in not allowing the burden of positive covenants to run is a policy against increasing the burdens on the land. In *Re Fawcett & Holmes Contract*[36] it was held that the deed creating the covenant must show an intention that the burden of it should run.

(2) Development or Building Schemes

As will be seen a below a special situation arises when it is proved that a building scheme, or scheme of development, *etc.* exists in law. The doctrine was developed in relation to the passing of benefit and is discussed in detail below, but it should not be forgotten that the judges in those cases speak of successors in title being able to sue and be sued by owners of other plots. However, it is worth pointing out in relation to the passing of the burden of a restrictive covenant that it does not seem that the concept of a building scheme constitutes a separate way in which the burden may run. If it did, then the burden would run, in effect, at law. *Tulk v. Moxhay*[37] is thought to express the outer limits of the passing of the burden of restrictive covenants, and the principal point here is that they only run in equity, not at law. On the other hand it is also true that if a

33 (1848) 2 Ph 774, 41 ER 1143 at 1144f.

34 (1881) 8 QBD 403.

35 *Shepherd Homes Ltd v. Sandham* (No 2) [1971] 1 WLR 1062.

36 (1889) 42 Ch D 150.

37 (1848) 2 Ph 774, 41 ER 1143 at 1144f.

building scheme is present then the requirements of *Tulk v. Moxhay*[38] are almost certainly met. The owner of a plot would have constructive notice of the covenant and the plaintiff would have to show that he or she owned a plot within the scheme which would benefit by the enforcement of the covenant.

4. Benefit

a) At Law

(1) Automatic Running

At first the common law did not recognise that the benefit of a contract could be assigned, since contracts were purely personal rights. But at an early date[39] it recognised that the benefit of covenants affecting land would pass to successors in title of the covenantee. Thus the common law began to regard such contracts as not being purely personal but as having some of the characteristics of a property right. When such contracts are contained in deeds conveying interests in land the common law recognises that the benefit of such covenants will run with the land, *i.e.* will pass automatically to successors in title of the land, if the following four conditions are fulfilled:

(a) Concern Covenantee's Land

The covenant must benefit the land of the covenantee, the person to whom the promise was made.[40] The common law enforces the benefit, but only if the covenant has the characteristic of a property interest. Here we see the extension of the original contract idea towards a property idea.

In *Gaw v. CIE*[41] the covenant was to keep the path clear of undergrowth, *i.e.* positive acts. The benefit of the covenant was held to pass at law to the successor in title of the covenantee together with right of way over the path. Another example of the benefit of a positive covenant passing at law, in that case a covenant to supply water to a bungalow, is afforded by *Shayler v. Woolf*.[42]

(b) Legal Estate

For the benefit to pass at common law the successor to the original covenantee has to show that he or she has a common law estate.[43]

---

38 *ibid.*

39 *The Prior's Case* (1369) YB 42 Edw III Pl 14 fol 3A; Co Litt 384a.

40 *Newton Abbot Coop Society v. Williamson* [1952] Ch. 286.

41 [1953] IR 232, Wylie, *Cases* p.622.

42 [1946] Ch 320, Eng CA.

43 *Webb v. Russell* (1789) 3 TR 393. This is no longer required in England after 1925: See below footnote 48.

(c) Same Estate

The successor must not only show that he or she has a legal estate, they must show that they have the same legal estate as the original covenantee.[44]

(d) Intention that Benefit Will Run

There must also be an intention that the benefit will run with the land. Such an intention is now presumed as a result of section 58(1) of the Conveyancing Act, 1881. Under that section covenants are deemed to be made with the covenantee, his heirs and assigns. as if the heirs and assigns had been expressly mentioned. At first it was thought that the section had a more radical effect: that it extended the passing of the benefit at law to all heirs and assigns, including those who did not take the same estate as the original covenantor. The case law, however, took a more restrictive view of the section, holding that it merely saved the use of some words in a deed.[45] It would seem that its effect is to presume intention, but not to relieve compliance with the other requirements mentioned above.

In England section 58 has been replaced by section 78 of the Law of Property Act, 1925 which contains the wider phrase "successors in title and the persons deriving title under him or them". In *Federated Homes Ltd v. Mill Lodge Properties*,[46] following *Smith and Snipes Hall Farm Ltd v. River Douglas Catchment Board*,[47] the English Court of Appeal held that this had a wider effect than section 58 of the 1881 Act. It held that the effect of section 78 was to annex the benefit of covenants to the land. It can be argued that this abolishes in England the requirement that the successor in title, in order to enforce the benefit, must have the same estate as the original covenantee.[48]

In *Roake v. Chadha*[49] the English High Court impliedly modified *Federated Homes*. It held that the benefit did not automatically pass where it was expressly stated that the covenant would not inure for the benefit of successors without express assignment. Thus, while under *Federated Homes*, implied assignment extended to successors regardless of their estate, according to *Roake v. Chadha* implied assignment could in any case be ousted by an express term to the contrary: it was only a presumption as to the parties' intention and so

44 *Gaw v. CIE* [1953] IR 232; Wylie, *Cases* p.622.

45 *Westhoughton UDC v. Wigan Coal & Iron Co Ltd* [1919] 1 Ch. 159.

46 [1980] 1 All ER 371.

47 [1949] 2 KB 500.

48 D.J. Hurst, "Transmission of of Restrictive Covenants" (1982) 2 Leg Stud 53; D. Hayton, "Revolution in Restrictive Covenants Law?" (1980) 43 MLR 445; G. H. Newsom, "Universal Annexation?" (1981) 97 LQR 32; and "Universal Annexation? A Postscript" (1982) 98 LQR 202; P. N. Todd, "Annexation after *Federated Homes*" [1985] Conv 177; Scammell, "Positive Covenants in Conveyances of the Fee Simple" (1954) 18 Conv 546 at 553–6. 1971 Survey NI para. 180. Wylie, para. 19.20.

49 [1983] 3 All ER 503.

could be rebutted. Thus, while *Federated Homes* had removed one impediment, *Roake* held that the new widened doctrine was only a presumption and could yield to an express term. The court in *Roake*, one may notice, took the market-oriented view that the role of law is not to extend the benefit of covenants as a matter of policy, but is confined to spelling out the intention of the parties to a bargain. *Federated Homes*, on the other hand, tends to the view that the benefit of covenants should be extended as a matter of general law and that those in a stronger bargaining position should not be able to use it to prevent a weaker party obtaining the benefit, or passing it on. Behind the technical dispute we find, yet again, that the more basic dispute is about the role of law in relation to the market.

The English cases after 1925 contrasted the more radical effect of section 78 with the earlier section 58 of the 1881 Act and in so doing accepted the English case law on section 58 before 1925. However, there is a possibility that courts in Ireland will not necessarily follow either set of English decisions and may hold that the earlier section 58 is not a mere word-saving provision. One cannot therefore categorically state that the law in Ireland is the same as that set out in the English cases on section 58. It was also held in England that for a successor to enforce the benefit at law he or she must show that they are a successor to the whole of the land and not merely a part. "At law, the benefit could not be assigned in pieces."[50] There is no decision in Ireland on the point. If this correct as to Irish law, then a successors would have to resort to the rules of equity as to the passing of the benefit. It should be noted that the conditions for the benefit to pass at law do not include:

(a) that the covenant must be negative. The benefit of positive covenants can pass at law;[51]

(b) that the covenant should benefit the land of the covenantor. Normally it does not, *e.g.* a promise not to build on the land.

(2) Express (Statutory) Assignment

The benefit of a contract can be expressly assigned as a chose in action under section 28(6) of the Judicature Act, 1877.[52] As to covenants affecting land this provision presents no particular difficulty where the defendant, *i.e.* the bearer of the burden, is the original covenantee or a personal representative of such (and so liable at law), but the better view seems to be that the statute does not permit an express assignee to enforce the benefit against a successor to the original covenantee except within the limits of the rule in *Tulk v. Moxhay*.[53] It

50 *Re Union of London* [1953] Ch 611, at p.630 per Romer J.

51 Scamell, "Positive Covenants in Conveyances of the Fee Simple" (1954) 18 Conv 546. Pritchard, "Making Positive Covenants Run" (1973) 37 Conv 194.

52 Replaced in England by s.136 of the Law of Property Act, 1925. See Cheshire p.589.

53 (1848) 2 Ph 774, 41 ER 1143 at 1144f.

would not therefore enable an express assignee to enforce the benefit against a successor who is a bona fide purchaser of the land without notice of the covenant. If this is correct the section does not create a separate statutory form of assignment overriding the rules of equity.

b) In Equity

In the following diagram A and B are two adjoining plots of freehold land. In the past they were also owned by A and B respectively. A and B entered into a covenant restricting the use of plot B. A could enforce it in contract. If A sells his plot to A2, can A2 enforce the benefit of the covenant?

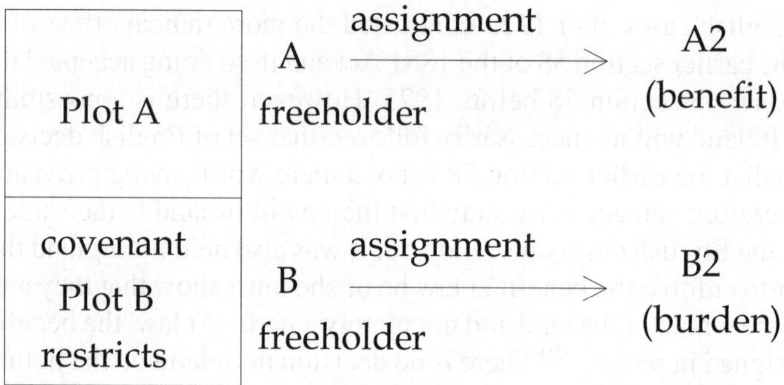

It has been seen that the benefit of covenants can run at common law and so A2 can often rely on the common law rules. But there are situations where the common law rules are inadequate, because one or more of conditions discussed above is lacking, namely:

(i) A2 wants an equitable remedy. This will frequently be the case because an injunction is usually the best remedy to enforce a covenant affecting the use of land.

(ii) A2 or the person from whom he bought the land is or was an equitable owner, *e.g.* a mortgagor having only an equity of redemption.[54] This is not uncommon in Ireland because mortgages can be created by conveyance of the fee simple.

(iii) Where A2 does not have the same estate as A.

(iv) If *Re Union of London*[55] applies in this jurisdiction and A has conveyed only part of the land.

(v) Where A2 relies on express assignment under section 28 of the Judicature Act, 1877 and the statute is not complied with. For example, no notice given to covenantor, or not made under the hand of the assignor.

54 *Rogers v. Hosegood* [1900] 2 Ch 388, [1900-3] All ER Reprint 915.

55 [1953] Ch. 611.

The benefit can pass in equity by three methods. It should also be noted, however, that:

a) they only apply to restrictive, not positive covenants;

b) the plaintiff must show that he or she is the current owner of the land. Equity only enforces the benefit on the basis that it benefits land, not a particular individual. Again it may be noticed that the rule in equity was developed here to protect property interests and not personal ones.

The three methods of passing the benefit in equity are:

(1) Annexation

It is not possible to draw a precise line between what courts may call express annexation and implied annexation, since courts have laid down general tests of when the benefit is held to have been annexed, but one may at least distinguish between the fairly clear tests and the residual category of cases which we may term implied annexation.

(a) Express Annexation

Here the person claiming the benefit has to show:

i) that there was an intention to benefit the land of the covenantee and his or her assigns and to burden the land nearby. Such an intention has been held to be present when the phrase used was "with intent that the covenant may inure to the benefit of the vendors, their successors and assigns and others claiming under them *to all or any of their lands adjoining*".[56] These rules again show that equity attempts to confine its intervention to the protection of property interests. At common law you do not have to show this because the burden does not pass as a general rule in any case;

ii) the land benefited must be ascertainable by conveyance or parol evidence;

iii) the covenant must be capable of benefiting the land; and

iv) there must have been no separation between the title to the covenant and the title to the land.

The reason for this rule is said to be that if a covenantee sold the land without the benefit of the covenant, then the covenant is not needed. Equity protects the covenantee's property interest. It is also said to be a requirement that if part of the land is assigned and is to have the benefit, then the covenant must have been taken with the intention to benefit parts as well as the whole of the land.[57] This is, however, a somewhat subjective, contractual type of test. It is suggested that there is some doubt today as to whether it would be applied. It is probable that once a covenant is assigned in equity it becomes annexed to the

56 *Rogers v. Hosegood* [1900] 2 Ch. 388, [1900-3] All ER Reprint 915.

57 Hayton (1971) LQR 539.

land, *i.e.* in future the benefit automatically passes in equity.[58] This again is an extension of the rules by which the passing of the benefit in equity is facilitated. A chain of assignments is a purely contractual notion while annexation to the land is a proprietary one.

(b) Implied Annexation

The English case of *Marten v. Flight Refuelling Ltd*[59] took the view that the benefit of a covenant is impliedly annexed where to ignore it would not only cause injustice but would depart from common sense. It is suggested that the first reason on its own is sufficient.

(2) Assignment

(a) Express Assignment

The difference between assignment and annexation is that assignment, at least originally, confers the benefit on people: annexation confers it on the land, or rather, so as to avoid reifying the concept, confers it on all the owners of the land for time being. For a person to show that they have the benefit of the covenant by assignment, they should show a complete chain of assignments from the original covenantee to themselves, but there are arguments that this is not in fact necessary:

(1) The cases suggest that the courts may be prepared to dispense with this strict requirement by holding that once the benefit of a covenant is assigned in equity, that has the effect of permanently annexing it to the land so that from then on the benefit of it will pass in equity without express assignment.[60]

(2) It can be argued that section 6 of the Conveyancing Act, 1881 acts as a kind of statutory assignment. Under the section: "a conveyance of land shall be deemed to include and shall... operate to convey with the land... all... privileges, easements, rights and advantages whatsoever appertaining... to the land".

The key question is whether the benefit of a covenant is a right or advantage pertaining to the land. On the face of it, if it touches and concerns the land, it should be.

---

58 *Re Pinewood Estate* [1958] Ch. 280 assumed that one would have to show a chain of assignments but later cases contain *dicta* to the opposite effect, *e.g. Stilwell v. Blackman* [1968] Ch. 508. Wade, (1957) CLJ 146.

59 [1962] Ch. 115 at 133. See also *Shropshire County Council v. Edwards* (1982) 46 P & CR 270.

60 *Stilwell v. Blackman* [1968] Ch. 508. *Re Pinewood Estate* [1958] Ch. 280 assumed that one would have to show a chain of assignments but Stilwell contains *dicta* to the opposite effect. Wade, (1957) CLJ 146.

The argument was considered in *Roake v. Chadha*,[61] which had to consider the equivalent section 62 of the English Law of Property Act, 1925, but rejected on the ground that there was an express provision in the original conveyance that the covenant should not pass except by express assignment, which had not occurred.

The judge, Paul Baker QC, did not therefore have to decide what the position would have been if no express clause had been included. He expressed the same doubts as Farwell J in the Chancery Division in *Rogers v. Hosegood*.[62] The question as to the effect of section 6 remains open in Ireland.

(b) Implied Assignment

If the covenant was annexed to the land when it was created, or, possibly, if the benefit was subsequently assigned, then the benefit of the covenant will pass automatically on subsequent conveyances. For this to happen it must be shown that:

(1) words in the deed creating the covenant show an intention to benefit the land,[63] as, for example, where the covenant is made with X, owner for the time being of Gortduff;

(2) the land benefited must be ascertainable;

(3) the covenant must be capable of benefiting the land; and

(4) it may be the case that if the benefit is annexed only to the whole of the land, only an assignee of the whole land can take the benefit.[64] If the covenant is annexed to the whole or any part of the land, then an assignee of part of the land can benefit.[65]

(c) Development or Building Schemes

The above rules extended the situations in which the benefit of covenants ran with the land, but there were still situations which fell outside their scope. We can illustrate one such situation as follows:

61 [1983] 3 All ER 503. See above.

62 [1900] 2 Ch. 388 at 398.

63 *Rogers v. Hosegood* [1900] 2 Ch. 388.

64 *Re Ballard's Conveyance* [1937] Ch. 473.

65 *Zetland (Marquess) v. Driver* [1939] Ch. 1.

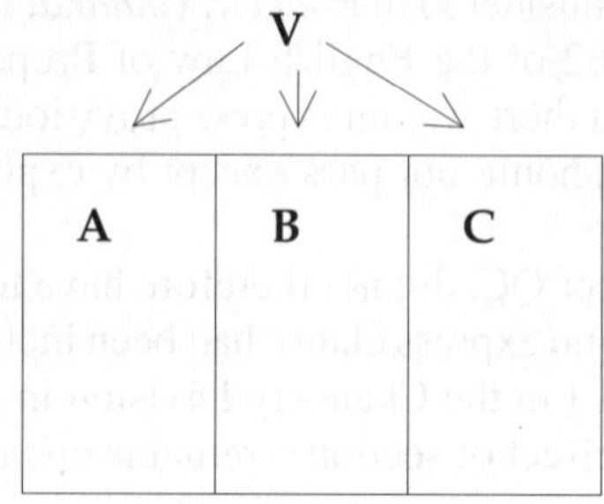

This is one situation. There may be others. V is the original covenantee. She sells first to A, then to B, then to C. All the purchasers enter into covenants with V as they buy their plots, for example, to use the land for residential purposes only. Can A enforce the covenant entered into by B with V since the amenity of plot A will be reduced if the covenant is broken? A cannot do so at common law because when V sold to B she had already parted with plot A. V could not covenant for the benefit of plot A because she no longer owned plot A. The covenant may have benefited the land of the covenantee, V, but plot A was not part of that land. Nor can A enforce the benefit in equity for the same reason. V could not have annexed the benefit of the covenant to plot A, and although it is possible for V to have assigned the benefit of her covenant to A it is unlikely to have occurred in practice.

One way of avoiding this problem was for V not to sell the fee simple in the plots but to sell long leases instead, thus retaining a reversion on all the plots. This was, however, unpopular with purchasers who usually wished to acquire the fee simple. Another method was for V to induce B to contract directly with A. There would thus be privity of contract between A and B. But this only works by the later purchaser contracting with the earlier one. It does not work the other way round. Suppose V sells plot C to C. Can C enforce the benefit of the covenant between V and B, or between V and A? How can later purchasers take the benefit of earlier covenants? A and B cannot contract with C at the time they buy their plots because he or she was not ascertained. Could the covenants have been assigned or annexed to C's plot? True, it was part of land retained by V at the time the covenants were created, but at common law one may not be able to assign part of the benefit, as we have already seen. In equity the problem may be that the covenant was annexed only to the whole of V's retained land or, frequently, that plot C was not capable of benefiting from the covenant at the time because no house had yet been built on plot C.[66]

66 It could be argued that in this situation a reverse of the rule in *Halsall v. Brizell* (see footnote 13) applies, so that if C is bound by his covenant with V which is for the benefit of A and B then he should be able to enforce the benefit of their covenants.

Problems such as this could lead to unfortunate results particularly in housing estates. In housing estates land has been laid out for residential purposes and its satisfactory use by all residents depends upon the observance of restrictions on land use by all residents. This is a problem which today is largely provided for by planning legislation and conditions as to user attached by the planning authority to the planning permission. The law of covenants shows how in the past private law was capable of being developed to serve not only the needs of individual property owners but more general needs of a social character. Even today, where planning legislation and conditions made under such legislation may have replaced the need to rely on the law of covenants, this law will still apply as to many covenants inserted by the developer for the general benefit of the estate and which have not been included in the planning conditions. A common example is a covenant not to erect television aerials in estates where cable television is available. This is intended simply to preserve the aesthetic appeal of the land and the buildings. Housing estates, schemes of development or building schemes as they are variously known, have been recognised as special cases.

In *Elliston v. Reacher*[67] Parke J held that a scheme of development creates a special legal regime. Each purchaser of a plot, and successors in title, can sue and be sued by every other purchaser and his or her successors in title. The scheme of development creates a kind of local law for the estate. Parke J laid down a number of legal tests to determine when a scheme of development would be held to exist:

- i) the plaintiff and defendant must derive title from a common vendor;
- ii) the vendor must have laid out the land for sale in plots subject to restrictions intended to be imposed on all the plots or consistent only with such a scheme;
- iii) the vendor must have intended the restrictions to benefit all the plots sold; and
- iv) the plots must have been purchased on the basis that the restrictions should benefit the other plots sold.

One more test was added later:

- v) the area of the scheme must be defined.[68]

Elliston v. Reacher has been applied in Ireland in *Fitzpatrick v. Clancy.*[69] Courts in England subsequently held that the tests in *Elliston* were too restrictive and have extended the definition of scheme of development to such an ex-

67 [1908] 2 Ch. 374 at 384.

68 *Reid v. Bickerstaff* [1909] 2 Ch 305.

69 Unreported, High Court, 1964; Wylie, *Cases* p.642.

tent that it now closely resembles planning restrictions detached from the notion of property rights created by mutual agreement.

In *Baxter v. Four Oaks Property*[70] there was no antecedent division into plots by the vendor, although there was a deed of mutual covenant. A scheme of development was nevertheless held to exist. In *Re Dolphin's Conveyance*[71] there was no common vendor, but the same principle was nevertheless applied. The court said there was a common intention by the several vendors to create such a scheme. In *Brunner v. Greenslade*[72] one of the plots had been subdivided so that plaintiff and defendant were not even successors in title to the two original contracting parties. No covenant had ever been expressly created as between the two parties. Nevertheless, the two parties were held to be bound by covenants similar in nature binding other plots. This is quite significant, for it shows that freehold covenants had become completely detached from contractual principles. Nevertheless, Megarry J strenuously denied he was creating a new equity. It is questionable whether the special regime of the development scheme applies to commercial developments.

In *Belmont Securities Limited v. Crean*[73] the first plaintiff was the developer of a small shopping complex, comprising three units. The third and fourth plaintiffs were the occupiers of the shop designated in the original scheme as grocer's shop. The plaintiffs brought an action against the defendants, who were occupiers of the shop designated as a newsagent, claiming damages for breach of a covenant contained in the original scheme restricting the use of the shop to that of a newsagent and claiming that the defendant was carrying on business as a grocer as well as a newsagent. The defendants argued that they had been carrying on business as a grocer since the beginning of the term and that it would be inequitable to enforce the covenant after such a lapse of time. O'Hanlon J held that the covenant was not enforceable by the third and fourth plaintiffs because it was not shown that it had been inserted in the original lease for their benefit or for the benefit of the particular parcel of land which they occupied. The first plaintiff, as original covenantee, was entitled to enforce the covenant, but as they had not retained any land they had only established a technical breach [of contract] and were only entitled to nominal damages of £5. The judge quoted Cozens-Hardy MR in *Reid v. Bickerstaff*[74] on the definition of a development scheme:

> "What are some of the essentials of a building scheme? In my opinion there must be a defined area within which the scheme is operative. Reciprocity is the foundation of the idea of a scheme. A purchaser of one parcel cannot be subject to an implied obligation to purchasers of an undefined and unknown area. He

70 [1969] Ch. 816.

71 [1970] Ch. 654

72 [1970] 3 WLR 891.

73 Unreported, High Court, O'Hanlon J, 17 June 1988.

74 [1909] 2 Ch. 305 at p.319.

> must know both the extent of his burden and the extent of his benefit. Not only must the area be defined but the obligations to be imposed within that area must be defined. A building scheme is not created by the mere fact that the owner of an estate sells it in lots and takes varying covenants from various purchasers. There must be notice to the various purchasers of what I may venture to call the local law imposed by the vendors upon a definite area. If on a sale of part of an estate the purchaser covenants with the vendor, his heirs and assigns, not to deal with the purchased property in a particular way, a subsequent purchaser of part of the estate does not take the benefit of the covenant unless (a) he is an express assignee of the covenant, as distinct from assignee of the land, or (b) the restrictive covenant is expressed to be for the benefit and protection of the particular parcel purchased by the subsequent purchaser . . . Unless either (a) or (b) can be established, it remains for the vendor to enforce or abstain from enforcing the restrictive covenant".[75]

It is suggested that this is a somewhat outmoded definition of a building scheme in view of the later English cases. It should not govern the limits of a building scheme in Ireland today unless there is a specific reason in policy or principle why the doctrine should not be extended to commercial schemes, or needs to be modified in relation to such schemes and if there is, then the judges should articulate it, rather than quoting outdated precedents.

E. Discharge and Modification

One of the problems associated with restrictive covenants in the Republic is that there is no really effective method of dealing with obsolete covenants.

a) Registered land

Under section 69(3) of the Registration of Title Act, 1964 the Registrar can discharge a covenant with the consent of all persons interested in its enforcement. It follows from this that one such person can prevent the discharge of the covenant or demand a large sum of money for their consent. If they all consent, then Registrar can discharge the covenant if it is beneficial to such persons.[76]

---

75 *ibid.*

76 In *Re An Application by Edwards* [1983] RVR 94 the covenant prohibited the of use of the land for business purposes. The English Lands Tribunal held that the covenant was not obsolete, but impeded the reasonable use of the land. The injury to objectors was slight and compensation would be awarded. In *Gilbert v. Spoor* [1982] 2 All ER 576 it was held that the objectors were not affected and consequently there was jurisdiction to refuse. In *Re 6,8,10 & 12 Elm Avenue, New Milton* [1984] 3 All ER 632 the land was voluntarily acquired by a local authority. It was held that the restrictive covenant could not be enforced so as to restrict the statutory purposes for which the land was acquired. This did not amount to discharge of the covenant.

b) Unregistered Land

In unregistered land there is no general provision for discharge of restrictive covenants. But the effect of some legislation may be to discharge covenants or suspend them in relation to some parties.

In *Whelan v. Cork Corporation*[77] it was held that one of the effects of a lessee acquiring the fee simple of land subject to a ground rent under section 8 of the Landlord and Tenant (Ground Rents)(No. 2) Act, 1978 was to discharge the burden of restrictive covenants binding the land, and this included not only those binding in privity of estate, *i.e.* as between the former tenant and the landlord, but also those binding under the doctrine of *Tulk v. Moxhay*.

The judge did not decide, as a constitutional issue, whether this contravened Article 40.2 as an unjust attack on property rights since the Attorney-General did not appear to argue the issue.

It seems likely that the provision is unconstitutional to the extent that it deprives third parties, without compensation, of the ability to enforce a covenant in equity under *Tulk v. Moxhay*. Such a result also appears to go beyond the evident purpose of the section which was to relieve the new fee simple from the burden of covenants contained in the original lease which might have been appropriate between landlord and tenant but which might unduly restrict a fee simple. The policy is the familiar one of preserving, primarily, the alienability of the fee simple estate. The burden of covenants in equity have, however, at least since *Tulk v. Moxhay*, always affected fees simple. It does not seem that the Renewable Leaseholds Conversion Act, 1849 has a similar effect. A grant in fee farm under the Act in substitution for a lease for lives renewable forever, or, in the case of a purported grant of a lease for lives renewable forever after the Act came into force, has the effect, as we have seen, of preserving covenants binding between landlord and tenant, but the provisions do not directly address the question of whether the burden of covenants running with the land under *Tulk v. Moxhay* in favour of third parties continue to bind the fee simple or not. The reference in section 10 of the Act to covenants the burden of which runs at law seems to be confined to covenants actually contained in the grant of the original lease. Commutation under section 3 is confined to covenants annexed to the reversion and does not refer to third parties. It can therefore be argued that restrictive covenants the burden of which ran in equity to affect the former lessee continue to affect the grantee of the fee simple under the fee farm grant.

---

77 [1991] ILRM 19, High Court Murphy J. The facts are set out in Chapter 20 above, p.663.

F. Technical Problems

There are two main problems with the law of freehold covenants in its current state:

1) the burden of positive covenants does not run at all in equity. It can only run at law if one of the devices mentioned earlier is employed;
2) as to restrictive (negative) covenants, the benefit may not run if the land is not within a development scheme. Furthermore, the burden only runs in equity, although this is usually a less serious problem than the benefit.

There is need to reform the position of covenants by providing a system for registration of covenants both positive and negative provided they are not unduly onerous. If registered, both the burden and benefit should pass to all successors. If not registered, the covenants would be void. There should also be a general provision for removal, on application to a court, of obsolete covenants or those which have become unduly restrictive or onerous.

G. Constitutionally Challengeable Covenants

Covenants which attempt to impose restrictions on alienation to particular groups, whether religious social or of any other description will, if they affect the simple estate, be liable to be held void as contrary to the principle of free alienation embodied in *Quia Emptores*, 1290 quite apart from constitutional implications.[78] Covenants which attempt to restrict ownership or occupation of land to members of a particular religious, racial, or other restricted social group are, quite apart from the question as to whether such covenants run at law or in equity, open to challenge on constitutional grounds as violating the right to equality as human persons under Article 40.1 of the Constitution. No case in the jurisdiction has dealt with the issues raised by racial or religious restrictions in the context of freehold covenants.[79]

In the United States the Supreme Court held in *Shelley v. Kraemer*[80] that racially discriminatory covenants which seek to prevent black persons using or occupying land are unenforceable by equitable remedies, and in *Barrows v. Jackson*[81] it held that such covenants are unenforceable by an action at law for damages, in both cases as violating the rights of prospective users of land to equal protection of the laws under the 14th Amendment. Local statutes which purported to make such covenants enforceable have also been held unconstitu-

78 See Chapter 6 Fee Simple.

79 As to covenants in leasehold tenure: see Chapter 19 Landlord and Tenant. As to conditional, determinable fees, see Chapter 6 Fee Simple.

80 (1948) 334 US 1.

81 (1953) 346 US 249, 97 L Ed 1586.

tional.[82] Such covenants are not in themselves illegal in the United States and voluntary compliance with them was not held to be contrary to the 14th Amendment which refers only to action by states. The United States courts have taken the view that for a state to lend its power to grant remedies for the breach of such covenants would cease to be a matter of individual choice: it would become the state's choice to deprive a section of the community of the right freely to purchase, own and enjoy property on the same terms as others, and this was precisely what the 14th Amendment proscribed. The court in *Barrows* held that their decision did not impair the obligation of contracts under Article 1 of the Constitution as that article referred to legislative action by states, not to the judgments of courts. The covenant in *Barrows* concerned only restrictions on use or occupation since restrictions on sale had long been held unenforceable in California as contrary to a public policy in favour of freedom of alienation.[83]

H. Northern Ireland

Article 34 of the Property (Northern Ireland) Order, 1997, which came into force on 10 January 2000,[84] replaces the rules of common law and equity with a statutory scheme. The scheme applies only to covenants between owners of estates on fee simple[85], and not to leasehold covenants, nor where there is privity of contract between the parties.[86] It applies to covenants in deed made on or after the date, including those in "pursuance of an obligation assumed" before the date.[87] The definitive list of covenants which are enforceable by the owner for the time being of the land benefited against the owner for the time being of the land burdened includes: covenants to maintain or repair party walls, and fences, covenants to do or permit or pay for works on the land benefited, or permit any activity on it, covenants not to us the land of the covenantor for specified purposes, including otherwise than as a dwelling house, covenants against causing nuisance, and covenants in relation to a body corporate formed for the management of land.[88] In relation to the specified covenants it is conclusively presumed that the benefit and burden attach permanently to the

82 *Buchanan v. Warley* (1917) 245 US 60, 62 L Ed 149.

83 *Wayt v. Patee* (1917) 205 Cal 46; *Title Guarantee & Trust Co v. Garrott* 42 Cal App 152.

84 SR 1999 No. 461.

85 Article 34(1); and so not where a head-landlord wishes to enforce a restrictive covenant against a sub-tenant.

86 Article 34(1) and (3).

87 Article 34(2).

88 Article 34(4).

whole and every part of the land of the covenantee and covenantor.[89] Article 34 also contains a sub-scheme in which, when a developer divides land into parcels and the parcel owners enter into covenants with the developer, covenants of the specified type apply as if they had been made between parcel owners themselves.[90]

89 Article 34(5).

90 Article 34(6), 34(7).

Tests: Re Ellenborough Park

Latimer, Copeland v Greenhalf

Blackburne v Somers

Gogarty v Hoskins

Doolan v Murray

Bulstrode v Lambert

Newman v Jones

Handel

William Aldred's Case

Liverpool City Council v Irwin

Heeney v Dub Corp

Sweeney v Duggan

CHAPTER 22

INCORPOREAL HEREDITAMENTS

A. Introduction

We have already seen that the classifications of real property law have changed over time and they have changed in response to social change. The classification "incorporeal hereditaments" is a good example. We have seen that the dominant legal concept in the feudal period in relation to land was seisin. The feudal law was obsessed with seisin because physical possession of land was necessary to the feudal method of extracting tribute from the villeins. Their surplus labour was extracted by force, or the threat of force, not through, in Adam Smith's phrase, the "invisible hand" of the market. Hence it was important to distinguish between interests in land which conferred seisin and those which did not. Incorporeal hereditaments originally were interests which did not entitle the owner of them to seisin. According to some writers incorporeal hereditaments can be subdivided into:

1) rights which will never mature into seisin, such as easements and profits; and
2) rights which would in time mature into interests giving the right to seisin, *i.e.* as future interests. If land was granted "to A for life, remainder to B in fee simple" A had a life estate giving seisin, an immediate right to possession of the land, *i.e.* a corporeal hereditament, and B, while A was alive, had an incorporeal hereditament. When A died, B's interest fell into possession and gave B the immediate right to possession, *i.e.* it became corporeal.

Other writers maintain that the rights in the second category were never incorporeal hereditaments: land is the corporeal object of estates and estates are either present or future, they are in possession, in remainder or in reversion.[1] Estates themselves are not incorporeal hereditaments: that which is held for an estate is either corporeal, *i.e.* land, or incorporeal, *i.e.* rights in land, such as easements.

Incorporeal hereditaments were hereditaments in that they were, and are, inherited under the rules of succession. They were said to be incorporeal because they did not give seisin itself, which was seen as corporeal, *i.e.* having a corpus, a body, or in other words, being a physical thing. Seisin was thus

1 Megarry & Wade, *Real Property* p.790. If future interests were ever classified as incorporeal it was probably because they did not carry seisin. Only present estates did that.

thought of as the same as land itself, which certainly is a physical thing. This was odd, because the common law was capable of distinguishing between rights in land and land itself. The doctrine of estates did exactly that and the feudal system of layers of tenure no doubt made it easier to think of property as a relation between people rather than a relation between people and things. However, the importance of possession seems to have made it difficult to maintain the clarity of this insight. At any rate, incorporeal hereditaments seemed to the lawyers of that time as in some way anomalous. They were real property, land, but not land. Blackstone, writing in the 18th century immediately before the Industrial Revolution, expressed the same fascination with the sophistication of abstract property rights when he described incorporeal hereditaments as not "the object of sensation, can neither be seen nor handled, are creatures of the mind, and exist only in contemplation".[2]

The importance of seisin was also evident in the formalities as to its transfer. The rule was "corporeal hereditaments lie in livery, incorporeal hereditaments lie in grant", *i.e.* a feoffment with livery of seisin was necessary to transfer corporeal rights, but a simple deed was enough to transfer incorporeal interests. As the agricultural basis of society gave way to an industrial one the importance of physical possession of land also declined. Force gave way to the market and tribute to wage labour. Seisin declined as a legal concept and after 1845[3] even corporeal rights could be transferred by grant.

Today seisin is no longer the all-pervasive concept it used to be, although possession is still important and probably always will be.[4] A classification which embraces both the types mentioned above is no longer necessary. Incorporeal hereditaments of the second type mentioned above have in any case already been dealt with in the chapters on future interests. This chapter is therefore concerned only with the first type. Rights of this type can broadly be defined, therefore, as interests in land which do not include the right of possession. Sometimes they are described as "rights over the land of another person". This again ignores the common law insistence that there is no single "owner" but merely persons having different estates and interests in the land. The subject of this chapter, then, is easements, such as rights of way, profits *à prendre,* such as shooting or fishing rights, rentcharges and other miscellaneous rights.

B. Incorporeal Hereditaments as the Subject of Estates

Incorporeal hereditaments are held for estates: freehold or leasehold. Leasehold easements can be granted. In Ireland leasehold tenants can acquire easements by

2 Bl Com vol. II p.17, Gray, *Elements of Land Law* p.32–3.

3 Real Property Act, 1845.

4 If X covenants today that he or she is seised of land it amounts to a covenant that no one is in adverse possession.

such methods as prescription (unlike many other common law jurisdictions) in which case that can also give rise to a leasehold easement. There are situations as we shall see where that can give rise to a freehold easement which will enable the landlord to take advantage of it and will bind the landlord of the servient tenement.

C. Categories Not Closed

Some easements have been recognised since feudal times, such as the right of way, for example. The Industrial Revolution with its mass movement of population to towns and cities and the new industrial uses of land created a need for different types of easements to be recognised. This caused a legal controversy in the early part of the 19th century as to the extent to which this need should be met. Resistance to the creation of many new types of easements was expressed by Lord Brougham in *Keppel v. Bailey*.[5] Brougham was progressive in that he saw the need that land be freely alienable as a commodity, but was concerned that owners should not be able to put any restrictions they liked on user that would make land subject to easements – servient tenements – less easily saleable. There was the suggestion that the category of easements should be fixed, but this was opposed by Lord St Leonards (Edward Sugden) in *Dyce v. Hay*[6]:

> "The category of servitudes and easements must alter and expand with the changes that take place in the circumstances of mankind".

The solution was not to refuse to recognise new easements but to develop tests to control them. These test were extensively discussed in *Re Ellenborough Park*.[7] That case was out of its time: it only summed up developments of doctrine that had occurred in the 19th century. Notice how a private right is used to meet a public need - planning occurs first in the guise of private rights. Restrictive covenants are another example.

D. Easements

An easement was defined by Monaghan CJ in *Hamilton v. Musgrove*[8] as follows:

> "An easement is an incorporeal right which may be defined to be a privilege, not conferring any right to a participation in the profits of the land over which it is exercised, which the owner of one tenement has over the neighbouring tenement, by which the owner of the servient tenement is obliged to suffer some-

5 (1834) 2 My & K 517 at 535, 47 ER 106.

6 (1852) 1 Macq 305.

7 [1956] Ch. 131.

8 (1870) IR 6 CL 129, CP.

thing to be done, or refrain from doing something, on his own land for the advantage of the dominant tenement. It must be imposed for the benefit of corporeal property, and imposed upon corporeal property".

1. Tests

a) Dominant and Servient Tenement

An easement is a right in land; it is a property right. The person who acquires it or holds it does not do so for their personal benefit but for the benefit of a piece of land. Easements cannot exist in gross *i.e.* they cannot exist as a benefit not connected to land. They must both benefit some land, known as the dominant tenement, and constitute a burden, *i.e.* reduce the usefulness, of some other land, known as the servient tenement.

It has been held that the dominant tenement need not be adjacent to the servient tenement. In *Latimer v. Official Co-operative Society*[9] there were three attached houses in a row belonging to A, B and C in that order. The house of A was demolished and rebuilt. Subsequently the wall of B's house, which supported C's adjoining wall, detached itself from C's wall causing it to crack. The evidence was that the new building on A's site had settled down after construction probably because it was heavier than the former building. It had pulled B's house with it, causing B's house to detach itself from that of C. The Court of Common Pleas held A liable to C without proof of negligence. An easement of support had been acquired at common law for the benefit of C's house from A's land.

If the dominant tenement is not specified, but an attempt is made to reserve the right to nominate in future unspecified land as the dominant tenement, the purported grant cannot be an easement.[10] If the potential dominant and servient tenements are ascertained, then a right to create an easement in future is valid as a property right, *i.e.* exercisable by a third party, provided its exercise is limited to the perpetuity period.[11]

b) Must Accommodate Dominant Tenement

The fact that other persons may benefit is not relevant. It is not enough that it enhance the value (price) of the dominant tenement. It must enhance its use value. This is really a test aimed at restricting the number of possible new easements and reflects the 19th century controversy mentioned above: new easements are to be recognised to meet social needs, in order to take account of new uses of land.

---

9 (1885) 16 LR Ir 305.

10 *London & Blenheim Estates Ltd v. Ladbroke Retail Parks Ltd* [1993] 4 All E R 157, [1994] 1 WLR 31, 67 P & CR 1, Court of Appeal.

11 *ibid.*

c) Ownership in Different Persons

At common law, at least as it developed in England, ownership of the dominant and servient tenements had to be vested in different persons. This rule was modified in Ireland because of the prevalence in the past of agricultural tenancies. Judges in Ireland allowed the acquisition of easements by tenants in a number of situations.[12]

d) Capable of Forming the Subject Matter of a Grant

It should be noted that all the methods of acquiring easements discussed below are based on the notion of grant: an express or implied grant, presumed grant, *etc.* To be recognised as an easement a right must be capable of being described in a deed of grant and so it must not be too vague. It must also be of such a nature that it is possible to tell if it has been interfered with by the owner of the servient tenement. In *Cochrane v. Verner*[13] it was held that there was no such easement as a right to shade and shelter for cattle provided by a hedge. It was too vague.

A grant intended to create an easement must not amount to ownership or possession.[14] In *Copeland v. Greenhalf*[15] a person obtained permission from neighbour to use his land to keep vehicles on them and come and go to repair them. It was held not to be an easement. The grant amounted to virtual possession of the land. It might create a contractual licence or a tenancy, but not an easement. Where land was granted for the purpose only of exercising troops thereon it was held[16] that it was the grant of a fee simple and not an easement.

2. Negative Factors

If the above tests are satisfied the court is still unlikely to recognise an asserted right as an easement if:

(1) it involves expenditure by the servient owner.[17] No recognised easement, with one exception, imposes such a burden. The exception is the easement to fence land. It is exceptional because it was recognised in the medieval period before the modern tests were developed;[18]

---

12 See s.22.8.

13 (1895) 29 ILT 571.

14 *London & Blenheim Estates Ltd v. Ladbroke Retail Parks Ltd* [1993] 1 All ER 307, [1992] 1 WLR 1278, at 1288B-C.

15 [1952] Ch. 488.

16 *White v. Baylor* (1846) 10 Ir Eq R 43.

17 *Regis Property v. Redman* [1956] 2 QB 612.

18 *Crow v. Wood* [1971] 1 QB 77.

(2) it is purely negative, *i.e.* it stops the servient owner doing something. But this is dubious because of the existence of two exceptions: easements to light and easements of support;

(3) it is contrary to public policy. In *Blackburne v. Somers*[19] it was held that there could not be acquired by prescription a right to pollute a stream in a way injurious to public health.

It should always be remembered that plaintiff a person claiming an easement not only has to show that it satisfies the above positive and negative tests: he or she has to show that he or she had acquired the easement by one of the methods discussed below, *i.e.* by express, implied or presumed grant.

3. Specific Easements

a) List of Examples

The following have been held to be capable of being easements:

(a) a right to throw spoil onto a neighbours' land;[20]

(b) a right acquired by prescription to a higher degree of light required for the normal use of a greenhouse and the benefit of the rays of the sun required to grow plants;[21]

(c) a right, acquired after 20 years' user, to the greater amount of light entering a new room which replaced an older one;[22]

(d) a right to run telephone lines over neighbouring land;[23]

(e) a right to use an airfield;[24]

(f) a right to use a lavatory and tap water for making tea on the servient tenement, a cinema, for the benefit of the dominant tenement, a shop in the cinema, exercisable by the lessee of the shop and her staff;[25]

(g) the right to use eel tanks on a river bed for the benefit of eel weirs reserved by a conveyance and of which the defendants were lessees;[26]

---

19 (1879) 5 LR Ir 1, V-C. See also *Goldsmid v. The Tunbridge Wells Improvement Commissioners* (1865) LR 1 Eq 161 at 169; *Attorney General* v *Richmond* (1866) LR 2 Eq 306 at 311; *The Staffordshire and Worcestershire Canal v. The Birmingham Canal* (1866) LR 1 HL 254.

20 *Middleton v. Clarence* (1877) IR 11 CL 499.

21 *Allen v. Greenwood* [1980] Ch. 119, CA.

22 *MacKey v. Scottish Widows Insurance Co* (1877) IR 11 Eq 541, Ch App, Christian LJ.

23 *Lancashire & Cheshire Telephone Exchange Co v. Manchester Overseers* (1884) 14 QBD 267.

24 *Dowty Boulton Paul Ltd v. Wolverhampton Corporation (No 2)* [1976] Ch. 13, [1973] 2 All E R 491.

25 *Jeffers v. Odeon (Ireland) Ltd* (1953) 87 ILTR 187. See also *Miller v. Emcer Products* [1956] Ch. 304 at 316.

26 *Ingram v. Mackey* [1898] 1 IR 272.

(h) the right to water cattle;[27]

(i) the right to dump lime and manure on the land of another;[28]

(j) the right to use a shoeing stone on the servient tenement for the benefit of a horse shoeing forge.[29]

b) Rights of Way

This is probably the most common easement.[30] A right of way may be by foot only and a grant of a right of way does not automatically carry with it the right to use vehicles. It is a matter of construction or implication as to the extent of the right.[31] A vehicular right of way, however, has been held to include the right to park for the time necessary to load and unload vehicles.[32]

c) Right to Park Cars

In *London & Blenheim Estates Ltd v. Ladbroke Retail Parks Ltd*[33] the English Chancery Division held[34] that the right to park cars may exist as an easement, provided that it is a general right to park within an designated area and not a right to park in a specific parking place only, which would leave the servient owner without any reasonable use of that piece of land.[35] In *Newman v.*

---

27 *Re the Estate of Harding* (1874) I R 8 Eq 620; Re *Tibbotstown and Cloneen Water Arbitration* (1897) 31 ILT 380.

28 *Redmond v. Hayes,* unreported, Kenny J, High Court, 7 October 1974.

29 *Calders v.* M*urtagh* (1939) 5 Ir Jur Rep 19.

30 *Head v. Meara* [1912] 1 IR 262; *Dunne v. Rattigan* [1981] ILRM 365; *Flanagan v. Mulhall* [1985] ILRM 134.

31 *Gogarty v. Hoskins* [1906] 1 IR 173; *Cannon v. Villars* (1878) 8 Ch D 415, see Jessel MR at 420–21; *Bulstrode v. Lambert* [1953] 2 All ER 728; *Doolan v. Murray*, unreported, High Court, Keane J, 21 December 1993.

32 *Bulstrode v. Lambert* [1953] 2 All ER 728.

33 [1993] 1 All ER 307, [1992] 1 WLR 1278 at p.1288 B-C, Chancery Division. The decision was upheld by the Court of Appeal, but on other grounds: [1993] 4 All E R 157, [1994] 1 WLR 31, 67 P & CR 1.

34 [1993] 1 All ER 307, [1992] 1 WLR 1278 at p.1288 B-C, Chancery Division. The decision was upheld by the Court of Appeal, but on other grounds: [1993] 4 All E R 157, [1994] 1 WLR 31, 67 P & CR 1. See also *Bilkus v. London Borough of Redbridge* (1968) 207 EG 803.

35 In *Esso Petroleum v. Epps* [1973] 1 WLR 1071 it was held that a right to park cars was not an overriding interest in registered land because it could not exist as an easement. This is now highly doubtful in view of *London & Blenheim Estates Ltd v. Ladbroke Retail Parks Ltd* [1993] 1 All ER 307. See footnote 10.

Jones[36] Megarry V-C said "... I feel no hesitation in holding that a right for a landowner to park a car anywhere in a defined area nearby is capable of existing as an easement". A right to park in a specific parking place could, of course, exist as a contractual right, as, for example, between employer and employee.

d) Right to a View

The right to a view has been held not to exist as an easement, on the ground that it is too vague.[37] Nevertheless in *Gilbert v. Spoor*[38] it was held that a view may be relevant in the discharge of a restrictive covenant, *i.e.* a court may not discharge the covenant if the result would be the grant it if results in loss of a view. In the Republic there is express jurisdiction only to discharge a restrictive covenant if the land is registered.[39]

e) Right to Protection from Weather

The English Court of Appeal in *Phipps v. Pears*[40] held that the right to have a wall of a house protected against the weather by the owner of the adjoining property could not exist as an easement, apparently on the ground that it was too vague. On the other hand, an easement of support gives the owner of the dominant tenement the right to support of buildings on the dominant tenement from the servient tenement.[41] However, weather proofing of adjoining buildings could be a condition of planning permission.

In *Treacy v. Dublin Corporation*[42] a local authority issued a statutory notice to demolish a dangerous building to the first floor level. The owner of the adjoining land sought an injunction to restrain the local authority exercising the power to demolish the dangerous building on the ground that an easement of support existed for the benefit of his building and binding the owner of the land on which the dangerous building stood. He argued that the statutory powers

36 Unreported, English Chancery Division, 22 March 1982, quoted in *Handel v. St Stephen's Close* [1994] 1 EGLR 70.

37 *Phipps v. Pears* [1965] 1 QB 76 per Lord Denning MR. The original case on the point denied the easement on the ground that a view was a matter of pleasure only: *William Aldred's Case* (1610) 9 Co Rep 57b, 77 ER 816 per Wray J:

> "for prospect, which is a matter only of delight, and not of necessity, no action lies for stopping thereof... the law does not give an action for such things of delight".

However, *Re Ellenborough Park* [1956] Ch. 131 held a *jus spatiandi* (right to walk about for recreation) to be an easement although pleasure is a large element in such a right.

38 [1982] 2 All ER 576.

39 Registration of Title Act, 1964 s.69(3). Wylie, *Irish Land Law* para. 19.47.

40 [1965] 1 QB 76.

41 See below.

42 [1993] 1 IR 305, [1992] ILRM 650.

did not authorise the local authority to interfere with this property right. Costello J in the High Court granted an injunction restraining the local authority from demolishing the building without providing a means of support for the adjoining building. The judge further ordered that the local authority could not proceed without providing wind and weather protection for the adjoining owner's building. The statute created duties as well as a power. This order was upheld in the Supreme Court, which nevertheless approved of *Phipps v. Pears, i.e.* that the right to protection from the weather for the benefit of a building could not exist as an easement.

f) Easements in High Rise Buildings

In *Liverpool City Council v. Irwin*[43] a local corporation was the owner of a tower block, which contained some seventy dwelling units including the maisonette of which the appellants were tenants. Access to the various units was provided by a common staircase together with two electrically operated lifts. Over the course of years the condition of the block deteriorated badly, partly due to the activities of vandals and the lack of co-operation on the part of tenants. The defects in the common parts of the block included (a) continual failure of the lifts, (b) lack of proper lighting on the stairs and (c) blockage of the rubbish chutes. The appellants together with other tenants protested against the condition of the block by refusing to pay rent to the corporation. The corporation sought an order for possession of the appellants' premises and the appellants counterclaimed against the corporation alleging, *inter alia*, a breach on the part of the corporation of implied covenants for repair and for the appellants' quiet enjoyment of the property and that there was an implied obligation on the corporation to keep the staircase and corridors of the block in repair and the lights in working order, and that the corporation was in breach of the obligation.

House of Lords held that easements for the use of the stairs, lifts, and rubbish chutes were implied into the tenancy agreements. Lord Wilberforce said:

> "There can be no doubt that there must be implied (i) an easement for the tenants and their licensees to use the stairs, (ii) a right in the nature of an easement to use the lifts and (iii) an easement to use the rubbish chutes".

The court also held that in the nature of the circumstances, the obligation to repair the common parts fell on the landlord. Lord Wilberforce quoted Bowen LJ in *Miller v. Hancock*[44]

> "The tenants could only use their flats by using the staircase. The defendant, therefore, when he let the flats, impliedly granted to the tenants an easement over the staircase… for the purpose of the enjoyment of the flats so let. Under those circumstances, what is the law as to the repairs of the staircase? It was

43 [1977] AC 239, [1976] 2 All ER 39, [1976] 2 WLR 562, [1985] Conv 66. House Of Lords.

44 [1893] 2 QB 177 at 180, 181, [1891-4] All ER Rep 736 at 738, 739.

> contended by the defendant's counsel that, according to the common law, the person in enjoyment of an easement is bound to do the necessary repairs himself. That may be true with regard to easements in general, but it is subject to the qualification that the grantor of the easement may undertake to do the repairs either in express terms or by necessary implication… It appears to me obvious, when one considers what a flat of this kind is, and the only way in which it can be enjoyed, that the parties to the demise of it must have intended by necessary implication, as a basis without which the whole transaction would be futile, that the landlord should maintain the staircase, which is essential to the enjoyment of the premises demised, and should keep it reasonably safe for the use of the tenants, and also of those persons who would necessarily go up and down the stairs in the ordinary course of business with the tenants…".

The House of Lords in the *Liverpool* case further held that, while it was not open to the court to imply terms simply because they were reasonable, the subject-matter of the agreement, *i.e.* a high-rise building in multiple occupation, and the nature of the relationship of landlord and tenant, necessarily required implication of the obligations by corporation. There was an implied term by the landlord/local authority to take reasonable care to maintain the common parts, in a state of reasonable repair and efficiency. The obligation was not, however, absolute, and required no more than was necessary or reasonable in the circumstances. The court concluded that it had not been shown that the local authority had failed on the facts. In so far as the appeal related to a failure on the part of the corporation to maintain the common parts, it was dismissed.

In *Heeney v. Dublin Corporation*[45] (the Ballymun lifts case) O'Flaherty J in an extempore judgment went further than the *Liverpool* case and held that in Ireland the constitutional guarantee in Article 40.5 of the inviolability of the dwelling gave rise to a constitutionally protected right of access by tenants to their dwelling in the tower block. A constitutional easement may require a higher standard than whatever was reasonable in the circumstances. It could also be argued that such an easement is only available against the State, although Article 40.5 is not expressly so directed.[46]

In *Sweeney v. Duggan*[47] Murphy J in the Supreme Court referred to Lord Wilberforce's judgment in the *Liverpool* case in the following terms:

> "In addition there are a variety of cases in which a contractual term has been implied on the basis, not of the intention of the parties to the contract but deriving from the nature of the contract itself. Indeed in analysing the different types of case in which a term will be implied Lord Wilberforce in *Liverpool City Council* v *Irwin* [1977] AC 239 preferred to describe the different categories which he identified as no more than shades on a continuous spectrum".

---

45 Unreported, Supreme Court, 17 August 1998, *The Irish Times*, 18 August 1998, City Edition.

46 Art. 40.5 states: "The dwelling of every citizen is inviolable and shall not be forcibly entered save in accordance with law".

47 [1997] 2 ILRM 211, Supreme Court , (Murphy J; Hamilton CJ and Barrington J concurring).

Although judges still use the language of consensual contract, the characterisation of high rise buildings, and other special forms of land use, such as shopping malls, are giving rise to modern regimes of land tenure in which the general law imposes the terms.

4. Future easements

If V conveys land to P and a covenant in the conveyance gives P the right, on buying additional land from V, to create an easement for the benefit of P's newly-acquired land (future dominant tenement) over V's land (future servient tenement), then:

1. the agreement is binding between V and P under the law of contract, even though the dominant tenement is left unspecified;
2. the contract is capable of creating an interest in land, *i.e.* an option, enforceable by P against successors in title of V, or by successors in title of P against V or V's successors in title, but only if:
   (a) according to the English Court of Appeal in *London & Blenheim Estates Ltd v. Ladbroke Retail Parks Limited*[48], the dominant tenement of the possible future easement is ascertained before V sells his or her land to a successor in title. The land in the hands of V's successor in title cannot be subject to an easement as to which the dominant tenement is unascertained: it would be tantamount to allowing an easement in gross[49] and would place undue burdens on land ownership;
   (b) the exercise of the option to create the easement is limited to the perpetuity period, because the contract creates a contingent interest in property.[50]

E. Profits *à Prendre*

A profit *à prendre* (Law French for "to take") is the right to take something from the land of another. The most usual examples are the right to fish[51] or shoot game[52] and remove the results. Other examples are the right to dig and remove turf[53] or minerals such as gravel. Unlike easements, profits *à prendre* may exist in gross, *i.e.* for the benefit of an individual person and not for the

48 [1993] 4 All E R 157, [1994] 1 WLR 31, 67 P & CR 1 (CA).

49 *Voice v. Bell* (1993) 68 P & CR 441, Court of Appeal (Civil Division).

50 *Dunn v. Blackdown Properties Ltd* [1961] Ch. 433; Gale paragraph 1–99. A possible exception would be an option in a lease to create an easement in conjunction with an option to renew the lease, the easement to last for the renewal period. See Chapter 11.

51 *Moore v. Attorney General* [1934] IR 44; Wylie, *Cases* p.5.

52 *Radcliffe v. Hayes* [1907] 1 IR 101.

53 *Convey v. Regan* [1952] IR 56; *Re Bohan* [1957] IR 49.

benefit of a dominant tenement.[54] The owner may leave the profit by will, sell it, or deal with it like any other property right.

Many shooting and fishing rights survived the Land Purchase legislation and continue to constitute qualifications on titles in Ireland in some areas.

1. Right of Turbary

The right to cut turf for fuel was former of great importance in Ireland, as judges have recognised[55], since people depended upon it to heat their houses and cook their food.

The right to cut turf may exist in a number of forms, only one of which is strictly a profit *à prendre*, *i.e.* a right vested in a person, or a number of identified persons, to cut turf on land the title to which is vested in another person. Prima facie the grant of a right of turbary includes the right to cut turf for fuel only, and not to sell it.[56] A right to cut turf for sale must be expressly granted.[57] When vested in more than one person the right is referred to as a common of turbary. Such rights have arisen in a number of ways. When an estate was sold under the Land Purchase Acts to a number of former tenants, there might be bog land on one of the purchaser's plots. The practice of the Irish Land Commission was in some cases to create commons of turbary vested in the other adjoining purchasers. In other cases the Irish Land Commission conveyed the bog in trust to be distributed among the purchasers.[58]

At common law a tenant has the right to cut turf for fuel where the land demised includes bog.[59] Section 29 of Deasy's Act, 1860 gave a statutory right to tenants to cut turf on their holdings for fuel.[60]

In Ireland[61] a right of turbary comprises the right to use bog turf for fuel and for other reasonable purposes such as to improve the soil[62], but dos not include

54 *Chesterfield (Lord) v. Harris* [1908] 2 Ch. 397 at 421, in House of Lords [1911] AC 623.

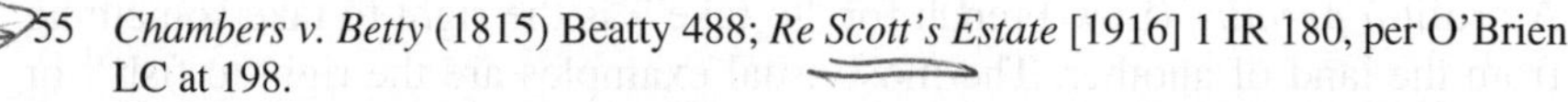

55 *Chambers v. Betty* (1815) Beatty 488; *Re Scott's Estate* [1916] 1 IR 180, per O'Brien LC at 198.

56 *Lifford (Lord) v. Kearney* (1883) 17 ILTR 30; *Douglas v. McLaughlin* (1883) 17 ILTR 84.

57 *Copinger v. Gubbins* (1846) 9 Ir Eq R 304; *Stevenson v. Moore* (1858) 7 Ir Eq R 462.

58 *Hickson v. Boylan,* unreported, High Court, Carroll J, 25 February 1993; Bland, *Easements* p.137.

59 *Howley v. Jebb* (1859) 8 Ir CLR 435; *McGeough v. McDermott* (1886) 18 LR Ir 217; (1886) 20 ILTSJ 459.

60 *Dobbyn v. Somers* (1860) 13 Ir CLR 293, 6 Ir Jur (ns) 57; *Lifford (Lord) v. Kearney* (1883) 17 ILTR 30; *Bruce v. Jackson* [1936] NI 192.

61 *Jameson v. Fahey* [1907] 1 IR 411. It may be otherwise in England.

62 *Dawson v. Baldwin* (1832) H & J 24; *Fitzpatrick v. Vershoyle* [1913] 1 IR 8; *Hutchinson v. Drain* (1899) 33 ILTR 147.

the right to scraws, *i.e.* surface turf,[63] or the soil left after the turf has been cut away.[64]

2. Sporting Rights

Wild game and fish belong to no one so long as they remain at large, but the owner of land at common law has the privilege of capturing and killing fish and game on his or her land.[65] This right can be severed from the other rights of ownership and vested in a person other than the owner of the land, in which case it becomes a profit *à prendre*. Since Deasy's Act, 1860 sporting rights had always been reserved, on the grant of a lease, to the owner of the realty.[66]

Sporting rights of the vendor[67] could be exempted from the overreaching effect of sale under the Land Purchase Acts by Irish Land Act, 1903 section 16. Section 13(2) of the same statute defines them as including "any right of hunting, shooting, fishing and taking game[68] or fish on any land. . . ". The rights could, by agreement, either be conveyed to the purchaser or expressly reserved to the vendor. In the absence of agreement they vested in the Land Commission and this default position means that many fees simple in Ireland in rural districts are subject to such rights. Sporting rights were also preserved on the resumption of a holding by the Land Commission.[69]

Where the title to land is registered, as it would be where a sale took place under the Acts, there is now provision for extinguishing sporting rights other than fishing rights where they were reserved to a person other than the registered owner.[70] Where such rights have not been exercised during a 12 year period after the coming into force of the Land Act, 1965 the Registrar may cancel the entry on the Register on application by any person interested in the land.[71]

3. Fishing Rights

If the owner grants to another person the exclusive right to fish, *i.e.* including the right to exclude the owner of the riverbed, the right granted is called a sev-

63 *Jameson v. Fahey* [1907] 1 IR 411.

64 *ibid.*

65 *Radcliffe v. Hayes* [1907] 1 IR 101;

66 Bland, *Easements* p.172.

67 Subject, under s.13(1) of the 1903 Act, to the Ground Game Act, 1880.

68 Game has the same meaning as in s.5 of the Land Law (Ireland) Act, 1881 and means "hares, rabbits, pheasants, partridges, quails, landrails, grouse, woodcock, snipe, wild duck, widgeon and teal" (s 5(5)) and the 1903 Act s.13(2) adds deer. Rabbits were not included in earlier legislation: see De Molyns, p.177.

69 See Chapter 15.

70 The Land Act, 1965 s.18.

71 *ibid.* s.18(c).

eral fishery.[72] The owner of a several fishery may or may not own the soil of the riverbed,[73] but even if he or she does not, may exclude the owner of the soil from fishing.[74] If the owner only grants the right to fish in common with the owner, or in common with others, it is known as a common of fishery or common of piscary.

Keane J in *Gannon v. Walsh*[75] recently confirmed the existence of a presumption that the grant of a several fishery carried with it the ownership of the riverbed up to its mid-point. Although there are many authorities[76] in favour of the presumption, no less than Lord Coke[77] expressed a contrary opinion, on the basis that it was illogical to presume that what appeared to be the grant of a mere incorporeal hereditament should carry with it the soil itself.[78]

Fishing and fishing rights have been controlled by statute and by-laws for many years in Ireland.[79]

F. Analogous Rights

1. Natural Rights

a) Common Law Right of Support

An owner of land enjoys as part of the rights of ownership a natural right of support for his or her land from adjoining land. The common law right only affects land in its natural state, so that if an adjoining landowner causes the soil on the neighbouring land to subside, the neighbour has an action.[80] But there is no natural right to the support of buildings from adjoining buildings or soil. Such a right can only exist as an easement.[81]

The common law rule developed in a predominantly agrarian society and the rule confining liability to subsidence caused by land in its natural state may

72 *Foster v. Wright* (1878) LR 4 CPD 438 at 449, per Lord Coleridge; *Malcomson v. O'Dea* (1863) 10 HLC 593. See generally: Longfield, *The Fishery Laws of Ireland*, Dublin: 1863.

73 *Malcomson v. O'Dea* (1863) 10 HLC 593.

74 Co Litt 122a.

75 Unreported, High Court, Keane J, 20 June 1996.

76 See Bland, *Easements* para. 9–08.

77 Co Litt 4b.

78 See also *Hindson v. Ashby* [1896] 2 Ch. 1, per Lindley LJ.

79 Fisheries Acts 1959–1998.

80 *Atkinson v. King* (1878) 2 LR Ir 320; *Backhouse v. Bonomi* (1861) 9 HLC 503.

81 *State (McGuiness) v. Maguire* [1967] IR 348; *Latimer v. Official Co-operative Society* (1885) 16 LR Ir 305; *Treacy v. Dublin Corporation* [1993] 1 IR 305, [1992] ILRM 650, Supreme Court (sanitary authority's statutory duty to demolish dangerous structures includes duty to support and protect adjoining buildings from weather).

have worked satisfactorily in such a context, but it is less satisfactory in urban settings where it may not be clear whether the building on the subsided land was partly responsible for the subsidence or whether it would have happened anyway.[82] Moreover there is a legal issue as to damages. Even if it could be proved that the affected land would have subsided even without the building on it, are damages to be confined to damage to the land, or do they extend to damage to buildings on the affected land? In the United States, all states extended damages to buildings if the excavator is negligent, but there is a difference where the excavator has not been negligent. In the late 19th century the courts in the United States tended to deny that liability extended to buildings.[83] The denial of liability favoured developers at a time of rapid urban expansion. In this century, however, the courts in the United States have tended to favour the English rule extending liability to damage caused to buildings.[84] Easements of support may be acquired at common law[85] as to ancient buildings and under the Prescription Act, 1832. It has been held that an easement of support may be breached not only by subsidence on the servient land but also by piling stones on it which causes cracks to appear in buildings on the dominant land.[86]

b) Water Rights

It has been seen[87] that owners of land have as one of the common law rights of ownership certain rights over water flowing in a defined channel[88] through the land. More extensive rights may be, however, be acquired as easements.[89]

2. Negligence

If an easement cannot be established then a party may have to rely upon the tort of negligence. A ready example is where an easement of support cannot be established. The injured party may try to establish a duty of care to support the building, plus breach of the duty and damage.

In *Kempston v. Butler*[90] a jury found that there was a custom in Dublin in the building trade that if a builder demolished a house he was under a duty of care to support adjoining houses, but the Common Pleas held such a custom to

82 Berger, *Land Ownership and Use* p.585.

83 *Moellering v. Evans* (1889) 121 Ind 195, 22 NE 989 ("The owner of the house is without remedy. It was his own folly to put it there.")

84 *Prete v. Cray* (1928) 49 RI 209, 141 A 609; Berger, p.585.

85 *Latimer v. Official Co-operative Society* (1885) 16 LR Ir 305.

86 *Green v. Belfast Tramway Co* (1887) 20 LR Ir 35, QB O'Brien J.

87 See Chapter 2.

88 *Thompson v. Horner* [1927] NI 191.

89 *Pullan v. Roughfort Bleaching and Dyeing Co Ltd* (1888) 21 LR Ir 73; *Hanna v. Pollock* [1900] 2 IR 664; Wylie, *Cases* p.329.

90 (1862) 12 Ir CLR 516.

be unreasonable and void. The custom may have developed because of the many Georgian terraces in Dublin consisting of tall houses supported on both sides by adjoining houses.[91] Today, such a duty would seem to be both reasonable and desirable.

3. Party Walls

There are four categories of party walls:[92]

(1) a wall of which two adjoining owners are tenants in common;

(2) a wall divided down its length into two, the half on one side belonging to the owner of the land on that side, and the half on the other to the owner of the land on that side;[93]

(3) a wall belonging entirely to the owner of land on one side, but subject to an easement of support in favour of the owner of the land on the other side;

(4) a wall divided down its length into two, the half on one side belonging to the owner of the land on that side, and the half on the other to the owner of the land on that side, but subject in each case to an easement of support in favour of one owner affecting the other.

The most usual forms are (a) and (d). There is a presumption at common law in favour of (a), *i.e.* co-ownership, which may be rebutted by evidence, for example, that the boundary line runs down the middle of the wall, which results in situation (b), or that the wall belongs to one owner alone.[94]

4. Public Rights

a) Navigation

The public have the right at common law to navigation in the tidal part of a river.[95] In the non-tidal part of rivers the public only have the right to navigation

91 *Bradburn v. Lindsay* [1983] 2 All ER 408; 268 EG 152. Defendant allowed her semi-detached house to become derelict and accumulate dry rot. It was vandalised. The local authority demolished it by order. A conveyance of the adjoining house described the party wall as repairable by each owner in equal shares. The adjoining house was damaged. The defendant was held liable. There was a duty of care. The defendant should have foreseen danger of dry rot and lack of support.

92 Cheshire, *Real Property* p.314; *Bond v. Nottingham Corporation* (1939) 1 Ch 847; 3 All ER 669.

93 *Hutchinson v. Mains* (1832) Alc & Nap 155; *Ingram v. Mooney* (1870) IR 5 CL 357.

94 *Hutchinson v. Mains* (1832) Alc & Nap 155. See generally Wylie, *Irish Land Law* para. 7.53–7.62; *Jones v. Read* (1876) IR 10 CL 315; Wylie *Cases* p.390.

95 *Attorney General v. Tomline* (1880) 14 Ch D 58; *Evans v. Godber* [1974] 1 WLR 137, [1974] 3 All E R 341.

if it has been dedicated as a public right, long use creating a presumption to that effect, or if it has been conferred by statute.[96]

b) Fisheries

The right to fish in the sea, *i.e.* territorial waters, and in tidal rivers belonged at common law to the Crown, and in the Republic this is now vested in the State.[97] This means that the public have the right to fish in these waters unless the State by legislation has vested them in some other body.[98] The public's right may be curtailed by the grant of aquaculture licences.[99]

The medieval common law recognised that the Crown had the right to grant the right to fish in defined parts of rivers and tidal waters to individuals or groups but the Crown lost this right by Magna Carta, 1215[100] which prohibited such grants after the date of the charter. Such fisheries as can be proved to have been granted before Magna Carta still exist today.[101]

The public have no right to fish in non-tidal rivers or lakes.[102] The Crown does not at common law have a prima facie right to the soil or the right to fish in the large non-tidal lakes of Ireland, which is prima facie is vested in the riparian owners, subject to any fisheries granted as profits *à prendre*.[103] As to non-tidal rivers, the right fish is vested in the owner of the river bed. The presumption is that the owner of the adjoining land owns the bed of the river *usque*

96 *Orr-Ewing v. Colquhoun* (1877) LR 2 App Cas 839.

97 *R (Moore) v. O'Hanrahan* [1927] IR 406 per Kennedy CJ; *Whelan v. Cork Corporation* [1991] ILRM 19; *Foyle and Bann Fisheries Ltd v. Attorney General* (1949) 83 ILTR 29, per Gavan Duffy P.

98 *ibid.* and *The Case of the Royal Fishery of the Banne* (1610) Davies 149.

99 Fisheries (Amendment) Act, 1997, Fisheries and Foreshore (Amendment) Act, 1998. Previous legislation was the subject of scrutiny in *Madden v. Minister for the Marine* [1997] 1 ILRM 136.

100 Cap 16. *The Case of the Royal Fishery of the Banne* (1610) Davies 149 denies this point but is erroneous: *Moore v. Attorney General* [1934] IR 44; Wylie, *Irish Land Law* 6.042 n 162.

101 *Little v. Cooper* [1937] IR 1 (several pre-Magna Carta fishery in River Moy, Co Mayo: discusses history of *Magna Carta Hiberniae); Moore v. Attorney General* [1934] IR 44 (several pre-Magna Carta fishery River Erne, Co Donegal); Wylie, *Cases* p.5.

102 *Murphy v. Ryan* (1868) IR 2 CL 143; *Bloomfield v. Johnson* (1868) IR 8 CL 68, Exch Ch (Loch Neagh); *Bristow v. Cormican* (1874) IR 10 CL 398 (Loch Neagh), (1878) 3 AC 641, Lord Cairns LC at 651; *Johnston v. O'Neill* [1908] 1 IR 358, [1909] 1 IR 237, [1911] AC 552; *Toome Eel Fishery (Northern Ireland) Ltd v. Cardwell* [1966] NI 1, CA.

103 *Bristow v. Cormican* (1878) 3 AC 641, per Lord Cairns LC. Lord Blackburn doubted whether the ownership of a small frontage on a lake would carry with it s strip of the soil of the lake out to the mid-point:

ad medium filum aquæ, i.e. up to the mid-point of the river.[104] The owner may grant the right to fish to another person, in which case it becomes separated from the other rights of ownership and exists as a profit *à prendre*. Such rights are discussed above.

c) Public Rights of Way

A public right of way may be acquired by statute or by dedication to and acceptance by the public.[105] If it is of ancient origin it may be presumed to have been so dedicated in the past.[106] Planning authorities have power to create and extinguish public rights of way.[107]

A private right of way is a right to pass from one terminus, *i.e.* entry or exit point, to another, although where land is under tillage or for other reasons the servient owner may vary the course from time to time.[108] In general a public right of way is a right in the public to pass from one public place to another public place, but may not be restricted to such a case.[109]

In *The Giant's Causeway Case*[110] a landowner granted a lease of the Giant's Causeway to a company set up to exploit it commercially. They put a fence around it and charged for admission. One issue was whether it was necessary for a public right of way to have a terminus at either end. It was accepted in argument that a cul de sac could be the subject of a public right in towns, but the court did not expressly decide that such could not be the case in the country, and held that any right over the causeway had failed through lack of evidence of dedication to the public.

That a right to walk about or promenade could exist as a public right was doubted in *Abercromby v. Town Commissioners of Fermoy*.[111] In that case a stretch of land called The Barnane Walk was held to be subject to the right in the inhabitants of Fermoy to walk about for the purpose of recreation, as had long been the case. Such a right could be acquired by custom or possibly dedication, but the court seems to have based its decision on a local customary right because it doubted that such a right could exist as a species of public right.

---

104 *Welsh National Water Development Authority v. Burgess* (1974) 28 P & CR 378 at 383; *Gannon v. Walsh*, unreported, High Court, Keane J, 20 June 1996.

105 *Neill v. Byrne* (1878) 2 LR Ir 287, CP.

106 *Carroll v. Sheridan* [1984] ILRM 451.

107 See Chapter 27. Where an authority intends to extinguish a public right of way it must advertise its intention by notice in a newspaper and hear objections: Roads Act, 1993 s.73.

108 *Flanagan v. Mulhall* [1985] ILRM 134.

109 (1905) 5 NIJR 301; (1898) 32 ILT 95, 211, per Holmes LJ.

110 (1905) 5 NIJR 301; (1898) 32 ILT 95, 211. Dawson, 'The *Giant's Causeway Case*: Property Law in Northern Ireland 1845–1995' in Dawson, Greer and Ingram (1996).

111 [1900] 1 IR 302; Wylie, *Cases* p.294.

Both these cases may have been affected by the decision in *Re Ellenborough*[112] which held that a *jus spatiandi*, the right to walk about for recreation, can exist as a private right, which had previously been thought not to be the case.[113] More recently, Costello J stated *obiter* in *Smeltzer v. Fingal County Council*[114] that a *jus spatiandi* could not exist as a public right.

d) Local Custom

Local customary rights are recognised at common law if they satisfy the tests of being ancient, certain, reasonable and continuous.[115]

Ancient means, at common law, proved to exist since time immemorial, *i.e.* since 1189,[116] but, as in the case of the acquisition of easements by prescription at common law, user for about 20 years[117] will give rise to a presumption of user since 1189, which can be rebutted by showing a modern origin. They will also be void if contrary to statute, such as *Quia Emptores*, 1290.[118]

Local customary rights must be local in the sense of being vested in the local community or sections of it, unlike public rights which are vested in the public in general[119]

G. Methods of Acquisition of Easements and Profits

1. Express Grant

An express grant occurs if V sells land to P and V grants an easement to P over land V retains. Words of Limitation are necessary *inter vivos*: the grantor must use the words "and his/her heirs" or "in fee simple" to grant the easement in fee simple.

If the easement is to be for a leasehold estate within Deasy's Act, 1860 it must comply with the Act, *i.e.* it must be at a rent (section 3), in writing and signed by the grantor or his agent authorised in writing, unless it is from year to year or a lesser period, in which case it may be made orally (section 4). One

---

112 [1956] Ch. 131.

113 The English Court of Appeal in *Re Ellenborough* overuled Farwell J in *Attorney General v. Antrobus* [1905] 2 Ch 188 and *International Tea Stores Ltd v. Hobbs* [1903] 2 Ch. 165.

114 [1998] 1 ILRM 24.

115 *Daly v. Cullen* (1958) 92 ILTR 127.

116 See below: "Prescription: at Common Law."

117 *Daly v. Cullen* (1958) 92 ILTR 127, Circuit Court, Wexford, Deale J, applying *Bright v. Walker* (1834) 1 Cr M & R 211 per Parke B, at p.217, 149 ER 1057; *DPP (Long) v. McDonald* [1983] ILRM 223.

118 *Merttens v. Hill* [1901] 1 Ch. 842; Chapter Tenure.

119 *Abercromby v. Town Commissioners of Fermoy* [1900] 1 IR 302; Wylie, *Cases* p.294.

should remember that these formalities only apply in practice to easements expressly granted because where an easement is claimed on other grounds such as prescription or estoppel it will be presumed that the formalities were complied with or the other party will be estopped from denying compliance with them, or may be bound to execute a valid grant.

If a purported grant of a leasehold easement fails to comply with Deasy's Act, 1860 but is supported by a memorandum under the Statute of Frauds (Ireland), 1695 or is partly performed, then it may be an easement in equity.[120]

2. Express Reservation

The common law made a distinction between exceptions and reservations in grants.[121] A grantor could except a physical part of the land, such as mines, minerals, stones or quarries, (things *in esse*) or a pre-existing right over it, and this is commonly done.[122] The common law used the word reservation to refer to a right which had not previously existed and which was intended to come into existence on the making of the grant. The general rule was that a grantor could not make a reservation in his or her own favour. Thus if V granted part of Gortbane to P, V could not reserve an easement over the part conveyed in favour of the part he retained. The common law saw a logical objection: such a right could only come into existence[123] once P had acquired the interest in the land, which would be after the grant had taken effect. The common law did, however, allowed a category of new rights to be reserved, namely those that issued out of the land granted, so that, for example, on a grant of Gortbane by V to P, V could reserve a rentcharge in his own favour charged on Gortbane.[124] This was probably because the feudal common law regarded rent as almost a physical attribute of land and therefore more in the nature of an exception.[125]

There are two ways to avoid the general rule against reservations. First, if the conveyance is executed by the purchaser of the land as well as the grantor the conveyance has a dual operation: it operates as a conveyance by V of the estate in the land to P, and as a grant by P of the easement to V.

A second method is for the vendor to convey the land to a feoffee to the use that the purchaser should have the land subject to the use and that the vendor should have the easement. The Statute of Uses, 1634 then executes the uses vesting a legal estate in the land in the purchaser and the legal estate in the

120 See Chapter 19 Landlord and Tenant: *Walsh v. Lonsdale.*

121 Co Litt 47a.

122 *McDonnell v. Kenneth* (1850) 1 Ir CLR 113; *Quinn v. Shields* (1877) IR 11 CL 254.

123 While the land was still vested in V it could only exist as a quasi-easement: *O'Donnell v. Ryan* (1854) 4 Ir CLR 44, at 59-60.

124 Co Litt 143a.

125 The income of the land, which is the source of the rent, is a thing in existence at the time of the grant.

easement in the vendor. There was a doubt about the effectiveness of this device before 1881, since the objection could be made that the Statute only operated where a person was seised to the use of another and it was doubted if the feoffee could be said to be seised of the easement before the conveyance was executed.[126] Section 62(1) of the Conveyancing Act, 1881 now provides that a conveyance of freehold to the use that a person should have an easement shall operate to vest the easement in that person.

3. Construction

Where a question arises as to the meaning or scope of a grant or reservation, the relevant principle of construction is that a grant is generally construed against the grantor, for a grantor may not derogate from his or her grant.[127] This has been described as "a principle which merely embodies in a legal maxim a rule of common honesty".[128] Where a reservation of an easement is made in the form of a re-grant by one of the methods described above, the courts have construed the re-grant of the easement against P, the purchaser of the land, on the basis that P is the grantor of the easement.[129] Nevertheless, this has been criticised.[130] The argument looks like sophistry rather than principle, since the whole deed is usually drafted by the vendor of the land.[131]

4. Implied Grant

Easements may arise by implied grant, for a grant is construed in favour of the grantee and against the grantor. This follows from the principle that a grantor may not derogate from his grant.[132] Not only may the original grantor not dero-

126 See Chapter 4 Equity: Statute of Uses: Seised.

127 See footnote 134.

128 *Harmer v. Jumbil (Nigeria) Tin Areas Ltd* [1921] 1 Ch. 200, per Younger LJ at p.225; Gale, *Easements* (16th ed.) p.207.

129 *Neill v. Duke of Devonshire* (1882) 8 AC 135, per Lord Selbourne LC at 149; *Dwyer Nolan Developments Ltd v. Kingscroft Developments Limited* [1999] 1 ILRM 141.

130 Brand, *Easements* p.206; NI Land Working Group *Final Report* (HMSO, 1990) (recommend reversal of the rule).

131 In *Doolan v. Murray* and *Dun Laoghaire Corporation*, unreported, High Court, Keane J, 21 December 1993, the judge quoted Wylie, *Irish Land Law* (2nd ed.), 1986, para. 6.058: "a grant of an easement will be construed against the grantor, whereas a reservation, being treated as a re-grant by the grantee, will be construed against him in favour of the grantor", but then the judge went on to construe the re-grant against the vendor of the land.

132 *Swanton v. Gould* (1860) 9 Ir CLR 234; *Donegall v. Templemore* (1860) 9 Ir CLR 374; *Lalor v. Lalor* (1879) 4 LR Ir 350, QB, 678, Appeal; *Ewart v. Belfast Poor Law Guardians* (1880) 5 LR Ir 536, V-C, (1882) 9 LR Ir 172, appeal. Lyall, "Non-Derogation from a Grant" [1988] 6 ILT 143; Elliott, " Non-Derogation from a Grant" (1964) 80 LQR 244.

gate, but those claiming through him or her are similarly barred and so the principle can give rise to a property interest.[133]

In *Connell v. O'Malley*[134] the defendant had a site near the River Boyne for sale with outline planning permission. Access was by a road, part of which ran over the defendant's land. The defendant entered into an agreement with the plaintiff to sell the land to him. The defendant then refused to go through with the sale. After protracted litigation resulted in the defendant being ordered to execute a conveyance, he erected two gates across the road and later a concrete wall. Barron J held that he was not entitled to do so as it would be a derogation from the grant. He continued:

> "Since [the doctrine] depends upon the presumed intention of the parties it cannot apply to a situation which could not have been anticipated. While the grantor must have knowledge of the particular purpose for which the property is acquired before any obligation arises, nevertheless he cannot have imputed to him more than ordinary knowledge of what such purpose was".

If the grantor anticipated or ought to have anticipated that the land would be rendered unfit or materially less fit for the purpose for which it was acquired, then conduct on his part which would have that effect would constitute a derogation.[135]

Easements have been held to arise in the past under various doctrines which are now regarded for the most part as examples of implied grant. It is now questionable whether the following categories, or the first two at any rate, are any longer distinct.

a) Easements of Necessity

If a grant is made of a plot of land and as a result the plot would become land-locked, then a court will find that a right of way is created in favour of the grantee as an easement of necessity. Although the doctrine generally concerns rights of way it does not appear to be limited to such rights.[136] The grantee must choose a convenient route and must not thereafter vary it.[137] Easements of necessity also arise where V sells part of his land to P and it is found that V's plot has become landlocked. This is discussed below under implied reservation.

---

133 *Ewart v. Belfast Poor Law Guardians* (1880) 5 LR Ir 536, V-C, (1882) 9 LR Ir 172, Appeal.

134 Unreported, High Court, Barron J, 28 July 1983; Lyall, "Non-Derogation from a Grant" [1988] 6 ILT 143; Wylie, *Irish Land Law* para. 6.059.

135 Note that in the case itself the issue was between the two parties to the agreement. The judge did not expressly decide that an easement had been granted, but that would seem to be the implication.

136 See *Wong v. Beaumont Property Trust* [1965] 1 QB 173, below.

137 *Donnelly v. Adams* [1905] 1 IR 154.

Megarry V-C in the English High Court held in the case of *Nickerson v. Baraclough*[138] that the doctrinal basis of easements of necessity was not the implied intention of the parties but a public policy in favour of the development of land, or against land being rendered unusable. The Court of Appeal rejected this view and asserted that the doctrine of easements of necessity was founded purely on the implied intention of the parties. It would follow from the latter position that such a right could be excluded by express agreement and that such an easement could only arise on a voluntary grant of land and not, for example, on escheat[139] or adverse possession[140].

Irish authorities even before *Nickerson* favoured the view that the doctrine is based on the intention of the parties. O'Connor LJ in *Maguire v. Browne*[141] said:

> "...a right of way of necessity rests on the supposed intention of the parties; that the law presumes that a man owning a parcel of land, and granting away all the land surrounding it, would not be so foolish as to leave himself entirely land-locked...; that, accordingly, it was taken that in such a case the parties would have understood or agreed that the owner of the otherwise land-locked land was to have a right of way...".[142]

In *Dwyer Nolan Developments Ltd v. Kingscroft Developments Ltd*[143] Kinlen J recently reaffirmed that the basis of the doctrine is the intention of the parties.[144] In holding that the vendor in that case was entitled to a way of necessity, the judge held that the court should take into account what each of the parties knew, all of the contractual terms concerning the conditions affecting the development and the area itself. The relevant factors in the case were that both vendor and purchaser were developers and knew the land was intended for development.

In *Wong v. Beaumont Property Trust*[145] three cellars in a house were let by B's predecessors in title to W's predecessors in title as a Chinese restaurant. Statutory regulations provided that no premises could be used as a restaurant unless they had a ventilation system. This could only be installed by fixing a duct to the outside wall of B's retained upper floors of the building. The English Court of Appeal held that Mr Wong was entitled to an easement to affix

---

138 [1981] 2 WLR 773, High Court; [1981] 2 All ER 269, Court of Appeal.

139 *Procter v. Hodgson* (1855) 10 Exch 824.

140 *Wilkes v. Greenway* (1890) 6 TLR 449.

141 [1921] 1 IR 148, 55 ILTR 149; affd. sub nom *Browne v. Maguire* [1922] 1 IR 23, 56 ILTR 17, House of Lords.

142 *ibid.* at 169.

143 [1999] 1 ILRM 141, High Court..

144 The judge cited *London Corporation v. Riggs* (1880) 13 Ch D 798, per Jessel MR and *Browne v. Maguire* [1922] 1 IR 23.

145 [1965] 1 QB 173.

and maintain a duct on the wall. The court classified this as an easement of necessity, although it was not a factual, but a legal, necessity.

The question has arisen as to whether the extent of an easement of necessity can be greater than the user of servient tenement at the time of the grant. If V sells part of his land to P, and P's plot would become landlocked, can P claim not only the use of a footpath over V's retained land, but to use it for vehicles also? On principle it should be possible to imply such an extended user, depending upon the purpose of the grant and the understanding of the parties, for the basis of the doctrine is implied grant, and therefore the question is what was intended to be granted, not what use the vendor made of the land before the grant. Irish authority supports this view.[146] Irish law may differ from English case law on this point.

b) Common Intention

Easements have also been held to arise even where they are not strictly necessary in the sense that the land could be used without them. In such cases the basis is usually said to be that they give effect to a presumed or implied common intention of the parties.

In *Latimer v. Official Co-operative Society*[147] a conveyance selling one of two semi-detached houses was held to imply an easement of support in favour of the house sold, even though the house could be used without the easement so long as the other house stood. Factual support does not supply the necessity of a right to support.[148]

c) The Rule in Wheeldon *v.* Burrows.

This rule derives from the case English case of *Wheeldon v. Burrows*.[149] The rule is to the effect that:

> "where an owner of land grants part of the land there will pass to the grantee all those quasi-easements which are continuous and apparent or which are reasonably necessary to the reasonable enjoyment of the property granted and which have been and are at the time of the grant used by the owner of the whole property for the benefit of the part granted".

Thus, if V owns two adjacent properties, A and B, and uses a path across A for the benefit of B and then sells B, the conveyance will pass a right of way over A without express mention in the deed. The right could not exist as an easement before the conveyance since both properties were within the ownership of V and his use of the path was no more than the exercise of the rights of an

146 *Maguire v. Browne* [1921] 1 IR 148, per Powell J.

147 (1885) 16 LR Ir 305.

148 As with rights of way: see footnote 175.

149 (1878) 12 Ch D 31 at 49. The rule is *obiter* even in England as the case itself involved implied reservation.

owner.[150] It may be doubted whether the fiction of the quasi-easement is at all useful. American courts have adopted a similar rule but as an easement implied from prior use.[151] Continuous should not be taken to mean incessant use or else rights of way, for example, would be excluded. Apparent implies that there must be some physical evidence of use. The judge in *Wheeldon* seems to have intended the phrase "reasonably necessary to the reasonable enjoyment of the property" to be an alternative to "continuous and apparent", but it has since been taken as an additional test to be satisfied.

In *Sovmots Investments v. Secretary of State for the Environment*[152] the English House of Lords held that the doctrine only applied to voluntary (*i.e.* in sense of being at the free will of parties) conveyances. The facts concerned the Centrepoint building in London. It was built in 1967. It was built as an investment and had remained unoccupied for many years. It included 36 maisonettes on the second floor level. The local authority issued a compulsory purchase order acquiring the 36 maisonettes in order to carry out its statutory duty of providing houses for the homeless. They included a schedule attached to the order claiming ancillary rights including rights of support and passage of water, sewage *etc.* The House of Lords held that the order was in excess of statutory powers. They also held that the ancillary rights had not passed under the rule in *Wheeldon* which did not apply to a compulsory purchase order. The rule was based on the rule that a grantor may not derogate from the grant because it was a voluntary act. The judgments indicate an attitude which is unfavourable to local authorities exercising compulsory powers aimed at providing housing for the homeless.

d) Section 6 of the Conveyancing Act, 1881

This section reads:

> "a conveyance of land shall be deemed to include and shall. . . operate to convey with the land. . . all . . . buildings, erections, fixtures, commons, hedges, ditches, fences, ways, watercourses, liberties, privileges, easements, rights and advantages whatsoever appertaining or reputed to appertain to the land, or any part thereof, or at the time of the conveyance demised, occupied, or enjoyed with, or reputed or known as part or parcel or appurtenant to the land or any part thereof".

This statutory provision is in some ways more extensive than the principle of *Wheeldon* and in other ways more restricted.

The section is the same as *Wheeldon* in that it does not operate to create new kinds of right, *i.e.* rights must satisfy existing tests of property rights, and

150 *Head v. Meara* [1912] 1 IR 262.

151 *Romanchuk v. Plotkin* (1943) 215 Minn 156, 9 NW 2d 421; and see Cunningham, Stoebuck and Whitman 1984 pp. 444–446.

152 [1979] AC 144.

so, if it is relied on to claim an easement, the easement must satisfy the usual tests.[153]

The section is wider than *Wheeldon* in that:

1) it applies to all kinds of rights, not only easements;
2) easements do not have to be continuous and apparent to fall within its scope;[154]
3) nor do they have to be reasonably necessary for the reasonable enjoyment of the property. For example, if a landlord grants a renewal of a lease to a tenant, section 6 operates to convert any licences[155] or privileges which the landlord allowed the tenant to exercise in the past into easements or profits, if they can qualify as such in law.[156]

It is narrower than Wheeldon in that:

1) it applies only to conveyances since 1881;
2) it applies only to conveyances and not to contracts;[157]
3) it may also not apply to an equitable lease under the doctrine of *Walsh v. Lonsdale* since it is not a conveyance;[158]
4) there is authority in England for the proposition that the section only applies where there was separate ownership of the two parts before the conveyance[159], *i.e.* it did not apply to rights which could only have been quasi-easements. This position was restated in the Court of Appeal in *Sovmots Investments v. Secretary of State for the Environment*[160] on the equivalent of section 6[161] but the point was not argued in the House of Lords[162] although *dicta* of Lord Wilberforce[163] appear to support it. It would follow therefore that if V owns and occupies land as a single plot and then sell part of it to P, the section will not pass to P, and convert to easements, any quasi-easements enjoyed by V. On the other hand, if P occupied part of V's land before the conveyance,

153 *Phipps v. Pears* [1965] 1 QB 76. Right to protection of a wall from the weather did not pass under s.62 of Law of Property Act, 1925 because it could not exist as an easement.

154 *Tichmarsh v. Royston Water Co Ltd* (1899) 81 LT 673; *Long v. Gowlett* [1923] 2 Ch 177.

155 *International Tea Stores Ltd v. Hobbs* [1903] 2 Ch 165.

156 *ibid.*

157 *McDonagh v. Mulholland* [1931] IR 110 at 122; *Peilow v. O'Carroll* (1972) 106 ILTR 29 Supreme Court.

158 *Borman v. Griffith* [1930] 1 Ch 493.

159 *Long v. Gowlett* [1923] 2 Ch 177, but see Harpum [1979] Conv 113; Megarry & Wade, *Real Property* 18–114.

160 [1979] AC 144, see above.

161 Section 62 of Law of Property Act, 1925, which was a re-enactment of s.6.

162 See Gale, *Easements* para. 3–97.

163 *Sovmots Investments v. Secretary of State for the Environment* [1979] AC 144 at 169.

whether as tenant or licensee[164], then any privilege *etc.*, which P enjoyed over V's land will pass to P as an easement, provided it is capable of existing as such. It is also clear that the principle, if it exists, is subject to at least two exceptions. It has been held that there need not have been separate ownership in the case of a right to light[165] and authorities on the original section 6 have recognised continuous and apparent quasi-easements as an exception,[166] although the authorities have not been recently reviewed either in England or Ireland. Continuous and apparent quasi-easements were also regarded as an exception to the principle that a person could not exercise rights over their his or her own land.[167] It is arguable that if V treated his land as two separate plots prior to the conveyance and in fact used the one which he was to retain in a way which was beneficial to the plot he later sold, then he treated his ownership of the two plots as distinct to that extent and such advantages should pass.[168]

Rights which do not pass under section 6, may of course, still pass under *Wheeldon v. Burrows*.

5. Implied Reservation

It is more difficult to established easements by implied reservation due to the principle that a grantor should not derogate from his grant. Barron J in *Connell v. O'Malley*[169] expressed the view that if a grantor wished to retain the benefit of quasi-easements for the land retained he would have to reserve them expressly, but there are examples of easements of necessity and easements of common intention arising in this way.

a) Common Intention

One case in Northern Ireland found that such an easement had arisen, although for the benefit not of the grantor but of his tenant. In *Re Flanagan and McGarvey and Thompson's Contract*[170] a person had two adjoining houses, A and B. He held B on a 989 year lease. He let out B on a quarterly tenancy. A path led from a road across the land attached to house A to the back door of the sub-let B. The path was convenient but not essential to the enjoyment of house B. The executors of the owner entered a contract, which did not mention the

164 *Lyme Valley Squash Club Ltd v. Newcastle under Lyme BC* [1985] 2 All ER 405.

165 *Broomfield v. Williams* [1897] 1 Ch. 602.

166 *Watts v. Kelson* (1870) 6 Ch App 166 (watercourse running through man-made culvert); *Bayley v. GWR* (1883) 26 Ch D 434 at 456; *Barkshire v. Grubb* (1881) 18 Ch D 616 (made up road).

167 Harpum [1979] Conv 113 at 114 *et seq*; Thompson [1995] Conv 239 at 241.

168 See also Bland, *Easements* 12–16.

169 Unreported, High Court, Barron J, 28 July 1983.

170 [1945] NI 32, High Court.

path, to sell house A to a purchaser. They claimed that they were entitled to reserve an easement for themselves over the path for the duration of the 989 year lease.

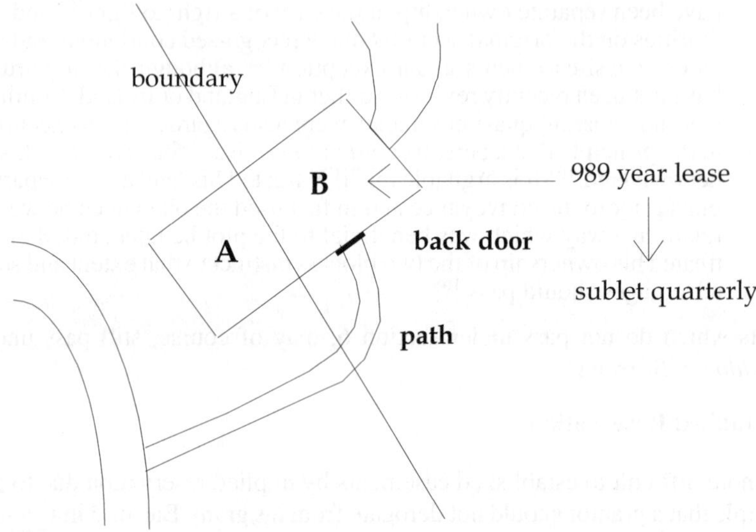

It was held by the High Court of Northern Ireland that they were not entitled to do so, but they were entitled to reserve a right of way for the benefit of the quarterly tenancy over house B and any statutory tenancy that might arise on its determination.

An alternative explanation of the result in the case which does not involve an exception to the rule against derogating from a grant is that when the sub-tenancy was granted over house B the quasi-easement over the path became an easement for the duration of the tenancy. As a legal right the tenant could have enforced it against third parties, including the present purchaser, regardless of notice. Thus the purchaser of A would be bound by it whether there was any mention of it in his contract or not and without any need to imply a reservation. The only right over A which the executors had power to convey to a purchaser was subject to a legal easement for the benefit of the sub-tenancy. On the other hand, this was not the reason given by the court for its decision and the case may therefore be some authority for the view that while a grantor cannot in general impliedly reserve easements for his or her own benefit, there may be circumstances in which they may do so for the benefit of their own tenants.[171] *Dwyer Nolan Developments Ltd v. Kingscroft Developments*

171 *Thomas v. Owen* (1887) 20 QBD 225 disapproved.

Limited[172] also seems to indicate that courts are more willing than in the past to find such easements and to regard them as based on a re-grant by the purchaser of the land in favour of the vendor.

b) Easements of Necessity

If a grantor, in conveying part of his land, leaves the land he or she retains without a means of access, *i.e.* it would be landlocked, an easement of necessity will be implied in favour of the grantor.[173] The right must be necessary at the time of the grant.[174] There will be no implied right if an alternative route is available, provided it is not by mere licence which may be revoked.[175]

6. Presumed Grant, or Prescription

Where a right which appears to be in the nature of an easement has been exercised for a long period of time, the court may presume that an easement was granted by deed at some time in the past. User which gives rise to such a presumption is known as prescription. Three methods of prescription exist:

1) at Common Law;
2) Lost Modern Grant;
3) Prescription Act, 1832.

a) General Tests

Certain requirements exist if a claim to an easement under any form of prescription is to succeed. There are some exceptions to these in particular doctrines, but they will be noted when we deal with the separate doctrines.

(1) User as of Right

The test here is derived from the Roman law of praedial servitudes and is expressed in the Latin maxim *nec vi, nec clam, nec precario*, *i.e.* the user must be without force, without secrecy, and without mere permission. To succeed in a claim based on prescription the claimant must show that he or she has exercised the easement as if they were entitled to it under a grant. Prescription may be contrasted here with acquiring title to land by adverse possession. Unlike adverse possession the user on which a claim to prescription is based must be lawful in origin. Adverse possession, it is true, is possession which is as of right in one sense, *i.e.* a right which is inconsistent with the right of thc original

---

172 [1999] 1 ILRM 141.

173 *Browne v. Maguire* [1922] 1 IR 23; *Re Flanagan and McGarvey and Thompson's Contract* [1945] NI 32, per Black J at p.42.

174 *Geraghty v. McCann* (1872) IR 6 CL 411; *Browne v. Maguire* [1922] 1 IR 23.

175 *Barry v. Hasseldine* [1952] Ch. 835.

owner but which, because of the concept of relativity of title in real property,[176] is a right good against later possessors. Prescription is as of right in the sense of a right consistent with the owner having granted the right to the claimant of the easement and which is not therefore exercised merely by permission or at the will of the owner of the servient tenement which can be withdrawn.

(2) Without Force

A claim to an easement by prescription cannot succeed if the servient owner has objected to the use continually and unmistakably.[177] The servient owner must have acquiesced in the use in the sense that he had knowledge of the acts constituting user, had the power to prevent them by his own acts or by suing in respect of them and had abstained from doing so.

(3) Without Secrecy

The servient owner cannot acquiesce without knowledge of the user. Using a path only in the dead of night will not establish a right of way.

(4) Without Mere Permission

The user must be consistent with a grant of a right. If user is by virtue of a bare licence then it is clearly precarious in that permission may be withdrawn by the owner of the land. User under a contract can be said to be as of right, but the right is then personal and is inconsistent with a right of property available against all owners of the land which is the kind of right conferred by a grant.[178] If user is under an express grant, user is, of course, as of right, and the claimant has no need to resort to prescription. Nevertheless, if user is under the mistaken belief that an express grant was made in the past that does not prevent user being as of right and does not rebut the presumption.[179]

(5) Continuous User

User must be continuous and not intermittent, but the meaning of continuous will depend on the type of easement claimed. A right to light is enjoyed uninterruptedly, at least while light is available, but the use of a right of way is necessarily from time to time and not constant. The Prescription Act contains exceptions to this requirement.

176 See Chapter 1 Introduction.

177 *Dalton v. Angus* (1881) 6 App Cas 740 Fry J at 773; Cheshire & Burn, p.513.

178 *Lowry v. Crothers* (1870) IR 5 CL 98 (right to cut turf enjoyed by permission for the whole of 60-year period. Tenant of the servient tenement who made the agreement had died before the period began).

179 *Bridle v. Ruby* [1988] 3 All ER 64, [1988] 3 WLR 191.

b) Prescription at Common Law

To succeed in a claim to prescription at common law the claimant has to show user from time immemorial, described by Coke[180] as a "time whereof the memory of men runneth not to the contrary".[181] It is also known as the time of legal memory.[182]

In the past, before the modern notion of limitation periods, the practice was to lay down from time to time by statute a date setting the limit for legal actions. No claim based on facts arising before that date would be entertained by the courts. The last statute to lay down such a date was the Statute of Westminster I, 1275 and it laid down 1189 as the year, the year of the coronation of Richard I.[183] The courts adopted the date by analogy in the law of prescription as a precise definition of time immemorial.[184] A plaintiff in an action claiming an easement at common law could not rely on facts prior to 1189. On the other hand, since user must be continuous, the plaintiff had to establish continuous user since 1189. Equally, a defendant to an action could successfully challenge the claim if he or she could prove that user began at any time after 1189, and this is still the law.

As time went by it became impossible to prove user back to that date and the judges adopted a second rule, consistent with the general principle of proof from time immemorial. They presumed user from 1189, which still remained the definition of time immemorial, on proof of user for as far back as the memory of living witnesses would go.[185] Later still a third rule was adopted by analogy to a statute[186] of James I which laid down a limitation period of 20 years for possessory actions. The courts thereafter presumed that the prescriptive right had existed from 1189 on proof of 20 years' user. Some cases in the Republic also take the view that user for a period of at least 20 years will also raise the presumption of user dating back to 1189.[187]

The weakness of common law prescription remains, however, that 20 years' user only raises a presumption of user since 1189 and not a fiction, so that it can be rebutted by showing that user cannot have been continuous since that date. This makes it particularly easy to resist a claim to a right of light based on the common law period. All one need show is that the building does

180 Co Litt 114b, 170. Coke also calls it time out of mind.

181 The phrase is used in the preamble to the Prescription Act, 1832.

182 *Knox v. Earl of Mayo* (1858) 7 Ir Ch R 563; Littleton, *Tenures* Section 170.

183 The time laid down was the limitation period of a writ of right: Co Litt 170.

184 Co Litt 170.

185 *Angus v. Dalton* 3 QBD 104. Carson *Real Property Statutes* p.21.

186 1623, 21 Jas I c 16.

187 *Daly v. Cullen* (1958) 92 ILTR 127, Circuit Court, Wexford, Deale J, applying *Bright v. Walker* 1 Cr M & R 211 per Parke B, at p.217, 149 ER 1057; *DPP (Long) v. McDonald* [1983] ILRM 223.

not date back to that year and that a similar building did not exist before, or that the land was not built on at some time since then.

A claim to a right of way based on prescription at common law succeeded in *Carroll v. Sheridan and Sheehan*.[188] The plaintiffs owned land abutting an ancient path a mile in length linking two public roads. The path formed a link between the main Dublin/Dundalk road and a road leading from Dundalk to Blackrock. The path was shown on a number of old maps, one dating from 1777. The ancient name of the path was 'An Bothar Maol' and according to folklore Queen Maeve traversed it in the course of her legendary cattle-raid on nearby Cooley. The path was overgrown, and it was no longer practicable to travel along it from end to end. The defendants, owners of land at one end of the lane, asserted that any right of way which may formerly have existed in favour of the plaintiffs' land had been extinguished by non-user. The plaintiffs sought a declaration that they were entitled to a right of way over the length of the lane. The plaintiffs failed in the Circuit Court, and appealed to the High Court on Circuit. Twenty witnesses gave evidence for the appellants. The defendants, owners of land at one end of the lane, claimed that any right of way which may have existed in favour of the plaintiffs' land had been extinguished by non-user.

O'Hanlon J, granting the appellants the declaration, held (i) that the evidence established that there was from time immemorial a road or lane, (ii) that the owners of the soil had dedicated the way to the use of the abutting landowners if not to the public in general, and (iii) that the plaintiffs had not originally claimed that the path was a public right of way, and could not amend their pleadings on appeal.

c) Lost Modern Grant

Because common law prescription could be defeated so easily in many cases, the courts created another fiction. If user could be shown for a considerable period they were prepared to assume that a grant had been made of an easement in modern times but had subsequently been lost. Twenty years' user has been held to be sufficient to raise the doctrine.[189] Some cases have held that the doctrine cannot be defeated by showing that no grant was in fact made.[190] More recently[191] the English Court of Appeal held user under the mistaken belief that a grant had been made in the past was not inconsistent with user as of right and so did not rebut the presumption of lost modern grant. The latter point seems consistent, for if the belief in the existence of the right was mistaken, user can

188 [1984] ILRM 451.

189 *Tisdall v. McArthur Steel & Metal Co Ltd* [1951] IR 228; Wylie, *Cases* p.375.

190 *Hanna v. Pollock* [1900] 2 IR 664; Wylie, *Cases* p.329; *Tehidy Minerals Ltd v. Norman* [1971] 2 QB 528.

191 *Bridle v. Ruby* [1988] 3 All ER 64.

still be carried on as if there were such a right and so the absence of a grant in fact does nothing to rebut it.

Nevertheless, it is not entirely clear what part the supposed lost grant plays in the doctrine. There is authority to the effect that the doctrine can be defeated by showing that during the period there was no person capable of making a grant[192] or that a grant would have contravened a statute.[193] Is the test whether the acts of user were done under a belief, even though mistaken, in the existence of a grant, in which case it should be irrelevant whether there was such a grant or even whether there could have been such a grant, or is it that the user must in fact be consistent with the existence of a grant even if it cannot be found? It is unclear whether the doctrine is really a presumption or a fiction or a form of hybrid between the two.

d) The Prescription Act, 1832

The Prescription (Ireland) Act, 1858 provided simply that the English Prescription Act, 1832 should apply in Ireland from 1 January 1859. The purpose of the Act is to provide alternative periods of prescription to those at common law or under the doctrine of lost modern grant. The Act provides different treatment for, on the one hand, easements other than that of light and profits and, on the other hand, easements of light.

As to easements other than that of light and profits there are two statutorily defined periods, the shorter period and the longer period. Somewhat confusingly these periods are different in duration in each case for, on the one hand, easements other than light and, on the other hand, profits, but it has to be remembered that the distinction between the shorter and the longer period is not only one of length, but also of the conditions that have to be met for them to be satisfied and these are the same for each period whether the right is an easement or a profit.

(1) Easements other than of Light and Profits

(a) The Shorter Period

Sections 1 and 2 of the Act deal with this general category. The shorter period in the case of easements other than of light has a duration of 20 years, whereas for profits it has a duration of 30 years. The other conditions to be satisfied are the same. Where the requisite duration of user is proved the claim cannot be defeated by showing that user began at some time since 1189 but before the period of user began, in other words the relevant period of user has been shortened to the duration of the shorter period. A claim can be defeated by proving an interruption as defined by the Act. This defence is dealt with below. A claim

192 *McEvoy v. Great Northern Railway* Co [1900] 2 IR 325 per Palles CB; *Oakley v. Boston* [1976] QB 270.

193 *ibid.*; *Neaverson v. Peterborough RDC* [1902] 1 Ch. 557.

could also be defeated by showing that the claimed right cannot qualify as an easement under the *Re Ellenborough* tests, or by showing that it was objected to by the owner of the land claimed to be the servient tenement, or that it was in secret, or that it was, during the period, only exercised by the mere permission or licence of the owner.

(b) The Longer Period

The duration of the longer period is, in the case of easements other than that of light, 40 years and for profits, 60 years. In either case, if the requisite duration is proved the right is "deemed absolute and indefeasible" unless enjoyed by written consent. It will be seen below, however, that there is one situation in which the right may not be indefeasible because of the statutory definition of deductions.[194]

(c) The Relevance of Permission under the Act

At common law even oral consent during the period would prevent the property being as of right and so the implication is that this is not the case in the longer period. However, the Act in this and other respects is not as clear as it might be. Sections 1 and 2 say that enjoyment must be that actually enjoyed by a person claiming right thereto and section 5 provides that it is sufficient to plead enjoyment as of right. It would seem in view of the earlier cases[195] that as of right only refers to the relevant period, whether the longer one or the shorter and even then it has a restricted meaning in the case of the longer period. In the case of the shorter period oral or written permission given during the period would defeat the claim. In the case of the longer period oral permission would never defeat it. It could only be defeated by showing written permission given during the period. In either case permission written or oral given before the period began is not relevant.

Permission		Short Period	Longer Period
Oral	before	no	no
	during	defeats	no
Written	before	no	no
	during	defeats	defeats

(d) "Next Before Action"

Section 4 of the Prescription Act states that both the longer and the shorter periods must be "next before. . . action", *i.e.* the periods may not be any periods in

194 See below.

195 For example, *Tickle v. Brown* (1836) 4 Ad & E 369, 5 LJKB 119, 111 ER 826.

the past but must immediately precede the bringing of the action in which the right is asserted. The significance of this will be seen shortly in the section on interruptions.

(e) Interruptions

If a claim is to succeed under the Act the period must not have been interrupted within the meaning of section 4 which states that "no act. . . shall be deemed to be an interruption, within the meaning of this statute, unless the same shall have been or shall be submitted to or acquiesced in for one year after the party interrupted shall have had or shall have notice thereof, and of the person making or authorizing" the interruption. An interruption must therefore be factual in that user must actually have been stopped, by, for example, a barrier being erected across a right of way, but to qualify as an interruption within the meaning of the Act the factual interruption must also have been submitted to or acquiesced in for a period of one year. Furthermore, the one year does not start to run until the claimant is aware of the interruption and of the identity of the person interrupting. In *Glover v. Coleman*[196] it was held that in order not to acquiesce in an interruption the claimant does not have to go so far as remove the factual interruption by, for example, removing a barrier, by force or even to sue the interrupter. It is enough to communicate his or her objection to the interruption to the interrupter with sufficient force and clarity.

In *Reilly v. Orange*[197] an English court held that the requirement of "next before. . . action" referred to an actual action and not merely a possible one. Thus, if X prescribes for 19 years and five days and is then interrupted by Y, X cannot claim the easement immediately on the argument that Y cannot complete the necessary one year's interruption before the 20 years expire. X must wait another 360 days and then bring an action. But it has been pointed out that this has the anomalous result that X then has only five days within which to bring his action. If he delays longer than that, Y will then have completed the one year interruption.[198] Equally, if X prescribes for 19 years and one day and is then interrupted by Y, X will still have to wait another 364 days to bring his claim, but will then only have one day in which to start a successful action. If X begins the action before then he will not be able to show 20 years' user "next before. . . action": if he delays until after the day has passed, Y can establish a one year interruption:

196 (1874) 10 CP 108.

197 [1955] 2 QB 112.

198 Cheshire, *Real Property (*13th ed.) p.520.

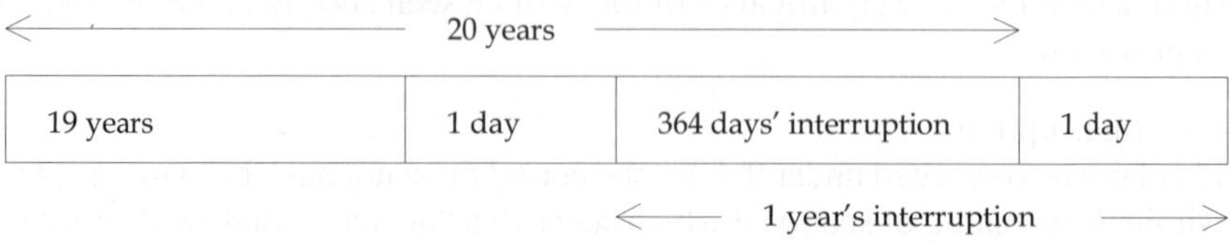

It would also follow that if X is interrupted after exactly 19 years he could not claim an easement at all, because he has to wait another 365 days, but by then Y would also have established a full one year interruption. However, these hypothetical situations are not so serious an objection as might at first appear, because X can stop the interruption at any time by indicating that he does not acquiesce in it. On the other hand it would seem that if a servient owner issues a writ before the shorter period of user has elapsed it does not rank as an interruption but will stop the period running and prevent the claim succeeding.[199]

(f) Deductions

The statute also allows deductions to be made from the relevant periods. These deductions do not count as interruptions, nor do they count as user. The period during which a deduction applies may simply be deducted and the remaining periods of user may be added together to make up the relevant period of user.

Section 7 provides that periods are to be automatically deducted from the shorter period during which the servient owner was a minor, mentally ill or a tenant for life. So also is a period during which an action is pending and has been diligently prosecuted.

Section 8 provides that periods are to be deducted from the longer period during which the servient tenement was held for "a term of life, or any term of years exceeding three years from the granting thereof" provided the claim is resisted by a reversioner on the term within three years of its determination. Section 8, in other words, provides (unlike section 7) for periods during which the servient tenement is held on leasehold to be deducted, but not automatically. They are only deducted if the landlord resists the claim to an easement within three years of the end of the lease. This provision is further considered in the next section.

Section 8 applies in the case of a "way or other convenient watercourse or use of water", but it appears that convenient is a misprint for easement, so that section 8 applies to all easements other than of light.[200]

199 *Reilly v. Orange* [1955] 2 QB 112, see above. The provision is contained in section 7 and there is no similar provision in s.8 dealing with the longer period.

200 *Laird v. Briggs* (1880) 50 LJ Ch 260 per Fry J, and 16 Ch D 440, on appeal at (1881) 19 Ch D 22 at p.33. Section 2 contains the phrase "any way or other easement, or to any

(g) Comparison of Sections 7 and 8

It is to be noticed that deductions under section 7 include periods during which the servient owner was a minor or mentally ill, whereas these do not give rise to deductions under section 8. Deductions under section 7 also include a period during which an action is being actively prosecuted, while section 8 does not include a similar provision. On the other hand, section 7 does not include in deductions any period during which the servient tenement was held under a term of years. Both sections include periods during which the servient tenement was held under a tenancy for life. Section 7 applies to profits à prendre, but section 8 does not.

The operation of the sections can be seen by taking some examples. If a path over land has been used by D, an adjoining owner, for 15 years while the land was held in fee simple, then 10 years while it was held by a tenant for life, and then another two years while it was held in fee simple again, the claim to an easement will fail. Only the shorter period can be relied on and, under section 7, the period while the servient land was held by a tenant for life must be deducted. This leaves 15 years which can be joined to the two years when it was again held by a tenant in fee simple, but this still does not add up to 20 years' user. If, however, user is continued for another three years while the land remains held in fee simple the claim can succeed, for the 15 years can be added to the five years making up the required 20 years' user and this is, for the purpose of the Act, 20 years user next before action.[201]

If D has used a right of way against the land of S for 10 years and then S becomes mentally ill, while user continues for another 12 years, the claim of D will fail, for only section 7 can be relied on and under that section the period of insanity must be deducted. But if user continued for 30 years after S became insane, S remaining in this condition throughout, the claim will succeed under section 8.

It has already been noted that the only provision for deducting leasehold terms is under section 8. If user continues for 15 years while the land is held in fee simple, then for 10 years while it is held under a lease, and then for a further three years while the land is held in fee simple, the claim succeeds under section 7 since leasehold terms are not deductible. It may be that the period must begin while the land is held in fee simple and also end while it is held in fee simple.[202]

(h) Is the Longer Period Absolute and Indefeasible?

It seems that the provisions of section 8 may work in a way which casts doubt on whether the longer period gives rise to a right deemed absolute and indefeasible. Suppose X prescribes for 33 years while the land is held in fee simple,

watercourse, or the use of any water".

201 *Clayton v. Corby* (1842) 2 QB 813.

202 *Palk v. Shinner* (1852) 18 QB 568; *Pugh v. Savage* [1970] 2 QB 373.

then 10 years while under a lease, and then a further two years while the land is held in fee simple. If the reversioner on the term sues after seven years of the lease have run, he will fail, for under section 8 the leasehold term cannot be deducted unless he sues within three years of the end of the lease. It would then seem that the prescriber has established the 40 year term which gives a right deemed absolute and indefeasible. But if the reversioner sues during the later two year period, he will defeat a claim under section 8 because then the leasehold term is deducted. Section 8 therefore seems to detract from the general rule in section 2.[203]

It may be thought that the prescriber could succeed under section 7 in either case, but it may be that such a claim would be defeated because of an oral permission given during the period, a fact which, as we have seen, is not an objection to the longer period. It seems that the principle which section 8 seeks to apply is that the longer term should not give rise to an easement against the reversioner on a term of years until the reversioner has had the opportunity, after the end of the term, of resuming occupation and challenging the use. Until that occurs the completion of the longer period only gives a right which is absolute and indefeasible against the tenant under the term of years.

(2) Easements of Light

Section 3 provides that were the use of light in a dwellinghouse, workshop, greenhouse[204] or other building has been actually enjoyed for a period of 20 years without interruption the right is deemed absolute and indefeasible, any local custom notwithstanding, unless it is enjoyed by some consent or agreement expressly made or given by deed or writing. Thus an oral consent given during the period will not defeat the claim.

It seems that the effect of section 3 is to make a 20 year period in the case of a right to light the equivalent of the longer period in the case of easements other than that of light.

Section 3, in contrast to sections 1 and 2, uses the phrase actually enjoyed without the further qualification that it must be by a person claiming right thereto. It seems therefore that the only element of as of right which continues to apply under the Act in the case of an easement of light is that a claim is defeated by written consent during the period. It has been held that the Act abolishes the presumption of a grant in the case of easements of light[205] although Irish authorities have taken the view that an easement of light can still be

203 *Beggan v. McDonald* (1878) 2 LR Ir 560.

204 *Allen v. Greenwood* [1980] Ch. 119 held that the dominant owner may acquire by prescription a right to an additional amount of light which is reasonably required for the use of a greenhouse, this being known to the servient owner.

205 *Jordeson v. Sutton, Southcoates & Drypool Gas Co* [1898] 2 Ch. 614 at 626, affirmed on appeal [1899] 2 Ch. 217.

claimed on the basis of lost modern grant apart from the Act.[206]

There is no deduction under sections 7 and 8 in the case of an easement of light on the ground that the servient owner was under a disability.

Light which is refracted through glass remains light within the Act and the refraction does not constitute an interruption within the meaning of the Act.[207]

Unlike sections 1 and 2, section 3 does not refer to the Crown and so it was not possible to acquire an easement of light under the Act over Crown land, but there is no presumption that the State in the Republic is not bound by a statute.[208]

7. Estoppel

In *Annally Hotel v. Bergin*[209] the plaintiffs owned a hotel and the defendant occupied an adjoining yard. The present hotel had been erected on the site of an earlier building and the owners of the hotel claimed ancient lights, *i.e.* a right to light acquired by presumed grant, as to windows overlooking the defendant's yard.[210] When the plans for the present building were drawn up they included two windows at a low level in the same position as windows in the earlier building. The plans were shown to the defendant's father who then occupied the yard and he made no objection to them at that time. When the construction reached the level of the proposed windows the defendant's father asked that they be put at a higher position in the wall as he might want to extend his own building in the yard at the lower level. The plaintiffs agreed although it caused considerable inconvenience. They asked that the agreement be put in writing but the defendant refused. Later, the defendant erected screens which obscured the hotel windows which had been put at the higher position.

Teevan J in the High Court held that where there was an agreement, however informal, to allow a right to light and, relying on that agreement, a person proceeds without a deed of grant to erect and spend money on erecting the windows in a building which, to be serviceable, must have the claimed right to light and the other person acquiesces in the acts of reliance, then the person who acquiesces will not be permitted to deny the right nor to rely on the absence of a grant.

206 *Hanna v. Pollock* [1900] 2 IR 664; *Tisdall v. McArthur & Co (Steel & Metal) Ltd* [1951] IR 228 at 241 although the Supreme Court did not decide the point on appeal: pp. 246-8. It was suggested in the English case of *Tapling v. Jones* (1865) 11 HLC 290 that the Act had abolished the doctrine as to easements of light.

207 *Tisdall v. McArthur* [1951] IR 228, (1950) 84 ILTR 173, Supreme Court.

208 *Howard v. Commissioners of Public Works* [1994] 1 IR 122.

209 (1970) 104 ILTR 65.

210 If such rights existed as to windows in the earlier building they would continue for the benefit of the present building as to windows in the same position.

The reason given by the judge is reason enough to justify an estoppel against the defendant's father, but not against the son. To explain that result one can only conclude that the estoppel gave rise to an equity, and specifically an easement of light applying to the windows at the higher level. The case should therefore be regarded as an instance of proprietary estoppel.

In *Crabb* v *Arun D C*[211] the executors of A owned a five and a half acre plot. They divided it into a three and a half acre plot and a two acre plot and sold the two acre plot to the plaintiff, Crabb. It was proposed to build a new road between the two plots which would give access to the main road. The conveyance to Crabb granted him an access point (point A) on the boundary of the two plots, which would give access onto the new road, and also a right of way over the site of the new road to the main road. Later, the executors conveyed the three and a half acre plot to the defendants, Arun District Council, expressly reserving the right of way at point A. Crabb later decided to divide his plot into two and to sell the northern portion which contained point A. At a meeting with a representative of the defendants in 1967 he explained his plan and pointed out that he would need access to the new road at another point (point B) to serve the southern portion. The defendants' representative gave the plaintiff an assurance that this would be acceptable to the defendants. Although no formal grant was made to the plaintiff of any exit at point B or easement over the new road from that point, the parties thereafter acted in the belief that he had or would be granted such a right. In early 1968 the defendants erected the boundary fence and constructed gates at points A and B. The gates were clearly intended to be permanent. In September 1968 the plaintiff agreed to sell the northern portion. In the belief that he had a right of access to the southern portion at point B, he did not reserve for himself as owner of the southern portion any right of way over the northern portion to point A.

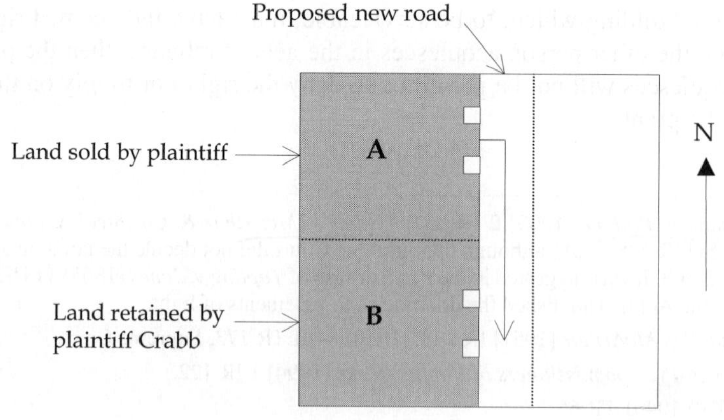

211 [1976] Ch. 179, [1975] 3 All ER 865, [1975] 3 WLR 847, 32 P & CR 70.

In January 1969, however, the defendants removed the gates at point B and closed up the access by extending the fence across the gap. They offered to grant a right of access and an easement on payment of £3,000 by the plaintiff. The plaintiff was unwilling to pay and so, without any access, the southern portion was rendered useless to him. In 1971 he began proceedings claiming a declaration that he was entitled to a right of way from the southern portion along the new road and an injunction restraining the defendants from interfering with his enjoyment of the right of way.

The trial judge held that although there was an "agreement in principle" at the meeting between Mr. Crabb and the council, there was no contract to grant an easement and an oral contract would in any case be unenforceable without written evidence under the English Land Act, 1925 which replaced the Statute of Frauds.[212]

In the English Court of Appeal Lord Denning MR, Lawton and Scarman LJJ held that this was not fatal to the claim. There was an assurance or expectation created by the council and the plaintiff had acted to his detriment in the belief that an easement would be granted. He had sold the other plot without reserving a right of way to point A. Lord Denning MR rejected the argument that the agreement in principle was conditional on a legal grant:

> "The judge found that there was 'no definite assurance' by the council's representative, and 'no firm commitment,' but only an 'agreement in principle,' meaning I suppose that, as Mr Alford said, there were 'some further processes' to be gone through before it would become binding. But if there were any such processes in the minds of the parties, the subsequent conduct of the council was such as to dispense with them. The council actually put up the gates at point B at considerable expense. That certainly led Mr Crabb to believe that they had agreed that he should have the right of access through point B without more ado".[213]

Scarman LJ agreed:

> "The nature of the legal right to be granted had to be determined. It might be given by way of licence. It might be granted by way of easement. Conditions might be imposed. Payment of a sum of money might be required. But those two men, the plaintiff and his architect came away from the meeting in the confident expectation that such a right would be granted on reasonable conditions".[214]

Lord Denning MR did not think it was relevant whether the council knew that Mr. Crabb intended to sell the other part of his land without reserving an easement himself:

212 Section 40 of the Land Act, 1925 has now been repealed in England by Law of Property (Miscellaneous Provisions) Act, 1989. Contracts for sale, *etc.* of land in England now have to be made by signed writing.

213 [1976] Ch. 179 at p.189.

214 *ibid.* at p.196.

> "The judge also said that, to establish this equity or estoppel, the council must have known that Mr Crabb was selling the front portion without reserving a right of access for the back portion. I do not think this was necessary. The council knew that Mr Crabb intended to sell the two portions separately and that he would need an access at point B as well as point A. Seeing that they knew of his intention – and they did nothing to disabuse him, but rather confirmed it by erecting gates at point B – it was their conduct which led him to act as he did; and this raises an equity in his favour against them".[215]

Scarman LJ came to the same conclusion on the point, but declined to erect it into a general principle:

> " in which it would be absolutely appropriate for a defendant to say: 'But you should not have acted to your detriment until you had had a word with me and I could have put you right.' But there are cases in which it is far too late for a defendant to get himself out of his pickle by putting on the plaintiff that sort of duty; and this in my judgment is one of those cases".[216]

The court came to the conclusion that the equity had been raised in favour of the plaintiff and that he was entitled to the easement. In view of the fact that the land had been rendered useless for a considerable period the plaintiff was not required to pay for the grant. There was no claim by the plaintiff in the original action for damages for loss caused by the sterilisation of the land and although it was held in later proceedings[217] before the English Court of Appeal that the court would have had power to grant such damages, the court held that since the issue had not been raised at the trial or the appeal of the original action, it was now too late to do so.

Atiyah[218] has criticised the case on the ground that it was unnecessary to decide it upon proprietary estoppel. In his view it could have been decided on contract. Was there really a difference between a verbal expectation or assurance intended to be acted upon and a promise? There was, as the court found, an agreement in *Crabb*. The absence of written evidence should not have been fatal to contract. There was part performance, the alternative to the Statute of Frauds accepted by courts of equity.

Millet,[219] who appeared as one of the counsel for the plaintiff in *Crabb*, replied to Atiyah's criticism. Counsel for the plaintiff had conceded in both courts that there was no enforceable contract, he pointed out, and therefore, although one could criticise the wisdom of this concession, one could not legitimately criticise the judges who were bound by it. Millet argues that there were difficulties with contract, namely (a) in establishing an agreement at all, (b) in

215 *ibid.* at p.189.

216 *ibid.* at p.198.

217 *Crabb v. Arun DC (No. 2)* (1977) 121 SJ 86, per Lord Denning MR, Lawton and Scarman LJJ.

218 (1976) 92 MLR 174–80.

219 (1976) 92 MLR 342–6. He later became a judge of the Chancery Division and is now a judge of the British House of Lords.

proving consideration, (c) in establishing that there was either writing or an act of part performance and (d) that the officers of the defendant council had actual or ostensible authority as agents to bind the council. He points out that the action of Crabb in selling the other plot without reserving an easement is not an act of part performance of the agreement, as Atiyah appears to believe. It was no part of the agreement that Crabb sell the land.

The last point is no doubt correct and to suggest otherwise is to confuse detrimental reliance in estoppel with part performance in contract. But it is arguable that there were other acts which were part performance, such as the use of point B by Crabb and possibly attaching a padlock to the gate. As to the other points, the Court of Appeal found that the parties actions were only explainable if there was an agreement, that it had been agreed that Crabb should pay a reasonable amount and therefore there was consideration, even if the amount had not been exactly quantified.

It is, nevertheless, questionable whether the parties in *Crabb* had reached an agreement as to the price to be paid for the grant sufficiently definite to form a contract, or, as Millet maintains, any agreement at all. Be that as it may, the case illustrates perhaps that estoppel as a sword may inevitably begin to occupy some of the ground previously covered by contract. One should not in any case accept the assumption that because the case could have been decided in contract it could not also have been decided on proprietary estoppel.

The principle in *Crabb* was applied by Gannon J in *Dunne v. Molloy*.[220] The plaintiff sought to assert a right of way over the defendant's land. The plaintiff failed to establish a right by prescription or lost modern grant and so attempted to establish his right to an easement on the basis of estoppel by conduct. Gannon J on appeal dismissed the claim on the ground that the plaintiff had failed to establish that the defendant encouraged him to act to his detriment.

H. Acquisition of Easements by Tenants

Before the Land Purchase legislation transformed rural landholding, agricultural tenancies were a feature of land holding in Ireland. Irish Courts in the 19th century, in contrast to some other common law jurisdictions, developed the notion that tenants could acquire easements in some circumstances.[221]

1. Tenants against Their Own Landlord

Tenants can probably prescribe against land held by their own landlord under the Prescription Act, but the cases imply that this can be done only as to the 40

220 [1976–77] ILRM 266.

221 *Hanna v. Pollock* [1900] 2 IR 664.

year period.[222] They may not do so under the doctrine of lost modern grant as this requires user as of right in the full sense.[223] There is no authority as to whether a tenant can prescribe against his own landlord at common law. The point was raised in *Timmons v. Hewitt*[224] but the case was decided on the ground of implied grant. Again, the problem is whether such user could be as of right.

2. Tenants against Another Tenant of the Same Landlord

Tenants may do so under the Prescription Act, but, again, the cases say only as to the 40 year period.[225] This would seem to imply that the period during which the servient tenement was held in leasehold is not deductible under section 8. In other words, a claim will bind the landlord's reversion only if he or she does not object, under the Act, within 3 years of the reversion falling in.[226]

Probably the tenant may also claim under lost modern grant,[227] and possibly also at common law.[228] In *Timmons v. Hewitt*[229] an easement was claimed by prescription at common law by a tenant entitled under an indefinite tenancy and Palles CB held that a grant could be inferred at some time in the past by one tenant to the other. Prescription at common law would seem to require an indefinite tenancy, or at least the presumption of one. Anything less than that could not give rise to a presumption of user since time immemorial.

3. Tenants against a Limited Owner or Tenant of Another Landlord

Tenants can prescribe under the Prescription Act under the 40 year period, it is said, whether or not the landlord of the servient tenement has acquiesced in the user.[230] Both sections 7 and 8, however, require the deduction of periods during which the owner of the servient tenement is a tenant for life. Tenants may also prescribe under the doctrine of lost modern grant provided the landlord of

---

222 *Beggan v. McDonald* (1878) 2 LR Ir 560.

223 *McNaughten v. Baird* [1903] 2 IR 731.

224 (1887) 22 LR Ir 627.

225 *Fahey v. Dwyer* (1879) 4 LR Ir 271.

226 See *Beggan v. McDonald* (1878) 2 LR Ir 560, footnote 230.

227 *Tisdall v. McArthur* [1951] IR 228 at 240.

228 *Timmons v. Hewitt* (1887) 22 LR Ir 627, per Palles CB at 637.

229 (1887) 22 LR Ir 627.

230 *Beggan v. McDonald* (1878) 2 LR Ir 560. The plaintiff had a lease for 45 years of which half a year had still to run. The defendant was a lessee of another landlord. The court held that the plaintiff had obtained an easement as against the defendant although the owner of the reversion had not acquiesced in the plaintiff's user.

the servient tenement knew and acquiesced.[231] There is no authority on whether there can be prescription at common law in this situation.[232]

I. Extinguishment of Easements and Profits

1. Statute

Several statutes provide for the extinguishment of easements and profits à prendre by public bodies or officials.[233] Section 18 of the Land Act, 1965 gives power to the Registrar of Lands to cancel the registration in the Land Register of sporting rights, other than fishing rights, where they have not been exercised for 12 years after the Act came into force. It follows that the Registrar has no power to cancel the registration of such a right where a period of 12 years disuse began after the Act came into force. This once-and-for-all effect of the provision is probably because it was seen as part of the land purchase legislation.

Section 29 of the Turf Development Act, 1946 gives Bord na Móna power to terminate "any easement, wayleave, water right or other right whatsoever over or in respect of land or water" in connection with the acquisition of land for its statutory purposes.[234] There is a similar provision in the Forestry Act, 1946 section 19.

A profit may be extinguished where the servient tenement is designated as a Special Area of Conservation (SAC) under the European Communities (Natural Habitats) Regulations, 1997.[235]

2. Release

In *O'Gara v. Murray*[236] the parties were two adjoining owners of premises in Connolly Street in Sligo. Since commercial access to the defendant's licensed premises was prevented by being blocked off, the only service access was by the rear of the premises using a way to which the defendant at that time admittedly had no title. A lease of 1912 showed a gap in the rear boundary wall and some form of way giving access to the rear. The right of way was used until sometime in the 1950's since when it had not been used and had become overgrown. Later, it was cultivated as a vegetable garden by the plaintiff. The de-

231 *Deeble v. Linehan* (1860) 12 Ir CLR 1 at 15 per Fitzgerald B.

232 *Timmons v. Hewitt* (1887) 22 LR Ir 627 per Palles CB at 637.

233 See Bland, *Easements* Ch. 15.

234 The constitutionality of the section was challenged, unsuccessfully, in *O'Brien v. Bord na Móna* [1983] IR 255, 314. In the High Court it had been argued that the Board only required a right of turbary, not the fee simple, but the argument was rejected.

235 SI 94 of 1997, made under European Communities Act, 1972, implementing Council Directive 92/43/EEC.

236 Unreported, High Court, McCarthy J, 10 November 1988.

fendant had at some time since 1912 enlarged the gap in the rear boundary wall without the permission of the plaintiff. The gap had been filled in at sometime since the 1950s. McCarthy J delivering judgment in the High Court stated the position as follows:

> "A right of way or other easement may be released expressly or impliedly; such implied release may arise where it is established that there was an intention on the part of the owner of the easement to abandon it. Mere cesser of user may not be enough; cesser of user coupled with incidents indicating abandonment may well be enough".

Among the factors indicating abandonment in the instant case were: (a) the use as a vegetable garden of the area over which the right existed, (b) the filling in of the wall, and (c) the creation of a way along a different area. The judge held that whatever right of way existed in 1912 had been released by "cesser of use and surrounding circumstances".

In *Carroll v. Sheridan and Sheehan*[237] O'Hanlon J held (i) that mere evidence of non-user is not sufficient to bring about the extinguishment of private rights of way[238], (ii) that a presumption of abandonment, which is not lightly to be inferred,[239] required to be supported by evidence of conduct or intention adverse to the exercise of the right.[240] He further held *obiter*[241] that public rights over highways cannot be lost by disuse. The judge considered the question of abandonment in relation to both public and private rights of way:

> "If one were dealing with a public way, this would appear to present no problem for the plaintiffs. Byles J said in *Dawes v. Hawkins* (1860) 8 CB (ns) 848: 'It is an established maxim – once a highway always a highway; for the public cannot release their rights, and there is no extinctive presumption or prescription'. A similar conclusion was reached in *Turner v. Ringwood Highway Board* (1870) LR 9 EQ 418, where it was held that a public right over any part of a highway was not lost by disuse. 'Where the sides of the way have become covered with furze and heath, and fir trees have been allowed to grow up for 25 years, the public have a right to have the trees removed and the whole width of the road preserved free from obstruction'. In *Representative Church Body v. Barry* [1918] 1 IR 402, where a road had been stopped for over 60 years, and the public excluded therefrom, and a new road made, the court was willing to act on a presumption that the necessary legal steps had been taken to extinguish a highway if one existed, under the Grand Jury (Ireland) Act 1836, but the evi-

237 [1984] ILRM 451. For the facts, see above Prescription at common law.

238 *R v. Choley* (1848) 12 QB 515 per Lord Denman CJ.

239 *Gotobed v. Pridmore* (1970) 115 SJ 78 (Eng CA).

240 *R v. Choley* (1848) 12 QB 515 per Lord Denman CJ; *Ward v. Ward* (1852) 7 Ex 838 (right of way held not to have been lost by mere non-user for a period much longer than 20 years – way not used because the owner had a more convenient mode of access through his own land). *Crossley v. Lightowler* (1866) LR 3 Ex 279, per Page Wood VC, (1867) 2 Ch App 478, per Lord Chelmsford LC.

241 The appellants had not alleged a public right of way in their pleadings and the judge refused to allow them to amend them on appeal.

dence of non-user in the present case falls far short of the extreme situation which arose in that case.

With regard to a private right of way, the authorities appear to establish that mere evidence of non-user is not sufficient to bring about the extinction of rights of way or other 'discontinuous' easements. In *Tehidy Minerals Ltd v. Norman* [1971] 2 QB 528, 533, the Court of Appeal held that abandonment of an easement or profit *a prendre* can only be treated as having taken place where a person entitled to it has demonstrated a fixed intention never at any time thereafter to assert the right himself or to attempt to transmit it to anyone else".

3. Unity of Ownership or Possession

If the dominant and servient tenements come into the same ownership then any easements and profits will cease to exist as such and will merge into the general rights of an owner as to his or her own property.

J. Rentcharges

1. Introduction

One form of rent is rent as a service of tenure, or a rent-service. The original form was a service of freehold tenure, but an analogous form was developed as to leaseholds, which is the form of rent most familiar to people today. We have seen that a lord of a tenure had as an incident of tenure the remedy of distress. Distress was therefore the remedy where a rent-service remained unpaid, and since the remedy was an attribute of tenure it applied automatically, *i.e.* by operation of law, and did not have to be expressly created. This again was a feature of a pre-market economy that it did not leave to the parties the creation of remedies but imposed them by general law.

It has been seen that freehold rent-services still exist in Ireland by the creation of new tenures in fee simple since *Quia Emptores*, 1290 under *non obstante* grants. Where land is held under such grants the power still exists to create such interests. In theory rent-services can still be created in relation to any land where the grantor creates a life estate or fee tail, since *Quia Emptores*, 1290 only applies to fee simple estates. Such rent-services are, however, rare, because life estates and fees tail are usually created, if at all, in family settlements and members of the same family do not usually charge each other rent.

Most rent-services today, however, are rents attached to the modern landlord and tenant relationship created under Deasy's Act, 1860. A peculiarity of Irish law is that the relationship of landlord and tenant can exist where the estate is freehold. This can occur under the Renewable Leasehold Conversion Act, 1849 and under section 3 of Deasy's Act.

Rents which were not the services of tenure, freehold or leasehold, were known as rents seck, or dry rents. They were dry because the remedy of distress did not automatically apply to them. Thus, if A conveys a fee simple to B and A reserves a rent for herself without creating the modern landlord and tenant relationship under section 3 of Deasy's Act, 1860, the rent is a rentcharge. Rentcharges have existed in Ireland since the Middle Ages.[242] At common law a person entitled to a rentcharge was not entitled to distress unless the right had been expressly granted. Statutory policy has undergone an evolution, from extending the right of distress to owners of rentcharges from the seventeenth century onwards, when legislation tended to embody the interests of landowners, towards a more recent and democratic tendency to restrict the remedy. The Statute of Uses, 1634 section 4 gives a statutory right of distress where the rentcharge is created by a conveyance to uses. Statutory reforms in this area have been superseded by later provisions which do not repeal the earlier provisions. The Distress for Rent (Ireland) Act, 1712[243] section 7 conferred a right of distress on all rents seck, while the Conveyancing Act, 1881 section 44(2) confers on rentcharge owners the right of distress as soon as the rent or any part of it is 21 days in arrear.

These provisions, and the importance of distress as a remedy has declined with the passing of section 19 of the Housing (Miscellaneous Provisions) Act, 1992 which provides that no distress shall be levied for a rent, including a rentcharge, of any premises let solely as a dwelling. While this removes the remedy from landlords of rented dwellings, its effect on rentcharges is less clear. The wording of the section would seem to require that the land be let, *i.e.* held on leasehold tenure and not merely held in fee simple. It could be argued therefore that if A holds a dwelling house in fee simple subject to a rentcharge vested in B, B may still levy a distress. In such a case A's only defence would be to claim that the distress is unconstitutional under Article 40.5 of the Constitution which protects the inviolability of the dwelling of every citizen.

2. Creation

a) Statute

Rentcharges can be created by statute, the most important examples in Ireland being rentcharges created for land drainage and improvements under the Landed Property Improvement (Ireland) Act, 1847[244] and land purchase annuities under the Land Purchase Acts.[245]

---

242 In 1333 Nicholas Taafe was granted a rentcharge by the prior for acting as seneschal to the Priory of Louth: Archdall, *Monasticon Hibernicum* p.482.

243 See also Distress for Rent Act , 1741 s.5.

244 The English statute is the Improvement of Land Act, 1864.

245 See Chapter 15 Land Purchase Acts.

b) Inter Vivos

Rentcharges may be created *inter vivos* for any estate for which a grant of land can be made. Words of limitation must be used to create an express legal rentcharge, so that, to create a rentcharge in favour of A for an estate in fee simple the deed must grant the rentcharge "to A and her his/her heirs" or "to A in fee simple".[246]

The common law rule that prevents a grantor reserving a easement in his or her own favour does not apply to a rentcharge.[247] G can therefore grant land to X in fee simple and in the same grant reserve a rentcharge to himself.

Grants of rentcharges for legal estates must be by deed,[248] but equitable rentcharges can be created by any of the methods recognised in equity, such as an agreement to create a legal rentcharge or by proprietary estoppel or constructive trust.

c) Wills

Under section 94 of the Succession Act, 1965, which replaces the same provision in section 28 of the Wills Act, 1837, the whole interest in a rentcharge passes in a will without words of limitation. In England section 28 was held to apply only to existing interests and not to interests created anew.[249] The point has not been considered in relation to section 94 of the Succession Act, 1965 and practitioners would no doubt err on the safe side and, until the point is decided, use the appropriate words of limitation as in an *inter vivos* deed.

3. No Rentcharge on a Rentcharge

There can be no rentcharge on a rentcharge: a rentcharge can only be charged on or attached to a corporeal hereditament.[250]

4. Enforcement

a) Person Liable

The person liable to pay a freehold rentcharge is the terre tenant (from Norman French terre meaning land) *i.e.* the freeholder in possession.[251] In possession is used in the technical sense, meaning, in the old sense, the person who has seisin of the land, or as it would be expressed today, the holder of the immediate free-

246 See Chapter 6 Fee Simple.

247 Co Litt 143a.

248 *Hewlins v. Shippam* (1826) 5 B & C 221, 108 ER 82.

249 *Nichols v. Hawkes* (1853) 10 Hare 342, 68 ER 958.

250 *Re The Alms Corn Charity* [1901] 2 Ch. 750 at 759. In England after 1925 a rentcharge on a rentcharge is valid: Law of Property Act, 1925 s.122.

251 *Swift v. Kelly* (1889) 24 LR Ir 478 per Palles CB at 485–6; Wylie, *Irish Land Law* para. 6.140.

hold estate. For example, if the land subject to a rentcharge in fee simple held by X is held by A in fee simple but has been let for 10 years to B, the terre tenant is A. A, not B, is liable to pay the rentcharge. X's action was originally one of the real actions and so lay against the terre tenant because he or she had seisin of the land. Furthermore, distress was levied against the person in actual occupation of the land. In freehold tenure the lord of a tenure could lawfully distrain against any goods he found on the land[252] and when the remedy was extended to persons entitled to rentcharges the same rules were applied, although of course the owner of a rentcharge was not the lord of the tenure.

The position as to rentcharges held for leasehold estates is less clear. If R holds land in fee simple and grants T a term of 99 years and reserves a rent, then the rent is a rent-service, not a rentcharge, but if the land in the hands of R was already subject to a rentcharge in favour of Y for a term of years, can Y sue, or distrain against, R or T or both? The law is no longer determined by the forms of action and therefore the owner of a leasehold rentcharge cannot be denied a remedy, but is Y to have a choice of suing either R or T? If so, Y would be in a more favourable position than if he or she had a freehold rentcharge, because then Y could only sue or distrain against R. There is some authority for the view that the owner of a leasehold rentcharge can proceed against the leaseholder of the land.[253] If so, then every person intending to enter into a lease or tenancy should ask whether the land is subject to any leasehold rentcharges or require the landlord to enter into an indemnity.

b) Methods of Enforcement

(1) Distress

At common law the owner of a rentcharge had no remedy of distress: this was the point of the distinction between a rent-service and a rentcharge. The Conveyancing Act, 1881 section 44(2) confers on rentcharge owners the right of distress as soon as the rent or any part of it is 21 days in arrear, subject to a contrary intention in the instrument.[254]

The remedy of distress was always open to constitutional challenge in the Republic.[255] The Housing (Miscellaneous Provisions) Act, 1992 by section 19 prohibits distress to be levied for the rent, including rent due under a rentcharge, of "any premises let solely as a dwelling".

252 See Chapter 3 Tenure.

253 *Re Herbage Rents* [1896] 2 Ch 811. Wylie, *Irish Land Law* para. 6.140.

254 The remedies in the 1881 Act are excluded from the rule against perpetuities: Conveyancing Act, 1911 s.6.

255 The remedy has been abolished in Northern Ireland, by the Judgments (Enforcement) Act (NI), 1969 s.122.

(2) *Action for Money*

At common law the owner of a rentcharge has an action for money due on the rentcharge. The remedy was originally one of the real actions and so the ability to sue runs with the rentcharge and the liability to be sued runs with the land.

In the case of freehold land we have seen that *Quia Emptores*, 1290 provides that services of tenure are automatically apportioned on sale, *i.e.* by substitution, of part of the land. Freehold rent services existing under *non obstante* fee farm grants would therefore be apportioned unless, of course, it could be argued that the grants are exceptions not only to the prohibition on subinfeudation in *Quia Emptores* but also to its other provisions as well. Leaseholds were never subject to *Quia Emptores* and so a subletting or assignment of part of the land did not cause an apportionment, but many statutory provisions deal with the complex issue of apportionment of leaseholds and often the lease itself will provide for it.[256] Similarly, apportionment does not apply at common law to rentcharges. The terre tenant of any part is liable for the full amount of the rent, so that if O owns in fee simple land the subject of a rentcharge and sells or lets part of it to B, O remains liable for the full amount.[257] The terre tenant is liable even if the rentcharge was not created by him or her[258] but is liable only to the extent of the profits, unless he is the original contracting party and has undertaken personal liability.[259]

A method of limiting the liability of assignees of part of land subject to a rentcharge is to create indemnity rentcharges between the assignor and assignee of the part whereby the assignor grants a rentcharge to the assignee to act as an indemnity if the assignee is sued for more than a proportionate part of the rent. Thus, if land is held in fee simple by O subject to a rentcharge in fee simple in R, then if O grants part of the land to P, P cannot resist an action by R to recover the whole rent, but can in turn rely upon an indemnity rentcharge created in favour of P by O on the sale of the part.

The right to sue and the liability to be sued run with the rentcharge and the land respectively. The benefit of an express covenant for payment, however, does not run with the rentcharge without express assignment.[260]

The Fee Farm Rents (Ireland) Act, 1851 extended all the remedies of a landlord and tenant under sections 20 and 21 of the Renewable Leasehold Conversion Act, 1849, except ejectment for non-payment of rent, to fee farm rents and other rents:

---

256 Wylie, *Landlord and Tenant* para. 10.15–10.27.

257 *Christie v. Barker (*1884) 53 LJQB 537.

258 *Thomas v. Sylvester (*1873) LR 8 QB 368.

259 *Re Harding* (1861) 11 Ir Ch R 29; *Odlum v. Thompson* (1893) 31 LR Ir 394, V-C. The suggestion to the contrary in *Sligo, Leitrim & Northern Railway Co v. Whyte* (1893) 31 LR Ir 316, MR, and *Pertwee v. Townsend (*1896) 2 QB 129 is dubious.

260 *Grant v. Edmondson* [1931] 1 Ch 1, criticised in (1931) 47 LQR 380.

> "reserved and payable under any grants. . . in fee simple, or for life or lives, or for years, or for a life or lives and a term of years, or for a life or lives concurrent with a term of years, and reserving or purporting to reserve thereout rent payable to the grantor. . . where the person to whom the rent is. . . payable has. . . no reversion".[261]

At the time the statute was enacted it would seem to refer primarily to rents reserved on the grant of a lease for lives, *etc.* Such rents in strict theory were freehold rent-services[262] and the tenure freehold tenure, but because of the obscurity of the law relating to the running of covenants and remedies in freehold tenure, they had been treated in Ireland as similar to, or identical with, leasehold rents and leasehold tenure.[263] If a grantor had made a grant of such an interest and reserved a reversion the law at the time would no doubt have regarded the grant as creating tenure and therefore attaching to the rent the usual remedies of leasehold landlords. However, if no reversion were retained by the grantor on such a grant there was a controversy at the time as to whether tenure could result.[264] If tenure did not result, then the usual remedies of a landlord would not apply to the rent. The controversy was not settled in Ireland until Deasy's Act, 1860. The purpose of the 1849 statute therefore seems to have been to apply the usual leasehold remedies to such rents. However, the wording of the statute also includes rents reserved by a grantor on making a grant in fee simple, *i.e.* normal rentcharge fee farm grants. In such a case there is no reversion, but neither is there tenure, because *Quia Emptores* precludes it. The wording of the statute does, however, exclude rentcharges not originally reserved in favour of the grantor. For example, if G holds land in fee simple and grants it to F, reserving a rent, the rent is a rentcharge and the terms of the 1851 Act apply to it the remedies in the 1849 Act. The same is true if G later conveys the rentcharge to D, since the rentcharge was originally reserved by G. But if G, on granting the fee simple, had at the same time granted a rentcharge over the land in favour of X, X would not have the remedies in the 1849 Act. No rent was reserved payable to the grantor. This state of the law creates an anomaly between different types of rentcharges.

(3) Ejectment

Since a rentcharge did not imply tenure between the owner of the rentcharge and the owner of the land, the owner of a rentcharge did not have the leasehold remedy of ejectment.

---

261 Fee Farm Rents (Ireland) Act, 1851 s.1.

262 See Chapter 9 Life Estates.

263 *ibid.*.

264 See Chapter 9 Life Estates: Lease for Lives, Chapter 19 Landlord and Tenant: Reversion.

(4) Right of Entry

Section 44(3) of the Conveyancing Act, 1881 confers a right of entry where the owner of the rentcharge when the rent is in arrear by 40 days. The right of entry entitles the owner of the rent to go into possession of the land without impeachment of waste and take the profits to defray the rent and costs.

(5) Right of Re-Entry

A right of re-entry is not to be confused with a right of entry. A right of re-entry is a right to put an end to the estate of the owner of the land by forfeiture for failure to pay the rent. Equity may grant relief against the forfeiture.[265] A right of re-entry must be created by the deed creating the rentcharge.[266]

(6) Demise to a Trustee

Section 44(4) of the Conveyancing Act, 1881 confers on a person entitled to a rentcharge, where the rent is 40 days in arrear, the right to create a lease of the land to a trustee for a term of years, with or without impeachment of waste, on trust to raise the money due plus costs. The trustee will raise the money by mortgaging the term of years.

5. Extinguishment

a) Limitation

If a rentcharge remains unclaimed for 12 years the title to it is barred by the Statute of Limitations, 1957 section 13(2)[267]

b) Merger

At common law if the possession or ownership of the land and the rentcharge vest in the same person the rentcharge is extinguished by merger, regardless of the intention of the parties.

c) Release

A rentcharge may be released by deed. At common law a partial release released the whole of the land from the rentcharge,[268] but section 10 of the Law of Property Amendment Act, 1859 provides now that a partial release bars only the right to recover any part of the rentcharge out of the land released and does not affect the right of a person interested in the land remaining unreleased and not concurring in or confirming the release.

265 *Brady v. Fitzgerald* (1847) 11 Ir Eq R 55, (1848) 12 Ir Eq R 273.

266 *Stevelly v. Murphy* (1840) 2 Ir Eq R 448.

267 Section 13(2) refers to land and s.2 defines land as including a rentcharge (but not other incorporeal hereditaments).

268 Co Litt 147b.

d) Discharge

Rentcharges created under fee farm grants may be redeemed under the Chief Rents Redemption (Ireland) Act, 1864 but under this Act an application has to be made to the court and redemption is voluntary. Where the rent qualifies as a ground rent under the Landlord and Tenant (Ground Rents)(No. 2) Act, 1978 the owner of the land has the right to acquire the fee simple free of the rent.

In addition to the above, under section 5 of the Conveyancing Act, 1881 the owner of land subject to an incumbrance, which includes a rentcharge, may sell the land free of it by obtaining the permission of the court to lodging a sum of money in court, the sum being sufficient to provide an income, after investment in government securities, to pay the annual amount.[269] An application may also be made under the Landed Estates Court (Ireland) Act, 1858 for redemption of the rentcharge or sale of the land.[270] Section 45 of the Conveyancing Act, 1881 which provided for redemption of rentcharges expressly did not apply to Ireland.[271]

In addition to the above, where a rentcharge is created in a grant also creating a settlement of the land within the Settled Land Acts, 1882-90 the rentcharge will be overreached on sale under the Acts and become a charge on the proceeds of sale in the hands of the trustees of the settlement.[272]

K. Franchises

The common law recognised that the Crown could grant exclusive rights, *i.e.* monopolies, to individuals, known as franchises. These were grants of part of the royal prerogative, such as the right to hold fairs or markets,[273] to wrecks[274] and to treasure trove[275] and the right to fish in rivers and tidal waters. The right to grant fishing rights was taken away from the Crown by Magna Carta, 1215[276]

---

269 *Re McGuiness's Contract* (1901) 35 ILTR 65.

270 See ss. 58–9, 68 and 71.

271 Section 45(7).

272 See Chapter 14 Settlements of Land: Trusts for Sale.

273 *Waugh v. Treasurer of The Grand Jury of Cork* (1847) 11 Ir CLR 451; *Russell v. Beakey* (1846) 8 Ir Eq R 559; *Cork Corporation v. Shinkwin* (1825) Sm & Bat 395; *Midleton (Lord) v. Power* (1886) 19 L R Ir 1.

274 *The Jeane Adolphe* (1857) 2 Ir Jur (ns) 285; W. N. Osborough, "Discoveries from Armada Wrecks" (1970) 5 Ir Jur (ns) 88; S. Dromgoole, "The Protection of Historic Wreck: The UK Approach" (1989) 4 Int J of Estuarine and Coastal Law 26 pt. 2, 95. See now Merchant Shipping (Salvage and Wreck) Act, 1993.

275 *Attorney General v. Trustees of the British Museum* [1903] 2 Ch. 598 at 608; The case is discussed above, Chapter 1 Introduction: Treasure Trove.

276 Cap 16, and see above footnote 100 and footnote 101.

which prohibited such grants after the date of the charter. Such fisheries as can be proved to have been granted before Magna Carta still exist today.[277]

In the 16th century the Crown attempted to extend the prerogative into the growing sphere of commerce, as a means of increasing its income, and to grant to individuals a monopoly over the production of given products, such as playing cards.[278] If this attempt had succeeded it would have created a barrier to the growth of capitalism, but it was opposed by the judiciary of the time who refused to allow such an extension of royal power. Franchises of markets and fairs had existed since the Middle Ages and so remained unchallenged. They also did not interfere with commerce.

L. Obsolete Hereditaments

1. Tithe Rentcharges

A tithe was the right of the church, usually vested in the rector of a parish, to one tenth of the produce of all land in the parish.[279] The dissolution of the monasteries under Henry VIII had the effect of secularising tithes and vesting them in lay proprietors, both individuals and educational institutions, who had purchased the rectories and vesting others in a church which was not the church of the majority of the Irish people.

Tithes in kind were abolished by the Tithes Composition Acts, 1823-36 which substituted money compositions charged on the land. The next change came with the Church Temporalities Act, 1833 which enabled tenants holding land from ecclesiastical bodies to acquire the fee simple subject to fee farm rents which were varied every seven years according to changes in the price of corn. The Tithe Rentcharge (Ireland) Act, 1838[280] abolished tithe compositions and replaced them with annual tithe rentcharges. The rentcharges were payable by the landlord of the land and not by the tenant who was legally relieved of the burden. Landlords could nevertheless pass on the cost to tenants in increased rents and so the legislative strategy was badly thought out. Tithe rentcharges still formed a significant part of the income of the Church of Ireland in the nineteenth century.

277 *Little v. Cooper* [1937] IR 1 (River Moy, Co Mayo); *Moore v. Attorney General* [1934] IR 44 (River Erne, Co Donegal); Wylie, *Cases* p.5.

278 *Darcy v. Allein (The Case of Monopolies)* (1602) 11 Co Rep 84b, 77 ER 1260; D. O. Wagner, "Coke and the Rise of Economic Liberalism" Economic History Review, 1st series p.30; Chrisopher Hill, *Intellectual Origins of the English Revolution* (Oxford, Clarendon, 1965) especially Chapter 5 "Sir Edward Coke – Myth-Maker".

279 Wylie, *Irish Land Law* para. 6.120–6.129.

280 See also Tithe Arrears (Ireland) Act, 1839 and the Tithe Rentcharge (Ireland) Act, 1848.

The Church of Ireland was disestablished by the Irish Church Act, 1869 which vested its property in the Commissioners of Church Temporalities in Ireland. The Commissioners were enabled to purchase the surrender of tithe rentcharges and so the owners of land subject to the charges could redeem them, although only with the consent of the Commissioners. The Irish Church Act (1869) Amendment Act, 1872 abolished the power to vary tithe rentcharge according to the price of corn. The Irish Church Act Amendment Act, 1881 dissolved the Commissioners and land held by them vested in the Irish Land Commission.[281] The next major development came with the Tithe Rentcharge (Ireland) Act, 1900, which took a backward step in, among other things, restoring the variation of tithe rentcharges, this time every 15 years according to fair or judicial rents fixed for tenanted land.

The Government of Ireland Act, 1920 apportioned the Church Temporalities Fund administered by the old Irish Land Commission between the two parts of Ireland. In the Republic the new Irish Land Commission took possession of the apportioned fund.[282] The Land Act, 1923, by section 39 gave owners of land the power to redeem tithe rentcharges as superior interests. The Land Act, 1931 ended the 15 year rent review.

Finally, tithe rentcharges and other payments into the Church Temporalities Fund were abolished in the Republic by the Land Act, 1984 section 7. Tithe rentcharges still subsist in Northern Ireland.[283]

2. Advowsons

An advowson (from Latin *advocatio,* to advise or call in aid) was the right of a landowner to appoint a clergyman, of the established church, to a living, *i.e.* to an ecclesiastical position, as priest of a parish, vicar *etc.*[284] They were one of the effects of the Dissolution of the Monasteries which turned the right to appoint priests to a parish into a secular property right vested in the local landowner. Advowsons were abolished by section 10 of the Irish Church Act, 1869 which disestablished the Church of Ireland.

---

281 See now Irish Land Commission (Dissolution) Act, 1992 s.4 (not yet in force). Land formerly held by the Commission is to vest in the Minister for Agriculture and Food.

282 See now Irish Land Commission (Dissolution) Act, 1992 s.4 (not yet in force).

283 For a more detailed account of tithe rentcharges see Wylie, *Irish Land Law* para. 6.120–6.130.

284 *Executors of Marquis of Winchester v. Bishop of Killaloe* (1846) 9 Ir LR 107, Smythe 125, CP; *Irish Society v. Bishop of Derry* (1841) 4 Ir LR 193, Ex Ch, (1846) 8 Ir LR 467, 12 Cl & Fin 642, 8 ER 1561, House of Lords.

3. Titles of Honour and Offices

Titles of nobility, or honour, such as peerages, were granted as part of the Royal prerogative. In the past they were usually accompanied by a grant of land and so they became themselves regarded as real property, specifically as incorporeal hereditaments.[285] They also resembled real property in that they were granted for estates, usually in fee tail male,[286] although sometimes in fee tail general so that in such cases the peerage could be held by a woman, *i.e.* a peeress in her own right. In the *Wensleydale Peerage Case*[287] the Committee of Privileges of the House of Lords decided that the Crown could not, in modern times, create a peerage for life at common law[288] so as to confer on the recipient the right to sit and vote in the House of Lords.

Peerages were used in Ireland as bribes to members of the Irish Parliament to vote for the Union[289] and this history led to the grant of titles of nobility being prohibited since 1922.[290] Article 40.2 of the present Constitution provides that:

1) titles of nobility shall not be conferred by the State;
2) no title of nobility or honour may be accepted by any citizen except with the prior approval of the Government.

---

285 Challis, *Real Property* p.468; *Berkeley Peerage Case* (1861) 8 HLC 21 at 118; *Buckhurst Peerage Case* (1876) 2 App Cas 1 at 20-1; *Re Rivett-Cranac's Will* (1885) 30 Ch D 136; *Cowley (Earl) v. Cowley (Countess)* [1901] App Cas 450, CA (reversed on other grounds by the House of Lords); Gadd, *Peerage Law* p.14.

286 Hence descent is traced from the original donee.

287 (1856) 5 HLC 958. Queen Victoria purported to create Sir James Parke, a baron (judge) of the Exchequer, a baron for life in the House of Lords. Strictly speaking the speeches in the Committee of Privileges support the view that the crown could create a life peerage, but the holder would not be entitled to sit or vote in the House of Lords. Parke B was later given a hereditary peerage. No attempt has been made since to create a life peer at common law. See Simpson, *Biographical Dictionary* p.401–3; Gadd, *Peerage Law* 8–9.

288 Life peerages may be created in the United Kingdom under the Life Peerages Act, 1958. Lords of Appeal in Ordinary, *i.e.* judges of the House of Lords, are also peers for life and are created under the Appellate Jurisdiction Act, 1876.

289 In the period between the appointment of Marquis Cornwallis as Lord Lieutenant in July 1798 and the Union, which came into effect on 1 January 1801, 28 Irish peerages were created, six Irish peers obtained British peerages and 20 Irish peers obtained peerages of higher status (Lecky, *History of England in the Eighteenth Century* vol. VIII p.398). Charles James Fox, speaking in the British House of Commons on 23 March 1797, commented that it was the policy of the Irish Government "by the sale of peerages to have a purse to purchase the representation, or rather the misrepresentations of the Irish people". See Macneill, *Studies in the Constitution of the Irish Free State* p.34–5.

290 Article 5 of the 1922 Constitution. Anon "The Constitution and the Acceptance of Honours" (1946) 80 ILT 165.

Peerages can therefore no longer be created. Existing ones no longer have legal consequences in the Republic.[291]

Offices were sometimes granted in the medieval period by the Crown to appointees as hereditaments, *i.e.* as hereditary offices in tail or, possibly, in fee simple, such as, in England, the office of Earl Marshall to the Duke of Norfolk. Offices were also granted for life, an example in Ireland being the grant in 1232 by Henry III of the Chancery of Ireland to the English Chancellor, Ralph Neville, Bishop of Chichester, for life.[292] Offices for life were not hereditaments but were similar to real property being granted for an estate. It is doubtful if any power now exists in the Republic to grant offices for estates.

291 The only attribute in the United Kingdom of an Irish peerage where the holder is not also a British peer is the right to attend a coronation.

292 Otway-Ruthven, *Medieval Ireland* p.154 *et seq*.

CHAPTER 23

MORTGAGES

"... the emergence of a property-owning, particularly a real-property-mortgaged-to-a-building-society-owning, democracy..."

– Lord Diplock in *Pettit v. Pettit* [1970] AC 777.

"No one... by the light of nature ever understood an English mortgage of real estate."

– Lord Macnaughten in *Samuel v. Jarrah Timber & Wood Paving Corporation Ltd* [1904] AC 323 at 326.

"Defence scientists have discovered a way of killing human beings in the most horrible way imaginable while leaving buildings perfectly intact: it's called a mortgage."

– Alexei Sayle

A. Introduction

The distinction incidentally pointed out by Lord Diplock is one full of implications, one of which is that the rights of mortgagees constitute the main limitation on the property-owning nature of modern Western societies. Owning one's own house is seen as an important aspect of a free society and yet the reality for most people is that for much of their lives they have a relationship with a building society or bank in which the lending agency has a dominant power. The average of 20 years is a long time to wait to own a fee simple outright and in the meantime continued ownership and possession are dependent upon keeping up the payments which fluctuate with changes in the interest rate, which is beyond the individual's control and largely beyond democratic control.

B. History

Feudalism was based upon the appropriation by feudal lords of the labour of the villeins, either in its natural form or in the form of useful products, products which the lord would consume or pass on to others to consume. Feudalism was largely based upon use values rather than upon commodities. A feudal lord did not receive his income by first advancing money to the villeins and receiving more money in return. Usury, the making of money out of money, appeared to be an unnatural and therefore evil practice. The classic statement of the feudal abhorrence of usury is that of Dante in his *Inferno* where he says that "all bankers will go to Hell because making money out of money is immoral".[1]

Usury was also condemned by the Church as sinful. As capitalism developed, however, methods were found of avoiding the feudal prohibition.[2] The borrower would lease land to the lender who would go into possession. The reason for this was that, in a society dominated by the feudal mode of production, capital, as a monetary profit derived from money invested, was, as we have seen, an abnormal form: income from land, on the other hand, even in the form of money, was not usury but the normal feudal service of tenure. Rather than risk the penalties attached to usury, the early money-lending capitalists went into possession of the borrower's land and so the return on their loan appeared instead as the return on the land, the normal and legitimate form.[3]

The lender would keep the income from the land. If the income was used to pay off the interest and the debt itself the transaction was known as *vivum vadium*, or living pledge. The debt was self-redeeming. In the other form, known as *mortuum vadium*, a dead pledge, or mortgage, the lender in possession still kept the income from the land, but it did not pay off the capital.[4] The income from the land was merely the interest on the loan. In this case the borrower would have to find the money to repay the loan from elsewhere. It was therefore a more oppressive form and could lead to the unfortunate borrower never being able to repay the loan, particularly if he was a small farmer or peasant and the land represented his main source of income. The Church still regarded this form as sinful for some time, but it ceased to be against the law.

In the original form of common law mortgage the fee simple was conveyed to the lender on condition that when the debt was paid on a given date the fee would be reconveyed to the borrower. This is still an important form of mortgage in Ireland. Originally, possession of the land was passed to the mortgagee by livery of seisin.

1 *Inferno,* Canto 6.

2 See R.H. Tawney, *Religion and the Rise of Capitalism* (London: 1926) pp. 36–55, 150–64; see p.297 n.69 for a description of devices to avoid the prohibition. It is interesting that a similar development took place in societies in which Islam was the dominant ideology. The Koran also condemns usury. Sûra 2, 276 reads:

> "Those who devour usury shall not rise again, save as he riseth whom Satan hath paralysed with a touch; and that is because they say, 'Selling is only like usury'; but God hath made selling lawful and usury unlawful;... But whosoever returns [to usury], these are the fellows of the fire, and they shall dwell therein forever". (Roberts, *The Social Laws of the Koran* (1925 London.)

Usury at first meant any return on capital but was later revised to denote only excessive interest: J.N.D. Anderson, *Islamic Law in Africa* (1955 London).

3 J.B.C. Murray, *History of Usury*, Chapter II.

4 Bl Com Sec III of Chapter X (Of Estates Upon Condition) p.156.

Later, as feudalism declined, capitalist forms came to be accepted and usury came to mean only an excessive return on money advanced. It was no longer necessary for the lender to resort to entering into possession of the land, but the old form of mortgage remained. Because it was used to accomplish a purpose for which it had not been designed, many harsh results flowed from it, for "...the common law knew of no better way to treat debtors than to make them live up to their bargains...".[5]

To the common law judges the date expressed in the deed as the date when the debt was to be repaid, known as the legal date of redemption, was decisive. If the debtor did not repay the debt on that date, then the condition for reconveyance could not be enforced and the lender was left with the fee simple absolute. If the debtor was only one day late, he or she could no longer redeem the property. To remedy this situation, Chancery evolved the equity of redemption by holding that although equity could not alter the legal effect of the forfeiture at common law, it could operate on the conscience of the mortgagee. Equity declared it unreasonable that he or she should retain for his own benefit what was intended as a mere security. In the words of Lord Nottingham:

> "In natural justice and equity the principal right of the mortgagee is to the money, and his right to the land is only as security for the money".[6]

Equity held that the mortgagor had an equity to redeem on payment of the debt and interest.[7] The equitable views finally made their way into the common law in the opinions of Lord Mansfield who took his approach from Scots law, where law and equity are not distinct systems of rules.

C. Financial Aspects: Repayment versus Endowment

From the financial point of view there are two main types of mortgage in use at the present time – the repayment mortgage and the endowment mortgage.

In the repayment form of mortgage the mortgagor pays back a sum each month which is partly composed of interest paid on the loan and partly of repayment of the capital, *i.e.* the loan itself. It is calculated in such a way that in the early years of the mortgage most of the monthly sum consists of interest and only a small part consists of capital repayment. Over the period of the mortgage, which is usually about 20 years, the proportion of the sum which is capital repayment increases and the proportion which is interest declines. In addition to these two elements of interest and capital the borrower will also pay a monthly life assurance premium to ensure that should he or she die before the end of the mortgage period, the building society or the bank will get their

5 Thomas, *Mortgages* p.6.

6 *Thornborough v. Baker* (1675) 3 Swans 628 at 630, 36 ER 1000 at 1001.

7 Coote, (1904) Chapter II (iii) pp. 12, 13.

money. Since the capital is being repaid throughout the period of the mortgage the annual amount of interest on the loan will decline each year. Thus the total amount of interest repaid over the 20 years, although substantial, is less than the cost of borrowing the total amount of the loan over 20 years. This is in fact the principal advantage of the repayment method from the point of view of the borrower. On the other hand, it is usual for the government to allow tax relief on mortgage interest repaid in given tax year and also on life assurance premiums. Since, in the repayment method, the amount of interest repaid each year declines, there will come a year in which the amount of interest repaid by the borrower equals the amount of tax relief allowed, and in subsequent years the interest repaid will be less than the tax relief, so that the borrower is not gaining the benefit of the full tax relief allowance. This is the principal disadvantage for the borrower in the repayment method.

In the endowment method none of the capital is paid off until the end of the mortgage. Thus the borrower borrows the entire amount of the capital over the whole period. The monthly sum paid in respect of the mortgage loan consists entirely of interest and this is so for the whole period of the mortgage. This is the principal disadvantage of this method from the point of view of the borrower, but the principal advantage of the method from the point of view of the building societies and the banks who lend mortgage money. Not surprisingly they will often try to persuade potential borrowers of the great benefits of endowment mortgages.

In addition to the monthly payment of the interest the borrower will also make a monthly contribution to an investment fund – the endowment fund. All the contributions of borrowers are invested by the building society or the bank and each contributor is credited with a number of units which increase over the period and which are themselves valued by the building society or bank. The total fund is thus a unit trust. It is the individual borrower's fund, consisting of units in the unit trust, which is used to pay off the entire loan at the end of the period of the mortgage. It also includes an element of life assurance. The growth of the value of the fund naturally depends on the growth of the stocks and shares in which it is invested and this has to be estimated so that the appropriate monthly sum to be paid into the fund can be decided on. It should be stressed that it is only a calculation as to how much invested each month will build up into a sum sufficient at the end of the period to pay off the loan. Thus, the expected percentage of growth in shares over the period is very conservatively estimated, so that if the annual growth in share prices has been 10 per cent a year in recent years, the growth in the value of the unit fund may be estimated at 7.5 per cent. This means that if the actual growth exceeds the estimated growth the fund at the end of the period will be more than sufficient to repay the mortgage loan and the borrower will be left with a surplus.

This expected surplus is an advantage of the endowment method, often stressed by those who sell them. A similar effect could, however, be produced by a repayment mortgage plus a separate investment/life assurance fund, on which tax relief is usually allowed and in fact may be treated as the same for tax purposes as a similar endowment fund which is part of a mortgage. On the other hand, it should not be forgotten that if the expected growth in the fund is less than the conservative estimate, then the borrower would be left at the end of the period with insufficient funds to pay off the mortgage.

In relation to any individual the advantages and disadvantages of the method will work in a different way, depending on their age, marital status and on whether they have dependants and may indicate that the repayment method is more advantageous, or less advantageous, than the endowment method.

D. Similar Interests

1. Pledges

A pledge is similar to a mortgage in that rights in an article of property are conferred on a lender (pledgee) as security for the repayment of a loan. But a pledge is unlike a mortgage in that (a) it applies to personal property and not land, (b) the pledgee takes possession as part of the transaction, but (c) the pledgee does not acquire any form of ownership in the pledged article.

The pledgee does acquire certain rights over the article in order to realise the security for the loan, such as a right to sell it. These rights are governed by the Pawnbrokers Act, 1964.[8]

2. Liens

Liens are institutions developed both by the common law and the courts of equity. They differ from mortgages in that they are not truly created by act of parties, but are in the nature of remedies imposed by a court consequent on some other transaction.

8 As amended by the Consumer Credit Act, 1995 s.154 & 8th Schedule. In Northern Ireland they are regulated by the Consumer Credit Act, 1974 (UK).

a) At Common Law

A common law lien arises by operation of law and is a mere right to retain possession of property until a debt, owed by the owner of the property, has been paid.[9] Unlike a mortgage or a pledge it carries with it no right to sell the property or indeed to deal with it in any other way. If the holder of the lien parts with possession of the property to anyone, except his or her own agent, the lien is at an end. The retention of possession is simply a lever which the creditor has which may induce the debtor to pay up. Common law liens have been held to apply to garage owners, giving them the right to retain possession of cars until a repair bill has been paid, to the owner of horse stables[10] and ship owners.[11] Solicitors have a lien over a client's documents while costs are unpaid.[12] The deposit of title deeds or a land certificate with a bank as security for a loan creates an equitable mortgage, but not a common law lien.[13]

b) In Equity

An equitable lien arises in situations in which equity confers on a party a means of protecting their interest. Thus, a vendor's lien for unpaid purchase money gives a vendor of land a lien on the property as soon as the contract is entered into and continues until the purchase money has been paid in full. If he or she has possession, which would normally be the case at least until the conveyance is executed, it may be retained,[14] but once possession has been given to the purchaser it cannot be reclaimed. Instead, the vendor is entitled to go to court for a declaration of a charge on the property which can be enforced by an order for sale.

A purchaser of land has an equitable lien to secure the return of any part of the purchase money paid if the contract is unenforceable through no fault of his own.[15] The effect of this is to give the purchaser priority, as secured creditor,

---

9 *Re Barrett Apartments Ltd* [1985] IR 350, 356, [1985] ILRM 679, Supreme Court per Henchy J.

10 *Lee v. Irwin* (1852) 4 Ir Jur (os) 372

11 *The Princess Royal* (1859) 5 Ir Jur (ns) 74; *Belfast Harbour Commissioners v. Lawther* (1866) 17 Ir Ch R 54.

12 *Re Galdan Properties Ltd (In Liquidation)* [1988] ILRM 559, Supreme Court; *Re Burrowes Estate* (1867) IR 1 Eq 445 (equitable lien before Judicature Act).

13 *Re Farm Fresh Frozen Foods Ltd (In Liquidation)* [1980] ILRM 131, High Court, Keane J. Bankers have a general lien over title deeds coming into their possession in the course of banking business, but this does not extend to deeds deposited as security for loans.

14 *Shaw v. Foster* (1872) LR 5 HL 321.

15 *Re Barrett Apartments Limited* [1985] IR 350 at 356, [1985] ILRM 679 Supreme Court per Henchy J, and see the judgment of McCarthy J approving of the statement of Keane J in the High Court [1985] IR 350; *Tempany v. Hynes* [1976] IR 101, Supreme Court; *Rose v. Watson* (1864) 10 HLC 672, 11 ER 1187; and see Appendix A in the

over the other creditors of the vendor should the vendor become insolvent.[16] Such a lien is to be distinguished from the purchaser's equity which arises when a contract has been entered into and part of the purchase money paid[17] where the contract is enforceable. The purchaser's equity gives the purchaser an equitable interest or estate in the premises, and he or she can join third parties in an action for specific performance of the contract and so obtain a conveyance.[18]

It is normal today for an intending purchaser to pay a booking deposit to the developer of a housing estate so that the house will be reserved for the purchaser. The arrangement is conditional on a contract being signed. Such an intending purchaser does not acquire an equitable lien for the return of the booking deposit. The Supreme Court in *Re Barret Apartments Ltd*[19] refused to recognise that such an intending purchaser had an equitable lien which would give the purchaser priority over the other creditors of the vendor. Equitable liens are the means by which the economic risks surrounding a market transaction are distributed by the legal system. If a policy is detectable behind the rules, it seems to be that parties to a land transaction are more favourably treated than ordinary commercial creditors if a contract has been entered into, but before a contract is formed the intending purchaser has to take the same risk as other commercial creditors. Some liens have been created by statute, such as the solicitor's right to apply to the court for a charging order over property of a client recovered or preserved in litigation.[20]

first edition of this work.

16 *Re Barrett Apartments Limited* [1985] IR 350 at 356 per Henchy J.

17 *Tempany v. Hynes* [1976] IR 101, Supreme Court.

18 *Rose v. Watson* (1864) 10 HLC 672, 11 ER 1187; *Whitbread & Co Ltd v. Watt* [1902] 1 Ch. 835.

19 [1985] IR 350 at 356, [1985] ILRM 679.

20 Legal Practitioners (Ireland) Act, 1876, s.3; *Re Legal Practitioners (Ireland) Act, 1876* [1951] Ir Jur Rep 1.

3. Judgment Mortgages

Judgment mortgages[21] in Ireland[22] are a means of enforcing a judgment. If B owes A a debt and does not pay, A may sue and obtain a judgment against B for the amount. If B does not pay the judgment debt then A may file in the court in which the judgment was entered an affidavit containing details of the judgment.[23] A copy of the affidavit is then registered in the Registry of Deeds,[24] or, if the title to the land is registered, in the Land Registry.[25]

If the land is misdescribed then it is likely that the affidavit will be held to be invalid, but the lack of any statutory formality is not necessarily fatal to the validity of the affidavit and the courts have tended to take a purposive approach.[26] The purpose of describing the judgment debtor's place of abode is to distinguish him or her from all other persons, not to provide an exact description of where he or she might be found.[27] The description of a person's title, trade or profession has been held not to be satisfied by a description of the person's marital status, such as widow[28], but satisfied where misdecribed as proprietor rather than building contractor.[29]

a) Priorities

A judgment mortgage is not a charge for valuable consideration and so in unregistered land a judgment mortgage registered in the Registry of Deeds is subject to all equities affecting the mortgagor at the time of registration of the judgment mortgage, including unregistered deeds.[30] This marks it out as distinct from ordinary mortgages.

In registered land the same principle applies and under the Registration of Title Act, 1964 section 71(4) a judgment mortgagee takes subject to unregistered

21 See the Judgment Mortgage (Ireland) Acts, 1850 and 1858 and the Judgments (Ireland) Acts, 1844 and 1849.

22 In Northern Ireland the procedure has been replaced by a form of charge: Judgments (Enforcement) (NI) Act, 1969 and Judgments (Enforcement) (NI) Order, 1981.

23 1850 Act s.6. See Wylie, *Irish Land Law* 13.163–13.182.

24 *Re Flannery* [1971] IR 10.

25 Registration of Title Act, 1964 s.71.

26 *O'Connor and Son Ltd v. Whelan* unreported, High Court, Denham J, 26 July 1991 (absence of "means of knowledge" clause not fatal where concerning issue not in dispute), distinguishing *Credit Finance Limited v. Hennessy* unreported, 25 May 1979; *Thorpe v. Browne* (1867) LR 2 HL 220, per Chelmsford LC at p.232.

27 *Irish Bank of Commerce Ltd v. O'Hara,* unreported, High Court, Costello J, 10 May 1989, upheld on appeal: unreported, Supreme Court, 7 April 1992.

28 *Allied Irish Banks plc v. Griffin* [1992] ILRM 590, High Court, Denham J.

29 *Ulster Bank* Ltd *v. Crawford*, unreported, High Court, Laffoy J, 20 December 1999, FL2147.

30 *Eyre v. McDowell* (1861) 9 HLC 619 at 620, 11 ER 87.

rights binding upon the mortgagor. Thus, in *Tempany v. Hynes*[31] the Supreme Court held that such a mortgagee of registered land takes subject to a purchaser's equity existing at the time of registration of the judgment mortgage.

A qualification on the foregoing is the principle in Ireland that a subsequent registered deed carries a judgment mortgage on its back, so that a subsequent registered deed for value secures priority not only for itself, but also for a judgment mortgage, over prior unregistered deeds, but only where the priority of the subsequent mortgage as against the unregistered deeds is in issue.[32] Whether this applies to registered land is open to question.

b) Effect

Section 7 of the Judgment Mortgage (Ireland) Act, 1850 provides that the registration of the affidavit of the judgment in the Registry of Deeds operates "to transfer to and vest in the creditor. . . all the lands, tenements and hereditaments mentioned therein, for all the estate and interest of which the debtor mentioned in such affidavit shall at the time of such registration be seised or possessed or have disposing power at law or in equity", subject to redemption on payment of the judgment debt. Where the land is subject to a joint tenancy the provision has the effect of severing the joint tenancy.[33]

In the case of registered title, on the other hand, registration of the judgment mortgage in the Land Registry does not have the same effect. It merely operates to charge the interest of the judgment debtor and the judgment creditor has such rights and remedies for enforcement as the court may order.[34]

The registration of a judgment mortgage only affects such property as the debtor possessed beneficially at the time of the judgment.[35] Hence, it cannot be registered against future interests.[36]

In *Containercare v. Wycherley*[37] Carroll J held that a judgment mortgage registered by a judgment creditor of a husband is not a conveyance by a spouse within section 3 of the Family Home Protection Act, 1976 and so could be registered without the consent of the non-conveying spouse.

The judge further held that section 7 of the 1976 Act, allowing proceedings to enforce the security of the mortgage to be adjourned where the other spouse is capable and willing to pay, only applied to instalment mortgages and so did not apply to judgment mortgages. However, on the principles discussed above

31 [1976] IR 101.

32 *Latouche v. Dunsany* (1803) 1 Sch & Lef 137; *Re Scott's Estate* (1862) 14 Ir Ch R 57; Wylie, *Irish Land Law* para. 13.181-2.

33 *McIlroy v. Edgar* (1881) 7 LR Ir 521; *Provincial Bank v. Tallon* [1938] IR 361.

34 Registration of Title Act, 1964 s.71(4).

35 1850 Act, s.6.

36 *Re Rea's Estate* (1877) 1 LR Ir 174.

37 [1982] IR 143.

a judgment mortgagee takes subject to equities affecting the husband and at least where the wife has an equitable interest in the premises, the court has a discretion.

c) Judgment Sub-Mortgages

It is possible for A to register a judgment mortgage against the land of B, which gives A an interest in the land, and then for C to obtain a judgment against A and to register a judgment mortgage against the interest which A has in the land of B under his, A's, judgment mortgage. This creates a sub-mortgage in C.[38]

4. Welsh Mortgage

A Welsh mortgage is an ancient form of mortgage still found in some common law jurisdictions.[39] It is now rare in Ireland. Its ancient and peculiar form is shown by the characteristic that the mortgagee goes into occupation of the land. The lender is entitled to take the rent and profits of the land instead of interest on the loan. Sometimes the loan itself remains outstanding and is not diminished by the income from the land. In other cases rent and profits may provide a way of paying back capital as well as interest.[40]

Where possession is in lieu of interest only, the mortgagee is not liable to account to the mortgagor for the rents and profits since he is entitled to whatever income the land produces.[41] The mortgage loan is not a simple debt for which the mortgagor can be sued.[42]

The mortgagee cannot force the mortgagor to redeem and the mortgagee does not have other remedies such as sale. The mortgagor, on the other hand, may redeem at any time, however remote,[43] although it was said in *Dunsany (Lord) v. Shaw*[44] that the right to redeem was equitable and could be defeated by a bona fide purchaser of the legal estate without notice of the mortgage.

38 *Rossborough v. McNeil* (1889) 23 LR Ir 409, V-C.

39 *Fidelity-Phoenix Fire Insurance Co v. Garrison* (1931) 39 Ariz. 277; 6 P.2d 47, Supreme Court of Arizona; *Humble Oil & Refining Co v. Atwood* (1951) 150 Tex 617; 1 Oil & Gas Rep 158, Supreme Court of Texas.

40 See Coote, (1904) vol. I pp. 30-35.

41 *Yates v. Hambly* (1741) 2 Atk 360 at 362, 26 ER 618 at 619 per Lord Hardwicke.

42 *Cassidy v. Cassidy* (1889) 24 LR Ir 577, QB.

43 *Conway v. Shrimpton* (1710) 5 Bro PC 187, 2 ER 617 (British HL) distinguishing *Hartpole v. Walsh* (1740) 5 Bro PC 267, 2 ER 670 (British HL on appeal from Ir Ch). *O'Connell v. Cummins* (1840) 2 Ir Eq R 251.

44 (1723) 5 Bro PC 262, 2 ER 667.

There is no right of foreclosure.[45] The mortgagee's remedy is possession and the entitlement to the profits. Since there is no fixed term the mortgagor may redeem at any time,[46] but he or she is at one considerable disadvantage: once the loan is paid off, whether automatically by the profits[47] or by the mortgagor, time begins to run under the Statute of Limitations, 1957.[48] It is a matter of construction whether a particular arrangement is a Welsh mortgage or not.[49]

The Welsh mortgage may be a variant of the obsolete *vivum vadium*[50], or simply a parallel development arising out of particular social conditions. It is a form which is appropriate to a stage in society when land produces either products in kind or monetary income but where interest rates have not crystallised into a market value. In a developed market economy lenders demand a greater degree of certainty on interest rates. It can also be a highly oppressive form where the borrower depends on the land for his income, for if the amount of land involved is large in relation to the land retained by the borrower, the handing over of possession to the mortgagee effectively deprives the mortgagor of any hope of redeeming the land. Even if this is not the case, and the income from the land is applied to repaying only the interest on the loan, that may amount to a punitive rate of interest. When the laws against usury were in force a court held that where the arrangement stipulated that the mortgagee was to have possession of the land rent free, any excess of the annual income over the legally fixed rate of interest was to be applied to repaying capital.[51] Mortgage lending is now controlled by the Consumer Act, 1995.[52]

---

45 *Balfe v. Lord* (1842) 2 Dru & War 480, 59 RR 786.

46 *Conway v. Shrimpton* (1710) 5 Bro PC 187, 2 ER 617 (British HL).

47 *Yates v. Hambly* (1741) 2 Atk 362, 26 ER 618 at 619 per Lord Hardwicke.

48 1957 Act, s.34(2).

49 *Re Cronin* [1914] 1 IR 23 (express power of sale negatives Welsh mortgage.)

50 See above, History.

51 *Gore v. Spotten* (1858) 7 Ir Ch R 508.

52 No. 24 of 1995.

E. Creation of Mortgages

1. Unregistered Land

a) Legal

(1) By Conveyance of the Fee Simple

This is the oldest form of mortgage and has been discussed earlier.[53]

(a) Conveyance and Reconveyance
Mortgage estates could have been created in the form of a determinable fee, so that the fee simple would automatically return to the mortgagor on repayment of the loan, but it was more convenient to create a conditional fee simple so that a reconveyance would be required to reconvey the fee simple. The reconveyance would be part of the title deeds. Since 1836, however, it has been provided by statute that a receipt endorsed on the mortgage deed is effective to reconvey the estate.[54] A purchaser investigating the title will only have to see whether the receipt is present or not, rather than having to make a separate check to see if the loan has been repaid.

(b) Legal Date of Redemption
A mortgage deed today is still a highly misleading document. The legal date of redemption is usually set at six months from the date of the deed, a date on which neither party intend the loan to be repaid. Nevertheless, the legal date is still of significance. The mortgagee cannot sue on the debt until the legal date has passed,[55] nor can the mortgagor redeem.

(c) Equity of Redemption
The mortgagor retains the equity of redemption, which is nowhere mentioned in the deed. The equity includes the equitable right to redeem the property, but also includes all the rights and remedies of the mortgagor and is a substantial interest in property comparable to, but by no means identical with, an equitable fee simple. It is also an interest capable of being valued. If a purchaser buys a house for £40,000 and raises a loan of £30,000 by a mortgage, conveying the fee simple to the mortgagee, then his equity of redemption is worth £10,000, *i.e.* if we assume that he can sell the house now for £40,000, then he can pay off the mortgage, and can retain £10,000. Let us say that he occupies the house for

---

53 See above, History.

54 See now the Building Societies Act, 1989 s.27 (where mortgagee a building society); Housing Act, 1988 s.18 (other mortgagees). See also s.23.12 "Discharge" below. The statute 6 & 7 Wm IV c.32 (1836) provided that a receipt endorsed on the mortgage deed was sufficient without an actual reconveyance. The 1836 Act was repealed with savings by the Building Societies Act, 1874 (c 42).

55 *Sinton v. Dooley* [1910] 2 IR 162; *Bradshaw v. McMullan* [1915] 2 IR 187.

10 years. The value of the house has risen to £47,000. In the 10 years he has also paid off part of the capital of the loan.[56] Let us assume that the loan has been reduced to £25,000. If he sold the house now he could pay off the mortgage and still have £22,000. In other words, his equity of redemption has risen in value to £22,000. Since the equity of redemption is a valuable interest it may itself be used to secure the repayment of further loans, so that the original mortgagee may create further mortgages if need be. Since the equity of redemption is a purely equitable interest any further mortgage or mortgages will necessarily be equitable as they will be mortgages of an equitable interest. The theory is less explicit beyond this point, but it must be assumed that the mortgagor then retains a new equity of redemption which, provided that the value of the property still exceeds the value of the existing mortgage debts, may itself be mortgaged, and so on. Equitable mortgages of this kind are usually by deed in order to attract the statutory remedies that apply to mortgages by deed, such as the power of sale.[57]

(2) By Demise or Sub-demise

(a) When the Mortgagor Has the Fee Simple

If the mortgagor has a fee simple a mortgage can be created by granting the mortgagee a lease. This is usually for a long period, *e.g.* 10,000 years. The advantage is that the mortgagee will not be liable under any covenants affecting the fee simple. This is especially important where the mortgagor has a fee farm grant,[58] for the mortgagee will not want to be liable to pay the rent due.

The term is subject to a clause for cesser on redemption, *i.e.* when the mortgage is redeemed the term comes to an end automatically.

One advantage of this form of mortgage is that, since the mortgagor retains a fee simple reversion, which is a legal interest, later mortgages can be legal. They are leases of the reversion.[59] The form is also used in Ireland where the fee simple is held under a fee farm grant. If the fee simple were to be conveyed to the mortgagee in such a case he or she would become liable to pay the fee farm rent.

(b) When the Mortgagor Has a Lease

If the mortgagor only has a lease and not the fee simple then a mortgage will necessarily be created by conveying a term of years to the mortgagee.

---

56 This is in practical terms the case whether the mortgage is of the non-endowment or of the endowment type.

57 Section 19 of the Conveyancing Act, 1881; see below.

58 *Re Sergie* [1954] NI 1.

59 See Chapter 19 Landlord and Tenant.

(i) By Sub-demise

The sub-demise is usually a number of days less than the mortgagor's lease so that the mortgagor retains a reversion.[60] Later mortgages can be legal, by leases of the reversion.

(ii) By Assignment

This is similar to a mortgage by conveyance of the fee simple where the mortgagor has a fee simple. The mortgagor conveys his or her lease subject to a proviso for redemption. It is rare for this form to be adopted as the mortgagee will become liable under the covenants in the lease to the mortgagor's landlord.

b) Equitable Mortgages

(1) Mortgages of an Equitable Interest

These are necessarily equitable, as for example mortgages of an equity of redemption where a fee simple owner has created a legal mortgage by conveyance of the fee simple. Another example would be where a beneficiary under a trust mortgages his or her interest. Under the Statute of Frauds, 1695 such mortgages can be created in writing signed by the assignor without a deed as an assignment of an equitable interest under a trust, but it is usual to create them by deed in order to confer on the mortgagee the remedies that apply to mortgages by deed.[61]

(2) Agreement for a Legal Mortgage

A specifically enforceable contract to enter into a legal mortgage operates itself as a mortgage in equity.[62] This is an example of the maxim of equity that "equity regards as done that which ought to be done". Thus, where L agrees to lend money to B and B agrees to give L security in the form of an interest in B's land, then once L advances the money[63] L can obtain specific performance of the agreement. In order to be enforceable the contract must comply with section 2 of the Statute of Frauds, 1695 *i.e.* there must be evidence of it in writing, signed by "the party to be charged", or alternatively there must be part performance of the contract.

---

60 Mortgage terms, not being at a rent, would seem to be outside s.3 of Deasy's Act. See Chapter 19 Landlord and Tenant.

61 For example, s.19 of the Conveyancing Act, 1881 (power of sale); see below.

62 *Card v. Jaffray* (1805) 2 Sch & Lef 374; *Abbott v. Stratten* (1846) 3 Jo & Lat 603; *Eyre v. McDowell* (1861) 9 HLC 619, 11 ER 871; *ACC Bank v. Malocco*, unreported, High Court, Laffoy J, 7 February 2000.

63 A contract to make a loan in future, whether secured by mortgage or not, cannot be the subject of specific performance by either party, since the common law remedy of damages is adequate: *Sichel v. Mosenthal* (1862) 30 Beav 371.

Various arrangements have been held to amount to a contract to create a mortgage and, provided the contract is specifically enforceable, to create an immediate equitable mortgage. In *Re Stewart's Estate*[64] creditors held a judgment mortgage which affected a life estate. When the land was sold by the Landed Estates Court the creditors agreed not to insist on immediate payment of the judgment debt on being satisfied as to the value of land held in fee simple and retained by the debtor. This agreement was held to give rise to a separate equitable mortgage of the land affecting the fee simple.

(3) Deposit of Title Deeds

An equitable mortgage may also be created by the owner of property depositing the title deeds to the fee simple, or other interest he or she possesses, or the land certificate, as security for the repayment of a loan. The deeds are usually, but not necessarily, deposited with the mortgagee. Deposit with the mortgagor's solicitor for the purpose of preparing a legal mortgage has been held sufficient, at least where the deposit implies an agreement to create a legal mortgage.[65]

If the mortgagee has been given possession of the deeds, he can retain them until the loan is paid, but if he parts with possession, the right to possession is lost.[66]

The act of deposit is sufficient in itself to constitute the equitable mortgage and therefore, since the doctrine is not based on the existence of a contract, the Statute of Frauds need not be complied with. In the case of an agreement for a legal mortgage, only a party who has signed the memorandum, or who has performed the act of part performance may enforce the mortgage, whereas here, since the enforceability of a contract is not in issue, the mortgagee can enforce the mortgage even though it is the mortgagor who has performed the act of deposit. The main security in practical terms is that, since the mortgagee has the title deeds, it will be difficult or impossible for the mortgagor to deal with the legal estate.

(4) Equitable Charge

Equity allows an owner of property to create a charge over it and this differs from an equitable mortgage properly so-called in that it does not have the effect of transferring an estate, legal or equitable, in the property.[67] It is an equitable lien rather than a mortgage. In *Re Kum Tong Restaurant (Dublin)*

---

64 (1893) 31 LR Ir 405, Monroe J. The case is discussed in detail in Chapter 4 Equity.

65 *Bulfin v. Dunne* (1861) 11 Ir Ch R 198 at 202, 204, citing *Ex Parte Bruce* (1810) 1 Rose 374, per Lord Eldon.

66 *Re Driscoll's Estate* (1867) IR 1 Eq 285.

67 *Shea v. Moore* [1894] 1 IR 158, per Walker C at 168; *Bank of Ireland v. Feeney* [1930] IR 457.

Limited[68] a company borrowed money and agreed by letter to secure the loan by holding the purchase money from the sale of its land for the benefit of the lender. The letter was held to create an equitable charge over the purchase money.

2. Registered Land

a) Legal (Registered) Charge

This is the equivalent in registered title of a legal mortgage of unregistered land.

(1) Deeds Inter Vivos

Section 62(3) of the 1964 Act provides that a mortgage in the old unregistered form *i.e.* by conveyance of the fee simple or by demise, does not in itself operate to charge the registered land. Section 62(2) provides that an instrument, if it is to charge registered land, must expressly charge the land or reserve out of the land the payment of the money secured. The charge comes into effect not from the date of execution of the instrument, but from the date of registration, as with a transfer of the registered title itself.

(2) Wills

No prescribed form is required, but the testator will have to avoid using words that apply only to unregistered land.

b) Equitable Mortgage

(1) By Deposit

Section 105(5) of the 1964 Act provides that the deposit of the land certificate [or charge certificate] has the same effect as the deposit of the title deeds in the case of unregistered land. It follows that such a deposit in itself creates an equitable mortgage binding the registered title without the necessity to register it as a burden on the title. Nor is it an overriding interest binding all purchasers regardless of registration.[69] It is an example of the survival of the equitable doctrine of notice in registered title. The practical protection of the mortgagee lies in the fact that it is impossible for the registered owner to convey the registered title without the land certificate.[70] Nor is it possible to create a registered charge without production of the land certificate.[71] This also means that it is unlikely that a later registered interest in the land could be created and unlikely

68 [1978] IR 446, High Court, McWilliam J.

69 1964 Act s.72.

70 1964 Act s.105(1), s.51.

71 Section 105(1).

therefore that the doctrine of notice would ever come into play. All that can be said is that if a registered interest were created after the equitable mortgage, the holder of it would be bound if he or she had notice of the equitable mortgage.[72]

The mortgagee can protect his or her interest by entering a caution on the register. Failure to do so might amount to negligence and deprive the mortgagee of priority[73] and so it is doubtful if the doctrine of notice in these circumstances is as extensive as in unregistered title.

(2) By Agreement

Equitable mortgages may also arise, as in unregistered title, by an agreement to create a registered charge, or by a mortgage of an equitable interest[74] but since they are not created by deposit, section 105(5) does not apply and they can only be protected by a caution entered by the person entitled to them. Mortgages of equitable interests are less frequently encountered in registered land because, since the creation of a legal charge does not transfer the legal title, subsequent charges can also be legal.

3. Mortgages by Estoppel

In *First National Bank plc v. Thompson*[75] T, who was neither the registered proprietor of the registered land concerned, nor entitled to be at that time, purported to execute a charge in favour of the bank. T then became registered as proprietor. The bank then attempted to register its charge. The English Court of Appeal held that before T became registered as proprietor a charge by estoppel had been created and when T acquired the legal estate the estoppel was fed by the legal estate giving the bank a legal charge, which they were entitled to register.[76]

F. The Position of the Mortgagee

1. Title Deeds

At common law the owner of an estate is entitled to possession of the title deeds. Thus, a mortgagee under a mortgage by conveyance of the fee simple is entitled to possession of the title deeds until redemption. This right is in itself a valuable part of the practical security, in that the mortgagor will not be able to

72 See above Chapter 24 Registration of Title.

73 *Tench v. Molyneaux* (1914) 48 ILTR 48.

74 Section 68(2).

75 [1996] Ch. 231, [1996] 1 All ER 140, 2 WLR 293.

76 The case was based upon the provisions on the English Land Registration Act, 1925, ss. 25 and 37, but the Republic's 1964 s.62 and 90 are in similar terms. For the doctrine of feeding the estoppel, see also Chapter 19.

deal with the legal estate in the land while he does not have the title deeds. It follows from this that if a mortgage is created by demise the mortgagee is only entitled to the document creating the leasehold term, unless the mortgagor expressly contracts to transfer the deeds to the freehold. Where a leasehold estate is mortgaged an analogous situation occurs. If the mortgage is by assignment of the lease, the mortgagee is entitled at common law to the document creating the lease, but if it is by sub-demise then the entitlement is only to the instrument creating the sub-lease unless a contract is made to transfer the main lease.

In the case of registered land the owner of a registered charge is entitled, by contrast, only to the charge certificate and not to the land certificate itself. The logical explanation is that a registered charge does not transfer the estate, but a more practical one is that the protection of the chargee lies in the fact that the charge is registered and so if the registered proprietor deposits the land certificate the equitable charge by deposit will not gain priority over the earlier registered charge. Moreover, the person taking deposit of the land certificate may search the register and discover the registered charge.

In the case of an equitable mortgage of unregistered land, if it is by deposit then by definition the mortgagee has the title deeds. If the equitable mortgage is created by other means the mortgagee has no right to the deeds, since he does not have the legal estate. The deeds will remain with the mortgagor or an earlier legal mortgagee if one exists.

Although the mortgagor must often surrender the title deeds to the mortgagee, the mortgagor now has by statute the right at all reasonable times to inspect and make copies or abstracts from the documents of title at his own expense and on payment of the mortgagee's costs and expenses.[77]

2. Insurance

If the value of the security were to be destroyed the mortgagee might be unable to recover the money lent, and so section 19 of the Conveyancing Act, 1881 confers on the mortgagees a statutory right to insure the property. The power is implied into mortgages by deed only, but the Registration of Title Act, 1964[78] confers on a owner of a registered charge all the rights and powers of a mortgagee implied in a mortgage by deed by the Conveyancing Acts.

In the past building societies usually inserted a term in the mortgage requiring that the insurance or other ancillary services be arranged through their own agents or insurance company. Mortgagors had little choice but to accept this term since it was found in most building society mortgages. It effectively prevented competition in the home fire insurance market. The mortgagor may

77 Conveyancing Act, 1881 s.16(1).

78 Section 62(6).

now[79] arrange his or her own insurance cover and other services and is not bound to accept an insurance policy arranged by the mortgagee. Mortgagees nevertheless can insist that the policy adequately insures their interest.

3. Fixtures

A mortgage of land includes all buildings and fixtures attached to the land.[80] The general test is that an article is prima facie a fixture if it is attached to the land by more than its own weight, unless it can be shown that it was not intended to be part of the land, and if it is only resting on the surface, it is prima facie not a fixture unless it can be shown that it was intended to be one[81] but courts may be more likely to conclude that an article is a fixture in a case between mortgagor and mortgagee than if the parties were otherwise.

In *Holland v. Hodgson*[82] looms were attached to the floor of a woollen mill by pegs driven through holes in the legs of the looms and into wooden beams set in the floor. They could be removed without damage to the floor. The Court of Exchequer Chamber was unanimous in the view that the looms were fixtures on the ground that they were attached to the land to improve its use as a factory and not merely as necessary to their use as machinery.[83] A more restrictive approach, if it is evident, has the effect, of course, of increasing the value of the security to the lender.

Although a tenant may sever and remove the class of tenant's fixtures such as ornamental, trade and agricultural fixtures,[84] a similar exception does not apply to mortgagors.[85]

79 Building Societies Act, 1989 ss. 35, 32(1)(b). Introduced by the Building Societies (Amendment) Act, 1986 s.6(1)(c).

80 Conveyancing Act, 1881 s.2, s.6.

81 *Maye v. The Revenue Commissioners* [1986] ILRM 377, High Court; *Holland v. Hodgson* (1872) LR 7 CP 328; *Leigh v. Taylor* [1902] AC 157; *Spyer v. Phillipson* [1931] 2 Ch. 183.

82 (1872) LR 7 CP 328.

83 Contrast *Webb v. Bevis* [1940] 1 All ER 247, a case of tenant's fixtures. A shed attached to the floor by being bolted to metal tags set in the floor was held not to be a fixture on the ground that it could be removed without damage to the floor. Also see *Spyer v. Phillipson* [1931] 2 Ch. 183.

84 Deasy's Act, 1860 s.17.

85 *Climie v. Wood* (1869) LR 4 Ex 328.

4. The Right to Possession

a) Mortgagees Entitled

(1) Legal Mortgages

At common law a mortgagee to whom the fee simple or any other legal estate had been conveyed had a right to possession of the land mortgaged since that was one of the rights of a legal owner.[86] The mortgagee could therefore take possession even though the mortgagor was not in default of the terms of the mortgage.[87] This essentially common law position was restated in the English High Court in *Four-Maids Ltd v. Dudley Marshall Properties Ltd*[88] by Harman J:

> "The right of the mortgagee to possession in the absence of some contract has nothing to do with default on the part of the mortgagor. The mortgagee may go into possession before the ink is dry on the mortgage unless these is something in the contract, express or by implication, whereby he has contracted himself out of that right. He has the right because he has a legal term of years in the property".

In Ireland, the mortgagee might, of course, have a legal fee simple.[89]

In the past the action by which a mortgagee sought to enforce this right was ejectment and in such a case, since it had the character of a common law action, the court had no discretion to refuse,[90] although it might adjourn the proceedings briefly if there was a prospect of the mortgagor redeeming the mortgage.[91]

Despite this, it is unusual for a mortgagee to seek possession except as a necessary step in enforcing the security by way of sale, since it would be difficult to sell the property without vacant possession.

Today where the mortgagee is usually a building society it is normal for the mortgage to provide that the mortgagee's right to possession is to be suspended, even after the legal date of redemption has passed, unless the mortgagor defaults in the periodic payments of interest and capital. The right to possession is conferred instead on the mortgagor by an attornment clause by which the mortgagor attorns or recognises himself or herself to be a tenant at

---

86 Unless the mortgagor had parted with the right before the mortgage was granted, as by granting a lease: *Moss v. Gallimore* (1779) 1 Doug KB 279 at 283, 99 ER 182. A lease granted after the mortgage would not bind the mortgagee.

87 *Four Maids Ltd v. Dudley Marshall (Properties) Ltd* [1957] Ch. 317, at 320 per Harman J; *Alliance Permanent Building Society v. Belrum Investment Ltd* [1957] 1 All ER 635, at 636 per Harman J.

88 [1957] Ch. 317 at 320, [1957] 2 All ER 35 at 36.

89 In England after 1925 a legal mortgage can still be created by a term of years, but not by conveyance of the fee simple.

90 *Ulster Bank v. Conlon* (1957) 91 ILTR 193.

91 *London Permanent Benefit Building Society v. De Baer* [1969] 1 Ch. 321.

will or periodic tenant of the mortgagee, so far as that is consistent with the mortgage.[92]

This then was certainly the position at common law before the Judicature Act, 1877 and probably remains the position today, although we consider in a section below whether there is now a discretion to refuse possession to a mortgagee when there is no default under the mortgage.[93]

(2) Equitable Mortgages

In the case of an equitable mortgage, the mortgagee has no legal estate and so has no right to possession at common law. The agreement could itself confer the right on the equitable mortgagee, but if there is a prior legal mortgage which confers the right to possession on the legal mortgagee, or on the mortgagor by a special provision, then this could only be done with the consent of whichever has the right vested in them. There is authority in Ireland for the view that an equitable mortgagee can claim possession in equity at least as against the mortgagor.[94] The mortgagee has a remedy of possession which is at the discretion of the court, as are all equitable remedies.[95]

The former procedure by which sale and possession of mortgaged property was sought was by an action claiming a declaration that the mortgagor's interest in the property was well charged with the mortgage and an order for sale if, within three months, the mortgagee did not pay the principal or interest due. The jurisdiction was therefore confined to where instalments or payments of interest or capital were due on the mortgage. At the same time, the jurisdiction also allows an order for possession to be made not merely as preliminary to an order for sale, but in any case where the court considers it proper to do so.[96] The sale was by the court itself, and this proved the main disadvantage of the action, since it was cumbersome and would realise less than a sale by private treaty.

Order 55 rule 7 of the 1905 Rules of Court,[97] now contained in the Rules of the Superior Courts, 1962, Order 54 rule 3, introduced a new procedure by originating summons.

---

92 Note that the Statute of Limitations, 1957 s.17(1)(a) provides that a tenancy at will comes to an end one year after it begins, for the purpose of the accrual of a right of action, but this does not apply to a tenancy at will created under a mortgage: s.17(1)(c).

93 See page 791.

94 *Antrim County Land, Building and Investment Co Ltd v. Stewart* [1904] 2 IR 357 per Palles CB, Wylie, *Cases* p.426, and see *Re O'Neill* [1967] NI 129 per Lowry J at 135.

95 *Bunyan v. Bunyan* [1916] 1 IR 70; *Royal Bank of Ireland v. O'Shea* (1943) 77 ILTR 4; *Irish Permanent Building Society v. Ryan* [1950] IR 12; *Re O'Neill* [1967] NI 129.

96 *Bank of Ireland v. Slattery* [1911] 1 IR 33, 40, applying Order 55, rule 7 of Rules of the Supreme Court (Ireland) 1905.

97 Rules of the Supreme Court (Ireland), 1905 Ord. 55 r.7.

The courts' view of when this discretion should be exercised has, however, undergone some change. It seems that the court may be more willing to grant possession than was the case in the past.

In *Doran v. Hannin*[98] possession was granted of licensed premises in order to prevent forfeiture of the licence, in *Bank of Ireland v. Slattery*,[99] in order to effectuate sale which was being frustrated by the interference of the mortgagor's family, and in *Bunyan v. Bunyan*[100] where no payment of principal money had been made and there was a large amount of interest in arrear. In each case there was something unusual on the facts, but more recently in *Irish Permanent Building Society v. Ryan*[101] a mortgagee had defaulted in repaying instalments of a building society mortgage and the High Court decided that possession would be granted merely on the ground that the property would fetch a higher price if sold with vacant possession, which is almost always the case. Gavan Duffy P emphasised, however, that the mortgage itself contained a clause for possession when money was due and unpaid:

> "Mortgagees have seldom sought possession under Order 55 r 7, and the Court has been slow to make an order. Nevertheless, I am of opinion that applications such as the present should be encouraged, rather than discouraged, in suitable cases, in view of the great saving in costs so far as the defendant is concerned. Having regard to the position of the defendant, I think this is a suitable case. The defendant executed an indenture of mortgage which contained a special clause, carefully drafted, enabling the mortgagees to enter into possession of the mortgaged premises if the mortgagor should be in default for the space of three calendar months in the payment of some instalment of principal and interest due under the mortgage deed. In the present case the defendant has been in default for the space of twelve months in the payment of the instalments and, in fact, has never paid any of the instalments due under the mortgage deed and has no prospect of paying any".[102]

(3) Registered Land

In registered land the registered chargee has no estate in the land and therefore no right to possession at common law,[103] but section 62(7) of the Registration of Title Act, 1964 gives the registered owner of a charge or his personal repre-

98 (1906) 40 ILTR 185.

99 [1911] 1 IR 33.

100 [1916] 1 IR 70.

101 [1950] IR 12.

102 *ibid.* at p.13-14.

103 Under s.62(6) of the Act a registered chargee has "all the rights and powers of a mortgagee under a mortgage by deed", but the phrase refers back to the earlier expression "a mortgage by deed within the meaning of the Conveyancing Acts", *i.e.* only the powers referred to in s.19 of the Conveyancing Act, 1881, hence the need for s.62(7). See also *Northern Banking Co Ltd v. Devlin* [1924] 1 IR 90.

sentative the right to apply in a summary manner for possession.[104] The power only exists where the principal sum has become due[105] and the court has a discretion to grant or refuse the order if it so thinks proper. The section was recently considered in *Bank of Ireland v. Smyth.*[106] Geoghegan J in the High Court held *obiter* that section 62(7) did not permit a discretion so wide that sympathetic factors could be taken into account.

(4) A General Discretion to Refuse Possession?

It has been seen that where the mortgagee's security is an equitable interest the mortgagee has no right to possession since the remedy he or she seeks is necessarily equitable and therefore discretionary. If, on the other hand, the mortgagee has the fee simple or a legal term of years, *i.e.* some common law right, we have seen that the common law courts before the Judicature (Ireland) Act, 1877 treated the mortgagee as any other owner of a fee simple for this purpose and upheld the right of the mortgagee to possession regardless of any default by the mortgagor, unless the mortgage limited that right. If the mortgage did not limit the right, the court had no jurisdiction to refuse an order for possession. There is some question, however, as to whether the court today is still bound by this position. Over a 120 years has passed since the Judicature Act. Should such distinctions still matter? Law and equity are now administered in the same courts. Moreover, the rule that a mortgagee who has a legal interest has a right to possession, not as a remedy even, but because it is seen as a characteristic of legal title, is a reifying concept, a conclusion not determined by the real social or economic relationship between the parties but by a supposed attribute of legal ownership. In the most common case of mortgages today, where a person is buying a house to live in and borrowing from a financial institution, the whole purpose of the mortgagor is to remain in possession and the principle interest of the mortgagee is in the return of capital and interest. Equity has long regarded the mortgagee's rights in other respects as accorded for the purpose of realising the security and not simply as an aspect of legal ownership as such. That is why equity allows redemption after the legal date of redemption has passed. Equity treats the mortgagor as the substantial owner of the property. Why should the right to possession be treated differently?

Lord Denning MR in English Court of Appeal in *Quennell v. Maltby*[107] thought there was a general discretion. The owner of a the fee simple in a house

104 The previous provision was s.13(a) of the Registration of Title Act, 1942. See *Norwich Union Life Insurance Society v. Jacks* (1953) 87 ILTR 73, Supreme Court.

105 Contrast Land Registration Act (NI), 1970 Schedule 7 part I para. 5(3)(b).

106 [1993] 2 IR 109, [1993] ILRM 790, The point was not considered in the Supreme Court judgment: [1996] 1 ILRM 241. See also *Barclay's Bank plc v. O'Brien* [1992] 4 All ER 983, where the court also scrutinised the reality of consent given by a married woman to a charge by her husband.

107 [1979] 1 WLR 318. [1979] CLJ 257 (R. A. Pearce).

mortgaged it to a bank as security for a bank overdraft. Although the mortgage contained a clause prohibiting lettings of the premises without the bank's consent, the mortgagor let the house to two university students. When the contractual period of the letting came to an end the mortgagor wanted to sell the house with vacant possession, but the students refused to leave, claiming they were statutory tenants whose possession was protected by the English Rent Acts. The mortgagor tried unsuccessfully to persuade the bank to bring an action for possession as mortgagee. He then asked the bank to transfer the mortgage to his wife on her paying off the overdraft, which she agreed to do. The bank transferred the mortgage to the wife who then brought the action, claiming that as mortgagee she had an absolute right to possession.

In these circumstances the English Court of Appeal refused to allow the Rent Acts to be evaded by the collusive device. It was accepted that the owner would not have been able to obtain possession under the Rent Acts. Denning MR pointed out that the wife had brought the action "simply for an ulterior purpose of getting possession of the house, contrary to the intention of Parliament, as expressed in the Rent Acts". Characteristically Denning MR went further and held that there was a more general equity today in relation to a legal mortgagee:

> ". . .in modern times equity can step in so as to prevent a mortgagee, or transferee from him, from getting possession of a house contrary to the justice of the case".[108]

In the judge's view this meant that a mortgagee – any mortgagee – could be restrained by the court from obtaining possession:

> "except where it is sought *bona fide* and reasonably for the purpose of enforcing the security and then only subject to such conditions as the court thinks fit to impose".[109]

The other judges in the court preferred a much more limited ground, namely that the wife was suing as agent of her husband.[110]

Lord Denning's judgment in *Quennell v. Maltby*[111] has not found favour with other English courts, partly because it rendered superfluous statutory provisions aimed at protecting mortgagors.[112] Recent English decisions have reasserted the general rule that the courts have no jurisdiction to refuse

108 [1979] 1 WLR 318 at 322G-H.

109 [1979] 1 WLR 318 at 322H.

110 Bridge and Templeman LJJ at [1979] 1 WLR 318 323E, 324F.

111 [1979] 1 WLR 318. [1979] CLJ 257 (R. A. Pearce).

112 See English Administration of Justice Act, 1970 as amended by s.8 of the Administration of Justice Act, 1973. The sections give power to the court to stay or suspend an order for possession.

possession to a legal mortgagee.[113] Nor would a cross-claim, even one exceeding the amount of the mortgage debt, by itself defeat the right of a legal mortgagee to possession,[114] although at common law a court had a residual jurisdiction to postpone an order for possession for a short time to enable the mortgagor to pay off the mortgage,[115] or to allow the mortgagor[116] or the mortgagee[117] to sell the property.

If the old position still holds, there is arguably a conflict between law and equity at the level of principle, and one which was intended to be resolved by the Judicature Act 1877. As Lowry J said in the High Court of Northern Ireland in *Re O'Neill*[118] in the context of the equitable jurisdiction to put a mortgagee in possession:

> "'The Court,' to use the words of Lord Cairns in *Pugh v. Heath* (1882) 7 App Cas 237 'is now not a Court of Law, or a Court of Equity, it is a Court of Complete Jurisdiction, and if there were a variance between what, before the Judicature Act, a Court of Law and a Court of Equity would have done, the rule of the Court of Equity must now prevail'".[119]

The common law, as we have noted, treated the owner of the fee simple as entitled to possession even where the owner was a mortgagee: equity treated the mortgagor as substantially the owner and the mortgagee as having only those remedies sufficient to enforce the security.

Apart from the equitable arguments, there is another issue that may affect the right of the mortgagee and that is the question of when a court would find an implied term in the mortgage conferring possession on the mortgagor.[120] In

---

113 *Mobil Oil Co Ltd v. Rawlinson* (1982) 43 P & CP 221 at 223f (right to possession regardless of default); *Barclays Bank plc v. Tennet,* unreported, Court of Appeal, 6 June 1984; *National Westminster Bank plc v. Jones* unreported, Court of Appeal, 3 December 1984 (right to possession *ab initio*); *Royal Trust Co of Canada v. Markham* [1975] 1 WLR 1416, Sir John Pennycuick V-C, 1420C; *Ashley Guarantee plc v. Zacaria* [1993] 1 WLR 62; *National Westminster Bank plc v. Skelton* [1993] 1 All ER 242, [1993] 1 WLR 72; *Midland Bank plc v. McGrath and Another* [1996] EGCS 61, Court Of Appeal (Civil Division).

114 *National Westminster Bank plc v. Skelton* [1993] 1 All ER 242, [1993] 1 WLR 72, CA; *Ashley Guarantee plc v. Zacaria* [1993] 1 WLR 62.

115 *Birmingham Citizens' Permanent Building Society v. Caunt and Another* [1962] Ch 883, 912 per Russell J.

116 *Royal Trust Co of Canada v. Markham* [1975] 1 WLR 1416, Sir John Pennycuick V-C, at 1420C; *Midland Bank plc v. McGrath and Another* [1996] EGCS 61.

117 *Cheltenham and Gloucester Building Society Plc v. Booker* [1997] 1 FLR 311, 73 P & CR 412, [1997] 19 EG 155, 29 HLR 634.

118 [1967] NI 129.

119 *ibid.* at p.133.

120 *Esso Petroleum Co Ltd v. Alstonbridge Properties Ltd* [1975] 1 WLR 1474 at 1484, [1975] 3 All ER 358 367; *Western Bank Ltd v. Schindler* [1977] Ch. 1, [1976] 2 All ER 393.

the case of a normal house-purchase mortgage the obvious intention of the parties is that the mortgagor is to take possession and remain there unless and until default is made.

(5) Family Home

In the case of a family home, under section 7 of the Family Home Protection Act, 1976 the court may adjourn proceedings for possession and sale where the other spouse is capable of paying the arrears due and is willing to do so. The adjournment may be for such a period and on such terms as are just and equitable. Thus, in the area of the family home, there is a legislative policy which regards the mortgagee's right to possession as only a means of enforcing the security and not an absolute right. In *McCormack v. Irish Civil Service Building Society*[121] Blayney J held that the mortgagee's right to possession is not absolute in relation to a family home. Sections 7 and 8 of the Family Home Protection Act 1976 may imply, the judge held, that a mortgagee of a family home may not enter into possession of the premises without first commencing legal proceedings, whether or not the mortgage contains an express power on the part of the mortgagee to enter into possession.

(6) Partial Restrictions

Where the mortgagee has the right to possession only after default in payment the mortgagee must allow a reasonable time for compliance before entry.[122] Where the mortgagee has the right of possession, whether after default or because there is no provision in the mortgage conferring it on the mortgagor, the mortgagee can exercise it directly without going to court, subject to what is said below as to the discretion of a court, but a mortgagee exercising the right would be subject to statutory restrictions in doing so.[123]

Where the mortgage also makes the mortgagor a tenant the restrictions as to notice etc., contained in section 14 of the Conveyancing Act, 1881[124] and the Conveyancing Act, 1892[125] also apply.

b) Strict Account

A mortgagee in possession may recoup interest due from the rents or profits of the property, and may also apply any surplus to the repayment of capital.

121 Extempore, Irish Times Law Reports, 17 April 1989, (Lexis: Transcript) High Court.

122 *Toms v. Wilson* (1863) 4 B & S 455, 122 ER 529.

123 Prohibition of Forcible Entry and Occupation Act, 1971. See Chapter 19 Landlord and Tenant.

124 Section 14, as amended by the Landlord and Tenant (Ground Rents) Act, 1967 s.35.

125 Sections 2, 4 and 5.

He or she may also recover money spent on necessary repairs or in paying rent to a landlord.[126] By statute[127] he or she may also cut and sell commercial timber. He is not liable for waste at common law, but will be restrained from committing equitable waste.

Apart from these rights the mortgagee must account strictly to the mortgagor, both for income actually received and for income which would have been received but for his default.[128]

Nor can a mortgagee in possession remunerate himself or herself as a receiver, and a provision in a mortgage which attempts to do so is void since it reduces the money available for redemption.[129] It should be noted that the possession of a mortgagee is an exception to the rule that possession must be adverse in order to extinguish title.[130]

5. Debt

The loan secured by a mortgage is also an ordinary debt and so one remedy of a mortgagee is to treat it as such and sue on the debt. The action cannot be brought before the legal date of redemption, since before then the debt is not due.[131] Equity, however, maintains the principle that the mortgagor is entitled to recover his or her interest in the land on payment of the money due under the mortgage and so will not permit the mortgagee to sue on the debt if the mortgagee has parted with his or her interest under the mortgage.[132]

6. Statutory Power of Sale

The mortgagee has the right to sell the mortgaged property in order to recover the security where the mortgagor is in breach of the terms of the mortgage. The mortgagee may exercise this right without going to court, but statute law places restrictions on the right. The exercise of the right is not effective unless the mortgagee can sell to a purchaser with vacant possession, and so, since the remedies of the mortgagee are cumulative, the mortgagee can go to court for an order for possession first. Furthermore, if the mortgagor has reason to believe that the proposed sale is in breach of the mortgagee's duty towards him, he can of course apply for an injunction to a court and to have the issue tried.

---

126 *Burrowes v. Molloy* (1845) 8 Ir Eq R 482.

127 Conveyancing Act, 1881 s.19(1)(v).

128 *O'Connell v. O'Callaghan* (1863) 15 Ir Ch R 31.

129 *Comyns v. Comyns* (1871) IR 5 Eq 583 per Sullivan MR; *Carew v. Johnston* (1805) 2 Sch & Lef 280 per Lord Redesdale LC at 301.

130 See Chapter 25 Adverse Possession.

131 *Sinton v. Dooley* [1910] 2 IR 162; *Bradshaw v. McMullan* [1915] 2 IR 187.

132 *Schoole v. Sall* (1803) 1 Sch & Lef 176, 149 RR 711 and see *Beamish v. Whitney* [1909] 1 IR 360.

At common law a mortgagee who had, under the mortgage, the fee simple, had the right to sell it, since the right to alienate is a characteristic, in reified terms, of a fee simple, but equity would force the purchaser to hold it subject to the mortgagor's equity of redemption. If the mortgagee had an equitable interest, then equity also recognised the right to sell it, but still subject to the equity of redemption.

One solution was to insert an express power of sale by executed use in the mortgage deed allowing the mortgagee to sell the fee simple free of the mortgagor's equity of redemption. Provided it allowed the mortgagee to retain, out of the proceeds of sale, only the amount of the outstanding mortgage debt and the expenses of sale, equity would recognise it as valid. But not all mortgages contained such a provision.

Section 19 of the Conveyancing Act, 1881 now confers[133] a statutory power of sale on all mortgagees where the mortgage is made by deed after 1881. The statutory power does not therefore apply to equitable mortgages by deposit of the title deeds or the land certificate and in such cases an application will have to be made to the court for an order for possession and sale out of court. Even if there is a deed, but the mortgage is of an equitable interest there may still be problems as the Act does not clearly apply to equitable interests.

a) Purchasers

So far as purchasers are concerned there is an important distinction between when the power arises and when it is exercisable. The purchaser is only concerned with when the power arises, not with whether it has become exercisable.

b) Power Arises

The power arises under Section 19(1)(i) when the mortgage money becomes due. In the case of a mortgage repayable by instalments, which is almost universal, the power arises when an instalment is in arrear.[134]

c) Power Exercisable

Under section 20 of the 1881 Act the power is not exercisable unless and until one of the three following conditions is satisfied:

(1) notice requiring repayment is served on the mortgagor and the mortgagor is in default for at least three months after service; or

(2) interest on the mortgage is in arrear and is unpaid for at least two months; or

---

133 The statutory power of sale was initiated by Lord Cranworth's Act, 1860 (23 & 24 Vict. c.145).

134 *Payne v. Cardiff RDC* [1932] 1 KB 241.

(3) there has been a breach of the provisions of the mortgage or of the Act, *i.e.* presumably, other than those requiring payment of the debt or interest. A common such provision is that prohibiting subletting of the mortgaged premises without the consent of the mortgagee.

One might notice here that if the mortgagor is not in arrear with payments of mortgage money, but has broken some other condition, such as that prohibiting subletting without consent, the power does not even arise.

d) Importance of the Distinction.

The importance of the distinction between the power arising and the power becoming exercisable lies in the passing of title to the purchaser.

If the power has not even arisen, then the mortgagee has no statutory power to convey the fee simple or other interest. If they have a common law power, as where the fee simple is vested in the mortgagee, then it is effective, but only to the extent it was before the Act, *i.e.* the purchaser acquires the fee simple, but subject to the mortgagor's equity of redemption, unless there is an express power of sale free of the equity in the mortgage itself.

If the power has arisen, but is not exercisable within the meaning of section 20, then the mortgagee has the statutory power to convey the fee simple free of the equity.[135]

The mortgagor's only remedy is an action for damages against the mortgagee. He has lost his proprietary remedy. The use of the term "exercisable" in the 1881 Act is therefore somewhat misleading. The power can be exercised in the sense of being effective to pass title, but not free of liability on the part of the mortgagee. Although the position is clear as to the remedies, the law is ambiguous here, recognising the legal effectiveness of the power in one sense, but not in another: he has the legal right to convey, but commits a legal wrong in doing so. This legal inconsistency is the expression of a moral ambiguity. Does the law approve or disapprove of the mortgagor selling in this case? The moral ambiguity shows through in the misuse of the word exercisable when it is said that the power has arisen, but is not exercisable. The power is indeed legally exercisable, but it may not be morally. The moral ambiguity is itself the result of the dominance of political economy, the concern to protect the purchaser on the market: to protect, therefore, the social relation of land as a commodity to be bought and sold with a minimum of risk. The law in the 19th century moved away from the jealous protection of mortgagors characteristic of early equity towards the protection of the purchaser.

The benefit which the purchaser enjoys here is that he need only satisfy himself that the power has arisen, which in the past could be done by examining the mortgage deed to see if the legal date of redemption had passed without the mortgage being redeemed. He did not have to inquire into the mortgage ac-

135 Section 21(2) and s.5(1) of the Conveyancing Act, 1911.

counts kept by the mortgagee. Nowadays, however, when most mortgages are repayable by instalments the purchaser will have to satisfy himself that a payment is in arrear which will require some enquiry of the mortgagee/building society, although it need not be of the extensive kind which would be the case if he had to satisfy himself that the conditions in section 20 were present. The courts have not allowed the act to be used a means of fraud and have held that the purchaser will not obtain title if he has actual knowledge of some irregularity.[136]

Section 22(1) of the 1881 Act provides that the receipt of the mortgagee discharges a purchaser from payment of the purchase money.

e) Family Home

Under section 7 of the Family Home Protection Act, 1976 a court has power to adjourn proceedings brought by a mortgagee suing for possession or an order for sale of a family home on the ground of non-payment of sums due by a spouse where the other spouse wishes to continue payments and is capable of paying the arrears within a reasonable time and future instalments. The section only applies, however, when the issue is before the court and would not apply to the mortgagee's statutory power of sale. But if application had to be made to the court for an order for possession preliminary to sale, the section would apply.

f) The Mortgagee's Duty of Care

(1) General

A mortgagee in exercising the statutory power of sale is acting in their own interest in that they are recovering the mortgage debt due to them. On the other hand, the mortgagor has an obvious interest in obtaining a good price for his property. This conflict has given rise to controversy in the case law. In the early 19th century Lord Eldon held that the mortgagee was a trustee for the mortgagor in exercising the power of sale,[137] but later in the century the mortgagee's own interest gained more recognition.

In *Farrar v. Farrars Ltd*[138] Lindley LJ held that the mortgagee had rights of his own which he is entitled to exercise adversely to those of the mortgagor. The mortgagee must act in a bona fide manner and take reasonable steps to obtain a proper price, but he is not under an obligation to postpone the sale in order to obtain a better price. In *Kennedy v. De Trafford*[139] it was said that:

136 *Bailey v. Barnes* [1984] 1 Ch. 25 at p.30 per Stirling J.

137 *Downes v. Grazebrook* (1817) 3 Mer 200, 36 ER 77.

138 (1889) 40 Ch D 395 at 398; and see *Haddington Island Quarry v. Huson* [1911] AC 722 at 727 per Lord de Villiers.

139 [1896] 1 Ch. 762, CA at p.772, affirmed [1897] AC 180, Eng HL; *Belton v. Bass, Ratcliffe & Gretton Ltd* [1922] 2 Ch. 449.

> "A mortgagee is not a trustee of a power of sale for the mortgagor at all; his right is to look after himself first. But he is not at liberty to look after his own interests alone, and it is not right, or proper, or legal, for him, either fraudulently, or wilfully, or recklessly, to sacrifice the property of the mortgagor. . .".

Section 21 of the 1881 Act, as amended by section 5 of the Conveyancing Act, 1911, provides that the mortgagee is not liable for any involuntary loss occurring in the exercise of the power of sale.

In *Holohan v. Friends Provident*[140] the mortgagees exercised their power of sale over the mortgaged premises.[141] They advertised it as an investment and without vacant possession. A lower price would be obtained for the land in such a case than if the premises were unoccupied. The mortgagor objected that they had failed in their duty in that they had made no effort to evict the tenants, that part of the premises, which had not been built on, could have been sold separately, and a mews at the back could also have been sold separately. In the Supreme Court O Dalaigh CJ held that there had been a breach of duty. The evidence did not show that the building society had given reasonable consideration to the alternative mode of sale, *i.e.* with vacant possession. The mortgagees were under a duty to act as reasonable people in considering the interests of the mortgagor. The position in *Farrar v. Farrars Ltd* may be questionable, in view of this case. If it is reasonable, in certain circumstances, to wait for a better price, the mortgagee may be under a duty to do so.

In *Casey v. Irish Intercontinental Bank Ltd*[142] the mortgagees accepted an offer of £110,000 which they considered to be a good price. They were later offered £190,000. The Supreme Court held that the mortgagees were not in breach of their duty in declining the later offer since they were bound by the first contract. Nevertheless, the fact that there exists a binding contract cannot relieve the mortgagees of any liability in damages to the mortgagor if the price under the contract is not a reasonable one. The question is whether it was reasonable to accept the offer which was accepted, as was emphasised by the Supreme Court in *Re Edenfell Holdings,*[143] a case involving the analogous duty of a receiver of a company appointed pursuant to a debenture. The court held in that case that it was not unreasonable for the receiver to accept an unconditional offer which was below the accepted value of the land in the absence of another unconditional offer of a higher amount and in the absence of a reasonable prospect of such an offer being forthcoming. It was also relevant that rejecting the offer could have incurred costs in bank interest and legal fees and might have left the receiver without a purchaser. It was not for the court to decide, with the benefit of hindsight, whether it might have been better to refuse the unconditional offer.

---

140 [1966] IR 1.

141 Raglan House, Clyde Road, Ballsbridge, Dublin.

142 [1979] 1 IR 364.

143 [1999] 1 IR 443, 458 (O'Flaherty, Keane and Barron JJ).

(2) Building Societies

The Building Societies Act, 1989 section 26 now[144] provides that building societies, if they exercise the power of sale as mortgagees "shall ensure as far as is reasonably practicable that the estate is sold at the best price reasonably obtainable".

g) Proceeds of Sale

Although the mortgagee is not a trustee of the power of sale, section 21(3) of the Conveyancing Act, 1881 provides that the mortgagee is a trustee of the proceeds of sale. The mortgagee must apply the proceeds of sale in the following order:

1. in discharge of prior incumbrances; then
2. in payment of the costs and expenses of the sale; then
3. in discharge of the mortgage money due under the mortgage; and then
4. in payment of the residue to the mortgagor, or if there is another mortgage, to the next mortgagee.

h) Effect of Sale

Section 21(1) of the Conveyancing Act, 1881 provides that the sale of the mortgaged property under the Act passes to the purchaser the estate or interest in the mortgaged property "freed from all estates, interests and rights to which the mortgage has priority, but subject to all estates, interests and rights which have priority to the mortgage". Thus, where the mortgage was created by conveyance of the fee simple, the fee simple passes under the sale. Where the mortgage was by demise, or sub-demise, the term or sub-term passes. In the case of a mortgage by demise the mortgagor may declare the fee simple reversion to be held on trust for the mortgagee in case of sale so that the mortgagee may then sell it.[145] In the case of a mortgage by sub-demise a similar declaration of trust may be made of the head term held by the mortgagor.

7. Court Order for Sale

The mortgagee may apply for an order for sale by the court without applying for possession at the same time. The order is in the form of a declaration that the sum is well charged on the mortgagor's interest in the property. The court will further order an inquiry into the amount due under the mortgage and will direct a sale if the amount due is not paid within three months of delivery of the examiner's certificate of the amount due. The court appoints an auctioneer and fixes a reserve price, and the purchase price is paid into court. Nevertheless,

144 The provision was introduced by the Building Societies Act, 1976 s.82(1)(a).

145 See for example *Re Sergie* [1954] NI 1; Wylie, *Cases* p.70.

the mortgagee is the vendor and if the sale is with vacant possession it is the mortgagee who must apply again to the court for an order of possession.[146] The procedure is generally less advantageous to a mortgagee than the summary procedure for possession and sale.[147]

8. Appointment of a Receiver

It has been seen that there are many disadvantages for the mortgagee in seeking possession of the property personally. Today most mortgagees are building societies who have no interest in managing the property. Their interest is a purely monetary one, in realising the interest and capital due. Before the Judicature (Ireland) Act, 1877 the courts of equity developed the remedy of appointing a receiver, on the application of the mortgagee, to manage the property. Naturally, the remedy was one which was available at that time only to equitable mortgagees, but section 28(8) of the 1877 Act conferred power on the court to appoint receivers in all cases, including legal mortgagees, and on such terms as it thinks fit.[148]

A receiver appointed by the court is not the agent of either party but is an officer of the court in carrying out the powers conferred. The remedy is infrequently used when the property is a dwelling house, since an order for possession and sale is more appropriate, but is more often used where the mortgaged premises consist of a business.[149]

Mortgage deeds in the past sometimes provided that the mortgagee was to have the right to appoint a receiver, which obviated the need to go to court. This is usually unnecessary now since section 19(1) of the Conveyancing Act, 1881 contains a statutory right to appoint a receiver without applying to the court.[150]

a) Mortgagees Entitled to Appoint a Receiver

The power to appoint a receiver under section 19(1) applies to mortgagees by deed, as with the case of the power of sale under the same section. Apart from

146 *Bank of Ireland v. Waldrow* [1944] IR 303.

147 See above.

148 *Butler v. Butler* [1925] 1 IR 185.

149 *Ardmore Studios (Ireland) Ltd v. Lynch* [1965] IR 1; *Kernohan Estates Ltd v. Boyd* [1967] NI 27; Wylie, *Cases* p.306.

150 The earlier Lord Cranworth's Act, 1860 (23 & 24 Vict. c.145) s.17–23 had contained a limited statutory right.

legal mortgages and registered charges[151] this will also include equitable mortgages or charges if made by deed. If they are not made by deed, application will still have to be made to the court.

b) The Power to Appoint

The power to appoint a receiver without application to a court arises when the mortgage money becomes due.[152] The power does not become exercisable until one of the three events in section 20 for the exercise of the power of sale has occurred.[153] The mortgagee must appoint the receiver in writing.[154] The mortgagee may also remove a receiver and appoint a new one, provided it is done in writing.[155]

c) Function of a Receiver

Section 24(3) of the 1881 Act gives power to a receiver to demand and to recover all the income from the property by action, distress[156] or otherwise to the extent of the estate mortgaged[157], and to give receipts. The receiver is entitled to deduct from the income costs, charges and expenses incurred and, in addition, a commission not exceeding five per cent of the gross amount of all money received.[158] The court may allow a higher rate of commission on application by the receiver. A mortgagee in possession, by contrast, may not charge a commission.[159]

The receiver must apply the money received by him in the following order:[160]

1. in discharge of rent, taxes and other outgoings;
2. in payment of annual sums and other payments and interest on capital sums having priority to the mortgage of which he is the receiver;
3. in payment of his commission and premiums on fire, life, or other insurances properly payable under the mortgage deed or under the 1881 Act and the cost of repairs;

---

151 Registration of Title Act, 1964 s.62(6).

152 1881 Act, s.19(1), as in the case of sale out of court.

153 *ibid.*, s.24(1).

154 *ibid.*.

155 Section 24(5).

156 Under the Housing (Miscellaneous Provisions) Act, 1992 s.19 it is illegal to levy a distress in the case of a dwelling house. It has been abolished in Northern Ireland by s.122 of the Judgments (Enforcement) Act (NI), 1969. See Chapter 19 Landlord and Tenant.

157 *Donohue v. Agricultural Credit Corporation plc* [1987] ILRM 26 (receiver appointed as to charge of part of dairy farm).

158 Section 24(6).

159 *Carew v. Johnston* (1805) 2 Sch & Lef 280 per Lord Redesdale LC at 301.

160 1881 Act, s.24(8).

4. in payment of interest due on principal money under the mortgage; and[161]
5. in payment of the residue to the person who would have been entitled to the income of the property but for the appointment of the receiver, *i.e.* normally the mortgagor.

Unlike a receiver appointed by the court, a receiver appointed by the mortgagee is now deemed to be an agent for the mortgagor.[162] The receiver is not therefore regarded as taking possession on behalf of the mortgagee, who is relieved of his duty to account strictly to the mortgagor. This strikes a balance between ensuring that the mortgagee receives what is due to him and protecting the interest of the mortgagor. The receiver is answerable to the mortgagor, but can, as we have seen, be removed by the mortgagee, not by the mortgagor.

Third parties paying money to a receiver are protected in that they are not concerned to inquire whether the power to appoint the receiver was exercisable.[163]

9. Foreclosure

a) The Jurisdiction

Foreclosure is a remedy developed in some jurisdictions whereby the mortgagor's right to redeem in equity is declared to be at an end, so that the mortgagee is left with the interest vested in him or her free of the right of redemption. As will be seen below, it is said never to be granted in Ireland although the jurisdiction may still exist.

The equitable right to redeem only arises once the legal date for redemption has passed, and so there is no question of foreclosure until that has occurred.[164]

In the case of a legal mortgage by conveyance of the fee simple, once the legal date for redemption has passed, a final order of foreclosure leaves the mortgagee with the fee simple free of the right to redeem in equity. In the case of an equitable mortgage the legal estate is in the mortgagor, and so the final order in such a case will direct the mortgagor to convey the legal title to the mortgagee free of the equity to redeem.

The order of the court is in two parts: a decree nisi which directs accounts to be drawn up to determine the amount due to the mortgagee and what other incumbrances may affect the land, and a decree absolute which forecloses the

161 The English Law of Property Act, 1925 s.109(8) added, after (4), in or towards the discharge of principal money due under the mortgage if so directed in writing by the mortgagee. There appears to be no power under the 1881 Act to do so.

162 1881 Act, s.24(2).

163 1881 Act, s.24(4).

164 *Burrowes v. Molloy* (1845) 2 Jo & La T 521, 7 Ir Eq R 49, 68 RR 243, per Sugden LC, cited in *Twentieth Century Banking Corp Ltd v. Wilkinson* [1976] 3 WLR 489 per Templeman J.

right of redemption. The first decree declares that unless (nisi) the mortgagor redeems within a certain period, usually three or six months from the date of the decree, the order will be made absolute.

It is curious in one sense that equity recognised the remedy of foreclosure at all, since the effect may well be that the mortgagor will obtain an interest in the property which is worth more than the amount due under the mortgage. It also means that subsequent mortgagees will not recover anything unless they redeem the earlier mortgage, because the mortgagee under an absolute order takes free of mortgages later than his own.[165]

Foreclosure can be seen as arising from the basic principle of equity that remedies are discretionary. That principle applies to the equitable right to redeem as to other equitable remedies.

Although the final order of foreclosure is called absolute, this is somewhat misleading. Such an order can, at the discretion of the court, be reopened and the foreclosure rescinded. The grounds on which this may be done were formulated down by Jessel MR in *Campbell v. Hoyland*.[166] The discretion may be exercised if

(1) the mortgagor was prevented by some misfortune from redeeming the mortgage between the order nisi and the order absolute; or

(2) if there would be a considerable difference between the amount due under the mortgage and the present value of the property.

The latter circumstance is most likely to occur under the present conditions of the market and would seem to constitute an additional reason for not granting foreclosure in the first place. It also makes it unlikely that foreclosure will be granted again by Irish courts. The only circumstances in which it would be equitable would seem to be either that the value of the property at the time the order is sought is equal, or approximately so, to the amount due on the mortgage, or that the value of the property has declined so that the mortgagee would not be able to recover the amount due by a sale, and would therefore prefer to have the property itself in the hope that it might again rise.

165 For this reason subsequent mortgagees must be joined in an action of foreclosure: *Rolleston v. Morton* (1842) 4 Ir Eq R 149; *Davis v. Rowan* (1843) 3 Dru & War 478; *Munster Bank Ltd v. Jervis* (1902) 26 ILTR 113. Mortgagees whose mortgages are prior to that of the mortgage seeking foreclosure would not be affected by an order in his favour and so need not be joined: *Perrot v. O'Halloran* (1840) 2 Ir Eq R 428.

166 (1887) 7 Ch D 166 at 169 and 172–5.

b) Never Granted in Ireland

Foreclosure is said to be a remedy that is never granted in Ireland.[167] In *Re Edwards*[168] Hargrave J in the Landed Estates Court said: "This contract is virtually a clause of foreclosure on a fixed day; and even in England, *where foreclosure is possible*, it only takes place after a bill has been filed. . ." [emphasis supplied]. More recently Lowry J in *Re O'Neill*[169] expressed the same view when he said: "In Ireland a mortgagee wishing to realise his security through the court applies for an order for sale and not, as in England, for foreclosure". Walker LC in *Bruce v. Brophy*[170] referred to the "settled practice for centuries of decreeing a sale and not foreclosure".[171] Nevertheless, there are *dicta* to the effect that the jurisdiction still exists and could be made in special circumstances.[172]

The Conveyancing Act, 1881 section 25 provided for a statutory power to order sale instead of foreclosure in a foreclosure action, but it did not apply to Ireland,[173] probably because, as we have just seen, the courts in Ireland asserted a jurisdiction at common law to do so.

---

167 *Re Power and Carton's Contract* (1890) 25 LR Ir 459 is sometimes cited as an example of foreclosure being granted in Ireland, but the original order in the case was made in England. See Wylie, *Land Law* para. 13.059. *Clinton v. Bernard* (1844) 6 Ir Eq R 355 per Sugden LC and cases there cited.

168 (1861) 11 Ir Ch R 367 at p.369.

169 [1967] NI 129.

170 [1906] 1 IR 611; Wylie, *Cases* p.456.

171 Fitzgibbon LJ in *Antrim County Land, Building and Investment Co Ltd v. Stewart* [1904] 2 IR 357 at 369 expressed the view that foreclosure fell into disuse in Ireland because there was a special procedure for appointing receivers and for sale in the Landed Estates Court. Wylie para. 13.060 doubts this, since it was the practice to order sale long before the Landed Estates Court was established. He suggests that a more likely explanation is that second and third mortgages were more common in Ireland than in England and such subsequent mortgagees would not recover their capital if foreclosure were granted unless they redeemed the prior mortgage.

172 Walker LC in the same case at p.616.

173 Section 25(7).

10. Remedies Cumulative

The mortgagee's remedies are cumulative. He or she does not have to choose between suing in debt or on the mortgage.[174] But if the mortgagee succeeds in debt the mortgagor does not have to pay until the mortgagee surrenders the title deeds.[175]

G. Consolidation

The two doctrines of consolidation and marshalling are similar in many respects. In either case the object of equity is to do justice between the parties. Where there are only two parties they may succeed in doing so, but it is open to question whether or not they do so when an innocent third party is introduced. Students may wish to consider whether, in such cases, greater justice would have been obtained without the doctrines.

1. The Doctrine

The equitable doctrine of consolidation applies to a mortgagee who has lent money to a single mortgagor on two occasions and the debts are secured on two different properties belonging to the mortgagor. In this situation it can happen that the value of one property declines to a point where it does not adequately secure the repayment of the debt charged on it, while the other is more than adequate to secure the debt originally charged on it. But for the doctrine the mortgagor could redeem the latter mortgage and leave the other debt inadequately secured. The doctrine gives the mortgagee the right to insist that the mortgagor redeems both mortgages or neither. It is an application of the maxim "He who seeks equity must do equity".

The doctrine applies to both legal and equitable mortgages and whether one is legal and the other equitable. It also applies to mortgages of personalty, and where one mortgage is of realty and the other of personalty.

2. Legal Date of Redemption Passed

The mortgagor is allowed to redeem after the legal date of redemption has passed only by the equitable jurisdiction, and so it follows from this that the legal date of redemption must have passed for all mortgages to which the right to consolidate is applied.

---

174 *Schoole v. Sall* (1806) 1 Sch & Lef 176, Lord Redesdale LC at 177, 149 RR 711. Before the Judicature Act, 1877 the mortgagee could sue on the common law debt and in equity at the same time, an exception to the general rule that one could not sue at law and in equity simultaneously.

175 *Schoole v. Sall* (1806) 1 Sch & Lef 176, 149 RR 711.

3. Mortgages Created by Same Mortgagor

It is clear that the right to consolidate applies only where there is a single mortgagor and a single mortgagee in relation to the relevant mortgages, but although the mortgages must have been created by the same mortgagor, they need not have been created in favour of the same mortgagee. There must, however, have been a time when both mortgages were vested in the same mortgagee and the right to redeem vested in one other person. Furthermore, the same mortgagee must have the mortgages vested in him or her at the time that person seeks to exercise the right to consolidate. It does not matter that they are no longer vested in that person at the time the action is brought. It also does not matter that the equities of redemption later became vested in different persons.[176]

The reason why the mortgages must have been created by the same mortgagor seems to be that it would not be fair to impose the doctrine of consolidation on a mortgagor unless the situation was foreseeable by him. Since he chose to take loans on more than one of his properties, he could foresee the situation to which the doctrine applies. But why then, it might be objected, does it not also arise where a mortgagor later buys mortgaged property? It may be suggested that the courts were unwilling to put a person who had mortgaged property at a disadvantage when it came to buying other property. The judges upheld the principles of a free market economy in favour of such a person. In this instance his position as a purchaser on the market was equated with other purchasers. This can be said to indicate the strong adherence of the judges in the 19th century to the market idea.

4. Right Expressly Reserved

Originally the courts of equity applied the doctrine as a means of doing justice between the parties outside the bargain they had made, but by the 19th century, with the development of a market economy, the notion took hold that parties should be left to themselves to bargain for what advantages they wished. The Conveyancing Act, 1881 placed a restriction on the right by providing that unless all the mortgages were all made before 1882 the right must be expressly reserved in the mortgage deeds. Section 17(1) provides:

> "A mortgagor seeking to redeem any one mortgage shall, by virtue of this Act, be entitled to do so, without paying any money due under any separate mortgage made by him, or by any person through whom he claims, on property other than that comprised in the mortgage which he seeks to redeem".

Section 17(2) qualifies this by providing that section 17(1) applies "only if and as far as a contrary intention is not expressed in the mortgage deeds or one of

176 *Re Thomson's Estate* [1912] 1 IR 460.

them".[177] The section does not appear to have excluded mortgages created without a deed, such as equitable mortgages by deposit, from the doctrine, since it is sufficient if one of the mortgages is by deed and that deed reserves the right.

5. Purchasers

Although the doctrine aimed to achieve equity as between mortgagor and mortgagee, it was less successful in this aim when a purchaser of the mortgaged property was involved. In the system of unregistered conveyancing in England it might not be possible for a purchaser of mortgaged property to discover whether the vendor had mortgaged other property and that the mortgage was owned or had later become owned by the same mortgagee. An innocent purchaser could be prejudiced in that he or she might be required by the mortgagee to redeem both the present property and the one previously mortgaged by the vendor, the mortgage of which is now held by the same mortgagee. He could not plead purchase without notice of a legal estate, because he normally only purchased the equity of redemption which, as a later equitable interest, was subject to the prior equity. Even when the mortgage was created by sub-demise, so that the mortgagor retained the freehold reversion, the purchaser's right to redeem is, after the legal date of redemption, purely an equitable right and so subject to the prior right to consolidate.

The problem is somewhat less acute in Ireland since the system of registration of deeds applies. To protect his right to consolidate against later dealings with the land mortgaged the mortgagee must ascertain that the mortgages involved are registered in the Registry of Deeds. But this would seem only to be necessary where the mortgages were capable of registration, *i.e.* where they were created by deed. Equitable mortgages by deposit may exist to which the right applies and which do not appear on the register. A purchaser could discover the existence of other registered mortgages created by the same mortgagor by searching the Index of Names of Grantors, but would not be able to discover the existence of equitable mortgages by deposit or of mortgages of personalty.

H. Marshalling

1. The Doctrine

The remedy of marshalling applies where one person owns an interest in two properties and another person has an interest in one of them. The latter has the right in equity to require the owner of the two interests not to deal with them in such a way as to prejudice him or her. The remedy applies to the administration

177 *Gore-Hickman v. Alliance Assurance Co Ltd* [1936] IR 721.

of the assets of a deceased person as well as to mortgages. In relation to mortgages it was explained by Cotton LJ in *Webb v. Smith*[178] as follows:

> "If A has a charge upon Whiteacre and Blackacre, and if B also has a charge upon Blackacre only, A must take payment of his charge out of Whiteacre, and must leave Blackacre, so that B the other creditor, may follow it and obtain payment of his debt out of it: in other words, if two estates, Whiteacre and Blackacre, are mortgaged to one person, and subsequently one of them, Blackacre, is mortgaged to another person, unless Blackacre is sufficient to pay both charges, the first mortgagee will be compelled to take satisfaction out of Whiteacre, in order to leave the second mortgagee Blackacre, upon which alone he can go".

In the case of mortgages the doctrine would apply in the following situation. A owns No. 1 Railway Cuttings and No. 2 Canal View. She mortgages them both to R to secure a loan of £30,000. Some years later she mortgages Railway Cuttings a second time, this time to S, for £6,000. Later, when A has defaulted on the mortgages to R, R wishes to exercise his right of sale to recover the loan. Let us say that Railway Cuttings is now worth £33,000. Canal View is worth £30,000. R could recover his loan by realising only the security on Railway Cuttings, but if he does so, S will not be able to recover the full amount of his loan, since if Railway Cuttings is sold and the £30,000 paid off to R, there will only be £3,000 left. R is therefore required to realise the security on Canal View alone, since it is adequate to repay his loan. This leaves S's mortgage intact.

It may be, however, that the value of Canal View is insufficient to cover the full amount of R's loan. Let us assume it is worth only £25,000. If R sells both properties the proceeds will amount to £58,000. R will recover his loan and will hold the balance of £28,000 on trust for S as to £6,000 and then the remaining £22,000 on trust for any other mortgagees and then, failing them, or if there is any money left after paying them, for A.[179]

In this situation, equity requires R to realise both securities in the way described. This does not have the effect of leaving S's mortgage intact, but at least he has recovered his loan. In this situation, R would wish to realise both securities in any case, without the doctrine, but the doctrine can be said to apply to the extent of holding that R has satisfied himself out of Canal View first, and only then resorting to Railway Cuttings to recover the balance of £5,000 due to him.

In the passage quoted above it was said that the owner of the single mortgage can compel the owner of the two mortgages to act as described, but there is also a line of cases which applies the doctrine of *subrogation*, holding that the owner of the two mortgages cannot be compelled so to act, but that if he resorts, without need, to the property mortgaged to the single mortgagee, the latter

178 (1885) 30 Ch D 192 at 200; and see *Aldrich v. Cooper* (1802) 8 Ves Jun 382, 32 ER 402.

179 Conveyancing Act, 1881 s.21(3) and see above.

will be entitled to a mortgage over the other property in priority to the double mortgagee. In the example, if R resorts to Railway cuttings unnecessarily, S has a mortgage as to the amount of his loan over Canal View in priority to R. S is subrogated to the position of R.[180] It is immaterial whether or not S had notice of R's mortgage at the time he took his.[181] It does not seem that it is necessary in Ireland for all the mortgages to be created by the same mortgagor,[182] nor is it necessary that the equities of redemption be vested in the same person when the right is invoked.[183] The right to marshal can be invoked not only by mortgagees, but also by purchasers of the equity of redemption in one of the plots mortgaged.[184]

2. Judgment Mortgages

In *Re Lynch's Estate*[185] there was a first mortgage by deed of plots A and B. A judgment mortgage was then registered against plot A and, later, a further judgment mortgage was registered against plots A and B. The first mortgagee having enforced the security, the judgment mortgagee of plot A claimed the right to marshal as against the judgment mortgagee of plots A and B. It was held that the doctrine applied. The judgment clearly establishes that a judgment mortgagee has the right to marshal against a later judgment mortgagee, but Dobbs J also held that a judgment mortgagee has the right as against all later charges, including ordinary mortgages, on the ground that registration enabled later chargees to discover the existence of the earlier judgment mortgage.

3. Third Parties

a) Mortgagees

A further complication arises if the mortgagor later mortgages the plot of land subject only to the double mortgage to another mortgagee. Thus, if A mortgages Plots 1 and 2 to B, and then mortgages Plot 1 to C alone, and then mortgages Plot 2 to D alone, does C have a right to marshal against B, requiring B to resort first to Plot 2, even though that may now prejudice D? The law is unclear as to the application of the doctrine where such third parties are involved and as to the relevance of notice on the part of such third parties.

---

180 *McCarthy v. McCartie (No. 2)* [1904] 1 IR 100; and see *Lanoy v. Duke of Athol* (1742) 3 Atk 444 at 446, 26 ER 668 at 669.

181 *Tidd v. Lister* (1854) 3 De G M & G 857 at 872, 43 ER 336; *Gibson v. Seagrim* (1855) 20 Beav 614, 52 ER 741; *Hughes v. Williams* (1852) 3 Mac & G 683 at 690, 42 ER 423.

182 Wylie, *Irish Land Law* para. 13.077.

183 *Ker v. Ker* (1870) IR 4 Eq 15.

184 *ibid.*, and see below.

185 (1867) IR 1 Eq 396, Landed Estates Court, per Dobbs J.

In *Re Archer's Estate*[186] Wylie J held that C still has a right to marshal, on the ground that A should not be able to deprive C of his right to marshal simply by creating another mortgage over Plot 2. In that case, however, all the mortgagees had notice of prior mortgages, so that D could be taken to have had notice, not only of C's mortgage, but of C's right to marshal also.[187] Wylie expressly left open the question as to whether the same result would follow if D had no notice of the prior mortgages.

On the other hand, *Dolphin v. Aylward*,[188] a decision of the House of Lords on appeal from Ireland, declined to recognise that the right to marshal could be exercised if it would prejudice a third party, such as D, whether the third party was a volunteer, *i.e.* had given consideration, or not. Later cases in Ireland seem to have ignored this decision, which was also inconsistent with earlier English authorities.[189]

In *Smyth v. Toms*[190] Ross J declined to follow *Re Archer's Estate*, which he held indistinguishable, and applied the English case of *Barnes v. Racster*[191] holding that C only had a right to marshal against the mortgagor and those claiming as volunteers through him. Where, in the above example, D is not a volunteer, the judge held that B must resort to both plots rateably, *i.e.* in proportion to their values. The equity to marshal is thus apportioned between C and D and C has to be content with whatever surplus Plot 1 produces after paying off its proportionate part of B's security.

The latter cases suggest that the test of whether the taker of a later interest takes free of the right to marshal is one of consideration, and that those giving such consideration take free of the equity, whether or not they have notice. However, the normal rule in equity is that only purchasers of a legal interest for value and without notice take free of equitable interests, the further exception being, in the case of mere equities, that a purchaser of an equitable interest for value and without notice would also take free. Assuming that the right to marshal is a mere equity, it is submitted that the proper test should be that only those who take for value and without notice should be free of the right to marshal.

---

186 [1914] 1 IR 285.

187 See also *Re Mower's Trusts* (1869) LR 8 Eq 110.

188 (1870) LR 4 HL 486.

189 Such as *Averall v. Wade* (1835) Ll & G t Sug 252, 46 RR 218 and *Barnes v. Racster* (1842) 1 Y & CCC 401, 62 ER 944.

190 [1918] 1 IR 338. See also *Re Lawder's Estate* (1861) 11 Ir Ch R 346.

191 (1842) 1 Y & CCC 401; *Tighe v. Dolphin* [1906] 1 IR 305; And see *Flint v. Howard* [1893] 2 Ch. 54 per Kay LJ at 72; *Bugden v. Bignold* (1843) 2 Y & CCC 377, 63 ER 167; *Wellesley v. Lord Mornington* (1869) 17 WR 355.

b) Purchasers from the Mortgagor

A owns Plot 1 and Plot 2 and mortgages them both to B. A then sells his equity of redemption in Plot 2 to P. It was held in *Ker v. Ker*[192] that in certain circumstances P has a right to marshal against B. He or she can insist that B enforces his security first against Plot 1, the equity in which was retained by A. P has the right to marshal if A sold Plot 2 subject to a covenant against incumbrances, or a declaration that the estate was free of incumbrances, or "the nature of the dealings shows that the land is sold or settled *as if* free from incumbrances..."[193]. P would clearly have a remedy in damages against A for breach of covenant, but Christian LJ in *Ker v. Ker*[194] maintained that the court will specifically perform the covenant, even so as to affect B. The right to marshal would bind everyone claiming through A except a purchaser for value without notice.[195]

I. The Position of The Mortgagor

A number of jurisdictions of the court protect the position of the mortgagor. These are: the equitable jurisdiction protecting the equity of redemption, which is a jurisdiction specific to mortgages; the equitable jurisdiction to strike down or modify unconscionable or oppressive contracts; and the common law rule against contracts in restraint of trade. The equitable jurisdictions are not mutually exclusive, and the relation between them is by no means clear. Sometimes the power to invalidate clogs on the equity of redemption is seen as an example of the general jurisdiction over unconscionable bargains, sometimes the courts treat it as an independent rule. We shall attempt to separate the jurisdictions for the sake of analysis, but it should be remembered that the cases do not always maintain the clear borderlines favoured by the writers of textbooks.

1. Redemption

a) The Rule against Clogs on the Equity of Redemption

The role of equity in relation to mortgages was, as has been seen, to ensure that the mortgagor retained the right to redeem the mortgage even after the legal date of redemption had passed, and created the equitable right to redeem for this purpose. Conveyancers acting for mortgagees on occasion responded to this by inserting covenants in mortgages aimed at or restricting or even taking away this right, and, as is often the case in property law, this dialectical conflict

192 (1870) IR 4 Eq 15.

193 (1870) IR 4 Eq 15 per Christian LJ at 30–31.

194 *ibid.*, and *McCarthy v. McCartie (No. 2)* [1904] 1 IR 100 per Walker LJ at 115.

195 *Averall v. Wade* (1835) Ll & G t Sug 252 at 259, 46 RR 218, 225; *McCarthy v. McCartie (No. 2)* [1904] 1 IR 100 at 119 per Walker LJ.

between the thesis of principle and the antithesis of the conveyancer's device led to a new synthesis of principles aimed at protecting the right to redeem while not interfering with parties dealing on equal terms. The main principle was stated by Walker LJ in *Browne v. Ryan*:[196]

> "When a transaction appears, or has been declared to be a mortgage, Courts of equity regard the instrument only as a security for the repayment of the principal, interest, and costs named and secured, and the mortgagor is entitled to get back his property as free as he gave it, on payment of principal, interest, and costs, and provisions inconsistent with that right cannot be enforced. The equitable rules, 'once a mortgage always a mortgage,'[197] and that the mortgagee cannot impose any 'clog or fetter on the equity of redemption,' are merely concise statements of the same rule".

In the 19th century and earlier judges tended to take a strict view of the principle, possibly because of the practice of owners of landed estates, or expectant heirs,[198] of entering into mortgage transactions which often had the effect of burdening the estate with debt. This meant that the income in the form of rent from the tenant farmers was used to repay loans to moneylenders rather than being available to invest in improving agriculture. Legislation in the 19th century, establishing the Landed Estates Court and later the Settled Land Acts resolved this problem over time, and there was less need for the intervention of the courts in mortgages transactions. Mortgages entered into between public companies and financial institutions were more often transactions between parties of equal bargaining strength and so the courts could retreat from intervention and leave the field to market forces. As Lord Macnaughten commented in the House of Lords in 1904, directors of a company in search of financial assistance "are certainly in a very different position from that of an impecunious landowner in the toils of a crafty moneylender".[199] Whatever the true explanation, it is certainly the case that a change in attitude on the part of the courts is detectable around the turn of the century.

The following provisions in mortgages have been held void as clogs on the equity of redemption:

1) an option to purchase the reversion on the mortgage term or the equity of redemption given to the mortgagee on the creation[200] or assignment[201] of the mortgage. An option in a later transaction has been held

---

196 [1901] 2 IR 653 at 676.

197 *Seton v. Slade* (1802) 7 Ves 265 at 273 per Lord Eldon LC.

198 *Rae v. Joyce* (1892) 29 LR Ir 500 at 509 per Walker C.

199 *Samuel v. Jarrah Timber & Wood Paving Corpn Ltd* [1904] AC 323 at 327.

200 *Brown v. Ryan* [1901] 2 IR 653; Wylie, *Cases* p.457; *Samuel v. Jarrah Timber & Wood Paving Corpn Ltd* [1904] AC 323.

201 *Lewis v. Frank Love Ltd* [1961] 1 WLR 261; [1961] 1 All ER 446; and see *Kevans v. Joyce* [1896] 1 IR 442, CA at 473.

valid, although the only consideration was a release of the mortgagor from the obligation to repay the mortgage loan;[202]

2) a clause attempting to make the mortgage irredeemable.[203] The mortgagor will be allowed to redeem notwithstanding such a clause;

3) a clause confining the equity of redemption to the life of the mortgagor,[204] or providing that if the mortgagor died before his father, the property was to belong absolutely to the mortgagee.[205]

(1) Postponement of Right to Redeem

A term which attempts to postpone the legal date of redemption beyond the customary six months, and which therefore attempts to postpone the equitable right to redeem, is not now[206] void unless it renders redemption illusory[207] or is otherwise unconscionable or oppressive.[208]

In *Fairclough v. Swan Brewery*[209] the mortgagor mortgaged a leasehold term of 17 years. Under the terms of the mortgage the right to redeem would only arise six weeks before the end of the lease. The Judicial Committee of the Privy Council held that the term rendered the mortgage virtually irredeemable and was void.

Modern cases, however, show a greater reluctance to interfere with contractual terms merely on the ground that they postpone redemption.

The case that exemplifies, and established, this new willingness to let the free market determine the terms of the mortgage is *Knightsbridge Estates Trust Ltd v. Byrne*.[210] In that case the Knightsbridge company had mortgaged a number of houses and shops to Prudential Assurance for £300,000 at 6 per cent interest. The loan could be called in at any time. The mortgagor company wanted to reduce the rate of interest and to spread the repayment of the loan over a period of years. They transferred the mortgage to the Royal Liver Friendly Society. This mortgage was for £310,000 at five and one quarter per cent and the loan was to be repaid over 40 years in half-yearly instalments. The loan was not to be called in by the mortgagees before that time provided the instalments were paid punctually. Several years later the mortgagors sought to

---

202 *Reeve v. Lisle* [1902] AC 461.

203 *Brown v. Ryan* [1901] 2 IR 653 at 676 per Walker LJ.

204 *Floyer v. Lavington* (1714) 1 P Wms 268, 24 ER 384.

205 *Salt v. Northampton (Marquess)* [1892] AC 1.

206 *Cowdry v. Day* (1859) 1 Giff 316, 65 ER 936 (postponed for 20 years, held too long a period)

207 *Fairclough v. Swan Brewery* [1912] AC 565.

208 *Knightsbridge Estates Trust Ltd v. Byrne* [1939] Ch. 441, affirmed on other grounds in [1940] AC 613.

209 [1912] AC 565.

210 [1939] Ch. 441.

redeem the loan on giving the usual six months notice and when the mortgagees refused, sued for a declaration that they were so entitled. The mortgagors claimed that the postponement of redemption for 40 years was unreasonable and void. The English Court of Appeal upheld the suspension, holding that reasonableness was not the test. Greene MR expressed the view that the agreement was "a commercial agreement between two important corporations experienced in such matters" and had "none of the features of an oppressive bargain where the borrower is at the mercy of an unscrupulous lender".[211] The agreement was a proper business transaction and any other result would place "...an unfortunate restriction on the liberty of contract of competent parties who are at arm's length".[212]

It might also be noted that the term had originally been sought by the mortgagors who at that time believed it to be in their own best interests. Later, when their circumstances changed, they saw their interests differently and wanted to retract their agreement. They should have bargained for a more flexible arrangement, but they only had themselves to blame for that. The court clearly considered that it was not their role to make their contract for them.

(2) Unconscionable Bargains

In equity there is a general jurisdiction to review unconscionable or oppressive bargains. Where parties to a contract are not on an equal footing that does not in itself invalidate the agreement or the unconscionable part of it, but the onus shifts to the dominant party to show that the agreement is fair and reasonable.[213]

The jurisdiction of courts of equity to set aside unconscionable or oppressive bargains was independent of the usury laws and survived their repeal.[214] There is still jurisdiction, therefore, to hold excessive rates of interest invalid as unconscionable.[215] The jurisdiction is still invoked from time to time. Thus, in *Chapple v. Mahon*[216] a covenant by a mortgagor to pay the mortgagee a commission of 5 per cent if the mortgage was paid off has been held illegal on

211 [1939] Ch. 441 at 455.

212 *ibid.*

213 *Kevans v. Joyce* [1896] 1 IR 442 at 463 per Monroe J, Court of Appeal at 473.

214 *Chapple v. Mahon* (1870) IR 5 Eq 225 per Chatterton V-C; *Rae v. Joyce* (1892) 29 LR Ir 500 at 516 per Walker C, at 520 per O'Brien CJ; *Kevans v. Joyce* [1896] 1 IR 442 at 463 per Monroe J, Court of Appeal at 473.

215 *Kevans v. Joyce* [(1896] 1 IR 442 at 463 per Monroe J, Court of Appeal at 473; *Miller v. Cook* (1870) LR 10 Eq 646.

216 (1870) IR 5 Eq 225.

this ground and in *Wells v. Joyce*[217] an unfavourable loan entered into by a Connemara farmer, said to be of rustic mind, was set aside.

(a) Variable Rate of Interest

Most mortgages today provide for a variable interest rate. The mortgagee may unilaterally vary the interest payable. The interest rate can thus be raised to a point at which the mortgagor is unable to afford the monthly payments and is forced to sell the house. It is possible that in the past such a term might be impugned as unconscionable, or on the ground of uncertainty in that the mortgagor agrees to any rate fixed by the mortgagee, but the term has not been successfully challenged on these grounds in modern times,[218] and it seems most unlikely that such a challenge would now succeed.[219]

Building societies alter the mortgage interest rate in response to changes in the base lending rate, *i.e.*, the rate of interest charged by the central bank in lending money to commercial banks. This rate, in Western market economies, is under the control of the minister of finance, and is the subject of political controversy and debate, and, in theory at least, the rate is subject to democratic control. A government which raises the rate to a point at which most home owners could no longer afford to make monthly mortgage payments, and maintained it at that level for a considerable period, runs the risk of losing the support of a sizeable proportion of the electorate and possibly the next election. It seems unlikely that courts would be willing to enter into the political arena and attract to themselves the consequent criticism on political grounds. Moreover, a decision that variable interest was unconscionable and void would have a major disruptive effect on the mortgage market. Mortgages might become more difficult to obtain than before, or the fixed rate of interest might be set at a level considerably above the base rate, so that a smaller section of the public than before would be able to contemplate buying a house on mortgage. These considerations might well lead a court to decline to hold variable interest rate terms invalid.

(b) Index-Linked Mortgages

Index-linked is a term used loosely to refer to some mechanism to offset the effects of inflation.[220] Without such a mechanism the value of the capital repaid will be worth considerably less than the origin loan in real terms, which is one of the principal attractions of the normal mortgage so far as the mortgagor is

---

217 [1905] 2 IR 134 at 142ff.

218 See Gray, *Elements of Land Law* p.959.

219 *ANZ Banking Group (NZ) Ltd v. Gibson* [1981] 1 NZLR 513 at 525 (variable interest rate in debenture not void for uncertainty).

220 Strictly it refers to values linked to the Retail Price Index, or to some other economic index such as the Financial Times Securities Index or the Dow Jones index of securities.

concerned, but one of its disadvantages from the point of view of the mortgagee. It is not clear in Ireland whether index-linked mortgages are illegal as contrary to public policy. Index-linking generally may be a self-fulfilling prophesy in that it tends in itself to increase inflation. It is also the case that capital in other forms of investment, such as stocks and shares, are not index-linked. In England they have been held legal.

In *Multiservice Bookbinding Ltd v. Marden*[221] commercial premises were mortgaged for a loan of £30,000 sterling. The mortgage specified that the loan could not be called in by the mortgagee, nor redeemed by the mortgagor, for a period of 10 years from the grant of the mortgage. The interest payable was to be calculated at 2 per cent above the Minimum Lending Rate on the entire loan over the whole period. The mortgage further stipulated that payments of interest or capital were to be linked to the Swiss franc and increased or decreased according to fluctuations in the exchange rate between the two currencies. As it turned out the pound sterling depreciated greatly over the period, so that at the end of the 10 year period the capital due was £87,588 and interest payable was £45,380. The mortgagor could nevertheless take some comfort in the fact that the property had trebled in value over the same period. It was held that the mortgage was not oppressive or unconscionable. The court held that "the parties made a bargain which the plaintiffs, who were businessmen, went into with their eyes open with the benefit of independent advice, without any compelling necessity to accept a loan on these terms and without any sharp practice by the defendant".[222]

(c) Penalties

Equity has long regarded clauses in contracts which impose a penalty on one party as being oppressive and has refused to enforce them. But it seems that here again the definition of what is a penalty has changed.

In *Chapple v. Mahon*[223] the mortgage provided that interest was charged at 10 per cent of the capital, but was to be only 8 per cent if the instalment was paid within 21 days of becoming due. This was held to be a penalty and the mortgagee was held entitled only to the lower rate. Later cases have nevertheless tended to regard such a provision as valid and as not being a penalty.[224]

It has been suggested that a distinction exists between clauses which provide that the normal interest is to be increased in the event of a default, and those which reduce the rate if the interest is paid on time, the former being void

---

221 [1979] Ch. 84, and see H.W. Wilkinson, "Index-Linked Mortgages" [1978] Conv 346; W.D. Bishop & B.V. Hindley; (1979) 42 MLR 338.

222 [1979] Ch. 84 at 110.

223 [1870] IR 5 Eq 225, Chatterton V-C.

224 *Re Rocella's Estate* (1898) 32 ILTR 8; *Re Carroll's Estate* [1901] 1 IR 78; *Re Jones' Estate* [1914] 1 IR 188.

and the latter valid.[225] but this is merely semantic and it seems likely that courts are less willing to strike down such a provision than previously was the case.[226] Recent cases in the United States have upheld variable interest in the case of default and refused to recognise that it is a penalty.[227] A covenant by a mortgagor to pay the mortgagee a commission of 5 per cent if the mortgage was paid off has been held illegal.[228]

(3) Collateral Advantages

A collateral advantage in a mortgage is any benefit conferred on the mortgagee other than the repayment of capital and the interest on the loan.

Before the usury laws were repealed in 1854[229] the courts tended to hold void any collateral advantage obtained by a mortgagee in a mortgage as being an indirect form of interest contravening the usury statutes. Since then a more liberal rule has been adopted which is accurately stated as follows:

> "A contract that grants a collateral advantage to a mortgagee is valid and enforceable unless it is oppressive and unconscionable or unless it is calculated to prevent or unduly hamper redemption".[230]

The new approach was outlined in the case of *Kreglinger v. New Patagonia Meat & Cold Storage Co Ltd.*[231] A meat company borrowed money from a firm of woolbrokers on mortgage by way of a floating charge on the assets of the company. The meat company agreed in the mortgage to let the woolbrokers have an option for five years to purchase any sheepskins the company had to sell. The woolbrokers agreed not to call in the loan for five years, but the company could redeem at any time. The company repaid the loan after two years, and claimed to take the property free of the option.

The House of Lords held that the option was still valid. Even though it was contained in the mortgage deed it was held to be a distinct and independent bargain. Lord Parker declared that:

---

225 Wylie, *Irish Land Law* para. 13.094.

226 *Chapple v. Mahon* [1870] IR 5 Eq 225 (above) does not fit this distinction.

227 *Vanston Bondholders Protective Committee v. Green* (1946) 329 US 156, Supreme Court; *Ruskin v. Griffiths* (1959) 269 F 2d 827, US Court of Appeals 2nd District; *Re White* (1988) 88 Bankr 498 (Lexis), US Bankruptcy Court for the District of Massachusetts.

228 *Chapple v. Mahon* (1870) IR 5 Eq 225.

229 By the Usury Laws Repeal Act, 1854 (17 & 18 Vict. c.90). Statutes of the Parliament of Ireland repealed by the Act were: 10 Chas I sess 2 c.22 (Ir); 2 Anne c.16 (Ir); 8 Geo I c.13 (Ir); 5 Geo II c.7 (Ir). See also *National Bank of Greece SA v. Pinios Shipping Co* [1989] 1 All ER 213, [1989] 3 WLR 185; *Cityland & Property Holdings Ltd v. Dabrah* [1968] Ch. 166; *Williamson v. Williamson* (1869) 7 LR Eq 542; *Mainland v. Upjohn* (1889) 41 Ch D 126 at 136.

230 *Biggs v. Hoddinott* [1898] 2 Ch. 307.

231 [1914] AC 25.

> "... there is now no rule in equity which precludes a mortgagee... from stipulating for any collateral advantage, provided such collateral advantage is not either [*sic*] (1) unfair and unconscionable, or (2) in the nature of a penalty clogging the equity of redemption, or (3) inconsistent with or repugnant to the contractual and equitable right to redeem".[232]

In recent years it had become the practice for building societies to insert into mortgages some terms which were intended to be beneficial to them, but were not of any benefit to the mortgagor, who had little choice but to accept them as building societies generally had standardised terms. One example was the term that the mortgagor should insure the property with the building society or its subsidiary insurance company. Another was that if the mortgagor paid off a part or whole of the mortgage before the agreed period had expired, a charge would be made for doing so. The jurisdiction to invalidate collateral advantages could have been used by the courts to invalidate the first of these standard terms, and the second could have been impugned as tending to inhibit the equity of redemption, but it was left to legislation to correct these abuses of the power of building societies. The Building Societies Act, 1989 section 36 gives mortgagors the right to arrange their own insurance.[233]

(4) Restraint of Trade

The common law doctrine of restraint of trade also applies to collateral advantages.[234] To the extent that restrictions are unreasonable they will be struck down by the courts. In the commercial context courts have sometimes found such restrictions to be separate contracts from the mortgage and so not a fetter on the equity of redemption.[235]

b) Who can Redeem

Redemption can be sought by any person interested in the equity of redemption,[236] such as assignees of the mortgagor or other successors in title, and subsequent mortgagees.[237] It even includes a lessee of the mortgagor where the lease itself is not binding on the mortgagee.[238]

---

232 [1914] AC 25 at 61.

233 Introduced by the Building Societies (Amendment) Act, 1986 s.6(1)(c).

234 *Irish Shell & BP Ltd v. Ryan* [1966] IR 75.

235 *Maxwell v. Tipping* [1903] 1 IR 498.

236 *Tarn v. Turner* [1888] 39 Ch D 456.

237 *Ocean Accident Corporation v. Collum* [1913] 1 IR 328.

238 *Tarn v. Turner* [1888] 39 Ch D 456.

c) Terms of Redemption

A mortgagor may redeem in or out of court, the former being necessary if the mortgagee unjustifiably refuses the tender of the money due under the mortgage.

(1) Notice

The mortgagor may redeem on the legal date of redemption in the mortgage and need not give any notice of his or her intention to do so, since the mortgage itself contains the term. After the legal date of redemption has passed (and it is normally one day) the mortgagor only has an equitable right to redeem and so it must be exercised equitably, *i.e.* reasonably and fairly. The mortgagor must give reasonable notice, usually six months, or pay six months' interest instead.[239] This is to allow the mortgagee a reasonably opportunity to reinvest his or her capital. Nevertheless reasonable notice is not required where the mortgage is temporary, which is usually the case with a mortgage by deposit,[240] or the mortgagee has demanded payment[241] or attempted to enforce the security.[242]

(2) Effect

Where only a single person is interested in the equity of redemption and the mortgage is the only incumbrance on the property, redemption discharges the mortgage and the property is then held free of it. Where more than one person is interested in the equity of redemption the effect of redemption is normally to transfer the mortgage to the person paying the money, as where property is mortgaged by A to X and Y and Y redeems X's mortgage. X will reconvey to Y, not A, and, since A still has the equity of redemption, Y still has a mortgage. Where there is more than one mortgage the first in order of priority has the best right to redeem.[243]

A mortgagee who has the right to redeem may, by Conveyancing Act, 1881 section 12, insist that the mortgagee conveys to a nominee of the mortgagor instead of to the mortgagor.

(3) Redeem Up, Foreclose Down

This is a principle of the courts in England where there are a number of mortgages affecting property and one mortgagee wishes to redeem one of the other mortgages. The principle is that a mortgagee who wishes to redeem a prior mortgage by action must not only redeem any other mortgages between him or

239 *Re Kennedy's Estate* [1889] 32 ILTR 115.

240 *Fitzgerald's Trustee v. Mellerish* [1892] 1 Ch. 385.

241 *Edmonson v. Copeland* [1911] 2 Ch. 301.

242 *Re Alcock* (1883) 23 Ch D 372.

243 *Teevan v. Smith* (1882) 20 Ch D 724 at 730.

her own mortgage and the one that is sought to be redeemed,[244] but must also foreclose all mortgages subsequent to his or her own mortgage and the mortgagor.[245] Thus, if property is mortgaged by X to A, B, C, D and E, the priority of those interested in the proceeds are, in order, A, B, C, D, E and X. X, as mortgagor, comes last because he is entitled to any surplus remaining after all the mortgages are paid off. The principle states that if D wishes to redeem B's mortgage then D must redeem C, who stands between himself and B, as well as B, and foreclose E and A. A and E can preserve their rights by paying off the other mortgages concerned in the action, but if they cannot, they will be foreclosed. Redeem up, foreclose down.

The basis of the principle is as follows. If B's mortgage is to be paid off, then C, D, E and A are all concerned because they are affected by the account of whatever is found to be due to B, since they all rank after B and take what is left over. The court would therefore insist that they be made parties to the suit for redemption, so that they can be represented. A is not concerned because he will be paid first in any case. It would, however, be unfair on C, E and A to put them to the expense of joining the suit merely as observers and also since the same situation might occur again in relation to some of them if one of them seeks redemption of another mortgage.

Since foreclosure is never granted in Ireland[246] and redemption suits rare, it is unlikely that the principle would ever be applied.[247]

2. Possession

This topic has been covered in the section on the position of the mortgagee.

3. Actions

It follows from what has been said earlier in this book about relativity of title that a mortgagor in possession, whether or not in possession as a tenant of the mortgagee or otherwise, is entitled to bring trespass and other common law actions such as nuisance against others with no better title.

Equity, rejecting the reification of the common law, always regarded the mortgagor and not the mortgagee as the substantial owner of the property and so a mortgagor may apply for equitable remedies such as injunction.

4. Sale

Under the Conveyancing Act, 1881 section 25 a person entitled to redeem could apply to the court for sale of the property instead, but the section does not

244 *ibid.*

245 *Farmer v. Curtis* (1829) 2 Sim 466, 57 ER 862.

246 See above.

247 Wylie, *Irish Land Law* para. 13.107.

apply to Ireland.[248] A court may nevertheless have an inherent jurisdiction to order sale in such a case.

J. Rights Common to Both Parties: Leases

1. Common Law

a) Mortgagor

At common law the mortgagor may grant leases which will be binding between the mortgagor and the tenant by estoppel.[249] They will not, however, bind the mortgagee in the absence of provisions in the mortgage granting power to lease to the mortgagor. Many mortgages prohibit the mortgagor from letting the premises without the consent of the mortgagee, since the mortgagee wishes to protect the right to enforce the security by sale with vacant possession. Where, in such a case, the mortgagor creates a letting of the premises with the mortgagee's consent, the lease binds the mortgagee and successors in title.[250]

b) Mortgagee

A legal mortgagee, as holder of a legal estate, has, under the principles discussed above, the right to possession of the premises and, consistent with this, was treated at common law as having the right to create leases.[251] Such leases, however, are subject to the mortgagor's equity of redemption and so liable to be destroyed by the mortgagor's paramount right to redeem in equity.

2. Statute

The Conveyancing Act, 1881 section 18 resolved the insecurities of leases created at common law by mortgagor or mortgagee by giving power to either of them to create binding leases, depending upon which of them is in possession. Provided they comply with the provisions of the statute[252] a lease made by the mortgagor will bind every mortgagee[253] and a lease made by the mortgagee will bind the mortgagor and prior mortgagees.[254]

---

248 1881 Act s.25(7).

249 See Chapter 19 Landlord and Tenant.

250 *Roulston v. Caldwell* [1895] 2 IR 136.

251 *Re O'Rourke's Estate* (1889) 23 LR Ir 497.

252 Contained in s.18 of the 1881 Act.

253 Section 18(1).

254 Section 18(2).

a) Conditions

Leases granted under the statutory power must not exceed 21 years for agricultural or occupational leases and 99 years for building leases.[255] The lease must be at the best rent reasonably obtainable.[256] It must contain a covenant by the lessee for payment of rent and a condition for re-entry if the rent is not paid within a time specified which must not exceed 30 days.

b) Exclusions

The statutory power to lease may be excluded[257] or extended[258] by agreement between the mortgagor or mortgagee. Many mortgage deeds contain a covenant binding the mortgagor not to let the premises without the consent of the mortgagee.

K. Transfer of Rights

1. By Mortgagor

a) Inter Vivos

A mortgagor may transfer his or her equity of redemption to another person. The mortgagor remains liable on the contractual covenant to pay the debt, unless there is agreement to the contrary.[259] The mortgagor would normally take an indemnity covenant from the assignee and such a covenant is implied in the case of an assignee for value.[260] A mortgagor may wish to sell the property free of the mortgage, as, for example, when a home owner wishes to sell his or her existing property and buy another one. In such a case the mortgagor must redeem the existing mortgage. A mortgagor may also discharge the mortgage by paying money into court under section 5 of the Conveyancing Act, 1881.

b) On Death

It has been seen that the original mortgagor is normally liable on a personal covenant in the mortgage to pay the debt. Formerly, on the death of the mortgagor, the mortgagee could call upon the personal representatives of the mortgagor to repay the debt out of the estate of the deceased mortgagor, as in the case of other simple debts, since they stood in the shoes of the deceased. Legis-

---

255 Section 18(5).

256 Section 18(6).

257 Section 18(13); *ICC Bank plc v. Verling* [1995] ILRM 123.

258 Section 18(14).

259 *Re Howard's Estate* (1892) 29 LR Ir 266.

260 *Adair v. Carden* (1891) 29 LR Ir 469.

lation known as Locke King's Acts[261] curtailed the right. Now the Succession Act, 1965 section 47 provides that charges on the property of a deceased person are to be paid primarily out of the property charged.

2. By Mortgagee

a) Inter Vivos

(1) Transfer

A mortgagee may transfer the debt or the mortgage security, or both, to a third person.[262] If the mortgagor does not join in the transfer then the transferee should give notice to the mortgagor, otherwise the transferee cannot complain if the mortgagor continues to pay money due to the transferor.[263] It is also advisable to obtain the concurrence of the mortgagor in order to obtain his or her agreement to the state of the accounts.[264]

(2) Sub-Mortgage

The mortgagee can create a mortgage of his or her mortgage, *i.e.* a sub-mortgage. Thus a mortgagee by conveyance of the fee simple may create a sub-mortgage by conveying a term of years created out of the fee simple to a sub-mortgagee.[265] The sub-mortgagee thus accepts the mortgagee/sub-mortgagor's rights as security for the repayment of the new loan. The sub-mortgagee for most purposes stands in the place of the original mortgagee to enforce the security.[266]

b) On Death

Under the Succession Act, 1965 section 10 all the property of a deceased person devolves on his or her personal representatives and so both the debt, which is personalty, and the mortgagee's interest in the property devolve on them in the same way.

261 Real Estate Charges Acts, 1854, 1867 and 1877.

262 *Simmons v. Montague* [1909] 1 IR 87.

263 *Dixon v. Winch* [1900] 1 Ch. 736, 742.

264 *Agnew v. King* [1902] 1 IR 471.

265 *Feehan v. Mandeville* [1890] LR Ir 90. *Rossborough v. McNeil* (1889) 23 LR Ir 409, V-C. (judgment sub-mortgage: see above Judgment mortgages).

266 Conveyancing Act, 1881 s.2(vi) mortgagee includes person deriving title from original mortgagee.

L. Priorities

1. Unregistered Principles

Priorities between mortgages of unregistered land is complicated by the effect of the registration of deeds system. The system does not entirely displace the rules developed by the common law and equity and so these must be understood first before the effect of the Registration of Deeds (Ireland) Act, 1707 is taken into account.[267]

a) First Legal, Second Legal

Successive legal mortgages are only possible if the first mortgage was created by demise or sub-demise and not by conveyance of the fee simple. Here the principle is "who is first in time is strongest in law", ("*qui prior est tempore, potior est jure"*), or "first made, first paid". Legal interests take effect prima facie according to the order of their creation. This is only so, however, if the equities are equal: the full maxim taking into account the impact of equity is "where the equities are equal the first in time prevails".

The equities will not be equal, and the first mortgagee will lose priority, in the case of fraud,[268] estoppel[269] or gross negligence[270] with respect to the title deeds. A first mortgagee who allows the mortgagor to retain the title deeds thereby enables an unscrupulous mortgagor to mislead a later mortgagee into believing that there is no prior mortgage[271] and is probably guilty of gross negligence unless he or she was given a plausible reason for not producing the deeds.[272]

b) First Legal, Second Equitable

If the first mortgage is legal it has two reasons to take priority. It is first in time. Secondly, where the equities are equal equity gives precedence to the legal estate under the maxim: "where the equities are equal the law prevails". The equities will not be equal in the case of fraud, estoppel or gross negligence.

c) First Equitable, Second Legal

This situation is the classic case of the doctrine of notice in equity. Here the principle is that a later purchaser of a legal interest, the mortgage estate, takes free of the earlier equity: "where the equities are equal the law prevails" but the

267 See also Wylie, *Irish Land Law* para. 13.127–13.162.

268 *Peter v. Russell* (1716) Gilb Eq 122, 25 ER 85.

269 *Dickson v. Muckleston* (1872) 8 Ch App 155 at 160.

270 *Re Greer* [1907] 1 IR 57.

271 *Re Ambrose's Estate* [1914] 1 IR 123.

272 *Agra Bank Ltd v. Barry* (1874) LR 7 HL 135.

equities are only equal if the later legal mortgagee is bona fide, takes for value and without notice of the earlier equitable mortgage (the Polar Star Rule). A later legal mortgagee normally will have notice where the earlier equity is a mortgage by deposit of title deeds, because he or she should have insisted on the production of the deeds.[273]

d) First Equitable, Second Equitable

Where both mortgages are equitable the first mortgage still has a good claim by being the first in time: "where the equities are equal, the first in time prevails".

Equity's attitude is that there are two equitable interests of equal value and neither party could have avoided putting themselves at risk. There is nothing to choose between them on this ground, and so the first in time is preferred. There is no real moral principle here, merely a pragmatic solution.

All this is on the assumption that the equities are indeed equal: the equities will not be equal in the case of fraud, estoppel or gross negligence. There may be negligence if the first mortgagee has parted with the title deeds without good cause.

e) Salvage

In Ireland a series of cases has held that salvage payments are paid first before the unregistered principles set out above are applied.[274] Salvage payments are payments which are necessary to save the property to the benefit of all those interested in it.[275] These are not generally payments to save the physical fabric of the premises[276] but, for example, to prevent a forfeiture of a leasehold interest[277] which has been mortgaged or to pay renewal fines.[278]

2. Unregistered Land

a) Deeds System Applies

(1) Registered v. Registered

The Registration of Deeds (Ireland) Act, 1707 by section 4 specifically provides that registered documents rank in the order in which memorials of them are lodged for registration. It makes no difference whether the mortgages are

273 *Re Stephen's Estate* (1875) IR 10 Eq 282.

274 *Re Power's Policies* [1899] 1 IR 6; *Munster and Leinster Bank Ltd v. McGlashan* [1937] IR 525; Wylie, *Irish Land Law* para. 13.158.

275 *Re Power's Policies* [1899] 1 IR 6.

276 See Chapter 14 Settlements of Land: Salvage.

277 *Kehoe v. Hales* (1843) 5 Ir Eq R 497.

278 *Hamilton v. Denny* (1809) 1 Ball & B 199, 12 RR 14.

legal or equitable for this purpose.[279] Fraud alone will deprive the earlier registered document of priority.

(2) Registered v. Registrable but Unregistered

Where the first mortgage is registered and the second is registrable but the second mortgagee has failed to register, the system applies and the registered interest takes priority.

(3) Registrable but Unregistered v. Registered

Section 5 of the 1707 Act provides that the registered document takes priority even if it is later. This is a basic principle behind the statute: the holder of a deed who can register it, but fails to do so, generally loses priority to a deed which has been registered.[280]

There is no distinction in this between legal and equitable interests.[281] Thus, if a person obtains a document conferring an equitable interest and registers it, a later purchaser of a legal interest in the same land cannot make the plea of bona fide purchaser for value without notice. There are two qualifications to this general rule.

(a) Actual Notice

The situation is within the acts with the proviso that actual notice of the unregistered right will, in certain circumstances, bind a registered transferee.[282] The courts do not allow the registration of deeds system to be used for fraud. Two situations are to be distinguished:

(a) in the first, A knows that B is entitled to some interest in land under a registrable but unregistered document. A obtains a similar or conflicting interest in the same land by deed and then registers it, with the intention of gaining priority over B. This is fraud and A will not gain priority,[283] but only if A has actual notice[284] or if the actual notice of

279 *Eyre v. Dolphin* (1813) 2 Ball & B 290, at p.300, 12 RR 94.

280 *Re McDonagh's Estate* (1879) 3 LR Ir 408, Land Js. *Cleary v. Fitzgerald* (1880) 5 LR Ir 351, V-C, (1881) 7 LR Ir 229, CA, see review of legislation by Deasy LJ at 250-255.

281 *Drew v. Norbury* (1846) 9 Ir Eq R 171.

282 See Chapter 5 Registration of Documents.

283 *Bushell v. Bushell* (1803) 1 Sch & Lef 92, 100, 9 RR 21 per Lord Redesdale LC; *Blades v. Blades* 1 Eq Cas Abr 358, 21 ER 1100 (English Yorkshire Registry).

284 *Forbes v. Deniston* (1722) 4 Bro PC 189, 2 ER 129, 2 Eq Cas Abr 482, 22 ER 409; *Delacour v. Freeman* (1854) 2 Ir Ch R 633; *Montgomery v. McEvoy* (1857) 5 Ir Ch R 126; *Clarke v. Armstrong* (1861) 10 Ir Ch R 263; *Re Flood's Estate* (1863) Ir Ch R 312; *Agra Bank v. Barry* (1874) LR 7 HL 135. On possible shift of opinion on definition of actual notice, see *Workingmen's Benefit Society v. Higgins* [1945] Ir Jur Rep 38. *Re Fuller* [1982] IR 161, High Court.

his agent, *e.g.* his lawyer, is imputed to him;[285]

(b) in the second situation A acquires an interest in land under a deed without knowledge at the time of its execution that B, under a prior document, had obtained a similar or conflicting interest. Having become aware of B's deed, A seeks to protect himself by registering his deed. This is not fraud but legitimate protection by A of his own position.[286]

An economic explanation is that in the first case A could have avoided any possible loss from being postponed to B by not taking a mortgage at all. In the second case A has innocently and unavoidably put himself at risk.

(b) Volunteers

If the owner of the document has not given consideration in the transaction to which the document relates, then he or she is bound by an earlier unregistered deed regardless of notice.[287] Here again equity intervened to protect the purchaser in a market who had advanced and risked money.

b) Deeds System Does Not Apply

(1) Registered v. Unregistrable

The later mortgage will be unregistrable if, for example, it is an equitable mortgage by deposit of title deeds.

The registration of deeds system does not apply because, it is said, one of the parties cannot register.[288]

(a) First Mortgage Legal

This is the same situation as "First Legal, Second Equitable". The first mortgage takes priority as both first in time and legal, the equities being equal.

Nevertheless, the registration system is not entirely irrelevant here. It provides a more satisfactory reason to prefer the first in time: the second mortgagee could have discovered the prior mortgage by examining the Register.[289]

---

285 If a solicitor actually knows of an unregistered deed, then that actual notice is imputed to the client. The client is bound even if an independent solicitor, exercising reasonable diligence, might not have discovered the unregistered deed: *Re Rorke's Estate* (1864) 14 Ir Ch R 442 at 446, Ch App; *Marjoribanks v. Hovenden* (1843) 6 Ir Eq R 238; *Espin v. Pemberton* (1859) 3 De G & J 547, 554, 44 ER 1380, per Lord Chelmsford.

286 Per Christian LJ in *Reilly v. Garnett* (1872) IR 7 Eq 1 at 25.

287 *Reilly v. Garnett* (1872) IR 7 Eq 1 at 27 per Christian LJ; *Eyre v. McDowell* (1861) 9 HLC 620.

288 *O'Connor v. Stephens* (1862) 13 Ir CLR 68 cited by Lord O'Hagan LC in *Reilly v. Garnett* (1872) IR 7 Eq 1. *Re Stephens* (1876) IR 10 Eq 282, L E Ct; *Cleary v. Fitzgerald* (1880) 5 LR Ir 351, V-C, (1881) 7 LR Ir 229, CA. *Re Burke's Estate* (1882) 9 LR Ir 24, CA.

289 *Re Greer* [1907] 1 IR 57.

Furthermore, even if the later mortgagee had been able to register it would have had no effect on priority.

(b) First Mortgage Equitable
The first mortgage may be equitable and registered where it is by deposit but a written memorandum exists, or it is by deed only.

This is the same situation as "First Equitable, Second Equitable" discussed above. Again, the registration system is not entirely irrelevant because the second mortgagee could have discovered the prior mortgage by examining the Register.

(2) Unregistrable v. Registered

If a transaction is not reduced to writing there is nothing that can be registered and the registration system has no effect.[290] An example of an unregistrable interest is an equitable mortgage created by deposit of the title deeds without any memorandum in writing. Priority is governed by principles of equity.

(a) Second Mortgage Legal
This is the same situation as "First Equitable, Second Legal". It is governed by the Polar Star Rule. Where the first mortgage is unregistrable because it is an equitable mortgage by deposit of title deeds it will normally have priority: the later legal mortgagee will usually have notice because he or she should have insisted on production of the title deeds.[291]

(b) Second Mortgage Equitable
This is the same situation as "First Equitable, Second Equitable". A second equitable mortgage will be registrable if it is by deposit but there is a written memorandum[292] or if it is an equitable mortgage by deed.

Registration by the later mortgagee, even if innocent, does not confer a better claim in equity because the earlier mortgagee could not have registered anyway.[293]

(3) Unregistrable v. Unregistrable

Here the registration system has no application since neither party can register. Unregistered principles apply. The mortgages are normally unregistrable because they are equitable mortgages by deposit and so the rules are those which

290 *O'Connor v. Stephens* (1862) 13 Ir CLR 68 cited by Lord O'Hagan LC in *Reilly v. Garnett* (1872) IR 7 Eq 1. *Re Stephens* (1876) IR 10 Eq 282, Landed Estates Court; *Cleary v. Fitzgerald* (1880) 5 LR Ir 351, V-C, (1881) 7 LR Ir 229, CA. *Re Burke's Estate* (1882) 9 LR Ir 24, CA.

291 *Re Stephen's Estate* (1875) IR 10 Eq 282.

292 *Re Stephens* (1876) IR 10 Eq 282, Landed Estates Court; *Rennick v. Armstrong* (1829) 1 H & B 727.

293 *Jennings v. Bond* (1845) 8 Ir Eq R 755 at 767.

relate to successive equitable mortgages: see "First Equitable, Second Equitable" above.

(4) Registrable but Unregistered v. Unregistrable

Priorities are governed by unregistered principles.

(a) First Legal, Second Equitable
See the corresponding section above.

(b) First Equitable, Second Equitable
See the corresponding section above.

(5) Unregistrable v. Registrable but Unregistered

This is the opposite situation to the previous section. Priorities are governed by unregistered principles.

(a) First Equitable, Second Legal
See the corresponding section above.

(b) First Equitable, Second Equitable
See the corresponding section above.

(6) Registrable but Unregistered v. Registrable but Unregistered

Priorities are governed by unregistered principles. All four situations discussed above may apply.

c) Tacking

Tacking will, when it applies, affect priorities. Tacking allows a mortgagee, when there are several mortgages affecting land, to secure greater priority for the mortgage by attaching or tacking it onto an earlier mortgage in the series and so gain priority over intervening mortgages.

There are two main doctrines by which this can be done at common law: (1) *tabula in naufragio*; and (2) tacking further advances.

(1) Tabula in Naufragio

(a) Application
Tabula in naufragio[294] (the plank in a shipwreck) applies where there are successive equitable mortgages following a legal mortgage. The doctrine cannot operate where the registration of deeds system applies, but only where unregistered principles still apply.[295]

---

294 The phrase was first used in *Brace v. Duchess of Marlborough* (1728) 2 P Wms 491, 24 ER 829.

295 *Tennison v. Sweeney* (1844) 7 Ir Eq R 511.

(b) The Doctrine
The doctrine is that, where there is a contest between the equitable mortgagees, in some circumstances one of them can tack his or her equitable mortgage onto the legal mortgage by obtaining a legal estate in the mortgaged land and so gain priority over the other equitable mortgage.[296] The basis of the doctrine is said to be that the equitable mortgagee who gets in the legal estate can, under the doctrine, take advantage of the principle that "where the equities are equal the law prevails".[297]

Thus, suppose X first mortgages land to A for £40,000 and then by equitable mortgage to B for £10,000 and then by another equitable mortgage to C for £10,000. X defaults on payment and the mortgagees enforce the security by sale of the land. Suppose that the land at the time of enforcing the security is worth only £55,000 which is insufficient to pay off all the mortgagees. This is the shipwreck. C would normally rank third in priority behind A and B and will only get the £5,000 which will remain after they are paid. Under the doctrine, if C can pay off A's mortgage and take a conveyance of the legal estate (which is vested in A under the legal mortgage) he can gain priority over B. The legal estate is the plank which C can seize to save himself.

(c) Equities Equal
C can only take advantage of the doctrine if the equities are equal. They have been held are only equal (a) if at the time C made his advance he had no notice of B's mortgage and (b) if he acquires some legal estate in the land or has a better right to it, as where it is held in trust for him.[298] Furthermore, if A held the legal estate on trust for B and C had notice of this when he acquired the legal estate, then C is bound by the trust and cannot take advantage of the doctrine.[299] B can prevent C gaining priority under the doctrine by acquiring herself the legal estate before C. B cannot, however, secure her priority by giving notice to C.[300]

(d) Criticism
Tabula in naufragio is said to owe its origin to the deference which the common law gave to the legal estate, but it might also be due to the deference which particular equity decisions paid to the common law. Cheshire[301] described it as "founded on technical and justly suspect reasoning". It also fa-

296 *Marsh v. Lee* (1671) 2 Ventr 337, 86 ER 473.

297 *Wortley v. Birkenhead* (1754) 2 Ves Sen 571 at 574, 28 ER 364 at 366; *Bailey v. Barnes* [1894] 1 Ch. 25, 36.

298 *Wilkes v. Bodington* (1707) 2 Vern 599 at 600, 23 ER 991 at 991-92.

299 *Workingmen's Benefit Society v. Dixon* [1908] 1 IR 582; Wylie, *Cases* p.467;

300 *Peacock v. Burt* (1834) 4 L J Ch 33, but see *West London Commercial Bank v. Reliance Permanent Building Society* (1885) 29 Ch D 954 at 963.

301 Cheshire, *Real Property* (9th ed.) p.599.

vours the equitable mortgagee who is sufficiently well-endowed with funds to be capable of buying the legal estate.

(e) Abolition and Restoration

The doctrine has had a chequered career: it was abolished in Ireland and England by section 7 of the Vendor and Purchaser Act, 1874 but was then restored again in Ireland[302] by section 73 of the Conveyancing Act, 1881.

(2) Tacking Further Advances

(a) Application

Tacking further advances has been held to apply in Ireland even where the mortgages involved are registered in the Registry of Deeds.[303]

(b) The Doctrine

Tacking further advances applies where a legal mortgagee lends more money, *i.e.* makes further advances, intended to be on the same security, unaware that another equitable mortgage has been created in the meantime.[304] Thus, if X mortgages land to A by legal mortgage, then to B by equitable mortgage and then A lends more money to X unaware of B's intervening mortgage, A can tack his equitable mortgage onto the legal one, if the equities are equal.

There is authority in Ireland for the view that an equitable mortgagee who is under an obligation to make further advances has a right to tack.[305]

(c) Equities Equal

The legal mortgagee can only tack if the equities are equal and they will not be if, at the time of making the further advance, he or she had notice of the intervening equitable mortgage.[306]

In an English case[307] it was held that notice on the part of the legal mortgagee excluded the right to tack even where the legal mortgagee had undertaken by a binding covenant to make further advances if required. Thus, if X mortgages land to A with a covenant by A to make further advances and then X mortgages by equitable mortgage to B and then A, with notice of B's mortgage,

302 It was restored in England by the Land Transfer Act, 1875 s.129, only to be abolished again in England, as to competing mortgages only, by the Law of Property Act, 1925 s.94(3). It still applies in England if one or neither of the competing interests is a mortgage. For example, an equitable mortgagee can gain priority over a prior unregistered option to purchase by acquiring the legal estate: Megarry, *Manual* (7th ed.) p.488.

303 *Re O'Byrne's Estate* (1885) 15 LR Ir 373; Wylie, *Cases* p.469.

304 *Morret v. Paske* (1740) 2 Atk 52, 26 ER 429 at 53.

305 *Re O'Byrne's Estate* (1885) 15 LR Ir 373; Wylie, *Cases* p.469; Wylie, *Irish Land Law* para. 13.161 n.56.

306 *Brown v. Lynch* (1838) 2 Jo 706; *Re Keogh's Estate* [1895] 1 IR 201; *Hopkinson v. Rolt* [1899] 2 Ch. 355.

307 *West v. Williams* [1899] 1 Ch. 132.

makes a further advance to X, A cannot tack the advance onto his first mortgage. The court nevertheless held that the creation of the equitable mortgage had relieved A of complying with the covenant.

(3) Other Cases of Tacking

The above categories may do not exhaust the possible cases of tacking. Thus, if a legal mortgagee lends more money to be secured on an equitable mortgage unaware that in the meantime an equitable mortgage has been created then the legal mortgagee may be able to tack the equitable mortgage onto the legal one.[308] Thus, X mortgages land to A by legal mortgage, then to B by equitable mortgage and then A lends more money to X on equitable mortgage unaware of B's intervening mortgage. This differs from *tabula in naufragio* in that A, as equitable mortgagee, already has the legal estate under the first mortgage at the time his equitable mortgage is created. It differs from tacking further advances in that the further loan by A was not intended to be on the same security.

3. Registered Land

a) General

(1) Registered v. Registered

Registered charges rank in priority according to the order in which they were registered[309] and not according to the order in which they were created.

Section 75 of the 1964 Act provides nevertheless that where a registered charge provides expressly for future advances to be secured on the charge the registered owner of the charge is entitled to priority to any subsequent charge, except where the further advance is made after the date of the subsequent charge and with express notice in writing of it. This is the equivalent of tacking further advances in unregistered title.

Registered charges, like registered interests, are subject to section 72 interests.

(2) Registered v. Registrable but Unregistered

Here the registered charge takes priority. This is clearly one of the intended effects of the system of registered title.

(3) Registrable but Unregistered v. Registered

The 1964 Act provides that the owner of a registered charge is not affected by unregistered rights.[310] This is clearly in accordance with the principle of regis-

308 *Morret v. Paske* (1740) 2 Atk 52 at 53, 26 ER 429.

309 1964 Act s.74.

310 Section 68(3).

tration: someone who can register, but does not do so, loses priority to someone who does. Nevertheless, actual notice on the part of a registered chargee may displace his or her priority, at least if acquired before entering the transaction by which he or she obtained the interest in the land.[311]

(4) Registered v. Unregistrable

The 1964 Act provides that the deposit of a land certificate or certificate of charge has "the same effect as the deposit of the title deeds of unregistered land or of a charge thereon".[312] Such mortgages nevertheless take effect subject to registered rights.[313] The prior registered mortgage will take priority, fraud apart.

(5) Unregistrable v. Registered

As has been noted in the previous section, the 1964 Act provides that the deposit of a land certificate or certificate of charge has "the same effect as the deposit of the title deeds of unregistered land or of a charge thereon".[314] This therefore has the effect of importing the Polar Star Rule with its doctrine of notice in equity.[315] The owner of the later registered charge will take subject to the prior unregistered charge if he or she has notice of it or is a volunteer.[316] In this instance the owner of the registered charge is likely to have notice since the land certificate will be deposited with the prior equitable mortgagee. Nevertheless, it is not easy to envisage how a registered charge could be created after a equitable mortgage by deposit because the land certificate would have to be produced in order for the later charge to be registered[317] and an equitable mortgagee who surrendered the land certificate to allow this to be done might lose the right to possession.[318] However, the equitable mortgagee might be held not to have given up the right to possession if he or she was tricked by the mortgagor into giving up the land certificate on some pretext and then got it back later.[319]

(6) Unregistrable v. Unregistrable

This situation is unlikely to arise because the registered owner can only create

311 See Chapter 24 Registration of Title.

312 1964 Act s.105(5).

313 *ibid.*.

314 1964 Act s.105(5).

315 See Chapter 24 Registration of Title.

316 1964 Act, s.52(2).

317 1964 Act s.68, s.105(1).

318 *Re Driscoll's Estate* (1867) IR 1 Eq 285, but see 1964 Act s.105(3).

319 See also Wylie, *Irish Land Law* para. 13.133.

an unregistrable charge by deposit of the land certificate.[320] Even if the first depositee was tricked into giving up possession in order to deposit it with the second mortgagee, the first mortgagee would be in danger of being held to have given up their right to possession and that would be an end of their mortgage.[321] If the first mortgagee gave it up only temporarily then the second mortgagee would be in the same position, because he or she would have surrendered it. Theoretically priorities are governed by unregistered principles.[322]

(7) Registrable but Unregistered v. Unregistrable

This situation would not arise in relation to mortgages or charges of registered land because the only way a registrable charge can be created is by registering it.[323]

(8) Unregistrable v. Registrable but Unregistered

Again, the situation cannot arise in relation to mortgages or charges of registered land because the only way a registrable charge can be created is by registering it.[324]

(9) Registrable but Unregistered v. Registrable but Unregistered

As with the previous category, the situation cannot arise in relation to mortgages or charges of registered land because the only way a registrable charge can be created is by registering it.[325]

b) Tacking

(1) Tabula in Naufragio

Tabula in naufragio cannot apply to registered land because there is no provision in the Registration of Title Act, 1964 to tack an unregistered charge onto a registered legal estate or charge.

320 1964 Act s.105(5).

321 But see s.105(3).

322 *Tench v. Molyneux* (1914) 48 ILTR 48.

323 1964 Act s.68, s.105.

324 *ibid.*

325 *ibid.*

(2) Tacking Further Advances

Section 75(1) of the Registration of Title Act, 1964 provides expressly for future advances to be secured on the charge the registered owner of the charge is entitled to priority to any subsequent charge, except where the further advance is made after the date of the subsequent charge and with express notice in writing of it.[326]

M. Discharge

1. Unregistered Land

Where a mortgage of unregistered land is created by conveyance of the fee simple or assignment of a lease the mortgage is discharged by reconveyance of the fee simple or reassignment of the lease and the deed should contain a receipt for the mortgage redemption money. A statutory form of receipt endorsed on the mortgage deed now operates in the Republic[327] both to discharge the mortgage and to reconvey the estate or interest without a formal reconveyance.[328]

Where the mortgage was created by demise or sub-demise, *i.e.* by a term of years created expressly for the purpose of mortgaging the land, the Satisfied Terms Act, 1845[329] also applies. The Act provides that where the purpose for which a term was created is fulfilled it becomes a satisfied term and automatically merges with the reversion expectant upon it. Since Deasy's Act, 1860 a reversion is not necessary in Ireland on the creation of a landlord and tenant relation but it is the practice to reserve one in mortgage terms probably so that it is clear that the 1845 statute will operate on discharge.

An equitable mortgage may be discharged by an ordinary receipt.[330]

2. Registered Land

A registered charge is discharged by the Registrar entering a note of satisfaction of the charge from the charge on the Register.[331] Part of the land may be

326 See Registered *v.s* Registered above.

327 See also Building Societies Act (NI) 1967 s.37.

328 Building Societies Act, 1989 s.27 (where mortgagee a building society); Housing Act, 1988 s.18 (other mortgagees).

329 8 & 9 Vict. c.112. The statute was mainly concerned with settled land and terms raised to pay portions: see Chapter 14 Settlements of Land.

330 *Firth & Sons Ltd v. CIR* [1904] 2 KB 205.

331 Registration of Title Act, 1964 s.65.

released from the charge in the same way.[332] The receipt or a signed release of the registered chargee is sufficient proof of the satisfaction or release.[333]

An equitable mortgage of a registered title may probably be discharged by an ordinary receipt in the same way as an equitable mortgage of unregistered land.[334]

3. Disposal

Housing (Miscellaneous Provisions) Act, 1992 section 13 provides that the Minister may make regulations in relation to the transfer, sale or assignment of mortgages. This power potentially may affect all mortgages.

332 *ibid.*

333 *ibid.*; Building Societies Act, 1989 s.27(2); Housing Act, 1988 s.18(2).

334 See *Firth & Sons Ltd v. CIR* [1904] 2 KB 205.

CHAPTER 24

REGISTRATION OF TITLE

"They love and revere the mysteries which they have spent so much time in learning, and cannot bear the rude hand which would wipe away the cobweb, in spinning which they have spent their zeal and their days for perhaps half a century."

– Lord Brougham quoted by Sir Robert Torrens.[1]

A. Origin

Registration of title was first introduced in a jurisdiction based on the common law[2] in 1858[3] in South Australia by Sir Robert Torrens, who was born in Cork in 1814 and educated at Trinity College Dublin. He was the first Premier of South Australia, but resigned this office to devote his energy to developing and refining the system. He developed it from the system of registering ships. In common law countries the systems of title registration are usually classified broadly into two basic types: the Torrens system and the English system. The English system is a modified version of the Torrens system.

The Torrens system is particularly suited to countries in which new titles were granted by the state and registered from their inception. It applies for example in Australia, most states of the United States, parts of Canada, New Zealand, and Jamaica. In many instances this view was based on the denial of aboriginal land rights, a position which is now being revised in some of the countries concerned.[4]

The English system, dating back to the Land Registry Act, 1862 and the Land Transfer Act, 1875, is suitable for countries in which land titles have existed for a long period and in which they have been operated on an unregistered

1 Simpson, *Land Law and Registration* para. 5.2.1.

2 See Simpson, *Land Law and Registration* para. 5.1.1.

3 By the Real Property Act, 1858 of South Australia. There is some question as to the originality of Torrens' scheme. He was accused at the time of some degree of plagiarism. The basic ideas behind the scheme may have been developed by Dr Ulrich Hübbe, a German lawyer living in South Australia in the 1850s who modelled it on the Hanseatic system of title registration: Gray, *Elements of Land Law* p.168 n.13.

4 See for example *Mabo v. Queensland* (1992) 66 ALJR 408 in which the High Court of Australia held, with some qualifications, that the native title claimed by Murray Islanders was recognised by the common law of Australia.

system before registration was introduced.[6] The English system applies for example in England, Nova Scotia, Ontario, Nigeria, Kenya and Tanzania.

The Irish system is basically the same as the English system but has some features typical of the Torrens system. For example, the register is public and may be inspected by anyone.[7] The first Irish Act was the Record of Title (Ireland) Act, 1865 and was drafted by Torrens himself. The purpose of the Act was to record the titles conveyed[8] or declared[9] by the Landed Estates Court,[10] which was to maintain the register, called the "Record of Title".[11] The record itself was not open to the public, but an index was to be made which could be inspected by anyone.[12] Recording of title under the Act was voluntary, even as to conveyances executed by the Landed Estates Court itself,[13] and this was one of the reasons why the Act proved ineffective. The English Land Registry Act[14] 1862 had been a failure for a similar reason.

The first effective act in Ireland was the Local Registration of Title (Ireland) Act, 1891. It introduced compulsory registration of freehold land bought by tenant farmers from landlords under the Land Purchase Acts. Compulsory registration was thus introduced in Ireland six years before it was introduced into England by the Land Transfer Act, 1897. Since registration in Ireland was introduced in the wake of the reform of agricultural tenure the areas where title is registered are predominantly agricultural rather than urban. In many countries the opposite is the case. The current legislation in the Republic is the Registration of Title Act, 1964 and the Land Registration Rules, 1972[15] and 1981.[16] In Northern Ireland the registers of deeds and of title were amalgamated in 1992 into a single register, called the title register.[17]

---

6 Simpson, *Land Law and Registration* Chapter 5.

7 Registration of Title Act, 1964 s.107.

8 Section 4.

9 Section 6.

10 Set up under 21 & 22 Vict. c.72.

11 Section 3.

12 Section 10.

13 Sections 4, 6, 7. Under s.7 the person to whom a title was conveyed by the court could decline to have it recorded.

14 25 & 26 Vict. c.53. See Simpson, *Land Law and Registration*.

15 SI 230 of 1972.

16 SI 258 of 1981.

17 Registration (Land and Deeds) (NI) Order 1992.

B. Compulsory Registration

Sections 23 and 24 of the Act make registration compulsory in the following cases where:

1) land is conveyed under the Land Purchase Acts; and
2) all freehold and leasehold land:
   a) where land is acquired by a statutory authority; and
   b) land in areas designated by the Minister of Justice by order.[18]

The counties of Meath, Carlow and Laois were declared compulsory areas with effect from 1 January 1970.[19] The registration of land in areas designated becomes compulsory:

(a) in the case of freehold land, upon conveyance on sale;

(b) in the case of a leasehold interest, *i.e.* a lease for a term of over 21 years,[20] on the grant or assignment on sale of the interest.[21]

Conveyance on sale and assignment on sale are defined[22] as an instrument made on sale for money or money's worth by virtue of which there is conferred or completed a title in respect of which an application for registration as owner may be made, and includes a conveyance or assignment by way of exchange where money is paid for equality of exchange. Interesting questions arise as to the nature of the sanction for failure to register after registration becomes compulsory. Section 25 provides that:

> "25.–In any case in which registration becomes compulsory, a person... shall not, under any conveyance on sale of freehold land or grant or assignment on sale of a leasehold interest executed *thereafter*, acquire the estate or interest purported to be conveyed... unless, within six months after such conveyance, grant or assignment (or at such later time as the Registrar or, in case of his refusal, the court may sanction in any particular case), he is registered as owner... but, on being so registered, his title shall relate back to the date of the execution of the conveyance... and any dealings with the land before registration shall have effect accordingly". [emphasis supplied]

Suppose Gortbane is land in County Meath. A conveyance on sale is executed in 1975 in favour of X. X dies in 1980 and leaves the land by will to Y. Y executes a conveyance on sale in favour of Z in 1985. Under section 24(2), it became compulsory to register the title on execution of the 1975 conveyance, since it was the first "conveyance on sale" after the county was designated a

---

18 Section 24(1).

19 Compulsory Registration of Ownership (Carlow, Laois and Meath) Order (SI 87 of 1969).

20 Section 3, 1964 Act.

21 Section 24(2), 1964 Act.

22 Section 24(3).

compulsory area in 1970. But what is the significance of the word thereafter in section 25? The natural meaning of the word is that it is Z who failed to acquire any interest under the conveyance of 1985, because section 25 relates to the conveyance executed after it became compulsory to register the title. The conveyance to X had the effect of making registration compulsory but it is the next conveyance after that which is ineffective until registration is carried out. It would also seem that, since the conveyance referred to in section 25 is that in favour of Z, then X acquired a good title under the conveyance of 1975 and could pass a good title to Y under the will. It was compulsory for X to apply for registration, but his failure to do so has no ill effects so far as he is concerned, except that he cannot pass a good title to anyone by conveyance on sale, except under section 25. It is Z who has not acquired any interest and will not do so unless she applies for registration within six months of the execution of her conveyance, or unless she can persuade the Registrar, with appeal to the High Court, to allow registration after that time. It is also arguable that although it is Z who must register in order to get title under the conveyance to her, the duty to register was imposed by statute on X and therefore Z should be able to recover the cost of doing so from X.

Once Z registers the title any dealings between the date of her conveyance in 1985 and the date when registration is effected are retrospectively validated and so too is her own conveyance. The retrospective operation of section 25, if this view is correct, does not relate to the conveyance to X, or to the will, because they are, and always were, valid. It must relate to other interests affecting the land. But should entries on the register of ownership start with X? Fitzgerald,[23] a former Registrar of Titles, is of the opinion that it should. Registration of the title became compulsory in 1975 as a result of the conveyance to X and it would seem that the state of the title should be recorded from that point on. One should remember that this is not registration of deeds: it is not a question of whether to include X's conveyance as such. It is not conveyances that are to be registered, but the state of the title, beginning at a specific point.

Registration became compulsory on the execution of X's conveyance and registration would seem to require the recording of the ownership of the title at that point. The proprietor at that point is X. The proprietorship register should therefore record X as the first proprietor, followed by Y. But what of Z? Z took no interest under the conveyance of 1985 and will not acquire one unless and until she applies for first registration within six months. During this time and until Z does so, who is the proprietor? The answer must be Y, subject to Z's power to divest him by registering the title. If, at the end of the six months, Z has failed to register the title, then Z has forfeited her power to divest Y and the land is again held by Y free of the liability to be divested by Z. It is interesting to consider whether Z would have any action for a new conveyance against Y

23 Fitzgerald, *Land Registry Practice* at 354.

after the six months have expired, or for registration of the title and then a registered transfer. On perusing Y's title Z should have discovered that the land in question had become subject to compulsory registration. If she then accepts Y's title and also neglects to remedy the situation herself under section 25, it seems unlikely that she can succeed against Y. But she might still persuade the Registrar to register the title. Y was always under the obligation to register the title, but no time limit applies to him, since he does not fall within the provisions of section 25. The only sanction so far as he is concerned is that until he does so he suffers from a disability in that he cannot pass a title by conveyance on sale to anyone which will be effective in itself. The grantee will only acquire title by, in addition, complying with section 25. Anyone to whom Y conveys or devises the property other than by conveyance on sale is under the same disability as Y.

C. Voluntary Registration

Where compulsory registration does not apply, the owner may still register the title voluntarily.

D. The Register

It is titles to interests which are registered, not pieces of land. There are three registers dealing with:

1) freehold interests in land;
2) leasehold interests in land; and
3) incorporeal hereditaments in gross and other rights.[24]

Other interests the title to which is not in itself registrable may appear as burdens against the title of other interests. The 1972 Rules provide that the register is to be kept in folios. The first part contains:

- (a) a description of the property the title to which is registered with a reference to the plan on the registry maps;
- (b) easements, covenants and other rights for the benefit of the property;
- (c) ownership of mines and minerals;
- (d) the boundaries of the property.

The second part contains:

- (a) the name and description of the owner of the property;

24 Section 8, 1964 Act.

(b) the classes of owner and of the titles (absolute, possessory, *etc.*) by which they hold. In the case of a fee simple the owner is registered as full owner.

The words fee simple do not appear on the register. If the owner has a legal life estate or fee tail the words life estate or fee tail do not appear on the register. In such cases, and where there are successive legal estate under a settlement, the owner of the first estate in possession is registered as limited owner;[25]

(c) the devolution of the property;

(d) special entries where there are co-owners, limited owners under the Settled Land Acts and infants;

(e) cautions and inhibitions restricting the registration of dispositions of the property.

The third part contains:

(a) burdens protected by registration under section 69 of the Act;

(b) registered charges not separately registered;

(c) notes of burdens protected without registration under section 72 or exemptions from them. Such burdens need not appear on the register at all[26] and so the absence of such a note will not protect a purchaser;

(d) cautions and inhibitions against dealing with registered burdens.

E. Effect of Registration

Registration of title is not merely procedural, but affects substantive law in a number of respects, as will be seen in dealing with specific topics. In general it can be said that:

1. it produces a new classification of interests in land;
2. it affects the legal relationship between people in relation to registered land. The principal case of this is that the equitable doctrine of notice is replaced by the principle of registration.

F. Conclusiveness of the Register

The basic principle behind registration of title is often called the mirror principle, *i.e.* the registration should be a mirror of the title, reflecting all the interests which affect the land in question so that a purchaser does not have to go behind the register to discover interests binding on him.

---

25 See below Chapter, Settlements of Land.

26 See below.

In actuality this principle is qualified by a number of exceptions as will be seen. The register is, in the words of section 31(1) conclusive evidence of the title of the owner to the land appearing on the register and to any right, privilege, appurtenance or burden appearing on the register, but this is subject to (a) section 72 interests which bind regardless of registration, (b) the register being rectified for fraud or mistake (sections 31,32).

In *Miscampbell v. McAlister*[27] the Northern Ireland Court of Appeal held that the corresponding section 34 in the Local Registration of Title (Ireland) Act, 1891 did not mean that the register was conclusive as to the existence or otherwise of incorporeal rights such as easements or covenants, but it is notable that section 34 did not include after the phrase "of the owner to the land" the later phrase "and of any right, privilege, appurtenance or burden". These words seem to have been included in the 1964 Act deliberately to exclude the holding in the case just referred to.

Registration of title was intended to abolish the equitable doctrine of notice and to replace it with the principle of registration. Registration of an interest makes it binding on a purchaser whether he or she bothers to consult the register or not. Whether this changes substantive law in any fundamental way is questionable, because in unregistered conveyancing a purchaser is bound in equity to make the reasonable enquiries which a prudent purchaser would make and is bound through constructive notice by any interests which he would have discovered had he made such enquiries. The registration statute confines such reasonable enquiries to the register. But even this cannot be stated without qualification. As we shall see, burdens within section 72 are binding on a purchaser without registration and even if he has no notice, actual or constructive, of them. The doctrine of notice is replaced in this aspect also and this does place an additional imposition on purchasers which is not found in unregistered conveyancing. Apart from such burdens a purchaser is not affected by actual notice of registrable but unregistered interests in the absence of fraud. The question of the conclusiveness of the Register is best understood after certain other topics have been dealt with and we shall therefore return to the issue later in the chapter.

G. Transfer

Conveyance of registered title is by registered transfer. Registered title differs from unregistered title in that the estate or interest in land does not pass to the transferee until the transfer is registered.[28] An executed transfer for consider-

27 [1930] NI 74.

28 Section 51(2). However, priorities are determined by the order in which the transferrs are lodged for registration: Land Registration Regulations, 1972 Art. 61; *Crumlish v. Registrar of Deeds and Titles* [1991] ILRM 37.

ation[29] which has been delivered but not registered is nevertheless valid against the registered owner and his devisee, as an unregistered right.[30] In principle it would extend to any transferee not for valuable consideration from the registered owner.

H. Rectification

1. Jurisdiction

Where an error occurs in the register (a) the registrar may, with the consent of the registered owner and any other interested persons, rectify the register on such terms as are agreed in writing by the parties, or (b) the court, if it is of the opinion that the register can be rectified without injustice to any person, may order the register to be rectified. Rectification of the register can be ordered by the court, or by the Registrar by consent, on the ground of fraud or mistake.[31] The error may be due to a misstatement, misdescription, omission or otherwise, and may be in the register itself or in a registry map.[32]

In *Crumlish v. Registrar of Deeds and Titles*[33] a plot of land in Co Donegal was transferred in November 1978 by a vendor for valuable consideration to SG and MG as joint tenants in fee simple, but it was not lodged for registration in the Land Registry until January 1980. The same vendor executed another transfer in February 1980 in favour of the applicant. This was lodged for registration in March 1980. In fact neither of the two transfers were registered until 20 August 1980, when by a mistake, both SG and MG and, in a separate folio, the applicant were registered as full owners of the property. Under the Land Registration Regulations 1972[34] transfers rank in priority in the order in which they are received in the central office of the Land Registry. The Registrar sought to rectify the error by cancelling the entry for the applicant as null and void. The applicant sought an order of *certiorari* to quash the Registrar's order as in excess of jurisdiction.

Lynch J in the High Court in granting the order held that the Registrar only had power to rectify the Register with the consent of the parties and the applicant in this case had specifically refused consent. The judge went on to consider section 19 of the 1964 Act, which provides that any person aggrieved by

29 It is otherwise if the transfer is voluntary: *Pim v. Coyle* [1907] 1 IR 330.

30 *Re Strong* [1940] IR 382; *Devoy v. Hanlon* [1929] IR 246, on ss. 35 and 44 of the Local Registration of Title (Ireland) Act, 1891. But unregistered rights only bind a transferee without consideration, apart from s.72.

31 Section 31(1).

32 Section 32.

33 [1991] ILRM 37, Lynch J.

34 Article 61.

an order of the Registrar may apply to the court, and section 30 which declares fraudulent and void any disposition for valuable consideration which, if it were of unregistered land would be fraudulent and void, and held that neither section conferred any powers on the Registrar.

In *Lac Minerals Ltd v. Chevron Mineral Corporation of Ireland & Others*[35] the High Court held that while privity of contract is not an essential precondition to a claim for rectification, there must be some nexus between the person claiming rectification and the document in respect of which the reformation is sought. The parties to the action in which rectification is sought must be privy to or affected by the same mistake in such a way that it would be unconscionable for the defendant in such proceedings to seek to rely on the document which erroneously recorded or mistakenly implemented the true agreement.[36]

2. Compensation

Compensation is payable under section 120 of 1964 Act by the State to a person adversely affected by a rectification. Section 120(2) extends compensation to any person who sustains loss provided the loss was not caused or contributed to by the neglect or default of that person or his or her agent.[37]

I. Classes of Title

Titles appearing on the Register may of different classes, *i.e.* qualities.

1. Absolute Title: Section 37

This is the highest class of title. Absolute title suggests a title absolutely guaranteed against interests not appearing on the register, but this is far from the case and the description is in fact quite misleading. A better description would be least qualified title.

Section 37 of the Act provides that absolute freehold title vests the estate in the registered holder subject to all express or implied rights, privileges but subject to: (a) The burdens registered against the title, and (b) The burdens affecting land without registration under section 72 (overriding interests).

Where the registered owner holds as trustee, the estate is also subject to the duties and liabilities of a trustee.[38]

Section 49 of the 1964 Act makes it clear that the Statute of Limitations, 1957 applies to registered land as it applies to unregistered land and a registered

35 [1995] 1 ILRM 161.

36 See also *Re Skelton*[1976] NI 132.

37 *Re Walsh* [1916] 1 IR 40; *Tomkin Estates Ltd v. O'Callaghan and Persian Properties Ltd*, unreported, High Court, McCracken J, 16 March 1995.

38 Section 37(3).

title may be lost by adverse possession and a new owner registered.[39] Section 72(1)(p) includes within the burdens affecting the title of a registered owner without registration "rights acquired or in the course of being acquired under the Statute of Limitations, 1957". Thus before an adverse possessor has become the new registered proprietor, his or her interest is protected under section 72.

In the Torrens system title begins with first registration, but it is by no means clear whether this is so under the 1964 Act. In England it has been held that interests acquired before first registration by adverse possession can affect even an absolute registered title.[40]

It has been seen in relation to unregistered land that all titles are subject in theory to the possibility of a better title. Such a theoretical possibility exists in that the ostensible fee simple may in fact be a long lease granted long ago and the reversion on the lease has not been barred by limitation either because (a) it has not yet fallen into possession or, (b) if it has, the 12 years have not yet expired.[41] It is not clear if this is also the case in registered title.

If the Registration of Title Act, 1964 changes either of the preceding points it can be said to have changed the nature of ownership in land.

2. Qualified Title: Section 39

This is the same as absolute title but subject to qualifications entered on the register. These are rights affecting the land at first registration.[42]

3. Possessory Title: Section 38

Where a person has claimed to have acquired title by possession the Registrar may enter their title on the register, but he can do so for absolute, qualified or possessory title.[43] The section does not expressly say that the Registrar may only make an entry after the 12 year limitation has run, and so, for example, a person occupying land of which there is no known better title might be registered. Thus, the Act does not exclude relative titles. Section 38(1) provides that registration for a possessory title shall not prejudice any right adverse to or in derogation of the title of the person registered.

---

39 Section 49(2). *Re Daily* (1944) NI 1, [1944] Ir Jur Rep 69 (husband registered owner, separates from wife. Wife and family continue in occupation).

40 *Chowood v. Lyall (No. 2)* [1930] 2 Ch. 156. See Chapter 25 Adverse Possession.

41 See Chapter 1 Introduction.

42 Note that such excepted interests are overriding interests under s.72.

43 Note that s.146 of the Finance Act, 1994 provides that the Registrar may not register a possessory title until the Revenue Commissioners issue a certificate stating that the property did not become chargeable to tax or that any tax has been paid: See Grogan [1995] *Gazette* (April) 125, but is now amended by Finance Act, 1996 s.128 to provide an exemption.

Section 38(2) says that the right referred to in section 38(1) includes right or equities existing by reason of the interest of the owner being deemed to be a graft upon his previous interest. This refers to the practice under the Local Registration of Title Act, 1891. When the Irish Land Commission[44] granted land to a former tenant, it vested the fee simple in the person who was apparently the tenant, but it did not investigate the tenant's title as it would have taken too long to complete the purpose of the Acts. The title was usually registered with a note as to equities which preserved any rights such as mortgages or charges affecting the tenants interest which had not been revealed by the investigation of the title. Section 35 of the 1964 Act provides that such titles are to be registered with possessory title. Where land was vested in a person by the Irish Land Commission[45] it was normally registered as possessory title, but could be registered as qualified or absolute title.[46]

4. Good Leasehold Title: Section 40

Registration of a leasehold interest with absolute title is only done when the title to the freehold and to any intermediate lease has also been investigated. If the title to the freehold and intermediate leases has not been investigated, the lease may be registered with good leasehold title.

J. Conversion of Titles: Section 50

1. Compulsory Conversion

Where land was vested in a person by the Irish Land Commission and registered with possessory title and has been so registered for 15 years the Registrar shall, provided he is satisfied that the registered owner is in possession, register the title as absolute in the case of freehold land and good leasehold in the case of leasehold land.

2. Voluntary Conversion

Where land was vested in a person by the Irish Land Commission and the title is deemed to be possessory and has been registered for 30 years the Registrar may convert it to absolute title on the registration of a disposition or on transmission on death. Where the title registered is deemed possessory and has been so registered for at least 12 years and the person entitled wishes to transfer for value, it may be converted to absolute or good leasehold title. The latter provi-

---

44 See now Irish Land Commission (Dissolution) Act, 1992, s.4.

45 1964 Act, s.26, Wylie, *Irish Land Law* para. 21.30, after 1 January 1967. See Irish Land Commission (Dissolution) Act, 1992 (not yet in force).

46 Section 26 of 1964 Act.

sion shows that a person who wishes to enter the market is placed in a more favourable position than is the case with non-market transactions.

K. Classification of Interests

Although the registration system introduces a new classification of interests the various categories are not mutually exclusive as will be seen.

1. Registered Interests: Section 8

a) Types of Interests

These are principally legal estates. They include:

1) Freehold estates.

   Where the freehold estate is less than a fee simple special provisions apply which are dealt with below.

2) Leaseholds for more than 21 years unexpired.

   Section 8 only refers to leasehold interests, but section 3 defines leasehold interest as an interest in land under a lease for a term of years of which more than 21 are unexpired at the date of registration. Tenancies created for any term not exceeding 21 years or for any lesser estate or interest fall within section 72(1)(i) where there is occupation under the tenancy and are binding without registration.

3) Incorporeal hereditaments in gross.

   This excludes easements and restrictive covenants since both such interests are always held for the benefit of dominant land. Such interests appear on the register as burdens registered against the servient land and as beneficial rights on the register entry of the register for the benefit of the dominant land.

   It includes:

   a) legal profits *à prendre*;

   b) legal rentcharges, including a fee farm rent created by rentcharge; and

   c) other, now rare, legal interests such as franchises (right to hold markets, fish in tidal waters) and fee farm rents created by feudal tenure.

b) Special Cases

(1) Co-Ownership: Section 91

Two or more persons can be registered as the owners of a single estate or interest. Under section 91(2) two or more such persons are deemed to be joint tenants unless there is an entry o the register to the contrary. Where persons are registered as tenants in common the register will also show the size of the share they each own.[47]

(2) Trusts: Section 92

Where there is a trust it is the trustees, as owners of the legal estate who are registered as owners.[48] Trust includes express, implied or constructive trusts.[49] The interests of the beneficiaries are not automatically entered on the register. They are classified as minor interests.[50] The normal practice is for the trustees to protect the interests of the beneficiaries by entering or applying for the entry of an inhibition or a caution. The Registrar may advise trustees to do so even if they do not apply themselves. Trustees who fail to do so may be liable to beneficiaries for any loss occurring through failure to do so. The effect of such an entry depends on whether the equitable interest is a minor interest of the type that is overreached on sale or not.[51] Such an entry will prevent or restrict dealing with the registered legal title. Trustees remain liable personally to beneficiaries.[52]

Beneficiaries who are in actual occupation of the land may be protected under section 72 without any entry on the register. This is particularly important in the protection of the interests of persons under implied or constructive trusts who may be unaware that they are entitled to such interests. Such a situation provides an example of the overlapping nature of the provisions of the Act, since a person entitled to an equitable interest who is in possession may be protected under section 72 without registration and also be able to enter an inhibition or caution.[53] There is nothing to prevent a person creating equitable estates and interests in the land or in a registered charge just as an unregistered owner may do.[54] Thus, not only may express equitable interests be created, but other equitable interests such as constructive trusts or interests arising under

---

47 Section 91(1).

48 *Re O'Doherty* [1894] 1 IR 58, Monroe J (on the 1891 Act).

49 Section 92(3).

50 See below.

51 Sections 96–98. See below Section 24.11.5 Minor Interests.

52 Section 37(4).

53 1964 Act s.105(5). See below Section 24.12 Overlapping Categories.

54 Section 68(2) Note that the section does not restrict the power to create interests to the registered owner.

the doctrine of proprietary estoppel may also be created. If the estate of a registered owner becomes subject to a trust after first registration then section 92(2) provides that none of the following persons shall be affected by notice of the trust merely by the receipt by the Registrar of an instrument, *e.g.* the trust deed, for registration:

(a) The Registrar;

(b) a registered transferee for valuable consideration;

(c) a registered owner of a charge created for valuable consideration;

(d) a person claiming an interest created for valuable consideration in a registered burden.

One should notice the qualification of for valuable consideration in (b), (c) and (d). Persons who take registered land otherwise than for valuable consideration are bound by more interests than those who pay valuable consideration for it, as will be seen below.

(3) *Settled Land*

(a) Successive Legal Estates

Where the settlement is created by successive legal estates the tenant for life or person having the powers of a tenant for life under the Settled Land Acts is registered as limited owner.[55] Section 37 provides that the effect is to vest the fee simple estate in the person so registered and in the other persons entitled to estates in remainder under the settlement "collectively, according to such estates and interests respectively". The meaning of this is far from clear. On the face of it converts successive legal estates into some form of co-ownership, although the intent is further obscured by the word respectively which suggests on the contrary that the estates are still successive and that all legal estates under the settlement continue to exist as before. One effect which it could arguably have is to require a transfer of registered settled land to be executed by all those having legal interest under the settlement, since the fee simple seems to be vested in them collectively. If so this would conflict with the Settled Land Acts which confer on the tenant for life, or person having the powers of a tenant for life, under the Acts the power to convey the fee simple without the consent of those entitled in remainder or reversion. This would radically alter the substantive law relating to settled land.

It could also arguably render much settled land inalienable, namely, where contingent interests exist under the settlement and where those interests are contingent for the reason that the persons who are to take them are as yet unascertained. How can the fee simple in such a case be vested in all the persons entitled to interests under the settlement? Is it only vested in those who are

---

55 Section 27.

ascertained at the date of the settlement? When, later, contingent interests vest in other persons when they become ascertained, does the fee simple re-vest in them together with the other persons in whom it was vested before? Here again, the section almost certainly did not contemplate such an effect. The names of other persons entitled under the settlement, *i.e.* other than the tenant for life or person having the powers of the tenant for life under the Acts, are not entered on the register. On the one hand it might seem odd not to do so in the case of a settlement by successive legal estates since they hold legal estates and the policy of the Act is to enter such estates, but these are future interests, not interests in possession. The anomaly of this situation is however, apparent particularly as the provision just dealt with, section 37, purports on the face of it to vest the fee simple in such persons. Nevertheless, in so far as such persons hold legal estates which will be overreached on sale the practice accords with theory because a purchaser is not concerned with the precise nature of their interests. The names of the trustees of the settlement are entered on the register in that capacity[56] since a purchaser must pay the purchase money to them or into court if he is to obtain a discharge from liability to the other persons entitled under the settlement.[57] The tenant for life remains liable as trustee of his powers to the other persons entitled under the settlement.[58]

We have seen that under section 27 in the case of a settlement the tenant for life or person having the powers of a tenant for life under the Settled Land Acts is registered as limited owner. The register does not contain a note as to the actual estate which he or she holds. This is said to be because a purchaser is not concerned with the information, it being sufficient for him or her to know that the land is settled land.[59] Under the 1891 Act similar provisions applied but it was the practice to include a marginal note as to the actual estate possessed by the person entitled in possession. This practice is not followed under the 1964 Act. It might, however, be essential for the Registrar to know exactly what estate is held by a person registered as limited owner, as, for example, where such a person claims to be entitled to a fee tail estate. Such a person might execute a disentailing assurance under the Fines and Recoveries (Ireland) Act, 1834 and then apply for registration as full owner. The practice in such a case is apparently for the Registrar to raise requisitions asking the applicant to state under what authority they exercise the power and to require the deed of settlement and the disentailing assurance to be submitted for examination. The implication of this is, however, that the whole title is not on the register, or that it exists partly on and partly off the register. This seems to contradict the mirror principle. Once first registration of the title is effected, title deeds should no

56 Section 99(1).

57 Section 40.

58 Section 37(4).

59 See page 877.

longer be relevant. Section 99(8) provides that a person is not affected by notice of any trusts of any settlement simply because a person is registered as limited owner or by any reference on the register to the land being settled. There is no real reason why a person should be so affected because the interests of those entitled in remainder or reversion are overreached on sale and a purchaser will take the land free of them if the sale is in accordance with the Settled Land Acts. The interests of those entitled under the settlement may be noted by inhibitions requiring notice to be given to them of any sale or other exercise of the tenant for life's powers, but such an entry may not restrict the powers in any way.

(b) Successive Equitable Estates

Section 27 appears to apply in the same way to settlements created by successive equitable estates, in that the tenant for life or person having the powers of the tenant for life under the Settled Land Acts, 1882-90 is registered as limited owner. The tenant for life has power to convey the fee simple and the curious provision of section 37(2), which declares that the registration of a person as limited owner vests the fee simple in the person and the other persons entitled under the settlement, may also have some significance here.

(c) Minors

Where land is settled land because the owner is an infant, *i.e.* a minor, the minor is registered as owner but is described as such on the register.[60] It is necessary for a potential purchaser to know that the registered owner is a minor because the powers under the Settled Land Acts, 1882-90 may be exercised on the minor's behalf by the trustees of the settlement.[61]

(4) Trusts for Sale

Where a trust for sale creates successive interests in the proceeds of sale it has already been seen that it is deemed to be settled land within the Settled Land Acts by section 63 of the Settled Land Act, 1882. Under sections 6 and 7 of the Settled Land Act, 1884, as has been seen, the trustees for sale can exercise their powers under the trust, including sale, unless the tenant for life has obtained an order of the court under section 7. Once such an order has been made only the tenant for life can sell the land and the trustees have only the powers of trustees of the settlement within the Settled Land Acts. Section 99(6) of the Registration of Title Act, 1964 provides that the provisions of the Act dealing with the registration of limited owners do not apply to trusts for sale unless the settlement itself confers the powers under the Settled Land Acts on the tenant for life or if the tenant for life has obtained an order of the court. If such an order is ob-

60 Section 101.

61 Sections 60, 100 Settled Land Act, 1882; *Re Conroy's Trusts* [1938] Ir Jur Rep 26, and see Chapter 14.

tained, section 99(7) provides that it shall be to the effect that the tenant for life shall be entered on the register as limited owner.

2. Burdens Affecting Land Without Registration

a) Introduction

These are usually referred to as section 72 interests or overriding interests. Section 72 interests, or overriding interests as they are often known in systems of land registration,[62] constitute the single most important qualification to the mirror principle, *i.e.* that a purchaser need only concern himself or herself with entries on the register and can ignore interests which do not appear there. Interests within section 72 are binding on the registered land whether or not they are on the register. The phrase whether or not indicates that the categories are not mutually exclusive and that interests falling within section 72 may also be protected in other ways, as in some cases, by being entered as burdens under section 69, or as inhibitions or cautions. It should also be noticed that interests within section 72 and which are not on the register are binding regardless of whether the person concerned has notice of them or not. This is not such a departure from unregistered conveyancing as it might first appear since most of them will be found to be interests of persons in actual occupation of the land which would give rise to notice in equity under the unregistered system, or to be legal interests which would be binding regardless of notice in the unregistered system.

b) Specific Interests

The following are the more important interests listed in section 72(1):

(a) succession duty, State rents arising under fee farm grants and payments in lieu of tithe rentcharges;[63]

(b) land improvement charges and drainage charges;

(c) annuities or rentcharges for the repayment of advances made under the Land Purchase Acts to enable agricultural tenants to buy the fee simple of a farm;

(d) rights of the Irish Land Commission[64] or of any person under a vesting order made by the Commission under the Land Purchase Acts;

(e) rights of the Irish Land Commission[65] on execution of an order for possession under section 37 of the Land Act, 1927;

62 The term does not occur in the 1964 Act.

63 Note that tithe rentcharges and other payments into the Church Temporalities Fund were abolished by the Land Act, 1984 s.7.

64 Now the Minister for Agriculture and Food: Irish Land Commission (Dissolution) Act, 1992, s.4.

65 Now the Minister for Agriculture and Food, *ibid.*

(f) public rights, *e.g.* public rights of way;

(g) customary rights arising from tenure. It is doubtful if any still exist;

(h) easements and profits à prendre unless created by express grant or reservation after first registration. If they are so created, they are registrable as a burden against the land under section 69;

(i) tenancies for a term not exceeding 21 years or for any less estate or interest, in cases where there is occupation under the tenancy. If the unexpired term exceeds 21 years the lease itself is a registrable interest under sections 3 and 8, and is also registrable as a burden on the fee simple under Section 69;

(j) rights of every person in actual occupation of the land or in receipt of the rents or profits unless inquiry is made of such person and they do not disclose their rights. This is the most important overriding interest since it is so general. It was intended to be the equivalent in registered land of the rule in *Hunt v. Luck*;[66]

(k) where the title is possessory, qualified or good leasehold title, all rights excepted from the effect of registration;

(l) a perpetual yearly rent superior to a rent registered as a burden on registered land;

This occurs when there are successive grants in fee farm, as under Deasy's Act. This facilitates first registration of the fee simple. The tenant in fee simple may register it with the rent reserved to the grantor registered as a burden and even if the fee farm grantor held subject to a rent, that need not be proved, but will still be protected under this section. Thus, if X made a grant in fee farm to A and later A makes a further grant under Deasy's Act in fee farm to B, A retains only a rent, having parted with the fee simple. B's fee simple may be registered with the rent B pays to A registered as a burden, but no investigation is made of the title further back to reveal the rent paid by A to X. This superior rent is nevertheless binding on B under this section. In Northern Ireland B would be registered with good fee farm grant title which similarly preserves the superior rents.[67]

(m) covenants and conditions contained in a deed or document creating a superior rent. This applies to the same situation to (l) above. Where the grantor of a fee farm grant himself held under a grant in fee farm, the grant to him may contain covenants and they are preserved by this section;

(n) a purchase annuity payable in respect of a cottage which is the subject of a vesting order under the Labourers Act, 1936;

(o) restrictions imposed by section 21 of the Labourers Act, 1936 on the

66 [1902] 1 Ch. 428; *Hamilton v. Lyster* (1844) 7 Ir Eq R 560.

67 1970 Act (NI) s.16(2).

mortgaging or charging of cottages purchased under that Act;[68]

(p) rights acquired or in the course of being acquired under the Statute of Limitations, 1957. When a person has acquired the land by adverse possession, then before the register is amended their interest binds the land under this section. The possible meaning of rights "in the course of being acquired" is discussed above under Absolute Title;

(q) statutory restrictions on assignment, subletting[69] or subdivision[70] which are specifically preserved by section 59, and, where the registered owner does not have the right to mines and minerals, the rights of persons who do;[71]

Section 59 provides that "nothing in this Act shall affect the provisions of any enactment by which the alienation, assignment, subdivision or subletting of any land is prohibited or in any way restricted". This would include not only such restrictions in leases[72] but also special conditions imposed on a sale of a dwelling by a housing authority.[73]

(r) covenants continued in force by section 28 of the Landlord and Tenant (Ground Rents)(No. 2) Act, 1978. Where a person enlarges a lease into a fee simple, some of the covenants under the lease are preserved.[74]

Under section 72(3) the registrar may enter a note of such burdens on the register when their existence is proved to his satisfaction and with the consent of the registered owner or the applicant for registration.

c) Overriding Interests under Section 72(1)(j)

(1) Included Interests

The most important category, potentially, of section 72 interests are the rights of persons in "actual occupation of the land or in receipt of the rents and profits thereof, save where, upon enquiry made of such person, the rights are not disclosed".

In Ireland there is less authority on these than in England, probably because registration in Ireland applies mostly to rural land, but in England the courts

68 See Chapter 6 Fee Simple.

69 Now under Landlord and Tenant (Amendment) Act, 1980 ss. 65 67.

70 Agricultural land may not be subdivided without the consent, formerly, of the Irish Land Commission: Land Act, 1965 s.45(12). Now the power vests in the Minister for Agriculture and Food: Irish Land Commission (Dissolution) Act, 1992, s.4.

71 Section 73.

72 See footnote 68.

73 Housing Act, 1966 s.89 as amended by the Housing (Miscellaneous Provisions) Act, 1992 s.25.

74 Section 28 of the Landlord and Tenant (Ground Rents)(No. 2) Act, 1978. The effect of section 28 does not appear to be limited to acquisition of the fee simple under the 1978 Act.

have found many types of interests to fall within the equivalent section[75]. This may indicate a judicial aversion to the registration principle. Among the interests found to be overriding have been the following:

(1) a purchaser's equity;[76]

(2) an option to purchase the freehold;[77]

(3) an unpaid vendor's lien;[78]

(4) a purchaser's lien for the deposit;[79]

(5) a tenancy under the doctrine of feeding the estoppel;[80]

(6) interests under constructive trusts;[81]

(7) a wife's equity acquired by contributions to the purchase of the matrimonial home;[82]

The English House of Lords in *Williams & Glynns Bank v. Boland*[83] came to the same conclusion. They also held that the wife was in actual occupation not withstanding the husband's occupation, disapproving of *Caunce v. Caunce.*[84] In England after 1925 co-ownership creates a statutory trust for sale and so the wife's equity might have been expected to be overreached on sale. In *Williams & Glynns* it was held that it would not be overreached because of section 2(1)(ii) of the Law of Property Act, 1925, *i.e.* that the trust for sale did not prejudice the rights of persons in occupation. In *City of London Building Society v. Flegg*[85] the House of Lords retreated from this position and explained *Williams & Glynns* on the basis that the equity was not overreached there because the purchase money had been paid only to a single trustee.

In Ireland there is no statutory trust for sale in the case of co-ownership and the reasoning in *Flegg* would not apply. This subject is pursued below.[86]

---

75 Section 70 of the Land Registration Act, 1925.

76 *Bridges v. Mees* [1957] Ch. 475.

77 *Webb v. Pollmount* [1966] Ch. 584.

78 *London & Cheshire Insurance Co v. Laplagrene Property Co Ltd* [1971] Ch. 499.

79 *Lee Parker v. Izzett* [1971] 1 WLR 1.

80 *City Permanent Building Society v. Miller* [1952] 1 Ch. 840.

81 *Hodgson v. Marks* [1971] 1 Ch. 892.

82 *Friends Provident Life Office v. Doherty* [1992] ILRM 372. The case is discussed below.

83 [1981] AC 487.

84 [1969] 1 WLR 286.

85 [1988] 1 AC 54, [1987] 2 WLR 1266. The property in the case was called Bleak House.

86 See Excluded Interests: A share of a tenant in common under a trust for sale.

(8) an occupational licence, perhaps;[87]

(9) the right to rectify the register.[88]

(2) Excluded Interests

Judges have expressed the view that section 72 does not create new types of property interest, it only classifies existing ones.[89]

(a) Spouse's Veto over Conveyance of Family Home

A spouse's power to refuse consent to a conveyance under the Family Home Protection Act, 1976 has been held not to be a section 72 interest. It is not a property interest.[90]

(b) Planning Permission

It seems unlikely that planning permission is a right within section 72(1)(j). Carroll J in the High Court in *Electricity Supply Board v. Gormley*[91] held that planning permission was not a right within section 52(1) of the Registration of Title Act, 1964. That section provides on the registration of a transferee of freehold land as full owner with an absolute title, the instrument of transfer vests in the registered transferee an estate in fee simple in the land transferred, subject to registered burdens under section 69 and unregistered burdens under section 72 but "free from all other rights, including rights of the State". Planning permission was, the judge said, just that: a permission and not a right. This probably means that it is not a right within section 72(1)(j) either.

Section 28(5) of the Local Government (Planning and Development) Act, 1963 provides that the grant of planning permissions "shall enure for the benefit of the land" and enforcement procedures also attach to the land.[92] In *Readymix Eire Ltd v. Dublin County Council*[93] Henchy J described planning permission as "an appendage to the title to the property". Nevertheless although the person having the benefit of a planning permission has something in the nature of a right to carry it out, they would not seem to have the right to

87 *Re Sharpe* [1980] 1 WLR 219, [1980] 1 All ER 198.

88 *Blacklocks v. JB Developments Ltd* [1981] 3 All ER 392.

89 In *Esso Petroleum v. Epps* [1973] 1 WLR 1071 it was held that intermittent parking of a car is not an overriding interest because it is not an easement, but see now *London & Blenheim Estates Ltd v. Ladbroke Retail Parks Ltd* [1993] 1 All ER 307, [1992] 1 WLR 1278, at 1288B-C, Chancery Division, where it was held, *inter alia,* that a right to park cars could be an easement if it did not deprive the servient owner of effective use of the land. See also Chapter 22 Incorporeal Hereditaments.

90 *Guckian v. Brennan* [1981] IR 478, High Court, Gannon J; *Murray v. Diamond* [1982] ILRM 113.

91 [1985] IR 129, Supreme Court, [1985] IR 129 at 144, appeal allowed on other issues.

92 Local Government (Planning and Development) Act, 1963 s.31(8), s.34.

93 Unreported, Supreme Court, 30 July 1974, cited with approval in *Dublin CC v. Jack Barrett Ltd* unreported, Supreme Court, 28 July 1983.

do so in a way which adversely affects the property rights of third parties in violation of the general law and therefore it can be doubted if it is a property right.

(c) A Share of a Tenant in Common under a Trust for Sale

A share in the beneficial interest in priority subject to a trust for sale is overreached on sale and so does not require protection against or priority over a purchaser and so does not fall within the section.

The House of Lords in England in *Williams & Glynns Bank v. Boland*[94] and *City of London Building Society v. Flegg*[95] considered the question of a spouse's equity in a matrimonial home acquired by contributions to the purchase of the home. In England a statutory trust for sale is created in such a case and this clearly has placed obstacles, no doubt unforeseen by those who drafted the legislation, in the way of judges who wish to protect the possession of a spouse, usually a wife, in the matrimonial home after the marriage relationship breaks down. In Ireland there is no statutory trust for sale and this must be borne in mind when considering the English cases, which are nevertheless worth examining because the issues raised are relevant in this jurisdiction.

In England, under the 1925 legislation, all cases of co-ownership create a statutory trust for sale.[96] This was done apparently in order to ensure unrestricted alienability of land in the market. It was the familiar policy which infuses much of the English 1925 legislation: the inclination to the market as the mechanism by which property interests change hands. The interests of tenants in common therefore take effect as beneficial interests under such a trust. The orthodox view is that beneficial interests under a trust for sale are notionally converted to interests in the eventual proceeds of sale from the moment the trust is created: equity regards as done that which ought to be done. In the view of equity the beneficiaries had interests in money and not in land at all. The doctrine was and still is a fiction. This old doctrine of conversion in equity also provided a justification or rationale for the more modern concept of overreaching: the notion that on sale of the land the beneficial interests are transferred into interests in the proceeds of sale and are so cleared off the title so that they no longer affect the legal title to the land and the purchaser is not concerned with them. In theory it can be seen that the two doctrines are not as readily compatible as it might seem. Conversion in equity takes place when the trust is created and so the actual point of sale has no notional effect on the interests: they have always been fictionally interests in money from the start. Overreaching on the other hand implies that a legal change takes place at the point of sale. The beneficial interests cease to affect the land at that point. Nevertheless

94 [1981] AC 487.

95 [1988] 1 AC 54, [1987] 2 WLR 1266.

96 Gray, *Elements of Land Law* pp. 526–36.

the older notion was seen as consonant with the market-oriented legal mechanism of overreaching.

One effect which was seen as following from this was that the beneficial co-owners had no right to possession of the land. Their interests were interests in money, not in land. Nevertheless the English courts did not adhere to this theory in all cases.[97] A further effect was that the orthodox theory would deny a right of occupation to a wife who had acquired an equity in a matrimonial home through contributions to the purchase price.

In *Williams & Glynns Bank v. Boland*[98] Lord Denning MR in the English Court of Appeal departed from the orthodox theory in holding that a spouse-beneficiary behind a trust for sale of a matrimonial home had an equitable interest in land[99] and that this meant that the spouse a right to possession while the trust subsisted. The House of Lords, on appeal, upheld the view that such a beneficiary had a right to occupy, but regarded the interest as merely subsisting in reference to land.[100] There seems little doubt that the position in *Williams & Glynns Bank* was adopted in order to protect the occupation of wives, and also resident children, against a mortgagee or chargee of the husband.

More recently the House of Lords in *City of London Building Society v. Flegg,*[101] while recognising that a beneficiary had a right of occupation, nevertheless held that it was capable of being overreached on sale of the land. They held, on a provision similar to section 72 of the Irish 1964 Act, that the share of a tenant in common under a trust for sale was not an overriding interest. They explained *Williams and Glynns Bank* by pointing out that the purchase money there had been paid only to one trustee which did not give the purchaser a good discharge. The decision in *Flegg* had the effect of reducing the protection of wives against third parties acquiring interests in a matrimonial home.

In Ireland a trust for sale does not automatically arise in the case of a wife's equity acquired by contributions and such an interest is not subject to the doctrine of automatic overreaching on a sale by the spouse-owner.[102] However, this does not mean that a spouse with an equity has a right to possession absolutely secure against third parties, other than those not acquired for valuable consideration.[103] The spouse's possession, as part of the equity, prima facie

97 The interests of beneficiaries under a trust for sale were held to be interests in land for the purpose of s.40 of the English Law of Property Act, 1925: *Cooper v. Critchley* [1955] Ch. 431 at 439, Court of Appeal. Gray, *Elements of Land Law* p.544.

98 [1981] AC 487, HL.

99 [1979] Ch. 312 at 331A, C.

100 [1981] AC 487.

101 [1988] 1 AC 54, [1987] 2 WLR 1266.

102 See above: Included Interests.

103 Where, for example, a husband is sole legal owner of a family home and a wife has an equity acquired by contributions the wife cannot prevent a creditor of the husband reg-

has priority, but only where the equities are equal and furthermore equitable remedies are in any case discretionary.

(3) Actual Occupation

In unregistered title a purchaser will be held to have constructive notice of the rights of persons in occupation of the land unless it would be inequitable to fix them with such notice.[104]

How do you tell if a person is in occupation? In *Kingsnorth v. Tizard*[105] the title to the land was unregistered, but the issue concerned the principle that a purchaser is taken in equity to have notice of the rights of persons in actual occupation.[106] A married couple occupied a matrimonial home of which the legal estate was in the husband's name. The wife had acquired an equity in the house. The marital relationship had broken down and the wife sometimes slept in her sister's house a few miles away and sometimes in the matrimonial home. On the occasions when she slept at the sister's house she would return to the matrimonial home to look after the children and prepare herself for work. She slept in the matrimonial home when the husband was away, which happened frequently. When she did so she occupied a spare bedroom. Her occupation of the bedroom would not have been obvious to someone who merely opened the door and looked in, although she kept cosmetics in various drawers. While this situation continued the husband applied to mortgage brokers for a loan. He said on the application form that he was not married. The mortgage brokers instructed a surveyor to examine the premises. The surveyor arranged with the husband to visit the house on a Sunday, at the suggestion of the husband. The surveyor visited the premises and saw evidence of occupation by the husband and the children but not of the wife who was not there at the time. In order apparently to explain the presence of the children the husband told the surveyor that he was married, but that his wife had left many months ago, that they were separated and that she lived with someone nearby. The surveyor reported the presence of the husband and the children and that no other persons appeared to be in occupation. The mortgage brokers advanced the loan to the husband. Shortly afterwards the husband emigrated, taking the son with him. The mortgage brokers sought to enforce their rights and in the present action sought to establish that their rights took priority over the wife's equity in the house.

---

istering a judgment mortgage against the husband's interest in the house: *Containercare (Ireland) Ltd v. Wycherley* [1982] IR 143, but the wife's equity still has priority over the judgment mortgagee's right to an order for sale under the Judgment Mortgage (Ireland) Act, 1850 since a judgment mortgagee is a transferee not for valuable consideration: *Curran v. Curran* unreported, High Court, McWilliam J, 10 March 1981.

104 *Hamilton v. Lyster* (1844) 7 Ir Eq R 560; *Hunt v. Luck* [1902] 1 Ch. 428.

105 [1986] 2 All ER 54, [1986] 1 WLR 783, 51 P & C R 296.

106 See Chapter 4 Equity: Doctrine of Notice:Rights of Persons in Occupation.

Finlay J in the English High Court held that the mortgage brokers had constructive notice of the wife's occupation. He held that she had not ceased to be in occupation, since that did not require exclusive, continuous or uninterrupted occupation. Nor was actual occupation negatived by regular and repeated absences. The wife was still present in the house virtually every day or part of every day. The occupation of the husband did not exclude the wife's occupation.[107] The judge held that the agent of the building society did not have to look into drawers in the bedroom, but that they had nevertheless not carried out such inspections as were reasonable in the circumstances.[108] A visit on a Sunday afternoon, particularly one arranged in advance with the applicant, was not such an inspection. It is questionable whether time-share leases would fall within the section. Is occupation for one or two weeks in the year sufficient to constitute actual occupation within the subsection? If a prospective purchaser inspects the land during the week leased to X and finds X in residence is X then within the subsection, but not the others who were not in occupation during that week? If the purchaser inspects it when X is not in residence and finds Y in occupation and Y says that he has a time-share, is that not enough to give notice to the purchaser that X has a time-share, or put the purchaser on inquiry? On the face of it an inspection which revealed a time-share should not then distinguish between the time-sharers merely on the basis of who happened to be present at the time, although whether the ones who were not could be described as in actual occupation must be open to doubt.

(4) Enquiries

The words "save where, upon enquiry made of such person, the rights are not disclosed" incorporate a test analogous in some respects to the doctrine of notice in equity. It is clear that if a purchaser or other party is to take free of an unregistered interest falling within the section then the enquiries must be made of the person entitled to the unregistered interest who does not then disclose it. Enquiries directed to their husband or wife will have no effect even if the husband or wife owns the legal estate in the land.

In *Friends Provident Life Office v. Doherty*[109] Mr D bought some land as the site of the matrimonial home. He was duly registered as proprietor of the land. Mrs D paid for the construction of the house. Some years later Mr D wanted to expand his potato business and applied for a substantial loan from the Friends Provident. They agreed to lend him the money on security of a mortgage of the house. Mr D made the usual statutory declaration to the effect that none of the burdens under section 72 of the 1964 Act affected the Folio. Mr and Mrs D together then made a statutory declaration to the effect that they

107 Following *Williams & Glynns Bank v. Boland* [1981] AC 487, HL.

108 See s.199(1)(ii) of the English Law of Property Act, 1925.

109 [1992] ILRM 372, High Court, N Circuit, Blayney J.

were lawfully husband and wife, that the house was a family home, that the land was in the sole name of Mr D, and that Mrs D consented to the mortgage. The mortgage was executed and Mrs D endorsed a consent for the purposes of the Family Home Protection Act, 1976 on the mortgage. Mr D fell behind in repayments and Friends Provident sued for and obtained an order for possession. Mr D appealed, but in the meantime Mrs D applied to the Circuit Court applying under section 12 of the Married Women's Status Act, 1957 for a declaration that she had an interest in excess of 50 per cent in the house.

The Circuit Court held against her and she then appealed. Blayney J in the High court held that she did have an equity in the house within section 72 and which existed before the mortgage was executed. The company had argued that her interest fell outside section 72 because they had made enquires of her in their requisitions on title and she had not revealed the interest. The judge rejected this as the requisitions were addressed to Mr D alone. He held that she therefore did have an interest within section 72. He nevertheless held that on the facts of the case she was estopped from pleading it because by her statements and conduct she had represented to Friends Provident that she had no interest in the house. The judge was led to this conclusion because Mrs D had stated that she consented to the mortgage and also that she had stated that the premises were in the sole name of her husband. The effect of the estoppel was not that she had no interest in the property, but was to postpone it to the interest of Friends Provident.

It was further argued by Mrs D that the company had not in fact made enquiries of her and so, in the terms of section 72, should be bound by her interest. The judge held that in the circumstances they had no reason to do so as she had volunteered the information which gave them the impression that she had no interest. Moreover, Mrs D was advised by a solicitor and there was no reason to suppose that Mrs D did not understand the effect of the mortgage. The case thus adds a gloss to section 72 in that a party who does not make enquiries of the person in actual occupation will not be bound by an interest if the person in occupation took the initiative in leading them to believe that no interest was being claimed, or no interest having priority to the one which they sought to register. Nevertheless, these situations can give rise to subtleties of interpretation and the danger is that the court may go to the extent of shifting the initiative fully to the occupier which the section does not appear to require. It may also have been the case that Mrs D was not aware that she had an equity in the house or that a court would have found such an interest if the issue had arisen. Ignorance of the law may not on its own be an excuse, but when the issue is whether a person deliberately mislead another as to their interests in property then the ignorance of law is relevant to their factual state of mind and must be taken into account.

In *Ulster Bank v. Shanks*[110] the Northern Ireland High Court arguably went too far in placing the onus on the occupier. In that case a house had been mortgaged by demise and the husband and wife later went to a bank to arrange a second mortgage, also by demise. The wife in the meantime had acquired an equity in the house through her contributions to the deposit and to paying off the first mortgage. The bank did not ask the wife if she had an equity and the wife did not volunteer the information. Murray J in the Northern Ireland High Court held that the wife's equity did not take priority over the second mortgage. It was, he thought, inequitable for a party to stand by and not mention an equity and then seek to rely on it later.[111]

Essentially the same point was also decided in *Northern Bank Ltd v. McNeill.*[112] Nevertheless, the corresponding provision to section 72(1)(j) in Northern Ireland which was in almost identical terms, did not place the onus on the person in actual occupation to reveal their right and neither does section 72(1)(j). The right of such persons are to be binding "*save* where, upon enquiry made of such person, the rights are not disclosed". The onus is clearly on the purchaser to inquire of the person in occupation what rights they have and only if they do not reveal them is the purchaser then free of the rights. This is essentially also the case in unregistered land where the decision in *Hunt v. Luck* and such cases was that constructive notice is normally to be imputed to the purchaser where a person is in occupation. There may be cases where the fact of occupation is difficult to discover and it may be unfair in those circumstances hold the purchaser bound by constructive notice, but in both the Northern Ireland cases the occupation by the wife was known to the bank. In the Ulster Bank case the judge quoted section 3 of the Conveyancing Act, 1882, which deals with constructive notice and evidently believed it supported his view:

> "3.(1) A purchase shall not be prejudicially affected by notice of any instrument, fact, or thing unless –
>
> (i) It is within his own knowledge, or would have come to his knowledge if such inquiries and inspections had been made as ought reasonably to have been made by him . . . .".

It is difficult to agree with the result in the case. The bank knew the wife was in occupation and once they had that knowledge there were obvious questions which should then have been asked. If they had asked her about her rights there is no reason to suppose they would not have been revealed. There seems to be no need for the courts to go out of their way to assist a bank which was so negligent as not to ask about the wife's contributions when she was in the manager's office and she and her husband were applying for a mortgage. One would ex-

110 [1982] NI 143.

111 See also *Paddington Building Society v. Mendelsohn* (1985) 50 P&CR 244, [1987] Fam Law 121, ([1986] Conv 57).

112 Unreported, NI Ch D, Murray J, 14 February 1986.

pect, given the state of the law, that the bank would have included such a question on the application form itself. The *Friends Provident* case is distinguishable on the ground that there the wife volunteered information which clearly represented that she claimed no interest in priority to the company.

3. Burdens affecting Land by Registration

a) General

These are interests under section 69 and, when registered, bind the title of registered interests. They are typically, but not exclusively, legal interests of minor importance:

(a) incumbrances existing at the time of first registration;

(b) a charge on land created after first registration. This is the equivalent in registered title of a legal mortgage. Under section 62 a charge confers the same remedies as a mortgage by conveyance with proviso for redemption or by way of demise, but does not transfer such an estate to the mortgagee.

In *Gale* v. *First National Building Society*,[113] the registered charge contained a term whereby the chargor agreed that if he defaulted in the repayments of a loan the chargee had the right to enter the land. After a default the chargee entered the land. Costello J refused an injunction to prevent the chargee continuing in possession, holding that the charge created a contractual licence, and that it was not necessary to register the right of entry other than in the charges register. It is unclear, however, if the judge intended to imply that the right would be effective against a transferee of the contracting party. If so, then contractual licences, at least ones of this type, would have achieved the status of property interests which they have yet to do in unregistered land;[114]

(c) a rentcharge or fee farm or other perpetual rent. The fee simple of a fee farm grant is registered as a registered interest and the rent reserved to the grantor is registered as a burden on the fee simple under this section;

(d) a power to charge land with the payment of money;

(e) a trust for securing money;

(f) a lien of a vendor on land for unpaid purchase money. (If the vendor is in actual possession then it is a section 72 interest and binding without registration[115]);

---

113 [1985] IR 609.

114 See Chapter 18.

115 *London & Cheshire Insurance v. Laplagrene* [1971] Ch. 499. And see s.72 interests.

(g) a lease for a life or lives or determinable on life or lives, or over 21 years, or where it is for a lesser term but occupation is not in accordance with the lease.

If the lease is for a term not exceeding 21 years or less and the tenant is in occupation, then the lease is a section 72 interest and is binding without registration under section 72(1)(i). No matter how long the original term, if more than 21 years are unexpired, the title to the lease is itself registrable under sections 8 and 3.

In *An Application of O'Sullivan, Folio 27742 Co Cork*[116] D'Arcy J held that a lease granting "week No. 25 in each year" for a total term of 1100 years did not fall within this section, since the term referred to had to be continuous. This leaves time-share leases on an insecure footing. Fitzgerald[117] has suggested that time-share leases should be included within section 72 burdens. A note under section 72(3) could then be entered. However, it would not seem desirable to increase that category since it detracts from the registration principle and since time-share leases are created expressly there seems no reason why leases such as that in the *O'Sullivan Case* could not be included in section 69. A total of 1,100 weeks is just over 21 years, which is no doubt why that total term was chosen and it is unfortunate that the judge did not feel able to interpret the section to allow this;

(h) a judgment or order of a court;

(i) a judgment mortgage, recognizance, State bond, inquisition or *lis pendens*. Judgment mortgages are discussed below;

(j) easements, profits *à prendre* created by express grant or reservation after first registration. If such interests are created otherwise than by express grant or reservation they are section 72 interests. It is only if such interests are expressly created that it is reasonable to provide that they must be registered by the parties;[118]

(k) restrictive covenants or conditions as to the use of land. Under section 69(3) any covenant or condition registered under the section can be modified or discharged by an order of the court on proof that the covenant does not run with the land or is not capable of being enforced against the owner of the land;

(l) [dower: abolished by the Succession Act, 1965]

(m) forestry Act;

(n) [right of Irish Land Commission[119] to lay pipes]

---

116 Unreported, High Court, D'Arcy J, 24 March 1983.

117 (1989) p.252.

118 Sections 97, 98 (easements by prescription).

119 Now the Minister for Agriculture and Food: Irish Land Commission (Dissolution) Act, 1992, s.4.

(o) power of appointment exercisable within the perpetuity period;

(p) power of distress or entry;

(q) right of residence in Irish law.

b) Judgment Mortgages and Other Rights

If a creditor obtains a judgment against a spouse they may register the judgment mortgage against the title to family home without the consent of the other spouse, since the spouse's right to refuse consent under the Family Home Protection Act, 1976 only applies to conveyances by the other spouse.[120]

A judgment mortgage is not a charge created on land for valuable consideration within the meaning of section 68 of the 1964 Act and therefore under section 71(4)(c) is subject to all unregistered rights subject to which the judgment debtor held the registered title at the time of the registration of the judgment mortgage.[121] In *Curran v. Curran*[122] it was apparently[123] held for this reason that a wife's equity prevented the judgment mortgagee obtaining an order for sale under the Judgment Mortgage Acts.[124]

In registered land a judgment mortgage does not effect a conveyance of the debtor-spouse's interest: it creates a charge on the interest.[125] It would seem to follow that a judgment mortgagee of registered land cannot apply for an order for sale under the Partition Acts because he or she is not a co-owner.

4. Cautions, Inhibitions and Notes

Section 69 does not exhaust all the interests which may be protected by an entry on the register. Other interests may be protected by a caution under section 97 or an inhibition under section 98. For example, if a tenant in common or joint tenant applies for an order for sale under the Partition Acts and the court

120 *Murray v. Diamond* [1982] ILRM 113; *Containercare (Ireland) Ltd v. Wycherley* [1982] IR 143.

121 *Tempany v. Hynes* [1976] IR 101.

122 Unreported, High Court, McWilliam J, 10 March 1981. Noted in [1981] ILRM 98.

123 The judgment sets out the principles to be applied and cites *Tempany v. Hynes* [1976] IR 101.

124 Judgment Mortgage (Ireland) Acts, 1850 and 1858 and the Judgments (Ireland) Acts 1844 and 1849.

125 Registration of Title Act, 1964 s.71(4). *Curran v. Curran* unreported, High Court, McWilliam J, 10 March 1981. In unregistered title a judgment mortgage does cause a conveyance of the interest of the debtor spouse, but if the judgment mortgagee applies for sale under the Partition Acts the court has a discretion to refuse: *O'D v. O'D* unreported, High Court, Murphy J, 18 November 1983, and the fact that the other spouse does not consent can be taken into account in exercising the discretion: *AL v. JL* unreported, High Court, 27 February 1984; *First National Building Society v. Ring* [1992] 1 IR 375.

refuses the order, the applicant joint tenant or tenant in common should enter an inhibition subject to a further application to the court.

Under section 12 of the Family Home Protection Act, 1976 a spouse may register a note on the register stating that they are married to the owner of the registered land. A note may also be entered on the register under section 72(3) as to any interest falling within section 72.

The differences between cautions and inhibitions are listed below:

Caution: section 97

1. Less serious. No dealing without notice given to the cautioner.
2. Entered by person entitled to interest.
3. By affidavit.
4. Temporary, unless Registrar specifies otherwise. If Registrar makes entry, can discharge entry.
5. Restricts registered owner only.

Inhibition section 98

1. More serious. No dealing without consent of specified person.
2. Entered by Court or Registrar.
3. On application by person interested.
4. More permanent: for specified time or until event occurs or further order.
5. May restrict dealings by any person able to deal with land.

In *State (Philpott) v. Registrar of Titles*[126] the prosecutor was registered as full owner with possessory title. The registrar registered an inhibition against all dealings in the land without his approval under section 121 of the 1964 Act. Before this, the prosecutor had entered into a contract to sell the land. The prosecutor was informed of the entry being made. The prosecutor claimed that he should have been informed in advance of the intention to make the entry and of the facts on which it was based so that he could have an opportunity to challenge it. The court held that the power under section 121 exists to protect the common fund out of which compensation is paid if the register is defective and any exercise of the power under that section should be capable of being identified as protecting the fund from a real possibility of a claim against it. The registrar in considering whether to register an inhibition was acting judicially. Unless urgency required otherwise, therefore, notice should be given to the person whose rights would be affected to show cause why the inhibition should not be registered.

126 Unreported, High Court, Gannon J, 29 July 1985.

5. Minor Interests

Sections 97 and 98 presuppose a residual category of interests which are not registrable interests nor burdens under section 69. They may be protected by a caution or inhibition, but even if they are, in some cases this will not even ensure that a purchaser takes subject to them, since it has been seen that this is not the effect of a caution. They may overlap as a category with section 72, so that if the person entitled to the interest is in actual occupation of the land the right may be protected without any form of registration under section 72(1)(j). In such a case it is a matter for the person entitled whether to protect them by a caution or inhibition or whether to rely on section 72. The interests are of two kinds, namely:

a) Interests Overreached on Sale

These are not classified either as registrable interests or as burdens affecting registrable interests because they do not affect the land in the hands of a purchaser, at least if he or she is careful to comply with legal requirements. They are:

(1) Legal Settlements

The life estate of the tenant for life and all other interests in remainder or reversion under strict settlements will be overreached on sale of the settled land under the Settled Land Acts, 1882-90. An inhibition may be registered requiring notice to be given to persons entitled to such interests if the tenant for life intends to exercise the powers under the Settled Land Acts.

(2) Equitable Settlements

Similarly, equitable interests under a trust, if it constitutes a settlement, will also be overreached by the operation of the Settled Land Acts.

(3) Equitable Interests under a Trust for Sale

Equitable interests under a trust for sale are converted to personalty in the eye of equity and will be overreached on sale.

b) Interests Not Overreached on Sale

These require to be noted on the register if they are to affect third parties taking for value.

(1) A Purchaser's Equity

A purchaser's equity arising under an enforceable contract to buy the land[127] would not protect the purchaser under the contract if it were to be destroyed by

127 *Northern Bank v. Devlin* [1924] 1 IR 90.

a sale to a third party. It is such a sale that the equity seeks to prevent. Such an equity, like other equities in accordance with the basic policy, does not automatically appear on the register: the purchaser under the contract will have to protect it as an inhibition. But if it is so protected, then it is not overreached on sale. No sale can take place while it appears on the register.

(2) Equitable Easements

An easement is intended to affect the beneficial use of the land and so overreaching is inappropriate. Equitable easements will, however, have to be noted on the register if they are to affect purchasers of the servient tenement.

(3) Interests under Bare Trusts

Equitable interests under trusts which are not settled land within the Settled Land Acts, 1882-90 are holding trusts to which the overreaching provisions of the Acts do not apply and so are not overreached.

L. Overlapping Categories

Minor interests which are not overreached may also constitute section 72 interests under section 72(1)(j). Furthermore, some burdens registrable under section 69 may also fall within section 72. It is doubtful in the case of minor interests whether entering a caution or inhibition confers any advantage. Cautions are only temporary and even inhibitions may be removed as the justice of the case requires under section 98(3). There is no provision for removing a section 72 interest - since there is nothing to remove. Paradoxically, therefore, the interest of a person in such cases may be better protected by not registering it. In one case[128] it was argued that priority between a purchaser's equity and a registered burden should be governed by section 69, *i.e.* on the assumption that the purchaser's equity could have been registered under section 69, and since section 69 provides that burdens take effect in order of their registration, the registered burden would take priority over the – assumed – registrable but unregistered burden. The court rejected the argument on the ground that a purchaser's equity is not registrable as a burden under section 69. Nevertheless, the decision suggests that one case of overlapping categories may be resolved by section 69, *i.e.* that any interest which falls within section 72 and also falls within section 69 and is therefore registrable as a burden, may lose priority to an interest which has been registered under section 69.

---

128 *Coffey v. Brunel Construction Ltd* [1983] IR 36. See below.

M. Conclusiveness of the Register and Transferees

The extent to which the Register mirrors the title depends upon the type of transferee.

1. Transferee for Value

A transferee of registered land who takes for valuable consideration takes the title subject to:[129]

1) registered burdens: section 69;
2) cautions and Inhibitions: sections 97, 98;
3) section 72 Interests (overriding interests). These bind despite not being registered and regardless of notice.

   The last category may include interests acquired by adverse possession before first registration.[130] Under section 72 they are overriding interests before the register is rectified;
4) equitable mortgages by deposit of the land certificate: section 105(5).[131]

   However, section 105(5) on the face of it is inconsistent with section 37(3) which provides that a person registered with absolute title takes subject to section 69 burdens and unregistered burdens under section 72 "but shall be free from all other rights, including rights of the State". It could nevertheless be argued that the specific provision of section 105 ousts the generality of section 37(3);
5) actual fraud or mistake.[132] The court may order the register to be rectified in such a case.

2. Transferees Not for Valuable Consideration

Such a transferee takes subject to:

1) all the interests mentioned in the preceding section, and in addition;
2) under section 52(2), any unregistered rights which bound the transferor. The same applies in the case of a charge obtained otherwise than for valuable consideration under section 68(3).[133]

---

129 See s.31 (conclusiveness of register), s.37 (effect of absolute title) and s.52(1) (transferees).

130 If *Chowood v. Lyall (No. 2)* [1930] 2 Ch. 156 is accepted in this jurisdiction.

131 See Survival of Unregistered Principles below, page 877.

132 Section 31(1).

133 Section 71(4)(c).

a) Judgment Mortgages

In *Tempany v. Hynes*[134] the Supreme Court held that a judgment mortgage is not a charge for valuable consideration and so the judgment mortgagee takes subject to unregistered rights affecting the judgment debtor. A judgment mortgage is merely a form of remedy. It would not be equitable to give to an unsecured debtor priority over earlier equities merely because the debtor chose a judgment mortgage as a remedy.

In *Curran v. Curran*[135] a husband was registered as full owner of a house. The wife claimed the whole or an undivided share of the beneficial interest. The wife had paid off part of the mortgage debt. The husband had got into debt and had agreed to the debt being secured by a legal charge over the house. None was ever executed. The creditor company sued on the debt and subsequently registered a judgment mortgage against the house. The judge held that the wife had a 50 per cent share of the beneficial interest in the house.[136] The judge held that the wife's equity acquired by contributions was an unregistered right within section 52(2) and that it therefore had priority over the judgment mortgage.

b) Lis pendens

In *Coffey v. Brunel Construction Ltd*[137] the plaintiff entered into a contract to buy land from B and paid the purchase money. A transfer was executed but not registered. The defendants then started an action in the High Court claiming that B held the land in trust for them. The suit was registered as a *lis pendens* against B's title. The Supreme Court held that the *lis pendens* was not a charge obtained for valuable consideration. Thus the purchaser's earlier unregistered equity prevailed over the registered *lis pendens*. The court held that the equity would not have prevailed against a transferee for valuable consideration nor against a chargee for valuable consideration but the holder of a *lis pendens* was not such. Priority between registered, or registrable, burdens was governed by section 69 which ranks them in the order in which they are registered, but the court held that a purchaser's equity was not capable of registration under section 69, since it did not feature in the list of interests in the section, and so it was unaffected by the section.

This position illustrates again that the courts tend to interpret the Act so as to provide protection for purchasers in the market who risk money, but do not

134 [1976] IR 101.

135 Unreported, High Court, McWilliam J, 10 March 1981.

136 The judge further held that the beneficial interest in the house was held by the wife and the company in equal shares, but this appears to have ignored section 71(4) which provides that the registration of a judgment mortgage in registered land does not transfer the debtor's interest in the house.

137 [1983] IR 36.

give such an extensive protection to those who do not risk money. One should note that the purchaser was not in actual occupation. If he had been, the right would probably have bound a transferee or chargee for valuable consideration under section 72(1)(j).

3. Is Notice Relevant?

a) Transferee Not for Value

Under section 52(2) a transferee not for valuable consideration is bound by unregistered interests which bound the transferor or chargor regardless of notice.[138] The principle in section 52(2) is intended to reproduce in registered land the result that would occur in unregistered title. In order to take free of equitable interests a purchaser or mortgagee of a legal interest would have to prove that they were a bona fide purchaser for value of a legal interest in the land without notice. If they fail as to any element of the plea, they take subject to the interest.[139] Hence, if they can prove they are a purchaser of a legal interest, but cannot prove consideration, they take subject to the equitable interest. The law assists the buyer of commodities in the market, but not those who take, even innocently, outside the market.

In the English case of *Peffer v. Rigg*[140] it was suggested that a transferee not for valuable consideration was bound by an unregistered express trust, *inter alia,* because she knew of it. Mr Rigg, the first defendant, and the plaintiff, his brother in law, bought a house mainly as a residence for their mother in law. The first defendant and the plaintiff were married to sisters. The house was transferred into the name of Mr Rigg alone to be held by him on trust for them both as tenants in common in equal shares. The mother in law lived in the ground floor flat until her death. The top flat was rented. Later Mr Rigg obtained a divorce from his wife, the second defendant, and as part of the arrangements then made he agreed to transfer the legal estate in the house to her. He executed a transfer to her as beneficial owner in consideration of £1. The second defendant was registered as proprietor. There was no note on the register as to the plaintiff's interest nor was the plaintiff in actual occupation.

Graham J in the English High Court held that the second defendant held the registered title subject to the plaintiff's share as equitable tenant in common. The judge gave two reasons for his conclusion. First, he held that since the second defendant had given only nominal consideration, she should be treated as a

138 There is one respect in which registered title may differ in this context from unregistered title. Section 52(2) is not expressly limited to equitable interests. A transferee not for valuable consideration of registered land may in principle, therefore, take subject to unregistered legal rights affecting the transferor if indeed there are any such things.

139 *Heneghan v. Davitt* [1933] IR 325.

140 [1977] 1 WLR 285.

transferee without valuable consideration.[141] Secondly, the second defendant actually knew of the plaintiff's interest. Referring to the equitable doctrine of knowing reception of trust property, the judge concluded that since the wife "knew... that the property was trust property when the transfer was made to her" she took the title "on a constructive trust in accordance with general equitable principles.[142]

Since the judge had already found that the wife was not a purchaser for valuable consideration the second reason was, it is suggested, erroneous. The wife would have been bound whether she had notice or not. On general equitable principles she could not establish the full plea of bona fide purchaser for value without notice, because she did not take for value. There is no reason why the position should be different under registered title.

b) Transferee for Value

Gray comments on *Peffer v. Rigg*:[143]

> "The factor which … made the decision in *Peffer v. Rigg* truly startling was the way in which Graham J cited the statutory definition of 'purchaser'[144] in support of his view that unprotected minor interests are rendered ineffective under section 59(6) only as against a purchaser 'in good faith'".

In the judge's view the wife could not claim to be such a purchaser because she knew quite well that her former husband held the property on trust.[145] The judge concluded that a purchaser "cannot... be in good faith if he has in fact notice of something which affects the title as in the present case".[146] This raises quite a distinct and, in Gray's view, a truly startling suggestion. That is that a transferee for valuable consideration takes subject to unregistered rights affecting the transferor if the transferee has actual notice of them. Gray[147] comments by saying that: "It is not usually thought to be 'bad faith' for a purchaser to take advantage of the folly of those who fail to effect the appropriate registration in protection of their interests".

Brightman J in *De Lusignan v. Johnson*[148] held that to register in the knowledge that unprotected rights existed was not bad faith and that it would be stretching the language to say that it was. He sought to draw a distinction between fraud and notice of the existence or possible existence of unprotected

---

141 [1977] 1 WLR 285 at 293F. The equivalent English section to section 52 is s.20(4) of the Land Registration Act, 1925.

142 [1977] 1 WLR 285 at 294E-F.

143 Gray, *Elements of Land Law* p.192.

144 English Land Registration Act, 1925 s.3(xxi).

145 [1977] 1 WLR 285 at 294E.

146 *ibid.*

147 Gray, *Elements of Land Law* p.192.

148 (1973) 230 EG 499.

rights. Only the former, he said, was a relevant ground of complaint against a purchaser of registered land. This position has now been reinforced in England by the decision in *Midland Bank Trust Co Ltd v. Green* .[149]

We have already seen that essentially the same issue arises in the registration of deeds system. In the context of that system the judges in the 18th and 19th centuries[150] made a distinction between two situations. If A entered into a transaction in ignorance of unregistered rights and then, having discovered them, registered her interest to protect herself this was not held to be fraud. On the other hand, if A, the prospective transferee, already had knowledge of the unprotected right before she entered into the transaction and then, after completing the transaction, registered in order to gain priority, that was regarded as fraud.

The Supreme Court in the Republic has not departed from this view in the context of the registration of deeds system, although it seems to have narrowed the definition of actual notice.[151] It is worth stressing that the issue is not a technical one, but a moral one, and the change of position exemplified by Brightman J in *De Lusignan v. Johnson*[152] and *Midland Bank Trust Co Ltd v. Green* [153] represents a shift to a standard of moral conduct which is more suited to the type of secular free-for-all capitalist market which has been asserted in recent years in Western countries and indeed may emerge in the former communist regimes of Eastern Europe. The older morality which established itself in the context of the registration of deeds system in the 18th century derived more from pre-capitalist notions reinforced by religious notions that one person was responsible morally for others. This was maintained in the 19th century by a judiciary which was still heavily influenced by religion. The decline of religious sentiment in the 20th century has now perhaps reached the point where fraud is redefined so that knowingly taking advantage of another's foolishness or weakness is regarded as acceptable.

It may also be noted that the harsher view of morality evident in the English cases just mentioned cannot be justified by arguing that it makes for a more efficient registration system, even assuming that such an aim would be sufficient to justify it. An intending purchaser who has actual notice of unregistered rights before he or she enters into a transaction does not require the protection of the registration system in order to avoid a loss. Indeed, this suggests perhaps the true reason for the new approach. A speculator who sees that a profit can be

149 [1981] AC 513 at 530A-B.

150 *Forbes v. Deniston* (1722) 4 Bro PC 189, 2 ER 129, 2 Eq Cas Abr 482, 22 ER 409; *Delacour v. Freeman* (1854) 2 Ir Ch R 633; *Montgomery v. McEvoy* (1857) 5 Ir Ch R 126; *Clarke v. Armstrong* (1861) 10 Ir Ch R 263; *Agra Bank v. Barry* (1874) LR 7 HL 135.

151 *Re Fuller* [1982] IR 161.

152 (1973) 230 EG 499.

153 [1981] AC 513 at 530A-B.

made on a piece of land would not be satisfied by being told not to enter into the transaction in the first place.

N. Survival of Unregistered Principles

1. Actual Notice

This topic has been dealt with in the previous section.

2. Limited Owners

We have already noted above[154] that where the registered owner has less than a fee simple the Act allows such a person to be registered simply as limited owner and the practice is not to note on the register the actual estate owned by such a person, on the ground that such estates are overreached on a sale under the Settled Land Acts and a purchaser is not therefore concerned with them. Nevertheless, a tenant in tail would probably wish to bar the entail instead and in such a case would have to adduce the settlement or will which created the entail. To this extent the estate itself remains unregistered.

3. Equitable Mortgages

It is possible to create an equitable mortgage of registered land by deposit of the land certificate or certificate of charge. Such a deposit, under section 105(5) has "the same effect as the deposit of the title deeds of unregistered land or of a charge thereon".[155] This would seem to mean that priority between the equitable mortgage and later interests, even if registered, is still governed by unregistered principles, *i.e.* by the Polar Star Rule, incorporating the doctrine of notice. A proprietor of a registered interest would therefore take subject to the charge unless he or she could show that they were a bona fide purchaser of a legal estate without notice of the charge, actual, imputed or constructive. However, section 105(5) on the face of it is inconsistent with section 37(3) which provides that a person registered with absolute title takes subject to section 69 burdens and unregistered burdens under section 72 but free from all other rights.

It is not easy for a such a conflict between an earlier unregistered equitable mortgage and a later registered interest to arise. The registered title could not be conveyed to a later purchaser, nor would a subsequent charge be created, without the production of the land certificate[156] which would be in the hands of the equitable mortgagee, who, if he or she parted with possession, would be in

154 See above, Limited Owners.

155 Section 105(5).

156 Section 105(1), s.68.

danger of losing the right to possession and therefore losing the mortgage since it is based upon possession. Nevertheless section 105(3) does provide that:

> "105(3).–The production of a certificate under this section shall not alter the right to the custody of the certificate, and shall not affect any lien of any person thereon".

The situation might be more likely to arise in the case of a subsequently-created lease, since an intending tenant is not generally entitled to examine title to the freehold.[157] The holder of the legal interest would be bound by the mortgage if they had notice of it. One issue that would arise in such a case would be as to what enquiries, apart from searching the register, the holder of the later legal interest would be under an obligation to make in order to take free of the earlier equitable mortgage.

4. Unregistered *v.* Unregistered.

Unregistered principles still apply as between the holders of two interests who have failed to register their interests.

In *Tench v. Molyneaux*[158] S, the registered owner, sold land to M. S had bought the land under the Land Purchase Acts and was told that there would be a delay in issuing the land certificate as there had been many such purchases and the registrar's office was unable to issue them all at once. S told M this and M paid the purchase money without taking a conveyance and without getting himself registered as the new owner. The land certificate was later issued to S who immediately deposited it with the plaintiff, T, to secure a loan. The issue was whether M, who had a purchaser's equity, took the land subject to the later equitable mortgage. M could have entered an inhibition on the register in respect of the equity. The court held that as between M and T priorities were governed by the principles of unregistered conveyancing. The equities were equal in this case and the first in time prevailed. M might have lost priority by negligence in not registering a caution, but there was no negligence on the facts because of the short time that had elapsed between the two events. In the case just discussed both the rights were equitable. If the later right were legal and the earlier one equitable it is possible that the doctrine of notice would still apply.

157 Section 105(1). If for a term exceeding 21 years the lease would be registrable. If for a term not exceeding 21 years then it would not be registrable but would be a section 72 interest: s.72(1)(i).

158 (1914) 48 ILTR 48.

O. Adverse Possession

1. General

The statute of limitations applies to registered land just as it applies to unregistered land.[159] While time is running against the registered owner the adverse possessor has an overriding interest under section 72(1)(p). This would not seem to give any protection to the adverse possessor against the registered owner or an assignee, just as in unregistered land an adverse possessor cannot resist a better title, and may only be intended to indicate that an adverse possessor has the right to evict those who attempt to set up a later possession. Where a person has acquired title to registered land by adverse possession they can apply to the Registrar to have their title registered.[160] Section 49(3) states that "upon such registration the title of the person whose right of action to recover the land has expired shall be extinguished".[161] In the English case of *Chowood v. Lyall (No. 2)*[162] purchasers of freehold land were registered as first proprietors with absolute title. Unknown to them, a squatter had acquired title by adverse possession to two strips of woodland. It was held that the squatter was entitled to have the register rectified in his favour. The same result would seem to apply in the Republic as under section 37(3) registration with absolute title is still subject to section 72 interests. In a sequel to the case[163] the purchaser was even held unable to obtain compensation as the court held that the loss was caused not by the rectification but by the failure to investigate the title prior to the sale by which the purchasers acquired the land before first registration. This was the result of the facts of the case which were that the purchaser before first registration who had failed properly to investigate the title was also the registered proprietor who stood to lose by rectification. If, however, they had been two different persons the result might have been different. An adverse possessor is not a transferee for valuable consideration, and so section 52 applies.

2. Leasehold

If an adverse possessor remains in possession of leasehold land for 12 years and then obtains registration as proprietor of the lease under section 49(3) the

159 Section 49(1).

160 Section 49(2).

161 Under the Act of 1891 an adverse possessor could only be registered by an order of court. But an owner registered subject to the equities – who might be an adverse possessor against another, unregistered, title — could have the note as to equities cancelled without an order of the court on showing that he had acquired the title under the limitation act: see *Dwyer v. Whitelegge* (1899) 33 ILTR 179.

162 1930] 2 Ch. 156.

163 *Re Chowood's Registered Land* [1933] Ch. 574.

title of the ousted lessee is then extinguished.[164] There can be no question of the ousted lessee retaining any interest which can be merged with or forfeited in favour of the lessor so as to affect the squatter in any way. Only the registered proprietor of an interest can transfer it or otherwise deal with it.[165] This suggests that as to registered title adverse possession does result, when the new title is registered, in a parliamentary conveyance.[166] This is correct apart from one possible qualification: the 1964 Act confers the right to apply for registration on the adverse possessor. If there was an automatic transfer by statute it would also be clear that the lessor could insist on treating the adverse possessor as the new tenant, whereas there is nothing specifically in the 1964 Act which confers on the lessor the right to have the adverse possessor registered.

---

164 See Walsh J in *Perry v. Woodfarm Homes* [1975] IR 104, and Chapter 25 Adverse Possession.

165 Section 51(2).

166 See Walsh J in *Perry* at p.120. And see *Spectrum Investments v. Holmes* [1981] 1 All ER 6.

CHAPTER 25

ADVERSE POSSESSION

A. Introduction

We have already dealt with the main principles of adverse possession in relation to freeholds since they are fundamental to understanding the concepts of possession and title to land under the common law system. We shall now deal with some aspects in more detail and also consider the principles relating to adverse possession of leaseholds which has recently given rise to controversy. The law relating to acquisition of title by adverse possession in the Republic of Ireland is governed by the Statute of Limitations, 1957. Many sections of the statute have been reproduced from earlier enactments and it is instructive to refer to these from time to time.[1]

B. The Policy Basis

Any system of law which sets as one of its goals the protection of private property needs a justification for rules which have the effect of depriving the original owner of his or her property. The following are possible theories:

1. Individual Initiative

One justification is that those who have rights should actively pursue them: it would be a misuse of the legal system to allow the holder of a right to be idle for many years until some accident or whim induces a recourse to the judicial system. This argument is essentially procedural: if A is dispossessed by B it would deny A an action to recover possession against B after a given period of time. However, if A were to get back into possession without resort to the courts, this argument would not justify preventing A defending his superior title against B.

2. Quieting Titles

A second justification is that of quieting of titles, that is to say the notion that there ought to come a time when defects in a title are cured. This policy is not

1 21 Jas I c.16; Real Property Limitation Act, 1833, 3 & 4 Wm IV c.27; Hewitt, *Limitations*. Real Property Limitation Act, 1874. And see also the English Limitation Act, 1939.

so much concerned with securing the title of the squatter as with innocent third parties who may buy titles in the market. It is therefore the quintessentially capitalist justification. Securing the title of the squatter, who has successfully bucked the market and got something for nothing is seen on this theory as a cost of reducing the risk of innocent purchasers. This argument would go further than the first and, in the example taken, justify the extinction of A's title after B had been in possession for the required period. The idea that A could recover possession and then be able successfully to defend an action by B would run contrary to this policy: after the period has run B's title should be secure.

3. Development

A third justification is that the doctrine of adverse possession favours the person who uses land at the expense of one who does not. The doctrine thus furthers the economic development of society. It favours the productive use of land as a social goal. This approach looks at the effects on society as a whole and implies that the law has a direct responsibility to further economic development. It can therefore be seen as a socialist or social democratic approach in the sense that it ascribes to law a role in allocating resources or furthering economic development.

4. Unadministered Estates

A fourth justification is a quite specific one which applies to Ireland and which is alluded to by Griffin J in *Perry v. Woodfarm Homes*:[2]

> Until comparatively recent years, raising representation in the case of small farms was quite rare, the occupiers preferring to rely on the Statute of Limitations, and there must be very few agricultural holdings in this country in which at some time in the past 140 years a tenancy was not 'acquired' under the statute. Again, leases for 999 years (such as the lease of 1947) are now quite common. . .".[3]

To say prefer suggests a deliberate choice and there may well be cases in which a family deliberately decides to save some money and not to apply for letters of administration in the case of intestacy, relying instead on the law of limitation to secure the titles of those who would take on intestacy. In other cases, however, there seems little doubt that the estate of a deceased farmer is left unadministered through ignorance of the legal formalities.

This policy supports limitation for a specific purpose and to solve a particular social problem.

---

2 [1975] IR 104, Supreme Court; see also *Gleeson v. Feehan* [1997] ILRM 522 per Keane J at 539.

3 *ibid.* at p.129.

C. The Movement of Policy

If one looks at the development of the law in Ireland, and indeed other Western common law countries, one can see that the law has moved from the first policy basis to the second: it has moved from a negative procedural approach to the notion of quieting titles, reinforced by the fourth policy in judicial interpretation. The third approach has not been adopted in such countries. The explanation, is it suggested, is that this stems from the dominance of the market as a means of distributing not only the products of labour, but also means of production such as land. The second policy has prevailed since it is most appropriate to reduce the costs of those buying land in a market: purchasers should be assured of obtaining secure titles. In the words of Lord St Leonards, formerly Edward Sugden, Lord Chancellor of Ireland and later of England:[4]

> "All statutes of limitation have for their object the prevention of the rearing up of claims at great distances of time when evidences are lost; and in all well-regulated countries the quieting of possession is held an important point of policy".[5]

This argument implies that it is more important to quiet titles than to protect that of the original owner. It is not surprising, therefore, that the adoption of this policy should have occurred in 1833 when the Industrial Revolution was beginning to have a major impact on society. On the other hand, in a capitalist economy the law limits itself to providing favourable conditions in which individual transactions can take place: it assumes that economic development is best attained by leaving the actors in a market to make their own bargains, and so the third justification is not adopted.[6] Such a policy would be more appropriate for countries in which the market is little developed and the State takes a more active role in promoting development.

D. The Effect on Title

Before 1833 if A possessed land adversely to the title of B and the limitation period had expired the effect was to bar B's right to recover possession, but it did not extinguish B's title. Thus, if B was able to regain possession without going to court, A could not recover possession. This was unsatisfactory in a number of respects but the principle cause of complaint was that the adverse possessor's title was precarious and although this might be quite acceptable in

4 Edward Burtenshaw Sugden, Lord Chancellor of Ireland 1834, 1841-46. Lord Chancellor of England 1852.

5 *Dundee Harbour Trustees v. Dougall* (1852) 1 Macq 317 at p.321.

6 Notice, in a different context, the rejection by the English Court of Appeal of the idea that rules of land law should favour development in a general social sense: *Nickerson v. Barraclough* [1981] Ch. 426 (in the context of easements of necessity.)

relation to the adverse possessor him or herself, it would be difficult for such a person or their successors in title to sell the land to purchaser, and even if they did the purchaser would acquire a precarious title. This would mean that the marketability of such land would be reduced. In a society which was passing through the Industrial Revolution it was regarded as desirable by those who made the law that land should be freely alienable through the market. One of the purposes of the 1833 legislation was to render titles more secure. Thus the 1833 Act provides that in future the effect of the expiry of the limitation period is to bar the title of the dispossessed party. Section 24 of the 1957 Act provides:

> "24.– Subject to section 25 of this Act and to section 52 of the Act of 1891, at the expiration of the period fixed by this Act for any person to bring an action to recover land, the title of that person to the land shall be extinguished".

Thus if the dispossessed person re-enters after the period has expired she or he is a trespasser.[7]

E. The Parliamentary Conveyance

The earliest judicial view of the 1833 Act was, in the words of Parke B, that: "The effect of the Act is to make a parliamentary conveyance of the land to the person in possession after that period of twenty years [as it then was] has elapsed".[8] Edward Sugden, later to become Lord St Leonards and the most distinguished property lawyer of his day, maintained the same view as Lord Chancellor of Ireland and later of England.[9]

This view was upheld in Ireland in relation to leasehold land in *Rankin v. McMurty*.[10] Holmes J in that case stated:

> "Whatever the mode of transfer, I am of [the] opinion that the estate and interest the right to which is extinguished, so far as the original owner is concerned, became vested in the person whose possession has caused such extinction".[11]

The judge felt that any other conclusion would cause uncertainty as to leasehold titles in Ireland. Gibson J added:

7 *Incorporated Society for Protestant Schools v. Richards* (1841) 1 Dru & War 258, 4 Ir Eq R 177.

8 *Doe d Jukes v. Sumner* (1845) 14 M & W 39 at 42, 153 ER 380.

9 *Incorporated Society for Protestant Schools v. Richards* (1841) 1 Dru & War 258 at 289, 4 Ir Eq R 177 at 197; *Scott v. Nixon* (1843) 3 Dru & War 388 at 405-8, 6 Ir Eq R 8, 61 RR 84 at 93-95; *Tuthill v. Rogers* (1849) 6 Ir Eq R 429, (1844) 1 Jo & La T 36 at 72, 66 RR 223 at 232; *Burroughs v. McCreight* (1844) 1 Jo & La T 290 at 303, 7 Ir Eq R 49, 68 RR 243 at 251; *Trustees of Dundee Harbour v. Dougall* (1852) 1 Macq 317 at 321; Sugden, *The New Property Statutes* p.8; Meredith "A Paradox of Sugden's" (1918) 34 LQR 253.

10 (1889) 24 LR Ir 290, QB. See also Wylie's comments on the case in *Irish Land Law* at para. 23.09.

11 *ibid.* at p.301.

> "If the statute has barred the right of the representative of the original lessee, in whom is the term now vested? I think it must be taken that the defendants, assuming the statutory bar has arisen, have in some way, whether by statutory estoppel, transfer, or otherwise, become owners of the lease".[12]

The court also approved of the passage in Darby and Bosanquet's book on limitations:

> "Though the title extinguished . . . is not directly transferred by the statute to the wrongdoer who has been in possession, yet the title gained by such possession, being limited by rights yet remaining unextinguished, is clearly commensurate with the interest which the rightful owners have lost by operation of the statute, and must, therefore, it is apprehended, have the same legal character, and be freehold, leasehold or copyhold accordingly".

It may be noticed that this statement falls short of saying that there has been a parliamentary conveyance of the former owner's title. It merely asserts that the dispossessor's title is similar in nature to the former title: it does not say it is identical.

In England, the view of Parke B and Sugden LC was rejected by the Court of Appeal in *Tichborne v. Weir*[13], a case on leaseholds. Lord Esher MR and Bowen LJ both held that the previous title was destroyed and not conveyed to the dispossessing tenant. The Irish decisions of Sugden LC were cited to the court but distinguished on the ground that they concerned freehold land.[14] Thus, even the court in *Tichborne* accepted the parliamentary conveyance theory in relation to freehold.

The holding in *Tichborne*, that the parliamentary conveyance theory did not apply to leaseholds, seems to have been accepted *obiter*[15] by the Irish Court of Appeal in *O'Connor v. Foley*.[16] The position in Ireland in relation to leaseholds has more recently been considered by the Supreme Court in *Perry v. Woodfarm Homes Ltd*[17] which is dealt with below. Suffice it to say at this point that the majority of the Supreme Court in *Perry* (a) did not accept that the ousted lessee retained an estate in the land, as opposed to contractual rights in relation to the lessor, but further (b) did not accept the parliamentary conveyance theory applied to unregistered land. It impliedly rejected the distinction in *Tichborne* and *O'*Connor between leasehold and freehold in this respect.

There is, however, a suggestion in *Perry* that the parliamentary conveyance theory may apply in registered title. Propositions (a) and (b) are not easy to reconcile and this issue is further considered below. At least in the case of free-

---

12 *ibid.* at p.303.

13 (1892) 67 LT 735, M & B 178, 709, followed in *Taylor v. Twinberrow* [1930] 2 KB 16.

14 *ibid.* at 737 per Bowen LJ.

15 In *O'Connor* the tenant was held to have become so by estoppel, not by adverse possession.

16 [1906] 1 IR 20.

17 [1975] IR 104, Supreme Court.

hold land it may not be easy to tell the difference between the parliamentary conveyance doctrine and a new title doctrine. The fact that the dispossessor's title is subject to rights which have not been extinguished is not consistent only with a conveyance having taken place. Equitable rights which bound the previous owner will bind the dispossessor because she or he, having taken by operation of law, is not a purchaser for value,[18] but this would be so whether there was a conveyance of the previous title or not. On the other hand the new owner will not be able to claim advantages enjoyed by the ousted owner under section 6 of the Conveyancing Act, 1881 or the Rule in *Wheeldon v. Boroughs*[19], since these have been held to apply only to voluntary conveyances.[20] This would equally be unaffected by whether the title was held to pass by operation of law or whether a new title was created. An implication of adopting the parliamentary conveyance theory in relation to section 24 of the 1957 Act would seem to be that such advantages would pass under that section.

The problem with the parliamentary conveyance theory is that it did not fit well with fundamental common law property theory. In theory a squatter, from the first moment of dispossession, has a fee simple relative to every one except the dispossessed title holder, or anyone with a better title than the dispossessed title holder.[21] This is a possessory title distinct from the title of the dispossessed title holder. After the 12 years have expired, the title of the dispossessed title holder is barred, leaving the squatter with a fee simple less vulnerable than before, but a fee simple based on the same title they had from the first day they entered the land.

F. The Elements of Adverse Possession

1. Meaning of Possession

a) Before 1834

Before 1834 there were a number of instances in which the law deemed the possession of one person to be possession by or on behalf of another. These cases were as follows:

(1) Younger Brothers

Possession by a younger brother (*possessio fratris*) was deemed to be possession by the heir at law. This was a rule which defended the principle of primo-

18 *Re Nisbett & Pott's Contract* [1906] 1 Ch. 386.

19 (1878) 12 Ch D 31.

20 *Sovmots v. Investments Ltd v. Secretary of State for the Environment* [1977] 2 WLR 951, English HL; and see Chapter 22 Incorporeal Hereditaments.

21 See above Chapter 1.

geniture. Even if the eldest son and heir was out of possession, a younger son would not obtain title by adverse possession. It never applied to entails.[22]

(2) Co-Owners

Possession by a co-owner was deemed to be possession by the other co-owners, unless there was express intention to possess the whole to the exclusion of the others.[23]

(3) Tenants at Sufferance

Possession by a tenant for years holding over at the end of the term (*i.e.* a tenant at sufferance) was deemed to be possession by the landlord.[24] Thus a tenant at sufferance was not in adverse possession.

b) After 1833

The effect of the Real Property Limitation Act, 1833 was to replace these cases of deemed possession with a test of actual or factual possession and to provide that the limitation period should begin to run from the time when a right of action to recover possession accrued to some person with a superior title.[25] Thus section 18(1) of the 1957 Act now provides:

> "18(1).– No right of action to recover land shall be deemed to accrue unless the land is in the possession (in this section referred to as adverse possession) of some person in whose favour the period of limitation can run".[26]

The special cases of possession have been dealt with as follows:

(1) Younger Brother

Since 1833 the possession of a younger brother (*possessio fratris*) is no longer deemed to be possession on the part of the heir at law. Since the Succession Act, 1965 has abolished the old rules of descent, except for estates tail, this change in the law only affects the descent of such estates today.

---

22 *Doe d Gregory v. Wichelo* (1799) 8 TR 211, 101 ER 1350, per Lord Kenyon CJ.

23 *O'Sullivan v. McSweeney* (1840) 2 Ir LR 89; *Scott v. Knox* (1841) 4 Ir Eq R 397.

24 *Howard v. Sherwood* (1832) Al & Nap 217.

25 See Denman CJ in *Culley v. Doe d Taylerson* (1840) 11 Ad & El 1008, 113 ER 697; *Paradise Beach & Transportation Co Ltd v. Price-Robinson* [1968] 2 WLR 873, [1968] AC 1072 per Lord Upjohn at p.879.

26 See *Dean of Ely v. Bliss* (1852) 2 De G M & G 459, per Lord St Leonards at 476–477, 42 ER 950 at 957:

> "It is perfectly settled that adverse possession is no longer necessary in the sense in which it was formerly used, but that mere possession may be and is sufficient under many circumstances to give a title adversely".

(2) Co-Ownership

Since 1833 possession by one joint tenant, tenant in common or coparcener is no longer deemed to be possession by all.[27] Thus, where one co-owner has been in possession of the whole of the land, or whose possession has in some sense been more extensive than an equal undivided share would justify, such possession is to that extent adverse to that of the others.

(3) Tenants at Sufferance

Since 1833 a tenant at sufferance is in adverse possession.[28] The landlord has, and always had, a right of action to recover possession accruing from the end of the contractual tenancy and this, now combined with the factual possession of the tenant without the consent of the landlord, makes the possession of the tenant adverse to the title of the landlord.

2. Dispossession or Discontinuance

Section 14(1) of the Statute of Limitations, 1957 provides that:

> "Where the person bringing an action to recover land, or some person through whom he claims, has been in possession thereof and has while entitled thereto been dispossessed or discontinued his possession, the right of action shall be deemed to have accrued on the date of the dispossession or discontinuance".

Thus the accrual of the cause of action arises on dispossession or discontinuance.[29]

a) Discontinuance

There can be no discontinuance by absence of use and enjoyment where the land is not capable of use and enjoyment.[30] Thus, in *Dundalk Urban District Council v. Conway*[31] a small plot of wasteland at a steep gradient beside a river was held incapable of actual use and enjoyment, even though it did not lack all value to the owner since it might have been required if it became necessary to repair an adjoining bridge. On the other hand, even where land is capable of use and enjoyment, mere non-use will not by itself necessarily amount to discontinuance of possession. This is so where the owner of land intends to use it

27 1957 Act, s.21.

28 *Doe d Bennett v. Turner* (1840) 7 M & W 226, 151 ER 749; *Remon v. City of London Real Property Co Ltd* [1921] 1 KB 49.

29 Lord Lindley MR in *Littledale v. Liverpool College* [1900] 1 Ch. 19 at p.21, quoted by Blayney J in *Dundalk Urban District Council v. Conway* unreported, High Court, 15 December 1987.

30 *Leigh v. Jack* (1879) 5 LR Exch 264 per Cotton LJ at 274, quoted by Blayney J in *Dundalk Urban District Council v. Conway* unreported, High Court, 15 December 1987.

31 Unreported, High Court, Blayney J, 15 December 1987.

for some purpose in future. This point is pursued in the section on *animus possidendi* below.

b) Dispossession

In *Leigh v. Jack*[32] Lord Bramwell said:

> "Acts of user are not enough to take the soil out of the Plaintiff, and vest it in the Defendant; in order to defeat a title by dispossessing the former owner, acts must be done which are inconsistent with his enjoyment of the soil, for the purposes for which he intended to use it".

and in *Wallis's Cayton Bay Holiday Camp Limited v. Shell-Mex and BP Ltd*[33] Lord Denning MR said:

> "Possession by itself is not enough to give a title. It must be adverse possession. The true owner must have discontinued possession or have been dispossessed and another must have taken it adversely to him. There must be something in the nature of an ouster of the true owner by the wrongful possessor... When the true owner of land intends to use it for a particular purpose in the future, but meanwhile has no immediate use for it, and so leaves it unoccupied, he does not lose his title to it simply because some other person enters on it and uses it for some temporary purpose, like stacking materials; or for some seasonal purpose, like growing vegetables. Not even if this temporary or seasonal purpose continues year after year for 12 years, or more".[34]

The character of the land, the nature of the acts done on it and the intention of the squatter are all relevant.[35] Where the owner did not for the time being use the land for the purpose for which he acquired it, a court will more readily conclude that acts done on it do not amount to adverse possession.[36] It is suggested that if the squatter's user is not inconsistent with the use to which the owner intends to put the land, then no amount of intention on the part of the squatter will render his possession adverse to the title of the owner.[37]

As for the acts done, whether they amount to adverse possession will also depend on the nature of the rights claimed. To possess adversely against a road reserved to the grantor of a lease it is not necessary to make it impossible to walk or move along the road. A fence with a stile for pedestrians has been held

32 (1879) 5 Ex D 264, cited with approval by Ross J in *Re Duffy's Estate* [1897] I IR 307 at 315.

33 [1974] 3 All ER 575.

34 *ibid.* at 580.

35 *ibid.*, Stamp LJ at 585.

36 *ibid.*

37 Blayney J in *Dundalk Urban District Council v. Conway* unreported, High Court, 15 December 1987 is equivocal on the point, first dealing with the issue of whether the squatter intended to claim ownership, and having decided that he did not, going on to consider whether the user was inconsistent with the purpose for which the owner intended to use the land.

sufficient to constitute adverse possession in such a case.[38]

3. Animus Possidendi by Occupier

Cases on dispossession sometimes refer to *animus possidendi* as a requirement of adverse possession. The concept is supposed to import an intention on the part of the occupier to possess the land in a way or for a purpose which is inconsistent with the owner's rights. But this does not imply that he or she must be aware that a title exists as to which their own possessory title is adverse. A person who occupies land mistakenly believing it to be their own can extinguish the title of the owner.[39]

Most of the cases in which such an *animus* is said to be necessary are cases in which the owner had acquired the land for a special purpose to be fulfilled in future and the claimant had occupied the land in the meantime. But even in such a case it is unclear to what extent the test is one of a state of mind, whether subjectively or objectively tested, or of objective facts.

In *Leigh v. Jack*[40] land had been acquired for the purpose of making a street which was to remain idle until the street was constructed. The defendant used the land to store scrap metal, making the land impassable except by pedestrians. It was held that the plaintiff owner had never been dispossessed. Cockburn CJ said[41] that the defendant did not intend to be a trespasser and knew that the land was intended for future use. Bramwell LJ indicated that had he built on the land or cultivated crops on it, the result might have been different. This suggests that the knowledge and intention of the claimant is relevant, not merely the actual use of the land by the owner. It also suggests that the intention of the owner is relevant, at least if known to the occupier. Some judges speak in more objective terms, such as Black J in *Convey v. Regan*:

> "When one claims a possessory title for whatever period of time may be necessary it is not enough to show mere non-user by the owner of his property if it be, say, a mine or a quarry. . . I think it is equally insufficient where, as here, the property is a patch of bog, the only practical use of which is the cutting of turf, which is a seasonal operation. . . There must be dispossession of the owner by acts inconsistent with his enjoyment of the soil for the purpose for which he intended to use it – in this case the purpose of cutting turf".[42]

This suggests that what matters is the use to which land is put in fact – and some land can only have certain uses – and whether the use to which the occupier put the land actually interfered with that use.

---

38 *Tottenham v. Byrne* (1862) 12 Ir CLR 376.

39 See remarks of Finlay P in *McMahon v. Kerry C C* [1981] ILRM 419; *Ramsden v. Dyson* (1866) LR 1 HL 129 on the impact of proprietary estoppel on this situation.

40 (1879) 5 Ex D 264.

41 *ibid.* p.271.

42 [1952] IR 56, at 59.

It is unclear whether a use by the occupier which is on the face of it temporary, such as stacking materials or cutting turf, can nevertheless be inconsistent with the use to which the owner intends to put the land in future if the occupier intends his apparently temporary activity to be permanent use. Subjective intention is hard to prove, and so if *animus* is a distinct element, it can normally only be inferred from the factual use.[43]

4. Successive Adverse Possessors

It has been seen[44] that possession constitutes the most basic form of title. It follows from this that if a dispossessor transfers his or her possessory title to a third party, the period of possession of such a transferor constitutes part of the title of the transferee. Suppose X dispossesses O and then, before the limitation period has expired, passes his possessory title to Y by *inter vivos* conveyance, by will or on intestacy. Y is then sued by O. Y can add the period of X's possession to his own and if the two added together make up 12 years or more, O's title is extinguished.[45] However, if X abandons his possession and Y enters into possession of the land immediately after X's departure, Y cannot make use of X's period of possession.[46] In those circumstances Y has not acquired X's possessory title.

G. The Limitation Period

1. Recovery of Land

The period laid down by the 1833 Act for actions to recover land was generally 20 years.[47] The Real Property Limitation Act, 1874 reduced it to 12 years[48] and this is retained by the 1957 Act.[49] The general period does not apply to the State.

2. Recovery of Rent

The period for the recovery of a rent or of arrears of a rentcharge is six years.[50]

---

43 *Seamus Durack Manufacturing Ltd v. Considine* [1987] IR 677, High Court.

44 See Chapter 1 Introduction.

45 1957 Act, s.15(4); *Clarke v. Clarke* (1868) IR 2 CL 395; *Mount Carmel Investments Ltd v. Peter Thurlow Ltd* [1988] 3 All ER 129, [1988] 3 WLR 1078, 57 P & CR 396, Court of Appeal (England); Cheshire, (13th ed.) p.827-28.

46 1957 Act s.18(3); Cheshire, (13th ed.) p.828.

47 1833 Act, s.2.

48 Section 1.

49 Section 13(2)(a).

50 1957 Act, ss. 27,28.

3. The State

Where the State seeks to recover land the period is 30 years[51] except for foreshore where it is 60 years.[52] Where land was once foreshore but has ceased to be so, the State has 60 years from the accrual of the right of action or 40 years from the date on which the land ceased to be foreshore, whichever first expires.[53]

4. Postponement of Period

Section 14(1) of the 1957 Act does not require knowledge of dispossession on the part of the dispossessed owner before the cause of action arises and time begins to run. The general rule is that time begins to run from the dispossession and dispossession can take place without the knowledge of the landowner. This derives from the crudity of the approach of the common law courts, but statute law has now mitigated this in the case of fraud and mistake.

a) Fraud

Section 71 of the 1957 Act now provides that where the dispossessed owner's right of action has been concealed by the defendant's fraud or that of his or her agent, time does not begin to run until the dispossessed owner discovers the fraud or could with reasonable diligence have discovered it.[54]

Subsection (2) provides that nothing in subsection (1) shall enable any action to be brought to recover, or charge or set aside any transaction affecting property which has been purchased for valuable consideration after the transaction giving rise to the fraud by a person who did not know or have reason to believe that the fraud was made. Here again it can be seen that where a choice has to be made between two equally innocent parties, the modern law prefers the purchaser in the market to the original owner.

As we have remarked before, the notion that modern capitalist systems protect private property has to be judged against this preference for those who act through the market.

b) Mistake

A mistake, such as a mistake as to where the true boundary lies, does not in general prevent time running against the dispossessed owner.[55]

51 1957 Act, s.13(1)(a).

52 Section 13(1)(b).

53 Section 13(1)(c).

54 1957 Act, s.71(1); *Morgan v. Park Developments Ltd* [1983] ILRM 156.

55 *Re Jones' Estate* [1914] 1 IR 188.

In *Palfrey v. Palfrey*[56] the Palfrey family had lived in No. 2 Hambros Cottages for several generations and Mrs Lily Palfrey had lived there since 1915, when she and her husband paid her husband's grandmother Sarah a rent of 2s 3d a week, rising to 2s 6d. Her husband died in 1917 and she stayed there paying rent until Sarah died in 1927 but she paid no rent from 1928 when the cottage became Edward Palfrey's (her father in law). He had then said to her "the property would have been Frank's" (her late husband) "and you are to have it". In 1968 some solicitors in Taunton discovered in their papers a conveyance of 1930 in which Edward conveyed the cottage to Lily's eldest son Clifford but Edward told no one. Lily continued to live there and Clifford claimed to be the owner in reliance on the 1930 conveyance.

The English county court judge found in Clifford's favour. He held that in 1928 the weekly tenancy had been surrendered and that from then on had been replaced by a contractual licence that Lily could stay in the house rent-free for the rest of their life.

The Court of Appeal unanimously reversed the decision on the ground that it was not supported by the evidence. Lily had been told that the cottage was hers, not that she was there on licence. In a sense her possession was not hostile but that was not necessary in order to constitute adverse possession. The fact that Clifford did not know of the conveyance to him did not make any difference to the question of whether time ran against him, and the time limit had expired many years ago.

In *Murphy v. Murphy*[57] a testator devised his farm to trustees on trust for his wife and his two sons, Thomas and Laurence, the plaintiff and the defendant. Under the will the land was to be managed for 10 years from his death and all profits put into a bank for the benefit of his widow and Laurence. Then his land on the south of a road was to be divided in a particular manner, that on the east (with its dwellinghouse) should be the property of Laurence and that on the west was for Thomas. The residue of his property was to go to his widow. He did not specifically dispose of the part on the north side. He died in 1936 and all three continued to live in the house and work at the farm. Laurence managed the farm and in 1949 Thomas left it and went to England. In 1954 he conveyed his part to Laurence. From then on Laurence closed the joint account and treated the entire farm as his own property. The widow lived there for some time and then went into an old people's home where she died in 1971, leaving her property to Thomas. In due course Thomas commenced an action in which he claimed the northerly part of the farm from Laurence. The defence was that Laurence had been in possession of that part from 1946 and that the

56 (1974) 229 EG 1593.

57 [1980] IR 183, Wylie, *Cases* p.696; *Hughes v. Griffin* [1969] 1 All ER 460, [1969] 1 WLR 23, 20 P & CR 113, 208 EG 1087, Court of Appeal.

claim was barred by lapse of time. It was not established that the widow was ever aware of his rights under her late husband's will.

It was held by the Supreme Court that from the expiration of the 10-year period in 1946 the widow became entitled to an estate in fee simple in the northerly land and that from at least 1954 Laurence had been in adverse possession of that land and that the widow's right of action was barred 12 years from that date. The possession of Laurence was established by his grazing his cattle there, payment of outgoings and improvement works of drainage on the land.

Kenny J cited Wylie's *Irish Land Law*[58] for the proposition that adverse possession may exist without either party being aware of it. Costello J in the High Court accepted that the inference that possession is by licence may be drawn more readily where there is a family relationship than where no family ties exist. However, this was not a case where the widow was entitled to the farm and land and lived there with her son who farmed it. In the present case the son Laurence was the legal owner of the farmhouse where the mother lived and of some land from which his mother had a right of residence. The land in dispute was owned solely by the mother and was part of an estate which he occupied and ran. Thus a possession of her land in denial of her right could more readily be inferred.

The harshness of the common law rule has been modified by section 72 which introduces a limited defence of mistake, but at the cost of clarity. Section 72(1) provides that:

> "Where, in the case of any action for which a period of limitation is fixed by this Act, the action is for relief from the consequences of mistake, the period of limitation shall not begin to run until the plaintiff has discovered the mistake or could with reasonable diligence have discovered it".

The defence of mistake only applies where the basis of the action is relief from the consequences of the mistake, such as a claim for rectification of a deed, or of the register in the case of registered title. It is not clear whether the subsection is intended to apply to all mistakes, or only those for which the dispossessor bears greater responsibility than the dispossessed owner. The test of reasonable diligence implies that time will still run against the dispossessed owner if he or she could have discovered the mistake with such diligence, whether or not the mistake was due to his or her fault or that of the dispossessor. Subsection (2) provides a similar exception as to innocent third parties to that in the case of fraud.

58 Wylie, *Irish Land Law* para. 23.22.

c) Disability

Where the dispossessed owner is under a disability[59] such as being a minor[60] or of unsound mind[61] the action may be brought within six years from the date when the owner ceased to be under the disability or dies, whichever first occurs, and this is regardless of whether the normal 12 year period has expired or not.[62] In the case of actions to recover land or money charged on land there is a maximum limit of 30 years from the date the right of action accrued.[63]

5. Fresh Accrual

Certain actions by the adverse possessor may cause time to start running afresh.

a) Acknowledgement

If someone in adverse possession indicates that they recognise that the dispossessed person is the lawful owner of the land this is inconsistent with their own adverse title. The effect is first to destroy their possessory title up to that point, but secondly their possession does not cease to be adverse as to the future: time begins to run afresh against the dispossessed owner. Time runs from the date of a written and signed acknowledgement by or on behalf of the defendant of the plaintiff's title.[64]

b) Part Payment

Payment of part of a debt secured on land may start time running again. Thus, if E is a mortgagee who has also acquired a right to enforce the security under the mortgage against R, the mortgagor, then if R pays part of the debt secured to E time begins to run against R afresh.[65] If E has gone into possession as mortgagee then any payment made by R on foot of the mortgage will set time running afresh as against M.[66]

---

59 1957 Act, s.48.

60 1957 Act, s.48(1)(a); *Currie v. Fairy Hill Ltd* [1968] IR 232.

61 1957 Act, s.48(1)(b); *Re Dowd* [1960] Ir Jur Rep 37; *Re Gill* [1964] IR 143.

62 1957 Act, s.49.

63 1957 Act, s.49(1)(d).

64 1957 Act, ss. 50, 51.

65 1957 Act, ss. 62, 68.

66 1957 Act, s.64.

H. Particular Cases

1. Future Interests

a) The General Rule

Adverse possession is possession adverse to some other possession, and so time does not begin to run against those entitled to future interests, whether in remainder or in reversion, until the interests vest in possession. At that point they also cease to be future interests at all, and so in general it can be said that there is no special rule as to future interests. But in one sense there is.

If the person entitled to a prior estate has been dispossessed, the owner of the future interest has no right of action until the prior estate has terminated, but when it does, the person entitled to the future interest has 12 years from when the adverse possession began, or six years from the end of the prior estate, whichever is longer.[67] Suppose land is settled on A for life, remainder to B in fee simple. X dispossesses A 10 years before A's death. B has six years from A's death in which to sue. If, on the other hand, X had dispossessed A three years before A's death, B would be able to sue at any time from A's death to a point nine years from that date, since the limitation period is measured as 12 years from the dispossession. This period is the correct one since it gives a longer period than six years from A's death.

If X completes 12 years' adverse possession before A dies, what then? Under the above rule A's title is barred, but not B's, and this is in accordance with principle. B has six years from A's death to bring an action against X. X extinguished A's title, but A's title was only a life estate. B claims by a title paramount to that of X. An interesting question is what estate did X acquire in the land? If the parliamentary conveyance theory applies[68] A's life estate would be conveyed to X, giving X an *estate pur autre vie* for the life of A. If not, then X would, as a squatter, have a relative fee simple which, after the 12 years, would be good against A, but not against B until six years after A's death.

If X had only taken possession after A's death, dispossessing B, B's interest would no longer be a future interest and the usual 12 year period would apply.

b) Interests After a Fee Tail

An exception to the preceding rules are interests in remainder or reversion after a barrable estate tail. The general rule that time does not begin to run until they become vested in possession does not apply: time runs against them from the time adverse possession is taken. This curious rule was adopted in order to avoid a defect in title similar to the one which still exists in the case of long

---

67 1957 Act, s.15(2)(a).

68 See above 884.

leases. In the past, if T were entitled in fee tail followed by a fee simple in F, and T was dispossessed by S, time did not begin to run against F until the fee tail came to and end which could be centuries later. By that time someone would possibly be in possession under a title which they believed to be a fee simple but which was in fact derived from the dispossessor. When the fee tail came to an end, *i.e.* by the heirs of T's body dying out, F or rather F's heirs would become entitled in possession and could defeat the supposed fee simple derived from S. Thus the new rule was adopted to prevent such a defect in title occurring. The effect is that, in the above example, F will now be barred 12 years after the dispossession even if the 12 years expire before the fee tail comes to an end.[69] Thus F may be barred before he ever acquires a right to possession. It is a moot point as to what F could do about it in the meantime. B cannot sue directly for possession as he is not entitled to it until the expiry of the estate tail. This case is similar to that of interests after a base fee.[70]

c) Interests After a Base Fee

Interests after a base fee constitute another exception. If a tenant in tail executes a disentailing assurance it may, through some defect, fail to produce a fee simple. If a tenant in tail in remainder fails to obtain the consent of the prior life tenant, who is the protector of the settlement under the Fines and Recoveries (Ireland) Act, 1834, the result is a base fee, which does not bar those entitled in remainder after the entail. Thus a person could have been in possession under a title which they believed to be a fee simple, whereas in fact it was only a base fee. When it came to an end those entitled in remainder would become entitled in possession. Time would only begin to run against them from that point. The second situation arose where the assurance suffered from some formal defect, such as failure to enrol the deed, resulting in a voidable base fee. This did not even bar the issue in tail, who had a right to put an end to the base fee immediately.

These situations constituted defects which in theory could affect all titles, at least in unregistered land, since such titles are usually traced back only 20 years.[71] Thus, A could hold land under a series of deeds which incorrectly showed the title to be a fee simple, whereas it really derived from a disentailing assurance executed 100 years before which had only produced a base fee. Since a base fee will only endure until the original issue in tail die out, that could occur at any time in the future and when it did, a right of action to recover possession would accrue to whoever was entitled to the estate in remainder,

---

69 1957 Act, s.15(3).

70 For example, where a person, other then a person entitled under the settlement, who could enlarge it, is in possession: see below. The fee is enlarged to a fee simple by 12 years possession by such a person.

71 See Chapter 4 Equity.

and time would begin to run against it from the moment it accrued. Thus a defect existed in A's title which could destroy it. A purchaser from A would not be able to discover the defect since the series of deeds would be examined going back for only 20 years. Lack of notice was no defence if the estate in remainder was a legal estate.

This defect has been avoided by section 19 of the 1957 Act.[72] Time now begins to run against those entitled in remainder or against the issue in tail from the time at which the assurance, if it had been executed by the person entitled in tail would have operated, without the consent of any person, such as the protector, to bar the issue in tail and the estates in remainder. The time period is 12 years.[73]

2. Equitable Interests

In general the provisions of the 1957 Act apply to equitable estates and interests in land, including interests under a trust for sale, as they do to legal estates and interests.[74]

a) Strangers

The rule is modified where trust property is possessed adversely by a stranger. The stranger does not bar the trustee's title until the interest of all the beneficiaries have been barred.[75] Thus if T holds land on trust for A for life, with remainder on trust for B in fee simple, 12 years adverse possession by X during A's lifetime bars A's life estate, but does not bar T's legal estate. Time does not run against B's future estate until it vests in possession at A's death. Under the 1957 Act the same protection is given to T's estate: time does not run against T until A's death, and it will only be barred when B's estate is barred, *i.e.* six years after A's death.[76] Thus after X has been in possession for 12 years T holds the land in trust for X for the rest of A's life, then on trust for B. This result creates a major problem for purchasers of a title acquired by adverse possession. They must inquire whether the land was held in the past under a settlement by way of trust, including a trust for sale.

---

72 See also the Real Property Limitation Act, 1833 s.22.

73 1957 Act, s.19(b); The limitation period only runs in favour of a person other than someone entitled to possession under the settlement, such as the original tenant in tail. This is because the original tenant in tail or some such person would be able to enlarge the base fee. See *Re Domvile* [1879] 3 LR Ir 282.

74 1957 Act, s.25(1).

75 1957 Act, s.25(2). For former rule see *Burroughs v. McCreight* (1844) 1 Jo & La T 290, 7 Ir Eq R 49, 68 RR 243.

76 See Chapter 10 Future Interests.

b) Trustees

In general trustees cannot bar the title of their own beneficiaries: there is no limitation period for an action by a beneficiary against his or her trustee to recover trust property where the claim is based upon fraud or for the recovery of property converted by the trustee to his or her own use.[77] If there is no fraud, such as a trustee paying money to the wrong person by mistake, the limitation period is six years.[78]

c) Beneficiaries

A beneficiary of land held on trust, including a trust for sale, cannot in general establish possession adverse to the trustees of the land or other beneficiaries.[79] An exception to this is where the beneficiary is entitled under a bare trust, *i.e.* where the beneficiary is solely and absolutely entitled to the whole beneficial interest.[80] In this case time begins to run against the trustees from the moment the beneficiary is in possession. In such a situation the beneficiary, under the principle in *Saunders v. Vautier*[81], is entitled to call upon the trustees to convey the legal estate to him. Thus if land is held by T on trust for A for life and remainder to B in fee simple, B being of full age and not under any disability, when A dies time begins to run against T in B's favour and in 12 years B's estate will become a legal one, extinguishing that of T. In the meantime, B can in any case call upon T for the legal estate. Another possible case is that of a purchaser under a contract of sale of a fee simple where the purchaser goes into possession. Time probably begins to run against the vendor from the moment the purchaser takes possession.[82] Here again, the possessor is entitled to call upon the holder of the legal estate to convey it. Nevertheless, the vendor is not a trustee for all purposes, and so it may be doubted if the purchaser can be said to be absolutely entitled to the beneficial interest.

d) Equitable Relief

The 1957 Act also contains a special provision as to equitable relief. Section 5 provides that nothing in the Act shall affect any equitable jurisdiction to refuse relief on the ground of acquiescence or otherwise. Equitable remedies may also, in equity, be refused on the ground of laches, *i.e.* undue delay in bringing the action.[83]

---

77 1957 Act, s.44.

78 1957 Act, s.43(1)(a).

79 1957 Act, s.25(4).

80 *ibid.*

81 [1835–42] All ER Rep 58, (1841) Cr & Ph 240, 4 Beav 115.

82 Wylie, *Irish Land Law* para. 23.39 and *Bridges v. Mees* [1957] Ch. 475.

83 See for example *Re Ffrench's Estate* (1887) 21 LR Ir 283.

3. Mortgages

a) Mortgagors

Where a mortgagee has gone into possession, which is rare nowadays, the mortgagor's right to redeem the mortgage is barred 12 years from the time when the mortgagee took possession provided the mortgagee during that time has not acknowledged the mortgagor's title or received any payment on account of principal or interest due under the mortgage.[84] The mortgagee's remedy of possession is to enable him or her to recoup arrears from the income of the land and the mortgagee is liable to account strictly for moneys received.[85] The treatment of such possession as adverse to the title of the mortgagor is therefore anomalous in principle, but principle here yields to practical considerations.

b) Mortgagees

The mortgagee's right to bring an action for sale or to sue for possession is barred after 12 years from the date when the repayment became due.[86] The mortgagee's title to the land then becomes extinguished.[87] The right to recover interest on principle is barred six years after the payment became due,[88] but the right to recover principal is barred after 12 years have expired from the time when it became due.[89]

c) Strangers

If a stranger is in adverse possession of the land at the time when a mortgage has been created, it has been held that if the stranger then completes the period, the title so acquired is valid not only against the mortgagor, but also against the mortgagee.[90]

d) Welsh Mortgage

A Welsh mortgage is one where the mortgagee goes into possession at the beginning of the mortgage and the income of the land is taken in lieu of interest,

84 1957 Act, ss. 33,34(1)(a),54,64.

85 See Chapter 23 Mortgages.

86 1957 Act, ss. 32,33.

87 1957 Act, s.33. *Cotterell v. Price* [1960] 1 WLR 1097. Under the 1957 Act, s.36(1)(b) the period is 30 years for certain mortgages, namely where interest on the mortgage is paid into the Church Temporalities Fund, a charge under s.31 of the Land Law (Ireland) Act, 1881, and a charge under the Housing (Gaeltacht) Acts, 1929 and 1934.

88 1957 Act, ss. 36,37; *Re Huggard's Estate* [1930] IR 532.

89 1957 Act, ss. 36,39.

90 *Munster & Leinster Bank Ltd v. Croker* [1940] IR 185.

or in lieu of both interest and capital.[91] Since the normal limitation rules would clearly be inappropriate to such mortgages, the 1957 Act provides that the right of redemption is lost after 12 years have expired from the time when the principal and interest have been satisfied. This provision, it must be admitted, is not exactly in accordance with the basis of a Welsh mortgage, under which the income of the land is not taken in repayment of interest or capital, but in lieu of repayment. Thus, a Welsh mortgagee is not liable to account strictly for the income as other mortgagees are.[92]

4. Deceased Persons' Estates

The limitation period in respect of estates of deceased persons is now six years and three years for recovery of arrears of interest on a legacy except for actions against personal representatives for fraud.[93]

It is not uncommon in Ireland, particularly in rural areas, for the estates of deceased persons to remain unadministered and for family members to remain in possession of the land after the death of the deceased. The possession of such family members is adverse[94] to the title of the President of the High Court, in whom the estate vests pending the appointment of personal representatives[95] and to the title of personal representatives when they are appointed.

a) Personal Representatives

The above social practice has influenced the development of the law in this area.[96] Generally, personal representatives are trustees for the beneficiaries under the will or for the intestate successors. As such, the rule was that they could not be in adverse possession as regards such persons. This caused a particular problem where a family member or members remained in occupation of

---

91 See page 778.

92 *ibid.*

93 1957 Act, s.45, substituted by Succession Act, 1965 s.126. *Drohan v. Drohan* [1981] ILRM 473. *Drohan* was distinguished in *Gleeson v. Feehan* [1993] 2 IR 113 Supreme Court, which held that s.45 applied to claims of persons beneficially entitled under a will, on intestacy or under s.111, against a personal representative administering the estate, but not to claims by personal representatives against the estate of the deceased. In Northern Ireland the periods remain 12 and six years respectively: 1958 Act (NI) s.46.

94 This altered the previous law. In *Martin v. Kearney* (1902) 36 ILTR 117 Pallcs CB had held that a family member in possession was an equitable tenant in common, not a trespasser (*i.e.* not in adverse possession) and would become a legal tenant in common when the estate was administered. See *Gleeson v. Feehan* [1997] ILRM 522, per Keane J at 529–30.

95 Succession Act, 1965 s.13, replacing s.3 Administration of Estates Act, 1959; *Gleeson v. Feehan* [1997] ILRM 522

96 See *Maher v. Maher* [1987] ILRM 582, High Court, below.

land and then, when the situation became clear to them, they applied for and were granted letters of administration. For some time Irish courts followed the rule as to trustees,[97] but then underwent a change of heart and decided that personal representatives could bar the claims of beneficiaries or intestate successors.[98] The law has been changed in both parts of Ireland to give legislative effect to this change. Section 2(2) of the 1957 Act[99] provided that a personal representative in that capacity is not a trustee for the purposes of the Statute of Limitations and this provision has now been replaced by a similar provision in section 123 of the Succession Act, 1965.

b) Family Members in Possession

Family members in possession under an unadministered estate have a possessory title which they hold as joint tenants and not as tenants in common.[100] After the expiry of the limitation period this will bar adverse titles, such as that of the President of the High Court, in whom the estate vests pending the appointment of personal representatives,[101] and that of personal representatives once appointed. This is so even if their own equitable interests in the estate, or that of absent members, were tenancies in common.[102] Survivorship applies to the title of family members acquired by adverse possession and so when one of them dies there is no share to pass to their successors. This simplifies title but at the expense of depriving other family members of a share.

5. Wives and Children

Suppose H and W, who are husband and wife, occupy a matrimonial home the title to which is vested solely in H. After disagreements H leaves the house and remains absent for at least 12 years. Does the wife, or do the wife and children, acquire H's title by adverse possession?

In the past the judicial acceptance of the inferior legal position of the wife tended to prevent the courts accepting that the wife could have a possession independent of and adverse to that of her husband. The decision of the Supreme Court of the Irish Free State in *Keelan v. Garvey*[103] is typical of this attitude. The tenant of a farm, having quarrelled with his wife, left the farm in 1897. A few days after leaving he wrote to his wife asking her to sell oats and pay some

97 *Nugent v. Nugent* (1884) 15 LR Ir 321; *Molony v. Molony* [1894] 2 IR 1.

98 *Vaughan v. Cottingham* [1961] IR 184; similarly in NI: *McNeill v. McNeill* [1957] NI 10; *Fagan v. McParland* (1977) 28 NILQ 201.

99 Northern Ireland: 1958 Act (NI) s.47(1).

100 Succession Act, 1965 s.125; *Maher v. Maher* [1987] ILRM 582, High Court, Circuit App; *Gleeson v. Feehan* [1997] ILRM 522.

101 See footnote 95.

102 Succession Act, 1965 s.125.

103 [1925] 1 IR 1.

money he owed and also giving directions about the treatment of the land. The wife remained in sole possession until her death in 1923. At some time during that period and before 12 years had expired, the wife purchased the farm under the Land Purchase Acts. The husband never returned to the farm during the wife's lifetime and she remained in possession until she died in 1923.

Molony LCJ held that the wife had acquired the tenancy of the farm by adverse possession, but was reversed by the Supreme Court. O'Connor J said:

> "It is true that the old doctrine of unity of ownership and possession as between husband and wife has been abolished by the Married Women's Property Act, but there still remains a relationship between them arising out of the marriage tie, and the mutual duties and obligations thereby imposed, which must be taken into consideration when the question arises between them as to the exclusive possession by either of the property of the other. . . It is the moral duty of the wife within certain limits to guard and manage her husband's property, and, in most cases, this is not merely recognised but cheerfully accepted and performed. . . His actual possession would no doubt cease during his absence, but there would still remain a certain unity between them which would make the possession of the wife the possession of the absent husband".[104]

Some features of this example of reasoning are worth commenting upon. At the end of the passage the judge restates the concept of unity, despite the fact that it had been abolished by statute and this had been acknowledged by the judge at the beginning of his judgment. There is also an implied stricture against the wife for not having cheerfully performed her subordinate role of managing the husband's property without any contact or support from the absent husband for 26 years. The judge nevertheless admitted that the unity was not absolute. It could be severed:

> "For instance, if the husband announced to his wife that he did not intend to return, that he had abandoned her and his family and farm, or if the circumstances showed that such was his intention, then the conclusion might fairly be drawn that the previous unity which made the wife the mere bailiff or agent of her husband was severed, and that her subsequent possession was not his possession but her own".[105]

This passage points up another feature of the genre: the carefully crafted impression that the rules operate equally as to both parties, are reasonable and provide exceptions. In the first passage quoted the judge speaks of the "exclusive possession by either of the property of the other" while the social facts, certainly at the time of the decision and even today, are almost universally that wives occupy property legally vested in their husbands. In the present quotation the judge stresses the reasonable exception, and yet the key element is not the abandonment of the property by the husband, which would have given the wife title to the farm on the facts, but the intention to abandon expressed at the time the desertion took place, which would be highly unusual in most cases,

104 *ibid.* at p.9.

105 *ibid.* at p.9–10.

and the effect of imposing this newly-discovered test, was to deprive the wife of the title on the facts. The husband's subsequent lack of interest in the land over the following 26 years was apparently regarded as irrelevant, although it could have been taken as evidence of an intention to abandon dating from his last contact or at some time thereafter. Surely it would have been reasonable to find that the husband had abandoned the farm at some time between his last contact and the start of a twelve year period expiring by the wife's death? The fact that the wife had purchased the freehold was also apparently irrelevant. The exception seems designed to justify a conclusion which is insupportable on the grounds of justice.

In *Re Daily*[106] Andrews LCJ also had to consider the case of a husband who had left home after quarrels with his wife. In this case there were children also present in the house and they remained with the wife. They also contributed to the working and improvement of the farm. The husband left the house in 1928 and did not return. The wife brought an action after the limitation period had expired claiming that the register should be amended in her favour. Andrews LCJ, delivering the judgment of the court, held that the husband's title had been extinguished by adverse possession, but not by that of the wife alone, but by that of the children as well, so that the wife and children had acquired title as joint tenants. *Keelan v. Garvey*[107] was not binding upon the judge but he chose to distinguish it on the facts. He found that the Supreme Court in *Keelan* was influenced by factors not present in the present case, particularly (a) the fact that the husband had written letters in which he treated the wife as a mere agent, (b) that the wife had become [fee simple] owner of the farm before the limitation period had expired and so before she could have claimed to extinguish his title by adverse possession and (c) that the judge found that there was an arrangement between the parties that the wife was to have the use of the farm during their separation and possibly for life. Andrews LCJ did not express any view as to when a wife's possession was still to be considered as that of the husband or whether social, or judicial, attitudes to the relationship had changed since *Keelan*.

It seems clear that judicial attitudes have undergone considerable change since *Keelan* and even since *Re Daily*. The courts in a number of contexts have stressed that marriage is to be regarded as an equal relationship.[108] It seems

106 [1943] NI 1, CA.

107 [1925] 1 IR 1.

108 *BL v. ML* [1989] ILRM 528, per Barr J, Supreme Court judgment reported sub nom *L v. L* [1992] ILRM 115 (property); *State (DPP) v. Walsh* [1981] IR 412 (act of wife in presence of husband); *McKinley v. Ireland* Irish Times Law Reports, 7 May 1990, Supreme Court unreported, (Transcript: Lexis) 27 July 1992 (action for loss of consortium); *W v. W* (1993) ILRM 294 (domicile of dependence held never to have been constitutional); *RF v. MF* unreported, Supreme Court, 24 October 1985, Henchy J nem diss (presumption of advancement).

more likely today that a court in the Republic would hold that a wife, or a wife and children, can acquire by adverse possession the title to property vested in a husband.

6. Forfeiture or Breach of Condition

Section 16 of the Statute of Limitations provides that a right to recover land by virtue of a forfeiture or breach of condition shall be deemed to have accrued on the date on which the forfeiture was incurred or the condition broken.

Suppose land is given to A subject to two conditions by which if either of two events occurs the land is to be forfeit. Both events occur. If an action is brought a short time after the second event, but more than 12 years after the first event occurred, then the action is barred. The occurrence of the second event does not give rise to a separate cause of action.[109] When the first event occurred the possession of A became adverse and those affected had 12 years from that point in which to bring an action.

7. Leaseholds

a) Running of Time against Lessor

Where land is subject to a lease time does not begin to run against the lessor until the termination of the lease.[110] When the lease comes to an end the lessor has 12 years within which to recover the land. We have seen that this still constitutes one of the defects which in theory can affect any title, at least in unregistered land, given that such titles in Ireland are investigated back for a limited period, usually 20 years. If V is selling land to P, the title deeds may indicate that V has a fee simple, but if the titles deeds were searched back 150 years they would show that V's title was in fact a lease for 160 years. There is thus a reversion outstanding on the term and it will fall into possession in 10 years' time. Time will not begin to run against the person entitled to the reversion until that time. Hence, V's title suffers from a defect which could destroy it.

b) Position of Dispossessor of Lessee

Where someone has dispossessed a lessee and has remained in possession for 12 years has the dispossessor acquired the remainder of the term so that they hold on the same conditions as the ousted lessee, or is their possession more precarious? We have seen that the landlord's right to possession is suspended until the termination of the lease. The lease may terminate by expiry or by breach of a condition or a forfeiture provided for in the lease. On the face of it the answer should therefore depend on whether the dispossessor has performed the

---

109 Section 20 Statute of Limitations, 1957. *Clarke v. Clarke* (1868) IR 2 CL 395; *Doe d Hall v. Moulsdale* (1847) 16 M & W 689, 153 ER 1367.

110 1957 Act, s.15(1).

covenants in the lease during the 12 year period and whether the landlord has accepted this performance. If the landlord has done so, then he or she should be estopped from denying the tenancy.[111] Unfortunately the issue has not come before the courts in the leading cases in this straightforward form. A common case of adverse possession arises when A encroaches on the adjoining land of B, unknown possibly to both parties. If B holds the land under a lease then B will continue to pay the rent and perform the other terms of the lease during the 12 year period. The lessor can of course bring an action for possession when the lease terminates and has, as we have seen, 12 years from that point in which to do so. But the question is as to the rights of the parties while the term continues. The question is whether the dispossessor's title is precarious during this time.

(1) The English Position in Fairweather

The English House of Lords in *Fairweather v. St Marylebone Property Co Ltd*[112] took the view that a dispossessor's title is precarious. In that case A had a garden shed which straddled the boundary line between his land and that of B, which B held on a 99-year lease. The dispossessed lessee purported to surrender his lease to the lessor. The lessor claimed that this had given him an immediate right to possession in the lessor which he could therefore enforce at once and that he did not have to wait until the 99-year term had expired.

The majority of the court, Lord Morris dissenting, held that he was entitled to do so. They held that the title of the dispossessed lessee was extinguished as against the dispossessor but not in relation to the lessor. The title of the ousted lessee to the lease remained as between the lessor and the ousted lessee so that the ousted lessee could surrender it to the lessor. They went on to hold that the effect of this was that the lessor's right to possession was no longer postponed by the lease and, more surprisingly, that this was so not only in relation to the ousted lessee but in relation to the dispossessor as well. The result was that the dispossessed lessee by surrendering the lease and the lessor by accepting the surrender could together oust the squatter even though the limitation period had expired.

Fairweather is open the criticism that the result involves an inconsistency in theory. The court begins by adopting a relative title approach in holding that the title to the lease is extinguished in relation to the squatter but not in relation to the lessor, but it ends by holding that a surrender of the lease by the lessee to the lessor can affect the squatter, which should only be so if it were an absolute title valid against all. It is also open to the criticism that it violates the provisions of the English statute of limitations which, just as the Irish Act, expressly

111 In *O'Connor v. Foley* [1906] 1 IR 20 and *Ashe v. Hogan* [1920] 1 IR 159 a squatter was held to be a tenant by estoppel, implying that a landlord could also be held bound to accept a squatter as a lessee on the same ground. See Wylie, *Irish Land Law* para. 23.13.

112 [1963] AC 510.

says that after the limitation period has expired the lessee has no title to the lease. It would seem to follow that if the lessee has no title to the lease he or she cannot surrender it or otherwise deal with it. A result which is on the face of it inconsistent in reasoning and contrary to the plain meaning of a statute may indicate that the judges were unwilling to follow the logic of the statute to its result in the case at hand. In *Fairweather* the willingness of the court to accept the theoretical inconsistency may have been motivated by a reluctance as a matter of policy to accept that squatters can acquire a lease as against lessors. In urban areas in Britain squatting in residential premises had become a growing consequence of homelessness.

The *Fairweather* case was extended in England by *Tickner v. Buzzacott*[113] which held that a lessor could forfeit the lease for non-payment of rent by the ousted lessee and this would give the lessor an immediate right to possession against the dispossessor. The court also held that the dispossessor had no right in equity to relief against forfeiture.

(2) The Irish Position in Perry

The question was considered in Ireland by the Supreme Court in *Perry v. Woodfarm Homes Ltd.*[114] The Irish judges did not accept the position in *Fairweather*. While they recognised that a contractual relationship can still exist between the ousted lessee and the lessor, they clearly held that the dispossessor's position is not as precarious as that in England after *Fairweather*. In *Perry* the northern extremity of the plaintiff's property was bounded by a lane which ran from east to west. A narrow strip of ground adjoined the northern side of the lane. In 1955 the plaintiff entered into adverse possession of a portion of the strip and continued in possession without acknowledging the title of any person to the portion. At the time the plaintiff entered possession the strip of ground was held, together with other land, by a lessee under a lease which created a term of 999 years from September 1947. In October 1970, the lessee purported to assign the lease to the defendants for the residue of the term. By that time the plaintiffs had clearly completed the 12 years period of adverse possession. A month later the lessors conveyed to the defendants the fee simple reversion in the land. The defendants claimed to be entitled to the possession of the strip of ground, including the portion possessed by the plaintiff. They argued that the leasehold interest in the portion of the strip had been determined by merger with the fee simple reversion when that had been acquired by the defendants. The plaintiff claimed an injunction restraining the defendants from entering upon the portion of the strip used by the plaintiff. O'Keefe P in the High Court granted a perpetual injunction.

The majority of the Supreme Court held on appeal that:

113 [1965] Ch. 426.

114 [1975] IR 104 at 117.

(1) After the expiry of the 12 year period the ousted lessee has no title to the lease and so no interest capable of being assigned.[115] Hence the purported assignment of the lease in October 1970 by Irish Life did not vest any estate in land in the defendants.[116]

(2) Hence also there was no interest vested in the defendants which could merge with the freehold reversion when it was conveyed in November 1970 and so the defendants did not acquire, by merger, an immediate right to possession enforceable against the plaintiff adverse possessors.[117]

(3) In unregistered land there is no parliamentary conveyance of the lease from the ousted lessee to the adverse possessor.[118] On this point the Supreme Court followed the Irish Court of Appeal in *O'Connor v. Foley*[119] and the English Court of Appeal in *Tichborne v. Weir*,[120] Griffin J observing that the latter case "has since been accepted as good law in England and as burying there, once and for all, the notion of a parliamentary transfer or conveyance".[121]

(4) The leasehold estate, although not the ousted lessee's title to it, continues to exist in a negative sense in that it forms an incumbrance on the freehold suspending the lessor's right to possession.[122]

(5) An ousted lessee cannot surrender the lease to the lessor and so cannot confer an immediate right to possession on the lessor, because the ousted lessee not longer has title to the lease.[123] The Supreme Court did not follow the English House of Lords in *Fairweather v. St Marylebone Property Co Ltd*[124] on this point. It followed from this that the lessor and the ousted lessee could not collude in this way to evict the adverse possessor.

(6) The lease still exists as a contract between the lessor and the ousted lessee and so, if the ousted lessee is an original contracting party,[125]

---

115 Per Walsh J at 119, Griffin J at 130, Henchy J expresses no view on assignment, but dissent would be consistent with his view on merger and surrender, at p.124.

116 Per Walsh J at 119, Griffin J at 130, 132.

117 Per Walsh J at 121 upholding the decision of O'Keefe P in the High Court; Griffin J at 130; Henchy J dissenting at p.124.

118 Per Walsh J at 120; Griffin J at 128, 129; Henchy J at 122; overruling *Rankin v. McMurtry* (1889) 24 LR Ir 290.

119 [1906] 1 IR 20, Fitzgibbon LJ at 26,

120 (1892) 67 LT 735, M & B 178, 709, followed in *Taylor v. Twinberrow* [1930] 2 KB 16.

121 At p.128.

122 Per Walsh J at 119, Griffin J at 129, Henchy J dissenting at 124.

123 Per Walsh J at 119, Griffin J at 130, Henchy J dissenting at 124.

124 [1963] AC 510.

125 If he or she is not then there is no privity of contract between the ousted lessee and the lessor and the lessee would not remain liable after parting with their estate: *Re Field* [1918] 1 IR 140. Section 14 of Deasy's Act provides that a landlord or tenant who is

> unless the original lease expressly provided otherwise, the ousted lessee remains bound, contractually, to the lessor to perform the covenants in the lease.[126] This follows from basic principles. A contract is a personal obligation not dependent upon the promissor having any estate in the land, unless the parties expressly say that it is.

The court is less clear as to the effect of the ousted lessee failing to perform the covenants in the lease. The court is clear that if the ousted lessee is an original contracting party he or she remains liable in privity of contract to the original lessor. If the contract contained a forfeiture clause then this would cause a forfeiture of the lease and the question then is as to the effect of this. Insofar as the lease remains a contractual obligation, on the face of it the only effect a forfeiture would have is to terminate this contract and release the parties to it from their mutual obligations. The adverse possessor would be unaffected. This result would also follow logically from the court's basic position that the ousted lessee's only remaining legal relations are in contract with the lessor. Griffin J is, however, equivocal on the point, saying on the one hand that "it is not necessary for the purpose of this case to decide what right, if any, has been gained by the squatter by reason of the title of the lessee having been extinguished", but goes on to say:

> "Nevertheless, it seems to me that, though there is no transfer or statutory conveyance to the squatter, what the plaintiff (as squatter) has gained is the right to possession of the premises in dispute as against the defendants (as fee simple owners) for the unexpired portion of the term of the lease, subject to the risk and possibility of a forfeiture".[127]

But a forfeiture brought about by whom? Earlier in his judgment, speaking of the decision of the English House of Lords in *Fairweather*, the same judge says:

> ". . . the effect of this decision is that by collusion between the lessee and the freeholder, the successors in title of a squatter on leasehold land can be ejected however long the lessee has been out of possession - be it 12 years, 120 years or 900 years. It seems to me that such a result would entirely defeat the object of the Statute of Limitations".[128]

This reasoning would seem to be as apt to the case of forfeiture as it is to assignment or surrender, but, again, later in his judgment the judge says:

---

such by assignment is only to have the benefit of or to be liable on the covenants so long as they retain the estate.

126 Per Walsh J at 119, Griffin J at 130.

127 At 129.The judge repeats this at 130:

> "In my view, the squatter has the right to possession not only as against the lessee and any stranger but also as against the lessor for the unexpired portion of the term, subject to the risk of a forfeiture;...".

128 At 129.

> "In the present case, at the time when the purported assignment by Irish Life was made [*i.e.* in 1970], there had been no forfeiture and the plaintiff was accordingly entitled to remain in possession against the lessor".[129]

The plaintiffs had completed 12 years' adverse possession in 1967 and so this could be taken to suggest that the ousted lessee, if they had failed to perform the covenants between 1967 and 1970, could have brought about a forfeiture, but the meaning is far from clear.

Walsh J, the other judge in the majority, seems to be more firmly of the view that the erstwhile squatter can prevent a forfeiture by performing the covenants personally:

> ". . . the squatter may be indirectly forced to carry out the covenants to preserve his possession from ejectment by forfeiture for non-observance of the covenants".[130]

Later he expresses the same view:

> "But because of the threat of re-entry hanging over the squatter in the event of failure to pay rent or to observe the covenants, the lessor is effectively in no worse position than he would have been with the original lessee. In fact he may find himself in a stronger position in so far as he can hold the original lessee to the terms while at the same time he is in a position to enforce indirectly all the covenants against the squatter by the threat of re-entry, if the lease provides for re-entry in the event of failure to observe the covenants".[131]

Certainly it must be correct that if the lessor has accepted the adverse possessor as a tenant the lessor cannot at the same time seek to evict the adverse possessor on the ground that the ousted tenant has failed to perform the covenants. Two problems that present difficulty occur where an adverse possessor, S has never performed the covenants in the lease, as where a strip was occupied and the adverse possessor only asserts a right after the expiry of the limitation period. Thus neither S nor the lessor, L, has acted on the basis that S is a tenant of L. The problems are:

(1) Can S force the lessor to accept performance from S?

(2) What happens if S remains in possession and does not perform the covenants?

and

(3) Can L force S to act as tenant and, if not, can S remain in possession free of rent for the rest of the term of the lease?

Neither judgment gives a definitive answer to these problems.

In (1) the problem is made more difficult by the equivocal nature of lease and tenancies generally: on the one hand they are property interests which can

129 At 130.

130 At 120.

131 At 120.

be conveyed or transferred but on the other hand they may involve at the least the lessee paying rent to the lessor who therefore has a legitimate interest in determining whether a proposed tenant is credit-worthy, and may involve a more personal relationship. Hence many leases provided for any assignment or subletting to be subject to the lessor's consent. It also underlines the unsatisfactory feature of the reasoning in *Perry* in following the English cases in holding that there is no parliamentary conveyance in the case of unregistered land which must mean that the squatter is not automatically entitled to the benefit or subject to the burden, of the leasehold interest. Registered land apart, it is difficult to see on what basis he or she could insist that the lessor accept him or her as the new tenant if the lessor is unwilling to do so and in the absence of a doctrine of a statutory conveyance.

Problem (2) points out a contradiction in the judgments in the Supreme court. Both judges agree that the lease continues to exist in a negative sense, suspending the right to possession of L until the end of the lease. In this case it is difficult to see what L can do if S fails to pay the rent or to perform the other covenants in the lease. Can it be that there is a kind of legal limbo in which S can remain for the remainder of the term of the lease and there is nothing either L or T can do about it? If L sues to enforce the terms of lease, may S not say "but I am not a tenant: I am a squatter, and you cannot evict me because you have no right to possession until the lease comes to an end!". Suppose also that S starts to commit what in a tenant would be waste? It may be that the odd equivocation on forfeiture on the part of Griffin J and to a lesser extent on the part of Walsh J may be due to their anticipating this type of problem. Griffin J suggests that if T does not continue to perform the obligations a forfeiture may occur affecting S, but this is surely inconsistent with the logic of the judgment. Walsh J suggests that L may have a choice of seeking performance from either T or S, implying that L can force S to comply with the lease or face forfeiture. Again, in the absence of a doctrine of parliamentary conveyance it is not immediately obvious why he can do so. The answer may be that if S remains without performing the covenants, L will sue for possession. S will then attempt to plead that there is a lease outstanding in a negative sense suspending L's right to possession. In such a case the court is likely to take the view that S cannot plead the lease to his own advantage unless he is also prepared to undertake the burdens of tenant. S cannot have it both ways: he cannot approbate and reprobate.[132]

132 *Corrigan v. Irish Land Commission* [1977] IR 317, Supreme Court; *O'Reilly v. Gleeson* [1975] IR 258, High Court; *Re Deighton's Will Trusts* (1952) 86 ILTR 127.

It remains to be decided whether in the Republic the acceptance of rent by the lessor from the adverse possessor is sufficient without more to estop the lessor denying that the adverse possessor is the new tenant. The English cases of *Tichborne v. Weir*[133] and *Tickner v. Buzzacott*[134] held that payment of a monthly rent, for example, would only give rise to a monthly tenancy and Walker LJ in *O'Connor v. Foley*[135] refers to the point in an exposition of the effect of the *Tichborne* case, but without comment. Since, in unregistered land, there is no parliamentary conveyance the adverse possessor is not automatically liable on the covenants in the lease to the landlord. This was certainly the view of Fitzgibbon LJ in *O'Connor v. Foley*[136] who said:

> "It appears to me to decide only this, that the Statute of Limitations operates by way of extinguishment, and not by way of assignment of the estate, which is barred; and that a person who becomes entitled to a leasehold interest by adverse possession for the prescribed period is not liable to be sued in covenant as assignee of the lease, unless he has estopped himself from denying that he is assignee".[137]

Nor is the lessor on expiry of the 12 year period automatically entitled to sue the adverse possessor for rent or on the other covenants.

c) Registered Land

Walsh J, in a *dictum* which was not dissented from by the other judges, said that he considered registered land to be on a different footing, due to the provisions of the registration Act. Section 49(2) of the Registration of Title Act, 1964 provides that where any person claims to have acquired a title by possession to registered land he may apply to the registrar to be registered as owner of the land and the registrar, if satisfied that the applicant has acquired the title, may cause the applicant to be registered as owner of the land with an absolute, good leasehold, possessory or qualified title. According to Walsh J:

> "This would appear to permit a squatter to have himself registered in the Land Registry as the owner of a leasehold, being registered land, where the squatter has dispossessed the registered owner of the leasehold".[138]

In fact it can be argued that this is more than a mere *dictum* since the title to the land in *Perry v. Woodfarm* was in fact registered.

This was held to be the position in the English case of *Spectrum Investment Co v. Holmes*.[139] The freehold had been registered in 1901. Under a lease

133 (1892) 67 LT 735, M & B 178.

134 [1965] Ch. 426.

135 [1906] 1 IR 20 at 33.

136 [1906] 1 IR 20.

137 *ibid.* at p.26.

138 At 120.

139 [1981] 1 All ER 6, [1981] 1 WLR 221, 41 P & CR 133.

granted in 1902 the leaseholder was granted a lease for 99 years. In 1939 the leaseholder granted a tenancy to Mrs H who lived there with her daughter, the defendant. Mrs H paid the rent until 1944. In that year the leaseholder assigned the lease to Mrs D who was registered as proprietor of the lease. Mrs D refused tenders of rent from Mrs H Mrs H died in 1951 and the daughter remained in occupation without paying rent. In 1957 the freehold was acquired by a company who were registered with possessory title. By 1963 the daughter had acquired title under the English Limitation Act as against the leaseholder, Mrs D. In March 1968 the defendant applied under the English Land Registration Act, 1925 to be registered as the leasehold proprietor of the house. Notice of the application was served on Mrs D's solicitors but they took no action. In June 1968 the daughter was registered as the leasehold proprietor and the entry in respect of Mrs D was removed. In 1975 the company's registration was later changed to absolute title. They and Mrs D then discovered that the defendant had been registered as the leasehold proprietor and in May 1975 entered into a transaction intended to defeat the defendant's title, by which Mrs D purported to surrender to the company her leasehold interest comprised in the title which had been closed in 1968. The company then applied to the county court for possession of the house and mesne profits, but these proceedings were stood over for a decision on the question of title to the house.

Browne-Wilkinson J in the Chancery Division held that the registration of the defendant as the leasehold proprietor had the effect, by virtue of section 69(1) of the English Act, of vesting the legal term of the lease in her as against Mrs D because, by virtue of section 69(4) of that Act, the registered leasehold estate could only be disposed of by a transfer under section 21(1) by the registered proprietor, and a transfer included a surrender. Since Mrs D's purported surrender had not been effected by a registered disposition it was invalid and the company's claim failed. The company could not claim under section 11 of the 1925 Act to be entitled to any estate, right or interest in the house as against the defendant until the lease expired. The court contrasted the position with that in *Fairweather*[140] and noted that a squatter who adversely possessed registered leasehold land differed from the rights such a person would have in respect of unregistered land since in the latter case the documentary lessee could effectively surrender the legal term to the freeholder to cause a merger.

As to Ireland, it would seem in the light of the similar provisions of the Irish Act of 1964[141] and the comments of Walsh J that there is nothing an ousted lessee can do to prevent the adverse possessor becoming registered as proprictor of the lease and can do nothing to affect the position once the adverse possessor is registered. In fact, even before that occurs but after the 12 year period

140 *Fairweather v. St Marylebone Property Co Ltd* [1962] 2 All ER 288.

141 Sections 49(2), 51.

is up, the situation would seem to be no different because the right of an adverse possessor is protected as an unregistered right under section 72.

d) Tenancy from Year to Year

Section 17(2) of the Statute of Limitations, 1957 provides that:

> "17.–(2)(b) The right of action of a person entitled to land subject to a tenancy from year to year[142] or other period, without a lease in writing, shall be deemed to have accrued at the date of the determination of the tenancy,[143] unless any rent or other periodic payment has subsequently been received in respect of the tenancy, in which case the right of action shall be deemed to have accrued on the date of the last receipt of rent or other periodic payment".

The section is a modified version of section 8 of the Real Property Limitation Act, 1833.[144] The phrase without a lease in writing clearly indicates that such leases are outside the section, presumably because where the parties have reduced a periodic tenancy to writing the written agreement will normally provide for the termination of the lease by notice. Nevertheless, if the parties omit to make such a provision the section is of no avail.[145]

One question which might arise is whether a document which fails to create a periodic tenancy at common law, but is effectual in equity under the doctrine of *Walsh v. Lonsdale*,[146] counts as a lease in writing for the purpose of the section. There is authority on the 1833 Act to the effect that it is not.[147] At common

142 A tenancy "for a year and so on from year to year" cannot be determined by notice until the end of the second year: *Doe d Chadborn v. Green* (1839) 9 Ad & E 658, 112 ER 1361. It is a tenancy for one year followed by a periodic tenancy. It is probable that such a tenancy does not terminate under the section until the end of the second year: Hewitt, *Limitations* p.97.

143 This phrase is equivocal, since a periodic tenancy is renewed automatically at the end of the first period. The tenancy therefore continues until terminated by notice. In view of the sections of other statutes cited below, on which the section is evidently based, it would seem that it means the end of the first year or other period.

144 3 & 4 Wm IV c.27. Section 8 reads:

> "When any person shall be in possession or in receipt of the profits of any land, or in receipt of any rent as tenant from year to year, or other period, without any lease in writing, the right of the person entitled subject thereto , or of the person through whom he claims, to make an entry or distress, or to bring an action to recover such land or rent, shall be deemed to have first accrued at the determination of the first of such years or other periods...".

And see also the English Limitation Act, 1939, section 9(2):

> "A tenancy from year to year or other period, without a lease in writing, shall, for the purposes of this Act, be deemed to be determined at the expiration of the first year or other period...".

145 *Foreman v. Mowlds* unreported, High Court, 28 January 1985, extempore judgment by Barrington J, noted in McHugh (1985) 3 ILT 47.

146 (1882) 21 Ch D 9.

147 *Archbold v. Scully* (1861) 9 HLC 360, 2 ER 769; *Drummond v. Sant* (1871) LR 6 QB 763.

law such a tenant was a tenant from year to year or other period according to how the rent was paid, but in equity such a person holds under the terms contained in the document. and this rule now prevails.[148] Time will not therefore run against such a tenant until the term in the document has expired.[149]

e) Tenancy at Will

Section 17 of the Statute of Limitations, 1957 provides that a tenancy at will is deemed to end one year after it begins unless previously determined. This means that after a year the possession of the tenant becomes adverse to that of the landlord, and time begins to run against him. O'Higgins CJ dissenting in *Bellew v. Bellew*[150] applied the provision to the facts of the case. The majority of the court preferred to regard the facts as having given rise to a licence.[151]

f) Licences

A licence[152] to occupy land, although it may imply more than this today, is at least a permission to occupy and so a licensee cannot be in adverse possession while the licence is in force.

In one English case a unilateral licence was held to have been created and to have had the effect of stopping time running against the owner of the paper title. In *BP Properties Ltd v. Buckler*[153] the Buckler family had been in possession of Great House Farm near Penarth from about 1916. For the purpose of the present case it is only relevant to say that in 1955 Western Ground Rents Ltd had obtained judgment against Mr Buckler for non-payment of rent. No attempt was made to enforce it as Mrs Buckler had recently come out of hospital after a serious operation and objected strongly to leaving the premises. In 1962 possession proceedings were again brought and a new possession order was obtained in December 1962. Again, no attempt was made to enforce the order. Mr Buckler died and Mrs Buckler remained in possession of the land. In 1974 BP Pension Trust Ltd, who had acquired the freehold, began an action for possession. This was adjourned and in the same year BP Trust applied for leave to enforce the original order made in 1962. This was granted, subject to a stay of execution until October 1974. A press campaign was then launched on behalf of Mrs Buckler, claiming that she was an elderly widow being evicted from the house she and her family had occupied for centuries. BP Properties, to whom

148 *Walsh v. Lonsdale* (1882) 21 Ch D 9.

149 *Archbold v. Scully* (1861) 9 HLC 360, 2 ER 769; *Drummond v. Sant* (1871) LR 6 QB 763.

150 [1982] IR 447.

151 See Chapter 19 Landlord and Tenant.

152 See Chapter 8 Licences, Estoppel and Constructive Trusts.

153 (1987) 284 EG 372, 55 P & CR 337, [1987] 2 EGLR 168, CA (Civil Division); *Pavledes v. Ryesbridge Properties Ltd* (1989) 58 P & CR 459, Ch D.

the freehold had been transferred, offered to allow Mrs Buckler to remain in occupation of the house and garden rent free for as long as she wished and "for the rest of your life if you so desire". Mrs Buckler did not reply. She was left in possession until her death in 1983. BP properties then began an action for possession against Mrs Buckler's son. He claimed to be entitled under a possessory title derived from the possession of his parents and subsequently himself.

Hollis J in the English High court held that Mr Buckler's possession was not adverse up to his death. Time did not begin to run against the landowner until then. He also held that from 1974 Mrs Buckler possessed the land under a licence from BP and so there was no 12 year period of adverse possession.

The unanimous judgment of the Court of appeal was delivered by Dillon LJ. He held that Mr and Mrs Buckler were in adverse possession from the end of the tenancy in 1955 and possibly from the last payment of rent two years earlier, although the point was not crucial to the judgment. The judge held that the possession order in 1962 had been obtained within 12 years of 1955 or 1953 and so was valid. He also held that as the enforcement order had been obtained within 12 years of the possession order, the enforcement order was also valid. Then there remained the significance of the offer contained in two letters from BP Pension and Properties on October 31, 1974 to Mrs Buckler. BP relied on section 10(2) of the 1939 Act which provided that when land ceased to be in adverse possession no fresh right of action shall accrue until adverse possession was resumed. They argued that she then became a licensee for life and time had ceased to run in her favour. But she had made no response (on her solicitor's advice) to the offer of a licence and was relying on the fact that, as the possession warrant issued in 1962 had been withdrawn by BP, her 12 years of adverse possession were completed by December 1974. Dillon LJ construed her silence as meaning "she was not asserting during the time from the receipt of the letters . . . any claim to ownership of the farmhouse and garden, or any intention to exclude the owner of the paper title".

Dillon LJ went on to say, with dubious reasoning, that the nature of Mrs Buckler's possession after receipt of the two letters could not be decided by looking at what was "locked up in her own mind". One must look at the position from the standpoint of the person with the paper title. What could that person have done? The rule that possession is not adverse if it can be referred to a lawful title applies even if the person in possession did not know of the lawful title. Dillon LJ took the view that, even though Mrs Buckler did not accept the terms of the letters, BP Properties would have been bound to treat her, in the absence by her of any repudiation of the two letters, as in possession as a licensee on the terms of the letters. They could not evict her (if they could have done so at all) without determining the licence. Even accepting that there was such a licence, however, one might point out that BP could easily have terminated it by another letter.

From the proposition that possession is not adverse if it is referable to a lawful title, and that a person may be in possession by virtue of a lawful title even if they are unaware of it, the judge leaps to the conclusion, which in no way follows from these propositions, that a person may be in possession by virtue of a licence when they had merely been offered a licence but had not accepted the offer. The judge has invented the concept of a unilateral licence, for which there was no previous authority. This unilateral licence had the effect, he found, of stopping time running against the licensor. In contract law silence does not constitute consent and an offer by one side which elicits no response from the other party does not constitute a contract. Yet the judge believed it could constitute a licence. In his favour it can be pointed out that not all licences are contracts, that a bare licence is in the words of Vaughn CJ in *Thomas v. Sorrell*[154] in 1674 merely permission to do something which otherwise is a trespass. Nevertheless, the company did not purport to grant the widow permission, but to offer her a licence and so phrased it in terms of a proposal. Furthermore, the judgment is tainted with the unjustifiable assumption that it was acceptable to put words into the widow's mouth. It is open to question whether a similar assumption would have been made about a person not tarnished by the illegality of trespass. Perhaps the underlying consideration was that the present action was not concerned with the widow's continued occupation, but that of the son, and the same sympathetic factors did not apply in his case, but in reaching the desired result the judge undermines the existing understanding of the law of adverse possession.

The Act of 1957 does not contain specific sections which deem licences to terminate after a specific period, as in the case of a tenancy at will. Nevertheless, once the licence is revoked[155] or terminates because it was only to last until a particular event occurred or purpose has been fulfilled[156] the licensee's possession becomes adverse to that of the licensor.

154 (1674) Vaugh 330, 351, 124 ER 1098 at 1109.

155 *Cullen v. Cullen* [1962] IR 268, High Court, Kenny J.

156 *Bellew v. Bellew* [1982] IR 447, [1983] 3 ILRM 128.

CHAPTER 26

SUCCESSION

"Let's talk of graves... Let's choose executors and talk of wills."
– Shakespeare, *Richard II* Act 3 scene 2.

A. Testamentary Succession

1. A Will takes Effect on Death

a) Will Revocable Till Death

A will has no effect until the death of the testator.[1] It is usually said to be ambulatory.[2] It merely declares the intention of the testator in the meantime.[3] The testator retains the power to revoke it and substitute other provisions, notwithstanding a declaration in the will to the contrary.[4]

There are a number of doctrines developed by the courts, namely, contracts by a testator to leave property by will and the doctrine of mutual wills, which appear to undermine the power of revocation, and in a practical sense they do, so that many writers deal with them under this heading. However, in a technical sense they do not and doctrinally they depend instead on contractual remedies. They are therefore really a distinct way by which property may be passed on death and are treated by the present writer under the topic of Informal or Non-Testamentary Succession below.

b) Will Speaks from Death

Section 89 of the Succession Act, 1965 provides that:

> "89.– Every will shall, with reference to all estate comprised in the will and every devise or bequest contained in it, be construed to speak and take effect as if it had been executed immediately before the death of the testator, unless a contrary intention appears from the will".

The section amends section 24 of the Wills Act, 1837 which excluded such

---

1 Wylie, *Irish Land Law* para. 14.01–14.03.

2 OED "ambulatory": *Cowel's Institutes* (1651) p.133: "A man's will... according the the Civil Law is ambulatory, or revocable, until death".

3 *Re Westminster's Deed of Appointment* [1959] Ch. 265 at 271.

4 *Vynior's Case* (1610) 8 Co Rep 81b, 77 ER 597.

rules as *Wild's Case*[5] from the ambit of the principle. Although a will speaks from death, in that it is construed according to its meaning at that time, there are still some exceptions. The armchair principle, discussed below, is one. Another instance is section 26(2) of the Adoption Act, 1952 which provides that:

> "26(2).–In any disposition of real or personal property made, whether by instrument *inter vivos* or by will (including codicil), after the date of an adoption order – any reference (whether express or implied) to the child or children of the adopter shall, unless the contrary appears, be construed as, or as including, a reference to the adopted person".[6]

The use of the word heirs as a word of purchase in some instances appears to be another example.[7]

2. Making a Will

a) Capacity

Section 77(1) of the Succession Act, 1965 (the 1965 Act) requires that, to be valid, a will must be made by a person who has attained the age of 18 or is or has been married and is "of sound disposing mind".[8] The court has an inherent jurisdiction, derived from the courts of equity, to refuse to grant probate of a will if it is not satisfied that the will was the free act of the testator, as where a testator was subject to undue influence.[9] A will made by a person suffering from a mental illness may still be valid if made during a lucid interval and is not invalidated by a subsequent relapse.[10]

b) Formalities

Section 78 of the 1965 Act sets out the formal requirements of a will. These are essentially the same provisions as those first contained in the Wills Act, 1837 which have been the subject of considerable case law. The presumption of due execution or compliance with formalities (*omnia praesumuntur rite esse acta*) operates here, but it does not cure all defects. It is discussed below.

5 See Chapter 8 Fee Tail.

6 But see *Re Stamp, deceased* [1993] ILRM 383, Lardner J, below.

7 See below and Chapter 6 Fee Simple.

8 *Banks v. Goodfellow* (1870) LR 5 QB 549 per Cockburn CJ at 567; *In bonis Farrell* (1954) 88 ILTR 57 (insane delusions).

9 See below Section 26.1.10.

10 Wylie, *Irish Land Law* para. 14.04.

(1) History

The Statute of Wills, 1634[11] required wills of realty to be in writing.[12] The Statute of Frauds, 1695[13] added the requirement that the will should be signed by the testator and witnessed in his or her presence by at least three witnesses. Nuncupative, *i.e.* oral, wills could be made of personalty, but the 1695 statute required them to be witnessed if the value of the property was over £30 and so it became the practice for wills of personalty to be in writing.[14] The Industrial Revolution of the late 18th century had as one of its consequences an increased concern for certainty in law. Businessmen and industrialists needed to be sure of the titles to the land they bought, needed to reduce the risks of their investment decisions and needed calculation of profit with some accuracy.[15] Some economic uncertainties were unavoidable, but the law could be rendered more certain, it was thought, by legislation. The Wills Act, 1837 set out to give greater certainty to wills of both real and personal property.

(2) Writing

Section 78 of the Succession Act, 1965 reproduces for the most part section 9 of the Wills Act, 1837 as amended by the Wills Act Amendment Act, 1852. For a will to be valid it must be (a) in writing, and (b) in accordance with the rules in the section, which are discussed below.

A will may be a number of documents.[16] An apparently inter vivos gift, if made conditional on donor's death, may be granted probate as a will, if it complies with the formalities.[17] A holograph will, *i.e.* one written in the testator's own handwriting, is not exempt on that ground from other formalities, as is the case in some jurisdictions.[18]

---

11 *ibid.* para. 14.06.

12 Section 1.

13 Short Titles Act, 1962. Following the English Statute of Frauds, 1677.

14 Megarry & Wade, *Real Property* p.476.

15 See Chapter 6 Fee Simple: words of limitation: history.

16 *Douglas-Menzies v. Umphelby* [1908] AC 224, 233, PC; *In bonis Wafer* [1960] Ir Jur Rep 19. (two wills, both admitted as last will).

17 *In the Goods of Morgan* (1866) LR 1 PD 214.

18 In some jurisdictions, particularly those based upon or derived from Roman law, such as Scotland, a holograph will is recognised as valid without further formalities: *McGinn v. Delbeke* (1927) 61 ILTR 117; *In the goods of Keenan* (1946) 80 ILTR 1. Holograph wills are not excluded from the formalities of the 1965 Act, nor were they excluded from the 1837 statute.

(a) Soldiers

Section 11 of the Wills Act, 1837 provided for informal wills to be valid in the case of soldiers[19] "in actual military service".[20] Soldier included female military personnel[21] and an Army nurse[22]. "Actual military service" has been held to extend to where orders of mobilisation had actually been issued and a person, knowing of them, had made a will in contemplation of actual military service.[23] It has also been held to extend to anti-terrorism activities in peacetime.[24]

These provisions have been repealed in the Republic.[25] This seems unfortunate in view of the continued involvement of Irish forces in United Nations peace-keeping roles. Indeed, the change from peace-keeping to peace-making strengthens the argument in favour of informal wills for those risking their lives in the cause of world peace. Donatio mortis causa may partly fill the gap, even more so if the decision in *Sen v. Headley,*[26] which holds that the doctrine applies to land, is followed. There are differences between the two doctrines. Donatio mortis causa only applies if the donor is actually contemplating death. Merely being in military service would not be enough. Donatio mortis causa also requires (a) the relinquishment of dominion by the donor over the property and (b) either the transfer of the thing itself or the *indicia* of title, although requirement (b) may be dispensed with if the donee is already in possession of the property.[27] Mere expression of intention, however, would not be sufficient.

---

19 Anon, "Soldiers' Wills" (1944) 10 Irish Jurist 8, 14.

20 The phrase was contained in s.19 of the Statute of Frauds, 1695. Critchley, "Privileged Wills and Testamentary Formalities: A Time to Die?" [1999] CLJ 49.

21 *Re Rowson* [1944] 2 All ER 36 (WAAF).

22 *In bonis Stanley* [1916] P 192; Anon "Soldiers' Wills" (1944) 10 Irish Jurist 8, 14. In *Doherty v. Mangan* [1943] IR 78 the provision was applied to an Irishman domiciled in Ireland but serving in the British forces during the Second World War.

23 *In bonis Schroeder* [1949] IR 89, Haugh J applying *In bonis Ryan* [1945] IR 174, *Doherty v. Mangan* [1943] IR 78.

24 *Re Jones* [1981] 1 All ER 1, [1981] Fam 7 (Northern Ireland).

25 Succession Act, 1965 Sch. 2.

26 [1991] Ch 425, [1991] 2 All ER 636, [1991] 2 WLR 1308, [1991] 2 FLR 449, 62 P & CR 277, [1991] Fam Law 373, CA. The case was settled before the appeal to the House of Lords was heard.

27 *Woodard v. Woodard* [1991] Fam Law 470, The Times, 15 March 1991, (Transcript: Lexis).

(b) Sailors

There was a similar relaxation of the normal formalities in the past for "mariners or seamen being at sea".[28] The phrase was held to include a female typist employed by the Cunard line on the *Lusitania*.[29] "At sea" must be interpreted consistently with the phrase "actual military service"[30] so that a sailor on shore leave but under orders to rejoin his or her ship is deemed to be at sea.[31] These provisions have also been repealed in the Republic.[32]

(c) Airmen and Airwomen

Not surprisingly the Wills Act, 1837 made no provision for informal wills by airmen. On the formation of the Royal Air Force in 1918 the privilege was extended to military airmen and airwomen.[33] These provisions have also been repealed in the Republic.[34]

(3) Succession Act, 1965 Section 78

Section 78 provides that to be valid a will shall be in writing and executed in accordance with the following rules:

1. signed "at the foot or end thereof" by the testator, or by some person in his or her presence and at his or her direction;
2. the signature shall be made or acknowledged by the testator in the presence of each of two witnesses and each witness shall attest by his or her signature the signature of the testator in the presence of the testator but no form of attestation shall be necessary nor shall it be necessary for the witnesses to sign in the presence of each other;
3. it is sufficient if the signature of the testator, or of the person signing for him under rule 1, is so placed at or after, or following, or under, or beside, or opposite to the end of the will, that it is apparent on the face of the will that the testator intended to give effect by the signature to the writing signed as his or her will.

Rules 4 and 5 concern the signature itself and are dealt with below.

---

28 The phrase is contained in s.19 of the Statute of Frauds, 1695. In *In the Goods of Hayes* (1840) 2 Curt 375, 163 ER 431 it was held that it included a purser and an admiral. See also *Re Rapley's Estate* [1983] 3 All ER 248, [1983] 1 WLR 1069, [1984] FLR 173, Ch D.

29 *In the goods of Sarah Hale, deceased* [1915] IR 362.

30 Wills (Soldiers and Sailors) Act 1918, s.2.

31 *Re Yates* [1919] P 93 [navy]; *Re Rapley* [1983] 1 WLR 1069 (merchant navy).

32 Succession Act, 1965 Sch. 2.

33 Wills (Soldiers and Sailors) Act 1918, s.5. *Doherty v. Mangan* [1943] IR 78.

34 Succession Act, 1965 Sch. 2.

Rule 1 of section 78 requires that the will must be signed by the testator or by some other person in his or her presence and by his or her direction. "Signed" has been given a wide interpretation and includes a mark,[35] as by an illiterate person, initials,[36] a name stamped[37] onto the will, as with a rubber stamp, a former or assumed name[38] or the signature of someone other than the testator but who signed the will at the direction of the testator, as Rule 1 allows.[39] The test is whether the testator intended the signature to execute the will. A seal is not enough.[40] A holograph will satisfies the requirement of signing if it contains the testator's name at the end, in an attestation clause or otherwise.[41]

(b) "At the Foot or End Thereof"

The signature must be at the foot or end of the will.[42] The phrase comes from the Wills Act, 1837. The courts after the enactment Wills Act, 1837 struck down a number of wills on the ground that this requirement had not been satisfied, and this led to the passing of the Wills Act Amendment Act, 1852 which contained specific rules as to the positioning of the signature.[43] These rules are re-enacted in section 78 Rule 4 of the Succession Act, 1965, as follows:

"4. No such will shall be affected by the circumstances –

(a) that the signature does not follow or is not immediately after the foot or end of the will; or

(b) that a blank space intervenes between the concluding word of the will and the signature;[44] or

(c) that the signature is placed among the words of the testimonium clause or of the clause of attestation, or follows or is after or under

35 *In bonis Kieran* [1933] IR 222; *Re O'Dea* [1932] LJ Ir 148; *In bonis Finn* (1936) 53 TLR 153 (thumb mark). The usual practise of a mark being in the form of a cross was said in *Bennett v. Brumfitt* (1867) LR 3 CP 28 to derive from the practise of the Anglo-Saxons of putting the sign of the cross in front of their names when signing, so that those who could not write their name simply put a cross: see also *In the Goods of Kieran* [1933] IR 222, per Hanna J.

36 *In bonis Emerson* (1882) 9 LR Ir 443.

37 *Jenkins v. Gaisford* (1863) 3 Sw & Tr 93, 164 ER 1208; *Re Bullock* [1968] NI 96.

38 *In bonis Glover* (1847) 11 Jur 1022; *In bonis Redding* (1850) 2 Rob Ecc 339, 163 ER 1338.

39 *In bonis Clark* (1839) 2 Curt 329, 163 ER 428.

40 *In bonis Emerson* (1882) 9 LR Ir 443; *In bonis Lemon* (1896) 30 ILTR 127.

41 *Re Rochford* [1943] Ir Jur Rep 71.

42 This requirement has been abrogated in England as to wills coming into effect after 1982: Administration of Justice Act, 1982 s.17, substituting a new s.9 of the Wills Act, 1837 as it applies in England.

43 The rules are contained in s.1.

44 *In bonis Rice* (1870) IR 5 Eq 176 (the text of the will was on the first page, second and third pages blank, signature of testator and witnesses on the fourth page. Held valid).

the clause of attestation, either with or without a blank space intervening, or follows or is after, or under, or beside[45] the names or one of the names of the attesting witnesses; or

(d) that the signature is on a side or page or other portion of the paper or papers containing the will on which no clause or paragraph or disposing part of the will is written above the signature; or

(e) that there appears to be sufficient space on or at the bottom of the preceding side or page or other portion of the same paper on which the will is written to contain the signature;

and the enumeration of the above circumstances shall not restrict the generality of rule 1.

5. A signature shall not be operative to give effect to any disposition or direction inserted after the signature is made".

The words at the end of rule 4 make it clear that the general rule that the signature must be at the foot or end still applies, although with a wider definition than before, so that, for example, rule 4(a) does not permit a signature to be at the beginning of the document. Rule 5 contains an ambiguity in that after could refer to time or place, but the other rules are clearly concerned with place and not time and after in rule 4(a) clearly refers to place. Rule 3 gives further clarity by providing that "it is sufficient if the signature is so placed at or after, or following, or under, or beside, or opposite to the end of the will" that it is apparent on the face of the will that the testator intended to give effect by the signature to the writing signed as his or her will. The rules would not therefore be satisfied by a holograph will which began "The Will of John Brennan. . ." John Brennan being the name of the testator.[46]

(5) Witnesses

(a) Presence

Rule 2 above requires that the testator's signature must be "made or acknowledged by the testator in the presence of each of two witnesses and each witness shall attest by his or her signature the signature of the testator in the presence of the testator". This means, in other words:

(1) the witnesses must both be present at the same time when they witness the making of the signature or the acknowledgement of the signature by the testator; but

(2) they need not be present when the testator signs the will, provided they are both present together when the testator acknowledges the signature;

45 *Derinzy v. Turner* (1851) 1 Ir Ch R 341.

46 See *Wood v. Smith* [1993] Ch 90, [1992] 3 All ER 556. In England after 1982 the signature need not be at the foot or end, see footnote 42.

(3) they need not both be present at the same time when they sign the will as witnesses (rule 2),[47] although each must do so in the presence of the testator.

The testator and witnesses need not be in the same room. It is enough if a line of sight exists, *e.g.* an open door, so that the witnesses could have seen the testator sign.[48] Presence does not, however, require that the testator see the witnesses[49], so a blind person can make a will.[50]

Under rule 2 it is not necessary to have a particular form of attestation clause, although it is desirable to have one.

(b) Signature of Witness

The signature of a witness may be initials,[51] a mark[52] or stamped.[53] It is not sufficient for a witness to acknowledge his or her signature: the witness must actually sign in the presence of the testator.[54]

(6) Attestation

The signatures of the witnesses attest the signature of the testator and not the will itself. Indeed the witnesses need not know that the document is a will, or be aware of its contents.[55]

It is also usual, although not necessary under rule 2, for witnesses to be present at the same time when they sign the will, as well as when they witness the testator's signature, and attestation clauses normally state this. A suitable attestation clause would be:

> *SIGNED* by [the testator's name]:
>
> [testator's signature]
>
> *in our joint presence and attested by us in the presence of* [testator's name] *and of each other:–*
>
> [signature of first witness]
>
> [description of first witness]

---

47 This seems to have been the case under the Wills Act, 1837: *Re Devlin* [1939] Ir Jur Rep 85; *In bonis Flynn* [1957] Ir Jur Rep 95.

48 *Shires v. Glascock* (1685) 2 Salk 688 (hole in the wall); *Winchilsea v. Wauchope* (1827) 3 Russ. 441 (if line exists, presumption of good attestation); Mellows, *Law of Succession* (5th ed.) para. 6.25.

49 *Tod v. Earl Winchelsea* [1826] 2 C & P 488.

50 *Re Piercy's Goods* (1845) 1 Robb Eccl 278.

51 *In bonis Strealey* [1891] P 172.

52 *In bonis Amiss* (1849) 2 Rob Ecc 116, 163 ER 1262.

53 *Re Bullock* [1968] NI 96.

54 *Wyatt v. Berry* [1893] P 5. In England acknowledgment by a witness is now permitted: Administration of Justice Act, 1982, s.17, substituting a new s.9 of the Wills Act, 1837.

55 *Re Devlin* [1939] Ir Jur Rep 85.

[signature of second witness]

[description of second witness]

Rule 2 does not prescribe any particular form of attestation clause or require one to be used, but it is desirable, because, as the next section shows, if one is lacking the benefit of the presumption of due execution may be lost.

(7) Presumption of Due Execution

When an issue as to compliance with the statutory formalities arises the courts have invoked the presumption *omnia praesumuntur rite esse acta*[56], which is not confined to wills, of proper execution.[57] The effect of the presumption is to shift the burden of proof onto those who assert that the formalities have not been complied with. However, it may not save the day in every case.

In *Clery v. Barry*[58] Palles CB attempted to confine the presumption, in cases on attestation by witnesses, to where the witnesses were dead or incapacitated or where their evidence was unreliable:

> "The principle is, that where upon the face of an instrument everything is regular, and there is nothing to awaken suspicion or call for additional inquiry, then, if the evidence is defective, either by reason of the death of witnesses or by lapse of time affecting their recollection, or of other circumstances which may affect their honesty, the same presumption arises as is usually acted on in the ordinary affairs of mankind".[59]

The case was applied in *Rolleston v. Sinclair*[60] in which there was no attestation clause in the will and the evidence of both living witnesses was to the effect that they were not present at the same time when the testator signed the will. O'Connor MR said:

> "In my opinion no such presumption arises in this case, because of two circumstances: 1, the will contains no attestation clause; and 2, the witnesses to the will are living and were available. Counsel for the executors were not able to produce a single authority in aid of the presumption in such a case".[61]

Referring to Palles CB in *Clery v. Barry*[62] the judge went on:

> "I consider this judgment to be an authority for the proposition that it is only when witnesses (or other persons who, though not official witnesses, were present) are dead, or cannot give evidence through incapacity, or their evidence cannot be accepted on account of unreliability, that the doctrine of *omnia rite esse acta praesumuntur* can be applied. It is to be called in aid only when there

56 "All things are presumed to be correctly done", Co. Litt. 6.

57 *Clarke v. Early* [1980] IR 223, Wylie, *Cases* p.496.

58 (1889) 21 LR Ir 152.

59 *ibid.* at p.167.

60 [1924] 2 IR 157.

61 *ibid.* at p.162.

62 (1889) 21 LR Ir 152.

is a void to be filled up. If there is really evidence, it must be acted on. . .".[63]

The benefit of an attestation clause was shown in *Kavanagh v. Fegan*.[64] The will contained an attestation clause but a surviving witness was unsure whether she had signed before or after the testator. Hanna J held that the presumption was not rebutted since the evidence was unreliable. The absence of an attestation clause is not necessarily fatal[65] but reliance will then have to be placed on the evidence. In *Clarke v. Early*[66] there was no attestation clause. The will contained a signature apparently of the testator. There were signatures of witnesses below. A witness was found who said he knew the name of the other witness and that he was a friend of the testator. The will was held invalid: the judge held there was a purported signature but no evidence the testator had signed will.

3. Incorporation by Reference

The doctrine of incorporation by reference is a means in relation to wills whereby documents not attested in accordance with the formalities required of wills are nevertheless incorporated into the will by a reference to them in the will. The document itself must be sufficiently identified, by parole evidence if necessary. It must also have existed in complete form at the time of execution of the will:[67] the doctrine does not allow for the incorporation of future documents.[68]

4. Secret Trusts

The doctrine of secret trusts[69] is closely related to the doctrine of incorporation by reference. As applied in Ireland, the doctrine of half-secret trusts may, by contrast, allow unattested documents[70] created after the will is made to be incorporated into it.[71]

---

63 [1924] 2 IR 157 at 163.

64 [1932] IR 566. Brady, *Succession* para. 2.40.

65 *Scarff v. Scarff* [1927] IR 13 (no attestation clause, will upheld).

66 [1980] IR 223.

67 *In bonis Mitchell* (1966) 100 ILTR 185.

68 *Blackwell v. Blackwell* [1929] AC 318 at 339 per Viscount Sumner. But see Secret Trusts.

69 Brady, *Succession* para. 1.52-79.

70 They will have to satisfy the formalities for trusts: Wylie, *Irish Land Law* para. 9.029-9.037.

71 *ibid.* and pp. 21–27.

a) Fully Secret

A fully-secret trust arises where A makes a gift of property in her will to B absolutely but tells B that he is to hold it on trust for C. In such a case equity will enforce the trust even though it does not appear on the face of the will. This is an exception to the formalities required of wills by statute. The courts have taken the view that equity will not allow a statute to be used for fraud. If B accepts the trust she cannot later plead the lack of statutory formalities in order to escape from the trust and claim the property for her own benefit.[72]

Both English and Irish cases agree that the objects of the trust may be communicated by the testator to the donee under the will at any time during the testator's lifetime, or by a sealed envelope containing a statement of the terms of the trust, to be opened on the testator's death.[73]

b) Half Secret

A half-secret trust arises where A makes a disposition by will to B and the will itself indicates that B is to take the property as trustee, but the objects of the trust are not disclosed in the will. The English courts in this case have required that the objects of the trust be communicated at or before the execution of the will[74] on the ground that to allow the objects to be communicated later would be to permit testators to reserve to themselves the power of making unattested dispositionsby will.[75] The English position has also been defended on the ground that the restriction in the doctrine of incorporation by reference to documents in existence at the date of the will would be made meaningless where trusts were concerned because the restriction could be avoided by half-secret trusts. However, the first objection also applies to the doctrine of fully-secret trusts and so the distinction seems anomalous. In Ireland there is a line of authority in favour of the view that the communication of the terms of a half-secret trust, as in the case of a fully secret trust, may be made after the execution of the will in the testator's lifetime.[76] This position was recently affirmed by Barron J in *In the Estate of Prendiville*.[77]

---

72 *Cullen v. Attorney General* (1866) LR 1 HL 190; *O'Brien v. Condon* [1905] 1 IR 51, Wylie, *Casebook on Equity* p.328; *Re Browne* [1944] IR 90, Wylie, *Casebook on Equity* p.322.

73 *Re Boyes* (1884) 26 Ch D 531; *Morrison v. McFerran* [1901] 1 IR 360; *Re Keen* [1937] Ch. 236.

74 *Johnson v. Ball* (1851) 5 De G & Sm 85, 64 ER 1029; *Re Keen* [1937] Ch. 236.

75 *Blackwell v. Blackwell* [1929] AC 318 at 339 per Viscount Sumner.

76 *Moss v. Cooper* (1861) 1 J & H 352, 10 ER 782; *Riordan v. Bannon* (1875) IR 10 Eq 469 at p.477 per Chatterton V-C; *Re King's Estate* (1888) 21 LR Ir 273; *Re Brown* [1944] IR 90 per Overend J.

77 *In the Estate of Prendiville* [1995] 2 ILRM 578, citing *Re King's Estate* (1888) 21 LR Ir 273 and *Re Brown* [1944] IR 90 per Overend J.

5. Lost Wills

a) Presumption of Intentional Destruction

What is the position where it is known that a testator made a will but it cannot be found when the testator dies? The courts have held that there is a presumption that it was destroyed intentionally.[78] The presumption may nevertheless be rebutted by evidence of the surrounding circumstances, such a proof of accidental destruction by fire, or the possibility that a disappointed relative had purloined it,[79] or that the testator's custody of his will was "anything but a close custody".[80]

b) Evidence of Contents

If the presumption of intentional destruction is rebutted the contents of the lost will may be proved by secondary evidence, such as a copy of it, but there may be other forms of such evidence. When the writer D H Lawrence died his will could not be found, but the court held that the presumption was rebutted by proof that the testator had asked someone to look for it shortly before he died. Probate was granted of it on proof that its contents were identical to that of another author.[81]

The contents of a lost will may also be proved by evidence of statements made as to its contents before or after the will was made whether the maker of the statement (such as the testator) is available as a witness or not, as an exception to the hearsay rule. This is the effect of the extraordinary case of *Sugden v. Lord St Leonards*.[82] Edward Sugden, later Lord St Leonards, had been Lord Chancellor of Ireland and later of England.[83] He was the most noted property lawyer of his time and a prolific author on the law of property, but when he died his will could not be found. He had certainly made one and had altered it from time to time. In his old age he often asked his daughter to recite the contents of it to him. His daughter had memorised the will and was able at the trial to write it out from memory. The Court of Appeal held that the presumption of intentional destruction was rebutted. This was not the only hurdle the court had to get over to prove the will. The daughter's evidence was hearsay. The majority of the court announced a new exception to the hearsay rule, namely statements as to the contents of a lost will.

---

78 *Welch v. Philips* (1836) 1 Moo PC 299, 12 ER 828, per Parke B; *Re Webb (deceased)* [1964] 2 All ER 91, [1964] 1 WLR 509.

79 *In bonis Coster,* unreported, Supreme Court, 19 January 1978, Wylie, *Cases* p.499.

80 *Sugden v. Lord St Leonards* (1879) 1 PD 154, per Cockburn CJ at 217.

81 The Times, London, 4 November 1932, and see Bailey, *The Law of Wills* p.94.

82 (1879) 1 PD 154.

83 Lord Chancellor Ireland 1834, 1841–46; Lord Chancellor Great Britain and Baron St Leonards, 1852.

The case is open to a number of criticisms. One is that the court may have been influenced by the identity of the testator.

The English Court of Appeal in *Sugden* had allowed in, under their new exception to hearsay, statements made by the testator after the execution of the will. In *Woodward v. Goulstone*[84] the House of Lords declined to express a view as to whether such statements were admissible to prove a lost will, thus throwing doubt on the decision in *Sugden*.[85] *Sugden* has nevertheless been approved of in Ireland.[86] There seems little reason to make the distinction, once the concession is made to admit hearsay evidence, apart from the fact that a testator's statements made after, perhaps long after, the will was made, may not be accurate, but arguably that should affect the credibility of the evidence rather than its admissibility.

6. Alterations

Section 86 of the Succession Act, 1965 provides that:

> "An obliteration, interlineation, or other alteration made in a will after execution shall not be valid or have any effect, unless such alteration is executed as is required for the execution of the will; but the will, with such alteration as part thereof, shall be deemed to be duly executed if the signature of the testator and the signature of each witness is made in the margin or on some other part of the will opposite or near to such alteration, or at the foot or end of or opposite to a memorandum referring to such alteration, and written at the end of some other part of the will".[87]

The words of the section differ from those of section 21 of the Wills Act, 1837 which contained the words "no obliteration... shall be valid... *except so far as the words of the will before such alteration shall not be apparent...* unless such alteration shall be executed in a like manner...[as a will]". Courts in England and Ireland had interpreted these words to mean that an unattested alteration was ineffective if the original words could still be read with the naked eye, assisted by any natural means such as holding the will up to the light or a magnifying glass.[88] If the alteration was ineffective, then probate would be granted with the original words. It seems clear that section 86, by omitting the words in italics, was intended to alter the law. If so, then alterations are now ineffective in the Republic unless attested in the same way as the will itself. This interpretation was adopted by Lardner J in *Re Myles, deceased*[89] in declining

84 (1886) 11 App Cas 469.

85 In England the Civil Evidence Act, 1968, s.9 gave statutory force to certain specified exceptions to the hearsay rule at common law. The exception in *Sugden* (footnote 82) is not mentioned.

86 *In bonis Ball* (1890) 25 LR Ir 556 per Warren J; *In bonis Gilliland* [1940] NI 125.

87 Wills Act, 1837 s.21; Wylie *Irish Land Law* paras. 14.14–14.16.

88 Cheshire *Real Property* p.778; *Re Itter* [1950] P 130, [1950] 1 All ER 68.

89 [1993] ILRM 34 at 36.

to grant probate of a holograph will which had been signed by the testator and witnessed but without a proper attestation clause. There were a number of deletions initialled by the testator but neither signed nor witnessed. It was also unclear whether the alterations had been made before or after the execution of the will and the judge held that the presumption that they had been made after execution, and so would be invalid on that ground also, had not been rebutted.

7. Revocation

It has been seen that generally a testator may revoke a will. It may be revoked in a number of ways.

a) Will or Codicil

A will may be revoked by a later will.[90] A mere declaration in the later will that "this is my last will" is not necessarily enough:[91] It is usual to insert a clause at the beginning in which the testator states "I hereby revoke all former wills. . .". The court may, however, hold that a will has been revoked by implication, as where a later will is inconsistent with an earlier one.[92] A later will, it may be noticed, does not, therefore, automatically revoke earlier ones, and so the testator's will may consist of more than one document.[93]

b) Destruction

Section 85(2) of the Succession Act, 1965 provides that a will may be revoked by "burning, tearing, or destruction of it by the testator, or by some person in his presence and by his direction, with the intention of revoking it".[94] There must therefore be both a physical act of destruction and a mental intention to destroy the will.

It would seem that destruction in section 85(2) is *ejusdem generis* with burning and tearing and so it must be physical destruction, not merely symbolic. In *Cheese v. Lovejoy*[95] the testator drew a line with a pen through the will, wrote revoked on the back and threw it into a waste paper basket. The housekeeper, who was present while this was done, later retrieved the will and produced it on the testator's death. The will was admitted to probate. It has been suggested that the word cancelling should be added to the list in section

90 Succession Act, 1965 s.85(2).

91 *In bonis Martin* [1968] IR 1.

92 *ibid.*; *In bonis Jennings* [1930] IR 196; *Pakenham v. Duggan* (1951) 85 ILTR 21; *O'Leary v. Douglas* (1879) LR Ir 323 (two identical wills. Held: later one revoked earlier one).

93 *In bonis McCarthy* [1965] Ir Jur Rep 56.

94 Wills Act, 1837 s.20, which contains the words "or otherwise destroying" in place of "destruction" in Succession Act, 1965 s.85(2).

95 (1877) 2 PD 251, 37 LT 295, on s.20 of Wills Act, 1837.

85(2) to allow for symbolic destruction, a course of action which was actually recommended by the Real Property Commissioners in their Report preceding the Wills Act, 1837 but was not implemented.

c) Marriage

Section 85(1) of the Succession Act, 1965 provides that a will is revoked by a subsequent marriage of the testator, except a will made in contemplation of that marriage "whether so expressed in the will or not".[96] The latter phrase is not found in section 18 of the Wills Act, 1837 which section 85(1) replaces. This appears to abolish the need for the will to be made *expressly* in contemplation of marriage to avoid being revoked by the subsequent marriage.

d) Conditional

A revocation may be made subject to a condition precedent.[97] This doctrine may be applied not only to revocation by another will or codicil but even to revocation by destruction if secondary evidence of the destroyed will exists.[98]

The doctrine of "dependent relative revocation" is invoked where a testator revokes an earlier will in the mistaken belief that other provisions will then take effect.[99] The situations are as follows:

1. a testator revokes an earlier will by a later will in the mistaken belief that the later will is valid.[100] If the second will is invalid, the doctrine invalidates the revocation of the earlier will. This is evidently on the ground that otherwise the purported testator will die intestate. It may be noticed that if the purported revocation is contained in the invalid later will so that it is also invalid, then no special doctrine is actually required to reach this result, other than that which invalidated the later will;

2. a testator revokes a will, which has itself revoked an earlier will, in the mistaken belief that the earlier will thereby automatically revives. This is apparently a common mistake for testators to make. Thus, in *In bonis Hogan*[101] the deceased, Mrs Hogan, made a will in 1977 and a later one in 1979 which revoked the 1977 will. On Mrs Hogan's death only the will of 1977 could be found. Mrs Hogan's daughter, the applicant and executor of the 1979 will, deposed that she believed that Mrs

96 Previously s.18 of the Wills Act, 1837.

97 *Re Plunkett* [1964] IR 259; *In bonis Coster,* unreported, Supreme Court, 19 January 1979; Wylie, *Cases* p.499.

98 *In bonis Hogan,* unreported, High Court, 18 February 1980; Brady, "A case of Dependant Relative Revocation" [1980] 75 ILSI Gazette 5.

99 For a critique of the doctrine see Newark, "Dependent Relative Revocation" (1955) 71 LQR 374, reproduced in Newark, McIvor ed., *Elegantia Juris.*

100 *Onions v. Tyrer* (1716) 2 Vern 741, 23 ER 1085; *Re McClintock* [1943] IR 83; *Re McMullen* [1964] Ir Jur Rep 33.

101 Unreported, High Court, 18 February 1980. See footnote 98.

Hogan had destroyed the 1979 will by burning it, although she had not seen this done. The applicant sought to have admitted to probate a copy of the 1979 will which had been kept by the testator's solicitor. The applicant contended that Mrs Hogan had only revoked the 1979 will by burning it in the belief that the 1977 will would automatically be revived. Gannon J accepted this argument and admitted the copy of the 1979 will to probate. He held that the attempted revocation of the 1979 will by burning was ineffective since it was dependent on a condition which had not been fulfilled, namely the revival of the 1977 will;

3. a testator revokes a will in the mistaken belief that the rules of intestacy will distribute his or her property in accordance with the testator's wishes.

Academic writers have criticised some judges for applying the doctrine where there was no real evidence of intention and in circumstances almost certainly unforeseen by the testator.[102] The justification has often been to give effect to an underlying intention of the testator not to die intestate.[103] Nevertheless the real intention of the testator is often more specific and is not implemented by the doctrine. The intention of Mrs Hogan in *In bonis Hogan*[104] was, on the evidence which the court accepted, to reinstate the provisions of the 1977 will. The decision failed to give effect to this intention. One solution would be to change the law so that it conforms more closely to what testators believe it to be: there could be a presumption against revival, but rebuttable by evidence of intention to revive the earlier will.

8. Revival

A will which has been destroyed with the intention of revoking it cannot be revived.[105] If it has not been destroyed a will can be revived by re-executing it or by executing a codicil showing an intention to revive the will.[106] The effect is the same as if a new will had been made on the date of revival. The importance of this is that the revived provisions can apply to people or property not in existence at the date of the original will. It has already been seen that if Will No. 1 is revoked by Will No. 2, then the revocation of Will No. 2 does not revive Will No. 1.[107] This is contrary to what most people expect or assume to be the case and there is some logic behind their assumption. A double negative is a positive, and so a revocation of a revocation would be expected to cancel the revocation.

102 Mellows, *The Law of Succession* p.94; Brady, *Succession* para. 4.52.

103 *ibid.*

104 Unreported, High Court, 18 February 1980. See footnote 98.

105 *Re Hall* [1943] Ir Jur Rep 25; Wylie, *Irish Land Law* paras. 14.22–14.23.

106 Succession Act, 1965 s.87; Wills Act, 1837 s.22.

107 *In bonis Hodgkinson* [1893] at 339.

The law does not, in any case, treat all cases of revocation as final since it recognises revival by re-execution.

9. Republication

A codicil republishes any previous will which has not been revoked.[108] The effect of republication is the same as revival: it is as if a new will has been made at the date of republication.[109]

10. Undue Influence

This doctrine has been discussed in the chapter on equity. In wills there is no presumption of undue influence, whatever the relationship between the testator and the beneficiary.[110] The burden is on the person alleging undue influence to prove it.[111] It must be shown not only that a person had power to overbear the will of the testator but that it was actually exercised and that the will was a result of the exercise of the power.[112]

11. Construction of Wills

a) The Intention of the Testator

The general principle of the construction of wills is that the courts attempt to carry out the intention of the testator as expressed in the will.[113] The will is read as a whole, so that a specific intention in one part of the will overrides a general one.[114] The court's duty is to give effect to the testator' intention, however peculiar or eccentric.[115] It is also a general principle that the court will not re-write a will.[116]

On the other hand the court may find it necessary to omit words which are

---

108 *Re Swiney* (1858) 6 Ir Ch R 455.

109 *Grealey v. Sampson* [1917] 1 IR 286, 296; *Mountcashell (Earl) v. Smyth* [1895] 1 IR 346.

110 *Healy v. Lyons*, unreported, High Court, 1978 (1975 No. 4631P); Wylie, *Irish Land Law* para. 9.075.

111 *Re Breen, deceased, Breen and Kennedy v. Breen*, unreported, High Court, Barr J, 5 May 1995.

112 *ibid.*; *Kelly v. Thewles* (1854) 2 Ir Ch R 510.

113 *Oliver v. Menton* [1945] IR 6; *Re Moore* [1947] IR 205; *Re McCready* [1962] NI 43; *Williams and O'Donnell v. Shuel and Barham*, unreported, High Court, Morris J, 6 May 1997; Hawkins and Ryder, *Construction of Wills* .

114 *Macandrew's Will Trusts* [1963] 3 WLR 822, per Ungoed Thomas J at 834; Fitzpatrick *v.* Collins [1978] ILRM 244.

115 *ibid.*

116 *Re Hogg* [1944] IR 244, 258.

shown not to express or to run contrary to the testator's intent.[117]

The testator is presumed to intend that words used are to be understood in their natural meaning unless something in the context or circumstances revealed by admissible evidence to the contrary.[118] However, this does not always require the court to apply the literal meaning of words where that would lead to a result which was clearly not the intention of the testator. As Porter MR put it in *Re Patterson*[119]:

> "It is the duty of a court of construction to ascertain, if it be possible, what the testator really meant fom the language he has used. That does not mean that the exact words he has used are in all cases to be followed in their literal meaning, even if it would be plain that to do so would frustrate the real intention. If, having considered the will and the whole will, it is plain that to place a literal meaning upon one clause would defeat the clear intent, it may be necessary to 'do violence' (as an eminent judge once expressed it), to the language used".[120]

The judge also quoted a passage from Hawkins, *Construction of Wills*:

> "... the intention of the testator, which can be collected with reasonable certainty for the entire will, with the aid of extrinsic evidence of a kind properly admissible, must have effect given to it, beyond, and even against, the literal sense of the particular words and expressions. The intention, when legitimately proved, is competent not only to *fix* the sense of *ambiguous* words, but to *control* the sense even of *clear* words, and to *supply* the place of *express* words, in cases of difficulty or ambiguity".

Both these passages were quoted in the Supreme Court in the peculiar circumstances of *Curtin v. O'Mahony*.[121] In that case a testator had left a dwelling house to a beneficiary absolutely. The will then provided that, in the event of the testator selling the house, his entire estate, both real and personal, was to be divided into shares for a number of charitable and other bequests. The house in fact remained unsold at the testator's death. It was argued that the testator did not actually intend the condition as to the sale of the house to apply to the division of the entire estate and therefore to the charitable and other legacies. It was argued that his true intention must have been that the legacies should take effect in any case, and that the proceeds of the house were to be included in the division if the house were to be sold by him in his lifetime. Counsel for the Attorney General urged the court to consider extrinsic evidence in the form of two previous wills. Lardner J in the High Court held that the will was clear and that the bequests must therefore fail. The argument based on extrinsic evidence

117 *ibid.*, Murnahan J at 251.

118 *Perrin v. Morgan* [1943] AC 399, 406, per Viscount Simon LC.

119 [1899] 1 IR 324.

120 *ibid.* at 331, cited in *Curtin v. O'Mahony* [1992] ILRM 7, per O'Flaherty J at 12.

121 [1992] ILRM 7.

was not pursued in the appeal.[122] The Supreme Court, allowing the appeal, held that the literal meaning of the words would lead to an absurd result clearly not intended by the testator. He clearly did not intend the residue of his estate to fall into intestacy. Furthermore, the court held that it was not necessary to resort to extrinsic evidence to reach that conclusion. The court held that a phrase limiting the operation of the condition could be supplied by construction. O'Flaherty J noted that the facts raised a direct conflict between two principles: that the court will not re-write a will and, on the other hand, that a will must be read so as to give effect to the testator's intention. The judge commented further on Porter MR's remarks cited above, specifically as to where the testator's intention can only be carried out by inserting words in a will by construction:

> "The Master of the Rolls went on to warn however that great care must be taken in applying this doctrine. It must be clear not alone that words have been omitted but also what the substance of the omitted clause is because otherwise the court would be not construing but making a will".[123]

Curtin v. O'Mahony must certainly be an extreme example of the doctrine of construction, but few would criticise the result.

b) Other Policies

The general principle of seeking the intention of the testator may on occasion give way to rules of construction which impose various policies on wills. The Rule in *Shelley's Case* is an example.[124] On the other hand there has long been a judicial tendency towards the testator's intent as primary and old rules have been modified in this direction, *Shelley's Case* in wills also being an example. In other cases, policies of a public nature were and may still be applied where the intention expressed in the will is unclear. We have seen that the class-closing rules favour the early vesting of property in the interests of the donee and the operation of a free-market where the testator has not been specific as to the definition of the class. In the case of extrinsic evidence, discussed below, the reluctance of the court in the past, and possibly still today, to admit such evidence where it would contradict or vary the terms of the will is partially attributable to a policy of discouraging litigation. Nevertheless, when the courts face the issue directly today the general trend is to re-assert the intention of the testator as the controlling principle.

c) Section 99 and Favor Testamenti

Section 99 of the Succession Act, 1965 provides:

---

122 It would have required the court to reconsider its own decision in *Rowe v. Law*. See below, "Extrinsic evidence".

123 [1992] ILRM 7 at 12–13.

124 See Chapter 6 Fee Simple: Shelley's Case.

"99.–If the purport of a devise or bequest admits of more than one interpretation, then, in case of doubt, the interpretation according to which the devise or bequest will be operative shall be preferred".

It has be argued that this introduced a new principle into the construction of will, similar to *favor testamenti* civil law systems,[125] although it is also arguable that the principle already existed in the common law.[126]

d) Extrinsic Evidence

(1) Before the Succession Act, 1965

Under the law in force before 1 January 1967 the general rule was that extrinsic evidence was inadmissible if its effect would be to contradict the terms of the will. The policy reason, when it was articulated, was usually said to be that if extrinsic evidence were admissible where the will itself was clear, disappointed relatives would frequently attempt to challenge wills and try to show by extrinsic evidence that the testator had intended to benefit them rather than the person to whom the will referred. This could give rise to protracted, expensive and probably inconclusive litigation. There were, however, a number of real or apparent exceptions to the principle and the law was in a far from satisfactory state.

(a) The Armchair Principle

First, the courts were prepared to put themselves in the position of the testator at the time he or she wrote the will, to sit in the testator's armchair.[127] They would do this for a number of purposes. Extrinsic evidence was admissible as to the state of the property itself and other material facts relating to it at the date of the will.[128] Extrinsic evidence was always admissible to explain a special meaning attached to the words by the testator himself. This did not contradict the meaning of the words, but rather established what the meaning was. It was a special application of the construction of documents. The meaning of the words in the will is not necessarily the ordinary meaning. Thus, in *Thorn v.*

125 See Brady, "The *Favor Testamentii* in Irish Law" (1990) Irish Jurist (ns) 1; Brady, *Succession Law* para. 5.44.

126 *Winter v. Perratt* (1843) 9 Cl & Fin 606 at 687, 8 ER 548 at 671 per Lord Brougham LC, cited in *In the Estate of Bayley* [1945] IR 224.

127 *Boyes v. Cook* (1880) 14 Ch D 53 at 56, James LJ: "you may place yourself, so to speak, in [the testator's] armchair, and consider the circumstances by which he was surrounded, when he made his will to assist you in arriving at his intention".

128 *Pierce v. McNeale* [1894] 1 IR 118, MR, citing *Innes v. Sayer* (1851) 3 Mac & G 606 at 614, 42 ER 393 at 397 per Lord Truro.

Amusing!

Dickens[129] the will, said to be the shortest on record, consisted only of the words "All to mother". Evidence was admitted to show that the gift was intended for the testator's wife, since the testator always referred to her as "mother". [130]Evidence was admitted in another case[131] to show that a testator, who had no children of whom he was the biological father, intended to benefit his step-children when he used the phrase "my children". Evidence could also be admitted to show that the testator had a closer relationship with one party or relative than to another.

Although it is sometimes said that the literal interpretation must first be applied before resort is had to the armchair principle, this is not always followed in practice, as *Thorn v. Dickens* demonstrates.

Evidence of the religious views of a testator could be admitted to explain a statement in a will which might bear a special meaning because of those views. In *Bunbury v. Doran*[132] a testator left the freehold of his house to beneficiaries "until I am able to live there and enjoy it myself". Extrinsic evidence showed that the testator held religious views, apparently peculiar to himself, to the effect that he would return to live on earth after his death for a period which he described as the millennium, and had said that he would live in his house during that period. The court indicated that evidence of more orthodox beliefs, such as Judaism or Islam, would be admissible for this purpose,[133] although they did not find it necessary to admit the extrinsic evidence to resolve the case. The event specified was rejected as impossible and the gift declared absolute, even though it appeared to be a determinable interest. Today, the State in the Republic is prohibited by Art 44.2.3° of the Constitution from imposing any disabilities or making any discrimination on the ground of religious belief. It is suggested that today a court would be bound to be to uphold the gift as a determinable interest.

Evidence was also admissible of the surrounding circumstances, habits and position of the testator's family. Thus in *In the Goods of Twohill*[134] the testator appointed as executor "my brother-in-law Edmund O'Kelly". He had no such brother-in-law. He did have a brother-in-law called Edward O'Kelly. Evidence was admitted to show that Edward was the only person to whom the name and description in the will could be applied.

---

129 [1906] WN 54.

130 It is a custom in some parts of England, and indeed in other parts of the world, for husbands to refer to their wives in this way after they have borne children.

131 *Re Jeans* (1895) 72 LT 834.

132 (1875) IR 9 CL 284, Ex Ch affirming Exchequer (1874) IR 8 CL 516.

133 *ibid.*, Fitzgerald B at 523.

134 (1879) 3 LR Ir 21. See also *Charter v. Charter* (1874) LR 7 HL 315.

(b) True Equivocation (Latent Ambiguity)
Where the description in a will applied, and applied accurately, to more than one person or thing there was said to be true equivocation or latent ambiguity. The ambiguity was latent because it only appeared when extrinsic facts were taken into account.

In a case of latent ambiguity it was said that the courts should first attempt to resolve the ambiguity by construction, using the armchair principle if required. Thus in *Healy v. Healy*[135] the testator gave a farm to "my nephew Joseph Healy", then a legacy to "Joseph Healy, the son of my brother Joseph Healy" and the residue to "the said Joseph Healy." There were two nephews called Joseph Healy, one the son of the testator's deceased brother James, and the other the son of the testator's living brother Joseph. It was held, on construction of the will itself, that Joseph the son of James took the farm and the residue. One reason given for the conclusion was that when the testator used the name Joseph Healy without further qualification he was thinking of Joseph the son of James. They also concluded that this displaced the normal inference that the word "said" referred to the immediately antecedent name.

If construction failed extrinsic evidence was admissible to determine which of the persons or things were intended to be referred to.[136]

In *Re Jackson*[137] the phrase was "my nephew, Arthur Murphy". The testator had three nephews called Arthur Murphy. Evidence of intention was admitted to show which one the testator had intended to benefit. The admission of extrinsic evidence did not infringe the main principle in such a case, since whichever person the evidence pointed to, it would not contradict the will.[138] Thus, if a devise referred to "my son John" and the testator left two sons called John, evidence was admissible to show that the testator believed one of them to be dead and intended to benefit the other.[139] Both sons were accurately referred to as "my son John".

---

135 (1875) 9 IR 418, Rolls.

136 *Phelan v. Slattery* (1887) 19 LR Ir 177, V-C.

137 [1933] 1 Ch. 237.

138 At the time the case was remarkable for the fact that one of the nephews was illegitimate under the law as it then stood. The extrinsic evidence indicated that it was the illegitimate nephew whom the testator intended to benefit. The court held that, once having admitted extrinsic evidence, they could not control its effect and so held the illegitimate nephew to be entitled. The implication was that, had there been only two nephews of that name, one legitimate and the other not, the court would have confined "nephew" to mean legitimate nephew and would have given the legacy to the legitimate one without resorting to extrinsic evidence. In the Republic today there is no such discrimination between marital and non-marital children: see the Status of Children Act, 1987.

139 *Lord Cheyney's Case* (1591) 5 Co Rep 68a at 68b, 77 ER 158 at 158.

(c) Patent Ambiguity

The courts took the view that true equivocation literally arose only if the ambiguity appeared when extrinsic facts were taken into account, such as the fact that there were two people of the same name. Hence it was also referred to as latent ambiguity. In the case of latent ambiguity extrinsic evidence was, as we have seen, admissible.

If, however, the description applied with equal accuracy to two or more persons or things and these were mentioned elsewhere in the will by descriptions which made their separate identity clear, the ambiguity was said to be patent. Extrinsic evidence was inadmissible since it would add something to the will. It would connect the ambiguous description with one of the two specific descriptions and this connection was not provided for by the will itself. This fine distinction was not universally adhered to and the cases on patent ambiguity were not consistent. Thus, evidence of intention was admitted in the case of a will in which the devise was to "George Gord, the son of Gord" even though it appeared from other parts of the will itself that there were two people called George whose fathers had the surname Gord.[140] Needs Case 1836

(d) Inaccuracy

Another distinct possibility was that the description in the will did not apply accurately to any one thing or person. The position was complicated by the fact that the courts did not always recognise this as a distinct category.

(i) One Candidate

In some cases there might only be one candidate to whom the description might, however inaccurately, be applied. In such a case the court might admit evidence to show that fact, supposedly on the armchair principle. *In the Goods of Twohill*[141] is probably an example of this.

In some cases the problem could be resolved by rejecting an inaccurate part of the description so that what remained then referred accurately only to one person. In *Dooley v. Mahon*[142] the gift was to "Monimia Mahon, the daughter of my brother Walter". The only daughter of Walter was called Monimia, but had married a man called Smith. She had also died before the date of the will, as the testator had been aware. The testator had another niece, called Monimia Mahon, who survived her. It was held that the gift went to the latter person. The testator had given a name and relationship which fitted only one person living at the time she made the will. The surplus description, naming the brother as "Walter", was rejected.

---

140 *Doe d Gord v. Needs* (1836) 2 M & W 129, 150 ER 698.

141 (1879) 3 LR Ir 21. See also *Charter v. Charter* (1874) LR 7 HL 315.

142 (1877) IR 11 Eq 299.

(ii) More Than One Candidate

A description in the will may not describe accurately any person or thing at all. Since this could only be known by taking account of facts extrinsic to the will the situation could probably be accurately described as a type of latent ambiguity. This was generally the situation in which the cases are most difficult or impossible to reconcile. On the one hand, it was often said that extrinsic evidence was inadmissible because its effect would necessarily be to contradict the will. The courts would not allow evidence to show that the testator had made a mistake and had really meant to refer to some thing or somebody whose description differed from that in the will. Some cases, however, while excluding evidence of instructions given by the testator to legal advisers, and their impressions of what the testator intended, admitted evidence of the armchair type to discover the true intention of the testator.

In *Re Noble's Trusts*[143] the testator, an 80-year-old lady, left property to "the five children of the late Post Captain Horatio Nelson Noble, my husband's son". The husband had two sons. One was called Horatio Nelson Noble, who, despite his first names, had been a major in the Indian Army and had died many years before. The other, Jeffrey Noble, had been a Post Captain in the Navy and had died shortly before the testator. Each son had five children living at the time the will was made. The testator had made the understandable mistake of thinking that the step-son called Horatio Nelson had joined the Navy. Sullivan MR refused to allow evidence of what had passed between the testator and her solicitor, and of the impressions of her solicitor and doctor as to her intentions. He did, however, admit evidence that she had been on terms of intimacy with Jeffrey and his children and had had little to do with the children of Horatio. He also admitted, more dubiously, evidence that the draft will had referred to the rank as Captain and she had instructed the solicitor to insert Post before it. The judge took this as evidence that she had clearly in mind the naval officer. The court held that the children of Jeffrey took under the will.

If the description applied with greater accuracy to one person rather than to another the courts were sometimes prepared to reject additional mistaken phrases if the remaining part of the description would accurately describe one person. On some occasions they did so after admitting extrinsic evidence, and sometimes without doing so.

In *Re Plunkett's Estate*[144] the testator left property "to FF and his sister MF, my granddaughter, share and share alike, said MF now living in France with her uncle M". MF was not then living with uncle M and had never done so. Her sister, CF, was living with uncle M and had done so for some time. The court held it to be a case of latent ambiguity so that extrinsic evidence was admissible, but the evidence was inconclusive and the case was decided in favour of

143 (1870) IR 5 Eq 140.

144 (1861) 11 IR Ch R 361.

MF on the ground that the name should control the description. The basic principle is to find the testator's dominant intention. In *Re Plunkett* the name came first and this may have pointed to the name being uppermost in the testator's mind.

In *Re Callaghan*[145] the gift was to "my god-daughter, JW". JW was not his god-daughter, but JW's sister, AW, was. Gavan-Duffy J held that the legacy should go to AW.[146] *Dooley v. Mahon*[147] might also be taken as an example of this situation.

A case which is difficult to explain satisfactorily is *Re Julian*.[148] A Protestant woman by her will bequeathed a sum of money to "The Seamen's Institute, Sir John Rogerson's Quay, Dublin". The bequest was claimed by two bodies: the Catholic Seamen's Institute, Sir John Rogerson's Quay, Dublin, and the Dublin Seamen's Institute, Eden Quay, Dublin, which was a Protestant body. The executors issued a summons to determine questions arising on the construction of the will and it was sought to prove the intention of the testator by the introduction of parol evidence of her religion, of her association with the Dublin Seamen's Institute, Eden Quay, and of a mistake, on the part of the solicitor who engrossed the will, in regard to the address of the institute as it appeared in the will. The testator in giving instructions to her solicitor had expressed her doubt as to the correct address of the institute and the solicitor had consulted a book of reference in which the only seamen's institute mentioned was the one at Sir John Rogerson's Quay, Dublin. It was held by Kingsmill Moore J in the High Court that the parol extrinsic evidence could not be admitted to show the intention of the testator because the institute which was to benefit had been clearly identified in the will. The intention of the testator was therefore frustrated and the benefit of her gift went to the Catholic Seamen's Institute, Sir John Rogerson's Quay, and not to the Seamen's Institute, Eden Quay, with which she had been associated.[149] Kingsmill Moore J said:

> "This is by no means the first – and, equally certainly, will not be the last – case in which a judge has been forced by the rules of law to give a decision on the construction of a will which he believed to be contrary to the intentions of the testator. The law reports are loud with the comments of judges who found themselves in similar plight; but I consider the law to be well established and conclusive. . .".[150]

It is nevertheless questionable, whatever the state of the law, whether the facts should have impelled the judge to a conclusion which was clearly not what the testator intended. The phrase in the will was "The Seamen's Institute, Sir John

145 [1937] IR 84.

146 *Re Blayney* (1875) IR 9 Eq 413; *Re Blake's Trusts* [1904] 1 IR 98.

147 (1877) IR 11 Eq 299.

148 [1950] IR 57.

149 As a matter of record, Kingsmill Moore J was a Protestant.

150 *ibid.* p.66.

Rogerson's Quay, Dublin", while the institute at that address was in fact called the "Catholic Seamen's Institute". This should have been enough to take it out of the clarity category to which the judge treated the facts as belonging, and to put it instead into the inaccuracy: more than one candidate category to which it properly belonged. Extrinsic evidence could then have been introduced.

In cases of inaccuracy with more than one candidate the extrinsic evidence might not resolve the issue, in which case the legacy would simply fail and the property would go to the residuary legatee if there was one, or on intestacy if there was none.

(e) Clarity: No Doctrine of Mistake

If the description in the will described accurately only one person or thing, extrinsic evidence was not admissible to show that a mistake had been made and that the testator had intended instead to refer to another person or thing. The intention which the court looked to was the intention as expressed in the will, *i.e.* as expressed in the words actually used, and they would only go beyond the words if the intention was unclear. The reason for excluding extrinsic evidence of this kind was probably a policy against "opening the flood-gates of litigation" as it was thought that many disappointed relatives would bring actions based upon such evidence which would often be inconclusive. Nevertheless, armchair evidence was sometimes admitted to indicate, not that the testator had made a mistake, but to show that the person apparently referred to was not the one to which the testator intended the description to apply. A dubious case is *Henderson v. Henderson*[151] in which the will referred to "my grandson, Robert William Henderson". The testator had such a grandson, but also a grandson William Robert Henderson. Kenny J admitted armchair evidence and held that the legacy went to William Robert. This seems to have gone too far, because admitting armchair evidence could only have had the purpose of showing that the testator had made a mistake.

(f) Equitable Presumptions

Extrinsic evidence was sometimes admissible to rebut equitable presumptions, as where two gifts were made in separate testamentary instruments to the same person. Equity presumed the second gift to be a repetition of the first and that only one gift was intended.[152]

(2) The Succession Act, 1965 section 90

Section 90 of the Succession Act, 1965 now provides that:

> "90.– Extrinsic evidence shall be admissible to show the intention of the testator and to assist in the construction of, or to explain any contradiction in a will".

But Rowe - no evidence if will is clear.

151 [1905] 1 IR 353.

152 *Hurst v. Beach* (1819) 5 Madd 351, 360, 56 ER 929 at 932.

It seems that this was intended to effect some change in the law, but it has been a matter of controversy as to how extensive the change is.[153]

The effect of section 90 was extensively considered in *Rowe v. Law*.[154] By her will made in 1967 a testator devised and bequeathed all her property, which she called her trust fund, to her trustees on trust (1) to discharge out of it her debts, funeral and testamentary expenses and subject to that (2) to set aside out of the capital of the trust fund a sum of £1,000 for the purchase and furnishing of a cottage for the use of the second and third defendants during their joint lives and the life of the survivor and subject to that "as to any balance then remaining" to invest it and pay the income to the second and third defendants during their joint lives and to the survivor during his or her life and subject to a further legacy to stand possessed of "the trust fund then remaining" and to pay and transfer it to the plaintiffs in equal shares. The testator died in 1972 and probate of her will was granted to the first defendant. The second and third defendants contended that, by her bequest of "any balance then remaining" in clause 2 of her will, the testator had intended to bequeath to them her entire estate less the payments of her debts, funeral and testamentary expenses, and the £1,000. Extrinsic evidence was available to support, and to controvert, that contention.

It was held by Kenny J in the High Court that the words used by the testator in the will were not ambiguous and did not raise any difficulty of construction. The testator had expressed clearly an intention to give the second and third defendants life interests in the balance of the £1,000 only, as distinct from the balance of the entire estate. The will being clear, the issue then was as to whether section 90 allowed extrinsic evidence to be admitted to prove a contrary intention expressed elsewhere. Kenny J held that section 90 of the Act of 1965 did not authorise the introduction of extrinsic evidence to establish an alleged intention on the part of the testator which conflicted with the intention expressed in the will.

The Supreme Court upheld Kenny J. The majority, Henchy and Griffin JJ, agreed with Kenny J that section 90, whatever changes it might have made, did not allow in extrinsic evidence if the will was clear. O'Higgins CJ, dissenting, thought that section 90 had changed the law in a more radical way:

> "It appears to me clear that Section 90 of the Act of 1965 was drafted to provide for two contingencies:- the first where there is a contradiction in the will itself and the second where there is a contradiction between the actual intention of the testator and what was said in the will, given its pre-1965 construction. This latter category would, of course, cover and include situations in which an error had been made by a solicitor or other person writing down the will".[155]

153 Wylie, *Irish Land Law* para. 14.40-14.41.

154 [1978] IR 55 at 62, (1980) 114 ILTR 86, Supreme Court.

155 [1978] IR 55 at 67.

The other two judges disagreed. Henchy J laid stress on the word "and" in the phrase "and to assist" in section 90:

> "I read Section 90 as allowing extrinsic evidence to be received if it meets the double requirement of (a) showing the intention of a testator and (b) assisting in the construction of, or explaining any contradiction in, a will. The alternative reading would treat the section as making extrinsic evidence admissible if it meets the requirement of either (a) or (b). That, however, would produce unreasonable and illogical consequences which the legislature could not have intended. If the section made extrinsic evidence admissible merely because it satisfies requirement (a), then in any case the court could go outside the will and receive and act on extrinsic evidence as to the intention of the testator".[156]

In O'Higgins CJ's view one of the aims of the legislation was to alter the law to prevent a recurrence of a case such as *Re Julian*.[157] The judge evidently assumed that the result in *Re Julian* was produced by the state of the law at the time, but this is open to doubt: the will was not unambiguous and the phrase did not accurately identify the beneficiary.[158] Henchy J appears to indicate that in his view *Re Julian* was a case of inaccuracy:

> "To sum up: Section 90 allows extrinsic evidence of the testator's intention to be used by a court of construction only when there is a legitimate dispute as to the meaning or effect of the language used in the will. In such a case (*e.g.*, *In re Julian* ((1950) IR 57)) it allows the extrinsic evidence to be drawn on so as to give the unclear or contradictory words in the will a meaning which accords with the testator's intention as thus ascertained".[159]

The decision of the Supreme Court in *Rowe v. Law*[160] means that, whatever change section 90 was intended to bring about, it does not allow the admission of extrinsic evidence where the will is clear. The change therefore appears to be that extrinsic evidence is now admissible in cases of patent ambiguity or inaccuracy.

The Supreme Court in *Rowe* upheld the earlier decision in *Bennett v. Bennett.*[161] The testator in that case had left farms to "my nephew Denis Bennett". The testator never had a nephew called Denis Bennett. He had a brother Denis Bennett, who renounced any claim under the will, and several nephews whose surname was Bennett but whose Christian names were not Denis. He had a nephew William Bennett whose claim was supported by the testator's brother and all the other nephews. The judge found that the extrinsic evidence showed that William had lived with his uncle and had worked the lands for some time before his uncle's death without any payment. The testator had also told William's father that the land was to go to William after his, the

156 *ibid.* at p.72.

157 [1950] IR 57. See footnote 148 above.

158 See above.

159 [1978] IR 55 at 73.

160 [1978] IR 55 at 62, (1980) 114 ILTR 86, Supreme Court.

161 Unreported, High Court, Parke J, 24 January 1977.

testator's, death. The whole family believed that William was to have the land. There was no explanation as to how the wrong name came to be inserted in the will. Parke J held that the testator's intention was that the land should go to William and so ordered. The judge held that section 90 had altered the common law so that extrinsic evidence could now be introduced where the will "cannot be construed literally having regard to the facts existing at the testator's death". The judge evidently believed that the section would produce a different result on the facts before him than would have been the case at common law, but this does not appear to be so, as *In the Goods of Twohill*[162] and *Re Noble's Trusts*[163] illustrate, for closeness of relationship was armchair evidence, but the view may have been influenced by *Re Julian*.[164]

In *Fitzpatrick v. Collins*[165] the High Court took the view that section 90 does not admit extrinsic evidence where a situation had not been foreseen by the testator at all. A testator left a will in which he provided that in the event of his wife "surviving me for the space of two months" he left all his property to her. He further provided that "in the event of my wife surviving me for the space of not more than two months" he left her only £500, with a further bequest for masses. He thus made no provision for what was to happen in the event of his wife dying before he did, so that if that occurred there would be an intestacy and the property would go to the next of kin. As it turned out, his wife died 8 years before he did. McWilliam J, applying *Rowe v. Law*, held that section 90 only applied where there was an ambiguity or contradiction in the terms of the will and there was no such ambiguity or contradiction here. The testator clearly had not directed his mind to the situation that might arise if his wife were to die before he did. Had he done so, he might well have made similar provisions as to those he had made in the event of her surviving him by not more than two months, but he had not done so, and it was not for the court to make a will for the testator to cover situations which he had overlooked.

In *Curtin v. O'Mahony and Attorney General*[166] Finlay CJ and O'Flaherty J in the Supreme Court indicated *obiter*[167] that a full court might reconsider the majority judgment in *Rowe v. Law*[168]. Counsel for the appellants in the appeal had disclaimed any request to the court to reconsider *Rowe v. Law*. It will be recalled[169] that the court in *Curtin* felt able to reach the result intended by the testator by supplying a phrase by construction.

162 (1879) 3 LR Ir 21. See also *Charter v. Charter* (1874) LR 7 HL 315, 150 ER 698.

163 (1870) IR 5 Eq 140.

164 (1950) IR 57. See above.

165 [1978] ILRM 244.

166 [1992] ILRM 7, Supreme Court (Finlay CJ and O'Flaherty J; McCarthy J concurring).

167 No extrinsic evidence was proffered in the case as to the testator's intention.

168 [1978] IR 55.

169 See above, p.936

Despite the obiter in *Curtin*, the Supreme Court in *Re Collins*[170] approved *Rowe v. Law*. In *Collins* the testator left the contents of her house to the plaintiffs. There was no specific devise of the house itself, but there was a residuary devise in favour of a charity. The plaintiffs sought to admit extrinsic evidence that the testator intended to leave the house as well as the contents to the plaintiffs. The evidence was conflicting, one plaintiff and another witness saying that the testator had said would leave the house to the plaintiffs, another witness saying merely that the testator said she would leave "most of her estate" to the plaintiffs and the testator's solicitor gave evidence that she had only given specific instructions as to the contents and had not mentioned the house. Barron J in the High Court dismissed the claim. Despite the fact that he preferred the evidence of the plaintiffs, he held the will was clear and unambiguous and there was therefore no basis for the admission of the evidence. The Supreme Court[171] dismissed the appeal and dismissed the submission of the plaintiffs that *Rowe v. Law* was wrongly decided. Keane J found, as Barron J in the High Court had done, that *Curtin* was distinguishable in that a partial intestacy would not be caused in the present case by an application of the literal meaning of the will. Keane J concluded:

> "S 90 of the 1965 Act was, at least, intended to alter the law by enabling extrinsic evidence to be adduced as to the intention of the testator where that would assist in the construction of, or explain contradictions in, the will. The submission on behalf of the plaintiff, however, is that it was intended to go radically further and enable such evidence to be adduced, not merely with the view to resolving ambiguities or uncertainty in the language used, but to supplement, and even to contradict, what the testator had actually said, however clear and unambiguously, in the will itself".

The court therefore endorsed the view of Hench J in the majority in *Rowe*, that there must either be a contradiction in the will, or at least something which creates the need for assistance, before section 90 comes into play. Keane J went on to consider *Re Julian*[172] and concluded that it might have been differently decided after section 90, even taking into account the ratios of *Rowe v. Law* and the present case on the interpretation of that section. As was pointed out in the first edition of this work, the will did not describe accurately and unambiguously the institution referred to.

---

170 *Re Collins, O'Connell v. Bank of Ireland* [1998] ILRM 465.

171 Keane J (Hamilton Chief Justice, O'Flaherty, Murphy, and Lynch JJ concurring).

172 [1950] IR 57.

e) Meaning of Children, Issue, *etc.*

The Status of Children Act, 1987[173] amended the Succession Act, 1965 so that the expression of a relationship in a will is now deduced irrespective of whether the relevant person's father or mother were married to each other[174] unless a contrary intention is shown.[175] Thus, a gift to "the children of X" now includes the non-marital as well as the marital children of X, while the a gift to "the legitimate children of X" would include only marital children.[176]

f) Gifts on Attaining a Given Age with a Gift Over.

The special rule which applied in this case, known as the Rule in *Edwards v. Hammond*[177] and which is now said to be a rule of construction, is discussed in Chapter 10 on Future Interests.[178]

g) The Rule in Wild's Case

This rule which used to apply where a testator left real property "to A and his/her children", has been abolished by the Succession Act, 1965.[179]

h) Die without issue

At common law if a testator left property "to A, but if he die without issue[180], to B. . ." the gift was presumed, in the case of land, to give A a fee tail and in the case of personal property, an absolute interest. The failure of issue was construed, in the absence of an intention to the contrary, to mean an ultimate failure of issue. B would take the property not only if A died without issue living at his death, but also if A had issue at his death, but they died out later.

Section 29 of the Wills Act, 1837 changed the law to give the phrase a more natural meaning. It provided that A would take a fee simple in the case of land and an absolute interest in the case of personalty, subject to a gift over to B if A

173 Enacted as a consequence of *Johnston v. Ireland* (1987) 9 EHRR 203, (Series A, No. 112; App No. 9697/82). See also Irish Law Reform Commission *Report on Illegitimacy*, September 1982.

174 Status of Children Act, 1987 s.3, and ss. 27, 29 adding s.4A to the Succession Act, 1965 and amending s.3.

175 See also Status of Children Act, 1987 s.28 adding to s.3 of the Succession Act, 1965 a definition of issue as including non-marital children (when read in conjunction with the new s.4A of the 1965 Act and s.3 of the Status of Children Act, 1987.

176 Explanatory Memorandum to Status of Children Bill, 1986.

177 (1684) 3 Lev 132, 83 ER 614.

178 See page 293.

179 See above Fee Tail.

180 For the meaning of issue and adopted chidren, see above.

had no issue living at his death.[181] This may have achieved greater fidelity to the intention of the testator, but was unsatisfactory in relation to A, since he could not be sure whether the gift would pass to B or not. Even if A had children or grandchildren, they might all die before he did. Section 10 of the Conveyancing Act, 1882 altered this result in the case of land by providing that, as soon as any of A's issue reached 21, the gift over to B became void. If there were issue of A living at his death but under age, and the gift over become void after A's death if the issue became 21 thereafter.[182]

Section 29 of the Wills Act, 1837 is repeated in section 96 of the Succession Act, 1965 but section 10 of the Conveyancing Act, 1882 is extended by section 100 of the 1965 Act to include personalty and also in that the issue need only be living at A's death.

The statutory provisions do not cover all situations in which "die without issue" needs to be construed. In *Re O'Donoghue (deceased), Mulhern v. Brennan*[183] the testator left the residue of his property to four sons, JA, JF, C, DG, and PP, as tenants in common and "in the event of any of my children dying without issue..." the surviving brothers or brother were to take the deceased brother's share but in the event of his leaving issue, the issue were to take the parent's share. All four sons survived the testator but died without issue. The judge found that there were two possible constructions: (a) the testator had not contemplated the possibility of all four sons dying without issue, and so there would be an intestacy, or (b) the last surviving brother took all. The judge applied the presumption that a testator does not intend an intestacy[184] and held that the surviving son took absolutely.

12. Legacies

In the past a distinction was made between gifts of real property in wills, called devises, and gifts of personal property in wills, called bequests or legacies. The Succession Act, 1965 abolished some important distinctions between real and personal property under the old law, but still refers to devises and bequests[185] and a gift of "all my real estate" may still be termed a devise.

Although the word legacy was used to mean a bequest, it is now more frequently used as a general word including devises and bequests and is so used here.

---

181 Section 29 of the Wills Act applied to issue and was limited to the use of that word, so that the section did not change the effect of the phrase "die without heirs of the body" which conferred an estate tail: *Re Sallery* (1861) 11 Ir Ch R 236.

182 *Re Booth* [1900] 1 Ch. 768.

183 Unreported, High Court, McCracken J, 26 May 1998.

184 *Re Harrison* (1885) 30 Ch D 390, per Lord Esher MR at 393.

185 See for example s.93 of 1965 Act.

a) Devises

A devise may be general, specific or residuary. A general devise would be a gift of "all my real estate" or "all my land". By section 92 of the 1965 Act a general devise now carries with it not only freehold estates which the testator held at death but also leasehold estates. The section repeats section 26 of the Wills Act, 1837.[186] A testator who had both land held in fee simple and leasehold estates devised "all my lands and tenements" to X. It was held that only the freehold land passed to X, but that if he had only leasehold land, the leasehold would pass. Section 26 reversed this artificial rule which depended upon the distinction insisted on at common law between real and personal property, leases being categorised as chattels real, a type of hybrid. Nevertheless, a devise today of "all my real property" probably still raises a presumption that it carries with it only freehold land since that is apparently the intention of the testator.

A specific devise is a gift of a specific piece of real property, *e.g.* a gift of "my house called Dunromin" or "my land in County Meath". A residuary devise is a gift of the residue of land after a specific devise, such as "the rest of my land I give to X". A residuary devise, or bequest, now constitutes a fund out of which the testator's funeral and testamentary expenses may be paid.[187]

b) Bequests

Bequests may also be general, specific or residuary. A general bequest is a gift of personal property by description, such as "one of my tables" when the testator has several, whereas a specific bequest refers to a particular piece of personal property, such as "the grandfather clock which my Aunt Betty gave me".[188] If a testator bequeaths a debt owed to the testator, that is a specific legacy.[189] If the testator bequeaths a sum of £50, or a sum of £50 to be paid out of a debt owed to him or her, then that is a general legacy. A gift of £50, without further qualification, is a gift to be paid out of the total amount of money in the testator's estate. The distinction between general and specific is significant in relation to ademption, discussed below.

---

186 That section was inserted because of the case of *Rose v. Barlett* (1506) Cro Car 292, 79 ER 856, 2 Atk 450, 26 ER 672.

187 Succession Act, 1965, 1st Schedule part II; Administration of Estates Act (NI), 1955; Wylie, *Irish Land Law* para. 14.25.

188 Wylie, *Irish Land Law* para. 14.26.

189 *Duncan v. Duncan* (1859) 27 Beav 386, 54 ER 151; *McCoy v. Jacob* [1919] 1 IR 134 at 138.

13. Failure of Benefit

Gifts in wills may fail for a number of reasons not all of which are dealt with here. The rules against remoteness have already been dealt with. The following are the main types of failure.

a) Ademption

Ademption is a term used to denote a failure of a gift in a will by some cause outside the will which affects the gift itself rather than the person who is intended to receive it. In the first case, the failure of property, the cause is that the property described in the will is no longer owned by the testator at his or her death. In the second case, that of ademption of legacies by portions, the failure is the existence of a gift outside the will and the application of the maxim of equity that "presumes an intention to fulfil an obligation".

Ademption may be contrasted with the doctrines of lapse and satisfaction. A gift is said to lapse when it fails because of the prior death of the intended beneficiary. Satisfaction is not easy to distinguish in all cases from ademption, and what word is used is not of great importance provided it is clear as to the effects in specific cases. Generally the term satisfaction is used to refer to the failure of some disposition of property by a gift within the will under consideration. In the case of the satisfaction of legacies by legacies the disposition of property may be within the will itself, *i.e.* the legacy is adeemed by another legacy within the same will.

(1) Failure of Property

Since a specific legacy refers to a unique item the gift will become void if the item ceases to be part of the testator's estate by the time of his or her death.[190] It is said to be adeemed.[191] A general legacy, on the other hand, is said not to be adeemed. This is correct if, for example, the gift is of "one of my tables" and the testator still has some tables at the time of death, even though he or she may have sold one or more of them before death, or bought others. If, however, the testator is found to have no tables in his or her possession at the time of death, it is suggested that such a general legacy would be adeemed, since the entire class or category out of which the legacy is to be taken has ceased to exist. A general legacy depends upon the existence at the testator's death of a category of property to which the description in the will can refer.

A specific legacy is not adeemed if there is an item corresponding to the description in the will at the testator's death. Thus a gift of "my grandfather clock" would not be adeemed if the testator had a grandfather clock at the time of making the will, then sold it later, but acquired another one which was the

190 *Fitzgerald v. Stirling* (1858) 6 Ir Ch R 198 (testator left a life interest in chattel to J, later conveyed it by deed to J absolutely).

191 Wylie, *Irish Land Law* para. 3.119–3.120; Brady, *Succession* para. 6.56.

only one in his possession at the time of his death. This is really just an illustration of the rule that a will "speaks from death".[192] In cases of doubt, judges tend to find that a legacy is general rather than specific when possible,[193] to avoid it being adeemed.[194]

(2) *Legacies by Portions*

The doctrine of ademption in this situation was explained by Sullivan MR in *Curtin v. Evans*:[195]

> "There is a presumption raised by the law against double portions; and accordingly, when a parent, or someone standing *in loco parentis,* gives by will a sum of money to a child, and afterwards a like or greater sum is secured by a settlement on the marriage of that child, the law presumes the legacy to be adeemed. But this is only a presumption, and therefore it may be rebutted by evidence of intention to the contrary. The burden of proof of intention to countervail the presumption rests on the person claiming the double portion. Parol evidence is admissible... [but] the Court ought to view and examine it with scrupulous care and great discrimination".[196]

A legacy given to a child will be adeemed by a portion given by a marriage settlement even though the portion is settled on husband and wife.[197] If the portion is of less value than the legacy, then the legacy is adeemed *pro tanto*.[198]

In the case of ademption of legacies by portions the child must take the portion and cannot claim the adeemed legacy.[199] This may be contrasted with satisfaction of portions by legacies in which the child has an election, *i.e.* he or she may choose between the portion or the legacy.

Ademption in this sense is not confined to persons *in loco parentis* and the children for whom they are responsible. If a testator leaves a legacy to a stranger, either an individual or an organisation, and after making the will gives the stranger a gift for the same purpose, the legacy is presumed to be adeemed by the later gift.[200] The presumption only arises, in the case of a stranger, however, where the legacy was given for a particular purpose and the

---

192 See page 919 above.

193 *Kelly v. Frawley* (1944) 78 ILTR 46, Brady, *Succession* para. 6.58.

194 *Re Gage* [1934] Ch. 536.

195 (1872) IR 9 Eq 553; Wylie, *Irish Land Law* para. 3.119; Wylie, *Cases on Equity* p.117.

196 (1872) IR 9 Eq 553 at p.557–58.

197 *Barry v. Harding* (1845) 7 Ir Eq R 317.

198 *Edgeworth v. Johnston* (1877) IR 11 Eq 326.

199 *Chichester v. Coventry* (1867) LR 2 HL 71; *Rentoul v. Fitzsimmons* (1900) 34 ILTR 194.

200 *Griffith v. Bourke* (1887) 21 LR Ir 92, per Porter MR at 95; Wylie, *Cases on Equity* p.122.

later gift was for the same purpose.[201] If the legacy was not a for a clearly expressed purpose, then the stranger may take both gifts.[202]

English decisions deny that the rule against double portions can be applied if the effect is to confer a benefit on a stranger.[203] Thus, if the residue of the estate is given to children A and B and to S, a stranger, and the testator later gives a portion to A, the stranger could not benefit from the rule against double portions. If the residue was £15,000 and the portion given to A £3,000, S will only get the original £5,000 share. The residue is adeemed by the portion to the extent of £3,000, leaving £12,000 as residue which is divided between A and B.[204] The English courts take the view that the principle behind the rule against double portions is to do justice between the children of the testator, or to preserve kinship solidarity, as we have put it.[205]

In *Re Bannon*[206] a testator left a legacy of £300 to a nephew J and the residue of his estate to another nephew, X. J later became engaged to a niece of the testator's wife. The testator gave £225 towards the purchase price of business premises for the couple. The Circuit Court held that, since the testator was *in loco parentis* to J, the legacy had been adeemed *pro tanto* by the portion of £225. The High Court, composed of only two judges, divided equally. Meredith J took the view that ademption should apply even though it would benefit X, who was in effect a stranger. Johnston J doubted this, but held that the presumption had in any case been rebutted. Since the High Court was equally divided the judgment of the Circuit Court stood. The Supreme Court reversed the decision of the Circuit Court, but on the ground that it had not been proved that the testator was *in loco parentis* to J, and so the presumption did not arise. Murnaghan J took the view that, in a suitable case, the presumption would apply even if it benefited a stranger. The difficulty on the facts of the case was that, if the presumption were to apply, the stranger would inevitably benefit, which is not always so, as the case discussed in the previous paragraph illustrates. Authority in the Republic must therefore be taken to be undecided on the point.[207]

201 *ibid.*

202 *ibid.*

203 *Meinertzagen v. Walters* (1872) LR 7 Ch App 670.

204 *Re Vaux* [1938] Ch. 581 at 590.

205 See the similar policy at work in class gifts.

206 [1934] IR 701.

207 But see Keane, *Equity* p.315.

b) Satisfaction

(1) Debts by Legacies

If a testator owes A a sum of money and dies without paying the debt, but leaves a legacy to B in her will equal to or greater than the debt, equity presumes "an intention to fulfil an obligation" and therefore presumes that the legacy was in satisfaction of the debt.[208] A legacy does not satisfy a debt *pro tanto*.[209] For the doctrine to operate the legacy must be equal or greater in value than the debt.

(2) Portions by Legacies

This is the opposite case to that in the second type of ademption. It also depends on the presumption of equity against double portions. If a parent, or someone *in loco parentis,* undertakes to provide a portion, *i.e.* financial provision for a child such as on marriage or for education or establishment in a trade or profession, dies without providing it, but leaves a legacy to the child, the legacy will be presumed to be in satisfaction of the portion.[210]

In the past the rule was not applied to a mother[211] but this may no longer the case in view of Article 40.1 of the Constitution. It may also be noticed that the formulation of the analogous rule in ademption of legacies by portions by Sullivan MR in *Curtin v. Evans*[212] speaks of parent.

It is said to be easier to rebut the presumption here than in the case of ademption of a legacy by a portion.[213] The reason is that if the will comes before the settlement, then, since the will is not binding until the death of the testator, the settlement is more easily read as substituting provisions, whereas if the settlement comes before the will, the settlement already creates a binding obligation and the beneficiary may in any case insist on taking the benefit under the settlement.[214] It also explains why there is an election in the latter case, but not in the former.

---

208 Wylie, *Irish Land Law* para. 3.115-3.116.

209 *Coates v. Coates* [1898] 1 IR 258, Wylie *Cases on Equity* p.114; *Humphrey v. Arabin* (1836) Ll & G t P 318.

210 Wylie, *Irish Land Law* para. 3.117 - 3.119.

211 *Warren v. Warren* (1783) 1 Bro CC 305, 1 Cox 41, 28 ER 1149; contrast *Re Eaderley's Will* [1920] 1 Ch 397.

212 (1872) IR 9 Eq 553; Wylie, *Irish Land Law* para. 3.119.

213 Brady, *Succession* para. 6.61.

214 *Chichester v. Coventry* (1867) LR 2 HL 71 at 87, per Lord Cranworth.

(3) Legacies by Legacies

Some writers[215] question whether this is a case of satisfaction. It may be more accurate to treat it as a special case of construction of wills. Where a will contains two legacies to the same person or institution it is a matter of construction whether the testator really intended to make two separate gifts to the same donee, or whether it was an oversight.[216]

(a) Same Instrument

Where the legacies are contained in the same will or codicil and are of the same value equity presumes that the testator did not intend both gifts to take effect, *i.e.* it was a mistake, and the legatee can take only one.[217] If they are of different value, the presumption is to the opposite effect, *i.e.* that they are both intended to take effect.

(b) Different Instruments

Where the legacies are contained in different wills or codicils equity presumes that both were intended to take effect.[218]

c) Election

Some cases of election in equity have already been dealt with. The more general principle known as the doctrine of election is, in effect, a means by which a testator may dispose of property which does not belong to him or her. If a testator purports to leave to A property in fact belonging to X, and also leaves a legacy to X, then if X wants to take the benefit of the legacy X must dispose of her own property in accordance with the will or compensate A for its loss. The principle is that if X wishes to take the benefit under the will, she must also accept the burden.[219]

The early cases placed the doctrine on the basis of the implied intent of the testator, but it was held by the British House of Lords in *Cooper v. Cooper*[220] that election applies even where the testator makes a mistake as to the ownership of the property. Even so, Lord Hatherley was prepared to construct a theory of intent in such a case: he held that the testator can be taken to have the ordinary intent implied in making a will, that he or she intends that every part of it should be effective.[221] The theory seems to be an artificial one, designed to disguise the fact that the court of equity is acting on the conscience of the

215 Wylie, *Irish Land Law* para. 3.121–3.124.

216 *Quinn v. Armstrong* (1876) IR 11 Eq 161; Wylie, *Cases on Equity* p.128.

217 *Garth v. Meyrick* (1779) 1 Bro CC 30, 28 ER 966.

218 *Walsh v. Walsh* (1869) IR 4 Eq 396; *Pakenham v. Duggan* (1951) 85 ILTR 21.

219 *Sweetman v. Sweetman* (1868) IR 2 Eq 141; Wylie, *Cases on Equity* p.109.

220 (1874) LR 7 HL 53.

221 *ibid.* at p.70.

donee, an intervention which in earlier centuries the courts found no need to disguise. There are signs that today the courts may prefer to base the principle again on the conscience of the donee.[222]

Election is said to lead to compensation and not forfeiture. The person who may be called upon to elect has a choice of three courses of action. They may:

(1) retain his or her own property and forgo the legacy; or

(2) take under the will and dispose of his or her property as the will directs; or

(3) retain his or her own property and take under the will, in which case he or she must compensate the other legatee for the loss of his or her property.

Not all of these options are rational in all cases. Thus, if X owns Gortbane which is worth £70,000 and the testator purports to leave it to A, and also leaves a legacy of £5,000 to X, X can keep Gortbane and forgo the legacy, or could take the £5,000 and hand over Gortbane to A, or keep Gortbane and the £5,000, but would then have to compensate A to the value of Gortbane. Most people in X's position in this case would prefer the first option. However, if the testator had merely purported to give A, his aged aunt, a right of residence in Gortbane, X might prefer to give the aunt a right of residence and take the £5,000.[223]

d) Lapse

The doctrine of lapse is in some respects the opposite of ademption. In ademption it is the non-existence of the property which causes the failure of the gift. In lapse it is the non-existence, *i.e.* death, of the intended recipient. Thus, if the testator leaves property to A and A dies before the testator, the general rule is that the gift does not take effect for the benefit of A's estate.

Co-ownership is a special case. If the testator leaves property to A, B and C jointly and A and B die before the testator, the rule of survivorship means that C is entitled to the whole interest at the testator's death and may take the gift. If all three are dead, then the whole legacy lapses. If, however, the gift had created a tenancy in common, the shares of A and B would lapse, but not that of C.

Where a legacy has lapsed the destination of the property will depend on the wording of the residuary clause,[224] if there is one. Thus, in *Re Swiney*[225] the clause gave the residuary devisee "the residue of my estate. . . not herein specifically devised. . .". The will devised property X to C. C died before the testator. The lapsed property X was held to pass not to the residuary devisee but on

222 *Re Mengel's Will Trust* [1962] Ch. 791.

223 *Re Gordon's Will Trusts* [1978] Ch 145; Brady, *Succession* para. 6.89.

224 Succession Act, 1965 s.91, reproducing Wills Act, 1837 s.25.

225 (1858) 6 Ir Ch R 455.

a partial intestacy, and at that time it went to the heir at law. Property X had been "specifically devised", even though the devise had failed. If there is no residuary clause the property will pass on a partial intestacy.

(1) Charitable Gifts

A gift to charity may not lapse if the charity is dissolved provided the testator has shown a general charitable intention and the court is willing to apply it *cy pres*.[226]

(2) Entails

Section 97 of the Succession Act, 1965, reproducing section 32 of the Wills Act, 1837, provides that the doctrine of lapse will not apply, unless there is a contrary intention, in the case of a gift of a fee tail or quasi-entail where the intended donee dies before the testator leaving issue capable of inheriting under the entail.[227]

(3) Gifts to Issue

Section 33 of the Wills Act, 1837 provided that where the testator made a gift in favour of his or her child or remoter issue and the child or issue predeceased the testator, then subject to a contrary intention, the gift would not lapse if the child or issue left issue living at the death of the testator.[228]

Section 98 of the Succession Act, 1965 repeats the provisions of section 33, but provides in addition that lapse will not apply where (a) the gift to the child or issue is made under a special power of appointment and (b) where the gift is made to a class. Section 33 of the Wills Act, 1837 applied, by its language, only to gifts made under general powers of appointment and so the Succession Act, 1965 abolishes the distinction in this respect. As to class gifts, the doctrine of lapse never applied. If a testator gave property "to my children", the class closed at the testator's death if there were children in existence at that point.[229] Thus, under the normal class-closing rule a child who died before the testator never became a member of the class, and so even if that child had had children who were alive at the testator's death, they did not participate. The Wills Act, 1837 did not remedy this situation. Although Section 98 states that in all cases within its scope "the gift shall not lapse", the effect of the section in this instance appears to be to alter the class-closing rule where the class consists of children or remoter issue of the testator.

---

226 Wylie, *Irish Land Law* para. 9.104–9.110.

227 *Re Pearson* [1920] 1 Ch. 247.

228 The section has been altered in England as to deaths after 1982 by the Adminstration of Justice Act, 1982 ss. 19, 73(6). See Megarry, *Manual* (7th ed.) 146–7.

229 See Chapter 12 Class Gifts.

In *Elliott v. Joicey*[230] an English court held that, under section 33 of the 1837 Act, the requirement that the issue of a deceased child be living at the testator's death was not satisfied by a child in the womb. However, section 3(2) of the Succession Act, 1965 now excludes the effect of the case by providing that "descendants and relatives of a deceased person begotten before his death but born alive thereafter shall, for the purposes of this Act, be regarded as having been born in the lifetime of the deceased and as having survived him".[231]

"Child" or "issue" includes non-marital as well as marital children or issue in wills made after 14 December 1987.[232] However, in *Re Stamp, deceased*[233] Lardner J held that "issue" prima facie does not include adopted children even in a will made after the Adoption Act, 1952. The will of John Stamp stated that should his son, Patrick Stamp, "die without leaving issue" the property bequeathed to him should be held in trust for the son of the testator's other son, Philip. Patrick was unmarried at the date of the will and at his father's death, married two years later. There were no biological children of the marriage and in 1965 Patrick and his wife adopted a daughter and in 1967 a second daughter. Patrick applied to have it determined, on is own and his daughters' behalf, whether the word issue in the will included adopted children or not. The plaintiff submitted, *inter alia,* that the Supreme Court had held[234] that the effect of an adoption order under the Adoption Act, 1952 was to take a child out of the family into which it was born and incorporate it into the adopting family and that the policy of the law and the Constitution is to regard adopted children for all purposes as equal to natural children of their parents. Lardner J, however, took the view that to hold that issue included adopted children would be to give the word a specialist meaning and not an ordinary meaning.

It is submitted that *Re Stamp* is wrongly decided. Section 26(2) of the act itself makes it clear that child or children of the adopter includes adopted children. Adoption is a legal fiction. The fiction is that the adopted person is legally the child of the adopter, even though the child is not biologically the offspring of the adopter. The legal fiction also reflects the social fact that such children are treated and accepted as the children of their adoptive parents and this has been implemented by the Supreme Court decision upholding the Adoption Act 1952. The ordinary meaning of such words as "child" or "issue"

230 [1935] AC 209.

231 Brady, *Succession* para. 6.17.

232 Status of Children Act, 1987 s.3, s.27, and s.29 adding s.4A to the Succession Act, 1965 and amending s.3. Section 4A provides that "in deducing any relationship for the purposes of this Act, the relationship between every person and his father and mother, shall... be determined in accordance with s.3 of the Act of 1987". This is subject to s.27A of the Succession Act, 1965 which deals with grants of probate and administration.

233 [1993] ILRM 383.

234 *Re The Adoption Act (No. 2) Bill 1987* [1989] IR 656.

etc. has therefore been changed both by social practice and Constitutional principle. It is consistent with the legal fiction to hold an adopted child to be the issue of the adopter, unless a testator expresses a contrary intention. For the same reason there seems to be no basis for the view of the judge[235] that an adopted child is not a "child of the marriage". Given that he or she is legally the child of adopter, consistency with the fiction surely requires that the child is the child of the marriage subsisting between the adopting parents at the time of the adoption order. To hold otherwise could create an absurd fiction that the child is a *non-marital* child. Furthermore, it is true that section 29(2) of the Adoption Act 1952 provides that a reference to "child" or "children" of the adopter in any disposition of real or personal property made by will or otherwise after the date of an adoption order are to be construed to include, unless the contrary intention appears, adopted children. The section makes clear the effect of an adoption order in one respect, but it should not be taken to require the corollary, *i.e.* that – as to all wills in the future – if no actual adoption order has been made at the time of the will, or by the testator's death, that child *etc.* does not include possible adopted children. It is possible, but seems unlikely, that the legislature intended that the word "child" could never be construed in future, prima facie, as including possible adopted children, when adoption and the possibility that someone might adopt a child is common experience. It would seem an unjustified discrimination against adopted children. The rules of construction should assume that testators are inclusive in their thinking until the opposite is proved, not that they intended be exclusive, or even prejudiced or bigoted, until it is proved otherwise. Furthermore, in *Stamp* itself the testator was referring to a future event, the death of his son, and the disposition of property was a future interest to take effect at that time.

e) Disclaimer

A beneficiary under a will cannot be forced to accept a gift under it and may disclaim it.[236] There is no formality for disclaimer which may be implied from conduct.[237]

f) Uncertainty

A gift in a will may fail for uncertainty if the property concerned or those who are to receive it are not identified with sufficient clarity to enable the court carry out its terms. The rules as to admitting extrinsic evidence have already been dealt with.

---

235 Lardner J in *Re Stamp* [1993] ILRM 383 at 387.

236 *Townson v. Tickell* (1819) 3 B & Ald 31, 106 ER 575 per Abbott CJ; Wylie, *Irish Land Law* para. 14.27; Brady, *Succession* para. 6.02.

237 *Re Birchall* (1889) 40 QBD 436.

Courts will attempt wherever possible to find the testator's meaning, even, sometimes, to the extent of giving specific content to a somewhat vague phrase. In *Jackson v. Hamilton*[238] the testator directed that the trustees should retain from time to time any reasonable sum or sums which would be enough to remunerate them for their trouble in carrying out the trust. The Master decided that £250 for each trustee would be reasonable and this was upheld by Sugden LC.[239]

It has been suggested that a gift fails for uncertainty not because the property or the recipient cannot be ascertained but because of uncertainty of concept.[240] This is difficult to maintain if one takes into account the relevance of admissible extrinsic evidence. If, for example, the gift is to "my nephew Arthur Murphy" and the testator has two nephews called Arthur Murphy then extrinsic evidence may show that the testator had in mind one of them rather than the other. On the other hand, extrinsic evidence may be inconclusive. The gift will then fail for uncertainty although the concept, in terms of its linguistic expression, is the same as before. A gift may fail for uncertainty not because the testator was unclear as to what he or she meant, but because the court is unable to discover what the testator's intention was.

g) Gifts to Witnesses

Section 82(1) of the Succession Act, 1965, repeating section 15 of the Wills Act, 1837, provides that:

> "82(1)– If a person attests the execution of a will, and any devise, bequest, estate, interest, gift or appointment, of or affecting any property (other than charges and directions for the payment of any debt or debts) is given or made by the will to that person or his spouse, that devise [*etc.*] shall, so far only as concerns the person attesting the execution of the will, or the spouse of that person, or any person claiming under that person or spouse, be utterly null and void".[241]

Subsection (2) makes it clear that the witness may nevertheless be admitted as a witness in court to prove the validity or invalidity of the will. The principle here is conflict of interest: the rule preserves the impartiality of witnesses and ensures that they have no improper motive in attesting the will. Since the main rule has this effect, there is no objection to their giving evidence as the attestation.

The general rule does not apply in the following cases:

238 (1846) 3 Jo & La T 702.

239 *Re Golay* [1965] 1 WLR 969; R.E. Megarry (1965) 81 LQR 481.

240 *Re Gape* [1952] Ch. 418; R.E. Megarry (1965) 81 LQR 481.

241 Wylie, *Irish Land Law* para. 14.34.

(1) Signed Not as a Witness

If the beneficiary signs not as a witness but in some other capacity, as where an executor signs above the attestation clause in the belief that it is necessary for an executor to sign the will.[242]

(2) Fiduciary Gifts

If the witness is to take the gift not beneficially but as a trustee the rule does not apply.[243]

(3) Secret Trusts

If the witness takes under a secret trust, the rule does not apply, presumably provided that the witness was unaware of the benefit at the time of attestation.[244]

(4) Subsequent Marriage

The rule does not apply to the spouse of an attesting witness who married the witness after the attestation of the will.[245]

(5) Confirmation

The rule does not apply if the gift to the witness is confirmed by a will or codicil which is not attested by the witness.[246]

(6) Sufficient Other Witnesses

The rule does not apply if the will would be validly attested even without the signature of the attesting beneficiary. In *In the Goods of Willis*[247] the testator asked his sister, to whom he had left all his property, to sign the will after the attesting witnesses. She had done so only to please her brother who was gravely ill. Sullivan P granted probate omitting the sister's signature. The Eng-

242 *Re Parker* (1905) 39 ILTR 6.

243 *Kelly v. Walsh* [1946] IR 388 (sum of money and residuary estate to a priest to say Masses for the repose of testator's soul. Dixon J: held charitable bequests, donee didn't take beneficial interest. Argued that he could indirectly benefit, because if he said the masses he would be entitled to claim honoraria. Held: no matter: he didn't have to say them himself, another priest could do so.

244 *O'Brien v. Condon* [1905] 1 IR 51; *Re Young* [1951] Ch 344.

245 *Tee v. Bestwick* (1881) 6 QBD 311.

246 *Re Marcus* (1887) 57 LT 399; *Gurney v. Gurney* (1855) 3 Drew 208, 61 ER 882; *In the Goods of Shaw* [1944] Ir Jur Rep 77.

247 (1927) 61 ILTR 48.

lish case of *In the Estate of Bravda*[248] had come to a harsher decision whose effect was only reversed in England in 1968.[249]

h) Unlawful Killing

Apart from the Succession Act, which will be considered shortly, if someone entitled to benefit from the estate of a deceased person is convicted of a crime in which the unlawful killing of the deceased was an element, then most jurisdictions would disqualify the potential beneficiary from obtaining the benefit, whether they are a beneficiary under a will[250] or on intestacy.[251] This was said to be based on the principle that a wrongdoer should not profit from his or her wrong.[252] In England and many states in the United States the principle is held to prevent the passing of the legal title to the beneficiary, but in some states of the United States the courts, in the absence of a statutory exception, prefer not to interfere with the passing of the legal title and hold that the beneficiary holds it on a constructive trust.[253]

Section 120 of the Succession Act, 1965 provides that:

> "120.–(1) A sane person who has been guilty of the murder or manslaughter of another shall be precluded from taking any share in the estate of that other, except a share arising under a will made after the act constituting the offence, and shall not be entitled to make an application under section 117".

The basis of the rule has been considered in the chapter on co-ownership. The common law rule was not based simply upon a concern to frustrate an evil de-

248 [1968] 1 WLR 492.

249 Wills Act, 1968 s.1.

250 *Riggs v. Palmer* (1889) 115 NY 506; 22 NE 188, Court of Appeals of New York, note the interesting dissenting judgment of Gray J. *Van Alstyne v. Tuffy* (1918) 169 NYS 173, comment in (1918) 16 Mich L Rev 561, (1918) 27 Yale LJ 964; *Matter of Sparks* (1939) 15 NYS 2d 926, comment in (1940) 40 Colum L Rev 327, 88 U Pa L Rev 628. *Cleaver v. Mutual Reserve Fund Life Association* [1892] 1 QB 147; *Borough Builders Ltd v. Dublin Corporation* [1966] IR 285, High Court; *Re Nevin*, High Court, Shanley J, 13 March 1997.

251 *Re Crippen's Estate* [1911] P 108, [1911–13] All ER Reprint 207.

252 *Riggs v. Palmer* (1889) 115 NY 506; 22 NE 188, Court of Appeals of New York; *Cleaver v. Mutual Reserve Fund Life Association* [1892] 1 QB 147, CA (Eng); *Re Crippen's Estate* [1911] P 108, [1911–13] All ER Reprint 207; Ames, *Lectures on Legal History* (1913) "Can a Murderer Acquire Title by his Crime and Keep It?"; Ague,"Homicide – Effect on Wrongdoer's Inheritance, Intestate and Survivorship Rights" (1953) 7 Miami LQ 524. Clary, "Crime Does Not Pay – Except for perhaps Murder: a Comment on *Bird v. Plunkett*" (1953) 27 Conn BJ 170; Youdan, "Acquisition of Property by Killing" (1973) 89 L Q Rev 235; "Disposition of Life Insurance Proceeds When Owner-beneficiary Murders the Insured" (1977) 29 Maine L Rev 126.

253 *Parks v. Dumas* (1959) 321 SW 2d 653, Texas, (murderer of parents); *Will of Wilson* (1958) 5 Wisc 2d 178, 92 NW 2d 282 (husband murdered wife). And see section 187 United States Restatement, Restitution.

sign, since it applied even where the killing was not intentional and even if the motive of the killing was not to obtain the benefit.

The notion that the rule is based upon the presumed intent of the testator is false since the principle has been applied in cases of intestacy.[254] What of a testator who was terminally ill and who had arranged with the legatee that she should kill him? Or, suppose a testator had given a number of people a good motive to kill him and had trusted that, given their character, they, or one of them, would do so? A court would surely not allow such legatees to take the property on the ground that it did not contradict the intention of the testator. Also, in other contexts, such as extrinsic evidence, courts have refused to give effect to the intent of the testator where it contradicts the express provisions of the will. One element in section 120 which points to its being based on intention is the exception of gifts made after the act constituting the offence, which suggests that the reason is that such a gift indicates forgiveness. If it is intended to incorporate a notion of forgiveness then it should also have made it necessary to prove that the testator was aware at the time of making the later gift that the act was caused by the intended beneficiary.

Another suggested principle is that to allow a person to benefit from killing another would be to encourage crime,[255] but this again would seem to justify the rule only as to deliberate killing motivated by thought of gain.

A more likely candidate for an explanation is that if the killer were to benefit directly from the crime it would outrage the feelings of ordinary law-abiding people.[256] Such a feeling of outrage, it could be argued, might tend to weaken adherence to the rule of law on the part of the otherwise law-abiding majority.

Section 120 does not provide expressly for exceptions to be made even in the case of manslaughter, which is an offence which can vary greatly in gravity from the deliberate to the unintentional.[257] Where, for example, a wife suffers years of domestic violence and finally snaps and kills her husband,[258] or from some other form of diminished responsibility[259] it is arguable that she should not automatically be deprived from benefiting from his estate or claiming her legal right.[260] Ordinary people would not necessarily be outraged by such a re-

254 *Re Crippen's Estate* [1911] P 108, [1911–13] All ER Reprint 207.

255 *Re H (deceased)* unreported, Ch D (Transcript:Lexis) 19 June 1987 per Peter Gibson J.

256 *Re Crippen's Estate* [1911] P 108 at 112, [1911–13] All ER Reprint 207 at 200, per Evans P.

257 Some English cases had refused to examine the degree of moral guilt in cases of manslaughter and applied the forfeiture rule: *In the Estate of Hall* [1914] P 1 per Hamilton LJ at p.7; *Re Giles* [1972] Ch. 544 per Pennycuick V-C at p.552.

258 *Re K (deceased)* [1985] 1 Ch. 85, [1985] 1 All ER 403, [1985] 2 WLR 262, [1985] FLR 558, [1985] Fam Law 130, [1985] Conv. 219.

259 *Re Giles* [1972] Ch. 544.

260 See s.120(4).

sult. It also creates the anomaly that if X knocks down and kills A through negligence, not knowing the identity of his victim, he is debarred from inheriting from under A, but if he knocks down and kills B under identical circumstances, it has no effect on his entitlement under A's will, yet his degree of moral culpability is the same. It seems incongruous that a rule which is based purely upon ethical considerations should be applied without regard to the justice of the case at hand.

Some of these difficulties have been removed in England by the Forfeiture Act, 1982, which expressly allows the forfeiture rule to be modified, except in the case of murder, to a range of benefits. After the Act the English courts have adopted the test in *Gray v. Barr*[261] that the forfeiture rule will not be applied if the killing is unintentional.[262] The Supreme Court of New South Wales in *Public Trustee v. Evans*[263] has declined to apply the rule in a case involving domestic violence. A wife, who had admittedly caused the death of her husband, had been acquitted of manslaughter, but the acquittal did not bar civil proceedings on the same facts and the Public Trustee had applied to the court to determine whether the rule of forfeiture should be applied. The court held that it should not on the ground that the rule in the jurisdiction was judge-made and should not be applied where death results after unintentional killing in the context of domestic violence.

In view of these developments it would seem right to amend section 120 to give a discretion to the court to set aside the general rule of forfeiture, either generally or in a number of specified circumstances.

i) Simultaneous Death

The problem of *commorientes* (Latin: those dying together), which refers to the legal rules applied when two or more people die in the same accident or in other circumstances when it is unclear which, if any, survived the others, has been dealt with in the context of the principle of survivorship in joint tenancy. At common law there was no special rule and so if A and B died in the same accident, it was for the personal representatives of A, if they alleged that A had survived B and had inherited B's property, to prove their case, and it was often impossible to do so. The personal representatives of B, if they wished to allege that B survived A, were in the same position. Thus there was, in effect, a presumption of simultaneous death.[264] Third parties could also be affected. Suppose that a husband left property in his will to his wife, but if she died in his

261 [1971] 2 QB 554.

262 *Re K (deceased)* [1985] 1 Ch. 85, [1985] Conv 219; [1986] 1 Ch. 180, [1985] 2 All ER 833, [1985] 3 WLR 202, CA; *Re H (deceased)* Ch D (Transcript: Lexis) 19 June 1987. But note *Ex parte Connor* [1981] QB 758, coming to a similar conclusion before the Act.

263 (1985) 2 NSWLR 188.

264 *Wing v. Angrave* (1860) 8 HLC 183.

lifetime, it was to go to X. The wife made a similar will leaving property to her husband, but to X if her husband died before she did. Both husband and wife were swept off a ship in a storm by the same wave. X could take nothing under either will because in neither case could she prove that the condition had been fulfilled.[265] The Succession Act, 1965 section 5 confirms that this is still the position in the Republic:[266]

> "5.– Where, after the commencement of this Act, two or more persons have died in circumstances rendering it uncertain which of them survived the other or others, then, for the purposes of the distribution of the estate of any of them, they shall all be deemed to have died simultaneously".[267]

Uncertainty was still held to exist in *Kennedy v. Kennedy*[268], a case of a car plunging into water, even though there was evidence that one person may have died almost immediately of a heart attack, while the other died minutes later from drowning.[269]

Other jurisdictions have attempted other solutions, such as a presumption that the younger person survived the elder,[270] but it is questionable whether such a rule achieves a better result. In this situation the intention of the testators is not really known since they did not express it. In the example above the testators, if they had been asked, might well have said that in the event of their dying together they would wish X to take the property of each of them, but this is speculation. Where an intention cannot be found in the will the courts prefer not to make a will for the testator but to allow the residuary clause or the rules of intestacy to take their course.

14. Freedom of Testation

Historically, freedom of testation, the right of the individual to leave property by will, was asserted, in the case of real property, in opposition to the control of feudal lords. As such, it was progressive in the sense that its attainment was part of the historical process of replacing feudal forms of property with individual property. Individual freedom can, however, be exercised capriciously and irresponsibly. Many jurisdictions have limited freedom of testation in a

---

265 *Underwood v. Wing* (1855) 4 D M & G 633, 43 ER 655; *Wing v. Angrave* (1860) 8 HLC 183; *In bonis Beynon* [1901] P 141.

266 In Northern Ireland the common law presumption still applies: Survey of the Land Law of Northern Ireland (1971) para. 406-7; Wylie, *Irish Land Law* para. 14.32. See also Article 3 of Succession (Northern Ireland) Order 1996 (SI 3163, NI 26).

267 Apparently taken from the German Civil Code, Art. 20, as amended in 1951. Also see the Swiss Civil Code, Art. 32 and McGuire p.10.

268 Unreported, High Court, Kearns J, 31 January 2000, FL2266.

269 According to the pathologist, the heart attack could also have been caused by a struggle to open the car door.

270 England: Law of Property Act, 1925 s.184.

new way, to ensure that testators do not entirely disinherit members of their own family. In *FM v. TAM*[271] Kenny J contrasted the provisions of the Succession Act, 1965 with those in other jurisdictions:

> "The concept underlying the legislation in New Zealand, New South Wales and England is that the testator owes a duty to make reasonable provision for the maintenance of his widow and of his dependants. Our Succession Act, however, is based on the idea that a testator owes a duty to leave part of his estate to his widow (the legal right) and to make proper provision for his children in accordance with his means. It is not based on a duty to provide maintenance for his widow nor is it limited in its application to children who were dependant on him".[272]

The provisions may also be compared to those in Scotland where the widow is entitled to a half share if there are no children, and a third share if there are children, hence the expression "the widow's part, the bairn's part and the dead's part". We have also seen that there was a similar law in Ireland before the Statute of Distributions (Ireland), 1695 known as "the custom of Ireland".[273] In the Republic today, however, the children are not entitled to a specific share but are entitled to apply under section 117 for reasonable provision. The policy reasons behind the provision of the Succession Act, 1965 are pursued further in the section dealing with section 117.[274]

a) Legal Right of the Spouse

Section 111 provides that if the testator leaves a spouse and no children, the spouse shall have a right to one-half of the estate;[275] if the testator leaves a spouse and children, the spouse shall have a right to one-third of the estate.[276] The right of the spouse is known as the legal right and has priority over devises and bequests by will and shares on intestacy (*i.e.* where there is a partial intestacy).[277]

The legal right of the spouse may be renounced by an ante-nuptial contract in writing between the parties to the intended marriage and also after marriage by a spouse in writing and during the lifetime of the testator.[278] A contract renouncing the legal right made after marriage need not be made between both parties to the marriage, but can be made between a spouse and a person due to

271 (1972) 106 ILTR 82.

272 *ibid.* at p.86.

273 Statute of Distributions (Ireland), 1695 s.10; *Re Urquart* [1974] IR 197, per Walsh J; Wylie, *Cases* p.516 at 519.

274 See page 983.

275 Section 111(1).

276 Section 111(2).

277 Section 112.

278 Section 113.

inherit from the other spouse.[279] Such contracts may be invalid on the ground of undue influence, or some other form of unequal bargaining power.[280] A legacy to a spouse is deemed, by section 114(2) of the Succession Act, 1965, to have been intended to be in satisfaction of the legal right of the spouse. A spouse nevertheless has the right to elect between a legacy and the legal right.

b) Election of Spouse

Where a person dies wholly testate a spouse has the right, under section 115 of the Succession Act, 1965, to elect between a legacy in the will and her, or his, legal right. Section 115(4) provides that the personal representatives of the deceased have a duty to notify the surviving spouse in writing of the right to elect under section 115. The election must be made either not later than six months from the receipt of notification, or within one year from the first taking out of representation of the deceased's estate, whichever is later.[281]

In default of election the spouse takes under the will and does not take her or his legal right under section 111.[282] This may reflect a policy that the Succession Act, 1965 only seeks to ensure that the testator leaves a part of his estate to his widow without seeking to dictate how much or how little he shall leave, so that the legal right is more in the nature of a guideline.[283] However, it can lead to the result that the surviving spouse takes nothing. In *Re Urquart*[284] a wife had left a legacy to her husband conditional on his surviving her for at least one month, the husband having made a similar provision for his wife. Both were involved in a car accident which caused their deaths. The husband survived the wife by only a day and did not recover consciousness. He therefore died without having made an election under section 115. The Revenue Commissioners nevertheless claimed that the husband's half share in the wife's estate, being his legal right was, in terms of the Finance Act, 1894, "property of which the deceased person was at the time of his death competent to dispose". Kenny J upheld this claim, but an appeal was allowed by a majority of the Supreme Court (Fitzgerald CJ and Walsh J, Henchy J dissenting). The view of the majority was that the husband was not "competent to dispose" of the legal right since he had not elected to take it in preference to the legacy. It was accepted that the reason for the husband's failure to elect was not relevant for this purpose. Henchy J, dissenting, did not accept that election was a condition precedent to being able to dispose of the interest, since, in his view,

279 *JH v. WJH* unreported, High Court, Keane J, 20 December 1979.

280 *ibid.*; Brady, *Succession* para. 7.08–12.

281 Section 115(4).

282 Section 115(1)(b). *JH v. WJH* unreported, High Court, Keane J 20 December 1979.

283 See *FM v. TAM* (1972) 106 ILTR 82, per Kenny J, quoted above.

284 [1974] IR 197; Wylie, *Cases* p.516.

both election and disposition could take place simultaneously.[285] He conceded that the consequence of holding as he did that the husband was competent to dispose of the interest at his death was that the husband's estate would be liable to pay tax on a share which he had not elected to take, and had never received. The majority decision avoided this result. In the event, the husband's estate took neither the legal right, since in the view of the court he had failed to elect, nor the legacy, since the condition precedent had not been satisfied.

In *Re Cummins*[286] the Supreme Court held that legal right does not depend upon the surviving spouse electing between it and a bequest in the will or a share on intestacy, so that, if the testator leaves a will which contains no provision for his or her spouse, the spouse still has the legal right share which vests on the death of the testator. The court distinguished *Urquart* on the ground that in *Urquart* the need to elect arose, whereas in *Cummins* it did not. Barron J quoted with approval a passage from the judgment Walsh J *Urquhart*:[287]

> "In my opinion, the whole of this structure presupposes and is based on an assumption implicit in the statute, in addition to what is expressly stated in s.111, that a legal right arises on the moment of the death of the testator. Where there is no legacy or devise or where there is a legacy or a devise expressed to be in addition to the legal share, the legal share vests upon the death. But when a testator in his will makes a devise or bequest to a spouse and it is not expressed to be in addition to the share as a legal right, then the spouse has a statutory right to take the share as a legal right – but that share does not vest until he takes it".

Where a person dies partly intestate, the surviving spouse may elect between (a) her or his legal right, and (b) her or his spouse's share on intestacy and, in addition, the legacy under the will.[288] In default of election, the spouse takes (b) and not the legal right.[289]

c) Spouse's Right to Appropriate Matrimonial Dwelling

Section 56 of the Succession Act, 1965 provides that where the estate of the deceased includes a dwelling in which at the time of the deceased's death, the surviving spouse was ordinarily resident, the surviving spouse may require in writing the personal representatives of the deceased to appropriate the dwelling under section 55 wholly or partly in satisfaction of any share of the surviving spouse.[290]

285 One objection to this is that property law, in its reifying way, would normally hold that election had preceded disposition by at least a nominal moment of time so that the interest could vest in the disponer.

286 [1997] 2 ILRM 401 (Barron J; Murphy and Lynch JJ concurring).

287 [1974] IR 197 at p.211.

288 Section 115(2)(a).

289 Section 115(2)(b).

290 *Re Hamilton, Hamilton v. Armstrong* [1984] ILRM 306 (application by spouse creates equity which can be enforced by spouse's personal representatives).

The same right applies to household chattels.[291]

As with the right to elect, the personal representatives of the deceased have a duty to notify the surviving spouse of her or his right to appropriate. The right must be exercised not later than six months from the receipt of notification or one year from first taking out representation of the deceased's estate, whichever is later.[292] The right to appropriate applies whether the deceased dies testate or intestate.

d) Proper Provision for Children

(1) General

Section 117 of the Succession Act, 1965 provides that:

> "117.–(1) Where, on application by or on behalf of a child of a testator, the court is of opinion that the testator has failed in his moral duty to make proper provision for the child in accordance with his means, whether by his will or otherwise, the court may order that such provision shall be made for the child out of the estate as the court thinks just.
>
> (2) The court shall consider the application from the point of view of a prudent and just parent, taking into account the position of each of the children of the testator and any other circumstances which the court may consider of assistance in arriving at a decision that will be as fair as possible to the child to whom the application relates and to the other children.
>
> (3) An order under this section shall not affect the legal right of a surviving spouse or, if the surviving spouse is the mother or father of the child, any devise or bequest to the spouse or any share to which the spouse is entitled on intestacy.
>
> . . .
>
> (6) An order under this section shall not be made except on an application made within six[293] months from the first taking out or representation of the deceased's estate".

As to subsection (3) it may be noted that it debars any claim by children where the testator left all his or her property to the surviving spouse where he or she is the mother or father of the children. The policy behind the section is presumably that the surviving spouse being the mother or father of the children, will provide for them out of the bequest. Since it can hardly be denied that the testator did not owe a moral duty to such children, the assumption behind the rule must be that a bequest of all the testator's estate to their mother or father discharges any moral duty to them. In *FM v. TAM*[294] Kenny J said as follows:

291 Section 56(2).

292 Section 56(4).

293 Previously 12 months; amended by Family Law (Divorce) Act, 1996 s.46.

294 (1972) 106 ILTR 82, High Court. See the similar statement by the same judge in *Re Moore, deceased,* unreported, High Court, Kenny J, 2 March 1970, cited in *MacNaughton v. Walker* [1976-77] ILRM 106.

> "...The existence of a moral duty to make proper provision by will for a child must be judged by the facts existing at the date of death and must depend upon (a) the amount left to the surviving spouse or the value of the legal right if the survivor elects to take this, (b) the number of the testator's children, their ages and their positions in life at the date of the testator's death, (c) the means of the testator, (d) the age of the child whose case is being considered and his or her financial position and prospects in life, [and] (e) whether the testator has already in his lifetime made proper provision for the child".[295]

In that case the testator had made no provision at all for his adopted son, who at the time of the testator's death was a married man "established in his profession", had two children of his own and owned his own house. He was in no sense dependent on the testator. He had never demanded, nor received, any financial or other assistance from the testator. Nor had the testator made any provision for him during the testator's lifetime. During the testator's life his wife had paid for the son's education, clothing and other incidental expenses. The testator had treated the boy with kindness but had told him he would not inherit the testator's farm in Co Meath. He had evidently agreed to the adoption to please his wife but had never treated the boy as his son. The testator had left the farm to his executors on trust for his wife and after her death to his two nephews. On these facts the judge decided that the testator had no made proper provision for his son and awarded him half the testator's estate, excluding immovable property in England.

In *Re IAC, deceased*[296] Finlay CJ[297] approved of these tests and added a number of further principles which, he said, could be seen as a qualification of them. These were:

1. The phrase "failed in his moral duty to make proper provision for the child in accordance with his means" placed a "relatively high onus of proof [*sic*][298] on an applicant". It was not enough to show that the provision was "not as great as it might have been, or that compared with generous bequests to the other children or beneficiaries in the will, it appears ungenerous". A court should not alter the terms of the will merely because on the facts proved it would have made different provisions.
2. Where the relationship between the testator and the children was one of care and kindness the court should "entertain some significant reluctance" to vary the will.

295 (1972) 106 ILTR 82 at 87.

296 *Re IAC, deceased, CC v. WC* [1989] ILRM 815 at 819, [1992] IR 143; *Re PC a Ward of Court, McGreevy v. AC*, unreported, High Court, Carroll J, 10 October 1995.

297 Griffin and Hederman JJ concurring.

298 This should be degree of proof. The concept was classically defined by Lord Brougham in his Speech in defence of Queen Caroline: "The evidence before us is inadequate even to prove a debt: impotent to deprive of a civil right: ridiculous for convicting of the pettiest offence: scandalous if brought forward to support a charge of any grave character: monstrous if to ruin the honour of an English Queen!" *Speeches* I.227.

3. Different considerations apply where there was a "marked hostility" between the testator and a particular child.

These tests probably represent an attempt to confine the jurisdiction of the court to where there is a marked difference between the provisions of the will and the provisions which a court would have substituted on the basis of the "proper and just parent" test and so to prevent a flood of applications under section 117.

(2) The Time of Applying the Tests

Kenny J in *FM v. TAM*[299] took the view that the proper time to apply the tests of failure in moral duty was the date of the testator's death, not the date on which the will was made. The judge repeated this view in *Re NSM deceased*[300] and added that the testator could also be taken to have knowledge, immediately before the will took effect, of the incidence of taxation on his or her estate and, even more artificially, of the costs of litigation incurred in defending the estate against claims which would in reality be unknown at that time. The notion that the tests under section 117 are applied at the testator's death is certainly consistent with section 89 of the 1965 Act which provides that wills "speak from death". This raises the possibility that a provision which was adequate to discharge the moral duty at the date the testator made the will may cease to be so by the time of the testator's death, or vice versa. For example, a testator might have provided equally for a number of children whose circumstances and needs at the date of the will were approximately equal, but had changed significantly by the time of the testator's death so that one or more had needs greatly in excess of those of the other children, as where one child suffers a catastrophic injury requiring constant medical and nursing care for the remainder of its life.

Alternatively, a testator may make no provision at all for a child either during the testator's life or by will. At the time the will was made this was morally insupportable, but by the time the testator died the child concerned had become a millionaire and had no need of provision, nor would a just and prudent parent have thought it necessary to make any provision for it.

In the first case the court would have jurisdiction to intervene. This may be justified on the ground that testators generally retain the power to alter the provisions of their wills up until their death and so the real failure of the testator was the failure to do so, but this is not entirely satisfactory as the testator may have ceased to have the capacity to make a new will by becoming senile, *etc.* Thus it indicates that the test becomes somewhat artificial in such circumstances, since the testator has not subjectively failed to understand his or her moral duty. In effect it gives power to the court to remake a will due to changed

299 (1972) 106 ILTR 82.

300 (1973) 107 ILTR 1, 6.

circumstances, whether or not the testator was responsible for the failure of the will to provide adequately or justly by the time of their death.

In the second case the court would lack jurisdiction to make provision for the child since at the time of the testator's death there could not be said to be a failure of moral duty, again on the basis of an objective test. In other words, the court would have to take into account not the testator's actual state of mind or assessment of moral obligations, but what a "prudent and just parent" would have done if they had written the will immediately before their death.

It is open to question as to whether a testator would be held to owe a moral duty to children of whose existence the testator was unaware at his or her death, such as posthumous children or children of a brief liaison. It could be argued that the degree of knowledge attributed to a testator under Kenny J's tests in *Re NSM deceased*[301] includes fictional knowledge of the existence of children. The testator would in any case have been aware that there was a possibility of such children existing.

(3) The Policy Basis of the Section

The decision in *FM v. TAM*[302] prompts some conclusions as to the meaning and purpose of section 117. It is worthwhile considering some alternative policies on which it might be argued that the section is based:

(1) There is a moral requirement on the testator to provide for dependents.

It is not necessary in order to succeed under the section for an applicant child to prove that he or she was dependant on the testator at the time of the testator's death. The child in *FM v. TAM* was not dependent and yet succeeded in an application under section 117.

(2) There is a moral requirement on the testator to provide for blood relatives, *i.e.* a blood is thicker than water principle.

The decision in *FM v. TAM* is against such a policy. The child in that case was not a blood relative, but was adopted, and yet succeeded under section 117. Moreover, in holding that the testator had not made proper provision in the circumstances of that case, Kenny J necessarily accepted that the testator was not justified in preferring his nephews to his adopted son, evidently on the ground that the nephews were related by blood.

(3) It is a public policy that the State should not have to provide for people who can be provided for by their own family?

This policy seeks to protect the Welfare State against unnecessary claims. Although taxpayers may be under a moral duty to provide for members of society who cannot provide for themselves, where parents can so provide they should do so. Again, this does not seem an ade-

---

301 (1973) 107 ILTR 1, 6.

302 (1972) 106 ILTR 82, Kenny J: see above.

quate explanation of section 117, since the child does not have to establish that but for the provision which they claim, they would be a charge on State funds. Kenny J perhaps suggests that this is an explanation for the New Zealand, Australian and English legislation, but it is doubtful whether it is any more satisfactory as an explanation in their case either.

(4) To allow a testator to ignore completely members of his or her family would weaken the nuclear family as a social unit and would be unconstitutional.

This, on the face of it, is more likely, given the importance which Article 41 of the Constitution attaches to the family as a social unit. One may note that the effect here of the Status of Children Act, 1987 is that the right to apply under section 117 is no longer confined to the family based on marriage, which the judges up to now have held to be the family referred to by the Constitution.[303]

(5) The section aims to promote kinship solidarity by reducing feelings of resentment between children of the same parent.

We have argued that such a policy in favour of kinship solidarity can be detected in other areas, such as the class-closing rules. We have also argued that in that context the policy takes second place to a policy favouring the right to deal freely with property on the part of persons entitled to such interests, where the two policies conflict. There is no possibility of such a conflict in the context of section 117 and so the law may favour kinship solidarity. There may be a policy conflict of another kind: between the policy of kinship solidarity and the policy of carrying out the testator's intention. In this case the legislature decided in favour of reducing tensions between living persons in preference to giving effect to the wishes of the testator.

(4) *Substantive Issues*

(a) General Considerations

In *MPD v. MD*[304] Carroll J laid down a general test of the kind of provision which would be considered proper:

> "I consider the proper provision for the children of the deceased according to his means should include provision not only to house, clothe, maintain, feed and educate them and ensure that medical, dental and chemists' bills are provided for until they finish their education and are launched into the world but should also include some provision by way of advancement for them for life".[305]

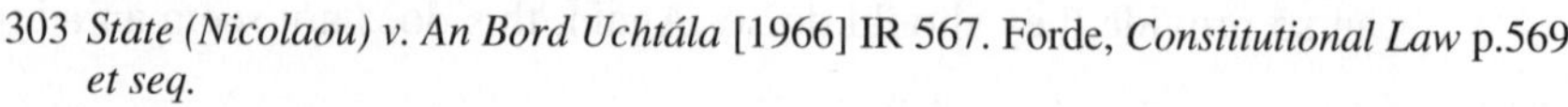

303 *State (Nicolaou) v. An Bord Uchtála* [1966] IR 567. Forde, *Constitutional Law* p.569 *et seq.*

304 [1981] ILRM 179.

305 *ibid.* at p.189.

This test would, of course, have to be considered in the light of the means of the testator, which might not, for example, allow for an advancement for life. The judge also considered how the testator should provide for two families, one of which was marital and the other not:

> "Proper provision by the deceased for his children by his wife should have ensured a reasonably equitable distribution of his property between his two families so that his children by his wife would not have to live in straitened circumstances while his children by the defendant could live to a high standard due to a large extent to the provision he had made for them and the defendant".[306]

There is nothing to suggest here that a testator would be justified in making a significantly greater provision for marital children as against non-marital children. In view of the fact that the Status of Children Act, 1987 was enacted in order to avoid discrimination against non-marital children, it does not seem likely that such a disparity would be held proper.

(b) Equal Shares

A bequest which gave equal shares to each child could be impugned by a child who had significantly greater needs than the others, as where it was in need of constant medical care.[307] On the other hand, if the deceased had died intestate the rules of intestacy would give equal shares to each child and the court would have no jurisdiction to alter them. Section 117 contemplates that an equal division between children may be improper while there is no such possibility recognised on intestacy. Having decided to place a legal obligation on testators in general to leave some property to each child,[308] if the provision is not to be easily evaded by testators making purely nominal bequests to disfavoured children, the legislation should include some method of assessing the value of a bequest in relation to the bequests given to other children and section 117 reaches this result. The anomaly which exists between testate and intestate succession in this regard could arguably be solved by providing for a jurisdiction of the court to intervene in cases of intestacy where an equal division would not be equitable. Proposals have indeed been made for reform to allow such a jurisdiction to be exercised.[309]

---

306 *ibid.* at p.189–90.

307 See *In the Estate of LB; EB v. SS* [1998] 2 ILRM 141.

308 This would, however, ignore the fact that no provision at all may be held reasonable in the circumstances under s.117. See below.

309 Brady, *Succession Law* para. 8.23–5. Deputy Harney moved an amendment on the Status of Children Bill to that effect, without success, (Dáil Debates, 28 October 1987, Col 1692) and the Law Reform Commission has recommended in favour of such a change: Report, Law Reform Commission 30–1989 p.23.

(c) Where No Provision is Made

If the testator makes no provision for a child does this necessarily mean that the testator has failed in their moral duty, or, which is not necessarily the same thing, does it mean that a child will necessarily succeed in an application under section 117? In *In the goods of JH*[310] the testator left his home to his wife for life with remainder to a grandson. He left is farm to one son but made no provision for his other children. Barron J in the High Court held that while a prudent parent might well decide not to divide the farm but to leave it to one child, it was a failure of his moral duty not to make any provision for his other children.[311] Nevertheless, there are certainly some cases where it seems clear that an application under section 117 will not succeed or may not succeed:

1) Under the discretion in section 117 itself, a testator may possibly be held to have acted as a just and prudent parent even though no provision was made for a child either by will or during the testator's life, taking into account the factors indicated by Kenny J in *FM v. TAM*. This might apply where one child is wealthy and requires no provision while the others are less so, and taking into account the means of the parent *etc*. This point is not settled by case law.

2) The phrase in section 117, "whether by his will or otherwise", indicates that the proper provision may be made in the testator's lifetime and this could justify an absence of provision in the will.

In *Re LB*[312] the plaintiff's mother had substantial property, including shares. She had four children, the plaintiff and his three sisters. The plaintiff had a history of alcoholism and drug abuse. The plaintiff had three children who, at the date of the trial, were still of school age. The plaintiff and his wife and children had lived in a house which had been given to the plaintiff and one of his sisters by their father. Two of the plaintiff's three sisters were married and all of the sisters were financially well off. At the time of the trial the plaintiff was aged 40 and unemployed. He was separated from his wife, who was a semi-invalid and unable to work. Some years before, the plaintiff's mother had transferred her shares to her children, dividing them equally between them, telling her solicitor at that time that she wished to make proper provision for them, and that she wanted to treat them all equally. The plaintiff sold his shares for about £275,000. In her last will the plaintiff's mother left £5,000 to each of her ten grandchildren, a nominal amount to the plaintiff and the rest of her estate to named charities. By the time she made the will the plaintiff had dissipated the £275,000 and plaintiff's mother indicated to her solicitor that she was aware of this and that he was experiencing financial hardship and marital prob-

310 *In the goods of JH, MFH and others v. WBN* [1984] IR 599, High Court, Barron J.

311 But see Blayney J obiter contra in *In the Estate of JH de B* [1991] 2 IR 105, High Court, that if the plaintiff had been a farmer, which he was not, he might have had a justifiable complaint in not being given any land.

312 *Re LB, EB v. SS* [1998] 2 ILRM 141.

lems. The plaintiff's mother died in 1992. The plaintiff claimed that since 1993 he had not taken alcohol or drugs. He instituted proceedings under section 117 claiming that his mother had failed in her moral duty to make proper provision for him and an order making such provision. On 5 July 1996 Lavan J held that the plaintiff had not established a failure of moral duty on the part of his mother. The plaintiff appealed.

The Supreme Court (Keane J; Lynch J concurring; Barron J dissenting) dismissed the appeal. Keane J noted that the case was unusual in that the plaintiff had no complaint as to the division of the shares between him and his three sisters in 1987. His claim was that having regard to his circumstances at the date of his mother's death, she should have made provision for him at the expense of the other beneficiaries, *i.e.* the charities. The court decided a number of points on the section: (a) that it was not entitled to take into account facts that arisen after the testator's death, *i.e.* in this case that the plaintiff had not taken alcohol or drugs since 1993. It could only become relevant if the court were to hold that she had failed in her moral duty and was then considering the extent of the provision that should be made for him; (b) the fact that a testator has treated all of his or her children equally is not an answer to an application under section 117, since a testator was not free to disregard the special needs of one of his or her children, *e.g.* due to physical or mental disability. The anxiety of parents to avoid friction among their children by treating them equally must be recognised. It was a relevant although not decisive factor; (c) generous financial provision having been made for the plaintiff during the testator's life, the choice facing her was whether to make further provision for him in the hope that this time it would not be dissipated, or whether to give it to more deserving causes. Moreover, the testator might have taken the view that to make further provision for the plaintiff, even by way of a trust, might not be in his best interests. This was clearly a view which a responsible and concerned parent could take; (d) in the circumstances there had been no breach of moral duty; (e) while the plaintiff's mother might be regarded as being under a moral duty to make some provision for the plaintiff's children, that was not a matter which the court could take into account under section 117. Barron J, dissenting, took the view that the plaintiff's mother had a moral duty to make some provision in favour of the plaintiff to enable him to fulfil his obligations to his dependants.

One might point out that even if the testator had made additional provision for the plaintiff with the notion of enabling him to provide for her grandchildren, there was no guarantee, given his history, that he would have done so. She could have done so by a direct provision to the grandchildren, in the form of a trust for their benefit, but her failure to do so could not be challenged by the grandchildren who have no claim under section 117. It is arguable that they should be able to claim.

3) It follows from section 117(3) that where the testator has bequeathed all his or her property to the surviving spouse and that spouse is the fa-

ther or mother of the applicant child, the child is debarred from claiming.

4) Under section 120 where the child has caused the death of the testator by murder, or manslaughter or had attempted to murder the testator, a claim is barred, unless the will was made subsequent to an act constituting the offence.[313]

(d) Behaviour towards Parent

Behaviour towards the parent is relevant. In *Re McDonald*[314] the testator made a nominal provision for his son, the plaintiff and the rest of his property on trust for the daughter of the defendant. The testator owned a farm and the plaintiff had worked on it from a young age. Relations between the testator and the plaintiff had broken down some years before the testator's death. The testator had become friendly with the defendant's family who had a farm in the area and to whom he was related and had gone to live with them some time before his death. The testator had obtained an injunction to recover possession of the farm from the plaintiff. The plaintiff had counterclaimed for the work done and had obtained judgment for £11,000. The plaintiff had remained in occupation in breach of the injunction and had been committed to prison for contempt at one point. The plaintiff's wife and children remained on the farm. The testator later regained possession of part of the farm and then transferred it to the plaintiff's brother. From then on a campaign was conducted in the locality, including threats and damage to property, which was directed against the testator and the defendant's family. McCracken J, in dismissing the plaintiff's claim under section 117, held that the behaviour of a child towards the testator was relevant to the issue of whether the testator had failed in his or her moral duty to the child. He also held it relevant that the plaintiff had had the use and benefit of the farm during the testator's life and that it had been against the testator's will. For many years, the testator had also run an account with a local shop from which his family could obtain their daily needs.

(e) Other Moral Obligations

The courts have emphasised that in determining whether the testator failed in his or her moral duty to an applicant child the court should take into account all the other moral duties of the testator. It has also been pointed out that for this purpose the testator may have moral duties to persons who could not themselves claim under section 117.

In *L v. L*[315] the testator was survived by his wife and children of his first marriage and by a woman and children of a union which the parties to it had apparently considered to be a second marriage. The testator's first wife had applied

313 See above page 963.

314 *Re McDonald, McDonald v. Norris* [1999] 1 ILRM 270.

315 [1978] IR 288.

for and obtained a divorce in the High Court in England. The testator left a will which made no provision for the first wife or the children of the first marriage. It left all the property to his second wife provided she survived him by at least six months, which she did. The first wife waived her legal right, but the children of the first marriage claimed under section 117 that proper provision had not been made for them. The claim was contested by the testator's second wife but not by the children of the second marriage who were in any case debarred by section 117(3), the testator having left all his property to their mother. It was not established that the divorce was valid in Irish law[316] and Costello J in ruling on preliminary points of law, held that in the circumstances of the case it was not necessary for him to decide as to the validity of the divorce nor consequently on the validity of the second marriage. The children of the second marriage did not contest the claim and could not have done so whether or not the second marriage was valid, because they were debarred by section 117(3). Nor did the judge have to decide who was the surviving spouse of the testator for the purpose of deciding who was entitled to the legal right, because the first wife had waived her right to the legal right and the second wife, having been left all the property had elected to claim her interest under the will. The judge pointed out that it was not therefore necessary to decide whether under the law in force at that time, illegitimate children as they were then called, could claim under section 117. He nevertheless held that in deciding whether the testator had made proper provision for the applicant children, the court should take into account all the testator's moral obligations and that they included moral obligations to illegitimate children,[317] to parents,[318] and to persons with whom the testator had lived as husband and wife whether or not the relationship constituted a marriage in law.[319] In relation to his own children it might be right to make greater provision for some children than others based upon their needs, as where a child had a special talent which it would be morally wrong to ignore, or where one child was an invalid in need of special medical care.[320] As to the children of the second marriage, although the testator clearly owed them

316 The report states that neither the wife nor the husband were domiciled in England. Domicile was, and still is, the test applied for the recognition of foreign divorces. At the time of the case the concept of domicile of dependence was applied to wives, whereby they were held to acquired automatically the domicile of their husbands. A wife who left her husband and obtained a foreign divorce would therefore usually be unable to obtain recognition of it in the Republic, while husbands were not under the same disability. The Domicile and Recognition of Foreign Divorces Act, 1986 purported to abolish domicile of dependence, but in *W v. W* [1993] ILRM 294 the Supreme Court held that domicile of dependence was, and had therefore always been, unconstitutional. See Kelly, *The Irish Constitution* (3rd ed.) pp. 1018–20.

317 [1978] IR 288 at 293, 294.

318 [1978] IR 288 at 294.

319 [1978] IR 288 at 296.

320 [1978] IR 288 at 294.

a moral duty and it was relevant to consider whether he had fulfilled this in considering whether the testator had fulfilled his moral duty to the applicant children,[321] the court could ignore them when considering what provision to make for the applicant children since the children of the second marriage had not made any claim to provision and none had been made for them in the will.[322]

In *In the Estate of JH de B, deceased*[323] Blayney J held that it was relevant to consider, in assessing the moral obligations of the deceased towards other children, an obligation arising from the deceased's having created or encouraged an expectation in another child that some of the deceased's property would be given to that child. This suggests that evidence which might fail if founding a claim based on proprietary estoppel might succeed as part of the evidence required under section 117. In some cases a claim might now be made under both heads, whereas in the past only a claim under section 117 would have been made, as for example *MacNaughton v. Walker*[324] which involved allegations that the testator had induced a child to believe that he would be left a stud farm and that the child had shaped his life accordingly by training in stud management. On the other hand, the fact that a beneficiary had been promised the land by the testator and had relied on it by expending labour on the land or looking after the testator might be a reason for leaving the will intact.[325]

(5) Status of Children Act, 1987

The Status of Children Act, 1987 provides[326] that non-marital children may apply under section 117 irrespective of whether the testator executed the will before or after the Act came into force, but it confers no right to apply under section 117 as to the wills of testators dying before the Act came into force.[327]

(6) Time limits

An application under section 117 must be made within 12 months of first taking out representation to the deceased's estate. Since applications will normally be made by children, the question arises whether the minority of the applicant is a disability which has the effect of extending the time limit. Section 127 of the Succession Act, 1965 provides that section 49 of the Statute of

321 The judge did not expressly do so, however. It is presumably the case that the testator fulfilled it by leaving all his property to their mother.

322 [1978] IR 288 at 293, 294.

323 [1991] 2 IR 105.

324 [1976-77] ILRM 106.

325 *Re PC, a Ward of Court, McGreevy v. AC*, unreported, High Court, Carroll J, 10 October 1995.

326 Succession Act, 1965 s.117(1A)(a) added by Status of Children Act, 1987 s.31.

327 1965 Act, s.117(1A)(b) added by Status of Children Act, 1987 s.31.

Limitations, 1957 "shall have effect in relation to an action in respect of a claim to the estate of a deceased person or to any share in such estate, whether under a will, on intestacy or as a legal right" as if three years were substituted for the six years mentioned in the section. If this applied to applications under section 117, then it would override the one year provision in the section itself and substitute for it the period of three years from the time the disability came to an end. The specific issue was whether an application under section 117 could come within the phrase "a claim. . . under a will, on intestacy or as a legal right". Carroll J in *MPD v. MD*[328] held that it could not. An application under section 117 could not, in her view, be described as a claim to a legal right which the judge took to refer exclusively to the legal right of a spouse.[329] The case is further discussed below in the next section.

This somewhat mechanical interpretation is unfortunate. As Brady has pointed out,[330] a child has to bring an action through their next friend, which could well be a person, such as a stepmother, with a conflicting interest of is or her own.

e) Disinheritance

Section 121 of the Succession Act, 1965 controls dispositions made within three years of death and intended to disinherit a spouse or children.

(1) Time Limits

The court may make an order (a) in the interest of a spouse or the personal representative of the deceased, within one year of the taking out of representation or (b) in the interest of a child, on an application under section 117.[331] The question of the time limit under section 117 is dealt with above.

(2) Scope

Section 121 deals with attempts by a testator, or an intestate, to disinherit his or her spouse or children or both. The section applies to "a disposition of property (other than a testamentary disposition or a disposition to a purchaser) under which the beneficial ownership of the property vests in possession in the donee within three years before the death of the person who made it or on his [or her] death or later".[332] The words seem apt to include a donatio mortis causa. In

328 [1981] ILRM 179.

329 One wonders, in this case, why s.121(5), in dealing with an application under that section by a spouse, refers to a period of one year from taking out representation, but in the case of an application by a child, to an application under s.117. If the period under s.117 is the same, why does s.121(5) distinguish the two cases?

330 Brady, *Succession* para. 7.76.

331 *ibid.*, s.121(5). For time limits under s.117, see Brady, *Succession* para. 7.75-79.

332 Succession Act, 1965 s.121(1).

fact, the section would seem to catch all such gifts, no matter when the subject matter was transferred and the words of gift spoken, because a donatio only vests the beneficial ownership, in the sense of the equitable interest, in the donee at a moment immediately preceding the death of the deceased.[333]

The section also contains an element of overreaching in that, if the donee has sold the property, the court order will be made against the consideration given by the purchaser in the hands of the donee.[334]

Where an application is made by a child it seems that a combined application should be made under sections 117 and 121 together.[335] This does not, however, mean that a child can only challenge a disposition under section 121 if the donor died testate, because, as Carroll J has pointed out, an application under section 121 has the effect, if successful, of deeming the disposition to have been made by will.[336] The applicant here gets the benefit of two fictions. The first is the statutory fiction that the disposition is made by will and the second is the declaratory theory of case law which in this instance maintains that a successful application was based upon grounds which were valid at the time the application was made.

In *MPD v. MD*[337] Carroll J had to decide a number of points on section 121. In that case the testator was survived by his wife and four children. For some time prior to his death the testator had been living with the defendant by whom he had had two other children. Within three years of his death the testator had transferred a half share in his business to the defendant and made her a joint tenant with him of the house they lived in. The defendant was granted probate of the testator's will. The plaintiff later brought an action under section 117 as next friend of the children of the marriage. It was this action which, as we have seen, the judge held to have been out of time. The judge also rejected the view that the widow could make an application on her own behalf under section 121 on the ground that it too would be out of time since it would not be made within the one year period. She also rejected two further arguments of counsel for the widow. The first was that time did not run against her under section 121 until she had been served with notice of her right to elect under section 115 by the personal representative of the deceased, who in this case was the defendant. The judge held that the wife was able to make an application under section 121 independently of any other provision. She also rejected the argument that, since an application under section 121 may be made on behalf of the spouse by the personal representative, that the personal representative, in this case the de-

333 See below.

334 Succession Act, 1965 s.121(8).

335 *MPD v. MD* [1981] ILRM 179. Carroll J concluded that this was the effect of s.121(5)(b).

336 *MPD v. MD* [1981] ILRM 179.

337 [1981] ILRM 179.

fendant, was under a duty to do so and consequently, having failed to do so, the defendant could not plead the time limit in section 121(5)(a). On this point the judge held that a personal representative was given power to apply but was not under a duty to do so. The failure of all these arguments might lead the sceptical lawyer to look to the facts for some further explanation of the judge's attitude. In this case the second union was a stable one, which in other jurisdictions might have been a second marriage, and this fact might account to some extent for the judge's apparently unsympathetic attitude to the widow.

(3) Effect

If the court is satisfied that the disposition was made in order to defeat or substantially to diminish the share of the spouse, whether as a legal right or on intestacy, or the share of a child on intestacy, or to leave a child insufficiently provided for, the court may order that the disposition be deemed to be a disposition by will, whether the maker of the disposition died testate or intestate.[338] The court may also order that the disposition, or part of it, shall be deemed never to have had any effect and the donee of the property, or any person claiming through the donee, shall be a debtor of the estate for such an amount as the court may direct.[339] The court may also make such further orders as may seem "just and equitable having regard to the provisions and the spirit of this Act and to all the circumstances".[340]

(4) Criticism

Section 121 is limited to dispositions which seek to disinherit the spouse or children of the deceased, but since it applies where the deceased died intestate the person entitled to the deceased's estate on his or her death may be neither a spouse nor a child, but remoter issue, such as a grandchild, or a collateral relation such as a cousin and this situation might have been foreseen by the deceased before he or she died. There is nothing in such a case to prevent a person disinheriting these remoter relations. This result may well have been intentional. It can be argued that while remoter issue may expect to inherit from a person who has neither spouse nor child, the deceased in such a case has no moral obligation to provide for them and so they correspondingly have no right to complain if the deceased chose to deprive them of their expectation. From a sociological point of view this result can also be seen as an example of how the law in this society concentrates moral obligations on the nuclear family at the expense of a wider extended family concept found in some other societies.

338 Succession Act, 1965 s.121(2).

339 *ibid.*, s.121(3).

340 *ibid.*, s.121(4).

B. Informal or Non-Testamentary Succession

1. Contracts

a) Contract by Testator

A contract to make[341] or not to revoke a will may be enforced against the personal representatives of a deceased person by an action for damages or for specific performance.[342] It may be noticed that the revocation of a will even in breach of contract is still effective: the remedy is a contractual one imposed on the personal representatives of the deceased.

b) Mutual Wills

The doctrine of mutual wills applies when two people, usually husband and wife, make wills in which they each leave their property to the survivor of them with remainders over, usually to their children, or they each leave their property to a third party directly, such as their child[343] in pursuance of an agreement[344] between them not to revoke their wills without the consent of the other party.[345] If one of the parties dies, then the courts will impose a trust on the surviving party or his or her personal representatives in favour of the beneficiaries under the will of the surviving party. As with a contract not to revoke, the revocation by the surviving party is not ineffective at law: the remedy is in equity by a constructive trust. Remarriage normally revokes a will automatically, and it seems that although this also applies to mutual wills, it does not affect the trust.[346]

2. Proprietary Estoppel

If A leads B to believe that A will leave property to B in his will and B relies on that expectation to her detriment, then, if the expectation is not fulfilled, the assurance may be held to be binding upon the personal representatives of A or

---

341 Lee, "Contracts to Make Wills" (1971) 87 LQR 358.

342 *ibid.*

343 *Re Dale* [1994] Ch. 31, [1993] 4 All ER 129, [1993] 3 WLR 652 (mutual will in favour of son: consideration was promise not to revoke will before death. Consideration must move from promisor, not necessarily towards the promisee. Dying without revoking it is performance of promise).

344 *Gray v. Perpetual Trustee Co Limited* [1928] AC 391, [1928] All ER 758; *Re Goodchild (deceased)* [1997] 3 All ER 63, [1997] Fam Law 660, [1997] 1 WLR 1216; see also See [1996] 1 All ER 670 at 678, [1996] 1 WLR 694 at 702.

345 *Dufour v. Pereira* (1769) Dick 419, 21 ER 332, 2 Hargrave's Juridical Arguments 304, 310 per Lord Camden: "…he, that dies first, does by his death carry the agreement on his part into execution". *Re Green* [1951] Ch 148; Brady, *Succession* para. 1.12.

346 *Re Goodchild (deceased)* [1997] 3 All ER 63, [1997] 1 WLR 1216.

the beneficiaries under a will made by A which defeats the expectation.[347]

It has been seen that an English court in *Re Basham*[348] held that proprietary estoppel applied to an assurance given by a property owner that property, in that case the residue of the estate, would be left to the plaintiff by will, so that, when the property owner later died intestate, an equity was raised in favour of the plaintiff to whom the assurance had been made and who had relied on it and this entitled the plaintiff to the property as against the personal representatives of the deceased intestate.

In *Re Basham* the deceased had died intestate but in *Smyth v. Halpin*[349] Geoghegan J upheld a claim based on proprietary estoppel where the property owner died testate and held that the equity entitled the plaintiff to the fee simple in the property despite the will. In that case the plaintiff's father was the owner of a house and farm. In a will in 1976 he left the property to his wife for life and then absolutely to the plaintiff subject to rights of residence in favour of his other children. In 1983 the plaintiff's father asked him whether he wanted the property and the plaintiff responded that he did. In a will in 1986 the plaintiff's father left the property to his wife for life and then to the plaintiff subject to rights in favour of his two daughters, each of whom would be entitled to choose a half-acre plot on the land for the building of a house. The plaintiff became engaged in 1987 and looked for a suitable site on which to build a house. The plaintiff asked his father to provide him with a site, but his father responded "This place is yours after your mother's day - what would you be doing with two places?". The plaintiff's father suggested that the plaintiff should build an extension on to the family home. An extension was designed by an architect on the assumption that the entire house would eventually belong to the plaintiff. The site on which the extension was built was transferred to the plaintiff so that he could use it as security to borrow the money required to build the extension. The plaintiff built the extension. In a later will the plaintiff's father left his land to his wife for life, then to the plaintiff absolutely, and left the house to his wife for life, then to the second named defendant (one of the plaintiff's sisters) absolutely. The will also gave the plaintiff a right of way over the land.

The plaintiff instituted proceedings seeking a declaration that he was entitled to the reversionary interest in the whole house following the life interest in favour of his mother and an order transferring that reversionary interest to him. He also claimed that the right of way referred to in the will was a right of way across the garden attached to the house and not an alternative right of way suggested by his mother and the second defendant. Geoghegan J held that there

347 *Re Basham* [1986] 1 WLR 1498.

348 [1986] 1 WLR 1498, see Chapter 18 Licences, Estoppel and Constructive Trusts: Estoppel by Reliance.

349 [1997] ILRM 38.

was an equity raised in favour of the plaintiff and that it could only be satisfied by a conveyance to him of the reversion in fee simple in the whole house. He also granted the easement. The judge first of all noted that the plaintiff did not argue the case on contract:

> "The plaintiff does not and indeed cannot ground his action upon contract. He does not suggest that there was any agreement on his part to confer any benefit on his father in return for making over the dwelling house. The fact that the plaintiff has not tried to make that very convenient case is to his overall credit in my view when assessing the credibility of his evidence. It might have been easy for him to have suggested that the father indicated that it would suit him if the plaintiff could look after him and his wife in their old age and that in return for that he would allow him build an extension to the house for immediate living in and give him the entire house in due course along with the land. Although such an agreement would not have been in writing or indeed evidenced by writing, it might have been quite a simple matter to establish it through acts of part performance".

As to proprietary estoppel, on which the action was based, the judge expressly recognised that granting the remedy "would effectively involve permitting the estoppel to be used as a sword and not merely a shield". On the facts, he found it "difficult to conceive" that the plaintiff "would ever have adopted his father's suggestion in relation to the extension to the house if it was not understood that he was to become the ultimate owner of the entire house". The case was within the principles set out in *Dillwyn v. Llewelyn*[350] and *Inwards v. Baker*[351]. One may note that other factors in the case made it a strong one: it was the father who persuaded the son to abandon his original plan of a separate site, and the evidence of the architect that that the design conceived the extension as an integral part of the house and not as a separate entity.

Re Basham was followed by the Court of Appeal in *Wayling v. Jones*.[352] In that case the plaintiff went to live with the deceased when the plaintiff was 21, and the deceased 56. The plaintiff helped him to run his businesses in return for living expenses and pocket money. The plaintiff was promised that he would inherit a particular hotel. The deceased made a will leaving the hotel to the plaintiff but by the time of his death had sold the hotel. The gift of the hotel had therefore been adeemed. The plaintiff nevertheless claimed that he was entitled to the proceeds of sale of the hotel by proprietary estoppel. The claim failed at first instance on the ground that the plaintiff had been unable to prove in cross-examination that the promises of the deceased influenced him to remain with the deceased. The Court of Appeal upheld the appeal. Balcombe LJ[353] stressed that:

350 (1862) 4 De GF & J 517.

351 [1965] 1 All ER 446.

352 [1995] 2 FLR 1029, [1996] Fam Law 88, [1996] 2 FCR 41, 69 P& CR 170.

353 [1996] 69 P& CR 170 at 173.

> "(1) There must be a sufficient link between the promises relied upon and the conduct which constitutes the detriment . . . (2) The promises relied upon do not have to be the sole inducement for the conduct: it is sufficient if they are an inducement[354] . . . (3) Once it has been established that promises were made, and that there has been conduct by the plaintiff of such a nature that inducement may be inferred then the burden of proof shifts to the defendants to establish that he did not rely on the promises . . .".[355]

More recently some doubt has been cast on the scope of *Re Basham* by a number of English decisions. In *Taylor v. Dickens*[356] an elderly lady promised to leave her house to her gardener, T. T thereafter refused to accept payment for his work. The lady made the will as she had promised, but soon afterwards T began to behave as if the house were already his, by leaving his things in sheds on the property. The testator found this both disturbing and unacceptable. Without telling T, she made a new will under which the house was left to a married couple who were friends of hers. She told friend that she was apprehensive about telling T of the new will and that she had "taken the coward's way out". There was also evidence that T's wife had told him he should not "count his chickens before they were hatched".

Weeks J held there was no equity raised in T's favour. It is well known that a testator can revoke his or her will. It was not sufficient for A to believe that he was going to be given a right over B's property if he knew[357] that B had reserved the right to change his mind. In that case, A must also show that B created or encouraged a belief on A's part that B would not exercise that right. The judge criticised the formulation of the principle by Mr Nugee QC in *Re Basham*[358] in that he did not mention the overriding requirement of unconscionability.

While the decision seems correct in not giving the claim priority over the testator's power of revocation, it is difficult to accept that an equity was not raised in T's favour by the fact of his declining to accept payment for his work, the testator's acceptance of that situation and her later failure to inform him of her change of mind, which would have enabled him to claim the lost wages, which she might in any case have offered to do. Surely he should have been entitled to his wages? She acquiesced in his reliance on her promise.

In *Gillett v. Holt*[359] G went to work on H's farm in 1956, and continued to work for H until 1995. Over the years H indicated to G that he intended to leave

354 Citing *Amalgamated Property Co v. Texas Bank* [1982] QB 84 at 104–105.

355 Citing *Greasely v. Cooke* [1980] 1 WLR 1306; (1980) 124 SJ 629, [1980] 3 All ER 710, Court of Appeal.

356 [1998] 1 FLR 806, [1998] 3 FCR 445, Chancery Division.

357 It is doubtful if the judge intends this to be an additional requirement, since he noted that it is common knowledge and, one might add, a matter of law on which T could have informed himself by taking legal advice at the time of the assurance.

358 [1987] 2 FLR 264 at 269D.

359 [1998] 3 All ER 917, [1998] 2 FLR 470; Milne [1999] CLJ 25.

most of his estate to G, and executed a number of wills giving effect to the intention. G had urged H to give him some immediate interest in the farm but H did not do so. By 1995 the personal and working relationship between G and H had broken down and H made a new will, in favour of the second defendant, which entirely excluded G. G brought an action against H based on proprietary estoppel claiming that he had devoted his entire working life to H's service on the understanding, fostered by H, that he would inherit his estate and that therefore H was under an obligation to leave the bulk of his estate to him. Carnwath J held that the claim failed. The plaintiff had failed to prove that the representations could reasonably be construed as an irrevocable promise that the plaintiff would inherit, regardless of any change in circumstances. Indeed. the judge did not accept that the plaintiff had so construed them. In cross-examination he had accepted that if circumstances had changed materially, for example if H had married and had children, he could not have complained if H had made some provision for them. The judge also held that the fact that the plaintiff had urged H to give him an immediate interest in the farm supported this conclusion. The judge concluded that "[the plaintiff] must have been well aware that his expectations, however reasonable, were dependent on Mr Holt's continuing goodwill, and had no legally enforceable foundation". The judge was careful to emphasise that it was not an unequivocal promise, nor one irrevocable in terms, which had to be proved, since proprietary estoppel was not necessarily based upon promise, but the genuineness and reasonableness of the plaintiff's belief that the representations were intended to be irrevocable and the defendant's knowledge that the plaintiff relied on them as such.

3. The Rule in Strong *v.* Bird

The Rule in *Strong v. Bird*[360] is to the effect that if A promises to make a gift of property to B but A fails to transfer title in his or her lifetime, then if B becomes the executor of A's estate, so that title vests in B in that capacity, the gift is perfected. B has common law title. Equity considers that no one has a better equity to the property than B and will not force B to hold it in a fiduciary capacity. It is sometimes said that the rule is an exception to the principle that equity will not perfect and imperfect gift, but equity really has no need to perfect the gift: the common law has done that and equity declines to intervene.

The rule does not apply if the donor intended a future gift.[361] Also, the intent to make the gift must continue until death. The rule has been extended in England to administrators.[362] This has been criticised on the ground that the executor is appointed by the testator, whereas an administrator is appointed by

360 (1874) LR 18 Eq 315, Jessel MR. The case itself is narrower than the principle for which it now stands.

361 *Re Freeland* [1952] Ch. 110.

362 *Re James* [1935] Ch. 449, Farwell J.

the court[363] and also that it may be pure chance who, among a small class of potential administrators, is appointed. It is arguable that the criticism is not well founded, in that it matters not how the donee obtains the legal title, provided the grounds of equity are satisfied. There is nevertheless one problem: if a person would benefit from the rule, if appointed, should that be taken into account by the court when appointing administrators?

4. Donatio Mortis Causa

a) The Doctrine

A donatio mortis causa is the relinquishment of dominion over property or the *indicia* of title to it by a donor who contemplates impending death, with the intention that it should be a gift[364], the gift only taking effect in the event of the donor's death, being revocable until death occurs and revoked automatically if the immediate danger recedes. The gift must be made in contemplation of death "by which is meant not the possibility of death at some time or other, but death within the near future, what may be called death for some reason believed to be impending".[365]

Donatio mortis causa was introduced into the common law from Roman Law. It has often been regarded as something of an anomaly. The anomaly is threefold:

(1) it avoids the formalities required of wills since the Wills Act, 1837 and for many centuries required by the Statute of Frauds, or required by more recent statutes prescribing formalities for the transfer of property;

(2) the doctrine is an exception to the rule that equity does not perfect an imperfect gift, although there are now an increasing number of exceptions to the rule including proprietary estoppel;

(3) the doctrine rests not upon the common law concepts of possession or the control of legal and equitable estates, but upon a modified version of the Roman concept of *dominium,* referred to in the cases as dominion.

b) Application to Land

The English Court of Appeal in *Sen v. Headley*[366] recently decided that the doctrine of donatio mortis causa applies to land. An appeal was to be taken to

363 *Re Gonin* [1979] Ch. 16, per Walton J at 34.

364 Deliver for safekeeping is insufficient: *Bentham v. Potterton*, unreported, High Court (appeal from Eastern Circuit, County of Meath), Barr J, 28 May 1998.

365 *Re Craven's Estate* [1937] Ch D 423 at 426 per Farwell J.

366 [1991] Ch. 425, [1991] 2 All ER 636, [1991] 2 WLR 1308, [1991] 2 FLR 449, 62 P & CR 277, [1991] Fam Law 373, CA.

the House of Lords but the parties settled the action before the appeal was heard.

It had long been thought that the doctrine of donatio mortis causa had no application to land. The sole authority in England in favour of the alternative view was said to be *Duffield v. Elwes*[367] in which Lord Eldon, delivering judgment in the House of Lords in 1827 after his retirement as lord chancellor, decided that the doctrine applied to a gift by a mortgagee, of money secured by mortgage, by the delivery of a mortgage deed, following Lord Hardwicke in *Richards v. Syms.*[368] Lord Mansfield in *Martin v. Mowlin*[369] had earlier held that a gift of money secured by mortgage carried with it the estate in the land held by the mortgagee as security. Lord Eldon nevertheless also maintained Lord Hardwicke's distinction between conditional mortgage estates and ordinary, absolute estates. Neither Lord Hardwicke nor Lord Eldon sought to justify the distinction in terms of deeper principle. They justified it on policy grounds, namely, the dangers of allowing informal transfers of property.

In *Sen v. Headley*[370] the plaintiff and the deceased had lived together as man and wife for 10 years and although they later separated, they remained on good terms. Some years later the deceased became terminally ill with cancer. He was told that his condition was inoperable and that it would deteriorate. The plaintiff visited the deceased in hospital every day. They discussed what would happen to the house when, as seemed inevitable, the deceased died before the plaintiff. The deceased had said to the plaintiff when they were alone together: "The house is yours, Margaret. You have the keys. They are in your bag. The deeds are in the steel box". The deceased died three days later. The plaintiff had always had a set of keys to the house. After the death of the deceased, the plaintiff found an additional and different set of keys in her bag. She believed the deceased must have put them in her bag. She used one of the keys from this bunch to open a cupboard containing the steel box. She used another key from the bunch to open the box and took possession of the deeds. That key, as it turned out, was the only key to the box.

The plaintiff brought an action against the deceased's estate claiming that she was entitled to the house on the basis that it had been given to her by the deceased under a valid donatio mortis causa. The plaintiff made no claim to the contents of the house. The deceased's nephew, one of the next of kin, who were the beneficiaries of the estate, opposed the claim. The judge held that there could not be a valid donatio mortis causa of land and dismissed the plaintiff 's action.

367 (1823) 1 Sim & St 239, (1827) 1 Bli (ns) 497; 57 ER 96.

368 (1740) Barn Ch. 90, 27 ER 567.

369 (1760) 2 Burr 969, 97 ER 658.

370 [1991] Ch. 425, [1991] 2 All ER 636, [1991] 2 WLR 1308, [1991] 2 FLR 449, 62 P & CR 277, [1991] Fam Law 373, CA.

The Court of Appeal (Nourse LJ, Purchas and Leggatt LJJ concurring), allowing the appeal, held that the doctrine did apply to land (a) if made in contemplation of death, (b) if the gift was made on the condition that it was to be absolute only on the donor's death, (c) that there was delivery of the essential *indicia* of title, such as the title deeds or land certificate, and (d) a parting with dominion over the land, by which the court appears to have meant the physical ability to deal with the land. The court further held that there had been a parting with dominion on the facts of the case.

Three factors seem to have influenced the decision. First, the judge indicated that while donatio mortis causa may be something of an anomaly, it would add to the anomaly to create an artificial distinction which was impossible to justify in terms of principle. Secondly, there had been developments in the law of choses in action which had established, in particular in *Re Dillon*[371] and *Birch v. Treasury Solicitor*,[372] that parting with dominion could occur in the case of an intangible thing such as a chose in action by the transfer of the *indicia* of title[373] and that the documents transferred need not set out the terms on which the subject matter was held. Thirdly, the law of constructive trusts had developed since 1827 and such trusts were excluded from the formalities generally required for a transfer of land.[374]

371 (1890) 44 Ch D 76, 59 LJ Ch. 420, 62 LT 614.

372 [1951] Ch. 298, [1950] 2 All ER 1198.

373 See the doctrine of constructive delivery in the United States. Thayer J in *Castle v. Persons* (1902) 117 F 835, US Circuit Court of Appeals, Eighth Circuit, (dissenting on the main issue):

> ". . . it is absolutely essential that the property or thing given should be delivered to the donee in the lifetime of the donor. Where the property given is bulky, a constructive delivery of the possession thereof may suffice; and where the thing given is a chose in action, and represented by a note, bond, or bill made by a third party, all the authorities agree that a delivery of the note, bond, or bill, unindorsed by the donor, will suffice. *Hill v. Stevenson*, 63 Me 364, 18 Am Rep 231; *Grover v. Grover*, 24 Pick 261, 35 Am Dec 319; *Corle v. Monkhouse*, 50 NJ Eq 537, 25 Atl 157; *Licey v. Licey*, 7 Pa 251, 47 Am Dec 513; *Hackett v. Moxley*, 65 Vt 71, 25 Atl 898. But it is equally well settled that when a chose in action is not thus represented by a note, bond, bill, or other instrument in writing, which can be delivered, but is merely a claim against a third party, which must be established by parol, a written assignment of the demand, by the donor to the donee, is essential to complete the delivery, whether the gift be one *inter vivos* or causa mortis. 2 Kent, Comm. (11th Ed.) 567; *Hooper v. Goodwin*, 1 Swanst 485; *Picot v. Sanderson*, 12 NC 309. See, also, *Sanborn v. Goodhue*, 28 NH 48, 56, 59 Am Dec 398; *Bond v. Bunting*, 78 Pa 210."

374 *Sen v. Headley* [1991] Ch 425, [1991] 2 All ER 636, [1991] 2 WLR 1308, [1991] 2 FLR 449, 62 P & CR 277, [1991] Fam Law 373.

(1) *Elements of the Doctrine*

(a) Dominion

The Court of Appeal in *Sen* held that there had been a parting with dominion and this was so notwithstanding that the deceased had retained keys of his own to the house. Nourse LJ conceded that in common law terms the deceased, by retaining his own keys to the house, had retained possession of the house it, but held that he had not retained "dominion" because "the benefits which thereby accrued to him were wholly theoretical",[375] since the deceased at the time was confined in bed in hospital. Dominon, it seems clear is used in the sense of physical control.

Dominion does not imply or not require legal control. Nourse LJ rejected the view accepted by Mummery J in the Chancery Division that donatio mortis causa could not apply to land because it would never be possible to say that a donor had relinquished *dominion* over the land, because, having parted with the title deeds or control over them, he or she could still create equitable interests, *e.g.* he or she could enter into a contract to sell the land, and so create a purchaser's equity, or by a declaration of trust, or by proprietary estoppel, constructive trust, and could create legal tenancies because an intending tenant is not entitled to inspect the title to the freehold.[376]

(b) Relinquishment

Nourse LJ statement that there had to be "a parting with dominion over the subject matter of the gift, *i.e.* with the ability to control it",[377] can be traced to the judgment of Lord Kenyon CJ in *Hawkins v. Blewitt*[378] where he said:

> "In the case of a donatio mortis causa, possession must be immediately given. That has been done here; a delivery has taken place; but it is also necessary that by parting with the possession, the deceased should also part with the dominion over it. That has not been done here".[379]

Lord Kenyon's choice of words are more equivocal than those of Nourse LJ. Nourse LJ reformulates the test of donatio mortis causa so that it relates (a) to dominion only and (b) that parting with, or relinquishment, is sufficient. The donor loses dominion but the donee does not have to acquire it.

(c) Time of Relinquishment

In *Sen v. Headley* the donor did not transfer the *indicia* of title nor relinquish dominion over the property at the time when he expressed the intention to make the gift. He had relinquished dominion in the subject matter of the gift

375 [1991] Ch. 438 H.

376 [1990] 1 All ER 898 at 907–908, [1990] Ch. 728 at 742–743.

377 *Sen v. Headley* [1991] Ch. 425 at 437.

378 (1798) 2 Esp 662 at 663, 170 ER 489 at 490.

379 *Sen v. Headley* [1991] Ch. 425 at 437.

sometime before, either when he entered hospital or when he put the keys to the cupboard and the steel box into the plaintiff's bag on one of her visits to the hospital. Yet this did not prevent the gift being a valid donatio mortis causa.

(d) Indicia of Title

It appears from *Sen* that relinquishment of dominion, and not possession, is the test in relation to the *indicia* of title. Nourse LJ remarked:

> "We do not suggest that there might never be a state of facts where there was a parting with dominion over the essential *indicia* of title to a chose in action but nevertheless a retention of dominion over the chose itself. . . But nothing comparable happened here".[380]

In *Mills v. Shields and Kelly (No. 2)*[381] Gavan Duffy P held that certificates of shares in public companies in Ireland, certificates of public companies registered in England and Post office savings certificates were not documents of such a nature that delivery of them could constitute a valid donatio mortis causa since they did not contain sufficient *indicia* of the terms of the contract under which they were held. This position is now in doubt following the English case of *Birch v. Treasury Solicitor* disapproving of the *dicta* on which Gavan Duffy relied.[382] A surer guide today is probably the necessity of production test adopted by the Australian courts.[383]

(2) Keys

Where the deeds are contained in a box it may not be sufficient to hand over a key to the box, rather than the box itself, if the donor retains a duplicate key.[384] The same is probably true where the donor gives the donee the combination to a safe, since the donor retains the knowledge of the combination. Even though the donor may not have the practical prospect of using the key, or combination, he or she could give it to someone else.

380 *ibid.* at p.438F-G.

381 [1950] IR 21.

382 These are *Delgoffe v. Fader* [1939] Ch 922 and *Duckworth v. Lee* [1899] 1 IR 405. See also Brady, *Succession Law* para. 1.34.

383 See Keane, *Equity and the Law of Trusts in the Republic of Ireland* at p.371 n.8 (the author is also a judge of the High Court of the Republic); Brady, *Succession Law* para. 1.34.

384 In *Sen v. Headley* the key to the box was unique. In *Hawkins v. Blewitt* (1798) 2 Esp 662 at 663, 170 ER 489 at 490, *Reddel v. Dobree* (1839) 10 Sim 244, 59 ER 607 and *Re Johnson* (1905) 92 LT 357, [1904–7] All ER Reprint 539 the alleged donor delivered a locked box to the alleged donee and either retained or took back the key to it. In *Reddel v. Dobree* he also reserved and exercised a right to take back the box. In each of them it was held that the alleged donor had retained dominion over the box and that there had been no donatio mortis causa. *Sen v. Headley* [1991] Ch. 425 at 437–8. *Re Craven's Estate* [1937] Ch. 423 at 427, [1937] 3 All ER 33 at 38.

In *Sen* the donor retained a key to the house itself, but this did not invalidate the donatio of the house. On the other hand, in the judge's view, it would have prevented a donatio of the contents of the house. At the beginning of his judgment Nourse LJ comments *obiter* that there could have been no claim to the contents of the house because there had been no delivery of them, apparently because the deceased had retained a key to the house.[385] Later, in dealing with the donation of the house itself, the judge comments that the retention of a key to the house by the deceased was not fatal to the gift of the house because the deceased was in no position to use the key since he was in hospital.[386] In which case, why did the same fact not negative a donation of the contents? It can be argued that there is no reason why a claim to the contents of the house should not have succeeded, had it been made.

(3) Donee in Possession

If the donee is already in possession of the land would this necessarily preclude the owner making a donatio of it? It seems not. Again, possession in itself is not the test.

In *Woodard v. Woodard,*[387] a case of a chattel, the deceased, on entering hospital where he subsequently died of leukaemia, said that he was giving his car to his son. The son, the defendant, was already in possession of the car, had a set of keys to it and was using it. Dillon LJ in the English Court of Appeal held that the fact that the son was already in possession of the car did not prevent the words of gift acting as a donatio mortis causa. In arriving at this conclusion, the judge relied on earlier cases[388] on immediate gifts which had held that the fact that the donee was in possession as bailee did not prevent the gift being valid. On the face of it this seems dubious: in donatio mortis causa the test is not as to possession. Nevertheless the elements of donatio mortis causa appear to be present. There was a relinquishment of dominion both over the car and over the keys. As in *Sen* they both occurred before the words of gift. Furthermore, neither appears to have been carried out with the intention of creating a gift. The intention then was to make a loan of the car to the son. The case reinforces the holding in *Sen* that donatio mortis causa can occur without the coincidence in time of the act of relinquishment with either (a) the words of gift, or (b) a specific intention to make the gift.

One further hypothetical suggests itself: suppose that A leaves his house to go into hospital, thereby relinquishing dominion over the land. The land is left in possession of X. A tells B that B is to have the land on A's death. B already

385 [1991] Ch. 431 F.

386 [1991] Ch. 438 H.

387 [1991] Fam Law 470, The Times, London, 15 March 1991, (Transcript: Lexis).

388 *Alderson v. Peel* VII Times Law Reports8, per Chitty J; *Re Stoneham* [1919] 1 Ch. 149, per Lawrence J.

has possession of the title deeds in some other capacity. Are words of gift alone sufficient in the case of land where the donee already has the title documents in his or her possession in some other capacity, the donor have previously relinquished dominion over the land?

(4) Donor in Possession

One other point may arise from *Sen*: can a donor relinquish dominion if he or she is still in possession of the land in the sense of being physically present on it, as where the donor is on his or her death bed in their own house on the land? One would expect that the deceased could still make a valid donatio since, as in *Sen*, their ability to exercise physical control over the land would be merely theoretical. It is hard to accept that a landowner could only make a donatio of their own land if they died in hospital.

(5) In Possession of a third Party

What is the position if the property is in possession of a third party at the time the words are spoken or instructions given? *Spratly v. Wilson*[389] posed a hypothetical. A who owns a watch which is in the possession of C, tells B to call at C's address and take away the watch, adding that it is to be a present. Is this a valid donatio mortis causa, there being no possession in A to begin with and no delivery by A to B? The key word here is possession. A does not have possession of the watch, but she does have dominion. She has the ability to dispose of the watch, to cause, in this instance, possession to pass from C to B. Possession itself is not relevant: what is relevant is dominion and that is, arguably, relinquished.

c) Revocation

(1) Express

The authorities are clear that the donor may expressly revoke the donatio during his or her life. It cannot be revoked by the donor by will since it takes effect notionally at a moment before death, so that the donee's title is complete before the will takes effect.[390]

(2) By Recovery

A donatio mortis causa is revocable until the death of the deceased and is automatically revoked if the donor recovers from the condition which caused him or her to contemplate death.[391]

389 (1815) Holt NP 10, 171 ER 142.

390 *Jones v. Selby* (1710) Prec Ch. 300, 24 ER 143.

391 *Castle v. Persons* (1902) 117 F 835, US Circuit Court of Appeals.

(3) By Subsequent Dealing

In the case of choses in action it has been seen that the donor may retain the power to make declarations of trust or assign them for value. In the case of land the donor could also, while having parted with the title documents, create a valid lease, since the prospective tenant may not usually inspect the title to the freehold, create equitable interests such as rights by proprietary estoppel, constructive trust, *etc.* He or she may also exercise the legal power to revoke the donatio mortis causa *inter vivos* or by will. What would the position be if the donor, having made such a donatio, then made a declaration of trust, or created a valid tenancy or validly assigned the benefit of a mortgage? Mummery J in the High court in *Sen* was clearly of the view that such a subsequent dealing would take priority over the earlier donatio:

> "The beneficiary under such a declaration of trust and the purchaser under such a contract would be entitled to an equitable interest in the house, which would take priority over any claim that Mrs Sen would have by way of donatio mortis causa on Mr Hewett's death".[392]

However, it is submitted that a later disposition would not necessarily display an intention to revoke the earlier donatio entirely. The donor might intend only to revoke the gift in part in the sense that he or she intended from then on that the donee take the legal title, or a reversion, in the land. Whether or not a later transaction revokes an earlier donatio or merely takes priority over it in a more limited sense might depend on the evidence in each case. For example if the deceased makes a donatio of the fee simple in favour of A and subsequently creates a tenancy in favour of B, the tenancy taking effect at once, then it seems clear that at a moment immediately before the deceased dies A will become entitled in equity to the fee simple subject to the tenancy.

(4) Death From A Different Cause

In *Mills v. Shields and Kelly*[393] it was held that if the donor contemplates death by one cause but dies from another, including suicide, that does not invalidate the gift. In *Mills* the deceased was concerned about the state of his health and was contemplating travelling to Dublin to have medical treatment which he believed posed a danger to his health. While in this state of mind he deposited a parcel of bank notes with a priest, telling the priest to give them to his brother who lived in South Africa should anything happen to him while he was in Dublin. He set out for Dublin three weeks later by train, but got off at a station before Dublin and committed suicide by hanging. Gavan Duffy P held that a donatio was not invalidated by the mere possibility[394] that the donor might

392 [1990] Ch. 728 at 742H.

393 [1948] IR 367; *Wilkes v. Allington* [1931] 2 Ch. 104.

394 Distinguishing *Agnew v. Belfast Banking Co* [1896] 2 IR 204.

have contemplated at the time of the gift that he might be overcome by an irresistible impulse to take his own life.

If the donor contemplated death by suicide it was held in the past that the gift is invalid on the ground of a public policy against suicide or assisting suicide.[395] However, those cases were decided at a time when suicide (and hence attempted suicide) was still a crime. Attitudes in this area have changed over the years and suicide is now regarded as more a matter for compassion than opprobrium. Suicide is no longer a crime in the Republic.[396] Clearly, the cases on this point will have to be reviewed.

C. Intestate Succession

The law of intestate succession has been radically altered in the Republic by the Succession Act, 1965. Before these new rules are discussed, some account will be given of the old law.

1. Before 1967

Before the Succession Act, 1965 came into effect on 1 January 1967 the common law made a distinction between realty and personalty.[397]

a) Personalty

The feudal common law did not recognise that a person had more than a life interest in personal property because it passed on the death of a person to the bishop of the diocese where the deceased lived to be used for charitable purposes.[398] It may be that the property was regarded as *bona vacantia* on the death of the owner and vested in the Crown which at some time had granted the prerogative to the Church.

The next stage in the development was that members of the family of the deceased person established their claim. The wife and children became entitled to one third of the estate each (*pars rationabilis*) and the deceased was able to dispose of the remaining third. This was confirmed by Magna Carta, 1225.[399]

A decisive change took place with the enactment of the Statute of Distributions (Ireland), 1695. Section 10 of the statute abolished the previous law and gave property owners total freedom to dispose of personalty. It was this provision which was castigated by the then Minister for Justice in introducing the

395 *Agnew v. Belfast Banking Co* [1896] 2 IR 204; *Re Dudman* [1925] 1 Ch. 553.

396 Criminal Law (Suicide) Act, 1993.

397 Wylie, *Irish Land Law* para. 15.10.

398 Wylie, *Irish Land Law* para. 15.03-4.

399 For Ireland and England.

Succession Act, 1965,[400] although his characterisation of freedom of testation as a peculiarly English phenomenon foisted on the Irish who were, impliedly, more caring and socially responsible, does not really accord with reality. The English had, after all, foisted a similar change on themselves, or, rather, the property owners who controlled Parliament had foisted the change on the rest of the population.

Personal property left by will, by contrast with real property, did not pass directly to the donee, but vested instead in the executors.

If the deceased did not make a will, personal property was still liable to pass to the Bishop. After the Reformation this meant the bishop of the established Church of Ireland, and so the rule in Ireland was a denial not only of the rights which the family otherwise enjoyed, as it was in England, but a denial also of the religious freedom of the deceased and his or her family. A will deprived the Bishop of the property, and apparently for this reason probate of a will was, until 1858, within the jurisdiction of the ecclesiastical court of the diocese. This jurisdiction was open to the objection that it involved a conflict of interest: the Church had an interest in the outcome of the case. "Probate" is an order of the court certifying that a will is valid. Probate jurisdiction was vested in a Court of Probate in 1858[401] and transferred to the High Court by the Judicature (Ireland) Act, 1877. The Circuit Court also has jurisdiction in some matters.[402]

On intestacy under the 1695 Act the widow took one third and the remainder went to the children or those representing them, such as grandchildren.[403] If there were no children, the widow took half, the rest going to those most closely related by blood.

Apart from some minor changes in 1890[404] the law remained unchanged in the Republic until the Intestates' Estates Act, 1954. Under that Act the widow became entitled to £4,000, or the whole estate if it were worth less than that figure, to be borne by both the real and personal property.

b) Realty

The feudal common law did not recognise that realty was devisable at all. The rules of descent, based on primogeniture, determined who would inherit the estate on the death of the present tenant. It has been seen that equity, through the means of uses, first permitted tenants to determine the destination of the estate after their death. Legal wills became possible after the Statute of Wills

400 Brady, *Succession* para. 7.02.

401 Probates and Letters of Administration Act (Ireland), 1857; Court of Probate Act (Ireland), 1859.

402 Succession Act, 1965 s.6.

403 Wylie, *Irish Land Law* para. 15.08.

404 Intestates' Estates Act, 1890.

(Ireland), 1634. The old rules then only applied if a tenant died without making a will or if the will, or part of it, failed.

Under the old rules realty passed directly to the heir-at-law. It continued to do so after the 1634 statute and even as to realty devised by will. At common law realty was not chargeable with the debts of the deceased, except for debts owed to the Crown and those which the deceased had specifically covenanted to bind the heirs as well as him or herself. This position was changed by the Administration of Estates Acts, 1833 and 1869 (Hinde Palmer's Act) which made realty generally available to pay debts.

(1) When The Old Rules Still Apply

Although in general the old rules of descent ceased to have effect from 1 January 1967, there are still some cases where they have to be applied. These are:

(a) Old Titles

It may be that when a piece of land is sold the vendor claims title as heir of a person who died intestate before 1967. In such a case the purchaser will have to ensure that the vendor is so entitled and in doing so will have to apply the old rules.

(b) Entails

The Succession Act, 1965 section 11(1) preserves the old rules in so far as they apply to fees tail.

(b) Heirs as Words of Purchase

The effect of the Succession Act, 1965 sections 15(2) is that if the words heir or heirs are used as words of purchase, then, as to "any. . . deed or instrument. . . executed" before 1967 the words have the same meaning as if the Act had not been passed.[405] The old rules therefore apply to such words used in wills executed before 1967, regardless of when the testator died.

Section 15(3) provides that, as to deeds or instruments executed after the Act came into force the words shall be construed to mean the intestate successors as now defined by Part VI of the Act "unless the contrary intention appears". The old rules will therefore still apply if there is such a contrary intention.

In these two instances the old rules still apply.

405 See Chapter 6 Fee Simple:Heirs as Words of Purchase.

(2) Fee Simple

The main rules of descent on intestacy before 1 January 1967 in the Republic as to fees simple were as follows.[406]

Rule (1) Descent Traced from Last Purchaser

Descent was traced at common law from the last person seised, but the technicalities of seisin were eliminated by the Inheritance Act, 1833, after which descent was traced from the last purchaser, *i.e.* the last person to acquire the land otherwise than by operation of law, *i.e.* otherwise than by descent, escheat, *etc.*[407] If the heirs of the last purchaser had died out the Law of Property Amendment Act, 1859[408] (Lord St Leonard's Act) allowed descent to be traced from the last person entitled as if he or she had been a purchaser.[409]

Rule (2) Males Preferred to Females

Males were preferred to females. The rules of descent were based on a patriarchal model of society. If X died intestate leaving a son and a daughter, the son inherited the real estate alone.

Rule (3) Primogeniture

Where there was more than one male of the same degree, *e.g.* brothers, the eldest male inherited realty alone. This was the rule of primogeniture, *i.e.* preference for the first born, but it applied only among males. Where there was no male, females inherited together as coparceners.

Rule (4) Representation

The doctrine of representation applied, whereby the lineal descendants of a person who, if they had lived, would have been heirs, represented that person.[410] Succession was *per stirpes*.[411] Thus, if X died intestate leaving daughters A and B, but had a daughter C who had died before X, the children of C, according to the preceding rules, would stand in place of C. If C had two sons, S1 and S2 and a daughter, D, the eldest son S1 would stand in place of C to the exclusion of S2 and D. S1 would represent C as coparcener with A and B. If,

---

406 The best modern discussion is in Cheshire, *Real Property* (9th ed.) 768-772. Cheshire's numbering of the rules follows Williams, *Real Property* and so does the discussion above.

407 1833 Act s.2.

408 Section 19.

409 This carried out the original proposal of the Real Property Commissioners in 1933.

410 *Valentine v. Fitzsimons* [1894] 1 IR 93, MR; *Blake v. Hynes* (1876) IR 10 Eq 419, MR, reversed (1882) 11 LR Ir 284, CA.

411 By the stock or family, *i.e.* the children divide their parent's share between them.

instead, C had two daughters, D1 and D2, they would take C's share together as coparceners. If Z, an intestate, had two sons, an elder son P and a younger son Q, and P had died before his father, P's eldest son would inherit as representing P.

Rule (5) Ancestors Took after Descendants

After 1833[412] ancestors or their representatives took after descendants. Ancestors were preferred to collaterals, *i.e.* brothers, first cousins, second cousins.[413] Thus the father of an intestate took in preference to a brother.

Rule (6) Paternal Ancestors Preferred to Maternal Ancestors

Paternal ancestors or their representatives were preferred to maternal ancestors.[414] This and the preceding two rules meant that if X died leaving a father, mother and brother the father took as the nearest male ancestor. If the father had predeceased X then the brother took as representing the father.

(a) Half Blood on the Male Side
Realty passed to blood relations of the deceased. After the Inheritance Act, 1833 relatives of the half-blood were admitted. Where the common ancestor was male (*i.e.* a man had married two wives) a relative of the half blood inherited after any relative of the whole blood in the same degree and his issue.[415] Suppose X died without descendants leaving a father F. F had married E and their children were X and X's sister. F later married A and they had a son John. X's sister, or her issue as representing her, took first, but if they failed, John took next. If Z died without descendants leaving a half-brother and cousin of the whole blood, after 1833 the half-brother inherited in preference to the cousin of the whole blood.

(b) Male Paternal Ancestors
If the intestate's father were dead and his issue either extinct or non-existent, then the inheritance went to the father's father and his representative issue, and so on to the father's father's father or his issue, up the paternal line.

(c) Female Paternal Ancestors
If there was no reasonable likelihood of ascertaining living descendants of male paternal ancestors[416] inheritance then went to female paternal ancestors or their representative descendants. In this instance the Inheritance Act, 1833 section 8 provided, oddly, that in tracing female paternal ancestors, recourse

412 Inheritance Act, 1833 ss. 6, 7.

413 This was only so after 1833: Williams, *Real Property* p.247.

414 Inheritance Act, 1833 ss. 7, 8.

415 Inheritance Act, 1833 s.9.

416 *Greaves v. Greenwood* (1877) 2 Ex D 289.

was first to be had to the mother of the remotest male paternal ancestor and her descendants.[417] Thus, if X's father, grandfather and great-grandfather were dead and their descendants extinct, the next person is the great-great-grandfather and descendants. If he or they were unknown, the next person was the mother of the great-grandfather. If there were no descendants, then one looked to the mother of the grandfather. If she and her descendants were dead then one looked to the mother and her descendants.

(d) Maternal Ancestors
If the mother and her descendants were all dead, then one had recourse to maternal ancestors, starting with the mother and working up the male and then down the female line, as in the case of the father.

(e) Half Blood on the Female Side
Where the person entitled to succeed was a female ancestor who was dead, the half blood took after the common ancestor.[418]

(3) Fee Tail

The rules of descent applied to entails with the following modifications:

(a) Descent from Donee
Descent of fee tail is traced from the original donee in tail.[419] This was a result of the statute *De Donis*, 1285.[420] If a grant is made "to X and the heirs of his/her body" anyone who takes by descent must answer that description.[421]

(b) Half Blood
Relatives of the half blood who were descendants of the original donee were always entitled to inherited entails, since the right to inherit was calculated by descent from the original donee, not by reference to the current tenant in tail or any other person.[422]

(c) Descendants Only
A fee tail passes to descendants only. Ancestors and collaterals are excluded.

(d) Males or Females May be Excluded
It has been seen that a fee tail may be created in various forms. A fee tail male excludes females from inheriting and a fee tail female excludes males. A fee

---

417 Cheshire, *Real Property* (9th ed.) p.770.

418 1833 Act s.9

419 *Doe d Gregory v. Wichelo* (1799) 8 TR 211, 101 ER 1350, Challis 244.

420 See Chapter 8 Fee Tail.

421 Williams, *Real Property* p.245.

422 *Doe d Gregory v. Wichelo* (1799) 8 TR 211, 101 ER 1350, per Lord Kenyon CJ, Challis 244.

tail special restricts inheritance to the descendants of the donee by a particular wife or husband. Other variations are also possible.[423]

(4) Escheat

If all these rules failed to produce anyone entitled to inherit, then before 1967 the freehold tenure came to an end by escheat and the land vested either in a mesne lord, if there was one, or in the Crown, or after 1922, in the State. This position was modified in the Republic by section 6 of the Intestates' Estates Act, 1954 which provided that if there were no other heirs a widow took in preference to escheat.

(5) Dower and Curtesy

It also has to be remembered that before 1967[424] a widow had the right of dower over one third of her deceased husband's land held for estates of inheritance and a widower had the right of curtesy over all his deceased wife's land similarly held.

2. Succession Act, 1965

Section 11 of the Succession Act, 1965 abolished "all existing rules, modes and canons of descent" including dower and curtesy, except in so far as they apply to a fee tail. The old rules were replaced with a new set of rules for determining inheritance of property. The new rules do not discriminate between real and personal property, or between male and female nor, since the Status of Children Act, 1987, between marital and non-marital children of the testator.[425] After payment of expenses, debts and liabilities and satisfying any legal right payable out of the estate, the property of the deceased is to be distributed in accordance with Part VI of the 1965 Act, the provisions of which are set out below.

a) Spouse and Issue

In the Republic where the intestate leaves a spouse but no issue surviving, the spouse is entitled to the whole estate.[426] If both spouse and issue survive the intestate, the spouse takes two-thirds of the estate and the rest is distributed among the issue.[427] Distribution among the issue is in equal shares, *i.e.* per capita, where they are of equal degree of relationship, otherwise it is *per*

423 See Chapter 8 Fee Tail.

424 Succession Act, 1965 s.11(2), see Chapter 9 Life Estates.

425 Succession Act, 1965, Pt VI; Wylie, *Irish Land Law* para. 15.16 intestate successors.

426 Succession Act, 1965 s.67(1).

427 *ibid.*, s.67(2).

stirpes.[428] If the intestate leaves issue but no surviving spouse, the issue take the whole estate, in equal shares if they are in equal degree of relationship, otherwise *per stirpes*.[429]

The law in Northern Ireland has been substantially affected by the Succession (Northern Ireland) Order 1996.[430] Under the Order the surviving spouse inherits on intestacy only if he or she survives the deceased by 28 days.[431] Subject to that, if there are issue, the surviving spouse takes the personal chattels[432] and the whole of the remaining estate where it does not exceed £125,000. If it does exceed this amount, the spouse takes, in addition to personal chattels, £125,000, plus one half of the residue where one child survives the intestate, or plus one third where more than one child survives.[433]

b) Per Stirpes

Section 3(3) of the Succession Act, 1965 defines *per stirpes* distribution as where "any issue more remote than a child of the deceased shall take through all degrees, according to their stocks, in equal shares if more than one, the share which the parent of such issue would have taken if living at the death of the deceased, and no issue of the deceased shall take if the parent of such issue is living at the death of the deceased and so capable of taking". In other words, the share of a child of the testator who predeceases the testator is shared equally among the children of that child, and similarly for later generations. *Per stirpes* is to be contrasted with *per capita* in which each member of a class takes an equal share. Thus, suppose an intestate, X, had three children, two sons, S1 and S2, and a daughter, D. X's spouse has predeceased him and so also have S1 and D. S1 leaves three children, GS1, GD1 and GD2. S2 is alive at X's death and has two children, GS2 and GD3. D leaves two children, GS3 and GD4. *Per stirpes* distribution is illustrated as follows:

428 *ibid.*, s.67(4).

429 *ibid.*, s.67(3).

430 SI 3163, NI 26.

431 *ibid.*, Art. 3(1) inserting s.6A in the 1955 Act.

432 Administration of Estates Act, 1955 s.7.

433 SI 3163, NI 26, Art. 7(2)(b).

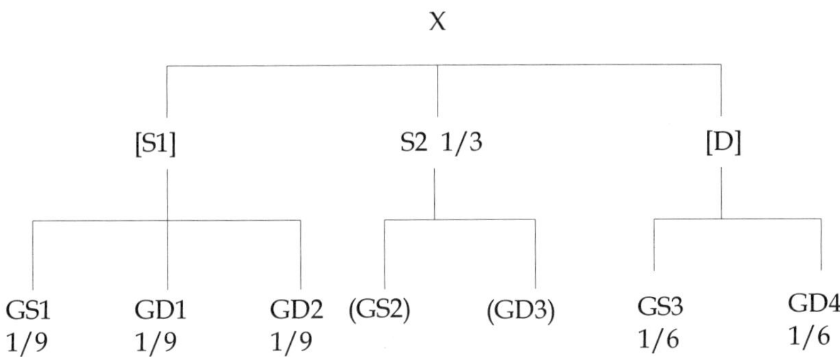

X's estate will be divided among his issue. The property is divided into three equal shares. These would have gone to S1, S2 and D if all three children had survived. However, S1 and D have both died before X and so their shares are further divided among their children in equal shares. S1 has three children and so S1's third share is divided again into three and the children each take 1/9th of the whole, while D has two children so D's 1/3rd share is further divided by only two, leaving each of her children with 1/6th of the whole. S2 is still alive at X's death and takes his share. His own children take nothing. They are irrelevant. The same result would obtain if S2 had no children.

If all the children of the intestate die before the intestate so that those due to inherit are all grandchildren of the intestate, then it would seem that they take *per capita*, since they are all, in terms of Section 67(3), in equal degree of relationship to the intestate. Thus, in the above example, if S1, S2 and D all died before the intestate, those due to take at the intestate's death are GS1, GD1, GD2, GS2, GD3, GS3, and GD4, all of whom are grandchildren. They are treated as a single class and distribution is made equally between them. This argument is reinforced by the consideration that this is what the Succession Act, 1965 itself prescribes in the situation, discussed below, namely where an intestate dies leaving neither spouse, issue nor parents, and brothers and sisters have all died leaving children. It seems that section 67(3) of the Succession Act, 1965 was intended to alter the position under the old law as to next-of-kin, in which distribution had been *per stirpes*, as decided in *Re Natt*.[434]

c) Non-Marital Children

Another discrimination made by the common law rules of descent was the exclusion of children born out of wedlock, or illegitimate children as they were

434 (1888) 37 Ch D 517; Megarry, *Manual* (3rd ed.) p.336.

then called. It was also clear from the provisions of the Succession Act, 1965 that the statute intended to discriminate against illegitimate children and that the word issue in the statute excluded such children, who were given only a limited right to inherit on intestacy from their mother, but not from their father.[435]

The discrimination in the Act was challenged in *O'B v. S*.[436] The plaintiff sister of the intestate applied for a grant of letters of administration of his estate. The application was opposed by the intestate's daughter, born out of wedlock, who claimed to be "issue" of the deceased within the Succession Act, 1965 and alternatively challenged the constitutionality of the Act if it were held to exclude non-marital children. Darcy J in the High Court held for the plaintiff and an appeal was taken to the Supreme Court.

The Supreme Court held that issue, especially in sections 67 and 69 of the Act, was intended to include only legitimate issue, since the Act, in section 110, provided separate succession rights for non-marital children. This view would seem to be in accordance with the intention of the legislature at the time of passing the Act. The court, however, held further that the provisions were constitutionally justified by Article 41 which declares the constitutional object of protecting the family. The judges in earlier cases had held family in Article 41 to mean the "family based upon marriage"[437] although marriage is only referred to in Article 41.3. It is difficult to accept Brady's comment that the legal conclusions in *O'B v. S* were "compelling and unavoidable".[438] The conclusions as to the intention of legislature at the time of the passing of the Succession Act, 1965 are certainly compelling, but the constitutional conclusions were certainly not so. The judges themselves have demonstrated the truth of this in holding that the constitutional protection of the family is now subject to "the exigencies of the common good", a phrase which does not occur in Article 41.[439] They have also held, when they felt called upon to do so, that Article 41 is an abstract statement of principle with few, if any, practical legal effects.[440] Moreover, it can be argued that the court in *O'B v. S* failed to take into account, in their reading of the Irish Constitution, of decisions of the European Court of Human Rights striking down similar discrimination against non-marital children. A more imaginative approach might have re-examined the "family based upon marriage" concept and examined the contradictions which it created. If

435 Section 110.

436 [1984] IR 316.

437 For example, *State (Nicolaou) v. An Bord Uchtála* [1966] IR 567. Kelly, *The Irish Constitution* (3rd ed.) pp. 997–98; Forde, *Constitutional Law* p.569 *et seq.*

438 Brady, *Succession* para. 8.19.

439 *Fajujonu v. Minister for Justice* [1990] 2 IR 151, [1990] ILRM 234.

440 *BL v. ML* [1992] 2 IR 77; sub nom *L v. L* [1992] ILRM 115, High Court, [1989] ILRM 528.

the protection of Article 41 is confined to families based upon marriage, then families not based upon marriage will be left without protection and subject to the whim of an irresponsible parent. The "family based on marriage" concept arguably makes marriage the the subject of protection of Article 41, not the family.

Whatever the rights and wrongs of *O'B v. S*, the result in the case was felt to be out of line with modern opinion and with the European Court of Human Rights. The Status of Children Act, 1987 inserted a new section 4A into the Succession Act, 1965 providing that in deducing any relationship for the purposes of the 1965 Act, the fact that a person's mother and father were or were not married to each other is not taken into account.[441] The constitutional issues raised in *O'B v. S* may yet have to be resolved since the 1987 Act could be challenged constitutionally by marital children or those claiming through them as a infringement of Article 41.

d) Child in the Womb

Descendants and relatives of an intestate conceived before his death, but not born until after it, now inherit as if they had been born in the deceased's lifetime and had survived the deceased.[442]

e) Half Blood

Descendants and relatives of the half blood are to be treated as, and inherit equally with, relatives of the whole blood of the same degree.[443]

f) Parents

Where the intestate dies leaving neither spouse nor issue, inheritance then passes to the parents, in equal shares if both are still alive.[444] If one survives the intestate, that parent takes the whole estate.[445]

g) Brothers, Sisters and their Issue

If the intestate dies leaving neither spouse, issue nor parents, inheritance now passes to the brothers and sisters of the intestate in equal shares.[446] If a brother or sister has predeceased the intestate, while other brothers or sisters survive,

441 Status of Children Act, 1987 s.3, and ss. 27, 29 adding s.4A to the Succession Act, 1965 and amending s.3. See also Children (Northern Ireland) Order 1995 (SI 755, NI 2) Art. 155–57.

442 Succession Act, 1965 s.3(2); Northern Ireland, 1955 Act, s.13.

443 *ibid.* s.72; Northern Ireland, 1955 Act , s.14.

444 *ibid.* s.68.

445 *ibid.*

446 *ibid.* s.69(1).

the children of the deceased brother or sister take their parent's share under the principle of representation.[447]

Representation of brothers and sisters is confined in the Republic to children and does not extend to other surviving issue such as grandchildren.[448] The children take the share *per stirpes*.

If no brother or sister survives the intestate the estate is distributed among the children of the brothers and sisters.[449] In this case, they take the estate in equal shares and not *per stirpes*.[450] The reason seems to be is that where there are no surviving brothers or sisters their children take as a distinct class whose members therefore take equal shares.

h) Next of Kin

If the intestate dies leaving neither spouse, issue, parents, brothers, sisters nor children[451] of brothers and sisters, then in the Republic inheritance passes to next-of-kin in equal shares.[452] The Succession Act, 1965 replaces the common law definition of next-of-kin with a new one. Next-of-kin in the Succession Act, 1965 section 71(1) is defined as "the person or persons who, at the date of death of the intestate, stand nearest in blood relationship to him" or her, and nearest is now defined by section 71(2) which provides that:

> "Degrees of blood relationship of a direct lineal ancestor shall be computed by counting upwards from the intestate to that ancestor, and degrees of blood relationship of any other relative shall be ascertained by counting upwards from the intestate to the nearest ancestor common to the intestate and that relative, and then downward from that ancestor to the relative; but, where a direct lineal ancestor and any other relative are so ascertained to be within the same degree of blood relationship to the intestate, the other relative shall be preferred to the exclusion of the direct lineal ancestor".

Representation does not apply among collateral next-of-kin.[453]

The effect of the above rules would be as follows. If an intestate, N, dies leaving only an uncle and a grandfather, the grandfather will take to the exclusion of the uncle. Counting up to the grandfather gives two as the degree of relationship, whereas to reach the uncle one must count up from N to N's father,

447 *ibid.*

448 *ibid.* s.69(2); contrast Northern Ireland, 1955 Act s.10(1).

449 *ibid.* s.69(2).

450 *ibid.*

451 NB The principle of representation does not extend in the Republic to remoter issue of brothers and sisters. See footnote 449.

452 Succession Act, 1965 s.70(1).

453 It has been seen that where some brothers and sisters predecease the intestate while others survive, the children of those who predecease represent their parents, but brothers and sisters are not next-of-kin in the strict sense used in the Succession Act, 1965. They take before resort is made to next-of-kin rules.

then the grandfather GF (as common ancestor) and down again to the uncle making a degree of relationship of three. In this case the degree of relationship is unequal and the grandfather, as nearest relative, takes to the exclusion of the uncle, who is more remote. Where, on the other hand, the relationship is equal, the above rule prefers the younger generation, so that as between uncles and aunts and great-grandparents, who are all three degrees remote from N, the uncles and aunts are preferred. The following diagram may be useful in following these points:

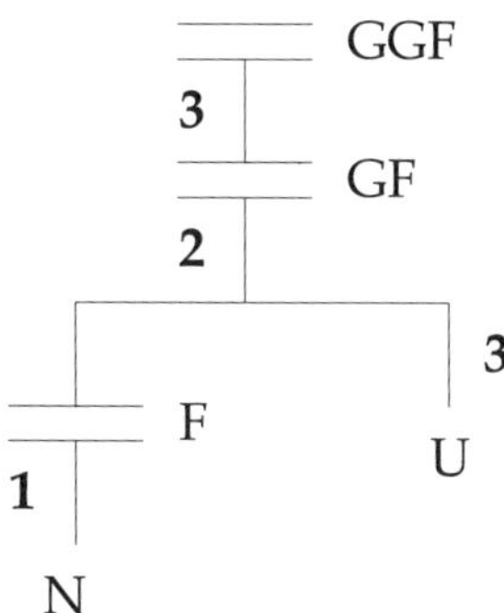

i) State as Ultimate Intestate Successor

In default of next-of-kin the inheritance passes to the State in the Republic as ultimate intestate successor under section 73(1) of the Succession Act, 1965. This replaces the feudal law of escheat in the case of real property, and the principle of *bona vacantia* in the case of personal property when owned by natural persons. Where property is owned by corporations or limited companies there is a survival of these doctrines, but the effect is similarly to vest the property in the State.[454]

j) Court's Discretion on Intestacy

An attempt was made by Deputy Harney during the passage of the Status of Children Bill to amend section 117 of the Succession Act, 1965 by including within the meaning of testator in that section any person dying intestate after the coming into effect of Part V of the Status of Children Act, 1987. Although it would have given a highly artificial meaning to the word, the idea was to give a discretion to the court in cases of intestacy to adjust the shares of children of the deceased in the same way that they now may do so in cases of testacy. The idea behind the proposal was that the rules of intestacy may be too rigid and may require adjustment in individual cases, bearing in mind the provision made by the intestate during his or her life for other children, *etc.* The

454 See Chapter 3 Tenure.

Government did not adopt the amendment and it failed, the Minister commenting that in any case that "the rules of distribution on intestacy guarantee a fair and suitable share to each child where no will has been made".[455] Not everyone would agree with this view. Nevertheless the effect of the rules of intestacy may be modified in other ways.

(1) Disinheritance

We have seen that section 121 of the Succession Act, 1965 controls attempts to disinherit and that it applies in cases of intestacy.

(2) Advancement and Hotch-Pot

Section 63 of the Succession Act, 1965 gives a limited exception to the rules by providing that an advancement made to a child of the intestate shall, subject to a contrary intention expressed by the deceased or to be inferred from the circumstances, be taken into account in determining that child's share of the estate. The section gives statutory form to the doctrine of "hotchpot" developed by courts of equity before the Act.[456] "Child" includes a person to whom the deceased was *in loco parentis*.[457] A child must bring advancements into account even in cases of partial intestacy,[458] but the principle does not apply to brothers or sisters or more remote descendants or relatives, unless the intestate stood *in loco parentis* to them. The principle was described by Lord Eldon as harsh for this reason.[459]

Advancement is given a statutory definition by section 63(6) of the Succession Act, 1965 as:

> ". . . a gift intended to make permanent provision for a child and includes advancement by way of portion or settlement, including any life or lesser interest and including property covenanted to be paid or settled. It also includes an advance or portion for the purpose of establishing a child in a profession, vocation, trade or business, a marriage portion and payments made for the education of a child to a standard higher than that provided by the deceased for any other or others of his children".

An advancement is deemed to be part of the deceased's estate and its value is that at the time of the advancement.[460] The value of the advancement is therefore added to the value of the estate at the deceased's death and the total divided into the number of shares. If the advancement is equal to or greater than the value of the share which the child is entitled to receive, the child takes

455 Dáil Debates, 28 October 1987, col 1695; Brady, *Succession* para. 8.

456 *Noblett v. Litchfield* (1858) 7 Ir Ch R 575; *Re Tyrell* [1894] 1 IR 267, V-C.

457 Succession Act, 1965 s.63(10).

458 *ibid.*, s.74.

459 *Ex parte Pye* (1811) 18 Ves Jun 140, at 151, 34 ER 271 at 275.

460 *ibid.*, s.63(2); Northern Ireland, 1955 Act, s.17.

nothing on distribution of the estate.[461] If it is less than the child's share on intestacy, the child is entitled only to the balance of the share left after deducting the amount of the advancement.[462] If the advancement is greater than the child's share on intestacy, the child is not a debtor to the estate of the balance in excess of the share, unless the advancement amounts, under section 121, to an attempt by the intestate to disinherit another potential beneficiary.

(3) Proprietary Estoppel

Nevertheless, the courts are adept at finding their way around unavoidable results. An English court in *Re Basham*[463] found a way, via proprietary estoppel, of readjusting property interests in a deserving case where the deceased had died intestate and had not provided for his daughter in the way he had led her to expect.

k) Partial Intestacy

A partial intestacy occurs where a person leaves a will which disposes of only part of their estate. This may occur for various reasons: the testator may have forgotten that he or she owned some property, or it may be that because of one of the rules already discussed, such as the perpetuity rule, a gift in the will is void and there is no residuary legatee, or only a legatee of part of the residue. In such a case section 74 of the Succession Act, 1965 provides that "the remainder shall be distributed as if he had died intestate and left no other estate".[464]

461 *ibid.*, s.63(3); Northern Ireland, 1955 Act s.17(1).

462 *ibid.*, s.63(5); Northern Ireland, 1955 Act s.17(1).

463 [1986] 1 WLR 1498, see above.

464 Repeating the provision in the Executors Act, 1830, as the marginal note to s.74 makes clear.

CHAPTER 27

PLANNING LAW

A. Introduction

Planning law consists of those laws which confer on planning authorities powers and obligations to control the use of land and the environment. The principal Act in the Republic is the Local Government (Planning and Development) Act, 1963. It is beyond the scope of this book to deal with planning law in detail, but since planning law both expresses a form of community or social property and limits the extent of private property, some account of it is both necessary and relevant. What follows is a general introduction.[1] At the time of writing the Planning and Development Bill, 1999 (the 1999 Bill) has not yet become law. It proposes to replace and consolidate existing legislation, including much of the European Communities (Environmental Impact Assessment) Regulations 1989 to 1999, as well as make certain changes to planning law. The more significant changes are noted in the text which follows. References are to the Bill as initiated.

Planning law can be seen as an attempt on the part of the community, or communities, to take control of the development of land rather than leaving it to private individuals or companies, and so as an attempt to produce a more coherent form of development which reconciles, through democratic institutions, the various needs of housing with public health, the preservation of the environment and the historic heritage, *etc.* In so far as this is so, planning law expresses a new kind of property in land. We have referred to this as communal property.

Nevertheless, this is both an idealised and a partial picture of planning law. The necessity to pay compensation for refusal of planning permission, where it is required, often imposes a severe limitation on the ability of the planning authority to exercise control over private development, although this has now been mitigated.[2] The larger developer often appears to have an advantage in practice for this and other reasons. It can be argued that it is too easy to re-zone areas and that this favours the large developer at the expense of local residents. The issue of compensation raises fundamental questions about the nature of property rights. Should private property rights be regarded as primary, so that

1 Those who wish to pursue the subject further may refer to O'Sullivan and Shepherd, *A Sourcebook on Planning Law in Ireland*. References in the text are to the first edition unless otherwise indicated.

2 See the Local Government (Planning and Development) Act, 1990.

planning powers would then be regarded as a detraction, so far as a given plot of land is concerned, from the rights of a private owner? If so, it would seem to follow that compensation should be paid for the loss of whatever profit would have been derived from the exercise of these primary private rights? Let us assume, for the sake of argument, that some such planning powers have always existed. If the right to compensation is asserted in such a case, then it is because the full right of a private property owner is assumed to have some natural law existence, or some reality other than in the actual legal system. Are some private uses of land regarded as primary in the sense of what has been termed substantive due process, in that they cannot be taken away, even with compensation? Or should the ultimate form of property be regarded as communal, so that the health and well-being of the community is regarded as the primary position and private property rights regarded as an exception or detraction from such rights, or as taking effect subject to them? Even if this is so, it can be argued that this merely justifies the taking away of private property for certain purposes, but does not justify imposing the cost on the private owner, so that, through compensation, the cost of giving effect to communal provision is spread throughout the community. Again, does this type of consideration apply to some communal rights but not others? If a landowner finds that his or her right to use land is restricted because an archaeological site is discovered on it, does that require compensation or not? These and similar questions recur again and again and form the fundamental issues in specific planning problems.

The increasing awareness of environmental issues has had its effect on planning law. McCarthy J in *The Attorney General (McGarry) v. Sligo County Council*[3] referred to a development plan as an environmental contract. In architecture there is a greater awareness of the dangers of wholesale destruction of existing communities under the name of modernisation.[4] One consequence of these cultural developments may be that the simple dichotomy between public and private rights, between private property and public interest, may come increasingly to be seen as crude and insensitive. In *Central Dublin Development Association Ltd v. The Attorney General*[5] Kenny J upheld the constitutionality of the planning laws. They had been challenged by local shop owners whose properties were to be acquired as part of a plan to renew an obsolete area. The judge held that the acquisition of the private rights was justified by the compensating benefit of the scheme to the community. A more sensitive approach to the concept of community might, on the other hand, have seen the incorporation of the existing shop owners and their businesses into the

3 Unreported, Supreme Court, 17 February 1989 (McCarthy J, Walsh and Hederman JJ concurring) per McCarthy J.

4 D. Harvey, *The Condition of Postmodernity: An Inquiry into the Origins of Cultural Change* (Oxford: Blackwell 1989).

5 (1969) 109 ILTR 69.

scheme as not only desirable but essential both in an architectural sense and in a legal sense.

B. Planning Authorities

1. Meaning

A "planning authority" is defined by section 2(2) of the Local Government (Planning and Development) Act, 1963 (the 1963 Act) as certain kinds of local authorities, namely, a county council, the corporation of a county borough or other borough, or an urban district council. It follows that not all local authorities are planning authorities and those that are not have to apply for planning permission to the planning authority in their area. Nevertheless although the local authorities mentioned are planning authorities and planning authorities are necessarily local authorities, the powers of the two types of body are not identical. The 1963 Act, for example, does not confer compulsory purchase powers on planning authorities[6] although it was held by McWilliam J in *Leinster Importing Co Ltd v. Dublin County Council*[7] that a planning authority may acquire land compulsorily under section 10 of the Local Government (Ireland) Act, 1898[8] pursuant to its general obligation under the Planning Acts, for the purpose, in the context of the case, of providing recreational open space and playing fields.

2. Functions

Planning authorities have the following functions:

(1) to prepare and revise a development plan;

(2) to grant or refuse planning permission to individuals who apply for permission to change the use of their land, where required;

(3) to enforce the need for planning permission where it is required, decisions on planning permission and compliance with conditions imposed on granting planning permission;

(4) to protect certain amenities outside the scope of the development plan; and

---

6 *Movie News Ltd v. Galway County Council*, unreported, High Court, Kenny J, 30 March 1975. It was accepted by the defendant in the case that s.10 of the Local Government (No. 2) Act, 1960 as substituted by s.86 of the Housing Act, 1966 did not confer compulsory purchase powers for the purposes of the 1963 Act; See O'Sullivan and Shepherd p.43; McDermott & Woulfe p.52.

7 Unreported, High Court, McWilliam J, 26 January 1977.

8 As amended by s.11 of the Local Government (No. 2) Act, 1960 and Housing Act, 1966 s.87.

(5) to develop community facilities.

C. The Development Plan

Planning authorities must draw up a development plan of their area. The development plan consists of a statement of objectives and a map.[9] The Planning Acts[10] lay down certain objectives which must be included in the plan.[11] The planning authority may also include other objectives which are not compulsory.[12] Once the plan is implemented it is binding on the planning authority itself although this principle has been modified.[13] At present, there is no time specified within which a plan must be made, but the 1999 Bill imposes a duty on planning authorities to make one every six years.[14] The plan must be reviewed at least every five years.[15] The 1999 Bill proposes to reduce this to four years. The planning authority may make variations to the plan or make a new plan.[16]

1. Variations

Section 21 of the 1963 Act[17] lays down the procedure for adopting variations to the development plan. A notice must be published stating that a copy of the proposed variation can be inspected at a stated places and times. Objections lodged within the required time must be taken into account in making the final version of the variation.

In *Finn v. Bray UDC*[18] Butler J held that if a draft revision of the development plan was varied after objections by members of the public, the whole stat-

9 1963 Act, s.19(2), as am. Local Government (Planning and Development) Act, 1999 s.33.

10 The principal Acts are the Local Government (Planning and Development) Acts, 1963, 1976, 1982, 1983, 1990, 1992. These have now been amended by the European Communities (Environmental Impact Assessment) Regulations, 1989, SI No. 349 of 1989 and the European Communities (Environmental Impact Assessment) (Amendment) Regulations, 1994, SI No. 84 of 1994 under the authority of the European Communities Act, 1972.

11 *ibid.*

12 1963 Act, s.19(3) and 3rd Schedule.

13 1963 Act, s.26(1), s.26(3) as substituted by s.39 of 1976 Act. See below.

14 Clause 9.

15 1963 Act, s.20. *Blessington Heritage Trust Limited v. Wicklow County Council*, unreported, High Court, McGuinness J 21 January 1998, .

16 *ibid.*. *Huntsgrove Ltd v. Meath County Council* [1994] 2 ILRM 36, High Court.

17 As amended by s.43(1)(g) of the 1976 Act. The revised section is reproduced in O'Sullivan and Shepherd p.15.

18 [1974] IR 169.

utory process of inviting objections had to be gone through again in relation to any new version of the draft revision. The effect of the decision was to make planning authorities reluctant to incorporate any objections into a draft revision, or a draft plan, since to do so could result in a potentially endless process. The new section 21A of the 1963 Act inserted by section 37 of the 1976 Act now largely avoids this problem by providing that variations to draft plans or revisions may be made without inviting representations unless they would, if made, be a material alteration. Where the variation would constitute a material alteration, representations must be invited, but the planning authority may thereafter make the plan or variation with or without the amendments, or incorporating new amendments (other than those concerned with preserving buildings or with public rights of way), which do not have to go through the same process.

2. Policy Directives

The Minister for the Environment may issue directives as to policy on planning and development and planning authorities must now have regard to such directives.[19] A directive in 1982 concerned new shopping areas and required consideration by the planning authority of the implications for existing communities, for employment and countering urban decline and for the elderly, infirm or disabled who might be dependent on existing shops. A Memorandum was issued by the Department of the Environment in 1982 setting out general guidelines for planning authorities.[20]

3. Binding Nature of The Plan

Section 26(3)(a)[21] of the 1963 Act did not permit a planning authority to grant planning permission which would materially contravene the development plan, except with the consent of the Minister. In *State (Pine Valley Developments Ltd) v. Dublin County Council*[22] the Supreme Court held that the Minister had no jurisdiction to give consent unless requested to do so by the planning authority. This had the unfortunate result of invalidating a number of planning permissions which had already been acted upon by the applicants. Section 6 of the 1982 Act retrieved the situation by retrospectively validating this category of permissions.

The 1976 Act substituted a new section 26(3) which now provides that the planning authority may grant a permission which materially contravenes the development plan provided they publish a notice of their intention to do so in a

19 1982 Act, s.7; SI No. 264 of 1982. O'Sullivan and Shepherd pp. 33, 487, 537.

20 The Memorandum is set out in O'Sullivan and Shepherd Appendix A.

21 Now amended by s.39(d) of the 1976 Act.

22 [1982] ILRM 196.

daily newspaper circulating in the area, that copies of the notice are given to the applicant and any person submitting an objection in writing, that any objection or representation received within 21 days after publication of the notice is considered and the proposal is approved by a resolution of the planning authority requiring the permission to be granted. Such a resolution must be passed by three quarters of the total number of elected representatives.[23]

4. Compulsory Objectives

The 1963 Act[24] requires the development plan to include the following:

a) Zoning

A compulsory element in development plans is the zoning of areas for use solely or primarily for particular uses, *i.e.* as residential, commercial, industrial, agricultural or otherwise.[25] This is the heart of the planning mechanism.

b) Roads and Parking

Other compulsory objectives are the greater convenience and safety of road users and pedestrians, by the provision of parking places, road improvements, *etc.* For these purposes a local authority is now a road authority under the Roads Act, 1993.[26]

c) Caravan and Halting Sites

The Housing (Traveller Accommodation) Act, 1998, makes the provision of accommodation for travellers a compulsory objective.[27] This is repeated in the 1999 Bill.[28] Halting sites are nevertheless subject to the notice and consulta-

---

23 Section 45 Local Government Act, 1991. There are further provisions where a "section 4" motion (a motion under s.4 of the City and County (Amendment) Act, 1955) is passed directing the manager to grant permission in a case where the manager considers it to be in contravention of the plan.

24 1963 Act, s.19(2), as am. European Communities (Natural Habitats) Regulations, 1997, SI No. 94 of 1997; Local Government (Planning and Development) Act, 1999.

25 1963 Act, s.19(2)(a).

26 Section 2. Roads Act, 1993 (Commencement) Order I993, SI No. 197 of 1993.

27 1963 Act s.19 as am. Housing (Traveller Accommodation) Act, 1998 s.26. Commencement: SI No. 328 of 1998; SI No. 428 of 1998; SI No. 448 of 1998; SI No. 37 of 2000. The provision of halting sites had been challenged as a contravention of plan in *O'Leary v. Dublin County Council*, unreported, High Court, O'Hanlon J, 16 May 1988 discussed in the first edition of this work.

28 Clause 10(2).

tion procedure under Part X of the 1994 Regulations.[29]

The 1963 Act included within "material change of use" the storing or keeping of caravans on land.[30] The 1994 Regulations now include within "exempted development" the parking of a caravan in the "curtilage of a dwelling", but on condition there is not more than one caravan and provided it is not used for residential purposes, except in rural areas where it may be occupied for not more than 10 days. [31]

d) Urban and Rural Areas

Objectives for urban areas include the development and renewal of obsolete (*i.e.* derelict)[32] areas, and extending amenities.[33]

Additional objectives in rural areas include the renewal of obsolete areas, extending amenities and the provision of water and sewerage services.[34]

The 1999 Bill makes no distinction between urban and rural authorities in relation to objectives.[35]

e) Protected Structures

Provisions now require the preservation of structures of artistic, architectural or historical, archaeological, artistic, cultural, scientific, social or technical interest.[36] The development plan must include a record of protected structures.[37] A notice must be to be served on the owner and occupier of a structure proposed to be preserved.[38] Owners are under a duty to ensure that they are not endangered[39] and planning authorities have power to require works to be carried out to preserve protected structures.[40] The Minister may issue guidelines to planning authorities including the criteria to be applied when selecting struc-

---

29 SI No. 86 of 1994, as am. SI No. 69 of 1995 and SI No. 124 of 1998.

30 Section 3 of the 1963 Act. See "Material Change of Use".

31 SI No. 86 of 1994, second schedule, Part I, Class 18, Part III, Class 1.

32 See also the Derelict Sites Act, 1990. The powers under the Act are vested in local authorities, not planning authorities.

33 *ibid.*.

34 1963 Act s.19(2)(b).

35 Clause 10(2).

36 1963 Act s.19(2)(vii), as inserted by the Local Government (Planning and Development) Act, 1999 s.33; Local Government (Planning and Development) (No. 2) Regulations, 1999 (SI No. 431 of 1999). The Act and the regulations came into effect on 1 January 2000.

37 1999 Act, s.2.

38 1963 Act s.21(1)(c) as substituted by the Local Government (Planning and Development), Act, 1999 s 34.

39 1999 Act, s.9.

40 *ibid.* s.10.

tures for the record.[41] These provisions are consolidated in Part IV of the 1999 Bill. A National Inventory of Architectural Heritage has been established[42] which may be used by the Minister to make recommendations to planning authorities as to specific structures.[43]

f) Other Objectives

The 1999 Bill sets out further compulsory objectives including conservation and protection of the environment, the conservation and protection of European sites, and the preservation of architectural conservation areas.

5. Optional Objectives

The 1963 Act[44] also lists objectives which may be included in a development plan, such as:

(1) establishing, extinguishing[45], or preserving[46] public rights of way and extinguishing private rights of way. Where in future a planning authority proposes for the first time to include a proposal to preserve a public right of way the 1999 Bill requires it to give notice to the owner of the land over which it exists;

(2) the construction of new roads[47], bridges, *etc.*, and alteration of existing ones;

(3) the laying down of building regulations specifying, for example, the minimum size of rooms in new houses, and the materials to be used in new structures, and removing or altering structures inconsistent with the development plan;

(4) community planning, such as regulating density, spacing and grouping of structures, the provision and siting of schools, churches and other community facilities;

(5) reserving land for public parks, burial grounds, game and bird sanctuaries;

(6) preserving sites of archaeological, historical, or geographical interest;

(7) preserving views or other features of natural beauty or interest;

---

41 *ibid.* s.3.

42 Architectural Heritage (National Inventory) and Historic Monuments (Miscellaneous Provisions) Act, 1999 s.2.

43 Local Government (Planning and Development) Act, 1999 s.4.

44 1963 Act, s.19(3) & 3rd Schedule.

45 See now Roads Act, 1993 s.73, SI No. 197 of 1993.

46 See Local Government (Planning and Development) Act, 1990 s.12 and Fourth Schedule para. 23.

47 *ibid.* The planning of national roads is the responsibility of the National Roads Authority established by the Roads Act, 1993, P. III.

(8) preserving woods, trees, shrubs plants and flowers;

(9) controlling advertising hoardings, *etc.*; and

(10) controlling waste disposal.

Additional objectives are set out in the first schedule to the 1999 Bill, including prohibiting or restricting, temporarily or permanently, the development of certain land, and the protection of the linguistic and cultural heritage of the Gaeltacht.

6. Local Area Plans

The 1999 Bill introduces local area plans, which a planning authority may make in relation to any part of its functional area.[48] Under the Bill, such a plan must be made as to an area designated as a town in the most recent census. More than one planning authority will be able to co-operate in the making of such a plan.

7. Regional Planning Guidelines

Under the 1999 Bill regional authorities may introduce regional planning guidelines and will be obliged to do so where the Minister directs.[49]

D. Other Powers

1. Special Amenity Area Orders

Section 42 of the 1963 Act empowers a planning authority to make a "special amenity area order" the purpose of which is to preserve the special features of an area of outstanding natural beauty, or of "special recreational value" or which needs nature conservation. A special amenity area order must be confirmed by the Minister.[50]

Where a special amenity area order is in force, a planning authority can make a further order, called a "conservation order", to preserve flora or fauna within the area.[51]

The existence of a special amenity area order also means that certain developments which were exempted cease to be exempted. For example, mining is exempted development, because there is a separate system of licensing, but if a

48 Clauses 18 to 20.

49 Clause 21.

50 See, for example, the Dublin County Council (Lucan Bridge to Palmerstown) Special Amenity Area Order (Confirmation) Order, 1990, SI No. 59 of 1990.

51 1963 Act, s.46, subss. (1) substituted by s.40(b) of the 1976 Act. Section 45 of the 1976 Act repealed subss. (2), (7) and (10.)

special amenity area order is in force, it will no longer be exempted and the developer will have to seek planning permission. One effect of this now is that an environmental impact statement will have to be provided and considered by the planning authority before a decision is made.

A further effect of a special amenity order is that when planning permission is refused on the ground that the land is within an area subject to such an order, no compensation is payable.[52]

2. Trees, Woodlands, Plants, Hedges

It is an offence to uproot or cut down a tree over 10 years old without giving notice to the Gardaí[53] and a prohibition order may be issued by the Minister.[54] Section 45 of the 1963 Act gives power to planning authorities to make orders protecting specified trees,[55] or woodland,[56] hedges[57] and plants.[58] Unlike section 46, section 45 does not require a special amenity area order to be in force before the power in the section can be exercised. Where trees are protected under the section the order may prohibit their being cut down, or lopped, *etc.*, without the consent of the planning authority.[59]

3. Appropriation and Disposal of Land

Where land is vested[60] in a planning authority for some purpose other than those in the 1963 Act, section 74 of the Act empowers the planning authority, with the consent of the Minister, to appropriate the land to any of those purposes. The power does not include the power of compulsory purchase[61] although, as it

52 The 1963 Act s.56(1)(h) as amended by the 1976 Act s.45.

53 Forestry Act, 1946 s.37. There are exemptions: s.37(4), *e.g.* a tree standing within one hundred feet of any building other than a wall or temporary structure, trees to be cut down or uprooted by a local authority for road widening.

54 *ibid.* s.39.

55 1963 Act, s.45; note that s.77 refers to a tree preservation order; Local Government (Planning and Development) Act, 1990 s.21 (compensation).

56 *ibid.*

57 1963 Act, s.44; 1990 Act s.20.

58 See Part V of 1963 Act.

59 1963 Act, s.45(1)(a).

60 The 1963 Act contains no power of compulsory purchase.

61 *Movie News Ltd v. Galway County Council,* unreported, High Court, Kenny J, 30 March 1975. It was accepted by the defendant in the case that s.10 of the Local Government (No. 2) Act, 1960 as substituted by s.86 of the Housing Act, 1966 did not confer compulsory purchase powers for the purposes of the 1963 Act; O'Sullivan and Shepherd p.43. If so, this nevertheless seems to make nonsense of s.74(4) of the 1963 Act which assumes that a planning authority has such powers by virtue of s.10 of the 1960 Act. See Planning Authorities: Meaning.

has been noted above, it was held by McWilliam J in *Leinster Importing Co Ltd v. Dublin County Council*[62] that a planning authority may acquire land compulsorily under section 10 of the Local Government (Ireland) Act, 1898 as amended by section 11 of the Local Government (No. 2) Act, 1960.

4. Development of Land

Section 77 of the 1963 Act gives power to planning authorities to develop land, particularly public roads, by widening them, *etc.*, and land in the vicinity of roads and bridges, *etc.*.

5. Views, Ecological, Archaeological Areas

Section 77 also empowers planning authorities to preserve "any view or prospect, any structure or natural physical feature [of land]" and "any site of geological, ecological or archaeological interest". These powers appear to be additional to the powers in relation to special amenity area orders under section 42 of the 1963 Act.

6. Public Rights of Way

Planning authorities may both create[63] and extinguish[64] public rights of way and may require their preservation by planning conditions, in some cases without compensation.[65] Where a public right of way exists, a road authority may declare the road over which it exists to be a public road, and the road authority then becomes responsible for its maintenance.[66]

7. Agreements

Section 38[67] of the 1963 Act provides that a planning authority may enter into an agreement with any person interested in land restricting or regulating the development or use of the land, either permanently or for a period specified in the agreement. Subsection (2) continues:

> "An agreement under this section . . . may be enforced by the planning authority or any body joined with them against persons deriving title under that person in respect of that land as if the planning authority or such body. . . were possessed of adjacent land and as if the agreement had been expressed to be made for the benefit of the land."

---

62 Unreported, High Court, McWilliam J, 26 January 1977.

63 1963 Act, s.48.

64 Roads Act, 1993, s.73; SI No. 197 of 1993.

65 Local Government (Planning and Development) Act, 1990 s.12 and Fourth Schedule para. 23.

66 Roads Act, 1993, s.11.

67 As amended by s.39(j) the 1976 Act.

The section is interesting in that it suggests an analogy between such agreements and easements or restrictive covenants and probably creates a statutory form of property similar to them.

One problem that might arise in relation to such agreements is as follows. X applies for planning permission. The planning authority proposes that X enters into an agreement restricting the use of the land and it is clear to X that planning permission will not be granted unless X enters into the agreement. Does this vitiate the agreement? Section 28(6) suggests that it does not, for it provides that where a condition is imposed as to the use of a dwelling house by "persons of a particular class or description" the condition "shall be embodied in an agreement pursuant to section 38". Section 38 therefore does not seem to use agreement in the normal sense of a voluntary contract. The applicant would often have the limited choice of accepting the planning permission subject to the agreement or not obtaining planning permission at all. However, this may be balanced by the courts having a greater scope to strike down agreements as being unreasonable, *etc.* under section 38.[68]

8. Miscellaneous Powers

Planning authorities also have powers to control noise, litter and advertisements.[69] They may also encourage tourist and planning studies,[70] enter land to carry out their other functions,[71] may enter into agreements over specific land[72] and may require members of the public to provide them with information regarding interests in land, *etc.*.[73]

E. The Register

Under section 8 of the 1963 Act planning authorities are required to maintain a register which records planning information, including planning permissions granted and conditions attached to them.

In *Readymix Eire Ltd v. Dublin County Council*[74] Henchy J described planning permission as "an appendage to the title to the property". He went on:

68 See Conditions below.

69 See Part V of 1963 Act.

70 1963 Act, s.15.

71 1963 Act, s.83.

72 1963 Act, s.38.

73 1963 Act, s.9.

74 Unreported, Supreme Court, 30 July 1974, cited with approval in *Dublin County Council v. Jack Barrett Ltd* unreported, Supreme Court, 28 July 1983.

> "When a permission issues in a case such as this, it enures to the benefit not alone of the person to whom it issues but also for the benefit of any one who acquires an interest in the property: section 28(5)[of the Local Government (Planning and Development) Act, 1963]. A proper record of the permission is therefore necessary. This is provided for by section 8, which prescribed that a planning authority shall keep a register of all land in their area affected by the Act. This register is the statutorily designated source of authoritative information as to what is covered by the permission. The Act does not in terms make the register the conclusive or exclusive record of the nature and extent of a permission, but the scheme of the Act indicates that anybody who acts on the basis of the correctness of the particulars in the register is entitled to do so. . ."

These registers are quite distinct from the Register of Title under the Registration of Title Act, 1964. The Register of Title is a register of property interests. The registers maintained by planning authorities under section 8 of the 1963 Act, on the other hand, record only planning permissions and conditions attached to them, neither of which are traditionally regarded as property interests, but a planning permission has been described by Henchy J as an appendage to the title[75] and conditions may impose burdens on the land similar in some ways to restrictive covenants whose function for some purposes they have replaced.

F. Constitutionality of the Planning Acts

In *Central Dublin Development Association Ltd v. The Attorney General*[76] several sections of the 1963 Act were challenged on constitutional grounds. It was argued that sections 19, 20 and 21 of the 1963 Act were unconstitutional on the ground that if a planning authority were to make and review development plans then private property could be devalued as a result and this would amount to an unjust attack on property rights contrary to Article 40.3.2°. While Kenny J accepted that property values might be affected, he rejected the argument that the provisions were unconstitutional. He commented:

> "If this argument were correct, many owners of houses would have been entitled to be paid compensation when the Rent Restriction Act, 1946 was passed."

The judge had also commented earlier in his judgment that no one had suggested that the Rent Restriction Acts or the Landlord and Tenant Acts were unconstitutional. This turned out to be a hostage to fortune. In *Blake v. The Attorney General*[77] the Supreme Court held parts of the Rent Restriction Act, 1960 were unconstitutional, specifically the sections which fixed rent without providing for a periodic review. While the case has cast doubt on the *Central*

---

75 *Readymix Eire Ltd v. Dublin County Council*, unreported, Supreme Court, 30 July 1974, cited with approval in *Dublin County Council v. Jack Barrett Ltd*, unreported, Supreme Court, 28 July 1983. See Chapter 24 Registration of Title.

76 (1969) 109 ILTR 19.

77 [1981] ILRM 34.

Dublin Development Association case, it is also true, as O'Sullivan and Shepherd point out,[78] that the specific constitutional objections in *Blake* do not apply to the 1963 Act, since the development plan is reviewed every five years. However, the 1963 Act may be open to objections which did not apply to the Rent Restriction Acts.

G. Estoppel

In general an estoppel cannot operate to make valid an invalid exercise of a statutory power.[79] In *Dublin Corporation v. McGrath*[80] the principle was applied to a planning authority. A planning inspector had represented to the defendant that he could proceed to erect a building without planning permission which in law required such planning permission. The inspector had said that he would look after the planning permission. The defendant completed the building. The planning authority maintained that it had been erected with planning permission. The defendant argued that they were estopped from denying that it was exempted development. The District Justice stated the case to the High Court. A number of English decisions[81] were cited to the court in which it had been held that the planning authority was estopped by a decision of a planning inspector made within his or her ostensible authority, but McMahon J pointed out that the legislation in the Republic does not give the planning authority power to decide whether a particular development is or is not exempted development. Exempted development is defined by section 4 of the 1963 Act and under section 5 of the Act any question as to whether a particular development is or is not exempted development must be referred to and decided by the Minister.

A planning authority may, however, be estopped by representations made or expectations created when acting within its statutory power, as where a planning authority represents or creates the expectation that it will grant an easement over its own land, which is something it has power to do.[82]

78 O'Sullivan and Shepherd p.5.

79 *Minister of Agriculture and Fisheries v. Hulkin*, unreported, English Court of Appeal per Greene MR, cited in *Minister of Agriculture and Fisheries v. Matthews* [1950] 1 KB 148, per Cassels J; *Rhyl UDC v. Rhyl Amusements Ltd* [1959] 1 All ER 257, per Harman J.

80 Unreported, High Court, McMahon J, 17 November 1978; O'Sullivan and Shepherd p.53.

81 *Southend-on-Sea Corporation v. Hodgson Ltd* [1961] 2 All ER 41; *Wells v. Minister of Housing* [1967] 2 All ER 1041; *Lever (Finance) Ltd v. Westminster Corporation* [1970] 3 All ER 496.

82 *Crabb v. Arun D C* [1975] 3 All ER 865, [1976] Ch. 179, [1975] 3 WLR 847, 32 P & CR 70. See Chapter 22 Incorporeal Hereditaments: Acquisition of Easements: Estoppel.

H. Development

Development within the Planning Acts is divided by section 3 of the 1963 Act, into two categories:

(1) the carrying out of any works on, in, or other land (hereafter "carrying out works"); or

(2) the making of any material change in the use of any structures or other land (hereafter "material change of use").

Section 2 of the 1963 Act defines use for the purposes of the Planning Acts as excluding "the use of land by the carrying out of works thereon" and therefore the two categories above are generally mutually exclusive. They may not be entirely so because of doubts as to whether thereon includes thereunder or therein.[83]

Section 56(1)(a) of the 1963 Act excludes payment of compensation under section 55 where there is a refusal of permission for development consisting of a material change of use. There is no such exclusion of compensation in the case of a refusal of permission for carrying out works. It may also be important to distinguish between the two categories in order to determine whether a particular development is exempted. Section 4(1)(g) of the 1963 Act, for example, exempts development consisting of carrying out works for specific purposes affecting the interior of the structure but there is no exemption for material change of use affecting the interior only.[84]

1. Carrying Out Works

Section 2 of the 1963 Act defines works as including "any act or operation of construction, excavation, demolition, extension, alteration, repair or renewal". If interpreted literally this seems to make irrelevant the issue whether the operations had any effect on the land concerned. In England it has been held that an operation only amounts to development if it has the effect of altering the physical character of the land,[85] but there is no decision in Ireland on the point and in view of the wording of section 2, the law may well be different in this jurisdiction.

2. Material Change of Use

Sections 3(2) and 3(3) of the 1963 Act specify certain changes which amount to changes of use for the purpose of the Act. These include using land for storing or keeping of vehicles or caravans, using the land for advertising, or for the

83 O'Sullivan and Shepherd p.56.

84 *Cork Corporation v. O'Connell* [1982] ILRM 505.

85 *Cheshire County Council v. Woodward* [1962] 2 QB 126; O'Sullivan and Shepherd p.57.

sale of goods. It is a matter for the courts to decide whether other changes amount to a material change of use. A change from a retail hardware shop to an amusement arcade has been held to be a material change of use, taking into account that the new use would attract large numbers of people to the area.[86] The opening of a public bar in a small hotel which previously only had a hotel bar for the use of guests has been held to constitute a material change of use, the court taking into account the substantial increase in traffic which had occurred as a result of the change.[87] Other examples of material change of use are a change from a dentist's surgery to residential flats[88] and a change from a gravel pit to an open rock quarry, the latter requiring a greater use of machinery and additional techniques such as blasting.[89] Permission to use principal buildings for a given use has been held not to imply permission to use outbuildings for the same use, so that where the principal buildings were destroyed by fire, use of the outbuildings for the same original purpose was a material change of use.[90]

If the original use is abandoned, then the resumption of the original use may constitute a material change of use.[91] It follows that any other use after an abandonment would constitute a material change of use and require permission.[92] A use is abandoned if there is both a period of cessation of the use and an intention to abandon.[93]

If the original use becomes more intense this can amount to a material change. In *Patterson v. Murphy and Trading Services Ltd*[94] a quarry had been

86 *Cork Corporation v. O'Connell* [1982] ILRM 505.

87 *Carrick Hall Holdings Ltd v. Dublin Corporation* [1983] ILRM 268, McWilliam J.

88 *Cusack & McKenna v. Minister for Local Government* unreported, High Court, McWilliam J, 4 November 1980; O'Sullivan and Shepherd p.66.

89 *Dublin County Council v. Sellwood Quarries* [1981] ILRM 23; O'Sullivan and Shepherd p.71.

90 *Galway County Council v. Connacht Proteins Ltd* unreported, High Court, Barrington J, 28 March 1980.

91 *Dublin County Council v. Tallaght Block Co Ltd*, unreported, Supreme Court, 17 May 1983; O'Sullivan and Shepherd p.62; *Cusack & McKenna v. Minister for Local Government*, unreported, High Court, McWilliam J, 4 November 1980; *Cork County Council v. Ardfert Quarry Products Ltd*, unreported, High Court, Murphy J 7 December 1982; O'Sullivan and Shepherd p.67–70.

92 *Cork County Council v. Ardfert Quarry Products Ltd*, unreported, High Court, Murphy J, 7 December 1982; O'Sullivan and Shepherd p.69.

93 O'Sullivan and Shepherd p.58; there appears to be no case law authority for a test of intention, but O'Sullivan and Shepherd's statement is consistent with similar legal tests.

94 Unreported, High Court, Costello J, 4 May 1978. See also *Cork Corporation v. O'Connell* [1982] ILRM 505 (retail hardware shop to amusement arcade held material change); *Dublin County Council v. Tallaght Block Co Ltd*, unreported, Supreme Court, 17 May 1983 Hederman J (nem diss) (crushing clay and gravel to concrete block manufacture material); *Carrick Hall Holdings Ltd v. Dublin Corporation* [1983] ILRM

used to extract shale by relatively primitive means. Later the use of the quarry was extended by the introduction of equipment for the processing of stone and by blasting. Costello J held that the change was material. The judge held that the three factors of scale, method, and purpose of use were significant.

3. Occasional or Transient Uses

Section 40(b) of the 1963 Act provides that planning permission is not required:

> "...in the case of land which, on the appointed day, is normally used for one purpose and is also used on occasions, whether at regular intervals or not, for any other purpose, in respect of the use of the land for that other purpose on similar occasions after the appointed day".

The sub-section contrasts "normal use" with "used on occasions...for any other purpose", *i.e.* an occasional use which is not the normal use, and appears to mean that where the occasional use has occurred before 1963, then it may continue to occur after 1963 without requiring planning permission. On the other hand, where the occasional use started after 1963, it will only require planning permission if it amounts to a material change of use. Thus, where the normal use is agriculture and the occasional use is a rock concert once a year, the occasional use has been held to require planning permission,[95] whereas if the normal use is a rugby ground but it is occasionally used for other sporting, social and musical events, including pop concerts, that has been held not to require planning permission.[96] The 1999 Bill proposes in Part XV to exclude events and funfairs from planning control[97] and instead to provide a special régime for licensing such events.

I. Exempted Development

Planning permission is not required for exempted development. Exempted development is defined by section 4 of the 1963 Act[98] and the Second Schedule of the 1994 Regulations.[99]

---

268 (hotel bar to public bar).

95 *Mountcharles (Earl) v. Meath County Council* [1996] 3 IR 417; [1997] 1 ILRM 446 (on 9 occasions in 15 years).

96 *Butler v. Dublin Corporation* [1999] 1 IR 565, [1999] 1 ILRM 481, Supreme Court (O'Flaherty and Keane JJ; Hamilton CJ, Murphy and Lynch JJ concurring).

97 Clause 217.

98 As am. by the Local Government (Planning and Development) Acts, 1976, 1980, and 1999; SI No. 86 of 1994; SI No. 349 of 1989.

99 Local Government (Planning and Development) Regulations, 1994, SI No. 86 of 1994. See also O'Sullivan and Shepherd pp. 72–73, 1987 Supplement pp. 2–3.

1. Statute Law

The following is a paraphrase of the subsections of section 4(1) of the 1963 Act[100]:

a) land used for agriculture, forestry; it is proposed by regulations under the 1999 Bill that the initial planting of forests and turbary will no longer be exempt, since they have significant environmental effects;[101]

b) development by the council of a county in the county health district;

c) development by the corporation of a county or other borough in such borough;

d) development by the council of an urban district in such district;

e) development consisting of the carrying out by the corporation of a county or other borough or the council of a county or an urban district of any works required for the construction of a new road, or the maintenance or improvement of a road;

f) development consisting of carrying out by a local authority or statutory undertaker of works for the purpose of renewing, altering or repairing, *etc.*, sewers, cables, overhead wires, *etc.*;

g) carrying out of works for the maintenance or improvement, *etc.*, of structures which affect only the interior and do not materially affect the external appearance of the structure so as to render the appearance inconsistent with the character[102] of the structure or of neighbouring structures. Nevertheless, under the 1999 Act the carrying out of works on a protected structure is exempted development only if the works would not materially affect the structure.[103] The owner may request in writing the planning authority to issue a declaration of the type of works which it considers would or would not materially affect the structure.[104] The carrying out of works specified in a notice requiring work to be done on a protected structure to prevent its endangerment, or restore it, is exempted development under the 1999 Act;[105]

h) use of land round a dwelling house for purposes incidental to the enjoyment of it, [*e.g.* garden shed, gazebo, patio];

---

100 See footnote 98.

101 Planning and Development Bill, 1999, Explanatory and Financial Memorandum p.4.

102 *Cairnduff v. O'Connell* [1986] ILRM 465, Supreme Court; O'Sullivan and Shepherd 1987 Supplement p.208 (character relates to shape, colour, design, ornamental features and the layout of the structure concerned and is not dependent upon the use to which it is put at any particular time).

103 Local Government (Planning and Development) Act, 1999 s.8.

104 *ibid.* s.8(2).

105 *ibid.* s.19.

i) use of the land as a casual trading area within the meaning of the Casual Trading Act, 1980; and[106]

j) development consisting of the carrying out of works referred to in the Land Reclamation Act, 1949,[107] not being fencing or the enclosure of land which has been open to or used by the public within 10 years preceding the date on which the works are commenced.

Under the 1999 Bill a person may seek a declaration from the planning authority on whether a particular development is or is not exempted.[108]

2. Regulations

Section 4(2)(a) gives power to the Minister to make regulations exempting further categories of use. The Local Government (Planning and Development) Regulations, 1994[109] contain an extensive list of exempted developments. These are set out in the Second Schedule. They are divided into classes and some classes have conditions attached to them. Space does not permit a complete list here, but they include, with conditions, extensions to dwelling houses, erection of walls and fences, boiler houses and oil tanks, satellite TV antennae, certain changes of use such as from a public house to a shop, the addition of antennae for mobile telephony to existing radio masts, and replacement of existing masts with limits as to height and radiation emissions.[110]

The developments in the Second Schedule are exempt provided they comply with any conditions specified in Article 9 or the Second Schedule itself and provided also that they do not fall within the restrictions specified in Article 10 of the Regulations.

A change of use within Part IV of the Second Schedule is exempt provided (a) it does not require the carrying out of works which are not exempt, (b) it does not contravene a condition attached to a planning permission under the Acts, and (c) it is not inconsistent with a use specified in such a planning permission.[111]

3. Loss of Exempt Status

There are cases in which development which is exempted loses its exempt status.

---

106 Inserted by s.7(3) of the Casual Trading Act, 1980.

107 The words following 1949 were added by s.43(1)(b) of the 1976 Act.

108 Clause 5.

109 SI No. 86 of 1994, as am. by SI No. 431 of 1999.

110 SI No. 86 of 1994, Second Schedule as am. SI No. 78 of 1997.

111 SI No. 86 of 1994, art. 11; O'Sullivan and Shepherd p.72.

a) Planning Conditions

O'Sullivan and Shepherd express the view that loss of exempt status would occur if the development contravenes a condition attached to a planning permission.[112] Thus, where planning permission is granted for a building and the interior of the building is not constructed in accordance with the permission, then the altered features cannot take advantage of exempt status under 4(1)(g) above even if they are outside the artistic, historic or architectural category. Thus in *Horne v. Freeney*[113] the respondent obtained planning permission for an amusement arcade, but departed from the permission by constructing a room with two rows of pillars instead of an open area for dodgem cars and by building the open area for the dodgem cars on the first floor instead of lavatories and other facilities. He argued that the altered features were exempt under section 4(1)(g) of the 1963 Act. The court rejected this argument on the basis that a planning permission was indivisible: it sanctions the carrying out of all the works and not merely some of them.

b) Special Amenity Area Orders

Development which is otherwise exempt also loses its exempt status if a special amenity area order is applied to the area.[114]

J. Planning Permission

Section 24 of the 1963 Act sets out the requirement of planning permission. Permission is required for any development unless it was begun before 1st October 1964 and not being exempted development. Section 25[115] empowers the Minister to make regulations as to planning applications and these are now contained in Part IV of the Local Government (Planning and Development) Regulations, 1994.[116] Section 26,[117] which has been described as "the most important section in the entire planning code",[118] sets out the powers and duties of the planning authority in relation to a planning application and the rights of appeal from a planning decision.The 1999 Bill makes provisions for the first time for third parties to make submissions.[119]

---

112 O'Sullivan and Shepherd p.72.

113 Unreported, High Court, Murphy J, 7 July 1982.

114 See Special Amenity Area Orders.

115 As amended, *inter alia,* by SI No. 84 of 1994.

116 SI No. 86 of 1994.

117 As amended, *inter alia,* by SI No. 84 of 1994.

118 O'Sullivan and Shepherd p.107.

119 Clause 33.

1. Who Can Apply?

In *Frescati Estates v. Walker*[120] the Supreme Court held that it was not necessary for an applicant for planning permission to be vested with a legal estate in the land. It is sufficient for the applicant to have the authority of the owner or of the person who has a reasonable prospect of carrying out the development for which planning permission is sought. O'Higgins CJ in *McCabe v. Harding Investments*[121] expressed the view that it was sufficient for a planning authority to have a general idea of the applicant's interest in the land.

In *State (Alf-a-Bet Promotions Ltd) v. Bundoran UDC*[122] McWilliam J decided that an application could be made on behalf of a company not yet in existence, but this was subsequently doubted *obiter* by Henchy J in *State (Finglas Industrial Estates Ltd) v. Dublin County Council*[123] on the ground that such a company is not a legal person and that this position was not altered by provisions in the Companies Act, 1963 validating acts done before incorporation.

2. Who is Exempt?

a) State Authorities

The repealed section 84[124] of the 1963 Act required that a state authority[125] shall consult the relevant planning authority to such extent as may be determined by the Minister before undertaking the construction or extension of a building. The 1963 Act did not mention the general requirement of planning permission contained in section 24, but the section had been assumed to mean that Government departments did not need to apply for planning permission.[126] In two cases in which the point was raised the High Court came to opposite conclusions.

---

120 [1975] IR 177.

121 Unreported, Supreme Court, 27 October 1982.

122 (1974) 112 ILT 9.

123 Unreported, Supreme Court, 17 February 1983; O'Sullivan and Shepherd p.224.

124 Repealed by the Local Government (Planning and Development) Act, 1993 s.5.

125 State authority was defined for the purposes of the section by subsection (2) as "a member of the Government" [*i.e.* Ministers] and the Commissioners of Public Works in Ireland. This is still the definition: Local Government (Planning and Development) Act, 1993 s.1. It also included "(c) the Irish Land Commission". See Irish Land Commission (Dissolution) Act, 1992, s.4. Public authority is defined in s.5 of the 1976 Act as including the Commissioners for Public Works, a harbour authority and any other body declared to be a public authority by the Minister by regulation. SI No. 65 of 1977 Art. 65 includes the Electricity Supply Board, Córas Iompair Éireann, and Bord Fáilte Éireann. See also Heritage Act, 1995 s.2, National Cultural Institutions Act, 1997 s.2.

126 O'Sullivan and Shepherd p.108.

Byrne v. Commissioners of Public Works[127] concerned an application by a group of plaintiffs who sought to halt the construction of an interpretative centre being carried out by the respondents at Ballinastoe, Luggala, Roundwood, Co Wicklow, as part of the Wicklow National Park project. Lynch J held that section 84 exempted the Commissioners from the necessity of obtaining planning permission. In *Howard v. Commissioners of Public Works*[128] the plaintiffs sought judicial review of the decision of the Commissioners to construct the Burren National Park Visitors' Centre and the development of a National Park at or near Mullaghmore, Kilnaboy, Co Clare. Costello J held that the proposed construction was illegal, *inter alia* because it lacked planning permission.[129] The conflict of precedent led to the Supreme Court to decide both appeals together.[130]

The Supreme Court held that section 84 did not impliedly exempt the Commissioners, as State authorities, from the requirement of planning permission. Much of the argument was concerned with the principle of statutory interpretation to be applied, and in particular, whether the State under the Constitution had the benefit of the common law principle that the Crown was not bound by a statute unless it expressly said so or by necessary implication. Finlay CJ held that no such principle applied under the Constitution and approved of a statement by the Indian Supreme Court[131] to the effect that such a principle was inconsistent with a republican form of Constitution with its guarantee of equality. The Chief Justice (Egan, Blayney and Denham JJ concurring) held that there was no presumption either way: the court had to decide on the basis of the statute whether or not it was intended to bind the State. On the specific point at issue, Finlay CJ held that the State, and so the Commissioners, were bound by the requirement of planning permission. Section 84 did not expressly exempt State authorities from section 24 which it could easily have done if this had been intended. This was concurred in by Blayney and Denham JJ, O'Flaherty and Egan JJ dissenting. One argument in favour of the State being exempt was that it would be absurd to require State authorities to apply to a planning authority for planning permission and to consult with the same authority as well, and similarly to consult, in the case of unresolved objections,

127 [1993] 1 ILRM 665.

128 [1993] 1 ILRM 665, interlocutory injunction unreported, High Court, O'Hanlon J, 3 December 1992.

129 Costello J also held that the Commissioners for Public Works lacked the powers to build, maintain or manage public buildings or supply public services. As a result the State Authorities (Development and Management) Act, 1993 was passed to confer such powers on state authorities.

130 *Howard v. Commissioners of Public Works* and *Byrne v. Commissioners for Public Works* [1993] 1 ILRM 665.

131 *State of West Bengal v. Corporation of Calcutta* [1967] All IR (SC) 997, per Subba Rao CJ at 1007.

with the Minister, who could also be involved in the decision as to planning permission. The majority rejected this argument essentially on the ground that to require State authorities to comply with both provisions, while awkward, was far from absurd. As Blayney J put it:

> "It is questionable in any event whether the enforcement of both sections creates an absurd situation. As a result of consulting with the local [*sic*] authority in regard to a particular development, the Commissioners would obtain information as to whether their application for planning permission would or would not be likely to be successful, and if it looked as if it would be successful, they could also ascertain, when consulting with the Minister, his attitude to any objections raised by the local authority and so be able to form a view as to whether, in the event of a refusal by the local authority, an appeal to the Minister would have a chance of success [and] so compliance with section 84 might in fact have been of benefit to the Commissioners enabling them to assess in advance whether it would be worthwhile seeking planning permission for a particular development.".

The judge concluded that section 84 could not be interpreted as relieving the Commissioners from the requirement of obtaining planning permission contained in section 24. There was also another reason for this conclusion:

> "Section 84 is very limited in its scope. It applies only to the construction or extension of a building. . . But the two interpretative centres they are constructing involve much more than just buildings. The Mullaghmore Centre includes a waste treatment plant, storage tanks, and a car park. . . and the Luggala Centre includes forecourts and parking facilities. . . No possible interpretation of section 84 could relieve the Commissioners from applying for planning permission for these additional entities which are not buildings but which clearly are development.".

As a result of the case the Local Government (Planning and Development) Act, 1993 conferred power on the Minister to make regulations providing that the Planning Acts shall not apply to certain types of development undertaken by state authorities.[132] State authority is defined by the Act as a minister of the Government or the Commissioners of Public Works.[133] The types of development are those connected with public safety, the administration of justice, defence or where the development has to be authorised under some enactment. Part XIII of the 1994 Regulations specifies these in detail. The 1993 Act and the Regulations provide for public notice, consultation, the preparation of environmental impact statements, and public inspection of documents.[134]

b) Local Authorities

Local authorities, whether they are planning authorities or not, who wish to undertake development outside their own functional area must apply for planning

---

132 Local Government (Planning and Development) Act, 1993 s.2.

133 Local Government (Planning and Development) Act, 1993 s.1; SI No. 86 of 1994, art. 3(3).

134 1993 Act s.2(1)(b); SI No. 86 of 1994 art. 160.

permission to the relevant planning authority in that area. Local authorities who are not planning authorities have to apply to the planning authority in their own area in respect of development they wish to undertake in that area.

On the other hand, development by local authorities who are planning authorities is exempt if carried out in their own area. It would hardly make sense for a local authority to apply, in effect, to itself in its capacity as planning authority. Local authorities are nevertheless bound by their own plan. In addition, Part X of the 1994 Regulations[135] establishes a procedure for notice, inspection and consultation for specified classes of development by local authorities.

Anyone can now apply for a planning injunction under section 27 of the 1976 Act as amended in 1992[136] to restrain a local authority from departing from their own plan.[137] The 1994 Regulations[138] lay down a procedure for public notice, consultation and inspection in the case of most forms of development by local authorities.

The 1999 Bill proposes to require planning authorities to take housing estates in charge, where requested by a majority of the residents, once the estate is complete.[139]

c) Motorways

In *Nolan v. Minister for the Environment*[140] it was held by the Supreme Court (Hederman and O'Flaherty JJ; Finlay CJ dissenting) that the Local Government (Roads and Motorways) Act, 1974 was[141] a self-contained piece of legislation which had to be regarded as separate from the planning code and planning permission could not be granted in respect of any land to which a motorway scheme related. That Act has been replaced by the Roads Act, 1993, section 49 of which deals with road and motorway schemes.

3. Who can Object?

Under section 21(2)(c) of the 1963 Act any ratepayer could object to the draft plan. It was assumed from this that only ratepayers could object to a planning application, but both the section and the assumption were constitutionally du-

135 SI No. 86 of 1994, art. 130-136; SI No. 124 of 1998 (halting sites not exempt).

136 Local Government (Planning and Development) Act, 1992 s.19(4)(g).

137 Grist, "The Planning Injunction" [1993] ILT 79; and see Unauthorised Development. See also *The Attorney General (McGarry) v. Sligo County Council,* unreported, Supreme Court, 17 February 1989 (McCarthy J, Walsh and Hederman JJ concurring).

138 SI No. 86 of 1994 Part X.

139 Clause 164.

140 [1991] ILRM 705, Supreme Court.

141 Since repealed by Roads Act, 1993 s.4 Sch. 1; SI No. 197 of 1993.

bious. In *De Búrca v. The Attorney General*[142] it was held that it was unconstitutional to restrict jury service to ratepayers. Courts in the United States have struck down similar restrictions.[143] There is greater awareness today than there was in 1963 of environmental issues and it is recognised today that a development plan affects not only property rights but the environment generally.[144] It would follow that anyone, or anyone likely to be affected, should be able to object both to the plan and to planning applications.

The issue is not a live one at the present time because total relief from rates on dwellings was granted by the Local Government Financial Provisions Act, 1978 section 3 and since then no distinction has in fact been made between ratepayers, which still exists as a legal category, and non-ratepayers in relation to objections to planning applications. Moreover, the valuation system on which rates in Ireland were based, known as the Griffith Valuation, was held to be unconstitutional by the Supreme Court in *Brennan v. The Attorney General*.[145] It would therefore not be possible to reintroduce rates on the old basis. If rates were reintroduced on a new and constitutional basis the issue of eligibility to object to plans or applications would be revived and its constitutionality would have to be considered.

4. Regulations

Section 26[146] of the Act is the most important section from the point of view of a planning authority since it lays down the procedure for applications for planning permission and the time limit within which a decision by the planning authority must be made.

d) Default Permission

(1) Statutory

Under section 26(4) a planning authority must notify the applicant as to its decision on the planning application within two months beginning on the day of receipt of the application. If they do not do so the section provides that "a decision by the planning authority to grant the permission or approval shall be regarded as having been given on the last day of that period". Permission is

142 [1976] IR 38.

143 *Turner v. Fouche* (1970) 396 US 346; *Cipriano v. Houma* (1969) 395 US 701.

144 *The Attorney General (McGarry) v. Sligo County Council,* unreported, Supreme Court, 17 February 1989 (McCarthy J, Walsh and Hederman JJ concurring) per McCarthy J.

145 [1984] ILRM 355. Kelly, *The Irish Constitution* (3rd ed.) p.1078; Forde, *Constitutional Law* pp. 635-7.

146 As amended, *inter alia*, by SI No. 84 of 1994.

therefore deemed to have been granted by default at the end of the period. Permission by default is not recognised in other jurisdictions, such as England.[147]

Section 26(4) nevertheless only applies to a planning application "in accordance with permission regulations". These are contained in the Local Government (Planning and Development) Regulations, 1994.[148] Planning authorities who have not made a decision within the requisite period have been anxious to defeat claims to permission by default and in such cases have argued that the original application was invalid as not in accordance with the permission regulations. Such arguments, where they are based on a technical failure, will not necessarily succeed. In *Dunne Ltd v. Dublin County Council*[149] Pringle J rejected the argument that a planning application was invalid because the applicant did not give his full name, did not indicate the nature of his interest in the land and failed to comply with one other minor requirements.[150] The judge held the particular requirements to be directory, and not mandatory, noting in the case of the second one that a person with no interest in the land could apply for permission.[151]

There are arguments for and against planning permission by default. It can be said in its favour that it puts pressure on the local government bureaucracy to come to a decision within a reasonable time and does not oblige the citizen to seek redress. On the other hand, it opens the possibility that a permission may be granted by default which contravenes the development plan.

(2) By the Court

A failure by the planning authority to comply with the application regulations can result in a grant of default permission by the court, but the court has shown a considerable reluctance to reach such a result since it would tend to undermine the planning process.[152]

e) Mandatory or Directory?

The judgment of Pringle J in *Dunne Ltd v. Dublin County Council*[153] indicates that the judges have adopted a piecemeal approach to the regulations, finding some of them to be mandatory and others merely directory. Failure to comply with Article 15 of the regulations, which require the notice in the newspaper to

---

147 Nowlan *Planning Acts* p.39.

148 SI No. 86 of 1994.

149 [1974] IR 45.

150 O'Sullivan and Shepherd p.108.

151 [1974] IR 45; O'Sullivan and Shepherd p.185.

152 *Creedoni v. Dublin Corporation* [1983] ILRM 339.

153 [1974] IR 45.

state "the nature and extent of the development" has been held to be fatal.[154] Failure to state as a heading the area, city, town, or county in which the land is situated under Article 9 is not fatal, provided it is indicated with sufficient clarity in the notice.[155] Nor is it fatal if a genuine error is made in stating the name of the applicant which did not in fact mislead those concerned.[156] A statement that the fee simple is vested in the applicant, whereas the applicant in fact is entitled to a conveyance of the fee simple under a contract, is not fatal.[157]

5. Powers of Planning Authorities

Provided a planning authority complies with the Regulations it has wide powers to impose conditions under section 26 of the 1963 Act. In *State (Abenglen Properties Ltd) v. Dublin Corporation*[158] it was argued that the conditions imposed by the planning authority on an outline planning permission had amounted to granting permission for a development that was not sought and that therefore the planning authority had not adjudicated on the application submitted. Darcy J rejected this argument and so impliedly sanctioned a wide interpretation of planning powers. The judge also held that the planning authority was not obliged to invite revised plans amounting to a modified application although they had a discretion to do so.[159] The Supreme Court on appeal decided the case on a different point.[160]

The wide powers of a planning authority nevertheless appear to be confined once an outline planning permission has been granted. In *State (Pine Valley Developments Ltd) v. Dublin County Council*[161] Barrington J in the High Court held that a planning authority had to consider the application in the light of an outline planning permission already granted. They could not re-open matters decided on the grant of the outline permission. In the Supreme Court the case was decided on the different issue of the validity of the appeal to the Minister on the outline permission.[162]

---

154 *Monaghan UDC v. Alf-a-Bet Promotions Ltd,* unreported, Supreme Court, 24 March 1980.

155 *Dunne Ltd v. Dublin County Council* [1974] IR 45, Pringle J.

156 *State (Toft) v. Galway Corporation* [1981] ILRM 439 ("Spirits Rum Co Ltd" instead of "Rum Spirits Ltd").

157 *McCabe v. Harding Investments Ltd* ,unreported, Supreme Court, 27 October 1982.

158 [1981] ILRM 54.

159 O'Sullivan and Shepherd p.215.

160 [1981] ILRM 590.

161 Unreported, High Court, Barrington J, 27 May 1981, Supreme Court, [1981] ILRM 169.

162 [1981] ILRM 169.

6. Outline Permission

Section 25(2) of the 1963 Act provides for outline applications to be made "for permission for development subject to the subsequent approval of the planning authority". The procedure enables an intending developer to avoid going to the expense of mounting a full application only to have it rejected. The 1963 Act does not refer to outline permission but the phrase is defined by Article 13 of the 1977 Regulations as "a permission for development subject to the subsequent approval of the planning authority". There is therefore evidently a distinction in terms between, on the one hand, planning permission, whether granted on a full or outline application, and, on the other hand, a subsequent approval of an outline permission which has been previously granted. Under section 30 of the 1963 Act a planning authority may revoke a planning permission, although not as to work that has already been carried out before the revocation. In *State (Cogley) v. Dublin Corporation*[163] it was argued that since, as was conceded, there was no power in a planning authority to revoke a subsequent approval of an outline permission, it followed that an outline permission which had subsequently been approved could not be revoked at all. Teevan J rejected this argument and held that the planning authority could revoke the outline permission itself, whether or not it had subsequently been approved.

Outline planning permission may not be applied for in respect of:

(1) the retention of structures or the continuation of use of a structure or other land;[164]

(2) development for which an environmental impact statement is required;[165] and

(3) development for which an environmental impact statement would have been required, but for its not exceeding some limit such as quantity, and in respect of which the planning authority has issued a notice in writing.

7. Retention of Structures or Use

Under section 27 of the 1963 Act a structure which existed immediately before the appointed day, *i.e.* the day on which the 1963 Act came into force, and which was an unauthorised structure can be the subject of an application to a planning authority to retain the structure. The danger of not doing so is that if the land is acquired compulsorily no compensation is payable for unauthorised structures on the land or for unauthorised use.[166]

---

163 [1970] IR 244.

164 Local Government (Planning and Development) Regulations, 1990 art. 12.

165 See below page 1042.

166 1990 Act ss. 5, 11 and First Schedule r.2(b)(v); formerly Fourth Schedule r.12 of the the 1963 Act, inserting rules into s.2 of the Land (Assessment of Compensation) Act,

The planning authority may grant permission subject to conditions. A grant of permission to retain a structure is not subject to the normal time limit applying generally to planning permission, since the development has already been carried out.[167]

Under section 28 of the 1963 Act a planning authority may grant permission to retain a structure erected on or after the appointed day, and may grant permission to retain an unauthorised use of land. If an application to retain the structure is not made, or is refused, the court may now order the removal of the structure if the application is made within five years of the erection of the structure.[168]

8. Environmental Impact Assessment (EIA)

On 27 June 1985 the Council of Ministers of the European Community adopted Council EIA Directive 85/337/EEC[169] which requires assessments to be made of the impact on the environment of certain public and private projects carried out within member states. The European Communities Act, 1972 gave power to the Minister for the Environment to make regulations giving effect to the Directive. The Minister did this by the European Communities (Environmental Impact Assessment) Regulations, 1989[170] (EIAR), which amended principal legislation in order to implement the Directive, and the Local Government (Planning and Development) Regulations, 1994[171] which lay down the procedures to be followed.

The contents of the Directive and Regulations concerning the various aspects of environmental impact statements (EIS) may be summarised[172] as follows:

1919.

167 The 1982 Act s.2(2)(a)(i). See below: Duration.

168 Local Government (Planning and Development) Act, 1992 s.19(4)(g), substituting a new s.27 of the 1976 Act. See below Enforcement.

169 O.J. No. L175/40, 5 July 1985, am. by EIA Directive 97/11/EC. O'Reilly, "Environmental Impact Assessment Reliance on Directive 85/337/EEC" in Irish Centre for European Law *Environmental Protection and the Impact of European Community Law.*

170 SI No. 349 of 1989; as amended by the European Communities (Environmental Impact Assessment) (Amendment) Regulations, 1994, SI No. 84 of 1994, and 1998, SI No. 351 of 1998, which also amend principal legislation. SI No. 84 of 1994 implements Council Directive 85/337/EEC, dealing with the assessment of the effects of certain public and private projects on the environment.

171 SI No. 86 of 1994, Arts. 24-28, 37, 59 Part IX (local authorities). The first regulations to implement the environmental impact assessment requirements were contained in SI No. 25 of 1990.

172 See B. Meehan, "Environmental Impact Assessment and Planning in Ireland" in Bradley, Skehan and Walsh eds, *Environmental Impact Assessment: A Technical Approach* (Brussels: DTPS, 1991).

9.

	EC Directive	Regulations
Projects requiring an EIS	Art. 4 (1) and Annex I (mandatory)	Art. 24 of EIAR, Art. 24 and Part IX of 1994 Regulations. (mandatory)
	Art. 4(2) and Annex II (discretionary)	Art. 24 of EIAR and Art. 24 of 1994 Regs. (mandatory)
Information to be contained in EIS	Art. 5(1) and Annex III	Art. 25 EIAR and Art. 28 of 1994 Regs.

The 1999 Bill provides in Part X a basis for EIA in primary legislation. These sections when enacted will therefore replace the EIAR in so far as they affect the planning acts.

f) Projects Requiring an EIS

Projects for which an EIS is mandatory under the Directive are oil refineries, power stations, chemical treatment plants, including plants for treating or storing radioactive and other hazardous waste, ports, railways and aerodromes. Article 4(2) of the Directive lists projects as to which member states have a discretion whether or not to require an EIS. Those projects, within Article 4(2) or otherwise, for which the Republic has chosen to require an EIS are listed in Article 24 of the EIAR and Article 24 of the 1994 Regulations. They include the extension of intensive agriculture, water management projects, afforestation, land reclamation, peat and mineral extraction and various other industrial uses. Local authorities must prepare an EIS in respect of certain developments that they propose to carry out.[173] Copies of EIS must be available for inspection free of charge at An Bord Pleanála (the Planning Board) and must be available for purchase.[174]

g) Information Required

Information that must be included in an EIS is set out in the EIAR in the Second Schedule paragraph 2.[175] Apart from a description of the development, it includes "data necessary to identify and assess the main effects which that development is likely to have on the environment"[176] and a description of the

173 SI No. 86 of 1994 Part IX, especially Arts. 116, 117.

174 *ibid.*, Art. 59; Local Government (Planning and Development) Act, 1963 s.78(2)(g) as amended by SI 84 of 1994.

175 See also SI No. 86 of 1994 Art. 28.

176 SI No. 349 of 1989 Sch. 2 para. 2(b).

likely effects on "human beings, flora, fauna, soil, water, air, climate, the landscape, the interaction between any of the foregoing, material assets, the cultural heritage".[177] Where significant adverse effects on any of those elements are identified, the statement must include a description of measures to be taken to avoid, reduce or remedy them.[178] The statement must contain a summary of the specified information in non-technical language.[179] The statement may also contain further information amplifying or explaining the specified information.

10. Duration

A planning permission inures for the benefit of the owner of an interest in the land for the time being.[180] Originally under the 1963 Act a planning permission was not limited in duration, but section 2 of the 1982 Act provides that in future a planning permission will normally be valid for five years.[181] There are two exceptions to the principle. First, the planning authority may grant a permission for more than five years.[182] Secondly, if the date of a permission has been extended beyond the five years under the provisions to be mentioned below, the later date applies.

Section 4 of the 1982 Act provides that the planning authority may extend the time limit where substantial works were begun before the period expired and can be completed within a reasonable time. A further extension can also be granted.

---

177 *ibid.* para. 2(c).

178 *ibid.* para. 2(d).

179 *ibid.* para. 2(e).

180 1963 Act s.28(5).

181 The introduction of the limit was phased: permissions granted before November 1976 did not expire before the end of October 1982, those granted between 1st November 1976 and 31st October 1982 expired on 31st October 1987 or seven years after the date of the grant, whichever is earlier and those granted after 1st November 1982 will normally last for five years.

182 Local Government (Planning and Development) Act, 1982 s.3.

11. Conditions

Under section 26 of the 1963 Act planning permission may be granted subject to conditions. The 1982 Memorandum[183] issued by the Department of the Environment sets out in Part V guidelines for planning authorities. The main tests set out in the memorandum are that conditions must be: (a) related to the planning policy for the area and the development for which permission is sought;[184] (b) reasonable;[185] (c) precise;[186] and (d) enforceable.[187] An English case added a fifth general test, namely, that the condition should not effect a fundamental alteration in the general law.[188] An example of a condition invalid on the latter ground would arguably be one which sought to restrict the alienability of the fee simple to an extent not permitted in general law.

Such tests are a basis for judicial control of over such conditions[189] as is Article 40.2 of the Constitution. Henchy J has pointed out that such tests are inherent in section 26 of the 1963 Act:

> "... It is necessary to look not only at the terms of the condition but also at the reason which the section requires to be given in support of it. If the reason cannot fairly and reasonably be held capable of justifying the condition then the condition is cannot be said to be a valid exercise of the statutory power.".[190]

Such a control is particularly important since planning conditions have the potential, if not strictly controlled, of altering the rights of ownership in a fundamental way.

The 1999 Bill provides for a new system of levying development contributions, which, as a condition of planning permission, are to be paid by the developer in respect of public amenities of benefit to the development.[191]

h) Occupation

Section 28(6) of the 1963 Act[192] provides that conditions may be imposed as to the purposes for which the structure may be used and in particular may specify

183 *"Development Control Advice and Guidelines."* The Memorandum is set out in O'Sullivan and Shepherd Appendix A.

184 1982 Memorandum (see footnote) para. 5.8, 5.9.

185 *ibid.*, para. 5.12.

186 *ibid.*, para. 5.11.

187 *ibid.*, para. 5.10.

188 *Mixnam's Properties Ltd v. Chertsey UDC* [1965] AC 735, [1964] 2 WLR 1210, per Lord Wilmer.

189 *Fawcett Properties Ltd v. Buckinghamshire County Council* [1961] AC 636, House of Lords.

190 *Killiney and Ballybrack Development Association Ltd v. Minister for Local Government and Templefinn Estates Ltd (No. 2)*, unreported, Supreme Court 24 April 1978.

191 Clause 47.

192 O'Sullivan and Shepherd p.122.

that a dwelling house may be used only by "persons of a particular class or description". The condition also states that such a condition as to a dwelling house "shall be embodied in an agreement pursuant to section 38".[193] On the other hand, the Memorandum of 1982 Part V in paragraph 5.22, concerning conditions about the occupation of buildings, says that:

> "The planning authority should not usually concern themselves with the question of who would occupy a proposed structure if they permit it to be erected. While section 28(6) of the 1963 Act, as amended,[194] allows for a condition limiting the use of a dwelling to use by persons of a particular class or description, this can have serious practical consequences. It could put a severe limitation on the freedom of the owner to dispose of his [or her] property and could make it difficult for the developer to finance the erection of the permitted dwelling by obtaining a mortgage loan. Generally, therefore, the use of such a condition should be avoided."

Paragraph 5.23 goes on to state that "in exceptional cases it may be necessary to impose an occupancy condition in the case of a house required for an agricultural worker, or a member of a farm family". Where such a house is required for a site on which a house would not normally be permitted, the paragraph states that "it may be a material planning consideration that the house would meet the particular need referred to in the application". Granting permission in such a case would create an exception to the general planning policy for the area and this justifies the imposition of the condition, the memorandum states.

Paragraph 5.23 of the Memorandum is clearly dealing with the situation where an applicant wishes to construct a house for the use of an agricultural worker or a member of a farm family, but what is the position if the applicant has no such intention and merely wishes to construct a house for sale and realise the profit? A condition restricting occupation to agricultural workers would have the effect of reducing both the market and the market value of the proposed house. Does such a person, as the owner of land, not have the right to its improved market value? On the other hand, if people from the town buy up houses in rural areas, for holiday homes or weekend cottages, *etc.*, then those who work in agriculture may find that there is no housing within their means. To what extent is this a matter of protecting agriculture as an industry, or of human rights? If people in an agricultural community have a right to be protected against the rigours of the market, should not someone who was born in a rural area have a similar right to enable them to buy a house and continue to live there? If conditions may protect agricultural workers, why not the local blacksmith, or a local artist? These are some of basic issues which such conditions raise. One might also note that Rule 30 in the Fourth Schedule to the 1990 Act

---

193 See above Agreements.

194 By the 1976 Act s.39(h).

appears to require compensation when a condition as to occupation is imposed, other than a temporary condition.

In *Fawcett Properties v. Buckingham County Council*[195] the English House of Lords came down on the side of protecting agricultural communities, even though the condition in the case was difficult to justify in these terms. A planning authority had given permission for the erection of a pair of farm workers' cottages, subject to the condition that: "The occupation of the houses shall be limited to persons whose employment or latest employment is or was employment in agriculture . . . or in forestry, or in an industry mainly dependent upon agriculture and including also the dependants of such persons as aforesaid.". The court held the condition valid as "fairly and reasonably related to the permitted development" and held that it did not impose an unreasonable restriction on the use of the cottages, even though, as Lord Jenkins pointed out, it would permit the occupation of the cottages by a retired farmer from New Zealand and would exclude local residents who were not employed in the industry.

In view of the remarks of Henchy J in the Supreme Court[196] it is unlikely that the condition in *Fawcett* would pass the more stringent test laid down by the judge in this jurisdiction.

Conditions aimed at restricting occupation to local residents may now be challenged under European Law as infringing the freedom of movement or right of establishment. Such conditions may also make it impossible to raise the money to pay for the construction by way of mortgage and so may infringe access to financial services.

i) Opening Hours

Paragraph 5.12. of the 1982 Memorandum recognises that a condition may be so unreasonable as to be held unlawful by the courts. It suggests that an example of an unlawful restriction would be one on the opening hours during which an industrial or other use can be carried out if it virtually nullified the permission. A permitted restriction on opening hours, it suggests, would be one which prevented a serious injury to the amenities of property in the area. It has been held that a planning authority, or the appeal body, may specify the opening hours of a shop as a condition in order to reduce nuisance.[197]

195 [1961] AC 636.

196 In *Killiney and Ballybrack Development Association Ltd v. Minister for Local Government and Templefinn Estates Ltd (No. 2)*, unreported, Supreme Court, 24 April 1978. See above text at footnote 190.

197 *Dublin Corporation v. Raso*, unreported, High Court, Finlay J, 1 June 1976.

K. Other Statutory Controls

Other statutory controls apply to development in the form of buildings and have a similar aim to planning law generally.

1. Building Control Act, 1990

a) Building Regulations

Under section 3 of the Building Control Act, 1990[198] the Minister may make Building Regulations specifying standards for the design and construction of buildings generally, the services, fittings and equipment in or in connection with buildings and as regards any material change[199] in the use of buildings. The regulations may be made for various purposes including the health, safety and welfare of persons using or affected by buildings, provision for disabled people,[200] the conservation of fuel and energy and the efficient use of resources, the encouragement of good building and other matters.

b) Building Control Authorities

The Building Control Act, 1990 defines building control authorities as county councils, corporations of county boroughs, the Corporation of Dún Laoghaire and the corporation of any other borough and the urban district councils if the latter two authorities are fire authorities.[201] The main function of building control authorities is to enforce the Building Regulations made under the Act.[202] Enforcement is by enforcement notice.[203]

2. Rented Houses

The Housing (Standards for Rented Houses) Regulations, 1993[204] are made under section 5 of the Housing Act, 1966.[205] These lay down standards for the

198 See Building Control Act, 1990 (Commencement) Order, 1991 SI No. 304 of 1991; Building Control Regulations, 1991 SI No. 305 of 1991; Building Regulations, 1991, SI No. 306 of 1991.

199 1990 Act s.3(1)(d). Under s.86(4)(b) of the 1963 Act, repealed by the Building Control Act, 1990, material change included the use of a building as a house where it had not been previously so used, and the use of a house constructed for use for one family to being used by two or more families.

200 See also the Housing (Disabled Persons and Essential Repairs Grants) Regulations, 1993 SI No. 262 of 1993.

201 The Building Control Act, 1990 s.2.

202 Building Regulations, 1991 SI No. 306 of 1991; see also Building Control Regulations, 1991 SI No. 305 of 1991.

203 1990 Act s.8.

204 SI No. 147 of 1993.

205 As amended by ss. 18, 24 of the Housing (Miscellaneous Provisions) Act, 1992.

state of repair of rented houses and are dealt with in the chapter on landlord and tenant.

L. Appeals

1. Appeal Structure

Under the 1963 Act any person refused planning permission could appeal from the planning authority directly to the Minister for Local Government, later the Minister for the Environment. This was thought to expose the planning process to the risk of political influence and section 14 of the 1976 Act transferred most of the Minister's appellate jurisdiction to An Bord Pleanála (the Planning Board, referred to in the Act simply as The Board).[206] The Minister retained appellate jurisdiction only as to appeals under section 66 (interim directions, now expired) and section 88 (application for relaxation of Building Regulations).[207]

The general duty and objective of the Board is set out in section 2 of the 1992 Act and is to ensure that appeals are "disposed of as expeditiously as may be" and to avoid delays. The Board consists of a chairman[208] appointed by the Government[209] and five ordinary members, the number of which may be increased by the Minister.[210] The 1999 Bill proposes to increase the minimum number to six.[211] It also provides for the Board to sit in divisions.[212]

2. Powers on Appeal

Most appeals are under section 26[213] of the 1963 Act, *i.e.* against refusal of permission, or against conditions imposed on a grant of planning permission. The Board determines the appeal as if it were an application to the Board in the first instance.[214] It may take into account matters other than those raised by the parties or third parties on the appeal.[215] The Board is to take into account envi-

206 The Board was also given jurisdiction to hear appeals under s.25 of the 1963 Act.

207 O'Sullivan and Shepherd p.237.

208 The 1983 Act s.3, s.5, s.6.

209 The 1983 Act s.5.

210 The 1983 Act s.3, as substituted by 1998 Act s.1.

211 Clause 89.

212 Clause 97.

213 As amended by Local Government (Planning and Development) Act, 1992 s.3; and now also by SI No. 84 of 1994.

214 The 1963 Act s.26 as amended by Local Government (Planning and Development) Act, 1992, s.3.

215 The Local Government (Planning and Development) Act, 1992 s.13.

ronmental impact statements submitted by the applicant under a legal duty to do so.[216]

Where the appeal is against conditions the Board may give directions to the planning authority as to the attachment, amendment or removal of the conditions.[217] The powers of the Board on an appeal against conditions are restricted to the same matters as it might consider under section 25(5) as if the application had been made to it in the first instance.

Any person other than a party may make submissions or observations in writing to the Board in relation to an appeal.[218] The Board may call upon the parties or any person who has made a submission or observation to the Board to make submissions[219] on any matters raised in the appeal and may require them to furnish documents.[220]

The Board may hold an oral hearing[221] of any appeal. A party to an appeal may in writing request an oral hearing by the Board.[222] The Board may re-open such a hearing and hear further submissions.[223] Documents relating to appeals are open to public inspection.[224]

3. Grounds of Appeal

In *State (Elm Developments Ltd) v. An Bord Pleanála*[225] the Supreme Court held that failure to state the grounds of appeal did not invalidate the appeal. The law has now been amended by section 4 of the Local Government (Planning and Development) Act, 1992 which requires that appeals be in writing and should state full grounds and the "reasons, considerations and arguments on which they are based". Failure to comply renders the appeal void.[226]

---

216 See European Communities (Environmental Impact Assessment) Regulations, 1989, SI No. 349 of 1989. Art. 8(c) and art. 11 were revoked by the Local Government (Planning and Development) Act, 1992 s.22(2).

217 The Local Government (Planning and Development) Act, 1992 s.15.

218 *ibid.* s.8.

219 *ibid.* s.9, s.11.

220 *ibid.* s.10, s.11.

221 *ibid.* s.12.

222 *ibid.* s.12(2).

223 *ibid.* s.13(1)(a).

224 Local Government (Planning and Development) Act, 1992 s.5; SI No. 69 of 1995.

225 [1981] ILRM 108; *State (Walsh) v. An Bord Pleanála,* unreported, High Court, Keane J, 19 November 1980; *State (Genport Ltd) v. An Bord Pleanála* [1983] ILRM 12.

226 Local Government (Planning and Development) Act, 1992, s.4(2); appeals are dealt with in Part IV of the 1994 Regulations, SI No. 86 of 1994 as amended by SI No. 69 of 1995; SI No. 75 of 1995; SI No. 100 of 1996.

If the Board, having considered the grounds of appeal, considers them to be vexatious, frivolous or without substance or foundation the Board may dismiss the appeal.[227]

M. Enforcement

1. Offences

Any person who carries out development which requires permission without obtaining planning permission commits an offence under section 24 of the 1963 Act.[228] Since the offence refers to development it does not include the retention of a structure or the continuation of a use.[229]

2. Breach of Conditions

Section 31 of the 1963 Act provides that if a planning permission has been granted but its terms and conditions are not complied with there is power to order compliance with planning permission or the removal of the structure by way of an enforcement notice. Section 31(1), however, provides that the notice can only be issued within five years of the development being carried out or, in case of a condition not being carried out, within five years of the appropriate date which is the date specified in the condition or in the notice.

3. Unauthorised Development

If a structure was erected without planning permission and no application had been made under section 31 of the 1963 Act to retain it, or such an application had been refused, there was previously no power to order the removal of the structure.[230] This was a major flaw in the legislation and created, as to such buildings, a legal limbo unless the land was compulsorily acquired.[231] Now the Local Government (Planning and Development) Act, 1992 section 19(4)(g), substituting a new section 27 of the 1976 Act, gives power to the High Court or Circuit Court to order the removal of the structure if necessary and to ensure "in so far as is practicable, that the land is restored to its condition prior to the

227 Local Government (Planning and Development) Act, 1992 s.14, 1983 Act, s.16.

228 As amended by Local Government (Planning and Development) Act, 1982 s.15, s.8 (made indictable). The penalties were amended by the 1976 Act s.30, s.36, the 1982 Act s.8, s.9 and the Local Government (Planning and Development) Act, 1992 s.20.

229 Nowlan, *Planning Acts* on s.24 of the 1963 Act.

230 Grist, "The Planning Injunction" [1993] ILT 79; *Morris v. Garvey* [1982] ILRM 177; *Dublin County Council v. Kirby* [1985] ILRM 325; *Dublin Corporation v. Bentham*, unreported, High Court, Morris J, 23 July 1992.

231 See Fourth Schedule rule 12 of the 1963 Act. See above Planning Permission: Retention of Structures.

commencement of the development or unauthorised use". However, section 27(6)[232] provides that this power does not apply, in the case of unauthorised development, to development carried out before the day on which the Act came into force,[233] *i.e.* 16 July 1992, and, as to unauthorised development started after that date, an application to exercise the power shall not be made more than five years after the development was completed.[234] The effect of these provisions, as to the power to order removal, is to grant an amnesty as to unauthorised development carried out before the Act came into force. There still seems to be a legal limbo, therefore, in relation to such structures.

N. Compensation

The whole question of compensation is a complex one and central to an application for planning permission which should not be made without considering the issue and obtaining advice from practitioners experienced in the day to day application of the rules. It is also central to an understanding of planning law generally since the rules themselves are based upon principles and policies which concern the relation between public and private interest and the relation between private property and communal property.

The broad principle behind the rules seems to be that compensation is payable where a legitimate private property interest is encroached upon in order to give effect to some aspect of communal property, or the public interest, which is the basis for either a refusal of planning permission to the individual or a grant of permission subject to conditions aimed at maintaining this pubic interest. Compensation is not payable when a individual seeks to develop his or her land in a way which encroaches upon communal property in a way which is regarded as illegitimate. In terms of the principles discussed at the beginning of this chapter, the law to this extent regards the communal or public interest as primary and private property as secondary: private property rights do not extend to these illegitimate uses.

---

232 Section 27(6)(a)(i) referring to 27(1)(a); the new s.27 is substituted by Local Government (Planning and Development) Act, 1992 s.19(4)(g).

233 Section 27(6) (c) substituted by Local Government (Planning and Development) Act, 1992.

234 Section 27(6)(a)(ii) substituted by Local Government (Planning and Development) Act, 1992.

1. Entitlement

a) Direct Compensation

The general right to compensation is now dealt with by the Local Government (Planning and Development) Act, 1990 section 11 and the Schedules to the Act.

(1) Arbitration

Section 5 of the 1990 Act provides that failure by the parties to reach agreement on the amount of compensation to be awarded shall be dealt with by arbitration under the Land (Assessment of Compensation) Act, 1919 subject to the provisions of the First Schedule and the proviso that an arbitrator may award no compensation. Statutes dealing with compulsory purchase and case law on those provisions are relevant in so far as they are consistent with the restrictions in section 5.[235]

(2) Refusal of Permission

Under section 11 the general right to compensation arises when, on refusal of permission or the grant of permission subject to conditions, the value of an interest of any person existing in the land is reduced. Section 11 also provides that occupier of the land is entitled to be paid the damage to his or her trade, business or profession.[236] The person concerned is entitled to compensation subject to the restrictions in section 12 and the Schedules to the Act.[237]

(a) Development

The Second Schedule sets out the types of development in respect of which refusal of permission will not give a right to compensation. The first and most general type is: (1) development that consists of or includes the making of any material change in the use of any structures or other land.

As Kenny J pointed out in relation to the similar provision in earlier legislation,[238] in *Central Dublin Development Association Ltd v. The Attorney General,*[239] it seems at first reading to exclude compensation in almost all cases, but the definition section[240] in the 1963 Act provides that "use in relation to land does not include the use of the land by the carrying out of any works thereon" and so limited the wide language of the Schedule. In *Re Viscount Se-*

---

235 O'Sullivan and Shepherd p379. *Owenabue v. Dublin County Council* [1982] ILRM 150.

236 1963 Act s.55(1).

237 1990 Act s.12.

238 1963 Act s.55 repealed by 1990 Act s.3.

239 (1969) 109 ILTR 69.

240 1963 Act s.2(1).

curities Ltd[241] Finlay P in the High Court held that the refusal of planning permission to build houses in an area zoned for the further development of agriculture nevertheless gave rise to a claim for compensation.

The other types of development are: (2) the demolition of a habitable house; (3) any development which would materially affect a protected structure or proposed protected structure;[242] (4) the erection of an advertising structure; (5) the use of land for advertisement; (6) development in an area as to which a special amenity area order relates; (7) development on land where there is available a planning permission under Part IV of the 1963 Act for development of a residential, commercial or industrial character, if the development consists wholly or mainly of houses, flats, shops or offices, hotels, garages and petrol stations, theatres or entertainment, or industrial buildings or any combination of them subject to no conditions or only to conditions in the Fourth Schedule; (8) development on land as to which compensation has already been paid in respect of a refusal of permission.

(b) Reasons for Refusal

In addition, compensation will also be excluded for any development where the reason for refusal of permission is one of those set out in the Third Schedule. These include development which is premature due to the deficiency in water or sewerage facilities or roads, development which would endanger public safety or health, cause a traffic hazard, cause air, water or noise pollution or pollution by waste disposal, interfere with a view of special amenity value or special interest, interfere with the safety of aircraft, injure or interfere with a historic monument, which would materially contravene a condition attached to an existing permission or a development objective in the development plan.

The 1990 Act altered the previous law[243] in that no compensation is now to be paid where (a) water or sewage capacity is not actually deficient but where increased capacity would be required for prospective development,[244] (b) where the development is premature by reference to the order of priority for development laid down in the development plan,[245] (c) where the development would interfere with a view,[246] (d) where it would a cause pollution,[247] (e) where the development would materially contravene an objective of the development plan which was in effect at the time the developer acquired the interest

241 (1978) 112 ILTR 17, High Court, Finlay P.

242 1990 Act Second Sch. para. 3 as am. Local Government (Planning and Development) Act, 1999 s.37.

243 Dáil Debates, 24 November 1988 cols 1833, 1834.

244 1990 Act s.13 Third Sch. para. 1.

245 *ibid.* para. 3.

246 *ibid.* para. 6.

247 *ibid.* para. 7.

in the land[248], or (f) where the planning authority serves notice on the claimant that in its view the land is capable of other development.[249]

The new provisions are aimed at avoiding the abuse of compensation when a developer applied for permission, or financed the application of the existing owner, with the knowledge that the application would be refused because the proposed development contravened the zoning of the area, or some other objective in the plan, and in the expectation of obtaining compensation. A similar situation can arise where permission is granted subject to conditions. Measures, discussed below, have been enacted in that context. Under the previous legislation the Supreme Court in *XJS Investments Ltd v. Dun Laoghaire Corporation*[250] had upheld such claims on the ground that the legislation did not at that time expressly exclude compensation in such a case. The court reached this conclusion apparently for the reason that the protection of private property required planning authorities to state their reasons for refusal precisely in the terms laid down by the legislation dealing with cases where no compensation was to be paid. Nevertheless, the decision was open to the criticism that it was based upon the assumption that the property interest acquired by the developer included an inherent right to develop the land contrary to the development plan, despite the existing zoning of the area. It can be argued that the protection of property rights does not require compensation for a loss which was entirely artificial because it was foreseen before the land was purchased and could easily have been avoided by the developer declining to buy the land in question.

The 1999 Bill includes some additional reasons for refusal of permission which exclude compensation, *i.e.* because there is a real and substantial risk that a development will not be completed; because the development adversely affects a landscape conservation area; because the development adversely affects a European site or other type of designated site; and because the development would contravene materially a zoning objective in the development plan.

(3) Grant Subject to Conditions

The Fourth Schedule sets out the conditions which may be imposed on a grant of planning permission and which do not give rise to a right to compensation. These include:

a) conditions requiring the giving of security for completion of the development, requiring a contribution towards the expenditure by the local authority;

b) conditions imposed on an application for permission for a temporary structure;

248 *ibid.* para. 11.

249 *ibid.* s.13.

250 [1986] IR 750, [1987] ILRM 659, Supreme Court; *Dublin County Council v. Eighty Five Developments Ltd* [1992] ILRM 815, Supreme Court.

c) conditions relating to the size and height of structures, the extent of parking places, the purposes for which structures may be used, and the materials used;

d) conditions reserving land for a specific class of structures or limiting the number of structures of a particular class, or reserving open space;

e) conditions relating to the supply of water, sewers, public lighting, sanitary facilities and roads;

f) conditions relating to the alteration or removal of structures;

g) conditions relating to the preservation of buildings of artistic, architectural or historic interest and features of such interest within such structures and to sites of archaeological, geological or historic interest;

h) conditions relating to the preservation of views and features of natural beauty or interest, and to the preservation of trees and other flora;

i) conditions controlling or prohibiting waste disposal or the filling of land;

j) conditions preserving public rights of way;

k) conditions reducing or preventing noise or vibration;

l) conditions prohibiting the demolition of a habitable house;

m) conditions as to the safety of aircraft;

n) conditions as to the sequence or period in which works are to be carried out;

o) conditions restricting the occupation of structures until the completion of other works, or until another conditions is complied with or until the consent of the planning authority to such occupation;

p) conditions which may be imposed under any other Act, rule or bye-law; and

q) conditions relating to a protected structure or proposed protected structure.[251]

It may be noted under (o) above that conditions imposing requirements as to occupation generally are not within the Schedule and so would attract compensation.[252]

The 1999 Bill provides that compensation shall not be payable where permission is refused because a new development plan has change the zoning of the area.[253]

---

251 Fourth Sch. para. 15 as substituted Local Government (Planning and Development) Act, 1999 s.37; Dáil Debates, 24 November 1988 cols 1833, 1834.

252 1990 Act s.12 and Fourth Sch. para. 30.

253 Clause 175(4).

b) Acquisition

A second method by which a disappointed applicant for planning permission may realise the value of his or her land is by forcing the planning authority to acquire it under section 29 of the 1963 Act.[254] In general the right to force acquisition arises where the owner can prove that the planning decision has rendered the land "incapable of reasonably beneficial use in its existing state" and that it cannot be made capable of such use by the carrying out of development for which planning permission has been obtained or as to which the planning authority has undertaken to grant permission.[255]

Statutes dealing with compulsory purchase and case law on those provisions are also relevant here.[256]

2. Measure

Detailed rules for assessing the reduction in the value of the interest in land affected by a planning decision are now contained in the First Schedule to the Local Government (Planning and Development) Act, 1990. Basically, the amount of the reduction in the value of the interest is the difference between what the land would have realised on a sale in the open market between a willing purchaser and a willing vendor before the planning decision and after the planning decision, but the provisions are detailed and advice would need to be taken.

Formerly the principles of compensation were contained in the rules in section 2 of the Acquisition of Land (Assessment of Compensation) Act, 1919,[257] which now only apply to cases of compensation falling outside the 1990 Act.[258] Those principles were considered in *Re Deansrath Investments Ltd*[259] in which the English decisions were reviewed and applied. It remains to be

254 See also 1990 Act s.18 (no compensation where value of an interest reduced as a result of removal or alteration in structure where planning authority under duty to acquire it).

255 1963 Act s.29(1).

256 O'Sullivan and Shepherd p.379. *Owenabue v. Dublin County Council* [1982] ILRM 150.

257 As amended by the Local Government (Planning and Development) Act, 1963 s.69 and Fourth Sch.: Section 69 was repealed by Local Government (Planning and Development) Act, 1990 s.3, but continues to apply, by virtue of s.3(2), to cases, other than cases under the 1990 Act, where compensation assessed is payable by a planning authority. Acquisition of Land (Assessment of Compensation) Rules, 1920 SRO 600 of 1921 as amended by Property Values (Arbitration and Appeals) Rules, 1961, SI No. 91 of 1961; O'Sullivan and Shepherd p.402 *et seq.*

258 1990 Act s.3(2).

259 [1974] IR 228; and see *McKone Estates Ltd v. Kildare County Council* unreported, High Court, O'Hanlon J, 24 June 1983; O'Sullivan and Shepherd p.428; *Holiday Motor Inns Ltd v. Dublin County Council* unreported, High Court, McWilliam J, 20 December 1977.

seen whether any of those principles will still be applied under the 1990 Act where the First Schedule is silent.

3. Registration

Where compensation is payable, a statement specifying the compensation and the reasons for the refusal or grant of permission is now to be registered in the Register maintained under section 8 of the 1963 Act.[260]

260 1990 Act s.9.

CHAPTER 28

HOUSING LAW

A. The Housing Acts

The basic Act in this area is the Housing Act, 1966 as amended,[1] especially by the Housing Act, 1988 and the Housing (Miscellaneous Provisions) Act, 1992.

B. Policy of the Acts

The policy of the 1966 Act was well stated by O'Higgins CJ in *McNamee v. Buncrana UDC*[2]:

> "The Housing Act, 1966 was a major legislative measure aimed at tackling, in a planned manner, the persistent problem of bad and inadequate housing – not only in the large centres of population but throughout the country. It envisaged the launching of a new and sustained housing drive, financed by loans and grants-in-aid to local bodies and handled by these bodies, as housing authorities, under the supervision of the Minister concerned.[3]"

The main policy was implemented by mandatory sections of the Act requiring housing authorities to draw up and implement a building programme.

The 1988 Act repealed the sections of the 1966 Act concerned with building programmes but nevertheless left in place the general power to provide housing. The 1988 Act also addressed directly for the first time the problem of homelessness. Earlier legislation had not done so explicitly. The 1988 Act gives powers to housing authorities to provide housing for homeless persons and to empower the Minister and housing authorities to make grants and other subsidies for that purpose.

The policies behind the housing legislation may now be said to be:

(1) the provision of public sector houses at a subsidised rent for those who could not otherwise afford housing;

(2) the improvement of housing standards in the private rented sector; and

---

1 Principally by the Housing Act, 1970; Housing (Miscellaneous Provisions) Act, 1979; Housing Act, 1988; and the Housing (Miscellaneous Provisions) Act, 1992. The 1988 Act repealed the Housing Act, 1969 and the Housing Act, 1984. The 1992 Act repealed the 1970 Act.

2 [1983] IR 213, [1984] ILRM 77.

3 *ibid.*; at 217.

(3) the encouragement, by grants and subsidies, of owner-occupation by those not previously owning their own homes.

C. Housing Authorities

The definition of housing authority, presently contained in section 23 of the Housing (Miscellaneous Provisions) Act, 1992 is complex and varies according to different sections in different Acts. Generally it comprises the council of county health districts, the corporation of county boroughs, the corporation of boroughs, the council of urban districts and town commissioners except in the case of certain sections, when it is the county council in which the various bodies are situated.

D. Powers of Housing Authorities

1. Power to Provide Housing

a) General

Section 56 of the 1966 Act[4] states that:

> "A housing authority may erect, acquire, purchase, convert or reconstruct, lease or otherwise provide dwellings (including houses, flats, maisonettes and hostels) and such dwellings may be temporary or permanent."

Section 56(2) provides that a housing authority "may, in connection with dwellings provided, to be provided or which . . . will in the future require to be provided . . . provide . . .other buildings or land and such other works or services, as will . . . serve a beneficial purpose either in connection with the requirements of the persons for whom the dwellings are provided or in connection with the requirements of those persons and of other persons". The Housing (Miscellaneous Provisions) Act, 1992 adds to section 20 of the 1988 Act subsection 1A which requires a housing authority to draw up and adopt within one year a written statement of their policy "to counteract undue segregation in housing between people of different social backgrounds".[5] The policy may be amended from time to time and the policy or any amendment is a reserved function.

Section 57 enables housing authorities to provide sites for building purposes, and section 58 deals with the management of houses provided by a housing authority. Under section 9 a housing authority must make housing assessments every three years of the needs of persons in their area who need housing either because they are homeless or are members of the travelling

---

4 As am. by the Housing Act, 1988 s.20.

5 Housing (Miscellaneous Provisions) Act, 1992 s.28.

community within section 13, discussed below,[6] or because they are living in housing which is unfit for human habitation or which is unsuitable for their needs.

Section 11 of the 1988 Act provides that a housing authority "shall. . . make a scheme determining the order of priority to be accorded to the letting of dwellings, provided by the authority under the Principal Act and of which they are the owner. . ." to persons in need of accommodation and who are unable in the opinion of the authority to provide it for themselves and whose need for accommodation has been included in the housing assessment made under section 9.

In *University of Limerick v. O'Reilly*[7] Barron J in the High Court held that section 56 applies to serviced halting sites as well as dwellings and that both section 56 and section 13, although they appear to give a discretion, it is a discretion "which must in appropriate circumstances be exercised". The issue in the case arose in the context of halting sites and the case is further discussed below.[8]

b) Emergency

Housing authorities have power to provide temporary accommodation and also temporary halting sites for the travelling community.[9] The powers are within the executive function of the manager of the local authority and are not reserved powers requiring the intervention of the elected members.[10]

2. Grants and Subsidies

The legislation provides for the Minister to make grants directly, or through bodies including housing authorities, subsidising various aspects of housing, including the provision of housing, sites for housing and caravans by housing authorities,[11] subsidies of the rent of houses leased by shared ownership lease[12] and of houses provided by voluntary bodies.[13]

---

6 See page 1066.

7 Unreported, High Court, Barron J, 21st February 1991.

8 See page 1066.

9 Housing Act, 1988 s.11(2) and s.27 of the Housing Act, 1988 amending the City & County Management (Amendment) Act, 1955 s.2(9) (emergency procedure applies to housing).

10 City and County Management (Amendment) Act, 1955 s.2(9).

11 Housing Act, 1988 s.15.

12 Housing (Miscellaneous Provisions) Act, 1992 s.4.

13 *ibid.* s.7.

Housing authorities with the consent of the Minister of Finance may also make grants to persons providing new housing[14] or improving houses.[15] They may also make loans for a number of housing purposes including the acquisition of interests in and the improvement of houses and the provision of hostel accommodation.[16] The Minister may make grants for the provision or conversion of housing for the elderly.[17] Grants may also be made to first-time buyers in the private sector towards the cost of purchase.[18]

3. Recovery of Possession

Section 62 of the Housing Act 1966 provides a summary procedure by which a local authority may apply to the District Court[19] for the issue of a warrant entitling it to recover possession, and applies the provisions of sections 86, 87 and 88 of Deasy's Act, 1860. Section 86 of Deasy's Act, 1860 provides in effect that a summons signed by a justice or justices having jurisdiction in the place in which the premises are situate may be served upon a tenant who has failed to deliver up possession to appear before them to show reasonable cause why possession should not be given. District court rules provide that a District Court clerk may issue the summons,[20] although the hearing must be before a judge.[21]

4. Squatters

The Garda Síochána have power to order illegal occupiers, other than a tenant holding over, to leave a house let by a housing authority in a peaceable manner on being notified by a housing authority that person is engaging in anti-social behaviour and that it is necessary in the interest of good estate management to remove them.[22]

---

14 Housing (New House Grants, *etc.*,) Regulations, 1990 SI No. 34 of 1990; SI No. 301 of 1990; Housing (New House Grants, *etc.*,) Regulations, 1990 (Amendment) Regulations 1993 SI No. 350 of 1993.

15 Housing (Miscellaneous Provisions) Act, 1979 s.6.

16 Housing (Miscellaneous Provisions) Act, 1992 s.11.

17 Housing (Miscellaneous Provisions) Act, 1979 s.7.

18 Housing (Miscellaneous Provisions) Act, 1979 s.4.

19 Courts of Justice Act 1924, ss. 77, 91.

20 District Court Rules 1948 r.30(1)(c), made under Courts of Justice Act 1924 s.91.

21 *Kerry County Council v. McCarthy* [1997] 2 ILRM 481, Supreme Court (O'Flaherty J, Barrington and Murphy JJ concurring); *Dublin Corporation v. Hamilton* [1998] 2 ILRM 542.

22 Housing (Miscellaneous Provisions) Act, 1997 s.20.

5. Housing Supply

The 1999 Bill as initiated provided in Part V for housing strategies to be prepared by planning authorities as part of the development plan so that sufficient land would be zoned for housing and would be available for social and affordable housing. The Bill provided that a planning authority could impose a condition requiring the developer to enter into an agreement with the authority. Under the agreement the developer would be required (a) to transfer a part of the land to the authority for social or affordable housing, the compensation to be the value of the land at its existing use value, *i.e.* prior to its being zoned for housing, or (b) the payment of sum equivalent to the value of the land. The authority would then draw up a scheme under which affordable housing would be sold to eligible persons at a discount. If the eligible person were to sell the house within 10 years, the authority could recover a proportion of the discount, *i.e.* of the difference between the market price of the house at the time of the purchase and the actual price paid. This proportion would be reduced by 10 per cent for each complete year of occupation. However, there are doubts as to the constitutionality of the provisions and they are likely to be modified.

E. Housing Standards

1. Building Control Act, 1990

a) Building Regulations

Under section 3 of the Building Control Act, 1990[23] the Minister may make Building Regulations specifying standards for the design and construction of buildings, the services, fittings and equipment in or in connection with buildings and as regards any material change[24] in the use of buildings. The regulations may be made for various purposes including the health, safety and welfare of persons using or affected by buildings, provision for disabled people,[25] the conservation of fuel and energy and the efficient use of resources, the encouragement of good building and other matters.

23 See Building Control Act, 1990 (Commencement) Order, 1991 SI No. 304 of 1991; Building Control Regulations, 1991 SI No. 305 of 1991; Building Control (Amendment) Regulations, 1994 SI No. 153 of 1994; Building Regulations, 1991 SI No. 306 of 1991; Building Regulations (Amendment) Regulations, 1994 SI No. 154 of 1994.

24 1990 Act s.3(1)(d) and Building Regulations, 1991 SI No. 306 art. 12. Under s.86(4)(b) of the 1963 Act, repealed by the Building Control Act, 1990 material change included the use of a building as a house where it had not been previously so used, and the use of a house constructed for use for one family to being used by two or more families.

25 See also the Housing (Disabled Persons and Essential Repairs Grants) Regulations, 1993 SI No. 262 of 1993 made under s.5 Housing Act, 1966 as amended by s.24 of Housing (Miscellaneous Provisions) Act, 1992 and by s.6 of Housing (Miscellaneous Provisions) Act, 1979.

b) Building Control Authorities

The Building Control Act, 1990 defines building control authorities as county councils, corporations of county boroughs, the Corporation of Dún Laoghaire and the corporation of any other borough and the urban district councils if the latter two authorities are fire authorities.[26] The main function of building control authorities is to enforce the Building Regulations made under the Act.[27] Enforcement is by enforcement notice.[28]

2. Rented Houses

a) General

The Housing (Standards for Rented Houses) Regulations, 1993[29] are made under section 5 of the Housing Act, 1966.[30] These lay down standards for the state of repair of rented dwellings. They come into force, except for houses let by housing authorities, on 1 January 1994. They are dealt with in Chapter 19 on Landlord and Tenant.

b) Houses Let by Housing Authorities

As to houses let by housing authorities the Housing (Standards for Rented Houses) Regulations, 1993[31] did not come into force until 1st January 1998.[32] Until then housing authorities' general liability was that set out in *Siney v. Dublin Corporation.*[33] The Supreme Court in that case held that the special circumstances of letting by housing authorities implied a warranty by the authorities that houses let by them were fit for human habitation at the date of the letting.

A tenant of a house let by a housing authority as well as a housing authority itself may now[34] apply to a District Court for an excluding order against another person (the respondent) excluding them from entering or being in the vi-

---

26 Building Control Act, 1990 s.2.

27 Building Regulations, 1991 SI No. 306 of 1991; Building Regulations (Amendment) Regulations, 1994 SI No. 154 of 1994; see also Building Control Regulations, 1991 SI No. 305 of 1991; Building Control (Amendment) Regulations, 1994 SI No. 153 of 1994.

28 1990 Act s.8.

29 SI No. 147 of 1993.

30 As amended by ss. 18, 24 of the Housing (Miscellaneous Provisions) Act, 1992.

31 SI No. 147 of 1993.

32 This discrimination could have been challenged on constitutional grounds under Art. 40.1: see first edition of this book.

33 [1980] IR 400. For the position in Northern Ireland see *Gallagher v. N McDowell Ltd* [1961] NI 26, CA.

34 Housing (Miscellaneous Provisions) Act, 1997 ss. 3, 4.

cinity of a specified house[35] or housing estate and may also prohibit threatening behaviour, harassment, *etc.*[36] The order is made on the ground that the respondent is engaging in anti-social behaviour[37], including dealing in drugs, intimidation, *etc.* A housing authority may also refuse to let[38] or sell[39] a dwelling to a person on the ground of anti-social behaviour or other grounds.

3. Unfit Houses

If a housing authority is of the opinion that a house is unfit for human habitation then under section 66 of the 1966 Act the housing authority can issue a repair notice requiring the owner to execute repairs within a specified period. If the repairs are not carried out in the specified time the housing authority may then issue a closing order[40] prohibiting the use of the house or a demolition order.[41] A sanitary authority has a positive duty under the Local Government (Sanitary Services) Act, 1964 to demolish a dangerous structure as defined by section 1 of the Act.[42]

4. Overcrowded Houses

Housing authorities have powers to prevent overcrowding of houses. Under section 65 of the 1966 Act a housing authority may serve a notice on the owner of a house specifying the maximum number of persons who may occupy a house or a room in a house. Failure to comply with the notice renders the owner guilty of an offence, but an exception is provided where a house which is not otherwise overcrowded becomes overcrowded because of an increase in the number of children of the person by whom the house is occupied.[43] It should be noted that section 65 can cause homelessness if those occupying the house in excess of the maximum number have nowhere else to live. It is questionable therefore whether a housing authority could exercise the power under the section without accepting responsibility for the consequences and therefore providing alternative accommodation.

---

35 House in the 1997 Act has the definition (s.1) given to it by the Housing (Miscellaneous Provisions) Act, 1992, s.1. It is not limited to houses let by housing authorities.

36 1997 Act s.3(4).

37 1997 Act ss. 3, 1.

38 1997 Act s.14(1).

39 1997 Act s.14(2), 14(3).

40 Housing Act, 1966 s.66(6)(a).

41 *ibid.* s.66(6)(b).

42 *Treacy v. Dublin Corporation* [1993] 1 IR 305, [1992] ILRM 650, Supreme Court (must support and protect adjoining buildings from weather).

43 1966 Act s.65(5).

5. Caravan and Halting Sites

Section 13 of the 1988 Act provides that a housing authority "may provide, improve, manage and control sites for caravans used by persons to whom this section applies".[44] Section 13(1) defines the person to whom the section applies as "applies to persons belonging to the class of persons who traditionally pursue or have pursued a nomadic way of life" and this is clearly intended to refer to the travelling people of Ireland.[45]

Although the section uses the word may, the courts in a series of cases interpreted it as imposing a duty on housing authorities.[46]

Section 8 of the 1988 Act on the other hand requires housing authorities to prepare a report within one year of the section coming into force setting out the housing needs of their area, including the needs of people who are "homeless or living in temporary or movable accommodation". Under section 9 a housing authority must assess the housing needs of the homeless and "persons to whom section 13 applies",[47] *i.e.* travellers, as well as persons living in unfit or unsuitable housing.

In *University of Limerick v. O'Reilly*[48] Barron J had to consider the effect of these provisions. The respondents were an extended family of travellers who had parked their caravans on land belonging to Limerick County Council near the main gates of the University of Limerick. The County Council declined to take action and so the University applied to the court under section 27 of the Local Government (Planning and Development) Act, 1976 for an order restraining the respondents' use of the land. Lynch J granted an interim order to the University and also granted leave to the respondents to join the County Council as third parties. By their third party notice the respondents claimed an order requiring the County Council to assess their needs and to provide them with a halting site within a reasonable distance of a local school.

Barron J reviewed the legislation. He noted that house is defined by section 1 of the 1988 Act and is restricted to dwellings rather than halting or caravan sites. He nevertheless found that section 56 of the 1966 Act giving power to supply dwellings was not so limited. It applied to serviced halting sites as it does to dwellings. He then continued:

---

44 As substituted by the Housing (Traveller Accommodation) Act, 1998 s.29.

45 See also Dublin Travellers Education and Development Group, Irish Council for Civil Liberties, Irish Traveller Movement *Anti-Racist Law and the Travellers* (Dublin: Irish Traveller Movement, 1993).

46 *McDonald v. Dublin County Council,* unreported, Supreme Court 23rd July 1980; *O'Reilly v. Limerick Corporation and Others* [1989] ILRM 181, discussed in the first edition of this work.

47 1988 Act s.9(2)(b).

48 Unreported, High Court, Barron J, 21st February 1991

> "The question to be answered is whether the enactment of Section 13 imposes a duty to provide such caravan sites or merely empowers the Council to do so. .
>
> The position of a traveller family which becomes entitled to be provided with a dwelling must be considered. It is uncontested that such a family must be offered a dwelling. If this is refused because the family belongs to a class of persons who traditionally pursue or have pursued a nomadic way of life, does this mean that the Council now has a discretion whether or not to provide that family with a caravan site? The answer to the question is no . . . Section 13 must be taken to intend that the obligation of the Council to provide for housing needs extends in the case of those to whom section 13 applies [to] the provision not of dwellings but of caravan sites."[49]

In commenting on both section 56 of the 1966 Act and section 13 of the 1988 Act the judge noted that "both appear to give a discretion, but this is a discretion which must in appropriate circumstances be exercised". These circumstances, it seems clear from the judgment, are that a family has become entitled to housing, so that once a family has become entitled to housing they are equally entitled to be provided, as an alternative, with a serviced halting site. The case therefore goes considerably further than *O'Reilly v. Limerick Corporation* in that it places the right of travellers to serviced halting sites on an equal footing with the right to settled housing. In fact it may be true to say that there not separate but equal rights, a right to settled housing and a right to a serviced halting site, but rather a general right to housing and that the form in which it is satisfied depends upon the mode of life of the person asserting it.

Although the case law has therefore held that a housing authority has a statutory duty to provide housing for homeless persons and sites for travellers, there may be valid grounds on which a housing authority may postpone it in priority to other duties.[50] The extent to which it may be postponed in priority to other duties was examined by Flood J in *County Meath Vocational Education Committee v. Joyce*.[51] The applicants were the owners and managers of a community school in Co Meath. A number of families from the travelling community had been encamped on the roadside near the school. The applicants sought an order under section 27 of the Local Government (Planning and Development) Act 1976 restraining the unauthorised use of the roadside near the school by the respondents and other families at the camp site. They claimed that the unauthorised camp site constituted a nuisance as members of the travelling community who frequented the site had trespassed on the school grounds and performed various acts of nuisance. The respondents denied nuisance and issued third party proceedings against Meath County Council. They claimed an indemnity against the applicants' claim, or alternatively a contribution to such an extent as the court might direct, on the grounds that the county council owed them a duty to provide serviced camp sites pursuant to section 13

49 *ibid.* at p.28.

50 See *O'Reilly v. Limerick Corporation and Others* [1989] ILRM 181, Costello J

51 [1994] 2 ILRM 210.

of the Housing Act 1988 and that the applicants' complaint had arisen by reason of the county council's breach of these statutory provisions.

Flood J granted an injunction against the respondents but also ordered Meath County Council to take steps to acquire suitable locations for camp sites, by compulsory purchase or otherwise, and to equip them, subject to the parameters laid down by the minister, within one year of the order or such longer period as the court might allow. He stated his view of the law as follows:

> "In my opinion the county council, as housing authority, have a duty to perform their functions under the Housing Acts in a rational and reasonable manner and to provide accommodation for persons defined as homeless in the Act of 1988 which, in my opinion, undoubtedly includes the travellers on this site. That obligation on the county council as housing authority is under the statute an obligation which arises in the precedence currently ascribed to the travelling community in the scheme of priorities under ss. 9 and 11 of the Act of 1988 in the first instance, but as the Supreme Court pointed out in *McNamee v. Buncrana UDC*[52] 'that irrespective of whatever scheme of priorities may from time to time be in operation each housing authority must have regard to those who in fact at any particular time are in its functional area and are in need of housing".

The Housing (Traveller Accommodation) Act, 1998[53] now requires a housing authority to adopt an accommodation programme which is to specify the accommodation needs of travellers and the provision of accommodation required to address those needs.[54] Section 6 provides for the triennial statutory assessment of needs under section 9 of the Housing Act, 1988 to be carried out in an integrated way in relation to and in consultation with travellers. Section 16 of the Act requires a housing authority to take such reasonable steps as are necessary for the purpose of implementing the programme. Section 25 gives power to local authorities to make loans for the purchase of caravans and sites for traveller use.[55]

6. Power to Sell or Lease

a) Letting

The ordinary power of housing authorities to let houses is contained in section 90 of the Housing Act, 1966 as replaced by section 26 of the Housing (Miscellaneous Provisions) Act, 1992. Section 11 of the 1988 Act requires a housing authority to draw up a scheme determining the order of priority in letting dwellings to prospective tenants. Housing authorities must also now to draw up and adopt within one year a written statement of their policy "to counteract

52 [1983] IR 213, [1984] ILRM 77.

53 Commencement: SI No. 328 of 1998; SI No. 428 of 1998; SI No. 448 of 1998; SI No. 37 of 2000.

54 Section 7.

55 SI No. 37 of 2000 (from 1 February 2000).

undue segregation in housing between people of different social backgrounds".[56]

b) Purchase Schemes

Section 90[57] of the Housing Act, 1966 contains the power of housing authorities to dispose of dwellings owned by the authority. A tenanted dwelling may only be sold to the tenant under a purchase scheme, although it may be sold to another housing authority or a voluntary body apart from such a scheme.[58] The Minister may direct a housing authority to adopt a purchase scheme[59] and in such a case the local authority has no option but to comply. Purchase schemes must be adopted as a reserved function. All other disposals of dwellings or land by a housing authority are still subject to the approval of the elected members of the local authority.[60]

(1) Terms of Sale

The method of disposal of a dwelling under section 90 is by "vesting of the fee simple in the dwelling", *i.e.* by a transfer order under subsection 5. The purchase price is the market value reduced by a discount.[61] The discount is 3 per cent of the market value for each year of the reckonable period of the tenancy, which is the aggregate of (a) the period of tenancy of the purchaser or his or her spouse, (b) a period during which the purchaser or spouse occupied the dwelling under the terms of a previous sale, and (c) a period of at least one year during which the purchaser or spouse was bona fide resident in the dwelling as a member of the household of the preceding tenant and succeeded to the tenancy.[62] The period can be rounded up to the next number of complete years if it would not add more than six months to the period.

A housing authority may refuse to sell a dwelling on a number of grounds including lack of need, anti-social behaviour and good estate management.[63]

There is no warranty implied as to the state of repair or condition or fitness for human habitation of the dwelling sold under section 90.[64] This is a new departure, since previously the housing authority had been under a duty to put

56 Section 20(1A) of the 1988 Act added by Housing (Miscellaneous Provisions) Act, 1992 s.28.

57 As replaced by the Housing (Miscellaneous Provisions) Act, 1992 s.26.

58 Housing Act, 1966 s.90(1)(a).

59 Housing Act, 1966 s.90(3) as replaced by the 1992 Act s.26.

60 Housing Act, 1966 s.90(4) as replaced by the 1992 Act s.26.

61 Housing Act, 1966 s.90(7)(e) as replaced by the 1992 Act s.26.

62 Housing (Sale of Dwellings) Regulations, 1993 SI No. 267 of 1993.

63 Housing (Miscellaneous Provisions) Act, 1997 s.14(3), amending s.90(12) of the 1996 Act, inserted by s.26 of Housing (Miscellaneous Provisions) Act, 1992.

64 Housing Act, 1966 s.90(1), (8) as replaced by the 1992 Act s.26.

dwellings in repair before sale.[65] This seems designed to avoid any liability from a possible extension by the courts of *Siney v. Dublin Corporation.*[66] The provision is curious and seemingly inconsistent with the role of housing authorities in enforcing housing standards on the private rented sector.

The 1966 Act in its original form provided for the sale of houses by a housing authority under its statutory powers to be by way of mortgage or charge.[67] The new replacement section inserted by the 1992 Act merely provides that regulations may provide for "the security (if any) to be taken for moneys owing to a housing authority and the manner of assessing its adequacy".[68] This move away from conventional mortgages as a means of finance is further discussed below.

On sale of a flat a housing authority may levy a management charge in respect of common areas.[69]

(2) Special Conditions

The interest sold may be made subject to special conditions defined by section 89.[70] These include a condition not to mortgage, charge or alienate the dwelling "otherwise than by devise[71] or operation of law" without the consent of the housing authority,[72] and conditions as to residence by the purchaser or a member of the purchaser's family, or a successor in title of the purchaser, or a member of the successor's family.[73] An attempted mortgage or charge without consent is void, but a consent subsequently obtained validates such a mortgage or charge retrospectively.[74]

The legislation creates yet another category of special fees simple subject to restrictions on alienation which would not be possible at common law in the case of fees simple conveyed by private individuals. The legislation on the one hand provides for privatisation of public sector housing while at the same time

---

65 Housing Act, 1966 s.106, repealed by Housing (Miscellaneous Provisions) Act, 1979 which replaced it with s.13.

66 [1980] IR 400. The case itself was concerned with a warranty as to the fitness of houses let to a tenant by a housing authority.

67 Housing Act, 1966 original s.90(5).

68 Housing Act, 1966 s.90(7)(h) as replaced by the 1992 Act s.26.

69 Housing Act, 1966 s.90(6) as replaced by the 1992 Act s.26.

70 Housing Act, 1966 s.89 as amended by the 1992 Act s.25.

71 This word may have been inserted to avoid the problem referred to above under the Labourers Acts.

72 Housing Act, 1966 s.89(c). Section 89 is amended by the 1992 Act s.25; Housing (Sale of Dwellings) Regulations, 1993 SI No. 267 of 1993.

73 *ibid.* s.89(b). Section 89 is amended by the 1992 Act s.25. See also Housing (Sale of Dwellings) Regulations, 1993 SI No. 267 of 1993, Sch. "Form of Transfer Order". The draft provides for the special conditions to apply for 20 years.

74 Housing Act, 1966 s.90(12)(c) as replaced by the 1992 Act s.37.

Where the housing authority consents to a mortgage of a house sold or leased by them the consent includes consent to any further mortgage or consolidation effected by the same mortgagor.[75] When the mortgage has been paid off, a receipt by a mortgagee, whether a building society[76] or not,[77] will operate to reconvey or surrender to the mortgagor the interest conveyed to the mortgagee under the mortgage without any other formal reconveyance or surrender.

Where a mortgagee exercises its power of sale any conditions under section 90 cease to apply.[78] Clearly a purchaser would prefer to buy a house free of restrictions and would no doubt pay more for a title free of them. These provisions therefore potentially raise the problem of collusion between a purchaser/mortgagor of such a house and the mortgagee in order to sell free of restrictions[79] or the possibility that a mortgagor might default in order to bring about a sale by the mortgagee on more favourable terms than the mortgagor might be able to secure by selling with consent. The difficulty in framing legislation in this area is that, without such an exemption, private sector building societies are unlikely to wish to lend money on the security of houses sold under the scheme. In fact, the absence of a warranty as to fitness and the meagre resources or insecurity of employment of many applicants means that such schemes are difficult to finance in the private sector and increasingly the emphasis is on loans by housing authorities themselves, as the new section 90 indicates.

Existing mortgages remain subject to the law before the 1992 Act.[80]

A housing authority or the Housing Finance Agency plc may transfer, sell, or assign mortgages held by the authority of the Agency in respect of loans made under the Housing Acts, 1966 to 1992 or the Housing Finance Agency Acts, 1981 to 1992.[81]

c) Shared Ownership Leases

The shared ownership lease was introduced by the Housing (Miscellaneous Provisions) Act, 1992 as a means of acquiring ownership open to those who cannot afford to buy the fee simple with a conventional mortgage but who can afford to buy, over a similar period, a share in the fee simple.

Section 2 of the 1992 Act defines a shared ownership lease as a lease:

---

75 Housing Act, 1988 s.17 as amended by 1992 Act s.37.

76 Building Societies Act, 1989 s.27.

77 Housing Act, 1988 s.18(3).

78 Housing Act, 1966 s.90(12)(b) as replaced by Housing (Miscellaneous Provisions) Act, 1992 s.26; previously the provision was contained in s.17(2) of the 1988 Act, repealed by 1992 Act s.37 & Schedule.

79 See above.

80 Housing (Miscellaneous Provisions) Act, 1992 s.37(2).

81 Housing (Miscellaneous Provisions) Act, 1992 s.14.

(a) granted for a term of more than 20 years but less than 100 years;

(b) granted on payment to the lessor of a sum of money not less than 25 percent and not more than 75 percent of the market value of the house; and

(c) which gives the lessee the right to acquire the lessor's interest in one or more instalments for a consideration provided for in the lease.

The intending purchaser will therefore have to raise at least 25 per cent of the purchase price. The notion is that if the purchaser is able to raise more than 75 per cent of the purchase price, by mortgage or otherwise, then purchase by vesting of the fee simple would be a more appropriate method. The normal period of a lease as envisaged by the scheme is likely to be 25 years, at the end of which the tenant will acquire a half share of the fee simple. The intention behind the legislation is that at the end of the first 25 years the tenant, or a family member, may enter into another such lease and at the end of a similar period will acquire the whole fee simple. It should be noted that the 1992 Act does not confer a right to a reversionary shared ownership lease on a tenant although specific leases may do so. During the first leasehold period the value of the half interest retained by the housing authority will probably increase along with other property values and this is a factor to be considered by intending purchasers. In the normal course of events it will take two generations to acquire the whole fee simple.

The perpetuity rule does not apply to the option[82] and such a lease may be entered into by any person, not necessarily a housing authority,[83] although the method is intended to be used by housing authorities as a means of selling houses provided by them to their lessees.

Since the purpose is the acquisition of the fee simple by the lessee, the lessee does not have the right to acquire the fee simple free of rent during the currency of the lease under the separate provisions of the Landlord and Tenant (Ground Rents)(No. 2) Act, 1978.[84]

A housing authority may subsidise the rent of a house leased to a person under a shared ownership lease[85] and if it does, the rent is reduced by the amount of the subsidy.[86]

d) Landlord and Tenant (Ground Rents) (No. 2) Act, 1978

Section 26 of the Landlord and Tenant (Ground Rents)(No. 2) Act, 1978 gives a tenant of a housing authority, other than a tenant under a shared ownership

---

82 *ibid.* s.2(2).

83 *ibid.* s.2(1).

84 *ibid.* s.2(3).

85 *ibid.* s.4.

86 *ibid.* s.4(2).

lease,[87] the right to acquire the fee simple. The fee simple is vested in the tenant by a transfer order under section 90 of the 1966 Act. The purchase price is calculated in accordance with section 7 of the Landlord and Tenant (Amendment) Act, 1984.

87 Housing (Miscellaneous Provisions) Act, 1992 s.3(8)(b)(ii).

POSTSCRIPT: PLANNING AND DEVELOPMENT BILL 1999

A number of changes were to the Planning and Development Bill 1999 in its course through the Oireachtas. The number of ordinary members of An Bord Pleanála was increased to seven. Modifications were also made to Part V of the Bill concerning the provision of social and affordable housing. Although the percentage of land to be reserved for social and affordable housing, as a matter of general policy, in the housing strategy remained at 20%, nothing was to prevent a local authority using more than 20% of land zoned for such housing (clause 94(4)(d)). Where ownership of land was to be transferred to a housing authority under an agreement entered into by the developer, then, where the land was acquired before August 25, 1999, the amount of compensation in the Bill, as initiated, was to be the amount actually paid for the land, rather than the value based on the existing value. This was to take account of the point that persons who acquired land before that date, and therefore in ignorance of the proposed change in the law, might have paid a somewhat higher price than the value based on existing use in anticipation of being able to develop the land. To deprive them of that extra value could cause the provision to be impugned as an unconstitutional attack on their property rights. This was amended to include the cases of persons who had acquired the land before that date by inheritance or by gift, or mortgagees in possession. In the case of inheritance or gift, the compensation would be the value of the land estimated in accordance with capital acquisitions tax. Mortgagees in possession would get the same amount as if they had been a purchaser. In any of those cases, if the existing use value is greater than that value, then compensation would be at the higher value (clause 96(6)).

On June 30, 2000 the President referred Part V of the Bill to the Supreme Court under Article 26 of the Constitution.

APPENDIX A

FUTURE INTERESTS IN IRELAND TODAY[1]

A. Estates

1. Legal Remainders

a) *Inter vivos*, no use or trust

The limitation must comply with the legal remainder rules at common law and comes within rule 4(b) so that one must wait-and-see.

An example of a remainder within Rule 4(b), the "wait-and-see" rule, is:

to A for life, remainder to his first grandson to marry and his heirs.

If A has no grandson then the remainder clearly breaks the perpetuity rule. It cannot therefore be allowed to take effect whenever it might occur. The Contingent Remainders Act does not therefore apply. It is still treated as a common law remainder and if A has a married grandson at his death the remainder takes effect. If not, the remainder is void. Arguably, if a remainder of this type complies with the perpetuity rule it falls within the Contingent Remainders Act, 1877 and can take effect despite a "gap" as an executory interest.[2]

This category includes the only kind of "gift over" possible at common law. The following creates a determinable life estate and a valid gift over.

to A for life or until she becomes a solicitor, then to B and his heirs.

The remainder breaks none of the common law remainder rules.

b) *Inter vivos, Purefoy v. Rogers*

The limitation falls within rule 4(b) and complies with the other legal remainder rules. Limitation does not comply with rule against perpetuities and so cannot take advantage of the Contingent Remainders Act, 1877. The rule in *Purefoy v. Rogers* still applies and so the insertion of a use does not relieve the limitation of the "wait-and-see" rule. It must comply with rule 4(b) or be void;

1 That is, after the Administration of Estates Act, 1959 (RI).

2 See 2(a).

e.g.

> *to X and his heirs to the use of A for life, remainder to his first grandson to marry and his heirs.*

If there is a married grandson when A dies, the remainder is valid. If not, it is void.

2. Legal Executory Interests

a) *Inter vivos* no use or trust, but the remainder complies with the rule against perpetuities

The limitation complies with the common law remainder rules 1, 2, 3, and 4(a) (or, rather, looks the same as common law remainders that do). It also complies with the rule against perpetuities, as all legal executory interests must. The Contingent Remainders Act applies, arguably;
e.g.

> *to A for life, remainder to his eldest son and his heirs at 21.*

This is the typical rule 4(b) situation. If A's eldest son was under the age of 21 at his father's death, the remainder was destroyed. The Contingent Remainders Act allows what appears to be a contingent remainder to be treated *as if* it were a legal executory interest because it complies with the perpetuity rule. The son may take the remainder even if he does not become 21 until after his father's death.

An alternative, conservative, view is that a limitation of this type does not fall within the Contingent Remainders Act, 1877 because no use is expressed. If that is so, then the son may only take the remainder if he becomes 21 at or before A's death. On this view the limitation comes within 1.(a) above.

b) Springing and Shifting Interests

Inter vivos by a use executed by the Statute of Uses and the limitation breaks the common law remainder rules 1, 2, 3, or 4(a). Purefoy v Rogers does not (and never did) apply because it is clear at the outset that the limitation does not comply with the common law remainder rules. The "springing" or "shifting" events must comply with the perpetuity rule:
e.g. legal "springing" interests;

> *to X and his heirs to the use of A and his heirs at the age of 21.*
>
> *to F and his heirs to the use of S when she becomes a solicitor.*

e.g. legal "shifting" interests;

> *to X and his heirs to the use of J and his heirs, but if A dies an infant, to the use of K and her heirs.*

The fee simple to K is an executory "gift over" after a conditional fee simple.

c) *Inter vivos* by a use executed by the Statute of Uses, and the remainder is of the Rule 4 type and complies with the rule against perpetuities

The limitation complies with rules 1, 2, 3, and 4(a) and falls within the scope of rule 4 (b), the wait-and-see rule. It complies with the rule against perpetuities. The Contingent Remainders Act applies;
e.g.

> *to F and his heirs to the use of A for life, remainder to his eldest son and his heirs at 21.*

The Contingent Remainders Act here has the effect of abolishing the rule in *Purefoy*. An eldest son who attains 21 even *after* his father's death still takes the remainder.

3. Equitable Interests

a) *Inter vivos* Trust

i.e. the limitation creates a use *not* executed by the Statute of Uses;
e.g.

> *unto and to the use of X and his heirs in trust for A for life, remainder in trust to his eldest son at the age of 21 and his heirs.*

The limitation must comply with the rule against perpetuities or be void. If the remainder fails to satisfy the rule it cannot in the alternative be subjected to the "wait and see" rule. So if the remainder had read "...remainder to his first grandson to marry and his heirs", it would have been void.

b) All limitations of future interests in Wills

For the purpose of determining their validity these are treated as future trusts, since initially they take effect as such. Hence they have to comply with the rule against perpetuities or be void.

B. Interests Less than Estates

a) Interests After Determinable or Conditional Fees at Common Law

(1) Possibilities of reverter

The perpetuity rule does not apply to possibilities of reverter at common law in Ireland.[3] The limitation:

> *to X and his heirs so long as the land shall be used for agriculture*

3 *Attorney-General v. Cummins* [1906] IR 406.

creates a determinable fee followed by a valid possibility of reverter in the grantor and his/her successors.

(2) Right of Entry for Condition Broken

Rights of entry for condition broken at common law in Ireland are not subject to the perpetuity rule.[4] The limitation:

> *to M in fee simple on condition that the land be used as a school*

creates a conditional fee simple followed by a right of entry in the grantor.

b) Corresponding Legal Executory Interests

These are interests corresponding in type to a)(1) and a)(2) above but taking effect under executed uses. They probably do not need to comply with the perpetuity rule in Ireland. It makes no difference whether the limitation is phrased as a determinable or conditional interest;
e.g.

> *to F and her heirs to the use of K and his heirs on condition that the land be used as a school.*

c) Corresponding Equitable Interests

These are interests corresponding in type to a)(1) and a)(2) above but taking effect under trusts. They probably do not need to comply with the perpetuity rule. It makes no difference whether the limitation is phrased as a determinable or conditional interest.
The following limitation:

> *unto and to the use of T and U and their heirs in trust for R and his heirs, on condition the land is used for agriculture*

creates an equitable conditional fee simple followed by a possibility of resulting trust in favour of the grantor and his/her successors.

4 *Walsh v. Wightman* [1927] NI 1.

BIBLIOGRAPHY

Alexander G. S., "The Dead Hand and the Law of Trusts in the Nineteenth Century" (1985) *Stanford Law Rev*, 1189.

Ames, *Lectures on Legal History*, 1913.

Anderson, J. Stuart, *Lawyers and the Making of English Land Law 1832–1940,* (Oxford: Clarendon Press, 1992).

Anderson, Perry *Absolutist State, Lineages of the Absolutist State* (New Left Books, London, 1974).

Archdall, Mervyn, *Monasticon Hibernicum,* (printed for Luke White, Dublin, 1786)

Atiyah, P. S., *Freedom of Contract: The Rise and Fall of Freedom of Contract,* (Clarendon Press, Oxford, 1979).

Baker J. H. *An Introduction to English Legal History,* (2nd ed., 1979).

Baker J. H., *Manual of Law French*, (2nd ed., Scolar, Aldershot, 1990).

Barton. B, "The Medieval Use" (1965) 81 L.Q.R. 562.

Bean, J. M. W. *The Decline of English Feudalism, 1215–1540,* (Manchester University Press, Manchester, 1968).

Berger, Curtis J., *Land Ownership and Use,* (2nd ed., Little Brown, Boston).

Bell, Andrew P. *Modern Law of Personal Property in England and Ireland,* 1989.

Bergin Thomas F. Bergin and Paul G. Haskell, *Preface to Estates in Land and Future Interests,* (Foundation Press, Brooklyn, 1966).

Bland, Peter, *The Law of Easements and Profits à Prendre*, (Round Hall Sweet & Maxwell, Dublin: 1997).

Blackstone, William, *Commentaries on the Laws of England,* (1st ed., London 1765–69).

Blom-Cooper, L., *The Language of the Law,* (Bodley Head, London,1965).

Bork, Robert, *The Tempting of America: the Political Seduction of the Law*, 1990.

Bracton, Henry de, *On the Laws and Customs of England,* (Belknap Press and Selden Society, Harvard, 1968).

Bradley, Skehan & Walsh, *Environmental Impact Assessment: A Technical Approach,* (DTPS, Brussels, 1991).

Brady J. C., *Succession Law in Ireland* (Butterworths, Dublin, 1989, 2nd ed., 1995).

Brand, P. A., "The Control of Mortmain Alienation in England, 1200–1300" in *Legal Records and the Historian.* (J. H. Baker, ed., 1978).

Browder, Cunningham & Smith, *Basic Property Law,* (St Paul, Minn, West, 1984).

Bryson ,W. H., *The Equity Side of the Exchequer* (Cambridge University Press, Cambridge, 1975).

Burby William E., *Handbook of the Law of Real Property* (3rd ed., St Paul, Minn: West, 1965).

Burke's, *Burke's Irish Family Records* (Burke's Peerage Ltd, London, 1976).

Burke's, *Burke's Genealogical and Heraldic History of the Landed Gentry of Ireland* (L. G. Pine, 4th ed.: Burke's Peerage Ltd, London, 1958).

Carson, T. H. and Bompas H. B., *Carson's Real Property Statutes (based on Shelford's Real Property Statutes)* (2nd ed., 1910, reprint by Professional Books, 1981).

The Case of Tenures upon Commission of Defective Titles, argued by all the Judges of Ireland , with their Resolution, and the Reason of their Resolution, (printed with the 1720 ed. of Wm. Molyneaux, *The Case of Ireland's Being Bound by Acts of Parliament in England, Stated*).

Casner A. J., "Class Gifts to Others Than to 'Heirs' or 'Next of Kin': Increase in The Class Membership" (1937) 51 Harvard Law Review, 254.

Challis, *Real Property Challis's Law of Real Property: Chiefly in Relation to Conveyancing,* 3rd ed., by C. Sweet, Butterworth, London, (1911).

Cheshire, *The Modern Law of Real Property* (9th ed., 1962, 13th ed., 1982, 15th ed., 1994, Butterworths, London, 1982).

Chesterman, M. R. "Family Settlements on Trust: Landowners and the Rising Bourgeoisie" in Rubin and Sugarman (1984).

Clark, Robert, *Contract,* (2nd ed., Sweet & Maxwell, Dublin, 1986).

Co Litt, Sir Edward Coke, *The First Part of the Institutes of the Laws of England: or a Commentary upon Littleton* (London, 1628, 11th ed.,1719).

Coote, *A Treatise on the Law of Mortgages* (7th ed., 1904).

Cullen L., "Catholics under the Penal Laws" (1986) 1 *Eighteenth Century Ireland* 23.

Cunningham, Stoebuck and Whitman, *The Law of Property* (West Publishing Co, St Paul 1984).

Dawson, Greer and Ingram (eds.), *One Hundred and Fifty Years of Irish Law* (Roundhall Sweet & Maxwell, Dublin,1996).

de Blacam, M., *Private Rented Dwellings*, (2nd ed., Roundhall Press, Dublin, 1993).

de Moleyns, Thomas, *The Landowner's and Agent's Practical Guide* (8th ed., by A. W. Quill and F. P. Hamilton, Dublin, 1899).

Delaney, V. T. H., "Equitable Interests and Mere Equities" (1957) 21 *The Conveyancer* 195.

Delaney, Hilary, *Equity and the Law of Trusts in Ireland* (Round Hall Sweet & Maxwell, Dublin, 1996).

Donaldson, A. G., *The Application in Ireland of English and British Legislation made before 1801*. (PhD. 2 vols. Queen's University, Belfast, 1952).

Donellan, E. J., *Energy and Mineral Resources Law in Ireland* (Round Hall Press, Dublin, 1985).

Dunlop, R, "The Plantation of Munster" (1888) 3 *English Historical Review* 250.

Dunlop, R, "The Plantation of Leix and Offaly" (1891) 6 *English Historical Review* 261.

E. St. Ir. H. F. Berry, ed., *Early Statutes, Ireland, John to Henry VI.*, Dublin, 1907.

Edmonds, *International Timesharing,* (Services to Lawyers Ltd, London, 1984).

Eekelaar & Katz, *Marriage and Cohabitation in Contemporary Societies* (Toronto, 1980).

Falconbridge, *Mortgages,* (4th ed. by W. Rayner and R. H. M. McLaren, Canada Law Book Ltd., Ontario).

Farrand, J. T. *Emmet on Title,* (18th ed., Oyez Longman, London, 1983).

Farwell, George *A Concise Treatise on Powers,* (2nd ed., Stevens, London, 1893).

Fearne, C., *Essay on the Learning of Contingent Remainders and Executory Devises,* (1st ed. 1772, 10th ed., by Charles Butler, Saunders, London, 1844. Reprint, Professional Books Ltd, Abingdon, 1982).

Filgate, William Henry, *A Popular Treatise on The Law of Landlord and Tenant in Ireland,* (Hodges and Smith, Dublin, 1849).

Firth, C. H. and Rait R. S., *Acts and Ordinances of the Interregnum 1642–1660*, (HMSO, London, 1911).

Fitzgerald, B., *Land Registry Practice,* (Round Hall Press, Dublin, 1989).

Forde, Michael, *Constitutional Law of Ireland* (Mercier Press, Dublin, 1987).

Furlong, J. S., *The Law of Landlord and Tenant as Administered in Ireland* (2nd ed., Dublin, 1869).

Gale, *Gale on Easements,* (16th ed. by S. G. Maurice, Sweet & Maxwell, London, 1997).

Gilbert, Lord Chief Baron, *The Law of Uses and Trust* (3rd ed., by Edward Burtenshaw Sugden, W. Reed, London, 1811).

Glanvill Rannulf de, *The Treatise on the Laws and Customs of the Realm of England Commonly Called Glanvill,* (G. D. G. Hall, ed., Nelson, London, 1965).

Goode W. J., *The Resistance of Family Forces to Industrialisation* in Eekelaar & Katz (1980).

Goodeve, L. A., *The Modern Law of Real Property* (4th ed., Sweet & Maxwell, London, 1897).

Gordon, W. M., *Scottish Land Law* (Green, Edinburgh, 1989).

Gray & Symes *Real Property and Real People* (Butterworths, London, 1981).

Gray Kevin J., *Elements of Land Law,* (Butterworths, London,1987, 2nd ed., 1993).

Hand G. J. *English Law in Ireland, 1290–1324,* (Cambridge University Press, Cambridge, 1967).

Hargrave, Francis, *Jurisconsult Excercitations,* (3 vols. London, 1811–13).

Hargreaves , "Terminology and Title in Ejectment" (1940) L.Q.R. 376.

Hargreaves, A. D., *An Introduction to the Principles of Land Law,* (2nd ed., Sweet & Maxwell, London, 1944).

Hawkins and Ryder, *Construction of Wills*

Hayton David J. Hayton, *Registered Land,* (3rd ed., 1981).

Hewitt E. P., *A Treatise on the Statutes of Limitations* (Sweet & Maxwell, London, 1893)

Heydon , *The Restraint of Trade Doctrine,* (Butterworths, London, 1971).

Holdsworth "Terminology and Title in Ejectment – A Reply" (1940) 56 L.Q.R. 479.

Holdsworth, Sir William, *A History of English Law,* (Methuen & Sweet & Maxwell, London, 1925. Reprint, 1966).

Hood Phillips, O., *Shakespeare and the Lawyers* (Methuen, London, 1972).

Howarth, *Wisdom's Law of Watercourses* (5th ed., Shaw & Sons., Crayford, 1992).

Jarman,Thomas , *A Treatise on Wills* (8th ed., by Raymond Jennings & John C. Harper, Sweet & Maxwell, London,1951).

Keane *Equity and the Law of Trusts in the Republic of Ireland.*

Kelly, J. M., *The Irish Constitution* (3rd ed., by Gerard Hogan and Gerard Whyte, Butterworths, Dublin, 1993).

Kelly, J. M. Kelly, "Hidden Treasure and the Constitution" (1988) *Dublin University Law Journal* 5.

Kelly, Fergus, *A Guide to Early Irish Law* (Dublin Institute for Advanced Studies, Dublin, 1988).

Kelly, J. M. , *A Short History Western Legal Theory* (Clarendon Press, Oxford, 1992).

Kolbert and O'Brien, *Land Reform in Ireland* (University of Cambridge, Department of Land Economy, Cambridge, Occasional Paper No. 3, 1975).

Landlord and Tenant Commission Report, Pr No. 9685, (1967).

Leach, W. Barton, "Perpetuities: Staying the Slaughter of the Innocents" (1952) 68 L.Q.R. 85.

Litt Littleton, *Tenures,* (first published *circa.* 1481).

Longfield, *The Fishery Laws of Ireland,* (Dublin, 1863).

Lyall, Andrew , "The Family Home Protection Act, 1976 and Conveyances Other Than by Spouses." (1984) 6 DULJ (ns) 158–165.

Lyall, Andrew, "Class-Closing Rules and Future Interests in Freeholds: Law and Political Economy." (1985) 20 *Irish Jurist* 66–108.

Lyall , Andrew, "Human Rights and Conditional and Determinable Interests in Freeholds." (1987) 22 *Irish Jurist* 250.

Lyall, Andrew, "Non-Derogation from a Grant" (1988) 6 *Irish Law Times* 143–147.

Lyall, Andrew, "The Purchaser's Equity: An Irish Controversy" (1989) 7 *Irish Law Times* 270–279.

Lyall, Andrew, "Freehold Covenants and What To Do With Them" (1991) 9 *Irish Law Times* 157–161.

Lyne, James, *A Treatise on Leases for Lives Renewable for Ever* (Hodges and Smith, Dublin, 1837).

MacCurtain & O'Dowd, *Women in Early Modern Ireland* (Edinburgh UP, Edinburgh, 1991).

McDermott & Woulfe *Compulsory Purchase and Compensation: Law and Practice in Ireland* (Butterworth, Dublin, 1992).

McEldowney, J.F., & O'Higgins, Paul, *The Common Law Tradition: Essays in Irish Legal History* (Irish Academic Press, Dublin).

Macfarlane, Alan, *The Origins of English Individualism: The Family, Property and Social Transition* (Blackwell, Oxford,1978).

McGuire, *The Succession Act* (Incorporated Law Society of Ireland, Dublin, 1981).

McMahon, Brian & Binchy, William, *The Irish Law of Torts* (2nd ed., Butterworths, Dublin, 1989).

McNeil, Kent, *Common Law Aboriginal Title* (Clarendon Press, Oxford, 1989).

Macnevin, *The Practice of the Landed Estates Court in Ireland* (3rd ed., 1859).

Madden, D. H., *A Practical Treatise on the Registration of Deeds, Conveyances and Judgment Mortgages* (2nd ed., W McGee, Dublin, 1901).

Maguire, J. A., *Compendium of the Law and Practice Relating to Registration of Deeds, Wills, Judgment Mortgages and other Facts Affecting Title to Land in Ireland* (Hodges, Figgis & Co, Dublin, 1900).

Maine, Sir Henry, *Early Law and Custom.*

Maitland, F. W., *The Forms of Action at Common Law* (Reprint, Cambridge UP, Cambridge, 1968).

Malcomson, A. P. W., *John Foster: The Politics of the Anglo-Irish Ascendancy* (Oxford University Press, Oxford,1978).

Martin J., *Note* [1980] *Conveyancer* 207.

Maudsley, *Note* (1965) 81 L.Q.R. 183.

Maudsley and Burn, *Maudsley and Burn's Land Law, Cases and Materals* (5th ed., E H Burn, Butterworths, London, 1986).

Maudsley, R. H., *The Modern Law of Perpetuities*, 1979.

Megarry, R. E. & Wade, H. W. R. *The Law of Real Property* (4th ed., Stephens, London, 1975).

Megarry R. E. *A Manual of the Law of Real Property* (Stevens, London, 3rd ed., 1962, 6th ed., 1982, 7th ed., 1993).

Milsom, S. F. C., *Historical Foundations of the Common Law* (2nd ed. London, 1981).

Moore, Barrington, *Social Origins of Dictatorship and Democracy: Lord and Peasant in the Making of the Modern World* (Penguin Books, London, 1967).

Morris J. H. C. & Leach, W. Barton, *The Rule Against Perpetuities* (2nd ed., Sweet & Maxwell, London, 1986).

Morris "The Rule Against Perpetuities and The Rule in *Andrews* v *Partington*" (1954) 70 L.Q.R. 61.

Murray, J. B. C., *History of Usury*.

Newark, F. H., *Elegantia Juris: Selected Writings of Francis Headon Newark*, (F. J. McIvor, ed. *Northern Ireland Legal Quarterly*, Belfast, 1973).

NI Survey Working Party of Faculty of Law, The Queen's University, Belfast *Survey of the Land Law of Northern Ireland* (Belfast, HMSO, 1971).

Nicholls ,K. W., "Some Documents on Irish Law and Custom in the Sixteenth Century" (1970) 26 *Analecta Hibernica* 105.

Nicholls, K. W. *Land, Law and Society in Sixteenth Century Ireland* (O'Donnell Lecture, University College Cork, Cork, 1976).

Nicholls K. W., *Gaelic and Gaelicised Ireland in the Middle Ages* (Gill & MacMillan, Dublin, 1972).

Nowlan, Kevin, *A Guide to the Planning Acts* (Incorporated Law Society of Ireland 1978, 2nd ed., under the title *A Guide to the Planing Legislation in the Republic of Ireland,* 1988).

O'Sullivan, P. O' & Shepherd, K, *A Sourcebook on Planning Law in Ireland* (1st ed., 1984, Supplement 1987, Professional Books, Dublin).

Otway-Ruthven, A. J., *A History of Medieval Ireland* (2nd ed., London, 1980).

Pawlisch, Hans S. *Sir John Davies and the Conquest of Ireland: a Study in Legal Imperialism* (Cambridge UP, Cambridge).

Plucknett, T. F. T., *A Concise History of the Common Law* (4th ed., Butterworths, London, 1948).

Plucknett, T. F. T., *Legislation of Edward I* (Oxford UP, Oxford, 1949).

Pollock, Sir Frederick & Maitland, F.W., *The History of English Law before the Time of Edward I* (2nd ed., Cambridge UP, Cambridge, 1968).

Potter, Harold, *Historical Introduction to English Law and its Institutions* (Sweet & Maxwell, London, 1958).

Powell R. R. B., "Determinable Fees" (1923) 23 Colum L .R. 207.

Radcliffe, G., *Real Property,* (Oxford University Press, Oxford, 1933).

Report on Ground Rents, *Report on Ground Rents* Pr. 7783 of 1964.

Rheinstein, (ed., *Max Weber on Law in Economy and Society* translated by Shils and Rheinstein, Cambridge, Harvard UP, Mass, 1954).

Rubin, G. R., & Sugarman, D., eds., *Law, Economy & Society* (Professional Books, Abingdon, 1984).

Sanders, Francis Williams, *An Essay on the Uses and Trusts, and on the Nature and Operation of Conveyances at Common Law and those Deriving their Effect from The Statute of Uses* (2nd ed., Privately Printed, London, 1799).

Sappideen,Carolyn, "Life After Death – Sperm Banks, Wills and Perpetuities" (1979) 53 *Australian Law Journal* 311–19.

Scamell, E.H., "Positive Covenants in Conveyances of the Fee Simple" (1954) 18 *Conv* 546.

Sheppard, William, *The Touchstone of Common Assurances* (6th ed. by Edward Hilliard Strahan & Woodfall, London, 1791).

Sheridan,"*Walsh v Lonsdale in Ireland*" (1952) 9 N.I.L.Q. 190.

Sherrin Christopher H., "The Application of the Class-Closing Rules to the Construction of Wills" (PhD thesis, University of London (Ext), 1972).

Simes, Lewis M., "Public Policy and the Dead Hand" (1955) .

Simes,Lewis M., *Handbook of the Law of Future Interests* (West, St Paul Minn,1966).

Simpson, A. W. M., *A Biographical Dictionary of the Common Law.*

Simpson, A. W. M., *An Introduction to the History of the Land Law* (Clarendon Press, Oxford, 1st ed. 1961. 2nd ed. 1986).

Simpson, S. Rowton, *Land Law & Registration* (Cambridge UP, Cambridge, 1976).

Smythe, H., *The Law of Landlord and Tenant in Ireland* (Milliken, Dublin, 1842).

Snell, *Principles of Equity* (28th ed. 1982, 29th ed. (1990).

Sugden, Sir Edward, *A Treatise of the Law of Property as administered by the House of Lords* (Sweet, London, 1849).

Sugden, Sir E Edward, *A Practical Treatise on the New Statutes relating to Property* (2nd ed., Sweet, London, 1862).

Sutherland, D. W. Sutherland, *The Assize of Novel Disseisin* (Oxford UP, Oxford, 1973).

Treitel, G. H., 'Jane Austen and the Law' (1984) 100 L.Q.R. 549.

Underhill, Sir Arthur and Hayton,David, *Law Relating to Trusts and Trustees* (14th ed. by David J Hayton, Butterworths, London, 1987).

Waite, "Disrepair and Set-off of Damages against Rent: the Implications of *British Anzani*" (1983) *Conv* 373.

Wigmore, *Evidence in Trials at Common Law*, (1981).

Wilkinson, H. W., "Index-Linked Mortgages" [1978] *Conv* 346.

Williams, Joshua and Williams, C. P. *Principles of the Law of Real Property* (23rd ed., Sweet & Maxwell Ltd, London, 1920).

Williams, Joshua, *The Seisin of the Freehold.*

Williams, Joshua, *The Settlement of Real Estates, being Twenty-four Lectures Delivered in Gray's Inn Hall in the Year 1876.* (London, 1879).

Wolstenholme, *Wolstenholme's Conveyancing and Settled Land Acts.*,10th ed., by Cherry, Russell and Rawlence. (Stevens, London, 1913) (Reprint Professional Books, 1981).

Wylie, J. C. W., *A Casebook on Irish Land Law,* (Professional Books Ltd, Abingdon, 1984).

Wylie, J. C. W., *A Casebook on Equity and Trusts In Ireland* (Professional Books Ltd., Abingdon).

Wylie, J. C. W., *Irish Conveyancing Law* (Professional Books, Abingdon).

Wylie, J. C. W., *Irish Land Law* (2nd ed., Professional Books, Abingdon, 1986).

Wylie, J. C. W., *Irish Landlord and Tenant Law* (Butterworths, 1990–92).

INDEX

Index